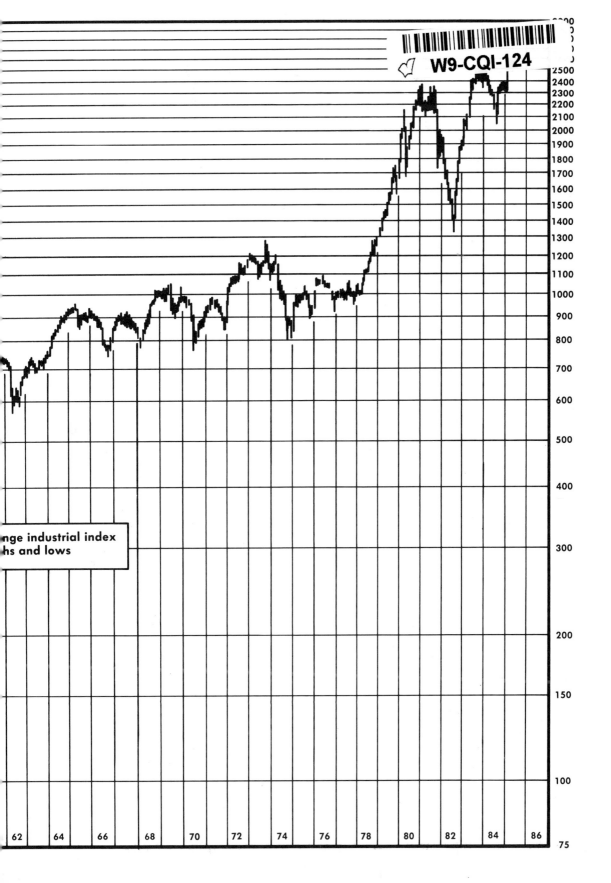

nge industrial index
hs and lows

INVESTMENTS
ANALYSIS AND MANAGEMENT

FIRST CANADIAN EDITION

INVESTMENTS
ANALYSIS AND MANAGEMENT

FIRST CANADIAN EDITION

JACK CLARK FRANCIS
BERNARD M. BARUCH COLLEGE
CITY UNIVERSITY OF NEW YORK

ERIC KIRZNER
ACCOUNTING GROUP
UNIVERSITY OF WATERLOO

McGRAW-HILL RYERSON LIMITED
TORONTO MONTREAL NEW YORK AUCKLAND BOGOTÁ CAIRO CARACAS
HAMBURG LISBON LONDON MADRID MEXICO MILAN NEW DELHI PANAMA
PARIS SAN JUAN SÃO PAULO SINGAPORE
SYDNEY TOKYO

INVESTMENTS: ANALYSIS AND MANAGEMENT

FIRST CANADIAN EDITION

ISBN: 0-07-549169-9

2 3 4 5 6 7 8 9 0   BP   6 5 4 3 2 1 0 9

Printed and bound in Canada

Care has been taken to trace ownership of copyright material contained in this text. The publishers will gladly take any information that will enable them to rectify any reference or credit in subsequent editions.

CANADIAN CATALOGUING IN PUBLICATION DATA

Francis, Jack Clark
  Investments : analysis and management

1st Canadian ed.
Includes index.
ISBN 0-07-549169-9

1. Investments. 2. Securities. 3. Financial futures. 4. Arbitrage. I. Kirzner, E. F. (Eric F.). II. Title.

HG4521.F73 1988   332.6   C87-095187-4

Cover Painting

  EWEN, Patterson Canadian 1925–
  Cloud Over Water, 1979
  acrylic and metal on plywood with gouged line
  224.0 × 335.0 cm (96 ^{1}/$_{16}$″ × 131 ^{7}/$_8$″)
  ART GALLERY OF ONTARIO, TORONTO: Purchase, 1980

ABOUT THE AUTHORS

Jack Clark Francis is professor of economics and finance at Bernard M. Baruch College, City University of New York. He was a Federal Reserve economist; a finance professor at the Wharton School of Finance, University of Pennsylvania; a U.S. army officer; and a finance and quantitative analysis instructor at the University of Washington in Seattle. Professor Francis has had articles published in the *Journal of Finance, Journal of Financial and Quantitative Analysis, Financial Management, Journal of Futures Markets, Journal of Monetary Economics, Journal of Economics and Business, Quarterly Review of Economics and Business, Review of Business, Journal of Portfolio Management*, and other academic and Federal Reserve periodicals. He has also authored a book entitled *Management of Investments*, co-authored *Portfolio Analaysis*, and co-edited *Readings in Investments*. Professor Francis lives in Stamford, Connecticut.

Eric Kirzner is assistant professor of finance in the Accounting Group at the University of Waterloo. He has had articles published in the *Journal of Business Research*, the *Canadian Journal of Administrative Sciences, CA Magazine*, the *CMA Journal, Your Money, The Financial Post*, and *Cost and Management*. He is the co-author of *The CCH Canadian Guide to International Investing* and *Global Investing: The Templeton Way* and is a contributing editor of the *MoneyLetter*. Professor Kirzner is a director of Equitable Trust and has served on the curriculum committee of the Society of Management Accountants and the editorial board of MD Management of the Canadian Medical Association. He lives in Toronto, Ontario, with his wife, Helen, his two daughters, Jennifer and Diana, and his faithful dog, Juno.

TO MY PARENTS
Sarah and Paul Kirzner

The two most progressive-thinking and socially conscious people that I have ever met. I hope that some of their attitudes have rubbed off on me.

CONTENTS

PREFACE

Jack Francis's *Investments: Analysis and Management* is now in its fourth edition. I have had the privilege of teaching investment courses with this text on numerous occasions at McMaster University, the University of Toronto, and the University of Waterloo and I was pleased when I received the opportunity to write the first Canadian edition of this thorough, lively, and comprehensive text.

Just the idea of Canadianizing an American text is in itself a controversial one. There is the implication of a patchwork or cut-and-paste process that may be offensive to some nationalists. However, there is a large and solid body of investment finance theory and knowledge that transcends geographic boundaries. Important and useful theories and models such as security valuation models, portfolio theory, the capital asset pricing model, arbitrage pricing models, option pricing models, international diversification, and the theory of efficient markets are not uniquely American; they can and should apply in any capital market. Nor, of course, were all of the theoretical developments and empirical tests in investment finance limited to American researchers; we, in the finance discipline, owe so much to the early French mathematicians and to the eighteenth-, nineteenth- and twentieth-century British economists.

In Canada, the theoretical and empirical work and contributions to the field of investment finance of Michael Brennan, Iain Morgan, Phelim Boyle, David Fowler, Myron Gordon, Larry Gould, John Hull, Vijay Jog, Alan Krause, Lawrence Kryzanowski, Allan Riding, Henry Rorke, David Shaw, Eduardo Schwartz, Seha Tinic, and Stuart Turnbull spring immediately to mind. Most importantly, I wish to pay tribute to the wonderful work of our late and dear colleague, Sanjoy (Joe) Basu, who, among many of the contributions that he made in his tragically short life, discovered one of the first of the efficient markets anomalies: the low P/E effect. The world only knows what additional and important contributions Joe might have made to the accounting, finance, and economics disciplines if he were still with us.

Text Coverage

The first seven chapters of the book provide the setting and background of investment finance in Canada. Chapter 1 provides a brief history of investment finance and the objectives of investing. Chapter 2 provides a complete overview of the basic types of securities issued and traded in Canadian capital markets. Chapter 3 describes the institutional structure of Canada's primary markets, the underwriting process, and the secondary markets. The evolution of our modern securities legislation, with its emphasis on full, true, and plain disclosure is the subject of Chapter 4. The ever-changing Canadian taxation system and its application to Canadian resident investors are discussed in Chapter 5. Chapter 6 sets out the important sources of investment information on Canadian investments, markets, and fundamental and economic data. Chapter 7 deals with security market indexes, their composition, and their applications.

In Chapters 8 through 10, fundamentally important concepts of valuation and risk are introduced. Chapter 8 explains what is meant by price, value, return, and risk and sets out the basic valuation model for detecting under- and over-valued securities. A quantitative discussion of the various types of risk is the subject of Chapter 9, while Chapter 10 introduces the capital asset pricing model and how a security's total risk may be positioned into unsystematic and systematic risk components.

Chapters 11 through 13 deal exclusively with bond valuation and interest rate determination. Chapter 11 provides a rigorous discussion of interest rate risk, immunization, and dedicated portfolios and introduces the basic bond valuation models. The effect of default and purchasing power risks on bond valuation is explored in Chapter 12, while in Chapter 13 the term structure of interest rates and the yield spread and their importance in forecasting interest rates are discussed.

The subjects of Chapters 14 through 18 are common share valuation and how risk and income interact to determine common share intrinsic values. Chapter 14 introduces stock valuation models, while Chapters 15, 16, and 17 deal with the two basic approaches to stock valuation — the fundamental (Chapters 15 and 16) and the technical (Chapter 17). Chapter 18 is a lengthy discussion of the behaviour of stock market prices and presents Canadian and American supporting and dissenting empirical evidence to the efficient markets hypothesis.

Chapters 19 through 22 discuss the marketable securities and derivative products that are used by experienced investors, traders, and business concerns for hedging, arbitrage, and speculative purposes. Chapter 19 explains long and short positions, describes hedges, and provides descriptive and analytic material on options, warrants, and convertible securities. Chapter 20 first introduces the nature of nonfinancial futures contracts and then provides a rigorous discussion of futures pricing and hedging applications. Chapter 21 extends Chapter 20 through an examination of the relatively new financial futures and options on financial futures contracts. Chapter 22 describes the potential benefits of and barriers to international diversification.

In Chapters 23 through 27, the book's focus shifts to portfolios of assets. Chapter 23 demonstrates how and why rational risk-averting investors should diversify their portfolios and sets out the analytic framework of portfolio theory. Chapter 24 extends the rigorous discussion to capital market theory and shows how, if investors act in the manner prescribed by the normative portfolio theory, risky capital assets shoud be priced in equilibrium. Chapter 25 is an economic analysis of risky decision making and sets out the basic principles of utility theory. Mutual funds and the various performance measurement criteria are the subject of Chapter 26, while Chapter 27 concludes this section with multiperiod wealth maximization and long-run portfolio revision stategies.

The final chapter of this book presents the most recent theoretical development in investment finance — the comprehensive multifactor arbitrage pricing theory. Canadian and American empirical studies are provided to present the current investigative state of this important model.

ACKNOWLEDGMENTS

I would like to thank the following people who helped me in shaping this first Canadian edition: Professor George Blazenko, University of Waterloo; Professor Phelim Boyle, University of Waterloo; William Burt, Freidberg Mercantile Group; Professor Ernie Cosgrove, Wilfrid Laurier University; Professor John Dickinson, University of Windsor; Professor Len Eckel, University of Waterloo; Mel Grossman, Soberman, Isenbaum, & Colomby; Ron Hutner, Dean Witter Reynolds (Canada) Inc.; Professor Alan MacNaughton, University of Waterloo; Sharon Midgely, Dean Witter Reynolds (Canada) Inc.; three anonymous referees; and especially Jack Clark Francis, Bernard M. Baruch College, City University of New York, for his enthusiastic encouragement, his technical advice, and his friendship all along the way of this lengthy but enjoyable project.

All errors, whether conceptual or technical in nature, are mine and mine alone.

I am grateful to the editorial team at McGraw-Hill Ryerson: Dave Scrimger, Jackie Kaiser, Betty Tustin, and especially Rosalyn Steiner, editor par excellence, who combined technical expertise with a marvellous sense of humour and managed to somehow keep me at least close to schedule using a firm, yet entirely gentle and amiable hand.

Eric Kirzner
Toronto
February 1988

Introduction

This is a book for investment managers and students of the investment management process. The book discusses marketable financial instruments such as common and preferred shares, bonds, puts, calls, and futures contracts—to name a few. These assets, the markets in which they are traded, the laws governing trading in Canada, valuation of the assets, construction of a diversified portfolio, and the important factors affecting investments management will be analyzed in the chapters that follow.

1-1 EVOLUTION OF INVESTMENTS TEACHING

The development of investments management can be traced chronologically through three phases, each corresponding to a specific stage in the development of Canadian financial markets and securities regulation. The first phase, spanning the mid-nineteenth century to about 1930, represented the haphazard beginnings of our modern financial market infrastructure. Probably the most notorious symptom of the early days was the widespread existence of ''bucket shop'' brokerage firms, which accepted orders from the public and then ''booked'' them (i.e., didn't place them). Whether or not the customer received his profit (if prices moved favourably) was determined by whether or not the brokerage firm was still in existence. And if prices moved unfavourably, the bucket shop operators pocketed the customer's loss! There was little regulation of the markets and stock exchanges then in existence. The Toronto Stock Exchange (founded in 1861), the Montreal Stock Exchange (1874), and the Standard Stock and Mining Exchange (founded in 1899, and merged with the Toronto Stock Exchange in 1934) all operated with little supervision.

Investments management then was a *skill* or an *art*. To make millions in the market, the traders of yesteryear needed to be steel-nerved gamblers who possessed a special cunning about the markets, who were pathologically greedy, who had the connections to raise large sums of capital, and who had the deadpan poker faces necessary to carry out these activities without tipping their hands. However, the daring speculative ventures, not to mention questionable trading practices, were at least partially stymied by the passage of securities legislation, such as Canada's Dominion Companies Act (1934), which prohibited door-to-door cold selling, and the Ontario Securities Act

(1945), which set out for the first time the basic principle of "full, true, and plain disclosure."

The unscrupulous skills used to make large investment trading profits around the turn of the century required an attitude best learned by observation and experience. Studying textbooks was not the most effective way to learn such nonintellectual skills, so no textbooks were written. The spine-tingling stories of how millions were made and lost by manipulating the markets are to be found only in the newspapers from the 1800s and early 1900s. One of the best sources from that period is *The Financial Post*, which, for example, published a series of exposés on fraudulent trading practices on the Toronto Stock Exchange in 1930.

During the 1930s and 1940s investments management entered its second phase, a phase of *professionalism*. The whole investments industry followed the lead previously taken by the Toronto Stock Exchange and seriously set about the task of upgrading its ethics, establishing standard practices, and cultivating a good public image. As a result, security and commodity exchanges tightened their entrance requirements; fair practice codes and self-policing bodies were set up to oversee investment activity; and investors busied themselves studying the fine print on their contracts, calculating financial ratios, and investigating the professional reputations of those with whom they dealt.

Since the professionalism of investments management began, investment textbooks writers have been busy. As the body of investments law has expanded — and investment markets became safer places, so that ordinary people began investing — numerous books have been written describing the laws and procedures investors must follow.

More recently, investments management has begun to be more *scientific*; this is the third phase in its development. It is impossible to specify the date when one stage ended and the next began, but some people point to a paper published by Harry Markowitz[1] in 1952 as the beginning of a scientific approach — although scientific analysis of investments can be found as far back as 1900.[2] Professionalism and scientific analysis are complementary and are, in fact, currently advancing simultaneously.

One of the most recent developments in the professionalization of investments management is the designation of chartered financial analyst (CFA) for investment analysts who have passed a series of examinations to demonstrate their proficiency. Interestingly, these exams have contained questions about economic theory and mathematical statistics — tools of the scientists. Thus, the professionalization of investments management is continuing, but assuming a more scientific bent. This book reflects that trend.

---

1 "Portfolio Selection," *Journal of Finance*, March 1952, vol. 7, no. 1, pp. 77–91. See also A.D. Roy, "Safety First and the Holding of Assets," *Econometrica*, vol. 20, no. 3, July 1952, pp. 431–449.
2 L. Bachelier, "Theory Speculation," *Ann. Sci. Ecole Norm. Sup.*, vol. 3, no. 1018 (Paris: Gauthier-Villars, 1900). Reprinted in Paul Cootner, *The Random Character of Stock Market Prices*, (M.I.T., Cambridge, Mass., 1964), pp. 17–78.

Since about 1960 the literature published about investments has expanded at an accelerating rate. As in the preceding decades, excellent books and articles appeared, explaining and rationalizing securities and other investments, the markets in which they were traded, and the relevant laws, procedures, and vocabulary. In addition, a whole new set of scientific research findings was published. Finance professors, security analysts, portfolio managers, economists, mathematicians, computer scientists, and others interested in investments management were partially dichotomized by the rapid publication of both traditional investments literature and the new esoteric scientific studies. Some people teaching investments seemed either to ignore the traditional institutional material and concentrate on the new scientific literature, or vice versa. The two groups have been almost mutually exclusive.

One of the aims of this book is to reverse the dichotomization by combining the most important elements from both the traditional camp and the new analytical group into one publication that suits the needs of both. The material is presented in such a fashion that those who want only the traditional material can find it—mostly in Chaps. 2 through 7, but elsewhere too. Those who want to confine their attention to analysis and exclude material about the investment institutions can do this by selecting relevant material from Chaps. 9 through 28.

1-1.1 Burgeoning Literature Dichotomized Investments Students

This text is written so that a beginning student can start at the front and move directly toward the back of the book. After Chap. 8, reference to the Mathematical Appendixes at the back of the book may be required to sustain progress. But the material does flow logically and increases in difficulty as the chapters pass, so that a front-to-back reading plan makes sense. However, too much material is included to be covered in most one-quarter or one-semester courses, so some chapters must be omitted. Which chapters are read is a matter of the professor's tastes. The book is laid out so that by picking and choosing among the chapters, many different courses can be formulated. Essentially, it is organized into nine main parts:

1-1.2 Organization

- Part 1, The Setting, explains the investment institutions found in Canada. Chaps. 2–7.
- Part 2, Introduction to Valuation and Risk-Return Theory, presents the theoretical foundation needed to make rational investment decisions. Chaps. 8–10.
- Part 3, Bond Valuation, shows how the time value of money affects security prices. Chaps. 11–13.
- Part 4, Common Stock Valuation, analyzes the procedures used by fundamental stock analysts. Chaps. 14–16.
- Part 5, Security Price Movements, reviews the debate between technical analysts and the random-walk theorists about the manner in which security prices fluctuate. Chaps. 17–18.
- Part 6, Other Investments, describes long and short positions, options, futures contracts, and international investing. Chaps. 19–22.
- Part 7, Portfolio Theory, explains the techniques of modern, scientific portfolio analysis and management. Chaps. 23–27.
- Part 8, Arbitrage Pricing Theory (APT), reviews the latest asset valuation theory. Chap. 28.

- Part 9, Mathematical Appendixes, explains various mathematical and statistical tools used in some later chapters and chapter appendixes.

These parts are fairly independent of one another. That is, they can be read without reference to the preceding parts; this is particularly true of Parts 1, 2, 3, and 5. Part 4 does assume a knowledge of Part 3, but those readers already familiar with the present value concept can read Part 4 independently. Part 3 presumes the reader has mastered Chap. 2. Part 6 uses tools that were developed in Part 2. Part 2 is not really essential to all parts of the book, but the material therein does touch on many important areas of financial investing.

All the parts are organized into related chapters that should usually be read in the order presented. But there is no reason why some of the later chapters in any part cannot be omitted. The end-of-chapter appendixes can certainly be skipped; most of them delve into a more detailed treatment of the material in the chapter. The majority of classes will read only those chapters that the professor feels might be particularly appropriate for the class within the time allotted.

The end-of-chapter appendixes are provided mainly for those students whose intellectual curiosity is not satiated by the chapter. The tiny bit of calculus that has crept into this book is confined to the appendixes; it is not essential for a basic grasp of the concepts under discussion. Instead, it is provided for those few readers who may want to see mathematical proof of some of the assertions made or to see how to use the tools under discussion to solve real problems. The Mathematical Appendixes (Part 9) are provided to help the student refresh his or her memory of mathematical procedures, which are quickly forgotten if not used regularly.

1-2 THE OBJECTIVE OF INVESTMENT

This book is written to develop investment managers who are interested in investing their funds in assets that have the maximum expected rate of return to any selected level of risk or, conversely, the minimum risk with a given expected rate of return. An example involving the six hypothetical assets listed below should make this clearer.

ASSET	EXPECTED RATE OF RETURN	RISK	DOMINATED?
M	0.1 = 10%	0.1	No
B	0.05 = 5%	0.1	Yes, by T and M
C	0.1 = 10%	0.2	Yes, by M and A
A	0.15 = 15%	0.2	No
T	0.05 = 5%	0.05	No
E	0.15 = 15%	0.3	Yes, by A

Figure 1-1 represents these six assets in risk-return space. That is, the six assets are plotted on the two-dimensional graph with their expected rate of return, denoted $E(r)$, on the vertical axis and their risk, measured numerically, on the horizontal axis.[3]

FIGURE 1-1   Assets graphed in risk-return space.

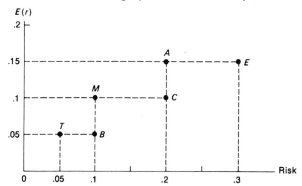

According to the investment objective assumed, assets T, M, and A dominate assets B, C, and E, respectively, because they have less risk for their given levels of expected return. Similarly, assets M and A dominate assets B and C, respectively, because they have the largest expected rates of return in their risk classes. Thus, the type of investor addressed by this book will prefer investing in assets T, M, or A rather than in assets B, C, or E.

Which of the dominant assets the investor prefers depends on his or her own personal investment preferences. A timid investor will prefer dominant investment T, whereas an aggressive investor will prefer dominant investment A. A "medium investor," halfway between timidity and aggressiveness, will prefer asset M, but the investment objective assumes that no rational investor would prefer assets B, C, or E.

Stating that the investment objective is to select assets that have the maximum expected rate of return in their risk class is like saying the objective is to maximize the investor's expected wealth at some preferred level of risk, since the larger the rate of return, the larger the terminal wealth.[4] It should be noted that this objective assumes the investor is essentially greedy.[5] Stated less crassly, this book is written for investors who prefer to have more wealth rather than less wealth. Other objectives, such as accumulation of power,

---

3 The quantitative risk measure used in Fig. 1-1 is explained in detail in Chap. 9. The analysis of diversified portfolios of assets is introduced in Chap. 23. Chapter 23 explains why the individual assets graphed in Fig. 1-1 will be dominated by portfolios and that some of the dominated assets may be held as fractional parts of dominant portfolios.

4 For a one-period time horizon the sentence is true. But for a multiperiod time horizon, the statement refers only to the geometric mean rate of return if the rates of return vary from period to period. The geometric mean return is explained in Mathematical App. F in Part 9 and/or Chap. 27.

5 In particular, this book assumes that the investor is greedy in the long-run sense, which implies observance of the law. Short-run greed is myopic and can lead to such self-destructive activities as theft and fraud (which, in turn, lead to jail, poor job prospects afterward, ad nauseam).

social reform, or attainment of prestigious position, may often be obtained through wealth if the manipulator has a sufficient amount of it. Therefore, we shall confine our attention to the wealth maximization objective within whatever risk class the investor prefers.

It is an oversimplification to assume that the objective of financial investing is pure and simple wealth maximization. There are constraints imposed by the law, and also by the investor's physical, financial, intellectual, and emotional resources. Limited personal resources frequently cause investors to select investments expected to yield only mediocre returns. *Risk aversion* is an important constraint on wealth maximization. The assumption of large financial risk can cause the investor to lose sleep, become irritable, develop ulcers, or even commit suicide. Time is another constraint that limits wealth accumulation. Many investors are only amateurs who "play the stock market" after work. These investors simply cannot find enough hours in the day to pursue every opportunity that may increase their wealth. Inadequate managerial skill can also limit people's achievements—many either cannot or do not want to manage a portfolio.

Most investors try to overcome the constraints imposed by limitations on their time, management skill, wealth, or other factors by confining their investments to a preferred risk level. By limiting the riskiness of their investments, these investors are usually able to limit the amount of time, managerial skill, and other factors that they must devote to investment management. Canadian federal government bonds are an investment that involves little risk or management effort if the investor is willing to earn uninspiring returns. The investment objective is covered in detail in Chap. 25 and its appendix—this material analyzes the rationale behind different investment objectives.

THE SETTING

These initial chapters explain in some detail the places, people, transactions, laws, and institutions that constitute the market place for security transactions in Canada. This material is presented first so that the reader may be able to understand the more abstract material that follows in terms of this basic institutional background.

CHAPTER 2

Securities

A *security* is a document that evidences specific claims on a stream of income and/or particular assets. Debt securities include bonds and mortgages. Ownership securities include common stock certificates and the titles to marketable assets (such as the bill of sale for an art object). In addition, preferred stock is a hybrid security that entitles its owner to a mixture of both ownership and creditor privileges. This chapter defines and discusses various features of both debt and equity securities.

Table 2-1 suggests a method of classifying the main types of securities. The table furnishes a compact summary of some of the salient points about the main categories of securities. This table should not be taken too literally, however. For example, the common stock issued by Bell Canada Enterprises is less risky than the bonds of many risky, little corporations. Table 2-1 refers only to the main categories of securities; it is not a true description of each and every individual security issue.[1]

TABLE 2-1   CLASSIFICATION OF SECURITY TYPES BY RISK, RETURN, AND DEGREE OF OWNER CONTROL OVER MANAGEMENT

SECURITY TYPE	CONTROL	RETURN	RISK
Common stock	1, most	1, most	1, most
Preferred stock	2	2	2
Corporate bonds	3	3	3
Government bonds	4, least	4, least	4, least

This chapter's discussion of securities begins with money market securities in Sec. 2-1 because they are the simplest kind of security. The Canadian government's debt securities are the topic of Sec. 2-2. Provincial and municipal

---

1 The existence of certain tax-exempt investors, the existence of different classes of common stock issued by the same corporation, and other real-world complications make Table 2-1 less than completely descriptive of reality. For these reasons Table 2-1 should be viewed as being a conceptual scheme rather than a specific case-by-case way to view the menu of investment securities.

bonds are examined in Secs. 2-3 and 2-4, and Sec. 2-5 delves into corporate bonds. Mortgage-backed securities are explained in Sec. 2-6. Equity instruments like common stocks are discussed in Sec. 2-7. Preferred stock is explained in Sec. 2-8. Convertible securities are the subject of Sec. 2-9. Then, some empirical market price data are presented in Sec. 2-10 in order to compare and contrast numerically the various securities.

Before turning our attention to specific debt securities, let's consider some general characteristics that apply to all debt securities. *Debt*, according to the dictionaries, is a condition that exists when one person owes something to another person. The dictionaries go on to explain that a *security* is a paper that is given as a pledge of repayment, or as evidence of debt or ownership. These definitions suggest that the phrase *debt securities* must refer to pieces of paper that evidence certain parties owe something to certain other parties. This chapter explores *marketable debt securities*—debt securities designed to be bought, sold, or traded in a securities market.

Investors buy debt securities in order to earn interest income from the security. That is, the investor lends money to the borrower who issued the debt security. But the investor expects to have the loan repaid with interest. The interest income is the inducement that causes the investor to give up the use of his or her funds and loan them at risk to some borrower who may be a total stranger.

There are many different kinds of marketable debt securities. They pay different rates of interest, they are available in different denominations, they have differing lengths of time until they come due for repayment, and some are more likely than others to be repaid. A wide variety of debt securities are discussed in this chapter. The discussion starts with the simplest kind of actively traded debt security—the money market securities.

2-1   MONEY MARKET SECURITIES

Dictionaries explain that things which are *liquid* flow freely from one place to another without being significantly compressed or expanded. Following this general definition, money (that is, cash) is the most liquid of all securities because it is readily acceptable at its face value in markets everywhere. Essentially, money is a *perfectly liquid asset* that flows freely from hand to hand without losing any of its value in the process. Money is more liquid than, say, long-term bonds, which have uncertain market prices that can deviate significantly from their face values and thus can be difficult to convert back into the amount of money that was paid for the bond. Thus, bonds may be an illiquid investment, especially if they are not traded in active markets.

Highly marketable securities that have short terms until they mature and involve little or no risk of default are said to be ''moneylike'' and are called *money market securities*. Money market securities are the most liquid of all securities except cash. Large corporate investors typically use money market securities as a place to invest cash temporarily available for a few weeks or months (for example cash held in anticipation of paying monthly income tax instalments), since money market securities pay varying rates of interest that reflect the supply of and demand for funds.

Money market securities are short-term debts. By definition of the Bank of Canada the money market includes securities with less than three years to maturity, although in practice the majority of money market issues and trades involve instruments with one year or less to maturity.[2]

Another attribute of money market securities is that typically they pay interest to their investors by selling at a discount from their face (or maturity) values. Consider for example, Canadian Treasury bills, which are sold by the Bank of Canada at regular auctions. Treasury bills are offered in denominations of $1,000, $5,000, $25,000, $100,000 and $1,000,000. A 91-day Treasury bill with a $100,000 face value might sell for $98,000 when it is first issued by the Bank of Canada. Then the buyer can either hold this security for ninety-one days or sell it in the secondary market any time before it matures. At maturity, whoever owns this T-bill can redeem it for its face value of $100,000. The $2,000 difference between the discounted purchase price of $98,000 and the maturity value of $100,000 is the interest paid (and treated as such, for tax purposes) to the T-bill investor (or series of investors).

Yields on money market instruments in Canada are normally calculated using a 365-day year (unlike the U.S. practice of using a 360-day year). Hence, in the example above, the annual simple yield on the 91-day $100,000 T-bill purchased at $98,000 would be:

$$\text{yield} = (\text{discount/market price}) \times (365/\text{days to maturity}) \times 100$$
$$= (2/98) \times (365/91) \times 100 = 8.18\%$$

Several other types of money market securities are discussed below.

Bearer Deposit Notes (BDNs) are issued by the chartered banks in minimum amounts of $100,000. Like T-bills, they are issued at a discount, to mature at par with the difference treated as interest income. BDNs are not cashable by the holder prior to maturity although they are transferable.

Certificates of Deposit (CDs), also referred to as term notes and term deposit receipts, are issued by the chartered banks in denominations ranging from $5,000 to $1,000,000. These instruments are both noncashable prior to maturity and nontransferable. However, the purchaser may acquire a put option (a put option is the right to sell; you will learn about options in Chapter 19) to cash in early according to a predetermined reduced interest-rate schedule.

Banker's Acceptances are drafts or written promises that borrowers give to banks promising to repay as yet unborrowed funds. Then, when the borrower takes down the loan, the lending bank will have accepted the banker's acceptance. Later, if the lending bank wants to withdraw the money that it has invested in the loan prior to the loan's maturity, it can sell the written promise to repay the loan to another investor. Banker's acceptances may be resold to any number of new investors before the loan becomes due and is repaid; there is a modest secondary market in these moneylike pieces of debt.

2 For more details about the money market and securities traded there see S. Sarpkaya, *The Money Market in Canada*, 3d ed., CCH Canadian, 1985.

The ultimate holder of the acceptance will collect the loan at maturity unless the borrower should default on the loan. The last investor has legal recourse in cases of default and can collect from the bank that originated the banker's acceptance.

Banker's acceptances have a maximum term of ninety days from date of acceptance and are drawn in amounts of $100,000 or multiples thereof. The issuer typically pays a fee of 1/2 to 1 percent of the face value of the debt to the accepting bank. Like most money market instruments, bankers' acceptances are issued at a discount to mature at par.

Commercial Paper refers to the short-term promissory notes issued by well-known companies with high credit ratings, such as Bell Canada Enterprises Inc., and Imperial Oil Ltd. Maturities range from overnight to one year; the majority of the paper is issued to mature in ninety days or less. These notes are not backed by any collateral, relying instead on the high credit rating of the issuing corporation. The minimum denomination is $50,000, although issues are typically much larger. By section 3(2) of the Ontario Securities Act (1985), registration is not required to trade in "negotiable promissory notes or commercial paper maturing not more than one year from the date of issue, provided that each such note or commercial paper traded to an individual has a denomination or principal amount of not less than $50,000." Hence, observed maximum maturities of one year and minimum denominations of $50,000.

It is usual for commercial paper issuers to maintain open lines of credit or standby bank lines (that is, unused borrowing power at chartered banks) sufficient to repay all of their outstanding commercial paper issued for working capital needs, in some cases temporary, in others as a permanent form of short-term financing.

Finance Paper is issued by sales finance companies and is similar to commercial paper with respect to terms, minimum denominations, and maturities. Typically, however, finance paper is secured with a pledge of accounts receivable.

Repurchase Agreements are devices used by securities dealers to help finance part of their multimillion-dollar inventories of marketable securities for one or more days. For instance, if a securities dealer ends a day of busy trading with an increase of $4 million in marketable securities in inventory but lacks the cash needed to pay for the additional securities, a buy-back may be sold to finance the $4 million of additional inventory overnight. In this case, at the same time that the cash-short securities dealer transacts to sell, he would also make an agreement to repurchase the $4 million worth of securities the next day at a slightly higher price. That slightly higher price would be the interest income for the overnight investor who purchased the buy-back. Alternatively, the securities dealers may sell and repurchase the securities inventory at the same price and simply make an explicit interest payment to the investor. This latter agreement is in fact the more common. In repurchase agreements the investor, normally a temporarily cash-rich corporation, is essentially making a very short-term loan to the securities dealer that employs part or all of the securities dealer's inventory as collateral for the loan.

Repurchase agreements lasting longer than overnight (or twenty-four hours) are not uncommon. These longer-term buy-backs can span thirty days, or even longer. Minimum denominations are $100,000.

Swapped deposits are short-term deposits made by Canadians in foreign banks or other financial institutions. The deposit is made in Canadian dollars and then converted to the foreign currency. The sponsoring Canadian domestic bank simultaneously agrees to reconvert the proceeds to Canadian dollars at a preset exchange rate at a specified future date. (The bank can offset its own foreign-currency risk exposure with the sale in the interbank forward market of an appropriate amount of foreign currency to match the amount and maturity of the deposit.) Canadian banks quote rates on swapped deposits. Bank swaps are typically of one- to six-month terms and are nontransferable.

The debt securities traded in money markets are all short-term securities that are largely free from the risk of default. If we expand our scope to include high-quality debt securities of all lengths of maturity, then Canadian government securities can be considered next.

2-2 CANADIAN GOVERNMENT SECURITIES

Since the Second World War, government securities have played an increasing role in the decisions of investors. At 1985 year-end, the total debt of the Canadian federal government was just under $200 billion. Almost every penny of this federal debt was interest-bearing debt; most of it in the form of Treasury bills, Canada Savings Bonds, and Canadian government marketable bonds. Demand for increased government services has also expanded the debt issues of provincial and municipal governments. These debt issues have been increasing not only in absolute amounts but also on a per capita basis. Government securities represent the amount of indebtedness of our governmental bodies. The owners of the securities are creditors; the government bodies are debtors.

A clear distinction should be drawn between the debts of the federal government and the debts of the provincial and municipal governments. In particular, the investor should be aware of the different levels of risk involved and the different features of each. Canadian federal government securities are discussed in this section. Provincial bonds are explained in Sec. 2-3.

Canadian government securities are of such high quality that their yield is often used as an example of a default-free interest rate. Indeed they are very safe, since the Canadian government has unlimited power to tax or to print money whenever such action becomes necessary to obtain the money to pay its bills.

2-2.1 Non-marketable Issues

Approximately 25 percent of the public debt consists of nonmarketable issues, namely Canada Savings Bonds (CSBs). First issued in 1946, there has been a new series each year (a total of forty-one series) numbered sequentially by year.

CSBs have interesting properties. They are nontransferable, hence there is no secondary market for CSBs. There is no penalty for cashing early before maturity (unless the holder cashes before December 31 of the year of purchase, in which case no interest is paid); any CSB can be cashed by the holder upon demand at any chartered bank at face value plus accrued interest. Thus, the holder has a put option (the right to sell) on the government that can be exercised at any time. CSBs can also be used as collateral for a loan, and, since the CSB is virtually a default-free instrument, such loans generally are made on terms favourable to the borrower.

Purchase of CSBs is currently limited to individuals, estates of deceased persons, trusts of deferred savings plans, and self-administered Registered Retirement Savings Plans. Canada Savings Bonds are sold each fall for issue on November 1 of the same year. CSBs issued in the early 1970s had terms (number of years to maturity) of twelve years. The 1975 through 1977 series had nine-year maturities; all issues since then have seven-year terms. The bonds are issued in two forms: regular interest bonds that pay the holder annual interest each November 1, and compound interest bonds for which the interest simply accrues to maturity. These compound interest bonds have characteristics similar to zero coupon or stripped bonds (described in Sec. 2-2.4).

The interest rate offered on each series reflects the prevailing level of interest rates at the time of issue; however, some of the series have special features. The government responded to the rising interest rates of the 1970s and early 1980s with a set of retroactive, cash bonus payments at maturity applied to previous CSB series up to series 31 (1976–1977), thus increasing the actual return for persons who held their bonds to maturity and thus forestalling substantial liquidations of CSBs. In some years a floor value return was designated for the issue. The 1982 series, for example, had a 12 percent rate of interest and a guaranteed minimum rate of 8½ percent.

2-2.2 Marketable Issues

Marketable issues make up 75 percent of the federal debt. Marketable bonds, as the name implies, can be traded in the secondary bond market prior to maturity. They bear a stated rate of interest (the coupon rate) and have a specific maturity date. Maturities at the issue date range from one to forty years.

These marketable bonds, normally called Government of Canada bonds, can be purchased from and sold to securities dealers that maintain inventories of such bonds. However, the purchaser can subscribe for new issues directly from the underwriter or underwriting syndicate. The holder of marketable government securities stands to gain not only from the interest paid on these bonds, like the owner of nonmarketable bonds, but also from possible price appreciation (higher selling price than purchase price), unlike the owner of nonmarketable bonds. Quotes for Government of Canada bonds are published in the financial press (e.g., *The Globe and Mail Report on Business* published daily, and *The Financial Post* published weekly). Prices are quoted in dollars and cents per $100 par value. For example, 98.88 means $98.88 market price per $100 par value, or more appropriately $988.80 per $1,000 par value (since minimum denominations are normally $1,000). Chapter 11 explains in detail how the yield on these marketable issues is calculated. For now, however, potential investors should become aware of the types and maturities of the various issues that are available.

Treasury bills are liquid, short-term notes that mature in 91 days, 182 days, and one year of issue. The Bank of Canada offers new 91- and 182-day bills every week, at a Thursday auction, selling them on a discount from face-value basis. One-year Treasury bills are sold at auctions every four weeks. T-bills are issued in bearer form in denominations of $1,000, $5,000, $25,000, $100,000, and $1,000,000.

T-bills are never sold at a premium over their face value—only at a discount. The discount to investors is the difference between the price that they have paid and the face amount that they will receive at maturity. For example, a $10,000 Treasury bill maturing in ninety-one days could be purchased for $9,750 if it were to yield 10.67 percent at an annual rate (or 2.56 percent = .0256 = $250/$9,750 on a 91-day basis).[3]

Bonds' One-Period Rates of Return   From the investor's point of view the most important outcome from an investment is the rate of income. The bond investor's one-period rate of return (or holding period return) is an important consideration to investors. Regardless of whether the period over which a bond's rate of return is calculated is a day, a week, a month, a quarter, a year, or five years, the definition of its one-period rate of return is given in Eq. (2-1a) below.

$$r_t = \frac{p_{t+1} - p_t + i_t}{p_t}$$

(2-1a)

The symbol r_t denotes the one-period rate of return in the *t*th period. The *t*th period can be whatever period you are interested in—this year, next week, or last quarter. The p_{t+1} and p_t terms are dollar quantities defined as the market price of the bond at the beginning of period $t + 1$ and period t, respectively. The i_t is the dollar amount of interest paid on the bond in period t. A numerical example should clarify all this.

If a bond sells at $995 on January 1 of some year and it sold at $950 on January 1 of the preceding year, then p_{t+1} = $995. If this hypothetical bond paid $50 interest per year, then its 1-year rate of return is 10 percent, as shown in Eq. (2-1b).

$$10.0\% = .1 = \frac{\$95}{\$950} = \frac{\$995 - \$950 + \$50}{\$950}$$

(2-1b)

3 The 91-day rate of 2.56 percent, or simply .0256, is annualized as follows:
$(1.0+qr)^4 = (1.0+ar)$
$\qquad = (1.0256)^{365/91} = 1.1067071$
where qr denotes the 91-day rate and ar denotes the annual rate of interest. Subtracting 1 from both sides of the equation results in: .1067071 = 10.67071 percent or approximately 10.67 percent per year. Then at the end of ninety-one days the buyer would be repaid $10,000 by the Bank of Canada. The $250 gain is the interest income for thirteen weeks; it equals the discount from the bond's face value when the bond was first sold.

If the bond's market price had fallen to $852.50 instead of rising to $995, the year's return would have been a negative 5 percent.

$$-5.0\% = -.05 = \frac{-47.50}{\$950} = \frac{\$852.50 - \$950 + \$50}{\$950} \tag{2-1c}$$

Equation (2-1a) is the one-period rate-of-return definition for a bond—this is also called the bond's holding period return.

Some people refer to a bond's one-period rate of return as its one-period yield. However, this language seems inadvisable because it could get confused with a bond's yield to maturity—a different concept that will be discussed later in Chapter 11.

**2-2.3
Stripped
Government
Bonds**

Stripped bonds are repackaged bonds. A brokerage firm or financial institution buys a large quantity of a particular issue of government bonds and then splits the bonds into two parts: the coupons or interest payments and the face or maturity value. The strips or coupons are then sold to investors seeking a semi-annual stream of interest payments; the remainder — the stripped bond is then sold separately. The investor who buys a stripped bond thus pays for an instrument that provides no return until maturity but which then provides the face value. Stripped bonds sell at large discounts to their maturity value to provide a suitable yield to the investor as the alternative to income receipts. Colourful acronyms are normally attached to these bonds, such as Merrill Lynch Canada Ltd's TIGRS and Guaranty Trust's COUGARS.

The various brokerage firms or institutions that originate their own stripped bonds usually promise their investors that they will create and maintain secondary markets where the certificates can be sold to another investor prior to maturity; this adds to the liquidity of the bonds. Nevertheless, since these repackaged investments are relatively new (started in 1982), there is no guarantee that a buyer will indeed surface if the holder wants to sell before maturity.

There is a disadvantage associated with investment in stripped bonds; taxable investors must pay income taxes on the implicit coupon interest every three years—even though they do not receive it. Stripped bonds, therefore, cannot be used to delay income tax payments—only the income that is being taxed is postponed. As a result, these interesting investments are normally suitable either for nontaxable investors or for investor self-administered Registered Retirement Savings Plans (RRSPs) where no tax is paid until the trust itself is matured.

**2-2.4
Price
Quotations
in
Newspapers**

Figure 2-1 shows an example of how government bond quotes appear in the financial press. In the case of every government bond listed, the first item beside the name Canada is the coupon rate. For the outlined entry this item is 12 or 12%; this bond will pay $120 in interest per year (actually $60 semi-annually) for every $1,000 of face value. Next in line is the maturity date, which for our example, is February 1, 1990, or just under four years from the date of these quotations. The *Bid* (third column from the right) represents the highest price that dealers were willing to pay at that date. For the Feb 1, 1990, bond this was 105.625, i.e., $105.625 per $100 par value or $1056.25 per

FIGURE 2-1   Bond price quotations.

Government bonds
As supplied by Wood Gundy

Canada and Canada guaranteed	Bid	Ask	Yield on bid
Feb 06, 1986			
Canada 10½ Mar 6 86	99.900	100.000	11.89%
Canada 10 Mar 15 86	99.800	99.900	12.14%
Canada 13 Jun 6 86	100.500	100.700	11.26%
Canada 12¼ Sep 5 86	100.600	100.800	11.10%
Canada 10 Dec 15 86	99.550	100.050	10.55%
Canada 15 Mar 15 87	104.350	104.550	10.65%
Canada 12¼ May 1 87	101.900	102.100	10.53%
Canada 14¾ Jun 1 87	104.750	104.950	10.72%
Canada 13 Jun 1 87	102.800	103.000	10.62%
Canada 10 Jun 6 87	99.500	99.700	10.40%
Canada 13½ Sep 1 87	104.000	104.200	10.63%
Canada 13 Oct 15 87	103.850	104.050	10.42%
Canada 12 Nov 15 87	102.400	102.600	10.46%
Canada 11 Dec 15 87	101.000	101.200	10.38%
Canada 10¼ Feb 1 88	99.500	100.150	10.30%
Canada 11¾ Feb 1 88	102.350	102.550	10.42%
Canada 10½ Mar 15 88	100.400	100.600	10.28%
Canada 10¾ Oct 15 88	101.050	101.250	10.28%
Canada 10 Nov 15 88	99.450	99.650	10.23%
Canada 9¾ Dec 15 88	98.950	99.150	10.18%
Canada 11 Feb 15 89	102.000	102.250	10.21%
Canada 12½ Mar 15 89	105.750	106.000	10.27%
Canada 9¼ Apr 15 89	97.500	98.000	10.19%
Canada 13¼ Jun 1 89	107.750	108.250	10.40%
Canada 13½ Jul 1 89	108.500	109.000	10.45%
Canada 13¾ Aug 1 89	109.250	109.750	10.51%
Canada 10 Oct 1 89	99.500	99.750	10.16%
Canada 10½ Oct 1 89	100.875	101.125	10.20%
Canada 12¼ Nov 1 89	105.750	106.000	10.34%
Canada 10¾ Nov 1 89	101.750	101.875	10.21%
Canada 11¼ Dec 15 89	103.250	103.500	10.20%
→ Canada 12 Feb 1 90	105.625	105.875	10.25%
Canada 13¼ Feb 1 90	109.250	109.500	10.36%
Canada 13¾ Mar 15 90	111.000	111.500	10.37%
Canada 13 May 1 90	109.000	109.250	10.31%
Canada 11¾ Jun 1 90	104.750	105.250	10.34%
Canada 10¾ Sep 1 90	102.125	102.375	10.15%
Canada 10½ Oct 1 90	101.375	101.625	10.11%
Canada 10¼ Dec 15 90	100.500	100.750	10.11%
Canada 12½ Feb 1 91	108.250	108.750	10.34%
Canada 9¼ 1 Mar. 91	97.125	97.375	9.99%
Canada 9¾ 1 May 91	98.875	99.125	10.03%
Canada 14½ May 1 91	116.125	116.625	10.41%
Canada 11 Jun 1 91	103.250	103.750	10.18%
Canada 18 Oct 1 91	130.625	131.125	10.62%
Canada 11½ Dec 15 91	105.250	105.750	10.28%
Canada 13½ Oct 15 92	114.500	115.000	10.42%
Canada 15½ Feb 1 92	121.875	122.375	10.48%
Canada 10¼ Jun 1 92	100.625	100.875	10.11%
Canada 15 Jun 1 92	119.625	120.125	10.64%
Canada 15 Jul 1 92	120.875	121.375	10.44%
Canada 14¼ Sep 1 92	117.875	118.375	10.41%
Canada 12¾ Nov 15 92	111.500	112.000	10.34%
Canada 11¾ Dec 15 92	107.375	107.625	10.22%
Canada 11¼ Feb 1 93	105.125	105.375	10.21%
Canada 10¾ May 1 93	103.000	103.250	10.15%
Canada 15¼ Jun 1 93	123.375	123.875	10.57%
Canada 14¾ Jul 1 93	121.250	121.750	10.54%
Canada 11¾ Oct 15 93	107.625	107.875	10.28%
Canada 11½ Dec 15 93	106.500	106.750	10.27%
Canada 12 Mar 1 94	108.750	109.000	10.37%
Canada 13 Apr 1 94	113.750	114.000	10.44%
Canada 13¾ May 15 94	117.625	117.875	10.50%
Canada 9½ Jun 15 94	96.875	97.125	10.06%
Canada 13½ Jul 15 94	116.500	117.000	10.50%
Canada 12¾ Oct 1 94	112.875	113.125	10.44%
Canada 12½ Dec 15 94	111.750	112.000	10.43%
Canada 11½ Feb 1 95	106.625	106.875	10.35%
Canada 12¼ Feb 1 95	110.500	110.750	10.42%
Canada 11¾ Mar 1 95	107.875	108.125	10.38%
Canada 10½ Jun 1 95	101.750	102.000	10.20%
Canada 11¼ Apr 1 95	105.375	105.625	10.32%
Canada 10 Oct 1 95	99.125	99.375	10.14%
Canada 10¼ 1 Mar 96	100.375	100.625	10.19%
Canada 9¼ May 15 97	94.000	94.500	10.16%
Canada 10¾ Dec 15 95	103.125	103.375	10.24%
Canada 9 Oct 15 99	91.375	91.875	10.18%
Canada 13½ Dec 1 99	119.500	120.000	10.75%
Canada 13¼ Mar 15 00	121.375	121.875	10.77%
Canada 15 Jul 1 00	129.375	129.875	10.91%
Canada 9¼ Dec 15 00	95.750	96.250	10.31%

Canada and Canada guaranteed	Bid	Ask	Yield on bid
Canada 15¾ Feb 1 01	135.250	135.750	10.92%
Canada 13 May 1 01	116.750	117.250	10.74%
Canada 9½ Oct 1 01	96.000	96.250	10.01%
Canada 8¼ Feb 1 02	90.000	90.500	10.02%
Canada 15½ Mar 15 02	134.375	134.875	10.92%
Canada 10 May 1 02	97.000	97.250	10.38%
Canada 11¼ Dec 15 02	105.250	105.500	10.57%
Canada 11¾ Feb 1 03	109.000	109.250	10.60%
Canada 9½ Jun 1 03	93.500	94.000	10.30%
Canada 10¼ Feb 1 04	100.000	100.250	10.25%
Canada 13½ Jun 1 04	121.500	122.000	10.78%
Canada 10½ Oct 1 04	100.500	101.000	10.44%
Canada 12 Mar 1 05	110.375	110.625	10.71%
Canada 12¼ Sep 1 05	111.375	111.625	10.84%
Canada 12½ Mar 1 06	114.375	114.625	10.74%
Canada 14 Oct 1 06	125.875	126.375	10.83%
Canada 13¾ Mar 1 07	124.125	124.625	10.82%
Canada 13 Oct 1 07	118.125	118.625	10.81%
Canada 12¾ Mar 1 08	116.375	116.875	10.79%
Canada 10 1 Jun 08	97.000	96.250	10.34%
Canada 11¾ Oct 1 08	109.000	109.250	10.68%
Canada 11½ Mar 1 09	107.125	107.625	10.66%
anada 10¾ Oct 1 09	102.000	102.250	10.52%
Canada 11 Jun 1 09	103.750	104.000	10.56%

Source: The Financial Post, February 15, 1986.

$1,000 bond. The *Ask* is the lowest selling price or $105.875 in our example. The *Yield* on *Bid* is the annual yield to maturity or 10.25 percent. (You will see in Chapter 11 that there are some crucial assumptions underlying this calculation.)

2-3   PROVINCIAL SECURITIES

All ten Canadian provinces issue bonds, and many provinces guarantee the bonds issued by provincial authorities and commissions and by municipal authorities. These instruments are priced and traded like federal government bonds, and a wide variety of coupon rates and maturities are available at any time in the secondary market.

Provincial bonds are issued monthly in minimum denominations of $500 in both bearer and registered form with interest paid semi-annually, typically on the fifteenth of the month.

Occasionally the provinces will issue T-bills or promissory notes with similar characteristics to those issued by the federal government. Issues are made on either a competitive tender basis or a tap (negotiated) basis.

2-4   MUNICIPAL SECURITIES

Municipal bonds are, by convention, called debentures and are issued by numerous Canadian municipalities. Municipal issues commonly are serial bonds or instalment debentures in which a portion of the bond matures each year according to a predetermined schedule. A $5 million issue to finance, for example, a new sanitary system (the benefits of which will extend long into the future) might be designed such that 10 percent of the issue matures each year making this serial issue effectively an issue of 10 one-year bonds. The societal benefits of the public project are thus at least partially matched to the financing and taxpayer "costs." Long-term municipal issues become money market instruments when their term to maturity is reduced to less than three years.

2-4.1   The Hierarchy of Government Bond Yields

In general, federal government bonds have the highest credit rating and the lowest yields followed by provincial and then municipal ones. However, on occasions the yields on some municipal issues, such as those of the City of Toronto or Montreal, have been lower than certain provincial issues, such as those of the Province of Newfoundland.

TABLE 2-2   THE TIERING OF CANADIAN GOVERNMENT BOND YIELDS

Issuer	Coupon	Maturity	Yield to maturity (Based on bid price)
Government of Canada	11¾%	Oct. 1993	9.73%
Ontario Hydro	12	Sept. 1993	10.10
Metro Toronto	11¾	Apr. 1993	10.19
New Brunswick Electric	11¾	Feb. 1993	10.23
Nova Scotia	12	Nov. 1993	10.25

At year end 1985, government bonds of similar maturity and coupon were quoted as shown in Table 2-2.

2-5 BONDS ISSUED BY CORPORATIONS

Essentially, a bond is what is commonly called an "I owe you" (or, more simply, an IOU). More particularly, a bond is a marketable, legal contract that promises to pay whoever owns it a stated rate of interest for a defined period and then to repay the principal at the specific date of maturity. Bonds differ according to their terms concerning provisions for repayment, security pledged, and other technical aspects. They represent the formal legal evidence of debt and are the senior securities of the firm.

2-5.1 The Indenture Contract

The *indenture,* or deed of trust, is the legal agreement between the corporation and the bondholders. Each bond is part of a group of bonds issued under one indenture. Thus, they all have the same rights and protection from the issuing company. Sometimes, however, bonds of the same issue may mature at different dates and have correspondingly different interest rates.

The indenture is a long, complicated legal instrument containing the restrictions, pledges, and promises of the contract. The trustee, usually a division of a trust company, ensures that the issuing firm keeps its promises and obeys the restrictions of the contract; the trustee also takes any appropriate legal action to see that the terms of the contract are kept and that the rights of the bondholders are upheld. Because the individual bondholders are usually not in a position to make sure that the company does not violate its agreements and because the bondholders cannot take substantial legal action if the firm does violate them, the trustee assumes these responsibilities. The trustee does the "watchdog" job for all the bondholders.

2-5.2 General Features of Corporate Bonds

Trustee The *trustee* is a third party to the contract between the issuer and the investor. It is the trustee's job to make sure that the corporate issuer lives up to the provisions contained in the indenture contract. The responsibilities and powers of the trustee are set out in the Canada Business Corporations Act, sections 77–88.

Bond Interest Bond interest is usually paid semiannually, although annual payments are also used. The method of payment depends upon whether the bond is a registered or coupon bond. The interest on *registered bonds* is paid to the holder by cheque. Therefore, the holders must be registered with the trustee of the bond issue to ensure proper payment. Registered bonds can be transferred only by registering the name of the new owner with the trustee and cancelling the name of the previous owner. In contrast, *coupon bonds* have a series of attached coupons that are clipped off at the appropriate times and sent to a bank for collection of the interest.

If the coupon interest is paid to whoever may happen to be the bearer of the bond without checking to see who is its registered owner, the bonds are called *bearer bonds.* The ownership of bearer bonds may be transferred simply by physically handing them over to the new owner. The ease of transfer enjoyed by bearer bonds increases the danger of loss to their owner—anyone who picks up a bearer bond is its legal owner and no registration records exist to verify the true owner's identity.

Coupon Rate   The coupon rate is the interest paid on the face value of a corporate or a Canadian government bond. It is one fixed dollar amount that is paid annually as long as the debtor is solvent. (Corporations' income bonds or adjustment bonds are the only exceptions.) The coupon rate is decided upon after the issuing corporation's underwriter has considered risk of default, the credit standing of the company, the convertible options, the investment position of the industry, the security backing of the bond, and the market rate of interest for the firm's industry, size, and risk class. After all these factors have been taken into account, a coupon rate is set with the objective that it will be just high enough to attract investors to pay the face value of the bond. Later, the market price of the bond may deviate from its face value as market interest rates change, while the contractual coupon rate remains fixed.

Generally, the higher the *yield* (or effective rate of return, as it is also called), the riskier the security.[4] Yield rather than coupon rate is more significant in buying bonds. If the bond is selling at a *discount*, its market price is below its face value. In this case, the yield is higher than the coupon rate. If it is selling at a *premium*, the market price of the bond is above its face value. In this case, the coupon rate is higher than the yield. In buying bonds, the investor should be aware of possible capital gains or losses resulting from changes in the market price of a bond, since this is as important as the interest income in calculating yield. Chapter 11 explains how to calculate bond yields.

Maturities   Maturities vary widely. The actual term to maturity of a new bond issue changes after the bond is issued because as long-term bonds approach their maturity dates, they become medium-term and then short-term bonds. Nevertheless, a bond is usually grouped by its maturity that existed on the date the bond was newly issued. *Short-term bonds* are any bonds maturing within three years. They are common in industrial financing and may be secured or unsecured. *Medium-term bonds* mature in three to about ten years. If a bond is originally issued as a medium-term bond, it is usually secured by a real estate or equipment mortgage, or it may be backed by other security. *Long-term bonds* may run ten years or more. Capital-intensive industries with long expectations of equipment life, such as railroads and utilities, are the greatest users of this form of bond financing.[5]

Call Provision   A call provision may be included in the indenture. This provision allows the debtor to call or redeem the bonds at a specified amount (above par) before maturity date. The difference between the par value of

---

4 The term *yield* is used synonymously with *yield to maturity* or *average rate of return compounded annually to maturity*. These terms refer to the effective rate of return to the owner if the bond is held to maturity. Bonds' yields to maturity are discussed in detail in Chap. 11.

5 For an analysis of the structure of corporate debt maturities see J. B. Silvers, ''Liquidity, Risk and Duration Patterns in Corporate Financing,'' *Financial Management*, Autumn 1976, vol. 5, no. 3, pp. 54–64.

the bond and the higher call price is called the *call premium*. The call provision is advantageous to the issuing firm but potentially harmful to the investor. If interest rates should decline, it may be wise for the firm to call in its bonds and issue new ones at the lower market interest rate. This action, however, leaves investors with funds they can invest only at the lower interest rate. To compensate for the undesirable callable feature, a new issue of callable bonds will sell at a higher interest rate than a comparable issue of noncallable bonds.

Sinking Fund   Sinking fund bonds are not special types of bonds but just a name given to describe the method of repayment. Thus, any bond can be a sinking fund bond if it is specified as such in the indenture. Sinking fund bonds arise when the company decides to retire its bond issue systematically by setting aside a certain amount each year for that purpose. The payment, usually a fixed annual dollar amount or a percentage instalment, is made to the sinking fund agent, who is usually the trustee. The agent then uses the money to call the bonds annually at some call premium, or to purchase them on the open market if they are selling at a discount.

Sinking fund bonds have been common in industrial financing that involves some risk because risky debt issues are more attractive to investors with a promise of faster payment. Where risk is lower (for example, in utilities), sinking fund bonds are less frequently used.[6]

Serial Maturities   Serial bonds are appropriate for issuers who wish to divide their bond issues into a series, each part of the series maturing at a different time. Ordinarily the bonds are not callable, and the bond issuer pays each part of the series as it matures. Municipalities issue serial bonds more frequently than do corporate bond issuers.

2-5.3 Secured Bonds

The most important classifying criterion of corporate bonds is whether they are secured or unsecured. That is, what security, if any, has been pledged to help pay investors if the company should be unable to live up to its obligations or should default?

If the indenture provides for a lien on a certain designated property, the bond is a secured bond. A lien is a legal right given to the bondholders, through the trustee, to sell the pledged property to obtain the amount of money necessary to satisfy the unpaid portion of interest or principal. Pledged security is used to make bonds more attractive to investors by making them safer investments. The reasoning is that if investors see the bonds as safer than similar nonsecured bonds, they will pay a higher price or accept

---

6 The potential investor in a sinking fund bond should investigate the provisions of the sinking fund's administration. Some bond issuers occasionally do not actually pass annual cash payments on to a third party who accumulates these monies safely in a sinking fund. Instead, only a bookkeeping entry may be made to indicate that some accounting category called "sinking fund" was credited—but no monies were actually set aside in a safe place to be cared for by a trustworthy third party. This latter type of sinking fund provides no protection for the investor.

a lower interest rate for them. In reality, the security is seldom sold in the case of default. The company is usually reorganized, with new securities issued for the defaulted bonds. The presence of a lien on the property has a very favourable influence on the treatment of the bondholders' interests in the reorganization, however.

Mortgage Bonds   A bond issue secured with a lien on real property or buildings is a mortgage bond. If all the assets of the firm are collateral under the terms of the indenture, it is called a *blanket mortgage*. The total assets need not be pledged, however; only some of the land or buildings of the company may be mortgaged for the issue. They can be first, second, or subsequent mortgages, each with its respective claim to the assets of the firm in case of default. A first mortgage is the most secure because it enjoys first claim to assets.

An *open-end mortgage* means that more bonds can be issued on the same mortgage contract. The creditors are usually protected by restrictions limiting such additional borrowing. The open-end mortgage will normally also contain an *after-acquired property* clause, which provides that all property acquired after the first mortgage was issued be added to the property already pledged as security by the contract. A *limited open-end mortgage* allows the firm to issue additional bonds up to a specified maximum (for example, up to 50 percent of the original cost of the pledged property). A *closed-end mortgage* means no additional borrowing can be done on that mortgage. This, with an after-acquired property clause, guarantees an increasing security base for the creditors. Investors should know the kind of mortgage they have and the provisions that are behind their mortgage bonds, since they determine the risk and return of the investment.

Collateral Trust Bonds   When the security deposited with the trustee of a bond issue consists of the stocks and bonds of other companies, these newly issued secured bonds are called *collateral trust bonds*. Since the assets of holding companies are usually largely in the form of stocks and bonds of their subsidiaries, holding companies are the main issuers of such bonds.

Collateral must, as a rule, be 25 to 33 percent greater than the value of the bonds in order to ensure adequate protection if liquidation is necessary. The borrower may remove this collateral and substitute other assets for it as long as the required margin of coverage is maintained. Such bonds are issued when the method is easier than issuing mortgage bonds or when the holding company wants to consolidate a number of smaller issues at a better market price. When mortgage bonds are further secured by a pledge of stocks and/ or bonds, the holder has a mortgage and collateral trust bond.

2-5.4 Unsecured Bonds

Debenture bonds, or more simply, *debentures*, are unsecured bonds. They are issued with no lien against specific property provided in the contract. They may be seen as a claim on earnings and not assets. This is not to say that the bondholders are not protected in case of default but, rather, that they are general creditors. All assets not specifically pledged or any balance remaining after payment of secured debts from assets previously pledged are available to pay the legal claims of general creditors. The debenture indentures usually take this added riskiness into account and contain specific protecting provisions. They may restrict any further issuing of debentures unless earnings over a certain number of years are two or three times what is needed to cover the original debenture interest. Another common clause says that if any secured debt is issued, the debentures will be secured by an equal amount. Sometimes working capital (that is, current assets minus current liabilities) must be maintained at a certain ratio to the principal amount of the debenture or the debtor is not allowed to pay dividends on its common stock.

Subordinated Debentures   Subordinated debentures are simply debentures that are specifically made subordinate to all other general creditors holding claims on assets. These other creditors are usually suppliers or financial institutions that have granted credit and loans to the firm. Many debentures, because they are unsecured, have in recent years been issued as convertible debentures. They then have all the characteristics of bonds, but under certain conditions they may be converted into a specified number of shares of common stock. This conversion privilege is a "sweetener" to make the unsecured debt more attractive. Convertible bonds will be discussed more thoroughly later in this chapter (in terms of the common stock into which they are convertible) and also in the appendix to Chapter 19 (where their conversion option is analyzed).

2-5.5   Bonds with Special Characteristics

Several types of bonds have general characteristics of bonds plus some special distinguishing characteristics. These types of bonds are given special names. For example, if a mortgage bond is secured so that it covers only part of the property of the firm or only a specific section of a railroad, it is called a *divisional bond*. It is the first mortgage on that operating division of the railroad or industrial firm. If the division is highly productive, the bonds will be strong; weak divisions will signify correspondingly weak bonds.

Direct Lien Bonds   These are special bonds secured by one piece of property such as a railroad terminal, dock, or bridge. Such a bond might then be referred to as a *terminal bond* or a *bridge bond*. If two or more companies own the property that is securing the bond, such as a railroad bridge, it is called a *joint bond*.

Prior Lien Bonds   These are bonds that have been placed ahead of the first mortgage, usually during the reorganization of a bankrupt firm. Only with the permission of the first mortgage bondholders can prior lien bonds be issued, taking priority over the first mortgage claim on assets.

Junior Mortgage Bonds   These bonds have a secondary claim to assets and earnings behind senior mortgage bonds. Because it is poor public relations for an issue to bear the title *second mortgage*, these issues typically have names such as *refunding mortgage, consolidated mortgage*, or *general mortgage*.

Assumed or Guaranteed Bonds   When a large firm takes over a small one in a merger or consolidation, the bonds of the small company must be recognized. If the small company is dissolved by the merger, the new entity assumes the liability represented by the bonds. These bonds are then covered not only by the specific property pledged in the indentures but also by the large firm's promise-to-pay clause.

If the merged company continues to operate as a unique division within the large company, its bonds will be guaranteed by the larger firm. Depending upon the willingness of the parent company to continue the guarantee through endorsement of the bonds, rental of its property, or some other legal agreement between the two companies, these bonds may be solid or very weak.

Income Bonds   These bonds share in the earnings of the firm up to a maximum rate of interest. If the bonds were issued prior to November 17, 1978, the "interest" payment is treated for tax purposes as a dividend receipt by the bondholder and a dividend payment by the issuer. If the bonds were issued after that date, the receipt and payment are treated as ordinary interest. Income bonds are rarely issued in Canada.

Stripped Bonds   Stripped bonds have had the coupon payments removed (and sold separately) and hence pay no interest prior to maturity. Instead, they are sold at large discounts from their face (or maturity) value so that the investor's price gain is the interest income. Thus, the investor has no worry about reinvesting coupon interest receipts, perhaps at disadvantageous interest rates, because there are none. The main disadvantage of these bonds is that Revenue Canada taxes the price gains "income" as if it were received in annual cash payments. The income taxes must be paid at least every third year, even though the stripped bonds produce no cash flow until maturity.

The zero coupon bond, popular in the United States and Europe, is an instrument with characteristics similar to the stripped bond. The only difference is that it is originally issued in a "stripped" state, that is, with no coupons. Like the stripped bond, it sells at a discount to mature at par value.

J. C. Penney was the first North American corporation to issue noninterest-paying bonds in 1981; then U.S. municipalities began to issue them in 1982. In Canada, stripped bonds became popular in 1983.

Retractable Bonds   These bonds have an early redemption option that allows the bond's investor to put (or sell) the bond back to the issuer before the bond's maturity date at a preset price (in option parlance, called the strike price), which is usually the par value. Investors benefit from this early redemption option because it essentially puts a floor under the bond's market price so that it cannot fall below the strike price as the redemption date approaches.[7] Typically such bonds are retractable three to five years before maturity.

---

7 Put options and the strike price of a put option are examined more deeply in Chapter 19. For a detailed description of fixed income option valuation see Robert W. Kopprash, "Contingent Take-Down Options on Fixed Income Securities", in Frank J. Fabozzi and I. M. Pollack (eds.), *The Handbook of Fixed Income Securities*, Homewood, Ill.: Dow Jones-Irwin, 1982. The put option component inherent in Canada Savings Bonds is discussed in Michael J. Brennan, "Canada Savings Bonds: Valuation and Redemptions," *Financial Research Foundation of Canada*, Proceedings of the Second Conference, April 17–18, 1979, pp. 27–29.

Extendible Bonds Extendible (or exchangeable) bonds allow the holder the right to exchange his bonds on a specific date for an identical amount of new debt at the same (or sometimes a higher) interest rate. For example, the Government of Canada 14.25 percent issue that matures September 1, 1987, contains an option to exchange the bonds on or before June 1, 1987, into an equal par value of 14.25 percent bonds due September 1, 1992.

2-6 MORTGAGE SECURITIES

The dictionary says that a mortgage is a "pledge of property to secure payment of a debt." There are two general categories of mortgages: commercial mortgages and home or residential mortgages. *Commercial mortgages* are usually bank loans that enable a growing business firm to buy more physical plant on credit. The new plant that is purchased becomes the collateral pledged against the commercial mortgage loan. In contrast, *home mortgages* are typically loans that a trust company makes to a family to buy a home on credit. Mortgages are like collateral bonds that have real estate pledged as collateral.

Billions of dollars of mortgage loans are made every year in Canada. Trust companies, chartered banks, life insurance companies, pension funds, and vendors originate most mortgage loans.

**2-6.1
Commercial
Mortgages
and
Conventional
Home
Mortgages**

Commercial mortgages are usually not bought and sold in active trading (or secondary) markets. The banks and other financial intermediaries that make these loans must hold them as long-term investments because active secondary markets in which to trade commercial mortgages do not exist. Most commercial mortgages are illiquid because they are usually of such a large denomination (namely, millions of dollars) that few investors are large enough to trade such securities easily. Furthermore, it is impossible for mortgage buyers to obtain credit insurance for commercial mortgages in order to protect themselves if the commercial borrower defaults on the mortgage payments.

Home mortgages are of much smaller denomination than commercial mortgages. They range in size from small mortgages of only a few thousand dollars up to million-dollar mortgage pools that are made up of numerous smaller individual mortgages.[8] No secondary market (i.e., a market for previously issued securities) for mortgages has developed in this country,

---

8 Mortgage-backed securities were first introduced in Canada by General Motors Corporation (GMC) Investors Corporation in August 1985 in the form of three- and five-year term investment certificates called Guaranteed Mortgage Certificates. Each certificate represents a percentage of a pool of mortgages packaged by the GMC Investors Corporation. The yield is preset for the term and principal and interest payments to certificate holders is guaranteed by Citibank Canada. All mortgages in the pool are CMHC (Canadian Mortgage and Housing Corporation) insured. The minimum investment is $10,000.

Although Guaranteed Mortgage Certificates are transferable and can be used as loan collateral, there is no secondary market for these securities at this time. GMC Investors Corporation will, however, buy back the certificates at any time after written notice within a maximum of 101 days at a price that reflects current mortgage rates, less an administrative fee.

despite the high level of home mortgage financing in Canada and despite numerous attempts to provide one, unlike the United States, where an active and liquid secondary market for insured residential mortgages exists. For some reason Canadian mortgage investors prefer to deal strictly in new mortgages.

The Canada Mortgage and Housing Corporation (CMHC) is a federal agency that, for a small fee, will guarantee home mortgages against default. Insurance is also available through private mortgage insurers, such as the Mortgage Insurance Corporation of Canada (MICC). That is, if a home buyer cannot or does not pay off an insured mortgage, the insuring agency will pay off the mortgage so that the mortgage investor is protected against large losses. The insuring agency must then foreclose on the defaulted mortgage and sell the home that was used as collateral in order to regain its investment.

Nearly all home and commercial mortgages are interest-bearing instalment loan contracts that fully amortize themselves, normally within twenty-five to thirty-five years.[9] The business or family that obtained the mortgage loan typically repays it in equal-sized monthly payments that extend over the life of the mortgage contract. If the real estate that the mortgage financed is sold before all the mortgage is paid off, then the portion of the mortgage still outstanding on the sale date must be paid off with the proceeds from the sale—this is called *prepaying* a mortgage. However, until the date it is all paid off, the mortgage remains a marketable debt security that may be sold to a new investor (unless the mortgage contract explicitly forbids the mortgage lender to sell the mortgage—a rare clause in mortgage contracts).[10]

2-6.2 Insured Home Mortgages

2-7 COMMON STOCK

Common stock is the first security of a corporation to be issued and the last to be retired. Common stock represents a share in the ownership of the firm. It has the last claim on earnings and assets of all other securities issued. But, it also has an unlimited potential for dividend payment through increasing earnings and for capital gains through rising prices. All other corporate securities (namely, corporate bonds and preferred stock) have a contract for interest or dividend payment not afforded to common stock. If the firm should fail, common stockholders get what is left after everyone else has been repaid. The chance of a common stockholder recovering anything from a bankrupt firm is highly unlikely. As shown in Table 2-1, the investor's risk is higher with common stock than with any other category of security. As a result of this risk, investors refuse to invest in common stocks unless those stocks

9 Mathematical formulas to determine the instalment payments necessary to amortize a loan with any given principal, interest rate, and term to maturity are shown and explained in various books. See chap. 18 app. B of *The Handbook of Fixed Income Securities*. The formulas for pass-through mortgage securities are explained there. Computer programs for home computers may also be purchased to calculate mortgage repayment schedules for any given interest rate and term to maturity.
10 Chaps. 17, 18, and 19 in *The Handbook of Fixed Income Securities*, discuss mortgage investing in more detail.

offer a rate of return sufficiently high to induce them to assume the possible losses that may result from the high risk.

When investors buy common stock, they typically receive certificates of ownership as proof of their part as owners of the firm. The certificate states the number of shares purchased, their par value, if any, and usually the transfer agent. When stock is purchased on the market (that is, when it is not a new issue purchased from the company), the new owner and the number of shares bought are noted in the stock record book of the transfer agent. The former shareholder's certificate is cancelled and the new certificate sent to the registrar, which is usually the same bank or trust company. The registrar checks to verify that no errors were made. When all checks are completed, the certificate is sent to the new shareholder.

2-7.1 Common Stockholders' Voting Rights

Common stock is usually voting stock.[11] The power to vote for the board of directors and for or against major issues belongs to common stockholders because they are the owners of the corporation. Most stockholders are not very much interested in the voting power they possess and will sign and return the proxies that are mailed to them by the company. A *proxy* allows a named person, usually part of the management, to vote the shares of the proxy signer at the stockholders' meeting. The use of proxies usually allows management, which normally by itself does not control enough votes to run the company, to be able to vote its decisions into effect.

A few corporate charters allow for *cumulative voting,* which permits a stockholder to have as many votes as he or she has shares of stock times the number of directors being elected. The stock owner may cast all these cumulative votes for only one director or divide them among several. This provision allows for stockholders with a significant minority of shares to gain representation on the board of directors. In most cases, however, voting is noncumulative and the majority of shareholders can elect the entire board (if they act together), regardless of how the minority votes. As mentioned before, small and large institutional stockholders are usually not interested in voting or will vote with management. However, in some unusual instances stockholders have banded together to oppose management. In 1970, for example, several groups of General Motors stockholders, including some large institutions, chose to vote against management on its air pollution proposal in favour of stronger measures. This disenchanted minority of shareholders came to the annual stockholders' meeting, moved and seconded an environmental protection motion that cost GM millions of dollars, and the motion was discussed and voted on by all shareholders who were present at the meeting. If the minority had not been allowed to have their costly

---

11 Some Canadian companies have issued two classes of common shares, voting and nonvoting. The two classes typically share equally in distributions and thus differ only by the voting privileges. As a result, the nonvoting common stock usually sells at a discount, sometimes quite substantial, to the voting shares. For example, on December 19, 1986, Canadian Tire Corporation Limited voting common shares were selling for $64.50 while the nonvoting shares were trading at $13.50, reflecting a takeover offer directed at the voting shares only. See sec. 2-7.4.

environmental proposal implemented as they desired, they could have used their cumulative voting power to fire a few people from the board of directors and elect environmentalists in their place. This threat enabled the minority interest to garner support for its motion by some shareholders who might not have supported it otherwise.

The *pre-emptive right* allows existing stockholders the right to subscribe to any new issue of stock so that they can maintain their previous fraction of total outstanding shares. In British Columbia, the preemptive right is a part of every corporate charter; in other provinces, its inclusion as part of the charter is optional. The reasoning behind the preemptive right is the recognition that stockholders are part owners of corporations and as such should have an interest in earnings and assets and a voice in management proportionate to the fraction of voting shares they own. The preemptive right, if exercised, prevents dilution of ownership control inherent in additional stock issues.[12] For example, if Charles Bronfman owned 30 percent of the Seagram Company Limited and the Seagram Company floats a stock issue that doubles the number of shares outstanding, Mr. Bronfman's share of ownership and control diminishes to 15 percent unless he has the preemptive right (and either the cash or the borrowing power) that allows him to buy 30 percent of the new issue. The preemptive right, then, if exercised, guarantees the undiluted maintenance of voting control, share in earnings, and share in assets.[13]

2-7.2 Pre-emptive Right

Par value is the face value of a share of stock. It was originally used to guarantee that the corporation receive a fair price for the value of the firm represented by a share of stock. The idea was to guarantee that the creditors' principal would be protected; however, in practice the concept did not work well. "Watered stock" was issued on many occasions; that is, stock was sold for less than its par value. Today most companies set no par value on their stock. As of 1975, the Canada Business Corporations Act expressly forbids the issue at par value of nominal value shares for federally incorporated companies.[14]

Investors must realize that the par value of the stock has very little to do with the value of their shares. They should be interested in the value of their stock as determined by earnings and capital gains and not by any value set as the par value of the stock.

The same misplaced concern is placed on *book value*. Book value per share can be calculated by adding the common stock and surplus accounts of the

2-7.3 Par Value

12 See R. J. Hay, ''The Shareholder's Pre-Emptive Right: Prevention of Director Abuse in New Share Issuance,'' *Canadian Business Law Journal*, vol. 9, no. 1, May 1984, pp. 2–43.

13 Occasionally a pre-emptive rights offering can be oversubscribed—that is, the existing shareholders submit pre-emptive bids for more than the underwriter had initially planned to offer. The so-called Green Shoe option, adapted from the United States, can be invoked to cover this problem. The Green Shoe option comes from an underwriting in the 1950s for a U.S. issue of stock in the Green Shoe Manufacturing Company. This option provides the underwriter the opportunity to buy more shares than initially planned from the issuer in the event that an oversubscription occurs.

14 Canada Business Corporations Act, s.24(1).

TABLE 2-3   COMPARISON OF 1984 PAR, BOOK, AND MARKET VALUES FOR SHARES OF RANDOMLY SELECTED CORPORATIONS

CORPORATION	PAR $	COMMON EQUITY (000),$	NUMBER OF COMMON SHARES OUTSTANDING (000)	BOOK VALUE PER SHARE, $	RANGE OF MARKET PRICE, $
Bank of Montreal	2	2,620,666	70,497	37.17	21–28
Guarantee Company Of North America	5	55,861	187	298.72	525–550
MacMillan Bloedel	NPV	987,500	29,063	33.98	22.75–35.50
Velcro Industries	1	38,906	3,762	10.34	47–57.75

Source: The Financial Post Survey of Industrials, 1985.

balance sheet and then dividing by the number of shares of common stock. Book value does give an indication of the assets of the corporation, but it has no real effect on stock prices. During the Depression of the early 1930s and again during the depressed stock markets of the 1970s, many companies had high book values but found that their stock was selling far below book value. Book and market values will probably be equal when the stock is issued, but after that, it appears that only coincidence will keep them equal at any given moment. Table 2-3 shows how book value and par value compare with the actual market price of the stock for a few randomly selected corporations. The variations in the three values for each corporation are wide.

2-7.4 Restricted Common Shares

Restricted shares have become more and more prevalent in Canada in recent years. These shares provide the holder with full participation in the earnings and assets of the company but have no (nonvoting shares) or limited voting rights (subordinated voting and restricted voting shares.)

Provision for the issuance of such shares is found in the Canada Business Corporations Act, s.24(4). Restricted common shares are treated as a separate class of shares and, as a result, holders may find that they are not entitled to participate in offers made in a takeover bid since the offer may not extend to the restricted shares. Some companies have terms in their by-laws extending all benefits of a takeover bid to the restricted shares. Restricted shares are identified in the financial press quotations with an "f" designation beside the company name.

Jog and Riding in a study of thirty-three Canadian firms, (carefully culled from an original sample of 130 firms) with dual classes of common shares, found that there were major perceived differences between regular (superior-voting common shares) and restricted-voting common shares and that Canadian investors were likely to avoid holding restricted-voting common shares, thus raising some interesting, relative valuation issues.[15] Robinson and White, and White, Robinson, and Chandra explored the relative valuation of voting and restricted common shares issued by the same company. They

---

15 Vijay M. Jog and Allan L. Riding, "Price Effects of Dual-Class Shares," *Financial Analysts Journal*, January–February, 1986, pp. 58–67.

found that the value of voting may derive from the ability of controlling share-holders to expropriate the wealth of other shareholders.[16]

Occasionally an investor encounters classified common shares. Some companies issue two, sometimes three different classes of common shares, distinguished by different dividend entitlements. A company may, for example, have Class A shares that allow the holder to receive cash dividends and class B shares that provide stock dividends. Otherwise, the two classes have identical provisions. The decision to hold either A or B shares may be entirely tax-motivated. (This is explored more fully in Chapter 5.) Classified shares are often interconvertible, allowing the holder to shift from class to class if his or her tax position changes. Marshall Drummond McCall Inc., traded on the Toronto Stock Exchange, has two classes of common shares: series A, which pays a quarterly cash dividend of 50¢/share (as of 1986), and series B, which pays an identical quarterly stock dividend. The two series often trade at slightly different prices, reflecting their particular appeal to different investors.

2-7.5 Classified Common Shares

According to their investment goals, some stockholders may be very much concerned about dividends. There is no rule regarding the size or regularity of dividends. Generally, however, rapidly growing corporations pay little or no dividends in order to retain as much capital as possible for internal financing. Established firms tend to pay out a larger portion of their earnings in dividends.

2-7.6 Cash Dividends

Some companies, for example, public utilities like Bell Canada Enterprises, take pride in their regular, substantial dividend policies. In contrast, other firms, such as Abermin Corporation, have no cash dividend payouts. At one time it was thought desirable to pay dividends and maintain some kind of stable policy toward them. Now most companies determine dividends according to the need of financing and investor expectation about growth. Dividends may or may not be important to the investor. If investors prefer regular income from large cash dividends, they will buy dividend-paying stock. If they are more concerned about making a capital gain, they will look at the growth prospects of the company and prefer a firm that retains its earnings rather than pay cash dividends.

Continuing the convention that p_t refers to the market price per security at the beginning of period t, the one-period rate of return from an equity share is defined in Eq. (2-2a).

2-7.7 Common Stocks' One-Period Rate of Return

$$r_t = \frac{p_{t+1} - p_t + d_t}{p_t} \qquad (2\text{-}2a)$$

16 Chris Robinson and Alan White, ''Ownership Structure and the Value of a Vote,'' working paper, Faculty of Administrative Studies, York University; Alan White, Chris Robinson, and Gyan Chandra, *The Value of Voting Rights and Restricted Common Shares*, Administrative Sciences Association of Canada 1985 Proceedings, vol. 1, Finance Division, pp. 1–9.

The d_t term in Eq. (2-2a) represents the cash dividends per share paid to shareholders of record during period t. Conceptually, p_t is the stock's purchase price if it had been bought at the beginning of the tth period and the quantity $p_{t+1} - p_t$ is called the capital gain or loss, depending on whether the stock appreciated or depreciated during the "period."[17] Calculating a stock's returns is more difficult if the corporation has split its shares or paid stock dividends.

2-7.8 Stock Dividends

Stock dividends are paid in shares of the issuing company's stock. When a stock dividend is paid, the stock account is increased and the capital surplus account is decreased. Except for these accounting entries, stock dividends and stock splits are identical. For this reason, the Toronto Stock Exchange has adopted a rule calling all distributions of stock under 25 percent per share *dividends* and distributions over 25 percent *splits*, even if the corporation involved calls its action something different.

2-7.9 Stock Splits

When a company divides its shares, it is said to have "split its stock." If a corporation had two million shares outstanding and split them 2 for 1, it would end up with four million shares outstanding. In a stock split, the firm must correspondingly reduce the par value of the common stock, but it does not change its stock and paid-in surplus accounts. If the firm's stock had a par of one dollar before the split, then the 2 for 1 split would give it a par of fifty cents.

A corporation's major reason for splitting its stock is to reduce the stock's market value. The split divides the market price per share in proportion to the split. For example, a $100 per share stock will sell at $50 after a 2 for 1 split, just as $100 per share stock will sell for $50 after a 100 percent stock dividend. In both cases there will be twice as many shares outstanding so that the total market value of the firm is unchanged by such paper shuffling. In essence, stock splits and stock dividends do not affect the value of the firm or the shareholder's returns (contrary to what many people think). In any event, most companies do not like the price of their stock to rise too high because the high cost may decrease its popularity. The $30 to $60 range seems to be most popular among investors. Thus, a stock split may be used to restore a popular market price.[18]

---

17 If p_t were used to denote *end*-of-period prices, Eq. (2-2a) must be modified as shown in Eq. (2-2b):

$$r_t = \frac{p_t - p_{t-1} + d_t}{p_{t-1}} \tag{2-2b}$$

Equations (2-2a) and (2-2b) produce identical results; they differ only by whether p_t denotes beginning- or end-of-period price.

18 This notion of an investor popular share price has been supported in some recent studies. See for example, J. Lakonishok and B. Lev, "Stock Splits and Stock Dividends: Why, Who, and When," working paper, Cornell University, September 1985.

Equation (2-2a) can be rewritten as (2-2c). To calculate a common stock's single-period return after a stock split or stock dividend, Eq. (2-2c) may be useful.

$$r_t = \frac{\text{capital gain or loss} + \text{cash dividends}}{\text{purchase price}} \qquad (2\text{-}2c)$$

Each share's price must be adjusted for stock splits and dividends before rates of return can be calculated. These price adjustments are needed to ensure that only actual changes in the investor's wealth will be measured, rather than the meaningless price changes that are associated with a stock dividend or split. For example, if a 2 for 1 split or a 100 percent stock dividend occurred, the share prices would be halved before the stock dividend or split (or doubled afterward) so that no changes in the investor's wealth would be attributed to it in calculating rates of return.

The following numerical example shows how a share of stock, originally selling for $100 per share, can fall to $50 per share owing to a 2 for 1 split or 100 percent stock dividend without changing the owner's 5 percent rate of return. The change in the unit of account (that is, the stock dividend or stock split) occurred between periods 2 and 3. Since the investor owns twice as many shares after the stock split but each share has half the previous market price, the investor's wealth is unchanged. And the investor's income in this simple example is $5 of cash dividends per period per $100 of investment both before and after the change in the unit of account, that is, a constant 5 percent rate of return per period.[19] This numerical example is summarized in Table 2–4.

TABLE 2-4 A 2 FOR 1 STOCK SPLIT, OR, EQUIVALENTLY, A 100 PERCENT STOCK DIVIDEND

TIME PERIOD (t)	t = 1	t = 2	t = 3	t = 4
Market price per share	$100	$100	$50	$50
Cash dividend per share	$5	$5	$2.50	$2.50
Earnings per share	$10	$10	$5	$5
Number of shares held per $100 original investment	1	1	2	2
Rate of return per period	5%	5%	5%	5%
Shares outstanding	100,000	100,000	200,000	200,000

2-8 PREFERRED STOCK

Preferred stock is just that: preferred stockholders have preference over common stockholders (but not bondholders) as to after-tax earnings in the form

---

19 The true economic effect of stock dividends and splits is analyzed later in Chap. 18 along the lines of E. Fama, L. Fisher, M. Jensen, and R. Roll, "The Adjustment of Stock Prices to New Information," *International Economic Review*, February 1969, vol. 20, no. 2, pp. 1–21.

of dividends and assets in the event of liquidation. Therefore, in terms of risk, the preferred stockholder is in a less risky position than the common stockholder but in a more risky position than the corporate bondholder. Preferred stockholders generally receive a higher rate of return on their investment than bondholders in compensation for the slightly greater risk they assume. However, they generally receive a lower rate of return than the common stockholder because they assume less risk. In fact, unlike common, preferred is limited (except with participating preferred) in the amount of dividends it can receive. If the firm is prosperous, the preferred receives only its stipulated dividend and all the residual earnings go to common stockholders.

2-8.1
Voting

Historically, preferred stockholders have had few, if any, voting rights. The theory was that as long as holders of this class of stock received their dividends, they should have no voice in the company. However, nonvoting preferred may become voting stock if preferred dividend payments are missed for a stated length of time. This is consistent with the idea that as long as dividends are paid, preferred stock should have no voice in management. Also, nonvoting preferred may be given voting rights for special circumstances, such as authorization of a new bond or stock issue or the merger of the company.

2-8.2
Pre-emptive
Right

Common law statute gives share owners, common or preferred, the right to subscribe to additional issues to maintain their proportionate share of ownership. However, as was explained in the section on common stock, the existence of the pre-emptive right depends on the law in the province where the corporation was chartered and the provisions of the company's articles of incorporation. The right is a bit more likely to be waived (unless the law forbids it) for preferred stock than for common, particularly if preferred is nonvoting.

2-8.3
Par Value

Most preferred stock has a par value. When it does, the dividend rights and call prices are usually stated in terms of par value. However, these rights would be specified even if there were no par value. It seems, therefore, as with common stock, that preferred that has a par value has no real advantage over preferred that has no par value.

2-8.4
Dividends

Dividends are the most significant aspect of preferred stock, since preferred stockholders invest more for gain from dividends than for gain from capital appreciation. The dividend paid is usually a stipulated percentage of par value, or for a stock with no par, stated dollar amount.

Most of the preferred issues outstanding today have a *cumulative dividend* clause. This means that the preferred stockholder is entitled to a dividend whether the firm earns it or not. If the corporation "misses" a preferred dividend, or any part of it, it is not lost but must be made up in a later year before any dividend can be paid to the common stock. For example, if a firm is unable to meet its $6 preferred dividend this year, but next year has $8 to disperse as dividends, all $8 will go to the preferred stock rather than $6 to preferred and $2 to common. After this payment, the firm will still owe $4 per share to its cumulative preferred stockholders.

Not all preferred stock is cumulative. *Noncumulative stock* is entitled to its dividends if they are earned. If they are not, the dividend is completely lost to the preferred stockholders. Of course, the corporation cannot legally pay dividends to its common stock if it has missed a preferred dividend during that dividend period (typically one year).

It should be noted that even with a cumulative provision, preferred stock carries no obligation to pay if the dividends are not earned. This provision may lead to difficulty if there is a question as to whether a dividend has been earned. If the directors decide to apply profits to a capital improvement (and who is to say what this is?) and not to pay a dividend, both the preferred stockholders and the common stockholders have no legal recourse; they are stuck with the directors' decision.

Fooladi and Roberts[20] demonstrated that there are stronger tax incentives in Canada than in the United States for preferred share issues.[21] They examined new issues of corporate debt and preferred and common stock, in both Canada and the United States, for the period 1975 through 1984, and found that preferred stock averaged 24.2 percent of total financing as compared to 6.4 percent for the United States.[22]

2-8.5
Call Feature

With many guarantees and "sweeteners" needed to make a preferred stock issue attractive, and with the preference and restrictions for dividend payments it demands, companies want to be in a position to call in these preferred shares if they become financially able. A redemption clause gives the company the right to redeem, or call in, the issues. As in a bond redemption, a preferred stock redemption is made at some time after the announcement of such action, and a call premium is paid above the par value of the stock and its regular dividend. Most preferred shares contain this redemption (or call) provision. The premium above par for utilities runs from 5 to 10 percent and from 5 to 15 percent for industrials. For both types of issuers, 5 percent is most common.

As with the bondholder, the call feature is seldom advantageous to a preferred stockholder. However, it is a desirable provision for the firm, since it allows a prospering corporation to bring an end to relatively high fixed charges, namely, preferred dividends. The call price has the effect of setting a ceiling price on preferred stock, since it is reasonable that an investor would be reluctant to pay a market price for a preferred share in excess of the amount for which the corporation could redeem it.

20 Iraj Fooladi and Gordon S. Roberts, "On Preferred Stock," *The Journal of Financial Research*, vol. ix, no. 4, winter 1986, pp. 319–324.
21 Dividends received by a Canadian corporation from another Canadian corporation are tax exempt. Furthermore, dividends received by individuals are eligible for a dividend tax credit. (These issues are discussed in Chapter 5.)
22 Iraj Fooladi and Gordon S. Roberts, "On Preferred Stock," *The Journal of Financial Research*, vol. ix, no. 4, winter 1986, p. 323.

**2-8.6
Sinking
Funds**

If a preferred stock issue is not convertible, it may include provisions for a *sinking fund*. This sinking fund may take the form of a simple accounting manipulation (debiting earned surplus and crediting a sinking fund for the preferred stock account), or it may entail an orderly annual retirement of the issue. If it is the latter, the shares will probably be redeemed at the call price unless the market price is significantly below the call price. In that case it might be less costly (even after brokerage commissions) for the firm to buy the preferred shares on the market.

A corporation's sinking fund for preferred stock has a much different legal status from that of a similar fund for bonds. A firm's inability to meet payments for a bond sinking fund may precipitate bankruptcy. Default on payments into a preferred stock sinking fund, though, has minor, if any, consequences. Occasionally, nonvoting preferred stock is given voting rights after a certain number of sinking fund payments have been missed.

**2-8.7
Participating
Preferred
Stock**

Participating preferred stock, like a participating bond, is uncommon. Both are entitled to a stated rate of dividends (interest) and then a share of the earnings available to be paid to the common stock. Since participating preferred stock is not very popular with the common shareholders, only weak firms will use such a provision as a ''sweetener'' to help sell this type of stock. Because preferred stock is basically a fixed-income investment like a bond but has few, if any, of the legal guarantees and recourses as to payment of interest that are inherent in a bond, the issuer may add protective clauses to the contract in order to make the stock safer and more salable.

**2-8.8
Floating
Rate
Preferred
Stock**

Preferred stock that had adjustable rather than fixed rates of cash dividend payments was marketed for the first time in Canada in 1982. These innovative new issues have dividend rates that are tied to the market interest rates on Treasury bills or the prime rate, and are adjustable daily or monthly, often subject to both a floor and ceiling rate. For example, some of the new issues allowed their rate of cash dividend payments to fall no lower than 7.5 percent and rise no higher than 15.0 percent. Adjustable rate preferred stock may be viewed as a successful modification of an old security to fit into today's more dynamic market conditions.[23]

**2-8.9
Conclusions
about
Preferred
Stock**

In sum, preferred stock is a curious hybrid between debt and equity. Although it is technically a form of equity investment, it has many of the characteristics of debt, such as fixed-income return, sinking fund provisions, and call provisions. Its one-period rate of return is calculated with Eq. (2-2a) on page 29, like common stock returns.

2-9 CONVERTIBLE SECURITIES

A *convertible security* is a security that can be converted into another security with different rights and privileges. More specifically, a convertible security

---

23 ''Variable Rate Preferred—The Tale of a Good Idea,'' *The New York Times*, March 6, 1983, p. 10.

is usually a preferred stock or a bond that can be converted into common stock. Once converted into stock, it cannot be changed back. If it is a bond, the convertible security provides the investor with a fixed interest payment; if preferred stock, with a stipulated dividend. The investor also receives the option to convert the instrument into common stock and thus has the speculative aspects of equity ownership.[24] The conversion option allows investors to participate in the residual earnings of the firm that are reflected in rises in the stock prices. They can earn their fixed return until (and if) they are assured of a capital gain, convert, and make a profit. The convertible may also be an inflation hedge. If inflation significantly reduces the real value of the fixed interest payment, the common stock price may also be inflated, and convertible holders can benefit from converting their security.

Many convertibles have a specific period in which the issue may be converted. For example, they may stipulate that conversion cannot take place until two or three years after the issue. This stipulation allows the money obtained through such financing to be used by the corporation for investment and growth that will show up in higher common stock prices only after a period of time. A limited issue will place a time limit as to when the conversion can take place, typically 10 to 15 years. Convertible preferred stocks are usually unlimited as to time horizon for conversion. An unlimited convertible bond is eligible for conversion for the entire time the bond is outstanding.

As a rule, convertible securities are callable. The call privilege allows the company to call in the security for redemption just as it permits the company to call in preferred stock or a straight bond. The purpose of the call provision is not to redeem the bonds or preferred stock but to force conversion of the issue when the conversion value of the security is well above the call price. In practice, few convertibles are ever redeemed.[25]

2-9.1 Conversion Ratio

The *conversion ratio* is the ratio of exchange between the common stock and the convertible security. For example, a $1,000 convertible bond may provide for a conversion to ten shares of common stock. The *conversion price* is then simply the $1,000 face value divided by the conversion ratio ($1,000/10 = $100 per share conversion price). This ratio may be stated as ten shares of stock for each bond.

There are instances when the conversion price is not constant over time. The conversion price might change simply with the length of time outstanding or with the proportion of the issue converted. A bond might have a conversion price of $100 per share for the first five years, $105 per share for the next five years, $110 for the third five years, and so on. Under a provision

---

24 Valuing the option portion of a convertible has been investigated. See M. H. Brennan and E. S. Schwartz, "Convertible Bonds: Valuation and Optimal Strategies for Call and Conversion," *Journal of Finance*, December 1977, pp. 1699–1715. J. E. Ingersol, Jr., "A Contingent Claims Valuation of Convertible Securities," *Journal of Finance*, May 1977, pp. 463–478.

25 Many of the convertibles issued in Canada have "trigger" provisions contained in the indenture. These provisions require that the price of the common stock trade above a specific ("trigger") price for a specified period before the convertible can be called.

stipulating increasing price with amount redeemed, a bond might have a conversion price of $100 per share for the first 25 percent of the shares converted, $105 for the second 25 percent, $110 for the third, and $115 per share for the final 25 percent converted. Such provisions for increasing conversion prices give the issuer some power to force investors to convert their issues as fast as possible when the market price has substantially exceeded the conversion price.

Conversion value is the market price per share of common stock times the conversion ratio. In the foregoing example, if the stock were selling at $105 per share, the conversion value of the bond would be 10 × $105 = $1,050. If the price were $95 per share, the conversion value would be $950 for the $1,000 face value bond.

The market price of a convertible security will usually be higher than its conversion value at time of issue. The difference between the two is the *conversion premium*. For example, suppose XYZ Corporation's convertible debentures are issued at par value of $1,000 per bond. Further, assume that the market price of the XYZ common stock was $88 per share on the date the convertible was issued and that the conversion ratio was $1,000/$100 = 10. The conversion value was thus 10 × $88 = $880. Subtracting the $880 conversion value from the convertible bond price of $1,000 gives a conversion premium of $120. Frequently the conversion premium is expressed as a percentage—for example, ($120/$880 equals) 13.6 percent conversion premium in this example.

2-9.2
Dilution

Dilution of an investor's position is possible on both sides of a convertible issue. If the firm splits its stock or declares a stock dividend, the conversion value of the convertible instrument is lowered appropriately. For example, if the conversion price of a bond were $100 per share and the conversion ratio were ten shares per bond, a 2 for 1 stock split would change the conversion ratio from ten to twenty (just as the number of shares would be doubled) and the conversion price from $100 to $50 (just as the market price of the common stock would be halved).

The existing investors in a company's stock also run the risk of dilution of their position. They usually recognize this well before conversion takes place, and on the announcement of a convertible issue the market price of the stock often declines. To keep the current stockholders' position stable, the convertible security can be covered by the provision for pre-emptive rights in the corporate charter. Under this provision, the convertible must be offered to the existing stockholders before it can be sold to the general public.

An example will illustrate the diluting effect of a convertible. We assume that a corporation issues $50 million of 7 percent convertible debentures at a conversion price of $25 per share. Upon conversion the total number of additional shares would be ($50 million/$25 =) 2 million new shares. Suppose that the company has four million shares outstanding originally and, for simplicity, no other debt. It expects earnings of $20 million in three years; the income tax rate is 50 percent. Table 2-5 shows what earnings per share would be before conversion and after conversion.

TABLE 2-5 DILUTION EFFECT OF CONVERSION

	DEBENTURES OUTSTANDING, $	CONVERTED, $
Earnings before interest and taxes	20,000,000	20,000,000
Interest on 7% debenture	3,500,000	0
Profit before taxes	16,500,000	20,000,000
Taxes at 50%	8,250,000	10,000,000
Profit after taxes	8,250,000	10,000,000
Shares outstanding	4,000,000	6,000,000
Earnings per share	$2.06	$1.67

Table 2-5 shows that, with conversion, the earnings per share are diluted. The impact of such dilution upon the market share price must be carefully considered by the investors. However, when the debentures are converted, the corporation is relieved of the interest burden of debentures or the dividends to preferred stock. Conversion has the effect of issuing equity to pay debt.

This method of delayed equity financing gives several advantages to the corporation.[26] One is a delayed dilution of common stock and earnings per share as shown in Table 2-5. Another is that the firm is able to offer the bond at a lower coupon rate, or preferred stock at a lower dividend rate, than it would have to pay on a straight bond or preferred stock. The rule usually is that the more valuable the conversion feature, the lower the yield that must be offered to sell the issue—the convertible feature is a sweetener.

Companies with poor credit ratings may issue convertibles in order to lower the yield necessary to sell their debt securities. The investor should be aware that some financially weak companies will issue convertibles just to reduce their costs of financing, with no intention that the issue will ever be converted. There are also corporations whose credit rating is weak but who have great potential for growth. Such a firm will be able to sell a convertible debt issue at a near-normal cost, not because of the quality of the bond but because of the attractiveness of the conversion feature for this "growth" stock. Times of tight money and growing stock prices will find even very credit-worthy companies issuing convertible securities in an effort to reduce their cost of obtaining scarce capital.

A definite disadvantage to the firm that is financing with convertible securities is that it runs the risk of diluting not only the earnings per share of its common stock but also the control of the company. If a large part of the issue

2-9.3 Reasons for Convertible Financing

26 The following are some in-depth studies about various aspects of convertible security financing for the interested reader: G. J. Alexander, R. D. Stover, and D. B. Kuhnau, "Market Timing Strategies in Convertible Debt Financing," *Journal of Finance*, March 1979, pp. 143–155; M. H. Brennan and E. S. Schwartz, "Convertible Bonds: Valuation and Optimal Strategies for Call and Conversion," *Journal of Finance*, December 1977, pp. 1699–1715; E. F. Brigham, "An Analysis of Convertible Debentures: Theory and Some Empirical Evidence," *Journal of Finance*, March 1966, pp. 35–54; R. W. Melicher and J. R. Hoffmeister, "The Issue Is Convertible Bonds," *Financial Executive*, November 1977, pp. 46–50.

is purchased by one buyer, typically an investment banker or insurance company, conversion may shift the voting control of the firm away from its original owners and toward the converters. This is not a significant problem for large companies with millions of stockholders, but it is a very real consideration for the small firm or one just going public.

2-9.4 Overhanging Issue

When a company is unable to force the conversion of an issue because the market price of the common stock has not risen to a point that will induce investors to convert, the issue is said to be an *overhanging issue*. Ordinarily a company will plan for the issue to be converted within a certain period of time. A growth company may expect conversion within eighteen months. The failure of the market price of the stock to rise sufficiently for conversion to occur might indicate a failure of the company to perform as expected. Such an overhanging issue can cause serious problems, since the company would find it difficult to gain market acceptance for another convertible issue or even for nonconvertible financing.

The possibility of an overhanging issue and the associated limitations on financial flexibility will definitely reduce the advantages of a convertible over an equity issue. A common stock issue brings in equity capital at the moment, where a convertible entails the uncertainty of whether it will ever be converted into common stock.

2-9.5 Reasons for Investing in Convertible Securities

The investor should be aware that the conversion option is not free. Convertible securities sell above the price of comparable nonconvertible securities. This additional cost may be worthwhile, however, for a convertible security has value in two forms rather than in just one. First, it has value as a bond or preferred stock. (Since convertible preferred stock and convertible bonds are so similar, the discussion will pertain equally to both.) Second, it allows the investor to hedge against the future. If the price of the stock rises, the convertible is valued at or near its conversion value. But if the market price should decline, the convertible value will fall only to its value as a straight bond.

To illustrate, assume a twenty-year, 7 percent convertible debenture has been issued by the XYZ Corporation. A straight twenty-year debenture for the same firm would require an 8 percent yield to maturity. The 7 percent bond must sell at a discount if it is to yield 8 percent to maturity. Consequently, $1,000 face value debenture must sell for about $902. Therefore, $902 is the value floor for XYZ's debenture. This means that if the market price of the stock should deteriorate to a point that makes the conversion value negligible, the bond price could not fall below $902. At that price, given that there is no significant change in the corporation's financial condition since the date of issue, the convertible will sell as if it were a straight bond. This bond ''floor'' is, of course, subject to the changes in interest rates and risk conditions of the firm, as are all bond prices. Bond valuation is covered in detail in Chapters 11, 12, and 13.

It is interesting to note that the popularity of convertibles with institutional investors has to some extent meant higher premiums over bond value. Many institutions are legally restricted from speculating in common stock. The convertible bond helps them enjoy the benefits of rising prices in the stock market without violating the law. The institution can buy the convertible as a bond and either sell it as its value rises with the climbing stock prices or wait to convert the bond and immediately sell the stock without penalty. Indeed, convertible securities are attractive to all classes-of investors, offering protection against falling stock prices and the speculative advantage of capital gains.[27]

2-10 EMPIRICAL EVIDENCE

Table 2-1, suggested that Canadian government bonds are the least risky investment and therefore have the lowest rate of income, on average, of the various types of securities. This chapter also suggested that, averaged over all of the different kinds of securities, common stock tends to have the highest risk and rate of return. Some explicit numerical analysis of empirical evidence is offered to substantiate these ideas.

A share of Canadian Pacific common stock and a marketable Canadian government bond are compared. These two securities were selected for comparison because they are so different. One is a residual-income security involving ownership risks; the other is a fixed-interest debt security involving no risk of bankruptcy.

2-10.1 Time Periods Analyzed

For purposes of this inquiry, the stock and the bond are observed for over a decade. A decade is long enough for about two complete business cycles and numerous smaller temporary market disequilibriums to pass so that the long-run equilibrium tendencies of the securities can be seen.

Rather than observe the securities only at the beginning and the end of the sampled period, they will be observed every six months. This will produce twenty observations per decade instead of only two. Essentially, it is assumed that the securities are purchased, held six months, sold, and then repurchased and held for the next six-month period, repetitively. This is a good framework in which to analyze a security's risk and return characteristics.

2-10.2 Raw Data for the Bond

The raw data for the marketable bond are shown in Table 2-6. The bond pays a 5.25 percent coupon rate on its face value of $1,000; that is, the owner of the bond receives $52.50 interest each year, or, actually, $26.25 every six months. When the bond matures in May 1990, its owner will receive the $1,000 face value. In the meantime, the market price fluctuates freely. The *income* to the owner of the bond is $26.50 interest every six months plus whatever capital gain or loss has occurred during the period. Thus, the owner's rate of income per period is calculated with Eq. (2-1a) on page 14.

---

27 The conversion option of convertible securities is analyzed further in Appendix A of Chap. 19 where call options and warrants are also analyzed. For further information about convertible bonds see *The Handbook of Fixed Income Securities*, chap. 22.

TABLE 2-6 HOLDING PERIOD RETURNS FOR A CANADIAN GOVERNMENT BOND

Name of issuer:	Federal government
Type of security:	Marketable bond
Fixed income:	5.25% of face per annum
Maturity date:	May 1990
Face value:	$1,000
Source of data:	*The Globe and Mail Report on Business*

			Rate of Return	
HALF-YEAR	MARKET PRICE, $	SEMI-ANNUAL COUPON, $	SEMI-ANNUAL	ANNUAL
1985–11	887.5	26.25	8.92%	17.85%
1985–1	838.88	26.25	6.81%	13.61%
1984–11	810	26.25	18.16%	36.31%
1984–1	707.75	26.25	−3.90%	−7.80%
1983–11	763.8	26.25	2.60%	5.21%
1983–1	770	26.25	9.83%	19.66%
1982–11	725	26.25	41.75%	83.49%
1982–1	530	26.25	4.46%	8.92%
1981–11	532.5	26.25	5.66%	11.33%
1981–1	528.8	26.25	−0.88%	−1.77%
1980–11	560	26.25	−12.83%	−25.65%
1980–1	672.5	26.25	8.33%	16.67%
1979–11	645	26.25	−7.41%	−14.83%
1979–1	725	26.25	5.81%	11.62%
1978–11	710	26.25	1.55%	3.10%
1978–1	725	26.25	1.18%	2.36%
1977–11	742.5	26.25	2.50%	5.00%
1977–1	750	26.25	2.81%	5.63%
1976–11	755	26.25	14.89%	29.78%
1976–1	680	26.25	7.82%	15.65%
1975–11	655	26.25	−3.37%	−6.74%
1975–1	705	26.25	2.99%	5.99%
1974–11	710	26.25	14.15%	28.29%
1974–1	645	26.25	−11.97%	−23.93%
1973–11	762.5	26.25	3.78%	7.57%
1973–1	760	26.25	−2.93%	−5.86%
1972–11	810	26.25	—	—

2-10.3 Raw Data for the Common Stock The raw data for the Canadian Pacific common stock are shown in Table 2-7. The data sheet is more complicated for the common stock than for the bond because of a stock split, that is, a change in the unit of account. Column 1 of both Tables 2-6 and 2-7 shows the dates on which the market price was observed. Columns 2 and 3 in both tables show the reported prices and cash flows (from either the stock's cash dividends or the bond's coupon interest). Column 4 in the two tables differs.

In Table 2-7 the fourth column indicates what changes occurred in the common stock's unit of account. There was a 3 for 1 stock split in May 1985. Columns 5 and 6 show the price and dividend data after they have been

TABLE 2-7   HOLDING PERIOD RETURNS FOR A CANADIAN PACIFIC STOCK

Name of firm:	Canadian Pacific Limited
Type of Security:	Common share
Industry:	Transportation; resources
Source of data:	*The Globe and Mail Report on Business: The Financial Post Corporation Service*

	Reported Data			Adjusted Data		
HALF-YEAR	MARKET PRICE, $	SEMI-ANNUAL CASH DIVIDENDS, $	CHANGE IN UNIT OF ACCOUNT	MARKET PRICE, $	SEMI-ANNUAL CASH DIVIDENDS, $	ANNUAL RATE OF RETURN
1985–11	18.75	0.24		18.75	0.24	– 6.47%
1985–1	19.625	0.7	3 – 1(5/11/85)	19.625	0.233	38.30%
1984–11	50	0.7		16.67	0.233	51.15%
1984–1	40.375	0.7		13.46	0.233	–37.33%
1983–11	50.5	0.7		16.83	0.233	10.59%
1983–1	48.625	0.7		16.21	0.233	74.98%
1982–11	35.875	0.7		11.96	0.233	92.60%
1982–1	25	0.95		8.33	0.317	–76.06%
1981–11	41.875	0.95		13.96	0.317	–10.72%
1981–1	45.25	0.95		15.08	0.317	12.41%
1980–11	43.5	0.95		14.50	0.317	28.68%
1980–1	38.875	0.9		12.96	0.300	2.68%
1979–11	39.25	0.9		13.08	0.300	38.81%
1979–1	33.625	0.8		11.21	0.267	70.00%
1978–11	25.5	0.6		8.50	0.200	84.08%
1978–1	18.375	0.5		6.13	0.167	18.84%
1977–11	17.25	0.485		5.75	0.162	–8.27%
1977–1	18.5	0.465		6.17	0.155	23.12%
1976–11	17	0.465		5.67	0.155	–4.59%
1976–1	17.875	0.395		5.96	0.132	70.67%
1975–11	13.5	0.435		4.50	0.145	–9.44%
1975–1	14.625	0.41		4.88	0.137	20.70%
1974–11	13.625	0.45		4.54	0.150	20.78%
1974–1	12.75	0.41		4.25	0.137	–30.19%
1973–11	15.5	0.41		5.17	0.137	–10.03%
1973–1	16.75	0.36		5.58	0.120	12.22%
1972–11	16.125	0.38		5.38	0.127	—

Note: First half ends June 30 and second half ends December 30.

adjusted for the changes in the unit of account. For example, all reported prices and dividends prior to the 3 for 1 split in May 1985 are divided by three before being entered in the columns for adjusted data. If these adjustments for changes in the unit of account had not been made, it would appear as if a $50 investment in Canadian Pacific in 1984 would have fallen to a market value of $19.625 in 1985. The owner's rate of income is calculated with the reported data using Eq. (2–2c) from page 31.

Table 2-8 compares the Canadian Pacific stock and the government bond with reference to several points. The Canadian Pacific stock earned more income per dollar invested than the bond, and its rate of income was more erratic or variable than the income from the bond. Thus, the stock was a riskier investment. Figure 2-2 is a smoothed approximation of the relative-frequency distribution of the returns from the two assets. This graph shows that the stock has considerably more *variability in its rate of income*—that is, risk—than the bond because its probability distribution is wider. The purpose of this numerical example is to add realism to the assertion that common stock is typically riskier and has higher average returns than bonds.

TABLE 2-8 COMPARISON OF CANADIAN GOVERNMENT BOND AND CANADIAN PACIFIC STOCK DATA, 1972–1985

	CANADIAN GOVERNMENT BOND, %	CANADIAN PACIFIC STOCK, %
Arithmetic average rate of return	9.29%	18.37%
Range of returns	−25.69 to 83.49	−76.06 to 92.60
Standard deviation	21.24	39.75

FIGURE 2-2 Smoothed relative frequency distributions comparing the rates of return from a bond and Canadian Pacific common stock, 1972–1985.

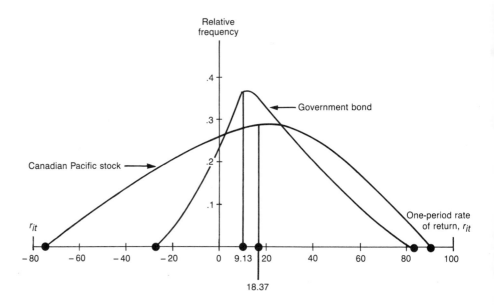

2-11 CHAPTER SUMMARY

Debt securities come in many forms. The debt securities traded in the money markets all mature in less than three years and involve virtually no risk of default. The securities issued by the Canadian government and its agencies are also free from default risk, but their maturities vary from one to forty years.[28] Municipal bonds, in contrast, involve elements of default risk if the issuing municipality falters. Corporate bonds are the most risky category of bonds. However, protective provisions in the indenture contract that governs the terms of a corporate bond issue can furnish some protection to the issue's investors if the issuer becomes bankrupt. Investors in residential mortgages can get relief from default risk by buying only insured mortgages. But no insurance is available to protect commercial mortgage investors.

The common stockholder has the right to receive a certificate to evidence share ownership, to receive dividends, usually to vote at the stockholders' meetings, and, in many provinces, the pre-emptive right to maintain a proportionate share in the corporation's assets, earnings, and voting control. But, in return for these advantages, the common shareholders are forced to accept (1) only a residual claim on the corporation's earnings after all other bills have been paid and (2) the last claim on the assets if the corporation goes bankrupt. If the corporation prospers, however, these last two claims can become very valuable investments.

Unlike common stockholders, preferred stockholders participate in the corporation's earnings to only a limited extent. Preferred stock offers (1) a secure cash dividend that has a prior claim on corporate earnings over the common stock dividend and (2) a fixed cash dividend return that is fairly secure. If the preferred issue is cumulative, then any missed cash dividend payments may be collected eventually, unless the issuer goes bankrupt. And, some issues of preferred stock allow their owners to vote at the common stockholders' meeting in the event that the preferred dividends are in arrears. Some issues of preferred are also backed by a sinking fund. High-grade preferred stock thus offers good security and a stable income if the issuing corporation flourishes.

Convertible preferred stocks combine all the features of ordinary preferred stock with the added benefit of being convertible into common stock in the event that the common appreciates nicely. Convertible preferred thus offers both safety features not found in common stock and the opportunity to participate in common stock's capital gains.

QUESTIONS

1. Differentiate between the coupon rate and a bond's one-period rate of return. Which should be more important to the potential investor? Why? *p 14*
2. Why can an issuer's call provision in the indenture be potentially detrimental to a bondholder? *p 33*
3. Why is an issue of income bonds rather infrequent? *p 23*
4. What characteristics do all money market securities have in common? *p 9*
5. What are the differences between Canadian government marketable and nonmarketable securities? Give examples of each. *p 12-14*

---

28 Econometrical analysis of the returns from Canadian bonds, bills, and stocks may be found in James E. Hatch and Robert W. White, "Canadian Stocks, Bonds, Bills and Inflation, 1950–1983," The Financial Analysts Research Federation, 1985.

6. What characteristics of municipal bonds are important to the potential investor?

7. Define the strike price of a retractable bond.

8. Compare and contrast commercial mortgages and residential mortgages.

9. Differentiate between the coupon rate of a bond and a preferred stock's rate of cash dividends.

10. Would you expect the market price of a corporation's common stock to fluctuate the same way as the price of its preferred stock? Why or why not?

11. What are the advantages of investing in the common stock rather than the bonds of a corporation? What are the disadvantages?

12. "Stock dividends and stock splits have no effect on the value of a company." True, false, or uncertain? Discuss.

13. How much importance should be attached to book value and par value in evaluating the investment qualities of a corporation's common stock?

14. Why may a firm wish to raise capital through a convertible securities issue? Why may a firm prefer not to issue convertible securities?

15. From the point of view of the investor, what factors would be considered before investing in a convertible security rather than a straight bond or preferred stock?

SELECTED REFERENCES

Brigham, E., A.L. Kahl, and W.F. Rentz. *Canadian Financial Management Theory and Practice.* Holt, Rinehart and Winston of Canada, 1983. Chapters 13 and 14 present a nonmathematical description of various types of securities.

Gardner, E.J., L.D. Schall, and C.W. Haley. *Introduction to Financial Management.* 1st Canadian ed. (revised). McGraw-Hill Ryerson, 1982. See chapters 19, 20, and 21 for an easy-to-read and informative discussion of common stock, long-term debt, preferred stock, convertible securities, and warrants.

Halpern, P., J.F. Weston, and E. Brigham. *Essentials of Canadian Managerial Finance.* 2d ed. Holt, Rinehart and Winston of Canada, 1983. Chapters 15, 16, and 18 present a nonmathematical description of various types of securities.

Kirzner, E. and J. Dickinson. *Guide to International Investing.* CCH Canadian 1984, 1985, 1986. The characteristics of Canadian bonds are described in paragraphs 40110 to 40225. Canadian preferred and common shares are described in 55150 through 55360. This reference book also contains information on the securities of Australia, France, West Germany, Hong Kong, Italy, Japan, Mexico, the Netherlands, Switzerland, the United Kingdom, and the United States.

Sarpkaya, S. *The Money Market in Canada.* 3d ed. CCH Canadian, 1984. A thorough examination of Canadian money markets and money-market instruments.

Securities Markets

After reading about the basic types of securities in Chap. 2, the next logical questions might be: Where do these securities come from? How are they subsequently bought and sold? Stated simply, the answers to these questions are that securities are originally issued by corporations, proprietorships, partnerships, and governments. Later, after the securities are initially issued, they are traded in various *securities markets*.

Securities markets are a multibillion dollar business today—a far cry from the auctioneers and merchants who bought and sold securities as the "Association of Brokers" in 1852. The markets have become so numerous and complex that they defy description in a few well-chosen words. It is the aim of this chapter to discuss the functions, operations, and trading arrangements available in securities markets in Canada and to evaluate briefly the efficiency of these markets. Indeed, the average university student has a vested interest in becoming knowledgeable on the subject: the Toronto Stock Exchange's 1984 census of share owners shows that 70 percent of the Canadian population owns — directly or indirectly — security investments, including real estate other than a principal residence.

3-1 UNDERWRITING

Billions of dollars worth of new securities are issued in the Canadian securities markets each year. These new issues are called *primary issues*. The agent responsible for finding buyers for these brand new securities is called the *investment dealer* or *underwriter*. The name "investment dealer" is rather unfortunate, for these persons are not primarily investors. That is, they do not typically make permanent investments of their own funds. What, then, do they do? Essentially, they purchase brand new issues from security issuers, such as companies and governments, and then they arrange for their immediate resale to the investing public.

Who are the underwriters? Perhaps the names listed below sound familiar.

Dominion Securities
McLeod Young Weir
Merrill Lynch Canada

Midland Doherty
Richardson Greenshields of Canada

A few large firms, such as those listed above, do much of the underwriting for the entire investment-dealing industry. The investment-dealing industry is made up of several hundred different firms in Canada—but most of them are small and not widely known. In addition to being investment dealers, almost all these firms perform brokerage services and other financial functions. In fact, most of the largest investment-dealing firms have diversified themselves into department stores of finance. Merrill Lynch Canada is a case in point. To name just a few of its activities, Merrill Lynch runs one of the largest brokerage operations in each of the following markets: government securities, securities issued by governmental agencies, commodities, options, financial futures, corporate bonds, preferred stocks, common stocks. Also, through its subsidiaries, Merrill Lynch provides real estate financing and investment advisory services. Thus, underwriting is only a small part of the huge Merrill Lynch operation. For instance, Merrill Lynch has far more stockbrokers who arrange trades between common stock investors in the secondary market than it has underwriters who originate common stock issues in the *primary market*.

3-1.1 Functions of the Underwriter

Advisory In a corporation's first confrontation with an underwriter, the underwriter will serve in an advisory capacity. The underwriter will aid the firm considering whether or not to issue new securities in analyzing its financing needs and make suggestions about various means of financing. The underwriter may also function as an adviser in mergers, acquisitions, and refinancing operations. Occasionally, following a securities issue, the investment dealer will be given a seat on the board of directors of the firm so that he or she may continue to give financial counsel to the firm and, in the process, help protect the underwriter's reputation as the sponsor of profitable, financially sound firms.[1]

Administrative The investigations, paperwork, and "general red tape" are quite voluminous in a securities issue. The investment dealer has the responsibility of seeing that they are all done in accordance with the relevant laws. Some of these specific administrative responsibilities will be discussed later.

Underwriting The brief period elapsing between the time the investment-dealing houses purchase an issue from the issuer and the time they subsequently sell it to the public is *risky*. Because of unforeseen changes in market conditions, the underwriters face the possibility of either not being able to sell the entire issue or of selling it at less than the purchase price.

Underwriting refers to the guarantee by the investment dealer that the issuer of the new securities will receive a specific minimum amount of cash for its new securities. Of course, inherent in this guarantee is some degree of risk for the underwriter. It is the underwriter's intention to buy the securities from the issuer at less than the expected selling price. This intention is sometimes frustrated, however.

1 The once common practice of a firm's placing "insiders," like its own underwriter, on its board of directors is a questionable practice. It is believed that a group of "outsiders" could bring a more objective and less biased view to the management of the firm.

Not all new security issues are underwritten. If the investment dealer finds one or more buyers for a new issue and arranges for a direct trade between issuer and investors, he or she is said to have made a *private placement*. Rather than perform the underwriting function, in a private placement the investment dealer is compensated for acting as the middle link in bringing buyer and seller together and for his or her skills and speed in determining a fair price and execution of the trade.

In a *public offering*, the investment dealer may not assume the role of underwriter; instead the investment dealer may agree to use certain facilities and services in distributing new shares on a *best efforts basis* while assuming no financial responsibility if all the securities cannot be sold. In these best efforts offerings the investment dealer's charges are typically more than they would have charged for a direct placement but less than they would have charged for a fully underwritten public offering. Best efforts offerings are the exception rather than the rule, however. Usually the investment dealer is the underwriter for public offerings.

Distribution   Distributing securities to investors is the central function of investment dealers. It is their primary concern to bring together buyer and seller, whether they actually buy and then sell the securities themselves, or whether they simply act as intermediaries in bringing together issuer and investors in a private placement. To gain understanding of how a primary distribution of securities materializes, consider the issuance of a $100 million debenture bond flotation by the XYZ Corporation.

Mr. X and his associates of the XYZ Corporation have agreed that they need $100 million to build another large new factory. They need advice about how to raise this much capital; therefore, they go to a nearby investment dealer house, say, ABC & Co., and seek counsel.

3-1.2 An Example of a Public Distribution

Early Conferences   The investment house that first reaches an agreement with the issuer is called the *originator or lead*; the originator ultimately manages the flotation and co-ordinates the *underwriting syndicate* and *selling group*. At the outset, however, the originator and the issuer must determine how much capital should be raised, whether it should be raised by debt or equity, and whether XYZ Corp. is in a sound financial position. Investigations are conducted by accountants, engineers, and lawyers. The accountants assess the firm's financial condition. If the funds are to be used to acquire new assets, ABC's engineering consultants investigate the proposed acquisition. Lawyers will be asked to give interpretations and judgments about various documents involved in the flotation. And ABC & Co. will make an investigation of the firm's future prospects. Finally, the originator will draw up a tentative underwriting agreement between the issuer and investment dealer house, specifying all terms of the issue except the specific price that will be set on the debenture.

The Banking Group   With most large issues, such as the one under discussion, the investment dealer will form a purchase syndicate made up of a group of investment dealers, numbering anywhere from two to sixty. There are at least three advantages to forming an underwriting syndicate. First, since it spreads around the purchase cost, ABC & Co. is not faced with an enormous cash drain while the securities are being sold. Second, it lessens the risk of loss, since several firms would bear the loss in case of failure. Third, the use of several underwriters and their selling groups encourages a wider participation of final ownership of the new securities. Figure 3–1 illustrates the relationship between issuer, originator, underwriting syndicate, selling group, and the ultimate investors.

FIGURE 3-1 Flowchart for a primary offering made through a syndicate of investment bankers.

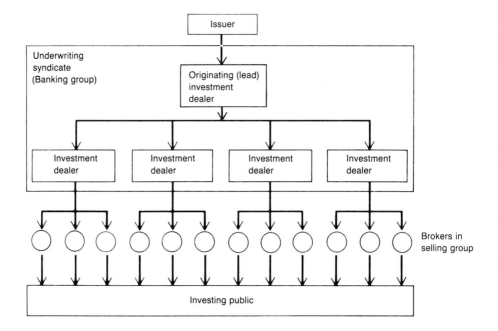

The Selling Group After the underwriters have purchased the issue from XYZ Corp., each uses its own selling group for distribution to the investing public. The selling group consists of other investment bankers, dealers, and brokers. Some firms, such as Merrill Lynch Canada, perform all these functions—from lead underwriter in some issues to brokers in others.

Disclosure Requirements The provincial securities law administered by the provincial securities commission in the provinces in which the securities will be offered for sale requires that a preliminary prospectus be filed with the commission. It must contain information for an investor to judge the investment quality of the new issue. After the filing of the statement, there is usually only a brief delay of at least ten days, until the new issue may be offered for sale. During this period the provincial securities commission analyzes the prospectus to determine if the relevant information was provided. The commission may act to delay approval or request amendments to the statement, in which case the waiting period may last days or weeks. In fact, most delays are caused by the large number of statements filed that must be processed by the commission staff.

The process culminates in the production of a final prospectus. After approval and after the price has been set, it is reproduced in quantity and delivered to potential investors. Investors must have a prospectus before they can invest. It contains information about XYZ's history, about those individuals who hold large blocks of XYZ stock, and other facts pertinent to the evaluation of the debentures offered. It should be emphasized that a securities commission approval of the registration statement and the prospectus within is not an endorsement by the commission of the investment value of the securities offered. Its approval implies only that adequate information has been revealed for investors to make their own judgment about the value of the security offer.

Not all issues must be registered with the securities commission. Included in this exempt classification are government issues and companies regulated by governmental agencies. Other issues that are likely to be exempt include (1) municipal offerings, (2) issues that are offered to only a few investors, and (3) issues by private mutual funds. Exemption does not make the issuer and underwriters immune from legal action if fraud is involved in the flotation, however.

Setting the Price   Perhaps the most difficult decision in a flotation is setting the "right" price. The right price is one that is not too low; this would be unnecessarily costly to the issuer. It also cannot be too high; this might cause losses for the underwriters. Therefore, a very delicate balance is necessary. Security valuation is too large a topic to delve into here; however, chapters in the latter part of the book are devoted to explaining how to estimate the value of securities.[2]

The price is generally set at the end of the registration period. The syndicate prefers to wait to set the final price until the issue is ready for marketing so that it may have the latest, most up-to-date information on the market situation. As a rule, when the price is right, market conditions are good, and the issuer and underwriters are reputable, the flotation will "go out the window"; that is, it will be sold in a few days or even hours. When one or more of these conditions is lacking, it may become a "sticky issue," taking a week, month, or even more to sell, and it may result in multimillion dollar losses for the underwriting syndicate if it is a big deal.

Market Stabilization   During the distribution period, the manager of an underwriting firm occasionally must *stabilize the price* of the issue to prevent its drifting downward. To achieve this objective, the underwriting syndicate's manager "pegs" the price by placing orders to buy the newly issued security at a specified price in the secondary market where the outstanding securities are trading. Although this procedure has been criticized as being a monopolistic price-fixing agreement, the commission has nodded approval as full, prior disclosure of intent to stabilize is made. It is defended on the grounds

---

2 Bond valuation is the topic of Chaps. 11, 12, and 13. Common stock valuation is the topic of Chaps. 14, 15 and 16.

that if price-pegging were not allowed, the risk of the underwriting syndicate would be greater; the underwriting cost to the issuer would increase correspondingly. The price-pegging activity usually continues for about thirty days after the issue begins.

If the issue has been badly priced, even the pegging operation does not help substantially. In the most extreme occurrence, the managing underwriter would start buying back everything that had been sold in an effort to keep the price up. In such a case, all the underwriters would experience severe losses.

3-1.3 Flotation Costs

Investment dealers earn their income as would any other merchants; that is, their selling price is greater than their purchase price. The difference is called the *spread.* In the case of XYZ Corp., let us assume there is a two-percentage-point spread. These percentage points are stated as a percent of the issue's face value. So, the investment dealer, ABC & Co., bought the bonds for $980 each and they were ultimately sold to the investing public for their face value of $1,000 each. That two points, then, is compensation for various costs, such as investigations, the discount given to the underwriting syndicate, and the additional discount given to the selling group members. The spread may very likely be divided as follows: ABC & Co., the managing underwriter, would keep one-half of one point of the two-point spread for originating and managing the syndicate; the banking group would earn about three-tenths of a point; and the members of the selling group would earn the remaining one and two-tenths of a point. If the managing underwriters should sell to an ultimate buyer, they would receive the full two-point spread—one-half point as originator, three-tenths of a point as part of the underwriting syndicate, and one and two-tenths of a point as a retailer.

Of the various types of securities issued, the selling costs for bonds are much less than for either preferred stock or common stock. The selling costs for common stock range from 2 to 4 times more than for bonds and about 1.1 to 2 times more than for preferred stock, depending on the size of the issue. It seems reasonable that flotation costs of bonds would be less than for preferred or common stock because bonds are usually sold in large blocks to a small number of large institutional investors, whereas a stock issue may be sold to thousands of stockholders. Thus, marketing costs and risk are significantly greater with stock issues.

Further, one need not look far to see why, as a percentage of gross proceeds, flotation costs for small issues are greater than for large issues. Fixed costs, such as registration fees and investigation expenses, account for about 85 percent of the cost of flotation. The greater the issue, then, the less the fixed cost per dollar of new issue. Moreover, as a general rule, small issues are made by less well known companies, and the less well known the company, the more obligated is the managing firm to make an extremely intensive investigation of the issuing firm. Also, marketing the issue of an unknown firm is much more difficult and thus more costly than launching the issue of a well-known firm. Therefore, flotation costs for small issues are higher than for large issues on a per-unit basis.

3-2   ORGANIZED SECURITIES EXCHANGES

The individual who is interested in investing may either arrange for the purchase of stock through a bank or go directly to a broker. Most investors prefer to go directly to a local brokerage house and request the services of one of its brokers. Either way, after the initial paperwork has been completed, the investor's order will be relayed to one of the dealers handling the securities in which the investor is interested, and the purchase will be consummated.

Individual investors most frequently use (through their brokers) the services of either the organized exchanges or the over-the-counter markets. These markets are called the *secondary markets*. Investors buy brand-new securities from their issuer (or the issuer's investment dealer) in the *primary market*. In the secondary market investors buy and sell securities among themselves so that the issuer never gets any direct cashflow from these trades. This discussion of the secondary markets begins with the organized exchanges, of which the largest and best known is the Toronto Stock Exchange (TSE). Table 3–1 shows that the TSE handled over 75 percent of all securities traded on organized exchanges during 1985, on a dollar volume basis. The Montreal Exchange followed far behind with only 18 percent of total volume. The Vancouver Stock Exchange, rich in low-priced mining stocks, had only 5 percent of total dollar volume but was the second largest in share volume in 1985. The other exchanges listed in Table 3-1 make up the balance (these are sometimes called regional exchanges).

TABLE 3-1   VOLUME OF 1986 TRADING BY CANADIAN STOCK EXCHANGES

	Number of Shares		Volume by Value, $	
	SHARES TRADED (000)	% OF TOTAL	VALUE ($000,000)	% OF TOTAL
TSE	4,906,702	49.7	63,684.1	75.3
ME	1,095,878	11.1	15,982.7	18.9
VSE	3,493,491	35.4	4,484.5	5.3
ASE	369,243	3.8	476.1	0.5
WSE	518	0.0	0.6	0.0
TOTAL	9,865,832	100.0	84,628	100.0

where:
TSE = Toronto Stock Exchange
ME = Montreal Exchange
VSE = Vancouver Stock Exchange
ASE = Alberta Stock Exchange
WSE = Winnipeg Stock Exchange

Source: Toronto Stock Exchange Factbook, 1986.

**3-2.1
Functions**

Probably the most essential function performed by any exchange is the creation of a *continuous market*—the opportunity to buy or sell securities immediately at a price that varies little from the previous selling price. Thus, a continuous market allows investments to be liquid and marketable, since the investors are not obligated to hold debt securities until maturity, or, if they have common stocks, infinitely long (since common stock never matures or expires unless the corporation is somehow dissolved).

An exchange also helps determine securities prices. Price is determined by buy and sell orders that flow from investors' demand and supply preferences. The exchanges bring together buyers and sellers from all over the nation and from foreign countries; anonymity between buyers and sellers is preserved as their agents transact whatever trades the investor orders.

The stock exchanges also provide a service to industry by indirectly aiding new financing. The ease with which investors can trade issues makes them more willing to invest in new issues.

The Canadian stock markets are relatively thin in terms of total trading volume by comparison with the large international markets, such as the New York Stock Exchange and the Tokyo Stock Exchange. This problem has been identified by Fowler et al.,[3] and Jorion and Schwartz.[4] Both studies analyzed price and volume data for stocks listed on the TSE and concluded that trading volume on the Toronto Stock Exchange was relatively low. Since the TSE is the largest of the Canadian exchanges in terms of trading volume, the problem is more severe on the smaller exchanges.

3-2.2 Organization

Since most of the other exchanges in Canada follow the organizational pattern of the Toronto Stock Exchange, this discussion will focus on the dominant features of the TSE.

The Toronto Stock Exchange has been described as a *voluntary association*. More specifically, it is a corporation that endeavours to maintain a smoothly operating marketplace. The Toronto Stock Exchange, like other exchanges, is directed by a board of governors elected by its members. The TSE board is composed of governors representing member firms and the public. The board is the chief policy-making body of the exchange. Among other duties, it approves or rejects applications of new members; it accepts or rejects budget proposals; it disciplines members through fines, suspension, or expulsion; it accepts or rejects proposals for new security listings; it submits requests to the Ontario Securities Commission (OSC) for changes; and it assigns securities to the various posts on the trading floor.

The main trading floor of the TSE is about thirty thousand square feet in size. There are five trading posts at which equities are traded, three trading posts for options, two trading pits for futures contracts, and a computer-assisted trading system (CATS) terminal. Around the edge of the room are telephone booths, used primarily to transmit orders from the broker's office to the exchange floor and back again to the broker's office after execution of the order. A number of the 1085 or so (it changes constantly) domestic corporations listed on the TSE are assigned to be traded at each of the posts on the trading floor.

---

3 D. J. Fowler, H. Rorke, and V. Jog, "Thin Trading and Beta Estimation Problems on the Toronto Stock Exchange," *Journal of Business Administration* 12, 1980, pp. 77–90.

4 Philippe Jorion and Eduardo Schwartz, "Integration vs. Segmentation in the Canadian Stock Market," *The Journal of Finance*, vol. 41, no. 3, July 1986, pp. 603–616.

There are seventy-two members of the TSE, as of December 1986. Memberships are frequently referred to as *seats*, although trading is conducted without the benefit of chairs. In 1981, seats sold at a record high of $166,000 but by 1986 they were down to only $37,000–$55,000. In most years there are about six transfers of exchange memberships. The composition of the membership varies as to function, but most are partners or employees of brokerage houses.

Commission Brokers Seventy-two seats on the TSE are owned by commission brokers. These seats are owned in the individual's name, but a brokerage house may be financing the individual's purchase of the seat and therefore controlling the seat indirectly. Some large brokerage houses control more than one seat. These exchange members act as agents who buy and sell securities for clients of the brokerage house and as dealers for their own position. Members whose functions differ from those of commission brokers include floor attorneys, floor governors, registered traders, and registered arbitrage traders.

Floor Attorneys Floor attorneys, or floor traders, are representatives of exchange member brokerage firms, entrusted with the responsibility of executing trades on behalf of the member firm clients. These floor traders are strictly employees of the brokerage firms. Fifteen of these floor traders are periodically selected by the board of governors of the TSE as floor governors, charged with the responsibility of overseeing the floor traders. Each member of the exchange is entitled to have six floor attorneys on the trading floor for each seat held, and all attorneys must be approved by the exchange.

Floor Governors Floor governors have powers vested by virtue of the by-laws of the TSE. These include the right to delay an opening in a stock in order to maintain an orderly market, to settle disputes among floor traders, to report floor violations, or even to recommend temporary expulsion from the floor of attorneys who are interfering with trading practices.

Registered Traders The TSE counterpart of the well-known *specialist* on the New York Stock Exchange is the registered trader. There are a number of differences in responsibilities and powers, however.

Registered traders are representatives of member firms of the TSE and are allowed privileges in return for fulfilling specific functions. The major privileges allowed are the right to trade for a firm account in which they have an equity interest or profit-sharing arrangement and an exemption from time-stamping requirements that apply to all other traders. This allows the registered trader considerable flexibility in trading and facilitates a "market-making" function.

In return, the registered trader has a number of responsibilities, such as the maintenance of a market quotation for at least one board lot in his/her stocks of responsibility (typically one to ten) at a maximum specified price spread. The registered trader is also required to maintain bids and offers for odd and broken lots at maximum allowable premiums and discounts according to the schedule at the top of page 54.

SECURITY PRICE	MAXIMUM ODD-LOT PREMIUM/DISCOUNT
Under $0.50	2¢
$0.50-under $1.00	3¢
$1.00-under $2.00	5¢
$2.00-under $5.00	10¢
$5.00-under $60.00	12.5¢
$60.00 and over	25¢

Finally, and foremost, the registered trader is expected to maintain an orderly market in his/her stocks of responsibility. The *Toronto Stock Exchange Members Manual* sets out these requirements specifically. Unless unwinding a position, "Registered traders are prohibited, alone or in concert with other non-client transactions (except where a liability by a member exists) from purchasing on the offering side (or selling on the bid side) of the market an amount of stock in excess of the greater of one-half the amount offered (bid) or ten board lots."[5] The registered trader is also expected to maintain a high proportion of stabilizing trades. A stabilizing trade is one in which purchases (sales) are made at a price below (above) the last preceding different-price trade. Destabilizing trades are the opposite. "It is expected that a maximum of 20 to 30% of a Registered Trader's trades will be destabilizing trades. If more than 30% of a Registered Trader's trades . . . are destabilizing trades, his performance will be deemed unsatisfactory."[6] Furthermore, in establishing or increasing a position in stocks outside his responsibility, the registered trader must always use stabilizing trades.

Registered Arbitrage Traders   Registered arbitrage traders have similar privileges, responsibilities, and functions as registered traders; however, their venue is intermarket trading. Like the registered trader, the registered arbitrage trader is expected to provide minimum spread quotations, buy odd and broken lots subject to maximum premia, and to maintain orderly markets through stabilizing trades. The only distinction is that the registered arbitrage trader is concerned with maintenance of trading on different markets (for example securities listed on both the Toronto Stock Exchange and Montreal Exchange).

Other traders found on the trading floor are designated registered options principals, market makers, options attorneys, designated registered futures principals, futures attorneys, and registered futures traders. These people have responsibilities related to options and futures contracts trading and will be discussed in Chaps. 19 and 20.

**3-2.4
Listing
Requirements**

All firms whose stock is traded on an organized exchange must have at one time filed an application for listing. Some firms, such as Bell Canada Enterprises, are listed on more than one exchange. The TSE has the most stringent

---

5 *Toronto Stock Exchange Members' Manual*, Division G, Part XIX, p. G19–2.
6 *Toronto Stock Exchange Members' Manual*, Division G, Part XIX, p. G19–3.

listing requirements of all the exchanges. For example, to be eligible the firm must have at least 200 stockholders who are holders of round lots; there must be a minimum of 200,000 shares outstanding or 100,000 shares owned by at least 400 different stockholders; and the company must demonstrate earning power of at least $200,000 in pre-tax cashflow or net tangible assets of $1,000,000 at the time of listing. Among its other obligations, a firm applying for TSE membership must be prepared to pay a listing fee and to make its financial statements continuously available to the investing public.[7]

Once a company has met all the requirements for listing and is allowed to have its securities traded on the TSE, it must meet certain requirements established by the exchange and the OSC in order to maintain that privilege. For example, the listed firm must publish quarterly earnings reports; it must fully disclose financial information annually; it must obtain OSC approval of proxy forms before they can be sent to stockholders; and insiders of the firm are prohibited from short selling.[8]

With the strict listing requirements and other requirements after membership, one wonders why firms seek listing on organized exchanges rather than settle for trading on the over-the-counter markets. Part of the answer lies in the fact that the listed firm benefits from a certain amount of "free" advertising and publicity, particularly if its stock is actively traded. This exposure probably has a favourable effect on the sale of its products to the extent that the company's name and its products are associated in the public's mind. Furthermore, some people claim that listing a stock on the TSE enhances the prestige of the listing corporation. If true, that would aid the listed corporations in obtaining capital at a lower cost. But scientific research in the United States has cast doubts on this.[9] However, the investor in a listed security may gain some small convenience from the large quantities of information published about the listed company (for example, the financial reports that the exchanges and securities commissions require the firms to distribute and news about dividends, new products, and new management) that are rapidly disseminated by the news media. Investors also can read in the financial pages the volume of trading that is being done in their companies and the daily high and low prices for shares traded.

In the final analysis, over half the total dollar volume of securities traded in Canada is accounted for by the over-the-counter (OTC) market rather than the organized exchanges, and most of the over-the-counter securities are not listed on any organized exchange. Thus, it would be erroneous to conclude that the OTC market is not also important as a security market in Canada.

---

7 The listing requirements for mining and oil and gas companies, foreign industrial companies, and real estate limited partnerships are different from these. See *Toronto Stock Exchange Members Manual*, vol. 2, pp. G7-3–G7-9.

8 Short selling is discussed in Sec. 19-1 of Chap. 19.

9 L. K. W. Ying, G. Lewellen, G. Schlarbaum, and R. C. Lease, "Stock Exchange Listings and Security Returns," *Journal of Financial and Quantitative Analysis*, September 1977, pp. 415–432. These researchers conclude that there are some immediate and temporary price increases associated with exchange listings. But later price declines appear to wipe out part or all of the earlier gains.

3-3 OVER-THE-COUNTER MARKETS

The term "over the counter" is a bit anachronistic. It originated in the days when securities were traded over the counters of various dealers from their inventories. Now, however, the over-the-counter market is more a way to do business than it is a place. It is a way of trading securities other than on an organized stock exchange. The broker-dealers who engage in the trades of these securities are linked by a network of telephones, telegraphs, teletypewriters, and computer systems through which they deal directly with one another and with customers. Thus, prices are arrived at by a process that takes place over communication lines spanning thousands of miles and allows investors to select among competing market-makers (instead of one monopolistic market-maker in each security, such as the TSE registered trader).

3-3.1 Securities Traded

The securities traded over the counter range from the most risk-free (that is, Canadian government) bonds to the most speculative common stocks. Historically, the OTC markets have been more important as bond markets than as stock markets. All Canadian government, provincial and municipal obligations are traded over the counter.

The OTC stock market is much smaller than the OTC bond market. Many of these OTC issues generate virtually no trading activity because they are shares in small, local corporations that may be closely held by members of the family of the firm's founder. Also, many bank, insurance, and investment company stocks are traded over the counter because in the past the OTC markets required less financial disclosure.

Furthermore, some companies voluntarily choose to have their shares traded over the counter either to save the annual listing fee or simply because the organized stock exchange secondary market format is of little or no perceived value to them.

Trading on the over-the-counter markets is reported daily in the financial press. However, there is far less data supplied on OTC trading than on exchange-listed trading. Reporting is confined to the sales volume, the final trade price, and the closing bid and ask price.

The introduction of electronic communications networks among the more active OTC broker-dealers has improved trading efficiencies; however, for many OTC issues, trading volume is light and the spread between the bid and ask price is wide. In some cases (most noticeably, junior mining companies) the spread can be as much as 100 percent. Such securities are said to be *thinly traded*.

3-3.2 Broker-Dealers

The over-the-counter market is dominated by broker-dealers. Some are wholesalers (that is, they buy from and sell to other dealers), some are retailers (selling mostly to the public), and some serve both functions. If the dealer buys and sells a particular security regularly, he or she is said to *make a market* in that security, serving much the same function as the registered trader on the Toronto Stock Exchange.

As mentioned previously, prices are determined by negotiated bid and asked prices on the OTC markets rather than by a monopolistic and market-making specialist, as on the organized exchanges. But only the bid, ask and closing prices of the OTC securities are published in most daily newspapers.

In the United States in 1971, a computerized communications network called NASDAQ (an acronym for National Association of Security Dealers automated quotations) became operative in the OTC market. NASDAQ (pronounced Naz' dak) provides up-to-date bid-and-ask prices for thousands of securities in response to the simple pressing of appropriate keys on a computer terminal. When an inquiry is made, the NASDAQ computer and telecommunications system instantly flashes prices on the screen of any computer terminal that is linked to NASDAQ's central computer. Thus, the OTC security sales representative can quickly obtain the bid-and-ask quotations of all dealers making a market in the stock he or she wishes to trade. After obtaining this information, the OTC broker then contacts the dealer offering the best price and negotiates a trade. The primary advantage to investors is the assurance that they are receiving the best price. Prior to the inception of NASDAQ, the investor was dependent on the stockbroker's diligence in acquiring bid-and-ask prices from several different market-makers; the broker would contact each individually. The investor could not be certain of receiving the best available price.

NASDAQ is designed to handle up to 20,000 stocks, but it currently lists only about 2,500 (which is still considerably more than the approximately 1,500 that are listed on the NYSE) because most of the other stocks are not active enough to be included within the system. Thus, NASDAQ has much unused capacity that may eventually be put to use by the inclusion of stocks listed on the exchanges. It is advantageous (for everyone except the NYSE specialists) to have all exchange-listed and OTC securities reported through NASDAQ; this makes it easier for investors to compare the prices from competing market-makers. Closer competition should minimize the costs and commission rates investors are charged to buy and sell securities.

Of the few thousand stocks quoted in NASDAQ, not all are published in *The Wall Street Journal* and other daily financial newspapers. In order to be included in the *national daily list* and be widely published, a stock must have at least three market-makers, a minimum of 1,500 stockholders distributed throughout the country, and command what is called "investor interest."

In order to measure investor interest, NASDAQ officials calculate the market value of trading in every issue at six-month intervals. They multiply the average weekly volume of shares traded in each issue by the price per share to estimate the market value of a security's trading activity. The top 1,400 stocks are placed on the "most active list" and the next 950 stocks are placed on the "supplementary list" of stocks for which trading data is to be published. Then the news media publish whatever they wish from these lists.

For those OTC stocks not included in the national daily list, a more comprehensive quotation service is provided by the National Quotation Bureau, an organization whose subscribers are primarily security dealers. It quotes prices of over 8,000 securities on its daily "pink sheets." Its information is derived chiefly from wholesale OTC dealer firms.

3-3.4 Over-the-Counter Quotations— COATS

In April 1986, the Ontario Securities Commission introduced the Canadian Over-the-Counter Automated Trading System (COATS), patterned after NASDAQ. Subscribers can obtain by computer terminal the current best bid and offering, last price and volume for approximately 300 issues that are quoted on a continuous basis by OTC market-makers. A quote on the COATS system by a market-maker is a commitment to buy (for the bid) or sell (for the ask) at least one board lot at the quoted price.

3-4   TRADING ARRANGEMENTS

Before a buy or sell order can be executed, the stockbroker must have explicit orders about the trading arrangements desired by the customer. For example, the broker must know whether the customer wants to specify a market order, limit order, or stop order and also whether the customer prefers to buy on margin or pay cash. These trading arrangements are explained below.

3-4.1 Types of Orders

Investors have several options when placing a buy or sell order. They may request that the broker place a market order, stop order, limit order, or open order to buy or to sell.

Market Orders   This type of order is the most common and most easily executed. With a market order, the customer is simply requesting that the securities be traded at the best possible price as soon as the order reaches the trading floor of the exchange. Market orders are usually traded very rapidly, sometimes in minutes after the order is given the broker, since no price is specified.

Stop Orders   Sometimes called stop loss orders, these are usually designed either to protect a customer's existing profit or to reduce the amount of loss. For example, if Ms. Investor buys a stock for $50 and its current market price rises to $75, she has a *paper profit* of $25 per share. If Ms. Investor fears a drop in the current market price, she could request a stop order to sell at, say, $70. This stop order would in effect become a market order after a board lot traded at $70, and it would be executed as soon as possible after the stock's market price reached $70. The $70 liquidating price is not guaranteed, however. The stock might be down to $69 or $68 or even lower by the time it could be executed. However, the investor's profit position is protected to a large extent. Of course, the danger of using stop loss orders is that the investor runs the risk of selling a security with a future of long-run price appreciation in a temporary decline.

To protect herself from excessive losses, our Ms. Investor may issue a stop order at a price less than the purchase price. For example, if she buys a stock for $50 but feels that it is a speculative investment, she may wish to request a stop order to sell at, say, $45 in order to minimize her loss.

Stop orders are executed in order of priority (as are limit orders). That is, the first stop order received at a given price is the first order executed. An accumulation of stop orders at a certain price can cause a sharp break in the market of the issue involved. In such an event, it is quite likely that the exchange would suspend the stop orders, just at the time the traders really needed the protection. Thus, the value of a stop order can be considerably diminished under such a contingency.

Stop Limit Orders These orders specify both the stop price and the limit price at which the customer is willing to buy or sell. The customer must be willing to run the risk that the security will not reach the limit price, resulting in no trade. If the trade cannot be executed by the floor trader when the order reaches the trading floor, the order will remain as an open order (stored in the TSE computerized Limited Order Trading System) to be executed if the limit price or better is reached.

Suppose that Mr. Morgan owns 2,000 shares of a stock currently selling at $40, but he fears that the price is poised for a decline. To allay his fears, Mr. Morgan places an order: "Sell 2,000 at $38, stop, and limit." As soon as the price of the stock falls to $38 the broker will attempt to execute the order at a price of $38 or better, but in no case at a price below $38. If the stock cannot be sold for $38 or better, there is no sale.

Mr. Morgan's stop limit order would have been more effective had it been placed as follows: "Sell 2,000 shares at $39 stop, $38 limit." If the price of the stock falls to $39, the broker will immediately endeavour to execute the stop portion of the stop limit order. If the stop order isn't executed at $39 for some reason, it may be executed at the $38 limit price or better. But, under no condition will the stock be sold at a price below $38. This second stop limit order is superior to the first stop limit order because there are more opportunities for it to be executed to Mr. Morgan's benefit.

A stop limit order to buy is executed in the reverse order of the stop limit order to sell. As soon as the stock's price reaches the stop level or higher, the stop order to buy is executed at the limit level or better — that is, at a price below the limit price, if possible. Unfortunately, the danger does exist that in a fast-moving market the prices may move so far so fast that even a well-placed stop limit order gets passed over without being exercised.

Open Order or Good-Till-Cancelled (GTC) Order These terms refer to the time in which the order is to remain in effect. An *open order* or a *GTC order* remains in effect indefinitely, whereas a *day order* remains in effect only for the day that it is brought to the exchange floor. The vast majority of orders are day orders, probably because the customer feels that conditions are right for trading on that specific day. Market conditions may change the next day. However, customers may prefer a GTC order, particularly for limit orders, when they are willing to wait until the price is right for trading. GTC orders must be confirmed at various intervals to remain in effect.[10]

Technically, margin trading includes both margin buying and margin short selling. However, only a small portion of total trading on the margin is short selling. (Short selling is discussed in detail in Chap. 19; for now, the concern is with buying on margin.)

3-4.2 Margin Buying

---

10 For more detail about the different kinds of orders and their meanings, read *How to Invest in Canadian Securities*, The Canadian Securities Institute, pp. 141–142.

TABLE 3-2   MARGIN REQUIREMENTS IN CANADA

Equities

TORONTO, MONTREAL, ALBERTA STOCK EXCHANGES*

SECURITY SELLING PRICE	MINIMUM MARGIN REQUIRED
Less than $1.50	100% (cash only—no margin)
$1.50–1.74	80%
$1.75–1.99	60%
$2.00 and over	50%

VANCOUVER STOCK EXCHANGE

$1.00 and over	50%

UNITED STATES UNLISTED SECURITIES

$3.00 and over U.S.	50%

Bonds

ISSUER	MINIMUM MARGIN REQUIRED†

GOVERNMENT OF CANADA

1 year or less to maturity	1% of market value multiplied by the fraction determined by dividing the number of days to maturity by 365
Over 1 year to 3 years	1% of market value
Over 3 years to 10 years	2% of market value
Over 10 years	4% of market value

CANADIAN PROVINCES

1 year or less to maturity	2% of market value multiplied by the fraction determined by dividing the number of days to maturity by 365
Over 1 year to 3 years	3% of market value
Over 3 years to 10 years	4% of market value
Over 10 years	5% of market value

MUNICIPAL BONDS

1 year or less to maturity	3% of market value multiplied by the fraction determined by dividing the number of days to maturity by 365
Over 1 year	5% of market value

*These rates also apply to certain securities traded over the counter in Canada, listed on recognized exchanges in the United States, the Stock List of the Stock Exchange (London), and on the Tokyo Stock Exchange (first section).

†These rates also apply to United Kingdom, United States, and other foreign government bonds with the highest credit ratings.

TABLE 3-2 **MARGIN REQUIREMENTS IN CANADA** (Continued)

Bonds

ISSUER	MINIMUM MARGIN REQUIRED†
CORPORATE BONDS	
1 year or less to maturity	3% of market value multiplied by the fraction determined by dividing the number of days to maturity by 365
Over 1 year to 3 years	6% of market value
Over 3 years to 10 years	7% of market value
Over 10 years	10% of market value

†These rates also apply to United Kingdom, United States, and other foreign government bonds with the highest credit ratings.

When investors buy stock on margin, they buy some shares with cash and borrow to pay for additional shares, using the paid shares as collateral. The shares paid for with the investor's money are analogous to the equity or down payment in an instalment purchase agreement. The stock exchanges control the amount that may be borrowed. For example, if the TSE stipulates a 55 percent margin requirement, the investor must pay cash equal to at least 55 percent of the value of the securities purchased. The buyer may borrow funds to pay for no more than 45 percent of the cost of the securities. The margin requirements on Canadian exchanges are shown in Table 3-2.

Common shares, preferred shares, and warrants listed on Canadian, United States, London and Tokyo (first section only) stock exchanges, certain equities traded over the counter (shares of insurance companies, banks, trust companies, and mutual funds sold by prospectus), and all Canadian bonds traded over the counter are eligible for margin trading in Canada. Table 3-2 indicates the minimum margin requirements for securities traded in Canada.

The investor who wishes to buy on margin is required to open a *margin account* with a stockbroker. Then the investor may be required by the brokerage firm to make a minimum deposit of $2,000 or more.[11] To see how things work, let us assume the margin requirement is 55 percent and Mr. Investor wishes to purchase 100 shares of a $100 stock. In other words, he wishes to make a total investment of $10,000, but assume he has only $5,500 cash of his own. Because of the 55 percent margin requirement, Mr. Investor can still buy 100 shares by paying cash for 55 shares and using them as collateral for a loan to pay for the other 45 shares. Assume Mr. Investor follows this procedure. Consider the position he will be in if his shares double in price to $200 each and, conversely, his position if the price of his shares drops by one-half, to $50 each.

---

11 Some of the most exclusive brokerage firms will not open even a cash account for a new client unless the client makes an initial deposit in excess of $250,000. The brokers at these brokerage firms are able to earn the largest commission incomes since they deal only with ''substantial individuals'' and institutional investors rather than small investors.

The Good News for Mr. Investor   If Mr. Investor's shares double in value from $100 to $200, his total profit will be $100 profit per share times 100 shares, or $10,000 before interest, commissions, and taxes. Compare this $10,000 gross gain with $100 profit per share times only 55 shares, or a $5,500 gross profit, if he has not bought on margin (that is, if he has invested only his $5,500 cash). Mr. Investor's gross profit increased because he bought on margin—as shown in the following T-accounts.

The Cash Purchase Summary follows:

Original Position without Margin

Market value	$5,500	Equity $5,500

Position without Margin after 100% Price Increase

Market value	$11,000	Equity $11,000

Total gain: ($100 per share) times (55 shares) equals $5,500— that is, 100 percent return on the invested cash.

The Margin Purchase Summary follows:

Original Position with Margin

(Assets)		(Liabilities and net worth)
Market value	$10,000	$ 4,500 Debit balance (the loan)
		$ 5,500 Equity
		$10,000 Total

Position with Margin after 100% Price Rise

(Assets)		(Liabilities and net worth)
Market value	$20,000	$ 4,500 Debit balance (the loan)
		$15,500 Equity
		$20,000 Total

Total gain: ($100 per share) times (100 shares) equals $10,000— that is, 182 percent return on the invested cash, an example of favourable financial leverage.

The Bad News for Mr. Investor   Next, let us suppose that Mr. Investor's shares decrease in price from $100 to $50 per share. The current market value of his investment has dropped from $10,000 to $5,000. Compare again his position as a margin buyer with that of a nonmargin buyer. As a margin buyer, he has a $50 per share loss times 100 shares, or a $5,000 loss. If he had not bought on margin and had purchased only 55 shares, his loss would have been $50 per share times 55 shares, or $2,750. Thus we see that by buying stock on 55 percent margin, he can increase his loss as well as his profit. Mr. Investor's losses are summarized in the following T-accounts.

The Cash Purchase Summary follows:

Original Position without Margin

Market value	$5,500	Equity $5,500

Position without Margin after 50% Price Decline

Market value	$2,750	Equity $2,750

Total loss: ($50 per share) times (55 shares) equals $2,750— that is, 50 percent of the invested cash is lost.

The Margin Purchase Summary follows:

Original Position with Margin

(Assets)		(Liabilities and net worth)
Market value	$10,000	$ 4,500 Debit balance (the loan)
		$ 5,500 Equity
		$10,000 Total

Position with Margin after 50% Price Decline

(Assets)		(Liabilities and net worth)
Market value	$5,000	$4,500 Debit balance (the loan)
		$ 500 Equity
		$5,000 Total

Total loss: ($50 per share) times (100 shares) equals $5,000— that is, 91 percent of the invested cash is lost because of adverse financial leverage.

The Worst News for Mr. Investor—A Margin Call   The transactions summarized in the preceding T-accounts do not tell the entire story an investor needs to know. If the stock decreases in value sufficiently, Mr. Investor will receive a *margin call* from his broker—brokers also call it a *maintenance call*. That is, the broker calls and informs the client that it is necessary to put up more margin (that is, to produce additional cash "down payment"). If Mr. Investor cannot come up with the additional cash immediately, the broker must liquidate enough of the stocks Mr. Investor owns at their depressed price in order to bring the equity in the account up to the required level. Selling the margined shares of Mr. Investor is easily accomplished, since margin customers are required to deposit their stock as collateral for the loan from their broker. If anything is left over after the sale and subsequent loan payment, the investor receives the balance.

   The primary benefit of buying on margin is that it allows investors to magnify their profits by the reciprocal of the margin requirement (that is, two times if the margin requirement is one-half, three times if it is one-third, and so forth). The major disadvantage is that it causes magnified losses of the same reciprocal if stock prices decline. There is the added disadvantage of fixed interest payments whether stock prices advance or decline. In sum, margin trading increases risk. Therefore it should be used only by those financially sophisticated individuals who can gracefully assume these added risks.

When an investor buys on margin, the one-period rate of return is defined in Eq. (3-1a).

$$r_t = \frac{p_{t+1} - p_t + d_t - i(1 - m)p_t}{mp_t} \qquad (3\text{-}1a)$$

Equation (3-1a) is different from Eq. (2-2a) for the nonmargin buyer's return. The percentage down payment, or margin, is denoted m in Eq. (3-1a). The denominator, mp_t, is the dollar amount of the margin buyer's equity investment, ignoring commissions. The margin buyer borrowed $(1 - m)p_t$ dollars at an interest rate of i, so the dollar amount of the interest expense, $i(1 - m)p_t$, is deducted from the numerator to obtain the net income return on equity.

For the sake of concreteness, Eq. (3-1a) is reproduced below as Eq. (3-1b) for the case from above in which Mr. Investor purchased a $100 stock on 55 percent margin and then its price doubled to $200. The interest rate Mr. Investor's brokerage firm charged him for the $45 per share loan is presumed to be 10 percent (or $i = .1$). No cash dividends were received while Mr. Investor held the stock.

$$\frac{\$200 - \$100 + 0 - [(.1)(1.0 - .55)(\$100)]}{(.55)(\$100)} = \frac{\$95.50}{\$55} = 1.736 \qquad (3\text{-}1b)$$

Equation (3-1b) shows that Mr. Investor made 173.6 percent return when the price of the stock he bought doubled. Stated differently, margin transformed a 100 percent price rise into a 173.6 percent gain for the lucky investor. (The rate of return is 182 percent if the interest expense is ignored, as it was in the same example above.)

3-4.3 Brokerage Services

The investor services provided by brokerage houses include the following:

1. *Free safe-deposit vaults for securities.* If investors leave their securities with the broker for safekeeping, they are relieved of the responsibility of renting a safe-deposit vault or finding some other means of storage, and they do not have to physically transfer their securities to and from the broker's office every time they wish to buy or sell. If the investor owns bonds and leaves them with the broker, the broker will clip the coupons, collect the interest due, and credit the customer's account.
2. *Free literature compiled and published by the research department.* This literature ranges from a booklet of essential information for the beginning investor to computer printouts of the most up-to-date information on securities compiled by the financial analysts of the firm's research staff. Some brokerage houses also provide free newsletters and brochures on commodity prices, foreign exchange, and various industries.
3. *A market for all types of trading.* The firm can arrange trades from the most speculative of commodities to the most risk-free investments.
4. *A credit agency.* When a customer is buying on margin, the broker will loan the funds. The rate of interest charged is usually at least 1 percent over the prime

rate; it varies with the amount of margin provided and the credit worthiness of the customer.

3-5 SUMMARY AND CONCLUSIONS

Primary securities markets are made by investment dealers who originate new issues of stocks and bonds. After the investment dealers' distribution is completed, the securities are traded in secondary markets. There are different types of secondary markets in Canada—organized exchanges like the TSE and the over-the-counter market. The types of brokers that work the secondary markets range from austere discount brokerages like Marathon Brown (these are discussed in the appendix to this chapter), which supply only the bare-bones services, to the most costly full-service brokerages, like Merrill Lynch Canada.

When an investor gives trading orders to his or her broker, instructions should be given about whether the transaction is to be a cash deal or on margin. Then the client must decide whether to issue a market order, a stop limit order, a stop order, a good-till-cancelled order, or a day order.

One of the most important modifications in the securities industry in recent decades went into effect in April 1983. On that date the TSE and ME abolished the fixed minimum commissions that, for more than a century, had given organized exchanges like the TSE market-making powers that subsidized their profits at the expense of investors. These developments and others are discussed in the appendix to this chapter for those who wish to study more detail about the structure of the stock markets in Canada.

QUESTIONS

1. What benefits do security exchanges provide for the country in which they reside?
2. What types of securities are most frequently traded over the counter?
3. How are selling prices determined over the counter and on the organized exchanges?
4. What are the advantages and disadvantages of trading on margin?
5. If the margin requirement is 65 percent and Mr. Investor intends to purchase 100 shares of $50 per share stock, what is the minimum down payment he will be required to make? Explain.
6. "Price-pegging assures the investment dealer syndicate that no losses will be incurred." Is the preceding statement true, false, or uncertain. Explain.
7. Do you see any conflict of interest between a stockbroker's roles as (a) a sales representative working to maximize commission income and (b) an investment adviser who is trying to give her or his clients advice to maximize their wealth? Explain.
8. What functions are performed by the investment dealer?
9. What is a "market order"?

10. Who are the people called "floor attorneys" within an organized exchange and what do they do?

Note: Questions number 11 and thereafter presume a knowledge of the appendix to Chap. 3.

11. Define the terms "breadth," "depth," and "resilience" as they relate to securities markets.

12. What are some of the benefits associated with efficient security markets?

13. In years past, the managers of large portfolios that spend thousands of dollars on brokerage commissions each year have been offered bribes (for example, free vacations, free research assistance, free prostitutes, gifts of various kinds, and other forms of illegal "payola," "under-the-table money," or "kickbacks") by unethical brokers in order to lure them into directing their portfolio transactions to the unethical brokers. What effect do you think negotiated brokerage commissions will have on such practices? Explain.

14. List the pros and cons of having Canada's stock market policed by, first, the OSC or some other government agency, and second, competition in one big national securities market that is all reported through one computer system like COATS and that has negotiated commission rates. Issues involved include: Would the OSC or competition be the least costly way for a nation to regulate its security markets? Are both needed? Are there certain types of problems that the OSC or competition is not suited to regulate?

15. Do the registered traders on the organized exchanges make those markets more or less efficient in your opinion? Why?

SELECTED REFERENCES

The Canadian Securities Institute. *How to Invest in Canadian Securities*, 1984, chap. 7. Elementary in style, nevertheless it provides a useful discussion of Canadian primary and secondary markets and trading procedures.

Cohen, Kalman J., Steven F. Maier, Robert A. Schwartz, and David K. Whitcomb. *The Microstructure of Security Markets*. Englewood Cliffs, New Jersey: Prentice-Hall, 1986. Chapter 2 of the book provides a comparison of equity markets, including trading methods employed and trading links. Chapter 3 includes considerable detail on electronic trading systems on major equity markets.

Garbade, Kenneth. *Securities Markets*. McGraw-Hill, 1982. The book provides an excellent economic analysis of the determinants of an efficient securities market system in chaps. 20 through 26. Mathematical statistics are used.

Hatch, James E. *Investment Management in Canada*. Prentice-Hall Canada, 1983. Chapter 7 provides some information on the history of exchanges in Canada.

Ross, Alexander. *The Traders*. Collins, 1984. A fascinating journalistic history of the development of stock exchanges and stock trading in Canada is presented.

Tewles, Richard J., and Edward S. Bradley. *The Stock Market*. New York: Wiley, 1982. This book describes in detail the institutions and practices that make up securities markets in the United States. No mathematics used.

Securities Markets Developments

Chapter 3 discussed the most important aspects of the securities markets in Canada. This appendix delves into more subtle and abstract market developments. These more sophisticated elements of the market's evolution are an extension of the basic concepts introduced throughout the chapter.

APP. 3A-1 BROKERAGE COMMISSIONS, FULL SERVICE, AND DISCOUNT BROKERS

The era of negotiated commissions began in April 1983 with two resulting effects: the intrusion of discount brokerage firms into the Canadian securities brokerage field and a new set of commission policies or guidelines for full service brokerage firms.

Discount Brokers

Discount brokers are no-frills operations. They offer order-taking capacity to clients for a commission. The registered representatives at discount brokerage firms are typically paid a salary rather than the commission income that their counterparts earn at full-service firms. The registered representatives are required under provincial securities laws to discuss specific trades with clients and to examine with them how requested trades will meet client objectives. However, this is conducted in the main, in a perfunctory and casual manner.

Discount brokerage firms typically do not provide research reports, recommendations, and the other services available at full-service firms.

Discount brokers have a published commission schedule from which, except for very large trades, they will not be willing to negotiate commissions further.

Full-Service Brokers

The full service brokerage firm offers its clients a wide range of investment and financial services including, among other things, specific company and industry research reports, advice and recommendations on specific trades, securities safekeeping, special interest accounts, and margin accounts. Registered representatives at these firms earn commissions on trades (typically 25 to 40 percent of the total client commission paid per trade) and are required to discuss carefully the suitability of each trade with clients before placing orders.

A full-service firm will have an internal commission schedule (usually not published) from which it will normally be willing to discount commissions for trades in excess of $3,000 to $5,000. Discounts can be as high as 40 percent from the base commission schedule. Registered representatives at most firms have some discretion in granting discounts; their willingness to negotiate will depend on the size of a customer's account and the frequency and size of trades.

The careful investor will recognize that he or she is paying for the additional services at the full-service brokerage firm through higher commissions than those paid at discount brokers. The table below sets out typical commissions at Canadian discount and full-service brokerage firms by size of trade and price of security. As can be seen, the larger the trade the greater the discount typically associated with dealing with a discount broker.

TABLE APP. 3A-1   TYPICAL COMMISSION RANGES FOR DISCOUNT AND FULL-SERVICE BROKERAGE FIRMS

	Full-Service Firms		
	PRICE OF SECURITY		
Size of trade	$2.50	$10.00	$25.00
$1,000	$25–35	$25–35	$25–35
2,000	45–65	45–55	40–50
5,000	80–170	80–150	80–100
10,000	110–325	110–275	110–200
20,000	150–625	150–525	150–375
	Discount Brokerage Firms		
	PRICE OF SECURITY		
Size of trade	$2.50	$10.00	$25.00
$1,000	$30–50	$30–45	$30–45
2,000	30–55	30–50	30–45
5,000	50–70	50–70	50–70
10,000	100–125	50–100	50–100
20,000	180–300	80–140	60–100

Source: CCH Canadian, *Guide to International Investing*, p. 24707.

APP. 3A-2   THE MARKET QUALITIES OF DEPTH, BREADTH, AND RESILIENCE

Perfectly *liquid* assets are *perfectly marketable* and suffer no shrinkage in value as a result of being liquidated hurriedly. Or, stated from a negative viewpoint, *illiquid* assets are not readily marketable — either price discounts must be given, or sales commissions must be paid, or both of these costs must be incurred by the seller in order to find a new investor for an illiquid asset. The less marketable an asset, the larger are the price discounts and/or the commissions that must be given up by the seller in order to effect a quick sale. The amount of such price concessions demanded from the sellers in a security market is one indicator of how much marketability risk investors are exposed to in that market.

Definition of the Bid-Asked Price Spread

Most securities markets have two prices posted for every security traded there — both a bid price and an asked (or offered) price. The TSE, for example, has bid and asked prices for every stock it lists. But only one price is printed for each security in the newspapers around the world each day. This single price is called the *execution price*; it is the price at which the last trade of the day was executed. Publishing only the execution price rather than both the bid and asked prices may be a public relations gimmick designed (1) to make things look simple, and (2) to conceal from casual observers the cut the brokers take out of every transaction.

You can sell an asset to the highest bidder at a price called its bid price. And you can buy an asset at the lowest price at which it is offered — called its asked (or offered) price. The bid price is always below the asked price. The bid-asked price spread is the cost of selling an asset quickly. Seen differently, the bid-asked spread is the dealer's reward for making a market in the asset.[12]

The bid-asked spread can be thought of as being (1) the price discount the seller had to give up to sell the asset quickly, or alternatively, (2) the broker's commission for handling the transaction. Or if the intermediary was a dealer instead of a broker, the bid-asked spread is the dealer's compensation for buying the asset and carrying it in inventory until another buyer can be found.

Figure App. 3A-1*a* and App. 3A-1*b* illustrate three different prices. The equilibrium price, P_E, is the price that would equate supply and demand in a perfect market. For example, in a perfect market, taxes, brokers' commissions, and other transactions costs would not exist. Thus, the equilibrium price is a theoretical price that will never emerge in a real-world market. The bid price, P_B, is the highest purchase price known available in the market; the asked (or offered) price, P_A, is the lowest price at which the asset is offered for sale.

FIGURE APP. 3A-1(a) and (b) Supply and demand schedules for the same asset in a weak market and a strong market.

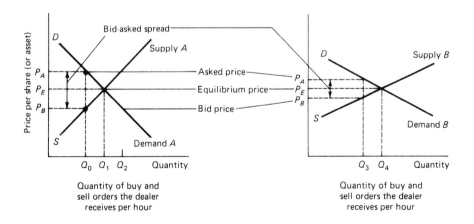

12 George J. Benston and Robert L. Hagerman, ''The Determinants of Bid-Asked Spreads in the Over-the-Counter Market,'' *Journal of Financial Economics*, vol. 1, December 1974, pp. 353–364; Harold Demsetz, ''The Cost of Transacting,'' *Quarterly Journal of Economics*, vol. 82, February 1968.

Strong and Weak Markets Contrasted

An asset may not be easily marketable for either or both of two basic reasons. First, the asset itself may be intrinsically undesirable. For an example of an undesirable asset, consider a corporation that issued a common stock while it was being sued in bankruptcy court—this stock would be risky to carry in inventory and hard to sell. As a result, if you were a securities dealer, for instance, you would charge your clients more to set up a trade in some shares of stock in a bankrupt corporation than if they wanted to trade the same number of shares in a blue-chip security. Second, and more to the point of this discussion of market qualities, the strength of the market in which the asset is traded can affect its bid-asked spread.

Figure App. 3a-1a depicts a weak market in which a large bid-asked spread is needed to sell the asset. Figure App. 3A-1b depicts a strong market where a small bid-asked spread is all that is needed in order to sell the same asset illustrated in Fig. App. 3A-1a within the same length of time. Stated more analytically, the market illustrated in Fig. App. 3A-1b is stronger and less fragmented, enjoys more trading volume, and is more internally efficient than the weak market in Fig. App. 3A-1a because the strong market has more *depth, breadth,* and *resilience*.

The terms "depth," "breadth," and "resilience" are defined in the remainder of this section. A securities market should have considerable depth, breadth, and resilience or else investors who trade securities there will be exposed to marketability risk.

Market Depth Defined

A market that is *deep* has buy and sell orders for the asset traded in that market that continuously exist both above and below the market price. As a result, when there is an imbalance in the quantity of buy and sell orders in a deep market, the resulting price changes are small. Markets that lack depth are called *shallow markets*. The market prices of assets traded in shallow markets typically jump about in an erratic and disconcerting fashion because there are few orders to buy and sell and the price range between these sparse orders is wide. The Toronto Stock Exchange provides a deeper market for most of the securities it lists than do many foreign security markets. For example, The Frankfurt and Milan bourses are particularly shallow.

Figure App. 3A-1b illustrates how the price changes necessary to find a buyer or seller for a given quantity of a specific security are smaller than are needed in the weaker market shown in Fig. App. 3A-1a. The strong market in Fig. App. 3A-1b enjoys more depth than the market in Fig. App. 3A-1a. That is, orders to buy or sell that are *quickly and easily found* extend far above and below the bid and asked prices in the strong market of Fig. App. 3A-1b, but they extend over only a limited range in the shallow market.

By definition, the transaction-to-transaction price changes are smaller in a deep market than in a shallow market. Therefore, a market-maker for an asset that enjoys a *depth of orders* instead of a shallow order flow is less likely to suffer losses on assets carried in inventory. As a result of this reduced risk of doing business, the bid-asked spreads that dealers charge are less in deep markets than they are in shallow markets.

In order for a market to have depth, it does not matter whether the market participants are all assembled at a single geographic location or widely dispersed around the world. But the market participants must have a good, fast, inexpensive communication system with each other so that they can locate and quickly act upon all bid and asked prices. *Fragmented markets* lack depth because, by definition, some bid and asked prices may go undiscovered for significant intervals of time — the buyers and sellers have trouble communicating their trading desires to each other in a fragmented market. In contrast, a geographically dispersed market that enjoys centrally reported offers to trade through computerized telecommunications (such as NASDAQ) is not a fragmented market — it can be a deep and unfragmented market if the requisite array of bid and asked prices are continuously present through computer hookups.

A market is said to be *broad* or have *breadth* if the bid and asked orders exist in substantial volume. Markets that operate with few buyers and sellers at any given moment and generate only a moderate volume of orders are called *thin markets*.[13] Comparing parts *a* and *b* of Fig. App. 3A-1 reveals that the market in Fig. App. 3A-1*b* has more breadth than its weak counterpart because the quantity of orders generated by the same equilibrium price is larger in the strong market, as indicated by the fact that $Q_4 > Q_1$ in the two figures. Dealers operating in a broad market should be willing to charge smaller bid-asked spreads than dealers in thin markets, because the broad markets provide more transactions on which the dealers can collect their bid-asked spread.[14]

Breadth and Resilience Defined

When an imbalance between the buy and sell orders arriving at the market arises, an appropriate price change is all that is needed to restore the proper order balance. When new orders pour in immediately after the price changes in a market, that market is said to be *resilient*. Fast and inexpensive market communications are necessary for a market to be resilient. And dealers in a resilient market should be willing to charge smaller bid-asked spreads because there is less risk that they will be stuck holding an inventory of assets they cannot sell if the price falls. Thus, resilience is a valuable quality for a market to possess.

As explained above in Sec. 3-2 of this chapter, TSE registered traders are monopoly market-makers in whatever stock the exchange assigns them. In their role as market-makers, one of their duties is to collect limit orders and stop orders from customers all over the world, record these orders in their *order book*, and execute these orders expeditiously ahead of their own orders

Marketability from the Viewpoint of a NYSE Specialist

13 For more detail see Kenneth Garbade, *Security Markets* (New York: McGraw-Hill, 1982), chap. 26.

14 Kalman Cohen, Steven Maier, Robert Schwartz, and David Whitcomb, "The Returns Generating Process, Returns Variance, and the Effect of Thinness in Securities Markets," *Journal of Finance*, vol. 33, March 1978; Thomas Epps, "Security Price Changes and Transaction Volume: Some Additional Evidence," *Journal of Financial and Quantitative Analysis*, March 1977, vol. 14.; Richard Rogalski, "The Dependence of Prices and Volumes," *The Review of Economics and Statistics*, May 1978; George Tauchen and Mark Pitts, "The Price Variability-Volume Relationship of Speculative Markets," *Econometrica*, vol. 51, March 1983.

at the time indicated on the customers' orders.[15] Table App. 3A-2 is a hypothetical bid page from the order book of a TSE registered trader who is making a market in a stock with a current market price of $68.50 per share. The figure shows four numerical examples of how breadth and depth might differ for the stock.

TABLE APP. 3A-2   FOUR NUMERICAL EXAMPLES OF DIFFERENT DEGREES OF BREADTH AND DEPTH IN A REGISTERED TRADER'S ORDER BOOK FOR A STOCK

BID PRICE	THIN AND SHALLOW	THIN BUT DEEP	BROAD BUT SHALLOW	BROAD AND DEEP
$68	100	100	500	500
$67	100.	100	500	500
$66	0	300	0	700
$65	0	300	0	900
$64	0	300	0	1,500

Summarizing, a market has *depth* when orders exist both above and below the price at which the security is currently trading. A market has *breadth* when the orders referred to in the preceding sentence exist in substantial volume. A market is *resilient* when price changes that are caused by order imbalances are immediately followed by an outpouring of new orders. Any given market will be more deep, broad, and resilient when information dissemination about prices and transactions costs is wide, fast, and accurate.

APP. 3A-3   EFFICIENT SECURITIES MARKETS

An *efficient capital market* can be defined as a market that will channel liquid capital quickly and accurately to where it will do the nation the most good. For example, if a competent woman discovers and patents a "better mousetrap," forms a mousetrap corporation, and sells shares of stock in it to the investing public, an efficient market will channel funds out of the stock of inferior firms and reallocate these funds so that they are invested in the securities of the manufacturer of the better mousetrap. This reallocation of capital funds will materialize only if two conditions are met. First, the woman who holds the patent on the better mousetrap must be able to obtain a fair appraisal of her product's value in the securities markets. This appraisal is essential in order for her to be able to sell common stock and thus raise the capital funds she requires to start producing the better mousetrap. However, in order for this first condition to occur a second condition must also be met. Second, the market-makers must charge brokerage commissions that are not

[15] A moment's consideration suggests to those familiar with computers that the registered trader job could probably be performed faster, cheaper, and more surely by using a computer. However, the exchange members are reluctant to computerize themselves out of a lucrative job. N. H. Hakansson, A. Beja, and J. Kale, "On the Feasibility of Automated Market Making by a Programmed Specialist," *Journal of Finance*, vol. 40, no. 1, March 1985, pp. 1–20.

too high, or the profit incentives that motivate the inventive woman and her potential investors to start to work will diminish.

Essentially, the Better Mousetrap Corporation, or any business, requires two kinds of market efficiencies in order to grow and prosper: (1) *external market efficiency*, that is, the existence of outsiders who can quickly and accurately appraise the true economic value of an enterprise so that they know what price to pay for a share in it, and (2) *internal market efficiency*, that is, the ability of a market to equate the supply of and the demand for its securities at a reasonable brokerage commission cost (or, equivalently, bid-asked spread). We will now discuss the two types of market efficiencies and their impact on the allocation of resources.

External efficiency "means that new information is widely, quickly, and cheaply available to investors, that this information includes what is knowable and relevant for judging securities and is rapidly reflected in their prices."[17] As a result of external efficiency, the price of a security should fully reflect available information.[18]

External or Pricing Efficiency[16]

Sometimes a securities market deemed to be externally efficient (the New York Stock Exchange, for example) is said to be a fair game for its participants. Essentially, the "fair game" label refers to the fact that no significant number of investors consistently uses inside information in order to earn profits by trading with other investors who do not have access to the same information. Of course, some investors in a market that is externally efficient may be "ripped off" because they were too lazy to investigate before they invested, but this represents an example of investor laziness rather than an external inefficiency. As long as all investors can get the same set of information if they work at it, the investors are participating in a fair-game market, which can also be called an externally efficient market.

Efficient security markets are very desirable. They allocate capital when and to where able business executives need it and reward the investors who provide this needed capital with adequate returns. On the other hand, incompetent business managers and investors will be disciplined by failure in an efficient market — the price of securities in a badly managed firm will fall because of lack of demand. As a result, attention will be drawn to the firm's incompetent management and the incompetents will be forced to seek other tasks for which they are better suited.

Impediments to External or Pricing Efficiency   Some of the major imperfections in the capital market mechanism are as follows:

1. *Uninterested shareholders*. Shareholders frequently assign their voice in management to the corporation's executives by signing proxy statements. Ineffective management may thus be perpetuated until such time as a majority of shareholders

---

16 R. R. West, "On the Difference between Internal and External Market Efficiency," *Financial Analysts Journal*, November-December 1975, pp. 30–34.

17 J. Lorie and R. Brealey, *Modern Developments in Investment Management* (New York: Praeger, 1972), p. 101.

18 E. F. Fama, "Efficient Capital Markets: A Review of Theory and Empirical Work," *Journal of Finance*, May 1970, p. 383.

become dissatisfied with their returns, refuses to sign proxy statements, and votes in new management.[19]

2. *Earnings retention used for financing.* Most corporations prefer to finance their expansion by retaining earnings rather than by using new securities. Such internal financing is cheaper than the issuance of new securities, but it allows management to ignore the price of the firm's securities in the financial markets and thereby avoid the discipline of the market.

3. *Investor ignorance.* Some investors buy securities on the basis of rumors or "hot tips" without investigating to determine whether the investment has true value.

4. *Mob speculation.* Hysteria temporarily determines security prices when mob speculation (such as that which followed the election of the Parti Québécois in Quebec) occurs. This condition results in incorrectly priced securities, which, in turn, leads to misallocation of capital to unproductive uses.

In the final analysis, the more diligently that investors investigate before they invest, the more externally efficient their capital markets will be. However, even after a market is externally efficient, it still cannot allocate resources efficiently unless it is also internally efficient.

Internal or Operational Efficiency

If a security market were perfectly efficient externally, then the market price of every security would equal the security's true economic value. However, it would still not be possible for the externally efficient market to allocate resources efficiently unless the cost and speed required to trade securities were reasonable; this is where internal efficiency becomes relevant. All the securities must be *immediately marketable* in order for a market to be internally efficient. Furthermore, the brokerage commission charges for trading securities (or what is often the same thing, the spread between the bid and the asked price) must not be so high that they will discourage the frequent transactions necessary to keep the market's trades reflecting current conditions.

In order for a securities market to continuously provide its investing customers with the opportunity to transact their buy and sell orders quickly at a low cost per transaction and thus be *internally efficient*, the market must have competing market-makers. The market-makers should stand ready to accommodate transactions by purchasing for their own inventories from investors who wish to sell and by being ready to sell to investors from their own inventories of securities. That is, the market-makers should continuously maintain bid (that is, their offering price to buy) and asked (their offer to sell) prices for all securities in which they choose to deal. And the brokerage commission, or the bid-asked spread, charged by these dealers should not be high—it should be only enough to provide a fair rate of return for competent market-makers.

19 One of the early classic studies documenting the phenomenon of stockholder apathy was A. A. Berle and G. C. Means, *The Modern Corporation and Private Property*, (New York: Macmillan, 1934). Also see Michael C. Jensen and W. H. Meckling, "Theory of the Firm: Managerial Behavior, Agency Costs and Ownership Structure," *Journal of Financial Economics*, October 1976, vol. 3, no. 4, pp. 305–360. A collection of studies dealing with this topic may be found in *Journal of Financial Economics*, vol. 11, April 1983.

The New York Stock Exchange provides an interesting case of improved internal efficiency. The NYSE's transactions efficiency was improved by a law that took effect on May 1, 1975—called "May Day" on Wall Street. Before May Day, the NYSE had refused to let its chosen securities be listed on any other exchanges. Furthermore, all the NYSE member firms agreed never to charge less than some fixed, minimum level of brokerage commission on every transaction they handled. Thus, although the securities prices on the NYSE fluctuated, the fee for the NYSE's brokerage service was not negotiable (that it, it had a fixed minimum level that was profitable for NYSE member firms to support). As a result, the NYSE was a monopoly market-maker and a noncompeting, price-fixing cartel.

However, the Securities and Exchange Commission decreed that the NYSE must cease its price-fixing cartel on May 1, 1975, and as a result, the NYSE's internal efficiency improved rapidly. The commission rate that NYSE brokerages charged for their service dropped approximately 25 percent immediately, and continued reductions of lesser importance followed.[20] Also, competition from other market-makers, who went into competition with the NYSE by making over-the-counter markets in the NYSE-listed stocks, probably also improved the depth, breadth, and resilience of the market for securities that benefited from having more than one market-maker. Almost everyone except the NYSE member firms benefited from the improvement in the NYSE's internal efficiency. Even noninvestors who have never owned a security benefit from increased market efficiency because resources are allocated more effectively.

In Canada, deregulated commissions were introduced in April 1983. By June of that year the average commission paid per share had fallen from 14.34¢ in April to 12.72¢. A trend was established, however. Small investors (trades of less than $20,000), were paying higher commissions than they were before deregulation, while the larger investors (trades of $20,000 and up) were paying less. This trend has continued.[21]

Resource Allocation

The labour and capital resources in an economy should be mobile so that they can go to the highest bidder. The highest bidder is presumably willing to pay more than lower bidders because of more urgent and/or more profitable uses for the resources. Thus, if labour and capital are mobile, they will be used at the time and the place that will tend to increase everyone's health, welfare, or happiness (as measured by gross national product per capita, for

---

20 R. O. Edmister, "Commission Cost Structure: Shifts and Scale Economies," *Journal of Finance*, vol. 33, no. 2, May 1978, pp. 477–486; J. L. Hamilton, "Competition, Scale Economies, and Transaction Costs in the Stock Market," *Journal of Financial and Quantitative Analysis*, vol. 11, pp. 779–802; J. L. Hamilton, "Marketplace Fragmentation, Competition, and the Efficiency of the Stock Exchange," *Journal of Finance*, March 1979, vol. 34, no. 1, pp. 171–187; Hans Stoll, "The Pricing of Security Dealer Services: An Empirical Study of NASDAQ Stocks," *Journal of Finance*, vol. 33, pp. 1153–1172; "Wall Street Is Finding after Ten Years, That It Enjoys Unfixed Rates," *Wall Street Journal*, April 22, 1985, pp. 1 and 18.

21 The Toronto Stock Exchange, RAMA Research (Revenue and Market Analysis), various dates.

example) the most. This is also true of investment funds, since they are one particular kind of capital.

Efficient security markets—in both the internal and the external senses—will make investment capital more mobile and thus help allocate resources so that they can be put to the best use. All this means simply that if someone does invent a truly better mousetrap, efficient markets will provide the capital financing needed to manufacture the product on a large scale and we will all be able to enjoy better mousetraps as a result. This benefit will not be obtained without some work, however. An investor can help develop internally efficient markets (and also save on commission costs) by negotiating with security brokers over the fees for their services.

APP. 3A-4   ELECTRONIC TRADING DEVELOPMENTS

A recent development in stock, options, and futures trading procedures has been the introduction of electronic order routing, placement, and quotation systems. In Secs. 3-3.3 and 3-3.4 you learned about the 1971 NASDAQ pioneering electronic quotation system introduced in the United States and the 1986 development of COATS in Canada. In the section below is a brief description of electronic *trading* systems introduced on the Toronto Stock Exchange.

Computer-Assisted Trading System (CATS)

In 1977 the Toronto Stock Exchange installed the first fully automated stock-trading system, called the Computer-Assisted Trading System (CATS), on a trial basis for thirty listed and inactively traded stocks. The experimental period ended September 30, 1979, and the system became fully operative with the number of inactive stocks traded through CATS increased to about 700. By June 1985, some 793 stocks, or over 52 percent of total TSE issues, were traded exclusively on the CATS system.[22] This system allows brokers to enter trading orders by computer terminal for execution from remote locations, including those outside Canada.[23] The two trading systems applications underlying CATS are MOST and LOTS.

Market Order System of Trading (MOST)

The Market Order System of Trading (MOST) allows for streamlined, automated trading for all stocks traded on the TSE for specific size, customer market orders. Toronto Stock Exchange members can electronically route market orders of 1,099 shares for the most liquid stocks and 599 shares for all other stocks for instantaneous execution on the Toronto Stock Exchange's computer system.

Orders are automatically treated as day orders, all or none and fill or kill by the system. No other order may be entered. No premium or discount is charged on odd-lot orders.

---

22 The Toronto Stock Exchange, *1985 Fact Book*.

23 The Paris Stock Exchange installed the TSE CATS system in 1986, after a trial period. The introduction of CATS creates the first continuous trading market and stock quotation system in France.

The Limit Order Trading System (LOTS) allows member-brokers to enter limit orders of any size for clients, either electronically from off the floor (e.g., from terminals in brokers' offices) or from the floor itself. The orders are entered directly to the TSE's list of orders for that stock (the TSE "Book"). These orders then compete with the orders placed from the floor.

Orders allowed are day, open, good till cancelled (GTC), or GTD (good till a certain date). Only customer orders can be entered through LOTS, i.e., professional or member orders cannot be routed in this way.[24] The introduction of computer-assisted trading has decreased trade execution time, lowered costs for odd-lot traders, and increased the number of "fills."

APP. 3A-5   LINKED TRADING

An important recent development has been the worldwide proliferation of trading links between secondary markets of different countries. In 1984 the Chicago Mercantile Exchange (CME) and the Singapore International Monetary Exchange (SIMEX) linked trading in 90-day Eurodollar and West German mark futures contracts on a mutual offset basis. As a result, investors could buy or sell contracts on one exchange and offset their position (sell or buy back) on the other. Thus the sleepless investor, worried about his or her mark futures, doesn't have to wait for the market to open in Chicago in the morning, but can trade contracts overnight!

Four trading hookups have taken place involving Canadian Exchanges in the 1980s: Montreal Exchange/Vancouver Stock Exchange/European Options Exchange/(Amsterdam)/Sydney Stock Exchange gold option trading link (1982 to 1985); Montreal Exchange/Boston Stock Exchange (1984) stock-trading arrangement; Toronto Stock Exchange/American Stock Exchange (AMEX) (1985) stock link; and the Toronto Stock Exchange/Midwest Stock Exchange (Chicago) stock link.

The TSE/AMEX link, for example, allows for two-way trading in the thirty-six Canadian-based stocks that are listed for trading on both exchanges. Orders can be routed either way between the exchanges, using the MOST system of the TSE or the AUTOPER (Post Execution Reporting) system of AMEX. The implication of these links for trading facilities and market efficiencies are most important, although whether these and other links add to market efficiencies in the long run is an empirical question.

---

[24] For more specific information on CATS, MOST, and LOTS, see Toronto Stock Exchange, *CATS Traders' Manual, Notices to CATS Traders, MOST Users' Manual,* and *LOTS Users' Manual.*

CHAPTER 4

Securities Law

Canada has one of the strongest economies in the world because it has reasonably efficient capital markets. Businesspeople in Canada can raise the funds they need to start new businesses or expand existing businesses by selling common stock, preferred stock, or bonds in a ready-and-waiting capital market. The capital markets in Canada channel billions of dollars from savers to investors every year. If these investment funds were not available to the business community, the Canadian economy would stagnate, unemployment would rise, and gross national product (that is, national income) per capita would fall. Strong capital markets are essential to maintain everyone's welfare.

To maintain and augment its capital markets, the provincial governments have taken various legal steps to ensure that the markets are fair and honest places where small savers and big investors alike can place their funds. In particular, laws forbidding fraud and price manipulation have been passed and agencies have been established specifically to enforce these securities laws. This chapter explains the various laws, legal agencies, and codes that govern capital markets and the investment industry in Canada. However, before examining these various programs, it will be helpful to consider the market disorders, fraudulent activities, and price manipulation schemes that led to regulation of securities markets.

4-1 THE ABUSES THAT MOTIVATED PASSAGE OF SECURITIES LAWS

Most of the worst abuses in the securities markets occurred before any strong security regulations existed. A number of provinces had passed so-called blue-sky laws, but they were deficient in many respects. Often by the time the provincial officials got around to prosecuting for the sales of worthless or fraudulent securities, the promoters had long since left the province and were not, therefore, subject to its jurisdiction. Mainly because of a lack of effective legal controls, scandalous activities using ''wash sales,'' ''corners on the market,'' ''churning,'' ''pools,'' and excessive ''pyramiding of debt'' preceded the great crash of the stock market, which lasted from 1929 to 1933. Since that time, more subtle problems involving ''insider information'' and fraud have occurred. Each of these disorders will be discussed briefly before the regulations that have been enacted to stop them are examined.

A *wash sale* is, essentially, no sale at all. For example, if a man sells securities to his child, this is a wash sale (assuming he can control his child). Or, someone may buy *and* sell a given quantity of some security in the same day; this, too, is a wash sale. The purpose of a wash sale is to establish a record of a sale. This may be done to establish a tax loss or to deceive someone into believing that the market price has changed.

4-1.1   Wash Sales

For example, suppose a dishonest investor were trying to purchase shares in the Ajax Corporation at less than the current market price of $40 per share. If Ajax shares were inactively traded, wash sales could be used to create the illusion of a falling price. The dishonest investor could buy and sell his or her own shares of Ajax at prices below $40, using fictitious names and several different securities brokers. The prices of these sales would be a public record. This would create the illusion that Ajax shares had fallen in price. Then the dishonest investor might be able to purchase shares in Ajax at less than $40 from an innocent party who owned shares but was unaware that the low prices from the wash sales were fraudulently generated.

The Criminal Code of Canada makes wash sales illegal. Swindlers who use wash sale schemes can be fined and/or sent to jail.

An investor who "corners the market" in some security or commodity buys all of that item that is for sale. This person then owns the only source of supply. This monopolistic seller who has the corner can then arbitrarily raise the price simply by withholding the supply of the item offered for sale. Eager buyers will bid up the price in hopes of coaxing some supply of the item out on the market so that they may purchase it. Price manipulators who obtain a corner on the market of some asset may then liquidate it at a high price for a capital gain. Or, a price-manipulating speculator might corner a market in hopes of trapping or "squeezing" short sellers by withholding the supply that is offered for sale, and then waiting while eager short sellers bid up the price as they try unsuccessfully to buy the item that they need to deliver. After the price is bid up to higher levels, the party that has the market cornered can sell the item to the short sellers at high prices that will throw them for substantial losses.

4-1.2   Corners

Short sellers are speculators who sell an asset they do not own.[1] They expect the price of that asset to fall, enabling them to purchase the asset at the new lower price and then deliver at the higher price at which they had *previously* arranged to sell it. Thus, short sellers profit from price declines.

The Criminal Code of Canada made price manipulation in securities markets illegal. By section 338(2) of the Criminal Code of Canada:

Every one who, by deceit, falsehood, or other fraudulent means, whether or not it is a false pretence within the meaning of this Act, with intent to defraud, affects the

---

1 Short selling is defined and discussed in detail in Sec. 19–1 of Chap. 19.

public market price of stocks, shares, merchandise or anything that is offered for sale to the public, is guilty of an indictable offence and is liable for imprisonment for ten years.

**4-1.3
Churning**

Law books define *churning* as the abuse of a customer's confidence for the personal gain of a securities broker by frequent and/or large transactions that are disproportionate to the size and nature of the customer's account. Churning is a very common and also a very safe way for securities brokers to steal funds from their clients' accounts while escaping detection by all but the most watchful of clients. Brokers are able to profit from churning a client's account because the broker earns a commission on every purchase and every sale regardless of whether the customer gains or loses on the trade. Churning occurs when a broker feeds clients "hot tips" that motivate them to buy and/or sell. Sales commissions are thus generated for the broker whether or not the client gains from the transactions. The practice is called "churning" because it involves *turning over* a client's account.

It is very difficult for a client who has been robbed by a broker to prove that churning occurred, provided the broker used some discretion. For example, if the broker merely plants the seed that blooms into a fruitless trade by giving the client worthless hot tips, it is difficult for the hapless client to even recognize that he or she was victimized. And furthermore, if the broker, who typically handles numerous accounts, does not churn any single account too frequently, it is difficult to prove that any churning occurred. There is, after all, no law that makes a broker liable for unprofitable trades a client may voluntarily undertake.

Successful civil lawsuits based on churning are rare; only the most obviously unscrupulous brokers and/or the brokerage houses end up paying damages to their clients. An example of an easy-to-win case of churning, for instance, occurs when a broker executes trades for a client's account without obtaining the client's permission to execute the trade.

To succeed in an action against a broker for churning, the wronged client must be able to demonstrate that the level of trading was excessive, that the broker in question had complete discretion over the client's account *while acting for a brokerage firm as a registered representative*, that the client was relatively naive, and that the type of trading conducted was at odds with the investment goals set out by the client when the account was opened.[2]

There have been few successful churning suits by Canadian investor/clients, possibly because clients and brokerage firms have willingly settled out of court.

4-1.4   Pools

A *pool* is a formal or informal association of two or more persons with the objective of manipulating prices and profiting from them. When this objective is completed, the pool is dissolved. A few manipulators may verbally agree to operate as a pool, or a contract involving many members can be drawn

2 See Claire Bernstein, "Churning Can Earn Brokers Contempt, Disdain, and Lawsuits", *The Globe and Mail*, July 21, 1986, p. B11.

up. Some of the pool members may provide capital; some may provide inside information; some may manage the pool's operations; or all may participate in all those functions. Some pools have hired managers for a fee or a percentage of the profits. Some pools even have had specialists from securities exchanges in collusion as hired managers or members of the pool. In general, pools do not tend to conform to any particular organizational format.

During the early 1900s there were basically two kinds of pools—trading pools and option pools. A *trading pool* purchased the shares in which it was interested in the open market. The trading pools usually tried to acquire the securities quietly and discreetly in order to keep from driving up the security's price they were buying by disseminating unfavourable publicity about the firm.

After a trading pool or an option pool had accumulated large quantities of the security at favourable prices, it would work to manipulate the price upward. Favourable information about the firm would often be disseminated in the form of rumours or hot tips. Pool members who were brokers would recommend the security to their customers. Pool members within the firm whose securities were being manipulated would issue favourable publicity about the firm. Radio commentators and news reporters were paid by some pools to recommend securities. Pools also churned the market in their security by transacting numerous wash sales to call attention to the security and make it appear to have an active market at rising prices. The pool's tactics were often successful in manipulating naive investors into bidding up the price of the pool's security.

When the market price of the pool's securities reached a high figure and was supported there by strong demand, the pool would liquidate its holdings as quietly as possible. Sometimes, pool members then went on to sell short in anticipation of the fall in price that was likely to ensue. Any profits earned by pools were losses for investors who were not in the pool.

An *option pool*, on the other hand, would arrange to acquire all or most of its securities at advantageous prices under option contracts. Many option pools had members who were on the board of directors of the firm whose securities were being manipulated. This board would vote to grant the pool options to buy blocks of new shares at a set price. When the market price rose above this option price, the pool would exercise its option to purchase the shares from the manipulated corporation and then turn around and sell these shares at the higher market price to the public. This manoeuvre diluted the profits accruing to the shareholders of the corporation who were not in the pool. The directors in the pool sometimes rationalized the income they derived from the pool by saying it was compensation for their services as directors.

The Criminal Code of Canada implicitly outlaws pool activities. By Section 340 of the Code:

Everyone who, through the facility of a stock exchange, curb market or other market, with intent to create a false or misleading appearance of active public trading in a security or with intent to create a false or misleading appearance with respect to the market price of a security,

(a) effects a transaction in the security that involves no change in the beneficial ownership thereof,

(b) enters an order for the purchase of the security, knowing that an order of substantially the same size and at substantially the same price for the sale of the security has been or will be entered by or for the same or different persons, or

(c) enters an order for the sale of the security, knowing that an order of substantially the same size at substantially the same time and at substantially the same price for the purchase of the security has been or will be entered by or for the same or different persons, is guilty of an indictable offence and is liable to imprisonment for five years.[3]

4-2 SECURITIES LEGISLATION PASSED FROM 1869–1911—THE UNITED KINGDOM'S INFLUENCE

Canadian securities legislation emanates from diverse sources and reflects its historical development, including the British and American influences and the unique character of our Canadian provincial/federal relations. The legislation comprises the various provincial securities acts, the Canada Business Corporations Act, the provincial business corporations acts, the Criminal Code of Canada, the rules and by-laws of the five stock exchanges, the by-laws and constitutions of the self-regulating bodies, including the Investment Dealers' Association and the Investment Funds Institute, and the Bank of Canada Act. Modern Canadian securities legislation is designed to provide investors with sufficient disclosure to make informed investment decisions in both primary and secondary markets and to protect the investing public against manipulative security practices, fraud and misrepresentation, and insider trading and takeover abuses. The most important of the security laws are outlined below. The laws are explained in chronological order to show how legislative thinking evolved and to familiarize the reader with specific acts.

The first form of Canadian securities legislation was introduced in 1869 and 1877 with the passage of the Canadian Joint Stock Companies Letters Patent Act and the Canada Joint Stock Companies Act. Modelled after the British Joint Stock Companies Act of 1844, these acts set out requirements of federal registration of companies and some (modest) corporate disclosure requirements, including material company contracts.

During the next decade, the provinces started to introduce similar provincial legislation, starting with Nova Scotia in 1883 and followed by the other two Maritime provinces. Rules were added to the acts and existing provisions broadened to include prospectus requirements upon the issue of securities, government inspection provisions, and director's liability for false statements made in prospectuses. The 1907 Ontario Companies Act not only expanded

---

3 See also *Toronto Stock Exchange Members' Manual*, vol. 1, section 11.26, which states, ''Every one who, by deceit, falsehood or other fraudulent means, whether or not it is a false pretence within the meaning of this Act, with intent to defraud, affects the market price of stocks, shares, merchandise or anything that is offered for sale to the public, is guilty of an indictable offence and is liable to imprisonment for ten years.''

prospectus requirements but also included a provision that allowed subscribers to rescind offers for new securities if they had not received a prospectus prior to the subscription.

The framework of future securities legislation was developed in this period; however, there was at this time only a modicum of protection for purchasers of new issues and virtually no regulation of secondary markets.

4-3   SECURITIES LEGISLATION PASSED BETWEEN 1912–1944—THE UNITED STATES'S INFLUENCE

Probably the most important event in the early development of Canadian securities legislation was Manitoba's enactment in 1912 of the Sale of Shares Act, similar in nature to the so-called "blue sky" law[4] introduced the previous year in Kansas. Manitoba's Act required that both new securities issued in Manitoba and salespersons trading these securities be registered. This bill placed major powers in the hands of the provincial regulators; it meant that a new issue of securities could be refused if deemed to be not in the public interest. The act applied only to nonresident issuers at time of passage but was extended to domestic issuers in 1914. Other provinces followed suit with similar legislation.

Meanwhile a parallel development was taking place: self-regulation, or the development of standards and codes of conduct within the industry itself.

The first noteworthy event toward industry self-regulation occurred in 1914 with the formation by a group of businessmen of the Bond Dealers' Section of The Toronto Board of Trade. Its aims were to develop and maintain standards of ethical business procedures for what was (and to a large degree still is) the unregulated bond market. In 1916 a Montreal group joined and the combined group was renamed the Bond Dealers' Association of Canada. In 1934 the name was changed again to the Investment Dealers' Association of Canada, a name it still retains. The IDA today is a national self-regulating body encompassing the entire investment industry. The current role of the IDA is discussed in section 4-5.4.

In 1928, Ontario introduced the Security Frauds Prevention Act, the first such legislation of its type. This act set out a number of activities considered to be fraudulent, provided for investigative powers to the regulators, and provided for denial of registration or suspension of salespersons who were in violation of the act. Most of the other provinces enacted similar legislation.

There was no major change in securities legislation in the aftermath of the Great Depression. Unlike the United States, The Canadian stock exchanges in existence at that time showed some willingness to self-regulate (for example, The Toronto Stock Exchange introduced compulsory audit of member's accounts), but the only real change was the prohibition of door-to-door selling of securities under the Dominion Companies Act of 1934.

---

4 The blue-sky law allows regulators to prevent the sale of securities if they believe that such a sale would not be in the public's interest. The public is thus protected against buying a "piece of the blue sky."

4-4 SECURITIES LEGISLATION ENACTED BETWEEN 1945 AND 1965

The first securities act in Canada was passed by the Ontario government in 1945. Its main feature was the introduction of the requirement that a statement be filed with the Ontario Securities Commission and a receipt issued therefor before primary distribution of a security could take place. The commission was given latitude to determine what, in fact, constituted primary distribution. The act emphasized full disclosure at the time of issue but the principle of continuous disclosure was strictly discretionary, and few companies provided interim reports to shareholders. Saskatchewan, Alberta, British Columbia, and Manitoba passed similar acts shortly thereafter.

The secondary market was still basically unregulated at this time, at least with respect to information provided to shareholders. Furthermore, there was no legislation with respect to insider trading, takeover bids or mergers to protect the investing public. In fact it was not until 1966 that continuous disclosure became a focus of provincial securities legislation. Some considerable developments in the industry self-regulation movement took place during this 1945 to 1965 period. In 1947, the Broker-Dealers Association of Ontario and the British Columbia Bond Dealer's Association were formed, and both introduced constitutions and by-laws that set out codes of practice and ethics. And once again the exchanges took a leading role; in 1958 The Toronto Stock Exchange introduced a rule requiring that junior resource companies file statements identifying changes in their affairs that could materially affect their share price. In 1962 the Investment Funds Institute was formed to regulate the rapidly growing mutual funds industry. In 1963 the Canadian Securities Course, under the auspices of the Investment Dealers' Association, was introduced and deemed a prerequisite for registration as a salesperson in Canada.

4-5 SECURITIES LEGISLATION PASSED SINCE 1966

4-5.1 Provincial Securities Legislation

The reports of two committees, the Attorney General's Committee on Securities Legislation in Ontario (The Kimber Report) and the Royal Commission to Investigate Trading in the Shares of Windfall Oils and Mines Limited had a major impact on Canadian securities legislation. Sweeping changes were made in the Ontario Securities Act in 1966, and new acts were introduced in British Columbia, Alberta, and Saskatchewan (1967), Manitoba (1968) and the Northwest Territories (1971). Attention now focused on continuous and full disclosure and regulation of secondary markets with new provisions to regulate takeover bids, proxy solicitation, and insider trading.

Annual amendments and revisions to provincial securities acts since 1966 have resulted in extensive, and in some cases rigorous, modern securities legislation. The modern emphasis in the provincial securities acts (most of which are similar to the Ontario Securities Act) is on full, true, and plain disclosure. Securities cannot now be sold to the public until the provincial securities commission is satisfied that such criteria have been reasonably met.

Each of the ten provinces and two territories have their own securities legislation although only British Columbia, Alberta, Saskatchewan, Manitoba, Ontario and Quebec have securities commissions. There are three basic aspects to modern Canadian securities legislation as embodied in provincial securities acts: registration, disclosure, and enforcement. These are discussed below.

Registration   All of the provincial securities acts have provisions requiring that both securities and salespersons and counsellors be registered for trading. These are the heritage of the early blue-sky laws. The gist of the provisions state:

- All persons who sell securities and/or act as security advisers, fund managers or underwriters, must be registered with the provincial securities commission (or other appropriate body) of their jurisdiction. Securities (including stocks, bonds, mutual funds, profit-sharing arrangements, resource and mining leases, collateral trust certificates, investment contracts, and the like) must also be registered with the appropriate provincial securities commission before they can be sold and traded.
- No person or entity can carry on business as a stock exchange unless that exchange is recognized in writing by the commission.

Disclosure   The basic principle of full, true, and timely disclosure is enacted through a number of provisions in the various provincial securities legislations and can be best explained using the Ontario Securities Act for illustration.

FULL AND TRUE DISCLOSURE—PROSPECTUS REQUIREMENTS

No person or company can sell or trade securities that have not been previously sold or distributed to the public unless a preliminary prospectus and a prospectus or a statement of material fact[5] have been filed with the commission and a receipt obtained from the director. (Ontario Securities Act, s. 52); or unless the securities or issuer are specifically exempt under the act.

The prospectus must provide "full, true, and plain disclosure" of all material facts relevant to the company including, among other things, an income statement, statement of surplus, and statement of financial changes of the issuer, for the last five financial years (or less, at the discretion of the director); a balance sheet as at a date no more than 120 days prior to the date of the preliminary prospectus, and a previous years' balance sheet at the corresponding date; the underwriting details and distribution plan; the share and loan capital of the issuer; a description of the issuer's business; the names of the promoters; the details of the issue (for equities identification of dividend, voting, pre-emptive, and conversion rights, if applicable, sinking-fund

---

5 The statment of material fact may be used by companies whose shares are already listed for trading on a recognized stock exchange or in some cases by Canadian natural resource companies. The statement of material fact contains much of the information required by a prospectus, but is less detailed.

provisions, etc., for debt securities interest rates, maturity, redemption features, collateral security, covenants, etc.); the names, addresses, and occupations of the directors and officers; and details of escrowed shares.

CONTINUOUS AND TIMELY DISCLOSURE

Material Changes   If a material change occurs, whether favourable or not, the company must immediately issue a press release describing the event or decision, unless the disclosure would be unduly detrimental to the interests of the issuer (and hence its shareholders). Material changes would include acquisition or disposition of a major asset, changes in the control structure, proposed takeovers or mergers, major revisions to previously reported or projected earnings, etc.

Financial Reporting   Issuers must supply quarterly interim financial reports, including an income statement and a statement of changes in financial position, within sixty days of the date of preparation, and annual financial reports, including an income statement, a balance sheet, a statement of surplus, and a statement of changes in financial position within 140 days of the end of its financial year, with comparative results (Ontario Securities Act s. 76[1] and s. 77[1]).

Proxy Solicitation   Ultimate control of a corporation abides in the voting shares. To protect the holders of voting shares from having their power usurped (meager as these powers may be for the minority shareholders of a large corporation), sections 83 through 87 of the Ontario Securities Act set out rules governing how and when proxies[6] are to be solicited. Unless the action might conflict with some applicable corporation law in the jurisdiction, management must send a proxy form and an information circular to shareholders of record in their province. The proxy form sets out who is soliciting the proxy, to whom the shareholder is allocating his votes (and a clear space where the shareholder can designate some other person), and how his votes would be allocated to particular issues or matters. The information circular includes, among other things, a statement of who is soliciting the proxy (normally this is management), whether the proxy can be revoked, the particulars and principal holders of the company's voting shares, how the directors are to be elected, and remuneration of directors.

Takeover Bids and Issuer Bids   Canadian capital markets have undergone a number of periods of frenzied takeover, and merger, and buy-back activity. Section 89 of the Ontario Securities Act states that all takeover bids or bids to buy back stock by the issuer company must be sent to all holders of record of the particular class of securities (or securities convertible into that class) sought under the offer. The shareholders must be given at least twenty-one days from the date of offer to accept, plus a ten-day cooling off period in which the acceptance can be withdrawn. If the offer is made for less than

---

6 A proxy provides the person or persons named in the document with the right to vote on behalf of the grantor at a meeting of shareholders. The right can be designated as restricted (instructing the proxy to vote in a particular manner) or unrestricted.

100 percent of the outstanding securities and an excess number of securities are deposited by holders, then the securities are to be taken up on as near a pro rata basis as possible. A takeover bid is accompanied by a takeover bid circular setting out the name of the offeror, the terms and conditions of the takeover bid, how payment is to be made for the deposited securities, and any recent material changes in the takeover target; an issuer bid is accompanied by a director's circular setting out the same type of information.

Insider Trading   Insiders of corporations include all directors and senior officers of the company or a company that is, in itself, an insider of the company, and any person or entity that owns directly or indirectly more than 10 percent of the voting shares of the company. Insiders are required to file within ten days of the end of the month in which they became shareholders, initial statements setting out their direct and indirect shareholdings.

They are also required to file statements of changes in their holdings in the underlying company within ten days of the end of the month in which the changes took place.

ENFORCEMENT

Securities commissions are granted fairly broad powers to enforce the respective securities acts and to regulate trading. In most provinces the commissions are empowered to conduct criminal investigations if they believe that a violation of the provincial act or the Criminal Code of Canada has been committed. The potential penalties are relatively severe. Section 118 of the Ontario Securities Act sets out the general enforcement powers and provides for fines of up to $25,000 for companies and up to $2,000 and/or imprisonment for up to one year for individuals for making misrepresentations in any document that must be filed under the act (such as a prospectus or information circular) or which in general contravenes the act. There are a number of specific prohibitions stemming from the types of practices referred to in this chapter in Sec. 4.1, including prohibitions against a salesperson or his/ her firm promising to repurchase a security purchased for a client (s. 37[1]), indicating that the security will sell for a specific price in the future (s. 37[2]), or suggesting that a security is about to be listed on a stock exchange (s. 37[3]), unless the director has consented to such a statement in writing.

Advisers, including writers in the financial press and financial newsletter contributors, must identify clearly and in type no less legible than that used in the text of the publication his or her holdings in any security recommended as a purchase, a sale, or a hold (s. 39). Other important aspects of current securities legislation are provided below.

In most provinces the purchaser of securities on a primary distribution is not bound to his purchase if he provides written or telegraphic notice to the investment dealer from whom he has purchased the securities that he will not be bound by the agreement. This notice must be provided by no later than midnight on the second business day after receipt of the final prospectus.

4-5.2   Rights of Withdrawal—The Cooling-Off Period

**4-5.3
Insider
Trading**

Under s. 124 of the Canada Business Corporations Act,[7] an insider of a corporation is strictly prohibited from selling short shares or buying or selling puts or call options of the shares of their own corporation or any of its affiliates.[8] Contravention of these prohibitions can lead to a fine of up to $5,000 and/or imprisonment for up to six months.

**4-5.4   Self-
Regulation in
the Canadian
Securities
Industry**

The Investment Dealers' Association of Canada (IDA) is a national body whose membership consists of stock exchange members and bond dealers. The IDA plays three roles: self-regulator through imposition and audit of minimum capital and insurance requirements of its members; lobbyist through interaction with government in the development of new securities legislation and enforcement; and educator through the Canadian Securities Institute. Generally, the objectives[9] of the IDA are

to foster and sustain an environment favourable to saving and investment, thus encouraging the accumulation of capital needed for continued economic development, for a rising standard of living, and for the productive employment of a growing population.

To accomplish these broad aims, the IDA also provides in its constitution for the maintenance of high standards of business conduct among its members, establishment and enforcement of capital, insurance, and other required minimums, co-operation with government in the development of financial legislation when it is deemed to be in the public interest, and provision of educational facilities to improve the professional competence of members.

The IDA sponsors the Canadian Securities Institute, the only recognized national organization providing financial education. Its most important offering is the Canadian Securities Course, which consists of three correspondence term assignments and a written study hall examination. New securities salespersons are required to complete and pass the course before they can be registered to trade for the public (Ontario Securities Act s.[110]).

The Institute also offers the Canadian Investment Finance Course, Parts I and II, and options and futures proficiency exams, in addition to a number of courses of general interest to the public.

INVESTMENT FUNDS INSTITUTE

This is a self-regulating body of the investment company or mutual fund industry[10] offering membership to all mutual funds operating in Canada and

---

7 The Canada Business Corporations Act became effective on December 15, 1975. The act applies to all corporations that are federally incorporated and deals with a wide range of issues from incorporation of a company to its liquidation and dissolution.

8 An exception is allowed if the insider owns a convertible security or option that can be transferred into the shares of the company and he or she exercises the privilege or transfers it to the purchaser within ten days of a short sale.

9 The Investment Dealers Association of Canada, Constitution, s. 2(a).

10 Mutual funds are also directly regulated by the various securities commissions that, among other things, require full disclosure in the fund's offering prospectus and registration of persons selling mutual funds or acting as fund advisers or counsellors.

offering the Canadian Investment Funds Course (a proficiency course). The institute has its own constitution and code of ethics and by-laws, providing for a Brokers Blanket Bond to protect the public against losses arising through fraud or other criminal acts of officers, employees, or sales representatives of investment companies. Its code of ethics counsels against salespersons overselling their clients, aggressive solicitation of prospective clients by denigration of their investments (a process known as twisting), or encouraging investors to borrow to buy mutual funds. The Investment Funds Institute also encourages salespersons to discuss the suitability of the investments with clients in light of their individual risk preferences and tastes.

Administration of futures trading falls under the aegis of provincial securities commissions, with one exception; grain futures traded on the Winnipeg Commodity Exchange are administered under the Federal Grain Futures Act.

4-5.5 Commodity Futures Trading

In general, the provinces have exempted futures contracts from registration and prospectus requirements so long as the trades are made by persons who are members of futures exchanges or by dealers registered under the provincial securities act. Only the provinces of British Columbia, Manitoba, and Ontario have passed commodity futures acts.

4-6 CONCLUSIONS ABOUT CANADIAN SECURITIES LEGISLATION

The regulatory system just outlined has greatly reduced the incidence of fraud and price manipulation, has increased market stability, and has fostered thoughtful investment analysis. Nevertheless, the regulatory environment is far from perfect and bears constant evaluation and improvement.

The proliferation of new investment types (such as instalment receipts, bond purchase warrants, and commodity-indexed, preferred shares), and new financial futures and option contracts (such as the TSE spot index futures contract), while increasing investment and hedging opportunities, means an even heavier burden on government regulators.

Securities commissions continue to walk a curious tightrope. On the one hand, there is a perceived need for investor protection through restrictive regulation: the type of regulatory process that the "blue-sky" laws provided. On the other hand, there is the pressure to provide a supportive environment for business financing through accommodating primary markets anchored by an active secondary market.

QUESTIONS

1. Briefly outline the background leading to the development of a system for regulating the securities markets after 1965.
2. What harm can come to a nation's financial markets and economy from corners on markets and pools?

3. What is a prospectus? What is its purpose? When should prospectuses be provided? When a securities commission releases a prospectus, does it imply that it recommends the issue for investment?

4. Is it illegal to trade securities on the basis of a hot tip from an employee of the firm that issues the securities? Explain.

5. What is meant by continuous disclosure? Why is it an important principle of securities legislation?

6. ''The Ontario Securities Commission's actions tend to ensure that investors will not lose their savings by investing them in securities.'' True, false, or uncertain? Explain.

7. What is meant by self-regulation? Trace its development in Canada.

8. ''If an insider of a company sells his or her shares just prior to the release of a poor earnings report, he or she will be liable to the shareholders for the difference in his or her selling price and the market price after the announcement.'' True or false? Explain.

SELECTED REFERENCES

Securities Law Reporter. Don Mills, Ontario: CCH Canadian, 1986. This four-volume reference work contains all provincial securities acts, stock and futures exchange charters and by-laws, acts of the self-regulating bodies, and securities court-case decisions.

Smythe, E. and D. Soberman. *The Law and Business Administration in Canada*. 4th ed. Prentice-Hall Canada, 1986. This textbook is designed for the undergraduate business student and is a clear, well-illustrated text on business law.

Taxes 5

The structure of income taxes in Canada encourages certain activities (for example, long term investing) and discourages other types of activities (such as tax-loss selling). This chapter explains the tax system so that judicious investors can postpone, reduce, or eliminate their tax payments. After all, postponing paying taxes for one year is similar to getting an interest-free loan. This chapter explains the essence of the tax system in Canada and provides legal and ethical ways to postpone and reduce income taxes.

Subsection 2(1) of the Income Tax Act states that "an income tax shall be paid as hereinafter required upon the taxable income for each taxation year of every person resident in Canada at any time in the year." This seemingly straightforward provision sets out the basic principle of who is subject to tax in Canada (subsection 2[3] defines tax payable by non-residents) but also underscores the fact that tax legislation in Canada is complex and interpretive (because nearly every word in section 2 requires explanation and amplification). The word "resident," for example, has been the subject of numerous legal cases argued in Canadian courts. The word "income" includes *world-wide* income, i.e., income earned from all sources, Canadian or otherwise. A Canadian resident who earns interest income on French bonds issued by the French government is nevertheless taxable on the income in Canada, although double taxation would be avoided through the foreign tax credit deduction.

Income tax legislation is normally in a state of flux in Canada. Amendmends to the Income Tax Act are proposed in annual budget addresses (and often at other times of the year, as well), and it usually takes months before the resulting bill (sometimes substantially altered) is introduced in Parliament, and months again before it is actually passed. This often makes tax-planning a difficult chore.

For example, on June 18, 1987, Finance Minister Wilson tabled his white paper on tax reform, which contained multistage and major changes to personal and corporate taxes and sales tax. At present, this tax reform legislation has not been introduced in Parliament, and it is likely that modifications may yet occur. Tax issues and treatments that may be affected by the proposed legislation are identified throughout the chapter.

5-1 FEDERAL PERSONAL INCOME TAXES

Federal income taxes are the largest tax that most people pay. Typical tax-payers pay more than twenty-five cents out of every dollar they earn to Revenue Canada, the tax collecting arm of the Canadian government. If someone refuses to pay, or pays late, or cheats on taxes, Revenue Canada can impose monetary penalties or can have the courts review the case. The courts can hand down fines of up to 200 percent of the taxes evaded or even sentences that involve years in jail, if tax evasion is uncovered.[1] Since such heavy penalties can be invoked, it behoves each of us to familiarize ourselves with the

TABLE 5-1 DERIVING TAXABLE INCOME

Total income: Includes wages, salaries, tips, training allowances, pension income, certain benefits as defined in section 6 of the Income Tax Act, Family Allowance receipts, unemployment insurance benefits, dividend (grossed-up in some circumstances) and interest income, rental income, taxable capital gains, net income from business, professional, commission, farming and fishing net income (after deducting allowable expenses), alimony and maintenance receipts

Less: Canada and Quebec Pension Plan contributions, Unemployment Insurance premiums, contributions to tax shelter plans (such as Registered Retirement Savings Plans), union and professional dues, tuition fees, child care expenses under certain conditions, interest expense related to investments, allowable business investment losses, among others

Equals: Net income

Less: Specific and itemized personal deductions such as
1. Basic Personal Exemption*
2. Age Exemption
3. Married exemptions subject to a threshold amount†
4. Exemptions for dependent children subject to a threshold amount†
5. Interest and dividend deduction (maximum of $1,000)
6. Pension income deduction
7. Medical expenses in excess of 3 percent of net income
8. Charitable deductions up to 20 percent of net income
9. Various other deductions

Less: Forward averaging elective income deduction††

Equals: Taxable income

---

*Many of the exemptions used to reduce net income to taxable income and the threshold amounts are subject to annual indexing in accordance with the annual change in the consumer price index as at September 30. Commencing in 1986, this annual indexing was reduced to the amount by which the September change in the consumer price index exceeds 3 percent. The allowable amounts for the 1986 taxation year are shown in Table 5-2.

†The married and dependent children deductions are subject to threshold amounts or minimum net income levels. If the dependant's net income is below the threshold the taxpayer is allowed the full deduction. The amount by which the dependant's net income exceeds this threshold reduces the taxpayer's exemption by fifty cents on the dollar.

††The June 18th White Paper on Tax Reform proposes that forward averaging be eliminated, commencing in 1988. Any amounts which were averaged in previous years will be eligible to be drawn down, up to 1997.

---

1 Prison sentences are rarely imposed upon tax evaders in Canada.

tax law. Remember, ignorance of the law is not a legally acceptable defence to an infraction.

Individuals (persons other than corporations) who earn wages, salaries, investment and other types of income are legally allowed to deduct certain of their expenses from their total income in order to determine their net income. Net income is then reduced to taxable income through the deduction of specified personal exemptions.[2] Table 5-1 summarizes the process used to derive a taxpayer's taxable income.

5-1.1 Federal Taxes on Taxable Income

TABLE 5-2   THE INDEXED EXEMPTIONS AND THRESHOLD AMOUNTS, 1986*

Basic exemption $4,180
Age exemption $2,610
(taxpayers 65 years or older as at December 31, 1986)
Married exemption $3,660
   threshold amount $520
Exemptions for dependent children†
Children born in 1969 or later $710
   threshold amount $2,760
Child born in 1968 or earlier $1,420
   threshold amount $1,340
Disability exemption $2,860

*Applicable to all Canadian taxpayers other than residents of Quebec
†The dependent children exemptions are reduced in 1987 and 1988.

For example, a single, healthy taxpayer, aged 35, who has no financial dependants and earns a net income of $25,000 per year is allowed a standard non-itemized exemption in 1986 of $4,180.

TABLE 5-3   CALCULATING TAXABLE INCOME FROM NET INCOME FOR TWO HYPOTHETICAL TAXPAYERS

SINGLE TAXPAYER	TAXPAYER WITH DEPENDENT SPOUSE AND CHILDREN
$25,000 net income	$25,000
− 4180 exemption	−9,090*
$20,820 taxable income	$15,910

*Exemptions:
Basic exemption $4,180
Married exemption $3,660
Exemptions for children
   18 and over [1,420 − ½ (net income − 1,340.00)] = [(1,420 − ½ (3,100 − 1,340)]
                =   540
   under 18   =   710
Total   = $9,090

2 The June 18 white paper on tax reform proposes that these personal exemptions be converted into nonrefundable but partially transferable tax credits, commencing 1988.

If the taxpayer in Table 5-3 were the sole supporter of a spouse and two children (one aged 19 and attending the University of British Columbia and earning $3,100 in 1986 after deductions including tuition, the other aged 17 with no income), then he or she would be entitled to larger deductions than a single person.

After a taxpayer has determined the amount of taxable income, the tax schedule can be consulted to find out the amount of taxes to be paid on it.

5-1.2 The Progressive Federal Income Tax Rates

There are two important characteristics about the Canadian federal income tax schedule. First, the taxes are stated as a percentage of the taxable income. Second, this percentage increases as the taxpayer's taxable income increases — this is called a *graduated* or *progressive tax*. Table 5-4 shows the federal tax rates for 1986,[3] the tax rates change each year due to indexing.[4]

1992

—$29590   17%
29591– 59180   26%
>59180   29%

TABLE 5-4   FEDERAL INCOME TAX SCHEDULE, 1986

IF TAXABLE INCOME IS	THE TAX IS
$1,305 or less	6% of taxable income
Over $ 1,305	$ 78 + 16% on next $ 1,306
Over $ 2,611	$ 287 + 17% on next $ 2,610
Over $ 5,221	$ 731 + 18% on next $ 2,611
Over $ 7,832	$ 1,201 + 19% on next $ 5,222
Over $13,054	$ 2,193 + 20% on next $ 5,221
Over $18,275	$ 3,237 + 23% on next $ 5,221
Over $23,496	$ 4,438 + 25% on next $13,054
Over $36,550	$ 7,702 + 30% on next $26,107
Over $62,657	$15,534 + 34% on remainder

In 1986 a federal surtax of 5.0 percent of basic federal tax in excess of $6,000 plus an additional 5 percent of basic federal tax in excess of $15,000 must be added to the calculation of tax payable. Commencing July 1, 1986, a flat surtax of 3 percent on individuals is imposed on the calculation of basic federal tax for all taxpayers, (including those with taxable income of less than $6,001) in addition to the surtaxes above, although this will replace the high income individual surtax in later years.

3 The June 18 white paper on tax reform proposes that, commencing in 1988, these ten brackets be reduced to three and that tax rates be lowered. Furthermore, starting in 1989, these tax brackets will be indexed to annual increases in the Consumer Price Index in excess of 3 percent. The federal income tax rate structure proposed for 1988 is as follows:

If taxable income is	The tax is
Up to $27,500	17%
$27,501–$55,000	$4,675 + 26%
$55,001 and over	$11,825 + 29%

4 See David B. Perry, "The Cost of Indexing the Federal Income Tax System," *Canadian Tax Journal*, vol. 33, no. 2, March-April, 1985, pp. 387–391, for an examination of the fiscal implications of the indexing.

Reconsider the two taxpayers shown in Table 5-3 in order to see examples of how to determine the amount of taxes due. The single person's taxable income of $20,820 incurs a federal income tax of $3,822.35, calculated as follows with Table 5-4.

	$3,237	from Table 5-4
Plus:	$585.35	equals 23% of the $2,545 excess over $18,275
Total	$3,822.35	federal income tax (not including surtaxes)

In contrast, the married person with the three dependants has taxable income of $15,910 from Table 5-3. Using table 5-4, the married person's taxes are found to be only $2,764.20, calculated as follows:

	$2,193	from Table 5-4
Plus:	$571.20	equals 20% of the $2,856 excess over $13,054
Total	$2,764.20	federal income tax (not including surtaxes)

5-2   PROVINCIAL PERSONAL INCOME TAXES

Income taxes are levied by each of the provinces and territories, with the exception of Quebec, and are collected by Revenue Canada. Provincial taxes are calculated as a stated and varying percentage of basic federal tax (federal tax before federal tax reductions). Provincial tax rates for 1986 are shown in Table 5-5.

TABLE 5-5   PROVINCIAL TAX RATES, 1986

Alberta 43.5%	Ontario 50%
British Columbia 44%	Prince Edward Island 52.5%
Manitoba 54%	Quebec*
New Brunswick 58%	Saskatchewan 50.5%
Newfoundland 60%	Yukon 45%
Nova Scotia 56.5%	Northwest Territories 43%

Ontario, Manitoba, and Saskatchewan have levied surtaxes for 1986 as well.

---

*The Province of Quebec has a unique system in that federal and provincial taxes are combined under the Quebec Taxation Act. The system of taxation is structurally similar to that levied on all other Canadian residents, however the actual schedules, exemptions, and other tables differ.

5-3   MARGINAL TAX RATES

Economics students are well familiar with the concepts of marginal revenues, costs and product, and their importance in determining pricing, sales and production levels for a firm.

Similarly, of particular interest to investors is the marginal tax rate or the amount of tax that an extra dollar of income attracts. In making investment decisions, the knowledgeable Canadian investor will want to adjust expected before-tax returns to an after-tax basis. To do so, one must use the appropriate tax rate. Employing the tax rates from tables 5-4 and 5-5, we can derive the 1986 marginal tax rates for Canadian investors in each province and territory

(Quebec excluded). Simply multiply the appropriate marginal federal tax rate from Table 5-4 by 1+ the relevant provincial tax rate in Table 5-5.[5]

An Ontario investor who has an estimated $25,000 in taxable income will have a marginal tax rate of 25 percent. His total marginal tax rate will be .25 × 1.50 = .375 or 37.5 percent. This same taxpayer living in the Yukon has a total marginal tax rate of .25 × 1.45 = .3625 or 36.25 percent.

5-4.1 Canadian Investment Income Deduction

5-4   TAXATION OF INVESTMENT INCOME

Canadian taxpayers are allowed up to a $1,000 interest and dividend deduction each year in the calculation of taxable income.[6] The amount allowed is calculated as the lesser of $1,000 or total interest and dividend income eligible for the deduction minus the interest on money borrowed to earn the income eligible for the deduction.

Income eligible for this deduction includes Canadian source interest income from Canada Savings Bonds; bank, trust company, and other financial institution accounts and term deposits; federal, provincial, municipal and corporate bonds, mortgages and notes; annuities; one-half of the bonus received on Canada Savings Bonds; Canadian source dividend income from taxable Canadian corporations. Since the effective marginal tax rate on this source of income is zero, up to the $1,000 exemption, investors should make the earning of sufficient income to generate the full deduction a top priority.

5-4.2 Taxation of Dividend Income

To encourage investment in equities and as part of the scheme to integrate corporate and shareholder income and eliminate double taxation of corporate distributions, dividend income earned by Canadian individuals from taxable Canadian companies are afforded a special treatment.[7] Investors include 133.33 percent of such dividends received in their computation of taxable income. The incremental 33.33 percent is called the gross-up. Federal tax is computed on this grossed-up amount. From the federal tax, the investor subtracts a dividend tax credit equal to 66.66 percent of the gross-up or equivalently 22.22 percent of the dividend. Provincial tax is then calculated on the residual net federal tax payable.

For example, assume that a resident of Nova Scotia with a marginal federal tax rate of 30 percent earns dividend income of $800 from taxable Canadian companies in 1987. The total income tax paid (assuming that the $1,000 exemption for interest and dividends has already been used up), and after-tax dividend retained is shown at the top of page 97.

---

5 The presence of the alternative minimum tax or AMT (introduced in 1986) can distort the calculation of marginal tax rates. However, the AMT is unlikely to affect more than a small percentage of Canadian taxpayers.

6 The June 18 white paper on tax reform proposes that this exemption be eliminated, commencing 1988.

7 The June 18 white paper on tax reform proposes a change to the method of calculation, commencing in 1988. The gross-up is to be reduced to 25 percent of the actual dividend received.

Dividend received	$800.00
Add: Gross-up	$266.66, i.e., 33.3% of dividend
Grossed-up dividend	$1,066.66
Federal tax payable	$320.00
Less: Dividend tax credit	$177.76, i.e., 66.66% × 266.66
Net federal tax payable	$142.24
Provincial tax payable	$80.37, i.e., 56.5% × 142.24
Total income tax payable	$222.61

The investor would pay $222.61 in tax and retain $577.39 or 72.17 percent of the dividend. In contrast, $800 of interest income earned by this same tax-payer would have resulted in $375.60 paid in total taxes. Beam and Laiken[8] have derived a convenient method of calculating after-tax equivalencies on investment income. The after tax dividend retained by an investor can be reduced to a workable formula, using the Beam and Laiken approach as follows:

$$D_a = D_b - [1.33D_bT_f - .666(.333)D_b][1 + T_p]$$
$$= D_b - [1.33D_bT_f - .2222D_b][1 + T_p]$$

where:
D_a = Dividend after tax
D_b = Dividend before tax
T_f = Marginal federal tax rate
T_p = Marginal provincial tax rate

Similarly the after-tax interest income equivalent to a before tax amount I_b is calculated as follows:

$$I_a = I_b - [I_bT_f][1 + T_p]$$

where:
I_a = Interest after tax
I_b = Interest before tax
T_f = Marginal federal tax rate
T_p = Marginal provincial tax rate

An investor living in Ontario who earns $1,500 in dividend income and has a 34 percent marginal federal tax rate and a 50 percent provincial rate would retain

$$D_a = D_b - [1.33D_bT_f - .2222D_b][1 + T_p]$$
$$= 1,500 - [1.33(1,500)(.34) - .2222(1,500)][1.50] = $982.50$$

Dividends received from other than taxable Canadian companies, e.g. foreign companies, are not subject to the gross-up, and are not eligible for the dividend tax credit or the $1,000 investment income deduction. Stock dividends

8 Beam, R. E. and S. N. Laiken, *Introduction to Federal Income Taxation in Canada*, 7th ed., 1985–1986 (Don Mills, Ontario: CCH Canadian Limited, 1986), chap. 6. Appropriate adjustments to the formula must be made if the white paper proposals to change the dividend tax credit calculation are passed.

received after May 23, 1985, are to be treated for tax purposes as dividends. The amount that the taxpayer includes is the pro rata increase in the paid-up capital of the firm.

A few large Canadian companies have special classes of shares on which the dividends are tax-deferred. The recipient of the dividend does not include the dividend in the computation of income. However, he or she must reduce the adjusted cost base of the underlying shares by the amount of the dividend, thus increasing (decreasing) the ultimate capital gain (loss). An example is the Brascan Limited 8½% Tax-Deferred Series A, for which the holder is entitled to a dividend of $2.125. The shares are convertible at the option of the holder into an equal number of Series B preferred shares (not tax-deferred) after April 15, 1988.

5-4.3   Methods of Reporting Interest Income

Taxpayers have three acceptable methods of reporting their interest income. These methods are:

1. *The cash basis.* With this method the taxpayer includes in income only the amounts actually **received** in the year. This cash method is subject to a maximum deferral period of three years. All interest income receivable or accrued after December 31, 1981, and not previously reported as income, must be included in income at least every three years.
2. *The receivable basis.* The taxpayer who elects to use the receivable method includes all amounts in income for a taxation year that are earned and **receivable**.
3. *The accrual basis.* The taxpayer includes all amounts for a taxation year that are **earned** but before they are received or receivable.

Investors may use any method. In practice, taxpayers are required to use one of the three methods consistently for each particular income property class. An investor might therefore use the cash basis for his term deposits and the accrual basis for his mortgage income.

5-4.4   Taxation of Capital Gains and Losses

Capital gains and losses arise out of the acquisition and disposition of capital assets, including such things as securities and real estate. In Canada there is no capital gains tax; more properly, there is a specific and preferential treatment afforded to gains made on the disposition of capital property.

It isn't always clear whether a particular transaction is capital or income in nature. For example, would the sale of the gravel deposits on land owned by a taxpayer be the sale of a portion of the land itself (a capital transaction) or a sale of the produce of the land (an income transaction)? See question 7 at the end of this chapter. The courts have frequently invoked the analogy of the fruit and the tree in deciding issues of this type. Capital is the tree that gives rise to the fruit, which is income. The sale of the tree is a capital transaction; the sale of the fruit is the sale of inventory and hence income.

Subject to a few exceptions and refinements, one-half[9] of the amount of capital gains (called a taxable capital gain) less one-half of capital losses (called

---

9 The June 18 white paper on tax reform proposes that this 50 percent portion of capital gain subject to tax be increased to 66.6 percent in 1988 and 75 percent in 1990.

allowable capital losses) is included in income and taxed in the ordinary way. Individual taxpayers, other than trusts, are allowed a lifetime exemption of $500,000 in capital gains or $250,000 in taxable capital gains.[10] The exemption is phased in on the following schedule.

changed lifetime $100,000 exemption

TABLE 5-6   PHASE-IN SCHEDULE FOR LIFETIME CAPITAL GAIN EXEMPTION

YEAR	CUMULATIVE LIMIT NET TAXABLE CAPITAL GAINS	CAPITAL GAINS
1985	$10,000	$20,000
1986	$25,000	$50,000
1987	$50,000	$100,000
1988	$100,000	$200,000
1989	$150,000	$300,000
1990	$250,000	$500,000

The exemption applies in any given year to the taxpayer's net taxable capital gain minus any net capital loss carryovers claimed in the year and less any allowable business investment losses realized in the year.

Capital losses realized after 1984 are only deductible against capital gains and are not deductible against other income. However, unused pre-1985 capital losses can be carried forward indefinitely, applied first against capital gains and then excess losses are deductible against other income up to a maximum of $2,000 per year.

The capital gain or loss on the disposition of capital property is calculated as follows:

Capital gain [loss] = proceeds of disposition − adjusted cost base − outlays or expenses on disposition

The adjusted cost base in general is the original purchase cost (including acquisition costs) of the property as adjusted up or down for specific transactions, such as the receipt of a tax-deferred dividend, superficial losses, or the prior sale of two or more identical properties.

---

10 The June 18 white paper on tax reform proposes that this $500,000 lifetime exemption be frozen in 1987 at $100,000 for most capital property, except qualifying farm property that remains at the $500,000 lifetime exemption as per the phase-in schedule in Table 5-6. However, it also proposes that, commencing in 1988, a $500,000 lifetime exemption will be allowed for capital gains made on the disposition of shares of small business corporations that have been held by the taxpayer or persons related to him throughout the immediately preceding 24 months. The net taxable capital gains available for the exemption will be reduced by the amount of cumulative and net investment losses claimed after 1987, including interest expense deductions in excess of interest income, taxable dividends, rental and property income, certain carrying charges on limited partnership income, losses from partnership and joint ventures, Canadian exploration and other resource expenses from flow-through shares, or partnership interests where the taxpayer is a passive investor. The restriction doesn't eliminate the exemption, but does defer the utilization rate for the exemption.

To illustrate, assume that an investor engages in the following transactions in the shares of company ABC:

June 22 1988: buys 300 shares at $5.50 a share plus $45 commission
August 17 1988: sells 200 shares at $6.25 a share less $40 commission
March 19 1989: buys 200 shares at $5.25 a share plus $35 commission
May 3 1989: sells 300 shares at $7.25 less $65 commission

The investor's capital gain for tax purposes is calculated as follows for the 1988 taxation year:
capital gain = proceeds of disposition – adjusted cost base – expenses re disposition

$$= 200 \times 6.25 - 200 \times 5.65^* - 40 = \$80$$

1989 taxation year:
capital gain = proceeds of disposition – adjusted cost base – expenses re disposition

$$= 300 \times 7.25 - 300 \times 5.50\dagger - 65 = \$460$$

$$*(300 \times 5.50 + 45)/300 = \$5.65$$
$$\dagger[(100 \times 5.65) + (200 \times 5.25 + 35)]/300 = \$5.50$$

The gain on the disposition of a principal residence is exempt from capital gains under all circumstances. In general, a principal residence is defined in paragraph 54(g) as "a housing unit, a leasehold interest therein, or a share of the capital stock of a co-operative housing corporation, owned, whether jointly with another person or otherwise, in the year by the taxpayer, if the housing unit was ordinarily inhabited in the year by the taxpayer, his spouse or former spouse, or a child of the taxpayer who, during the year, was dependent on him for support . . ." A taxpayer may only designate one property as a principal residence for a given taxation year.

5-4.5 Allowable Business Investment Losses

Investors who have incurred a loss on the disposition of shares or debt in Canadian-controlled private corporations can write off 50 percent of this loss, called an allowable business investment loss, against other sources of income. However, the loss claimed will reduce the lifetime capital gain exemption outlined in sec. 5-4.4. As of 1986, only losses incurred on the disposition of debt or equity securities from a Canadian-controlled private corporation eligible for the small business deduction will qualify as allowable business investment losses.

5-4.6 Futures Trading

Gains and losses incurred in trading in futures contracts are treated as capital gains or losses for tax purposes unless the taxpayer trades such contracts as part of a business hedging operation or is an officer or director of a company actively engaged in business related to the underlying commodity. In such cases the gains or losses must be treated as ordinary income or loss.

Speculators may elect to have their gains or losses treated as ordinary income or loss. However this is a *lifetime* election, hence the taxpayer must treat such gains or losses in this way each year. Revenue Canada will not allow the taxpayer to change. Such an election would presumably be made by an investor who sustained large losses in a given year and intended to refrain from futures trading henceforth.

An option contract gives the holder the right to buy (a call option) or to sell (a put option) a specified quantity of an underlying asset. The purchaser pays a price, normally called a premium, for this right. Three outcomes are possible, each giving rise to specific tax consequences. If the option contract itself is sold, the resulting profit or loss is a capital gain or capital loss in the year of disposition. If the option contract is exercised, then the premium is added to the cost base of the property that is acquired and thus affects the eventual determination of the capital gain or loss when the property is finally sold. Finally, if the option is allowed to expire, the premium paid for the option is a capital loss in the year that the option expires.

**5-4.7
Trading
in Option
Contracts**

To discourage investors from artificial transactions designed solely to avoid or limit tax liability, paragraphs 53(1)(f) and 54(i) set out the rule that an investor or his spouse or a corporation controlled by the investor, who acquires the same or identical capital properties during a period commencing thirty days before to thirty days after the sale of the property will be denied the deduction of any resulting capital loss. Instead, the loss is added to the cost base of the reacquired property.

**5-4.8
Superficial
Losses**

In the next section, tax shelters for individual's contributions to their own retirement funds are described. These represent an example of tax incentive programs designed to encourage specific personal behaviour.

5-5 TAX-SHELTERED RETIREMENT PLANS

Practically all adults save in order to be able to enjoy a few luxuries in their retirement years. Furthermore, the federal government does not want a large pool of elderly people to be suffering because of inadequate retirement funds. For these reasons, several tax-sheltered retirement plans have been passed into law. Although these plans are essentially savings plans, they offer two additional tax incentives. First, the money saved from current income and put in these retirement plans may be deducted from gross income to determine net income. That is, administered retirement savings qualify as a legal tax deduction.[11] Second, the interest income, cash dividends, and any capital gains from retirement funds are not taxable until the taxpayer retires (and typically falls into a lower tax bracket) and actually receives the retirement funds.

To see how tax-sheltered retirement savings plans work, consider an individual who has $10,700 in taxable income. Let's now assume this individual saves $1,500 in a tax-sheltered retirement plan. Table 5-7 shows calculations

---

11 Only specified retirement plans are entitled to this treatment. Employee profit-sharing plans, for example are not.

indicating that this retirement saver enjoys an income tax savings of $300 by saving $1,500 for his or her own retirement.

TABLE 5-7   TAX SAVINGS FROM AN INDIVIDUAL'S $1,500 RETIREMENT SAVINGS

WITHOUT RETIREMENT PLAN		WITH RETIREMENT PLAN
$10,700	Taxable income	$10,700
0	Contribution to retirement plan	− 1,500
$10,700	Taxable income	$ 9,200
× .20	Assumed average tax rate of 20%	× .20
$ 2,140	Income taxes	$ 1,840
− 1,840	Subtract lesser tax ←	
$ 300	Income tax savings from plan	

There are different types of tax-sheltered retirement plans. The best known is the Registered Retirement Savings Plan, which is discussed below.

5-5.1 Registered Retirement Savings Plans

RRSPs, the most widely used form of tax deferral and planning for the future in Canada are plans registered with the government, and administered directly or indirectly by a bank, trust company, life insurance company, credit union, mutual fund, or brokerage firm.

Taxpayers may make annual contributions to such plans subject to specific amounts, or contribution limits up to the year in which the taxpayer turns 71. The income and gains on the investments held within the trust are exempt from tax and the annual contributions are tax deductible. At the maturity of the plan which can be at any time, but must occur by the taxpayer's seventy-first year, the RRSP holder has a number of options for the allocation of the funds within the trust (these are described presently). The taxpayer may also, subject to the contribution limits, make payments to a plan in favour of his/her spouse. The annual contribution limits for RRSPs are as follows:

For 1986, persons who are not members of employer sponsored pension plans are entitled to annual contributions to a limit of the lesser of $7500 or 20 percent of earned income;

Persons who are members of employer sponsored pension plans are entitled to annual contributions to a limit of the lesser of $3,500 minus the employee's contribution to the registered pension plan or 20 percent of earned income;
Earned income includes income from employment, net business income, and net income from real estate rentals.

In 1987 and subsequent years the contribution on limits change as shown in Table 5-8.

Types of Plans   There are two types of RRSPs: managed and self-administered. The former, by far the more widely used, are fully managed plans of the financial institutions that offer RRSPs. These range from straight debt plans to aggressive equity funds. The latter is a plan also set up at a financial institution but fully directed by the investor. The investor selects the portfolio

TABLE 5-8   PHASE-IN SCHEDULE FOR NEW RRSP LIMITS

TAXPAYER NOT A MEMBER OF A REGISTERED PENSION PLAN OR DEFERRED
PROFIT-SHARING PLAN

1987 the lesser of 20% of earned income or $7,500
1988 the lesser of 20% of earned income or $7,500
1989 the lesser of 18% of earned income or $8,500
1990 the lesser of 18% of earned income or $10,500
1991 the lesser of 18% of earned income or $11,500
1992 the lesser of 18% of earned income or $12,500
1993 the lesser of 18% of earned income or $13,500
1994 the lesser of 18% of earned income or $14,500
1995 the lesser of 18% of earned income or $15,500
1996 the lesser of 18% of earned income or $15,500 subject to indexing

---

TAXPAYER A MEMBER OF A MONEY PURCHASE REGISTERED PENSION PLAN

1987 the lesser of 20% of pensionable earnings or $7,000*
1988 the lesser of 20% of pensionable earnings or $7,000
1989 the lesser of 18% of pensionable earnings or $10,500
1990 the lesser of 18% of pensionable earnings or $11,500
1991 the lesser of 18% of pensionable earnings or $12,500
1992 the lesser of 18% of pensionable earnings or $13,500
1993 the lesser of 18% of pensionable earnings or $14,500
1994 the lesser of 18% of pensionable earnings or $15,500
1995 the lesser of 18% of pensionable earnings or $15,500 subject to indexing

---

MEMBER OF DEFINED BENEFIT REGISTERED PENSION PLAN

1987 the lesser of† 20% of preceding year's earned income or $7,000
1988 the lesser of 20% of preceding year's earned income or $7,000
1989 the lesser of 18% of preceding year's earned income or $10,500
1990 the lesser of 18% of preceding year's earned income or $11,500
1991 the lesser of 18% of preceding year's earned income or $12,500
1992 the lesser of 18% of preceding year's earned income or $13,500
1993 the lesser of 18% of preceding year's earned income or $14,500
1994 the lesser of 18% of preceding year's earned income or $15,500
1995 the lesser of 18% of preceding year's earned income or $15,500 subject to indexing

---

*Combined Registered Pension Plan and Registered Retirement Savings Plan contributions including both the employer and employee portions.
†These amounts are reduced by a pension adjustment that is a proxy for the benefit received from the employer's contribution.

composition subject to the constraints that no more than 10 percent of the market value of the plan be in foreign securities and that the securities be qualified ones for inclusion. Qualified securities include, among others, deposits and term deposits in financial institutions, as well as foreign currency deposits in Canadian banks and trust companies; federal, provincial, municipal and corporate bonds (these are subject to restrictions); notes and similar issues; common, and preferred shares, warrants and rights listed on the five Canadian stock exchanges; foreign shares listed on prescribed foreign stock exchanges (subject to the 10 percent rule); mutual funds; shares of mortgage investment companies; mortgages secured by Canadian real estate. Specifically excluded are collectibles, precious metals, foreign currencies, and futures contracts.

A taxpayer can contribute to an RRSP in the name of his/her spouse. The payments are tax deductible by the payor while the RRSP trust itself will legally belong to the recipient spouse. Payments made to a spousal plan reduce the amount eligible for RRSP contribution by the person making the payment.

Maturity Options RRSP holders have a number of choices with respect to their RRSP at maturity or deregistration of their plan (which can take place at any time, but must be before the end of the year in which the taxpayer turns 71). The holder can purchase an annuity with all or a portion of his RRSP at any time; he or she can cash in the plan taking the full proceeds into income; or the holder can buy a Registered Retirement Income Fund.

Upon the maturity of the Plan the holder can purchase the following types of annuities: a life annuity for the life of the purchaser (annuitant) or for the lives of the annuitant and the spouse, with or without a guaranteed term, such term not to exceed the number of years computed as (90 – age of the annuitant at the maturity of the RRSP), or a fixed-term annuity that provides payments to age 90. Life annuities, available only from insurance companies, provide monthly payments for the life of the purchaser (annuitant) or for the lives of the annuitant and the spouse (joint and survivor annuity). At the death of the annuitant (or the last survivor, in the case of a joint and last survivor annuity), all payments cease. The purchaser can guarantee that at least a minimum number of payments are received by buying an annuity with a minimum term of, say, five or ten years. On the death of the annuitant before this minimum period, payments continue to the spouse for the remaining term or are paid as a commuted lump sum to a nonspousal beneficiary. Special features, such as guaranteed terms or joint and survivor clauses, reduce the monthly receipts. Fixed term annuities simply provide payments of principal and interest over the term (up to age 90) of the annuity.

A Registered Retirement Income Fund (RRIF) has characteristics similar to an annuity. The investor transfers his or her RRSP funds to a trustee and then receives annual payments to age 90 based on the fair market value of the trust at the beginning of the year at an interest rate specified by the annuitant, such rate not to exceed 6 percent. Hence the annuitant receives gradually increasing amounts each year to age 90.

A Registered Retirement Income Fund can be purchased with RRSP funds from 60 years of age to December 31 of the year the holder turns 71. RRIFs can be cashed in by the holder at any time, although the taxpayer would then be subject to tax on the entire proceeds. RRIFs must be maintained by a trustee but can, like RRSPs, be self-administered.

5-6 INVESTMENT AND TAXATION

The obvious question is "How should I manage my investments so as to minimize tax payments?" in view of the numerous tax laws described earlier in this chapter, you might expect that it would be impossible to give one simple answer to this question. While it is true that one simple tax strategy that will minimize each investor's tax payments cannot be articulated, one simple rule of considerable applicability and value is shown in Box 5-1.

Don't liquidate assets that are accumulating capital gains as long as they continue to gain. However, when an investment turns bad and starts losing, realize the loss as quickly as possible by selling the loser.

Box 5-1
A Good Tax
Strategy for
Many
Investors

The tax strategy recommended above is a buy-and-hold strategy that was extended to include a provision for the speedy recognition of losses. The buy-and-hold policy for investments that are gaining in value is predicated on the preferential treatment of capital gains, combined with an obvious reluctance to liquidate a good investment. There is no reason to sell an investment if you expect continued capital gains. Furthermore, the buy-and-hold strategy will minimize the brokerage commissions that accompany every buy or sell transaction. And whatever taxes on capital gains must be paid can be put off until the sale actually occurs.

In contrast to the buy-and-hold-the-gainers strategy, it is usually wise to sell investments that register disappointing losses as quickly as possible. Losers should be liquidated hastily for two reasons: to stop the losses from increasing and to recognize the losses in the short term (that is, one year or less) so that they may be written off against capital gains and thus reduce the tax bill. This latter portion of the recommended strategy is called *taking advantage of tax losses.*

5-7   SUMMARY AND CONCLUSIONS

Both private individuals and corporate entities are required by law to pay income taxes in Canada. However, capital gains and dividends on common and preferred shares are taxed at a lower rate in order to encourage investing behaviour. Also, various tax-deferred pension plans are available to encourage private individuals to plan for their own retirement.

The preceding outline of federal taxes may elicit three different reactions. First, the laws seem unfair; that is, they distribute the tax burden over different classes of taxpayers in such a way as to hurt certain groups and benefit other groups. Some possible solutions to this problem are usually examined in a full-semester course in welfare economics.

A second common response to the tax laws is that the tax system seems overpowering. The complex array of tax regulations requires specialized training in order to operate under them without overpaying. This problem can be overcome by hiring a tax accountant.[12]

---

12 This chapter presents only a thumbnail sketch of the tax laws in Canada. Many details were omitted to make for easier reading. As a result, this chapter cannot be used to train tax experts. There are many university-level tax accounting courses that must be mastered in order to become a tax expert.

A third common reaction to the tax laws is the belief that taxes are simply too high. One result is a large and growing "subterranean economy" of tax evaders who work for income they do not report to the federal government.[13] In any event, analysis of these problems is beyond the scope of this text.

QUESTIONS

1. Identify three allowable deductions from net income in arriving at an individual's taxable income.
2. Elvira Quesada has a federal marginal tax rate of 34 percent and a provincial tax rate of 50 percent and in 1987 must choose between a Bell Canada Enterprises bond, selling at par and yielding 12 percent to maturity and a Bell Canada Enterprises preferred share yielding 8 percent. Assuming all other factors are equal, which security should she choose? Why?
3. What are the major benefits derived from investing in an RRSP?
4. What are the disadvantages of investing in an RRSP?
5. What is the difference between marginal and average tax rates?
6. Do you believe that the tax schedule should be graduated (or progressive), as it is in Canada? Explain.
7. Wally Fatima purchased a 100-acre tract of land in northern Manitoba in 1986. Two years later he sold the rights to large gravel deposits on the land to Acme Extractors Ltd., a resident Manitoba corporation for a price based on the tonnage of gravel removed. The company made payments to Wally of $28,000, $34,000 and $58,000 in 1988, 1989, and 1990 respectively. How should Wally treat the proceeds from this sale of gravel deposits, for tax purposes?
8. Jack Lind, an Ontario resident, purchased 100 shares of Bell Canada Enterprises at $38.00 a share on November 15, 1984. The brokerage commissions were $105. He sold the shares on December 17, 1984, at $35.50 each less $98 in brokerage commission. On January 3, 1985, he repurchased the shares at $34 plus $97 in commission. Determine the tax consequences for 1984 and 1985. What is the adjusted cost base of his 100 shares of Bell as of January 3, 1985?
9. Mike Reynolds, a resident of Nova Scotia, sold his tool and die business in 1986, and declared that he was moving to Mexico to pursue a life of leisure. He and his wife, Sally, subsequently purchased a villa in Acapulco, but retained the family cottage in Antigonish, Nova Scotia, so that they could spend the summer months with their grown children and grandchildren and escape the hot Mexican summers. The Reynolds maintained most of their wealth in Mexico, however they kept some $20,000 at the Bank of Nova Scotia (Antigonish Branch) for their use in Canada. Mike, an avid tennis player retained his membership in the Antigonish

---

13 Peter M. Gutmann, "The Subterranean Economy," *Financial Analysts Journal*, November-December 1977; P. M. (Gutmann, "Are the Unemployed, Unemployed?" *Financial Analysts Journal*, September-October 1978; P. M. Gutmann, "The Subterranean Economy Five Years Later," *Across the Board* (the Conference Board Magazine), vol. 20, no. 2, February 1983.

Lawn and Tennis Club, although his annual membership fee was reduced by 50 percent since the club considered him a nonresident member. Sally kept up her membership in the local theatre group and in fact occasionally appeared in minor roles in the theatre productions during the summer. The Reynolds filed income tax returns in Mexico each year. Are the Reynolds liable to tax in Canada? Why or why not?

SELECTED REFERENCES

Beam, R. E. and S. N. Laiken. *Introduction to Federal Income Taxation in Canada*. 7th ed. 1985–1986. Don Mills, Ontario: CCH Canadian, 1986.

Canadian Income Tax Act with Regulations, 1985. Don Mills, Ontario: CCH Canadian, 1985.

Harris, Edwin C., *Canadian Income Taxation*, 4th ed. Toronto: Butterworths, 1983.

Hore, John E. *Trading on Canadian Futures Markets*. Canadian Securities Institute, 1985. Chapter 14 discusses tax issues concerning futures trading.

Peat Marwick. *Tax Reform 87, Analysis and Commentary*. June 1987.

Price Waterhouse. *Oil and Gas Taxation*, March 1986.

Price Waterhouse. *Canadian Mining Taxation*, October 1986.

Stikeman, H. H., *Income Tax Act: Annotated*, 15th ed. Don Mills, Ontario: Richard de Boo, 1985.

CHAPTER 6

Sources of Financial Information

This chapter describes various sources of financial news and information. These sources are useful to professional financial analysts and amateurs alike. Studying the information sources described in this chapter can give investors insights and broaden their exposure to valuable information.

Usually, an investment inquiry should begin with an inquiry into *world affairs*. Wars, epidemics, international tensions—all affect nations' economies and securities markets. A financial analyst should develop a picture of world conditions and then an estimate of the impact of these conditions on the *national economy*. At that point, the analyst can focus on *specific industries*. Labour negotiations, changes in legislation, sales, and the competition within the industry must be considered. Only after all this background investigation has been completed is the financial analyst ready to examine a particular *firm*. Obviously, a good financial analyst must consult many sources of news and other information.

The remainder of this chapter discusses information sources about world affairs, national economies, industries, and industrial firms — in that order. Computer facilities that may be used to assist economists and financial analysts are discussed at the end of the chapter. Subscription prices of some of the publications are provided. These prices are of course subject to change.

6-1 WORLD AFFAIRS

Five of the most useful financial newspapers are *The Financial Times* (of London), *The Globe and Mail Report on Business*, *The New York Times*, *The Wall Street Journal*, and *The Financial Post*. These papers carry complete and current reports on political and economic conditions around the world.

6-1.1 The Financial Times

The Financial Times is published daily except Sunday and holidays. The paper provides extensive coverage of world economic and financial developments, with special emphasis on Europe. Section II contains considerable world market data, including U.S. and U.K. daily futures and options contracts quotes, selected company quotations on over twenty different exchanges, and a four-day moving set of market indexes for all major bourses. See Figure 6-1. The major drawback is the cost: $365 U.S. per year. Many university and business libraries receive the newspaper, however.

FIGURE 6-1 Representative daily sample from *The Financial Times*.

Indices

NEW YORK

DOW JONES	Dec. 31	Dec. 30	Dec. 29	Dec. 26	Dec. 24	1986 High	1986 Low	Since Comp High	Since Comp Low
◆Industrials	1895.95	1908.61	1912.12	1930.40	1926.88	1955.57 (2/12)	1502.29 (22/1)	1955.57 2/12/86	41.22 2/7/32
H'me Bnds..	93.43	93.21	93.37	93.36	93.43	93.65 (19/12)	83.73 (14/1)	—	—
Transport...	807.17	810.20	813.23	819.65	820.37	866.74 (4/12)	686.97 (9/1)	866.74 4/12/86	12.32 8/7/32
Utilities	206.01	205.78	208.03	209.47	209.19	219.15 (20/8)	169.47 (22/1)	219.15 20/8/86	10.5 8/4/32

◆Day's High 1920.42 (1920.70) Low 1885.40 (1894.69)

STANDARD AND POOR'S	Dec. 31	Dec. 30	Dec. 29	Dec. 26	Dec. 24	1986 High	1986 Low	Since Comp High	Since Comp Low
Composite ‡	242.17	243.37	244.67	246.92	246.75	255.3 (27/8)	203.49 (22/1)	253.3 27/8/86	4.40 1/6/32
Industrials .	269.93	271.31	272.58	275.13	275.31	282.77 (2/12)	224.48 (22/1)	282.77 2/12/86	3.62 21/6/32
Financials ..	26.92	27.09	27.29	27.54	27.59	31.13 (14/3)	25.19 (22/1)	31.13 14/3/86	8.64 1/10/74
N.Y.S.E. COMPOSITE	138.58	139.12	139.89	141.14	141.00	145.75 (4/9)	117.75 (22/1)	145.75 4/9/86	4.464 25/4/27
AMEX. MKT VALUE	263.27	261.54	262.39	264.10	263.75	285.19 (26/6)	240.30 (4/2)	285.19 25/6/86	29.13 9/12/74
NASDAQ OTCCOMP.	348.83	347.32	348.03	350.01	349.62	411.16 (3/7)	323.01 (9/1)	411.16 3/7/86	54.87 3/10/74

DIVIDEND YIELDS	Dec. 26	Dec. 19	Dec. 12	Dec. 5	year ago (approx)
Dow Industrial	3.59	3.59	3.61	3.58	4.12
	Dec. 24	Dec. 17	Dec. 10	Dec. 3	
S and P Industrial....	3.00	2.99	2.94	2.90	3.45
S and P ind P/E ratio	17.71	17.74	17.99	18.23	14.60

TRADING ACTIVITY

Millions Volume †	Dec. 31	Dec. 30	Dec. 29
New York.....	139.17	126.18	99.80
Amex	15.82	14.18	14.41
O.T.C.	(u)	126.40	102.02

New York	Dec. 31	Dec. 30	Dec. 29
Issues Traded...	2,076	2,071	2,022
Rises	792	475	409
Falls	817	1,131	1,183
Unchanged	467	465	430
New Highs	(u)	21	18
New Lows	(u)	47	28

CANADA

TORONTO	Dec. 31	Dec. 30	Dec. 29	Dec. 26	Dec. 24	1986 High	1986 Low
Metals & Minerals	(u)	1958.2	1957.5	(c)	1958.53	2442.8 (21/3)	1917.4 (5/8)
Composite	3066.1	3050.4	3045.1	(c)	3046.65	3129.1 (18/4)	2754.0 (17/2)
MONTREAL							
Portfolio	1533.5	1534.6	1533.7	(c)	1538.86	1623.3 (18/4)	1386.6 (22/1)

NEW YORK ACTIVE STOCKS

Wednesday	Stocks traded	Closing price	Change on day		Stocks traded	Closing price	Change on day
BellSouth	4,641,900	57¾	−0⅜	Walt Disney ...	1,896,700	43⅛	+0¾
S. Cal. Edison	3,167,700	33⅞	−0¼	AT and T.	1,510,600	25	—
Amer. Info. ...	3,147,600	132½	−0⅜	IBM	1,509,000	120	−0⅞
May Dpt. Strs.	2,437,100	35½	+0⅛	Owens-Illinois .	1,448,900	53	+1
Illinois Power .	2,004,300	29⅜	—	Niag. Mohawk .	1,364,200	16¾	+0¾

	Dec. 31	Dec. 30	Dec. 29	Dec. 26	1986 High	1986 Low
AUSTRALIA						
All Ord. (1/1/80)	1473.1	1470.5	1467.5	(c)	1473.1 (31/12)	1010.8 (2/1)
Metals & Mnls. (1/1/80)	714.8	714.5	717.2	(c)	720.1 (23/12)	481.1 (20/1)
AUSTRIA						
Creditbk Aktien(30/12/84	(c)	231.99	231.25	(c)	266.64 (23/4)	226.58 (5/3)
BELGIUM						
Brussels SE (1/1/84)	(c)	4095.61	4081.51	(c)	4131.69 (9/12)	2768.91 (15/1)
DENMARK						
Copenhagen SE(3/1/83/)	(c)	(u)	(u)	(c)	250.70 (18/4)	186.28 (11/11)
FINLAND						
Unitas Genl. (1975)	(u)	425.4	424.9	(c)	432.9 (18/12)	258.3 (2/1)
FRANCE						
CAC General (31/12/82)	397.8	398.4	405.8	407.10	414.3 (15/12)	267.8 (2/1)
Ind 'ı endance (31/12/82)	157.0	156.6	160.2	161.00	165.0 (15/12)	101.1 (2/1)
GERMANY						
FAZ Aktien (31/12/58)	(c)	676. 37	678.07	(c)	753.88 (17/4)	583.92 (22/7)
Commerzbank (1/12/53)	(c)	2046.4	2049.0	(c)	2278.8 (17/4)	1762.4 (22/7)
HONG KONG						
Hang Seng Bank(31/7/64)	2568.30	2559.36	2552.45	(c)	2568.30 (31/12)	1559.94 (19/3)
ITALY						
Banca Comm. Ital.(1972	722.78	716.86	716.37	(c)	908.20 (20/5)	454.67 (24/1)
JAPAN**						
Nikkei (16/5/49)	(c)	(c)	(c)	18,820.65	18936.2 (20/8)	12881.0 (21/1)
Tokyo SE New (4/1)68)	(c)	(c)	(c)	1562.55	1583.35 (20/8)	1025.85 (21/1)
NETHERLANDS						
ANP.CPS General (1970)	(c)	278.4	279.5	(c)	301.0 (5.9)	240.4 (3/3)
ANP.CBS Indust (1970)	(c)	273.2	275.1	(c)	303.9 (19/8)	234.0 (3/3)
NORWAY						
Oslo SE (4/1/83)	(c)	357.76	354.84	(c)	402.91 (16/1)	331.61 4.8)
SINGAPORE						
Straits Times (30/12/66)	891.30	891.21	898.20	901.20	940.64 (3/11)	563.34 (28/4)
SOUTH AFRICA						
JSE Gold (28/9/78)	—	—	1907.0	(c)	2061.0 (19/9)	1104.1 (21/4)
JSE Indust (28/9/78)	—	—	1416.0	(c)	1419.9 (12/11)	1019.3 (214)
SPAIN						
Madrid SE (30/12/85)	(c)	208.31	207.80	205.25	208.83(19/12)	100.83 (3/1)
SWEDEN						
acobso ⊐ & P (31/12/56)	(c)	2459.19	2443.85	(c)	2672.78 (7/11)	1729.57 (29/1)
SWITZERLAND						
SwissBankCpn (31/12/58)	(c)	588.9	588.3	(c)	625.5 (8/1)	497.2 (4/8)
WORLD						
M S. Capital Intl.(1/1/70)	—	357·0	358.6	357.4	360.8 (1/9)	249.8 (23/1)

** Saturday December 27: Japan Nikkei 18,701.3. TSE 1,556.37.

Base value of all Indices are 100 except Brussels SE—1,000, JSE Gold—255.7, JSE Industrial—264.3, and Australia. All Ordinary and Metals—500. NYSE All Common—50; Standard and Poors—10; and Toronto Composite and Metals—1,000. Toronto Indices based 1975 and Montreal Portfolio 4/1/83. † Excluding bonds. ‡ 400 Industrials plus 40 Utilities, 40 Financials and 20 Transports. c Closed. u Unavailable.

Source: *The Financial Times*, January 2, 1987, p. 21.

6-1.2 The Globe and Mail Report on Business

The Globe and Mail Report on Business is published daily except Sundays and holidays. *The Globe and Mail* is Canada's best-known and most extensive daily financial newspaper. Although the reporting emphasis is on the Canadian economy and financial markets, there is also some information provided on the international scene. Monday's *Report on Business* also contains a two- to four-page international section. Regular features include ''Options futures,'' ''International Business,'' ''Bonds,'' ''U.S. Report,'' and ''Statistical Trends.'' Daily quotations are provided for the Toronto, Vancouver, and Alberta Stock Exchanges, the Montreal Exchange, the New York Stock Exchange (selected basis only), the American Stock Exchange (selected basis only), Canadian open-ended mutual funds, and Canadian and U.S. futures and options markets.

6-1.3 The New York Times

The New York Times (NYT) is a daily newspaper noted for its objective coverage —''All the news that's fit to print'' is the *NYT*'s slogan. The *NYT* has a large business and financial section toward the back of every edition that some people judge to be superior to those of some purely business newspapers. This section reports financial news, market data from various markets, and stories about individual firms and industries. With the exception of certain regular features, the *NYT* carries much of the same financial news as *The Wall Street Journal*. The *NYT*'s coverage of world affairs is probably among the best in the world.

6-1.4 The Wall Street Journal

The Wall Street Journal (WSJ) is published five days a week. It is written for a national audience interested in finance and, in particular, investments.[1] The *WSJ* reports world, national, and financial news and news about industries and firms. It also reports the opinions of economists and various financial experts about the course of future events.

Regular *WSJ* items useful to investors include feature-length articles and columns such as ''Outlook,'' ''Labor Letter,'' ''Tax Report,'' ''Dividend News,'' ''Earnings Digest,'' ''Abreast of the Market,'' and ''Bond Markets.'' The paper also reports price and volume data daily for assets traded on the NYSE, AMEX, the OTC markets, the bond markets, foreign exchange markets, the options exchanges, and other financial markets.[2]

6-1.5 The Financial Post

The Financial Post is published weekly[3] and is Canada's most comprehensive financial newspaper, containing information on Canadian and international capital markets. The first section is devoted primarily to Canadian business and economic news. The second section, called, ''The Investor's Guide'' has a complete set of market quotations, journalistic articles on Canadian stocks, bonds, and mutual funds, and analysts' stock and bond recommendations. Special features include ''Inside the Markets,'' ''Western Markets,'' ''Talisman Fund,'' monthly comprehensive, mutual fund performance reports, and tax reports. The third and fourth sections are generally devoted to business affairs and special business reports.

6-1.6 Other Financial Newspapers

Other financial newspapers that carry useful financial news and information are *The Northern Miner*, a weekly newspaper that provides market data and journalistic articles on the Canadian mining industry, *The Financial Times*, a weekly newspaper that carries general economic news, financial analysts' comments, mutual fund reports (including a comprehensive quarterly survey), market quotations, and other financial and economic information; *Barron's*, a weekly U.S. financial newspaper that makes no attempt to report world, national, or local news. *Barron's* ''Statistical Section'' typically fills

---

1 Subscriptions to the *WSJ* cost $236 U.S. per year for second-class postage delivery to your door. Instructors interested in using the *WSJ* in class may contact Educational Service Bureau, Dow Jones & Company, P.O. Box 300, Princeton, New Jersey, 08540, for information about student subscription programs and various free teaching materials.

2 Dow Jones & Company publishes the *WSJ* and *Barron's* financial newspapers and prepares the Dow Jones Industrial Average, the Dow Jones Transportation Average, and the Dow Jones Utility Average. These three averages are very popular and receive wide coverage through the Dow Jones & Company newspapers.

3 Subscriptions to *The Financial Post* cost $39.95 a year. Write to *Financial Post*, Circulation, 777 Bay Street, Toronto, Ontario M5W 1A7.

about half this fifty-page newspaper; it includes security price and volume quotations, mutual fund statistics, commodity market data, the "Market Laboratory," the "Pulse of Industry and Trade," and other compilations of market data. The title "Statistical Section" can be misleading, however, because only raw data are published.

6-2 NATIONAL AFFAIRS

Price movements of most securities are highly attributable to movement in the price level of the entire securities market. Thus, if the level of market indexes can be forecast, much information about the future prices of most securities will be provided. Changes in market indexes tend to precede changes in the national economy by two to six months and sometimes more. Thus, forecasting the level and direction of the national economy accurately a year in advance is extremely useful in predicting the direction of security price movements.[4] Some large banks publish economic forecasts that can be useful.

Some of Canada's chartered banks publish newsletters on economic conditions. Reports in these newsletters usually focus on the general economic outlook, and they often refer to the expected effects on the securities and foreign exchange markets. For example, The Royal Bank's *International Money Markets*,[5] the Royal Bank's *Econoscope*[6] and the Toronto Dominion Bank's *Canadian Business Climate*[7] are all available free upon request. A short letter to these banks is all that is needed. These bank newsletters are easy to read. Graphs and tables may be included, but mathematics and technical terms are used sparingly.

6-2.1 Bank Newsletters

Several summaries of macroeconomic data may be obtained from Canadian government sources. These sources contain data that can be used in forecasting.

The Bank of Canada Review is published monthly by the Bank of Canada. The first section contains a number of charts of economic activity spanning the past five to ten years. The second section contains statistical tables that include money, stock, and bond market data, foreign exchange statistics, general economic statistics, financial institution asset and liability holdings, and Bank of Canada press releases.[8]

6-2.2 Canadian Government Publications

4 Geoffrey H. Moore, *Business Cycles, Inflation and Forecasting*, National Bureau of Economic Research, study number 24, Ballinger Publishing Company, Cambridge, Mass., 1980, pp. 187–202.

5 Write to IMM research, Economics: Investment Banking and Money Markets Group, The Royal Bank of Canada, 18th floor, Royal Bank Plaza, 200 Bay Street, Toronto, Ontario M5J 2J5.

6 Write to Economics Department, The Royal Bank of Canada, Head Office, P.O. Box 6001, Montreal, Quebec H3C 3A9.

7 Write to the Department of Economic Research, The Toronto Dominion Bank, P.O. Box 1, Toronto Dominion Centre, Toronto, Ontario M5K 1A2.

8 Annual subscription is $10.00 and may be obtained by writing *The Bank of Canada Review*, Public Information Division, Bank of Canada, 245 Sparks Street, Ottawa, Canada K1A 0G9.

FIGURE 6-2   Sample page from bank newsletter.

What the economic indicators say

Royal Bank Trendicator*

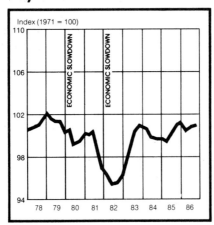

Competitiveness index

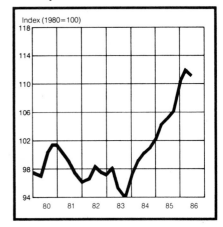

Decline reverses

The Royal Bank's Trendicator* edged up at an annual rate of only 0.2% during the third quarter of this year, following a 0.8% rise in the second quarter, but has yet to fully recover from its decline during the first quarter of 1986.

As well as indicating near-term sluggishness Trendicator* provides insight into developing strengths and weaknesses in the various broad sectors of the economy. The significant decline in the length of the manufacturing workweek suggests that the slowdown in that sector, which had shown vibrant growth during the 1983-1985 period, will likely continue into 1987, owing partly to the expected retrenchment in consumer spending, a view supported by the decline in the new-orders/inventory ratio for industries producing consumer durables. The component for residential construction rose much more slowly during the third quarter, indicating that this sector, which has been an important source of growth during the past year, is now close to its peak. On the plus side, the forward-looking indicator for exports suggests a further recovery in this area during the coming months.

First dip since 1983

After steady improvement since the third quarter of 1983, the Canadian Competitiveness Index deteriorated slightly in the second quarter of 1986, reflecting largely the appreciation of the Canadian dollar relative to the U.S. dollar. (The United States is Canada's largest trading partner and therefore the U.S. dollar is heavily weighted in the index.) Relative unit labour costs dropped in the same period, but this improvement was fully offset by a deterioration in relative industrial selling prices.

On a case-by-case basis, Canada alone registered a drop in annualized unit labour costs as output per worker rose faster than the average wage rate. Germany registered the smallest increase, followed by the United States, Japan, and the United Kingdom. As for industrial selling prices, Japan posted the largest annualized gain, followed by the United States and Germany; but prices rose in the United Kingdom and Canada with the latter registering only a modest increase.

Trademark

Source: *The Econoscope,* The Royal Bank of Canada, December 1986.

S 86

FIGURE 6-3 Sample page from *Bank of Canada Review*.

F4

Stock market statistics: Canada and United States
Statistiques boursières : Canada et États-Unis

Canadian stock market indicators
Indicateurs des cours et de l'activité des bourses au Canada

Toronto Stock Exchange Bourse de Toronto
Stock price indexes 1975 = 1000 Indices des cours des actions, 1975 = 1000

Month / Mois	Composite (300) Indice synthétique (300) — Closing quotations / Cours de clôture au cours du mois			Closing quotations at month-end / Cours de clôture en fin de mois							Stock dividend yields (composite) Rendement de dividendes (indice synthétique)	Price/earnings ratio (composite) Taux de capitalisation des bénéfices (indice synthétique)	Montreal Stock Exchange price indexes 4 January 1983 = 100 Month-end close / Bourse de Montréal 4 janvier 1983 = 100	
	High Haut	Low Bas	Close Dernier jour	Oil and gas Pétrole et gaz	Metals and minerals Métaux et minéraux	Utilities Services d'utilité publique	Paper and forest products Papiers et produits de la forêt	Merchandising Entreprises de distribution	Financial services Services financiers	Golds Or			Market portfolio (25) Indice du marché (25)	Banks (6) Banques (6)
	B4235	B4236	B4237	B4238	B4239	B4240	B4241	B4242	B4243	B4244	B4245	B4246	B4287	B4288
1982 J	1,956.3	1,704.6	1,786.9	3,226.4	1,682.2	1,358.3	1,625.1	1,387.0	1,234.0	2,558.9	4.92	7.85	88.1	79.8
F	1,750.0	1,164.8	1,671.3	2,801.6	1,612.2	1,350.6	1,476.8	1,364.0	1,187.3	2,454.3	5.37	7.54	83.7	74.8
M	1,681.0	1,537.6	1,587.8	2,573.9	1,463.3	1,402.5	1,349.8	1,385.6	1,176.8	2,198.7	5.62	7.61	78.5	74.3
A	1,634.8	1,548.2	1,548.2	2,669.3	1,395.0	1,458.3	1,349.6	1,367.1	1,087.3	2,116.5	5.70	7.81	75.9	68.8
M	1,592.6	1,497.5	1,523.7	2,781.3	1,334.1	1,472.7	1,294.3	1,307.1	1,047.8	1,933.7	5.65	8.32	74.4	66.7
J	1,496.0	1,355.7	1,366.8	2,383.3	1,206.7	1,310.5	1,176.4	1,157.6	947.3	1,608.0	6.31	7.86	66.8	60.5
J	1,454.8	1,346.4	1,411.9	2,390.9	1,309.8	1,285.9	1,228.7	1,215.8	1,006.9	1,678.7	5.79	8.78	68.7	64.0
A	1,613.3	1,392.5	1,613.3	2,763.0	1,500.8	1,399.1	1,399.9	1,334.1	1,180.0	2,344.9	5.00	11.38	81.2	76.5
S	1,658.2	1,602.0	1,602.0	2,740.9	1,430.0	1,430.1	1,355.2	1,442.4	1,127.5	2,555.9	4.93	12.53	79.2	72.8
O	1,803.5	1,578.2	1,774.0	2,939.3	1,601.1	1,574.8	1,382.9	1,615.9	1,295.1	2,754.7	4.41	14.82	88.5	83.2
N	1,887.3	1,790.7	1,838.3	2,800.6	1,585.6	1,668.1	1,385.5	1,621.4	1,420.8	3,212.9	4.28	17.33	92.3	94.1
D	1,958.1	1,845.3	1,958.1	2,683.3	1,857.3	1,802.5	1,496.2	1,694.6	1,527.2	4,217.6	4.03	19.12	100.5	102.7
1983 J	2,122.6	1,926.4	2,031.5	2,774.8	2,026.1	1,681.7	1,706.0	1,783.8	1,463.1	5,247.4	3.87	20.87	103.5	100.3
F	2,147.6	2,022.3	2,090.4	2,650.9	2,026.7	1,828.6	1,811.8	1,866.7	1,603.8	3,833.2	3.76	24.00	107.8	109.2
M	2,170.1	2,110.5	2,156.1	2,770.8	2,046.8	1,851.3	1,860.5	1,954.3	1,766.6	3,989.3	3.65	24.72	110.9	120.3
A	2,340.8	2,151.1	2,340.8	3,125.6	2,141.5	2,018.3	1,948.0	2,106.5	1,903.9	4,346.4	3.32	27.93	121.0	130.7
M	2,457.7	2,318.8	2,420.7	3,458.7	2,344.0	1,940.2	2,158.0	2,126.1	1,894.7	4,897.2	3.28	28.78	122.4	130.3
J	2,467.0	2,371.7	2,447.0	3,695.2	2,295.7	1,889.5	2,110.3	2,126.2	1,817.6	4,550.1	3.25	28.79	122.6	122.4
J	2,517.8	2,439.6	2,477.6	3,830.9	2,492.5	1,882.7	2,010.9	2,149.8	1,819.6	4,708.2	3.22	28.11	121.9	121.6
A	2,483.1	2,387.2	2,483.1	3,755.7	2,593.4	2,024.8	2,017.6	2,149.4	1,754.9	4,901.8	3.22	26.67	120.6	118.8
S	2,598.3	2,499.6	2,499.6	3,710.8	2,465.9	2,065.0	2,060.9	2,174.9	1,819.0	4,045.0	3.22	25.73	123.0	122.3
O	2,522.8	2,332.9	2,361.1	3,263.2	2,217.3	2,092.4	1,965.8	2,146.5	1,747.9	3,487.3	3.41	25.15	115.3	118.2
N	2,540.9	2,358.3	2,540.9	3,486.4	2,511.6	2,270.4	2,145.5	2,274.4	1,781.8	4,148.5	3.23	23.15	125.0	122.2
D	2,558.0	2,500.7	2,552.4	3,468.6	2,491.8	2,299.8	2,199.3	2,368.6	1,818.4	4,161.4	3.22	22.41	125.0	121.5
1984 J	2,585.7	2,468.9	2,468.9	3,342.3	2,283.4	2,203.5	2,319.1	2,221.2	1,815.2	3,993.9	3.34	20.22	120.8	121.0
F	2,471.5	2,357.0	2,419.8	3,439.2	2,214.5	2,181.7	2,202.3	2,119.5	1,755.0	4,565.2	3.47	18.52	119.1	118.2
M	2,436.2	2,310.5	2,382.1	3,450.8	2,326.3	2,081.4	2,243.0	2,150.7	1,590.5	4,659.5	3.54	18.27	116.1	106.3
A	2,386.4	2,184.8	2,323.3	3,487.7	2,085.2	2,120.8	2,247.3	2,083.6	1,572.6	4,213.5	3.63	15.91	112.5	104.2
M	2,359.2	2,208.4	2,229.7	3,316.0	1,956.9	2,058.6	1,987.3	2,011.1	1,517.1	4,132.1	3.86	15.32	108.1	100.5
J	2,289.8	2,077.4	2,220.9	3,201.6	1,862.4	2,120.5	1,945.3	1,972.8	1,474.4	3,909.5	4.03	15.28	104.6	97.4
J	2,220.8		2,140.0	2,853.7	1,714.2	2,218.1	1,856.5	1,954.5	1,474.9	3,050.1	3.63	14.30		96.5
A	2,389.8	2,381.8	2,388.8	3,407.0	2,019.4	2,283.1	2,025.5	2,105.0	1,591.9	3,527.6	3.63	15.19	117.1	104.7
S	2,407.0	2,332.9	2,392.7	3,521.1	1,989.0	2,204.6	1,966.6	2,100.2	1,617.6	3,693.8	3.70	15.07	117.8	108.1
O	2,417.6	2,347.7	2,353.3	3,188.5	1,926.4	2,302.7	1,998.1	2,098.7	1,628.8	3,451.0	3.70	14.72	116.0	108.3
N	2,427.0	2,350.5	2,368.5	3,094.5	1,873.0	2,408.4	1,984.5	2,033.4	1,680.8	3,374.5	3.73	14.95	117.4	113.2
D	2,403.2	2,333.6	2,400.3	2,989.9	1,932.0	2,449.0	2,031.9	2,034.3	1,773.0	2,921.2	3.70	15.24	119.8	119.3
1985 J	2,609.1	2,347.5	2,595.1	3,127.1	2,179.3	2,556.3	2,298.4	2,235.8	1,864.3	3,118.6	3.43	15.38	131.5	126.2
F	2,640.5	2,578.7	2,595.0	3,152.4	2,075.3	2,584.1	2,221.0	2,222.4	1,829.2	3,090.9	3.46	16.17	130.3	123.5
M	2,652.7	2,577.5	2,612.8	3,479.8	2,020.2	2,664.5	2,104.9	2,188.4	1,761.4	3,750.2	3.46	15.43	129.1	118.6
A	2,668.8	2,592.8	2,635.3	3,544.5	2,010.6	2,670.1	2,053.1	2,266.7	1,853.6	3,733.9	3.42	14.43	130.1	124.9
M	2,750.3	2,599.6	2,736.3	3,453.0	1,984.7	2,906.3	2,084.7	2,477.2	1,950.7	3,697.8	3.29	14.73	133.5	133.5
J	2,766.1	2,687.5	2,712.5	3,207.2	1,897.7	2,944.5	2,049.4	2,603.7	2,005.1	3,647.7	3.32	13.85	132.3	138.8
J	2,810.0	2,711.7	2,778.6	3,189.3	2,096.0	2,867.5	2,166.6	2,700.8	2,015.3	4,395.5	3.25	14.54	136.7	138.7
A	2,820.9	2,749.6	2,820.0	3,467.3	2,115.4	2,931.1	2,080.6	2,695.2	2,105.8	4,691.3	3.20	14.68	136.9	145.5
S	2,817.0	2,610.4	2,632.3	3,258.3	1,883.6	2,768.1	1,879.8	2,619.5	1,963.5	4,180.8	3.42	13.57	128.3	136.0
O	2,675.9	2,606.5	2,674.8	3,196.7	1,740.8	2,817.2	1,942.2	2,789.1	2,068.7	4,141.8	3.32	13.70	128.7	143.4
N	2,857.7	2,848.6	2,857.2	3,443.2	1,929.9	2,927.8	2,071.3	2,961.4	2,227.7	4,419.1	3.16	14.80	138.4	155.7
D	2,902.2	2,347.5	2,900.6	3,297.8	2,079.4	2,893.5	2,350.3	3,113.2	2,241.0	4,449.1	3.13	14.54	141.9	157.2
1986 J	2,888.6	2,758.8	2,843.0	2,998.4	2,268.8	2,656.3	2,529.6	3,194.0	2,134.4	4,805.8	3.21	14.19	139.3	148.6

Source: Bank of Canada Review, February 1986.

Weekly Financial Statistics, also published by the Bank of Canada, provide numerous data on security yields in financial markets, Bank of Canada and chartered bank balances, and foreign exchange reserves.

Statistics Canada is the federal government statistical agency responsible for collecting, compiling, and publishing national and regional economic, demographic, and sociological statistical data. The *Canadian Statistical Review*[9] is a monthly publication that contains basic economic statistics in tabular and graphic form. *Catalogue of Current Publications*, published by Statistics Canada, provides a complete index of all Statistics Canada publications.

Annual financial, economic, demographic, and exchange rate data for Canada and most other countries can also be found in the Organization for Economic Cooperation and Development (OECD) publication, *OECD Main Economic Indicators*,[10] and the International Monetary Fund (IMF), *International Financial Statistics*.[11]

6-2.3 Securities Commissions and Self-Regulating Bodies Publications

The various provincial securities commissions publish *Bulletins* on a weekly basis. These deal with such matters as cease-trading orders, insider reports, new issues, takeover bids, and other issues covered in the provincial securities acts.

The Investment Dealers Association (the IDA) publishes a quarterly report, *The IDA Report*, that includes financial industry data, as well as bond and money market trading reports and dealer news issues.[12]

6-2.4 Stock Exchange Publications

The Toronto and Vancouver Stock Exchanges and the Montreal Exchange publish monthly reviews that provide, among other things, statistical reports that set out new listings, volume of trading, historical records of trading, price and volume quotations, earnings and P/E multiples for all listed securities, index data, interlisted trading summary, market indexes, board lot sizes, short positions, and other data and material.[13]

The Toronto Stock Exchange also publishes an annual *Factbook*, which contains a recent chronology of important exchange- and market-related events, market index summaries, actively traded stocks, etc. There are numerous other publications of the exchanges, including the TSE's *Daily Record*, which provides a complete report on each day's trading in all listed stocks; the TSE's

9 Statistics Canada, Ottawa, Canada K1A 0Z8.

10 OECD Publications and Information Center, Suite 1207, 1750 Pennsylvania Avenue, N.W. Washington, D.C., 20006-4582.

11 International Monetary Fund, 700 19th Street, N.W., Washington, D.C. 20431.

12 Investment Dealers Association of Canada, Suite 350, 33 Yonge Street, Toronto, Ontario M5E 1G4; Tour de la Banque Nationale, 27ᵉ etage, 600 rue de la Gauchetiere ouest, Montreal, Quebec H3B 4L8.

13 *The Toronto Stock Exchange Review* can be ordered from TSE Circulation Department, Exchange Tower, 2 First Canadian Place, Toronto, Ontario, M5X 1J2. It costs $146.20 a year. *The Vancouver Stock Exchange Review* can be ordered from The Vancouver Stock Exchange, Stock Exchange Tower, P.O. Box 10333, 609 Granville Street, Vancouver, B.C., V7Y 1H1. It costs $65.00 per year. *The Montreal Exchange Monthly Review* is available from The Montreal Exchange, The Stock Exchange Tower, P.O. Box 61, 800 Victoria Square, Montreal, Quebec, H4Z 1A9. It costs $45.00 per year.

Short Position Report, compiled at the middle and end of each month; and the TSE's *Daily Bulletin*, which provides daily changes for all listed securities in issued capital of listed securities, rights offerings, stock splits, and capital reorganizations.[14]

6-3 INVESTMENT INFORMATION SERVICES

Syntheses of fundamental financial information about industries and individual firms are published by investment information services. Such firms offer subscriptions to their daily, weekly, and monthly publications. The cost of a subscription is deductible from an investor's income, according to federal personal income-tax regulations. Large public libraries usually carry the publications of one or more of these services, which may be consulted free of charge. The leading services that provide fundamental information on Canadian companies are as follows:

The Financial Post Information Service
Maclean Hunter Building
777 Bay Street
Toronto, Ontario M5W 1A7

Canadian Business Service
Marpep Publishing Limited
Suite 700
133 Richmond Street W.
Toronto, Ontario, M5H 3M8

Moody's Investors Services, Inc. (owned by Dun & Bradstreet)
99 Church Street
New York, New York, 10007

The Financial Post publishes a massive amount of corporate data, available in a number of formats. *The Financial Post* Corporation Service is the most extensive data bank of fundamental information on Canadian companies. Marpep Publishing publishes a comprehensive set of financial data on companies and security yields. Moody's (in particular *Moody's International Manual*) provides extensive data on Canadian companies interlisted on U.S. exchanges.

The major sources of U.S. corporate data are:

Standard & Poor's Corporation (owned by McGraw-Hill)
25 Broadway
New York, New York, 10004

Moody's Investors Services, Inc. (see above)

14 These items are available from the Toronto Stock Exchange, Exchange Tower, 2 First Canadian Place, Toronto, Ontario M5X 1J2. The *Factbook* is $3.50 to $5.00 per year, The *Daily Record* is $357 per annum (cheaper if picked up at the exchange), the *Short Position Report* is $18 per annum, the *Daily Bulletin* is $150 per annum. The Vancouver Stock Exchange and the Montreal Exchange also publish similar reports.

FIGURE 6-4
Sample page from
The Financial Post
Information
Service.

Canada Packers Inc.

Revised January 16, 1986 (IC)

Destroy àll previous Basic and White
cards on this Company

CUSIP Number 135177

Stock Symbol CK

Head Office — 95 St. Clair Ave. West, Toronto, Ont. M4V 1P2

Telephone — (416) 766-4311

THE COMPANY is the largest food producer in Canada. Directly and through subsidiaries is engaged in the production and processing of meats, poultry, vegetables, dairy products, edible oils and non-food products with processing and manufacturing facilities in Canada, West Germany, Great Britain, Australia and Mexico.

COMPARATIVE DATA

Fiscal Year	Total Assets	L.-Term Debt	Shldrs.' Equity	Net Sales	Net Inc. Oper.	Earns. Per Sh.	Divds. Paid	Price Range■ High	Low
			——— 000's ———			—Common Shares▲—			
	$	$	$	$	$	$	$	$	$
1985....	619,492	39,046	311,128	3,051,089	25,039	2.08	0.92	30.00	24.00
1984....	596,311	40,621	297,437	3,175,963	25,275	2.10	0.86	28.25	16.50
1983....	558,941	27,301	281,764	3,001,447	20,961	1.75	0.80	16.75	14.13
1982....	544,747	44,219	270,407	2,943,099	30,039	2.51	0.80	18.50	14.75
1981....	522,789	47,817	249,986	2,842,369	24,485	2.18	0.77	18.00	14.25

■ Previous calendar year. ▲Adjusted throughout for 2-for-1 stock split on July 8, 1983.

CONSOLIDATED CAPITALIZATION AS AT MARCH 30, 1985

	——— Outstanding ———	%
Long-term debt	$39,046,000	11
Common stock .... 12,039,000 shs.	10,819,000	3
Retained earnings*	300,309,000	86

*Net of $175,000 in unrealized foreign currency adjustment.

SUMMARY STATEMENT

For the six months ended September 28, 1985, net income more than doubled to $15,925,000 or $1.31 per share from $7,735,000 or 64 cents per share for the similar period in 1984. Net sales rose 3% to $1,541,342,000 from $1,496,107,000. Cash flow was up $30,995,000 from $21,549,000. The substantial improvement in net income reflected the strike during the second quarter in the preceding year, when profit was significantly reduced. Earnings in the meat product segment were mixed and continued to be affected by unsatisfactory beef margins. Operations outside Canada were satisfactory with the exception of the company's German operations which were depressed. Processed foods earnings were at a satisfactory level, and non-food products segment showed improvement despite depressed margins in the oil seed crushing industry and lower tallow prices.

Financial results for the year ended March 30, 1985, included a 1% decline in net income and a 4% decrease in net sales compared with results for fiscal 1984. The meat products and processed food segments were severely affected by a strike during the second quarter. To emphasize the impact, the return on net sales for meat products and processed food segments was 0.64% and 2.64% respectively, compared with 1.03% and 4.59% respectively for fiscal 1984.

Capital expenditures in fiscal 1985 totaled $26,518,000 compared with $35,810,000 in fiscal 1984. Major projects concluded in the past year or were under construction at March 31, 1985, included the Food Service plant expansion in Bramalea; the research facility at Maple, Ont. for Shur-Gain Dairy; and the expansion of the National Edible Oils refinery in Toronto.

Acquisitions for fiscal 1985 included the purchase of the controlling interest in a feed mill; and the grocery products business of Burns Meats Ltd. for total cash consideration of $6,500,000.

Joint venture to open salmon hatcheries and ocean farms, in the Maritimes and British Columbia, worth $25,000,000 was undertaken with Sea Farm of Bergen, Norway.

N.B.—For quick reference data, see page 2.

The Financial Post
INFORMATION SERVICE Copyright© 1986 — Maclean Hunter Limited

The Value Line Investment Survey (owned by Arnold Bernhard & Co.)
711 Third Avenue
New York, New York, 10017

Most of Standard & Poor's and Moody's information is based on the reference volumes *S&P Corporation Records* and *Moody's Industrial Manuals*. *Moody's Industrial Manuals* are thick, bound volumes that give complete investment data for a period of years and the financial history of hundreds of companies. They are specialized: there are different books for industrial, transportation, utility, bank and financial, and government securities. Unlike Moody's manuals, *S&P Corporation Records* are arranged alphabetically by the names of the companies rather than by industry. Frequent bulletins keep the six-volume set of *S&P Corporation Records* up to date. Twice weekly, Moody publishes a report to keep its manuals current.

The Financial Post supplies Canada's largest financial and economic data bank. The Corporation Card Service is a library of extensive coverage of over 600 publicly owned companies. An annual yellow card for each company includes a brief history of the company since incorporation, the company's operations, the directors and officers, detailed financial data for at least the past five years, dividend payment history, stock price range, and historical financial summary from date of incorporation. The service is updated with white cards that provide brief interim reporting on major developments and interim financial reports. *The Financial Post* Service is very expensive but is available at virtually all business reference, college, and university libraries.[15]

6-3.1   The Financial Post

The Financial Post also publishes three annual surveys: *The Survey of Mines and Energy Resources*, *The Survey of Industrials*, and *The Survey of Predecessor and Defunct Companies*. The most widely used is *The Survey of Industrials*, which contains information on over 6300 Canadian companies, including operating histories, capital structure, dividend record, the management team, and abridged information from the financial reports, as well as market indexes and eight-year price ranges for all of the securities listed on Canadian stock exchanges.[16]. Other publications include *The Complete Dividend Service*, which consists of an *Annual Dividend Record* of payments of publicly held shares, trust and fund units, foreign stocks listed on Canadian exchanges, and details on purchase offers, stock splits, consolidations, redemptions, rights offerings, and name changes. Monthly and weekly dividend records are available as well. *The Canadian Bond Prices* is an annual compilation of bond yields and prices for all public and some private company bonds.[17] *Preferred Shares and Warrants* is a listing of preferred shares and warrants traded in Canada. Information on preferred shares includes the number of

---

15 The annual cost of the full service is $3,297.00.

16 *The Survey of Industrials* can be purchased from *The Financial Post* Information Service, Maclean Hunter, 777 Bay Street, Toronto, Ontario, at a cost of $43.95. *The Survey of Mines and Energy Resources* and *The Survey of Predecessor and Defunct Companies*, cost $59.95 and $39.50, respectively.

17 Available for $75.00 per copy.

shares outstanding, annual dividend rate and payment dates, retraction dates, conversion and redemption features, stock symbols, and exchange listings. Warrants are listed by both company name and by expiry date, with both listings providing exercise prices, subscription terms, expiry dates, and

FIGURE 6-5 Sample page from *The Blue Book of CBS* stock reports.

THE BLUE BOOK OF CBS STOCK REPORTS
CANADIAN BUSINESS SERVICE
Suite 700-133 Richmond St. W., Toronto M5H 3M8

Norcen

CBS quality rating: CONSERVATIVE

August, 1987

Price: $25.25 per voting share

Earnings: 1986 fiscal:$0.64 (p/e 39.5)

1987 CBS fiscal est.: $0.95 (p/e 26.6)

Indicated dividend: $0.50   Yield: 2.0%

Recommendation: Hold

Performance relative to market:
Near term: Likely to match indices.
Long term: Likely to outperform indices.
Last 6 months: NCN +14.8%; CBS Oils +28.5%.

Recent developments and outlook: Norcen will redeem all of the outstanding 7.75% convertible Junior preference shares, 1983 series on Sept. 1, 1987 at $26 per share. Junior preference shares are convertible into approximately 1.282 non-voting ordinary shares. Earlier, Norcen issued $150 million 5% adjustable rate convertible subordinated debentures, series B due March 30, 2007. The debenures are convertible at the option of the holder into voting ordinary shares of the company at $25 per voting share and will not be redeemable before May 15, 1992. Net proceeds from the financing were used to reduce lines of credit. For the first quarter of 1987, Norcen reported a net income of $27.72 million or $0.46 per share compared with a net income of $21 million or $0.35 per share in the year-earlier period. Sales and other revenue rose 25.1% to $185.8 million from $148.5 million. Oil and liquid production increased to average 39,700 barrels per day from 36,200 barrels daily. Average price received per barrel of oil declined to $19.08 from $22.01 while average price received for natural gas dropped to $1.90 per mcf. from $2.57 per mcf. The long-term outlook for Norcen is positive. We expect earnings growth to reflect firm world oil prices and higher production. We would continue to hold Norcen shares for long-term capital appreciation.

Current performance: For the year ended Dec. 31, 1986 net income, before extraordinary items, declined 58.2% to $50 million or $0.64 per share from $119.7 million or $2.03 per share in 1985. Total revenue declined 7.6% to $615.3 million from $665.9 million. Cash flow from operations amounted to $204.9 million or $4.19 per share compared with $228.9 milllion or $4.29 per share. Lower results for 1986 were attributed to an approximately 50% decline in crude oil prices from their 1985 levels.

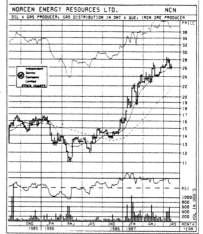

PRICE OUTLOOK: *Norcen Energy shares remain in a long-term rising trend, and have good support in the $22 to $24 range.*

Previous fiscal year: For the year ended Dec. 31, 1985, net income increased 14.8% to $119.7 million or $2.03 per share from $104.3 million or $1.65 pershare in 1984. Operating revenues rose 8.9% to $621.1 million from restated $559.4 million. Improved results for 1985 were attributed mainly to increased contirubtions from the oil and gas division and to increases in investment and other revenues.

WHAT THE COMPANY DOES

Norcen Energy Resources Limited is engaged in oil and gas exploration, production and exploration of coal and the operating of oil and gas gathering and transmission pipelines. Oil and gas operations are carried out in Alberta, British Columbia, Saskatchewan, the Beaufort Sea and offshore East Coast, and in the United States and in Australia. Norcen's mineral resources assets consist mainly of a 28% interest in Hanna Mining Company (a diversified natural resource company); a 10.47% equity interest in Iron Ore Company of Canada (largest producer of iron ore in Canada); a royalty interest on iron ore produced by IOC; and royalties on ore mined by Pamour Inc. from two gold properties in the Timmins district of Ontario. In 1986, a new company, Superior Propane Inc. was formed to operate all of Norcen's propane holdings including former operations of Cigas Products Ltd., Monarch Propane Ltd., and Superior Propane. On March 7, 1986, Hollinger Inc. transferred its 37.7% interest in Norcen to Hees International Corp. for notes and shares of that company.

stock exchange listings.[18] *The Record of New Issues*, published on annual, monthly, and weekly bases is a listing of new issues offered by Canadian companies. It includes information on debt equity and rights financings, principal/agent underwriters, gross proceeds of the issue, offer date and price, commissions, and currency.[19] *The Research Evaluation Service* contains forecasts for Canadian stocks as prepared by research analysts at Canadian brokerage firms. The service consists of individual forecasts, which contrast company earnings, cash flow, and dividend forecasts by different analysts. Projected returns and a consensus forecast are derived from the individual forecasts. Allied products are *The Consensus Summary*, a summary of the consensus forecasts and a measure of dispersion of these forecasts, and the *Analyst's Analyser*, which compares the forecasts to actual prices.[20]

The Blue Book of CBS (Canadian Business Service) *Stock Reports* is published every two weeks by Marpep Publishing. Data sheets on individual Canadian companies include quality ratings, buy, hold, or sell recommendations, a description of the company's business, recent developments and outlook, past and projected performance relative to the market, a five-year analysis of performance, key financial ratios, and other fundamental data. The service is available at an annual cost of $195. Most university and public business reference libraries are subscribers to the service. Marpep also publishes weekly *The Money Reporter*, which contains current data and recommendations on Canadian bonds, preferred shares, and deposit rates. An annual subscription to *The Money Reporter* is $145.

6-3.2 Marpep Publishing

The voluminous *Moody's Industrial Manuals* contain fundamental financial information about hundreds of firms. For each firm information is presented under the following headings and subheadings: Capital Structure, with subheadings on long-term debt and capital stock history, subsidiaries, business and products, and principal plants and properties; Management, with subheadings on officers, directors, general counsel, auditors, stockholders, employees, general office address, and unfilled orders; Income Accounts, with subheadings on comparative income account, supplementary P & L (profit and loss) data, comparative balance sheets, property account, and a description of reserves; Financial and Operating Data, with subheadings on statistical records, data adjusted for stock splits and stock dividends, financial and operating ratios and analysis of operations; Long-Term Debt, with subheadings on authorized debt, call dates, sinking fund, security, sales and leasebacks, dividend restrictions, rights on default indenture modification, term loans, notes payable, revolving credit agreement, and other notes; and Capital Stock, with subheadings on authorized stock, dividend restrictions, voting rights, pre-emptive rights, transfer agent, registrar, stock subscription rights, and debenture subscription rights.

6-3.3 Moody's

18 Cost is $26.95 per copy.
19 The annual edition is $19.95, the monthly is $95 per issue, the weekly is $55 per issue.
20 The full package costs $5,000 per annum. *The Consensus Summary* alone sells for $750 per quarter.

FIGURE 6-6
Sample page from *Moody's Handbook of Common Stocks.*

Note: The information was current when published, but, since conditions can change rapidly, later reports may give different opinions about the same security.

Source: Moody's Handbook of Common Stocks, Fall 1986.

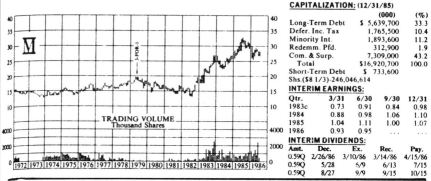

BELL CANADA ENTERPRISES, INC.

LISTED	SYM.	LTPS•	STPS•	IND. DIV.	REC. PRICE	RANGE (52-WKS.)	YLD.
NYSE	BCE	95.8	84.3	$2.36•	27	32 - 26	8.7%

UPPER MEDIUM GRADE. THE LARGEST TELECOMMUNICATIONS COMPANY IN CANADA, THE COMPANY MANUFACTURES AND SELLS TELECOMMUNICATION PRODUCTS.

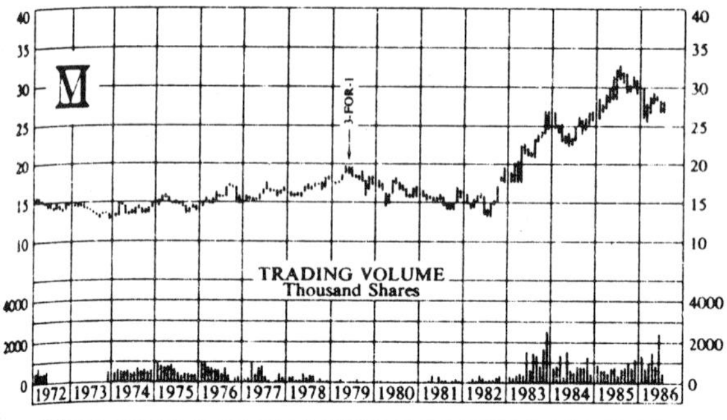

CAPITALIZATION: (12/31/85)

	(000)	(%)
Long-Term Debt	$ 5,639,700	33.3
Defer. Inc. Tax	1,765,500	10.4
Minority Int.	1,893,600	11.2
Redemm. Pfd.	312,900	1.9
Com. & Surp.	7,309,000	43.2
Total	$16,920,700	100.0
Short-Term Debt	$ 733,600	

Shs.($8 1/3)-246,046,614

INTERIM EARNINGS:

Qtr.	3/31	6/30	9/30	12/31
1983c	0.73	0.91	0.84	0.98
1984	0.88	0.98	1.06	1.10
1985	1.04	1.11	1.00	1.07
1986	0.93	0.95	...	...

INTERIM DIVIDENDS:

Amt.	Dec.	Ex.	Rec.	Pay.
0.59Q	2/26/86	3/10/86	3/14/86	4/15/86
0.59Q	5/28	6/9	6/13	7/15
0.59Q	8/27	9/9	9/15	10/15

BACKGROUND:

Bell Canada Enterprises, Inc. is a holding company whose subsidiaries and associated companies provide telecommunications services. Bell Canada, an operating telecommunications subsidiary, supplies network voice, data and image communications in Ontario, Quebec, and the Northwest Territories. BCE owns 52% of Northern Telecom, a manufacturer of telecommunications equipment. TransCanada PipeLines operates natural gas pipelines and is 48% owned by BCE. Other subsidiaries are engaged in printing, packaging, publishing, and real estate. In 1985 revenues were derived: 45.5% telephone operations, 43.5% telecommunications equipment manufacturing, and 11% other businesses.

RECENT DEVELOPMENTS:

For the quarter ended 6/30/86, net income fell 8% to $253.6 million from $274.5 million in the comparable period a year ago. Revenues increased 2% to $3.42 billion from $3.35 billion. Earnings per share fell 14% to $0.95 from $1.11 on an 8% increase in average share outstanding. In the six month period, net income declined 7% to $493.7 million on revenues of $6 62 billion, up 4% from $6.35 billion. The Company declared a regular quarterly dividend of $0.59 per share, payable 10/15/86.

PROSPECTS:

BCE's Bell Canada telephone operations will continue to grow. The unregulated telecommunications business of Northern Telecom faces increased competition and weakening demand in the large digital switching equipment market. Low oil and gas prices continue to adversely affect gas pipeline operations of TransCanada PipeLines. Through BCE Development Corp. the Company has returned as a major participant in the U.S. real estate market. This should provide significant returns in the long-term.

STATISTICS:

YEAR	GROSS REVS ($ MILL.)	% OP. INC TO NET PLT	GROSS FOR COM. %	NET INCOME ($ 000)	COMMON EQUITY %	SHARES (000)	BOOK VALUE PER SH. $	EARN PER SH $	DIV. PER SH. $	DIV. PAY. %	PRICE RANGE	P/E RATIO	AVG. YIELD %
76	3,130.1	13.7	8.3	289,600	40.6	121,861	18.85	2.15	1.19	55	17 - 14¼	7.3	7.6
77	3,513.1	12.8	7.3	288,500	40.0	131,281	19.19	1.99	1.36	68	18⅞ - 15½	8.6	7.9
78	4,374.3	13.6	8.1	395,100	36.7	141,194	20.11	2.49	1.43	57	21⅞ - 17⅜	7.9	7.3
79	5,264.7	13.0	7.6	433,200	51.5	158,478	29.98	2.64	1.55	59	18⅜ - 14½	7.1	8.0
80	6,037.3	12.0	3.9	367,700	48.8	167,303	f20.70	1.45	1.64	N.M	19⅞ - 15⅞	16.4	10.0
81	7,389.9	12.4	5.9	c550,700	49.2	177,481	21.74	c2.97	1.80	61	17⅛ - 14⅛	5.3	11.5
82	8,411.3	15.5	6.8	c622,200	49.7	187,681	22.67	c3.11	1.96	63	[illegible]½ - 13¼	5.3	12.0
83	8,874.7	16.8	8.8	c745,200	54.8	215,038	24.68	c3.46	2.04	59	27⅛ - 18⅛	6.5	9.4
84	10,578.7	16.0	7.7	940,300	56.4	233,482	27.06	4.03	2.18	54	27⅛ - 22⅜	6.1	8.8
85	**13,257.4**	**18.5**	**7.6**	**1,050,800**	**53.6**	**246,047**	**29.71**	**4.23**	**2.28**	**54**	**33 - 26**	**7.0**	**7.7**

•Long-Term Price Score — Short Term Price Score, see page 4a. STATISTICS ARE AS ORIGINALLY REPORTED. Canadian dollars unless otherwise stated. c-Before $8.7 million ($0.05 per share) credit in 1981; before $3.9 million ($0.02 per share) credit in 1982, and before $84.6 million ($0.39 per share) credit in 1983. f-1980 and subsequent years includes deferred income tax. Including deferred income taxes 1980, $29.46; 1981, $29.25; 1982, $30.34; 1983, $31.80, 1984, $34.31; 1985, $36.88.

INCORPORATED:
April, 1880 – Canada

PRINCIPAL OFFICE:
800 Square Victoria
44th Floor
Montreal, Quebec, H3C 3G4
Canada

ANNUAL MEETING:
In April

NUMBER OF STOCKHOLDERS:
332,440

TRANSFER AGENT(S):
Royal Trust Co., Canada
Morgan Guaranty Trust, N.Y., N.Y.
Royal Trust Co., London, England

REGISTRAR(S):
Montreal Trust Co., Canada
Morgan Community Trust, N.Y., N.Y.
Williams & Glyn's Registrars Ltd., London, England

INSTITUTIONAL HOLDINGS:
No. of Institutions: 193
Shares Held: 16,676,088

OFFICERS:
Chmn. Pres. & C.E.O.
A. Jean de Grandpre
Vice Pres Finance
J.S. Spalding
Secretary
G. Houle
Treasurer
D.O. Jarvis

FIGURE 6-7
Sample page from Moody's International Manual.

Source: Moody's Investors Services, Moody's International Manual, vol. 1, 1986.

CANADIAN PACIFIC LIMITED
(Canadian Pacifique Limitee)

CAPITAL STRUCTURE

LONG TERM DEBT

Issue	Rating	Amount Outstanding	Times Charges Earned 1985	Times Charges Earned 1984	Interest Dates	Call Price
1. Equipment trust, 8½s, 1989	[2]	$12,405,000			F&A1	......
2. Equipment trust, 10¼s, 1990	[2]	19,600,000			J&J2	......
3. Equipment trust, 8s 8⅝s, 1992	[2]	22,863,000			J&J15	......
4. Equipment trust, 8¼s, 1993	[2]	3,812,000			J&D20	......
5. Equipment trust, 14⅝s, 1991	[2] Aa1	105,000,000			J&D15	Text
6. Equipment trust, 10½s, 1988	[2] Aa1	70,000,000			M&S15	......
7. Perpetual 4% consol. debt stk.	[2] A1	[12] 184,981,000			J&J1	N.C.
8. Retractable debenture, 12½s, 1999	[2] A2	105,000,000			Oct. 15	......
9. Collateral trust, 8½s, 1989	[2]	4,547,000			M&N1	[4] ....
10. Collateral trust, 14⅝s, 1992	[2]	105,000,000	N.A.	N.A.	......	......
11. Collateral trust, 8⅞s, 1992	[2]	36,403,000			F&A1	......
12. Collateral trust, 10.35s, 1994	[2] A1	60,850,000			J&D1	104.90
13. Collateral trust, 11¼s, 1995	[2]	47,215,000			M&N15	[3] 105.20
14. Collateral trust, 9¾s, 1989	[2] A1	59,486,000			M&N15	[3] 100.75
15. Debenture 10⅝s, 1990	[2] A2	75,000,000			Oct. 1	N.C.
16. Eurobonds, 10¾s, 1993	[2] A2	100,000,000			Jan. 15	101.25
17. Eurodebentures, 6¾s, 1996	[2] A2	10,000,000			Jan. 23	N.C.
18. Maple Leaf Mills deb. 11s, 1998	[2] B1	20,700,000			Monthly	103.00
19. Loans & other	[2]	47,032,000			......	......
20. Subsidiary debt	[2]	5,769,252,000			......	......

CAPITAL STOCK

Issue	Par Value	Rating	Amount Outstanding	Earned per Sh. 1985	Earned per Sh. 1984	Divs. per Sh. 1985	Divs. per Sh. 1984	Call Price
1. 4% preference	No par	......	13,275,585 shs.	$18.58	$84.98	4%	4%	......
2. Ordinary	No par	......	[7] 297,705,933 shs.	[8] 1.11	[8] 1.75	[6] $0.47	[6] $0.47	......

[1] Held privately. [2] U.S. issue. [3] Subject to change, see text. [4] Not reported. [6] Adj. for 3-for-1 split. [7] Year-end shares. [8] Based shares as reported by Company adj. for 3-for-1 split May 17, 1985. [11] Canadian prices. [12] At Dec. 31, 1984-1985, the net amount o with the change in acctg. policy for foreign currency translation, been translated at current rates of exchange.

HISTORY

Incorporated by an Act of the Dominion Parliament of Canada, February 16, 1881, as Canadian Pacific Railway Company for the purpose of completing a transcontinental railway as provided for in the terms under which British Columbia entered the Canadian Confederation in 1871. Although under the terms of the contract with the Dominion Government, the Company had ten years to complete the project, it did so in less than half that time and the construction of the main line was completed in 1885.

For much of its history the majority of the Company's owners resided outside the borders of Canada. However, after the end of World War II, Canadians began to invest in the Company in increasing numbers and by 1965 the majority of its owners resided in Canada. The percentage of voting rights held in Canada is now 79.44%.

Under the terms of the contract to build Canada's first transcontinental railway line, Canadian Pacific received a 25 million acre land grant. It subsequently added to these natural resource assets. For example, among interests acquired in 1898 was British Columbia Smelting and Refining Company, the assets of which included a smelter at Trail Creek, British Columbia. Some eight years later this smelter and other properties were merged into The Consolidated Mining and Smelting Company of Canada Ltd., now Cominco Ltd., which is a principal producer of lead and zinc with production from mines in Canada, United States, Australia, Greenland, Spain and South Africa. The Company also added to its timber land resources in 1905 when it purchased 1.5 million acres on Vancouver Island,at the same time as it purchased the Esquimalt and Namaimo Railway.

In 1956, The Company undertook a comprehensive survey and cataloguing of its natural resource and real estate assets. The survey took some seven years to complete, but it quickly became evident that there was justification to depart from traditional policy and the Company should set about developing these assets itself.

The survey of petroleum resources was completed first, and wholly-owned Canadian Pacific Oil and Gas Ltd., was incorporated in January 1958 to explore and develop the mineral rights on 11.9 million acress of land in Western Canada. The forest and real estate surveys were then completed, and two wholly-owned subsidiaries set up to develop these areas. Pacific Logging Company Limited was re-activated in 1962 to tree farm and reforest some half million acres of Canadian Pacific timberland on Vancouver Island and in the Kootenay district of the British Columbia mainland. Marathon Realty Company Limited was incorporated in 1963 to develop Canadian Pacific's nationwide real estate holdings. At the same time, Canadian Pacific decided to put its long experience in hotel management to fuller use and Canadian Pacific Hotels Limited was incorporated.

It became apparent early that the development of the non-transportation assets of the Company would be optimized if it were centralized under a special holding company. Accordingly, a wholly-owned subsidiary Canadian Pacific Investments Limited was incorporated in July 1962 with two purposes: to administer the development of Canadian Pacific's natural resources and real estate and to operate as an investment holding company.

Following its incorporation, the parent's interests in Cominco, C.P. Oil & Gas, Pacific Logging, Marathon Realty and C.P. Hotels were transferred to Canadian Pacific Investments. Moreover, the parent proceeded to sell its remaining non-transportation assets to C.P.I. in return for shares in that company. C.P.I. would then sell such assets to the appropriate subsidiary in return for shares in that subsidiary.

In Nov. 1967, Canadian Pacific Investments Limited successfully offered to the public $100 million of convertible preferred shares. This was, at that time, the largest single stock issue in Canada's financial history, and it provided Canadians an opportunity to share more directly in the development of their country's resources. Proceeds from the issue were used to make major equity investments, principally in Canada in resource-oriented enterprises, and to finance further expansion of C.P.I.'s subsidiaries. The conversion privilege terminated Nov. 1, 1977.

Effective May 5, 1980 name of Canadian Pacific Investments Limited was changed to Canadian Pacific Enterprises Limited to reflect more accurately its nature as a management company involved in strategic planning.

In 1980 Enterprises sold 6,500,000 common shares in U.S. and 1,200,000 shares outside North America. Late in 1982 CPE Ltd. made a public issue of 3.4 million shares in Canada. Concurrently Canadian Pacific Ltd. purchased 7.9 million common shares at the public offering price. As a result of these and other subsequent stock transactions, ownership by CP Limited of Enterprises common stock represented a 69.86% share at end of 1984. In 1980 Enterprises began paying dividends on a quarterly basis, common stock was divided on a two-for-one basis and Corp. instituted a shareholder dividend reinvestment and share purchase plan.

Effective Dec. 6, 1985 C.P. Ltd. and Enterprises were merged with the approval of the shareholders of both companies. Under the merger in which Enterprises became wholly-owned subsidiary of the Corporation, the holders of Common Shares of Enterprises were issued 1.675 ordinary shares of the Corporation for each Common Share of Enterprises. This resulted in the issue of 78,942,444 additional ordinary shares of the Corporation with a value of $1,401,228,000.

Today, Canadian Pacific Limited, which is the name adopted July 3, 1971, is an extensively diversified company with world-wide ramifications.

PRINCIPAL SUBSIDIARIES

Percentage Ownership

	December 31 1985	1984	1983
Rail Transportation			
[1] CP Rail			
[3] Soo Line Corporation	55.75%	55.74%	55.69%
Non-Rail Transportation			
CP Air			
Canadian Pacific Air Lines, Limited	100	100	100
Eastern Provincial Airways Limited	100	100	.....
Nordair Inc.	52	.....	.....
[1] Canadian Pacific Hotels			
CP Ships			
Canadian Pacific Steamships, Limited	100	100	100
Centennial Shipping Limited	100	100	100
Racine Terminal (Montreal) Limited	100	100	100
Canadian Pacific (Bermuda) Limited	100	100	100
CP Trucks			
Canadian Pacific Express & Transport Ltd.	100	100	100
CanPac International Freight Services Inc.	100	100	100
Oil and Gas			
[2,7] PanCanadian Petroleun Limited			
Mines and Minerals			
[2,7] Cominco Ltd.			
Fording Coal Limited			
[2] CP Limited			
Cominco Ltd.			
[2] Processed Minerals Incorporated			
[2,7] [8] Steep Rock Resources Inc.			
Forest Products			
[2] [5] CIP Inc.			
[2] [7] Great Lakes Forest Products, Limited			
[2] Commandant Properties, Limited			
Steel and Industrial Products			
[2] The Algoma Steel Corporation, Limited			
[6] AMCA International Limite			
[2] CP Limited			
[7] The Algoma Steel Corporation, Limited ...			
Real Estate			
[2] Marathon Realty Company Limited			
Other Businesses			
[2,7] Maple Leaf Mills Limited			
[1] CP Telecommunications			
[2] Syracuse China Corporation			
Financial and Miscellaneous			
[2,14] Canadian Pacific Securities Limited			
[2] Chateau Insurance Company			
[2] Canadian Pacific Enterprises Limited			
Corporate Activities			
Canadian Pacific Limited			
Corporate Activities			

[1] CP Rail and CP T departments of CP Limite Hotels is a department o Lines, Limited.

[2] Ownership percentages reflect CP Limited's indirec ties through Canadian Pac (Enterprises) of whose com held 69.86% at December December 31, 1983. Own 1985 reflect the results o December 6, 1985, of Ente (see Note 3 to the financial s

[3] See Moody's Transporta

[4] See Moody's Bank and F

[5] Prior to acquisition on Company was Canadian In pany.

[6] Prior to June 1, 1981 Dominion Bridge Co. Ltd.

[7] See Alphabetical index.

[8] Prior to April 27, 1983 ration was Steep Rock Iron

BUSINESS

Canadian Pacific Limited tion) directly and through transportation, the developr ral resource properties, ma activities in Canada and quent to the merger of Cor Pacific Enterprises Ltd. it tions in nine segments: Rai

Moody's Handbook of Widely Held Common Stocks is issued four times a year and gives a brief summary of about 1000 firms. Figure 6-6 shows a sample page. For each firm the price is charted and compared with the industry's price trend. Financial background, current developments, and future prospects are reported, along with the financial statistics for several years. *Moody's International Manual* contains extensive information on virtually all industrialized countries. The section on Canada contains demographic data and considerable detail on federal, provincial, and municipal debt and levered Canadian companies. Sample pages are provided in Figure 6-7.

6-3.4   Other Canadian Sources

The Northern Miner Press publishes an annual reference text, *The Canadian Mines Handbook*, on Canadian mining companies, which includes financial data on Canadian mining companies, historic share price information, mining maps, and production data.

The Canadian Bond Rating and the Dominion Bond Rating Services are the two Canadian firms that evaluate the default risk of Canadian bond issues and publish quality ratings. Both firms publish their ratings procedures and definitions. For each company that pays an annual subscription fee for the service, the rating agencies provide a specific rating, a summary of the factors underlying the rating, basic financial data, and some analysis. Figure 6-8 provides a sample page from the Dominion Bond Rating Service.

6-3.5 Standard & Poor's for U.S. Companies

Standard & Poor's (S&P) massive *S&P Corporation Records* discusses the affairs of each company listed, using the following topic headings: Capitalization and Long-Term Debt; Corporate Background, with such subheadings as sales backlogs, subsidiaries, affiliates, principal properties, capital expenditures, employees, officers, directors, and executive officers; Bond Descriptions, with such subheadings as trustee, purpose of issue, sinking fund, redemptions, security, dividend restrictions, and price range; Stock Data, with such subheadings as voting power, capital changes, capital stock offered through rights, stock issued under convertibles, capital stock sold, stockholders, transfer agent, listings, and dividends; and Earnings and Finances, with such subheadings as auditors, consolidated earnings statements, adjusted earnings, quarterly sales, property account analysis, maintenance and repairs, consolidated income statement, and consolidated balance sheet.

The Outlook is a weekly publication of S&P. It surveys market conditions and recommends common stocks to investors. It also contains special articles, reports on individual firms, discussions of stocks currently in favour, a report on overall business conditions, a market forecast and recommendations, and sometimes a "stock for action." A special annual issue of *The Outlook* is published with a forecast for the coming year. This forecast is divided into such categories as best low-priced stocks, candidates for dividend increases, rapid growth stocks for long-term profits, and stocks for action in the year ahead. Figure 6-9 shows a sample page of investment recommendations from *The Outlook*. In addition to investment recommendations, market index data are published in both tabular and graphical form. Standard & Poor's also publishes an annual paperback book, *Security Price Index Record*, which contains data back to 1928 for all ninety of the Standard & Poor's different industry stock price indexes. The *Stock Price Index Record* also contains other financial market data from past years. Moody's publishes the *Stock Survey,* which is a weekly publication that is similar to Standard & Poor's *The Outlook.*

FIGURE 6-8   Sample bond rating from Dominion Bond Rating Service.

April 10, 1986   **BOND RATINGS**   Report # 101693

RATING: BBB	AMCA INTERNATIONAL LIMITED	**DBRS** BOND RATINGS

SUMMARY: The rating on all Series of Debentures issued by AMCA is being reduced to BBB from A (low) for the following reasons: (1) The earnings recovery which is occurring is not strong enough to hold the rating at A (low) for this stage of the economic cycle.   We estimate that AMCA would have to average earnings of $60-$80 million through the cycle to carry an "A" rating and is far from approaching this level of earnings. (2) 1985 was the third straight poor year, and 1986 is expected to be better, but not enough.   Structural changes have affected AMCA's main industry segments including catchup in technology by foreigners, and the lingering effects of a still strong U.S. dollar. (3) The balance sheet, although improved, has: (a) Too much debt. (b) Too much debt is variable rate. (c) Too much in preferred shares. (d) Too much retractable debt and preferred shares coming due by 1990.   Thus, although earnings in 1986 are expected to rise, and the revaluation of the yen will help earnings, this is not enough to hold the rating.

EARNINGS: In 1985, AMCA's pre tax earnings from continuing operations rose to $9.6 million compared to an adjusted loss of $25.9 million in 1984. With tax recoveries, net income was $16.8 million versus a loss of $4.7 million before extraordinary items a year earlier. Sales of continuing operations increased 9% to $1.6 billion. Profitability, as measured by return on equity, however, was a weak 3% compared to 19% at the peak of the cycle in 1981. Generally, the recovery is taking much longer than we expected.   While some areas such as construction and packaging equipment, pulpwood machinery and aerospace parts performed well, key areas such as engineering services and·machine tools/systems, which were expected to be strong in 1985, continued to lag. The weakening of the U.S. dollar since the fall of 1985 made the Company more competitive in areas such as machine tools. Strong North American demand for compaction equipment, excavators and pile drivers, and slightly better prices helped operating income of the Construction Products segment rise 69% to $22 million. In the Engineering and Construction Services segment, however, the effects of a continuing lack of petroleum/ petrochemical or marine projects worldwide (major sources of business in the past), virtually offset a slightly stronger pre engineered buildings area. Operating income of this segment was virtually unchanged at $21 million.   At $30 million, operating income of another key segment, Industrial Products, was only 11% better than the previous year.   The weak area here was machine tool/systems, which nearly neutralized the strong performance of aerospace parts and processing/packaging equipment areas.   A swing from a loss in 1984 to operating income of $3 million in 1985 in the Steel Products segment was due to good performances in the Manitoba mini-steel mill and eastern Canadian structural steel areas.   In addition, a 13% decrease in interest expense and a $6 million income tax recovery helped in the recovery of earnings. Better demand and slightly reduced competition are expected to be the key factors in the combined recovery of earnings in 1986, but interest and preferred share dividend costs are still too high.

LIQUIDITY: There was a relatively small degree of improvement in AMCA's liquidity ratios in 1985, as the positive effects of a recovery in earnings, asset sales, and a U.S. $53 million preferred share issue were largely offset by a much higher level of capital expenditure and receivables. Cash flow after dividends was $19 million compared to a negative $32 million in 1984, but was sufficient to finance less than one half of a substantially higher $43 million of capital expenditure. The shortfall and increase in receivables (net of a decline in inventories) were met by the proceeds from the $53 million preferred share issue and sale of assets, enabling liquidity ratios to improve slightly.

The Company: AMCA International Limited is an operating company engaged worldwide in the design, engineering, manufacturing, installation, marketing and financing of a broad range of steel related products and services. These include industrial products, machine tools, construction equipment and engineering and construction services. Geographically, 70% of sales are in the U.S. Algoma Steel owns 34.5% of the common shares, and the Canadian Pacific Group controls 50.7% of the shares.

Debt Rated:	All Series of Debentures	BBB
	Cumulative Redeemable Retractable Preferred Shares	Pfd-3

FIGURE 6-9 Sample page from S&P's *The Outlook*.

Group 1: Foundation stocks for long-term gain

These issues are basic building blocks for a portfolio. They offer the prospect of long-term appreciation, along with moderate but growing income. The investor seeking to build an estate should start with stocks from this list, augmenting them with issues from other groups according to one's objectives and temperament.

Earnings Per Share ($) 1983	E1984	E1985	Indicated Div. $	1982-84 Price Range	Recent Price	P/E Ratio	Yield %		Annual Growth Rates—for Latest 5 Years— Sales	Earn.	Div.	▼Price Action vs. Mkt. 11-28-80 to 8-12-82	Since 8-12-82	Listed Options Traded	Last Page Ref.
4.31	A5.95	7.00	2.60	71 1/2-23 5/8	60	8.6	4.3	Assoc. Dry Gds. (Jan.)	20%	16%	7%	1.86	1.21	..	645
3.95	4.40	4.70	2.20	44 7/8-27 3/4	39	8.3	5.6	CPC Int'l	4	6	11	1.35	0.76	..	599
1.50	↓3.40	4.00	1.80	39 -19 5/8	28	7.0	6.4	Dow Chemical	8	−18	10	0.81	0.90	C	645
3.01	A3.40	↓3.80	1.40	42 1/2-15 1/4	42	11.1	3.3	Heinz (H.J.) (Apr.)	11	16	15	1.58	1.52	..	711
9.04	10.75	12.50	3.80	134 1/4-48 3/4	125	10.0	3.0	•Int'l Business Machines	14	11	4	1.29	1.22	C	711
5.22	A5.35	↓5.50	2.60	63 1/4-38 7/8	57	10.4	4.6	•Procter & Gamble (Jun.)	13	11	12	1.68	0.82	A	711
3.73	4.25	5.00	1.20	78 1/2-30	45	9.0	2.7	Schlumberger Ltd.	17	19	22	0.55	0.80	C	599
7.23	7.85	8.50	2.44	55 3/8-20 1/2	49	5.8	5.0	•Security Pacific	12	9	10	1.32	1.31	..	545
5.20	[1]5.20	5.40	1.85	39 5/8-19 7/8	38	7.0	4.9	Sonat Inc.	22	17	20	0.97	0.94	..	599

Group 2: Stocks with promising growth prospects

These stocks promise to enjoy well above average growth rates in earnings per share for the foreseeable future. Although most of the issues command relatively high P/E ratios, the premiums are, in our view, justified. Income is not a consideration here.

Earnings Per Share ($) 1983	E1984	E1985	Indicated Div. $	1982-84 Price Range	Recent Price	P/E Ratio	Yield %		Latest 5-Year Growth Rates Sales	Earn.	No. of Earn. Gains '78-'83	Interim ■Earn. Trend	▼Price Action vs. Mkt. 11-28-80 to 8-12-82	Since Aug. 12, '82	Listed Options Traded	Last Page Ref.
2.86	3.35	3.70	1.20	53 3/8-25 3/8	43	11.6	2.8	Abbott Laboratories	15%	18%	5	+18%	1.51	0.91	Ph	699
3.00	3.45	3.95	1.60	50 3/8-25 3/8	46	11.6	3.5	•Bristol-Myers	10	14	5	+17	1.70	1.01	C	583
4.37	5.20	6.25	2.30	70 1/2-39 7/8	68	10.9	3.4	•Emerson El. (Sept.)	10	9	5	+16	1.96	0.76	A	635
1.47	A1.74	2.10	0.44	32 3/8- 9 7/8	22	10.5	2.0	Nat'l Med. Ent. (May)	51	29	5	+16	1.08	1.18	A	635
†2.05	†2.70	†3.15	†0.40	49 1/8-10 7/8	38	15.9	0.8	•Northern Telecom	1.	..	4	+17	1.62	2.09	T	595
3.85	A4.08	4.40	1.60	62 1/2-28 5/8	46	10.5	3.5	Syntex (July)	19	25	5	− 2	1.62	0.75	C	583
1.74	2.60	3.25	1.24	38 1/4-19 1/8	32	9.8	3.9	•Thomas & Betts	7	−2	4	+52	1.03	1.01	...	583
1.09	A1.25	1.70	0.20	36 7/8-10 11/16	29	17.1	0.7	•Unitrode Corp. (Jan.)	29	26	5	+27	0.87	1.37	...	635

A bullet (•) before the name of a stock in the group indicates that the issue is currently considered to be among the best situated in the group.

*↑Upward change in earnings estimate or dividend rate since last publication of the Master List; ↓downward change. E-Estimated. A-Actual. *Of following year.*

Listed options traded: C-Chicago Board Options Exchange; A-American Stock Exchange; Pac-Pacific Stock Exchange; Ph-Philadelphia Stock Exchange; T-Toronto Stock Exchange.

Price/Earnings Ratios are based on latest shown estimated or actual earnings.

▼A figure above 1.0 indicates that the stock outperformed the S&P industrial stock price index in this period. It is computed by taking the ratio of the stock's price at the end of the period vs. the beginning of the period and dividing it by the corresponding ratio of the index. The time periods covered are updated periodically to conform to the latest major market cycle.

■This column compares share earnings of the latest six months with those of the corresponding year-earlier period.

††This figure shows the degree to which the stock's dividend and price change offset the sharp increase in the consumer price index in the five years through 1983. A figure of 1.0 would indicate that the impact of inflation was completely offset.

[1]Including a $0.39 reversal of reserves for refunds, but excluding the $1-$1.25 potentially favorable effect of the Boise Cascade joint venture cancellation. [2]Not calculable; company was formed in May 1981. [3]Before nonrecurring gain. [4]Excl. $1.30 a share write-off. [5]Not available; company spun off from AT&T effective January 1, 1984. [6]Company went public in October 1983. [7]Includes certain non-operating items relating to recent California public utility commission decisions. †Canadian funds.

546 October 3, 1984 The Outlook

Source: *The Outlook*, a Standard & Poor's publication.

FIGURE 6-10   Standard & Poor's explanation of its common stock quality rating categories.

EARNINGS AND DIVIDEND RANKINGS FOR COMMON STOCKS

The investment process involves assessment of various factors—such as product and industry position, corporate resources and financial policy—with results that make some common stocks more highly esteemed than others. In this assessment, Standard & Poor's believes that earnings and dividend performance is the end result of the interplay of these factors and that, over the long run, the record of this performance has a considerable bearing on relative quality. The rankings, however, do not pretend to reflect all of the factors, tangible or intangible, that bear on stock quality.

Relative quality of bonds or other debt, that is, degrees of protection for principal and interest, called creditworthiness, cannot be applied to common stocks, and therefore rankings are not to be confused with bond quality ratings which are arrived at by a necessarily different approach.

Growth and stability of earnings and dividends are deemed key elements in establishing Standard & Poor's earnings and dividend rankings for common stocks, which are designed to capsulize the nature of this record in a single symbol. It should be noted, however, that the process also takes into consideration certain adjustments and modifications deemed desirable in establishing such rankings.

The point of departure in arriving at these rankings is a computerized scoring system based on per-share earnings and dividend records of the most recent ten years—a period deemed long enough to measure significant time segments of secular growth, to capture indications of basic change in trend as they develop, and to encompass the full peak-to-peak range of the business cycle. Basic scores are computed for earnings and dividends, then adjusted as indicated by a set of predetermined modifiers for growth, stability within long-term trend, and cyclicality. Adjusted scores for earnings and dividends are then combined to yield a final score.

Further, the ranking system makes allowance for the fact that, in general,

corporate size imparts certain recognized advantages from an investment standpoint. Conversely, minimum size limits (in terms of corporate sales volume) are set for the various rankings, but the system provides for making exceptions where the score reflects an outstanding earnings-dividend record.

The final score for each stock is measured, against a scoring matrix determined by analysis of the scores of a large and representative sample of stocks. The range of scores in the array of this sample has been aligned with the following ladder of rankings:

A+	Highest	B+	Average	C	Lowest
A	High	B	Below Average	D	In Reorganization
A−	Above Average	B−	Lower		

NR signifies no ranking because of insufficient data or because the stock is not amenable to the ranking process.

The positions as determined above may be modified in some instances by special considerations, such as natural disasters, massive strikes, and non-recurring accounting adjustments.

A ranking is not a forecast of future market price performance, but is basically an appraisal of past performance of earnings and dividends, and relative current standing. These rankings must not be used as market recommendations; a high-score stock may at times be so overpriced as to justify its sale, while a low-score stock may be attractively priced for purchase. Rankings based upon earnings and dividend records are no substitute for complete analysis. They cannot take into account potential effects of management changes, internal company policies not yet fully reflected in the earnings and dividend record, public relations standing, recent competitive shifts, and a host of other factors that may be relevant to investment status and decision.

Source: Standard & Poor's Stock Guide, 1984.

S&P publishes the monthly pocket-sized *Stock Guide* and the similar *Bond Guide*. These two booklets contain many of the salient financial statistics from the voluminous *S&P Corporation Records*. Each of these booklets is a concise summary of investment information about various issues. Figure 6-10 is an explanation of S&P's stock ratings. The *Stock Guide* also contains lists under the categories "stock for potential appreciation," "recommended stocks primarily for appreciation," "candidates for dividend increases," "candidates for stock splits," and "25 of the best low-priced stocks." The back pages of the *Stock Guide* contain data about the hundreds of publicly available mutual funds.

Standard & Poor's *Commercial Paper Rating Guide* is a monthly booklet. The booklet briefly discusses every major issuer of commercial paper and indicates a quality rating for the issuer's money market security.

6-3.6 Mutual Fund Information

Two excellent sources of mutual fund information in Canada are *The Financial Post* and the *Financial Times*, which publish regular mutual fund surveys in their respective newspapers. *The Financial Post's Survey*, published once a month provides, for each mutual fund, the launch date; the names of the fund managers; the total assets; ten-, five-, three-, and one-year rates of returns; standard deviations about the returns; reward-to-risk ratios; management fees and commissions. The quarterly *Funds Survey* of the *Financial Times* includes net asset values; percentage of portfolio invested in foreign securities; total assets; sales fees; and ten-, five-, three-, one-year, and three-month rates of returns. Funds are grouped by objectives, and then placed in subgroups by three measures of variability.[21]

The Financial Post also publishes a quarterly *Survey of Funds*, which contains information for over 225 funds located in Canada; descriptive data including the names, addresses, and telephone numbers of managers and sponsors; investment objectives; purchase plans; tax-deductibility status; management fees; and redemption and dividend policies. Performance measures include ten-year compounded rates of returns; annual rates of returns for the ten-year period; median, high, and low returns for all of the funds within a particular objectives grouping; and market index data including the historic returns on Canadian, U.S., and foreign markets and instruments.[22]

The Canadian Securities Institute publishes *Canadian Mutual Funds*, a booklet on the Canadian mutual funds industry, types of mutual funds, organization of mutual fund corporations, and other such descriptive material.

Most Canadian newspapers publish, on a daily or weekly basis, the net asset values of Canadian mutual funds.

---

21 The three measures of variability are high, intermediate and low. Intermediate variability funds have rate of return fluctuations that are similar to the general market. Low (high) variability funds fluctuate less (more) than the market.

22 Single copies are $40.00, annual subscription for four quarterly copies is $99.00.

FIGURE 6-11   Sample page from *The Financial Post's* Survey of Funds.

TAX DEDUCTIBLE EQUITY FUNDS

FUND NAME	TAX REF	FUND CODE	MILS OF $	10 YR	9 YR	8 YR	7 YR	6 YR	5 YR	4 YR	3 YR	2 YR	1 YR	CURRENT QUARTER	YEAR TO DATE
AGF PFD (JUL/84)	***	9195	348.0	****	****	****	****	****	****	****	****	11.9	9.7	1.8	4.6
RANK												77	87	10	71
AIC ADVANTAGE	1	9196	1.0	*****	*****	*****	*****	*****	****	****	*****	*****	*****	-0.5	8.5
RANK				***	***	***	***	***	***	***	***	*****	*****	-23	38
ALLIANCE MUTUAL	1	9019	5.6	15.7	17.8	16.2	13.9	12.8	17.4	22.4	14.1	21.7	29.8	-5.0	16.2
RANK				36	28	32	32	26	25	27	29	18	11	77	9
ALLIED CANADIAN FUND	1	9154	1.8	*****	*****	*****	*****	*****	*****	*****	*****	*****	10.5	1.3	7.9
RANK				***	***	***	***	***	***	***	***	***	84	77	48
AMD CANADIAN BLUE CHIP	1	9197	5.8	*****	*****	*****	*****	*****	*****	*****	*****	*****	*****	-5.3	4.3
RANK				***	***	***	***	***	***	***	***	***	***	81	73
ASSOCIATE INVESTORS	1	9018	6.6	15.1	15.2	14.0	11.6	9.8	14.0	20.0	11.7	15.7	12.1	-2.1	2.7
RANK				46	60	53	56	56	57	43	49	58	82	31	84
BC CENTRAL CR. UNION RRSP EQUITY	12	9032	3.1	10.2	11.9	9.4	5.0	1.6	5.4	13.3	6.0	9.4	5.9	-3.4	-0.4
RANK				76	75	76	79	78	79	74	78	84	93	55	97
BISSETT CANADIAN FUND	1	1010	0.9	*****	*****	*****	*****	*****	*****	*****	11.8	17.0	18.4	-7.0	9.8
RANK				***	***	***	***	***	***	***	47	48	45	99	29
BULLOCK DIVIDEND FUND	***	9149	8.0	*****	*****	*****	*****	*****	*****	*****	*****	*****	12.4	1.8	5.0
RANK				***	***	***	***	***	***	***	***	***	81	11	69
BULLOCK GROWTH FUND	12	1001	10.0	12.9	12.6	11.5	8.8	2.6	6.5	13.2	2.1	9.8	17.3	-10.2	8.2
RANK				67	74	70	72	75	78	75	85	82	51	112	43
CAMBRIDGE GROWTH	1	7020	0.9	15.7	16.8	15.4	16.0	17.0	20.3	24.8	20.2	28.3	35.4	-2.6	17.8
RANK				38	43	39	15	2	9	10	3	5	4	39	5
CANADA CUMULATIVE	1	9031	108.2	16.2	16.2	14.3	12.6	9.9	12.0	18.4	6.7	9.4	14.8	-5.5	2.5
RANK				29	48	52	50	54	70	54	76	85	69	84	86
CANADA LIFE E.2	1	7019	6.8	17.0	18.6	17.6	15.4	13.8	18.8	22.6	15.6	20.1	23.1	-5.9	9.2
RANK				26	20	18	18	19	14	24	15	31	23	90	31
CANADA LIFE S.9	1	7018	85.4	15.8	17.4	16.4	14.1	12.3	17.1	20.9	13.9	17.6	19.4	-5.2	6.7
RANK				35	33	29	28	28	30	36	30	41	38	80	59
CANADA TRUST EQUITY G FUND	1	9038	25.3	*****	16.6	15.5	12.9	11.3	14.3	18.1	10.6	16.4	18.2	-4.9	6.9
RANK				***	45	38	46	39	53	55	56	54	48	76	58
CANADA TRUST RSP EQUITY	12	9029	314.8	14.3	16.0	14.6	11.6	9.3	12.8	17.5	8.7	13.4	13.2	-7.6	2.4
RANK				55	51	47	58	60	65	58	69	73	77	103	87
CANADIAN ANAESTHETISTS	1	9017	48.6	19.0	20.3	18.7	15.1	11.8	14.8	19.9	12.4	16.1	16.2	-3.8	7.2
RANK				12	13	13	21	31	50	46	43	56	61	63	56
CANADIAN DENTAL COMMON STOCK FUN	1	9142	27.1	15.1	17.2	16.1	14.5	14.1	18.8	22.5	15.7	21.5	23.3	-2.9	11.1
RANK				47	35	33	25	25	13	26	21	22	22	44	22
CANADIAN GAS & ENERGY	13	1014	29.2	10.9	8.9	5.8	-0.4	-7.3	-3.6	1.7	-8.7	-7.7	-9.3	6.4	-10.6
RANK				75	78	79	84	86	88	86	94	98	99	3	108
CANADIAN INVESTMENT FUND	12	7017	105.4	13.0	14.1	12.9	11.4	10.4	14.4	17.1	8.8	12.8	11.9	-5.8	0.6
RANK				65	66	66	60	51	52	63	68	75	83	89	96
CANADIAN PROTECTED FUND	1	9157	7.0	*****	*****	*****	*****	*****	*****	*****	*****	*****	14.1	-3.8	7.2
RANK				***	***	***	***	***	***	***	***	***	73	62	55
CANADIAN SECURITY GROWTH	1	1018	311.1	20.8	21.9	19.8	18.3	16.0	20.4	26.7	17.5	22.5	24.1	-4.1	11.0
RANK				4	4	4	4	7	4	5	8	15	20	66	23

UNANNUALIZED RATES OF RETURN — CURRENT QUARTER, YEAR TO DATE (9/30/86)

TAX DEDUCTIBLE EQUITY FUNDS

Survey of Funds

FIGURE 6-12 Sample mutual fund net asset value quotation from a daily newspaper.

CANADIAN MUTUAL FUNDS

Recent prices of investment funds supplied by the Investment Funds Institute of Canada. They are the net asset value per share or unit last circulated by the fund, in accordance with its pricing practice as contained in the prospectus of the fund. n—no sales charge; y—delayed NAVPS; xd—ex-dividend.

MEMBERS

AGF Group
yInternatn'l	10.34
yVenture Fnd	4.61

Amer Grth 9.01
Cdn Gs Enr 10.43
Cdn SecGth 10.32
Cdn Trustd 4.39
Corp Inv 12.80
Crp Inv Stk 9.88
Excel Am Eq 4.95
Excel Cd Bd 4.98
Excel Cd 4.99
Ex MMF 7.30 5.00
Global 9.54
GreenL (Cdn) 6.89
GreenL (US) 6.34
Grth Eqty 12.37
HiTech 15.00
Japan 6.15
nMMF 8.31
Optn Eqity 4.52
Pfd Inc 9.99
Special 5.52
ADVANTAGE 12.53

ALL-CANADIAN
Compound 17.59
Dividend 13.75
Natural Res 6.90
Revenue Gth 3.63
Univest 7.34

Allied Captl Mgmt.
nCanadian 6.02
nDividend 4.80
nIncome 5.25
nInternt'lCdn 8.35
nInternt'lU.S. 6.34
nMMF (7.82) 5.00

A.M.D
Am Bl Chip 12.17
CD Bl Chip 12.11
Dividend 9.64
Fix Inc. 9.48
MMF 8.21 1.00
MMF US 6.23 1.00
Resc Can. 13.95
T-Bill (8.40) 10.00
nAssoc Inv 7.38

Bolton Tremblay
Cda Cum 17.23
Intern'tl 9.18
yMny Fd 8.24 1.00
Ptd. Income 10.69
Pld. Rsces 14.49
Taurus 6.03

Calvin Bullock
American 9.98
CIF 8.13
Dividend 10.17
Growth 2.78
Income 7.37

Canada Trust
ynCTNAF 32.92
ynEquity 64.84
ynIncome 9.30

CGF Group
yFund 4000 7.25

Chou Assoc Mgt
yAssociates	27.67
yRRSP	11.79

Confed Group
Dolph Eqty	10.07
yDolph Mtge	5.05

CT Invest Counsel
nE-S Tm 7.97	10.03
Ev Spec Eq	13.52
Everest Bn	9.79

Cundill Group
Security	15.84
Value	14.53

Desjardins Group
ynActions	20.85
ynEquilibre	10.36
ynHypo	4.38
ynIntern'tl	24.09
ynOblig	4.37

Dynamic Group
yAll Dyn IV	5.18
yAll Dyn V	5.10
D Income	5.50
yMMF (8.37)	1.00
yDy Global	6.06
DyAm US	8.12
DynAmCn	10.68
DyCdn	15.67
DynPrec Met	1.59
Mgd P'folio	6.98
nSav'g (7.75)	10.00

Eaton Group
yV MMF 8.06	10.00
yViking Cdn	17.52
yViking Com	15.30
yViking Div	7.78
yViking Gth	19.52
yViking Inc	3.99
yViking Int	20.48

EP Mon 8.34 1.00
nFirst CdM 11.19

First City Funds
Growth	5.69
Income	4.49
yReal	5.72

Fonds SNF
yEquilibree	11.58
yQuebecoise	10.73

Future Fund Shares
nFood Fund	6.81
nGolden Fund	9.14
nLife Fund	6.60
nSilver Fund	5.76
nTechno Fund	4.95
nValue Fund	6.21

Galcor Group
yMortgage	10.07
yRealty Gwth	12.17

Global Strategy
Amercas Fd	11.65
Europe Fd	10.94
Far East Fd	12.22

yGlobal S Cp 20.81
Global S Fd 18.87

Guaranty Trust Gr
ynInv Equity	6.97
ynInv Income	4.50
ynMortgage	10.42
yProp Fnd	92.04

Guardian Group
yCanada	7.31
yEnterprise	1.56
yGrth Fund	21.81
yNorth Amer	5.97
Pac. Rim.	22.65
xdyPfdDiv(7.95)	9.33
S Mny (8.45)	10.18
yStrat Inc	10.17
World Eqty	5.05

Gd Amer Sec USF
yFully Mgd	10.17
US MMF 6.31	9.88
yG Mort Shul	10.14

Heartland Group
yBond	9.98
yEquity	10.05
yGrowth	9.99

HUME GR.
ynHume Fund	13.77
ynHume RRSP	13.74

Investors Group
yBond	4.06
yCdn Equity	6.91
yDividend	8.95
yGlobal	6.33
yGrowth	10.69
yIntern'tl	15.77
yJapan	15.74
yMMF (8.37)	1.00
yMtge	4.96
yMutual	9.23
yProv Stk	13.48
yReal Prop	5.29
yRetiremnt	25.04
ySumma	5.28

J. Heward Group
y JHAmer Cdn	8.97
y JH Amer US	6.81
y JH FundLt	9.46
ynLotus Fund	13.14

MER Group
yEquity	17.42
yGrowth	14.20
ynMMF (5.91)	10.00

Metropolitan Gr
yBond	3.08
yCdn Mutl	7.18
yCollective	20.82
yGrowth	9.08
ySpeci.	8.25
yVenture	12.05

Montreal Trust Gr.
ynDividend	9.72
ynEquity	31.04
ynIncome	8.18
ynInternatl	33.76
ynMtge	9.96

Morgan Trust
yDividend	5.87
yGrowth	13.66
yIncome	11.54
yResource	9.22
yWorldwide	17.51
yMult. Opp. Fd.	4.15

Mutual Group
Amerifund	13.36
Diversifd 25	12.33

Diversifd 40 13.27
Diversifd 55 13.67
Dividend 9.99
Equifund 15.49
nMMF (7.78) 1.00

MYW Inv Funds
yCdn Balanc	10.27
yCdn Growth	10.72
yDefensv Inc	9.99
yN Am Grth	10.30
yNoram Conv	13.45
yOne DecisnFd	11.61

Ont. Teachers Gr.
ynAgresive	13.28
ynBalanced	11.54
ynDiversifd	13.05
ynFixVal 8.15	10.00
ynMtge	11.47
yOptiml Cdn	7.78

Pagebrook RF 9.50

Prudential Group
Dividend	5.19
Growth	10.56
Income	9.99
nMMF 8.03	10.00
yPtnm Hlth Sci	16.96

Rabin Budden Gr.
ynCapital Fd	8.52
ynIncome Fd	5.93

Realgrowth Fds
yA.Trend (US)	7.73
yActive Inc.	9.26
yCdn Equity	18.92
yRen Can B+B	5.30

Royal Trust Gr.
ynAdv. Bal	10.61
ynAdv. Grwth	11.21
ynAdv. Inc	9.88
ynAmerican	26.52
ynBond	8.68
ynCanadian	37.98
ynEnergy	8.86
ynGlobal Inv	10.19
yGovt Bond In	8.54
ynJapanese	24.09
ynMMF 8.00	10.00
ynMortgage	10.38
ynPreferred	9.67

Royfund Group
nBond Fnd	4.99
nEquity	23.31
nMMF (7.57)	10.00

Saxon Group
nBalanced	11.10
nSmall Cap	12.59
nStock	10.95
nWorld Gwth	14.47

Sceptre Funds
ynBalanced	12.05
ynCap Protect	10.57
.ynEquity	13.24
ynInt'l	14.17

Scotia Funds
Income	9.39
Stock Bond	9.75

Sentinel
yAm Eq Cdn	9.73
yAm Eq U.S.	7.39
Cda Bond	8.98
Cda Equity	12.19
Global	11.95
ynMMF(7.91)	10.00

SPECTRUM
nCash (8.01)	1.00
nCdn Equity	10.31

nDiversified 9.96
nDividend 9.66
nInterest 9.49
nIntl Equity 10.09
nSaving (8.15) 1.00
ySterling Mtge 5.14
yTD GrnL Mtge 10.43

Templeton Grp
Temp Cdn	6.66
Temp Gr Cdn	21.41
Temp Gr USF	16.28

Trimark Group
Income Gth	5.02
Interest 8.48	10.00
Trimark	14.66
Trimark Cdn	12.62

Trust General
ynAction Am	18.54
ynAction Can	28.87
ynEquilibre	9.99
ynHypo	10.67
ynMar. Mon.	10.00
ynOblig	9.34

20-20 Group Fin
yCdn ConvDeb	10.09
yCdn ConvPfd	10.80
ySS World	10.27
Sunset	12.65
yUnivAve Gth	15.73

Waltaine Funds
nBalanced	10.45
nConv. Ped.	9.97
nInstant $$	10.03
riPfd. Inc.	9.27

Walwyn Group
ynBond	9.55
ynCd Equity	12.00
ynIntern'tl C	12.71
ynIntn'tl US	9.65
ynMMF	10.00
ynOption	10.04
ynPreferred	10.00
ynVenture	12.64

NON-MEMBERS
ynAltamira	6.17
ynC-Anaes	11.82
Can Nat Res	6.64
Canwst RSP	97.92
yCapital Gwth	8.91
nCapstone	7.32

Co-op Trust Group
ynGrowth	15.64
ynIncome	9.49

CSA MGMT Gr.
Goldfund	8.06
Goldtrust	10.00

Dixon, Krog Gr.
D K Amn	24.67
D K Ent.	18.04
Heritage	4.74
yDomequity	12.78
yEthical Gwth	5.63

FIDUCIAIRES
yAction	11.62
yOblig	9.94
yFiscon	10.21
yGyro Equity	15.79
yHall Bond	10.15
Harvard	8.98

Industrial Gr.
CS Mgt (7.91)	10.00
Indust Am	9.24
Indust Div	12.35
Indust Eq	22.57
Indust Global	7.08

Indust Gwth 15.95
Indust Hor 5.21
Indust Inc 10.06
Indust Pens 6.73
Mack Eq 2.90
Mack Mtge 1.22
yMar Equity 6.84
yMarlboro 9.74

Md Mgmt Fd
ynCMAIF	30.16
ynMD Grth	19.81
ynPerp G. I	1.99
ynPerp G. II	9.87
nNatrusco	9.16

NW Group
yCanadian	9.02
yEquity	12.16
yNW Trust Eq	21.56

Pacific Group
Growth	8.37
Ret Bal.	5.20
US Growth	5.73

PHN Group
Bond	8.52
Canadian	21.37
Div Inc	14.87
Fund	31.40
MMF 8.15	10.00
Pooled	49.66
RRSP	60.75
Vintage Fd	13.36

PMF Mgt. Ltd.
nPension	6.90
nXanadu F	5.68

Pret et Revenu Gr
yAmerican	32.80
yCanadian	12.22
yFonds H	5.19
yRetraite	20.99

Principal-US Gr.
yEquity	7.78
yWorld	10.61

Sagit Group
yCam. Bal.	6.34
yCam.	8.25
yCam. Res.	3.52
yTns. Can. Eq.	8.03
yTrans B	87.88
yTrans C	15.12
ySynchrovest	8.28

Timvest Funds
yAmerican	6.16
yBond	9.66
yDiversfd	5.67
yGrowth	10.10
yIncome	10.47
yMMF 7.29	10.00

United Group
Accum	12.20
Accum. R.	11.91
American	7.44
Mortgage	5.15
Security	4.34
Venture	11.13
Venture Ret	14.09

Universal Group
American	11.48
Equity	11.88
Global	6.22
Income	5.03
Pacific	12.31
Resource	8.28
yWestrn Grth	4.38

The Globe and Mail, Friday, September 18, 1987.

The two main sources of tax information for investors are Revenue Canada publications and tax reference books.

Revenue Canada Taxation publishes a series of pamphlets on income tax matters including those dealing with capital gains, income from property, and registered retirement savings plans. These are available free of charge to Canadians.[23] Interpretation bulletins are published on various Canadian tax issues. These bulletins, which are also available free to Canadian taxpayers, provide the tax department's interpretation of important tax issues in the Income Tax Act.[24] The CCH Canadian *Master Tax Guide*[25] and De Boo's *Canada Tax Manual*[26] are comprehensive reference texts on Canadian federal income tax, covering all aspects of tax including income from business and property, capital gains and losses, pensions and retirement savings plans, corporation and shareholders.

The major Canadian accounting firms publish regular tax letters. Some are available free to students on request; others are provided to clients only. Examples are Peat Marwick's *Canadian Tax Letter*, and Ernst and Whinney's *The Letter*.

6-3.7 Tax Information

The Canadian and U.S. options exchanges publish considerable descriptive and promotional material on options and futures contracts and trading processes. One of the most useful is *montreal options* published monthly by the Montreal Exchange,[27] containing descriptive material on Montreal Exchange options contracts and trading and hedging recommendations. See Figure 6-14. Other publications of the Montreal Exchange, ranging in price from $0.50 to $3.00, include: *A Guide to the Stock Options Market*, *Understanding Gold Options*, *Trading Options Contracts on the Canadian Dollar*, *Trading Options on Currencies*, *The Index Options Market*, *IOCC Gold Options*, and *Fact Sheet: Eastern Lumber Futures*.

Publications of the Toronto Futures Exchange, available at a cost of $2.75 each or less include:[28] *Understanding Financial Futures*, *Interest Rate Futures Reporting Guide*, *Trading Silver Options*, *Trading the U.S. Dollar Futures Contract*, *Trading Oil and Gas Stock Index Futures*, *The TSE 300 Index Option*.

Futures is a monthly publication that contains information on new futures and options contracts, trading strategies, contract specifications, and recent developments on futures exchanges.[29] Emphasis is on U.S. exchanges and contracts. A U.K. publication, *Futures and Options World*,[30] provides similar information with emphasis on the U.K. options and futures contracts.

6-3.8 Information on Options and Futures Contracts

23 Write to Department of National Revenue Canada, Ottawa, Canada, K1A 0G7.

24 Write to Department of National Revenue Canada, Ottawa, Canada, K1A, 0G7.

25 CCH Canadian Limited, 6 Garamond Court, Don Mills, Ontario, M3C 1Z5.

26 Richard de Boo Limited, 70 Richmond St. East, Toronto, Ontario, M5C 2M8.

27 Available free from The Montreal Exchange, The Stock Exchange Tower, P.O. Box 61, 800 Victoria Square, Montreal, Quebec H4Z 1A9.

28 The Toronto Futures Exchange, The Exchange Tower, 2 First Canadian Place, Toronto, Ontario M5X 1J2.

29 *Futures*, 219 Parkade, Cedar Falls, Iowa, 50613-9985. Annual subscription is $34.00 U.S.

30 *Futures and Options World*, c/o Expediters of the Printed Word Ltd., 515 Madison Avenue, New York, New York, 10022. Free to persons in the futures and options industry; otherwise $59.00 U.S. per annum.

FIGURE 6-13   Sample tax letter published by an accounting firm.

F O C U S   O N

TAXATION

January/February 1987

1987 Federal Budget Promises Sweeping Reforms

The next federal budget is expected to be delivered sometime in February. It promises to be one of the most significant budgets since the last major reforms to the Canadian tax system in 1971. One of the main reasons for this is the recent wave of tax reforms taking place around the world, most notably the far reaching tax reform package recently enacted in the United States. Furthermore, the whole process of tax reform in Canada has been under study for a number of years. It picked up a full headed steam in late October 1986 when Finance Minister Wilson announced the commencement of his pre-budget consultation process and simultaneously tabled guidelines for comprehensive tax reforms to the Canadian tax system.

Thorne Ernst & Whinney
Member of **EW** Ernst & Whinney International

FIGURE 6-14   The Montreal Exchange monthly, *montreal options.*

THE MONTREAL EXCHANGE

montreal options
monthly strategy supplement

July 1986, Vol. 2, No. 4

PLEASE CIRCULATE TO:

TBA: OPTIONS ON T-BILLS

On Friday August 15, 1986, Canada's first Treasury bill options began trading at the ME. These are also Canada's first European-style options with exercise only possible at expiry.

The symbol for T-bill options is "TBA". Series expiring in September, October and November with strike prices of 91.50 and 92 were listed for trading. The strike prices are based on the ME's T-bill index which is equal to 100 minus the yield of Canadian 91-day Treasury bills.

Strike Price Codes

The table below contains the strike price codes for the new T-bill options (TBA). The exercise prices are set at intervals of 50 basis points (e.g., 90 and 90.50). Market quotes are available on the CMQ and Can-quote systems using the ticker symbol "TBA" and the standard expiry month codes. Telerate carries the T-bill market on page 3105, the Government of Canada T-bill auction details on page 3111 and TBA option quotes on page 3138.

Strike Price	Code	Strike Price	Code
88.00	G	90.50	Q
88.50	I	91.00	S
89.00	K	91.50	U
89.50	M	92.00	W
90.00	O	92.50	B

Specialist

McLeod Young Weir is the specialist for this new option class.

TBA Cross-Canada Tour

The ME will be hosting seminars during September on its new T-bill options and their hedging applications. Details are as follows:

AT A GLANCE

- Launch of T-bill options
- Trading Strategy
  Cascades covered write
- TBA: value of a basis point
- IOCC Order Book
- Hiram Walker update

Date	City	Location	Time
Sept. 3	Quebec City	Hilton International, Le Beaumont Room	4:30 pm
Sept. 4	Montreal	Montreal Exchange Auditorium	4:30 pm
Sept. 8	Ottawa	Château Laurier, Palladian Room	4:30 pm
Sept. 9	Toronto	Commerce Court West, Commerce Hall	4:30 pm
Sept. 10	Kitchener	Valhalla Inn, Historian Suite	4:30 pm
Sept. 11	London	Holiday Inn, Edinburgh Room	4:30 pm
Sept. 15	Winnipeg	To be announced	3:30 pm
Sept. 16	Regina	Regina Inn, York Room	3:00 pm
Sept. 17	Calgary	Calgary Convention Centre, McIntyre Room	3:00 pm
Sept. 18	Vancouver	Hyatt Regency, Cypress Room	2:00 pm
Sept. 24	Halifax	Halifax Board of Trade, Room no. 1	9:00 am
Sept. 25	St.John	Delta Hotel, Manchester Room	9:00 am

A TBA slide presentation and pamphlet have been prepared. For further informa- tion or to reserve a place for the seminar, please call local 471 at the ME.

Source: *montreal options,* The Montreal Exchange, July 1986, vol. 2, no. 4.

Canadian newspapers publish daily futures quotations in the financial section. Figure 6-15 is an example.

FIGURE 6-15 Sample newspaper futures quotation.

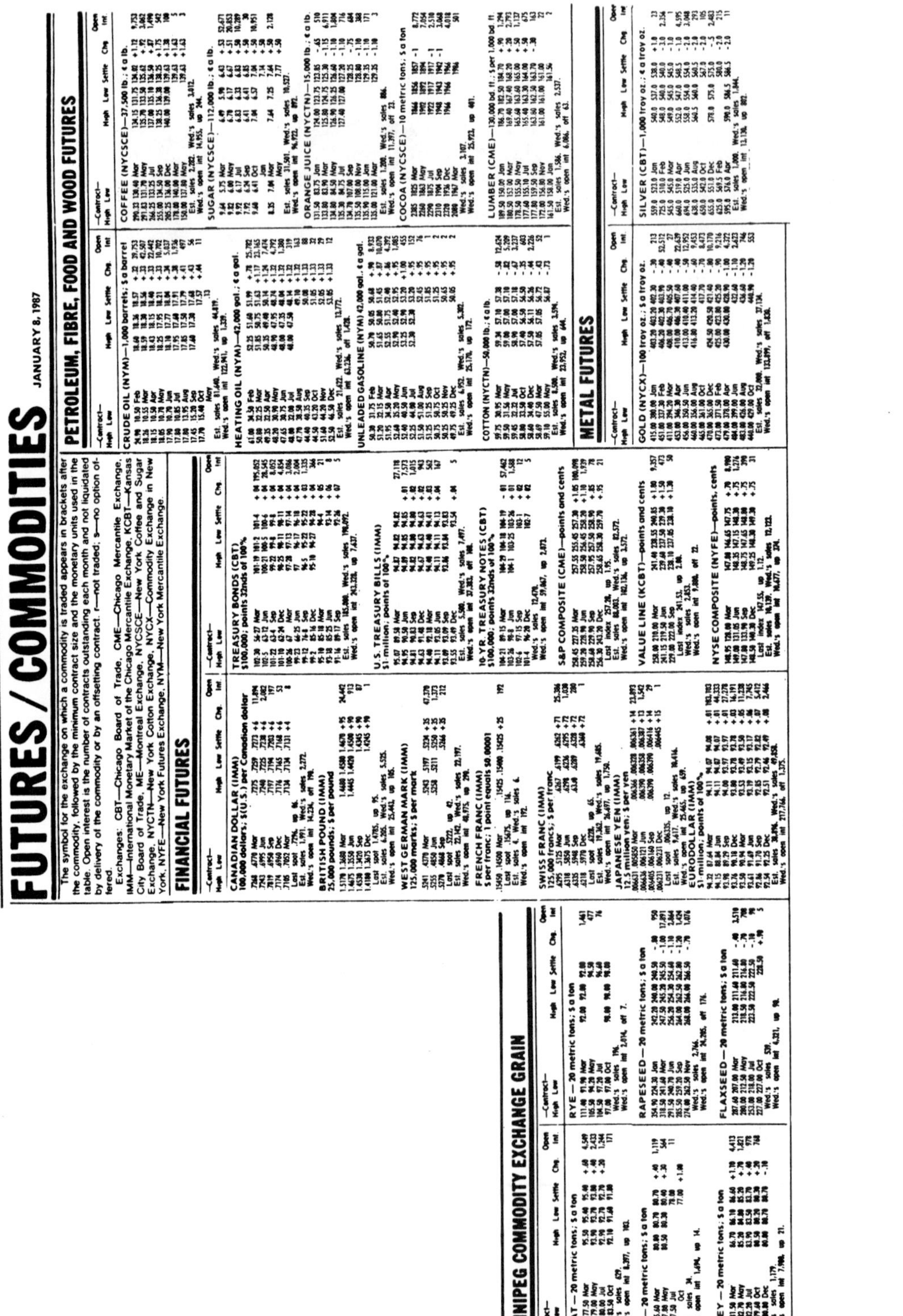

Source: The Globe and Mail, Report on Business, January 9, 1987.

In the United States, Standard & Poor's publishes a paperback book entitled *Options Handbook* that primarily provides information about the corporation that issued the securities to which the option applies. In this respect, the *Options Handbook* is similar to Standard & Poor's *Stock Market Encyclopedia*. In addition to information about the corporation on which the options are traded, the *Options Handbook* contains pieces of essential information about the options themselves.

Value Line Inc. publishes a weekly magazine named *Value Line Options and Convertibles* that contains much valuable information about the corporation that issued the securities on which the options are written, along with valuable information of particular interest to option buyers and writers. In the opinion of some observers, the *Value Line Options and Convertibles* periodical provides option traders with the best available information that can be obtained at a modest price.

6-4   BROKERAGE HOUSES

Brokerage houses are the offices of securities brokers and dealers. In order to expedite their sales efforts these brokerage offices usually carry one or more of the leading investment surveys for their customers' use. However, large brokerages maintain their own research departments, which generate information for their customers. A broker's research department disseminates publications, usually in the form of market newsletters or reviews, upon request. The department makes analyses of industries and individual companies. Upon request some research departments will also analyze portfolios and make specific recommendations tailored to a customer's investment goals. A brokerage that is too small to maintain a research staff may use a research company; sometimes small brokerages even use newsletters from the larger brokerage houses.

Most of the major brokerage firms in Canada have research departments. Each brokerage firm's research department produces reports in the form of booklets that are mailed to anyone requesting them. The reports are sent at no cost in order to attract customers.

Some brokerages have the reputation of being "retailers," as opposed to being primarily institutional brokerages or investment dealers. These retail brokerages sell primarily to individual investors—the "little people." In order to attract the small investor, they provide numerous services either free or at a minimum charge. Merrill Lynch, and Dominion Securities are two of the more prominent retail brokerages. Among the free services such firms frequently provide for their customers are up-to-the-minute financial news, information about commodities and bonds as well as common stock, and safekeeping of securities.

Although the large retail brokerages strive to maintain a good reputation for fair dealing, their salespeople's advice should not be followed blindly. The brokerages' publications enable investors to get a quick look at the market and the particular brokerage's feelings about it. Wise investors, however, will never rely on the report of just one firm or investment service but will examine other views before investing.

Some of the Canadian brokerage firm newsletters include Midland Doherty's *Market Dialogue,* Dean Witter Canada's *Perspective,* Davidson Partners' *Focus,* Dominion Securities' *Equity Review,* and Merrill Lynch Canada's *Spotlight.*

6-5 INVESTMENT NEWSLETTERS

Both independent and brokerage firm–related companies publish and sell advisory newsletters to the public. *The Money Reporter* provides rankings and

FIGURE 6-16 Sample market letter from a Canadian brokerage firm.

and should add approximately 150,000 oz. of production initially ... most liquid, best-managed and cheapest of Canadian gold plays ... 1984 EPS \$0.68; 1985 and 1986 estimates \$0.80 and \$1.60, assuming gold price of U.S. \$325 and U.S. \$350 respectively.

POWER CORPORATION
(POW — \$18.63) (A — 2:1:7)
Management holding company dominated by its 70% interest in recently-formed Power Financial, in turn dominated by Great-West Life which now derives over half its strongly growing earnings from U.S.A. ... 40% stake in Consolidated-Bathurst also very valuable ... recent sale of Canadian Pacific investment has left POW with no debt, \$200 MM in the bank and a market-adjusted shareholders' equity in the \$1.4 billion range ... remains a relatively cheap stock backed by solid fundamentals and has outstanding continuing growth possibilities.

RIO ALGOM
(ROM — \$23.13) (B — 2:1:9)
Continues to demonstrate superior earnings based on solid performance from uranium and steel distribution ... 68%-owned Lornex, North America's second largest open pit copper mine had much improved first half 1985 ... higher copper price would provide major earnings boost ... look for continued earnings growth, 1985 and 1986 estimates are \$2.05-\$2.30 and \$2.50-\$3.50, up strongly from \$1.65 in 1984.

SHELL CANADA
(SHC — \$26.63) (A — 2:1:7
Canada's third largest integrated energy resource company whose operations include exploration for and development of crude oil, natural gas, oil sands and coal properties ... also refines and markets products derived from these natural resources ... following 1984 EPS gain of 55% over the previous year, we expect SHC to continue to show strong earnings growth over the next several years through continued oil product profit margin improvement, higher sales volumes, increased chemicals earnings and gains in resource earnings ... 1985 and 1986 EPS estimates are \$1.74 and \$2.54.

SPAR AEROSPACE
(SPZ — \$29.50) (B — 2:1:7)
1984 unusually profitable as company earned 8.4% on each revenue dollar, resulting in earnings per share of \$1.73 ... expect 1985 profit to head back toward more traditional 4%-6% return on each sales dollar ... 1985 EPS estimate \$1.75 fully-diluted and 1986 estimate is \$1.75 — \$2.00 ... current contract inventory and contract potential give SPZ largest potential order book in its history.

QRQ KEY

Suitability:
A — Investment Grade
B — Good Quality
C — Speculative

Investment Opinion:
Time Frame:
1st Number: Int. Term
2nd Number: Long Term

1 — Buy
2 — Above Average

7 — Qualified for Income
8 — Not Qualified for Income
9 — Pays no cash dividend

MERRILL LYNCH CANADA'S TOP DOZEN

		Price: 08/29/85		Earnings Per Share								
	QRQ	Close	52 Week Range	Last Year Fisc.	Last Year Actual	Curr. Yr. Est.	P/E Est.	5 Yr. EPS Growth Est. (%)	Book Value	ROE Est. 1985	Ind. Div.	Cur. Yld.
Bank of Nova Scotia	A 2:1:7	13.63	14¾-11¼	Oct. 84	1.72	1.90	7.2	11	14.50	13.10	0.68	5.0
CAE Industries	B 1:1:7	15.63	18¾-12⅝	Mar. 85	0.86	1.05	14.9	30	2.72	38.60	0.28	1.8
CDC Life Sciences	B 1:1:9	22.00	26 -12⅝	Dec. 84	1.08	1.35	16.3	24	5.73	23.56	Nil	Nil
Hees International	A 1:1:7	22.75	23½-17⅝	Dec. 84	1.60	2.00	11.4	20	11.84	16.89	0.60	2.6
Int'l. Thomson Org.	A 2:1:7	9.63	9¾-7⅝	Dec. 84	0.52	0.70	14.5	17.5	2.60	26.92	0.165*	2.3
Laidlaw Transportation	B 1:1:9	15.00	16¾-7⅝	Aug. 84	0.52	0.78	19.2	28	5.82	13.40	0.16	1.1
Lonvest	A 2:1:7	17.88	18⅞-16⅞	Dec. 84	1.60	1.84	9.7	11	14.00	13.14	0.17	1.0
Placer Development	C 2:1:9	25.75	27⅞-21⅛	Dec. 84	0.68	0.80	34.3	36	13.54	5.53	0.30	1.2
Power Corp. of Canada	A 2:1:7	18.63	19¾-10⅛	Dec. 84	1.68	2.25	8.28	13	14.70	15.30	0.75	3.2
Rio Algom	B 2:1:9	23.13	25½-18	Dec. 84	1.65	2.05	11.3	16.2	13.83	14.82	0.60	2.6
Shell Canada	A 2:1:7	26.63	29⅞-21¼	Dec. 84	1.27	1.74	15.3	39	19.54	8.90	0.60	2.3
Spar Aerospace	B 2:1:7	29.50	30¾-21¼	Dec. 84	1.73	1.75	39.3	20	7.46	23.45	0.48	1.6

* U.S. Funds.

Source: Merrill Lynch Canada's *Spotlight.*

recommendations on bonds, annuities, preferred shares, the money market and tax shelters such as RRSPs. The *MoneyLetter* features Morton Shulman and Andrew Sarlos columns and provides stock, futures, and personal investing recommendations. The *Investor's Digest of Canada*, a bi-monthly news sheet, supplies stock analyses by brokerage house researchers. One major feature is ''The Forecaster'' in which earnings projections for various companies are compared. Other well-known market letters are *The Polymetric Report* and *Consensus*.

Investors may also obtain information about a firm by reading its annual report or interviewing its executives. However, both these sources may be biased. Only events that have a favourable impact on the firm's prospects are discussed in most cases, for management is reluctant to publicize its errors.

**6-5.1
Annual
Reports and
Interviews
with
Executives**

6-6 PROFESSIONAL JOURNALS

Various professional organizations and publishing companies publish periodicals containing articles relevant to financial investing. Some of the more prominent journals are briefly discussed here.

The *Financial Analysts Journal (FAJ)* is a bi-monthly publication of the Financial Analysts Federation, which is an association of financial analysts and others devoted to the professional advancement of investment management and security analysis.[31]

**6-6.1
Financial
Analysts
Journal**

  The *FAJ* addresses itself to the field of financial investments. It typically contains articles on economic viewpoint, investment management, and investment analysis. It also publishes articles on industry reviews, corporation finance, bond analysis, accounting, and similar investment topics. The articles are written primarily by finance professors, finance executives, and financial technicians.

Financial Management is published quarterly by the Financial Management Association. It is intended for executives interested in the financial management of business firms, but it also contains investment-related articles on such topics as stock splits, dividend policy, mergers, and stock listings.[32]

**6-6.2
Financial
Management**

Institutional Investor is published monthly and is aimed at professional investors and portfolio managers, with emphasis on what is happening in the investment industry.[33] The magazine is full of promotional literature and is written by a paid professional staff. No intellectual material or mathematical formulas are used in the articles in *Institutional Investor*. This magazine and

**6-6.3
Institutional
Investor**

31 Subscriptions are $51 U.S. per year and may be obtained from *Financial Analysts Journal*, Financial Analysts Federation, P.O. Box 3726, Charlottesville, Virginia, 22903.
32 Subscriptions are $25 U.S. per year and may be obtained from Financial Management Assoc., Executive Director, College of Business Administration, University of South Florida, 4202 Fowler Avenue, Tampa, Florida, 33620.
33 Subscriptions are $95 U.S. per year and may be obtained from *Institutional Investor*, Inc., 488 Madison Avenue, New York, New York, 10022.

the one discussed next specialize in publishing articles for busy investment executives.

**6.6-4
Journal
of Portfolio
Management**

The *Journal of Portfolio Management* is published quarterly.[34] The intent of the journal is to function as a forum for the publication of academic research of use to the practicing portfolio manager. Over half the articles are written by academics, designed to be read by investment executives.

**6-6.5
Journal
of Finance**

The *Journal of Finance* is published five times a year by the American Finance Association, a professional organization primarily for finance professors, finance executives, and business economists. An annual membership fee of $25 U.S. entitles members of the association to receive a subscription to the *Journal of Finance (JF)* at no additional fee.[35] The *JF* typically contains about a dozen studies done by finance professors, a few comments on previously published articles, and reviews of recently published finance books. The papers published range from sophisticated mathematical analysis to descriptions of finance institutions. All phases of finance are covered—investments, corporation finance, public finance, real estate finance, international finance, and money and banking.

**6-6.6
Journal
of Financial
and
Quantitative
Analysis**

The *Journal of Financial and Quantitative Analysis (JFQA)* is a quarterly academic finance journal that also publishes a few applied mathematics papers. The *JFQA* is published jointly by the Western Finance Association and the graduate school of business of the University of Washington. Subscriptions cost $20 U.S. per year in the United States and $25 U.S. per year for foreign mailings.[36] Each issue of the journal contains about ten articles submitted by professors of finance, business economics, statistics, and econometrics. Analytical articles employing mathematical and statistical studies of financial problems are found in the *JFQA*.

**6-6.7
Canadian
Journal of
Administra-
tive Sciences**

The *Canadian Journal of Administrative Sciences* is a bi-annual academic journal that publishes research papers in the various administrative science fields, including finance. Most issues contain about ten to fifteen articles of which at least one deals with a finance topic. The journal is sponsored by the Administrative Sciences Association of Canada, the Max Bell Foundation, and the Faculty of Administrative Sciences, York University.[37] Finance articles are also found in the *Collected Papers* from the Annual Conference of the Administrative Sciences Association of Canada, Finance Division, published

---

34 Subscriptions are $90 U.S. per year and may be obtained from *Journal of Portfolio Management*, Subscription Department, 488 Madison Avenue, 14th floor, New York, New York, 10022.

35 Subscribers should write to Professor Michael Keenan, American Finance Association, 100 Trinity Place, New York, New York, 10006.

36 Subscriptions may be obtained from the *Journal of Financial and Quantitative Analysis*, Graduate School of Business Administration, Mackenzie Hall, University of Washington, Seattle, Washington, 98195.

37 Subscriptions cost $30 a year and are available from Faculty of Management, McGill University, 1001 Sherbrooke Street West, Montreal, Quebec N3A 1G5.

annually. The articles are typically at varying stages, ranging from preliminary version working papers to papers about to be published in academic journals.

6-6.8 Journal of Financial Economics (JFE)

The *Journal of Financial Economics (JFE)* is a quarterly academic journal essentially managed by the finance faculty of the University of Rochester and published by Elsevier Science Publishers.[38] Each issue contains about seven articles that usually employ mathematics and/or statistics to investigate investments problems. Practically all the articles are written by professors of finance.

6-6.9 Journal of Business (JOB)

The *Journal of Business (JOB)* is a quarterly academic journal published by the University of Chicago.[39] The journal typically contains about six analytical articles dealing with a wide range of business topics; investments studies seem to be the most popular topic. Professors of business and economics author the articles in most cases.

6-7   DATA FILES FOR COMPUTERS

As computers have developed, the cost per computation has dropped. At the same time, equipment and programs have advanced and become easier to use. As a result, financial analysis in various forms is now being done by computer. Some firms market financial information in a form that may be read directly into a computer as raw input data.

6-7.1   The Financial Post On-Line Databases

The Financial Post provides on-line and fixed databases on magnetic tape for a wide range of Canadian and U.S. securities. Data offered include weekly and month-end prices and yields for over 1600 Canadian bond issues;[40] annual financial statement data, stock prices, volume, industry classifications, etc., for over 470 Canadian companies (quarterly data available for 115 companies);[41] dividend data, including shareholders' record date, tax status, indicated annual payment, exdividend dates, etc., for all Canadian listed and leading unlisted securities;[42] mutual fund data, including net asset value per share, total assets, fund type, monthly history for over five years, etc., on over 300 Canadian mutual funds;[43] stock price, options, and futures information including bid/ask, volume, high/low, close, and splits for all equities

---

38 Subscriptions cost $45 U.S. per year and are available from Elsevier Sequoia S.A., P.O. Box 564, CH-1001, Lausanne 1, Switzerland.

39 Subscriptions cost $25 U.S. per year and may be obtained from *Journal of Business*, The University of Chicago Press, Journals Division, P.O. Box 37005, Chicago, Illinois 60637.

40 The Canadian Bond Database, weekly service is $250 per week, monthly service is $250 per month. The service is also available on-line at a fixed monthly or annual rate or a charge per item.

41 The Corporate Database is available on-line, at an annual subscription fee of $6,000. It can also be obtained on-line on a per-item basis. An updated magnetic tape with information back to 1959 is also available.

42 The Dividend Database is available on magnetic tape on a daily, weekly, or monthly basis.

43 The Mutual Fund Database is available on magnetic tape on a monthly or quarterly basis.

traded on Canadian exchanges and the New York and American Stock Exchanges, and Canadian equity options, futures, and indexes.[44] Other services offered include a U.S. pricing services database and a stock profile database.

FIGURE 6-17   Page from *The Financial Post's* corporate debenture descriptive material.

I. P. Sharp Associates Limited | 2 First Canadian Place,
Suite 1900,
Toronto, Ontario M5X 1E3
(416) 364-5361
Telex 0622259

Financial Post Securities   FPSTOCK

Category: Finance   Documentation Revision Date: July 1985
                                                             Data Base Creation Date: July 1973
Description:
      Stock trading statistics for securities traded on the Canadian exchanges, the New York Stock Exchange, and the American Stock Exchange. The data base contains the daily volume, high, low, and closing prices for about 3,800 Canadian securities. It has 30,000 time series. The Canadian information is a composite of Montreal, Toronto, Calgary, and Vancouver exchanges.

      Data for the New York Stock Exchange (NYSE) consists of daily closing prices for about 3,000 securities listed on NYSE. Data for the American Stock Exchange (AMEX) consists of daily closing prices for about 1,700 securities listed on AMEX.

      The data base also contains weekly price and volume data for the Canadian securities, and both weekly and monthly closing prices for the AMEX and NYSE securities.
Frequency/History:
      The data base is updated daily. There is daily data available for the past 260 trading days for all exchanges; weekly data from January 1965 for Canadian exchanges, from July 1974 for NYSE, and from September 1973 for AMEX; and monthly data from July 1974 for NYSE, and from September 1973 for AMEX.
Updates:
      Daily from tapes containing the previous day's data.
Source:
      The Financial Post Investment Databank.
Access:
      Through 39 *MAGIC* via *FPDAILY*, *FPWEEKLY*, or *FPMONTHLY*; or through 51 *FP* for Canadian, 51 *FPNY* for New York, and 51 *FPAM* for American data. There is also 51 *FPPLOT*, which contains functions for creating graphs. For example, in 39 *MAGIC*:
          1 2 3 4 5 *DAILY DATED* 1 12 84 *TO* 31 12 84
          AUTOLABEL
          TABLE '*C/VO,N/IBM*' *FPDAILY* 4
      gives the daily closing prices of Seagrams on the Canadian exchanges and IBM on the New York Exchange in December 1984.
Online Documentation:
      Type *DESCRIBE* in 51 *FPSTOCKLIST* or 51 *FPPLOT*.   To obtain a listing of the directory, type *STOCKLIST* in 51 *FPSTOCKLIST*.
Printed Documentation:
      Financial Post Data Base
      Financial Data Bases Reference Guide
Mail System Contacts:
      MONQ, FIN
Notes:
      There is no subscription fee for using this data base.

---

44 The Securities Database is offered on an exchange by exchange basis, on-line or on magnetic tape.

Standard & Poor's Compustat Services, Inc., sells a financial database called Compustat. Compustat is a magnetic tape to be read by a computer's tape-drive input device or through an authorized time-sharing vendor. The Compustat tape contains 20 years of annual data for more than 6000 stocks. Quarterly data on 2700 stocks from 1972 are also available. There are 173 annual data items and 65 quarterly data items for each company on the tapes. The tapes are updated 12 times a year at no charge over the basic subscription price of $60,000 per year for corporate customers.

The Compustat Canadian File contains data, available in either Canadian or U.S. dollars, on approximately 225 large Canadian companies. Canadian universities can obtain the Compustat Files at a substantially lower price than corporate customers.[45]

6-7.2 Compustat tapes

The Center for Research in Security Prices (CRSP) file is a magnetic tape that may be used as raw input data. There are two different versions of the CRSP tape for sale—the monthly and the daily versions. The CRSP monthly tape contains monthly prices, quarterly cash dividends, and stock dividend and split information for every firm listed on the NYSE since 1926.[46] A daily prices version of the CRSP tape may also be purchased, but the daily tape goes back only to the 1960s. The CRSP tape costs tens of thousands of dollars per year to rent, so usually only large, well-funded institutions that are dedicated to ongoing research can afford them. However, educational institutions can rent the CRSP tape at much lower prices.

6-7.3 The CRSP File

Interactive Data Corporation (IDC) sells a quarterly magnetic computer tape with daily stock trading volumes and prices and quarterly dividends and earnings for all NYSE and AMEX securities and some OTC securities; it is called the ISL tape. ISL tapes may be purchased and updated periodically.[47] The same data are also available in book form. Standard & Poor's publishes them in volumes entitled *Daily Stock Price Records*; each volume contains one quarter of data for hundreds of companies. Data management can be a problem with ISL tapes because, for example, twenty different quarterly tapes must be used to obtain five years of observations on one stock.

6-7.4 The ISL Data

Standard & Poor's Compustat Services, Inc. also has the prices, dividends, and earnings (PDE) file, which contains monthly stock prices, quarterly dividends per share, quarterly earnings per share, monthly trading volume, stock dividend or split information, book value per share, the stock exchange

6-7.5 The PDE File

---

45 One year subscription for annual tapes for 225 Canadian companies and 2400 U.S. companies, including research files is approximately $4,800 U.S. Write to: Standard & Poor's Compustat Services, Inc., 1221 Avenue of the Americas, 33rd Floor, New York, New York, 10020.

46 The tape may be purchased from the Center for Research on Security Prices, University of Chicago, 1101 East 58 Street, Chicago, Illinois 60607.

47 IDC is a subsidiary of Chase Manhattan Bank. The ISL tape may be purchased from the Interactive Data Corporation, 1114 Avenue of the Americas, 6th floor, New York, New York 10036.

where the stock is traded, the Compustat file code number, the CUSIP number, the industry number, and the stock exchange ticker symbol for about 5500 stocks. The tape also contains price, dividend, and earnings data on the various Standard & Poor's and other stock market indexes. Purchasers of the Compustat annual and quarterly tapes and other interested parties may obtain the PDE tape at a modest price; the PDE are nearly all taken from the Compustat tapes.

6-7.6   The Value Line Database

Value Line maintains machine-readable data files on the 1650 corporations it analyzes and publishes in its *Value Line Investment Survey*. The complete data files containing stock prices and financial statement data, some of it going back as far as 1954, may be purchased from Value Line in the form of magnetic tapes for several hundred dollars. Value Line also sells an abbreviated version of these data on floppy disks called Value/Screen for $495 per year. These floppy disks are available for personal computers like the IBM-PC Compaq, other IBM-PC compatibles, Apple, Franklin Ace, and others. Contact Value Line at the address given above on page 117 to obtain their data.

6-7.7   The Berkeley Options Database

The University of California at Berkeley obtains market data from the Chicago Board of Trade about the options traded there and compiles them to be sold. Daily bid and asked prices are available from 1976 to the present. These data may be purchased by contacting the business school at the Berkeley campus.

6-7.8   The Chicago Board of Trade Commodity Data

The Chicago Board of Trade (CBT) has been compiling commodity price information in machine-readable form since 1981. These data are available on a transaction-to-transaction basis or on a daily basis and may be purchased in the form of magnetic tapes. The data are also available in booklets that have been printed and sold by the CBT for many years. These sources of data may be acquired through the CBT itself.

The computer-accessible financial data files discussed above are far too expensive for most individual investors to purchase. However, some large universities and corporations provide these useful facilities for their students and employees at no cost to the individual user in order to expedite financial research. In addition to access to these data files, the financial researcher must either be able to program the computer to use the data or be able to employ the services of an able computer programmer.

In this section, we have identified a number of commercially available data files for computers. The list is by no means exhaustive. For example, Canadian stock price data bases have been prepared by researchers at both the universities of Laval and Western Ontario, by the Financial Research Institute (FRI), and by the Toronto Stock Exchange.

6-8   SOFTWARE SERVICES FOR COMPUTERS

Computer programs (sometimes called software packages) are available to do some clerical-type analysis and statistical work. Most of these programs can use one of the data files discussed above as raw input data. The program reads the data file, performs the requested work, and prints out the results.

These software packages can usually be adapted to different computer systems. They calculate financial ratios, make inter-firm and inter-industry comparisons, do various kinds of statistical analyses, and perform other repetitive tasks.

The Statistical Package for the Social Sciences (SPSS) is a large package of computer programs for statistical analysis that is well documented, with an easy-to-read users' manual. The package contains routines to compile descriptive statistics and perform many kinds of sophisticated statistical analyses. These programs are written in various forms and are ready for use with IBM, CDC, Univac, or Xerox Sigma computers of various sizes.[48]

6-8.1 The Statistical Package for the Social Sciences (SPSS)

The Bio-Med package, originally prepared for medical research at the University of California, Los Angeles (UCLA), is now a widely used software package containing programs to do several different kinds of sophisticated statistical analysis. The excellent book of documentation that accompanies the Bio-Med programs rounds out a useful package employed in many business schools. It may be obtained at a low cost from UCLA.

6-8.2 The Bio-Med Package

INVESPAK is a package of twenty-five different computer programs, written in the BASIC language, that perform various kinds of financial analysis computations. These include such tasks as calculating risk and return statistics for investment assets as well as brokerage commissions and margin requirements; estimating the value of stocks, bonds, convertible securities, warrants, and put and call options; and performing Markowitz portfolio analysis to create an efficiently diversified portfolio.[49]

6-8.3 INVESPAK

Software Arts Inc., the computer software company that is most famous for creating the VisiCalc spreadsheet program, has also written other programs, that it sells. TK!Solver is an equation-processing program that sells for $500 and will solve complex equations (for example, the Nth degree polynomials used in present value work) for the value of any one variable in the program.[50]

6-8.4 The TK!Solver Program

One of the most sophisticated econometric packages that has been available in recent years is called the Time-Series Package (TSP). The program was originally written for large computers, but more recently a version for personal computers has been published for sale by McGraw-Hill Book Company. Written in collaboration with the original authors of the TSP program, the

6-8.5 The Time-Series Program (TSP)

---

48 See N. Nie, C. H. Hull, J. G. Jenkins, and D. H. Bent, *SPSS*, 2d ed. (New York: McGraw-Hill, 1975). This is a large, easy-to-read paperback book dealing with practically every phase of the SPSS package.

49 See William B. Riley, Jr., and Austin H. Montgomery, Jr., *Guide to Computer Assisted Investment Analysis* (New York: McGraw-Hill, 1982). If you don't want to go through the labour of typing the programs into your personal computer yourself, you can obtain floppy disks with all twenty-five programs from McGraw-Hill for a fee.

50 The TK!Solver program is available from Software Arts Inc., 27 Mica Lane, Wellesley, Massachusetts 02181.

new scaled-down program is called Micro-TSP. The Micro-TSP package will run on an IBM-PC; it transforms variables, links up with other unrelated programs (like VisiCalc), calculates statistics (like the Durbin-Watson) that are unique to time-series analysis, prepares plots for a line printer, and performs sophisticated econometric algorithms (like the Cochrane-Orcutt auto-regressive first-order scheme to overcome serial correlation problems and two-stage least-squares analysis). The program may be obtained on a floppy disk with a booklet of documentation telling how to use it from McGraw-Hill.[51]

6-8.6 Bookstaber's Complete Investment Book

Richard M. Bookstaber is the author of the book entitled *The Complete Investment Book*, published by Scott-Foresman in 1985. The book includes listings of many computer programs that perform investment analysis. The computer programs are written in the Microsoft BASIC language (which is commonly used with IBM-PCs). The book has four main sections, entitled "Bonds," "Stocks," "Technical Systems," and "Options." Each chapter within the sections addresses a different trading strategy. The computer programs may be copied out of the book itself, or Dr. Bookstaber will sell the programs on floppy disks at a low price for those who do not desire to spend hours entering the code.[52]

6-9   SUMMARY

The Globe and Mail Report on Business and *The Financial Post* are the most accessible sources of news concerning business in Canada. Also, investors can read about the Canadian economy in periodic newsletters sent free by major banks and in Canadian government publications, such as those of Statistics Canada. Information on world affairs and foreign markets can be found in *The Financial Times* (of London), *The New York Times*, and *The Wall Street Journal*.

Information on selected industries and individual firms is available by subscription to an information service, such as *The Financial Post* or Moody's. The major brokerage houses disseminate free publications giving their investment opinions. And investors can obtain audited financial statements from the firms themselves.

51 Quantitative analysis is, in addition to being respected, becoming increasingly popular among professional investment analysts. See Barbara Donnelly, "Wall Street's Quants Come into Their Own," *Institutional Investor*, November 1984, pp. 181–187. To get Micro-TSP write: MICRO-TSP Editor, College Division, McGraw-Hill Book Co., 1221 Avenue of the Americas, New York, New York 10020.

52 There is approximately one program for each chapter in Bookstaber's book. For $70 Dr. Bookstaber will mail a disk containing every one of these programs entered separately on a disk and a manual explaining how to use the software. Or, for $90 Bookstaber will send a larger program that is menu-driven and links all the separate programs together with a graphics capability to form a sophisticated investments analysis package that entails every aspect discussed in his book. Those who wish to acquire Bookstaber's programs on a disk and the accompanying documentation can send their cheque to: The Complete Investment Software, P.O. Box 205, Short Hills, NJ 07078. These programs would cost hundreds of dollars to have keypunched commercially and many thousands of dollars to have created commercially.

Professional financial analysts who seek to fully analyze massive economic and financial data may buy the raw data in machine-readable form from
various vendors. To complete the analysis, computer hardware and software
can be obtained from a number of suppliers.

QUESTIONS

1. "The financial newspapers contain rigorous analytical studies aimed at
   determining the cause-and-effect relationships between various economic
   variables." Is this true, false, or uncertain? Explain.
2. Select a publicly traded security and compare the reports on it found in
   The Financial Post Corporation Service and in *Moody's Handbook of Common
   Stocks*. Write a page about the significant differences among these two
   sources.
3. Write a short essay contrasting the bond ratings system of the Dominion
   Bond Rating Service with the Canadian Bond Rating Service. (This will
   require outside research, since bond ratings are explained only briefly in
   this book. See Fig. 6-8.)
4. Where could an investor interested in buying shares in a mutual fund
   find information that would help in choosing a fund?
5. If you had to prepare a graph of AAA-grade corporate bond yields showing the path of the interest rate time series monthly for the last ten years,
   where could you find the raw data quickly, easily, and inexpensively?

CHAPTER

7

Security Market Indicators

Investors who follow the market want to know, "How's the market doing?" Security market indicators have been constructed to answer this question quickly and easily. The Dow Jones Industrial Average (DJIA) is an example of a well-known, widely quoted U.S. stock market indicator. The DJIA is widely quoted, if for no other reason, because *The Wall Street Journal* and *Barron's* are two widely read financial newspapers that are published by Dow Jones & Company—the same firm that compiles the DJIA.

Technically speaking, the DJIA is an average, not an index. A stock market *average* is merely a weighted or unweighted average stock price for a specified group of stocks. In contrast, an index, such as the TSE 300 Composite Index, is a series of pure index numbers. Stock market indexes usually employ more refined methods to measure the general level and changes in stock prices than do stock market averages.

Index numbers are void of dollar values or other units of measure. Stock market indexes are usually calculated as ratios of dollar values. They are "pure numbers" that are used for making comparisons between different index numbers in the same series or other index numbers. An index is usually a weighted average ratio that is calculated from an average of a large number of different stocks. The index numbers in a particular time series of index numbers are all constructed from the same base date and base value (which is usually set to be 100, 10 or 1) to make them directly comparable. Some year in the past is selected as the base year from which the index's base value is calculated in order to impart a sense of time perspective to the index.

7-1 DIFFERENT AVERAGES AND INDEXES EXIST FOR DIFFERENT USES

Many different security market indexes and averages exist and are published. Some stock market averages and indexes are listed below.

CANADA

- TSE (Toronto Stock Exchange) 300 Composite Index
- TSE 35 Index
- TSE Oil and Gas Index
- TSE High Technology Index

- Canadian (Montreal Exchange) Market Portfolio Index
- Canadian Banking Index
- Canadian Forest Products Index
- Canadian Industrial Products Index
- Canadian Mining and Minerals Index
- Canadian Oil and Gas Index
- Canadian Utilities Index
- VSE (Vancouver Stock Exchange) Index

UNITED STATES

- The Dow-Jones Industrial Average
- The Dow Jones Transportation Average
- The Dow Jones Utility Average
- Moody's Industrial Average
- Moody's Railroad Stock Average
- Moody's Utility Stock Average
- Standard & Poor's Stock Averages from 90 different industrial categories
- Standard & Poor's 400 Industrial Stocks Average
- Standard & Poor's 20 Transportation Stocks Average
- Standard & Poor's 40 Utility Stocks Average
- Standard & Poor's Financial Stocks Average
- Standard & Poor's Composite 500 Stocks Average
- *The New York Times* Index
- Value Line Average
- Wilshire 5000 Equity Index
- New York Stock Exchange Average
- Center for Research on Security Prices (CRSP) Index
- National Quotation Board Index of Over-the-Counter Stocks
- American Stock Exchange (ASE) Index
- *Barron's* 50 Stock Average
- Russell 2000 Index
- Russell 3000 Index

FOREIGN AND WORLD

- Australian Stock Exchange All-Ordinaries Share Price Index
- CAC (France) Industrial Ordinary Share Index
- Commerzbank (West Germany) Composite Share Index
- FAZ-Atkien (West Germany) Index
- Hang Seng (Hong Kong) Bank Index
- Nikkei–Dow Jones (Japan) Index
- Tokyo Stock Exchange Index
- Swiss Bank Corporation Index
- *The Financial Times* (United Kingdom) Ordinaries Index
- *The Financial Times*–Stock Exchange (FTSE) 100
- Morgan Stanley Capital International World Composite Index

Bond indexes follow:

CANADA

- McLeod Young Weir 40 Bond Index
- McLeod Young Weir Long-Term Bond Index
- McLeod Young Weir Medium-Term Bond Index

UNITED STATES

- Dow Jones 40 Bonds Index
- Salomon Brothers Corporate Bond Index
- Standard & Poor's Municipal Bond Index
- Standard & Poor's U.S. Government Bond Index

The following commodity indexes are available.

- Dow Jones Indices of Spot Commodity Prices
- Dow Jones Futures Commodity Index

The security market indicators listed above are published in daily and financial newspapers (such as *The Globe and Mail, The Financial Post, The Financial Times, Le Devoir,* and *The Vancouver Sun* in Canada, *Barron's* and *The Wall Street Journal* in the United States, *The Financial Times of London* and *Le Monde* abroad) and periodicals (such as *The Bank of Canada Review, The Economist* and the various Moody's publications).

The averages and indexes above are indicators of different things and are useful for different purposes.[1] For example, someone who is searching for a growth industry would be more interested in the Toronto Stock Exchange's indexes of stocks from forty-three subgroup categories than in the TSE 300 Composite Index from all industries. Figure 7-1 illustrates values for all the TSE indexes, which are published with other information monthly in its publication, *The Toronto Stock Exchange Review.*

Market indexes furnish a handy summary of historical price levels in the markets from which they were derived. This type of information has several uses. First, a person who owns several securities in some given market or industry can quickly get an indication of how market movements have affected the market value of his or her portfolio. Curious investors need only check the value of an index of similar securities and determine the percentage change in it in order to get an indication of how their own portfolios fared. This is much faster than checking the prices of each security separately. Second, indexes are useful for historical analysis. By analyzing market indexes

---

1 Stock market indexes have been used as a basis for constructing the so-called index funds. This interesting application is discussed in A. F. Ehrbar, ''Index Funds—An Idea Whose Time Is Coming,'' *Fortune*, June 1976, pp. 145-154; Harvey Shapiro, ''How Do You Really Run One of These Index Funds?'' *Institutional Investor*, February 1976; K. P. Ambachtsheer and J. L. Farrell, ''Can Active Management Add Value?'' *Financial Analysts Journal*, November-December 1975, pp. 39-48.

FIGURE 7-1   TSE Composite 300 stock price index data.

Table for the Month

TSE 300

INDEX	12-Month Earnings $ (000s)	Price/Earnings Ratio	Earnings Adjusted to Index $	Indicated Dividends Year $ (000s)	Yield %	Dividends Adjusted to Index $	INDEX RANGE FOR MONTH High	INDEX RANGE FOR MONTH Low	INDEX RANGE FOR MONTH Close	Net Change	% Change	Relative Strength Against Group	Relative Strength Against Composite	Total Volume	Total Return Index
Integrated Mines	14,687	99+	3.65	167,656	1.98	41.62	2335.17	2098.71	2102.10	-219.75	-9.46	99.27	68.27	12,809,968	2766.24
Metal Mines	20,553-	44.23-	56.67-	15,264	1.31	32.83	2689.21	2428.27	2506.63	-197.68	-7.31	118.37	81.41	5,530,413	3086.48
Uranium and Coal	67,085	10.09	208.20	39,167	5.78	121.42	2434.04	2012.88	2100.76	-296.78	-12.38	99.20	68.23	4,667,230	2791.60
METALS/MINERALS	61,219	99+	12.60	222,086	2.15	45.52	2346.54	2114.71	2117.51	-220.32	-9.42	—	68.77	23,007,611	2757.53
GOLD/SILVER	86,297	63.13	62.19	55,714	1.02	40.04	4122.53	3884.03	3926.33	-130.52	-3.22	—	127.52	18,573,304	5063.20
Integrated Oils	379,036	10.16	261.70	144,010	3.73	99.17	2927.11	2629.17	2658.93	-243.50	-8.39	103.16	86.36	5,728,336	3841.83
Oil/Gas Producers	329,034	15.39	173.63	92,255	1.82	48.63	2959.97	2665.57	2672.23	-212.53	-7.71	103.68	86.79	27,174,305	2269.42
OIL AND GAS	708,071	12.59	204.71	236,265	2.64	68.04	2824.37	2574.21	2577.35	-218.40	-7.81	—	83.71	32,902,641	2834.42
PAPER/FOREST PRODUCTS	121,077	24.35	133.53	53,539	1.81	58.85	3331.05	3100.35	3251.63	+135.74	+4.36	—	105.61	5,062,395	5052.12
Food Processing	63,184	15.40	331.95	24,997	2.56	130.87	5180.71	4618.37	5112.16	+503.55	+10.93	102.98	166.03	695,496	8365.55
Tobacco	133,802	16.07	594.99	176,315	2.24	214.17	9958.23	8049.79	9561.60	+1148.97	+13.66	192.61	310.55	2,870,007	16542.12
Distilleries	480,373	15.04	325.55	48,275	2.43	118.98	5122.73	4633.94	4896.40	+168.11	+3.56	98.63	159.03	83,969,964	6875.71
Breweries	80,588	21.44	188.58	44,766	2.59	104.72	4088.85	3638.90	4043.28	+366.57	+9.97	81.44	131.32	601,981	4822.50
Household Goods	9,041-	N/A	81.07-	8,037	2.32	71.83	3190.12	2739.75	3096.29	+281.48	+10.00	62.37	100.56	2,493,076	6225.86
Autos and Parts	66,075	14.83	367.06	23,914	2.44	132.82	5745.17	5041.13	5443.62	+328.06	+6.41	109.65	176.80	2,681,744	10104.46
Packaging Products	47,235	19.16	366.08	16,606	1.83	128.35	7404.65	6718.60	7014.19	-113.48	-1.59	172.73	227.81	2,174,358	8406.11
CONSUMER PRODUCTS	862,216	16.59	299.22	342,909	2.39	118.64	5103.67	4621.18	4964.14	+289.65	+6.20	—	161.23	95,486,626	3049.42
Steels	173,748	17.12	101.36	97,527	3.27	56.74	1850.25	1721.58	1735.45	-21.71	-1.24	76.78	56.36	3,352,399	4433.28
Metal Fabricators	26,604	18.64	184.58	11,169	2.25	77.41	3588.01	3039.65	3440.58	+402.22	+13.24	152.23	111.74	1,646,418	385.83
Machinery	29,276-	N/A	19.60-	5,347	.77	3.54	487.18	424.54	460.99	+21.79	+4.96	20.39	14.97	5,874,973	8663.00
Transport. Equipment	16,296	16.25	211.02	6,100	2.30	78.86	3470.68	3070.98	3429.10	+368.93	+12.06	151.72	111.37	308,465	3551.10
Electrical/Electronic	230,324	18.57	203.90	51,331	2.52	98.37	3903.58	3564.79	3786.48	+89.09	+2.41	167.53	122.98	8,663,919	5346.94
Cement and Concrete	8,474	52.69	74.09	11,271	1.93	46.94	4022.58	3637.19	3903.93	+84.25	+2.21	172.73	126.79	465,502	4020.85
Chemicals	17,896	25.76	99.59	8,483	1.83	58.62	2599.27	2442.20	2565.54	+104.79	+4.26	113.51	83.32	692,753	4590.68
Business Forms/Equipment	207,152	17.50	130.86	93,080	2.56	48.36	2376.07	2134.06	2290.18	+105.61	+4.83	83.32	74.38	3,248,453	3427.98
INDUSTRIAL PRODUCTS	651,591	20.32	111.22	284,308	2.14	49.44	2328.47	2159.66	2260.00	+54.38	+2.47	—	73.40	24,252,882	5264.20
Developers/Contractors	4,004-	N/A	48.43-	4,146	.94	49.49	5519.52	4580.47	5265.16	+561.35	+11.93	51.98	171.00	3,239,887	16352.30
Property Mgt./Investment	66,529	29.43	367.87	14,889	.76	82.28	10844.44	9711.27	10826.59	+1011.39	+10.30	106.89	351.63	2,748,271	12059.32
REAL ESTATE/CONSTRUCT	62,483	38.39	263.82	19,035	.79	80.01	10203.07	9064.16	10128.15	+970.69	+10.60	—	328.95	5,988,158	5478.30
TRANSPORTATION	40,649	26.59	158.56	13,954	1.29	54.38	4378.67	3978.44	4216.20	+129.19	+3.16	—	136.93	4,082,192	2581.63
Oil Pipelines	54,255	11.65	265.46	29,248	1.62	50.10	3217.78	3039.01	3092.64	+125.14	+4.22	137.37	100.44	635,998	2875.87
Gas Pipelines	215,315	9.28	226.18	140,989	7.05	147.98	2305.60	2056.06	2099.00	-181.33	-7.95	93.23	68.17	11,580,141	3277.98
PIPELINES	269,570	9.76	230.66	170,237	6.46	145.43	2428.23	2220.49	2251.31	-125.85	-5.29	—	73.12	12,216,139	3358.81
Gas Utilities	75,251	10.78	200.28	44,019	5.42	117.02	2192.21	2067.94	2159.04	+1.68	+0.08	76.85	70.12	1,531,162	4844.26
Electrical Utilities	220,342	9.45	377.18	120,518	5.78	206.02	3604.23	3397.24	3564.38	+101.15	+2.92	126.94	115.76	3,718,861	5200.84
Telephone Utilities	1,158,662	9.62	278.69	660,047	5.92	158.72	2731.02	2605.87	2681.04	+41.01	+1.55	402.62	87.07	9,452,219	5053.11
UTILITIES	1,454,254	9.65	290.96	824,584	5.87	164.81	2851.30	2720.16	2807.80	+54.37	+1.57	—	51.19	14,702,242	7047.55
Broadcasting	5,916-	90.99-	53.73-	15,562	1.73	84.59	4890.80	4571.51	4889.43	+29.07	+0.60	72.27	158.80	917,784	11556.54
Cable/Entertainment	211,979	23.50	318.56	76,664	.00	.00	7631.22	7319.70	7486.10	+274.09	+3.80	110.66	243.14	1,897,698	10766.61
Publishing/Printing	248,108	25.65	278.15	92,225	1.44	102.74	7224.49	6243.35	7134.58	+687.37	+10.67	105.46	231.72	4,001,168	10158.50
COMMUNICATIONS	21,857	24.40	277.25	35,391	2.46	166.42	6827.62	6035.67	6764.89	-25.75	-0.38	—	219.71	6,816,650	5137.38
Wholesale Distributors	161,958	16.34	215.58	35,347	1.33	46.85	3874.42	3449.56	3522.57	+179.57	+5.37	50.43	114.41	556,846	12032.65
Food Stores	25,759	33.65	77.49	16,137	1.86	48.50	6258.28	5801.28	6167.93	+141.04	+5.72	158.35	200.32	1,558,887	4653.75
Department Stores	66,021	15.80	481.48	14,189	1.35	35.20	2799.40	2435.00	2607.54	+144.39	+1.93	66.95	84.70	2,594,044	11909.27
Clothing Stores	63,883	27.10	75.40	23,011	1.32	26.97	7878.04	6984.28	7607.54	+237.10	+13.13	52.46	247.08	3,084,115	2905.01
Specialty Stores	29,000	24.36	89.32	7,487	1.05	22.85	2102.04	1788.85	2043.32	+129.87	+6.35	402.62	66.36	1,200,348	17222.68
Lodging, Food, Health	368,377	19.83	196.41	103,963	1.42	55.30	2237.24	2082.77	2175.89	+234.90	+6.44	126.50	509.34	16,716,014	6425.67
MERCHANDISING	—	17.29	273.35	—	—	—	3936.49	3607.02	3894.90	+152.18	+3.33	—	84.70	—	4083.51
Banks	1,905,421	7.96	361.39	746,316	4.91	141.24	4892.86	4360.64	4725.18	+143.52	+5.23	92.79	70.67	20,126,013	8690.11
Trust, Savings, Loan	109,925	15.91	213.46	45,466	2.59	87.96	2924.30	2713.52	2876.64	+124.67	+3.83	201.52	153.47	1,458,717	6722.12
Investment Companies	12,475	52.83	34.39	12,008	1.82	33.07	3436.13	2991.34	3396.20	+196.39	+12.13	12.67	110.30	1,898,439	5249.59
Insurance	57,785	14.53	160.68	15,967	1.90	44.36	1863.91	1653.79	1816.88	+172.48	+7.96	144.84	59.01	9,068,753	3069.73
Financial Management	138,852	9.43	443.43	45,872	1.79	74.85	2396.82	2222.09	2334.73	+175.38	+4.38	77.48	247.08	35,255,674	4399.02
FINANCIAL SERVICES	2,224,959	13.45	—	865,630	4.12	—	4358.37	4121.60	4181.58	+103.48	+2.30	—	76.15	28,251,796	6859.24
MANAGEMENT COS.	853,978	—	—	288,491	2.51	—	—	—	—	-163.78	-3.77	—	135.81	—	4539.68
TSE 300 COMPOSITE	8,012,345	15.15	203.22	3,572,941	2.94	90.51	3134.49	3074.42	3078.89	+31.63	+1.04	—	—	323,314,324	4539.68

Source: *The Toronto Stock Exchange Review*, April 1986, p. 60. The Toronto Stock Exchange, 2 First Canadian Place, Toronto, Ontario.

and other economic indicators, an analyst can detect some consistent relationships between different indexes and sectors of the economy. These types of relationships can be useful. If an index is a dependable leading index, it may be useful for forecasting.

Some people suggest that indexes have other important uses. Some believe, for example, that by charting an index over time it is possible to detect patterns that are repeated at various phases of the market's rise and fall. Then the patterns from this one index can be used to forecast that market's future direction. These charting activities, called *technical analysis,* are discussed in more detail in Chaps. 17 and 18.

7-2 CONSTRUCTION OF INDEXES

Every market index is constructed differently. A well-constructed market index will give an indication of the prices of the entire population under consideration. A poorly constructed index will indicate only what an unrepresentative sample of the population is doing.

In the selection of a market index with which to work or the design of a new index, analysts should consider such factors as sample size, representativeness, weighting, convenient units.

Sample Size   The sample should be a significant fraction of the population studied because larger samples generally give clearer indications about what the underlying population is doing. On the other hand, if the sample is too large, it will be too costly to compile.

Representativeness   The sample should contain heterogeneous elements representing all sections of the population. For example, a sample of securities should not be limited to large firms or firms that are all in the same industry.

Weighting   The various elements in the sample should be assigned weights that correspond to the actual investment opportunities in the population under study. For example, a security's weight in some index might be proportional to the fraction of total market value represented by all the firms' shares outstanding. Or equal weights could be used to represent the probability of selecting any given security with random sampling—this would be like selecting stocks by throwing an unaimed dart. The equal weights could represent the results of a ''no skill'' investment strategy, for instance. The two weighting methods most commonly encountered are the equal or price weighted and the capitalization weighted.

With the former method, the index or average is simply computed as the sum of the prices of the securities in the index divided by an appropriate base number. As a result, equal percentage changes in price of higher-priced stocks have a proportionately greater effect on the index than the lower-priced ones. As illustration, imagine a price-weighted index comprised of two securities only; security A selling for $50 a share, and security B selling for $5 per share. This simple ''index'' has a value of $(50 + 5)/2 = 27.50$ on day one. Assume on day two that the price of security A rises by 10 percent while that of security B is unchanged. The new index value would be $(55 + 5)/$

2 = 30, a 9.1 percent increase. Now suppose instead that on day two the price of security B had risen by 10 percent while that of A had remained unchanged. The index level would have been (50 + 5.50)/2 = 27.75, a mere .9 percent increase.

Capitalization weighted indexes on the other hand use both the price and the number of shares outstanding in the computation. In general, the price of each security is multiplied by the number of shares outstanding, and this resulting *market value* or capitalization is divided by a base period *market value*. Using the example above, suppose that there were 10,000 shares of security A and 100,000 shares of security B outstanding giving each company a market value of $500,000. In this case an equal percentage change in the price of securities A and B would have an identical effect on the index value.

Convenient Units An index should be stated in units that are easy to understand and that can be easily used to answer relevant questions.[2]

7-3 COMPARISON OF STOCK MARKET INDEXES

So many security market indexes exist that it isn't practical to describe each different one. However, it is instructive to examine specific indexes. A useful method is to compare and contrast indexes in pairs to identify positive and negative features. In the next two subsections, you will find two sets of comparisons. In Sec. 7-3.1 one of the "worst" U.S. indexes, the popular and highly publicized Dow Jones Industrial average (DJIA), is contrasted with one of the "best"—the more sophisticated but relatively unheard of Centre for Research on Security Prices (CRSP) Index—in light of the criteria listed in Sec. 7-2.

In Sec. 7-3 the two most widely followed broad-based market indexes in Canada, the Toronto Stock Exchange's 300 Composite Index and the Montreal Exchange's Canadian Market Portfolio Index are compared. Although the two indexes have different features, they both reflect broad market movements relatively carefully, and as well, are highly correlated.[3]

---

2 Other factors should be considered in the design of a sample or an index, but they are beyond the scope of this discussion. The interested reader may find entire courses and books on the subject of experimental design and sampling: H. A. Latane, D. L. Tuttle, and Wm. E. Young, "Market Indices," *Financial Analysts Journal*, September–October 1971, pp. 75–85; J. H. Lorie and M. T. Hamilton, "Stock Market Indices," in *Modern Developments in Investment Management*, 2d ed., James Lorie and Richard Brealey (eds.) (Hinsdale, Ill.: The Dryden Press, 1978), pp. 78–93; P. H. Cootner, "Stock Market Indexes: Fallacies and Illusions," *Commercial and Financial Chronicle*, Sept. 29, 1966 [reprinted in *Modern Developments in Investment Management*, James Lorie and Richard Brealey (eds.), pp. 94–100]; H. Working, "Note on the Correlation of First Differences of Averages in a Random Chain," *Econometrica*, vol. 28, no. 4, October 1960, pp. 916–918; L. Fisher, "Some New Stock Market Indexes," *Journal of Business*, supplementary issue of January 1966, pp. 191–225; P. L. Cheng and M. K. Deets, "Statistical Biases and Security Rates of Return," *Journal of Financial and Quantitative Analysis*, January 1971, pp. 977–994; Barr Rosenberg, "Statistical Analysis of Price Series Obscured by Averaging Measures," *Journal of Financial and Quantitative Analysis*, September 1971, pp. 1083–1094.

3 From January 1983 to September 1985, the TSE 300 Composite Index and the Canadian Market Portfolio Index had a correlation coefficient of .965 indicating an extremely high degree of co-movement during that period. *Source*: The Montreal Exchange, *The Canadian Stock Indices*, February 1986, p. 8.

**7-3.1
Comparison
of the Two
U.S. Indexes**

The CRSP index is sold commercially to businesses. College researchers get substantial discounts, but the CRSP data are still costly. The data are updated only every three months; thus they are never sufficiently current to be useful for current events analysis. The CRSP tape is used primarily by academic researchers who are performing statistical analysis on decades of data. In contrast, the DJIA is published daily by Dow Jones & Company, owner of *The Wall Street Journal* and *Barron's* newspapers — both newspapers discuss the DJIA liberally.

Sample Size   The CRSP index contains every NYSE stock (approximately 1300) so that the sample equals the entire NYSE population. The DJIA is an average of thirty securities listed on the NYSE. Thus, the DJIA samples 2.3 percent of the population.

Representativeness   The DJIA contains only securities of the large, old, blue-chip firms. No small firms and no new firms are in the DJIA. In contrast, the CRSP includes every security listed on the NYSE. The disadvantage of using large samples, such as the CRSP index employs, is the cost. Since computers are now being used to do the clerical work, however, such costs are not as big a problem today as they used to be.

Weighting   The CRSP weights each security equally.[4] Thus, if 1300 securities are listed on the NYSE at a given date, the CRSP assigns each a weight of 1/1300. The equal weights used in the CRSP represent the proportions that would result if a portfolio were selected in a random manner, for example, with an unaimed dart. That is, every security has an equal chance of being selected by an unskilled person.

The DJIA presently uses an arbitrary weighting system. In 1928, when the DJIA was expanded to thirty stocks, the thirty market prices were simply summed up and divided by thirty to obtain the DJIA. Thus, equal weights (of 1/30) were assigned to the thirty securities used in 1928. Over the years, however, as some of the thirty securities underwent stock splits and stock dividends, the weights of 1/30 for each asset became inappropriate. To adjust for these changes, the weights of all thirty shares were increased.

Let us assume, for example, that the first of the thirty securities to be split was split 2 for 1. This split would leave two shares, each worth half as much, so the prices of the twenty-nine original shares plus one of the new smaller shares would be summed up and the total would be divided by 29½ instead of thirty.[5] This weighting system is equivalent to selling the split share and investing the proceeds evenly in all thirty remaining shares.

The adjustment process described in the preceding paragraph was not particularly rational in 1928, but it became more irrational and meaningless as

4 The CRSP also has an index in which each security is weighted by its importance (that is, market value-weighted) in the total NYSE market.

5 Split shares often increase in value, but this is due to retained earnings or growth in earnings and unrelated to the split. The effects of stock splits and stock dividends, analyzed in Chap. 19, are seen to be nil, on average. The Dow Jones Industrial Average is explained in "Revised Dow Jones Industrials to Add IBM and Merck, Delete Chrysler and Esmark," *The Wall Street Journal*, June 28, 1979, p. 5.

some securities in the sample grew more than others. In the 1980s the thirty securities in the average were divided by 1.314 and the DJIA was in the 800 to 1300 range; the average price of the thirty shares was about $65. As a result, the weights used in the DJIA do not relate to any relevant values or market opportunities.

Convenient Units   The DJIA has ranged between 800 and 2400 points in recent years. Dow Jones & Company has explained that each of these points equals about a seven-cent change in the market value of an ''average share of stock.'' The points themselves are void of any intrinsically meaningful economic interpretation.

Unlike the DJIA, the CRSP index contains market prices, percentage changes in the prices, and two different rates of return—one that includes cash dividends and one that omits cash dividends.[6] Since the rate of return is the most important outcome for most investment and since it is the best standard for investment comparisons, the percentages and rates of return are quite convenient.

The TSE 300 Composite Index and the Montreal Exchange Canadian Market Portfolio Index are both computed on a regular basis during the day (the former every fifteen minutes, the latter every three minutes) and are published each day in the financial press.

7-3.2 Comparison of Two Canadian Indexes

Sample Size   The TSE 300 Composite Index is a market value weighted index of 300 stocks that are traded on the Toronto Stock Exchange. There are fourteen major group and forty-three subgroup indexes. As at June 1985, the TSE 300 represented about 20 percent of the quoted market value of all securities listed for trading on the TSE and about 51 percent of the quoted market value for Canadian-based firms.[7]

The Montreal Exchange Canadian Market Portfolio Index is comprised of twenty-five large capitalization stocks listed on the Toronto Stock Exchange, the Montreal Exchange, and the Vancouver Stock Exchange with a total market value, as at December 31, 1985, of over $80 billion representing about 40 percent of the total market value of all listed Canadian securities.[8] The Montreal Exchange also publishes six subindexes, not all of which are contained in the Market Portfolio Index. The two indexes therefore have radically different sample sizes but represent similar amounts of the Canadian equity market.

Representativeness   The TSE 300 Composite Index contains the 300 largest securities, in terms of quoted market value, traded on the TSE. The Canadian

---

6 The file is actually a magnetic computer tape that contains price relatives (*PR*) rather than rates of return (denoted *r*). The relationship between price relatives and rates of return is shown below, where p_t denotes the dollar price at time period *t*.

$$PR = (p_{t+1}/p_t) = (1 + r_t)$$

7 The Toronto Stock Exchange, *1985 Fact Book*, p. 35.

8 The Montreal Exchange, *The Canadian Stock Indices*, February 1986, p. 6.

Market Portfolio Index contains only twenty-five of the most heavily capitalized companies in Canada.

Weighting   The TSE 300 Composite Index weights each security selected by market value i.e., the capitalization method.

To calculate the index value each day the following formula is used:

$$\text{Index value} = \frac{\text{aggregate quoted market value} \times 1,000}{\text{base value}}$$

where:

aggregate quoted market value = current market price of security times the company's total outstanding preferred or common shares, not including control blocks of 20% or more.

Base value = aggregate quoted market value for 1975, set at 100.

The TSE 300 Composite Index is calculated and published every fifteen minutes during the trading day. The TSE also computes and publishes total return indexes that reflect absolute index changes *plus* reinvestment of dividends. These are computed once a day. The base period was set at 1,000 as of December 31, 1986.

The index is comprised of 300 securities selected according to a number of criteria. To be eligible for inclusion,[9] the underlying company must be incorporated in Canada, or be substantially Canadian owned, must have a quoted market value of at least $3,000,000, not including control blocks of 20 percent or more, must have traded at least 25,000 shares for a value of $1,000,000 in aggregate transactions on all Canadian stock exchanges in the previous year, and must have been continuously listed on the TSE for twelve consecutive months. In addition, the stock must have a three-year average quoted market value of at least $3,000,000. The average quoted market value is computed as the trade-weighted average price of the stock for each of the three preceding twelve-month periods multiplied by its float outstanding at the end of each of the periods. The trade-weighted average price is the total value traded for the twelve-month period divided by the total volume of shares traded for the same period. The stocks that otherwise meet the criteria, but are not in the top 300, form a pool from which replacements are selected.

From the list of eligible securities, the 300 with the largest quoted-market value over the last three years are included, regardless of industry group. If a stock falls lower than 325th in the quoted market value rankings at the time of the annual qualifying calculations then it is replaced by the stock that is highest in rankings in the unused pool. Similarly, a stock not included in the index that rises above 275 in the eligible pool replaces the stock that has fallen furthest below the 300 level.

---

9 *Source*: The Toronto Futures Exchange, *What is the TSE Composite Index?* undated brochure, pp. 2–4.

The Canadian Market Portfolio Index, on the other hand, is an equally weighted or price-weighted arithmetic average index. Thus the index assigns a weight of 1/25 to each security in the index. Accordingly, in contrast to the TSE index, changes in price of higher-priced securities have a greater proportionate effect on the index than equal percentage price changes of lower-priced securities.

The index is calculated as the sum of the security prices that comprise the index divided by the sum of the stock prices on the base day. The result is multiplied by 1,000. More specifically:

$$I_t = I_o \times \frac{\left(\sum_{i=1}^{n} P_{it}\right)}{\left(\sum_{i=1}^{n} P_{io}\right)}$$

where:
I_t = index value on day t
I_o = index value on day o
P_{it} = price of stock i on day t
P_{io} = price of stock i on day o, the base day
n = number of stocks in index = 25

Convenient Units   Both indexes are expressed in index points and can be easily related to their base periods. Unlike the Montreal Exchange, The TSE also publishes a total return index that includes cash dividends. Since the rate of return is the most important outcome for most investments, and since it is the best standard for investment comparisons, the percentage and rates of return are quite convenient.

The Canadian Market Portfolio Index was changed from an equally weighted geometric average with base of 100 (as of January 4, 1983), to its current structure on March 3, 1986. By changing the base to 1000, the Montreal Exchange thus placed the Canadian Market Portfolio Index on a comparable scale basis to that of the TSE 300 Composite Index and the Dow-Jones Industrial Average. Furthermore, the arithmetic averaging formula is used in the computation of most of the North American indexes including the TSE 300, the S&P 500, and the NYSE Composite Index.

7-4 MAINTENANCE PROBLEMS WITH SECURITY MARKET INDEXES

After a security market index is constructed, situations periodically arise that require its revision. The three main problems that make index revision necessary are (1) stock splits, (2) a change in the number of stocks in the sampled list, and (3) substitutions to replace unsatisfactory securities. The way these three problems affect the DJIA, the CRSP index and the TSE 300 Composite Index are considered below.

Stock Splits The strange way that stock splits are reflected in the divisor of the DJIA was explained above in the section entitled ''Weighting.'' As a result of the Dow Jones procedure, the relative importance of stocks that split decreases and the importance of nonsplit stocks increases in the computation of the DJIA. There is no logic behind these shifts in the relative weights of the stocks in the DJIA.[10]

The CRSP index, on the other hand, handles stock splits more logically. This index is constructed from prices and returns that are adjusted to nullify any changes in the unit of account (namely, stock dividends or splits). Then, each different security in the index is assigned either an equal weight or a market value weight that is unaffected by stock splits.

Stock splits have no effect per se on the TSE index calculation. After a stock split the increased number of shares outstanding, when multiplied by the reduced share price, should, ceteris paribus, leave the aggregate market value of the security unchanged and the index unaffected.

Change in Sample Size When the DJIA was first constructed in 1884, it contained twelve stocks. The sample size was increased to twenty stocks in 1916. The present sample size of thirty stocks was adopted in 1928. As for the CRSP index, selection of a sample size has never been a problem because the entire population has been used to compute the index since its inception.

The Toronto Stock Exchange has changed the size and the composition of its major index a number of times. The first index introduced in 1934 contained twenty stocks in the industrial index. In 1963 the exchange adopted the current system of capitalization weightings and set the sample size at 108. The sample size had reached 202 by 1968. In 1977, the TSE Composite 300 Index was introduced. The sample size has not been changed since then.

Substitutions Substitutions can be a recurrent and troublesome problem for an index computed from a small sample—like the DJIA. There have been many substitutions in the DJIA over the decades. One of the more interesting substitutions involved IBM stock. IBM was added to the DJIA in 1932 and then deleted in 1939 in order to make room for American Telephone and Telegraph (AT&T). The logic behind this substitution was too tortured to understand in hindsight.[11] In 1979 IBM was added back into the DJIA. More specificially, Chrysler and Esmark were deleted and replaced by IBM and Merck & Co. It was felt that the two new stocks were more ''blue-chip'' than the two that were eliminated.

Substitutions in the CRSP are more logical and of only minor importance because of the small weight given to each individual stock. Stocks are added

---

10 H. L. Butler and J. D. Allen, ''Dow Jones Industrial Average Re-Examined,'' *Financial Analysts Journal*, November–December 1979, pp. 23–32. Butler and Allen discuss the effect of stock splits and substitutions on the DJIA. Andrew T. Rudd examines the DJIA statistically in ''The Revised Dow Jones Industrial Average,'' *Financial Analysts Journal*, November–December 1979, pp. 57–63.

11 The sample used in the DJIA is not only small, it doesn't even contain all industrial stocks, as the DJIA title implies it should. More specifically, the public utility stock of AT&T in the DJIA is obviously not an industrial stock. It appears that a substitution for AT&T is in order.

to or deleted from the CRSP index only when they are listed or delisted from the NYSE.

The TSE formula is designed to immunize the index from substitutions. When a new stock is added to the TSE list and/or an existing stock removed, the aggregate market value of that stock is added to or deleted from the aggregate market value of all of the stocks in the index. The index level, however is, ceteris paribus, unaffected by the substitutions. The following formula is employed to adjust the numeraire or base aggregate market value:

$$B = \frac{A \times (C + D)}{C}$$

where:

B = base aggregate market value
A = old average base aggregate market value
C = unadjusted current aggregate market value
D = current aggregate market value of the capital to be added or withdrawn
$C + D$ = adjusted current aggregate market value

7-5 RATES OF RETURN ON MARKET INDEXES

Market indexes are used to answer many different investment questions. One of the most common questions in the minds of potential investors is "What kind of return can I earn if I invest in common stocks?" The answer to this question is shown in Table 7-1.

Table 7-1 shows the annual rate of return from holding Canadian stocks over every year from 1960 to 1983. Three sources are shown: the Ibbotson/Carr/Robinson study, which utilized Morgan Stanley Capital International Perspective data, the Hatch/White monograph, which used a large sample of Toronto Stock Exchange, Montreal Exchange and Vancouver Stock Exchange data, and the Boyle/Panjer/Sharpe annual report, which used the Statistics Canada CANSIM data base using the TSE industrial Index and the TSE 300 Composite Index.

These rates of return show what an investor who reinvested all cash dividends and paid no income taxes or brokerage commissions would have earned if he or she neither suffered unusually bad luck nor enjoyed unusually good luck. The returns in Table 7-1 are sometimes referred to as the returns from a *naive buy-and-hold strategy*. That is, the returns in Table 7-1 are what might have been earned by a naive investor who selected a diversified portfolio of Canadian stocks randomly and then simply held onto them while reinvesting all the cash dividends in the portfolio.

Table 7-1 is useful in answering the question often asked by new investors, "What can I expect if I invest in a portfolio of diversified common stocks?" But no index can answer every question an investor might ask. For instance, Table 7-1 gives only vague clues about what to expect from an investment in only one particular stock instead of a diversified portfolio. (Such an undiversified investment would probably yield more variability than the returns from the diversified "portfolio" shown in Table 7-1.) Various different market indexes exist with which a wide variety of investor questions can be answered.

TABLE 7-1
CANADIAN COMMON STOCKS—ANNUAL RATES OF RETURN, 1960–1983

YEAR	IBBOTSON-CARR-ROBINSON	HATCH-WHITE	BOYLE-PANJER-SHARPE
1960	−1.16	1.58	1.78
1961	39.03	33.93	32.75
1962	−6.84	−7.11	−7.09
1963	14.39	15.07	15.60
1964	24.36	24.59	25.43
1965	4.81	6.61	6.68
1966	−9.24	−6.3	−7.07
1967	7.18	20.26	18.09
1968	26.61	22.45	22.45
1969	3.21	−1.73	−0.81
1970	15.81	−4.63	−3.57
1971	14.13	8.51	8.01
1972	33.12	27.02	27.38
1973	−3.11	−2.67	−0.27
1974	−26.52	−27.23	−25.93
1975	15.07	22.61	18.48
1976	9.71	11.51	11.02
1977	−1.37	14.01	10.71
1978	20.55	29.24	29.72
1979	52.26	51.48	44.77
1980	22.00	27.86	30.13
1981	N/A	−8.18	−10.25
1982	N/A	4.15	5.54
1983	N/A	37.38	35.49

Sources: Roger G. Ibbotson, Richard C. Carr, and Anthony W. Robinson, "International Equity and Bond Returns", *Financial Analysts Journal*, July–August 1982, p. 69.

James E. Hatch and Robert W. White, "Canadian Stocks, Bonds, Bills and Inflation: 1950–1983," The Financial Analysts Research Foundation, Monograph 19, 1985, p. 58.

Phelim P. Boyle, Harry H. Panjer, and Keith P. Sharp, "Report On Canadian Economic Statistics 1924–1986," Canadian Institute of Actuaries, June 1987, p. 6.

7-5.1 Comparing Indexes from Different Markets

Table 7-2 shows the correlation coefficients between investment returns from several different investment assets in Canada. Table 7-2 illustrates that the stock market returns are not so highly correlated with the returns from other assets. Investment managers need to know how the price of each assets category reacts to the same basic economic forces if they are going to manage their investments well.

Table 7-3 contains summary statistics calculated from the different investment assets for which correlation coefficients were shown in Table 7-2. The geometric mean rate of return, the arithmetic average rate of return, and the standard deviations of the year-to-year rates of return for each different asset

TABLE 7-2   CORRELATIONS AMONG STOCK RETURNS AND OTHER ASSET RETURNS, 1950–1983

ASSET	TREASURY BILLS	LONG CANADA BONDS	INDUSTRIAL BONDS	CANADIAN EQUITIES	U.S. EQUITIES
Treasury bills	1.0000	0.2341	0.2405	0.0306	−0.0139
Long Canada bonds	0.2341	1.0000	0.8514	0.2787	0.2605
Industrial bonds	0.2405	0.8514	1.0000	0.3228	0.3055
Canadian equities	0.0306	0.2787	0.3228	1.0000	0.7464
U.S. equities	−0.0139	0.2605	0.3055	0.7464	1.000

Source: James E. Hatch and Robert W. White, "Canadian Stocks, Bonds, Bills and Inflation: 1950–1983," The Financial Analysts Research Foundation, Monograph 19, 1985, pp. 102–103.

TABLE 7-3   CANADIAN AND U.S. CAPITAL MARKET TOTAL ANNUAL RETURNS AND INFLATION RATES, 1950–1983

	COMPOUND RETURN	ARITHMETIC RETURN	STANDARD DEVIATION
Treasury bills	5.47	5.55	4.18
Long government bonds	4.14	4.52	9.66
Industrial bonds	5.23	5.6	9.45
Canadian equities	11.46	12.95	18.34
Canadian inflation rate	4.76	4.83	3.97
U.S. equities	11.96	13.41	18.12
U.S. inflation rate	4.75	4.87	5.03

Source: James E. Hatch and Robert W. White, "Canadian Stocks, Bonds, Bills and Inflation: 1950–1983," The Financial Analysts Research Foundation, Monograph 19, 1985, p. 8.

are in Table 7-3.[12] The geometric mean and the arithmetic mean are two similar, but slightly different, ways of calculating the average rate of return. The standard deviation is a statistic that measures the variability of returns (or the range of returns) over which the investment experienced fluctuations—riskier investments have larger standard deviations of returns.

By comparing the summary statistics in Table 7-3 with the correlation coefficients between the different indexes shown in Table 7-2, an inexperienced investor can gain insights into different investment possibilities that would take a lifetime of practical experience to accumulate. However, care must be taken in interpreting such statistics.

7-6   CHAPTER SUMMARY AND CONCLUSIONS

There are two major categories of security market indicators—the average, and the more scientific index. Market indexes (like the TSE 300 Composite

12 The geometric mean rate of return is defined and discussed in Mathematical App. F at the back of this book.

Index and the CRSP index) are more sophisticated than market averages (like the DJIA) for three main reasons: (1) indexes have base years to facilitate comparisons, (2) indexes can employ some meaningful weighting system if it is appropriate, and (3) indexes are usually measured in more useful units of measurement than are averages.

Dozens of different security market averages and indexes are tabulated and published worldwide every day. Stock market indicators for each different market and for various categories of stocks within each market, bond market indicators for different categories of bonds, commodity indexes for different categories of commodities (such as grains, metals, and meats) and for each commodity exchange, and foreign exchange indexes are all prepared daily. Numerous economic indexes, such as the consumer price index, which is used to measure inflation, are also used by businesspeople. Each different index is supposed to give a valid indication of the level of the prices of some important group of market assets. Each index should be scrutinized before using it for exacting purposes, however, because some are biased and unrepresentative.

A well-constructed index uses a statistically significant sample of the population being surveyed; this sample is selected so that it provides a representative indication of the entire population being studied. A good index also employs a weighting system founded on economic logic—such as an equally weighted securities index—to show how the average random investor should do without any good or bad luck. Also, it is always better to use an index that is reported in convenient units rather than in numbers that don't lend themselves to making meaningful comparisons.

After a good index is selected, it must still be watched to ensure that it is properly maintained. Securities markets indexes must adjust properly for stock dividends and splits. Changes and substitutions in the list of assets being sampled should be made judiciously too.

In the final analysis, it is fairly easy to construct a satisfactory stock market index for Canada. To a large extent the prices of all common stocks are simultaneously and systematically affected by the basic economic forces so that they all move through the alternating bull (that is, appreciating price trend) and bear (namely, price decline) market periods together. Thus, a price-weighted index, like the Canadian Market Portfolio Index, is highly positively correlated with the capitalization-weighted TSE 300 Composite Index. Different markets, such as the commodity and bond markets, however, require the selection of separate market indexes because these markets "march to a different drummer."

QUESTIONS

1. What is the difference between a stock market average and a stock market index?
2. Compare and contrast the two following weighting systems frequently used in the construction of stock market indexes: (1) Equal weights —

every stock in the index is assigned an equal weight or proportion; (2) Value-weighted — every stock is assigned a weight that corresponds to its total market value stated as a proportion relative to the aggregate market value of all securities in the market in which it is traded.

3. What tasks are stock market indicators used for?
4. What considerations are relevant when either constructing a new market indicator or selecting an existing one to use? Explain.
5. What are the major criticisms made against the popular Dow Jones Industrial Average?
6. How are the so-called value-weighted weights calculated when constructing a stock market index? What is the value weighting system of weights supposed to represent?
7. Consider the three following NYSE stock market indicators:
   a. CRSP Value Weighted Index
   b. CRSP Equally Weighted Index
   c. DJIA
   Which of these three NYSE market indicators is best? Explain why.
8. Make a list of the twenty-five stocks that are used in the construction of the Canadian Market Portfolio Index. Of what segment of stocks traded in Canada do you think this index is representative? Explain.

SELECTED REFERENCES

Fabozzi, Frank J., and Gregory M. Kipnis (eds.) *Stock Index Futures*. Homewood, Ill.: Dow Jones–Irwin, 1984. Chapter 5, entitled "Stock Market Indicators," explains details about stock market index construction.

Hatch, James E., and Robert W. White. *Canadian Stocks, Bills, and Inflation: 1950–1983.* Charlottesville, Va.: The Financial Analysts Research Foundation, 1985. This empirical study provides data on the annual and multi-period, nominal, and real returns from common stocks, federal, provincial, and municipal bonds, industrial bonds, and Treasury bills. The easy-to-read monograph contains many tables of informative data from the 1950 to 1983 sample period and various risk factors.

Ibbotson Associates. *Stocks, Bonds, Bills, and Inflation: 1985 Yearbook.* Chicago, 1985. This 151-page book updates the similar book by Ibbotson and Sinquefield that is also in this reference section.

Ibbotson, Roger G., and Rex A. Sinquefield. *Stocks, Bonds, Bills and Inflation: The Past and the Future.* Charlottesville, Va: Financial Analysts Research Foundation, 1982. This small book presents an easy-to-read explanation of how different security market and economic indicators are constructed, with the aid of a little first-year college algebra. Graphs and tables of the summary statistics yield themselves to comparisons that will be insightful to astute investors.

Teweles, Richard J., and Edward S. Bradley. *The Stock Market.* 4th ed. New York: Wiley, 1982. Chapter 19 is an easy-to-read, nonmathematical discussion of stock market averages and indexes. The chapter ends by explaining how the Dow theory (about charting stock prices in hopes of finding revealing patterns) uses stock market averages.

INTRODUCTION TO VALUATION AND RISK-RETURN THEORY

PART 2

Part 2 introduces the basic valuation model and relates it to the various investment risks. The intrinsic economic value of a market asset is the present value of the future income.

$$\text{Present value} = \sum_{t-1}^{T} \frac{\text{income}_t}{(1 + k)_t}$$

where k is the appropriate risk-adjusted rate for the asset. CHAPTER 8—Price = ? = Value explains the basic principles of valuation that are used to discern underpriced and overpriced securities.

CHAPTER 9—Total Risk and Its Factors defines total risk quantitatively and discusses the various risk factors that contribute to an asset's total risk.

CHAPTER 10—The Characteristic Line and The Capital Asset Model shows how to statistically partition an asset's total risk from all factors into two mutually exclusive portions called diversifiable (or unsystematic) risk and undiversifiable (or systematic) risk and traces the asset pricing implications of this analysis.

The three chapters that make up Part 2 introduce fundamentally important valuation and risk concepts that are used throughout the later chapters.

CHAPTER 8

Price = ? = Value

Stock prices fluctuate endlessly. Figure 10-1 on page 215 illustrates the fluctuations in stock prices. All the chapters that follow this one are addressed either directly or indirectly to answering the question, "What determines security prices?" To answer this question it will be necessary to study abstract concepts about price, value, return, and risk. Before discussing the meanings and implications of these words, it may be best to consider the essence of the economic process that determines security prices.

8-1 COMPARING PRICE WITH VALUE

A security's *value* determines its price. But not all the 3.2 million people in Canada who own securities know that fact; the ones who don't are the unfortunate investors who are most likely to be "ripped off." Professional and semiprofessional investors follow the more scientific procedure of forming estimates of a security's value (which are sometimes called intrinsic-value estimates, present value estimates, or economic value estimates) before they make a decision to buy or sell a security. To see how these value estimates determine security prices, consider the buy-sell decision rules summarized in Box 8-1.

The buy-sell decision rules in Box 8-1 are simple to understand, but they are difficult to implement because it is hard to obtain good estimates of an asset's true economic value. Some security analysts earn annual salaries in excess of $100,000 per year for merely providing and explaining their value estimates for a few securities. For example, an expert integrated mines analyst might be responsible for only the following four stocks—Cominco, Falconbridge, Inco, and Noranda. But if this analyst can correctly predict the direction in which the prices of these four stocks move over an extended period of time, he or she will develop a "track record" for making good predictions and will develop a "following of investors." As a result, some stock brokerage can profit from paying this analyst a six-figure annual salary because the expert's following will generate trading commissions for the brokerage firm in excess of the high salary. In addition, the analyst can earn some nice trading profits for his or her own account. This example suggests the economic worth of being able to prepare good value estimates for a security.

Box 8-1
The Buy-Sell
Decision
Rules
for Investors

The Buy Rule If a security's price is below its value, it is underpriced and should be bought and held in order to reap capital gains in the future. More succinctly, if the actual market price of security i at the tth instant in time is p_{it} and its intrinsic economic value is v_{it}, then the buy rule is stated as follows:

   If $(p_{it} < v_{it})$, buy

The Sell Rule If the ith security's actual market price at time t is above the security's true value estimated at the same time, then sell the security to avoid losses when its price falls down to the level of its value.

   If $(p_{it} > v_{it})$, sell

The Don't Trade Rule If the ith asset's market price equals its economic value, then the price is in equilibrium and is not expected to change. That is, the asset is correctly priced and there is no profit to be made from buying or selling it.

   If $(p_{it} = v_{it})$, don't trade

8-2 THE BASIC VALUATION MODEL

The chapters that follow explain how to estimate security values in order to detect overpriced and underpriced securities. The specific valuation process used to find the value of the different kinds of securities varies with the type of security. But, the valuation process outlined in Box 8-2 is the basic economic mechanism employed to value all securities.

Box 8-2
The Present
Value Model

The present value of a market asset is the discounted present value of the income the investor may expect to receive from the asset.

$$\text{Present value} = \frac{\text{Income}_1}{(1 + i)^1} + \frac{\text{Income}_2}{(1 + i)^2} + \frac{\text{Income}_3}{(1 + i)^3} + \ldots \quad (8\text{-}1)$$

The equation gives the present value of a stream of income returns expected to start at time $t = 1$. These future dollar returns are discounted at discount rate i (the discount rate is like a risk-adjusted interest rate).

The static present value model shown in Box 8-2 illustrates how a security's value (or present value, economic value, or intrinsic value) is calculated. After the security's present value is determined, a buy-sell investment decision can be made by comparing the security's price to its intrinsic value, as suggested in Box 8-1.

8-3   THE DYNAMICS OF VALUATION AND INVESTMENT

In practice, the valuation process is more complex than suggested in Boxes 8-1 and 8-2. One problem encountered in practice involves the amount of confidence to give the security analyst's value estimate. A security analyst's value estimate is rarely in the form of a single specific price estimate. More often, the estimate is given with a *margin for error*. For example, an expert analyst might estimate that XYZ stock is worth $30 per share plus or minus a $5 per share margin for error. This means the analyst estimates the equity share's value to be within the $25 to $35 range. Thus, the buy-sell rules shown in Box 8-1 are a bit oversimplified.

Another practical problem results from the fact that a security's risk and return, and thus also its value, will probably change with the passage of time. For example, selling a security puts downward pressure on its market price (if market supply exceeds market demand at the moment of the sale), and buying a security may bid up its price (if the market's supply-for-sale of the security does not increase simultaneously). As a result of any change in its price level, the security's expected future capital gains or losses must be revised, and this affects its estimated future income.

Also, the security's risk may change. The risk of a stock or bond would increase, for example, if the issuing corporation borrowed funds (and thereby increased the ratio of the firm's debt to its total assets) in order to undertake a new venture that involved possible losses. Any increase in risk raises the risk-adjusted discount rate in the present value formula and thus lowers the security's value (as illustrated in Box 8-2). The step-by-step reaction of a vigilant investor to the increased riskiness of the investment described above is summarized below.

1. Estimate both the estimated dollar income from the security if you should buy it and the appropriate risk-adjusted discount rate to be used in the present value formula shown in Box 8-2. (The risk-return relationship is illustrated in Fig. 9-3 on page 183.)
2. Estimate the security's present value using the discount rate and income forecast obtained from step 1.
3. Use the three buy-sell decision rules in Box 8-1 to decide whether to buy, sell, or do neither.
4. See if the market price changes as a result of buy and sell orders from you and other investors. If changes occur, return to step 1 and repeat the process to determine if further action is advisable.

Security analysts must continually reevaluate the securities they are assigned to follow. Thus, the valuation process is more realistically represented by the dynamic valuation process illustrated in Fig. 8-1. The flow chart

FIGURE 8-1   Flow chart of the continuous valuation process.

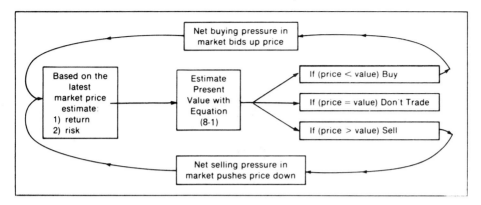

in Fig. 8-1 is a never-ending loop of reconsidering the value, comparing the price and the value, and then reconsidering the buy-sell decision based on the latest estimates. Every time a new piece of information about a security is obtained, that security's value may change. Thus, values fluctuate continuously. And the buying and selling pressures in the marketplace keep market prices in continuous motion as they pursue the *continuously changing values*. This is what makes being a security analyst a fast, exciting, and dangerous job.

8-4   COOTNER'S PRICE-VALUE INTERACTION MODEL

In order to explain how stock prices would fluctuate in a market where price-value comparisons were continuously being made, Paul Cootner suggested that security prices can be viewed as a series of constrained random fluctuations around their true intrinsic value.[1] Cootner hypothesizes the existence of two groups of investors. The first group can be referred to as the "naive investors," those who have access only to the public news media for their information. They might be amateur analysts, or people who select stocks by throwing unaimed darts. They might be speculators, or people who base their investment decisions upon their interpretations of the public news and their financial circumstances. Naive investors will recognize few, if any, divergences from intrinsic values. They are more likely to invest on the basis of hot tips when they have excess liquidity and at other times when the investment may or may not be wise.

The second group of investors are the "professional investors," those who have the resources to discover news and develop estimates of intrinsic value before the naive investors even get the news. As a result, the professionals will recognize significant deviations from intrinsic value and initiate trading that tends to align the market price with the intrinsic value.

---

1 P. H. Cootner, "Stock Prices: Random versus Systematic Changes," *Industrial Management Review*, Spring 1962, vol. 3, no. 2, pp. 24–45.

FIGURE 8-2 Hypothetical charts of random stock price fluctuations within fixed limits: (a) no change in intrinsic value; (b) intrinsic value changes at periods t and $t + 1$.

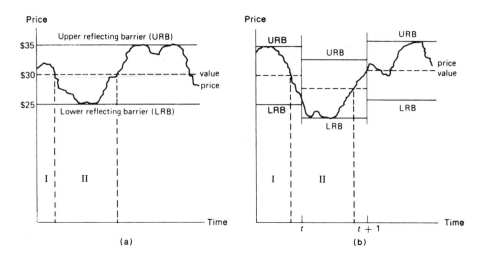

(a)   (b)

Figure 8-2 illustrates how security prices might fluctuate over time in the hypothetical market Cootner describes. The dashed lines represent the professional investors' *consensus value estimate*. Note that the intrinsic value of the security illustrated in Fig. 8-2*b* changes at times t and $t + 1$, while the value remains unchanged at $30 in Fig. 8-2*a*. Since trading by naive investors is not necessarily based on correct interpretation of the latest news, these investors may ineptly buy securities whose market prices are above their intrinsic values. Such naive buying is illustrated in Fig. 8-2*a* and 8-2*b* by the price fluctuating above the value in phase I. After this initial overoptimistic buying, naive investors may ineptly sell the stock when its price is below its value, as shown in phase II of Fig. 8-2*a* and 8-2*b*. Unprofitable speculative trades by naive investors and trades made to obtain needed liquidity (for example, to pay for an emergency) are responsible for the aimless price fluctuations that can cause prices to diverge from values.

When a security's price does differ significantly from its true intrinsic value, the professional investors find it profitable to correct this disequilibrium. Small deviations are not profitable to correct because the profits are not sufficient to pay for the brokerage commissions. But when prices are significantly out of line, the professionals bid up low prices or liquidate overpriced securities. In effect, the professionals erect "reflecting barriers" around the true intrinsic value.[2] These reflecting barriers are represented by the solid lines above and below the intrinsic value lines in Fig. 8-2. The upper reflecting barrier is denoted URB and the lower reflecting barrier is labelled

2 William Feller, *An Introduction to Probability Theory and Its Applications*, 3d ed., vol. 1 (New York: Wiley, 1968), pp. 436–438. These pages provide a discussion of a random walk with reflecting barriers.

LRB. Prices will fluctuate freely within the reflecting barriers. But when prices reach these barriers, the professionals' action will cause prices to move toward their intrinsic value. Such a market has been called an intrinsic-value random-walk market.[3]

8-5   EQUILIBRIUM PRICES FLUCTUATE EFFICIENTLY

Economists who have studied the movements of security prices and considered Paul Cootner's theory have accepted and modified it in varying degrees. Paul Samuelson, for example, has theorized about how Cootner's model would perform if securities markets were what economists call "perfectly competitive."

Nobel Prize–winning economist Paul Samuelson has extended Cootner's model by defining *perfectly efficient prices* to be market prices that reflect all information.[4] Samuelson suggests that a security with perfectly efficient prices would be in "continuous equilibrium." This continuous equilibrium will not be static through time, however. Every time a new piece of news is released, the security's intrinsic value will change and the security's market price will adjust toward the new value. It is the speed of this price adjustment process that gauges the efficiency of a price. A perfectly efficient security's price is in a "continuous equilibrium" such that the intrinsic value of the security vibrates randomly and the market *price equals the fluctuating intrinsic value* at every instant in time. If any disequilibrium (of even a temporary nature) exists, then the security's price is less than perfectly efficient.[5] Of course, actual market prices are not perfectly efficient because different security analysts typically assign different value estimates to any given security.

**8-5.1
Samuelson's
Continuous
Equilibrium**

Actual market prices can pursue only a *consensus estimate* of any given security's intrinsic value, since security analysts' value estimates differ. If most security analysts' value estimates happen to be similar at a point in time, then the consensus value estimate may vary only within a small range. In this case, the security's price will be almost perfectly efficient as it fluctuates in a narrow range around its changing equilibrium economic value, as shown in Fig. 8-3a. In Fig. 8-3 a security's intrinsic value falls at time period $t + n$ when some bad news about the security emerges.

In contrast to the situation illustrated in Fig. 8-3a, consider Fig. 8-3b, which represents another security with an identical intrinsic value at every point in time. However, this second security of equal value "fell in disfavour" (a Bay Street bit of jargon which means that few investors were interested in buying it), and large divergences between the security's price and its value occurred. As shown in Fig. 8-3b, the second security's price fluctuated far below its

3 Eugene Fama, "The Behavior of Stock Market Prices," *Journal of Business*, January 1955, p. 36.

4 Paul Samuelson, "Proof That Properly Discounted Present Values of Assets Vibrate Randomly," *The Bell Journal of Economics and Management Science*, Autumn 1973, pp. 369–374.

5 Eugene Fama, "Efficient Capital Markets: A Review of Theory and Empirical Work," *Journal of Finance*, May 1970, pp. 383–417; Eugene Fama, "The Behavior of Stock Market Prices," *Journal of Business*, January 1965, pp. 34–105.

FIGURE 8-3   More and less efficient security prices: (a) efficient price fluctuations: (b) weakly efficient price fluctuations.

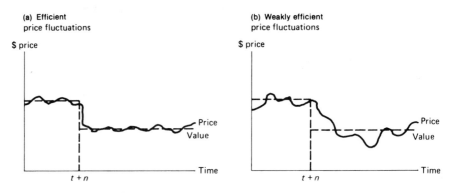

value (that is, inefficient price movements occurred) as a result of insufficient interest from investors who would continuously estimate the security's value, compare value and price, and make buy-sell decisions rapidly.

8-5.2 The Random-Walk Theory

For years, security analysts and financial economists have studied and discussed what is sometimes called the *random-walk theory* of security prices. According to the random-walk theory, a security's market price should fluctuate randomly around its intrinsic value because (1) the new information arrives at random intervals throughout every day, (2) this new information causes security analysts to reestimate the values of the securities affected by the new information, and (3) market trading based on the buy-sell rules shown in Box 8-1 causes security prices to fluctuate randomly as they pursue constantly changing intrinsic values.

The random-walk theory of stock prices is like Paul Cootner's model, illustrated in Fig. 8-2, without the reflecting barriers.[6] Or, in a more idealistic model, the prices of securities in a random-walk market might fluctuate in continuous equilibrium if investors were continuously informed and were in uniform agreement (an admittedly heroic assumption) about the securities' intrinsic values. In any event, the valuation process underlying both Cootner's model and the random-walk model is summarized by the continuous flow chart shown in Fig. 8-1.

Detailed statistical studies of security prices discussed in later chapters (see, for example, Chap. 18) reveal that security price changes do tend to fluctuate randomly, as described in the models above.[7] These statistical findings attest to the realism of the market mechanism illustrated above in Figs. 8-2 and 8-3. Readers who are interested in learning more about how

[6] Paul Cootner (ed.), *The Random Character of Stock Market Prices* (Cambridge, Mass.: M.I.T., 1964).

[7] Eugene Fama, Harry Roberts, and others have given the name *efficient markets* to security markets in which the prices fluctuate randomly around their intrinsic values in a narrow range. Eugene Fama, op. cit.

security analysts prepare their estimates of a security's intrinsic value can read Chaps. 9 through 18. Those chapters discuss the determination of the intrinsic value estimates, which in turn determines the market prices of bonds, common stocks, and preferred stocks.

8-6 CHAPTER SUMMARY

The present value model shown in Box 8-2 provides the intrinsic value estimates that should be used as the basis for rational, well-informed, wealth-maximizing investment decisions. The buy-sell investment decision rules presented in Box 8-1 are simple to use after the estimate of a security's intrinsic value is obtained. The intrinsic value estimates and the buy-sell decisions must be used more than once for each security, however. Securities' intrinsic values change continuously because every time a piece of new information becomes available it may cause security analysts to change their assessment of the intrinsic value of one or more securities. It is these changes in the intrinsic value estimates that motivate investors to buy and bid up or sell and push down the ever-changing securities prices. The continuous flow chart shown in Fig. 8-1 illustrates the never-ending series of investment decisions that keep security analysts busy.

QUESTIONS

1. Look up the dictionary definitions of the words "value" and "price." Compare and contrast these two words in a short essay.
2. Why must a security analyst have estimates of a security's risk and return before preparing estimates of the security's value? *Hint*: What determines the value of the appropriate discount rate in the present value model?
3. Should the value of a security be stable or should it fluctuate? What should change the value of a security?
4. Define the term "efficient price." Explain it.
5. Suppose the chairperson of the board of Cadillac Fairview (CF) appeared on the late night news of every television station in Canada tonight and announced that CF had discovered an oil well on every parking lot it owned around the world. Assuming the executive would not distort the truth, how would the announcement affect the market price of CF stock? Would the price of CF move upward in a trend as more and more investors learned of the CF discovery each day and then bid the stock's price up day after day as they reached their decisions to buy the stock after a learning lag? Explain.
6. Investor naivete is a source of inefficient price movements (as explained in Paul Cootner's model of market price determination). Briefly discuss five other factors that probably cause prices to differ from values.
7. There are tens of thousands of part-time amateur investors in Canada. However, there are only a few thousand members of the Financial Analysts Federation (FAF); these constitute most of the full-time professional

investment managers. Given that there are tens of thousands of amateur investors and, in contrast, only a few thousand professional investors, which group do you think dominates the market? That is, do you think that security prices fluctuate randomly because there are mostly part-time amateur investors in the market? How can a small number of professional investors have a significant impact on security prices?

SELECTED REFERENCES

Brealey, Richard A. *An Introduction to Risk and Return from Common Stocks*. 2d ed. Cambridge, Mass: M.I.T., 1983. Chapter 1 of this easy-to-read book is entitled "Technical Analysis and Random Walks." It is particularly relevant to the discussion in this chapter. No mathematics.

Working Holbrook. "A Theory of Anticipatory Prices." *American Economic Review*. May 1958, pp. 188–99. The late Professor Working was one of the most important theoreticians and econometric researchers in the area of security prices. (He usually discussed commodity futures rather than stocks or bonds, but the logic is the same.) The paper provides an articulate review of this scholar's thoughts about the determination of market prices. No mathematics.

Total Risk and its Factors

"Risk" is an important word as it applies to financial investments. In fact, "risk" is more than just a word—it is a concept. There are different factors that cause different types of risk. This chapter defines investors' *total risk* and analyzes the factors that contribute to total risk.

This chapter defines total risk *quantitatively* so that it may be treated in an analytical manner. Chapter 10 goes on to show how to statistically divide the total risk of an asset into two parts—diversifiable risk and undiversifiable risk. Chapter 28 presents a new theory, called the arbitrage pricing theory, that can be used to isolate and measure the various *risk factors* that may be present in any particular asset's total risk.[1]

The risk analysis techniques of this chapter and Chap. 10 provide an important foundation for understanding many topics throughout the rest of this book.

9-1 DEFINING TOTAL RISK ANALYTICALLY

Webster's dictionary defines *risk* as "the chance of injury, damage, or loss." This is an intuitively pleasing definition, and few people would disagree with it. However, this verbal definition is not very analytical. Verbal definitions are interpreted in different ways by different people. They can be made clearer only by means of other verbal definitions or by examples that are not always entirely appropriate and are rarely concise. Such definitions do not yield to measurement. Frequently, they are not even exact enough to allow objects possessing the defined characteristic (here, "risk") to be ranked in terms of that characteristic. Thus, it seems desirable to develop a surrogate for the dictionary definition of risk that is amenable to quantification.

---

1 This chapter suggests that an asset's total risk is the sum of various "risk factors" defined in the chapter. This discussion is informative and insightful, and it introduces the concept of linear additive risk factors that is the basis for the new arbitrage pricing theory explained in Chap. 28.

9-1.1
Quantitative
Surrogates

If risk analysis is to proceed, a quantitative financial risk surrogate is needed.[2] However, if this surrogate is to be intuitively pleasing, it must measure, either directly or indirectly, "the chance of injury, damage, or loss" so that it may be used synonymously with the word "risk." The quantitative financial risk surrogate used in this text is measured from the investment's probability distribution of rates of return.

9-1.2
Probability
Distribution
of Rates of
Return

The rate of return is the single most important outcome of an investment. Therefore, the quantitative risk surrogate focuses on rates of return. Considerations of whether a stock is a growth stock, whether the company's "image is pleasing," or whether the firm's product is "glamorous" are relevant only to the extent they affect its rate of return and riskiness.

In an uncertain world, investors cannot tell in advance exactly what rate of return an investment will yield. However, they can formulate a probability distribution of the possible rates of return. Figure 9-1 shows three probability distributions of returns for Bell Canada Enterprises, Canadian Tire, and Dylex common stock.

A probability distribution may be either subjective or objective. An *objective probability distribution* is formed by measuring objective historical data. A *subjective probability distribution* is formed by simply writing down someone's hunches and assigning probabilities to them. Of course, what occurred historically may influence hunches about the future. But if the probability distribution is not stationary over time, historical probability distributions of rates of return are not much help in forecasting the future probability distributions upon which investment decisions are based. Luckily, most firms' probability distributions of rates of return and the statistics describing them do not seem to change very much as time passes.[3] Thus, objective distributions almost always influence the development of subjective distributions and in many cases are good estimates of what the future holds.

---

2 Quantification is occurring in many fields. For example, a biology student may now major in biometrics at most universities. Biometrics involves measuring biological phenomena. By testing new drugs and detecting subtle cause-and-effect relationships (for example, lung cancer and smoking), biometricians are extending the ability of the medical profession. Within the social sciences, quantification progress is accelerating, too. Most psychology departments today offer programs in psychometry—that is, the measuring of mental traits. The IQ test is probably the best-known psychometric instrument. However, psychometric tools measure many subtle traits besides intelligence. Economics departments are offering majors in econometrics. Econometricians develop mathematical economic models, which they test statistically. Econometricians are expanding the study of economics from rationalization of observable phenomena to a science of measuring, testing, and predicting, and they are winning Nobel prizes.

3 Balvir Singh and Abdul H. Rahman, "An Econometric Analysis of the Variability of Security Returns," *Administrative Sciences Association of Canada, Annual Proceedings*, Finance Division, vol. 1, 1985, pp. 19–27. They demonstrate that the variances of Canadian stock prices display stability over time; Marshall Blume, "On the Assessment of Risk," *Journal of Finance*, March 1971, pp. 1–10; O. A. Vasicek, "A Note of Using Cross-Sectional Information in Bayesian Estimation of Security Betas," *Journal of Finance*, December 1973, pp. 1233–1239; R. C. Klemkosky and J. D. Martin, "The Adjustment of Beta Factors," *Journal of Finance*, September 1975, pp. 1123–1128; B. Rosenberg and J. Guy, "Beta and Investment Fundamentals,"

FIGURE 9-1   Subjectively derived finite probability distributions of rates of return.

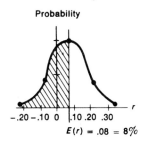

Bell Canada Enterprises

$E(r) = .08 = 8\%$

i	p_i	r_i
1	.05	.38 = 38%
2	.2	.23 = 23%
3	.5	.08 = 8%
4	.2	-.07 = -7%
5	.05	-.22 = -22%
	1.0	

$E(r) = .08 = 8\%$

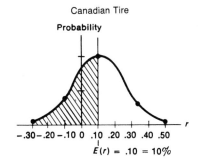

Canadian Tire

$E(r) = .10 = 10\%$

i	p_i	r_i
1	.1	.5 = 50%
2	.2	.3 = 30%
3	.4	.1 = 10%
4	.2	-.1 = -10%
5	.1	-.3 = -30%
	1.0	

$E(r) = .10 = 10\%$

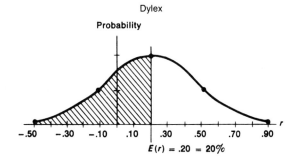

Dylex

$E(r) = .20 = 20\%$

i	p_i	r_i
1	.1	.9 = 90%
2	.25	.5 = 50%
3	.3	.2 = 20%
4	.25	-.1 = -10%
5	.1	-.5 = -50%
	1.0	

$E(r) = .20 = 20\%$

Probability distributions of returns are essential in deriving a quantitative financial risk surrogate. Investors tend (consciously or subconsciously) to focus on the probability distribution of rates of return. In particular, investors want to know the average rate of return they can expect from each potential investment and the risk associated with that investment.

Financial Analysts Journal, May–June 1976; F. J. Fabozzi and J. C. Francis, "Beta as a Random Coefficient," *Journal of Financial and Quantitative Analysis*, March 1978, pp. 101–115; J. C. Francis, "Statistical Analysis of Risk Surrogates for NYSE Stocks," *Journal of Financial and Quantitative Analysis*, December 1979, pp. 981–997. Several of these articles are reproduced in *Readings in Investments*, edited by J. C. Francis, Cheng-Few Lee, and Donald Farrar (New York: McGraw-Hill, 1980).

9-1.3
Expected
Return

The expected return is a weighted *average return* using the probabilities for weights; it measures the average or central tendency of the probability distribution of returns (see Box 9-1).

BOX 9-1
Definition of
the Expected
Rate of Return
$E(r)$

The *expected return* is the sum of the products of the various one-period rates of return times their probabilities. Equation (9-1) defines the expected return symbolically.

$$E(r) = \sum_{t=1}^{T} p_t r_t$$

(9-1)

$$= p_1 r_1 + p_2 r_2 + p_3 r_3 + p_4 r_4 + p_5 r_5$$

where r_t denotes the tth rate of return from the probability distribution, p_t is the probability that the tth rate of return occurs, and there are T possible rates of return.

The calculations below are for the expected value of Canadian Tire probability distribution in Fig. 9-1.

$$E(r) = p_1 r_1 + p_2 r_2 + p_3 r_3 + p_4 r_4 + p_5 r_5$$

$$= (.1)(.5) + (.2)(.3) + (.4)(.1) + (.2)(-.1) + (.1)(-.3)$$

$$= .05 + .06 + .04 - .02 - .03$$

$$= .1 = 10\%$$

The expected return is the mathematical expectation or the mathematical expected value of the different rates of return that are possible. Mathematical statisticians call the expected value the *first moment* of the probability distribution. The second moment (about the mean) of a probability distribution is called the variance.[4]

9-1.4
Variance
and
Standard
Deviation of
Returns

The wideness of a probability distribution of rates of return is a measure of uncertainty or risk. That is, the more an investment's return varies around its expected return, the larger is the investor's uncertainty. The risk or width of the probability distribution can be measured with the variance of returns defined in Eq. (9-2) at the top of page 175. The calculations are for Canadian Tire data from Fig. 9-1.

4 The first four statistical moments are the mean, variance, skewness, and kurtosis. These four moments are discussed in Mathematical App. C at the end of the book. Expectation operators are explained in Mathematical App. B.

(9-2)

$$\sigma^2 = \sum_{t-1}^{5} p_t[r_t - E(r)]^2$$

$$= p_1[r_1 - E(r)]^2 + p_2[r_2 - E(r)]^2 + p_3[(r)_3 - E(r)]^2 +$$
$$p_4[r_4 - E(r)]^2 + p_5[r_5 - E(r)]^2$$

$$= (.1)(.5 - .1)^2 + (.2)(.3 - .1)^2 + (.4)(.1 - .1)^2 +$$
$$(.2)(-.1 - .1)^2 + (.1)(-.3 - .1)^2$$

$$= .016 + .008 + 0 + .008 + .016$$

$$= .048 \text{ rate of return squared}$$

The standard deviation is defined in Box 9-2. Canadian Tire's standard deviation is calculated below.

$$\sigma = \sqrt{\sigma^2}$$

$$= \sqrt{.048}$$

$$= .22 = 22\% = 22 \text{ percentage points}$$

The standard deviation is stated in rates of return, but the variance is stated in terms of the "rate of return squared." Since it is more natural to discuss rates of return rather than rates of return *squared*, risk is sometimes measured with the standard deviation of returns. However, for statistical purposes it is sometimes more convenient to use the variance rather than the standard deviation when discussing risk. Conceptually, either risk definition is appropriate since they are simply positive mathematical transformations of each other.[5]

An asset's *total risk* equals its total variability of returns. Total variability of returns is measured using either the variance or the standard deviation of the one-period rates of return. The standard deviation is defined in Eq. (9-3); it is the square root of the variance.

Standard deviation of returns $= \sqrt{\text{variance}\,(r)} = \sigma$ (9-3)

The standard deviation and the variance both equate dispersion around the expected value—the wideness of the probability distribution—with total risk.

Box 9-2
Definition of
Total Risk

---

5 The standard deviation and the variance are what mathematicians call positive monotone transformations of each other. Other risk measures exist that differ more markedly. For a discussion of different quantitative risk surrogates and why the "variability of return" definition that is inherent in the standard deviation of returns was selected, see J. C. Francis and S. H. Archer, *Portfolio Analysis*, 1st ed. (Englewood Cliffs, N.J.: Prentice-Hall, 1971), chap. 11. See also Harry Markowitz, *Portfolio Selection* (New York: Wiley, 1959), chap. 9.

**9-1.5
Symmetric
Probability
Distribution of
Returns**

If risk is defined as the chance of loss or injury, it seems more logical to measure risk by the area in a probability that is *below* its expected return. This procedure can be difficult, and it is unnecessary if the probability distribution is *symmetric*.

Figure 9-2 shows three probability distributions of returns—one skewed left, one symmetric, and one skewed right. The symmetric distribution has no skewness. The area on one side of the expected return of a symmetric distribution is the mirror image of the area on the other side of the expected return.

FIGURE 9-2   Three probability distributions with different types of skewness.

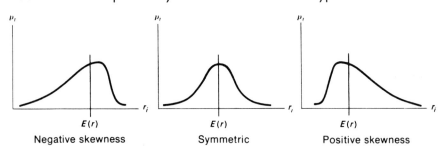

Negative skewness   Symmetric   Positive skewness

Empirical studies of historical probability distributions of returns indicate they are not significantly skewed if short differencing intervals (for example, if one month elapses between p_t and p_{t+1}) are used.[6] Consequently, it is not important whether variability of returns is measured on one or both sides of the expected return.

Measuring total variability of return (that is, risk) on both sides of the expected return with the standard deviation and variance includes surprisingly good returns (that is, returns above the expected return) in the risk measure. But as long as the probability distributions of returns are fairly symmetric, the way the risk of a group of assets is measured does not change in any meaningful way. Measurements of each asset's *total* variability of return will be twice as large as measurements of that asset's variability below the expected return if its probability distribution is symmetric. As long as total variability of return on both sides of the expected return is used consistently as a risk surrogate, the risk measurements of all assets will still result in the same risk rankings for a group of assets. Since the standard deviation and variance are such common statistics and will rank assets' risk in the same

---

6 J. C. Francis, "Skewness and Investors' Decisions," *Journal of Financial and Quantitative Analysis*, March 1975, pp. 163–172. Also, see the first part of the appendix to Chap. 18 for an intuitive explanation with graphs. L. Fisher and J. H. Lorie, "Some Studies of Variability of Returns on Investments in Common Stocks," *Journal of Business*, April 1970, pp. 99–134. J. C. Francis and S. H. Archer, *Portfolio Analysis*, 2d ed. (Englewood Cliffs, N.J.: Prentice-Hall, 1979); see tables 14-2 and 14-3 and chaps. 14 to 16 about nonsymmetric distributions of returns. Alan Kraus and Robert H. Litzenberger, "Skewness Preference and the Valuation of Risk Assets," *Journal of Finance*, September 1976, pp. 1084–1100.

order as a more complicated measure (for example, of variability below the expected return), they will be used as quantitative financial risk surrogates.[7] This approach will also be simpler than trying to measure only the lower half of the distribution. Measuring risk by the standard deviation and variance is equivalent to *defining risk as total variability of returns* about the expected return or, simply, as variability of returns.

In essence, it is the accuracy with which future (subjective) probability distributions of rates of returns are forecast that determines the value of the quantitative risk surrogate. Since investment decisions are based on future returns, much care must go into estimating the expected return and expected risk statistics for all assets under consideration. This is the job of the securities analyst.[8]

The remainder of this chapter introduces some of the various factors or sources of investment risk that an investment manager must be prepared to analyze.[9] Each of the remaining sections in this chapter is devoted to one investment risk factor. These different investment risk factors are referred to throughout the rest of this book.

9-1.6   The Factors That Make Up an Asset's Total Risk

Default risk arises because firms may eventually go bankrupt. Some default risk is systemically related to the business cycle, which affects almost all investments. However, some default risk is caused by changes that are unique to the afflicted company.

Interest rate risk arises from changes in the level of market interest rates. Interest rate risk is predominantly an undiversifiable risk because the levels of all interest rates tend to rise and fall together and to affect the values of all assets similarly.

Market risk arises because bull and bear market conditions tend to affect all securities systemically.

Management risk arises when the people who manage an investment asset make errors that decrease the asset's value. Thus, management risk is that part of total risk caused by bad business decisions.

Purchasing power risk is caused by inflation, which erodes the purchasing power of invested dollars.

Marketability risk is that portion of an asset's total risk caused by discounts and selling commissions that must be given up to sell an illiquid asset.

Political risk is that portion of an asset's total variability of return caused by changes in the political environment (for instance, a new tax law) that affect the asset's market value.

---

7 Harry Markowitz, *Portfolio Selection* (New York: Wiley, 1959), chap. 9. Markowitz explains the use of the variance instead of his semivariance (svr), which measures variability below the expected return. By his definition:

$$\text{svr} = \sum_{t-1}^{n} P_t [\text{bar}_t - E(r)]^2$$

where bar_t is the *t*th *below average rate of return*. The bars are shaded in Figure 9-1.

8 Gordon Alexander and J. C. Francis, *Portfolio Analysis*, 3d ed. (Englewood Cliffs, N.J.: Prentice-Hall, 1985), deals explicitly with procedures the security analyst can use to estimate risk and return statistics. See chaps. 5 and 6 of the book in particular.

9 Stephen A. Ross, ''The Arbitrage Theory of Capital Asset Pricing,'' *Journal of Economic Theory*, December 1976, vol. 13, pp. 341–360.

Callability risk is variability of return caused by the fact that a security may legally be called for a forced sale.

Convertability risk is variability of return caused by the fact that a market security (such as a bond) may be converted to another security (such as a common stock).

The above types of risk are independent but can occur simultaneously, nevertheless. For example, a management error that occurs when interest rates are low may be overcome; the same error could bankrupt the firm if it were to occur when interest rates (and thus interest expenses) were high. In this example management risk interacts with interest rate risk. The above list of risk factors is not exhaustive. Empirical research is under way to identify the factors that make up an asset's total risk.[10] The remainder of this chapter and its appendix introduce those risk factors that are likely to contribute to the total risk of an asset.

9-2   THE DEFAULT RISK FACTOR

Default risk is that portion of an investment's total risk resulting from changes in the financial integrity of the investment. For example, when a company that issues securities moves either further away from or closer to bankruptcy, these changes in the firm's financial integrity are reflected in the market prices of its securities. The variability of return that investors experience as a result of changes in the credit-worthiness of a firm that issues investment securities is their default risk.[11]

An investor who purchases common stocks, preferred stocks, bonds, or other corporate securities must face the possibility of default and bankruptcy of the issuer. Financial analysts usually can foresee bankruptcy because deteriorating financial ratios and default on debt (when the firm is unable to pay its bills) almost always precede it. Occasionally an act of God, such as a flood or earthquake, may destroy, for instance, all a manufacturing company's assets. And if this firm were to have no insurance to cover the losses, a sudden bankruptcy could result.

Almost all the losses suffered by investors as a result of default risk are *not* the result of actual defaults and/or bankruptcies. Investor losses from default risk usually result from security prices falling as the financial integrity of a healthy firm that issued the securities *weakens*. By the time an actual

---

10 Richard Roll and Stephen A. Ross, "An Empirical Investigation of the Arbitrage Pricing Theory," *Journal of Finance*, December 1980, vol. 35, no. 5, pp. 1073–1104. Arbitrage pricing theory, the subject of Chap. 28 of this book, explains how to evaluate the individual elements that combine to form an asset's total risk.

11 Default risk may be further divided into two subcomponents. The two parts of a security's default risk might be called business risk (from the assets on the issuing firm's balance sheet) and financial risk (from the liabilities on the issuing firm's balance sheet).

It is tempting to say that default risk is proportional to the probability of not getting back the principal of the investment. But, this is not a satisfactory concept, because this probabilistic definition differs from the variability of return definition that underlies modern risk analysis. We can say, however, that an asset's variability of return and its probability of not returning the investor's principal both increase monotonically as the asset's default risk increases.

bankruptcy occurs, the market prices of the troubled firm's securities will have already declined to near zero. So, the bankruptcy losses would be only a small part of total losses resulting from the process leading up to the default. Nevertheless, since losses due to default risk occur as a firm's financial integrity deteriorates in a way that increases the likelihood the firm may some day go bankrupt, it is useful to begin by reviewing the legal bankruptcy proceedings.

When a corporation fails to make a scheduled payment of interest or principal on a debt, the firm is said to be in *default* on that obligation.[12] If payment is not made within a relatively short period, a lawsuit almost inevitably follows.

9-2.1 Bankruptcy Law

A question that arises in most bankruptcy hearings is whether the firm's assets should be liquidated and the proceeds divided among the creditors or whether a reorganization should take place. A *liquidation* occurs if the bankruptcy court feels the resulting value would exceed that likely to be obtained if the firm were to continue in operation.

If the firm's assets are liquidated in a bankruptcy, the proceeds of the liquidation are paid out to creditors according to the following list of legally established priorities:

Prior to the establishment of claims: Secured creditors (mortgagees, lienholders, etc.) can appoint a receiver to seize and sell the assets specifically secured under their contract or indenture. Secured creditors are not impeded by the Bankruptcy Act.

First priority: In the case of a deceased bankrupt, all reasonable funeral and testamentary expenses are paid first.

Second priority: The next payments go to pay the trustee in bankruptcy's expenses and fees, followed by the legal costs associated with the bankruptcy proceedings.

Third priority: The next priority is to pay a special federal government levy for supervising the bankruptcy. The levy, paid to the Superintendent of Bankruptcy is 2 percent of the first $1,000,000; $\frac{1}{2}$ percent on the next $1,000,000 and $\frac{1}{10}$ percent of amounts in excess of $2,000,000.

Fourth priority: Any remaining proceeds from the bankruptcy go to pay back wages, salaries, commissions, and other compensation due to workers earned within the three months prior to the bankruptcy (to a maximum of $500 per employee), plus up to an additional $300 to travelling salespersons for unpaid expenses incurred in that three-month period.

Fifth priority: Any remaining proceeds are used to pay up to two years of back municipal taxes.

Sixth priority: The bankrupt's landlord is now entitled to up to three months' rent arrears and accelerated rent up to three months subsequent to the bankruptcy.

Seventh priority: Any remaining proceeds go to pay the legal costs of the petitioner into bankruptcy, including sherriff's fees and land registration fees.

12 A corporation unable to meet its obligatory debt payments is said to be *technically insolvent*. If the value of a firm's assets falls below its liabilities, it is said to be insolvent in the *bankruptcy* sense. While details differ from case to case, the typical bankruptcy situation begins with a default of one or more required payments. If agreements with creditors cannot be obtained, the corporation itself usually files for bankruptcy. Subsequent developments involve the bankruptcy courts, court-appointed officials, representatives of the firm's creditors, the management of the firm, and others.

Eighth priority: Any remaining proceeds are paid toward amounts owed to the federal government under the Income Tax Act, the Workers' Compensation Act, and the Unemployment Insurance Act.

Ninth priority: The next payments made are for federal or provincial government debts not covered above.

Tenth priority: Remaining proceeds are next paid to special claims resulting from injuries to employees of the bankrupt company not covered by the Workers' Compensation Act and only to the extent of monies received from third-party insurers.

Eleventh priority: If any funds remain, the company's general or unsecured creditors are paid. Unsecured creditors include debenture holders, secured creditors whose claims were not fully satisfied upon sale of the specific assets, trade creditors, etc. This class of creditor often receives only a portion of the money owed to them by the bankrupt firm.

Twelfth priority: Preferred stockholders are paid if proceeds from auction are left. Normally the amount available is either a paltry sum or nothing at all.

Thirteenth priority: Common stockholders are paid last; they usually receive nothing from their investment.

Reorganization If the value of the firm's assets when employed as a going concern appears to exceed the value in liquidation, a technically insolvent firm may instead propose a reorganization to its creditors. The proposal in the form of an *arrangement* (the firm is given additional time to meet its obligations) or *composition* (the firm's creditors agree to forego some of their debt) is provided to a licensed trustee and then presented to the creditors at a duly constituted meeting of the creditors. At least 50 percent of the firm's creditors, present in numbers or by proxy and representing 75 percent of the creditors in terms of dollar value of the debts, must concur with the proposed reorganization. Creditors will agree to a proposal if they perceive that the present value of the expected cash flows accruing to them upon reorganization exceeds the actual payments that they will receive now. If the proposal is accepted, it must be approved by the courts who will rule generally on the basis of fairness, the treatment of junior creditors, and the conduct of the debtor. If, for example, before or during the insolvency period, the debtor fails to keep proper books of account, engages in wild speculations, provides special treatment to specific creditors or commits fraud, the court will strike down the proposal.[13] Acceptance by the court is binding on all creditors. If bankruptcy proceedings have already taken place, the acceptance of a proposal annuls the bankruptcy.

Typically, creditors are given new claims in the reorganized firm, intended to be at least equal in value to the amounts that would have been received in liquidation. For example, holders of debentures might receive preferred stock in the reorganization, while holders of subordinated debentures might become common stockholders. Stockholders might be left without any interest in the firm; that is, they might lose their entire investment if the bankruptcy judge decrees it.

Among the goals of reorganization are a fair treatment of various classes of securities and the elimination of impossible debt obligations. Presumably,

13 The Bankruptcy Act, s.107(1).

a plan that the troubled firm's debt and equity investors might agree upon among themselves could be considered equitable.

Financial services, such as the Dominion Bond Rating Service and the Canadian Bond Rating Service in Canada and Standard and Poor's, Moody's, and Fitch's in the United States, continuously study thousands of different corporations and analyze their financial situations. Box 12-1 on page 289 demonstrates the quality ratings that the Dominion Bond Rating Service assigns to the bonds that it rates. The other financial services assign similar quality ratings.[14]

9-2.2 Quality Ratings for Bonds and Stocks

Determinants of Quality Ratings The financial services assign quality ratings that measure the default (or bankruptcy) risk of bond and stock issues and then sell these ratings to the rated companies and the financial services' subscribers. A firm's default risk is essentially determined by (1) the amount of funds available to the issuer relative to the amount of funds required by contract to be paid to bondholders (or expected to be paid to the stockholders) modified by (2) the strength of the security owner's claim for payment. To differentiate among securities in terms of default risk and quality ratings, the investor can analyze the firm's financial statements and financial ratios. But the following section sketches how the financial services assign quality ratings to an issue of securities.

Ratios. To analyze corporate bonds, the single most important factor is probably some "times fixed charges earned ratio."

$$\text{Times fixed charges earned ratio} = \frac{\text{income earned by firm}}{\text{firm's fixed charges}} \qquad (9\text{-}4)$$

For this ratio, some measure of earnings for a period of time is taken as the amount of income available with which to pay fixed charges. And the amount of interest on bonds and/or cash dividends on common stock for that period is the amount required. The greater the amount of earnings relative to the amount of interest and/or cash dividends, the greater the ratio and the greater the ability to pay during that period. Different financial analysts calculate the times fixed charges earned ratio using quantities that are defined differently.[15]

The requirement to pay. The other main element considered in determining a security's quality rating is the strength of the requirement to pay. The relative strength of the requirement to pay is largely determined by the terms of the indenture contract between the company and its bondholders. A company that has issued bonds has a

---

14 The different rating agencies seldom give different ratings for the same security. If two financial services do give the same security different ratings, it is referred to as a *split rating*. The few differences that do occur are rarely more than one rating grade level apart. This attests to the similarity of the different bond and stock rating services' ratings.

15 For common stocks, for instance, the usual measure of how much funds are available is earnings per share; the amount of funds "required" is the amount of cash dividends generally expected by investors. When a company has paid a certain amount of cash dividends per share in the past, the amount may be considered the expected amount. If the trend has been upward, the usual expectation is that it will continue upward.

   Common stock analysis is the topic of Chaps. 14, 15 and 16. Bond default risk analysis is studied in Chap. 12.

contract with its bondholders to pay specified amounts on particular dates. If it fails to make payments, it violates its contract, and the bondholders have the legal remedies of creditors, such as instituting receivership or trusteeship for a company. In contrast, stockholders enjoy no such legal promise to pay dividends, and accordingly the consequences to the company of nonpayment of dividends are much less severe. In particular situations there are many different circumstances that affect the strength of the requirement to make payments to security holders. But the contrast between the legal positions of bondholders and stockholders is sufficient to illustrate that financial risk is related to the strength of the requirement to pay.

Meaning of Quality Ratings   The bond ratings published by such investment information services as the Dominion Bond Rating Service (DBRS), the Canadian Bond Rating Service (CBRS), Moody's, and Standard & Poor's (S&P) indicate the default risk associated with the purchase of securities by assigning individual issues of securities to risk classifications. The term "high grade" is applied to issues with low financial risk. The highest-grade bonds are designated "A + +" by CBRS and "AAA" by DBRS. The next-highest grade (that is, the next-lowest level of financial risk) is designated "A +" by CBRS and "AA" by DBRS, and the third level is designated "A" in both systems. There are three "B" classifications and three "C" classifications for bonds, differentiated in the same manner as the A classifications and representing higher levels of risk. CBRS has a "D" classification for bonds in default, which DBRS does not use.

There are several rating or ranking systems for preferred stocks. The Canadian Bond Rating Service, for example, explains its ratings with respect to both the ability of the firm to pay its dividends and the asset protection of the share. The highest rating that DBRS assigns, P1, is described as "Highest Quality." The preferred shares have excellent asset protection and a strong capacity to pay dividends. P5, on the other hand, are described as "Speculative." The company's ability to maintain adequate coverages in the future is not well assured. The other major Canadian rating service, the Dominion Bond Rating Service, ranks preferreds from Pfd-1, described as "prime credits, with strong earnings and balance sheet characteristics," to Pfd-5: "Companies with Pfd-5 ratings are speculative." The ratings scales used by the two agencies are shown in Table 9-1. Although DBRS uses a more conservative set of titles to designate their rankings than CBRS, the two agencies use essentially the same approach to evaluation. The two scales are not directly comparable but are shown in descending order for convenience.

TABLE 9-1   PREFERRED SHARE RATING SCALES

DESIGNATION CBRS/DBRS	CBRS RATING	DBRS RATING
Highest quality/Above average	P1	Pfd-1
Very good quality/Average	P2	Pfd-2
Good quality/Medium grade	P3	Pfd-3
Medium quality/Lower grade	P4	Pfd-4
Speculative/Speculative	P5	Pfd-5
Dividend in arrears or not currently paid		D

It would seem that investors should require issuers of high-risk securities to pay higher rates of return than issuers of low-risk securities; otherwise, why should investors assume the greater risk of loss or even bankruptcy?

Figure 9-3 shows the relationship between risk and corporate bond yields at different times. Corporate bonds yield progressively higher interest rates

9-2.4 Risk and Return

FIGURE 9-3   The default risk structure of market interest rates on (a) September 1970 and (b) July 1981. Note that (i) the level of all interest rates rose, (ii) the positive risk-return trade-off does not disappear as the level of interest rates changes, and (iii) the yields (and thus, the prices) of defaulted bonds are negotiable within a wide range.

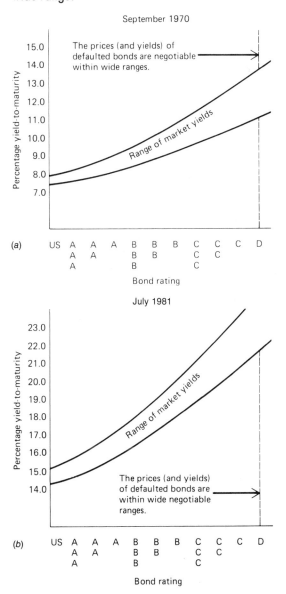

as their financial integrity and quality ratings deteriorate. Bond prices vary inversely with interest rates; therefore, the quality ratings directly affect bond prices because the ratings affect the bond's risk-adjusted interest rates. Bank of Canada policy, fiscal policy, the supply of and demand for loanable funds, and other factors that constantly change cause the relationship between discount rate and bond ratings to shift every day. But high-risk bonds must always pay the highest returns in order to attract investors.

The trade-off between the risk that investors undertake and the rate of return they are paid is not limited to bonds. Stock investors also try to avoid risk. As a result, common stocks must, on average, pay higher rates of return than bonds because common stockholders have only a residual claim against whatever assets (if any) the business has left over after all higher priority debts are paid. Default risk is examined more closely in Chap. 12.

9-3 THE INTEREST RATE RISK FACTOR

A bond is a legal contract. Most bonds require the borrower to pay the lender (that is, the bond investor) a fixed annual coupon interest payment every year until the bond matures. Thus, the owner of a coupon bond receives cashflows, as does the beneficiary of an annuity contract.

At maturity, the bond issuer must repay the principal amount (also called the face value) of the bond. This is true for both corporate bonds and Canadian government bonds. But corporate bonds and government bonds differ in an important respect: corporations can default or even go bankrupt, but government bonds are free from default risk.[16]

Federal government bonds are sometimes called default-free bonds because the Canadian government cannot go bankrupt as long as Canadians own assets and the Canadian government has enforcement procedures that, if necessary, could be used to collect taxes. Therefore, the government (which collects federal income taxes through its Revenue Canada branch) is not likely to become bankrupt even if hard times arise. Nevertheless, Canadian bonds experience interest rate risk. In fact, interest rate risk is the main risk that Canadian government obligations are subject to, since they are free of default risk. This interest rate risk can be substantial. In the past decade, for example, long-term federal government bonds have fluctuated in price from as low as 50 percent to as high as 120 percent of their face values solely because of interest rate risk.

9-3.1 Changes in the Market Prices of Bonds

Federal government bonds are usually sold in denominations of $1,000, $5,000, and $25,000. Larger face values are sold, but the minimum face value is $1,000.[17] However, the market prices of these default-free bonds vary minute by minute and rarely equal their face values, except at maturity, when the face value must be repaid to the lender. The factor that makes a $1,000

---

16 See Chap. 2 for a description of different types of bonds. Section 9-3 and the rest of this book presume that the reader understands the present value concept explained in Mathematical App. A at the end of the book.

17 Some of the older issues, prior to 1970, have minimum denominations of $500.

government bond with decades to maturity vary in price from $800 to $1,200 is the changing market interest rates.

The market price of a bond can be calculated to the penny by observing the current market interest rate—or yield to maturity, as it is more properly called—and using it to find the present value of the bond's cashflows. The cashflows are all known in advance — they are the annual coupon interest payments plus the face value at maturity. For example, a $1,000 government bond with a 10 percent coupon rate will pay $100 per year up to and including the year of its maturity, and then it will also repay the $1,000 principal. The various present values this default-free bond may assume as its time to maturity varies from zero years to infinity are illustrated in Fig. 9-4 for market interest rates of 9 percent, 10 percent, and 11 percent. The market price of a bond will always exactly equal its present value, so these calculated values are informative.

FIGURE 9-4 How a change in interest rates affects market prices for bonds of varying lengths of maturity.

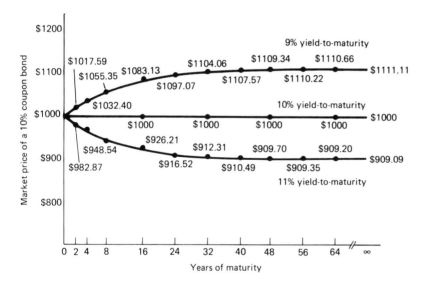

The present values illustrated in Fig. 9-4 (and the prices of all coupon-paying bonds for that matter) are calculated with Eq. (9-5) below.

$$\text{Present value} = \sum_{i=1}^{T} \frac{\text{coupon}_t}{(1.0 + \text{yield})^t} + \frac{\text{face value}}{(1.0 + \text{yield})^T} \tag{9-5}$$

9-3.2 Determinants of Interest Rate Risk from Price Fluctuations

18 Strictly speaking, a bond's yield to maturity can be defined as the discount rate that equates the present value of all the bond's future cashflows to the bond's current market price. A bond's yield to maturity is discussed in more detail in Chap. 11. The yield to maturity is called the internal rate of return from the asset in most capital budgeting discussions. Sometimes the yield to maturity is called the dollar-weighted rate of return.

The word "yield" in Eq. (9-5) is short for the bond's yield to maturity, a rate of return measure that is compounded over the expected life of the bond.[18]

Changes in Market Interest Rates   The two present value theorems shown in Box 9-3, below, can be discerned from Fig. 9-4, or by mathematically analyzing Eq. (9-5).

Present value theorem one is illustrated in Fig. 9-4. The present value of the bond is higher along the curve calculated with the 9 percent interest rate than it is along the lower curve, which represents the same bond's present values calculated with an 11 percent rate. That is, the bond's present value at any given time to maturity moves inversely with the interest rate used to discount the cashflows.[19]

Present value theorem two is also relevant to Fig. 9-4. The 10 percent government bond's present values fluctuate over a much wider range at the longer maturities than at the shorter maturities. That is, the bond has more interest rate risk as the *futurity* of its cashflows increases.

BOX 9-3
Two Basic
Bond Price
Theorems

> The following two theorems about the relationship of bond prices and yield to maturity may be discerned from graphs like Fig. 9-4.*
>
> *Theorem one*: Bond prices (or the present value of anything) move inversely to the yield to maturity (that is, the discount rate used).**
>
> *Theorem two*: For any given difference between the coupon interest rate and the yield to maturity of a bond, the associated price change will be greater the longer the bond has until it matures.†
>
> ---
>
> * These theorems were derived formally by B. G. Malkiel, "Expectations, Bond Prices, and the Term Structure of Interest Rates," *Quarterly Journal of Economics*, May 1962, pp. 197–218.
>
> ** Taking the partial derivative of Eq. (9-5) furnishes proof of theorem one. This partial derivative must be negative in sign, because all the numerical quantities are positive and thus the negative sign determines the derivative's sign. Similar differential calculus analysis of Eq. (9-5) can provide proof of some of the other bond price theorems. Or, more simply, most of these theorems can be seen visually by studying and comparing Figs. 9-4 and 9-5.
>
> † Theorem two is not true for some long-term discounted bonds, but it is true for most bonds. And theorem two is never horribly misleading—it merely oversimplifies for a few long-term bonds that are discounted.

---

19 Chen, Roll, and Ross have found a statistically significant relationship between asset returns and the (orthogonalized) market interest rates from long-term bonds (and several other economic variables, too). See Nai-Fu Chen, Richard Roll, and Stephen A. Ross, "Economic Forces and the Stock Market: Testing the APT and Alternative Asset Pricing Theories, "CRSP Working Paper Number 119, December 1983. Their results are also referred to in Richard Roll and Stephen A. Ross, "The Arbitrage Pricing Theory Approach to Strategic Portfolio Planning," *Financial Analysts Journal*, May–June 1984, pp. 14–29. The relationship between the individual risk factors and the total risk of an asset are discussed more fully in this book's Chap. 10 and most particularly in the chapter about arbitrage pricing theory (APT), Chap. 28.

Coupon Rate Changes   A bond investor seeking to avoid the interest rate risk arising from price fluctuations (described by present value theorems one and two) may do so by investing in short-term bonds (say, bonds with one year to maturity) rather than in bonds with more futurity (that is, longer maturities). Then, however, another kind of interest rate risk is encountered, coupon rate risk.

If an investor keeps funds invested over a number of years by buying a new one-year bond every time an old one-year bond matures, each of these successive one-year bonds will bear a different coupon interest rate. Bonds' coupon interest rates can vary over just as wide a range as their market interest rates. Thus, an investor who buys only short-term bonds must buy a succession of bonds with varying coupon interest rates.

Coupon interest rates that fluctuate year to year (which are the source of the only cashflows from a bond before it matures) create *coupon rate risk*. This risk that arises from changing coupon interest income can take its toll, for example, on retired people who depend on coupon income to buy their food each month. However, the coupon rate risk will at least reduce the other kind of interest rate risk (that is, the risk of price fluctuations) associated with bonds with long periods to maturity. Each investor must decide which type of interest rate risk is easier to bear—the risk arising from price fluctuations or coupon rate risk.[20]

Unlike government bonds, corporate bonds are subject to the risk of default and even bankruptcy. If a company that has bonds outstanding goes bankrupt, the bonds can become worthless. Bond quality ratings are useful in assessing the bankruptcy risk associated with particular bond issues.

9-3.3 Corporate Bonds

Bond ratings essentially rank issues in order of their probability of default. Many defaulted bonds eventually resume their scheduled interest payments. But for some firms, bond default results from irreversible insolvency and is an early step along the path to bankruptcy.

Figure 9-3 above shows the nature of the relationship between bond ratings and the appropriate discount rate (that is, the bond's yield to maturity or market interest rate) existing at two dates. Note that all bonds are discounted at progressively higher discount rates as their ratings deteriorate. Since bond prices are determined by the discount rate, the ratings have a direct effect on bond prices.

Bank of Canada policy, fiscal policy, supply and demand for loanable funds, and other factors that constantly change cause market interest rates to change. Changing credit conditions can turn bond markets into speculative markets, because present value theorems one and two apply to corporate bonds in exactly the same way they apply to government bonds. Thus, corporate bonds are also subject to the two kinds of interest rate risk—coupon rate risk and price change risk. The only difference between the default-free

20 If bond investments can be held for years until they mature (this is how pension funds and life insurance companies invest most of their funds), then price fluctuations are easy to bear. But if bond investments might need to be liquidated in an emergency when bond market prices are low, then the risk from price fluctuations is unbearable, and short-term bonds would be the less risky investment alternative.

government bonds and the more risky corporate bonds is that the corporate bonds must pay higher rates of interest in order to induce investors to assume their risk of default. However, since all interest rates tend to rise and fall together, the corporate bonds' interest rates merely fluctuate at a level higher than the level at which government bonds' interest rates fluctuate.

9-3.4 Common Stocks

Even preferred and common stocks experience interest rate risk. Preferred and common stocks usually pay cash dividends. The dividend yield from a share of preferred or common stock is defined below.

$$\text{Dividend yield} = \frac{\text{cash dividend per share}}{\text{market price per share}}$$

The coupon yield (or current yield) from a bond is defined below.

$$\text{Coupon yield} = \frac{\text{coupon interest per year}}{\text{market price per bond}}$$

The dividend yield from a share of stock and the coupon yield from a bond are both rates of periodic cashflow that make up part of the investors' total rate of return. Yet these two cash yield measures are different, because of bankruptcy considerations.

A bond's coupon interest payment is a contractual payment that cannot vary in amount or timing, or else the issuing company will be sued. Cumulative cash dividends on preferred stocks in arrears must likewise be paid before the issuing firm can pay dividends on the common shares. But some preferred stock issues have noncumulative cash dividends, which may be skipped if the issuing corporation experiences hard times. Cash dividends are paid to common stockholders only if the issuing firm's board of directors sees fit. Common stockholders' cash dividends can be cancelled completely if the firm's profitability is dubious and if paying dividends might increase the chance of bankruptcy. This bankruptcy risk makes the cash dividend yield paid to common stockholders considerably more risky than bondholders' coupon yield. Nevertheless, the present value model is still relevant in determining the prices of stocks. It is through the present value mechanism that interest rate risk affects the prices of preferred and common stocks. Considering how cash dividend yields tend to move with interest rates as time passes can help in understanding why stocks experience some interest rate risk.

Figure 9-5 illustrates how the average dividend yields of preferred and common stock fluctuate together with the average market interest rate of bonds over a period of years. Common stock has the lowest average dividend yield because some industrial common stocks pay little or no cash dividends —their stockholders receive most of their return in capital gains. The preferred stock has the highest average dividend yield because preferred stockholders receive only cash dividend income; furthermore, the preferred stock must pay a higher yield than bonds pay because preferred stock involves more default risk than do bonds. In spite of these differences, the various yields shown in Fig. 9-5 tend to fluctuate together; this similarity is the result of interest rate risk.

FIGURE 9-5   Cash dividend yields on common stock averages and bond average yield moving together.

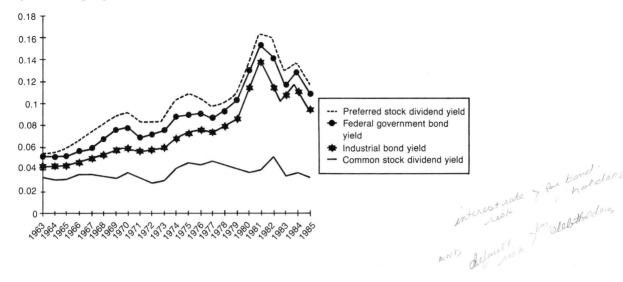

Common stocks and preferred stocks have interest rate risk because their estimated values are the present values of all future cash dividends. Thus, when the prevailing level of interest rates changes, the present values of these securities can change too. Preferred and common stock prices do not change exactly together with bond prices because stocks are more affected by default risk than are bonds. Also, common stocks have less interest rate risk than do preferred stocks because common stock dividends are so affected by the firm's financial prospects. That is, the profit prospects of a firm affect financial analysts' cash dividend expectations so strongly that the effect of interest rates on the present value of these uncertain cash dividends is minor. In contrast, interest rate risk is more evident in bonds than in stocks because bonds' coupon payments are contractually specified and thus known in advance. As a result, interest rate risk is the main type of risk for bondholders but only a minor risk for stockholders. Interest rate risk is studied more closely in Chap. 11.

9-4   THE MARKET RISK FACTOR

Market ups and downs are usually measured by using a security market index. The Toronto Stock Exchange 300 Composite Index of common and a few preferred shares is a good index for stock markets in Canada. It resembles a portfolio made up of 300 stocks randomly selected from fourteen industry groupings. Some of these 300 stocks are from large corporations, and some are from small corporations. A portfolio of common stocks picked randomly should perform like the TSE 300 Composite Index. This means that when the TSE 300 falls 20 percent, the average common stock investor loses twenty cents of every dollar invested in common stocks. This could be a bitter pill to swallow, especially considering that investors can earn between 5 and 10 percent simply by putting money in a riskless savings account.

9-4.1 Bull Markets are Punctuated by Bear Markets

When a security index rises fairly consistently (from a low point, or a *trough*) for a period of time, this upward trend is called a *bull market*. The bull market ends when the market index reaches a peak and starts a downward trend. The period of time during which the market declines to the next trough is called a *bear market*. *Market risk* arises from this variability in market returns, which results from the alternating bull and bear market forces.

The effects of these alternating bull and bear markets can be seen most clearly in a graph illustrating the behaviour of security prices over time. Figure 9-6 shows the bull and bear markets for Canadian stocks over the period 1924–1985.

Figure 9-6 shows that bull markets predominate over bear markets. Over the period 1924–1985, bull markets have lasted anywhere from a few months to over five years with an average duration of about thirty months, while bear markets have spanned a few months to four years with an average duration of about seventeen months. During bull markets, prices have risen by a little over 30 percent, while, in bear market years, prices fell on average by about 12 percent. The fact that there were about twice as many bullish years as bearish years helps explain the long-run upward trend in stock market prices that is clearly shown in Fig. 9-6. Of course, to a certain extent, these statistics about bull and bear markets are influenced by the arbitrary parameters employed in delineating the bull and bear years.[21]

It is a pleasure for stock market investors to fantasize about the stock market's long-term upward trend and about those bullish times during which the market value of a portfolio could be more than doubled quickly with virtually no effort (as was the case in the 1933 to 1936, 1948 to 1951, or 1982 to October 1987 bull markets). However, the thought of losing more than 84 cents out of every dollar invested in common stocks in less than four years (as was the case in the 1929 to 1932 bear market) brings a person's feet back down to the ground with a discomforting thud. The obvious question is, ''What causes the stock market indexes to rise and fall like a breathtaking roller coaster?''

9-4.4 Buying Low and Selling High—Good Investment Timing

According to a definition formulated by two experts on economics, a *business cycle* is

. . . a type of fluctuation found in the aggregate economic activity of nations that organize their work mainly in business enterprises; a cycle consists of expansions occurring at about the same time in many economic activities, followed by similarly general recessions, contractions, and revivals which merge into the expansion phase of the next cycle; this sequence of changes is recurrent but not periodic; in duration business cycles may last from more than one year to ten or twelve years; they are not divisible into shorter cycles of similar character with amplitudes approximating their own.[22]

---

21 Any year in which there was a market increase in excess of 10 percent was designated a bull market year; any year in which prices fell was a bear year.

22 W. C. Mitchell and A. F. Burns, *Measuring Business Cycles* (New York: National Bureau of Economic Research, 1946).

FIGURE 9-6   Canadian stocks fluctuate through bull and bear markets.

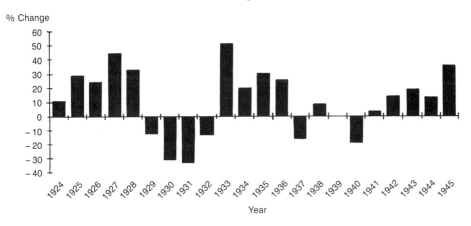

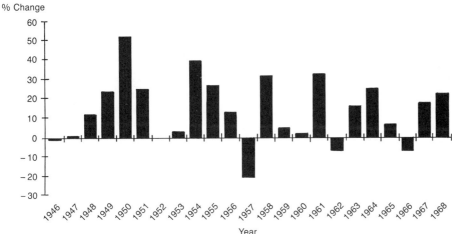

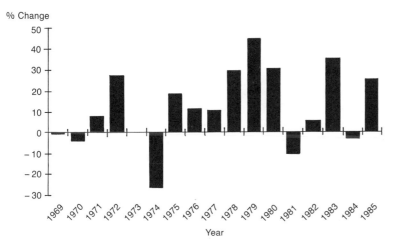

Source: P. Boyle, H. Panjer, and K. Sharp, *Report on Canadian Economic Statistics,* Canadian Institute of Actuaries, June 1986, p. 10, Table 1A. Published by permission.

The main element that causes the stock market to rise bullishly and then fall bearishly again and again is the fact that the nation's economy follows a cycle of recessions and expansions.[23]

The stock market appears to fall into a bear market *before* almost every recession. The bear market that started in early 1973, for instance, preceded the recession that started later that year. Occasionally, the stock market falls into bearish periods when no recession is at hand. For example, the bear markets in 1962 and 1966 did not precede recessions. However, many of the bear markets shown in Fig. 9-6 anticipated actual recessions that were evidently correctly predicted by security analysts.

Since the *anticipation of recessions* appears to be the cause of most bear markets, it behooves investors to study past recessions so that they can attempt to forecast recessions. Investors can protect their portfolios by withdrawing invested funds before the onset of the bear market. Buying just before security market prices rise in a bull market and selling just before the start of a bear market—that is, buying low and selling high—is called good *investment timing.*

9-5 THE MANAGEMENT RISK FACTOR

Most people know that high-level executives earn princely salaries, occupy luxurious offices, and wield enormous power within their organizations. None of this should make us forget, however, that even the very highest executive is merely mortal and capable of making a mistake or a poor decision. This section assesses how the errors business managers sometimes make can affect investors who buy shares in their firms. Investors must be wary of these managers; they are in a position to make both gross and subtle errors. There are so many different kinds of management errors that it is not feasible to enumerate all the management risks to which investors expose themselves.

Only a few management errors will be discussed below. These difficulties are reviewed to broaden your appreciation of some of the problem areas a security analyst must consider. Watching for management errors requires an attitude of vigilance and sensitivity rather than an uncanny ability to forecast specific incidents.

9-5.1 Acts of God

An *act of God* is an extraordinary interruption of events by a natural cause. Floods, earthquakes, hordes of destructive insects, and bolts of lightning are examples. These events can be neither prevented nor foreseen, and they usually entail great costs to those involved. Conscientious business managers can, however, reduce the risk of great financial loss by insuring their plant and equipment and taking other steps to prepare for such catastrophes.

When an act of God wreaks disaster upon a business firm, the costs of the misfortune typically fall on the firm's insurance company (if the firm has insurance), on any employees who may be harmed, and, ultimately, on the

---

23 For a detailed and expert discussion, see Geoffrey H. Moore, *Business Cycles, Inflation and Forecasting* (Cambridge, Mass.: Ballinger, 1980), chap. 9. National Bureau of Economic Research Studies in Business Cycle Number 24.

firm's investors. Consider, for example, the terrible winter that buried the eastern portions of Canada under a record snowfall during January and February 1977. This heavy snowfall was accompanied by extremely cold temperatures and soaring demand for natural gas, electricity, and oil for heating purposes. In some areas, there were power failures caused by snow and ice. Thousands of businesses and schools were closed for weeks, and thousands of workers were furloughed. The nation's gross national product was reduced by millions of dollars. Since most businesses were not insured against or otherwise prepared for this catastrophe, their investors suffered stock price declines totalling millions of dollars.

Many of the losses from the cold weather of 1977 would have been averted if business managers and governmental planners had ordered better insulation for their buildings, stockpiled extra heating supplies and other raw materials, made contingency plans to allow for foul weather, and purchased insurance against such losses. Shortsightedness caused many companies to suffer financial losses that reduced the value of their securities in the market. Thus, investors in those firms also suffered losses that could have been transferred to insurance companies which were better equipped to handle them. Many investors attempted to have inept business managers fired — but this is like closing the door to the chicken coop after the fox has eaten the hens. In any event, this is one sort of management risk to which investors expose themselves.

Losses can occur if management allows a firm's product to become obsolete. Theoretically, a business corporation will live forever if it is well managed. When shareowners sell out or employees change jobs, die, or retire, new people take their places. This transfer of roles enables businesses to survive for generations. Products, too, must sometimes be replaced if they grow old, go out of style, suffer decreasing usefulness, or otherwise become obsolete.

9-5.2 Product Obso- lescence

It is up to management to overcome the problem of obsolescence by developing and maintaining active research and development (R&D) programs. Annual expenditure for R&D to generate new products for the firm to produce and sell is a sign of a farsighted top management. For example, if the buggy manufacturers of 1900 had reinvested some of their profits in R&D, they might have survived in the 1930s as horseless carriage manufacturers. The steam engine manufacturers of the 1940s had to learn how to manufacture diesel locomotives to survive in the 1960s. The American Locomotive Corporation and Baldwin Locomotive Corporation, for example, used to be huge steam engine manufacturing companies; then General Motors pulled away their customers with diesel engines and drove them out of business. Television manufacturers in the 1950s had to develop colour sets in order to compete in the markets of the 1960s. The Detroit automotive giants must produce smaller, more fuel-efficient cars if they are to stand up to foreign car competition in the 1980s.[24] Clearly, management must make changes to avoid *product obsolescence*.

24 See "Despite Losses, GM Could Emerge Even Bigger and Stronger than Ever," *The Wall Street Journal*, Aug. 7, 1980, p. 19.

The road to corporate success is littered with bankrupt corporations that did not develop new products to replace obsolete ones. In many cases, blame can be directly attributed to management error. Not enough of the firms' profits were spent on R&D to develop new products. Instead, nearsighted top management tried to make bigger short-run profits by cutting R&D budgets. The resulting permanent losses to these firms' investors were management's fault.

**9-5.3
Loss of
Important
Customers**

A product usually becomes obsolete over a period of years. However, it is commonplace for a business firm to lose a customer with no prior warning. Competitors constantly win customers from each other. A firm that suddenly loses a *large* customer can go bankrupt rapidly.

It is a management error to let a company become dependent on one customer or a few customers whose loss could financially embarrass the firm. Every firm's top management should strive to develop a broad and diversified group of customers. Ideally, no single customer will be capable of ruining a supplying firm merely by changing suppliers.

It is easy to obtain a diversified customer group in some industries. Retail department stores, supermarkets, dry cleaning stores, filling stations, airlines, and theatres, for example, usually do not depend on any one customer to maintain a profitable level of sales. However, some businesses are dependent upon one customer or a few.

Any small firm that supplies parts (say, rearview mirrors, floor carpets, or radio antennas) to an automobile firm is likely to be entirely dependent on the auto giant for its existence. Small firms often lack the diversified sales force and manufacturing technology needed to obtain new customers and may exist solely to supply one customer. This precarious position could indicate that the firm is poorly managed.

Of course, some industries are composed of oligopolistic competitors who dominate the buying of raw materials for that industry. If a firm finds itself selling to only a few monopsonistic or oligopolistic customers, the firm might consider diversification into another industry to help prolong its existence.

**9-5.4
Agency
Theory**

Reading about management errors can leave one with a cynical outlook. It is possible, for example, to hastily conclude that conscientious business executives are merely mortal people who make mortal errors because they become tired, are too busy, or may not be sufficiently well-educated to make better decisions. However, a theory is developing to replace this cynicism with informed insight. Doctors Jensen and Meckling have hypothesized an economic theory about *principal-agent relationships* that can explain some of the management errors discussed above.[25] Knowledge of this theory is worthwhile because the insights it yields may enable security analysts to make better forecasts and predictions. Let us consider this theory.

25 The roots of agency theory can be traced back many years. See, for example, A. A. Berle and G. C. Means, *The Modern Corporation and Private Property* (New York: Macmillan, 1934).

An agent-principal relationship exists whenever decision-making authority must be delegated. Corporations are an example of a common principal-agent relationship — a corporation's shareholder/owners delegate the day-to-day decision-making authority to managers who are hired employees rather than substantial owners. Jensen and Meckling argue that corporate managers who have little or no ownership interest in the corporation that employs them have more incentive to consume certain nonpecuniary benefits than they would if they were substantial owners of the firm.[26] The nonpecuniary benefits to which Jensen and Meckling refer might include nonsalary benefits like company-supplied luxury cars for executives, liberal expense accounts, corporate jets, some personally gratifying corporate acquisition, and other comforts and ego-bolsterers for managers. Jensen and Meckling suggest that owners work harder to maximize the value of the firm than employees, if all other factors are equal. That is, to the extent that ex post rewards and punishments are not perfect and just, employed managers may not expend as much ex ante effort to generate profitable investment opportunities as they would if they owned the firm where they worked.

The Jensen-Meckling agency theory reasons that many stock market investors are rational, intelligent people who can discern the conflict of interest existing between the economic welfare of the corporate owners and the corporation-employed managers. Jensen and Meckling maintain that this conflict of interest is more or less built into the corporate decision-making process because corporate managers who are merely employees can, and sometimes do, abuse the powers vested in them to act as agents for the owners. As a result of this conflict of interest, investors will discriminate by paying more for shares in an owner-managed firm than they would pay for shares in an identical corporation managed by employees who own little or no ownership interest in the firm. This difference in the value between the owner-managed and the employee-managed corporations is defined as the *agency cost*.

Eugene Fama argues against the Jensen-Meckling agency theory.[27] Fama contends that in a well-functioning market for productive resources (such as managers and capital), significant agency costs should not exist. Fama reasons that corporation managers must seek employment in competitive markets, compete against their peers within the corporate environment, and thus face the discipline of the competitive marketplace. Furthermore, Fama points out, managers face the harsh discipline and also enjoy the opportunities provided by competitive markets for managerial talent. More specifically, to the extent that good managers see a market for their services that provides alternative employment opportunities, good managers should be motivated by

26 Michael C. Jensen and William H. Meckling, "Theory of the Firm: Managerial Behavior, Agency Costs and Ownership Structure," *Journal of Financial Economics*, 1976, vol. 3, pp. 305–360. See also Michael C. Jensen and William H. Meckling, "Rights and Production Functions: An Application to Labor-Managed Firms and Codetermination," *Journal of Business*, 1979, vol. 52, pp. 469–506.

27 Eugene F. Fama, "Agency Problems and the Theory of the Firm," *Journal of Political Economy*, 1980, vol. 88, pp. 288–307.

any other more lucrative opportunities to work up to their full potential in an effort to gain positions that will pay them more.

Barnea, Haugen, and Senbet,[28] and also Haugen and Senbet,[29] have presented a third view that rationalizes the existence of the Jensen-Meckling agency theory and, at the same time, acknowledges the insights provided by Fama's critique of the agency theory. Barnea, Haugen, and Senbet argue that the issuing of complex securities (namely, executive stock options and puts) can resolve the inherent conflicts between the shareholders and the managers of a corporation.

In analyzing the normative issues of agency theory, researchers have recognized different motivating factors (that is, different arguments in the utility function) between the owner/principals and the agent/employees. Recognizing these differences has enabled researchers to develop optimal incentive contracts that minimize agency costs.[30] More recently, Fama and Jensen — who had previously opposed each other concerning agency theory — have co-authored studies that note the survival of the "open corporation" even in the face of agency costs. They suggest that corporate survival may be attributable to benefits that professional managers bring to the corporation.[31]

Agency theory is still evolving. Economic researchers are currently investigating various aspects of the theory in an effort to validate, refine, or reject it. Some of these studies delve into events (for example, a large sample of corporation mergers) to see if the event raises or lowers the value of the owners' equity shares. If this research determines that a significant agency cost does exist, that would explain how management errors like those reviewed above continue to occur in a competitive business world. And it would suggest that owner-managed corporations are better investments than employee-managed firms.[32]

9-6   THE PURCHASING POWER RISK FACTOR

Webster's dictionary states that *inflation* is "an increase in the amount of currency in circulation, resulting in a relatively sharp and sudden fall in its

28 Amir Barnea, Robert A. Haugen, and Lemma W. Senbet, "A Rationale for Debt Maturity and Call Provisions in the Agency Theoretic Framework," *Journal of Finance*, vol. 35, December 1980, pp. 1223–1224.

29 R. A. Haugen and L. W. Senbet, "Resolving the Agency Problems of External Capital through Options," *Journal of Finance*, June 1981, pp. 569–581.

30 D. W. Diamond and R. Verrecchia, "Optimal Managerial Contracts and Equilibrium Security Prices," *Journal of Finance*, May 1982, vol. 37, pp. 225–288; S. Grossman and O. Hart, "Takeover Bids, the Free-Rider Problem, and the Theory of the Corporation," *The Bell Journal of Economics and Management Science*, Spring 1980, pp. 42–64; Bengt Holstrom, "Moral Hazard and Observability," *The Bell Journal of Economics and Management Science*, Spring 1979, vol. 10, pp. 74–91; Bengt Holstrom, "Moral Hazard in Teams," *The Bell Journal of Economics and Management Science*, Autumn 1982, vol. 12, pp. 324–340; Steven Shavell, "Risk Sharing and Incentives in the Principal and Agent Relationship," *The Bell Journal of Economics and Management Science*, Spring 1979, vol. 10, pp. 55–73.

31 Eugene Fama and Michael C. Jensen, "Separation of Ownership and Control," *Journal of Law and Economics*, June 1983a, vol. 26; Eugene Fama and Michael C. Jensen, "Agency Problems and Residual Claims," *Journal of Law and Economics*, June 1983b, vol. 26.

32 The April 1983 issue of the *Journal of Financial Economics* is devoted to articles about different aspects of agency theory. Interested readers may see vol. 11, nos. 1–4.

value and rise in prices." Economics textbooks often characterize inflation simply as an increase in the general level of prices. This section focuses on the effect that inflation has on investment decisions. It behooves investors to try to deal rationally with purchasing-power risk because inflation will erode their wealth if they don't.

Purchasing-power risk denotes the fact that an investor's money assets (such as cash, savings, and bond investments) may lose their purchasing power because of inflation. An investment may lose its purchasing power even though its price is continually rising. Many investors do not understand how an investment may suffer purchasing-power losses when its market price moves upward—these investors have *money illusion*, a phrase economists use to describe a certain type of naive behaviour. People who have money illusion mistakenly believe that if they have more money, they must be richer. This belief does not take into account the way money can lose its buying power because of inflation. For example, if the amount of wealth you have doubles during a period when the price level quadruples, you are poorer even though you have more money.

Investor losses to inflation can be measured. However, one should understand how inflation is measured before studying purchasing-power losses.

Economists measure the rate of inflation by using a price index that they construct. The consumer price index (CPI) is a popular price index in Canada. It is tabulated by Statistics Canada and measures the cost of a representative basket of consumer goods. This basket contains specified quantities and qualities of various items of food, clothing, housing, and health care bought by the average urban household. Statistics Canada employees go to stores around Canada every month and note the prices of consumer goods to obtain realistic CPI data.

Of course, the price of this hypothetical basket of goods changes from month to month. The amount of that change is stated as a percentage of the CPI for the previous month, and this figure is the rate of inflation.

In other words, the rate of inflation between month 1 and month 2 is the difference between the CPI for those months, divided by the CPI for month 1, as shown below in Eq. (9-6a). The inflation rate is denoted q.

$$q = \frac{\text{CPI for month 2} - \text{CPI for month 1}}{\text{CPI for month 1}} = \text{rate of inflation between months 1 and 2} \qquad (9\text{-}6a)$$

If the cost of the market basket goes from \$200 to \$202 in 1 month, the rate of inflation would be 1 percent, as shown below.

$$q = \frac{\$202 - \$200}{\$200} \qquad (9\text{-}6b)$$

$$= \frac{\$2}{\$200} = .01 = 1.0\%$$

An inflation rate of 1 percent per month is equivalent to about 12 percent per year. More precisely, if the CPI increases by 1 percent in some month,

9-6.1
Money
Illusion

9-6.2
Measuring
the Rate
of Inflation

this monthly rate of 1 percent is converted to an annual rate by adding 1 to the rate of price increase and then raising that quantity to the power 12 to get the annual rate of inflation of 12.68 percent, as shown below.

$$(1.0 + 1.0\% \text{ per month})^{12} = 1.01^{12} = 1.1268 = 1.0 + 12.68\%$$

It is the common practice to report inflation rates on an annual basis (as well as interest rates) so that they can be compared easily.

There is more than one rate of inflation relevant to each period of time. Goods that enjoy strong demand, such as homes, will usually experience faster rates of inflation than goods that aren't in strong demand. Also, the rate of inflation for each good varies from month to month. Table 9-2 contains data for the CPI showing month-over-month and year-over-year rates of inflation.

9-6.3 Real Returns Versus Nominal Returns

After inflation has been measured, it should be compared to investment returns. To avoid money illusion, an important question is, ''Are your investments' rates of return higher than the rate of inflation?''

When you read in a newspaper that a savings account pays an annualized rate of return of 6 percent, for example, that is the investment's *nominal rate*

TABLE 9-2 CONSUMER PRICE INDEX (CPI) DATA

YEAR AND MONTH 1984	INDEX [1981 = 100]	CHANGE OVER 1-MONTH SPAN, %	CHANGE OVER 1 YEAR SPAN, %
January	120.2	0.5	5.3
February	120.9	0.6	5.5
March	121.2	0.2	4.7
April	121.5	0.2	4.9
May	121.7	0.2	4.8
June	122.2	0.4	4.1
July	122.9	0.6	4.2
August	122.9	0.0	3.7
September	123.0	0.1	3.8
October	123.2	0.2	3.3
November	124.0	0.6	4.0
December	124.1	0.1	3.8
1985			
January	124.6	0.4	3.7
February	125.4	0.6	3.7
March	125.7	0.2	3.7
April	126.2	0.4	3.9
May	126.5	0.2	3.9
June	127.2	0.6	4.1
July	127.6	0.3	3.8
August	127.8	0.2	4.0
September	128.0	0.2	4.1
October	128.4	0.3	4.2
November	128.9	0.4	4.0
December	129.5	0.5	4.4

Source: Statistics Canada, February 1986, S126.

Heading above table: **Consumer Prices, All Items**

of return. Nominal rates of return are *money rates of return*; that is, they are not adjusted for the effects of inflation. A numerical example should clarify this.

For purposes of illustration, assume that a savings deposit earns a nominal interest rate (or nominal rate of return) of 6 percent, $r = .06 = 6\%$, during some one-year period. Thus, if $100 were deposited, it would grow to $100(1.0 + r) = \$100(1.06) = \$106$ in that year. However, if we also assume that the rate of inflation during that year is $q = .06 = 6$ percent, then the real value (in terms of current purchasing power) of the $100 savings at the end of the year is still only $100 after we divide the nominal rate by the inflation rate to get the real rate, as shown below.

$$\frac{(\$100)(1.0 + r)}{1.0 + q} = \frac{(\$100)(1.06)}{1.06} = \$100$$

In this example the nominal rate of return was eroded by an equal inflation rate so that the savings account's purchasing power didn't increase, even though there were 6 percent more dollars in it.

Generally speaking, an asset's nominal future value after earning a nominal rate of r for one period is related to its present value as shown below:

Nominal future value = (present value) $(1.0 + r)$

$$(\$106) = (\$100)(1.06)$$

And an asset's *real* (or *inflation-adjusted*) *future value* is calculated as shown in the following equation:

$$\text{Real future value} = \frac{\text{nominal future value}}{1.0 + \text{inflation rate}}$$

An investment's "real rate of return" during some time period is calculated by dividing 1 plus the asset's nominal rate of return, $(1.0 + r)$, by 1 plus the rate of inflation $(1.0 + q)$, during the same time period. Equation (9-7a) defines this *real rate of return*, denoted *rr*. Equation (9-7a) is similar to the preceding dollar value equation.

$$1.0 + rr = \frac{1.0 + r}{1.0 + q} \tag{9-7a}$$

Equation (9-7a) can be equivalently restated as Eq. (9-7b).

$$rr = \frac{1.0 + r}{1.0 + q} - 1.0 \tag{9-7b}$$

For example, if a common stock earns a 10 percent nominal rate of return, $r = .1 = 10\%$, for a year when the inflation rate is 8 percent, $q = .08 = 8\%$, the stock's real rate of return is less than 2 percent in that year.

$$1.0 + rr = \frac{1.10}{1.08} = 1.0185, \text{ or } rr = 1.85\% \tag{9-7c}$$

This investment in common stock results in a 1.85 percent increase in *real* purchasing power. The only portion of an investment's nominal rate of return that results in increased consumption opportunities for an investor is the real rate of return. The rest of the investment's nominal rate of return is wasted on compensating for purchasing power lost to inflation. Investors who suffer from money illusion fail to realize this and erroneously believe that the investment in this example yields more than a 1.85 percent gain.

You can now see how it is possible for an investment that earns a positive nominal rate of return to earn a *negative* real return. Consider a savings account that pays 6 percent interest in a year when inflation is 8 percent. This savings account has a *negative* real rate of return, as shown in Eq. (9-7d) below.

$$rr = \frac{1.0 + r}{1.0 + q} - 1 = \frac{1.06}{1.08} - 1 = .9815 - 1 = -.0185 \tag{9-7d}$$

Investors with money illusion would think that the savings account has increased their wealth by 6 percent when, in fact, their purchasing power has decreased by 1.85 percent.

If an investment has a negative real rate of return, that does not necessarily mean that the investor would have been better off without the investment. After all, if money is held in cash (earning no interest, so that $r = 0$) instead of being invested in, say, a 6 percent savings account, as in the previous example, the investor will suffer a 7.4 percent loss in purchasing power.

$$rr = \frac{1.0 + r}{1.0 + q} - 1 = \frac{1.0}{1.08} - 1 = .926 - 1 = -.0740$$

Thus, it is better to earn 6 percent than to hold cash, even though both alternatives earn a negative real return. Of course, the objective of wise investors is to earn a positive real return.[33] Box 9-4 shows a shortcut method for calculating real or nominal rates of return to expedite attainment of the objective.[34]

---

33 Canadian evidence on the effect of inflation on stock prices is found in Yalagruesh B. Yalawar, "Common Stocks as Hedges Against Inflation," *Administrative Sciences Association of Canada, Annual Proceedings*, Finance Division, vol. 1, 1981, pp. 106–115.

34 Some other detailed studies on the effect of inflation on stock prices are as follows: (1) A. A. Alchian and R. A. Kessel, "Redistribution of Wealth Through Inflation," *Science*, September 1959, pp. 535–539. (2) M. Arak, "Inflation and Stock Values: Is Our Tax Structure the Villain?" *Quarterly Review Federal Reserve Bank of New York*, Winter 1980–1981, vol. 5, pp. 3–13. (3) Z. Bodie, "Common Stocks as a Hedge against Inflation," *Journal of Finance*, May 1976, vol. 31, pp. 459–470. Z. Bodie and V. I. Rosansky, "Risk and Return in Commodity Futures," *Financial Analysts Journal*, May–June 1980, pp. 27–39. (4) R. A. Brealey, "Inflation and the Real Value of Government Assets," *Financial Analysts Journal*, January–February 1979, vol. 35, pp. 18–21. (5) P. Cagan, *Common Stock Values and Inflation—The Historical Record of Many Countries*, National Bureau of Economic Research, Report No. 13, March 1974. (6) E. F. Fama and G. W. Schwert, "Asset Returns and Inflation," *Journal of Financial Economics*, 1977, vol. 5, pp. 115–146. (7) J. Jaffee and G. Mandelker, "'The Fisher Effect' for Risky Assets: An Empirical Investigation," *Journal of Finance*, May 1976, vol. 31, pp. 447–470. (8) H. Hong,

Although they understand the economic logic of calculating real rates of return, some people dislike using Eq. (9-7a) because it requires a division that must be calculated with tedious decimal point accuracy.

$$1.0 + rr = \frac{1.0 + r}{1.0 + q} \tag{9-7a}$$

These folks have simplified Eq. (9-7a) by multiplying both sides of the equation by the quantity (1.0 + q) and rearranging to obtain the mathematically equivalent Eqs. (9-8a), (9-8b), and (9-8c) below.

$$1.0 + r = (1.0 + rr)(1.0 + q) \tag{9-8a}$$

$$1.0 + r = 1.0 + rr + q + (q)(rr) \tag{9-8b}$$

$$r = rr + q + (q)(rr) \tag{9-8c}$$

Equations (9-8a), (9-8b), and (9-8c) show that the nominal rate of return, r, can be defined in three different but mathematically equivalent ways. Furthermore, a close look at Eq. (9-8c) reveals an easy shortcut calculation that yields fair approximations of the nominal rate of return.

The people who are looking for a shortcut for calculating the nominal rate of return reason that the product of q times rr in Eq. (9-8c) will often be a tiny value that can probably be ignored with little loss of accuracy. Therefore, they restate Eq. (9-8c) in the simplified form shown in Eq. (9-9) to expedite their calculations.

$$r = rr + q \tag{9-9}$$

Equation (9-9) is a good approximation of Eq. (9-8c) if the values of q and rr are so small that their product is not significantly different from zero. More specifically, when the inflation rate is not up into the double digits Eq. (9-9) is an easy way to calculate the nominal rate of return without creating an approximation that is terribly misleading.

BOX 9-4
An Easy Approximation for Calculating Nominal Returns

"Inflation and the Market Value of the Firm: Theory and Empirical Tests," *Journal of Finance*, September 1977, vol. 32, pp. 1031–1048. (9) J. Lintner, "Inflation and Security Returns," *Journal of Finance*, May 1975, vol. 30, pp. 259–280. (10) F. Modigliani and R. A. Cohn, "Inflation, Rational Valuation and the Market," *Financial Analysts Journal*, March–April 1979, vol. 35, pp. 24–44. (11) B. Moore, "Equity Values and Inflation: The Importance of Dividends," *Lloyds Bank Review*, July 1980, pp. 1–15. (12) S. A. Moosa, "Inflation and Common Stock Prices," *Journal of Financial Research*, Fall 1980, vol. 3, pp. 115–128. (13) C. R. Nelson, "Inflation and Rates of Return on Common Stocks," *Journal of Finance*, May 1976, vol. 31, pp. 471–483. (14) B. A Oudet, "The Variation of the Return on Stocks in Periods of Inflation," *Journal of Financial and Quantitative Analysis*, March 1973, vol. 8, pp. 247–258. (15) F. K. Reilly, G. L. Johnson, and R. E. Smith, "Inflation, Inflation Hedges and Common Stocks," *Financial Analysts Journal*, January–February 1970, vol. 26, pp. 104–110. (16) G. W. Schwert, "The Adjustment of Stock Prices to Information about Inflation," *Journal of Finance*, March 1981, vol. 36, pp. 15–29. (17) J. C. Van Horne and W. F. Glassmire, Jr., "The Impact of Changes in Inflation on the Value of Common Stocks," *Journal of Finance*, September 1972, vol. 27, pp. 1081–1092.

Next, let us investigate the nominal rates of return that the typical investor earns from different types of investments with the concurrent rate of inflation. The purpose of making this comparison is to discern those types of investments that yield the best *real* returns.

**9-6.4
Comparing
Investment
Returns
with Inflation
Rates**

After learning how to see through the "illusory veil of money" and discern the real dollars, the next question that investors typically ask is, "What should I invest in to earn the best real rate of return?" To determine the average inflation-adjusted investment experience with different types of assets, financial analysts have prepared various hypothetical portfolios. A common stock portfolio, a portfolio of federal government bonds, and a portfolio of Treasury bills were prepared by randomly selecting a representative sample of each of these types of securities. These portfolios were formed without any attempt to pick either the best or the worst securities in each

FIGURE 9-7   Wealth indexes of investments in Canadian capital markets, 1950–1983.

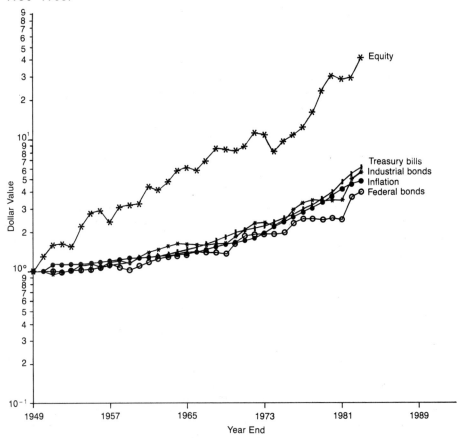

Source: James E. Hatch, and Robert W. White, *Canadian Stocks, Bills, and Inflation: 1950–1983,* Charlottesville, Va.: The Financial Analysts Research Foundation.

category. The portfolios thus represent indexes of average investment performance. These investment indexes are useful by themselves, for comparison with each other, and for comparison with the rate of inflation.

Figure 9-7 shows how $1 invested at the end of 1949 would probably have grown if it had been invested in each of the four different types of investment portfolios and then continually reinvested for the next thirty-three years. The different investments' annual rates of return and the concurrent inflation rate were calculated as explained below.

Common Stocks   The University of Western Ontario equity data base of diversified common stocks with all cash dividends reinvested was used as an index of normal stock market returns. Each common stock's rate of return was calculated as follows:

$$r = \frac{\text{capital gain or loss} + \text{cash dividend}}{\text{purchase price at beginning of year}} \qquad (9\text{-}10)$$

Adjustments were made to compensate for any stock that had a stock split or stock dividend, so that these changes would not distort the returns. Then, all 763 stocks' annual rates of return were averaged together each year using their relative market values as weights. Thus, stocks in the larger companies were given larger weights to represent the fact that there are more investment opportunities (namely, more shares of stock outstanding) in a large firm than in a small firm. Figure 9-7 shows that this hypothetical common stock portfolio had a greater value after thirty-three years than most of the other hypothetical portfolios.[35]

Common Stocks in Small Corporations   A hypothetical portfolio of the common stocks with the smallest total value of all issues listed in the University of Western Ontario equity data base was prepared. The 50 percent of all listed stocks that had the smallest total values were selected at the start of each year to create a new (but similar, since only a few of these stocks changed each year) portfolio of stocks issued by small corporations. The annual rates of return from these small stocks were calculated using Eq. (9-10) above, just as the returns from the other common stock portfolio were calculated.

Government of Canada   A hypothetical portfolio composed of Canadian government bonds with over ten years to maturity was prepared. All the bonds were outstanding on the date the index's return was prepared. Every bond in this portfolio had its rate of return calculated as follows:

$$r = \frac{\text{capital gain or loss} + \text{coupon interest}}{\text{purchase price at beginning of year}} \qquad (9\text{-}11)$$

Then, the returns of all the bonds outstanding each year were averaged together to calculate the index's annual returns.

---

[35] For a deeper analysis of the effects of inflation on common stocks see Zvi Bodie, "Common Stocks as a Hedge Against Inflation," *Journal of Finance*, May 1976, pp. 459–470.

Treasury Bills   A portfolio of Treasury bills, which have an average of ninety-one days to maturity, was constructed. As explained in Chap. 2, these debt securities pay no coupon interest; they are sold at a discount from their value at maturity (or principal) to provide interest income for their investors. Their rates of return were calculated as follows:

$$r = \frac{\text{capital gain or loss}}{\text{purchase price}} \tag{9-12}$$

Then, the average of all outstanding Treasury bills was calculated to obtain the yearly returns for the index.

Inflation Rates   The rate of inflation was calculated using Eq. (9-6) for each of the thirty-three years illustrated in Fig. 9-7. Figure 9-7 was prepared by starting with $1 in each investment category as of December 1949. Then, each investment's annual return was used to increase or decrease the value of the investment at the end of the preceding year, and this was done for thirty-three years.

9-6.5 Concluding Remarks About Purchasing Power Risk

A wise investor should compare the inflation rate with the nominal rates of return from different investments to see if the investments' real rates of return are positive or negative. Investors should focus on these real returns (1) to avoid being fooled by the money illusion fallacy and (2) to detect those investments that will maximize their purchasing power.[36]

The common stocks issued by the small corporations had the highest long-run gains of any of the securities considered. Figure 9-7 indicates that a $1 investment in common stock grew to $153.13 in thirty-three years. The Treasury bills had the weakest performance. The T-bills' original dollar grew to $3.98 in thirty-three years, a return that was below the cumulative inflation rate over the same thirty-three years. The CPI (which reflects the rate of inflation) grew from a level of $1 in December 1949 to $4.86 at the end of 1983. This means that the cost of a representative basket of consumer goods cost 4.86 times as much in 1983 as it did at the end of 1949. Since the hypothetical portfolio of Treasury bills increased by less than this amount, it may be concluded that the T-bills had a positive nominal rate of return, but a negative real rate of return. Table 9-3 contains summary statistics to help clarify this picture.

The summary statistics in Table 9-3 are averages measured over thirty-three years. These averages should be useful in planning investments. But if basic economic conditions change, these historical averages may become irrelevant or even misleading. For example, the inflation rate and market interest rates

---

36 For an empirical analysis of agricultural commodities as an inflation hedge and a comparison with investments in common stocks and bonds see Zvi Bodie and Victor I. Rosansky, ''Risk and Return in Commodity Futures,'' *Financial Analysts Journal*, May–June 1980, pp. 27–39. Essentially, this study reports that the nominal returns from a portfolio of futures contracts on agricultural commodities and the portfolio's risk were about the same as the return and risk from Standard & Poor's 500 Stocks Index. But, the agricultural commodity futures were a better inflation hedge than the stocks. Furthermore, the returns from the commodities were negatively correlated with common stock returns.

TABLE 9-3   ANNUAL RETURN SERIES, 1950–1983

SERIES	GEOMETRIC MEAN*	ARITHMETIC MEAN	STANDARD DEVIATION
Treasury bills	5.47%	5.55%	4.18%
Long Canada bonds	4.14	4.52	9.66
Common stocks	11.46	12.95	18.34
Small stocks	15.95	18.61	24.65
Inflation	4.76	4.83	3.97

*The geometric mean rate of return is explained in Mathematical App. F at end of this book.

Source: James E. Hatch and Robert W. White, *Canadian Stocks, Bills, and Inflation: 1950-1983*, Charlottesville, Va.: Financial Analysts Research Foundation, p. 8, exhibit 4.

in Canada doubled between the early 1960s and the early 1980s. Furthermore, these changes did not occur smoothly—there were erratic year-to-year fluctuations. Dealing profitably with changes such as these requires constant vigilance. In the final analysis it is *unanticipated inflation* rather than the well-known historical rates of inflation that is the essence of purchasing power risk.[37]

9-7   CONCLUSIONS ABOUT RISK AND RISK FACTORS

The *total risk* of an asset may be defined as the total variability in the asset's one-period rates of return. The total risk of an asset may be perceived as being the sum of several different contributing risk factors that each increase the asset's total variability of return in some way, as shown below.[38]

 Default risk factor (if present)
Plus: interest rate risk factor (if present)
Plus: market risk factor (if present)
Plus: management risk factor (if present)
Plus: purchasing power risk factor (if present)
Plus: marketability risk factor (if present)
Plus: political risk factor (if present)
Plus: callability risk factor (if present)
Plus: convertibility risk factor (if present)
Plus: other risk factors (if present)

Equals: total risk

---

37 Ross and Roll's empirical research indicates that unanticipated inflation is a significant risk factor. Other significant risk factors also exist. Richard Roll and Stephen A. Ross, ''The Arbitrage Pricing Theory Approach to Strategic Planning Portfolio Planning,'' *Financial Analysts Journal*, May–June 1984, pp. 14–26. Arbitrage pricing theory, the topic of Chap. 28 of this book, shows how the different risk factors that make up total risk can be statistically evaluated.

38 The various risk factors are additive only under certain conditions that are discussed with reference to the arbitrage pricing theory, in Chap. 28. The appendix to Chap. 9 discusses the callability, convertibility, and political risk factors for those who are interested.

The risk factors present in any individual asset are different from the risk factors in most other assets — every combination of risk factors is unique. Bonds, for instance, usually derive the largest portion of their total risk from the interest rate risk factor. In contrast, many common stocks are affected only slightly by the interest rate risk factor and, instead, are affected primarily by the default and management risk factors.

It is assumed throughout this text that rational investors are risk-averse — they dislike risk from whatever factor or combination of factors it may be derived.[39] As a result, financial analysts, security analysts, and portfolio managers labour to perceive the risk factors present in whatever asset they are analyzing and to delineate the significance of each risk factor that is present in that asset's make-up.[40] The following chapters will explain how these risk factors interact and how they affect asset values.

QUESTIONS

1. What are the advantages and the disadvantages of research and development expenditures in the corporate budget?
2. Define the terms below:
   a. Bull market
   b. Bear market
   c. Market risk
   d. Business cycle
3. Archibald Scott observed that some common stocks experienced good price rises during the last bear market. Therefore, he plans to continue to be a consistently active investor in the future regardless of whether the stock market is experiencing a bullish trend or a bearish trend. Scott says that he has studied past bear market stock prices and "found several good price-gaining stocks during every month of the last two bear markets." Comment on Scott's investment plans for the future.
4. Sally Overton heard two economists predict that the current economic boom would peak and turn downward into the beginning of a recession. This recession was expected to start five months ahead. On the basis of the two forecasts, Overton has decided to invest her life savings in a widely diversified portfolio of common stocks and then to liquidate four months from now, one month before the forecasted recession starts. Overton reasons that this strategy will allow her to take advantage of the last few months of bullish price rises before the bear market starts. How do you evaluate Overton's strategy?
5. On Friday, November 22, 1963, President John F. Kennedy was assassinated as he rode in a car in a parade in Dallas, Texas. News of the

39 Rational people may undertake small risks, such as gambling for the sake of entertainment. The appendix to Chap. 25 shows that people who have positive but diminishing marginal utility of wealth (that is, are economically rational) tend to avoid significant risks, however.
40 Richard Roll and Stephen A. Ross, "An Empirical Investigation of the Arbitrage Pricing Theory," *Journal of Finance*, December 1980, vol. 35, no. 5, pp. 1073–1104. This is a pioneering study that attempted to isolate and identify the risk factors using empirical data. See Chap. 28 of this book for a discussion of this study.

killing flashed around the world. When the news reached the NYSE, hysterical selling began that caused officials to close the exchange early. In the 27 minutes between the arrival of the news of the assassination and the closing, many stock prices dropped by as much as $5 or $10 per share. The DJIA fell 24.5 points in those 27 minutes. However, when the exchange reopened on the following trading day (that is, on Monday, November 25) the shares were at the prices they had been *before* the tragic news. On the first trading day following the funeral, the DJIA leaped 32 points. In your opinion, did the market temporarily collapse because of default risk, management risk, interest rate risk, market risk, or what? Explain.

6. Write a short essay defining total risk verbally and explain how this definition is consistent with using the variance of returns as a quantitative risk surrogate.

7. Write one-sentence definitions of each of the following:
   a. Purchasing power risk
   b. Interest rate risk
   c. Market risk
   d. Management risk
   e. Default risk
   f. Total risk

   For additional credit, define political risk, callability risk, convertibility risk, and marketability risk, which are discussed in the appendix to Chap. 9.

8. How do bankruptcy proceedings relate to the default risk of investment securities?

9. Compare and contrast the following terms:
   a. Expected value
   b. Weighted average
   c. Arithmetic mean
   d. Median

   Write a short essay that compares these statistics phrases with each other, giving special reference to the random variable in a probability distribution of possible returns from an investment. *Hint*: Consult a textbook about mathematical statistics and/or mathematical probabilities.

10. If such bond rating agencies as the Dominion Bond Rating Service and Moody's raise the rating of a bond issue from B + + or BBB to A, what effect is this likely to have on the stock and bond prices of the firm? Explain.

11. Does purchasing power risk pose more of a threat to people who are working and saving for their retirement or to retired people? Explain.

12. Which of the following two categories of investment assets is the best hedge against inflation — real assets (such as real estate, homes, diamonds, gold, silver, and rental property) or monetary assets (such as savings account deposits, cash in a lockbox, and bond investments)? Why? What factors unrelated to purchasing power risk should also be considered in selecting between these two categories of investment assets?

13. Suppose that a representative basket of consumer goods cost $200 on January 1, 1988, and that the same basket cost $242 on January 1, 1990. What was the rate of inflation per year for 1988 and 1989? Show your calculations.

14. Why do the market prices for Canadian federal government bonds decline as interest rates rise? Why do they rise as interest rates decline? *Note*: The following questions apply to the material in the appendix to Chap. 9.

15. What are the disadvantages of investing in a market asset that is not easily marketable?

16. Compare and contrast the marketability risk of two different TSE stocks. Select a blue-chip stock that has thousands of shares traded each day for one of your stocks. Select another TSE stock traded only infrequently with which to compare the high-volume stock. In your comparison, consider the following factors: the daily high and low prices, and the bid-asked spreads. *Hint*: You may have to ask a stockbroker to obtain this information for you—or you could write to the TSE and request it.

17. Why do convertible bonds from a given firm sell at a different yield to maturity than nonconvertible bonds issued by the same firm that are identical in every respect except the convertibility?

SELECTED REFERENCES

Agmon, Tamir, and M. Chapman Findlay. "Domestic Political Risk and Stock Valuation." *Financial Analysts Journal*. November–December 1982, pp. 3–6. This article defines *political risk* and shows how it can affect security values.

Bodie, Zvi. "Common Stocks as a Hedge Against Inflation." *Journal of Finance*, May 1976, pp. 459–470. Mathematical statistics are used to analyze the effects of *inflation* on equity shares. Empirical data are also used to test the models derived.

Boyle, Phelim P., Harry H. Panjer, and Keith Sharp. *Report on Canadian Economic Statistics, January 1, 1924–December 31, 1985*, Canadian Institute of Actuaries, June 1986. An empirical study that provides return and variance data for common stocks, federal and provincial government bonds, industrial bonds, savings instruments, mortgages, Treasury bills, and a number of economic indicators for the period 1924 to 1985.

Brennan, M. J., and E. S. Schwartz. "Convertible Bonds: Valuation and Optimal Strategies for Call and Conversion." *Journal of Finance*, December 1977, pp. 1699–1716. The paper mathematically derives guidelines for finding the value of convertible bonds and highlights some *convertibility risk* considerations.

Garbade, Kenneth. *Securities Markets*. New York: McGraw-Hill, 1982. This textbook focuses on the economic analysis of security markets. In particular, chaps. 20, 24, and 26 discuss the concepts of a market's breadth, depth, resiliency, thinness, the bid-asked spread, and other characteristics useful in analyzing *marketability risk*. The book also devotes a few pages in chap. 17 to explaining callable bonds that are relevant to *callability risk*.

Hatch, James E., and Robert W. White. *Canadian Stocks, Bills, and Inflation: 1950–1983*. Charlottesville, Va.: The Financial Analysts Research Foundation, 1985. This empirical study compares the returns from common stocks, federal, provincial, and municipal bonds, industrial bonds, and Treasury bills with the consumer price index. The easy-to-read monograph contains many tables of informative data from the 1950 to 1983 sample period and various risk factors.

Ibbotson, R. G., and R. A. Sinquefield. *Stocks, Bonds, Bills and Inflation: The Past and the Future*, Monograph 15. Charlottesville, Va.: Financial Analysts Research Foundation, 1982. This empirical study compares the returns from common stocks, corporate bonds, Treasury bills, and T-bonds with the consumer price index.

Markowitz, H. *Portfolio Section*. New York: Wiley, 1959. This classic book explains portfolio analysis. Chapters 2 and 4 delve into probability distributions, standard deviations, expected returns, and the characteristic line. Chapter 9 discusses the semivariance. Algebra and finite probability are used in these chapters to rationalize quantitative surrogates for total risk.

Sauvain, H. *Investment Management*. 3d ed. Englewood Cliffs, N.J.: Prentice-Hall, 1967. Chapters 5 through 7 discuss financial, purchasing power, and interest rate risk. No mathematics used.

Teweles, Richard J., and Edward S. Bradley. *The Stock Market*. 4th ed. New York: Wiley, 1982. Chapter 26 provides a good description of convertible bonds that sheds light on *convertibility risk*.

Appendix 9A

OTHER RISK FACTORS

The major risk factors are interest rate risk, purchasing power risk, market risk, default risk, and management risk. These risk factors were discussed in Chap. 9. In addition to these major risk factors there are some other significant risk factors that are usually of lesser importance. This appendix discusses some of these other risk factors.

APP. 9A-1   THE MARKETABILITY RISK FACTOR

Marketability risk, as differentiated from the market risk of bull and bear markets, is that portion of an asset's total variability of return resulting from price discounts given or sales commissions that must be paid in order to sell the asset in a hurry.

Perfectly liquid assets are perfectly marketable and suffer no marketability risk. Or, stated from a negative viewpoint, illiquid assets are not readily marketable—either price discounts must be given or sales commissions must be paid, or both these costs must be incurred by the seller, in order to find a new investor for an illiquid asset. The more illiquid an asset is, the larger are the price discounts and/or the commissions that a seller must give up in order to effect a quick sale.

You can buy an asset at its bid price and sell it at its asked (or offered) price. The bid price is always below the asked price, as shown in Fig. App. 3A-1 on page 69. The bid-asked spread is the cost of selling an asset quickly. Seen differently, the bid-asked spread is the dealer's reward for making a market in the asset.

The bid-asked spread can be thought of as the sum of (1) the price discount the seller has to give up to sell the asset quickly and (2) the broker's commission for handling the transaction. Or, if the intermediary is a dealer instead of a broker, the bid-asked spread is the dealer's compensation for buying the asset and (it is hoped, only temporarily) carrying it in inventory until another buyer can be found.

APP. 9A-2   THE POLITICAL RISK FACTOR

Political risk may be thought of as the exploitation of a politically weak group to benefit a politically strong group, with the efforts of various groups to improve their relative positions increasing the variability of return from the affected assets. Whether the changes that cause political risk are sought by political or by economic interests, the resulting variability of return is called political risk if it is accomplished through legislative, judicial, or administrative branches of the government that can be manipulated politically.

International investors face political risk in the form of expropriation of nonresidents' assets, foreign exchange controls that prohibit foreign investors from withdrawing their funds, disadvantageous tax and tariff treatments, a requirement that nonresident investors give partial ownership to local residents, and unreimbursed destruction of foreign-owned assets by hostile residents of the foreign country. Foreign investors are forced to deal with *international political risk* by requiring higher expected rates of return from foreign investments than from domestic investments, by obtaining guarantees from high-level government officials in writing, and by using nonrecourse financing provided by the foreign country before undertaking any foreign investing. Although most political risk discussions focus only on international political risk, domestic political risk should not be overlooked.

Domestic political risk takes the form of environmental regulations, zoning requirements, fees, licences, and, most frequently, taxes of one form or another. The taxes may be property taxes, sales taxes, income taxes, or employment taxes. Taxes are levied on a readily identifiable, politically weak group, such as owners of real estate, buyers of luxury goods or "sinful goods" (the consumers of liquor), high-income earners, or employers. The passage of new tax laws or the modification of previously existing taxes can be foretold only probabilistically, if at all. The tax proceeds are transferred from the readily identifiable, politically weak group to a more politically powerful group. The tax and the transfer of the wealth are accomplished through the jurisdiction of some governmental unit that can be manipulated politically.

The effects of political risk on investment values can be traced explicitly through the discounted present value of cash dividends model. Equation (App. 9A-1) indicates that the present value of a share of stock equals the discounted present value of all cash dividends the equity share is expected to pay to its owners from now (that is, time period $t = 0$) to infinity.

$$p_0 = \frac{d_1}{(1 + k)^1} + \frac{d_2}{(1 + k)^2} + \frac{d_3}{(1 + k)^3} + \ldots \qquad \text{(App.9A-1)}$$

where

d = cash dividend per share paid in time period t

k = risk-adjusted discount rate

p = stock's present value

Political risk can change the value of the share of common stock in Eq. (App. 9A-1) in two different ways. First, if a new corporate income tax were imposed on the corporation or an old income tax were raised, for example, the firm would not be able to pay its investors cash dividends as large as expected before the income tax increase. This politically legislated tax would reduce the investment's value—an example of political risk at work.

The second way that political risk can cause variability in the common stock's value is through risk changes. Care must be taken to avoid "double-counting" when risk adjustments are made, however. If cash dividends were correctly adjusted in the numerator of Eq. (App. 9A-1), only pure risk changes justify a further adjustment to the discount rate in the denominator of the equation. When political change does cause a pure change in risk, however, this change will pass through the discount rate and cause political variability of return for investors who bought the stock.[41]

APP. 9A-3 THE CALLABILITY RISK FACTOR

As explained in Chap. 2, some issues of bonds and preferred stock are issued with a provision that allows the issuer to call them in for repurchase if the issuer desires. Issuers like these call provisions because it allows them to refund outstanding fixed-payment securities with a newer issue if market interest rates drop to a level below the level being paid on the outstanding securities. But whatever the issuing company gains by calling in an issue is gained at the expense of the investors who had the misfortune to have their securities called. Investors should view the call provision as a threat that may deprive them of a good investment at a time when their funds can be refunded only at a lower rate of yield.

That portion of a security's total variability of return derived from the possibility that the issue may be called commands a risk premium that comes in the form of a slightly higher expected rate of return. This additional return should increase in proportion to the risk that the issue is called. The following array of categories shows how callability risk varies with the terms attached to the call provision.

1. Securities that are noncallable at any time during their life have no callability risk.
2. An issue that is noncallable for refunding, but that can be recalled for redemption with funds from sources other than a refunding (such as retained earnings), is the second safest category.
3. The third category is the largest and most difficult to define because it involves one or both of two different kinds of call protection. One kind of call protection is a stipulation that the issue may not be called for a certain number of years (such as five, ten, fifteen, or twenty) after the issue is new; the issue is then callable on short notice after the protected period is past. The other kind of call protection is a call premium that allows the issuer to call the securities at any time, but only at a premium (of 10 percent, for example) over their face value. The risk protection from these provisions increases with the number of years before the call may be allowed to occur and/or with the size of the call premium.
4. Callability risk is the greatest with those issues that are callable at any time on short notice. These securities may yield as much as seventy or eighty basis points more than an equivalent issue not callable under any conditions.[42]

41 This section draws from an article by Tamir Agmon and M. Chapman Findlay, "Domestic Political Risk and Stock Valuation," *Financial Analysts Journal*, November–December 1982, pp. 3–6.
42 F. Jen and J. Wert, "The Effect of Call Risk on Corporate Bond Yield," *Journal of Finance*, December 1967; Zvi Bodie and Benjamin Freidman, "Interest Rate Uncertainty and the Value of Bond Call Protection," *Journal of Political Economy*, February 1978; Edwin Elton and Martin Gruber, "The Economic Value of the Call Option," *Journal of Finance*, September 1972; Gordon Pye, "The Value of a Call Option on a Bond," *Journal of Political Economy*, April 1966; Gordon Pye, "The Value of Call Deferment on a Bond: Some Empirical Results," *Journal of Finance*, December 1967.

APP. 9A-4   THE CONVERTIBILITY RISK FACTOR

Callability risk and convertibility risk are similar in two respects. First, both these provisions are contractual stipulations included in the terms of the original issue. Second, both these provisions alter the variability of return (that is, the risk) from the affected security. *Convertibility risk* is that portion of the total variability of return that an investor in a convertible bond or a convertible preferred stock experiences because of the contractual possibility that the investment may be converted into the issuer's common stock.

Sometimes bonds and preferred stocks are issued with the stipulation that they may be converted into the issuing corporation's common stock if the investor wishes to do so, as explained in Chap. 2. Essentially, the convertibility right attached to some bonds and/or preferred stocks gives their investors the option to buy shares of the corporation's common stock at some future date and fixed price by using the bond or preferred stock valued at its face value to pay for the purchase. The value of the conversion right of a security can be assessed by comparing the price of a nonconvertible security with the price of a similar convertible security.[43]

---

43 Convertible securities are discussed in E. O. Thorp and S. T. Kassouf, *Beat the Market: A Scientific Stock Market System* (New York: Random House, 1967), chap. 10. See also M. J. Brennan and E. S. Schwartz, "Convertible Bonds: Valuation and Optimal Strategies for Call and Conversion," *Journal of Finance*, December 1977, pp. 1699–1716.

CHAPTER

10

The Characteristic Line and Capital Asset Pricing Model (CAPM)

Chapter 9 defined the *total risk* of an asset as the asset's total variability of return then went on to show how to measure total risk statistically with the "variance," or the "standard deviation of returns." This chapter expands on the material presented in Chap. 9 by showing that the total risk of an asset can be statistically divided into two parts: diversifiable risk and undiversifiable risk.

Undiversifiable risk
Diversifiable risk
Total risk

Partitioning total risk into these two mutually exclusive segments yields an important insight called the capital asset pricing model (CAPM hereafter), or, synonymously, the security market line (SML). Let us begin this chapter's exploration of the new facets of risk by defining diversifiable risk and undiversifiable risk.

Undiversifiable Risk Stems from Systematic Variability *Undiversifiable risk* is that portion of total variability of return caused by factors that *simultaneously* affect the prices of all marketable securities.[1] The systematic nature of these price changes immunizes them from much of the risk-reducing effects of diversification. Thus, *systematic risk* is synonymously called undiversifiable risk.

Changes in the economic, political, and sociological environment that affect securities markets are sources of systematic risk. Systematic variability of return is found in nearly all securities in varying degrees because most securities move together loosely in a systematic manner.

1 The simultaneity of systematic stock price movements was first documented using monthly data by J. C. Francis, "Intertemporal Differences in Systematic Stock Price Movements," *Journal of Financial and Quantitative Analysis*, June 1975, pp. 205–219. A later study refines Francis' measurements by using daily data; see G. A. Hawawini and A. Vora, "Evidence of Intertemporal Systematic Risks in the Daily Price Movement of NYSE and AMEX Common Stocks," *Journal of Financial and Quantitative Analysis*, 1979. The Hawawini-Vora study suggests that sometimes there is a one- or two-day lead or lag in the speed with which some stock prices react to systematic changes.

FIGURE 10-1   Canadian market indexes fluctuating together.

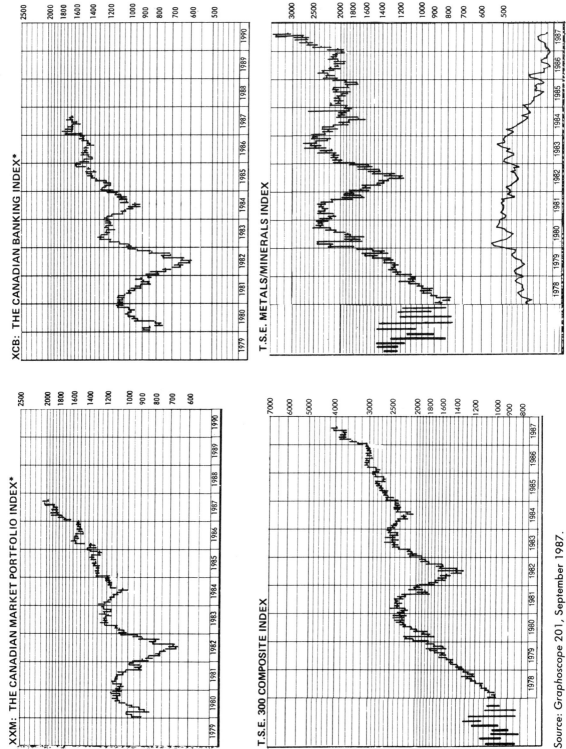

Source: Graphoscope 201, September 1987.

Figure 10-1 shows how the Montreal Exchange's Canadian Market Portfolio Index of 25 widely held Canadian stocks and the Canadian Banking Index of 6 large banks' stocks, and the Toronto Stock Exchange's 300 Composite Index of 300 representative stocks and the Metals and Minerals Index of 21 mining company stocks all tend to vary in price together: this is systematic variability. The prices of nearly all individual common stocks tend to move together in the same manner; that is why many stocks listed on the major Canadian exchanges are significantly positively correlated with one another. In fact, Hatch and White[2] found that the underlying index explained about 26.7 percent of the variation in the price movements of a large sample of stocks listed on the Toronto Stock Exchange, the Montreal Exchange and the Vancouver Stock Exchange over the period 1950–1983.[3]

Canadian firms that have a high proportion of systematic risk include: Bow Valley Industries, Brascan, CP Enterprises, Canadian Pacific, Copperfield Mining, Denison Mines, Dofasco, Falconbridge Nickel, Genstar, Gulf Canada, Husky Oil, Imperial Oil, Nova, an Alberta corporation, Placer Development, Power Corp, Rio Algom, Teck Corp, Trimac, and United Corp.

It will be noted that the firms with high systematic risk tend to be those providing basic industrial goods (such as railroads, tool companies, and rubber companies), firms engaged in the natural resource industry and highly levered firms that have cyclical sales (like the airlines and home builders), and small firms with high-technology products that might become rapidly obsolete (like the computer companies). The sales, profits, and stock prices of these firms follow the level of economic activity and the level of the securities markets to a high degree. As a result, these firms tend to have high degrees of undiversifiable risk.

Diversifiable Risk Comes from Unsystematic Changes *Diversifiable risk* is that portion of total risk that is unique to a firm or industry. Changes, such as labour strikes, management errors, inventions, advertising campaigns, shifts in consumer taste, and lawsuits, cause unsystematic variability of returns in a firm. Since unsystematic changes affect one firm, or at most a few firms, they must be forecast separately for each firm and for each individual incident by any security analyst who is attempting to predict the price movements of an asset. And, more importantly, since unsystematic security price movements are statistically independent from one another, they may be reduced via diversification. Thus, unsystematic risk is synonymously called *diversifiable risk*.

The proportion of total variability which is unsystematic varies widely from firm to firm. The total risk of a few firms is all unsystematic risk. Consumers

---

2 James E. Hatch and Robert W. White, *Canadian Stocks, Bonds, Bills and Inflation: 1950–1983,* Monograph 19 (Charlottesville, Va.: The Financial Analysts Research Foundation, 1985) p. 121.

3 These are similar to the reported findings in the United States that the New York Stock Exchange indexes explain about 30 percent of the variation in the price movements of the (approximately) 1700 listed stocks. See Marshall Blume, "On the Assessment of Risk," *Journal of Finance,* March 1971, pp. 1–10. J. C. Francis "Statistical Analysis of Risk Surrogates for NYSE Stocks," *Journal of Financial and Quantitative Analysis,* December 1979.

Distributing, Daon Developments, Irwin Toy, Laidlaw Transportation, Toronto Sun Publishing, and Westinghouse Canada, are firms that have large proportions of unsystematic risk and small proportions of systematic risk.

Many of the firms with low proportions of systematic risk and high proportions of unsystematic risk produce nondurable consumer goods. Sales, profits, and stock prices of these firms do not depend on the level of industrial activity or the stock market. As a result, these firms might have their best years when the economy is in a recession.

Contributing Risk Factors   Table 10-1 lists various risk factors that were introduced and defined as possible components of an asset's total risk in Chap. 9. Table 10-1 categorizes these risk factors under headings which indicate that they may contribute to an asset's diversifiable risk and/or its undiversifiable risk. The makeup of every asset's risk is unique. For instance, default risk may impact on the total risk of some asset in a systematic manner that would contribute to that asset's undiversifiable risk. Or, some assets (like federal government bonds, for example) have no default risk at all. The categorization hypothesized in Table 10-1 is thus not appropriate for every asset's risk.

Table 10-1 shows how the risk factors discussed in Chap. 9 are related to the risk partition explained in Chap. 10.

TABLE 10-1   SOURCES OF RISK

1. Sources of Undiversifiable Risk:
   - Systematic interest rate risk (if present)
   - Plus: Systematic purchasing power risk (if present)
   - Plus: Systematic market risk (if present)
   - Plus: Systematic management risk (if present)
   - Plus: Systematic default risk (if present)
   - Plus: Systematic marketability risk (if present)
   - Plus: Systematic callability risk (if present)
   - Plus: Systematic convertibility risk (if present)
   - Plus: Other systematic risk factors (if present)
2. Sources of Diversifiable Risk:
   - Plus: Unsystematic interest rate risk (if present)
   - Plus: Unsystematic purchasing power risk (if present)
   - Plus: Unsystematic market risk (if present)
   - Plus: Unsystematic management risk (if present)
   - Plus: Unsystematic default risk (if present)
   - Plus: Unsystematic marketability risk (if present)
   - Plus: Unsystematic callability risk (if present)
   - Plus: Unsystematic convertibility risk (if present)
   - Plus: Other unsystematic risk factors (if present)

Aggregate: Total risk

**BOX 10-1
The Categories of Risk Factors that Make Up Total Risk**

10-1 THE CHARACTERISTIC LINE

Chapter 9 argued that the standard deviation (or the variance) of rates of return was a quantitative surrogate for *total risk*. Then, this chapter began with a nonquantitative explanation of systematic and unsystematic risks and their sources. Do not be misled by the nonquantitative discussion at the beginning of this chapter, however. It is possible to measure the systematic and unsystematic risks of an asset by using quantitative risk surrogates. A statistical tool, which we shall refer to as the *characteristic line*, is employed to measure systematic, or undiversifiable, risk and unsystematic, or diversifiable, risk.

FIGURE 10-2   Characteristic line for Kaiser Aluminum and Chemical common stock.

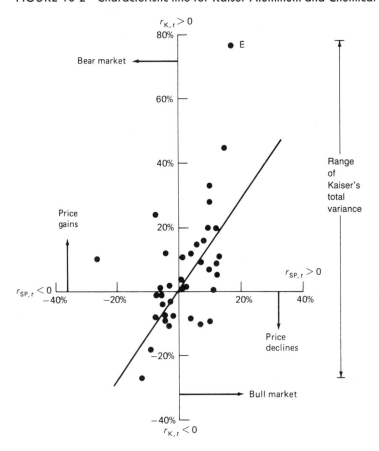

$$r_{K,K} = a_K + b_K r_{m,t} + e_{k,t}$$
$$r_{k,t} = .29 + 1.45 r_{m,t} + e_{k,t}$$
$$\bar{r}_k = 4.78\%$$
$$\bar{r}_m = 3.58\%$$
$$\sigma_k = 19.54\%$$
$$R^2 = .47$$
$$T = 38$$

Figure 10-2 illustrates the characteristic line for the common stock issued by the Kaiser Aluminum and Chemical Corporation.[4] Statistically speaking, characteristic lines are ordinary least-squares regression lines of the form shown in Eq. (10-1). Statistics books sometimes call our characteristic line the simple linear regression model.[5]

$$r_{it} = a_i + b_i r_{mt} + e_{it}$$
(10-1)

where

a_i and b_i = the regression intercept and slope statistics, respectively

e_t = the random error around the regression line which occurs in period t

A characteristic line graphically represents the nature of systematic and unsystematic risks; it shows the relationships of some assets with the market. Each characteristic line is thus a *market model* for one security.

The action of the stock market is measured along the horizontal axis of Fig. 10-2 in terms of rates of change or rates of return from the market at different time periods, denoted r_{mt}. Equation (10-2) shows how rates of change in the market are calculated, using Standard & Poor's (SP) market index.[6] A number of other market indexes could also have been used.

10-1.1 Market Returns: The Characteristic Line's Independent Variable

$$r_{mt} = \frac{SP_{t+1} - SP_t}{SP_t}$$
(10-2)

where

SP_{t+1} = the dollar amount of the S&P index at the beginning of period

$t + 1$

SP_t = the value of the index at the beginning of period t

These period-by-period rates of change in the market index are downward-biased estimates of average returns available in the market because cash dividends are excluded. There is no reason why dividends should not be included in r_{mt} or why other market indexes should not be used in determining characteristic lines. However, once a market index is adopted, it should be used *consistently* in determining all characteristic lines if they are to be comparable.

4 The term *characteristic line* is from Jack L. Treynor, "How to Rate Management of Investment Funds," *Harvard Business Review*, January–February 1965, pp. 63–75. Mr. Treynor appears to be the first person to perceive the concept of undiversifiable risk: Jack L. Treynor, "Toward a Theory of Market Value of Risky Assets," unpublished manuscript, 1961.

5 Mathematical App. D, in Part 9, provides a brief review of the definitions of terms such as regression line, correlation coefficient, and standard error.

6 Appendix 10B provides some empirical market returns that were calculated with Standard & Poor's 500. See *Standard & Poor's Trade and Securities Statistics*, an annual book of statistics which is updated with monthly supplements.

**10-1.2
Asset
Returns—
The
Characteristic
Line's
Dependent
Variable**

Rates of return for which the characteristic line is being prepared are calculated by using Eq. (2-2) for stocks.

$$r_{it} = \frac{p_{t+1} - p_t + d_t}{p_t} \qquad (2\text{-}2)$$

where

d_t = cash dividend in period t from stock i

p_t = market price at beginning of period for ith stock

p_{t+1} = end-of-period price for period t or, equivalently,

the beginning price for period $t + 1$

Returns on the ith asset are the dependent variable on the vertical axis of Fig. 10-2. If the ith asset has any systematic risk, part of its variation in rates of return is dependent upon the independent variable—returns on the market. Monthly, quarterly, semi-annual, or annual returns may be used to prepare a characteristic line.[7]

**10-1.3
Estimating
a
Characteristic
Line**

The characteristic line is a line of "best fit." It may be estimated intuitively; it may be fit to historical data by hand; or ordinary least-squares (OLS) regression may be used. If historical data are to be used, the first step in estimating the characteristic line for some asset is to calculate the periodic returns on the asset as defined in Eq. (2-2) and the returns on the market as defined in Eq. (10-2). The time periods used for calculating returns on the asset and the market must be *simultaneous* because the characteristic line model measures an investment asset's simultaneous reactions to market pressures.

Table 10-2 shows the quarterly data used to fit the characteristic line for Kaiser Aluminum and Chemical Corporation's common stock. These data can be obtained from the sources of financial information discussed in Chap. 6. After the rates of return on the ith asset and some market index data have been gathered, they can be arranged as shown in Table 10-3.

The rates of return from the market and the asset may be plotted as shown in Fig. 10-2. Point E in this figure, for example, is a point where the market return was 17 percent and Kaiser's return was 77 percent during the same time period. Each dot represents the rate of return on the asset and the market during a given time period. A line of best fit can be "eyeballed" through these points, or a regression line can be calculated. The dependent variable

---

7 It is desirable to have at least thirty observations over a sample period of no longer than a decade when estimating the characteristic line. Thirty observations are suggested because that is where small sample theory typically ends and the large sample theory begins. For example, the T distribution may be dropped and the normal distribution used in its place. The reason a decade is suggested as an upper limit for the sample period is because sample periods that are too long encompass time periods during which the firm may change.

TABLE 10-2   KAISER ALUMINUM & CHEMICAL CORPORATION RETURN DATA

YEAR/ QUARTER	Raw Data, $		Adjusted Data, $		QUARTERLY DIVIEND YIELD, %	QUARTERLY PRICE CHANGE, %	QUARTERLY RATE OF RETURN, %
	BEGIN PRICE	CASH DIVIDEND	BEGIN PRICE	CASH DIVIDEND			
1974.1	20.000	0.188	10.000	0.094	0.094	11.88	12.82
1974.2	22.375	0.188	11.188	0.094	0.840	−25.14	−24.30
1974.3	16.750	0.250	8.375	0.125	1.49	−13.43	−11.94
1974.4	14.500	0.250	7.250	0.125	1.72	−11.20	−9.47
1975.1	12.875	0.300	6.438	0.150	2.32	74.74	77.07
1975.2	22.500	0.300	11.250	0.150	1.33	43.89	45.22
1975.3	32.375	0.300	16.188	0.150	0.926	−28.18	−27.26
1975.4	23.250	0.300	11.625	0.150	1.29	19.35	20.64
1976.1	27.750	0.300	13.875	0.150	1.08	19.81	20.90
1976.2	33.250	0.300	16.625	0.150	0.902	10.52	11.42
1976.3	36.750	0.300	18.375	0.150	0.816	−0.68	0.1360
1976.4	36.500	0.300	18.250	0.150	0.821	.0	0.8219
1977.1	36.500	0.300	18.250	0.150	0.821	−2.39	−1.572
1977.2	35.625	0.350	17.813	0.175	0.982	3.856	4.839
1977.3	35.000	0.350	18.500	0.175	0.945	−12.83	−11.89
1977.4	32.250	0.350	16.125	0.175	1.08	−4.260	−3.175
1978.1	30.875	0.400	15.438	0.200	1.29	−5.667	−4.372
1978.2	28.125	0.400	14.563	0.200	1.37	9.441	10.81
1978.3	31.875	0.400	15.938	0.200	1.25	15.29	16.54
1978.4	36.750	0.400	18.375	0.200	1.36	−2.721	−1.360
		FEBRUARY 1, 1979; a 2 for 1 split was effective					
1979.1	17.875	0.250	17.875	0.250	1.39	11.18	12.587
1979.2	19.875	0.250	19.875	0.250	1.25	−7.547	−6.289
1979.3	18.375	0.300	18.375	0.300	1.63	13.60	15.23
1979.4	20.875	0.300	20.875	0.300	1.43	−9.580	−8.143
1980.1	18.875	0.300	18.875	0.300	1.58	0.662	2.251
1980.2	19.000	0.300	19.000	0.300	1.57	4.605	6.184
1980.3	19.875	0.350	19.875	0.350	1.76	32.07	33.83
1980.4	26.250	0.350	26.250	0.350	1.33	−11.90	−10.57
1981.1	23.125	0.350	23.125	0.350	1.51	9.729	11.24
1981.2	25.375	0.350	25.375	0.350	1.37	−10.83	−9.458
1981.3	22.625	0.350	22.625	0.350	1.54	−19.88	−18.34
1981.4	18.125	0.350	18.125	0.350	1.93	−11.72	−9.793
1982.1	16.000	0.350	16.00	0.350	2.18	−10.93	−8.750
1982.2	14.250	0.150	14.250	0.150	1.05	−11.40	−10.35
1982.3	12.625	0.150	12.625	0.150	1.18	7.920	9.108
1982.4	13.625	0.150	13.625	0.150	1.10	10.09	11.19
1983.1	15.000	0.150	15.000	0.150	1.00	6.666	7.666
1983.2	16.000	0.150	16.000	0.150	0.937	27.34	28.28

r_i is regressed onto the independent variable r_m. It is best to fit the regression line because additional statistics, such as the correlation coefficient, can be obtained once the regression line is determined.

TABLE 10-3 RETURNS TO CALCULATE CHARACTERISTIC LINE

TIME PERIOD, t	INDEPENDENT VARIABLE, RETURNS ON MARKET	DEPENDENT VARIABLE RETURNS ON ASSET i
$t = 1$	r_{m1}	r_{i1}
$= 2$	r_{m2}	r_{i2}
$= 3$	r_{m3}	r_{i3}
$= 4$	r_{m4}	r_{i4}
.	.	.
.	.	.
.	.	.
.	.	.
.	.	.
$t = T$	r_{mT}	r_{iT}

Regression model: $r_{it} = a_i + b_i r_{mt} + e_{it}$ Eq. (10-1)

Characteristic line: $r_i = a_i + b_i r_m$ Eq. 10-3a)

10-1.4 Interpreting the Characteristic Line

Equation (10-3a) represents the characteristic line for the ith asset. Equation (10-3a) is like Eq. (10-1) except that the residual return left unexplained by the regression, e, has been averaged out to zero when summed up over all the observations, and thus it does not appear in the equation. The time subscripts in Eq. (10-1) have also been deleted because Eq. (10-3a) was fit through the multiple time periods over which the returns were observed.

$$r_i = a_i + b_i r_m \qquad (10\text{-}3a)$$

The term a_i is called the *alpha coefficient* for security i; it is the intercept point where the characteristic line intercepts the vertical axis.[8] Alpha is an estimate of the ith asset's rate of return when the market is stationary, $r_{mt} = 0$. The term b_i is called the *beta coefficient*; it measures the slope of the characteristic line.

The beta coefficient in the characteristic line is defined mathematically in Eq. (10-4a) and (10-4b) below.

$$b_i = \frac{\text{cov}\,(r_i, r_m)}{\text{var}(r_m)} \qquad (10\text{-}4a)$$

$$= \frac{\text{units of rise}}{\text{units of run}} = \text{slope of characteristic regression line} \qquad (10\text{-}4b)$$

where

$\text{cov}(r_i, r_m) =$ the covariance[9] of returns of the ith asset with the market

$\text{var}(r_m) =$ the variance of returns for the market index

The beta coefficient is an *index of systematic risk*. Beta coefficients may be used for (ordinal) rankings of the systematic risk of different assets. However,

---

8 Statistically speaking, the alpha intercept statistic is defined as follows:
$a_i = \bar{r}_i - b_i \bar{r}_m = E(r_i) - b_i E(r_m)$

the beta coefficient is not a (cardinal) measure that may be compared directly with total or unsystematic risk. If the beta is larger than one, that is, if $b > 1.0$, then the asset is more volatile than the market and is called an *aggressive asset*. If the beta is smaller than one, $b < 1.0$, the asset is a *defensive asset*: it is less volatile than the market. Most assets' beta coefficients are in the range from 0.5 to 1.5. But, Kaiser is an aggressive stock with a high degree of systematic risk. Kaiser's beta of 1.50 indicates that its return tends to increase 50 percent more than the return on the market average when the market is rising. When the market falls, Kaiser's return tends to fall 150 percent of the decrease in the market. The characteristic line for Kaiser has an above-average correlation coefficient of $\rho = .68$ indicating that the returns on this security follow its particular characteristic line slightly more closely than the average stock. This tendency may be determined by visually noting that the points tend to fit around the characteristic line in Fig. 10-2.

Statistically, total risk is measured by the variance of returns, denoted $\text{var}(r)$. This measure of total risk may be partitioned[10] into the systematic and unsystematic components as follows:

**10-1.5
Partitioning
Risk**

$\text{var}(r_i)$ = total risk of ith asset

$\quad = \text{var}(a_i + b_i r_m + e)$ substituting $(a_i + b_i r_m + e)$ for r_i

$\quad = \text{var}(b_i r_m) + \text{var}(e)$ since $\text{var}(a_i) = 0$

$\quad = b_i^2 \text{var}(r_m) + \text{var}(e)$ since $\text{var}(b_i r_m) = b_i^2 \text{var}(r_m)$

$\quad = \text{systematic} + \text{unsystematic risk}$ \hfill (10-5)

The unsystematic risk measure, $\text{var}(e)$, is called the *residual variance* (or *standard error squared*) in regression language.

The percentage of systematic risk is measured by the coefficient of determination (ρ^2) for the characteristic line. The percentage of unsystematic risk equals $(1.0 - \rho^2)$. More specifically,

$$\frac{\text{Unsystematic risk}}{\text{Total risk}} = \frac{\text{var}(e)}{\text{var}(r_i)} = (1.0 - \rho^2) \tag{10-6a}$$

$$\frac{\text{Systematic risk}}{\text{Total risk}} = \frac{b_i^2 \text{var}(r_m)}{\text{var}(r_i)} = \rho^2 \tag{10-6b}$$

---

9 The covariance is defined as follows:

$$\text{cov}(r_{ij} r_m) = \left(\frac{1}{T}\right) \sum_{t=1}^{T} [(r_i - \bar{r}_i)(r_m - \bar{r}_m)] = \rho_{im} \sigma_i \sigma_m$$

10 Used in this context, *partition* is a technical statistical word that means to divide the total variance into *mutually exclusive* and *exhaustive* pieces. This partition is only possible if the returns from the market are statistically independent from the residual error terms that occur simultaneously, $\text{cov}(r_{mt}, e_{it}) = 0$. The mathematics of regression analysis will orthogonalize the residuals and thus ensure that this condition exists.

Studies of the characteristic lines of hundreds of stocks listed on the NYSE indicate that the average correlation coefficient is $\rho = .5$, approximately.[11] This means that about $\rho^2 = 25$ percent of the total variability of return in most NYSE securities is explained by movements of the entire market; that is, systematic risk averages about one-fourth of total risk for most NYSE stocks.

Average systematic risk	25% = ρ^2
Average unsystematic risk	75% = $1 - \rho^2$
Total risk	100% = 1.0

The systematic changes are common to all stocks and are impossible to diversify away; they are *undiversifiable*.

Kaiser Aluminum's common stock is a riskier-than-average common stock when we consider total risk and systematic risk, as indicated by the statistics in Table 10-4.[12]

TABLE 10-4 RISK AND RETURN STATISTICS FROM CHARACTERISTIC LINE REGRESSION

	KAISER	MARKET PORTFOLIO
Total risk variance of returns = var(r)	0.038	0.008
Unsystematic risk = residual variance = var(r_e)	0.020	0*
Systematic risk measure = b_i^2 [var(r_m)] = ρ^2[var(r_i)]	0.018	0.008
Beta coefficient = index of systematic risk	1.45	1.0
Systematic risk percentage = ρ^2 =	0.47 = 47%	1.0 = 100%

  * Chapter 22 shows that by diversifying internationally, risk that was considered undiversifiable within the domestic context can become, in whole or in part, diversifiable within the context of multinational investments.

10-2 THE CHARACTERISTIC LINE: A CLOSER EXAMINATION

The characteristic line describing the period-by-period interaction between the rates of return of asset i and the rates of change in some market index

11 Mathematical App. D discusses correlation, regression, and the characteristic line and defines the residual variance, coefficient of determination, and other regression terms. See also B. F. King, "Market and Industry Factors in Stock Price Behavior," *Journal of Business*, January 1966, p. 151. King says, in effect, that the average market effect is 50 percent of total risk; this implies $\rho = .7$. Marshall Blume, however, found an averge ρ of about .5 in "On the Assessment of Risk," *Journal of Finance*, March 1971, p. 4. See also O. A. Vasicek, "A Note on Using Cross-Sectional Information in Bayesian Estimation of Security Betas," *Journal of Finance*, December 1973, pp. 1233–1239. J. C. Francis, "Statistical Analysis of Risk Surrogates for NYSE Stocks," *Journal of Financial and Quantitative Analysis*, December 1979.

12 Statements about the relative degree of total risk are made in the context of a long-run horizon—that is, over at least one complete business cycle. Obviously, an accurate short-run forecast which says that some particular company will go bankrupt next quarter makes it more risky than Kaiser, although the latter may have had more historical variability of return.

was defined in Eq. (10-1); it is a model of market forces as they affect the *i*th asset. The characteristic line is also called the *market model* or the *single-index model* by some financial economists.[13]

For prediction purposes, the *conditional expectation* of Eq. (10-1), which was previously shown above as Eq. (10-3*a*) is useful. The conditional expectation is restated equivalently as Eq. (10-3*b*) below.

10-2.1 Graphing Characteristic Lines

$$E(r_i \mid r_m) = a_i + b_i r_m \qquad (10\text{-}3b)$$

Equations (10-3*a*) and (10-3*b*) are like Eq. (10-1) except that the residual return left unexplained by the regression, *e*, has been averaged out to zero when summed up over all the observations, and thus does not appear in conditional expectation. Stated differently, the mathematical expectation of the residual term is zero, $E(e) = 0$. The time subscripts in Eq. (10-1) have also been deleted because Eq. (10-3*a*) is an ex ante (or future expectation) model. In contrast, Eq. (10-1) is an ex post (or historical, data-oriented) model that employs time subscripts to refer to the time series of single period rates of return represented by the model.

The characteristic line's alpha intercept term may have a positive, zero, or negative value for any given asset. But the statistic is usually very near zero in value for most assets. This alpha has no asset-pricing implications and cannot be used for investment-performance evaluation.[14]

The beta regression slope coefficient has an average value of unity. Most betas lie in a range between 0.5 and 1.5, and the betas which lie the farthest away from unity have a tendency to regress back toward unity with the passage of time.[15]

---

13 The first printed discussion of the characteristic line was by Harry Markowitz, *Portfolio Selection* (New York: Wiley, 1959), pp. 97–101: Markowitz called it an *index model*. The next printed record of the model was in the doctoral dissertation of William F. Sharpe at University of California at Los Angeles. Markowitz was on Sharpe's dissertation committee and apparently passed his ideas on to Sharpe. Sharpe referred to the model as the *single-index model* in an article that summarized his dissertation entitled ''A Simplified Model for Portfolio Analysis,'' *Management Science*, vol. 9, no. 2, pp. 277–293, January 1963. Working independently of Markowitz and Sharpe, Jack L. Treynor published an article entitled ''How to Rate Management of Investment Funds,'' *Harvard Business Review*, vol. 43, no. 1, pp. 63–75, January–February 1965. Treynor referred to the model as the *characteristic line*, and this book has adopted Treynor's name for the model because it seems the most descriptive. Professor Eugene Fama appears to be the first to have referred to the model as the *market model*, and his students at the University of Chicago have followed his choice of term in many instances.

14 The alpha intercept term of the characteristic line in terms of risk-premiums does have investment performance implications that are explained by M. C. Jensen, ''The Performance of Mutual Funds in the Period 1945 through 1964,'' *Journal of Finance*, May 1968, pp. 389–416.

15 M. Blume, ''Betas and Their Regression Tendencies,'' *Journal of Finance*, June 1975, pp. 785–795. W. F. Sharpe and G. Cooper, ''Risk-Return Classes of NYSE Stocks, 1931–67,'' *Financial Analysts Journal*, March–April 1972. J. C. Francis, ''Statistical Analysis of Risk Coefficients for NYSE Stocks,'' *Journal of Financial and Quantitative Analysis*, vol. XIV, no. 5, December 1979, pp. 981–997.

FIGURE 10-3   Two different characteristic lines: (a) regression line for an asset with cyclical returns; (b) regression line for an asset with countercyclical returns.

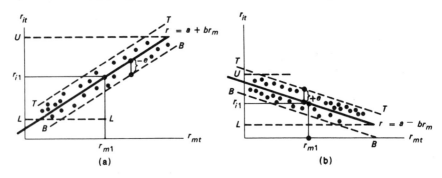

Two possible forms that Eq. (10-1) may assume are shown in Fig. 10-3. Equation (10-1), or equivalently Eq. (10-3b), has been fitted to (1) a firm which has returns that are positively correlated with the returns on the market and (2) a firm whose returns are negatively correlated with the market. For these two firms, the characteristic lines indicate that when the rate of return for the market portfolio is r_{m1}, the security is expected to earn a return of r_{i1}. In statistical language, $E(r_{i1})$ is called the conditional expectation that is conditional on the value of r_{m1}.

In the language of capital market theory, the asset in Fig. 10-3a has more systematic risk than the asset in Fig. 10-3b. It has a positive slope coefficient b_i, positive covariance of returns with the returns from the market portfolio m, and positive correlation of returns with returns on m. The firm in Fig. 10-3b has a negative regression slope coefficient b_i, negative covariance, and negative correlation coefficient. Thus the asset in Fig. 10-3b will decrease the risk of a portfolio that is correlated with m (as most portfolios are) more than the asset in Fig. 10-3a. Most simply, the asset in Fig. 10-3b is the better candidate for risk-reducing diversification purposes.

**10-2.2
Unsystematic
Risk Is
Residual
Variance**

Any time Eq. (10-1) results in a correlation coefficient below positive unity, the observations will not all lie on the regression line; of course, this is the typical case graphed in Figs. 10-2 and 10-3. The vertical deviations of the observations from the regression line are called *residual errors* and are denoted e in Eq. (10-1). Although the least-squares regression technique used to derive Eq. (10-1) or (10-3b) minimizes the sum of the squared errors (that is, minimum Σe_{it}^2) over all the observations, the sum is still a positive value. The term $\sigma^2(r_i | r_m)$ is called the *residual variance around the regression line* in statistical terms, or *unsystematic risk* in financial market theory language.

$$\sigma^2(r_i | r_m) = \frac{\sum_{t=1}^{T} e_{it}^2}{T}$$

(10-7a)

$$= \frac{\sum\limits_{t=1}^{T} (r_{it} - a_i = b_i r_{mt})^2}{T} = \text{var}(e) \qquad (10\text{-}7b)$$

In Fig. 10-3 the *total* range over which the returns varied is represented graphically by the vertical distance between the upper (U) and the lower (L) horizontal dashed lines. The *residual* or *unsystematic* range of variability is represented graphically by the vertical distance between the top (T) and bottom (B) dashed lines, which are parallel to the characteristic line. These dashed lines (U, L, T, and B) are not any kind of boundary lines; they are merely added to depict graphically the total risk (between U and L) and unsystematic risk (between T and B).

If a firm were to experience a change in earning power, its characteristic line might or might not move. Suppose a technological breakthrough occurred that increased a firm's income at every level of sales. If the increased earnings raised the firm's expected rate of return at any given sales volume by one percentage point, the characteristic line might shift upward by one percentage point on the vertical axis. Figure 10-4 represents one possible shift.

10-2.3 Comparative Statics for a Change in Profitability[16]

FIGURE 10-4   Comparative statics of a change in earning power with a change in systematic risk.

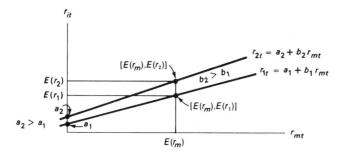

In Fig. 10-4 the rise in the characteristic line is measured by the change in the intercept coefficients, $a_2 - a_1$. If the firm is to *continue* to yield a higher rate of return to its shareholders, it must experience an increase in systematic risk in order to maintain an equilibrium tradeoff relationship between expected return and systematic risk. Thus, the slope of the firm's characteristic line must increase from b_1 to b_2, as shown in Fig. 10-4.

If an increase in systematic risk does not accompany the rise in earnings, a once-and-for-all capital gain will result from the increase in earnings. This capital gain will raise the firm's purchase price enough so that its expected

---

16 Comparative statics involve comparing different static equilibriums. Thus, Fig. 10-4 does not depict the once-and-for-all capital gain and unusually large one-period rate of return that would occur because of the increased earning power.

return will not change, although future dividends may be expected to remain higher. That is, both the numerator and the denominator in Eq. (10-8) will increase proportionally so that the expected return does not change.

$$E(r) = \frac{E(\text{capital gains} + \text{dividends})}{\text{purchase price}} \tag{10-8}$$

Thus the firm's systematic risk and expected return will be unchanged, and the original characteristic line will still describe the characteristic pattern for the firm's rates of return. Investors who owned the stock at the time the once and-for-all capital gain occurred will have captured the capitalized value of the earnings increase (that is, the big one-time capital gain).

10-2.4 Firms with Different Beta Coefficients

All simple linear regression lines pass through the *centroid* where the expected value (or mean) of both variables occurs. Since the characteristic line is a regression line, it must pass through this point $[E(r_m), E(r_i)]$. The centroids and three different characteristic lines are shown graphically in Fig. 10-5.

FIGURE 10-5 Comparison of three firms with different systematic risks.

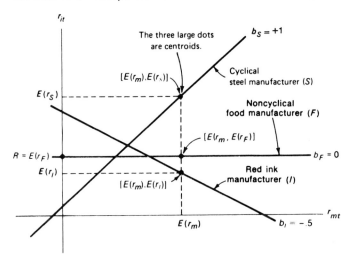

Suppose one firm depicted in Fig. 10-5 is a steel manufacturer, denoted S. Such a firm's sales and profits will likely follow the level of activity in the national economy. As a result, the steel firm has a beta regression slope (systematic risk) coefficient of unity. The second firm is the noncyclical firm denoted F, which might be a food manufacturer; its beta coefficient is zero, and so its returns are not expected to vary owing to systematic risk factors. The third hypothetical firm shown in Fig. 10-5 is a red ink manufacturer, denoted I. This firm is unique in that its returns characteristically co-vary inversely with the rate of return from the market. Supposedly, red ink sells better in recessions and depressions when accountants make more entries in red ink; so the red ink manufacturer has a beta coefficient of $-\frac{1}{2}$.

As a result of the basic difference in the characteristic of each business, the three firms in Fig. 10-5 all have drastically different beta coefficients, $b_S > b_F = 0 > b_I$. Since expected returns are a function of systematic risk for all assets, the three firms' expected returns also differ as follows: $E(r_S)$ > $E(r_F) = R > E(r_I)$, where R denotes the risk-free rate of return. Figure 10-5 depicts these facts graphically.

10-3 THE CAPITAL ASSET PRICING MODEL (CAPM)

Studies of the probability distributions of returns indicate that firms with high total risk and high systematic risk tend also to have high average rates of return. This is what financial economists would intuitively expect. Investors demand high rates of return to induce them to invest in risky assets, reminding one of the widely quoted axiom that "there is no such thing as a free lunch." This "free lunch" principle asserts that you cannot expect to get something for nothing. This is also true of investment returns. Investors who want to earn high average rates of return must take high risks and endure the associated loss of sleep, the possibility of ulcers, and the chance of bankruptcy.

In Chap. 1 it was suggested that wealth-maximizing, risk-averting investors will seek investments that have the maximum expected return in their risk-class. Their expected happiness (or utility) from investing is derived as indicated from the unspecified function below.

$$E(U) = f[E(r), \sigma]$$

The investment preferences of wealth-seeking, risk-averse investors represented by the function above cause them to maximize their expected utility (that is, happiness), which is a function of an investment's expected return $E(r)$ and total risk σ. Such investors will seek to (1) maximize their expected return in any given risk-class, or conversely, (2) minimize their risk at any given rate of expected return. However, in selecting individual assets, investors will not be particularly concerned with the asset's total risk, σ. The unsystematic portion of total risk can be easily diversified away by holding a portfolio of several different securities. However, systematic risk affects all stocks in the market and is therefore undiversifiable. Clearly, it is much more difficult to eliminate undiversifiable systematic risk than it is to eliminate diversifiable unsystematic risk.

In the search for assets that will minimize their risk exposure at a given level of expected return, investors will tend to focus on assets' undiversifiable systematic risk. They will bid up the prices of assets with low systematic risk (that is, low beta coefficients). On the other hand, assets with high beta coefficients will experience low demand and market prices that are low relative to assets' income. That is, assets with high levels of systematic risk will tend to have high expected returns. This may be seen by noting in Eq. (10-9a) that the expected return is higher after the purchase price for the asset falls. Obviously, the expected return ratio, denoted $E(r)$ in Eq. (10-9a), will be larger after the denominator decreases as shown at the top of page 230.

$$E(r) = \frac{E(p_{t+1}) - p_t + d_t}{p_t} \qquad (10\text{-}9a)$$

$$E(r) = \frac{\text{expected income}}{\text{market purchase price}} \qquad (10\text{-}9b)$$

An asset with high systematic risk (that is, a high beta) will experience price declines until the expected return it offers is high enough to induce investors to assume this undiversifiable risk. This price level is the *equilibrium price*, and the expected return is the *equilibrium rate of return* for that risk-class.

Figure 10-6 shows the capital asset pricing model (CAPM), or security market line (SML), as it is also called, which graphically depicts the results of the price adjustments (that is, the equilibrium prices and expected returns) from this risk-averse trading.

The CAPM, or SML, is a linear relationship in which the expected average rate of return of the ith asset is a linear function of that asset's systematic risk as represented by b_i. Symbolically, Eq. (10-10) represents the CAPM.

$$E(r_i) = R + cb_i \qquad (10\text{-}10)$$

where

b_i = the independent variable representing the systematic risk of the ith asset; it determines the dependent variable $E(r_i)$, the average expected rate of return for asset i

R = the vertical axis intercept

c = the slope of the CAPM[17]

R is the rate of the interest appropriate when risk is zero.[18] Canadian Treasury bill yields would be a good estimate of R, since these instruments come closer to having zero risk than other marketable securities.

Any vertical line drawn on Fig. 10-6 is a *risk-class* for systematic risk. The CAPM relates an expected return to each level of systematic risk. These expected returns can be interpreted as the appropriate discount rates or the cost of capital that investors expect for that amount of systematic risk.

---

17 The slope of the CAPM is defined as follows:

$$c = \frac{\text{rise}}{\text{run}} = \text{slope of CAPM}$$

$$= \frac{E(r_m) - R}{b_m} = E(r_m) - R \qquad \text{since } b_m = 1.0$$

This slope is the risk-return tradeoff in the security market and is called the ''market price of risk.''

18 Black has suggested a model in which it is not necessary to assume the existence of a riskless rate; see Fischer Black, ''Capital Market Equilibrium with Restricted Borrowing,'' *Journal of Business*, July 1972, pp. 444–454. In Black's model the riskless interest rate is replaced by a portfolio that has a beta equal to zero but still has positive variance of returns. The zero-beta portfolio is uncorrelated with the market portfolio, so that its total risk and its unsystematic risk are identical and both are positive quantities. This portfolio is created by holding

FIGURE 10-6   The security market line (SML), or capital asset pricing model (CAPM).

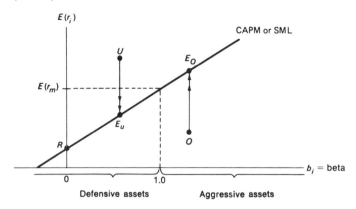

Systematic or undiversifiable risk is the main factor risk-averse investors should consider in deciding whether a security yields enough rate of return to induce them to buy it. Other factors, such as the "glamour" of the stock and the company's financial ratios, are important only to the extent they affect the security's risk and return. The CAPM graphically represents the tradeoff of systematic risk for return that investors expect and are entitled to receive. This implies that the CAPM has asset-pricing implications.

After an asset's average return and systematic risk have been estimated, they may be plotted in reference to the CAPM. In equilibrium every asset's $E(r)$ and beta systematic risk coefficient should plot as one point on the CAPM. To see why this is true, consider Fig. 10-6, which shows two assets denoted O and U. Asset U is underpriced because its average rate of return is too high for the level of systematic risk it bears. Asset O is overpriced because its expected rate of return is too low to induce investors to accept its undiversifiable risk. These two assets should move to the CAPM, as shown by the arrows to their equilibrium positions at the points marked E.

10-3.1 Asset's Price Movements

To see why assets O and U are incorrectly priced, reconsider Eq. (10-9a), which defined the expected rate of return for a common stock.

$$E(r) = \frac{\text{expected capital gains or loss} + \text{expected cash dividends}}{\text{purchase price}} \qquad (10\text{-}9c)$$

risky securities and leveraging and selling short. Some preliminary empirical estimates of the rates of return on the zero-beta portfolio have been published; see F. Black, M. C. Jensen, and M. Scholes, "The Capital Asset Pricing Model: Some Empirical Tests," published in *Studies in the Theory of Capital Markets*, a book of unpublished studies edited by M. C. Jensen and published by Praeger, New York, 1972. Professor G. Alexander has shown an algorithm that could be used to obtain estimates of the returns from a zero-beta portfolio: "An Algorithmic Approach to Deriving the Minimum Variance Zero-Beta Portfolio," *Journal of Financial Economics*, March 1977.

To reach their equilibrium positions on the CAPM, assets O and U must go through a temporary price readjustment. Assuming the assets' systematic risk remains unchanged, the expected return of U must fall to E_U and the expected return of O must rise to E_O. To accomplish this move to an equilibrium rate of return, the denominator of Eq. (10-9c) must rise for asset U and must fall for asset O. Assets O and U or any marketable capital asset (such as a portfolio, stock, bond, or real estate) will be in disequilibrium unless its risk and return lie on the CAPM. Supply and demand will set to work as outlined above to correct any disequilibrium from the CAPM.

10-3.2 Market Imperfections

The operation of the rational forces of supply and demand can be expected to move assets lying off the CAPM toward the CAPM, but because of market imperfections, all assets' risk-return characteristics never lie exactly on the CAPM. Some market imperfections that preclude attainment of a complete equilibrium are

1. *Transaction costs.* The stockbroker's commissions and transfer taxes associated with each security transaction drain away investors' incentive to correct minor deviations from the CAPM.
2. *Differential tax rates on capital gains.* Since capital gains are taxed differently from dividends and interest, the after-tax rate of return (atr) defined in Eq. (10-11) differs with the investor's tax bracket. Thus, each investor envisions a slightly different CAPM in terms of after-tax returns:

$$\text{atr}_t = \frac{d_t(1 - t_0) + (p_{t+1} - p_t)(1 - t_g)}{p_t} \tag{10-11}$$

where

t_0 = the effective tax rate on dividends

t_g = the effective tax rate on capital gains

3. *Heterogeneous expectations.* Different investors assess the systematic risk of any given asset differently and therefore perceive different equilibrium rates of return as being appropriate for any given asset.
4. *Imperfect information.* Some investors are irrational; some are uninformed; and some receive financial news later than others.

Because of market imperfections, all assets are not expected to lie exactly on the CAPM. Therefore, in practice, the CAPM is actually a band rather than a thin line. The width of this band varies directly with the imperfections in the market. As a result, the CAPM cannot be used to pinpoint an asset's equilibrium price. Instead, it can suggest only a range of prices for an asset.

10-4   EMPIRICAL RISK-RETURN ESTIMATES

Section 9-1 explained how to measure an asset's expected rate of return and its total risk, and Sec. 10-1 showed how to measure an asset's systematic risk and unsystematic risk. Economic logic, suggesting that investors should demand higher returns to induce them to buy investments with high systematic risk, was explained too. The next logical question is: If stocks' betas and average returns are actually measured over a period of time, will the high beta stocks really have higher rates of return? Or, put more crassly: Is this CAPM theory really any good? Empirical tests of the CAPM theory were published by William F. Sharpe and Guy Cooper; their work is described in the following paragraphs. Similar studies by other researchers have both extended the CAPM to embrace other variables and reached conclusions that coincide with the basic CAPM reviewed here.[19]

In the Sharpe-Cooper study, monthly stock prices for hundreds of NYSE stocks from 1926 to 1967 provided the raw data. Monthly rates of return were first calculated by using Eq. (2-2) for every stock and every month. Second, betas were calculated with Eq. (10-4a), using five years (or sixty monthly observations) of rates of return. Third, an annual rate of return was calculated for each stock. Fourth, the stocks were grouped into risk deciles based on their beta coefficients. The risk-classes were based on the five years *preceding* the year in which the annual return was calculated to simulate picking stocks for future investment based on five years of past data — a procedure that assumes betas are stable over time.

10-4.1 The Sample and the Statistics

The procedure was replicated for hundreds of stocks every year from 1931 to 1967. Betas were calculated from five years of data, risk deciles formed from the betas, annual returns measured during the sixth year, and then the procedure was repeated for the next year. When the procedure had been repeated once for each (5 + 1 = 6) six-year period from 1931 to 1967, the ten risk deciles from each of the thirty-seven years were averaged to obtain average risk deciles and average annual returns. Figure 10-7 shows the beta coefficients averaged over all stocks in all years for the ten risk-classes. The annual returns averaged over all stocks and all years in each risk decile are shown in Fig. 10-8.

---

19 Empirical tests of the CAPM include: M. Blume and I. Friend, ''A New Look at the Capital Asset Pricing Model,'' *Journal of Finance*, March 1973, pp. 19–34; F. Black, M. C. Jensen, and M. Scholes, ''The Capital Asset Pricing Model: Some Empirical Tests,'' in M. C. Jensen (ed.), *Studies in the Theory of Capital Markets* (New York: Praeger, 1972); M. Blume and F. Husic, ''Price, Beta and Exchange Listing,'' *Journal of Finance*, May 1973, pp. 283–299; M. Miller and M. Scholes, ''Rates of Return in Relation to Risk: A Re-Examination of Some Recent Findings,'' in M. C. Jensen (ed.), *Studies in the Theory of Capital Markets*, (New York: Praeger, 1972), pp. 47–78; E. F. Fama and J. MacBeth, ''Risk, Return and Equilibrium: Empirical Tests,'' *Journal of Political Economy*, May/June 1973, pp. 607–636; M. R. Reinganum, ''Misspecification of Capital Asset Pricing: Empirical Anomalies Based on Earnings Yields and Market Values,'' *Journal of Financial Economics*, March 1981, pp. 19–46; R. Litzenberger and K. Ramaswamy, ''The Effect of Personal Taxes and Dividends and Capital Asset Prices: Theory and Empirical Evidence,'' *Journal of Financial Economics*, June 1979, pp. 163–195; R. W. Banz, ''The Relationship between Return and Market Value of Common Stocks,'' *Journal of Financial Economics*, March 1981, pp. 3–18; deficiencies in the preceding empirical tests are pinpointed by Richard Roll, ''A Critique of the Asset Pricing Theory's Tests,'' *Journal of Financial Economics*, March 1977, pp. 129–176.

FIGURE 10-7 Average betas for risk deciles, 1931–1967.

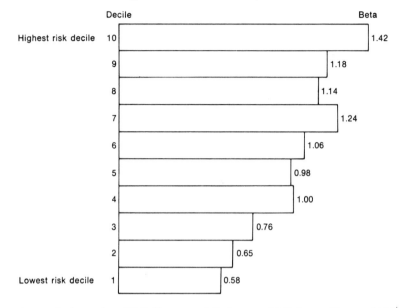

Source: Redrawn from W. F. Sharpe and G. Cooper, "Risk-Return Classes of N.Y.S.E. Common Stocks, 1931–67," *Financial Analysts Journal*, March–April 1972.

FIGURE 10-8 Average annual rates of return by risk deciles, 1931–1967.

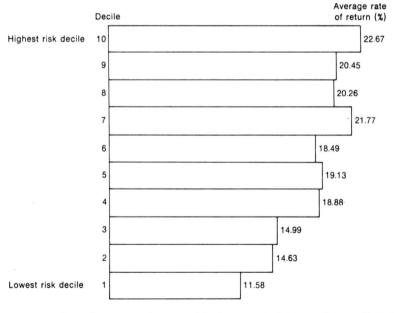

Source: Redrawn from W. F. Sharpe and G. Cooper, "Risk-Return Classes of N.Y.S.E. Common Stocks, 1931–67," *Financial Analysts Journal*, March–April 1972.

A simple linear regression of the form shown in Eq. (10-12) was fitted through the ten average betas, denoted b_i from Fig. 10-7, and their associated average annual returns, denoted $\bar{r}_i$ from Fig. 10-8, for $i = 1, 2, \ldots, 10$ deciles.

**10-4.2
CAPM
Estimates**

$$\bar{r}_i = a + b(b_i) \tag{10-12}$$

Figure 10-9 shows a graph of the risk-return relationship delineated by the study.

FIGURE 10-9   Regression line through 10 average betas and 10 average returns.

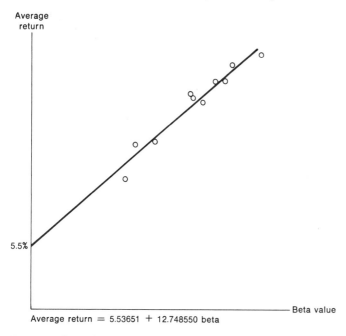

Average return = 5.53651 + 12.748550 beta

Source: Redrawn from W. F. Sharpe and G. Cooper, ''Risk-Return Classes of N.Y.S.E. Common Stocks, 1931–67,'' *Financial Analysts Journal,* March–April 1972.

The Sharpe-Cooper study is a scientific investigation which was painstakingly constructed so as to avoid introducing bias. Some sampling error exists in the study as it does in every statistical study, but the statistics do support the theory. In the long run, buying stocks with high (or medium or low) degrees of systematic risk was shown to yield portfolios with high (or medium or low) average future rates of return. On a single-stock basis, this may not occur because the single stock selected may go bankrupt, experience a change in its systematic risk, or undergo some other change that was not representative of the behaviour of most stocks. However, by using hundreds of stocks and decades of data, such sampling problems are eliminated and the market's equilibrium tendency emerges.

10-5   CONCLUSIONS ABOUT RISK

The total risk of any asset can be assessed by measuring its variability of returns. Total risk can be partitioned into two main parts — systematic risk and unsystematic risk. Each can be estimated by using the characteristic regression line. The characteristic regression line of an asset explains the asset's systematic variability of return in terms of factors related to a market index. The sources of systematic risk include changes in the purchasing power of money, interest rate fluctuations, swings in the security market prices called bull and bear markets, and other systematic factors.

The portion of total risk that is not explained by an asset's characteristic regression line is called unsystematic risk. Unsystematic variability of returns is unique to each asset and is caused by management errors, financial problems in the firm, which might cause it to default on a debt obligation, and/or other unsystematic factors that disturb the firm's security price fluctuations.

Since unsystematic variations are unique to each firm; they can be easily diversified away to zero by spreading the funds to be invested across the securities of several unrelated firms. Systematic risk, on the other hand, is more difficult to diversify because it is common to all assets in the market to some extent. Within a given market (for example, the stock market), assets with high degrees of systematic risk must be priced to yield high rates of return in order to induce investors to accept high degrees of risk that are essentially undiversifiable within that market. The CAPM illustrates the positive relation between assets' systematic risks and their expected or average rates of return. Empirical tests support the validity of the CAPM.

QUESTIONS

1. Write a short essay defining total risk verbally, and explain how this definition is consistent with using the variance of returns as a quantitative risk surrogate.
2. Make a probability distribution of your starting salary per month when you graduate. What quantitative risk surrogate would you use to measure the risk of these dollar quantities? What problems are presented by simply using the standard deviation of your dollar salary as a quantitative risk surrogate?
3. Write one-sentence definitions of each of the following: (a) total risk, (b) systematic risk, (c) unsystematic risk, (d) diversifiable risk, and (e) undiversifiable risk.
4. Gather ten years of quarterly data from 1974-IQ to 1983-IVQ inclusive for Kaiser Aluminum common stock and prepare a regression like the one shown in Fig. 10-2. The needed stock market index data are in Appendix 10B. Calculate rates of return for the asset and estimate the characteristic line for the asset. Is it a defensive or an aggressive asset? Does the characteristic line for the asset have much predictive power? Is

the asset good for diversification purposes? Has the beta coefficient for Kaiser shifted during the latest four quarters?

5. How do you expect the total risk of a mutual fund to be divided between systematic and unsystematic risk?

6. Assume that a firm added a new product to its line that decreased the overall riskiness of the firm. For example, a highly cyclical rubber company began producing red ink. How would this affect the value of a share of the firm's stock? Use a diagram of the CAPM to show the asset-pricing implications of this change in the firm.

7. Could you as a security analyst expect to find any worthwhile information by studying the residual error from the characteristic line regression? Explain.

8. Are the beta coefficients in the characteristic line stable through time? Explain. Is it worthwhile to study betas if they are intertemporally unstable?

9. Do you believe that an asset's unsystematic risk should have no effect on its market price, as the capital asset pricing model (CAPM) suggests? Explain.

SELECTED REFERENCES

Breeden, D. T. "An Intertemporal Asset Pricing Model with Stochastic Consumption and Investment Opportunities." *Journal of Financial Economics*, September 1979, pp. 265–296. Advanced calculus is employed to develop an extension of the capital asset pricing model (CAPM) that maximizes the investor's expected utility from consumption. Breeden's model maximizes the investor's lifetime utility from consumption over multiple time periods and explains consumption-investment decisions. As a result, asset prices depend on their co-variances with aggregate *consumption* rather than with any market index.

Sharpe, W. F. "Capital Asset Prices: A Theory of Market Equilibrium under Conditions of Risk." *Journal of Finance*, September 1964, pp. 425–552. Reprinted in *Readings in Investments*, J. C. Francis, Cheng-Few Lee, and Donald Farrar (eds.). New York: McGraw-Hill, 1983. This classic article suggests the asset pricing implications of systematic risk. Sharpe develops the risk-return relationship for portfolios (that is, the capital market line, or the CML) and for individual assets (namely, the CAPM). Calculus is used only in the footnotes. A knowledge of elementary statistics is assumed.

Beta Stability

The statistics from a security's characteristic line contain much information about various aspects of the stock's price movements and can be useful in predicting how the security will react to changes in the condition of the market from bullish rises to bearish declines. However, when the data points (that is, the dots in Fig. 10-2) do not fit closely around it, the characteristic line's predictive power diminishes accordingly. Since the correlation coefficient, ρ, is a goodness-of-fit statistic that measures how well the data points fit around the characteristic line (or any regression line), this statistic gives some indication of how much faith should be placed in its associated beta coefficient.

The characteristic line statistics shown at the bottom of Table App. 10A-1 for Homestake Mining, for example, have a correlation coefficient of .01 for the sample period from January 1927 through June 1935. Table App. 10A-1

TABLE APP. 10A-1   BETA COEFFICIENTS CHANGE OVER TIME

FIRM	TIME PERIOD, MONTH/YEAR	BETA	ρ^2*
Union Oil of California	1/27-6/35	0.55	0.58
	7/35-12/43	0.57	0.49
	1/44-6/51	0.97	0.45
	7/51-12/60	0.98	0.32
IBM	1/27-6/35	0.49	0.49
	7/35-12/43	0.25	0.26
	1/44-6/51	0.56	0.29
	7/51-12/60	0.86	0.23
May Department Stores	1/27-6/35	0.83	0.74
	7/35-12/43	0.64	0.49
	1/44-6/51	0.72	0.35
	7/51-12/60	0.82	0.32
Atlantic Coast Line Railroad	1/27-6/35	1.2	0.73
	7/35-12/43	1.26	0.7
	1/44-6/51	1.7	0.43
	7/51-12/60	1.63	0.57
Homestake Mining Corporation	1/27-6/35	0.042	0.01
	7/35-12/43	0.235	0.07
	1/44-6/51	0.333	0.09
	7/51-12/60	0.465	0.11

*ρ^2 = coefficient of determination for characteristic regression line
    = correlation coefficient squared
    = percent of variation explained

Source: Marshall E. Blume, ''The Assessment of Portfolio Performance: An Application of Portfolio Theory,'' unpublished doctoral dissertation, University of Chicago, March 1968.

shows that the squared coefficient of correlation is called the *coefficient of determination*. The coefficient of determination tells what percent of the total variance in the stock's price is explained by the regression. The coefficient of determination for Homestake for the 1927–1935 sample of only 1 percent (that is, .01) documents the fact that the data points did not fit Homestake's characteristic line closely.

Securities that have very low goodness-of-fit statistics for their characteristic lines (like the early Homestake data, for example) frequently have beta coefficients that are *random coefficients*. These random coefficients are essentially wild beta coefficients that move up and down over a wide range in a spurious fashion as the characteristic line is fit over and over during different sample periods. Furthermore, a firm's beta may change drastically if, for instance, it undertakes production of new products with a complete new management team. But year after year most firms' probability distributions of returns and betas are similar (that is, they are relatively stable through time). Table App. 10A-1 shows how the betas for a few firms have behaved with the passage of time. Considering that the data for these calculations span thirty-three years, the stability of the statistics over time for May Department Stores, for instance, is impressive.[20]

APP. 10A-1 FRANCIS'S STUDY OF INTERTEMPORAL STABILITY OF RISK STATISTICS

It is important to ask whether the beta coefficient and the standard deviation statistics for different securities are stable through time or whether they jump around randomly (like the Homestake Mining statistics shown at the bottom of Table App. 10A-1, for instance). If the statistics gyrate wildly, they have little value to financial analysts because today's historical statistics are a poor predictor of the future riskiness of an investment.

Dr. J. C. Francis analyzed 750 NYSE stocks over a decade in order to assess the stability of three statistics that measure the riskiness of financial assets. The three statistics Francis analyzed are (1) the beta coefficient from the characteristic line, (2) the correlation coefficient, which measures how closely the

---

20 Explicit studies of beta stationarity include W. F. Sharpe and G. Cooper, "Risk-Return Classes of New York Stock Exchange Common Stock, 1931–67," *Financial Analysts Journal*, March–April 1972; M. E. Blume, "On the Assessment of Risk," *Journal of Finance*, March 1974, pp. 1–10; Nancy Jacob, "The Measurement of Systematic Risk for Securities and Portfolios: Some Empirical Results," *Journal of Financial and Quantitative Analysis*, March 1971, pp. 815–834; R. C. Klemkosky and J. D. Martin, "The Adjustment of Beta Factors," *Journal of Finance*, September 1975, pp. 1123–1128; J. C. Francis, "Statistical Analysis of Risk Surrogates for NYSE Stocks," *Journal of Financial and Quantitative Analysis*, December 1979. A Canadian study of beta stationarity is A. L. Calvet and Jean Lefoll, "A Varying Parameter Model for the Estimation of Systematic Risk and its Application To Canadian Equity Data," *Administrative Sciences Association of Canada 1981 Conference*, Finance Division, vol. 1, pp. 130–135. They found that there was a definite tendency for betas on Canadian companies to become unstable in the period 1973 to 1979.

TABLE APP. 10A-2   TRANSITION MATRIX, PERCENTILE IN YEAR t VERSUS PERCENTILE IN YEAR $t + 5$

DECILES	1	2	3	4	5	6	7	8	9	10
Beta1	0.4267	0.2533	0.0800	0.0400	0.0533	0.0400	0.0533	0.0000	0.0400	0.0133
StdD1	0.5067	0.1867	0.0800	0.0667	0.0667	0.0400	0.0267	0.0133	0.0133	0.0000
Corr1	0.1867	0.200	0.1067	0.1600	0.0667	0.0400	0.1067	0.0667	0.0533	0.0133
Beta2	0.1867	0.2933	0.1600	0.0933	0.0800	0.0267	0.0533	0.0533	0.0267	0.0267
StdD2	0.2267	0.2400	0.2133	0.1467	0.0800	0.0267	0.0267	0.0267	0.0000	0.0133
Corr2	0.2000	0.1600	0.1600	0.1600	0.0800	0.0133	0.0400	0.0400	0.1067	0.0400
Beta3	0.1733	0.1200	0.2000	0.1333	0.1067	0.1333	0.0667	0.0267	0.0133	0.0267
StdD3	0.1200	0.1867	0.2000	0.1867	0.0800	0.0800	0.0400	0.0667	0.0267	0.0133
Corr3	0.1200	0.1067	0.1200	0.0800	0.0400	0.1867	0.0933	0.1200	0.0800	0.0533
Beta4	0.0933	0.0667	0.1867	0.1733	0.1733	0.1067	0.0267	0.0667	0.0800	0.0267
StdD4	0.0800	0.1467	0.2267	0.0667	0.1200	0.1600	0.0933	0.0533	0.0533	0.0000
Corr4	0.0933	0.1467	0.1333	0.0267	0.1067	0.1467	0.0800	0.0933	0.0933	0.0800
Beta5	0.0667	0.1067	0.1067	0.1467	0.1200	0.1200	0.1067	0.0933	0.1067	0.0267
StdD5	0.0533	0.1333	0.0667	0.1467	0.2267	0.0800	0.1467	0.1067	0.0400	0.0000
Corr5	0.1200	0.1067	0.0933	0.0800	0.0933	0.0400	0.1333	0.1467	0.0667	0.1200
Beta6	0.0400	0.0667	0.0933	0.1067	0.0933	0.2000	0.1600	0.1467	0.0667	0.0267
StdD6	0.0000	0.0533	0.0800	0.2400	0.1600	0.1200	0.1600	0.0800	0.0667	0.0400
Corr6	0.0667	0.0800	0.1067	0.1333	0.0667	0.1867	0.0533	0.0933	0.1200	0.0933
Beta7	0.0000	0.0533	0.0533	0.1200	0.0933	0.0800	0.1600	0.2000	0.1600	0.0800
StdD7	0.1033	0.0267	0.0933	0.0933	0.1200	0.2000	0.1867	0.1333	0.0933	0.0400
Corr7	0.0667	0.0667	0.0667	0.0933	0.1200	0.0667	0.1600	0.0933	0.1333	0.1333
Beta8	0.0000	0.0267	0.0667	0.1067	0.1600	0.1733	0.1333	0.0800	0.0667	0.1867
StdD8	0.0000	0.0267	0.0400	0.0267	0.1067	0.1467	0.1733	0.1867	0.1333	0.1600
Corr8	0.0667	0.0533	0.0667	0.1200	0.1733	0.1467	0.1333	0.1333	0.0000	0.1067
Beta9	0.0133	0.0133	0.0400	0.0533	0.0667	0.0933	0.1467	0.2267	0.1600	0.1867
StdD9	0.0000	0.0000	0.0000	0.0267	0.0400	0.1067	0.0667	0.2133	0.2400	0.3067
Corr9	0.0400	0.0400	0.0933	0.0667	0.0933	0.1067	0.1067	0.1333	0.1867	0.1333
Beta10	0.0000	0.0000	0.0133	0.0267	0.0533	0.0267	0.0933	0.1067	0.2800	0.4000
StdD10	0.0000	0.0000	0.0000	0.0000	0.0000	0.0400	0.0800	0.1200	0.3333	0.4267
Corr10	0.0400	0.0400	0.0533	0.0800	0.1600	0.0667	0.0933	0.0800	0.1600	0.2267

Source: J. C. Francis, "Statistical Analysis of Risk Statistics for NYSE Stocks," *Journal of Financial and Quantitative Analysis*, December 1979, vol. XIV, no. 5, p. 992, table 4.

data points fit around the characteristic line, and (3) the standard deviation, which measures the asset's total risk.

Francis divided the decade he studied up into two 60-month subsamples and measured the three statistics he analyzed for 750 different stocks. After calculating all these statistics over the first five years (or sixty months) and also over the second five years, he arranged them into *arrays* with the largest values at the top of the list and the smallest statistics at the bottom of the list. Six arrays were thus constructed, as listed below.

1. An array of 750 betas over the first 60 months.
2. An array of 750 betas over the second 60 months.
3. An array of 750 standard deviations over the first 60 months.
4. An array of 750 standard deviations over the second 60 months.
5. An array of 750 correlation coefficients over the first 60 months.
6. An array of 750 correlation coefficients over the second 60 months.

Then Francis divided each of the six arrays of 750 statistics up into ten equal-sized deciles with seventy-five stocks' statistics in each *decile*. He then arranged these six arrays of deciles of statistics into the transition matrix shown in Table App. 10A-2 in order to see how stable the statistics were from one 5-year subsample until the next 5-year subsample. Table App. 10A-2 is actually three different transition probability matrices—one for betas, one for standard deviations, and one for correlation coefficients — all assembled in one matrix.

The transition probability matrix for betas in Table App. 10A-2 shows, for example, that .4267 (or 42.67 percent) of the betas in the top decile in the first five years turned up in the top decile in the next five-year period. Slightly over a quarter (.2533 or 25.33 percent, to be exact) of the betas in the top decile declined in value enough to be in the second decile in the second five-year period. Note that betas in the top decile in the first sixty-month sub-sample dropped into every one of the deciles except the eighth decile in the following sixty-month subsample. But only .0133 (or 1.33 percent) fell clear down into the tenth decile in the next five-year subsample. After studying the entire transition matrix, it appears that very few betas rose or fell more than two or three deciles during a five-year period. The betas in the deciles around the median (that is, the fiftieth percentile) moved into the farthest deciles.[21]

Further study of Table App. 10A-2 reveals that the standard deviations are the most stable of the three statistics analyzed by Francis. For example, .2267 (or 22.67 percent) of the standard deviations that started out in the fifth decile in the first sixty-month subsample ended up in the same decile in the next five-year subsample. This finding means that most common stocks' total risk,

---

21 The median betas probably changed deciles more than the extreme betas because the values of the statistics in the fourth, fifth, and sixth deciles were compressed into a narrow numerical range. In contrast, the highest and lowest deciles included a wider range of values so that larger numerical changes were needed to move out of these extreme deciles.

and also the width of the probability distributions of returns shown in Fig. 9-1, are fairly stable through time.

The correlation coefficients were the least stable statistics analyzed by Francis. Only .0933 (or 9.33 percent) of the correlations that started in the fifth decile in the first subsample were still in the fifth decile five years later, for example. Findings like this mean that simply because an asset's data points fit closely around the asset's characteristic line in one 5-year period does not mean that that asset will experience the same goodness-of-fit in the following five-year period.

The three transition matrices in Table App. 10A-2 suggest that betas, standard deviations, and correlations may not be as stable as financial analysts might desire. Nevertheless, these risk statistics do appear to exhibit sufficient intertemporal stability to make it worthwhile for serious financial analysts to study them.[22]

APP. 10A-2   THE RANDOM COEFFICIENT MODEL

The classic characteristic line model of Eq. (10-1) must be modified slightly to embrace the securities that experience changing betas. Equation (App. 10A-1) is identical with Eq. (10-1) in every respect except one—the beta in Eq. (App. 10A-1) has a time subscript.[23]

$$r_{it} = a_i + b_{it}r_{mt} + e_{it} \qquad \text{(App. 10A-1)}$$

The time subscript on the beta indicates that the beta may assume a different value in each time period—that is, $\text{var}(b_{it}) > 0$ as t changes—if appropriate. Empirical research indicates[24] that the unstable characteristic line model of Eq. (App. 10A-1) is appropriate for some of the stocks listed on the NYSE,

---

22 The Francis study also presents models that are useful in predicting the future values of betas, standard deviations, and correlations that yield better predictions than merely extrapolating historical values into the future. See J. C. Francis, "Statistical Analysis of Risk Statistics for NYSE Stocks," *Journal of Financial and Quantitative Analysis*, December 1979, vol. XIV, no. 5, Eqs. 5 and 6.

23 P. A. V. B. Swamy, *Statistical Inference in Random Coefficient Regression Models* (Berlin: Springer-Verlag, 1971). H. Theil, *Principles of Econometrics* (New York: Wiley, 1971), sec. 12-4.

24 F. J. Fabozzi and J. C. Francis, "Beta as a Random Coefficient," *Journal of Financial and Quantitative Analysis*, March 1978, F. J. Fabozzi and J. C. Francis, "Stability Tests for Alphas and Betas over Bull and Bear Market Conditions," *Journal of Finance*, September 1977. F. Fabozzi and J. C. Francis, "The Effects of Changing Macroeconomic Conditions on Alphas, Betas, and the Single Index Model," *Journal of Financial and Quantitative Analysis*, June 1979. S. J. Kon and G. C. Jen, "Estimation of Time Varying Systematic Risk and Performance for Mutual Fund Portfolios: An Application of Switching Regression," *Journal of Finance*, May 1978. B. Rosenberg, "A Survey of Stochastic Regression Parameters," *Annals of Economic and Social Measurement*, vol. 2, no. 4, pp. 381–397, 1973. B. Rosenberg and J. Guy, "Beta and Investment Fundamentals," *Financial Analysts Journal*, May–June 1976.

for example. Making continual adjustments for these changing betas creates much additional work for the security analysts.[25]

Francis and Fabozzi published the first study suggesting that beta was a random coefficient in a significant minority of the common stocks listed on the NYSE.[26] Some financial analysts argued that practically all betas were stable.[27] Professors Lee and Chen joined the debate by publishing arguments which tend to support the Francis-Fabozzi position that beta coefficients do move about erratically.[28] No definitive consensus has been reached about the stability of the beta coefficient. However, a scholarly debate on the topic is proceeding.[29]

25 Practically all preceding empirical research with the characteristic line has been limited to a partial-equilibrium analysis in which individual securities interactions with some stock market index are measured. Professor Roll has suggested that a general equilibrium analysis would be a more appropriate context in which to test the risk-return capital market theory. Richard Roll, ''A Critique of the Asset Pricing Theory's Tests; Part 1: On Past and Potential Testability of the Theory,'' *Journal of Financial Economics*, vol. 4, no. 2, pp. 129–176, March 1977. Roll would include commodities, bonds, art objects, real estate, and investments in human capital in the market index. The validity of Roll's general equilibrium suggestion is acknowledged. However, at the present time no general market index of the scope Roll visualizes is generally accepted. Furthermore, the validity and importance of the *partial-equilibrium analysis* with the characteristic line is in no way diminished by Roll's suggestion.

Published estimates of a broad-based portfolio have been prepared by R. G. Ibbotson and Carol L. Fall, ''The U.S. Wealth Portfolio: Components of Capital Market Values and Returns,'' *Journal of Portfolio Management*, Fall 1979; and, more recently, R. G. Ibbotson and L. B. Siegel, ''The World Market Wealth Portfolio,'' *Journal of Portfolio Management*, Winter 1983, pp. 5–17, and R.G. Ibbotson, L.B. Siegel, and K.S. Love, ''World Wealth: Market Values and Returns,'' *The Journal of Portfolio Management*, Fall 1985, pp. 4–23.

26 F. J. Fabozzi and J. C. Francis, ''Beta as a Random Coefficient,'' *Journal of Financial and Quantitative Analysis*, March 1978.

27 Rodney L. Roenfeldt, Gary L. Griepentrog, and Christopher C. Pflaum, ''Further Evidence of the Stationarity of Beta Coefficients,'' *Journal of Financial and Quantitative Analysis*, March 1978, pp. 117–121. See also Gordon J. Alexander and P. George Benson, ''More on Beta as a Random Coefficient,'' *Journal of Financial and Quantitative Analysis*, vol. 17, March 1982, pp. 27–36.

28 Cheng Few Lee and Son N. Chen, ''A Random Coefficient Model for Re-Examining Risk-Decomposition Method and Risk-Return Relationship Tests,'' *Quarterly Review of Economics and Business*, vol. 20, Winter 1980, pp. 58–69.

29 J. M. Jog and A. L. Riding, ''Some Canadian Findings Regarding Infrequent Trading and Instability in the Single Factor Market Model,'' *Journal of Business Finance and Accounting* 13(1), Spring 1986, pp. 125–135. See also G. J. Alexander, P. G. Benson, and C. E. Swann, ''Random Coefficient Models of Security Returns: A Comment,'' *Quarterly Review of Economics and Business*, vol. 23, no. 1, Spring 1983, pp. 99–106. Cheng Few Lee and Son-Nan Chen, ''Random Coefficient Models of Security Returns: A Comment,'' *Quarterly Review of Economics and Business*, vol. 23, no. 1, Spring 1983, pp. 106–109. Shyam Sunder, ''Stationarity of Market Risk: Random Coefficient Tests for Individual Common Stocks,'' *Journal of Finance*, vol. 35, September 1980, pp. 883–896. Kenneth Garbade and Joel Rentzler, ''Testing the Hypothesis of Beta Stationarity,'' *International Economic Review*, vol. 22, no. 3, 1981, pp. 577–587. Gabriel Hawawini, ''Why Beta Shifts As the Return Interval Changes,'' *Financial Analysts Journal*, May–June 1983. Diana R. Harrington, ''Whose Beta Is Best?'' *Financial Analysts Journal*, July–August 1983, pp. 67–74. Meir I. Schnellr, ''Are Better Betas Worth the Trouble?'' *Financial Analysts Journal*, May–June 1983, pp. 74–77.

Firms that undergo drastic changes in their product mix, financial structure, and management team will probably experience changes in average return, standard deviation, and systematic risk. For the majority of firms, however, the probability distributions of returns are stationary enough that a rational investor should be willing to pay money to find out what they are. This does not imply perfect stability — just sufficient stability to make the information valuable for investment decisions.[30]

30 Evidence about the stability of the beta coefficient has been published; see R. L. Roenfeldt, G. L. Griepentrog, and C. C. Pflaum, ''Further Evidence of the Stationarity of the Beta Coefficient,'' *Journal of Financial and Quantitative Analysis*, March 1978. In addition, suggestions have been offered about how to adjust beta coefficients in order to obtain more useful statistics. Kalman Cohen, Gabriel Hawawini, Steven Maier, Robert Schwartz, and David Whitcomb, ''Estimating and Adjusting for the Intervaling-Effect Bias in Beta,'' *Management Science*, 1984. Elroy Dimson, ''Risk Measurement When Shares Are Subject to Infrequent Trading,'' *Journal of Financial Economics*, 1979, pp. 197–226. Myron Scholes and Joseph Williams, ''Estimating Beta from Non-Synchronous Data,'' *Journal of Financial Economics*, 1977, pp. 309–327. J. C. Francis, ''Statistical Analysis of Risk Statistics for NYSE Stocks,'' *Journal of Financial and Quantitative Analysis*, December 1979, vol. 14, no. 5, pp. 981–987.

Data for the TSE 300 Composite Index and for Standard & Poor's Composite Index

In order to calculate characteristic lines, it is necessary to have rates of change of specific market indexes. Tables App. 10B-1 and 10B-2 list quarterly observations on the Toronto Stock Exchange (TSE) 300 Composite Index and Standard & Poor's (S&P) 500 Stocks Composite Index for several years. These data can be used to calculate the rate of price changes or rates of return for both the U.S. and Canadian equity markets.

The TSE 300 Index is composed of 300 stocks divided into 14 industry groups. The S&P 500 Index is made up of 425 industrial, 20 railroad, and 55 utility stocks. These indexes are like portfolios of 300 and 500 different stocks, respectively.

The percentage changes in the price indexes are good estimates of the average rate of price change for marketable common shares listed on the New York and Toronto Stock Exchanges.

The dividend rates for the TSE were estimated by calculating the average annual dividend yields for the three months of each quarter and then dividing by four to express the yields on a quarterly basis.

The quarterly dividend series for the S&P 500 Index is like a cash dividend paid on one of the hypothetical shares in the S&P 500 portfolio. It represents the weighted average cash dividend for all 500 shares in the portfolio. This dividend is divided by the S&P 500 price index to obtain the weighted average dividend yield for the 500 firms in the sample. This dividend yield is at an annual rate, that is, four times the quarterly rate.

Quarterly observations of an empirical surrogate for the riskless rate are also shown in Tables App. 10B-1 and 10B-2. Canadian and American Treasury bills with three months to maturity were observed monthly, and then three-months' yields were averaged to obtain the yield reported for the quarters.

TABLE APP. 10B-1 TSE COMPOSITE 300 INDEX RATE OF RETURN DATA

YEAR/QUARTER	TSE 300 BEGIN OF QUARTER	TSE 300 END OF QUARTER	TSE QUARTERLY DIVIDEND YIELD, %	TSE 300 QUARTERLY PRICE CHANGE RATE, %	TSE 300 TOTAL RETURN, %	RISK-FREE RATE QUARTERLY, %
1975.1	835.4	989.6	0.795	18.46	19.253	1.58
1975.2	989.6	1055.3	1.15	6.64	7.789	1.73
1975.3	1055.3	976.4	1.17	-7.48	-6.307	1.98
1975.4	976.4	953.5	1.24	-2.35	-1.105	2.11
1976.1	953.5	1054.1	1.10	10.55	11.651	2.20
1976.2	1054.1	1055.6	1.08	0.14	1.222	2.24
1976.3	1055.6	1028.4	1.10	-2.58	-1.477	2.28
1976.4	1028.4	1011.5	1.20	-1.64	-0.443	2.15
1977.1	1011.5	1022.1	1.19	1.05	2.238	1.94
1977.2	1022.1	1031.2	1.21	0.89	2.100	1.81
1977.3	1031.2	1000.1	1.21	-3.02	-1.806	1.78
1977.4	1000.1	1059.6	1.21	5.95	7.159	1.81
1978.1	1059.6	1063.3	1.23	0.35	1.579	1.85
1978.2	1063.3	1126.2	1.14	5.92	7.056	2.05
1978.3	1126.2	1284.7	1.03	14.07	15.104	2.22
1978.4	1284.7	1309.0	1.10	1.89	2.991	2.56
1979.1	1309.0	1466.4	1.07	12.02	13.094	2.72
1979.2	1466.4	1618.4	1.04	10.37	11.406	2.70
1979.3	1618.4	1751.9	0.998	8.25	9.247	2.86
1979.4	1751.9	1813.2	1.040	3.50	4.539	3.41
1980.1	1813.2	1797.6	0.958	-0.86	0.098	3.52
1980.2	1797.6	2061.4	1.01	14.68	15.685	3.09
1980.3	2061.4	2260.0	0.931	9.63	10.565	2.63
1980.4	2260.0	2268.7	0.894	0.38	1.279	3.55
1981.1	2268.7	2333.1	0.933	2.84	3.772	4.18
1981.2	2333.1	2361.1	0.922	1.20	2.122	4.55

1981.3	2361.1	1883.4	1.07	-20.23	-19.162	5.04
1981.4	1883.4	1954.2	1.14	3.76	4.899	3.95
1982.1	1954.2	1587.8	1.33	-18.75	-17.419	3.66
1982.2	1587.8	1366.8	1.47	-13.92	-12.449	3.87
1982.3	1366.8	1602.0	1.31	17.21	18.518	3.47
1982.4	1602.0	1958.1	1.06	22.23	23.288	2.64
1983.1	1958.1	2156.1	0.940	10.11	11.052	2.33
1983.2	2156.1	2447.0	0.821	13.49	14.313	2.30
1983.3	2447.0	2499.6	0.805	2.15	2.955	2.31
1983.4	2499.6	2552.4	0.822	2.11	2.934	2.37
1984.1	2552.4	2382.1	0.863	-6.67	-5.809	2.51
1984.2	2382.1	2220.9	0.943	-6.77	-5.824	2.83
1984.3	2220.9	2392.7	0.941	7.74	8.677	3.07
1984.4	2392.7	2400.3	0.923	0.32	1.241	2.65
1985.1	2400.3	2612.8	0.863	8.85	9.716	2.60
1985.2	2612.8	2712.5	0.836	3.82	4.652	2.38
1985.3	2712.5	2632.3	0.823	-2.96	-2.134	2.23
1985.4	2632.3	2900.6	0.801	10.19	10.994	2.22

TABLE APP. 10B-2 STANDARD & POOR'S 500 STOCKS COMPOSITE INDEX RATE OF RETURN DATA

YEAR/ QUARTER	S&P BEGIN OF QUARTER	S&P END OF QUARTER	S&P LATEST 12-MONTH DIVIDEND	S&P QUARTERLY DIVIDEND	S&P QUARTERLY DIVIDEND YIELD, %	S&P QUARTERLY PRICE CHANGE RATE, %	S&P TOTAL RETURN, %	RISK-FREE RATE, %
1974.1	97.68	93.25	3.44	0.8600	0.880	-4.53	-3.654	7.462
1974.2	93.25	86.02	3.50	0.8750	0.938	-7.75	-6.815	7.600
1974.3	86.02	63.39	3.59	0.8975	1.04	-26.30	-25.26	8.268
1974.4	63.39	70.23	3.60	0.9000	1.41	10.79	12.21	8.286
1975.1	70.23	82.64	3.67	0.9175	1.30	17.67	18.97	7.336
1975.2	82.64	94.85	3.71	0.9275	1.12	14.77	15.89	5.873
1975.3	94.85	82.93	3.71	0.9275	0.977	-12.56	-11.58	5.401
1975.4	82.93	90.90	3.68	0.9200	1.10	9.61	10.71	6.337
1976.1	90.90	102.24	3.69	0.9225	1.01	12.47	13.49	5.684
1976.2	102.24	103.59	3.76	0.9400	0.919	1.32	2.239	4.953
1976.3	103.59	104.17	3.85	0.9625	0.929	.559	1.489	5.169
1976.4	104.17	107.00	4.05	1.012	0.971	2.716	3.688	5.169
1977.1	107.00	99.21	4.19	1.047	0.978	-7.280	-6.301	4.698
1977.2	99.21	100.10	4.36	1.090	1.09	0.897	1.995	4.624
1977.3	100.10	96.74	4.50	1.125	1.12	-3.356	-2.232	4.829
1977.4	96.74	93.82	4.67	1.167	1.20	-3.018	-1.811	5.472
1978.1	93.82	88.46	4.80	1.200	1.27	-5.713	-4.434	6.137
1978.2	88.46	95.09	4.91	1.227	1.38	7.494	8.882	6.408
1978.3	95.09	102.96	5.02	1.255	1.31	8.276	9.596	6.481
1978.4	102.96	96.73	5.07	1.267	1.23	-6.050	-4.819	7.315
1979.1	96.73	100.90	5.20	1.300	1.34	4.310	5.654	8.680
1979.2	100.90	101.99	5.34	1.335	1.32	1.080	2.403	9.358
1979.3	101.99	108.56	5.51	1.377	1.35	6.441	7.792	9.377
1979.4	108.56	105.76	5.65	1.412	1.30	-2.579	-1.278	9.631
1980.1	105.76	102.18	5.80	1.450	1.37	-3.385	-2.014	11.80
1980.2	102.18	114.93	5.94	1.485	1.45	12.47	13.93	13.45
1980.3	114.93	127.13	6.07	1.517	1.32	10.61	11.93	10.04
1980.4	127.13	136.34	6.16	1.540	1.21	7.244	8.455	9.235
1981.1	136.34	136.57	6.28	1.570	1.15	0.168	1.320	13.71
1981.2	136.57	129.77	6.39	1.597	1.16	-4.979	-3.809	14.36
1981.3	129.77	117.08	6.52	1.630	1.25	-9.778	-8.522	19.61
1981.4	117.08	122.74	6.63	1.657	1.41	4.834	6.250	15.08
1982.1	122.74	113.79	6.72	1.680	1.36	-7.291	-5.923	12.02
1982.2	113.79	108.71	6.81	1.702	1.49	-4.464	-2.968	12.89
1982.3	108.71	121.97	6.85	1.712	1.57	12.19	13.77	12.35
1982.4	121.97	138.34	6.87	1.717	1.40	13.42	14.82	9.705
1983.1	138.34	153.02	6.91	1.727	1.24	10.61	11.86	7.935
1983.2	153.02	168.91	6.94	1.735	1.13	10.38	11.51	8.081

BOND VALUATION

Bonds are the simplest type of security on which to make a value assessment. And, most of the major risk factors affect bond investors. Chapters 11, 12, and 13 discuss the interaction between investment risk factors and bond valuation.

CHAPTER 11—Bond Valuation shows how to determine a bond's economic value and how to measure its interest rate risk with mathematics. The basic valuation model furnishes the fundamental engine for the analysis:

Basic Valuation Model The intrinsic economic value of market asset is the present value of the future income.

$$\text{Present value} = \sum_{t=1}^{T} \frac{\text{income}_t}{(1 + k)^t}$$

where k is the appropriate risk-adjusted discount rate for the asset.

CHAPTER 12 — Default and Purchasing Power Risk in Bonds analyzes the effects of these two risk factors on bond values.

CHAPTER 13—Market Interest Rates interprets empirical interest rate data within the economic theory of interest.

CHAPTERS 11, 12 and 13 explain how to value bonds and also set the stage for the common stock valuation discussion of Chaps. 14, 15, and 16.

CHAPTER 11

Bond Valuation

In order to decide whether to buy or to sell a security, an investor must compare the security's market price with its value to determine if the security is over- or underpriced. The *value* of a bond is simply the present value of all the security's future cashflows.[1] The buy or sell decision can be made as soon as the value of the bond is known.

The buy or sell decision rules were introduced in Box 8-1, on page 163. In terms appropriate for both stocks and bonds, Chap. 8 explained how to use the present-value model (see Box 8-2, on page 163) to find the value of a security. The purpose of the present chapter is to show how to use the present value model to calculate the value of a bond, which is the simplest type of security to analyze.

Of all the different kinds of bonds in existence, the Canadian federal bond is the easiest to value, because there is presumably no chance that the Canadian government will go bankrupt. Corporate bonds, which can go bankrupt, are a little more complicated to analyze. They are analyzed after the default-free government bonds are examined.

Let us begin by considering the numbers that are used in the present value model.

11-1 THE PRESENT VALUE MODEL AND BOND VALUATION

Chapters 8 and 9 discussed the time value of money and interest rate risk and introduced the present value model. The present value formula is given again in Eq. (11-1*a*).

$$\text{Present value} = \frac{\text{coupon}_1}{(1 + \text{interest rate})^1} + \frac{\text{coupon}_2}{(1 + \text{interest rate})^2} +$$
$$\dots + \frac{\text{coupon}_T + \text{face value}}{(1 + \text{interest rate})^T} \qquad (11\text{-}1a)$$

---

1 This chapter presumes a knowledge of the present-value model which was explained in Chap. 9 under the heading Interest Rate Risk. See Mathematical App. A at the end of this book for present value tables.

The three terms that appear on the right-hand side of Eq. (11-1*a*) are discussed below.

Market interest rate: The interest rate, or discount rate, or yield to maturity, is an interest rate that changes constantly; thus, it must be obtained from current market reports.[2] Assume an interest rate of 10 percent (which is also stated as .10). The yield to maturity is represented by the abbreviation ytm.

Face value: The bond's face value (or principal value) and the time when it is due to be repaid (its maturity date) are printed on the bond and are fixed throughout the bond's life. Assume that a $1,000 face value bond is to be repaid in three years (that is, $T = 3$).

Coupon: The coupon is the product of the coupon rate and the face value. The timing of coupon interest payments is also important. Assume a coupon rate of 6 percent; thus the bond pays $60 (equals $1,000 times 6.0 percent or .06) on the last day of each year of its three-year life.

Substituting the values assumed in the preceding paragraphs into Eq. (11-1*a*) yields the following formula:

$$\text{Present value} = \frac{\$60}{(1 + .10)^1} + \frac{\$60}{(1 + .10)^2} + \frac{\$60 + \$1000}{(1 + .10)^3}$$

$$= \$54.545 + \$49.586 + \$796.393$$

$$= \$900.52$$

The present value calculation above suggests that the bond is worth $900.52. One of the convenient aspects of bond valuation is that everyone uses this formula; thus, everyone would agree that this bond is worth $900.52.

The information needed to use the present value formula to value a bond is easy to obtain. The bond's principal amount, its coupon interest payments, and the dates of these cashflows are all printed on the bond: they never change. The only difference of opinion likely to arise in valuing a bond is in selecting the appropriate interest rate to use for discounting the cashflows. At any given time, different discount interest rates are appropriate for different bond issues. These differences exist because different bonds have different risks of default, but default risk is an issue we will postpone until we discuss corporate bonds later in this chapter.

11-2 VALUING A RISKLESS BOND

There is a large, active market in federal government bonds (which are different from the nonmarketable Canada Saving Bonds). The prices of these marketable pieces of the national debt vary from day-to-day; they are widely published regularly in varying formats. Figure 11-1 is an excerpt from a newspaper that shows the prices of marketable Canadian federal government bonds.

2 The effective interest rate for a bond is the same as the bond's yield to maturity. The yield to maturity is the discount rate that equates the present value of all the bond's future cashflows with the current market price of the bond.

FIGURE 11-1   Price quotations for federal government bonds.

Weekly Bond Prices

QUOTATIONS AT THURSDAY CLOSE BY WOOD GUNDY INC.

GOVERNMENT OF CANADA

Issue	Coupon	Maturity	Bid price	Ask price	Bid yield	Ask yield
CANADA	10½	6 MAR. 86	100.25	100.45	9.01	7.90
CANADA	10	15 MAR. 86	100.10	100.30	9.44	8.45
CANADA	13	6 JUN. 86	101.60	101.80	9.14	8.67
CANADA	12¼	5 SEP. 86	102.05	102.25	9.05	8.75
CANADA	10	15 DEC. 86	100.90	101.40	9.00	8.45
CANADA	15	15 MAR. 87	106.40	106.60	9.25	9.08
CANADA	12¼	1 MAY 87	103.70	103.90	9.24	9.09
CANADA	14¾	1 JUN. 87	107.05	107.25	9.33	9.18
CANADA	13	1 JUN. 87	104.80	105.00	9.31	9.16
CANADA	10	6 JUN. 87	101.15	101.35	9.12	8.98
CANADA	13½	1 SEP. 87	106.35	106.85	9.29	8.98
CANADA	13	15 OCT. 87	105.90	106.10	9.33	9.21
CANADA	12	15 NOV. 87	104.50	104.70	9.33	9.22
CANADA	11	15 DEC. 87	103.10	103.30	9.24	9.12
CANADA	10¼	1 FEB. 88	101.95	102.15	9.19	9.08
CANADA	11¾	1 FEB. 88	104.50	104.70	9.31	9.20
CANADA	10½	15 MAR. 88	102.45	102.65	9.24	9.14
CANADA	10¾	15 OCT. 88	103.65	103.85	9.22	9.14
CANADA	10	15 NOV. 88	102.00	102.20	9.19	9.11
CANADA	9¾	15 DEC. 88	101.55	102.05	9.14	8.94
CANADA	11	15 FEB. 89	104½	104⅞	9.29	9.20
CANADA	12½	15 MAR. 89	108½	108¾	9.36	9.27
CANADA	9¼	15 APR. 89	100½	100¾	9.06	8.98
CANADA	13¼	1 JUN. 89	110¼	111¼	9.49	9.32
CANADA	13½	1 JUL. 89	111½	112	9.57	9.41
CANADA	13¾	1 AUG. 89	112⅜	112⅞	9.58	9.42
CANADA	10	1 OCT. 89	102¼	102½	9.27	9.19
CANADA	10½	1 OCT. 89	103½	103¾	9.36	9.28
CANADA	12¼	1 NOV. 89	108⅜	108⅞	9.51	9.43
CANADA	10¾	1 NOV. 89	104⅜	104⅝	9.36	9.29
CANADA	11¼	15 DEC. 89	106	106¼	9.40	9.32
CANADA	12	1 FEB. 90	108¼	108½	9.51	9.44
CANADA	13¼	1 FEB. 90	111⅞	112⅜	9.65	9.51
CANADA	13¾	15 MAR. 90	113⅝	114⅛	9.72	9.58
CANADA	13	1 MAY 90	111¾	112	9.62	9.55
CANADA	11¾	1 JUN. 90	107¾	108¼	9.55	9.42
CANADA	10¾	1 SEP. 90	105¼	105½	9.33	9.27
CANADA	10½	1 OCT. 90	104⅜	104⅝	9.33	9.27
CANADA	10¼	15 DEC. 90	103¾	104	9.29	9.23
CANADA	12½	1 FEB. 91	111¼	111¾	9.64	9.52
CANADA	9¼	1 MAR. 91	100⅛	100⅜	9.22	9.16
CANADA	14½	1 MAY 91	119⅝	120½	9.70	9.59
CANADA	11	1 JUN. 91	106⅜	106⅞	9.47	9.35
CANADA	18	1 OCT. 91	134⅜	135⅛	9.93	9.84
CANADA	11½	15 DEC. 91	108½	109	9.59	9.49
CANADA	13½	15 OCT. 92	117½	118	9.89	9.80
CANADA	15½	1 FEB. 92	125⅛	125⅝	9.90	9.80
CANADA	10¼	1 JUN. 92	103⅞	104⅛	9.43	9.38
CANADA	15	1 JUN. 92	123¼	123¾	10.00	9.91
CANADA	15	1 JUL. 92	124⅛	124⅝	9.89	9.80
CANADA	14¼	1 SEP. 92	121⅛	121⅝	9.85	9.75
CANADA	12¾	15 NOV. 92	114½	115	9.80	9.71
CANADA	11¾	15 DEC. 92	110¼	110½	9.69	9.64
CANADA	11¼	1 FEB. 93	108⅛	108⅜	9.64	9.59
CANADA	10¾	1 MAY 93	105⅞	106⅛	9.61	9.57
CANADA	15¼	1 JUN. 93	127	127½	10.00	9.92
CANADA	13½	15 OCT. 93	117½	118	9.89	9.80
CANADA	14¾	1 JUL. 93	124⅜	125¼	9.99	9.91
CANADA	11¾	15 OCT. 93	106⅜	107⅞	9.76	9.72
CANADA	11½	15 DEC. 93	109⅜	109⅞	9.73	9.69
CANADA	12	1 MAR. 94	111⅞	112⅛	9.85	9.80
CANADA	13	1 APR. 94	116⅞	117⅛	9.95	9.91
CANADA	13¾	15 MAY 94	120⅞	121⅜	10.01	9.93
CANADA	9½	15 JUN. 94	99¾	100	9.54	9.50
CANADA	13½	15 JUL. 94	119¾	120¼	10.00	9.92
CANADA	12¾	1 OCT. 94	116	116½	9.96	9.88
CANADA	12½	15 DEC. 94	114⅞	115⅜	9.95	9.87
CANADA	11½	1 FEB. 95	109¾	110	9.85	9.81
CANADA	12¼	1 FEB. 95	113¾	114	9.91	9.88
CANADA	11¾	1 MAR. 95	111¼	111½	9.85	9.82
CANADA	10½	1 JUN. 95	105⅛	105⅜	9.66	9.62
CANADA	11¼	1 APR. 95	108⅜	108⅞	9.81	9.77
CANADA	10	1 OCT. 95	102¼	102½	9.64	9.60
CANADA	9¼	15 MAY 97	97¼	97¾	9.65	9.58
CANADA	10¾	15 DEC. 95	106⅜	106⅝	9.74	9.70
CANADA	9	15 OCT. 99	94⅜	95⅛	9.71	9.64
CANADA	13½	1 DEC. 99	122⅜	122⅞	10.42	10.36
CANADA	13¾	15 MAR. 00	124⅜	124⅞	10.42	10.36
CANADA	15	1 JUL. 00	132½	133	10.58	10.52
CANADA	9¾	15 DEC. 00	98½	99	9.95	9.88
CANADA	15¾	1 FEB. 01	138⅜	138⅞	10.59	10.54
CANADA	13	1 MAY 01	119¾	120¼	10.40	10.34
CANADA	9½	1 OCT. 01	98⅞	99⅛	9.64	9.61
CANADA	8¾	1 FEB. 02	92⅞	93⅜	9.63	9.56
CANADA	15½	15 MAR. 02	137¾	138⅛	10.59	10.54
CANADA	10	1 MAY 02	100	100¼	10.00	9.97
CANADA	11¼	15 DEC. 02	108¼	108½	10.22	10.19
CANADA	11¼	1 FEB. 03	111⅞	112⅛	10.26	10.23
CANADA	9½	1 OCT. 03	96½	97	9.92	9.86
CANADA	10¼	1 FEB. 04	102⅜	103⅛	9.90	9.87
CANADA	13½	1 JUN. 04	124¼	124¾	10.50	10.45
CANADA	10½	1 OCT. 04	103½	104	10.08	10.02
CANADA	12	1 MAP	113½	113¾	10.36	10.34
CANADA	12¼	1 SF		115⅞	10.40	1
CANADA	12½	1		77⅞	10.42	
	14					

Source: *The Sunday Star*, December 29, 1985, p. F6.

The first column contains the name of the issuer; here, all the bond quotes are Government of Canada issues.

The second column gives each bond issue's coupon interest rate, denoted i hereafter. The coupon interest rate applies to the bond's face value. Most Government of Canada bonds are sold in $1,000 denominations; that is, their face value (F) is $1,000. Thus a $1,000 face value bond (that is, F = $1,000), which has a 12 percent coupon rate (namely $i = .12 = 12$ percent) pays $120 [$iF = 12.0$ percent $\times$ ($1,000)] per year every year until the bond matures and repays its principal of F = $1,000 to its owner.

The third column shows the bonds' maturity dates as day, month, and year. If a split year is shown (as it is in some financial newspapers), such as 86/91, the particular issue is extendible, exchangeable, or retractable, and the holder has in fact an option as to which date to accept the principal payment from the government.

The fourth and fifth columns in Fig. 11-1 give the bid and asked prices (that is, the highest price a potential buyer has bid and the lowest price a potential seller has offered) stated as a percentage of each bond's face value. A price of $106.60 translates into a market price of $1,066.00 per $1,000 face value bond; a price of $124¾ means $1,247.50 per $1,000 face value.

The sixth and seventh columns give the bond's yield to maturity based on its current bid and ask prices, respectively.

A bond's yield to maturity (ytm) can be interpreted as the bond's average compounded rate of return if the bond is bought at the current asked price and held until it matures and the face value is repaid. That is, the *yield to maturity* is the discount rate that equates the present value of all cashflows to the purchase price of the bond. (The ytm is called the internal rate of return in capital budgeting discussions.)

To show how to determine the value of a bond, the Canadian government 12, October 1, 1995, will be analyzed.[3] This bond's present value will be found, assuming that 12 percent is the yield to maturity; that is, the market

---

3 If the bond were purchased between the dates when the semiannual interest payments occurred, the seller would receive accrued interest from the party purchasing the bond. For example, if the bond were sold three months after a semiannual interest payment, the purchaser would pay the market price of the bond on that date plus half the $60.00 interest earned but not yet received by the party selling the bond. For the sake of simplicity, accrued interest will not be discussed in this chapter. Ignoring the accrued interest introduces an approximation into the calculations.

The following formula is used in determination of accrued interest.

$$\frac{\text{Accrued}}{\text{interest}} = \frac{\text{days since last interest payment}}{\text{days between last and next coupon payments}} \times \frac{\text{semi-annual interest payment}}{}$$

Note that the "days" are counted from the delivery date instead of the transaction date. For a more detailed discussion see Robert W. Kolb, *Interest Rate Futures* (Richmond: Robert F. Dame Publishing, 1982), pp. 76–79. Or, Sidney Homer and Martin L. Leibowitz, *Inside the Yield Book* (Englewood Cliffs, N.J.: Prentice-Hall, 1972), chap. 13. Or, see Marcia Stigum, *Money Market Calculations* (Homewood, Ill.: Dow Jones-Irwin, 1981), pp. 87–105; the 1983 revised edition discusses this on pp. 56–57.

yield of 12 percent will be used as the discount rate. The interest per year paid on the bond is i times F (that is, 12 percent × $1,000) or $120 per year. The bond pays its 12 percent coupon rate in semiannual payments of $60 when the face value F is $1,000. Thus the bond's compounding interval or "period" is six months. Assume that there are exactly twenty 6-month periods until the bond matures and the face value of $1,000 is received. The appropriate market rate of interest or discount rate is the bond's yield to maturity, ytm = 12 percent per annum, or 6 percent per 6-month period.[4]

The *discount factor* for cashflows received t periods in the future and discounted at the interest rate ytm is the quantity $1/(1 + ytm)^t$. Present value tables (for example, Table A-1 in the Mathematical App. A at the rear of the book) contain the discount factors for a wide range of time spans and different rates of discount (or interest). The cashflows in the tth period, denoted c_t, are $c_t = \$60.00$ for periods $t = 1, 2, \ldots, 19$ half-years plus $c_{20} = \$1,060.00$ when the bond matures at the end of 10 years. The present value of these cashflows is calculated in Eq. (11-1a). Mathematically, the problem is to find the present value, denoted p_0.

$$p_0 = \sum_{t=1}^{10 \text{ years}} c_t/(1 + ytm)^t \qquad (11\text{-}1a)$$

Equation (11-1a) is restated to allow for semi-annual payments.

$$p_0 = \sum_{t=1}^{20 \text{ half years}} 60/(1+.05)^t + \$1,000/(1.05)^{20}$$

$$= \$747.73 + \$376.89$$

$$= \$1,124.62$$

The present value of $1,124.62 will be the asked price for the 12 percent coupon federal government bond maturing in 1994, assuming that there are twenty 6-month periods (or ten years until maturity) if the market-determined yield to maturity is 10 percent. The market price of the bond should not deviate one single penny from its present value if the market interest rate equals the ytm of 10 percent and no other factors change.

In practice, a bond may actually be traded at any price between the bid and asked prices. The reason is that the actual yield may vary a few hundredths of 1 percent from day to day as the market rates fluctuate randomly from minute to minute. These hundredths of a percentage point are called *basis points*. Sometimes a basis point is lightly referred to as an "01." However, the teaching point has been made and is restated succinctly: Since all the cashflows from a federal government bond investment are known in advance, the bond's value (and thus its market price) is determined by the

---

4 The ytm's of 12 and 6 percent were assumed so that easy-to-find present value tables could be used to check the calculations.

market interest rates (that is, the yields to maturity). The bond's market price will not remain above its value because investors will sell and drive its price down until the price equals its present value. Similarly, the price will not be below the bond's present value because the price would be bid up until it equalled the present value by investors who know how to calculate bond values. These buying and selling pressures were illustrated in Box 8-1, on page 163.

11-3 A BOND'S YIELD TO MATURITY

Federal government bonds contain no default risk and offer no opportunity for growth in their contractual income; therefore, the default and growth factors do not affect their prices. However, the discount rate (or, equivalently, the yield to maturity, ytm) and the term to maturity T do vary and do affect the prices of government and other bonds. The following discussion shows how bond prices are affected by the discount rate and the term to maturity, and how to calculate a bond's yield to maturity.

Tables have been prepared to show the correct price for a bond of any given term to maturity and any appropriate market interest rate. Figure 11-2 shows the page from a book of bond tables for bonds with 10.0 percent coupon rates.[5] The values in this table show the percentage of face value for which bonds with a 10.0 percent coupon rate should sell if they are to yield the rate shown in the left column. Books of bond tables have a separate page for various rates of coupon interest. These books of bond tables have been the most popular way to find a bond's yield to maturity for decades. However, inexpensive hand-held calculators are available today that can quickly calculate an exact yield to maturity.

11-3.1 Bond Tables

The values in Fig. 11-2 were calculated using Eq. (11-1a), as shown in the preceding example. By the use of bond tables, however, the tedious present value calculations may be avoided. The bond tables may be used for two problems. If the term to maturity is known, the bond tables can be used to look up (1) the bond price if the yield to maturity is known or (2) the yield to maturity if the market price is known.

When it is necessary to determine the yield to maturity of a bond, three methods may be used. First, if a bond table is available, the yield may be quickly and easily found for a given price and maturity. The second way to determine yields is more cumbersome. The *yield to maturity* for a bond is the discount rate that equates the present value of all net cashflows to the cost of the investment. Since the coupon interest iF, the face value F, the purchase price p_o, and the cashflows c_t are known quantities (that is, they are printed on the bond and written in the issue's indenture contract), Eq. (11-2a) may

11-3.2 Solving the Formula for a Bond's Yield to Maturity (ytm)

---

5 Technically, these bond tables are appropriate for bonds for which the coupon is paid exactly half-yearly. However, the differences are worth considering only for transactions involving millions of dollars of bonds. This difference is the reason that calculated present values may differ slightly from the values found in the appropriate bond table.

FIGURE 11-2 Sample page from book of bond tables for 10 percent coupon bonds.

YEARS TO MATURITY

yield	1	2	3	4	5	6	7	8	9	10	11	12	13	14	15	16
0.0	110.00	120.00	130.00	140.00	150.00	160.00	170.00	180.00	190.00	200.00	210.00	220.00	230.00	240.00	250.00	260.00
1.00	108.93	117.78	126.53	135.20	143.79	152.29	160.70	169.03	177.28	185.44	193.53	201.53	209.46	217.30	225.07	232.76
2.00	107.88	115.61	123.18	130.61	137.89	145.02	152.01	158.87	165.59	172.18	178.64	184.97	191.18	197.27	203.93	209.08
3.00	106.85	113.49	119.94	126.20	132.28	138.18	143.90	149.46	154.85	160.09	165.17	170.11	174.90	179.54	184.06	188.43
4.00	105.89	111.42	116.80	121.98	126.95	131.73	136.32	140.73	144.98	149.05	152.97	156.74	160.36	163.84	167.19	170.41
4.25	105.57	110.91	116.04	120.95	125.66	130.17	134.50	138.65	142.63	146.45	150.11	153.62	156.98	160.90	163.30	166.96
4.50	105.32	110.41	115.27	119.93	124.38	128.64	132.71	136.61	140.34	143.90	147.31	150.57	153.69	156.67	159.52	169.25
4.75	105.07	109.90	114.52	118.92	123.12	127.13	130.96	134.61	138.09	141.41	144.58	147.60	150.49	153.94	155.87	158.38
5.00	104.82	109.40	113.77	117.93	121.88	125.64	129.23	132.64	135.88	138.97	141.91	144.71	147.38	149.91	152.33	154.62
5.25	104.57	108.91	113.03	116.94	120.65	124.18	127.53	130.71	133.72	136.59	139.31	141.90	144.35	146.68	148.89	150.99
5.50	104.32	108.41	112.29	115.96	119.44	122.73	125.85	128.81	131.61	134.26	136.77	139.15	141.41	143.54	145.56	147.48
5.75	104.07	107.92	111.56	115.00	118.24	121.31	124.21	126.95	129.54	131.98	134.29	136.48	138.54	140.49	142.33	144.07
6.00	103.83	107.43	110.83	114.04	117.06	119.91	122.59	125.12	127.51	129.75	131.87	133.87	135.75	137.53	139.20	140.78
6.25	103.58	106.95	110.12	113.09	115.89	118.53	121.00	123.33	125.52	127.58	129.51	131.33	133.04	134.65	136.16	137.59
6.50	103.34	106.47	109.40	112.16	114.74	117.16	119.44	121.57	123.57	125.44	127.20	128.85	130.40	131.86	133.22	134.50
6.75	103.09	105.99	108.69	111.23	113.60	115.82	117.90	119.84	121.66	123.36	124.95	126.44	127.84	129.14	130.36	131.50
7.00	102.85	105.51	107.99	110.31	112.47	114.50	116.38	118.14	119.78	121.32	122.75	124.09	125.34	126.50	127.59	128.60
7.25	102.61	105.04	107.30	109.40	111.36	113.19	114.89	116.47	117.95	119.39	120.60	121.79	122.90	123.94	124.90	125.79
7.50	102.37	104.56	106.61	108.50	110.27	111.90	113.42	114.84	116.15	117.37	118.50	119.56	120.53	121.44	122.29	123.07
7.75	102.13	104.10	105.92	107.61	109.18	110.64	111.98	113.23	114.39	115.46	116.45	117.37	118.23	119.02	119.75	120.43
8.00	101.89	103.63	105.24	106.73	108.11	109.39	110.56	111.65	112.66	113.59	114.45	115.25	115.98	116.66	117.29	117.87
8.25	101.65	103.17	104.57	105.86	107.05	108.15	109.17	110.10	110.97	111.76	112.49	113.17	113.80	114.37	114.90	115.39
8.50	101.41	102.71	103.90	105.00	106.01	106.94	107.79	108.58	109.30	109.97	110.58	111.15	111.67	112.14	112.58	112.99
8.75	101.17	102.25	103.24	104.14	104.98	105.74	106.44	107.09	107.68	108.22	108.72	109.17	109.59	109.98	110.33	110.66
9.00	100.94	101.79	102.58	103.30	103.96	104.56	105.11	105.62	106.08	106.50	106.89	107.25	107.57	107.87	108.14	108.39
9.25	100.70	101.34	101.93	102.46	102.95	103.40	103.80	104.17	104.51	104.83	105.11	105.37	105.61	105.82	106.02	106.20
9.50	100.47	100.89	101.28	101.63	101.95	102.25	102.51	102.76	102.98	103.18	103.37	103.54	103.69	103.83	103.96	104.07
9.75	100.23	100.44	100.64	100.81	100.97	101.12	101.25	101.37	101.48	101.57	101.66	101.75	101.82	101.89	101.95	102.01
10.00	100.00	100.00	100.00	100.00	100.00	100.00	100.00	100.00	100.00	100.00	100.00	100.00	100.00	100.00	100.00	100.00
10.25	99.77	99.56	99.37	99.20	99.04	98.90	98.77	98.66	98.55	98.46	98.37	98.30	98.23	98.16	98.11	98.05
10.50	99.54	99.12	98.74	98.40	98.09	97.82	97.56	97.34	97.13	96.95	96.78	96.63	96.50	96.37	96.26	96.16
10.75	99.31	98.68	98.12	97.61	97.16	96.75	96.38	96.04	95.74	95.47	95.23	95.01	94.81	94.63	94.47	94.33

11.00	92.55	92.73	92.94	93.17	93.42	93.71	94.02	94.38	94.77	95.21	95.69	96.23	96.83	97.50	98.25	99.08
11.25	90.82	91.04	91.29	91.57	91.88	92.22	92.61	93.04	93.52	94.05	94.65	95.32	96.06	96.89	97.82	98.85
11.50	89.14	89.39	89.68	90.01	90.37	90.77	91.22	91.72	92.29	92.92	93.63	94.41	95.30	96.28	97.39	98.62
11.75	87.50	87.79	88.12	88.48	88.89	89.35	89.86	90.44	91.08	91.80	92.61	93.52	94.54	95.68	96.96	98.39
12.00	85.92	86.24	86.59	87.00	87.45	87.96	88.53	89.17	89.89	90.71	91.62	92.64	93.79	95.08	96.53	98.17
12.25	84.37	84.72	85.11	85.55	86.04	86.60	87.23	87.93	88.73	89.62	90.63	91.77	93.05	94.49	96.11	97.94
12.50	82.87	83.24	83.66	84.14	84.67	85.27	85.95	86.72	87.58	88.56	89.66	90.91	92.31	93.90	95.69	97.72
12.75	81.42	81.81	82.25	82.76	83.33	83.97	84.70	85.52	86.46	87.51	88.71	90.06	91.59	93.32	95.28	97.49
13.00	80.00	80.41	80.88	81.41	82.01	82.70	83.47	84.35	85.35	86.48	87.76	89.22	90.87	92.74	94.86	97.27
13.25	78.62	79.05	79.54	80.10	80.73	81.45	82.27	83.20	84.26	85.46	86.83	88.39	90.15	92.16	94.45	97.05
13.50	77.28	77.73	78.24	78.82	79.48	80.23	81.09	82.07	83.19	84.46	85.91	87.57	89.45	91.59	94.04	96.82
13.75	75.98	76.44	76.97	77.57	78.26	79.04	79.94	80.97	82.14	83.48	85.01	86.75	88.75	91.03	93.63	96.60
14.00	74.71	75.18	75.73	76.35	77.06	77.88	78.81	79.88	81.11	82.51	84.11	85.95	88.06	90.47	93.23	96.38
14.25	73.47	73.96	74.52	75.16	75.89	76.74	77.70	78.82	80.09	81.55	83.23	85.16	87.37	89.91	92.82	96.16
14.50	72.27	72.77	73.34	73.99	74.75	75.62	76.62	77.77	79.09	80.61	82.36	84.38	86.69	89.36	92.42	95.95
14.75	71.10	71.61	72.19	72.86	73.63	74.53	75.56	76.74	78.11	79.69	81.51	83.60	86.02	88.81	92.02	95.73
15.00	69.96	70.47	71.07	71.75	72.54	73.46	74.51	75.73	77.15	78.78	80.66	82.84	85.36	88.27	91.63	95.51
15.25	68.85	69.37	69.97	70.67	71.48	72.41	73.49	74.75	76.20	77.88	79.83	82.08	84.70	87.73	91.23	95.29
15.50	67.77	68.30	68.90	69.61	70.43	71.38	72.49	73.77	75.26	77.00	79.00	81.34	84.05	87.19	90.84	95.08
15.75	66.72	67.25	67.86	68.58	69.41	70.38	71.51	72.82	74.35	76.12	78.19	80.60	83.40	86.66	90.45	94.86
16.00	65.70	66.23	66.85	67.57	68.41	69.40	70.55	71.88	73.45	75.27	77.39	79.87	82.76	86.13	90.06	94.65
16.25	64.70	65.23	65.85	66.58	67.44	68.44	69.60	70.97	72.56	74.42	76.60	79.15	82.13	85.61	89.68	94.44
16.50	63.72	64.26	64.89	65.62	66.48	67.49	68.68	70.06	71.69	73.59	75.82	78.44	81.50	85.09	89.30	94.22
16.75	62.77	63.31	63.94	64.68	65.55	66.57	67.77	69.18	70.83	72.77	75.05	77.73	80.88	84.57	88.91	94.01
17.00	61.85	62.39	63.02	63.76	64.64	65.67	66.88	68.31	69.99	71.96	74.29	77.04	80.26	84.06	88.54	93.80
17.25	60.95	61.48	62.12	62.86	63.74	64.78	66.01	67.45	69.16	71.17	73.54	76.35	79.65	83.56	88.16	93.59
17.50	60.07	60.60	61.24	61.98	62.87	63.91	65.15	66.61	68.34	70.39	72.81	75.67	79.05	83.05	87.78	93.38
17.75	59.21	59.74	60.38	61.12	62.01	63.06	64.31	65.79	67.54	69.62	72.08	74.99	78.45	82.55	87.41	93.17
18.00	58.38	58.91	59.54	60.28	61.17	62.23	63.49	64.98	66.75	68.86	71.36	74.33	77.86	82.06	87.04	92.96
18.25	57.56	58.09	58.71	59.46	60.35	61.41	62.68	64.18	65.97	68.11	70.65	73.67	77.27	81.56	86.67	92.76
18.50	56.76	57.29	57.91	58.66	59.55	60.62	61.89	63.40	65.21	67.37	69.95	73.02	76.69	81.08	86.31	92.55
18.75	55.99	56.51	57.13	57.87	58.77	59.83	61.11	62.63	64.46	66.64	69.26	72.38	76.12	80.59	85.94	92.34
19.00	55.23	55.74	56.36	57.11	58.00	59.06	60.34	61.88	63.72	65.93	68.57	71.75	75.55	80.11	85.58	92.14
20.00	52.37	52.87	53.47	54.20	55.08	56.14	57.43	58.99	60.88	63.17	65.93	69.98	73.33	78.92	84.15	91.32
25.00	41.38	41.75	42.22	42.81	43.55	44.50	45.69	47.20	49.11	51.53	54.60	58.48	63.38	69.60	77.46	87.41
30.00	34.09	34.34	34.66	35.09	35.66	36.41	37.41	38.72	40.46	42.76	45.79	49.81	55.13	62.16	71.45	83.74

be solved for the only unknown value in the equation. The only unknown value in Eq. (11-2a) is the exact yield to maturity (ytm).

$$p_0 = \sum_{t=1}^{T} \frac{\text{cashflow}_t}{(1 + \text{ytm})^t} \tag{11-2a}$$

$$= \sum_{t=1}^{T} \frac{iF}{(1 + \text{ytm})^t} + \frac{F}{1 + \text{ytm}^T} \tag{11-2b}$$

It is difficult to evaluate a Tth root polynomial like those given in Eq. (11-1a) and (11-2a). Such Tth root equations are usually solved by a laborious trial-and-error procedure using different values of the discount rate until the one is found which yields the desired mathematical equality. Such computations may be expedited by using a calculator. Appendix 11A also gives two computationally efficient formulas to estimate the ytm.

Someone who invests in a coupon-paying bond will earn the yield to maturity promised on the purchase date if and only if all of the following three conditions are fulfilled.

1. The bond is held until it matures rather than being sold at a price which differs from its face value before its maturity.
2. The bond does not default on any of its cashflows. That is, the bond issuer pays all coupons and the principal in full at the scheduled times.
3. All cashflows (namely, the coupon payments) are immediately reinvested at an interest rate equal to the promised yield to maturity.

11-3.3 About the Reinvestment Rate

As mentioned above, a bond's yield to maturity is based on the assumption that all cashflows throughout the bond's life (namely, the coupon interest) are immediately reinvested at the yield to maturity. Of course, this assumption is not always true; the interest income might be consumed, for example, rather than reinvested. This is equivalent to reinvesting the funds at a zero rate of return, and the realized yield to maturity will be reduced accordingly by such disinvestments.

Table 11-1 illustrates the effects of different reinvestment rates on a bond's realized yield to maturity. The table shows the total realized compounded rate (that is, the effective yield to maturity) for an 8 percent coupon (i = 8 percent = .08) bond bought at face value twenty years before it matured. Table 11-1 shows that only 4.84 percent total yield to maturity is realized if the coupon interest is consumed instead of being reinvested. Essentially, the bond's yield to maturity is reduced by consuming the coupons rather than reinvesting them because the investor will not get to earn the *interest on the interest*. But the same bond has a realized total yield of 9.01 percent if the coupons are reinvested at 10 percent. This shows the importance of the reinvestment opportunities and highlights an often-ignored source of a bond risk: the *reinvestment rate risk* can cause a bond's realized yield to vary.

TABLE 11-1   AN 8 PERCENT NONCALLABLE 20-YEAR BOND BOUGHT AT 100 TO YIELD 8 PERCENT

REINVEST-MENT RATE, %	Interest on Interest		COUPON INCOME, $	CAPITAL GAIN OR DISCOUNT	TOTAL RETURN, $	TOTAL REALIZED COMPOUND YIELD, %
	% OF TOTAL RETURN	AMOUNT, $				
0	0	0	1600	0	1600	4.84
5	41	1096	1600	0	2696	6.64
6	47	1416	1600	0	3016	7.07
7	53	1782	1600	0	3382	7.53
8*	58*	2201*	1600*	0	3801*	8.00*
9	63	2681	1600	0	4281	8.50
10	67	3232	1600	0	4832	9.01

*Yield from yield book.

Discussions about bonds are complicated by the fact that every bond has different ways to measure its yield. More specifically, every bond has two ways to measure its yield and also two ways to measure its rate of return. These four different bond yield concepts are briefly compared and contrasted below.

11-3.4 Different Bond Yield and Return Measures

1. *Coupon rate.* The coupon rate or nominal rate, denoted i, is that fixed rate of interest which is printed on the bond certificate. Coupon rates are contractual rates that cannot be changed after the bond is issued. (Coupon rates cannot be calculated for Treasury bills and other zero coupon or stripped bonds.)
2. *One-period rate of return.* The single period (for example, the one-month or one-year period) rate-of-return formula for a coupon bond is shown below. [Equation (11-3) can also be used to calculate the one-period rate of return for zero-coupon bonds like Treasury bills simply by putting a zero in for the coupon interest.]

$$r_t = \frac{\text{capital gain or loss} + \text{coupon interest}}{\text{purchase price}} \tag{11-3}$$

The one-period rate of return r varies from positive to negative in each period as the bond experiences capital gains and losses, respectively.
3. *Current yield.* Every bond that pays coupon interest has the current yield or coupon yield, defined below

$$\text{Current yield} = \frac{\text{dollars of coupon interest per year}}{\text{current market price}} \tag{11-4}$$

For example, a 6.0 percent coupon bond with $1,000 face value which is selling at the discounted price of $900 has a current yield of ($60/$900 = .0666 =) 6.66 percent. The current yield is an annual cashflow measure based on current market prices.
4. *Yield maturity.* The internal rate of return or yield to maturity, designated ytm, of a bond is the discount rate that equates the present value of a bond's cashflows to the bond's current market price. The ytm is a compounded multiperiod effective rate of return that is earned if the bond is held to its maturity date and does not default.

FIGURE 11-3   The relation between different yield measures for a 6% coupon bond.

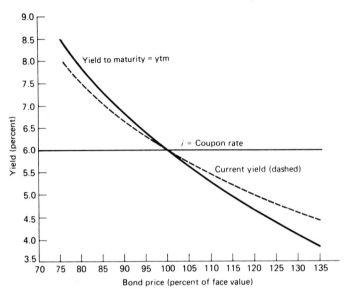

Figure 11-3 illustrates how three of these four different interest rate measures interact with the market price of their related bond.[6] Figure 11-3 illustrates three price-interest rate relationships for a default-free bond with $1,000 face value, 6.0 percent coupon rate, and twenty-five years until maturity. The one-period rate of return is not shown in this figure because it depends on both the beginning- and the end-of-period prices of the bond, which are not conveyed in the figure. Figure 11-3 depicts graphically the fact that the market price of a bond varies inversely with both its yield to maturity and its current yield.

Thus far we have only discussed one measure of a bond's *time dimension* —a bond's term (or time or years) to maturity. There is another, less obvious, time dimension to a bond—it is called the bond's *duration*.

11-4   MACAULAY'S DURATION (MD)

In 1938, F. R. Macaulay suggested studying the *time structure* of a bond by measuring its *average term to maturity*, or *duration*, as it is more commonly called.[7] A bond's *duration* may be defined as the weighted average number of years until the cashflows occur, where the relative present values of each cash payment are used as the weights. The formula for Macaulay's duration (MD hereafter) is given in Eq. (11-5).

---

6 The mathematical relationship between the true yield to maturity and the approximate-yield to maturity as well as the relationship between the current yield are examined by G. A. Hawawini and A. Vora, ''On the Theoretic and Numeric Problems of Approximating the Bond Yield to Maturity,'' *Engineering Economist*, vol. 25, no. 4, 1980, pp. 301–325.

7 F. R. Macaulay, *Some Theoretical Problems Suggested by the Movement of Interest Rates, Bond Yields and Stock Prices in the United States Since 1856* (Columbia, New York: National Bureau of Economic Research, 1938.)

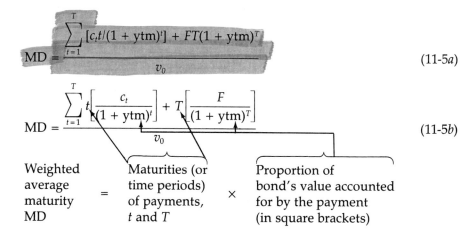

$$MD = \frac{\sum_{t=1}^{T}[c_t t/(1 + ytm)^t] + FT(1 + ytm)^T}{v_0} \qquad (11\text{-}5a)$$

$$MD = \frac{\sum_{t=1}^{T} t\left[\dfrac{c_t}{(1 + ytm)^t}\right] + T\left[\dfrac{F}{(1 + ytm)^T}\right]}{v_0} \qquad (11\text{-}5b)$$

$$\begin{array}{ccc}
\text{Weighted} & & \text{Maturities (or} & & \text{Proportion of} \\
\text{average} & = & \text{time periods)} & \times & \text{bond's value accounted} \\
\text{maturity} & & \text{of payments,} & & \text{for by the payment} \\
\text{MD} & & t \text{ and } T & & \text{(in square brackets)}
\end{array}$$

A small numerical example should clarify the duration calculations. Consider a hypothetical bond with the characteristics listed below:

11-4.1 A Numerical Example

Face value = F = $1,000
Yield to maturity = ytm = 6.0 percent = .06
Coupon rate = i = 7.0 percent = .07
Annual coupon payments = iF = .07 ($1,000) = $70 = c_t
Number of years to maturity = T = 3 years
Market price = p_0 = $1,026.73
Premium over face = $p_0 - F$ = $1,026.73 - $1,000 = $26.73

The present value of this bond is calculated with Eq. (11-1a) to obtain the value of $1,026.73 shown below. This bond's duration is calculated by using the numerical values from the present value calculations above inserted into Eq. (11-5). The three-year bond's duration is 2.8107 years, as shown below.

As Eq. (11-5) and the computations above show, a bond's duration is simply the weighted averaged time that elapses until the bond's various cashflows are received, using the relative present values of each payment as a weight.

(1) YEAR, T	(2) CASHFLOW	(3) $1/(1 + YTM)^t$	(4) = (2) × (3)
1	$ 70	$0.9434 = 1/(1.06)^1$	$ 66.04
2	70	$0.8900 = 1/(1.06)^2$	62.30
3	1,070	$0.8396 = 1/(1.06)^3$	898.39
			$1,026.73 = v_0

(1) YEAR, T	(2) PRESENT VALUE OF CASHFLOW FROM COLUMN 4 ABOVE	(3) PRESENT VALUE AS PROPORTION OF v_0	(4) COLUMN 3 × COLUMN 1
1	$ 66.04	0.0643	0.0643
2	62.30	0.0607	0.1214
3	898.39	0.8750	2.6250
		1.0	2.8107 = MD

FIGURE 11-4A   Duration and term to maturity for discount and zero coupon bonds.

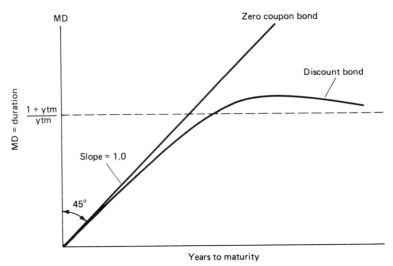

**11-4.2
Contrasting
Duration
with Years
to Maturity**

In all cases, a coupon-paying bond's duration is less than or equal to its term to maturity (that is, MD ≤ T). If a bond's only cashflow is made to repay the principal and interest on the bond's date of maturity, then the bond's term to maturity is identical with its duration. More succinctly, if $iF = 0$, then MD = T. However, as stated above, for bonds with periodic coupon interest payments (which most bonds have) the duration of the bond will be less than the bond's term to maturity. In the numerical example above, for instance, the annual coupons of $70 caused the three year bond to have an average term to maturity or duration of 2.8107 years. Earlier and/or larger cashflows always shorten the duration (or average life) of a bond investment. Figures 11-4A and 11-4B illustrate the relationship between the term to maturity and the duration of a bond, and Table 11-2 shows the number of years' duration for several different bonds which are priced to yield 6.0 percent if held to maturity.

TABLE 11-2   BOND DURATION IN YEARS FOR BOND YIELDING 6 PERCENT UNDER DIFFERENT TERMS

YEARS TO MATURITY	Various Coupon Rates			
	0.02	0.04	0.06	0.08
1	0.995	0.990	0.985	0.981
5	4.756	4.558	4.393	4.254
10	8.891	8.169	7.662	7.286
20	14.981	12.980	11.904	11.232
50	19.452	17.129	16.273	15.829
100	17.567	17.232	17.120	17.064
	17.667	17.667	17.667	17.667

Source: L. Fisher and R. L. Weil, "Coping with the Risk of Interest Rate Fluctuations: Returns to Bondholders from Naive and Optimal Strategies," *Journal of Business*, October 1971, p. 418.

FIGURE 11-4B An illustration of duration versus time to maturity for some
hypothetical bonds.

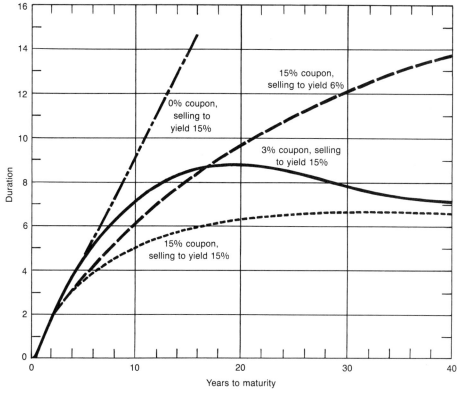

Source: William L. Nemerever, "Managing Bond Portfolios Through Immunization Strategies,"
reprinted in *The Revolution in Techniques for Managing Bond Portfolios* (Charlottesville, Va.: The
Institute of Chartered Financial Analysts, 1983), p. 104. Reproduced from *The Revolution in
Techniques for Managing Bond Portfolios,* The Institute of Chartered Financial Analysts, 1983.
By permission.

A bond's years of duration are considered to be a better measure of the
time structure of an investment's cashflows than its years to maturity, *T,*
because the duration reflects the amount and timing of every cashflow rather
than merely the length of time until the final payment occurs. Furthermore,
Macaulay's duration is a measure of the bond's *interest rate risk*.[8] An interest
rate risk measure for bonds, called interest rate elasticity, and the relationship
between a bond's elasticity and its duration are explained in the following
paragraphs.

8 It has been shown that

$$MD_{it} = \frac{dp_{it}}{p_{it}} \frac{-d(\text{ytm})_{it}}{1 + \text{ytm}_{it}}$$

M. H. Hopewell and G. G. Kaufman, "Bond Price Volatility and Term to Maturity: A
Generalized Respecification," *American Economic Review,* September 1973, pp. 749–753; and
R. A. Haugen and D. W. Wichern, "The Elasticity of Financial Assets," *Journal of Finance,*
September 1974, pp. 1229–1240.

BOX 11-1
The
Relationship
Between a
Bond's Term to
Maturity and
Macaulay's
Duration

The following theorems describe the relationship between Macaulay's duration (MD) and the number of years until a bond matures (denoted T):

MD Theorem 1   A bond's duration equals its term to maturity if and only if it is a zero-coupon bond (that is, a pure discount bond) or a one-period coupon-bearing bond.

MD Theorem 2   A coupon-bearing bond with a finite maturity of more than one period ($1 < T < \infty$) has a duration which is less than its term to maturity.

MD Theorem 3   The duration of a perpetual bond (for example, British Consuls have $T = \infty$) is equal to $[1.0 + (1.0/\text{ytm})]$ irrespective of its coupon rate.

MD Theorem 4   The duration of a coupon-bearing bond selling at or above its face (or par) value increases monotonically with its term to maturity and approaches the quantity $[1.0 + (1.0/\text{ytm})]$ as its term to maturity approaches infinity.

MD Theorem 5   The duration of a coupon-bearing bond selling at a market price below its face value reaches a maximum before its maturity date reaches infinity and then recedes toward the limit $[1.0 + (1.0/\text{ytm})]$.

MD Theorem 6   The duration of a coupon-bearing bond selling below its par (or face) value reaches its maximum value when T reaches the value indicated in Eq. (11-6) below.

$$T = \frac{1.0}{\log(1.0 + \text{ytm})} + \frac{1.0 - \text{ytm}}{\text{ytm} - i} + \frac{\text{ytm} - i}{i(1.0 + \text{ytm})^T \log(1.0 + \text{ytm})} \quad (11\text{-}6)$$

MD Theorem 7   The duration of a coupon-bearing bond selling below par reaches its maximum at a maturity which is directly related to the bond's coupon rate and inversely related to the bond's yield to maturity.

MD Theorem 8   The longer a coupon-paying bond's term to maturity, the greater the difference between its term to maturity and its duration.

The theorems above are illustrated in Fig. 11-4. These theorems were derived mathematically; see Gabriel Hawawini, ''On the Relationship between Macaulay's Bond Duration and the Term to Maturity,'' *Economic Letters*, vol. 12, 1984.

11-5   INTEREST RATE ELASTICITY (IE) AND INTEREST RATE RISK

Economists call a bond's price elasticity with respect to a change in the bond's yield to maturity its *interest rate elasticity*. Interest rate elasticity is denoted IE_{it} for the ith bond; it is defined in Eq. (11-7a).[9]

---

9 The Greek letter delta Δ in Eq. (11-7a) denotes change.

$$\text{IE}_{it} = \frac{\text{percent change in price for bond } i \text{ in period } t}{\text{percent change in yield to maturity for bond } i} \qquad (11\text{-}7a)$$

$$\text{IE}_{it} = \frac{\Delta p_0/p_0}{\Delta \text{ytm}/\text{ytm}} < 0 \qquad (11\text{-}7b)$$

A bond's interest elasticity will always be a negative number since a bond's price and its yield to maturity always move inversely. If the ith bond's yield to maturity, say, doubles during any time period, this percent change is a positive 100.0 percent ($= + 1.0$), as shown below:

$$\text{Percent change in yield} = \frac{\Delta \text{ytm}}{\text{ytm}} = 100.0\% = + 1.0$$

If the bond's price simultaneously drops by 70 percent (that is, $- .7 = -70.0$ percent), then this bond's elasticity is a negative seven-tenths:

$$\text{IE}_{it} = \frac{\Delta p_0/p_0}{\Delta \text{ytm}/\text{ytm}} = \frac{-70.0\%}{+100.0\%} = \frac{-.7}{+1.0} = -.7$$

A bond's elasticity of negative seven-tenths means that *any* percentage change in the bond's ytm will cause a simultaneous inverse percentage change in the bond's price which is seven-tenths as large.

A bond's price elasticity can be calculated directly with Eq. (11-7a). Alternatively, one can use the mathematical relationship between a bond's elasticity and its duration shown in Eq. (11-8) to find IE_{it} if MD_{it} is already known.[10]

11-5.1 How Duration Determines Interest Rate Elasticity

$$(-1.0)\,\text{IE}_{it} = \text{MD}_{it}\,\frac{\text{ytm}}{1 + \text{ytm}} \qquad (11\text{-}8)$$

Equation (11-8) indicates that anything which causes the ith bond's duration to increase (such as more years to maturity and/or a lower coupon rate) also increases the bond's elasticity. For example, increasing a bond's term to maturity tends to increase its duration, as shown in Fig. 11-4, and therefore its elasticity is increased as shown in Eq. (11-8).

Interest rate risk may be defined as price fluctuations in a security caused by simultaneous changes in its discount rate (which is the yield to maturity for a bond). Thus, bonds with high levels of interest rate risk will experience larger price changes than bonds with less interest rate risk from any given change in the bond's yield to maturity.[11] A bond's elasticity measures its interest rate risk.

11-5.2 Measuring a Bond's Interest Rate Risk

10 Equations (11-7), (11-8) and other insights were provided by Robert A. Haugen and Dean W. Wichern, ''The Elasticity of Financial Assets,'' *Journal of Finance*, September 1974, pp. 1229–1240. See also J. R. Hicks, *Value and Capital*, 2d ed. (New York: Oxford, 1965), p. 186.

11 Bonds with high levels of interest rate risk will experience larger price changes than bonds with low levels of interest rate risk in all cases when the yield curve experiences parallel shifts. However, if the yield curve changes slope, then sometimes bonds with low levels of interest rate risk could experience the larger price changes.

To show how a bond's percentange price fluctuations from any change in its yield are inexorably determined by the bond's elasticity, Eq. (11-7b) is rewritten as Eq. (11-9) below.

$$\left(\frac{\Delta p_0}{p_0}\right)_{it} = \mathrm{IE}_{it}\left(\frac{\Delta \mathrm{ytm}}{\mathrm{ytm}}\right)_{it} \tag{11-9}$$

Equation (11-9) is derived simply by solving Eq. (11-7b) for the instantaneous percentage price change, denoted $(\Delta p_0/p_0)_{it}$. Equation (11-9) shows mathematically that, at the tth instant in time, the ith bond's elasticity will determine the size of its percentage price change when its yield to maturity changes.

11-5.3   Bond Price Theorems   After learning about the interrelationship between a bond's term to maturity, its duration, and its elasticity, five bond price theorems can be introduced to summarize these interrelationships.[15] The five bond price theorems are

**BOX 11-2
Five Bond Price Theorems**

BP Theorem 1   Bond prices move inversely against bond yields.[12]

BP Theorem 2   For any given difference between the coupon rate i and the yield to maturity, the accompanying price change will be greater the longer the term to maturity T.[13]

BP Theorem 3   The percentage price changes described in theorem 2 increase at a diminishing rate as T increases.

BP Theorem 4   For any given maturity, a decrease in yields causes a capital gain that is larger than the capital loss resulting from an equal increase in yields.[14]

BP Theorem 5   The higher the coupon rate i on a bond, the smaller will be the percentage price change for any given change in yields (except for 1-year and perpetual bonds).

12 Taking the following partial derivative of Eq. (11-2a) furnishes proof of theorem 1.

$$\frac{d(p_0)}{d(\mathrm{ytm})} = \sum_{t=1}^{T} \frac{-tc_t}{(1+\mathrm{ytm})^{t+1}} < 0$$

This partial derivative must be negative in sign, because all the numerical quantities are positive, and thus the negative sign determines the derivative's sign. Similar differential calculus analysis of Eq. (11-2a) can provide proof of some of the other bond price theorems.

13 BP theorem 2 is not true for very long-term bonds that are selling at a discount. However, theorem 2 is true for all other bonds, and it is not far from being true for the long-term discounted bonds. Considering the simplicity of the theorem, it contains enough valuable information to be worthy of study with the caveat about long-term discounted bonds in mind.

14 This assumes yields change from the same starting value whether they move up or down.

15 These theorems were derived formally by B. G. Malkiel, "Expectations, Bond Prices, and the Term Structure of Interest Rates," *Quarterly Journal of Economics*, May 1962, pp. 197–218.

shown in Box 11-2; these theorems can also be discerned from the definition of interest rate elasticity and also from Fig. 11-5.

FIGURE 11-5 Market prices for a 3% coupon, $1,000 face value bond at various maturities at 2%, 3%, and 4% discount rates (compounded annually).

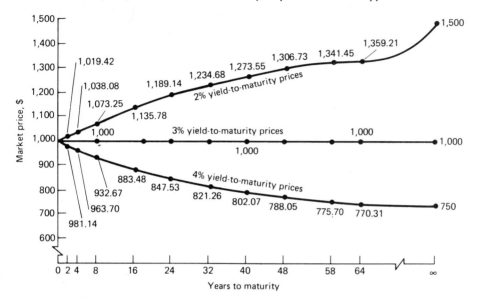

Figure 11-5 illustrates the price analysis applied to a bond with a 3 percent coupon rate. The infinite number of different prices that a 3 percent coupon, default-free bond could assume when market interest rates were 2, 3, or 4 percent are graphed over all possible terms to maturity. Figure 9-4, on page 185, shows the same analysis of a bond that has a 10 percent coupon rate at market interest rates of 9, 10, and 11 percent, for purposes of comparison.

Theorems 1 and 2 were explained in Chap. 9 on page 186 when interest rate risk was introduced. Theorem 3 is true because a bond's duration (and thus, its elasticity) increases at a diminishing rate as its term to maturity increases, as illustrated in Fig. 11-4. Theorem 3 (and several other theorems as well) can be discerned more directly from Figs. 9-4 and 11-5. Theorem 4 is true because the quantity ytm (1.0 + ytm) in Eq. (11-8) changes more when the bond's yield to maturity decreases than it does when the bond's yield increases by any given amount (assuming both the increase and the decrease started from the same yield to maturity). As a result, the bond's elasticity (that is, interest rate risk) changes more when the bond's yield falls than when it rises by the same amount. And finally, theorem 5 is true because a bond with a high coupon rate (that is, larger cashflows early in the bond's life) will have a shorter duration, smaller price elasticity, and less interest rate risk than a bond that is similar in every respect except for a lower coupon rate.

11-5.4 Price Speculation with Riskless Government Bonds

The quotes shown in Fig. 11-1 show that the market prices of Government of Canada bonds vary significantly from their face values. For example, the Government of Canada 9 percent coupon bonds maturing in 1999 were selling at the asked price of 95⅛ or $951.25 per $1,000 face value. This $951.25 was discounted below the bond's face value because market interest rates were above the coupon rate. If purchased at $951.25 and held to maturity, the bond offers a capital gain ($1,000 − $951.25) = $48.75.

The bond can also be sold to another investor before it matures at whatever the market price is at the time. In any event, there is an opportunity for price speculators to profit by trading in government bonds. Consider the implications of the five bond price theorems for a bond price speculator.

As theorem 1 stated, the market prices of government bonds move inversely with interest rates. Equation (11-2a) shows mathematically and Fig. 11-5 illustrates graphically how this price fluctuation comes about. If a price speculator foresees a drop in market interest rates, he or she anticipates a rise in the market prices of Treasury bonds (and other bonds too). In this case, the speculator would buy (that is, take a long position in) marketable Government of Canada bonds. On the other hand, the speculator who expected a rise in interest rates would expect bond prices to fall. In this latter case, the speculator would sell marketable Government of Canada bonds short to profit from the expected price fall.

Theorem 2 states that the price fluctuations are larger in bonds that have longer terms to maturity. This is true for all bonds except a few long-term bonds selling at discounted prices. Figure 11-5 illustrates this graphically. However, it is difficult to discern the slight divergence from theorem 2 for the long-term discounted bonds (that is, the bonds that have ytms above their coupon rate). Speculators in bond prices should prefer long-term to short-term bonds for this reason, but theorem 3 implies that speculators need not go to the very longest term bonds to obtain large price fluctuations.

Theorem 4 implies that speculators can profit more by buying bonds (that is, taking a long position) during a decline in interest rates than by selling short during a period when an equal rise in interest rates (starting from the same level) is expected. Theorem 5 explains that bonds with small coupon rates will undergo larger capital gains (or losses) to attain a high (or low) yield to maturity than similar bonds with higher coupon rates because their prices are more valuable.[16]

11-6 IMMUNIZING AGAINST INTEREST RATE RISK

Duration is useful to financial managers, analysts, and economists; it measures both the time structure of a bond and the interest rate risk. Duration is a key concept in structuring a bond portfolio. One of the most popular applications of the duration measure occurs when a bond investor wants to use "immunization" in order to "lock in" an interest rate. Immunization will provide a compound rate of return over the period immunized that equals

---

16 Table 2-5 on page 37 shows the market prices of a bond as market interest rates vary.

the portfolio's yield to maturity regardless of fluctuations in the market interest rates. An example is instructive.

Suppose that current interest rates are at an all-time peak. Bond investors who expect market interest rates to fall in the future will want to buy bonds at the peak in interest rates for two reasons. First, as bond price theorem 1 explained, bonds will enjoy capital gains if their market interest rates do decline. Second, yields are most enticing and rewarding to bond investors at a time when market rates are high. So, bond investors who expect interest rates to decline attempt to buy bonds at the peak in interest rates, when their market prices are the cheapest.

Suppose that Ms. Carol Reed, controller of the Palmer Corporation, wanted to invest $1,000 of Palmer's cash in a Government of Canada bond with a 9 percent coupon rate and face value of $1,000 and suppose that this bond would mature in ten years. Let us also assume that Ms. Reed needs exactly $1,000 to pay a bill the Palmer Corporation has coming due in exactly

11-6.1 Immunization—The Single Bond Case

TABLE 11-3 TOTAL RETURN ON A 9 PERCENT, $1,000 BOND DUE IN 10 YEARS AND HELD THROUGH VARIOUS REINVESTMENT RATES

INCOME SOURCE	REINVESTMENT INTEREST RATE, %	Holding Period In Years					
		1	3	5	6.79*	9	10
Coupon income	5	$ 90	$270	$450	$611	$ 810	$ 900
Capital gain or loss		287	234	175	100	39	0
Interest on interest		1	17	54	105	191	241
Total return (and yield)		$378 (37.0%)	$521 (15.0%)	$679 (11.0%)	$816 (9.0%)	$1,040 (8.5%)	$1,141 (8.2%)
Coupon income	7	$ 90	$270	$450	$611	$ 810	$ 900
Capital gain or loss		132	109	83	56	19	0
Interest on interest		2	25	78	149	279	355
Total return (and yield)		$224 (22.0%)	$404 (12.0%)	$611 (10.0%)	$816 (9.0%)	$1,108 (8.6%)	$1,255 (8.5%)
Coupon income	9	$ 90	$270	$450	$611	$810	$900
Capital gain or loss		0	0	0	0	0	0
Interest on interest		2	32	103	205	387	495
Total return (and yield)		$ 92 (9.0%)	$302 (9.0%)	$554 (9.0%)	$816 (9.0%)	$1,197 (9.0%)	$1,395 (9.0%)
Coupon income	11	$ 90	$270	$450	$611	$810	$900
Capital gain or loss		−112	−95	−75	−56	−18	0
Interest on interest		2	40	129	261	502	647
Total return (and yield)		−$ 20 −(2.0%)	$215 (6.7%)	$504 (8.5%)	$816 (9.0%)	$1,294 (9.7%)	$1,547 (9.8%)

*Duration of a 9 percent bond bought at par and due in 10 years.

Source: Peter E. Christensen, Sylvan G. Feldstein, and Frank J. Fabozzi, "Bond Portfolio Immunization," in Frank J. Fabozzi and Irving M. Pollack (eds.), *The Handbook of Fixed Income Securities* (Homewood, Ill.: Dow Jones-Irwin, 1983), chap. 36, p. 808, exhibit 1.

ten years. From our study of duration we learned that an investor like Ms. Reed cannot protect the Palmer Corporation from changes in interest rates with the purchase of a ten-year bond. Synchronizing the date when the $1,000 bill must be paid with the date the $1,000 bond matures will not assure the Palmer Corporation of having the correct amount of cash on hand to pay the bill. This surprising conclusion arises partly as a result of the reinvestment problem.

A reinvestment problem arises when the reinvestment of future coupon interest occurs at future market interest rates that are expected to be further and further below the original target yield if market rates decline as expected. Note from Table 11-3 that as interest rates shift and remain at their new levels for the rest of the ten-year period, the total "holding period return" on a 9 percent par bond due in ten years varies significantly. The initial effect of a change in market interest rates appears in the value of the asset, a capital gain (or loss) occurs immediately.

After an initial change in interest rates that is presumed to occur right after the Palmer Corporation buys the $1,000 bond, the remainder of the decade proceeds without further changes in market interest rates. However, as the decade progresses, the *interest-on-interest* component of a bond's total return exerts a stronger influence.[17] Table 11-3 shows that by the end of the decade the interest on interest dominates the capital gain (or loss) in determining the bond's total return over the decade. This outcome makes sense. Capital gains occur quickly, whereas changes in reinvestment rates take time to exert their effect on the bond's total return gradually over the decade.

Two opposing forces operate on the total return of a bond—first, interest on interest, and, second, the bond's market price fluctuations. After considering these opposing forces, the natural question to ask is: At some point in the future, do the opposing forces of capital gain and reinvestment returns exactly equal or offset one another? More specifically, if market interest rates jump from, say, 9 to 11 percent and a capital loss occurs right after the $1,000 bond is purchased, at what point in the future will that capital loss be made up by reinvesting the coupon income payments at the higher future interest rate of 11 percent? The two offsetting forces of capital value and reinvestment return exactly offset each other when the bond investment has been continuously maintained for the *duration* of the bond. In this case the ten-year bond's duration is 6.79 years. Stated differently, in order to earn the 9 percent target return (the original yield to maturity at the time of purchase), it is necessary to hold the bond investment for the period of its duration—6.79 years. In contrast, to lock in a market rate of 9 percent for a ten-year period, Ms. Reed must invest the Palmer money in a bond with a *duration* of ten years. The time to maturity for a par bond with a duration of 10 years is approximately twenty-three years.

From Table 11-3 we note that the calculations are worked out for interest rate fluctuations as high as 11 percent and as low as 5 percent. The interesting point, however, is that as the interest rate fluctuates from 5 to 11

17 To be more precise, the interest on interest equals the interest on reinvested coupons plus interest on interest from interest on reinvested coupons.

percent, the Palmer Corporation is still able to earn the 9 percent total return if the investment position is maintained for 6.79 years—the duration of the bond.

The objective of a portfolio manager who immunizes a portfolio is to totally eliminate the portfolio's interest rate risk. Immunization does not attempt to reduce any risk other than interest rate risk.

Immunization is said to exist if the total value of a portfolio of bonds at the end of some specified planning horizon is equal to the ending value the portfolio was expected to have when it was purchased. If the portfolio is fully immunized, the returns from it will be no less than the returns promised over the planned holding period at the time the investment was made. A simple example of a company that owns a two-bond portfolio should help clarify the meaning of this definition.

Consider again the hypothetical Palmer Corporation, which is presumed to have a loan that is scheduled to be repaid in one lump sum ten years in the future. However, let us increase the assumption about the size of the portfolio. Assume in the paragraphs below that the Palmer Corporation has a $200,000 debt coming due in ten years that Ms. Carol Reed wishes to immunize by using $200,000 of the corporation's cash to purchase 200 government bonds that have ten year maturities and face values of $1,000 each. Call the $200,000 liability the first item in the Palmer portfolio. Assume that the Palmer Corporation also has $200,000 in cash. Call this starting cash asset the second item in the company's portfolio of only two items. To invest the cash in the Palmer portfolio for ten years without taking any chance of suffering losses because of interest rate risk, the firm might purchase a $200,000 zero-coupon or stripped default-free bond that matures in ten years. If this default-free bond could be selected so that its maturity date occurred simultaneously with the due date of the outstanding $200,000 debt, it would be convenient for the Palmer Corporation. By matching the maturity date of an asset and a liability of the same size, Ms. Reed could eliminate all interest rate risk in Palmer's two-item portfolio. This is the simplest kind of portfolio protection or immunization against interest rate risk. The portfolio would be fully protected from interest rate risk for the ten years until the $200,000 lump sum loan is repaid.

The example of the Palmer Corporation's two-item $200,000 portfolio is so simple that it is unrealistic. The example is unrealistic in the following three respects: (1) The needed zero-coupon bonds (or simply "zeros" as they are sometimes called) may not be available. This makes simply matching the maturity dates of assets and liabilities impractical. (And, if the asset is a coupon bond, its duration will be less than its term to maturity.) (2) It is typically impossible to find fixed-income assets of any kind that have maturity dates synchronizing with the due dates of the existing liabilities. (3) Assets do not typically come in the exact denomination (such as $200,000) that equals the liability that is to be paid with the proceeds. As a practical matter it is usually necessary to construct a portfolio of coupon bonds that have differing maturity dates and different denominations. Solving the problems created by these three realities leads to the *duration-matching immunization strategy*.

11-6.2 Immunizing a Bond Portfolio

The Duration-Matching Immunization Strategy A portfolio of bonds can be immunized, essentially, by selecting the bonds in the portfolio so that the *weighted average* value for their Macaulay's duration (MD) exactly equals the duration of an equal-sized offsetting liability. For instance, if the Palmer Corporation had a $200,000 liability that was coming due in ten years and had to be repaid in one lump sum, this liability would have Macaulay's duration of ten years (MD = 10 years) since no payments occur before the lump sum repayment date. The corporation's controller might immunize this $200,000 liability by purchasing two bonds with a weighted average duration of ten years and a combined value of $200,000 at their duration (as differentiated from their maturity). This transaction would fully immunize the $200,000 Palmer portfolio. The duration of a portfolio equals the dollar-weighted average of the durations of the bonds that make up the portfolio, as shown in Eq. (11-10).[18]

$$MD_p = \frac{V_1(MD_1) + V_2(MD_2)}{V_1 + V_2} \tag{11-10}$$

where

V_1 and V_2 = the dollar values of the two bonds in the portfolio

MD_1 and MD_2 = the two bonds' respective durations

MD_p = the weighted average duration of the two bonds

in the Palmer portfolio.

It has been shown in Table 11-3 and elsewhere[19] that even if the market interest rates fluctuate up and down during the life of a portfolio, the portfolio can nevertheless be fully immunized against interest rate risk losses. This immunization operates as explained by Bierwag and Kaufman below.[20]

If interest rates change after the bond is purchased, the investor is subject to two risks: (1) a price risk arising from the possibility of selling the bond at a price different from the amortized bond book basis and (2) a coupon reinvestment risk arising from reinvesting the coupons at interest rates different from the yield to maturity of the

18 Equation (11-10) is not exact, it is an approximation. Since the yield to maturity is an input to the duration calculation, every asset that has a different ytm will have its duration affected differently by a change in the level of the market interest rates. To be accurate in calculating the duration for a portfolio, the aggregate cashflows for the entire portfolio must be used to calculate the portfolio's duration.

19 Redington first showed how Macaulay's duration worked for the assets and liabilities of a firm in F. M. Redington, "Review of the Principle of Life Office Valuations," *Journal of the Institute of Actuaries*, vol. 78, 1952, pp. 286–340, which is reprinted in Gabriel A. Hawawini (ed.), *Bond Duration and Immunization: Early Developments and Recent Contributions*, (New York: Garland, 1982). Fisher and Weil went on to show that a duration-matching strategy would almost perfectly immunize the value of a portfolio even though market interest rates fluctuated, see Lawrence Fisher and Roman L. Weil, "Coping With the Risk of Market Interest Rate Fluctuations: Returns to Bondholders from Naive and Optimal Strategies," *Journal of Business*, October 1971, pp. 408–431.

20 Quotation from G. O. Bierwag and George G. Kaufman, "Coping With Interest Rate Fluctuations: A Note," *Journal of Business*, vol. 50, no. 3, July 1977, p. 365.

bond at the time of purchase. The impact of these risks on realized returns varies in opposite directions with changes in interest rates. Increases in interest rates will reduce the market value of a bond below its amortized basis but increase the return from reinvestment of the coupons. Conversely, decreases in interest rates will increase the market value of a bond above its amortized basis but decrease the return on the reinvestment of the coupons. In order for a bond to be immunized from changes in interest rates after purchase, the price risk and the coupon reinvestment risk must offset each other. It follows that duration must be the time period at which the price risk and the coupon reinvestment risk of a bond or bond portfolio are of equal magnitude but opposite in direction.

The duration-matching immunization strategy described in the preceding quotation converts a portfolio of assorted coupon-paying bonds into what is essentially a single zero-coupon bond with a maturity equal to the desired investment period. By thus keeping the weighted average duration of the assets equal to the duration of the liability, the bond portfolio manager is able to immunize the portfolio against interest rate risk.

"Duration Wandering" and Rebalancing The duration of a bond will not move in one-to-one correspondence with the passage of time, as shown above in Fig. 11-4. Therefore, Ms. Reed, or any investment manager, must monitor and "rebalance" the bonds in a portfolio on an annual or as-needed basis in order to maintain the portfolio's duration at the value that will eliminate its interest rate risk. To illustrate, suppose the remaining life in the planning period for the Palmer portfolio has declined by a year—from a decade to nine years. The duration of the original ten-year bond in the Palmer portfolio will have declined by less than a year—to approximately 9.2 years. To neutralize the risky effects of this "duration-wandering" tendency, Ms. Reed should rebalance the portfolio in order to match the duration of the bond with the remaining time in the planning period. *Rebalancing* the portfolio, in this case, would consist of selling off the original ten-year bond and buying a different bond that had a shorter duration to keep the duration of the portfolio in line with the debt's maturity date. Left unchecked, unavoidable duration-wandering will cause the market value of the Palmer portfolio to fluctuate significantly in a fashion that may be costly. However, by monitoring and adjusting the portfolio's duration, Mr. Reed can immunize it in the face of multiple shifts in interest rates.

Problems with Immunization Immunizing a portfolio of debts is not as simple as it may seem initially.[21] First of all, it is important not to forget that the duration of a bond portfolio and the remaining length of the investment period will decrease at slightly different rates with the passage of time. Figure 11-4 illustrates how a bond's duration does not decrease in a one-to-one correspondence with the passage of chronological time. As a result of the difference between decreasing time until a debt matures and the duration measure, the bond portfolio will need to be rebalanced periodically to keep

---

21 "Pension Funds Switch to Bonds Helps Securities Firms but Isn't without Risks," *Wall Street Journal*, August 21, 1984.

its duration equal to the remaining term of the investment horizon. If the portfolio is not rebalanced periodically, an initially perfect immunization will become increasingly imperfect as time passes.[22]

Market interest rates fluctuate continuously during every hour of every day. These fluctuations cause a second problem for portfolio managers who are endeavouring to immunize their portfolios. Since the yield to maturity is one of the determinants in every formula for duration, the constantly changing yields to maturity in the financial markets cause fluctuations in bonds' durations. Dealing with these random and unexpected changes in the durations of the assets and liabilities in their portfolio causes a source of constant concern that portfolio immunizers refer to as "stochastic process risk." Essentially, *stochastic process risk* refers to uncertainty arising from the shape of and shifts in the yield curve. This stochastic process risk is a second problem that can render a fully immunized portfolio imperfect and in need of rebalancing.[23]

A third possible problem arises from future inflation rates, which could accelerate and create the need to increase certain liabilities (such as future pension fund payments) accordingly. However, if an immunization strategy has the investment assets that were purchased to meet the future liabilities shackled down to a specific rate of return, the future value of the offsetting assets may prove to be inadequate to fund the inflating future liabilities.

A fourth disadvantage of establishing an immunized portfolio is that the funds invested in bonds (or bondlike) assets cannot be invested in common stocks or other investments that may be more lucrative. If future common stock returns continue to exceed bond returns by as much as they have over

---

22 The experiences of different portfolio managers who are attempting to immunize their portfolios is discussed superficially by Diane Hal Cooper, "To Immunize, or Not To?" *Institutional Investor*, February 1982, pp. 89-94. A more scientific discussion of how to immunize by using interest rate futures is found in Robert W. Kolb, *Interest Rate Futures* (Richmond: Robert F. Dame, 1982), pp. 164-180.

23 Immunization, rebalancing immunized portfolios, and dealing with the "stochastic process risk" that results from changes in the yield curve that affect bonds' durations is all discussed in the following easy-to-read survey article. G. O. Bierwag, George G. Kaufman, and Alden Toevs, "Duration: Its Development and Use in Bond Portfolio Management," *Financial Analysts Journal*, July-August 1983, pp. 15-35.

The article discusses the implications of the definition of duration that explicitly recognizes the term structure of interest rates. The duration definition below, for example, which differs from the duration definition in Eq. (11-5), recognizes the term structure by appending a time subscript to each period's interest rate.

$$MD = \frac{\sum_{t=1}^{T} [c_t t / (1 + ytm_t)^t] + FT/(1 + ytm_t)^T}{v_0}$$

In discussing how to deal with changes in the term structure of interest rates that cause "stochastic process risk" in measuring duration, the authors state (on their p. 15) that "the evidence suggests that the Macaulay measure of duration performs reasonably well in comparison to its more sophisticated counterparts and, because of its simplicity, appears to be cost-effective." However, readers who wish to learn more about this problem should read the survey article and the references it cites. In particular, see pp. 19-24.

past decades, the opportunity cost of high stock market returns that are lost by investing in an immunized portfolio could be significant.[24]

Finally, a fifth problem that some people cite as a reason not to immunize a portfolio is the default risk that occurs when bonds other than government obligations are put into the portfolio. The introduction of default risk into a portfolio that is immunized against interest rate and funding risks is seen as being counterproductive. Municipal and corporate bonds can default and even become bankrupt and, in so doing, disrupt an otherwise effective immunization strategy.

Immunization is a new scientific tool that portfolio managers added to their box of work tools during the 1980s. Numerous researchers are labouring over further developments in the procedure.[25] Strategies already exist to overcome most of the objections listed above.

11-7 CHAPTER SUMMARY

The introduction to interest rate risk in Chap. 9 explained the present value model initially. The present chapter started by showing how to calculate the value of a default-free bond with that present value model. Then the yield to maturity was defined as the discount rate that equates the present value of a bond's future cashflows with its current market price. Different methods for obtaining yield-to-maturity estimates were discussed. The yield to maturity was then contrasted with other bond return and bond yield concepts.

Macaulay's duration (MD) was introduced and defined as the average length of time that the funds remain tied up in an investment. The MD formula revealed that a bond's duration is simply the weighted average length of time until each cashflow is received, using each cashflow's relative present value as the weights. MD was shown to be a different measure of the time structure of a bond's cashflows than was the bond's term to maturity. Then a bond's interest rate elasticity (IE) was defined and shown to be a measure of a bond investment's interest rate risk. The exact mathematical relationship btween MD and IE was reviewed to show that MD was also a measure of a bond's interest rate risk. MD was then used to create immunized portfolios to reduce the portfolio owner's interest rate risk.

QUESTIONS

1. What is the duration of a bond that has a yield to maturity of 6 percent and a perpetual maturity? British consols are an example of such bonds;

---

24 In the long run common stock returns exceed bond returns so much that some investors may be well advised to avoid an immunized portfolio that yields a specified rate of return in favour of riskier but higher common stock returns. Adopting an immunization strategy is more desirable when high market interest rates can be locked in.

25 H. Gifford Fong and Frank J. Fabozzi, *Fixed Income Portfolio Management*, Dow Jones-Irwin, Homewood, Ill., chap. 6.

these bonds are issued by the United Kingdom. They pay coupon interest forever, but the principal is never supposed to be repaid.

2. What is the relationship between a bond's coupon rate and its duration?

3. "It is possible for a bond portfolio manager to immunize the portfolio against any interest rate risk." True, false, or uncertain? Explain.

4. What happens to a bond's duration if the bond's yield to maturity rises?

5. "Duration does not correspond with the exact date of any particular cashflow that a default-free bond may experience. Therefore duration is a worthless measure of the time structure of a bond's cashflows." True, false, or uncertain?

6. Calculate the present value and duration of a bond paying an 8.0 percent coupon rate annually on its $1,000 face value if it has eight years until its maturity and has a yield to maturity of 9.0 percent. Show your computations. What is this bond's interest rate elasticity? (*Hint:* Read App. 11B for a simple formula to ease your computation.)

7. Reconsider the bond described in Question 6 above. If the bond's yield to maturity was 8.0 percent, what would be its present value? Duration? Elasticity? What can you conclude from this problem about the relationship between (a) the level of market interest rates and (b) interest rate risk?

8. Under what conditions would a bond's coupon rate be larger than its current yield? Explain.

9. What is the bid-asked spread for the 9's of 1999 listed in Fig. 11-1? Does anyone profit from this spread? Explain.

10. Would you prefer to invest in (a) a ten-year bond with a 4.5 percent coupon rate that is selling at 89.89 percent of its face value or (b) a similar ten-year bond that is selling at par and has a 5.85 percent coupon rate? Assume that both bonds are issued by the same firm and have the same provisions in every respect, except that their coupon rates differ. Explain why you prefer one bond over the other. (*Hint:* Read App. 11A for computational shortcuts.)

SELECTED REFERENCES

Barnes, Tom, "Corporate Bonds and Capital Market Theory—Some Issues." *Administrative Sciences Association of Canada 1983 Conference*, Finance Division, vol. 1. pp. 265–272. This paper discusses problems with data collection on Canadian bond issues and raises some interesting issues on Canadian bond betas.

Bierwag, G. O., George G. Kaufman, and Alden Toevs. "Duration: Its Development and Use in Bond Portfolio Management," *Financial Analysts Journal*, July–August 1983, pp. 15–35. An easy-to-read survey of the research that led to duration as a useful tool for bond portfolio managers. Only a little elementary algebra is used.

Bookstaber, R., *The Complete Investment Book* (Glenview, Ill.; Scott, Foresman, and Company, 1985). Chapter 8 explains immunization graphically, formulates the linear program problem to do immunization, and publishes a computer program written in BASIC language to perform the algorithm.

Fisher, Lawrence, and Roman L. Wiel, "Coping With the Risk of Market-Rate Fluctuations: Returns to Bondholders from Naive and Optimal Strategies," *Journal of Business*, October 1977, pp. 408–431. This study investigates the effectiveness of immunization in reducing interest-rate risk. Portfolio management with a shifting term structure of interest rates is simulated. Only elementary algebra is used.

Haugen, R. A., and D. W. Wichern, "The Elasticity of Financial Assets," *Journal of Finance*, September 1974, pp. 1229–1240. Algebra and differential calculus are used to derive both the duration and elasticity measure of interest rate risk from the present model of security valuation. Bankruptcy risk is also considered in the analysis so that it is relevant for both stock and bond valuation.

Hopewell, M. H., and G. G. Kaufman, "Bond Price Volatility and Term to Maturity: A Generalized Respecification," *American Economic Review*, September 1973, pp. 749–753. Differential calculus is used to show that Macaulay's duration is a measure of interest risk for bonds.

John McCallum, "The Expected Holding Period Return, Uncertainty and The Term Structure of Interest Rates," *Journal of Finance* 30, May 1975, pp. 307–323. This paper examines the relationship between bond betas and terms to maturity for Government of Canada bonds.

Appendix 11A

Bond Valuation: Calculating the Yield to Maturity Expeditiously

This appendix explains how to calculate a bond's yield to maturity (YTM) quickly and with considerable accuracy.

If the bond analyst does not have the time to find the precise discount rate to fit into Eq. (11-2) (from page 258), an approximate yield to maturity can be obtained with fewer computations. Two easy-to-calculate approximation techniques are explained below.

APP. 11A-1 AN EASY-TO-UNDERSTAND FORMULA FOR YIELD APPROXIMATIONS

An intuitively logical method may be used to find a bond's approximate yield to maturity, denoted aytm. Equation (App. 11A-1a) defines this approximate yield-to-maturity formula.

$$\text{aytm} = \frac{\text{average capital gain or loss per year} + \text{annual coupon interest}}{\text{average investment}}$$

$$= \frac{[(F - p_0)/T] + iF}{(p_0 + F)/2}$$

where

T = number of years until the bond's maturity   (App. 11A-1a)

P_0 = purchase price (or present value)

i = coupon interest rate per annum

For example, for a 3½ percent coupon bond maturing in twenty-five years, the approximate yield to maturity is calculated as shown below. Assume the market price is $770 for a F = $1,000 face value bond.

$$\text{aytm} = \frac{(\$1,000 - \$770)/25 + (.035)(\$1,000)}{(\$770 + \$1,000)/2}$$

$$= \frac{(\$230/25) + \$35}{(\$770 + \$1,000)/2} \qquad \text{(App. 11A-1b)}$$

$$= \frac{\$9.20 + \$35}{\$885} = \frac{\$44.20}{\$885}$$

$$= .0499 = 4.99\% \text{ approximate yield to maturity}$$

As pointed out previously, bond analysts and monetary economists who work with bonds regularly refer to 1/100 of one percentage point as a *basis point*. The error of sixteen basis points calculated below is why Eq. (App. 11A-1a) is said to yield only approximations.

.0515 The bond's exact yield to maturity
− .0499 Approximation calculated in the example above
.0016 Error from example with Eq. (App. 11A-1*b*)

Equation (App. 11A-1*a*) may also be solved for P_0 and used to estimate the market price for a given yield to maturity.

Equation (App. 11A-1*a*) is easy to understand because it aligns with one's economic concept of the yield-to-maturity measure. The numerator is a measure of the average income per year, and the denominator is the amount of funds invested each year averaged over the bond's life. It seems intuitively correct to measure the yield to maturity by taking the ratio of these two quantities. Unfortunately, the intuitively pleasing Eq. (App. 11A-1*a*) produces answers that are only approximately correct.

APP. 11A-2   A BETTER YIELD-TO-MATURITY APPROXIMATION

Doctors Hawawini and Vora surveyed decades of work by various analysts and reported several formulas that yield better approximations to a bond's exact yield to maturity than does Eq. (App. 11A-1*a*) above.[26] Equation (App. 11A-2*a*) produces easy-to-calculate approximations that are quite close to the exact yield to maturity.

$$\text{aytm} = \frac{[(F - p_0)/T] + iF}{.6p_0 + .4F} \qquad \text{(App. 11A-2}a\text{)}$$

where

i = coupon rate of the bond

T = number of years left until the bond matures

p_0 and F = purchase price and face value of the bond, respectively

Note that the numerators of Eq. (App. 11A-1*a*) and (App. 11A-2*a*) are identical — they both define the average income per year. The denominator of Eq. (App. 11A-2*a*), however, differs from that of Eq. (App. 11A-1*a*). The present value is given more weight in the denominator of Eq. (App. 11A-2*a*) than in Eq. (App. 11A-1*a*). Thus Eq. (App. 11A-2*a*) gives better estimates of the true ytm.

Using the same values employed above with Eq. (App. 11A-1*a*), an analogous numerical example calculated with Eq. (App. 11A-2*a*) is shown below.

$$\text{aytm} = \frac{\$230/25) + \$35}{.6(\$770) + .4(\$1000)} = \frac{\$44.20}{\$862} = 0.513 = 5.13\% \qquad \text{(App. 11A-2}b\text{)}$$

---

26 Gabriel A. Hawawini and Ashok Vora, "Yield Approximations: A Historical Perspective," *Journal of Finance*, vol. 37, no. 1, March 1982, pp. 145–156 (see Eq. 11-5 in table II).

The error of two basis points from Eq. (App. 11A-2b) is smaller than the error of sixteen basis points obtained using the same hypothetical values in Eq. (App. 11A-1a) above.

.0515 The bond's exact yield to maturity
− .0513 Approximate yield to maturity with
_____ Eq. (App. 11A-2b)
.0002 Error from Eq. (App. 11A-2b)

APP. 11A-3 COMPUTER PROGRAMS

Computer software to calculate the yield to maturity (ytm) can either be written, or it can be purchased commercially. One of the best software packages to calculate the ytm that is available commercially is sold for several hundred dollars by Software Arts Inc. It is called TK!Solver. Some colleges and corporations have the TK!Solver program available to be used cost-free.

Software Arts Inc. is a computer software company that is best known for its famous spreadsheet program named Visi-Calc that sold thousands of copies during the early 1980s. However, Software Arts has other, completely different programs for sale too. TK!Solver is a computer program that does equation processing in a personal computer—on a IBM PC or on an Apple, for instance. TK!Solver solves Nth degree polynomials, trigonometric functions, and other complex equations for any single variable in the equation. Then the program will either save and/or print out the solution in various formats, such as lists or graphs.

Dr. Richard Bookstaber has also written computer programs in BASIC language that calculate a bond's yield to maturity, present values at different selected discount rates, and the realized yield over a multiyear holding period if the bond is sold before it matures. These programs are listed in a book by Dr. Bookstaber entitled *The Complete Investment Book*, published and sold by Scott, Foresman, and Company of Glenview, Illinois.[27]

---

27 See chap. 2 of *The Complete Investment Book* by Richard Bookstaber (Glenview, Illinois: Scott, Foresman, and Company, 1985), p. 173 for more information about Bookstaber's computer programs.

Default Risk and Purchasing Power Risk in Bonds

Bond investors face several different kinds of risks. First, there is the *interest rate risk*, which affects all bondholders every day as the market prices of all outstanding bonds move inversely to their market yields. Interest rate risk was introduced in Chap. 9 and discussed in more detail in Chap. 11. *Market risk* is a second risk factor to consider; it is caused by the fluctuations in market interest rates. Market risk was introduced in Chap. 9 and will be considered again, as it applies to bonds, in Chap. 13.[1] Unlike common stocks, the fluctuations in market interest rates are the most powerful driving force behind fluctuations in the market prices of bonds. Third, there is the *risk of default* and perhaps even bankruptcy. Default risk was introduced in Chap. 9. Fourth is *purchasing power risk*, which was also introduced in Chap. 9. Some additional aspects of default risk and purchasing power risk that are of special interest to bond investors are the subject of this chapter. Bond default risk is examined first.

The general procedure used to develop bond quality ratings and the effect of bond ratings on the market prices of corporate bonds will be discussed in the following section.

12-1 DETERMINING CORPORATE BOND QUALITY RATINGS

The Dominion Bond Rating Service (Toronto) and the Canadian Bond Rating Service (Montreal), in Canada, and Moody's Investor Services, Standard and

---

1 Market risk and interest rate risk are sometimes difficult to differentiate when analyzing bonds. This separation is most easily seen with bonds by considering what happens when a bond's quality rating is raised and, simultaneously, market interest rates are pushed up by rising inflationary expectations. As a result of the increased quality rating, a bond's price tends to rise because bond prices move inversely with the lower bond yield that typically results from higher quality ratings. At the same time, however, the same bond's price may actually fall because inflationary expectations rose and drove up the general level of market interest rates enough to offset the tendency for the bond's price to rise because its quality rating was raised. In order to statistically measure interest rate risk separately from market risk, the arbitrage pricing theory (APT) is used. The APT, presented in Chap 28 explains how different risk factors can be "extracted" by using factor analysis to "orthogonalize" them. The more subjective distinctions made between the default risk and the purchasing power risk factors in this chapter are established to set the stage for those who are endeavouring to conceptualize the nature of APT risk factors.

Poor's (S&P), and Fitch's, in the United States, are the major North American firms that evaluate the default risk of bond issues and publish their quality ratings. For an annual subscription fee, a rating agency will periodically re-evaluate its ratings of specific bonds and continuously publish these ratings year after year. Such continuous ratings make the bond issue easier to trade in the bond markets than if it were not continuously rated, so the issuer is glad to pay for this service, which helps provide an active market for its own securities.

Box 12-1 on page 289 lists and defines the Dominion Bond Rating Service's various quality ratings. The bond rating procedures used at the Dominion Bond Rating service are similar to that of the Canadian Bond Rating Service. The next section explores the factors that determine corporate bond ratings. There are two main considerations: the issuer's financial condition and prospects, and the indenture contract that governs the issuing firm.

**12-1.1
The Issuer's
Financial
Condition**

Rating agencies assign quality ratings indicating the probability of a continued and uninterrupted stream of interest payments and principal repayment by considering, among other things:

- The short- and long-term liquidity of the firm as measured by financial ratios
- The issuer's past, present, and future earnings
- Specific features of the bond indenture
- Qualifying factors, such as the assessment of management, the size of the company, and the quality of accounting

Financial Ratios   Here is an example of how a firm's financial ratios can affect the market prices of the firm's bonds:

1. The firm's coverage ratios fall (or rise), indicating an increased chance that the firm will (or will not) default on its bonds. As a result, the bond quality rating agencies lower (or raise) the rating they publish.
2. When a firm's quality rating falls (or rises), the appropriate interest rate to use in Eq. (11-1a), on page 254, rises (or falls), as shown in Fig. 9-3, on page 183.
3. When the interest rate changes in the present value calculations, the bond's value moves inversely with the interest rate (as explained by bond price theorem 1 in Box 11-2). Since bond values and bond prices are based on the same present value calculations, bond market prices also move inversely with the interest rate. Thus, a bond's price moves in the same direction as the bond's quality rating when there is a rating change.

Bond traders seeking to profit from bond quality rating changes and the associated price changes can get advance warning of these changes by studying the financial ratios and their trends for different corporate bond issues. This enables the traders to buy bonds that can be expected to enjoy price rises and to sell bonds whose prices are expected to fall. Such aggressive trading can yield profits if the forecasted changes on which the trends are based actually occur. But an investor whose forecasts are wrong can go bankrupt.

In forecasting bond rating changes, it is wise to consider coverage ratios, financial leverage ratios, liquidity ratios, and profitability ratios.

Coverage Ratios   Most bond analysts and bond raters who sit on rating committees would probably agree that the main determinant of the quality rating of a bond issue is its *coverage ratio*. A coverage ratio is a measure of how many times the issuing company's earned income could pay the interest charges and other costs related to the bond issue. A coverage ratio is a ratio of the earnings available for the payment of bond charges to the bond charges themselves. The available earnings are usually defined to be the total corporate operating income before taxes, with interest expenses included. A coverage ratio greater than 1 indicates that the issuing firm has more than enough income to pay its interest expense. The DBRS generally prefers to see this ratio above 3.0 times. This is an important consideration because it is information about the probability of the firm defaulting on its interest payments. Table 12-1 summarizes the method used by one U.S. analyst in evaluating coverage ratios to see what quality rating to assign to bond issues.

TABLE 12-1   COVERAGE RATIOS AND QUALITY RATINGS

COVERAGE RATIO	STABILITY OF EARNINGS	RELATIVE QUALITY
6 and over	Cyclical	Very high
4 and over	Stable	Very high
3 to 6	Cyclical	Medium to high
2 to 4	Stable	Medium to high
Under 3	Cyclical	Low
Under 2	Stable	Low

Source: Jerome B. Cohen, Edward D. Zinbarg, and Arthur Zeikel, *Investment Analysis and Portfolio Management*, 4th ed. (Homewood, Ill.: R. D. Irwin, 1982), p. 481.

As Table 12-1 indicates, bond analysts consider not only the issuer's earnings as measured by its coverage ratios but also the stability of the earnings, because stable earnings provide a more consistently available amount than do unstable earnings for meeting the fixed interest expenses arising from the firm's debts.

The trend of the ratios is also important. An upward trend suggests that better times lie ahead, assuming the ratios will continue to rise. A flat trend portends little change. A downward trend causes bond analysts and bond raters who project the decline into future years to warn potential investors that troubled times may lie ahead and to suggest lower quality ratings for the bond issuer.

Different bond analysts may compute coverage ratios differently. For instance, the coverage ratios may be calculated on income on a before-tax or an after-tax basis. Or, some bond analysts may prefer to include lease payments, preferred dividends, and sinking fund payments with interest payments and calculate a ratio called the *times fixed charges earned ratio*. Such changes would lower the ratios in Table 12-1, since including taxes, lease payments, preferred dividends, and/or sinking fund payments lower a firm's ratios if everything else remains unchanged. This ratio is widely used in Canada because of the larger number of preferred share issues outstanding.

A low times interest earned ratio may be the result of two causes. First, earnings may be too low. If so, the firm's poor profitability would also show up as low rates of return on assets and as rates of return on equity that are below those of most other firms. Second, the firm may be too deeply in debt and thus incur too much interest expense. If so, this will also show up as high financial leverage ratios. The section below explains financial leverage ratios.

Financial Leverage Ratios Companies that use borrowed funds (rather than the owner's equity) to expand are said to be using *financial leverage*. Ideally, money will be borrowed at a low interest rate and reinvested within the firm at a rate of return that exceeds the interest rate on the debt: the difference is profit. It is possible, however, for a firm to get too deeply into debt. If a firm uses too much financial leverage (that is, borrows too much), its fixed interest expense will grow to such a high level that if profits fall even slightly, the firm will not be earning enough to pay its contractual interest expense. This can lead quickly to bankruptcy; that is why bond investors are interested in evaluating the indebtedness of issuing firms.

Three of the most popular ratios used to measure financial leverage are the total debt to equity ratio, the long-term debt to capitalization ratio, and the long-term debt to equity ratio. The terms used in these three ratios are standard items from a firm's balance sheet, except for capitalization, a financial term that accountants no longer employ in their statements. A firm's *capitalization* is the total short-term debt (except current liabilities), long-term debt, and equity (or net worth)—that is, the capital funds committed to the firm.[2]

Each bond analyst usually has a favourite leverage ratio, though most bond analysts use more than one leverage ratio to assess the firm's level of indebtedness from different perspectives. The above ratios tend to increase or decrease together as a firm uses more or less, respectively, borrowed money.

Certain problems arise with the use of financial leverage ratios. Some of these problems relate to what is called off-balance-sheet debt. The items used to calculate the ratios above may ignore guarantees made by the firm and other types of long-term liabilities that do not normally appear on balance sheets. This results in understated leverage ratios. Some financial analysts simply ignore this problem. However, most analysts handle the problem by adding an amount to the firm's liabilities equal to the present value of its future lease payments and other off-balance-sheet debt. A difficulty is that different bond analysts may make different types of adjustments and thus come up with different leverage ratios for the same firm. This complicates interfirm comparisons of the ratios.

---

2 There is no one sacrosanct definition of a firm's capitalization. The definition varies substantially from industry to industry, but also, to a lesser degree, from one financial executive to the next. These disagreements are not all taken lightly. In enforcing capital adequacy requirements on banks, bank examiners get into heated discussions with bankers—because the stakes are high.

Another problem with the calculation of financial leverage ratios is how to decide whether to use book values or market values because, for example, the market prices of bonds fluctuate from day to day and thus differ from the book value shown in the liability section of the issuing firm's balance sheet. When the two methods produce quite different ratios, the financial analyst usually calculates the leverage ratios using both book and market values. Either way, it is possible to get an idea about whether or not the firm is too deeply in debt and to discern the trend of its indebtedness over time.

Liquidity Ratios   If a firm is too deeply in debt, the associated high interest expenses may consume all the firm's earnings and keep it teetering on the edge of insolvency. Financial analysts can use any of several *liquidity ratios* to evaluate the solvency of a firm and thus to determine whether the firm will be able to pay its bills on time.

Solvency Ratios   The two most common liquidity ratios are the current ratio and the quick ratio:

$$\text{Current ratio} = \frac{\text{current assets}}{\text{current liabilities}} \tag{12-1}$$

$$\text{Quick ratio} = \frac{\text{current assets} - \text{inventories}}{\text{current liabilites}} \tag{12-2}$$

These solvency ratios evaluate the ability of a firm to pay bills currently coming due.

Current liabilities are bills due to be paid within one year. Current assets include cash, marketable securities, accounts receivable, inventory, and any other asset that should, in the normal course of business, turn into cash within one year.

Some analysts say that a normal, healthy firm should have a current ratio of 2 (the firm has $2 of current assets for every $1 of current liabilities). However, other values are commonly considered safe; the norm varies from industry to industry.

Critics of the use of the current ratio point out that the portion of current assets held in inventory is not liquid unless customers are eagerly waiting to buy it and pay cash for it. These analysts prefer to use the quick ratio. A quick ratio of one is sometimes suggested as a minimum standard because it means there is one dollar of cash, marketable securities, and accounts receivable (all of which are more liquid than inventory) for each dollar of bills due to be paid in the current year. Other ratios measure liquidity indirectly; these are called *turnover ratios*.

Turnover Ratios   Turnover ratios are used to measure the *activity* within a firm. Use of these ratios is based on the premise that assets not being actively employed must not be very useful and are therefore probably not very liquid or profitable. Illustrated at the top of page 286 are four ratios that measure asset turnover and thus give an indirect indication of how liquid and profitable are the assets.

$$\text{Accounts receivable turnover} = \frac{\text{annual sales}}{\text{average accounts receivable}} \tag{12-3}$$

$$\text{Collection period in days} = \frac{\text{accounts receivable}}{\text{average day's sales}} \tag{12-4}$$

$$\text{Inventory turnover ratio} = \frac{\text{annual sales}^3}{\text{average inventory}} \tag{12-5}$$

$$\text{Total asset turnover} = \frac{\text{annual sales}}{\text{total assets}} \tag{12-6}$$

The accounts receivable turnover ratio and the collection period in days ratio give some indication of the liquidity of the current asset called accounts receivable. The inventory turnover ratio measures how rapidly a firm sells out and replaces its inventory. The total asset turnover ratio is designed to gauge whether all the assets owned by a firm are being used or whether some are lying dormant. Bond rating agencies, bond investors, and others who have loaned the firm money can get different perspectives on the firm's liquidity and how well managed the firm is by studying the turnover ratios.

The use of turnover ratios can be illustrated by example. Suppose that the *ABC Corporation* has an accounts receivable turnover ratio of 6 and an inventory turnover ratio of 12. Since there are twelve months in one year, the turnover ratio of 6 means that ABC's accounts receivable turn over once every two months, averaged over the entire year. ABC's inventory turnover of 12 means that the inventory turned over once each month, on average. Stated differently, we can conclude that ABC allows its customers an average of two months to pay their bills and has an inventory that averages one month old. Assume that ABC's total asset turnover ratio is 3; this is no easy interpretation. The asset turnover ratio must be compared with its own historical values to determine the trend and also compared with the asset turnover ratios of ABC's competitors to gain perspective. The next question is: Are these turnover ratios high or low? A standard of comparison is needed to answer this question.

Accounts receivable collected within two months might be normal for a neighbourhood grocery store that sells on credit or for a public utility that issues monthly bills to its customers. But a one-month collection time would be absurdly fast for a trust company's home mortgage department, because home mortgage loans have their payments spread out over an average length of twenty-five years in Canada. As far as the inventory is concerned, a one-month-old inventory would simply be impossible for the products produced by quality whisky distilleries, construction companies that build skyscrapers, or shipyards that assemble ocean liners. However, a fresh-fish market or a

---

3 This ratio is sometimes expressed as:

$$\frac{\text{cost of goods sold}}{\text{average inventory}} \quad \text{or} \quad \frac{\text{net operating costs}}{\text{average inventory}}$$

vegetable dealer had better never be caught with an inventory as old as a month; health inspectors would probably close the business for selling unfit food. Thus, each industry has its own normal turnover ratios, and so a firm's turnover ratios may usually be compared only with those of competing firms and the firm's own historical ratios.

Cashflow Ratios   The cashflows generated by a firm are divided by the firm's total long-term debt to measure *cashflows as a percentage of debt*. If such cashflow ratios indicate that a firm's interest expense cashflow stated as a percent of its debt is less than the firm's interest rate paid on total long-term debt, the firm may default on its interest payments. Unless the firm has liquid assets to sell off or is willing to incur new debts to pay interest on its old debts, the troubled firm faces imminent financial disaster. The determinants of a firm's cashflows are listed below.

Adjusted income: Adjusted income is the firm's normal operating income before taxes minus the extent to which equity earnings exceed dividends received.
Interest expense on long-term debt: Interest expense is added back into the firm's income after interest expense because the resulting income-before-interest expense is a cashflow that may be used to pay interest expense.
Depreciation: Depreciation is an expense item deducted from the firm's revenue to allow for replacement of plant and equipment that declines in value because of fair wear and tear. But the replacements and/or repairs need not actually be made simply because the bookkeeping entry deducting depreciation expense is made. Thus, depreciation is a noncash expense that financial analysts view as a cashflow that can be used for interest expense or to repair the firm's physical assets, whichever is most needed.

Another cashflow ratio is found by calculating the total of the three cashflow items listed above and then dividing this total cashflow by the total interest expense on the firm's long-term debt. Solvency cannot be maintained in the long run unless this latter cashflow ratio exceeds 1.

Profitability Ratios   It may not be apparent why bond quality rating agencies and bond investors should be particularly concerned with a firm's profitability. After all, even if a company's profits were to double, only the firm's common stock would appreciate in value. Since bonds earn only their fixed interest rate, an increase in profitability does not directly imply capital gains for bonds. Nevertheless, bond ratios and bond investment analysts are interested in the profitability of firms issuing bonds because profitability is probably the single best indicator of a firm's financial health. One of the more useful profitability ratios is the rate of return on total assets ratio.

$$\text{Rate of return on total assets} = \frac{\text{net profit before taxes}}{\text{total assets}} \tag{12-7}$$

The rate of return on assets will be lowest for firms in any given industry that have too many assets, high debt levels, low earnings, or some combination of these problems.

A profitability ratio that can reveal more about an earnings' weakness is the operating margin ratio (as shown at the top of page 288).

$$\text{Operating margin} = \frac{\text{operating income}}{\text{sales}} \qquad (12\text{-}8)$$

Operating income is a firm's pretax earnings before depreciation and interest expense (that is, before nonoperating expenses) are deducted to obtain the firm's taxable income. Dividing operating income by sales gives the percentage of every sales dollar available to pay overhead expenses and to contribute toward profits. If this ratio is too low, it means the firm should either raise its sales price per unit or cut its direct manufacturing (or operating) costs, or do both.

Another popular profitability ratio is the pretax rate of return on permanent capital ratio:

$$\frac{\text{Pretax rate of return}}{\text{on permanent capital}} = \frac{\text{pretax income} + \text{interest}}{\text{permanent capital}} \qquad (12\text{-}9)$$

The sum of pretax income and interest is the total amount a firm has available to pay its interest expenses. *Permanent capital* is a firm's permanently committed capital funds and is the sum of short-term debt not currently coming due, long-term debt, and net worth (or total equity).

The pretax rate of return on permanent capital ratio states the firm's income as a percent of its permanent capitalization. It is useful for comparison with current interest rates. If the ratio does not exceed current interest rates, the company is probably not earning enough to pay its interest expense; this condition will result in low bond quality ratings.

Profitability ratios are useful both for historical comparisons with the firm's own ratios in order to discern trends within the firm and for comparisons with the firm's competitors in order to find strengths or weaknesses.[4] These ratios are also used by bond raters in assigning quality ratings to the firm's bond issues.

Financial Ratios and Bond Quality Ratings In explaining how it rates industrial bonds, the Dominion Bond Rating Service (DBRS) made the statement shown in Box 12-1.[5] When examining Box 12-1, remember that different ratios are favoured by each bond analyst and each bond rating agency and that for any given set of ratios, different values are appropriate for each industry. Also, do not forget that through the ups and downs of the normal business cycle the values of every firm's ratios vary in a cyclical fashion. Thus, bond rating is not as simple as Box 12-1 may appear to suggest.

Here is how the Dominion Bond Rating Service describes its ratings classifications:

---

4 Financial service firms like *The Financial Post*, Standard & Poor's, Moody's and Value Line calculate numerous financial ratios every year for at least ten years back. These ratios are then published in tabular form and sold. Such ratios are calculated every year for thousands of large and medium-sized firms. (See Chap. 6, pp. 115–133.)

5 Readers who desire detailed numerical examples of financial ratio calculations should consult a book written about that topic. For a modern treatment of the topic see George Foster, *Financial Statement Analysis* (Englewood Cliffs, N.J.: Prentice-Hall, 1978.) For a more traditional discussion of the topic see *Standard & Poor's Rating Guide* (New York: McGraw-Hill, 1979).

BOX 12-1
Rating
Classifica-
tions for
Bonds

BOND RATINGS

Rating Classifications — Bonds

(1) Four main factors go into a rating—liquidity, earnings (past, present and future), covenants and qualifying factors.

(2) To attain a rating in the AAA category, a company has to be "near perfection", and definitely only a very small proportion of companies will attain this rating.

(3) The ratings of most companies will fall into A and BBB categories. Companies rated A could be viewed as being up to high average credits while BBB companies would be viewed as being up to low average credits. Please note that we are also using high and low sub-categories, i.e. A(low), BBB(high), and the greatest proportion of these sub-categories will be found in the A and BBB categories. Note that a BBB rating is the category which divides the higher rating categories above it (all the A's) from the speculative categories lying below.

(4) The BB, B and CCC categories define difference degrees of speculation. The BB are mildly speculative, the B are "middle" speculative and the CCC are highly speculative. Note that if a company is maintaining payments of principal and interest, the lowest rating it could receive from DBRS is CCC, if it is rated.

(5) Once a company is in default, it would receive a CC rating. The single C category is reserved for the second tier of debt which a company in default might have.

Thus, the following summaries should be noted:
AAA – "near perfection".
AA   – Well above average.
A   – Up to high average, upper medium grade.
BBB – Up to low average, medium grade.
BB   – Mildly speculative.
B   – Middle speculative.
CCC – Highly speculative.
CC   – In default.
C   – Second tier of debt of a company in default.

Source: Dominion Bond Rating Service, Bond Ratings, July 1986. Reprinted with permission.

**12-1.2
Economic
Significance,
and Size of
the Issuer
and Other
Qualifying
Factors**

Suppose that financial ratios had been calculated for the XYZ Corporation and that the members of the bond rating committee agreed that the XYZ Corporation was highly profitable, very liquid, and, on the basis of the criteria shown in Box 12-1, deserved a rating of AAA. However, then suppose a financial analyst suggested, "Even though XYZ's financial ratios indicate its bonds should be AAA rated, I predict the company will be driven into bankruptcy next year. The product XYZ produces has recently been made obsolete by a new invention that was just patented by one of XYZ's competitors."

The bond rating committee adjourns for a week to do more research before assigning the XYZ bond issue a rating.

This example shows that bond raters and other financial analysts must consider more than a company's financial ratios. The bond issuing firm's competition, its size, its importance in its industry, recent changes in the industry, and many related factors must also be considered before assigning a quality rating or making an investment in a bond. This analysis of factors external to the bond-issuing firm should start with the firm's competitors.

The Issuer's Industry In an effort to discern important facts about the industry within which a bond issuer operates, analysts will study the following types of points:[6]

Position in the economy: Is the firm in the capital-goods sector (such as machinery production), the consumer-durables sector (such as automobile production), or the consumer-nondurables sector (such as food processing)?

Life cycle of industry: Is the industry in a growth, stable, or declining phase?

Competitive nature: What is the nature and intensity of the competition in the industry? Is it on a regional, national, or international basis? Is it based on price, quality of product, distribution capabilities, image, or some other factor? Is the industry regulated (as in broadcasting), providing some competitive protection?

Labour situation: Is the industry unionized? If so, are labour contracts negotiated on an industrywide basis, and what is the recent negotiating history?

Supply factors: Does the industry generally have good control of key raw materials, or is there a dependence upon questionable foreign sources?

Volatility: Is there an involvement with rapidly developing or changing technologies? Is there a dependence upon a relatively small number of major contracts (as is sometimes the case in the aerospace industry)?

Major vulnerabilities: Is the industry likely to be a prime target for some form of political pressure (such as the jawboning over prices to which the steel industry has often been subjected)? Are substantial environmental expenditures likely to be mandated (as has been the case in the metals industry)? Are near-term energy shortages possible? What is the ease of entry into the industry?

Answers to the questions above inform the bond analyst about the industry's growth potential, problems that may plague the industry, and the stability of the industry's sales. After these questions are answered, the analysis of the bond issuer can move on to a consideration of the issuer's competitive situation within its industry. These points must be investigated in this order before a bond issue can be meaningfully evaluated.

The Issuer's Competitors The key questions that S & P raters consider when evaluating an issuer's competition are listed below.[7] The questions are primarily about the firm whose bonds are being rated in order to keep the research into competition from becoming an aimless and costly inquiry into each of the bond issuer's competitors. The cost of the research on competition can be limited by inquiring only into how the competition affects the bond issuer.

---

6 *Standard & Poor's Rating Guide* (New York: McGraw-Hill, 1979), p. 28.
7 *Standard & Poor's Rating Guide* (New York: McGraw-Hill, 1979), pp. 29–30.

Market share: Does a company have a large enough portion of the market share (be it regional, national, or international) to significantly influence industry dynamics? This may be especially important in a market dominated by only a few producers. Does the company have the opportunity to exercise price leadership? Does the company offer a full range of products or have proprietary products or a special niche in the market?

Technological leadership: Is the company usually among the first with new developments, or is it typically a follower? How do research and development expenditures compare with the industry average?

Production efficiency: Is the company a relatively low-cost producer? Are its facilities newer or more advanced than the average? Is it more or less vertically integrated than the average? If mandated expenditures (such as for pollution control) are required, has the company already complied to a greater or lesser extent than its competitors? Does the company face a more onerous labour situation than its competitors?

Financial structure: How does a company's use of leverage and various types of financing vehicles compare with that of others in the industry?

After the bond raters have answered the questions above to their satisfaction, they are ready to turn their attention to the last phase of bond rating, studying the new issue's indenture contract. Essentially, the bond rating committee endeavours to gauge the impact of the various protective provisions provided to enhance the safety of the bond buyer's investment.

12-2   THE PROVISIONS IN THE ISSUE'S INDENTURE

The bond owner's rights are spelled out in the legal instrument called the *indenture*. The various protective provisions spelled out in the indenture can raise the quality rating for an issue if a strong issuer grants liberal provisions. For example, if the bond issue's indenture pledges as collateral a large, modern office building that could be easily rented or sold, this protects the bond investors if the issuer should go bankrupt. The bond investors could get ownership of the collateral in a bankruptcy proceeding and sell it to recover the funds they invested in the issuing firm. In spite of the importance of these provisions, however, they are less important than the issuer's earning power. All the liberal protective provisions in the world will not get a high quality rating for a firm that faces a future of continuing losses.

The bond issuer commonly provides the following types of protective provisions to ensure the safety of the bondholder's investment.

- The issuer pledges specific assets as collateral.
- The issuer subordinates other legal claims on its assets or income.
- The issuer provides for a sinking fund with which to pay off the bonds even if the issuer defaults on its other debts.
- The issuing firm's management promises to operate the firm in certain ways to protect the bondholders.

These provisions are considered in more detail below.

Collateral   A paragraph in a bond indenture that specifies that specific assets of the issuing company become the property of the bond investors to do with as they wish if the issuer defaults on the interest or principal payments of the bond issue is called a *collateral provision*. Many bond issues have no collateral provision, but those that do are rated somewhat higher (other factors being equal).

Debentures are bonds that have no assets pledged as collateral to help guarantee the bondholders that they will be repaid in case of a bankruptcy (see Chap. 2). If the issuer does go bankrupt, the debenture owners will find themselves placed in the undesirable category of "general creditors" in the priority of claims. General creditors include the public utilities, suppliers of raw materials who sold on credit, and other junior-level creditors. It is common for general creditors to be repaid only ten cents of every dollar they are owed when a bankruptcy suit is settled. To avoid this disheartening prospect, bond investors can buy mortgage bonds, for example, in order to obtain a collateral provision. Mortgage bonds have a prior claim in bankruptcy on the specific asset (for example, a new factory financed by the proceeds of the bond issue) pledged as collateral.

Bondholders do not get a collateral provision for nothing. Such a provision increases the bond issue's price per bond slightly, and it lowers the interest income yield. So by buying collateralized bonds, the investor gives up some money in order to get a safer investment; this is a risk-return tradeoff.

Subordination In order to make safety-conscious investors more willing to buy bonds, clauses can be included in the indenture that subordinate certain claims or assets. A *subordination clause* places the bond issue or other bond issues or specified creditors in an inferior or secondary legal position with respect to the issuer's assets if the issuer defaults on the interest or principal payments.

The so-called *after-acquired property clause* is an example of a subordination clause. Such a clause states that if an issuer acquires additional assets after a first mortgage bond (or other type of collateralized bond, as specified) is outstanding, these new assets will automatically become part of this first mortgage bond's collateral. Such a clause protects the first mortgage bondholders from having the firm acquire newer assets with later mortgage bond issues against which the first mortgage bond owners would hold no claim. In effect, this clause subordinates the claim of any later mortgage bond buyers to the first mortgage bondholders' claim: first mortgage bondholders can claim their old assets plus all the newer assets as collateral, too.

Another fairly common subordination is the *dividend test clause*. Such a clause limits the claim of the common stockholders (who essentially run the corporation through their voting power at annual stockholders' meetings) on corporate profits. Profits might be used to pay either cash dividends to stockholders or interest to bondholders. This clause specifies that the issuer cannot pay annual cash dividends in excess of annual earnings. Such a clause helps ensure that if the firm suffers losses, its borrowing power and liquid assets will be retained to pay bondholders rather than used to pay cash dividends to the common stockholders. Several other similar clauses also subordinate maximization of common stockholders' profits to bondholders' safety.

Sinking Funds A sinking fund provision also subordinates the common stockholders' interest in maximizing corporate profits to the bondholders' desire for safety. A *sinking fund* is a fund into which the bond issuer is required to pay every year. The sinking fund provision in some indentures requires that the sinking fund deposits be held by a third party (for example, a bank that holds them in escrow) to be used solely to repurchase the bonds at some future date. This type of sinking fund guarantees bondholders that the money needed to repay their loan is being safely accumulated. But this accumulation of funds does not maximize the issuer's profit. Thus, aggressive common stockholders who want their profits maximized may object to sinking fund provisions.

A sinking fund clearly provides increased safety of repayment for bond-holders. After a number of years' annual payments have been safely accumulated in the sinking fund, the rating agencies may acknowledge the protection provided to investors by raising the issue's quality rating. An improved quality rating will increase the bond's market price and thus enrich the bondholders. Furthermore, sinking funds that are well funded may provide price supports for their bonds. That is, if the sinking fund has a policy of repurchasing bonds in the market when their market prices fall sufficiently low, this policy constitutes a price support that keeps the bonds' prices from falling below a specific price. This way of holding up bond prices benefits the bondholders, but sinking funds can also work to the detriment of bond-holders, in two significant respects.

First, some sinking fund provisions provide that bonds may be redeemed at stipulated dates before the issue matures. Thus, an investor may have gone to the trouble of evaluating a bond issue and purchasing a bond at what is considered to be an attractive yield to maturity only to have the investment snatched away by a sinking fund prematurity-date purchase. Such sinking fund purchases are most likely to occur when interest rates are low and the investor has no good reinvestment alternative. Second, issues with sinking funds pay lower yields because they offer their bondholders greater safety. This is an example of the risk-return tradeoff: The lower-risk investments can attract buyers at lower rates of return.

Other Protective Provisions   Some indenture contracts forbid the issuer to sell off its own assets in order to lease the same assets back again later. The purpose of such a sale-and-leaseback arrangement is to free capital invested in plant and equipment so that it may be spent for other purposes. Meanwhile, the use of the asset is ensured because the seller of the asset contracts to lease it back as part of the sales agreement. Bondholders want provisions against sale-and-leaseback transactions because they deplete the issuer's collateral assets; a leased asset is no collateral.

Debt test clauses are common in issues of speculative grade bonds. Such provisions limit the issuer's ability to create additional debt and thereby protect bondholders in two ways. First, they limit the issuer's ability to undertake rapid expansion, which is usually risky. Second, if the issuer should go bankrupt, such clauses limit the number of creditors who must quarrel over the remaining assets.

Negative pledge clauses limit the issuer's ability to pledge assets as collateral for any future borrowings. This protects existing bondholders from having to face senior bankruptcy claims that might have arisen with later issues of other collateralized bonds.

Prohibitions against the sale of subsidiary corporations are common. Such provisions allow the issuer to sell major subsidiaries only if they immediately repay the previously outstanding debt. This protects bondholders from losing important sources of income or collateral assets that the issuer owns through its subsidiaries.

It should now be apparent that there is an almost unlimited variety of provisions that can be inserted in an indenture. The ingenuity with which safety-seeking bondholders encumber issuers' management is refreshing. Remember, however, that nothing is granted for free. Every protective provision bondholders obtain reduces the rate of return they can expect to earn from their bonds. There are rare exceptions to this rule, but generally the natural economic order of things requires a tradeoff of risk for return.

12-3   BOND PRICES AND BOND QUALITY RATING CHANGES

When profits turn into consistent losses, a company is forced to deplete its liquid assets to pay its bills as they come due. When both profitability and liquid assets are gone and the firm cannot borrow any more money, it defaults on its debt payments. Furthermore, the bond quality ratings of a company that is moving from good health to bankruptcy will decline as the firm's financial ratios deteriorate.

12-3.1 Empirical Analysis of Bond Rating Changes and Bond Prices

Dr. Mark Weinstein analyzed the monthly market price changes of 132 different bonds which were associated with 100 different bond rating changes occurring between July 1962 and July 1974.[8] He studied 32 (that is, 132−100) more bonds than rating changes because some bond issuers had more than one bond issue outstanding at the time of their rating change, and the prices of all outstanding bonds were analyzed for each rating change. Dr. Weinstein investigated to find if bond prices reacted to quality rating changes with a lead or a lag, or simultaneously; or if they did not react at all.

Of the 132 bonds Weinstein analyzed, 60 had rating increases and 72 had decreases. He found small price reactions that occurred *before* the rating changes. These bond price changes were symmetrical and were in opposite directions for the quality rating increases and the decreases — just as you might expect. The negative monthly percentage price changes associated with the rating decreases were reversed in sign and added to the positive monthly percentage price changes associated with the rating increases. Weinstein did this in order to determine the average bond price response pattern month by month before and after a rating change without regard to the direction of the change.

8 Mark I. Weinstein, ''The Effect of a Rating Change Announcement on Bond Prices,'' *Journal of Financial Economics*, December 1977, vol. 5, no. 3, pp. 329–350.

As explained in Chaps. 9 and 11, all bond prices fluctuate inversely with market interest rates. Therefore, the systematic bond price movements that are caused when the level of all market interest rates is rising or falling must be filtered out of the bond price changes in order to discern the price reactions that may be attributed purely to rating change. Weinstein used three bond price change measures defined in Eqs. (12-10), (12-11), and (12-12) to accomplish this task.

$$u_{it} = r_{it} - r_{pt} \tag{12-10}$$

where

u_{it} = unsystematic or abnormal percentage price change that may be attributed to the rating change of bond i in month t

$$r_{it} = \frac{p_{it} - p_{i,t-1}}{p_{i,t-1}} \tag{12-11}$$

where

r_{it} = percent price change per month for the ith rating-changed bond in the tth month

p_{it} = market price of bond at the end of the tth month

$p_{i,t-1}$ = market price at the beginning of the tth month

$$r_{pt} = \frac{p_{pt} - p_{p,t-1}}{p_{p,t-1}} \tag{12-12}$$

= percent price change per month in month t from a diversified portfolio of bonds (denoted by the subscript p) all of which have the same quality rating as the ith bond

The abnormal percentage price change for the ith bond in the tth month measured by Eq. (12-10) may also be affected by unsystematic factors other than rating change. For example, the ith bond might experience unsystematic price gains (that is, $u_{it} > 0$) or losses (namely, $u_{it} < 0$) from an abnormally large purchase or sale, respectively, of the bonds by some substantial investor that was totally oblivious of the ith bond's rating change. In order to isolate these causes of abnormal bond price changes and focus only on rating change reactions, Dr. Weinstein averaged the unsystematic percentage price changes over all 132 bonds studied, as shown in Eq. (12-13).

$$U_t = \frac{1}{N} \sum_{i=1}^{N} u_{it} \tag{12-13}$$

where

N = 132 = the number of bonds studied

U_t = average unsystematic or abnormal percentage bond price change t months from the rating change month

Note: t was set to zero for the rating change month for all 132 bonds.

In addition to summing over all 132 bonds in order to average out to zero all unsystematic changes not caused by rating changes, Weinstein adjusted the time subscripts, denoted t. He set $t = 0$ for the rating change month for all the 132 bonds studied regardless of the month in which their rating change occurred. Thus the statistic U_0 measures the average unsystematic risk-adjusted price change reaction from dozens of different months—all of which have been averaged over 132 different bonds. As a result, the value of U_t is void of any date in time; it is stated relative to the sampled bonds' rating change month.

To further average out any unsystematic reactions that were unrelated to the rating changes, Dr. Weinstein cumulated the monthly U_t from B months before the rating change month to A months afterward. The formula for these cumulative abnormal returns is shown in Eq. (12-14).

$$\text{Cumulative abnormal returns} = \sum_{t=B}^{A} U_t = \sum_{t=B}^{A} \left(\frac{1}{N} \sum_{i=1}^{132} u_{it} \right) \tag{12-14}$$

Table 12-2 shows the results Dr. Weinstein obtained from various applications of his procedure. Next, Weinstein divided the sum of the averages defined in Eq. (12-14) by the quantity $(B - A)$ months to obtain a mean monthly abnormal return over the period near the rating change month, as shown in Eq. (12-15).

$$\text{Mean monthly abnormal return} = \frac{1}{A - B} \sum_{t=B}^{A} U_t \tag{12-15}$$

The eight portfolios shown in Table 12-2 represent eight different summations of the average monthly unsystematic percentage price changes U_t. They are called portfolios because each one represents the results of holding a different portfolio of diversified bonds all of which experienced rating

TABLE 12-2 UNSYSTEMATIC PRICE CHANGE STATISTICS FOR BONDS THAT EXPERIENCED RATING CHANGES

	VALUE OF B	A	FROM B TO A CUMULATION OF U_t RETURNS	MEAN MONTHLY ABNORMAL RETURNS	STANDARD ERROR	t STATISTIC OF MEAN MONTHLY ABNORMAL RETURN
1	−7	−1	0.009	0.002	0.133	0.01
2	−1	0	0.623	0.623	0.396	1.59
3	0	+6	0.162	0.027	0.137	0.20
4	−7	+6	0.442	0.034	0.096	0.36
5	−19	−13	0.385	0.064	0.113	0.69
6	−13	−7	0.358	0.060	0.123	0.48
7	−19	−7	1.204	0.100	0.071	1.41
8	−19	−1	1.278	0.278	0.061	1.16

Source: Mark I. Weinstein, ''The Effect of a Rating Change Announcement on Bond Price,'' *Journal of Financial Economics*, December 1977, vol. 5, no. 3, pp. 329–350, table 4.

changes at different calendar dates from July 1962 to July 1974. The second and seventh portfolios are the most interesting because they experienced the most statistically significant abnormal price reactions.

Portfolio 2 summarizes the results from buying bonds one month before their rating was changed (that is, at time $B = -1$) and then selling the bonds one month later (that is, A months after the change, so $A = 0$). This strategy yielded an average abnormal return that was positive on average; its value was 623/1000 of 1 percent. Using the standard deviation of the abnormal returns around their mean (called the standard error of the estimate by statisticians) as a measure of sampling errors allows the t statistic defined in Eq. (12-16) to be computed:

$$t \text{ statistic} = \frac{\text{mean monthly abnormal return} - \text{zero}}{\text{standard error}} \qquad (12\text{-}16)$$

The second portfolio's t statistic of 1.59 indicates that the portfolio's mean monthly abnormal return was 1.59 standard errors above a mean value of zero. The mean value of zero was assumed in order to test the hypothesis that the abnormal price response differed significantly from zero. This outcome would happen infrequently (that is, with only a probability of 0.0559) as a result of mere sampling distribution. Essentially, there is a slightly abnormal price reaction in the month of the rating change. But this rating change response is so small, on average, that it would not even pay the brokerage commissions associated with buying and selling the bonds to obtain the abnormal return.

Portfolio 7 is the only other portfolio that appears to have experienced a rating change price reaction which differs from zero sufficiently to be of interest. The data in Table 12-2 show that bond portfolio strategy 7 earned a cumulative abnormal return of 1.204 percent over the one-year period from nineteen months before to seven months before the rating change. This is equal to $1/10$ of 1 percent per month abnormal return over the year from $1\frac{1}{2}$ years to $\frac{1}{2}$ year prior to the rating change.[9]

Implications of the Weinstein Study   In summary, the statistics in Table 12-2 are consistent with the hypothesis that (1) bond prices do not react after their ratings have been changed, (2) bond prices experience a tiny abnormal reaction in the rating change month, and (3) bond prices accomplish most of their price change reactions about one year in advance of having their ratings changed. The implication of (1) and (2) is that, after you allow for the brokerage commissions to buy and sell, it would not be worthwhile to trade bonds because their quality rating was changed if you did not trade until after the change was announced to the public.

Overall, Dr. Weinstein's findings imply that bond investors should not waste their time and money on Moody's, Standard & Poor's, Dominion and

---

9 Dr. Weinstein's results refine the conclusions presented in an earlier empirical analysis of bond price reactions to bond rating changes. Paul Grier and Steven Katz, "The Differential Effects of Bond Rating Changes among Industrial and Public Utility Bonds by Maturity," *Journal of Business*, April 1976, vol. 49, no. 2, pp. 226–239.

Canadian Bond Rating Services or any other bond ratings. Changes in the quality rating of the issuing corporation largely lag, and thus they appear to be a delayed reaction to changes in a bond issuer's actual quality as reflected in the bonds' market prices.[10]

The Weinstein study suggests that bond market prices are unbiased and efficient estimators of bonds' true economic values. Apparently, when the quality of a bond-issuing company changes, both the price and value of its bonds change together in advance of any changes in published bond ratings. This evidence suggests that bond market prices fully reflect all publicly disseminated information. In fact, Weinstein's results suggest that as a result of the buying and selling done by astute bond analysts the prices *anticipate* the publicly announced rating changes. Only detailed financial analysis and planning should yield any bond trading profits as a result of bond rating changes.

Trading bonds that have already had their quality ratings changed does not seem to offer any chance of earning easy trading profits. However, the common stock of the bond-issuing corporation may react significantly to the change in the bond issuer's quality rating. That is a subject worthy of further research.

12-4 BOND RETURNS AND PURCHASING POWER RISK

Bonds are called dollar-denominated assets because they promise to make their payments in dollars rather than in real goods such as food or clothing. This means that any coupon interest payments and the principal repayment that are contractually promised to the bonds' owners are fixed dollar quantities which do not increase with the inflation that will almost surely occur during the bonds' life. As a result of any inflation, bondholders are repaid in dollars that have less purchasing power over real (that is, physical) goods than the dollars that were originally invested in the bonds. This loss in purchasing power over real goods, which all bond investors will most likely experience, is the *purchasing power risk* from bond investing. Purchasing power risk is often larger than investors realize because they are unaware of the rate of inflation and its implications.

It is surprising that most investors are not better informed about inflation, because various Canadian government agencies prepare and freely disseminate inflation estimates to the public media. Although it is not perfect, the most popular price index in Canada is the *Consumer Price Index (CPI)* prepared by Statistics Canada. The CPI measures the cost of a representative market basket of different goods and services that are regularly consumed by representative Canadians. Current prices for these goods are gathered from different areas around the country and then assigned weights based on the

---

10 Professor Holbook Working suggested that a price change may anticipate the event which causes the price change if market analysts foresee the future with any success; see ''A Theory of Anticipatory Prices,'' *American Economic Review*, May 1958, pp. 188–199.

areas' relative proportions of the total population. The prices of most of the items that make up the CPI are observed regularly. Table 9-2, on page 198, shows CPI statistics published by the Canadian government.

The main conceptual problems with the CPI involve how the commodities, which make up a representative consumer's market basket, are selected, how changes in people's buying preferences are reflected, and how services and capital goods for use in the index are priced. Even though it is imperfect, the CPI is probably the most representative index of price changes for Canadian investors. It will be used in this chapter to measure inflation in Canada.

As explained earlier in Sec. 9-4, inflation measurements are fundamental to dealing with purchasing power risk. The relation between the value of the CPI in the tth time period (denoted CPI_t), and the rate of price inflation (denoted q) is shown in Eqs. (12-17a) and (12-17b).

$$q_t = \frac{CPI_t - CPI_{t-1}}{CPI_{t-1}} \text{ for one period} \tag{12-17a}$$

$$(1 + q_t)^n = \frac{CPI_{t-n}}{CPI_t} \text{ for } n \text{ periods} \tag{12-17b}$$

Equation (12-17a) measures the one-period rate of inflation. The quantity in Eq. (12-17b) is called a *value relative* for measuring inflation over multiple periods. Column 5 of Table 12-3 shows the annual rates of inflation in the CPI over the years from 1950 to 1983.

Table 12-3 also shows the market rates of return for both long-term industrial and federal government bond indexes that were calculated with Eq. (12-18).

$$r_t = \frac{(p_t - p_{t-1}) + c_t}{p_{t-1}} \text{ for 1 year} \tag{12-18}$$

where

c_t = coupon interest payment in the tth year

p_t = price level of the portfolio of bonds that make up the index

r_t = money rate of return per period = nominal return

12-4.1 Long-Term Bond Yields Exceed Inflation

The annual rates of return for long-term industrial and federal government bonds calculated with Eq. (12-18) are shown in columns 3 and 4, respectively, of Table 12-3.

Bear in mind that these returns are all stated on a before-commissions and before-tax basis. The returns after the transactions costs are deducted would be less.

Column 5 of Table 12-3 indicates the results of a series of reinvestments in one-month Treasury bills. Equation (12-19) defines how these Treasury bill returns were computed.

12-4.2 Treasury Bill Yields

$$r_t = \frac{p_t - p_{t-1}}{p_{t-1}} \tag{12-19}$$

TABLE 12-3 YEAR BY-YEAR TOTAL RETURNS, 1950–1983

YEAR	EQUITIES	INDUSTRIAL BONDS	GOVERNMENT BONDS	TREASURY BILLS	CHANGE IN CPI,q	INFLATION ADJUSTED			
						EQUITIES	INDUSTRIAL BONDS	GOVERNMENT BONDS	TREASURY BILLS
1950	0.2997	0.0268	-0.0011	0.0051	0.0601	0.2260	-0.0314	-0.0577	-0.0519
1951	0.2262	-0.0644	-0.0301	0.0071	0.1073	0.1074	-0.1551	-0.1241	-0.0905
1952	0.0238	0.0449	0.0205	0.0095	-0.0173	0.0418	0.0633	0.0385	0.0273
1953	-0.0644	0.0399	0.0376	0.0154	0	-0.0644	0.0399	0.0376	0.0154
1954	0.436	0.1034	0.0978	0.0162	0.0035	0.4310	0.0996	0.0940	0.0127
1955	0.2701	0.0218	-0.0043	0.0122	0.0035	0.2657	0.0182	-0.0078	0.0087
1956	0.044	-0.0758	-0.0354	0.0263	0.0315	0.0121	-0.1040	-0.0649	-0.0050
1957	-0.2001	0.0758	0.066	0.0376	0.0203	-0.2160	0.0544	0.0448	0.0170
1958	0.3281	0.0299	-0.0582	0.0227	0.0266	0.2937	0.0032	-0.0826	-0.0038
1959	0.0356	-0.0428	-0.0444	0.0439	0.0129	0.0224	-0.0550	-0.0566	0.0306
1960	0.0158	0.1194	0.0688	0.0366	0.0128	0.0030	0.1053	0.0553	0.0235
1961	0.3393	0.0891	0.0975	0.0286	0.0032	0.3350	0.0856	0.0940	0.0253
1962	-0.0711	0.0495	0.0316	0.0381	0.0157	-0.0855	0.0333	0.0157	0.0221
1963	0.1507	0.0538	0.0459	0.0358	0.0186	0.1297	0.0346	0.0268	0.0169
1964	0.2459	0.0471	0.0674	0.0373	0.0182	0.2236	0.0284	0.0483	0.0188
1965	0.0661	-0.0058	0.0104	0.0379	0.0298	0.0352	-0.0346	-0.0188	0.0079
1966	-0.063	-0.0153	0.0172	0.0489	0.0348	-0.0945	-0.0484	-0.0170	0.0136
1967	0.2026	-0.0034	-0.0227	0.0438	0.042	0.1541	-0.0436	-0.0621	0.0017
1968	0.2245	0.0243	-0.0062	0.0622	0.0403	0.1771	-0.0154	-0.0447	0.0211
1969	-0.0173	-0.0104	-0.0236	0.0683	0.0465	-0.0610	-0.0544	-0.0670	0.0208
1970	-0.0463	0.1397	0.227	0.0689	0.0148	-0.0602	0.1231	0.2091	0.0533
1971	0.0851	0.1448	0.1179	0.0386	0.0487	0.0347	0.0916	0.0660	-0.0096
1972	0.2702	0.0951	0.0159	0.0344	0.051	0.2086	0.0420	-0.0334	-0.0158
1973	-0.0267	0.024	0.0196	0.0478	0.0927	-0.1093	-0.0629	-0.0669	-0.0411
1974	-0.2723	-0.0586	-0.0098	0.0768	0.1232	-0.3521	-0.1619	-0.1184	-0.0413
1975	0.2261	0.0835	0.0274	0.0705	0.0953	0.1194	-0.0108	-0.0620	-0.0226
1976	0.1151	0.2332	0.1965	0.091	0.0591	0.0529	0.1644	0.1297	0.0301
1977	0.1401	0.1058	0.0619	0.0764	0.0946	0.0416	0.0102	-0.0299	-0.0166
1978	0.2924	0.0516	0.0147	0.079	0.0836	0.1927	-0.0295	-0.0636	-0.0042
1979	0.5148	-0.0155	-0.0277	0.1105	0.098	0.3796	-0.1034	-0.1145	0.0114
1980	0.2786	0.0293	0.0246	0.1216	0.1119	0.1499	-0.0743	-0.0785	0.0087
1981	-0.0818	-0.0078	-0.0202	0.1909	0.121	-0.1809	-0.1149	-0.1260	0.0624
1982	0.0415	0.4335	0.4581	0.1525	0.0926	-0.0468	0.3120	0.3345	0.0548
1983	0.3738	0.1389	0.0969	0.0945	0.0455	0.3140	0.0893	0.0492	0.0469

Source: James E. Hatch, and Robert W. White. *Canadian Stocks, Bonds, Bills and Inflation: 1950–1983.* p. 58, table 7. Note that real annual returns differ slightly (generally by no more than 0.0001) from Hatch and White's table 8 on p. 59. The differences are attributable to different rounding procedures.

Comparing the annual yields from the Treasury bills with the annual rates of inflation in the CPI reveals that the Treasury bill investment's yield slightly exceeded the rate of inflation, on average, as shown in Fig. 9-7.

To provide more perspective on the bond returns, the returns from a common stock index also are shown in Table 12-3 and Fig. 9-7. The University of Western Ontario equity data base of 763 Canadian stocks was used. The annual rates of return for a diversified portfolio of common stocks that were selected randomly were calculated from this stock price index. The cash dividend index was included to obtain total returns. Equation (12-20) shows how the rates of return for the stock market index were calculated.

12-4.3 Common Stock Comparison

$$r_i = \frac{(I_t - I_{t-1}) + (I\text{ cash dividends}_t)}{I_{t-1}} \tag{12-20}$$

where:

I_t = Index level in period t

The data in Table 12-3 and the summary statistics in Table 9-3 show that, on average, the common stocks earned much greater returns than any of the bond investments. One should not hastily conclude from this difference, however, that common stock investments are better than bond investments. The common stocks must pay higher returns to compensate their investors for assuming the greater risks associated with common stock investing.

Comparing the risk statistics in Table 9-3 for common stocks with the bonds' risk statistics is informative. An investment's risk or variability of return can be measured by its standard deviation of returns or the range over which its returns fluctuate. Comparing the fluctuations of the common stock index's returns in Table 12-3 (from a high of 51 percent to a low of -27 percent is a range of 78 percent) with the bonds' risk statistics indicates that the stock index is a far more risky investment than any of the bond indexes. Thus common stock investors do get higher returns than bond investors, on average. However, they must suffer lost sleep and the greater possibilities of a nervous breakdown or of bankruptcy because their investment is riskier. Thus, the common stock investors earn the higher return they typically obtain.

As explained previously in Sec. 9-6, "money illusion" is a phrase economists attribute to individuals who are so naive as to think they are wealthy merely because they have *more money* than other people. This belief is naive because it ignores the effects of inflation on the money's purchasing power. People who have a money illusion have not learned to distinguish between real wealth and nominal wealth. Real wealth is what truly matters; nominal wealth can be illusory during inflationary times.

12-4.4 Real Versus Nominal Returns

Equations (12-18) through (12-20) define the one-period nominal rates of return on long-term bonds, Treasury bills, and common stocks, respectively. None of the equations measures real returns, however. Table 12-3 and Fig. 9-7 were prepared to suggest comparing nominal investment returns to the inflation rate in order to form estimates of the real returns. But to calculate each security's real (that is, inflation-adjusted) rate of return, Eq. (12-21) is used.

$$rr_t = r_t - q_t \tag{12-21}$$

The term r_t in Eq. (12-21) is the one-period nominal rate of return for the tth time period calculated with Eq. (12-18), (12-19), or (12-20). The inflation rate for the tth period, q_t was defined in Eq. (12-17a). After the inflation rate is subtracted from the nominal rate of return as shown in Eq. (12-21), a good approximation of the *real rate of return* for time period t, denoted rr_t, is obtained. (See Box 9-4 on page 201 about the approximation.)

The real rate of return measures the percentage increase in real purchasing power an investment yielded in a given period rather than its nominal (or dollar) return. Columns 7 through 10 of Table 12-3 show the annual real rates of return from various investment averages. An investment asset will have a positive nominal return, $r_t > 0$, and a negative real return, $rr_t < 0$, during any period in which its nominal return was less than the inflation rate, $r_t < q_t$.

12-5 CHAPTER SUMMARY

The present-value model of Eq. (11-1) is used in bond valuation. Sometimes the most difficult part of the bond-rating process is determining the appropriate market interest rate to use as the discount rate; this is where the bond quality rating is useful.

Bond rating committees and bond investors use financial ratios and guidelines, such as the ones given in Box 12-1, to place a bond issue tentatively into a quality category. This tentative rating is re-examined in light of the issue's economic significance and competitive position, and the tentative rating may be shaded upward or downward as deemed appropriate. Finally, the protective provisions are evaluated to determine the final quality rating, with guidelines gained from years of experience helping analysts assess the impact of the various clauses. (For example, if a profitable issuer has outstanding at the same time a debenture bond and a mortgage bond, the collateralized bond will typically be rated one notch above the unsecured debenture if the two issues are about equal in all other respects.)

The relationship between the appropriate discount rate and a bond's quality rating changes continuously through time. Bank of Canada policy, fiscal policy, the supply and demand for loanable funds, and many other factors cause this relationship to change from day to day. The only difference between default-free government bonds and industrial bonds is that industrial bonds must pay higher rates of interest in order to induce investors to assume the default risk. Since interest rates tend to rise and fall together, corporate bonds' interest rates merely fluctuate at a slightly higher level than do government bonds' interest rates.

Bond rating agencies like Dominion Bond Rating Service, Canadian Bond Rating Service, Standard & Poor's, Moody's, and Fitch's spend considerable resources assessing the quality of individual bond issues. These bond ratings seem to have some validity because (1) they vary directly with the market interest rates available in the bond markets on any given date, (2) the bond quality ratings are written into the investment guidelines handed down by most provincial governments, and (3) bond issuers pay thousands of dollars annually merely to have their bond issues rated currently.

Purchasing power risk is like a hidden tax. Inflation takes away from (or, if you prefer, taxes) the creditors and tends to give what it takes to debtors. If the debtors pay a nominal interest rate that is below the rate of inflation, inflation definitely benefits debtors at the expense of their lender. Therefore, bond investors, who are essentially lenders, cannot afford to overlook the purchasing power risk, which rises with the inflation rate.

The default risk is greatest on low-grade industrial bonds, and the purchasing power risk is worst in the high-inflation economies of the world. In the final analysis, however, one of the wonderful things about bond investment (as opposed to bond price speculation) is that investors can be relatively free from worry about interest income fluctuations if they so desire. By simply buying a high-grade bond with little risk of default, which offers contractual interest payments and repayment of the principal at specified times, the investor can have peace of mind and earn a yield to maturity that is known in advance. However, for the brave-hearted security analysts who do default risk analysis and monetary economists who forecast inflation and interest rates, the bond markets offer opportunities for profitable speculating, too.

QUESTIONS

1. Assume that in July 1987 the Bell 6's of 2005 bonds have a 10 percent yield to maturity. That is, the Bell Canada Enterprises' issue of bonds that paid 6 percent and will mature in 2005 were yielding 10 percent. Assuming that the bond matured in exactly 18 years, how could you calculate its present value?

2. Compare and contrast Bell 6's of 2005 selling at 75 with Daon Development's 10¼'s of 2005 quoted at 87¾ on July 20, 1987. Express your ideas in terms of risk and return of these two bonds. Explain the reasons for the differences between them.

3. Compare home mortgages to collateralized bonds with a sinking fund.

4. Why would an investor prefer to buy bonds with a sinking fund provision? Why might investors tend not to want a sinking fund provision for bonds they owned?

5. Explain why the yields on short-term bonds fluctuate more than the yields on long-term bonds, and yet the prices of long-term bonds nevertheless fluctuate more than the prices of short-term bonds.

6. Dr. Weinstein's study of bond price movements showed that substantial gains could be earned by buying corporate bonds a day or two after their quality rating was upgraded. True, false, or uncertain? Explain.

7. What did Dr. Weinstein use as a standard for comparison or yardstick against which to gauge the price movements of the corporate bonds that had their ratings changed?
8. Do you think that bond rating agencies like Dominion Bond Rating Service, Standard & Poor's, and Moody's give any heed to the market prices of the issuer's bonds and/or common stock when they change the quality ratings to outstanding issues? (*Hint:* Consider the research results of Dr. Weinstein and Professors Griffin and Sanvicente.)

SELECTED REFERENCES

Boyle, Phelim P., Harry H. Panjer, and Keith Sharp, *Report on Canadian Economic Statistics, January 1, 1924–December 31, 1985.* Canadian Institute of Actuaries, June 1986. An empirical study that provides return and variance data for common stocks, federal and provincial government bonds, industrial bonds, savings instruments, mortgages, Treasury bills, and a number of economic indicators for the period 1924 to 1985.

Hatch, James E. and Robert W. White. *Canadian Stocks, Bonds, Bills and Inflation: 1950–1983,* Monograph 19. Charlottesville, Va.: The Financial Analysts Research Foundation, 1985. An easy-to-read empirical analysis of market premiums for default risk and purchasing power risk in stock and bond indexes. The empirical work is well grounded in the received theory of financial economics.

Ibbotson, Roger G. and Rex A. Sinquefield, *Stocks, Bonds, Bills and Inflation: The Past and the Future.* 1982 ed. Charlottesville, Va: The Financial Analysts Federation. A similar study to Hatch and White using U.S. data.

Appendix 12A

Rating Corporate Bonds Statistically

Professors Pinches and Mingo (P&M)[11] have shown how to use a statistical procedure called multiple discriminant analysis (MDA) to estimate bond ratings based on six statistics for a firm. Essentially P&M fit four linear equations like Eq. (App. 12B-1) to classify bonds into one of five categories.

$$z_{ij} = f_{i1}x_{1j} + f_{i2}x_{2j} + f_{i3}x_{3j} + f_{i4}x_{4j} + f_{i5}x_{5j} + f_{i6}x_{6j} \qquad \text{(App. 12A-1)}$$

where

$i = 1, 2, 3, 4, 5$ ratings

$J = 1, 2, \ldots, n$ bonds issues

The six explanatory variables are defined below for firm J's bonds:

x_{1J} = subordination of the issue is measured by setting x_1 to zero or unity to indicate whether or not it is subordinated

x_{2J} = years of consecutive cash dividends, a measure of stability

x_{3J} = size of the bond issue, a measure of the issue's marketability

x_{4J} = 5-year average of net income divided by interest expense, a coverage ratio

x_{5J} = 5-year average of long-term debt over net worth, a leverage measure

x_{6J} = net income over total assets, a measure of profitability for the J company

The f_i coefficients in Eq. (App. 12A-1) are numbers estimated statistically so that the discriminant score, denoted z_J for the jth bond, would give the best indication of whether that bond issue is in the ith quality rating. For example, for the first category ($i = 1$), which is the AAA-grade rating, if a bond issue's discriminant score is not high enough, that bond is not classified in the first category. Instead, the bond's discriminant score is next calculated for the second function ($i = 2$) to see whther z_J is high enough to qualify the bond to be in category 2 (that is, an AA-grade bond). This process goes on through the third and fourth discriminant scores, respectively. If a bond's discriminant score is not high enough to qualify for any of the first four

11 G. E. Pinches and K. A. Mingo, "A Multivariate Analysis of Industrial Bond Ratings," *Journal of Finance*, March 1973, pp. 1–32.

categories (that is, $i = 1, 2, 3$, or 4), the bond is assigned to category 5, which is grade B and below.[12]

In testing their model, P&M correctly classified 92 out of a sample of 132 bonds; that is, 70 percent were correctly classified. Multiple discriminant analysis appears to be a useful statistical tool for rating bonds. Multiple regression models can also be employed fruitfully in rating bond issues statistically.[13]

12 R. A. Eisenbeis and R. B. Avery, *Discriminant Analysis and Classification Procedures* (Lexington, Mass: Lexington Books, 1972).

13 Robert S. Kaplan and Gabriel Urwitz, "Statistical Models of Bond Rating: A Methodological Inquiry," *Journal of Business*, vol. 52, no. 2, April 1979, pp. 231-262. Kaplan and Urwitz developed a model to estimate bond ratings that works very well. However, when testing their model against a common multiple regression model, they report that the multiple regression model is nearly as accurate at classifying bond issues' ratings as their more sophisticated model.

The Level and Structure of Market Interest Rates

The price of a bond moves inversely to its yield to maturity with decimal point mathematical precision. Therefore, the best approach to predicting bonds' prices is to first explain their yields to maturity. The yields to maturity of all bonds are market interest rates that fluctuate minute by minute. These fluctuations in bond market interest rates may be viewed as arising from two sources — those that are internal and those that are external to the issuing firm.[1]

1. Changes *inside* the issuing firms alter the probability that the bond investors might suffer losses from default or bankruptcy. This risk factor is peculiar to corporation and municipal bonds; it is called *default risk*. Default risk was introduced in Chap. 9 and analyzed further in Chap. 12.
2. Changes *outside* the issuing firm affect similar bonds simultaneously. Changes in the supply and demand for credit, changes in the inflation rate (which was introduced in Chap. 9 under the heading of Purchasing Power Risk), and changes in the macroeconomic environment (which was also introduced in Chap. 9 under the heading of Market Risk), are factors external to the individual corporations that affect their bond yields and prices. Those factors which are external to the firm determine the level and structure of market interest rates and, thus, bond prices.

The market interest rates, or yields to maturity, which are the focus of this entire chapter, were called the appropriate discount rate for finding a bond's present value in Chaps. 11 and 12. These rates are sometimes also called the risk-adjusted cost of debt capital or the investor's required rate of return.[2] However, regardless of what you call the yield to maturity, explaining bond values is easy once the appropriate yield to maturity is known: just use Eq. (11-2) to find any bond's exact value.[3]

---

1 In order to reap the full benefit from Chap. 13, the reader should fully understand Chap. 11, Bond Valuation, and Chap. 12, Default Risk and Purchasing Power Risk in Bonds.

2 Care should be taken not to become confused about bonds' *one-period rates of return* as defined in Eq. (2-1). Chapter 11 discusses only bonds' *yields to maturity*, and these multiperiod rates of return are different from the one-period rates of return.

3 Some bond analysts stress the similar and simultaneous way in which the market price and market yield to maturity of a bond are determined. This approach is technically valid because, as a glance at the present value model of Eq. (11-1) will show, the present value of a bond and its yield to maturity are merely different sides of the same coin. The approach used in this book does not deny the simultaneity of the present value and *yield*; however, it does not emphasize this simultaneity either. Instead, it explains the present value of a bond as being determined by *yield to maturity*. That is, the *yield* is treated as an explanatory or causal variable that determines the bond's price. This latter approach is followed because it avoids the cumbersome discussion of bonds with different face values and focuses more expeditiously on the common denominator that can be used to compare and contrast all debt securities — namely, the investment's market-determined interest rate.

13-1 THE LEVEL OF INTEREST RATES

The term structure of interest rates (that is, the shape of what is called the *yield curve*) refers to the relationship between yields for bonds that are identical in every respect except their term to maturity. Studying the term structure of interest rates addresses questions like: ''Why are the yields of some issuers' bonds that have twenty years to maturity usually higher than the same issuers' bonds with fewer years to maturity, if all other factors are equal?'' Such questions are addressed later in this chapter. This section deals with the *level*, but not the structure, of interest rates. It answers questions about why all interest rates are high or low, rising or falling.

Market yields to maturity are determined by many things. The most basic determinant of interest rates is what economists call the *real rate of interest*, or the rate at which capital grows in the physical sense. For example, consider a stock of capital that consists of ten coconut trees on an island. If the ten coconut trees produce enough nuts and leaves to maintain the fertility of their soil, sustain the people who tend them, and increase to eleven coconut trees in a year, the trees may be viewed as a stock of capital that grew at 10 percent per year. Economists call this basic rate of interest the real rate of interest. The real rate of interest is not published in newspapers, as are the nominal interest rates.

In addition to the real rate of interest, market interest rates are also affected by various risk-premiums that investors may demand. In order to undertake risky investments, lenders (such as bond investors) my require one or more *risk-premiums* to be paid over and above the real rate of interest to induce them to lend their funds when the risk of loss exists. The determination of default risk-premiums for bonds and the relationship between bond yields and bond quality ratings was explained in Chap. 9. Other kinds of risk-premiums, which bond investors may demand, will be explained below.

Since interest rates and loans are typically in nominal money quantities rather than real physical quantities, the nominal interest rate must contain an allowance for the rate of price change so that lenders' wealth will not be eroded away by inflation. For example, if a lender loans $100 for a year at 5 percent interest, the lender will be repaid $105. But, if inflation at a rate of 10 percent exists, $E(\Delta P/P)$ = 10 percent, this $105 will have the purchasing power a year later of 1/1.1 = 90.9 percent of $105, or $95.45 because of the inflation.[4] Thus, the lender must charge 5 percent interest plus 10 percent inflation allowance, or 15 percent per year to allow for the inflation. In this case, the lender will be repaid $15 [= $100 times (100 percent + 5 percent + 10 percent)]. After 10 percent inflation, the $115 has a real purchasing power of 1/1.1 = 90.9 percent of $115, or $104.54. The lender thus gained only a $4.54 increase, or 4.54 percent, in purchasing power by loaning money

---

4 The symbol E denotes the mathematical expectation; it is defined in Mathematical App. B. The Greek letter delta, Δ, means *change* when it is used in economics. The symbol P might represent the consumer price index (CPI), for example. Therefore, ΔP means price change, and $E(\Delta P/P)$ represents an expected percentage price change, that is, the expected inflation rate.

at 15 percent interest during a year in which inflation was 10 percent. This shows that lenders need to raise interest rates by at least the rate of inflation in order to maintain the real purchasing power of their wealth. This inflation adjustment is called the *Fisher effect*, after an economist named Irving Fisher, who first explained it decades ago.[5]

The manner in which the three determinants of interest rates (that is, the real rate of interest, risk-premiums, and the rate of expected price change) are combined is summarized symbolically in Eq. (13-1).

$$\begin{pmatrix} \text{Nominal,} \\ \text{or market} \\ \text{interest,} \\ \text{rate} \end{pmatrix} = \begin{pmatrix} \text{real} \\ \text{rate of} \\ \text{interest} \end{pmatrix} + \begin{pmatrix} \text{various} \\ \text{possible} \\ \text{risk-} \\ \text{premiums} \end{pmatrix} + \begin{pmatrix} \text{expected} \\ \text{rate of} \\ \text{inflation} \end{pmatrix} \qquad (13\text{-}1)$$

Equation (13-1) is a model of how the *level* of interest rates is determined.

The level of interest rates refers to how high interest rates tend to be. For example, suppose that the real rate of interest is 3 percent per year (3 percent $= .03$), that lenders require a 2 percent risk-premium for loans of some given risk-class (2 percent $= .02$), and that expected inflation is 2 percent per year $[E(\Delta P/P) = 2 \text{ percent} = .02]$. According to Eq. (13-1), this implies that the nominal interest rate for loans of this given risk-class is (3 percent + 2 percent + 2 percent =) 7 percent per year. If inflationary expectations rise from 2 to 4 percent per year, Eq. (13-1) implies that nominal interest rates will rise to (3 percent + 2 percent + 4 percent =) 9 percent per year. This increase from 7 to 9 percent is a change in the *level* of interest rates that would increase all interest rates.

An economist named Dr. William Gibson, among others, published scientific evidence showing how the public's inflationary expectations, $E(\Delta P/P)$, determine market interest rates.[6] Gibson estimated a series of regressions of the form shown in Eq. (13-2).

**13-1.1
Measuring
the Effects of
Inflationary
Expectations**

$$\text{ytm}_{it} = A_i + B_i E(\Delta P/P)_t + z_{it} \qquad E(z_{it}) = 0 \qquad (13\text{-}2)$$

---

5 Irving Fisher discussed the effects of inflation on market interest rates in *Appreciation and Interest* (New York: Macmillan, 1896), pp. 75–76. The ideas were expanded later in Fisher's book *The Theory of Interest* (New York: Macmillan, 1930). For a different view which is critical of Fisher's well-received theory see Steven C. Leuthold, "Interest Rates, Inflation and Deflation," *Financial Analysts Journal*, January–February 1981, pp. 28–41.

6 W. E. Gibson, "Interest Rates and Inflationary Expectations: New Evidence," *American Economic Review*, December 1972, pp. 854–865. A more sophisticated study was done by W. P. Yohe and D. S. Karnosky, "Interest Rates and Price Level Changes, 1952–69," *Review*, St. Louis Federal Reserve Bank, December 1969. This readable survey and empirical test is available free in pamphlet form as reprint no. 49 from the St. Louis Fed. A more esoteric study is by M. Feldstein and O. Eckstein, "The Fundamental Determinants of the Interest Rate," *Review of Economics and Statistics*, November 1970, pp. 303–374. See also E. Fama, "Short-Term Interest Rates as Predictors of Inflation," *American Economic Review*, June 1975, pp. 269–282, and Udayan P. Rege, "Inflationary Expectations as a Source of Variation in Nominal Interest Rates," *Administrative Sciences Association of Canada, 1985 Conference Proceedings*, Finance Division, vol. 1, pp. 122–129.

In Eq. (13-2), ytm_{it} designates the market interest rate or yield to maturity of the ith bond issue in time period t, and $E(\Delta P/P)_t$ denotes inflationary expectations in period t. The A_i and B_i terms are the regression intercept and slope coefficients (see Mathematical App. D about regression) for the ith bond issue. Regression Eq. (13-2) tries to explain the market yield of the ith bond in the tth period in terms of the rate of inflation that was expected in that period.

Gibson used surveys taken at different times from dozens of economists' inflation forecasts for one year in the future to find the consensus of inflationary expectations. Surveys of U.S. economists from coast to coast were taken every six months for eighteen years; $E(\Delta P/P)_t$ denotes their average forecast for the tth time period's inflation. Table 13-1 shows the regression results.

TABLE 13-1   GIBSON'S REGRESSION STATISTICS FOR EQ. (13-2)

i	YIELDS (R'S) FROM:	INTERCEPT A_i	SLOPE B_i	$\bar{R}^2$
1	3-month Treasury bills	2.20	.93	.76
2	6-month Treasury bills	2.04	1.09	.78
3	9- to 12-month Treasury bills	2.19	1.06	.79
4	3- to 5-year Treasury notes	2.92	.89	.83
5	10-year Treasury bonds	3.23	.67	.85

Regression Eq. 13-2 was fitted for five different bond issues. The coefficients of determination, denoted $\bar{R}^2$ in Table 13-1, measure the percentage of variation in the bond yields to maturity explained by the concurrent inflationary expectations variable, $E(\Delta P/P)$. Since the lowest $\bar{R}^2$ is .76 (= 76 percent for 3-month Treasury bills), this means that over three-quarters of the changes in interest rates can be explained with inflationary expectations. All five slope coefficients, B_i, approximate unity, indicating that if the rate of inflation changes by a certain amount, interest rates change by about the same amount. The smaller regression slope coefficients for the bonds with longer terms to maturity may be interpreted to mean that one year's inflation expectations have a smaller effect on long-term bond yields than on the yields of short-term bonds. The intercept terms A_i in Eq. (13-2) are estimates of the real rate of interest plus the risk-premium (which should be zero for U.S. Treasury bonds) in Eq. (13-1). For example, for Treasury bonds with ten years and over to maturity, the intercept is A = 3.23 percent during the sampled period.

These regression statistics attest to the importance of inflationary expectations in the determination of market interest rates during the period sampled. The annual inflation rate and interest rate data shown in Table 12-3 furnish further evidence of the way interest rates move up and down with inflation.

Although both the regression statistics in Table 13-1 and the data in Table 13-2 present strong evidence that rising rates of inflation pushed up interest rates during the 1960s and 1970s, there are changes in interest rates that were not related to inflationary factors. These as-yet-unexplained changes are the result of various risk-premiums (which will be explained in the next section) and changes in the supply of and demand for loanable funds caused by disintermediation, "crowding out," the ebb and flow of the business cycle, and other factors.[7]

**13-1.2
Supply and
Demand for
Credit**

TABLE 13-2   **AVERAGE YIELDS OVER RECENT SAMPLE PERIODS**

YIELDS TO MATURITY PERIOD	1956–1965	1966–1975	1976–1985
Government of Canada Bonds	4.77%	7.35%	11.49%
Provincial Bonds	5.28	8.26	12.23
Industrial Bonds	5.38	8.55	12.46

Source: Phelim P. Boyle, Harry H. Panjer, and Keith P. Sharp, *Report on Canadian Economic Statistics, January 1, 1924–December 31, 1985* (Canadian Institute of Actuaries, 1985), p. 16, table 3A. Published with permission of the Canadian Institute of Actuaries.

The business cycle affects credit conditions by affecting the supply and demand for funds. Business economists at banks, bond portfolio managers, and others who must forecast day-to-day changes in interest rates study flow-of-funds tables that show where credit inflows (namely, savings) and credit outflows (that is, borrowings) originate in an effort to ascertain the effects of short-run changes in the supply and demand for loanable funds. During a period of economic expansion, the unemployment rate falls, business activity quickens, and businesses borrow money to build bigger plants and to finance more inventory, accounts receivable, and equipment purchases. The resulting credit demands bid up interest rates. In contrast, during slowdowns and recessions, unemployment increases, manufacturing activity slows, and demand for credit shrinks; thus interest rates fall, if all other factors are constant.

**13-1.3
Market
Interest
Varies
with the
Stage
of the
Business
Cycle**

In 1983 the Canadian economy was emerging from a recession and businesses were starting to demand bank loans and other forms of credit to expand their factory operations and to finance larger inventories. Thus, businesses and the government were both trying to borrow whatever loanable

---

7 *Intermediation* refers to the activity of financial intermediaries like banks and trust companies as they intermediate between savers and investors. Financial intermediaries accept many small savings deposits, pool them, and then make large loans to finance business expansion and home building. *Disintermediation* is the reverse; savers withdraw their savings from financial intermediaries and thus cause a reduction in loanable funds. Rising interest rates cause disintermediation because banks and savings and loan associations are reluctant to accept deposits that obligate the institution to pay high interest rates on their savings accounts. Credit crunches are a result of interest rates pushed up by tight credit conditions and inflation rather than the cause of the high interest rates themselves.

funds were available. The resulting demand for credit exceeded the available supply of loanable funds, and some hopeful businesses were *crowded out* of the credit markets by the massive borrowing demands of the Canadian government. This crowding out — that is, the borrowing competition between businesses and the federal government — bid up market interest rates to levels above what they would have been if the government had balanced its budget. More concisely, crowding out caused high interest rates during 1983 and 1984.

Essentially, market interest rates may be viewed as being the *"price"* of *credit*. When the demand for credit exceeds the supply of loanable funds, market interest rates are bid up by those who are seeking to borrow.

The level of inflationary expectations and the phase of the business cycle are two of the main factors usually affecting interest rates. But, various kinds of risk-premiums, which rise and fall, can also have an important effect on market interest rates.

13-2   YIELD SPREADS

Yield spreads are the differences between the yields of any pair of bonds — usually a default-free Canadian federal government bond and another, more risky, bond. Yield spreads are defined in Eq. (13-3) for the *t*th time period.

$$\begin{pmatrix} \text{Yield on} \\ \text{risky bond} \end{pmatrix}_t - \begin{pmatrix} \text{Canadian federal} \\ \text{government bond yield} \end{pmatrix}_t = (\text{yield spread})_t \qquad (13\text{-}3)$$

Yield spreads like the one in Eq. (13-3) may also be called *risk-premiums* because they measure the additional yield that risky bonds pay to induce investors to buy more risky bonds rather than less risky bonds.

13-2.1
The Cyclical
Portion of the
Yield Spreads

Table 13-2 shows some yield spread statistics for different classes of bonds. The table shows that over the period 1956–1965, for example, industrial bonds paid an average risk premium of .61 of 1 percent, or 61 basis points (that is, 5.38 percent less 4.77 percent) over similar term federal government bonds.

The data in Table 13-2 show that yield spreads averaged larger in the 1966 to 1975 sample period than they did from 1956 through 1965. However, Table 13-3 shows that yield spreads vary with the business cycle.[8] The right-hand column of Table 13-3 shows, for example, how the average risk-premiums on provincial-grade bonds varied over the business cycle. Other yield spreads may be calculated from the data, which show that all risk-premiums tend to

8 Chen, Roll, and Ross have found a statistically significant relationship between common stock returns and the (orthogonalized) market interest rate yield spreads (and several other economic variables, too). See Nai-Fu Chen, Richard Roll, and Stephen Ross, "Economic Forces and the Stock Market: Testing the APT and Alternative Asset Pricing Theories," CRSP Working Paper no. 119, December 1983. Their results are also referred to in "The Arbitrage Pricing Theory Approach to Strategic Portfolio Planning" by Richard Roll and Stephen Ross in the May–June 1984 issue of *Financial Analysts Journal*, pp. 14–29. The relationship between the individual risk factors and the total risk of an asset are discussed more fully in this book's Chap. 28, about the arbitrage pricing theory (APT).

TABLE 13-3   MARKET RATES AND YIELD SPREADS AT ECONOMIC PEAKS AND TROUGHS

DATE	Rates and Yield Spreads in Percent, for Securities as Follows				
	GOVERNMENT OF CANADA BONDS	PROVINCIAL BONDS	INDUSTRIAL BONDS	INDUSTRIAL-GOVERNMENT SPREAD	PROVINCIAL-GOVERNMENT SPREAD
Dec. 1969 (peak)	8.33	9.19	9.29	0.96	0.86
Nov. 1970 (trough)	7.50	8.83	9.02	1.52	1.33
Nov. 1973 (peak)	7.64	8.48	8.71	1.07	0.84
March 1975 (trough)	8.47	9.67	10.15	1.68	1.20
Jan. 1980 (peak)	12.13	12.66	12.78	0.65	0.53
July 1980 (trough)	12.32	13.15	13.21	0.89	0.83
July 1981 (peak)	17.07	18.08	18.05	0.98	1.01
Apr. 1982 (trough)	14.75	16.28	16.76	2.01	1.53
Dec. 1983 (peak)	12.02	12.86	12.95	0.93	0.84

be larger at economic troughs than at the peaks in economic activity. This cyclical fluctuation can be forecast and used to establish profitable hedges between bonds in different classes that are expected to have opening or closing yield spreads.

Risk-premiums are higher at economic troughs for two main reasons. First, unemployment, fear of job loss, and risk-aversion are higher during recessions. Therefore, most investors demand larger risk-premiums to induce them to buy risky bonds. Second, the corporations that issue bonds typically experience reduced sales and profits during recessions. Since the issuers are more subject to bankruptcy during recessions, investors require larger risk-premiums.[9] These cyclical changes in the risk-premiums in Eq. (13-1) are one more reason why market interest rates fluctuate. However, there are other noncyclical causes for risk-premiums to change.

The yield spreads between different debt securities open and close from year to year for some reasons that are not cyclical and easy to predict. Investors may demand risk-premiums of varying amounts for any of the following reasons.

**13-2.2
The
Noncyclical
Risk-
Premiums**

1. *Fears of future inflation.* Table 13-1 shows regression statistics from Gibson's regression Eq. (13-2). These statistics indicate that Gibson's inflation model explained the variations in market interest rates very well during the 1960s and 1970s in

9 Lawrence Fisher, "Determinants of Risk Premiums on Corporate Bonds," *Journal of Political Economy*, June 1959, pp. 217–237; W. Braddock Hickman, *Corporate Bond Quality and Investor Experience*, Princeton University Press for the National Bureau of Economic Research, 1958; *Statistical Measures of Corporate Bond Financing Since 1900*, Princeton, 1960; George E. Pinches and Kent A. Mingo, "A Multivariate Analysis of Industrial Bond Ratings," *Journal of Finance*, March 1973, pp. 1–18. In addition to the risk-premiums which investors demand that *vary over the business cycle*, the current supply of and demand for loanable funds also affects yield spreads; see Ray C. Fair and Burton G. Malkiel, "The Determination of Yield Differentials between Debt Instruments of the Same Maturity," *Journal of Money, Credit and Banking*, November 1971, pp. 733–749.

terms of the concurrent rates of inflationary expectations. This was a period of steadily accelerating rates of inflation to higher and higher levels to which the public was unaccustomed; thus each new higher rate of inflation was unanticipated. But, Gibson's inflation model did not explain why market interest rates remained at double-digit levels during the period 1980–1984, for example, while the inflation rate crashed down from 12 percent to only 4 percent. Gibson's inflation model could not explain this phenomenon because it did not allow for investors' *fears* that double-digit rates of inflation might not be easy to extinguish. As a result of widely held fears during the early 1980s that double-digit inflation would resume, investors largely ignored the fall in the actual rate of inflation. Instead, investors demanded new high "fear of inflation" risk-premiums during the early 1980s to induce them to buy bonds at a time when they were afraid of renewed double-digit inflation.

2. *Domestic political fears.* The daily purchases and sales of bonds by hundreds of bankers and investment managers has a continuous and substantial impact on yield spreads. Most of these professional financial people scrutinize the current events news for political developments that have economic and financial implications. The political expectations and fears of these money managers are thus reflected in yield spreads. For instance, if the financial community thinks that a liberal government might get elected in Canada and raise taxes to finance liberal spending programs in the years ahead, political fears that the higher taxes might stifle people's incentive to work would tend to increase yield spreads. Financial newspapers like *The Financial Post* frequently report that the financial community appears to have reached some consensus forecast of the future based on its current assessment of political eventualities and even explain how the financial community's political expectations influence yield spreads and other aspects of the economic environment.

3. *Foreign political fears.* International investors face the risk that the governments of foreign countries in which they wish to invest may be suddenly overthrown, the risk that the existing government may swing far to the right or left in its political policies, the risk that the foreign currency may be devalued, the risk of civil uprising, ad nauseam. As a result of these perplexing uncertainities, some investors demand risk-premiums from foreign investments over and above the risk-premiums they expect from domestic investments to induce them to assume the risks of foreign investing.

4. *Fears of military upheaval.* When a country becomes involved in a war, it usually causes the country to spend more on the war effort than can be collected in tax revenues, and federal deficits result. Most governments do not finance their war deficits by selling federal debt obligations. Instead, governments usually finance war deficits by printing new money at an inflationary rate that is sufficient to cover the deficit spending. The resulting rates of inflation undermine and destroy the country's security values and eventually the country's general economy, if the war lasts very long. Experienced financial economists have observed this wartime phenomenon over and over again in modern history. Furthermore, when a country is engaged in a war, the chance always exists that the country may suffer domestic damage if the enemy invades it. Fears of this financially bleak and physically scary environment cause investors to require high risk-premiums to invest in either corporate or government bonds from countries that are about to enter a war or are already engaged in a war.

In addition to changes in the level of interest rates that result from changing rates of inflation, changing credit conditions, cyclical changes in yield spreads, and unusual risk-premiums, there are also changes in what economists call the "term structure of interest rates." These changes in the term structure of interest rates result from a different set of influences, which are examined in the next section.

13-3   THE TERM STRUCTURE OF INTEREST RATES

The combined effects of changes in inflationary expectations and changing credit market conditions cause the *level* of market yields to vary over a wide range from year to year. However, these facts reveal nothing about the term structure of interest rates. Different bonds have different terms to maturity. For example, the federal government, corporations, such as Bell Canada Enterprises, Inco, and other organizations that borrow in the bond markets, have different bond issues outstanding with maturities ranging from three months to over thirty years. Moreover, any given bond issuer usually has, on any given day, *different yields to maturity* on its various bond issues that differ only with respect to their *term to maturity*. For a given bond issuer, the structure of yields for bonds with different terms to maturity (but no other differences) is called the *term structure of interest rates*. *Ceteris paribus* the term to maturity of a bond, will affect its yield. Thus, Eq. (13-1) must be extended as shown below in Eq. (13-4) to reflect how the market interest rate of the ith bond at the tth time period is affected by varying the bond issue's term to maturity.

$$\begin{pmatrix} \text{Nominal, or} \\ \text{market interest,} \\ \text{rate for } i \text{ at } t \end{pmatrix} = \begin{pmatrix} \text{real} \\ \text{rate of} \\ \text{return} \end{pmatrix} + \begin{pmatrix} \text{risk-} \\ \text{premiums} \\ \text{for } i \text{ at } t \end{pmatrix} + \begin{pmatrix} \text{expected} \\ \text{rate of} \\ \text{inflation} \\ \text{at time } t \end{pmatrix} + \begin{pmatrix} \text{term} \\ \text{structure of} \\ \text{interest rates} \\ \text{for } i \text{ at } t \end{pmatrix} \quad (13\text{-}4)$$

This section of the chapter focuses on the term structure of interest rates, or, if you prefer, the *yield curve*. By eliminating all variables that do not affect this term structure, the analysis is simplified and expedited. This can be done by limiting the discussion to the various maturities of Canadian government bonds. All Canadian government bonds have identical *default risk*-premiums of zero. By restricting discussion to marketable Canadian government bonds we have, in financial parlance, limited our discussion to the Canadian government *yield curve*.

FIGURE 13-1   Yield curve shapes.

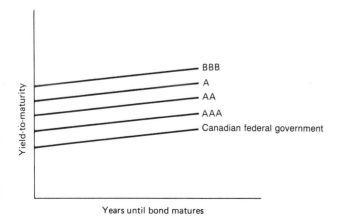

The *term structure of interest rates* for Canadian government bonds, or the *yield curve* as it is also called, may be defined as the relationship between yields and maturities for bonds in given default risk-classes. The yield curve changes a little every day, and there are different yield curves for each risk-class of bonds. The yield curve for AAA corporate bonds, for example, is different from the yield curve for federal government bonds on any given day. Figure 13-1 illustrates the risk differentials between several hypothetical yield curves for bonds from different risk-classes in Canada. The yield curves for the riskier classes of bonds are at a higher level than the yield curve for less risky bonds — the difference in levels is due to the difference in risk-premiums. Further, the yield curves for riskier bonds are not so stable as the yield curve for federal government bonds. Therefore, we shall confine our attention to the yield curve for federal government bonds throughout the remainder of this chapter to expedite the discussion.

13-4 THREE MAIN THEORIES ABOUT DETERMINATION OF YIELD CURVES

Traditionally, there have been three main theories about how the shape of the yield curve is determined:

1. The *liquidity premium theory* asserts that long-term yields should average higher than short-term yields. This theory maintains that investors pay a price premium (resulting in lower yields) on short maturities to avoid the interest rate risk that is more prevalent in the long maturities. Thus, an upward sloping curve is considered ''normal.''
2. The *expectations theory* asserts that long-term yields are the average of the short-term yields prevailing during the intervening period. This implies that, if all investors expected rates to (*a*) rise, the yield curve would slope upward, (*b*) remain unchanged, the yield curve would be horizontal, or (*c*) fall, the yield curve would slope downward.
3. The *segmentation (or hedging) theory* asserts that the yield curve is composed of a series of somewhat independent maturity segments. For example, the commercial banks predominantly demand short maturities, savings and loans mainly demand intermediate maturities, long-term bonds are purchased mostly by life insurance companies. Thus, yields on each segment of the yield curve are determined independently by the supply-and-demand conditions existing in that maturity segment.

Five bond price theorems were listed in Box 11-2 and discussed in Chap. 11. With the bond pricing theorems as a background, consider each of the three theories about the term structure of interest rates in some depth. After these theories have been explained, a discussion will integrate them into one unified theory. It should be pointed out, however, that some people adhere rigorously to only one of these theories and believe that it alone explains the term structure of interest rates.[10]

---

10 Chen, Roll, and Ross have found a statistically significant relationship between common stock returns and the (orthogonalized) slope of the yield curve (and several other economic

Assume, as we shall throughout this book, that risk is related to variability of return or dispersion of market value. Using this risk definition, interest rate risk increases with the term to maturity of a bond. The long-term bonds have more interest rate risk than short-term bonds because their duration and interest elasticity are larger values, as explained in Chap. 11. As a result, the prices of long-term bonds do fluctuate more than the prices of shorter-term bonds (even though long-term rates fluctuate less than short-term rates).[11] The large price fluctuation in the longer-term bonds is the basis for the *liquidity premium hypothesis*. Accordingly to this hypothesis, the yield curve should be typically sloping upward at longer maturities because investors demand higher returns to hold the risky long-term bonds.

**13-4.1
Liquidity
Premium
Hypothesis**

> Liquidity preference produces asymmetry in the relationship between short-term and long-term rates at cycle peaks and troughs. It accounts for the failure of short-term rates to exceed long-term rates at peaks by as much as they fall below long-term rates at troughs.[12]

Advocates of the liquidity premium theory support their opinion by taking yield curves from each phase of several business cycles and showing that the average of short-term government bond rates is less than the average of long-term government bond rates.[13] Graphically speaking, this means that, on average, the yield curve is upward sloping at the longer maturities. Although this is usually true, it is not conclusive proof of the validity of the liquidity premium theory; reasons do exist to suggest that one might doubt the liquidity premium theory.

Four reasons why the liquidity premium theory might be reversed (that is, why higher rates should be observed for short-term bonds) have been suggested by those who doubt the theory.[14] First, with the passage of time, short-term rates fluctuate in an uncertain manner. Investors in short-term maturities must, therefore, face a series of reinvestments at risky and uncertain returns. Second, increased transaction and information costs required to

---

variables too). See Nai-Fu Chen, Richard Roll, and Stephen Ross, "Economic Forces and the Stock Market: Testing the APT and Alternative Asset Pricing Theories," CRSP Working Paper no. 119, December 1983. Their results are also referred to in "The Arbitrage Pricing Theory Approach to Strategic Portfolio Planning," by Richard Roll and Stephen Ross, in the May–June 1984 issue of *Financial Analysts Journal*, pp. 14–29. The relationship between the individual risk factors, such as the slope of the yield curve, and the total risk of an asset are discussed in this book's Chap. 28, about the arbitrage pricing theory (APT).

11 J. B. Yawitz, G. H. Hempel, and W. J. Marshall, "The Use of Average Maturity as a Risk Proxy in Investment Portfolios," *Journal of Finance*, vol. XXX, no. 2, May 1975, tables 1 and 2.

12 R. Kessel, *The Cyclical Behavior of the Term Structure of Interest Rates*, National Bureau of Economic Research, occasional paper no. 91, 1965.

13 Howe and McCallum apply term structure tests to Government of Canada bond data for the period 1949 to 1978. They found evidence to support the liquidity premium theory in the intermediate term maturity range. See Maureen E. Howe, and John S. McCallum, "The Term Structure of Interest Rates in Canada: The Empirical Evidence", *Journal of Business Administration*, vol. 12, no. 1, Fall 1980, pp. 137–145.

14 F. Modigliani, Richard Sutch, et al., *Supplement to Journal of Political Economy*, August 1967. B. P. Malkiel's book *The Term Structure of Interest Rates*, Princeton, 1966, also discusses the liquidity premium hypothesis.

refinance frequently in the short-term maturities (instead of in fewer longer-term bond issues) reduce net returns from such investments. Third, investors in long-term bonds can reduce their risk by hedging (that is, by synchronizing their assets and libilities to mature simultaneously). For example, there is no uncertainty about the maturity value or maturity date of long-term high-quality bonds. Thus, long-run fund requirements can be hedged by buying long-term bonds that mature when the investor expects the funds will be needed. Fourth, the yield curve could slope downward because investors expect lower inflation premiums, and consequently lower interest rates, in the future than at present. Here, then, are four possible reasons why the long-term bonds might sell at higher prices and lower yields.

Although the case for the existence of liquidity premiums is weakly made, it still contains some truth, and most economists give it some weight in their thinking.

13-4.2 The Expectations Hypothesis

The expectations hypothesis asserts the long-term rates are the average (or, more precisely, the geometric mean) of the short-term rates expected to prevail between the current period and the maturity date of the bonds.[15] For example, using the simple arithmetic average, if one-year rates are now 10 percent and are expected to be 11 percent next year, then rates on two-year bonds today will be approximately 10.5 percent.

$$10.5\% = \frac{10\% + 11\%}{2 \text{ years}} = \text{2-year average}$$

If we assume that the forward interest rate that we expect to exist three years ahead is 15 percent, then we can calculate the current (or spot) rate on a three-year loan to be the average of the next three consecutive one-year future rates, as shown below.

$$12\% = \frac{10\% + 11\% + 15\%}{3 \text{ years}} = \text{3-year average}$$

In developing the expectations hypothesis, two general types of interest rates will be discussed. These interest rates are sometimes referred to as the spot and the future rates; or, some people use the phrase ''forward rate'' in place of ''future rate,'' the words future and forward being synonymous. The terms *spot* and *future*, or, if you prefer *spot* and *forward*, are used in the same way they are used in discussing commodities to distinguish between items for current delivery and items for future delivery, respectively. Think of money as being simply another commodity, think of the price of money for future delivery as being the principal plus interest—denoted [(principal) $(1 + r)$].

---

15 Mathematical Appendix F explains the geometric mean rate of return, or time-weighted rate of return, as it is also called. The geometric mean return is contrasted with the yield to maturity, or dollar-weighted rate of return, as it is called. See also Appendix 13B.

Future (or forward) rates, denoted $_tF_{t+1}$, refer to the yield to maturity for bonds that are expected to *exist in the future*. More specifically, F_{t+1} denotes the yield to maturity (or market interest rate or future rate) that is currently expected to apply to some future one-year bond that will exist during time period t. Spot rates, denoted $_0S_t$, refer to the interest rates for bonds that *currently exist* and are being currently bought and sold at time $t = 0$. More specifically, $_0S_n$ denotes the market interest rate (or yield to maturity) for a currently existing bond that matures n periods in the future. These conventions are used in making the rigorous statement of the expectations hypothesis shown as Eq. (13-5) in Box 13-1.

BOX 13-1
Mathematical
Statement
of the
Expectations
Hypothesis

$_0S_n =$ Spot rate published in daily newspaper for a loan that starts immediately (at time $t = 0$) and is repaid n periods in the future.

Date the money is actually loaned: the left-hand subscript

Repayment data: the right-hand subscript

$_tF_{t+n} =$ Forward rate for a loan that starts at time period t and is to be repaid n periods later at time period $(t + n)$; this interest rate is implicit and cannot be observed directly.

Using the mathematical conventions defined above, a rigorous statement of the expectations theory is given in Eq. (13-5) below.

$$1 + {}_0S_1 = (1 + {}_0F_1)$$

$$(1 + {}_0S_2)^2 = (1 + {}_0F_1)(1 + {}_1F_2)$$

$$(1 + {}_0S_3)^3 = (1 + {}_0F_1)(1 + {}_1F_2)(1 + {}_2F_3) \qquad (13\text{-}5)$$

$$\cdots\cdots\cdots\cdots\cdots\cdots\cdots$$

$$(1 + {}_0S_n)^n = (1 + {}_0F_1)(1 + {}_1F_2) \ldots (1 + {}_{n-1}F_n)$$

The forward rates $_1F_2, {}_2F_3, \ldots, {}_{n-1}F_n$ are implicit; that is, these future rates cannot be observed. In contrast, the spot rates $_0S_n$'s can be observed; they are printed in the newspapers daily. This means that the implicit future rates can be determined for any future period or series of future years by solving Eq. (13-5) for the appropriate value of $_nF_{n+1}$. This is not a statement of economic behaviour; it is simply a mathematics problem. The implicit market interest rate for a one-period loan which is expected to exist t periods in the future, can be found by solving Eq. (13-6a) for $_tF_{t+1}$ as shown below.

$$(1 + {}_tF_{t+1}) = \frac{(1 + {}_0S_{t+1})^{t+1}}{(1 + {}_0S_t)^t} \qquad (13\text{-}6a)$$

$$= \frac{(1 + {}_0S_1)(1 + {}_1F_2)(1 + {}_2F_3)\ldots(1 + {}_tF_{t+1})}{(1 + {}_0S_1)(1 + {}_1F_2)(1 + {}_2F_3)\ldots(1 + {}_{t-1}F_t)} \qquad (13\text{-}6b)$$

It is similarly possible to determine the implicit future rates for multiperiod bonds. For a bond with a life of n periods, which starts in period t and ends in period $t + n$, the yield over the life (that is, over the n periods) of this bond can be derived from Eq. (13-7a).

$$\left(\frac{(1 + {}_0S_{t+n})^{t+n}}{(1 + {}_0S_t)^t} \right)^{(1/n)} = \tag{13-7a}$$

$$= \sqrt[n]{(1 + {}_tF_{t+1})(1 + {}_{t+1}F_{t+2}) \ldots (1 + {}_{t+n-1}F_{t+n})} \tag{13-7b}$$

$$= (1 + {}_tF_{t+n}) \tag{13-7c}$$

where

$\quad {}_tF_{t+n}$ = market yield for an n-period bond that starts in future period t and matures in the farther future period $t + n$

The relations suggested by the expectations hypothesis will not hold exactly in the "real world" because transactions costs (such as sales commissions and taxes) will inhibit trading. However, ignoring transactions costs, arbitrage ensures that Eq. (13-5) will tend to hold if many bond traders are profit seekers. Recall that arbitrage is a series of transactions that yield a certain return; arbitrage is not uncertain or risky. Arbitrage between maturities will tend to maintain the expectations theory as it is represented in Eq. (13-5). This is an economic theory based on a mathematical identity.

13-4.3
Arbitrage

Some investors will rearrange their bond portfolios and cause bond prices and yields to be revised according to Eq. (13-5) because they expect to profit from such a move. For example, suppose inequality (13-8) occurs; this violates Eq. (13-5).

$$(1 + {}_0S_T)^T > (1 + {}_0F_1)(1 + {}_1F_2) \ldots (1 + {}_{T-1}F_T) \tag{13-8}$$

Some profit-seeking investors who have money to invest for T periods will buy the existing long-term bond yielding ${}_0S_T$. This will drive up its price and drive down its yield until Eq. (13-8) becomes an equality that aligns with Eq. (13-5).

After profit-maximizing investors purchase the long-term bond yielding ${}_0S_T$, its price may later drop because of changing credit conditions and/or changing expectations. In this case, the investor must hold the long-term bond until it matures to attain the yield ${}_0S_T$. Since it is not always possible for profit-seeking investors to hold long-term bonds until they mature, they may sell them after their price has fallen and inequality (13-8) exists again. In this case, the sale will lower the bond's price and increase inequality (13-8). As a result of such disadvantageous sales (which even a profit-seeking speculator may sometimes be forced to make), the arbitrage process cannot be expected to maintain Eq. (13-5) as an exact equality. However, the actions of these profit seekers will *tend* to make current yields (that is ${}_0S_t$) a function of expected future yields (that is, the $_tF_{t+1}$'s) as suggested by the expectations theory of Eq. (13-5).[16]

One empirical test that supports the expectations theory as designated by Eq. (13-5) is simply to compare the interest rate forecasts inherent in the yield curve of some past date with the record of business activity after that date. Assuming that the professional investors have worthwhile ideas at any moment about the future level of business activity, and also assuming that they believe the level of interest rates follows the level of business activity, it then follows directly from the definition of the expectations hypothesis that the yield curve should usually slope up preceding economic expansions and down preceding contractions. Without recognizing the implicit reasoning, a business executive's version of the expectations theory would be: "Declining business activity during the period of time presented by the yield pattern will result in a negatively sloped yield pattern," or vice versa for rising rates.

The pure segmentation theory asserts that lenders and borrowers confine themselves to certain segments of the yield curve for the following reasons:

**13-4.4
The
Segmenta-
tion Theory**

1. Legal regulations, such as "basket-clauses," which limit the investments that banks, trust companies, insurance companies, and other institutions are allowed to make.
2. The high cost of information, which causes investors to specialize in one market segment.
3. The fixed maturity structure of the liabilities that various bond investors tend to have (for example, life insurance companies and pension funds tend to have long-term liabilities, which may be forecast by an actuary), which lead them to hedge their liabilities with assets of equivalent maturity.
4. Simply, irrational preferences.

As a result, the rates on different maturities tend to be determined independently by the supply-and-demand conditions in the various market segments.

The segmentation theory is also referred to as the *hedging theory*. The implication of this name is that investors are typically obligated by some particular maturity pattern of liabilities. Given the maturity of an investor's liabilities, he or she can hedge against capital losses in the bond market by synchronizing asset and liability maturities. Thus, each investor is confined to some maturity segment that corresponds to his or her liability maturities. Figure

---

16 Rigorous monetary economics makes a distinction between spot rates and the yield to maturity of a bond that explains why arbitrage will not maintain inequality (13-8) as an equation continuously and why some bonds will never lie exactly on the yield curve. The difference is that a bond's spot rate is a time-weighted (or geometric mean) rate of return, while the yield to maturity is a dollar-weighted rate of return that differs from the time-weighted rate of return whenever the yield curve is not horizontal at the bond's yield to maturity. The implicit reinvestment rate is the key to this difference. Mathematical Appendix F at the end of this book explains the difference between the dollar-weighted and the time-weighted rates of return. Appendix 13B discusses the economics of the difference. Or, see the following article, Willard T. Carleton and Ian A. Cooper, "Estimation and Uses of the Term Structure of Interest Rates," *Journal of Finance*, September 1976, vol. XXXI, no. 4, especially pp. 1067–68.

FIGURE 13-2 Segmented yield curve.

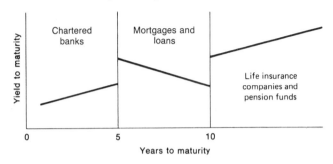

13-2 shows a grossly simplified conception of how the yield curve might be segmented.

Those individuals who do interpret the yield curve as being completely determined by independent markets dealing in different maturities are usually persons who deal solely in one of those market segments. Such individuals may be overimpressed by the sheer dollar volume of the transactions and the immediate price reactions they witness. It is possible that to some extent these persons are victims of their own myopic activities; they may be unaware of the constant activities of professional profit-seeking arbitrageurs who are risk-indifferent and view all securities as substitutes.

Some profit-seeking arbitrageurs earn their living by smoothing out irregularities in the yield curve. Although these professional arbitrageurs may be few in number, their presence and effectiveness are attested to by the relative smoothness of the yield curve of any date. That is, sharp kinks, such as those shown in Fig. 13-2, are nonxistent: The actual turns in the yield curve are smoother and less exaggerated.[17]

**13-4.5
Riding the
Yield Curve**

Some bond portfolio managers attempt to increase their portfolio's yields by undertaking a bond investment strategy called "riding the yield curve." This strategy may be undertaken whenever the yield curve is upward-sloping (that is, the long-term rates are higher than the short-term rates) regardless of whether the yield curve is smooth or kinky.

Riding the yield curve is a buy-and-hold strategy in which the bond investor purchases an intermediate- or long-term bond when the yield curve is sloped upward and is expected to maintain that slope and level. The purchased bond

17 Traditionally, yield curves have been estimated by hand simply by "eyeballing" a line of best fit through data points representing bonds in a homogeneous default risk-class. More recently, however, more scientific models have been developed. Some of the algorithms tend to generate smooth yield curves; see S. W. Dobson, "Estimating Term Structure Equations with Individual Bond Data," *Journal of Finance*, March 1978, pp. 75–92. However, some other algorithms generate more kinky estimates of the yield curve; see J. H. McCulloch, "Measuring the Term Structure of Interest Rates," *Journal of Business*, January 1971, pp. 19–31. Michel Houglet, "Estimating the Term Structure of Interest Rates for Non-Homogeneous Bonds," Ph.D. dissertation (Berkeley: University of California, 1980). Gary S. Shea, "Pitfalls in Smoothing Interest Rate Term Structure Data: Equilibrium Models and Spline Approximations," *Journal of Financial and Quantitative Analysis*, vol. 19, no. 3, September 1984, pp. 253–270.

is then simply held in order to obtain the capital gains that occur as the bond moves closer to its maturity date and thus rides down the yield curve. That is, in addition to the bond's coupon interest, the bond investor earns capital gains resulting from the lower market yields that are encountered as the bond matures. Of course, the danger inherent in this strategy is that the level of interest rates may rise or that the short-term end of the yield curve may swing upward. Either development would cause the bond investor to suffer a capital loss. Profit opportunities such as these prompt professional bond investors to study monetary economics on a regular basis and work at forecasting the yield curve.

13-5 CONCLUSIONS ON TERM STRUCTURE

There is no consensus among businesspeople and economists about which of the preceding theories concerning the term structure is descriptive of reality. There is an undeniable element of logic in each of the three theories, and each is supported to a certain extent by empirical data. In fact, a combination of all three theories probably furnishes the best description of the elements determining the term structure of interest rates.

In essence, expectations of future rates determine a yield curve. However, the yield curve based on pure expectations (denoted EE in Fig. 13-3) is unobservable. Liquidity premiums that increase with the term to maturity are superimposed on top of the yields that are purely a function of expectations. Thus, a yield curve, such as YY in Fig. 13-3, which is observable, represents a combination of the rates determined by expectations plus liquidity premiums (the liquidity premiums are equal to the vertical distance between YY and EE). This means that the liquidity premium theory is not invalidated by the occasional existence of a downward-sloping yield curve.

The long-term end of the yield curve is determined by the expectations and liquidity premiums that investors demand to induce them to hold these bonds. The stationary nature of the long-term end of the yield curve over the years reflects the constancy of long-term expectations and liquidity premiums.

The segmentation theory explains the frequent movements in the short-term end of the yield curve. The Bank of Canada endeavours to control the money supply and exert pressures on market interest rates by buying and

FIGURE 13-3 A yield curve determined by expectations and liquidity premiums.

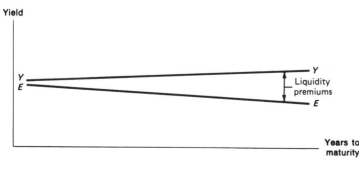

selling millions of dollars of Treasury bills on a day-to-day basis. Thus, the Bank of Canada interacting with the liquidity needs of chartered banks are the primary supply and demand forces at work on the short-term end of the yield curve. The wide and frequent swings in that portion of the yield curve that has less than one year to maturity may be largely attributed to changes in these supply and demand factors. The effects of these forces on the yield curve are segmented and therefore diminish rapidly in the intermediate- and long-term maturities.

13-6 CONCLUSIONS ABOUT THE LEVEL OF RATES

The determinants of the level of interest rates are easier to discern than the determinants of the term structure of interest rates. Inflationary expectations, crowding out, and risk-premiums associated with fears of possible inflation upturns in the future have been the important factors in the determination of the level of market yields since the mid-1960s. However, at certain times shifts in the credit supply and demand can result in faster interest rate changes than shifting inflationary expectations alone would dictate. Changes in the risk-premiums that occur as the phases of the business cycle change can contribute significantly to movements in the level of market rates of interest, too.

Since bond prices are strongly affected by market interest rates, forecasting interest rates is an important task of a bond portfolio manager. Therefore, bond portfolio managers should be monetary economists as well as bond analysts if they hope to maximize profits.

QUESTIONS

1. Compare and contrast (*a*) changes in bond prices caused by changes in the level of interest rates with (*b*) those caused by changes in the term structure of interest rates.
2. How should the inflationary expectations of investors in one-year bonds and investors in twenty-year bonds differ?
3. If you managed a bank's multimillion-dollar portfolio of bonds, what would you do if you were convinced a credit crunch, which would send market interest rates skyrocketing, was beginning? How might other bond portfolio managers behave if they also expected a credit crunch, and how would their actions affect your job?
4. When actual Government of Canada bond yields for a given day are plotted against the terms to maturity to draw a yield curve, why do all the data points not lie exactly on the yield curve if it is drawn to be smooth? Does the fact that not all of the data points lie on the yield curve refute the expectations theory of interest rates in any way? Explain. *Hint*: Think about income taxes.
5. Define the term yield curve. What financial variables which affect interest rates are held constant throughout the length of the yield curve? Why are these variables held constant?
6. Cut out the section of a recent newspaper which has the yields to maturity for Government of Canada bonds. Prepare a yield curve from these

data. Write separate paragraphs using each of the following three theories to rationalize this particular yield curve: (*a*) expectations theory, (*b*) liquidity premium theory, and (*c*) segmentation theory.

7. Assume that four-year bonds are currently yielding 7 percent and three-year bonds are yielding 6 percent. What is the implied yield for one-year bonds starting three years from now? Show your work. *Hint*: Use the expectations theory.

8. Give two reasons why the yield curve might be expected to slope upward most of the time, and also give two reasons why it might slope downward.

9. Why should government economic policymakers care about the yield curve? A portfolio manager? An investment dealer?

10. Bond dealers define a bear hedge as a transction in which "a short sale of longs is hedged by going long shorts"; that is, a short position of long-term bonds is hedged by taking a long position in short-term bonds. Why would a bond dealer enter such a bear hedge? (Refer to Chap. 19 for an explanation of long and short positions.)

SELECTED REFERENCES

Culbertson, J. A. "The Term Structure of Interest Rates," *Quarterly Journal of Economics*, November 1957, pp. 485–517; also, Michaelson. "Comment." Ibid., February 1963, pp. 166–174; and J. A. Culbertson. "Reply." Ibid., November 1963, pp. 691–696. This series of nonmathematical articles articulates the viewpoint of advocates of the segmentation theory.

Federal Reserve System, Board of Governors, Historical Chart Book Washington. This monthly pamphlet may be purchased for 60 cents by writing to the Federal Reserve. It provides a valuable summary of financial and economic data in chart form.

Financial Research Foundation, Proceedings of the Fourth Conference, Spring 1980. The theme of the conference was interest rates. See for example: Peter Jones. "Predicting Interest Rates: A Survey of Current Methodology Used in Practice," pp. 5–9; James Pesando. "Predicting Interest Rates, Part II: A View on the Predictability of Short- and Long-Term Interest Rates," pp. 9–11.

Howe, Maureen E., and John S. McCallum. "The Term Structure of Interest Rates in Canada: The Empirical Evidence." *Journal of Business Administration*, vol. 12, no. 1, Fall 1980, pp. 137–145. An empirical study of the term structure of Government of Canada bonds over a lengthy data period.

Malkiel, B. G. "Expectations, Bond Prices, and the Term Structure of Interest Rates." *Quarterly Journal of Economics*, May 1962, pp. 197–218. A discussion and analysis of the relation between yield changes and bond prices. This article uses differential calculus and utility theory. It develops bond pricing theorems and explains the simple behavioural assumptions behind the expectations hypothesis.

Meiselman, D. *The Term Structure of Interest Rates*. Englewood Cliffs, N.J.: Prentice-Hall, 1962. The book explains the expectations hypothesis and supporting data using regression analysis and elementary difference equations.

Yohe, W. P., and D. S. Karnosky. "Interest Rates and Price Level Changes, 1951–69." *Review*. St. Louis Federal Reserve Bank, December 1969. A readable survey of relevant literature and explanation of Almon distributed-lag regression analysis that shows the positive relation between inflation and market interest rates.

Bond Swaps

As a result of the ever-changing yield spreads that exist in the bond markets, the managers of bond portfolios sometimes attempt to profit from a bond-trading tactic called bond swaps. In general, a *bond swap* may be defined as the purchase and sale of equal amounts of similar bonds that are undertaken in an effort to increase a bond portfolio's rate of return. The four most common types of bond swaps are explained below; they are called:

1. Substitution swaps
2. Intermarket spread swaps
3. Rate anticipation swaps
4. Pure yield pickup swaps

The substitution swap is explained first because it is the simplest of all four types of bond swaps.[18] In the following discussion of bond swaps, the bond that is to be sold (TBS) if the swap is consummated is called the *TBS bond* and the bond that is to be purchased (TBP) to complete the swap is called the *TBP bond*.

APP. 13A-1 THE SUBSTITUTION SWAP

The substitution swap involves bonds that are perfect substitutes (in theory, at least) in every respect except their prices (or equivalently, their yields to maturity). In order for two bonds to be perfect substitutes, both the TBS bond and the TBP bond must have identical quality ratings, identical numbers of years to maturity, identical coupon interest payments, the same sinking fund provisions, the same marketability, and equivalent call features and must be identical in every other aspect described in their respective indenture contracts. The TBS bond and the TBP bond can differ only with respect to their yields (and prices), and that key difference is the basis for the substitution bond swap.

All bond swaps are based on faith in one of the basic economic axioms. The particular axiom that forms the basis for bond swaps states that the same good cannot sell at different prices in the same marketplace. Such a price disparity between homogeneous goods would not endure if it temporarily emerged, because the economic *law of one price* suggests that profit-seeking price speculators would buy the homogeneous good (for example, shares of some particular security) from the cheapest supplier and sell it to the highest bidder as long as it was profitable to continue to do so; this is called simple *arbitrage*. The price speculators would continue this arbitrage until they bid

---

18 Richard Bookstaber, *The Complete Investment Book* (Glenview, Illinois: Scott, Foresman, and Company, 1985). See chap. 7 about bond swaps. Bookstaber lists a BASIC language computer program to analyze bond swaps; see Bookstaber's pp. 77–79. The program may also be purchased from Dr. Bookstaber on a floppy disk as explained on p. 173 of this book.

up the cheapest supplier's selling price with their purchases and/or drove down the highest bidder's offering price through repeated selling. When the cheapest seller's price was bid up and/or the highest buyer's price was driven down to the point where the buy and the sell prices were equal throughout the marketplace (except for the shipper's charges for transportation allowance to get the goods from the seller to the buyer, the salesperson's commissions, etc.), then and only then would the arbitrage become unprofitable and therefore cease. Thus, when potential arbitrage profits are detected in the bond markets, substitution bond swaps go on until bonds that are perfect substitutes have equal market prices.

To further clarify the nature of a substitute bond swap, consider a hypothetical example. Suppose that a bond swapper has a TBS bond which has thirty years to maturity, yields 7 percent if held to maturity, and is currently priced at its par value (so that its coupon rate equals its yield to maturity). Then the bond swapper finds another bond issued by an almost identical corporation that has identical provisions. That is, this TBP bond has thirty years to maturity, a 7 percent coupon rate, and the same quality rating as the TBS bond and is identical in every other respect except the market price (or, equivalently, the yield). Because of what economists call a temporary market imperfection or because the bond swapper is unable to see that the TBS bond is not really a perfect substitute for the TBP bond, the TBP bond is priced to yield 7.10 percent. The 10-basis-point yield pickup opportunity between the two presumably identical bonds will motivate profit-seeking arbitrageurs to swap the TBP bonds for their TBS bonds. Furthermore, this arbitrage should continue profitably for the bond swapper until the yields and prices of the two bonds are equal or until the bond swapper bankrupts himself by continuously undertaking poorly conceived swaps that cause him to suffer repeated losses. The latter would occur if the TBS and TBP were not perfect substitutes, as the swapper has erroneously thought.

APP. 13A-2   MEASURING GAINS FROM THE SUBSTITUTION SWAP

Bond swaps are undertaken because some bond portfolio manager or bond speculator expects to profit in the future as the price of the TBS bond is realigned with the price of the TBP bond. The time that elapses while the prices of the two swapped bonds become realigned is called the *workout time*. The workout time can be as short as a few weeks if the bond swapper is rewarded by the market for detecting a true market imperfection that is corrected quickly by a rush of profitable arbitrages, or the workout time can be as long as the period before the bonds mature. Assuming that the two swapped bonds do not default, they will mature with prices equal to their face values and yields equal to their yields to maturity as of the day they were purchased. Thus, in the hypothetical example of a substitute swap above, the workout time might drag on for as long as thirty years.

It is impossible to know the length of the workout time for a swap before the swap is undertaken. Therefore, some workout time assumption must be made in order to calculate the additional rate of return that is expected to be gained from any potential bond swap. For purposes of illustration a one-year workout time will be assumed and used to analyze the substitution swap example explained above.

The substitution swap of two bonds, each of which had 7 percent coupon rates and thirty-years to maturity, was undertaken because the TBP bond yielded a modest 10 basis points more than the presumably identical TBS bond, which was priced at par to yield 7 percent. The present value of the TBP bond was thus $987.70, calculated with Eq. (11-1) or by using a book of bond yields. In order to construct a concrete example for further analysis, it is assumed that the two bonds are in fact identical and that their yields converge on 7 percent within a one-year workout time. Thus, both the TBS bond and the TBP bond will be selling for their face values of $1,000 at the end of the workout time. Of course, the TBS bond will yield 7 percent over the workout year because its price always equals its face value of $1,000, and its yield to maturity never varies from 7 percent. However, the TBP bond will experience capital gains as its yield falls from 7.1 to 7.0 percent and causes it to earn a compound yield of 8.29 percent during the one-year workout time. In other words, this hypothetical swap yielded 1.29 percent, or 129 basis points, yield improvement on a one-time basis during the workout year. The profitability calculations for this bond swap are shown in Table App. 13A-1.

TABLE APP. 13A-1 PROFITABILITY CALCULATIONS FOR A HYPOTHETICAL SUBSTITUTION SWAP

Assumptions:

1. The TBS bond was a 30-year bond that continuously sold at its par value to yield its coupon rate of 7%.
2. The TBP bond was purchased at $987.70 to yield 7.1% over its 30-year life, but its price rose to $1,000 as its yield fell to 7.0% during the year after it was purchased.
3. The workout time was 1 year.
4. All cashflows were reinvested at 7%.

	TBS bond	TBP bond
Original bond investment	$1,000.00	$987.70
Two $35 semiannual coupons	$70.00	$70.00
Interest at 7% for 6 months on first coupon	$1.23	$1.23
Bond's price at end of workout year	$1,000.00	$1,000.00
Total dollars at end of workout	$1,071.23	$1,071.23
Total dollar gain during workout	$71.23	$83.53
Gain per dollar of investment	0.07123	0.08458
Year's realized compound yield	7.0%	8.29%

Conclusion: The swap earned 129 basis points for one year.

Source: S. Homer and M. L. Leibowitz, *Inside the Yield Book* (Englewood Cliffs, N.J.: Prentice Hall, 1972), table 29.

APP. 13A-3 THE RISKS INHERENT IN BOND SWAPS

The calculations in Table App. 13A-1 assume a one-year workout time. If the workout takes longer, then the capital gains must be spread over more years and the realized gain per year of workout time diminishes. Speaking approximately, the realized compound yield during the workout period varies inversely to the length of the workout time. Table App. 13A-2 shows several different realized compound yield gains if the substitute swap of two 30-year bonds is consummated and the yield is calculated as outlined in Table App. 13A-1. The results are shown in Table App. 13A-2 under different assumptions about the workout time. At the very worst, the swap would take the entire thirty-year lives of the bonds to work out. In this case, only an additional 4.3 basis points per year from the thirty workout years would be obtained. This small increase in the additional yield does not seem sufficient to induce a risk-averse bond swapper to undertake the risks associated with the swap.

The risks associated with a bond swap are too substantial to ignore. The swap should promise a sufficiently large gain in realized yield to (1) pay for the bond brokerage commissions generated by the swap and also (2) compensate the bond swapper for the risks incurred. There are four types of risks involved in a bond swap; they are listed below.

1. The workout time is longer than anticipated. This lowers the realized additional yield per workout (as shown in Table App. 13A-2).
2. The yield spreads may move adversely (that is, in a direction opposite to that anticipated). For example, in the substitution swap example above, if the yield spread opened up to more than 10 basis points rather than closing toward zero as anticipated, the bond swappers could suffer losses from the swap. Such losses might result if, for example, the quality rating of the TBP bond were downgraded during the workout time, which would cause the yield to maturity to rise above 7.1 percent.
3. The overall level of all interest rates may change in an adverse movement. For example, if accelerating inflation caused the interest rates of the TBP bond, the TBS bond, and all other bonds to rise appreciably, then the substitution swapper could suffer losses. Even if the yield spread narrowed to zero as hoped, a rise in interest rate levels would cause all thirty-year bonds to plunge in price (because they have long durations and high interest rate elasticities, as explained in Chap. 11). If interest rates are expected to rise, the portfolio manager should switch to cash holdings or bonds with shorter maturities and, thus, less interest rate risk in order to minimize losses.
4. The TBP bond may not be the type of substitute for the TBS bond that was wanted. To use the substitution swap for another example, if the TBP bond was intrinsically a more risky bond than the TBS bond, then the yields could never be expected to converge and produce additional yield. Thus, the bond swapper should analyze the bonds carefully before entering into a swap if the desired gains are ever going to materialize. The intermarket spread swap explained below is particularly vulnerable to this type of risk.

APP. 13A-4 THE INTERMARKET SPREAD SWAP

A second major category of bond swaps is the intermarket spread swaps. These swaps involve a TBS bond and a TBP bond that are different in some respect. The swapped bonds may have different coupon rates but may be issued by the same corporation or governmental organization and may be similar in every other respect, for example. Tables 13-2 and 13-3 above present some summary statistics that can be helpful in planning intermarket spread swaps.

TABLE APP. 13A-2   THE RELATION BETWEEN THE WORKOUT TIME AND THE REALIZED YIELD GAIN FOR THE HYPOTHETICAL SUBSTITUTION SWAP

WORKOUT TIME, YEARS	REALIZED COMPOUND YIELD GAIN, BASIS POINTS PER YEAR
30	4.3
20	6.4
10	12.9
5	25.7
1	129.0
½	258.8
¼	527.2

Source: A. Homer and M. L. Leibowitz, *Inside the Yield Book* (Englewood Cliffs, N.J.: Prentice-Hall, 1972), table 30.

For an example of an intermarket spread swap consider swapping a twenty-five-year TBS federal government bond with a 7 percent coupon rate that is selling at par to yield 7 percent. The TBS bond is to be swapped for another twenty-five-year federal government TBP bond. The TBP bond has a 5 percent coupon rate and is selling at a discount from par to yield 6.60 percent if held to maturity. The 40-basis-point spread is adverse for the holder of the TBP bond; but if the yield spread opens further to 50 basis points, the swap is nevertheless advisable. If the 7 percent TBS bond is sold and replaced by the TBP bond (that is, the two are swapped), there are three ways the yield spread could increase from 40 to 50 basis points:

1. The 7 percent TBS bond's yield could rise from 7.0 to 7.10 percent.
2. The 5 percent TBS bond's yield could drop from 6.60 to 6.50 percent.
3. Some combination of both (1) and (2) could occur.

If the expected yield spread increase materializes from any of these three possibilities, the lower-coupon TBP bond will outperform the higher-coupon TBS bond because the TBP bond has more interest rate risk (as measured by its duration or elasticity) than the TBS bond.

To see the advisability of the hypothetical intermarket spread swap, consider the three possible outcomes listed in the preceding paragraph.

1. If the high-coupon 7 percent TBS bond experiences a 10-basis-point increase in its yield as the yield spread widens, the resulting capital loss would be avoided because the TBS bond would have been liquidated in the swap.
2. If the low-coupon 5 percent TBP bond experienced a 10-basis-point decrease in its yield as the yield spread widens, then a significant capital gain would occur for the benefit of the swapper who acquired the bond.
3. If some combination of both (1) (that is, some increase in the TBS bond's yield) and (2) (namely, some capital gain on the TBP bond) occurs, then the swap yields some of each of the associated benefits.

The bond swapper suffers by earning the lower yield of only 6.60 percent on the TBP bond rather than the higher 7.0 percent yield on the TBS bond.

However, if the workout time for this swap is short, then the bond swapper only suffers this reduced yield a short time. After the workout time, the swap can be reversed (that is, the TBS bond can be repurchased and the TBP bond sold), and two benefits will thereby occur: (1) the swap will have realized a "pickup" of about 1.0 percent of the value of the bonds because of the realized capital gain on the TBP bond and/or the capital loss that was avoided on the TBS bond and also (2) the higher yield to maturity offered by the TBS bond will be regained when the swap is reversed and the TBS bond is repurchased. Of course, these benefits are obtained only if the bond swapper's expectations for the yield spread's widening 10 basis points do in fact materialize. If the yield spread narrows unexpectedly or all interest rates rise significantly, then the bond swapper would have been better off holding cash that paid no interest income at all.[19]

APP. 13A-5   THE RATE ANTICIPATION SWAP

If a bond investor foresees a probable change in the level of all interest rates, then a rate anticipation swap should be considered. For example, if the national economy is advancing toward a boom (or falling into the trough of a recession) so that the rate of inflation and thus all interest rates may be expected to rise (fall), then long-term bonds should be sold (bought) and swapped for holdings of cash or short-term bonds in order to avoid capital losses (earn capital gains) from the anticipated changing level of interest rates. Other types of rate anticipation swaps also exist. But risks associated with these as well as almost all other bond swaps are inversely proportional to the ability of the bond swapper to forecast market interest rates.

APP. 13A-6   THE PURE YIELD PICKUP SWAP

The fourth category of bond swaps is the pure yield spread pickup swap; it is a simple transaction based on no expectation of market changes, so that the risks associated with erroneous forecasts are absent. This swap is accomplishd by selling a bond that has a given yield to maturity and simultaneously buying a similar bond that offers a higher yield to maturity.

19 Most bond swap suggestions are offered, as might be expected, by bond brokers who hope to earn trading commissions if the swaps occur. Since a bond broker gains commission income regardless of whether the swap is profitable for the bond investor, the advice of a broker may be biased and self-serving. Furthermore, the broker probably will not explain the risk of the significant losses that are possible. Thus, the advice of all security brokers should be scrutinized.

COMMON STOCK VALUATION

The value of a share of common stock, like the value of a bond, is the present value of all the income flowing to the owner of the stock. Common stockholders, however, are owners of the corporation who receive an uncertain stream of residual income. That is, stockholders are not at all like debtors, who receive contractual streams of income. Therefore, common stock valuation must deal with measuring the riskiness of the investment. The riskiness of a common stock is important because that is what determines the discount rate to be used in finding the stock's present value. This risk is involved in common stock investing because there is uncertainty about the stream of residual income a stockholder can expect. Chapters 14 through 16 explain the concepts of risk and income as they interact to determine the value of a share of stock. Each of the chapters in Part 4, except Chap. 16, relies on material explained in the preceding chapter; therefore they should be read in the order presented. These chapters show how to estimate the value of an individual asset so that the investor will be able to tell whether the asset is overpriced or underpriced.

Common Stock Valuation Theory*

Chapters 11, 12, and 13 explained how to find the value of bonds. Bond valuation is simple because a bond's cashflows are unambiguously known in advance, and the discount rate can be determined within a narrow range. In contrast, several ambiguities and uncertainties frustrate the exact determination of common stock values. This chapter examines the most important of these problems. Several common stock valuation models will be the focus of this chapter.

14-1 DEFINITION OF A MODEL

Models have been described as simplified versions of reality. The models with which this chapter deals are mathematical models. Like airplane models, they represent reality. They relate certain independent variables, such as dividends and earnings, to a dependent variable, the value of the common stock. Symbolically, the models studied will be of the form $V = f(X_1, X_2 \ldots, X_n)$, where V denotes the value of the asset and $X_1 X_2, \ldots, X_n$ represent those independent variables that determine value. These models will explicitly depict each variable's interaction with the other variables. They are simplified versions of the financial processes that actually determine asset prices.

In an effort to keep things simple, models abstract from many variables and instead focus only on the main determinants. For example, none of the models contains variables representing political scandals, changes in Bank of Canada monetary and credit policy, the timing and impact of changes in the level of economic activity, and numerous other variables that do not directly affect the value of common stock. All the models do, however, contain a variable representing the asset's income, since income is the most important determinant of value. In this chapter, the important conceptual issues related to the valuation of equity shares in a nonlevered firm are explained. Chapters 15 through 18 deal with common stock valuation on a more pragmatic level.

---

* Readers who wish to omit the abstract theory and go to more directly applicable techniques of common stock analysis may skip Chap. 14 and go on to Chap. 15. However, Chap. 11 is needed as background for Chaps. 14 and 15.

The value of a common stock is simply the present value of all future income the owner of the share will receive. This valuation model is the same for all stocks and all bonds. It is summarized symbolically in Eq. (14-1).

$$\text{Value} = \sum_{t=1}^{T} \frac{\text{income for period } t}{(1.0 + \text{appropriate discount rate})^t} \qquad (14\text{-}1)$$

Using this valuation model on stocks is more difficult than using it on bonds because of two main problems. First, it is not known in advance what a stock's income will be in each future period, and, second, it is not clear what the appropriate discount rate should be for a particular stock. This chapter examines suggested solutions to these problems that have been offered by various financial analysts and economists. Before getting into these different valuation models, however, a brief review of the symbols used is provided.

The mathematical models in this chapter use the following symbols, which are defined here for easy reference.

v_t = present value of one share of common stock at period t

e_t = earnings per share at time period t

d_t = dividends per share at time period t paid to stockholders of record at the start of period t

r_t = *average* internal rate of return of all investments within the firm during time period t

k_t = appropriate discount rate at time t = firm's cost of capital as determined by its risk

f = retention ratio (which is assumed constant) = fraction of e which is retained inside the firm

$1 - f$ = payout ratio = (dividends/earnings) = fraction of e paid out to investors as a cash dividend

g = fr = rate of growth in earnings, which is assumed to remain constant

t = a counting index indicating time period, for example, a quarter or a year

n_t = number of shares of stock outstanding at time period t

Δn_t = $n_{t+1} - n_t$ = number of new shares (if any) sold during period t at the ex-dividend price per share.

Capital letters are used to denote total amounts for the firm as a whole.

V_t = total value of firm at tth time period = $\sum v_t = n_t v_t$

D_t = total dividends paid to all stockholders of record at start

of tth period = $\sum_{}^{n} d_t = n_t d_t$

E_t = total earnings of firm in period t = $\sum_{}^{n} e_t = n_t e_t$

T = the last time period, or the terminal period

I_t = total investment in tth period = $E_t - D_t + \Delta n_t v_t$

$D_{t+1/t}$ = total dividends payable at period $t + 1$ to stockholders of record at period t (but not to new stockholders) = $n_t d_t$

14-2 CAPITALIZING DIVIDENDS

J. B. Williams and M. J. Gordon have developed a model relating an equity share's value to its dividend income.[1] They hypothesized that the value v of a share of stock equals the present value of the infinite ($t = \infty$) stream of dividends d to be received by that stock's owner.

$$v_0 = \sum_{t=1}^{\infty} \frac{d_t}{(1 + k)^t} = \frac{d_1}{1 + k} + \frac{d_2}{(1 + k)^2} + \cdots + \frac{d_\infty}{(1 + k)^\infty} \tag{14-2}$$

In Eq. (14-2), k is the capitalization rate that is appropriate for the firm's risk-class. Retained earnings are assumed to increase future dividends in this model. Thus, it does not ignore retained earnings: it treats them indirectly.

The logic of the dividend model is undeniable. Cash dividends are the only income from a share of stock that is held to infinity. So, the value of a share of stock that is held to perpetuity could only be the present value of its stream of cash dividends from now until perpetuity. But, you may ask, what if the share is sold in a few years? The model includes this possibility.

**14-2.1
Selling Shares**

If an investor sells a share after, say, three periods, the present value of that share is as shown in Eq. (14-3a), according to the logic of the dividend model.

$$v_0 = \sum_{t=1}^{3} \frac{d_t}{(1 + k)^t} + \frac{v_3}{(1 + k)^3} \tag{14-3a}$$

$$= \frac{d_1}{1 + k} + \frac{d_2}{(1 + k)^2} + \frac{d_3 + v_3}{(1 + k)^3} \tag{14-3b}$$

The v_3 term represents the value of the share in period $t = 3$ when it is sold. Further, according to the logic of Eq. (14-2), v_3 is the present value of all dividends from period $t = 4$ to infinity; this is represented symbolically as Eq. (14-4).

$$v_3 = \sum_{t=1}^{\infty} \frac{d_{t+3}}{(1 + k)^t} \tag{14-4a}$$

$$= \frac{d_4}{(1 + k)^1} + \frac{d_5}{(1 + k)^2} + \frac{d_6}{(1 + k)^3} + \cdots + \frac{d_\infty}{(1 + k)^\infty} \tag{14-4b}$$

1 M. J. Gordon, *The Investment, Financing and Valuation of the Corporation* (Homewood, Ill: Irwin 1962). J. B. Williams, *The Theory of Investment Value* (Cambridge, Mass: Harvard, 1938).

To show how the dividend model encompasses situations in which a share is sold before infinity, Eq. (14-4b) is substituted into Eq. (14-3b) to obtain Eq. (14-3c):

$$v_0 = \frac{d_1}{1 + k} + \frac{d_2}{(1 + k)^2} + \frac{d_3}{(1 + k)^3} + \frac{d_4/(1 + k)^1 + \ldots + d_\infty/(1 + k)^\infty}{(1 + k)^3} \qquad (14\text{-}3c)$$

Since

$$\frac{d_{n+3}/(1 + k)^n}{(1 + k)^3} = \frac{d_{n+3}}{(1 + k)^n(1 + k)^3} = \frac{d_{n+3}}{(1 + k)^{n+3}}$$

Eq. (14-3c) can be equivalently rewritten as Eq. (14-3d):

$$v_0 = \frac{d_1}{1 + k} + \frac{d_2}{(1 + k)^2} + \frac{d_3}{(1 + k)^3} + \frac{d_4}{(1 + k)^{3+1}} + \frac{d_5}{(1 + k)^{3+2}} \qquad (14\text{-}3d)$$

$$+ \ldots + \frac{d_\infty}{(1 + k)^\infty}$$

Comparison of Eqs. (14-3d) and (14-2) will reveal that they are equal. This shows the indirect manner in which the dividend model considers retained earnings and capital gains. That is, v_0 includes v_3, the value of the share in the future. And v_3 includes capital gains that result from retained earnings. Thus, the dividend model does not ignore the effects of capital gains or retained earnings.

In order to show the interaction of earnings, dividends, retained earnings, and the growth rate of the firm, the model treats these variables explicitly as shown below. Dividends are related to earnings by defining dividends to be equal to the payout ratio $(1 - f)$ times earnings, as shown in Eqs. (14-5a) and (14-5b).

14-2.2 Definitions and Relationships in Dividend Model

$$D_t = (1 - f)E_t = \text{total cash dividends} \qquad (14\text{-}5a)$$
$$d_t = (1 - f)e_t = \text{cash dividends per share} \qquad (14\text{-}5b)$$

Total corporate retained earnings of fE dollars are assumed to be reinvested within the all-equity firm at a rate of return of r. Since the firm we are discussing here has borrowed no money, it can only grow from retained earnings. This allows earnings to grow at the rate of $g = fr$ per period as shown in Eq. (14-6a), assuming no new outside capital is invested.

$$\left.\begin{aligned} E_t &= (1 + g)^t(E_0) \\ &= (1 + fr)^t(E_0) \end{aligned}\right\} \quad \text{total earnings growth} \qquad (14\text{-}6a)$$

$$\left.\begin{aligned} e_t &= (1 + g)^t(e_0) \\ &= (1 + fr)^t(e_0) \end{aligned}\right\} \quad \text{per share earnings growth} \qquad (14\text{-}6b)$$

As long as the retention ratio is a positive number ($f > 0$), dividends per share will grow as shown in Eq. (14-7a) if no new shares are issued.

$$d_t = (1 - f)(1 + fr)^t(e_0) \tag{14-7a}$$

$$= (1 - f)(1 + g)^t(e_0) \tag{14-7b}$$

$$= (1 - f)(e_t) \quad \text{since } e_t = e_0(1 + g)^t \tag{14-7c}$$

In the case where some fraction f of earnings is retained and earns a return of r within the firm, the present value of a share of stock is determined by substituting Eq. (14-7a) into Eq. (14-2) to obtain Eq. (14-8). In Eq. (14-8) the beginning cash dividend per share is restated in terms of the beginning earnings per share by substituting $e_0(1 - f)$ in place of d_0 to produce:

$$v_0 = \sum_{t=1}^{\infty} \frac{e_0(1 - f)(1 + fr)^t}{(1 + k)^t} \tag{14-8}$$

Equation (14-2) may be rewritten equivalently as Eq. (14-9a) by using Eq. (14-7a)[2]

$$\sum_{t=1}^{\infty} \frac{d_0(1 + fr)^t}{(1 + k)^t} = \sum_{t=1}^{\infty} \frac{d_0(1 + g)^t}{(1 + k)^t} = \frac{d_1}{k - g} \tag{14-9a}$$

Equation (14-8) may be rewritten equivalently as Eq. (14-9b) by substituting $e_0(1 - f)$ for d_0 in Eq. (14-9a), as shown below.

$$v_0 = \sum_{t=1}^{\infty} \frac{e_0(1 - f)(1 + g)^t}{(1 + k)^t} \tag{14-8}$$

$$= \frac{d_1}{k - g} \tag{14-9a}$$

$$= \frac{e_1(1 - f)}{k - g} \tag{14-9b}$$

One of the advantages of the dividend model is that it may be rewritten equivalently in different forms. For example, Eqs. (14-2), (14-8), (14-9a), and (14-9b) are all useful representations of the same model. Equation (14-8) explicitly shows the relationship of earnings e_0, dividend policy f, internal profitability r, and the firm's cost of capital k in the determination of the value of the stock. This model may be used to determine the value per share by defining all the variables on a per-share basis as shown, or the model may be used to value the entire firm by using the total quantities represented by the variables in capital letters.

---

2 See footnote 1 in Chap. 15 for the details of the mathematical proof that Eq. (14-9a) is an equality and not merely approximately true.

Equation (14-9c) is particularly useful for studying the effects of dividend policy (as represented by the variable f) on value. First, consider the normal firm where the internal rate of return on new investment equals the discount rate (that is, $r = k$).

$$v_0 = \frac{e_1(1 - f)}{k - fr} = \frac{e_1(1 - f)}{k - g} \quad \text{since } g = fr \tag{14-9c}$$

$$= \frac{e_1(1 - f)}{k(1 - f)} \quad \text{if } r = k$$

$$= \frac{e_1}{k} \tag{14-10}$$

Equation (14-10) shows that regardless of the firm's initial earnings, e_1, or riskiness (which determines k), the firm's value is not affected by dividend policy. That is, when $r = k$, dividend policy is irrelevant since f, which represents the firm's dividend policy, cancels completely out of Eq. (14-10).

Equation (14-10) is also proof that capitalizing earnings is equivalent to capitalizing dividends when $r = k$, regardless of the payout ratio. Equation (14-10), which capitalizes only earnings, was derived from Eq. (14-8). Equation (14-9a), which capitalizes dividends, was also derived from Eq. (14-8).

TABLE 14-1   NUMERICAL SOLUTIONS FOR DIVIDEND MODEL

$V = \dfrac{e_1(1 - f)}{k - fr}$ for $k > fr = g$ $\hfill$ (14-9c)

growth firm, $r > k$	declining firm, $r < k$	normal firm, $r = k$
$r = 15\%$ $k = 10\%$ $e_1 = \$5$	$r = 5\%$ $k = 10\%$ $e_1 = \$5$	$r = 10\%$ $k = 10\%$ $e_1 = \$5$
If $f = 60\%$, $v = \$200$. $v = \dfrac{5(.4)}{.1 - (.6)(.15)}$ $= \dfrac{2}{.01} = \$200$	If $f = 60\%$, $v = \$28.57$ $v = \dfrac{5(.4)}{.1 - (.6)(.05)}$ $= \dfrac{2}{.07} = \$28.57$	If $f = 60\%$, $v = \$50$. $v = \dfrac{5(.4)}{.1 - (.6)(.1)}$ $= \dfrac{2}{.04} = \$50$
If $f = 20\%$, $v = \$57.14$. $v = \dfrac{5(.8)}{.1 - (.2)(.15)}$ $= \dfrac{4}{.07} = \$57.14$	If $f = 20\%$, $v = \$44.44$. $v = \dfrac{5(.8)}{.1 - (.2)(.05)}$ $= \dfrac{4}{.09} = \$44.44$	If $f = 20\%$, $v = \$50$. $v = \dfrac{5(.8)}{.1 - (.2)(.1)}$ $= \dfrac{4}{.08} = \$50$
Conclusion: v increases with the retention rate f for firms with growth opportunities, $r > k$.	Conclusion: v increases with the payout ratio $(1 - f)$ for declining firms, $r < k$.	Conclusion: v is not affected by dividend policy when $r = k$.

This shows mathematical proof of the equivalence of capitalizing dividends and capitalizing earnings when $r = k$. When $r = k$, the quantity $1/k$ is the same as the price-earnings ratio (or earnings multipliers shown in Table 15-3).

Table 14-1 uses the dividend model Eq. (14-9c) to show the effects of various dividend policies, as represented by the value assigned to f, on the value of a hypothetical share. The values in Table 14-1 are computed on the assumption that earnings per share are $e_1 = \$5$, the firm's cost of capital is constant at $k = 10$ percent, and the internal profitability of the firm varies, that is, $r = 5$, 10, and 15 percent.

Table 14-1 shows the effect of various values of r, k, d, and e in determining v. Inspection of Eq. (14-9c) and Table 14-1 reveals that the optimal dividend policy depends on the relationship between the firm's internal rate of profit r and its discount rate k.

14-2.4 Growth Firms

Firms that earn a return on invested funds r that is higher than their cost of capital or discount rate k are *growth firms*. Growth firms have $r > k$, and maximize their value by retaining all earnings for internal investment. For example, IBM has been a growth stock because of technological breakthroughs combined with a marketing and service strategy that gave the company profitable market penetrating powers. As a result of the strong marketing position it attained, IBM was able to operate very profitably. This enviable position allowed IBM to raise capital at a cost of k percent per year and reinvest it internally at a higher rate of r percent per year. Firms with such profitable investments available would be foolish not to reinvest all their earnings if they could not raise capital externally. The model accurately depicts this situation and shows that paying dividends would decrease such a firm's value (unless the firm could borrow).

14-2.5 Declining Firms

Firms that do not have profitable opportunities to invest may be called *declining firms*. A firm typically declines because its product becomes obsolete, its sales continue to decline, and no further investment within the firm is profitable. Examples of declining firms can be found in the buggy-whip industry from 1930 to 1960. Declining firms have so few, if any, profitable investment opportunities that their return on investment r remains below their cost of capital or discount rate k. In this case, the firm maximizes its value (that is, the value of its owners' shares) by paying out everything it earns to its shareholders as cash dividends. In fact, the optimal financial decision would be for the firm to liquidate itself and pay one big final cash dividend as soon as possible. In a capitalistic system, the recipients of these dividends will either spend them or search out better investments. Either way, the capital will be used more productively.

14-2.6 Normal Firms

The vast majority of firms have precious few growth opportunities (that is, investments with $r > k$). These firms operate in a tedious (but nevertheless worthwhile) static equilibrium where the internal rate of return from their investments just equals their cost of capital or discount rate, $r = k$. For these firms, dividend policy has no effect on value in the dividend model. That is, the value of the firm is unchanged whether it pays out 10 percent of its earnings as dividends, or 90 percent, or any other percentage. The numerical example in Table 14-1 portrays this case too.

It is easy to be deceived into thinking that a firm which is getting bigger is a growth firm. For example, consider a hypothetical chemical company that experiences an increase in its total sales, enlarges its labour force, increases profits, and sees its stock price rise. Does this make the chemical company's stock a growth stock? No, not necessarily. This hypothetical company may be getting physically larger by retaining earnings and selling new issues of common stock to the public. These funds are raised at a weighted average cost of capital of k. Then they are reinvested and earn a rate of return of r. However, if $r = k$, the *present* value of dollars invested does not grow. The value of funds invested in the chemical company tends to increase only enough to compensate investors for bearing the risk and inconvenience of postponing consumption in order to make the investment.

14-2.7 Growth in Size not Equivalent to Growth in Value

Increases in the chemical company's share prices are due to earnings retention. The retained earnings earn a rate r, causing earnings and dividends per share to grow. However, future dividends and capital gains must be discounted at the appropriate discount rate k to find their present value. As long as $r = k$, the *present value* of further dividends and capital gains just equals the present value of the earnings that were retained to finance this expansion. Thus, the company gets physically bigger in size and the price of its shares rises, but the *present value* of an investment in it does not increase. If it paid out 100 percent of its earnings in dividends, the firm could still continue to get bigger by issuing new securities instead of retaining earnings. Either way, the present value of the benefits received from a dollar invested would be unchanged because $r = k$. Therefore, simply getting bigger does not make a corporation a growth firm.

The present value of cash dividends model is a valuable teaching device to show the effects of dividend policy on an all-equity firm under different assumptions about profitability. However, the *simplified* nature of the model can lead to conclusions that are true for the model but not true *in general*. Consider the simplifying assumptions that underlie the dividend model.

14-2.8 Simplifications in Dividend Model

1. There is *no external financing*. The dividend model contains no debt and interest expense variables or allowance for new shares to be issued. As a result, every penny of dividends comes directly out of retained earnings in the model, and, since retained earnings are the only funds with which the firm may expand, dividend policy and investment must compete for the firm's earnings.
2. The internal rate of return r of the firm is *constant*. This ignores the diminishing marginal efficiency of investment that would normally reduce r as a firm's investment was increased.
3. The appropriate discount rate k remains *constant*. Thus, the model ignores the possibility of a change in the firm's risk-class and the resulting change in k.

4. Since the firm and its stream of earnings are *perpetual*, T goes to infinity.
5. *No taxes* exist. This simplification will be relaxed later.
6. The growth rate $g = fr$ is *constant forever*.
7. The following relationship must not be violated: $k > fr = g$. If $g > k$, the value of a share would be infinite. However, it is *realistic to assume* that $k > g$.
8. The firm's dividend policy, as represented by the symbol f, is presumed to remain *fixed to infinity*.

Let us consider the problems that are introduced by these eight assumptions. The analysis will provide a review of capital budgeting and financing (that is, corporation finance) and of how such matters affect dividend policy and the value of the firm.

No Outside Financing   The dividend model *confounds* dividend policy with the investment program of the firm. Since the model does not include sources of funds from external financing, every dollar of dividends takes away a dollar from earnings retained for investment. When such a situation exists, either the firm's investment program, its dividend policy, or both will be suboptimal. This problem is represented graphically in Fig. 14-1. A review of the optimum investment program shows the result of ignoring external financing.

FIGURE 14-1   A firm's investment opportunities.

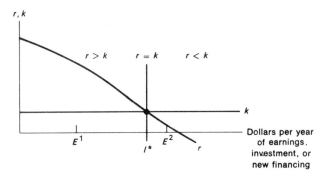

Figure 14-1 shows dollars per year on the horizontal axis and the values of r and k on the vertical axis. The exhibit depicts some hypothetical firm's investment opportunities as it makes its financial plans for the next year. Both the corporation's total profit and its total investment are measured on the horizontal axis in dollars per year. The firm's marginal cost of capital equals its average cost of capital k, as represented by the horizontal line at k percent per year.[3] The rates of return r on each investment open to the firm are shown

---

3 Capital budgeting students will notice that investments up to I^* have positive net present values, but investments over I^* (for example, E^2) have negative net present values. Figure 14-1 is oversimplified for the sake of brevity. Actually, because of corporate income taxes, the real firm's cost of capital decreases if debt capital is used, *ceteris paribus*, and the average rate of return on investment is not shown. The discussion omits the difference between the

as decreasing as more investment occurs; this reflects the assumption that the most profitable investments will be made first and the poorer investments made last. The total dollar value of the annual investments is also measured along the horizontal axis. In Fig. 14-1 I^* dollars of investment occurs where $r = k$. I^* is the optimal investment regardless of whether the capital to finance this investment is raised by selling stocks, bonds, or preferred stock, by retaining earnings, or by obtaining a loan (assuming k does not change).

To the left of I^* dollars of investment, the internal rate of return is larger than the firm's cost of capital, $r > k$, and the firm could increase its value by expanding investment to I^*. If earnings are only E^1, I^* still is the amount of investment that will maximize the firm's value. The firm should invest I^* if it has to sell new securities to raise the needed funds. However, in the dividend model, outside financing is not included. Thus, for this situation the model would show that the owner's wealth (that is, v) was maximized by retaining and investing the firm's total earnings of E^1 and paying no dividends. In a more comprehensive model allowing for outside financing, the firm should sell new securities to finance the I^* investment; only this investment would truly maximize the owner's wealth. A more comprehensive model that allows new financing is explicated later in this chapter.

Constancy of r   Assuming that the most profitable investments are made first, common sense indicates that eventually no more profitable investments will be left. This is correctly represented graphically in Fig. 14-1 by a declining investment r curve. However, the dividend model assumes that r is constant (an assumption that is true, if it is ever true, only over a tiny range of investments).

If total earnings in Fig. 14-1 were E^2 dollars, for example, the dividend model indicates that they should all be paid out in dividends because $r < k$ at E^2. In a more comprehensive model that recognizes that r declines, the optimal policy would be to retain earnings of I^* for investment and pay dividends of $E^2 - I^*$ dollars. Since the model always indicates that the optimal dividend payout is either one of three policies (namely, zero, 100 percent, or irrelevant), the dividend policy that actually maximizes the owner's wealth will rarely be indicated by this oversimplified model.

Constancy of k   A firm's cost of capital or appropriate discount rate k varies directly with the risk of the firm. Figure 14-2 is a graph of the capital asset

---

marginal return and the average return, but some writers have shown the importance of this distinction in terms of such models. See Douglas Vickers, "Profitability and Reinvestment Rates: A Note on the Gordon Paradox," *Journal of Business*, July 1966, pp. 366–370. The assertions made in this chapter that firms that have $r = k$ are not growth firms are true only if r is the average rate of return. If $r' = k$, where r' is the marginal rate of return, then $r > r' = k$, and the firm is a growth firm. Strictly speaking, $r' = k$ is the optimum condition. If $r = k$, this implies $r' < k$, which is suboptimal because some investments have been undertaken that have marginal returns less than the marginal cost of capital. See E. Lerner and W. Carleton, "The Integration of Capital Budgeting and Stock Valuation," *American Economic Review*, September 1964, pp. 683–702. Lerner and Carleton examine the effects of a diminishing marginal efficiency of investment on the dividend model.

pricing model (CAPM), or security market line (SML), as it is also called, which shows that as the risk of a firm (or any asset) increases, the appropriate discount rate rises too. The present value of the firm's income moves inversely with the discount rate. By assuming that the discount rate k is constant, the model abstracts from these effects of risk on the value of the firm. Risk measurement and the appropriate discount rate were discussed in Chaps. 9, 10, and 12.

FIGURE 14-2 The discount rate k is determined by risk.

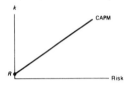

Infinite Life It is usually realistic to assume that a modern corporation endures perpetually. It will have new managements, and probably new products, too, as time passes, but the legal corporate shell can live forever.

No Taxes This unrealistic simplifying assumption is relaxed in a more comprehensive model developed later in this chapter. The differential tax rates on dividends and capital gains are considered.

Constant Growth Rate This assumption is merely a simplification of reality. It can be easily changed without changing the conclusions. The assumption that g does not change is made merely to simplify the mathematics of the model.

Cost of Capital Exceeding Growth Rate, k > g This assumption is realistic. Although a firm could sustain very high growth rates over the period of a few years, no firm could double or triple its earnings every year indefinitely. If a firm's earnings doubled annually for very many decades, its total profit would grow to exceed the gross national product (GNP) of Canada.

Constant Dividend Payout Ratio. (1 − f) The assumption that the firm has a constant retention rate f is merely another effort to simplify the mathematical form of the model. If f did change far in the future, the conclusions of the model would not be changed because the present value of future dollars is smaller. Furthermore, this assumption is fairly realistic. Many firms do tend to maintain a fixed retention rate when it is *averaged* over several years.

Beginning social scientists should not become discouraged about the dividend model because it is built on eight more or less (mostly less) realistic assumptions. Remember, a model is supposed to be a simplified version of reality. The simplifications were made for good reasons: to keep the mathematics as simple as possible and to focus only on the main issues in the valuation theory of equity shares. The model yielded some fascinating insights; for example, would you have believed that dividend policy does not affect the value of most normal firms? This issue is analyzed further below.

Dr. Gordon has studied the effects of relaxing the simplifying assumptions of the dividend model, and he has performed econometric tests using empirical data.[4] He concludes that dividend policy is irrelevant when $r = k$ and all the simplifying assumptions are maintained. However, when these assumptions are realigned to conform more closely with reality, Dr. Gordon concludes that dividend policy *does* affect the value of a share even though $r = k$. The introduction of risk into the model is Gordon's way of reaching the conclusion that dividend policy does matter in the "real world."

14-2.9 Gordon's Bird-in-the-Hand Model

With the introduction of risk and uncertainty, the appropriate discount rate k *varies* as risk and uncertainty vary.[5] Gordon suggests that risk and uncertainty increase with futurity; that is, the further one looks into the future, the more uncertain things (namely, dividends) become. Therefore, Gordon suggests that k should not be held constant. Rather, k increases further in the future. Future dividends should be discounted at a higher discount rate than current dividends. Symbolically, Gordon says $k_t > k_{t-1}$ for $t = 1$, $2, \ldots$, because of increasing risk and uncertainty in the future.[6] He rewrites his basic model Eq. (14-2) as Eq. (14-11) with a subscript on the discount rates to represent uncertainty by specifying that $k_t > k_{t-1}$. The subscripts on k change to represent Gordon's assumptions that k changes in the future.

$$v_0 = \sum_{t=1}^{\infty} \frac{d_t}{(1 + k_t)^t}$$

(14-11)

$$= \frac{d_1}{(1 + k_1)} + \frac{d_2}{(1 + k_2)^2} + \frac{d_3}{(1 + k_3)^3} + \cdots + \frac{d_t}{(1 + k_t)^t} + \cdots$$

Equation (14-11) is sometimes lightly referred to as the "bird-in-the-hand" model, since near dividends are valued above distant dividends.[7] If the average of the discount rates in Eq. (14-11) equals the constant discount rate in Eq. (14-2), then Eq. (14-2) and the bird-in-the-hand model, Eq. (14-11), are equal. However, it is unlikely the k_t's average out to equal k in Eq. (14-2).

To show the impact of uncertainty on dividend policy, Dr. Gordon suggests that the first cash dividend, namely, d_1 in Eq. (14-11), be *retained and reinvested* to earn a constant internal rate of return r into perpetuity. The

---

4 M. J. Gordon, op. cit. chaps. 6–14.

5 "Risk" and "uncertainty" are used synonymously in this book to refer to probabilistic outcomes where the probability distribution is known. Uncertainty is not used here in the Knightian sense that the probability distribution is not known, as suggested by Frank H. Knight, *Risk, Uncertainty, and Profit* (Boston: Houghton Mifflin, 1921).

6 The first article to correctly analyze the implicit behaviour of the risk-adjusted discount rate over time was A. A. Robichek and S. C. Myers, "Conceptual Problems in the Use of Risk-Adjusted Discount Rates," *Journal of Finance*, vol. 21, December 1966, pp. 727–730.

7 The phrase comes from an old saying: "A bird in the hand is worth two birds in the bush."

earnings from this reinvestment are rd_1 dollars per period per share into perpetuity. If these additional earnings are paid out as increases to the other regular dividends (that is, d_2, d_3, . . .), the value of the stock is represented by Eq. (14-12).

$$v'_0 = \frac{0}{1 + k_1} + \frac{d_2 + rd_1}{(1 + k_2)^2} + \frac{d_3 + rd_1}{(1 + k_3)^3} + \cdots + \frac{d_t + rd_1}{(1 + k_t)^t} + \cdots \qquad (14\text{-}12)$$

Even though r equals the average of all the k_t's, the value of the stock in Eq. (14-12) is less than the value of the stock in Eqs. (14-2) and (14-11). Symbolically, $v_0 > v'_0$ because the average of the k_t's for $t = 1, 2, \ldots$, is a smaller average discount rate than the average of the k_t's for $t = 2, 3, \ldots,$.

If the cash dividends were the same dollar amount and the discount rate had remained constant, as in Eq. (14-2), the value of the firm would be unchanged by shifting dividends with regard to time. Equation (14-13) shows the present value of the income from the reinvested d_1 if $r = k$.

$$\sum_{t=1}^{\infty} \frac{rd_1}{(1 + k)_t} = \frac{rd_1}{k} = d_1 \qquad \text{if } r = k \qquad (14\text{-}13)$$

Thus, if $r = k_t$ for all time periods, shifting d_1 to a later period does not affect v_0 because the present value of the perpetual income rd_1 is d_1. However in $k_t > k_{t-1}$, as in Eq. (14-12), the income from the reinvested dividend (that is, rd_1) is discounted at a higher average discount rate, since the average of k_t for $t = 2, 3, \ldots$, is larger than the average of k_t for $t = 1, 2, 3, \ldots,$. Thus $v'_0 < v_0$, which shows how dividend policy can affect value in a world of uncertainty.

By merely introducing uncertainty into the model, Gordon has shown how dividend policy can affect the value of a common stock.[8] Uncertainty explains why some investors value a dollar of dividend income more than a dollar of capital gains income. These investors value dividends above capital gains because dividends are easier to predict, less uncertain, and less risky, and are therefore discounted with a lower discount rate. When uncertainty of the type shown in Eq. (14-11) exists, the present value of a dollar of dividends is larger, the sooner the dividend is received.

14-3 MM'S DIVIDEND IRRELEVANCE ARGUMENT

Two financial economists, Dr. Franco Modigliani and Dr. Merton Miller (called MM hereafter, for brevity), disagreed with Dr. Gordon's bird-in-the-hand model, which shows that a firm's dividend policy affects its value.[9] MM constructed the simpler one-period dividend valuation model developed below from Eq. (14-2) as a basis for their dividend irrelevance argument.

8 M. J. Gordon, "Optimal Investment and Financing Policy," *Journal of Finance*, May 1963, pp. 264–272.
9 M. H. Miller and F. Modigliani, "Dividend Policy, Growth and the Valuation of Shares," *Journal of Business*, October 1961, pp. 411–433.

The multiperiod dividend valuation model, Eq. (14-2) or (14-3b), can be simplified to a one-period dividend valuation model by assuming that the share of stock is sold after one period, as shown below in Eq. (14-14):

$$v_0 = \frac{d_1}{1 + k} + \frac{d_2}{(1 + k)^2} + \cdots + \frac{d_\infty}{(1 + k)^\infty} \quad \text{(14-3d)}$$

$$= \frac{d_1 + v_1}{1 + k} \quad \text{(14-14a)}$$

because, if a share is sold after one period (at $t = 1$), the term v_1 can be substituted in place of the share's future dividends.

$$\sum_{t=1}^{\infty} \frac{d_{1+t}}{(1 + k)^t}$$

To find the value of the entire firm in period t, MM merely multiply both sides of Eq. (14-14a) by the number of shares outstanding in period t, denoted n_t, to obtain Eq. (14-14b), as shown below.

$$v_t = \frac{d_t + v_{t+1}}{1 + k_t} \quad \text{(14-14a)}$$

$$n_t v_t = V_t = \frac{n_t(d_t + v_{t+1})}{1 + k_t} = \frac{D_t + V_{t+1}}{1 + k_t} \quad \text{(14-14b)}$$

To expedite mathematical manipulation, MM base their model on the following simplifying assumptions:

1. *Perfect capital markets.* In a perfect capital market, no buyer or seller is large enough for his or her individual transactions to affect prices, financial information is freely available to everyone so that uninformed investors may be ignored, and no taxes, brokers' commissions, or other transfer costs exist to deter investors from seeking a profit-maximizing equilibrium.
2. *Investors value dollars of dividends and dollars of capital gains equally.* This assumption is partially the result of assuming that no tax differential exists between dividends and capital gains.
3. *No risk or uncertainty.* Investors can forecast future prices and dividends with certainty, and therefore one discount rate is appropriate for all securities and all time periods. In this case $r = k = k_t$ for all t.

Under the assumptions just listed, the price of each share must adjust so that the rate of income (that is, the rate of dividends plus capital gains) on every share will be equal to the appropriate discount rate and be identical for all assets over any given interval of time. This *fundamental theorem of valuation* means that the rate of return from a share of common stock, as defined in Eq. (14-15), is equal for all firms over any given period of time.

$$r_t = \frac{d_t + v_{t+1} - v_t}{v_t} \quad \text{(14-15)}$$

$$= \frac{\text{cash dividends} + \text{capital gains or loss}}{\text{purchase price}}$$

**14-3.1
One-Period
Dividend
Valuation
Model**

**14-3.2   MM
Fundamental
Principle of
Valuation**

The fundamental theorem says that the rate of economic income defined in Eq. (14-15) will be equal for all shares in perfect markets that are at equilibrium when no differences in risk exist. This fundamental valuation model is true because MM assumed away everything that might interfere with its validity.[10]

The important implication of MM's fundamental principle of valuation is that all firms in all periods will have the same cost of capital k. This is true because a firm's cost of capital k equals the investor's rate of return r. So, if all firm's r_t's must be equal by the fundamental principle of valuation, their k_t's must all be equal too ($r = k$). The quantities r and k are just two different sides of the same coin.

14-3.3
MM's Proof of Dividend Irrelevance

If a firm has a change in the number of shares outstanding, this change is denoted $\Delta n_t = n_{t+1} - n_t$. In the case that new shares are issued (or old ones repurchased as treasury stock), Eq. (14-14b) should be rewritten as Eq. (14-16) to reflect possible changes in the value of the firm.

$$V_t = \frac{D_t + V_{t+1} - \Delta n_t v_{t+1}}{1 + k_t} \tag{14-16}$$

The quantity $\Delta n_t v_{t+1}$ is subtracted from V_{t+1} in the numerator of Eq. (14-16) to reflect the change in the number of shares outstanding. The total value of all these *new* shares is defined in Eq. (14-17).

$$\Delta n_t v_{t+1} = n_{t+1} v_{t+1} - n_t v_{t+1} \tag{14-17}$$

$$= v_{t+1}(n_{t+1} - n_t)$$

Since MM's model allows for the issuance (or retirement) of shares, the firm can raise (or repay) capital to pay dividends and *also* undertake the optimal investment program (as explained in Fig. 14-1). Thus, dividend and investment policies are not perversely intertwined in MM's model as they were in Eq. (14-2), the multiperiod dividend model. As a result, MM's model yields more valid conclusions about the effects of cash dividends than does the dividend model.

Changes in the firm's investment in total assets, denoted I_t, may be financed through either earnings retention ($E_t - D_t$) or the issuance of new shares ($\Delta n_t v_{t+1}$). It follows that the proceeds of any new common stock issue must therefore equal the new investment less any retained earnings, as shown by Eq. (14-18).

$$\Delta n_t v_{t+1} = I_t - (E_t - D_t) \tag{14-18}$$

$$= I_t - E_t + D_t$$

10 Some people object to the models that social scientists like MM build because the models are based on simplifying assumptions. However, the objection is not valid. Social scientists seek basic economic truth by assuming away realistic details like taxes and uncertainty and by employing the powerful logic of mathematics to their simplified models. This approach has just as much credibility as do the experiments conducted by the physical scientists who conduct their gravity experiments, for instance, in sealed vacuum chambers where winds do not blow and birds do not fly.

If Δn_t is negative, this represents the case where assets are sold or earnings are retained to purchase outstanding shares (that is, treasury stock).

Using these symbols, MM show that the value of the firm is unaffected by its dividend policy by substituting Eq. (14-18) into Eq. (14-16) to obtain Eq. (14-19a), as shown below.

$$V_t = \frac{D_t + V_{t+1} - \Delta n_t v_{t+1}}{1 + k_t} \qquad (14\text{-}16)$$

$$= \frac{D_t + V_{t+1} - (I_t - E_t + D_t)}{1 + k_t}$$

$$= \frac{V_{t+1} - I_t + E_t}{1 + k_t} \qquad (14\text{-}19a)$$

The restatement of the total value of the firm with external financing in Eq. (14-19a) is consistent with the previous statement of the firm's value in Eqs. (14-16) and (14-14b). However, since it is possible to restate the value of the firm Eq. (14-19a) without dividends, D_t, this proves that dividends have *no effect* on the value of the firm when external financing is used. As shown in Fig. 14-1, dividends affect the firm's value only when the firm finances all investment *internally*. When external financing is utilized, dividend policy has no effect on the value of the firm under MM's simplifying assumptions.

Some students of finance are not impressed by Modigliani and Miller's dividend irrelevance model. Therefore, to supplement Dr. Gordon's bird-in-the-hand model, these people have dissented with MM by offering the following subjective arguments for the relevance of dividend policy in valuing equity shares.

**14-3.4
Subjective
Arguments
for
Dividend
Relevance**

Resolution of Uncertainty   Some advocates of dividend relevance have supported the bird-in-the hand model by pointing out that investors prefer to receive cash dividends because the payout resolves their uncertainty. If a firm retains its earnings, there is uncertainty about when and if those retained earnings will cause capital gains.

Clientele Theory   The popular clientele theory is a second subjective theory which suggests that dividend policy affects stock prices. It asserts that certain stocks attract certain kinds of investors because the investors prefer the firm's dividend payout policies. For example, widows who are counting on their investment income to keep them out of the poorhouse are supposed to buy public utility stocks that tend to pay good cash dividends. In contrast, high-income investors are assumed to want growth stocks that pay no cash dividends and instead have large capital gains which enjoy a preferential income tax treatment.

The differential tax treatment of capital gains and dividends requires that the before-tax rate of return as defined in Eq. (14-15) be rewritten as shown at the top of page 350.

$$\text{atr}_t = \frac{d_t(1 - T_0) + (v_{t+1} - v_t)(1 - T_g)}{v_t} \qquad T_0 > T_G \qquad (14\text{-}20)$$

where

atr$_t$ = after-tax rate of return at period t

T_0 = tax rate on dividends

T_g = tax rate on capital gains

Since MM's fundamental principle of valuation and all their models are based on the definition of the rate of return, dropping the assumption of no taxes will change all their models. MM freely state that "the tax differential in favour of capital gains is undoubtedly the major systematic imperfection in the market."[11] Nevertheless, MM still conclude that dividend policy has no effect on share values.

MM reason that the lower rate of tax on capital gains is not important for several reasons. First, some investors' capital gains and dividends are taxed equally (namely, charitable and educational institutions, foundations, and pension trusts). Second, MM begin their own clientele theory by pointing out that all stocks have a long-run average payout ratio between zero and 100 percent (or, equivalently, 1.0). Figure 14-3 shows a hypothetical relative-frequency distribution of the payout ratios *supplied* by all the firms issuing stock. If investors have preferences for given payout ratios, they could be surveyed and the clientele for each payout ratio could be ascertained. Figure 14-4 shows

FIGURE 14-3 Hypothetical relative-frequency distribution of payout ratios supplied by firms.

FIGURE 14-4 Hypothetical relative-frequency distribution of payout ratios desired by investors.

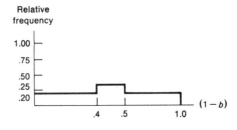

11 M. H. Miller and F. Modigliani, op. cit., p. 432.

a hypothetical relative-frequency distribution of payout ratios *desired* by investors. A comparison of the supply and demand for various payout ratios represented by Figs. 14-3 and 14-4 reveals a shortage of payout ratios in the 40 to 50 percent range and an oversupply of all other payout ratios.

MM reason that the market prices of stocks with payout ratios in the scarce 40 to 50 percent range will be bid up. The other firms' prices will be relatively lower because of lack of demand. If the managements of these firms are perceptive, they will note how much more demand exists for firms whose payout ratios are in the 40 to 50 percent range, and they will change their payout ratios until supply equals demand at each payout ratio. Thus, each firm will attract a *clientele* of investors who prefer its payout policies. For example, a consistent dividend-paying firm like Bell Canada Enterprises would not have as many high-income investors who prefer capital gains as growth stocks like IBM. MM[12] go on to point out that

even if there were a shortage of some particular payout ratio, investors would still normally have the option of achieving their particular savings objectives without paying a premium for the stocks in short supply by buying appropriately weighted combinations of the more plentiful payout ratios.

Informational Content   Some people have argued that information is conveyed from a corporation's top management to its stockholders through the firm's dividend policy. Stockholders are viewed as outsiders who are not fully aware of what is going on in their firm.[13] Therefore, they look for signals about their firm, and a corporation's cash dividend policy is one of the easiest places to find information from top management.

For example, if a corporation announces a cash dividend reduction, some investors may interpret this change as evidence that the firm's earning power has been permanently reduced. Some of these bearish shareholders may sell the stock and drive its price down because they think earnings may never recover their upward trend. This appears to be what happened to General Motors in 1980, as shown in Fig. 14-5, when the company did not earn enough to pay its cash dividends out of current earnings. In fact, GM's stock price declined until early 1982. Many other illustrations like Fig. 14-5 could be drawn to support the notion that cash dividends convey valuable investment information to both past and potential investors.

Investors' Liquidation Costs   A final argument in support of cash dividends as a means of increasing owners' wealth is based on stockbrokers' commissions. If a shareholder must liquidate some shares to obtain needed cash, a brokerage commission must be paid to sell the shares. Many of the commission costs could be avoided if corporations would all pay cash dividends regularly.

12 Ibid.
13 Frank H. Easterbrook, ''Two Agency-Cost Explanations of Dividends,'' *American Economic Review*, vol. 74, no. 4, September 1984, pp. 650–659.

FIGURE 14-5 Dividends and earnings per share for General Motors Corporation.

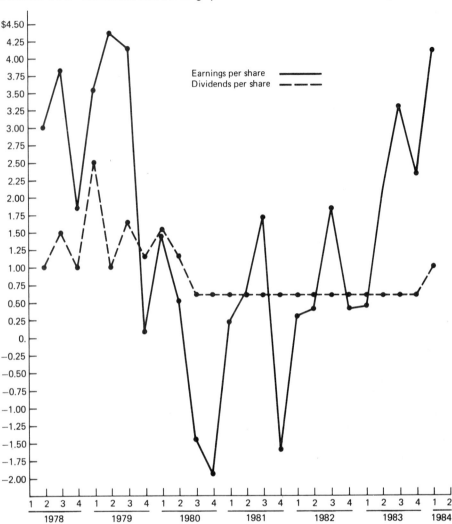

**14-3.5
Arguments
Favouring
Dividend
Retention**

Among those who believe that a firm's dividend policy does affect the value of its shares, there is a group that argues *for* and another group which argues *against* cash dividends. The latter group disagrees with the subjective arguments that cash dividends are desirable because they resolve uncertainty, convey information, and provide cashflows for needy clientele. This group offers the following points in support of earnings retention (which tends to cause capital gains).

Tax Differential The most powerful and undeniable argument against cash dividends is the fact that they are taxed at a higher rate than capital gains [see Eq. (14-20) above]. This tax differential is a good rationale for earnings retention.

The Flotation Costs of Issues Those who favour earnings retention point out that the firm can expand on retained earnings instead of on new security issues. This allows the firm to avoid paying a fee to an investment dealer to float new security issues to raise capital with which to finance expansion.

Sale of Stock at Lower Price   A subjective argument favouring dividend relevance is that new shares of stock which are sold to replace money paid out in cash dividends will drive down the market price of the outstanding shares.[14] The point of this position is that investors should prefer the stock of firms that retain earnings. The value of the shares will not be depressed by diluting sales of new shares to obtain cash with which to pay cash dividends.

The preceding discussion embraced many aspects of the intellectual discussion about dividend policy. Valuation models were introduced. Models showing the relevance and the irrelevance of dividend policy were analyzed. The arguments for and against cash dividend payment were reviewed. What is the final answer? Are dividends really irrelevant?

14-3.6 Conclusion About Dividend Policy

MM's dividend irrelevance model is more general than Gordon's bird-in-the-hand model because the MM model allows external financing. Further, MM's clientele theory (see Figs. 14-3 and 14-4) is more logical than stories about widows' cash needs and other subjective arguments. However, the burden of heavier taxation on cash dividends is difficult to dismiss. Overall, it seems that dividend policy is probably irrelevant, but investors in high tax brackets logically dislike cash dividends. The problem with reaching this conclusion is that most business persons and amateur investors believe the opposite: they think cash dividends are desirable. So, alas, the dividend debate continues unresolved.

Several statistical studies with empirical data have endeavoured to discern whether or not a corporation's cash dividend policy affects the market value of its common stock shares.[15] The results of these studies suggest that dividends may have a positive effect on stock prices, but the results are generally of marginal significance.

14 John Lintner, ''Dividends, Earnings, Leverage, Stock Prices, and the Supply of Capital to Corporations,'' *Review of Economics and Statistics*, August 1962. This article is a classic piece of research about cash dividends.

15 The following empirical studies using U.S. data more or less reach the conclusion that cash dividends have a positive but marginally significant effect on the market value of equity shares: F. Black and M. Scholes, ''The Effects of Dividend Yield and Dividend Policy on Common Stock Prices and Returns,'' *Journal of Financial Economics*, May 1974, vol. 1, pp. 1–22. M. J. Brennan, ''Taxes, Market Valuation and Corporate Financial Policy,'' *National Tax Journal*, 1970, vol. 23, pp. 417–427. E. J. Elton and M. J. Gruber, ''Marginal Stockholder Tax Rates and the Clientele Effect,'' *Review of Economics and Statistics*, February 1970, vol. 52, pp. 68–74. R. H. Litzenberger and K. Ramaswamy, ''Dividends, Short Selling Restrictions, Tax-Induced Investor Clienteles and Market Equilibrium,'' *Journal of Finance*, May 1980, vol. 35, pp. 469–481. R. H. Litzenberger and K. Ramaswamy, ''The Effect of Personal Taxes and Dividends on Capital Asset Prices,'' *Journal of Financial Economics*, June 1979, vol. 7, pp. 163–195. M. H. Miller and M. Scholes, ''Dividends and Taxes,'' *Journal of Financial Economics*, December 1978, vol. 6, pp. 333–364. W. F. Sharpe and H. B. Sosin, ''Risk, Return and Yield, New York Stock Exchange Common Stocks, 1928–1969,'' *Financial Analysts Journal*, March–April 1976, vol. 32, pp. 33–42.

Morgan reached a similar conclusion with respect to Canadian equity shares, at least for the period after the 1971 tax reform. He found that ''. . . the Canadian stock market behaved

In a different vein, an important common stock valuation question that ignores the long-run effects of dividend policy is: Do cash dividend payments cause short-term stock price fluctuations?

14-4   EFFECTS OF CASH DIVIDENDS

It was explained above that the value of a common stock equals the present value of its future income. If this is true, the market price of a share of common stock should drop when cash dividends are paid by an amount equal to the present value of that dividend, since a cash dividend payment decreases the present value of the share. Let us denote this dropoff in market price associated with payment of cash dividends as DO, which is defined in Eq. (14-21).

DO = (closing price before dividend) − (closing price ex-dividend)   (14-21)

Dr. D. Durand and A. May of Massachusetts Institute of Technology published a study of the behaviour of American Telephone and Telegraph (AT&T) stock after cash dividends were paid.[16] AT&T was chosen for the study because (1) its stock had a broad, orderly, active market and (2) its $2.25 quarterly cash dividend was large in relation to the 12.5 cents stock price

TABLE 14-3   DROPOFFS IN AT&T STOCK AT 43 QUARTERLY DIVIDENDS OF $2.25

DO, $	DO/$2.25, %	MAR. '48–SEPT. '52	DEC. '52–MAR. '57	JUNE '57–MAR. '59	ROW TOTALS
1¼	50		1		1
1⅜, 1½	55, 60				
1⅝	72		2		2
1¾	78	2	1	1	4
1⅞	83	3	2		5
2	89	5	2	1	8
2⅛	94	3	3	1	7
2¼	100	2	1	2	5
2⅜	106		3	1	4
2½	111				
2⅝	117	1	1	1	3
2¾	122	1			1
2⅞	127		1		1
3, 3⅛, 3¼	133, 138, 144			1	
3⅜	150			8	2
Totals		18	17	$2.34	43
Average		$2.15	$2.07	104%	$2.16
DO/$2.25		96%	92%		96%

as though dividends and capital gains were imperfect substitutes in the period 1968–1971, and more or less perfect substitutes afterwards.'' See I. G. Morgan, ''Dividends and Stock Price Behaviour in Canada'', *Journal of Business Administration*, vol. 12, no. 1, Fall 1980, pp. 91–105. The quote above is found on p. 105.

16 D. Durand and A. May, ''The Ex-Dividend Behavior of American Telephone and Telegraph Stock,'' *Journal of Finance*, March 1960, pp. 19–31.

changes (that is, only ⅛ point changes are posted), which facilitated measuring the DO. A total of forty-three quarterly dividend dates from 1948 to 1959 were examined. The average of the forty-three DOs was $2.16, which was 96 percent of the $2.25 cash dividend paid. The data for all forty-three quarterly dividends are shown in Table 14-3.

The data in Table 14-3 strongly support the theory that the value of a stock is the present value of its future income. Tax effects account for the small difference between the dropoff and the dividend; that is, shrewd investors who intend to sell the stock prefer to sell it shortly before the dividend is paid so that they may recognize their income as capital gains (rather than dividends, which are taxed at the higher ordinary income tax rate). This tendency drives the price down slightly before cash dividends are paid and keeps the DO from being as large as the cash dividend.[17]

Figure 14-6 shows the price action of AT&T around the time of its quarterly dividends from 1948 to 1952. The line through the points traces the average dollar amount the market price fluctuated around the ex-dividend market price.

FIGURE 14-6   Graph of price drop-off on AT&T stock.

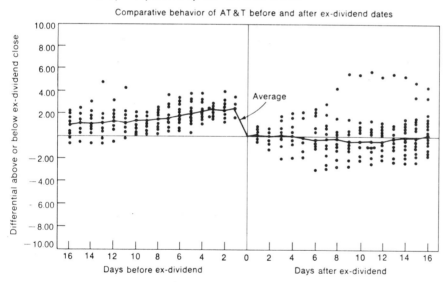

Comparative behavior of AT & T before and after ex-dividend dates

Source: From D. Duran and A. May, "The Ex-Dividend Behavior of American Telephone and Telegraph Stock," *Journal of Finance,* March 1960, pp. 19–31.

17 In a study of Canadian security price behaviour, Booth and Johnston found that on the ex-dividend date, the drop-off, as measured by the ratio of the ex-dividend price change divided by the dividend per share, was significantly different from zero or one, implying a market preference for capital gain income over dividend income. This is consistent with a tendency to sell prior to the ex-dividend date to recognize capital gain rather than dividend income. See L. D. Booth, and D. J. Johnston, "The Ex-Dividend Behaviour of Canadian Stock Prices: Tax Changes and Clientele Effects," *Journal of Finance,* vol. XXXIX, no. 2, June 1984, pp. 457–476.

This line rises gradually as the dividend date approaches and the present value of the dividend increases. Then the dropoff occurs simultaneously with the dividend. It is clearly not advisable to purchase a stock a few days prior to its dividend date (unless the purchaser is tax-exempt). The price would drop after the dividend, and the new investor, having received the dividend, must pay ordinary income tax on it. Thus, the after-tax dividend income is less than the capital loss. Trading shares to capture cash dividends is no way to beat the market.

14-4.1 Conclusions About Cash Dividend Effects

Cash dividends are a source of real income to the investor. The market recognizes the present value of cash dividends and adjusts the price of the stock accordingly. The data compiled by Durand and May indicate that the market has a slight preference for capital gains over dividends, but in view of the income tax structure, this is rational.

It seems that on the average the market views dividends in a rational manner and cannot be beaten or fooled into erroneous values by dividend gimmicks. The data seem to support the Modigliani-Miller thesis (explained in Sec. 14-3) that dividend policy is irrelevant, except for possible tax effects.

The tax advantage gained by purchasing stocks just after cash dividends are paid and selling them shortly before the next cash dividend is useful only to investors in very high income tax brackets. When the risks associated with holding the security between dividend dates and the sales commissions incurred in buying and selling are considered, this strategy is not likely to beat the market.[18]

14-5 DIFFERENT APPROACHES TO VALUATION

Finance professors, fundamental security analysts, economists, and others have suggested several approaches to determining the values of common stocks. Three of the more popular approaches involve capitalizing (that is, finding the present value of) three different streams of money.

1. *The cashflow approach.* The advocates of this approach—mostly finance professors and economists—suggest that the value of a security is the present value of the cashflows it produces. Chapter 11 stressed this approach in valuing bonds, since their cashflows are known in advance.
2. *The dividend approach.* This approach suggests that the value of a common stock is the present value of all its expected cash dividends.
3. *The stream-of-earnings approach.* This approach suggests that the value of a security is the present value of all its future earnings. This approach is supported by many fundamental security analysts.

At this point, the obvious question is: What do investors capitalize—net cashflows, dividends, or earnings? MM have shown that, properly formulated, all three approaches are identical.

18 For a review of other investigations of cash dividend dropoffs and a more detailed analysis of this phenomenon, see Kenneth M. Eades, Patrick J. Hess, and E. Han Kim, ''On Interpreting Security Returns during the Ex-Dividend Period,'' *Journal of Financial Economics*, March 1984, vol. 13, no. 1, p. 34.

MM start to equate these three seemingly divergent valuation approaches by extending Eq. (14-19a) to cover longer time spans. Thus, Eq. (14-19a) may be rewritten as Eqs. (14-19b) and 14-19c).

$$V_t = \frac{E_t - I_t + V_{t+1}}{1 + k} \tag{14-19b}$$

$$= \frac{E_t - I_t}{1 + k} + \frac{V_{t+1}}{1 + k} \tag{14-19c}$$

Looking beyond one period to T periods in the future causes Eq. (14-19c) to expand to Eq. (14-22):

$$V_0 = \sum_{t=1}^{T-1} \frac{E_t - I_t}{(1 + k)^t} + \frac{V_T}{(1 + k)^T} \tag{14-22}$$

When T is infinitely large, $V_T/(1 + K)^T$ becomes zero and Eq. (14-22) can be rewritten as Eq. (14-23):

$$V_0 = \sum_{t=1}^{\infty} \frac{E_t - I_t}{(1 + k)^t} + 0 \tag{14-23}$$

14-5.1 The Cashflow Approach

Consider for a moment the cashflow in period t, denoted C_t. The cashflow is the difference between cash inflows and cash outflows. More specifically, the cashflow from a firm is its earnings less the investments necessary to maintain the firm, as shown in Eq. (14-24).

$$C_t = E_t - I_t \tag{14-24}$$

According to the advocates of the discounted cashflow approach, the value of the firm is given by Eq. (14-25).

$$V_0 = \sum_{t=1}^{\infty} \frac{C_t}{(1 + k)^t} \tag{14-25}$$

Substituting Eq. (14-24) in Eq. (14-25) yields Eq. (14-23). This shows the equivalence of the cashflow valuation model to Eq. (14-23) and its predecessors, Eqs. (14-19a), (14-14a), and (14-16).

14-5.2 The Stream-of-Earnings Approach

Those who do not approve of the discounted stream-of-earnings approach typically attack it on two points. First, these detractors charge that stockholders cannot withdraw earnings from the corporation as they are earned; they must wait for cash dividends to be paid, and the retained earnings may never be received. When $r = k$ and markets are perfect, this argument is empty. In this case the market value of a share increases by an amount equal to retained earnings. Thus, stockholders who want their earnings can have them by liquidating some of their holdings.

Second, the earnings approach is sometimes attacked for "double counting." The double-counting advocates charge that all earnings are counted as income when they are earned. Then *earnings on retained earnings* are counted as income again later. The problem with some double-counting advocates is that they define income inappropriately.[19] The earnings E_t less new investments I_t required to maintain future earnings, as defined in Eq. (14-26), correspond with economists' definition of truly *consumable* income.

$$\text{True economic earnings} = E_t - I_t \tag{14-26}$$

Economists and many others correctly assert that the retention of accounting profits in the firm to maintain its future income (but not increase it) is not the retention of true income, although the accounting profession calls it "retained earnings." Thus, the stream-of-earnings approach, properly formulated, says the value of the firm is the present value of all *true economic earnings* as defined in Eq. (14-23)

$$V_t = \sum_{t=1}^{\infty} \frac{E_t - I_t}{(1 + k)^t} \tag{14-23}$$

Thus, MM show that if it is properly formulated (that is, if earnings are defined properly), the stream-of-earnings approach is equivalent to the other valuation approaches. In practical applications, it is the responsibility of the financial analyst to adjust accounting profit to conform to the true economic income if the stream-of-earnings approach is to be used.

To see the necessity of adjusting accounting earnings to conform to the concept of economic income, consider, say, the colour television industry. The RCA Corporation dominated the industry in the 1960s because it developed the technology to mass-produce the only good colour TV tubes in the world. Thus, when RCA went into mass production of colour television sets, RCA's competitors who wanted to avert bankruptcy and possibly even maintain their future income undiminished had to invest much or all their *accounting profit* internally to develop the technology to produce colour TV sets. The depreciation flows provided by the firms' old assets were not sufficient to finance these new assets for colour television production. This investment of accounting profit most certainly was not the retention of true income — true income is something that its recipients should be free to consume if they please. The so-called retained earnings could not be withdrawn from the firm and consumed without decreasing the firm's ability to compete and earn in the future. Any television manufacturer that did not move into the production of colour sets in the 1960s would more than likely be unable to compete in the television industry of the 1970s. This RCA case shows (1) the need for the financial analyst to adjust reported accounting income, (2) the rationale behind valuation Eq. (14-23), and (3) the weakness of the accounting definition of income as it compares with the economic concept of income.

---

19 Section 16-5 explains in more detail how accountants' definition of income is distorted and misleading and can actually lead to "double counting."

The dividend approach, properly formulated, says that the discounted value of the dividends coming to a *given share* of stock equals the value of that share. This is equivalent to taking the present value of *all* future dividends of the firm only if *no* new shares were issued or old ones retired. Let $D_{t,1}$ denote total dividends of the firm *paid in period t to stockholders of record at period t = 1*. Dividends paid on new shares issued after $t = 1$ should not be included in present value of $D_{t,1}, D_{t+1,1}, D_{t+2,1}, D_{t+3,1}, \ldots, D_\infty$. The present value of the firm to stockholders of record at $t = 1$ is given by Eq. (14-27a).

$$V_1 = \sum_{t=1}^{\infty} \frac{D_{t,1}}{(1+k)^t} \tag{14-27a}$$

$$= \frac{D_{1,1}}{1+k} + \sum_{t=2}^{\infty} \frac{D_{t,1}}{(1+k)^t}$$

$$= \frac{1}{1+k}\left[D_{(t,1)} + \sum_{t=2}^{\infty} \frac{D_{t+1,1}}{(1+k)^t}\right] \tag{14-27b}$$

The present value at $t = 2$ of the future dividend stream $D_{t,1}$ equals the present value at $t = 2$ of the dividend stream $D_{t,2}$ times a fraction $[1 - \Delta n_1/n_2]$ representing the ratio of the number of shares outstanding at $t = 1$ to the number of shares outstanding at $t = 2$. Equation (14-28) represents this symbolically.

$$\sum_{t=1}^{\infty} \frac{D_{t+1,1}}{(1+k)^t} = \left[\sum_{t=1}^{\infty} \frac{D_{t+1,2}}{(1+k)^t}\right]\left(1 - \frac{\Delta n_1}{n_2}\right) \tag{14-28}$$

Substituting Eq. (14-28) into Eq. (14-27b) yields Eq. (14-29):

$$V_1 = \frac{1}{1+k}\left\{D_{1,1} + \left[\sum_{t=1}^{\infty} \frac{D_{t+1,2}}{(1+k)^t}\right]\left(1 - \frac{\Delta n_1}{n_2}\right)\right\} \tag{14-29}$$

Multiplying the quantity inside the brackets by the quantity inside the large parentheses in Eq. (14-29) yields

$$n_2 v_2\left(1 - \frac{\Delta n_1 V_2}{n_2 v_n}\right) = V_2 - \Delta n_1 v_2$$

by using the definitions below in Eq. (14-30).

$$V_2 = n_2 v_2 \tag{14-30}$$

$$= \sum_{t=1}^{\infty} \frac{D_{t+1,2}}{(1+k)^t}$$

Substituting the quantity $V_2 - \Delta n_1 v_2$ in place of the product of the quantity in brackets and the quantity in parentheses in Eq. (14-29) yields Eq. (14-31).

$$V_1 = \frac{1}{1+k}(D_{1,1} + V_2 - \Delta n_1 v_2) \tag{14-31}$$

$$V_t = \frac{D_t + V_{t+1} - \Delta n_t v_{t+1}}{1+k} \tag{14-16}$$

Since $D_{1,1} = D_t$ at $t = 1$, Eq. (14-31) is equivalent to the basic valuation Eq. (14-16), from which Eq. (14-23) and others were derived. Thus, MM show that, properly formulated, the dividends approach is equivalent to the earnings and net cashflow approaches.

14-6 SUMMARY AND CONCLUSIONS

The theory of finance is not definitive about the effect of dividend policy on the value of an equity share. Dr. Gordon's so-called "bird-in-the-hand" model demonstrated how uncertainty about the future can make a share that pays cash dividends more valuable than a share that is identical in every way, except that its cash dividend policy is more restrictive. Doctors Modigliani and Miller, in turn, developed a more general dividend valuation model that permits external financing. MM, using their model, prove that dividend policy has no effect on the value of a share. The fact that MM's model is more general (that is, it allows outside financing) makes it more acceptable than more restrictive models. However, when differential income taxes on dividends and capital gains are considered, a good case can be made for retaining all earnings to maximize the value of normal and growth firms. Thus, the theory is at odds with the popular notion among many business executives that cash dividends have the ability to affect the value of common stock.

Theoretical analysis of several commonly used valuation models was highly informative. Valuation models based on cashflows, earnings, and dividends were all shown to be equivalent when properly formulated. Moreover, the analysis of these models was helpful in clarifying exactly how they should be formulated to yield consistent results. In the next chapter, the dividend valuation model embraced by Gordon, MM, and other analysts as well—that is, Eq. (14-2)—is reformulated in a more pragmatic manner, and fundamental security analysis methods that have been popular on Bay and Wall Streets for decades are analyzed within the context of this model.

QUESTIONS

1. Define the phrase *financial model*.
2. For a firm with earnings per share of $10, dividends per share of $6, a cost of equity capital of 10 percent, and an internal rate of return of 15 percent, calculate its value by using the dividend model.

3. Discuss the simplifying assumptions that MM's and Gordon's models have in common. Can any problems arise from using such simplifications?

4. Do investors capitalize dividends or earnings in estimating the value of a stock?

5. "Dividend policy is irrelevant." True, false, or uncertain? Explain.

6. Compare and contrast the importance of dividend policy with and without the preferential tax rates on capital gains by using any model you prefer. Assume that the internal rate of return r equals the firm's cost of capital k and that capital gains are taxed at half the rate for dividend income.

7. How can the present value of a share's cash dividends be equal to the present value of the share's earnings when dividends are almost always less than earnings?

8. Critically analyze the proposition on which Gordon's bird-in-the-hand model is based, that is, that uncertainty increases with futurity.

9. Why do Modigliani and Miller use the same discount rate k to find the value of three different income streams: dividends, earnings, and cashflows?

10. "A common stock that never pays any cash dividends is worthless." True, false, or uncertain? Explain.

SELECTED REFERENCES

Friend, Irwin and Marshall Puckett. "Dividends and Stock Prices," *American Economic Review*, September 1954, pp. 656–682. An empirical test to determine whether investors capitalize dividends or earnings. Regression analysis is used.

Gordon, M. J. *The Investment, Financing and Valuation of the Corporation.* Homewood, Ill.: Irwin, 1962. A full discussion of Gordon's model for capitalizing dividends and a review of some of the literature. Some calculus used, mostly algebra.

Gordon, M. J. "Why Do Corporations Pay Dividends?" Working paper, Faculty of Management Studies, University of Toronto, 1986, pp. 1–30. The pages contain Gordon's current views on the relevance of dividend policy within the context of the long-run growth and survival of the corporation and immunity from takeover.

Miller, M. H. and F. Modigliani. "Dividend Policy, Growth and the Valuation of Shares." *Journal of Business*, October 1961, pp. 411–433. The theory of valuation for shares in an all-equity corporation is analyzed with some analysis and review of relevant theories. First-year college algebra used.

Modigliani, F. and M. H. Miller. "The Cost of Capital, Corporation Finance and the Theory of Investment; Corporate Income Taxes, and the Cost of Capital: A Correction," *American Economic Review*, June 1958, pp. 433–443. More recently, see Miller's "Debt and Taxes," *Journal of Finance*, May 1977, vol. XXXIII, no. 2, pp. 261–276. The valuation of a corporation that uses debt is explained. First-year college algebra is used.

Fundamental Common Stock Analysis

Security analysis is the basis for rational investment decisions. If a security's estimated value is *above* its market price, the security analyst will recommend buying the stock. If the estimated value is *below* the market price, the security should be sold before its price drops. This buying and selling process is what determines the market price of a security. Underpriced stocks are purchased until their price is bid up to equal their value. Overpriced stocks are sold, which drives their price down. Astute analysts continue to give "sell" instructions until the price is driven down to their estimate of its value—that is, until it is down to what they think it is "worth." In a perfectly efficient securities market, prices always equal values as a result of the buying and selling pressure just described. However, the values of securities are continuously changing as news about the securities becomes known, and this flux is what makes life exciting for security analysts. They must keep up-to-date value estimates for the securities with which they are working, or they will make bad (that is, unprofitable) buy and sell recommendations and lose their invested funds and/or their job.

This chapter explains how fundamental common stock analysts—that is, analysts who study the fundamental facts affecting a stock's value rather than follow fads or charts—do their investment research. Fundamental analysts delve into companies' earnings, their managements, the economic outlook, the firm's competition, market conditions, and many other factors. However, all their research is based on the valuation model explained below.

15-1 THE PRESENT VALUE OF CASH DIVIDENDS

The true economic value or *intrinsic value* of a share of common stock, like the value of a bond or other asset, equals the present value of all cashflows from the asset. Letting d_{it} denote the ith shares' (for example, Inco) cash dividends per share paid in the tth period (say, the third quarter of 1989 might be used as one of the time periods), and letting k_i represent the ith stock's risk-adjusted discount rate (or cost of equity capitalization rate) means that the ith share's value, denoted p_i, is given by the present value formula in Eq. (15-1a), or equivalently by Eqs. (15-1b) and (15-1c).

$$p_{i0} = \sum_{t=1}^{\infty} \frac{d_{it}}{(1 + k_i)^t} \tag{15-1a}$$

$$= \sum_{t=1}^{\infty} \frac{d_{i0}(1 + g_i)^t}{(1 + k_i)^t} \quad \text{since } d_{it} = d_{i0}(1 + g_i)^t \tag{15-1b}$$

$$= \frac{d_{i1}}{k_i - g_i} \tag{15-1c}$$

The growth rate for dividends, the g symbol, is presumed constant in writing Eqs. (15-1b) and (15-1c); therefore $d_{it} = d_{i0}(1 + g_i)^t$. This simplification allows the algebraic manipulation necessary to derive Eqs. (15-1c) and (15-1b).[1]

15-2 FUNDAMENTAL ANALYSTS' MODEL

Most common stock analysts prepare their estimates of intrinsic value per share by multiplying the ith stock's normalized earnings per share, denoted

---

1 If dividends grow at some constant rate, denoted g, then future dividends are related to current dividends as shown below. First note that Eq. (15-1a) can be rewritten as Eq. (a).

$$p_0 = \sum_{t=1}^{\infty} \frac{d_0(1 + g)^t}{(1 + k)^t}$$

$\Sigma d_0 x = d_0 \Sigma x$ because d_0 is a constant. This relation means that Eqs. (15-1b) or   (a)
  (a) may be rewritten as shown below.

$$p_0 = d_0 \sum_{t=1}^{\infty} \frac{(1 + g)^t}{(1 + k)^t} \tag{b}$$

$$= d_0 \left(\frac{1 + g}{1 + k} = \frac{(1 + g)^2}{(1 + k)^2} + \frac{(1 + g)^3}{(1 + k)^3} + \cdots \right) \tag{c}$$

Multiplying Eq. (c) by $[(1 + k)/(1 + g)]$ yields Eq. (d).

$$p_0 \frac{1 + k}{1 + g} = d_0 \left[1.0 + \frac{1 + g}{1 + k} + \frac{(1 + g)^2}{(1 + k)^2} + \cdots \right] \tag{d}$$

Subtracting Eq. (c) from the preceding equation yields Eq. (e).

$$\left(\frac{1 + k}{1 + g} - 1 \right) p_0 = d_0 \tag{e}$$

By assuming that $k > g$, the preceding equation can be rearranged as

$$\left[\frac{(1 + k) - (1 + g)}{1 + g} \right] p_0 = \left[\frac{k - g}{1 + g} \right] p_0 = d_0 \tag{f}$$

Multiplying Eq. (f) by the quantity $(1 + g)$ and rearranging yields Eq. (g).

$$p_0(k - g) = d_0(1 + g) = d_1 \tag{g}$$

where $d_0(1 + g)^1 = d_1$ denotes "next period's" dividends per share. Equation (15-1c) can be obtained by rearranging the preceding equation as follows.

$$p_0 = \frac{d_1}{k - g} \tag{15-1c}$$

e_{it} for the tth period, times the share's earnings multiplier, m_{it}, as shown in Eq. (15-2)

$$p_{it} = e_{it}m_{it} \tag{15-2}$$

The security analyst gets the earnings per share from the corporation's accountants and then normalizes it, as explained in Chap. 16, to obtain e_{it}.

15-2.1
The
Earnings
Multiplier

The economic theory to explain the earnings multiplier is obtained simply by dividing both sides of Eq. (15-2) or (15-1b) by normalized earnings per share, e_{it}, as shown in Eq. (15-3a):

$$m_{i0} = \frac{p_{i0}}{e_{i0}} = \sum_{t=1}^{\infty} \frac{(d_{i0}/e_{i0})(1 + g_i)^t}{(1 + k_i)^t} \quad \text{at time } t = 0 \tag{15-3a}$$

$$= \frac{p_{i0}}{e_{i0}} = \frac{d_{i0}}{e_{i0}} \sum_{t=1}^{\infty} \frac{(1 + g_i)^t}{(1 + k_i)^t} \tag{15-3b}$$

$$= \frac{d_{i1}/e_{it}}{k_i - g_i} \tag{15-3c}$$

The earnings multiplier is frequently called the *price-earnings ratio*.[2] The ratio d_{it}/e_{it} in Eqs. (15-3a) and (15-3b) is called the *dividend payout ratio*; it is about 50 percent for most corporations.

The remainder of this chapter focuses on the pragmatic approaches security analysts use to estimate a stock's appropriate earnings multiplier as defined in Eqs. (15-3a) and (15-3c) and the intrinsic value of the share. The factors that determine a security's dividend growth rate g are explained first. However, the primary topics for the remainder of the chapter are the factors that cause securities markets to value a stock like, say, Domtar at eight times its earnings per share in 1973 after valuing the same share at twenty-two times its earnings in 1967. However, before discussing earnings multipliers, a more direct approach to the valuation of a corporation is considered, that is, simply appraising its assets to find their sales values. This approach is not recommended because a corporation should not be considered to be merely a collection of physical assets. A viable corporation is one that produces some product of value and earns income. If the corporation's assets cannot produce income, they have no economic value.

15-2.2
Asset
Values

The asset value of a security is determined by estimating the liquidating value of the firm, deducting the claims of the firm's creditors, and allocating the remaining net asset value of the firm over the outstanding junior securities

---

2 The equity share valuation model represented by Eqs. (15-1), (15-2), and (15-3a) has been developed by B. G. Malkiel, "Equity Yields, Growth, and Structure of Share Prices," *American Economic Review*, December 1963, pp. 1004–1031, and "The Valuation of Public Utility Equities," *Bell Journal of Economics and Management Science*, 1970, pp. 143–160, and by B. G. Malkiel and J. G. Cragg in "Expectations and the Structure of Share Prices," *American Economic Review*, September 1970, pp. 601–617.

(namely, shares of stock). The asset value of a firm is usually estimated by (1) consulting a specialist in appraising asset values and/or (2) consulting an accountant about the book value of the firm.

Asset values are important in determining the market value of a company when it may go bankrupt, but that is about the only time asset values are important. In the case of probable bankruptcy, the firm's income and dividends will probably not be continued and will therefore have negligible value: the firm's value is dependent upon the prices its assets will bring at sale. But for prosperous firms asset values need not be considered. The intrinsic value of a prosperous firm or ''going concern'' typically far exceeds the value of the firm's physical assets.

TABLE 15-1 SELECTED FINANCIAL DATA FOR DOMTAR INC. COMMON STOCK ON A PER-SHARE BASIS

YEAR	BOOK VALUE, $	RANGE OF MARKET PRICE, $ LOW	HIGH	PER-SHARE EARNINGS, $	AVERAGE PRICE-EARNINGS RATIO, TIMES	PER-SHARE CASH DIVIDEND, $	DIVIDEND PAYOUT RATIO, %
1984	$41.39	$29.00	$35.25	$2.44	13.17	$1.20	49.18%
1983	$34.51	$19.63	$32.50	$1.09	23.91	$1.00	91.74%
1982	$33.55	$15.38	$22.00	($0.05)	undefined	$1.50	undefined
1981	$35.47	$20.00	$37.63	$1.80	16.01	$2.50*	138.89%
1980	$34.06	$21.75	$30.75	$2.83	9.28	$1.95	68.90%
1979	$31.36	$22.38	$29.25	$3.28	7.87	$1.80	54.88%
1978	$26.60	$14.00	$25.00	$2.12	9.20	$2.10†	99.06%

*Includes five dividend payments due to change in payment dates.
†Regular dividend of $0.90 plus extra dividend of $1.20.

Source: *The Financial Post* Information Service, The Financial Post Company Limited, 777 Bay Street, Toronto, Ontario.

Table 15-1 shows some of the data for Domtar that would be used in estimating the intrinsic value of a share of the firm's common stock. The lack of relationship between book asset values and market values is apparent in these data: this is typical. In most cases, asset values may be ignored when valuing common stock (except for a nonoperating asset that may be sold affecting the firm).

15-3 EARNINGS MULTIPLIERS: A PRAGMATIC APPROACH

Much of the fundamental security analyst's work centres on determining the appropriate capitalization rate or, equivalently, the appropriate multiplier to use in valuing a particular security's income. The main factors that must be considered in determining the correct multiplier are (1) the risk of the security, (2) the growth rate of the dividend stream, (3) the duration of any expected growth, and (4) the dividend payout ratio. Also, as the national economy and credit conditions change, interest rates, capitalization rates, and multipliers change. Table 15-2 suggests the general nature of the relationship between capitalization rates, multipliers, and risk when growth in income is zero. With this general background in mind, the determinants of intrinsic values are examined below. First, earnings multipliers are analyzed.

TABLE 15-2   CAPITALIZATION RATES AND THEIR EQUIVALENT MULTIPLIERS WHEN INCOME IS CONSTANT

CAPITALIZATION RATE (K), %	RISKINESS	EQUIVALENT MULTIPLIER (1/K)
1	Negligible risk	100 times
2		50
4		25
6		16.7
8		12.5
10	Medium risk	10
15		6.7
20		5
25		4
33		3
50	High risk	2

**15-3.1
Earnings
Multipliers**

In determining the price-earnings ratio to use in valuing a firm's securities, three factors must be estimated: the capitalization rate, the dividend growth rate, and the dividend payout ratio. As shown in Fig. 15-1, capitalization rates vary with the firm's risk-class and the prevailing market conditions. This inquiry into earnings multipliers begins with the multipliers for a normal market; later, the effects of bull or bear markets will be examined.

A *normal market* is a market in which most security prices are experiencing slow, steady growth and the average price-earnings ratio is in the low to mid-teens. Table 15-3, and Figures 15-2 and 15-4 show the cyclical fluctuations in

FIGURE 15.1   Capitalization rates and multipliers are affected by risk and economic conditions.

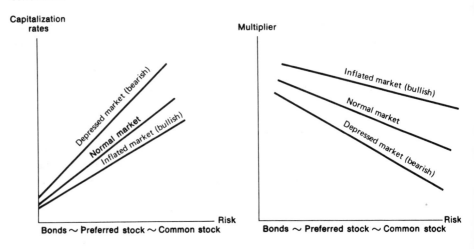

TABLE 15-3 THE TSE 300 COMPOSITE INDEX AND RELATED ECONOMIC STATISTICS

	CONSUMER PRICE INDEX	REAL GNP INDEX	REAL CORPORATE PROFITS BEFORE TAX INDEX	REAL RESIDENTIAL CONSTRUCTION INDEX	REAL NON-RESIDENTIAL CONSTRUCTION INDEX	TSE 300 COMPOSITE INDEX
1972	1.05	1.06	1.24	1.13	0.99	1.19
1973	1.13	1.14	1.78	1.24	1.08	1.26
1974	1.25	1.18	2.31	1.23	1.16	0.97
1975	1.38	1.20	2.27	1.14	1.31	1.05
1976	1.49	1.27	2.30	1.37	1.28	1.07
1977	1.61	1.29	2.41	1.30	1.34	1.04
1978	1.75	1.34	2.96	1.27	1.36	1.27
1979	1.91	1.38	3.92	1.24	1.54	1.71
1980	2.11	1.39	4.34	1.15	1.70	2.28
1981	2.37	1.44	3.76	1.19	1.84	2.16
1982	2.62	1.38	2.43	0.94	1.71	1.70
1983	2.77	1.42	3.77	1.18	1.45	2.67
1984	2.89	1.49	4.56	1.13	1.42	2.47

Source: Derived from Statistics Canada, various years.

the stock market and some market-related economic statistics during recent years. Table 15-3, for example, shows the TSE 300 Composite Index and some economic statistics, all expressed as index values with 1971 as the base year, arbitrarily set at 100.0.

When average earnings multipliers drop below 13 times, many market prices are deflated. When average earnings multipliers rise above approximately 18, it is the result of a bull market, and many stocks are overpriced.

FIGURE 15-2   TSE 300 Composite Index and Related Economic Statistics.

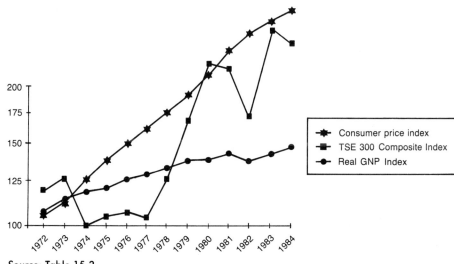

Source: Table 15-3.

The definitions of bear and bull markets are not based on particular market levels alone, however, but rather on the *direction of changes* as well as the *level* of the market.

Since future expectations are influenced by past experience, a good way to estimate a firm's risk-class is to examine historical data. Studies of securities listed on the New York Stock Exchange (NYSE) have shown that their historical average earnings capitalization rate varies directly with the security's volatility coefficient (measuring systematic or undiversifiable risk). Figure 15-3 depicts the risk-return relationship called the capital asset pricing model (CAPM).[3] The CAPM illustrates the positive relationship between an asset's undiversifiable risk (as measured by its beta coefficient, from Chap. 10) and the appropriate discount rate (or expected rate of return) for the asset. The fundamental analysts can measure the risk of the company in recent periods, adjust these historical risk statistics for any expected changes, and then use these forecasted risk statistics to obtain capitalization rates from Fig. 15-3.[4]

The capitalization rates in Fig. 15-3 are for normal markets. If the analysis is being performed during an inflated market, for example, the capitalization rates in Fig. 15-3 should be adjusted downward to increase the earnings mul-

FIGURE 15-3 The capital asset pricing model (CAPM) or security market line (SML) for normal market conditions.

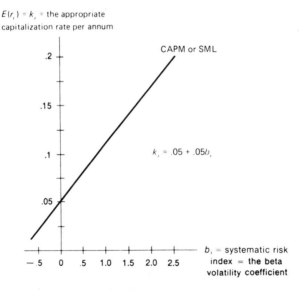

$E(r_i) = k_i$ = the appropriate capitalization rate per annum

CAPM or SML

$k_i = .05 + .05b_i$

b_i = systematic risk index = the beta volatility coefficient

3 The capital asset pricing model (CAPM) or, as it is also called, the security market line (SML) in Fig. 15-3 is the authors' subjectively adjusted estimate based on empirical regressions. Empirical estimates of the SML may be found in F. Black, M. C. Jensen, and M. Scholes, "The Capital Asset Pricing Model: Some Empirical Tests," in M. C. Jensen (ed.), *Studies in the Theory of Capital Markets.*

4 Chapters 10, 16, and 28 explain how to measure a stock's risk in more detail. The following footnote cites research studies about how to measure systematic risk with the beta coefficient in order to impute a capitalization rate.

tiplier in line with prevailing conditions. The reverse is true if pessimism prevails and the market is depressed. After the capitalization rate has been determined, the growth rate in dividends per share must be estimated.

If a security is expected to become more valuable in the future, this anticipated rise in value will tend to make it more valuable now. In order to place a current value on future growth in value, that growth must be estimated before it occurs. The growth rate in dividends or earnings per share is a good measure of growth in a firm's earning power in most cases. It is usually fairly simple to estimate the growth rate in cash dividends or earnings per share. Measuring these growth rates is discussed in Chap. 16.

15-3.2 Estimated Growth Rates Affect Multipliers

It is important to develop accurate estimates of the firm's dividend (or earnings) growth rate and the period of time this growth may be expected to continue. Table 15-4 contains numerical values that need to be multiplied by the common stock's dividend payout ratio, d/e, to obtain the appropriate earnings multiplier. Table 15-4 shows that the growth rate and the expected duration of growth in dividends have an important influence on the earnings multipliers. In fact, the growth rate is as important as the capitalization rate in preparing estimates of the appropriate earnings multipliers.

Estimating Intrinsic Value with Zero Earnings Growth To see how the multipliers in Table 15-4 are used to estimate intrinsic values, consider a hypothetical example. Suppose that security markets were normal and that a security analyst had estimated the risk and growth statistics for the ABC Company. Assuming ABC's beta systematic risk coefficient, which measures its undiversifiable risk, was estimated to be $b = 1.0$, Fig. 15-3 indicates that the appropriate capitalization rate for the firm is $k = 10$ percent.

Two different security analysts' estimates of a security's beta systematic risk coefficient should not differ appreciably since the betas tend to be fairly stationary over time.[5] However, when a difference does occur, the security

5 See the following research about beta coefficients—an index of systematic risk. Papers by Frank J. Fabozzi and J.C. Francis include (1) "Beta as a Random Coefficient," *Journal of Financial and Quantitative Analysis*, March 1978, pp. 101–116. (2) "Stability Tests for Alphas and Betas over Bull and Bear Market Conditions," *Journal of Finance*, September 1977. (3) "The Effects of Changing Macroeconomic Conditions on Alphas, Betas, and the Single-Index Model," *Journal of Financial and Quantitative Analysis*, June 1979. (4) "The Stability of Mutual Fund Systematic Risk Coefficients," *Journal of Business Research*, 1980, pp. 263–275. (5) "Heteroscedasticity in the Single-Index Model," *Journal of Economics and Business*, Spring 1980, vol. 32, no. 3, pp. 243–248. (6) "Industry Effects and the Determinants of Beta," *Quarterly Review of Economics and Business*, vol. 19, no. 3, Autumn 1979, pp. 61–74. See also the following articles by J. C. Francis: (1) "Analysis of Equity Returns: A Survey with Extensions," *Journal of Economics and Business*, Spring/Summer 1977, vol. 29, no. 3, pp. 181–192. (2) "Statistical Analysis of Risk Coefficients for NYSE Stocks," *Journal of Financial and Quantitative Analysis*, vol. XIV, no. 5, December 1979, pp. 981–997. See also the following research. (1) G. J. Alexander and N. L. Chervany, "On the Estimation and Stability of Beta," *Journal of Financial and Quantitative Analysis*, March 1980, vol. 15, pp. 123–137. (2) E. K. Altman, B. Jacquillat, and M. Levasseur, "Comparative Analysis of Risk Measures: France and the United States," *Journal of Finance*, December 1974, vol. 29, pp. 1495–1511. (3) M. E. Blume, "Betas and Their Regression Tendencies," *Journal of Finance*, June 1975, vol. 30, pp.

TABLE 15-4   PRICE-EARNINGS RATIOS FOR VARIOUS RISK-CLASSES AND VARIOUS RATES OF DIVIDEND OR EARNINGS GROWTH IN NORMAL MARKETS

TYPE OF RISK	CAPITALIZATION RATE (k), %	GROWTH RATE IN DIV, (g), %	Appropriate P/E Ratio if Earnings Growth Continues for:					
			5 YEARS	10 YEARS	15 YEARS	20 YEARS	25 YEARS	FOREVER
Outcome fairly certain, low risk: example: high-quality preferred stock	2	0	50 (d/e)	50 (d/e)	50 (d/e)	50 (d/e)	50 (d/e)	50 (d/e)
		1	52.4 (d/e)	54.8 (d/e)	57	59.0 (d/e)	61.1 (d/e)	101 (d/e)
	4	0	25 (d/e)	25 (d/e)	25 (d/e)	25 (d/e)	25 (d/e)	25 (d/e)
		1	26.2 (d/e)	27.2 (d/e)	28	28.8 (d/e)	29.5 (d/e)	33.7 (d/e)
		2	27.4 (d/e)	29.6 (d/e)	31.6 (d/e)	33.3 (d/e)	35	51 (d/e)
Some uncertainty, medium risk: example: an established business	6	0	16.7 (d/e)	16.7 (d/e)	16.7 (d/e)	16.7 (d/e)	16.7 (d/e)	16.7 (d/e)
		2	18.2 (d/e)	19.5 (d/e)	20.5 (d/e)	21.4 (d/e)	22.1 (d/e)	25.5 (d/e)
		4	19.9 (d/e)	22.8 (d/e)	25.5 (d/e)	27.9 (d/e)	30	52 (d/e)
	10	0	10 (d/e)	10 (d/e)	10 (d/e)	10 (d/e)	10 (d/e)	10 (d/e)
		3	11.3 (d/e)	12.3 (d/e)	13	13.5 (d/e)	13.8 (d/e)	14.7 (d/e)
		6	12.8 (d/e)	15.1 (d/e)	17	18.6 (d/e)	20	26.5 (d/e)
	14	0	7.1 (d/e)	7.1 (d/e)	7.1 (d/e)	7.1 (d/e)	7.1 (d/e)	7.1 (d/e)
		4	8.3 (d/e)	9 (d/e)	9.6 (d/e)	9.8 (d/e)	9.9 (d/e)	10.4 (d/e)
		8	9.7 (d/e)	11.7 (d/e)	13.2 (d/e)	14.3 (d/e)	15.2 (d/e)	18 (d/e)
High degree of uncertainty, high risk: example: new business	20	0	5 (d/e)	5 (d/e)	5 (d/e)	5 (d/e)	5 (d/e)	5 (d/e)
		4	5.8 (d/e)	6.1 (d/e)	6.3 (d/e)	6.3 (d/e)	6.3 (d/e)	6.5 (d/e)
		8	6.6 (d/e)	7.6 (d/e)	8.2 (d/e)	8.3 (d/e)	8.3 (d/e)	9 (d/e)
		12						
	26	0	3.8 (d/e)	3.8 (d/e)	3.8 (d/e)	3.8 (d/e)	3.8 (d/e)	3.8 (d/e)
		4	4.4 (d/e)	4.6 (d/e)	4.6 (d/e)	4.6 (d/e)	4.6 (d/e)	4.7 (d/e)
		8	5 (d/e)	5.5 (d/e)	5.6 (d/e)	5.6 (d/e)	5.6 (d/e)	6 (d/e)
		12	5.7 (d/e)	6.7 (d/e)	7.2 (d/e)	7.2 (d/e)	7.2 (d/e)	8 (d/e)

Formulas to derive multipliers:
(d/e) = payout ratio

$$M = \left[\sum_{t=1}^{p}\frac{(1+g_1)^t}{(1+k)^t} + \sum_{t=p+1}^{\infty}\frac{(1+g_1)(1+g_2)^{t-p}}{(1+k)^t}\right]\left(\frac{d}{e}\right)$$

$$M = \frac{(d/e)(1+g)}{(k-g)}$$

analyst must rely on experience and judgment in selecting a capitalization rate if the discrepancies cannot be attributed to errors in the risk forecasts. Usually two estimates of the appropriate capitalization rate will not diverge very much, and the analyst can simply use their average as a capitalization rate. However, if a significant divergence is present that cannot be rationalized, the analyst may have found a security whose price is significantly out of equilibrium. Such disequilibrium situations can result in considerable profits for an investor who is willing to assume the risks associated with such uncertainties.

785–796. (4) M. E. Blume, ''On the Assessment of Risk,'' *Journal of Finance*, March 1971, vol. 26, pp. 1–10. (5) Dimson, ''Risk Measurement When Shares Are Subject to Infrequent Trading,'' *Journal of Financial Economics*, June 1979, vol. 7, pp. 197–226. (6) E. Dimson and P. R. Marsh, ''The Stability of UK Risk Measures and the Problem of Thin Trading,'' *Journal of Finance*, forthcoming. (7) A. A. Eubank, Jr., and J. K. Zumwalt, ''An Analysis of the Forecast Error Impact of Alternative Beta Adjustment Techniques and Risk Classes,'' *Journal of Finance*, June 1979, vol. 34, pp. 761–776. (8) L. Fisher and J. Kamin, ''Good Betas and Bad Betas,'' unpublished paper, Center for Research into Security Prices, University of Chicago, November 1971. (9) N. Jacob, ''The Measurement of Systematic Risk for Securities and Portfolios: Some Empirical Results,'' *Journal of Financial and Quantitative Analysis*, March 1971, vol. 6, pp. 815–834. (10) R. C. Klemkosky and J. D. Martin, ''The Adjustment of Beta Forecasts,'' *Journal of Finance*, September 1975, vol. 30, pp. 1123–1128. (11) S. J. Kon and W. P. Lau, ''Specification Tests for Portfolio Regression Parameter Stationarity and the Implications for Empirical Research,'' *Journal of Finance*, May 1979, vol. 34, pp. 451–465. (12) M. Scholes and J. Williams, ''Estimating Betas from Nonsynchronous Data,'' *Journal of Financial Economics*, December 1977, vol. 5, pp. 309–328. (13) W. F. Sharpe, ''The Capital Asset Pricing Model: *under Uncertainty* (New York: Academic Press, 1977). (14) W. F. Sharpe and G. M. Cooper, ''Risk-Return Classes of New York Stock Exchange Stocks, 1931–1967,'' *Financial Analysts Journal*, March–April 1972, vol. 28, pp. 46–54. (15) O. A. Vasicek, ''A Note on Using Cross-Sectional Information in Bayesian Estimation of Security Betas,'' *Journal of Finance*, December 1973, vol. 28, pp. 1233–1239. The following studies discuss the use of accounting data to estimate risk: (16) W. Beaver, P. Kettler, and M. Scholes, ''The Association between Market-Determined and Accounting-Determined Risk Measures,'' *Accounting Review*, October 1970, vol. 45, pp. 654–682. (17) W. Beaver and J. Manegold, ''The Association between Market-Determined and Accounting-Determined Measures of Systematic Risk: Some Further Evidence,'' *Journal of Financial and Quantitative Analysis*, June 1975, vol. 10, pp. 231–284. (18) G. Foster, *Financial Statement Analysis* (Englewood Cliffs, N.J: Prentice-Hall, 1978). (19) N. J. Gonedes, ''Evidence on the Information Content of Accounting Numbers: Accounting-Based and Market-Based Estimates of Systematic Risk,'' *Journal of Financial and Quantitative Analysis*, June 1973, vol. 8, pp. 407–444. (20) B. Rosenberg, ''Extra Market Components of Covariance among Security Prices,'' *Journal of Financial and Quantitative Analysis*, March 1974, vol. 9, pp. 263–294. (21) B. Rosenberg and J. Guy, ''Beta and Investment Fundamentals,'' *Financial Analysts Journal*, May–June 1976, vol. 32, pp. 60–72, and July–August 1976, vol. 32, pp. 62–70. (22) B. Rosenberg and W. McKibben, ''The Prediction of Systematic and Specific Risk in Common Stocks,'' *Journal of Financial and Quantitative Analysis*, March 1973, vol. 8, pp. 312–334. Roll's paper contains a theoretical discussion of the importance of choosing the appropriate market measure: (23) R. Roll, ''A Critique of the Asset Pricing Theory's Tests: Part 1: On Past and Potential Testability of the Theory,'' *Journal of Financial Economics*, March 1977, vol. 4, pp. 129–176. (24) D. Fowler, H. Rorke, and V. Jog, ''Heteroscedasticity, R^2 and Thin Trading on the Toronto Stock Exchange,'' *Journal of Finance*, vol. 34, no. 5, December 1979, pp. 1201–1210. (25)V. M. Jog, and A. L. Riding, ''Some Canadian Findings Regarding Infrequent Trading and Instability in the Single Factor Market Model,'' *Journal of Business Finance and Accounting*, 13 (1), Spring 1986, pp. 125–135.

For ABC Company (the same hypothetical firm), the capital asset pricing model (CAPM) in Fig. 15-3 indicated a capitalization rate of 10 percent.[6] If no dividend growth is expected for ABC, the appropriate earnings multiplier from Table 15-3 is ten times the payout ratio d/e. The price-earnings ratio was derived by finding the present value of unity each year to infinity and multiplying this value by the payout ratio, as shown in Eq. (15-4a).

$$\text{Zero-growth earnings multiplier} = \sum_{t=1}^{\infty} \frac{1}{(1 + \text{capitalization rate})^t} \frac{d_1}{e} \qquad (15\text{-}4a)$$

$$= \frac{d_1/e}{\text{capitalization rate}} \qquad (15\text{-}4b)$$

Equation (15-4b) is a simplified but equivalent version of Eq. (15-4a).

Assume that ABC's normalized earnings per share are currently $4 per year and that its average payout rate is 50 percent of earnings. Applying the earnings multiplier of $(1/.1 =)$ 10 times to these earnings implies that the intrinsic value of ABC is about $(10 \times \$4 \times .5 =)$ $20 per share.

Of course, there are numerous places where errors may creep into estimates of normalized earnings, the dividend payout ratio, the capitalization rate, and the dividend growth rate. Therefore, it is not certain that the intrinsic value is exactly $20 per share. It is possible that an error of plus or minus 10 percent, which is the range from $18 to $22, could occur in a carefully prepared analysis of a mature company. Therefore, if the stock were selling at $15, it would seem to be underpriced and therefore a good buy. However, if it were selling at $18.50 or $21.75, it might be correctly priced and thus not as interesting.

Estimating Intrinsic Value with Perpetual Earnings Growth   If it is assumed that ABC's earnings are currently $4 per share but will grow with cash dividends forever at, say, 3 percent per year, the intrinsic value estimate will be quite different from what it was with zero growth. Table 15-3 shows that for a capitalization rate of 10 percent and a growth rate of 3 percent, the correct multiplier is 14.7 times d/e. This multiplier is derived by finding the present value (using a capitalization rate of $k = .1 = 10$ percent) of a stream of numbers starting at unity and growing at a rate of $g = 3$ percent per year into infinity. Equation (15-5a) at the top of page 373 shows the mathematical model representing these computations. Equation (15-5b) is equivalent to Eq. (15-5a). Note that Eq. (15-5b) is also equal to Eq. (15-4b) when the earnings growth rate is zero.

For beginning earnings of $4 per share, a perpetual growth rate of 3 percent, and a cash dividend payout rate of one-half (that is, $d/e = .5$), the intrinsic value estimate is $(14.7 \times \$4 \times .5)$ for the intrinsic value to be in the range from $(\$29.40 \pm 10$ percent $=)$ $32.34 to $26.46.

---

6 The theoretical capital asset pricing model (CAPM) is defined as follows: $E(r_i) = R + [E(r_m) - R]b_i$. It is assumed in Fig. 15-3 that $R = .05 = 5.0$ percent and $E(r_m) = .1 = 10.0$ percent and thus the CAPM assumes the specific form $E(r_i) = .05 + (.1 - .05)b_i$. See Chap. 10 for details about the CAPM.

$$\text{Earnings multiplier for perpetual growth} = \sum_{t=1}^{\infty} \frac{(1 + \text{earnings growth rate})^t}{(1 + \text{capitalization rate})^t} \frac{d_1}{e} \qquad (15\text{-}5a)$$

$$= \frac{d_1/e}{(\text{capitalization rate} - \text{growth rate})} \qquad (15\text{-}5b)$$

$$= \frac{d_1/e}{k - g}$$

Estimating Intrinsic Value with Temporary Growth It is not likely that a well-managed firm's growth will remain zero, nor is it likely that a firm can mainain its dividend growth at a high level forever. Therefore, suppose ABC's dividends are expected to grow at 3 percent for five years and then level off. In this case, Table 15-4 indicates that the appropriate price-earnings multiplier is 11.3 times d/e. This implies that a most likely estimate of the intrinsic value is (.5 × 11.3 × $4 =) $22.60. But the intrinsic value could range from ($22.60 ± 10 percent =) $20.34 to $24.86, allowing the 10 percent margin for error.

As seen above, the intrinsic value of ABC is highly dependent on its dividend growth. Zero growth implies ABC is worth $20 per share, while perpetual growth at 3 percent implies a value of $29.40. Between these two extremes a value of $22.60 is implied if dividends grow at 3 percent for five years and then level off and have zero growth thereafter.[7]

The preceding examples demonstrated the effect that the size and duration of the growth rate in dividends can have on the earnings multiplier.[8] The effects of the dividend payout ratio are more direct than the effect of growth rate and thus easier to see. The theoretical analysis that led up to the values shown in Table 15-3 indicates that, if other things remain constant, reducing a corporation's dividend payout cuts its multiplier and thus its intrinsic value proportionately. The important question related to the payout ratio is how to evaluate it. That is, since corporations' dividends per share are a different percentage of their earnings per share practically every quarter, what is the best estimate of a firm's payout ratio? A glance at the right-hand column of Table 15-1, for example, shows how Domtar's payout ratio fluctuated widely from 1978 to 1984. Most corporations' payout ratios fluctuate more than this because the firms endeavour to maintain undiminished cash dividends while their earnings fluctuate violently at times. And when a corporation incurs a loss (that is, negative earnings per share), its payout ratio is simply undefined for that period. Stated differently, negative payout ratios have no rational economic interpretation.

15-3.3 The Payout Ratio and the Multiplier

---

7 Tables of price-earnings ratios computed under numerous growth rates and discount rates are available in Joe Lavely and Paul E. Ruckman, *Simultaneous Compounding and Discounting* (Lexington, Mass., Lexington Books, 1979).

8 Robert A. Haugen and Dean W. Wichern, ''The Elasticity of Financial Assets,'' *Journal of Finance*, September 1974, pp. 1229–1240. C. C. Holt, ''The Influence of Growth Duration on Share Prices,'' *Journal of Finance*, September 1962, pp. 465–475.

Estimating the payout ratio that a stable public utility like Bell Canada Enterprises seeks to maintain is simple. Table 15-5 shows that no losses were incurred and the payout ratio fluctuates symmetrically around 60 percent from year to year. For a more risky company, such as Domtar, which we examined in Table 15-1, it is necessary to estimate the corporation's *normalized earnings* per share averaged over the complete business cycle. Earnings analysis is investigated in Chap. 16, and the procedure for finding normalized earnings is explained there. After a share's normal earnings are estimated, all that need be done is divide normalized earnings per share into the corporation's regular cash dividend per share to find the payout for use in the determination of an earnings multiplier. Unfortunately, in a few cases this straightforward procedure is inappropriate.

TABLE 15-5　SELECTED FINANCIAL DATA FOR BELL CANADA ENTERPRISES COMMON STOCK ON A PER-SHARE BASIS

YEAR	RANGE OF MARKET PRICE, $ LOW	RANGE OF MARKET PRICE, $ HIGH	PER-SHARE EARNINGS, $ (OPERATING)	AVERAGE PRICE-EARNINGS RATIO, TIMES	PER-SHARE CASH DIVIDEND, $	DIVIDEND PAYOUT RATIO, %
1984	$29.00	$35.75	$4.03	8.03	$2.205	54.71%
1983	$22.13	$33.75	$3.46	8.08	$2.105	60.84%
1982	$16.63	$24.50	$3.11	6.61	$1.990	63.99%
1981	$16.88	$20.00	$2.97	6.21	$1.840	61.95%

Source: The Financial Post Survey Of Industrials, The Financial Post Corporation Service Group, 1985. MacLean Hunter Limited, 777 Bay Street, Toronto, Ontario.

Some large corporations have adopted the policy of reinvesting all corporate earnings in order to maximize their internally financed growth—that is, their dividend policy is to have a zero payout ratio. Although this payout ratio is logical if the corporations have profitable investment opportunities, it means Eq. (15-3a) cannot be used for those multipliers without some adjustments. Other pathological cases exist for which the model in Eq. (15-3a) also will not work. For example, what if a corporation keeps borrowing funds with which to pay cash dividends that bear no relation to its earnings? The once mighty Penn Central Railroad did so when it continued to pay cash dividends year after year until its $5 billion bankruptcy in 1970. For these unusual cases, the fundamental security analyst must use the corporation's past earnings multipliers as a starting point. Then past multipliers can be adjusted to derive earnings multipliers with which to estimate a share's intrinsic value. Past earnings multipliers are useful in estimating future earnings multipliers for those corporations that have unusual payout ratios, because the past multipliers implicitly contain the market's estimate of the payout. Even normal corporations with positive dividend payout policies and dividend payments that are highly positively correlated with earnings, as shown in Fig. 15-4, may be analyzed more effectively sometimes by making reference to historical earnings multipliers.

FIGURE 15-4 P/E multiples and industrial bond yields, 1970–1985.

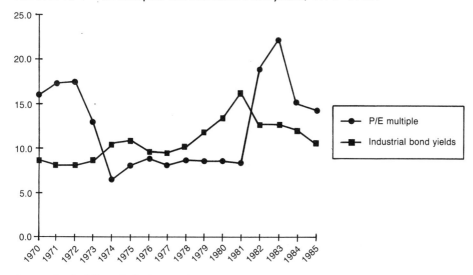

Source: Bank of Canada Review, various years.

In the estimation of a stock's intrinsic economic value, there are many subjective considerations. Care must be taken in weighting the different impacts of these subjective factors on d_t, e_t, g, and k so as not to double-count the effect of one change in d_t, e_t, g, or k unless it truly affects more than one of these variables. Unfortunately, many changes (for example, the addition or deletion of a product line, mergers, or a new competitor) can affect the expected values of d_t, e_t, g, and k simultaneously; this is the time when special care must be used to incorporate the change into all the affected variables properly without double counting or overcompensating. The firm's management and financial position are two of the more important factors that involve subjective evaluations which can affect d_t, e_t, g, and k.

15-3.4 Subjective Factors Affect Multipliers

Management Evaluation In forecasting the risk and earnings of a given corporation, fundamental analysts also consider management. The depth and experience of management; its age, education, and health; the existence of personalities that are bottlenecks in an organization; and management's ability to react effectively to changes — all affect the firm's risk and its future income. The research and development (R&D) program should also be considered. For example, if a company has new discoveries or advanced technology that will give it a competitive advantage in the future, the potential benefit tends to have a favourable effect on the forecasted intrinsic value of its securities by decreasing risk and/or increasing earnings growth. Section 9-5 (pages 192–196) discussed these and other problems involved in assessing the qualifications of a corporation's management under the heading Management Risk.

Assessing the ability of management and the value of ongoing research is difficult. Capable managers do not fit an easily recognizable stereotype, and the most trivial technological development can be extremely profitable. Making such evaluations is more of a personal skill than a science. The more widely educated, experienced, and sensitive the analyst is, the better he or she will be able to recognize significant factors and assess their value.

Analysis of Financial Ratios   In an effort to forecast earnings, dividends, and their multipliers, financial statements must be considered. Financial analysis can also shed light on how well-managed the firm is, what its growth areas are, and how risky its operations are. These factors affect the multipliers used to derive the intrinsic value estimates.[9] Financial analysis starts by adjusting the financial statements to overcome inconsistencies and "window-dressing" gimmicks. In Chap. 16 some cases are analyzed in which corporations misrepresent their annual income. These misleading accounting practices must be detected and corrected so that meaningful financial ratios can be calculated and evaluated.

Working capital ratios (such as the current ratio and inventory turnover ratio) are used to determine the firm's liquidity and to measure the efficiency of its current assets. Capitalization ratios (such as the debt of equity ratio) measure the proportions of borrowed funds and equity used to finance a company. A firm which is heavily in debt will have poor capitalization ratios, high fixed-interest expense, a high break-even point, less financial flexibility, and more volatile profit rates, and it will generally be a greater risk than an all-equity corporation. All these factors tend to lower the multipliers used in valuing the firm.

Income ratios (for example, the rate of return on assets and return on equity) measure the productivity of the money invested in the enterprise and are useful in detecting ineffective uses of capital. If the income ratios are all high, the firm is in the enviable position of having weak or nonexistent competition. On the other hand, low income ratios indicate low productivity of capital and a significant possibility that the firm might default on its debt contracts. Low income ratios will tend to lower the firm's multipliers.

---

9 Empirical evidence showing how firms' financial ratios affect their beta systematic risk coefficients are contained in Ben Amoako-Adu and Uri Ben-Zion, "Determinants of Risk of Stocks Traded on the Toronto Stock Exchange," *Administrative Sciences Association of Canada, Proceeding, 1983 Conference, Finance Division*, vol. 1, pp. 58–66; Ahmed Belkaoui, "Accounting Determinants of Systematic Risk in Canadian Common Stocks: A Multivariate Approach," *Accounting and Business Research*, Winter 1978, pp. 3–10; W. H. Beaver, P. Kettler, and M. Scholes, "The Association between Market-Determined and Accounting-Determined Risk Measures," *Accounting Review*, October 1970, vol. 45, pp. 654–682; D. J. Thompson II, "Sources of Systematic Risk in Common Stocks," *Journal of Business*, April 1976, vol. 49, no. 2, pp. 173–188. Essentially, these studies show that more risky firms have higher beta systematic risk coefficients. In turn, the betas determine the firms' cost of capital (that is, k) as shown in the security market line (SML), or capital asset pricing model (CAPM), of Fig. 15-3. The betas and the cost of capital are thus seen to be positive transformations of each other, and both move inversely with the present value (or intrinsic value) of a security. For a summary of how a firm's fundamental factors affect its beta (and thus its discount rate and intrinsic value) see J. C. Francis and S. J. Archer, *Portfolio Analysis*, 2d ed. (Englewood Cliffs; N.J.: Prentice-Hall, 1979), chap. 4, and app. A, chap. 4. For a popular book about analysis of financial ratios see L. A. Bernstein, *Financial Statement Analysis*, 3d ed. (Homewood, Ill: Irwin, 1983).

Standards of Comparison for Financial Ratios After financial ratios are calculated, they are of more value if they can be measured against some standard of comparison. The common standards against which financial ratios are measured are (1) the firm's own historical ratios (longitudinal analysis), (2) competitors' ratios (cross-sectional analysis), and (3) published industry average ratios. Competitors' ratios and industry ratios may be used to detect significant deviations from the normal way of doing business. A historical trend in a firm's ratios indicates that some change is occurring within the firm. Once these items of interest are detected, additional analysis will reveal the source of the deviation and whether the deviation is desirable.[10]

Industry ratios are published in Canada in Dun & Bradstreet, *Key Business Ratios* (eleven different ratios for over 150 different types of businesses), and Statistics Canada, *Corporation Financial Statistics, Industrial Corporations*, and *Manufacturing Industries of Canada*. Unfortunately, there is a long preparation time of the data and typically the ratios, when published, are lagged by about two years. U.S. company and industry ratios are published in *Moody's Industrial Manual*, Standard & Poor's *Corporation Records, Value Line Investment Survey*, and other sources.

Numerous studies of varying degrees of sophistication have sought to determine the major factors that determine stock prices. One study used a mathematical statistics process called *multivariate analysis*. This study of 63 firms listed on the NYSE found that, on the average, 31 percent of the variation in a stock's price could be attributed to changes in the level of the whole stock market; 12 percent to changes peculiar to each firm that were assumed to come from within the firm. These percentages varied from industry to industry. The average percentages for six industries are shown in Table 15-6. This study indicates the necessity for the fundamental analyst to look beyond the firm itself in estimating future earnings, dividends, and multipliers.

Figures 15-4 and 15-5 show how yields, P/E multiples and E/P ratios in Canada varied over recent years. The aggregated data concealed many radical

**15-3.5
Factors
Affecting
Intrinsic
Value**

---

10 Altman and Levalee have shown how to use financial ratios in Canada to foretell bankruptcy. Their failure classification model had an 80 percent accuracy level and, as they conclude ''. . . respectable accuracy for two statements prior to failure (over two years) but the accuracy falls off dramatically as the data become more remote.'' Edward I. Altman and Mario Y. Levallee, ''Business Failure Classification in Canada,'' *Journal of Business Administration*, vol. 12, no. 1, Fall 1980, pp. 147–161.

Altman's original work on bankruptcy predictions was conducted on U.S. data. See: Edward I. Altman, ''Corporate Bankruptcy Potential: Shareholder Returns and Share Valuation,'' *Journal of Finance*, December 1969. Also see Altman's ''Financial Ratios, Discriminant Analysis, and the Prediction of Corporate Bankruptcy,'' *Journal of Finance*, September 1968. For a more complete review of Altman's work see E. I. Altman, *Corporate Financial Distress* (New York: Wiley, 1983). For an investigation of stock price behaviour see S. Katz, S. Lillien, and B. Nelson, ''Stock Market Behavior Around Bankruptcy Model Distress and Recovery Predictions,'' *Financial Analysts Journal*, January–February 1985, pp. 70–74.

FIGURE 15-5   Stock and bond yields.

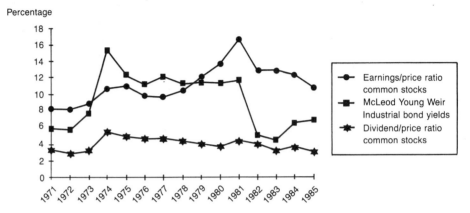

Source: Adapted from *Bank of Canada Review*, various years.

fluctuations that affected some firms' multipliers and earnings. Neverthe-less, these two figures show that earnings, dividends, and the reciprocals of their multipliers all vary considerably. Fundamental analysts must be able to forecast these and the other factors that introduce this volatility into the deter-minants of market value if they are to *time* their purchases and sales advantageously.

TABLE 15-6   **PROPORTION OF STOCK PRICE VARIATION DUE TO VARIOUS FACTORS, 1927 TO 1960**

INDUSTRY	FIRM	MARKET	INDUSTRY	INDUSTRY SUBGROUPS
Tobacco	.25	.09	.17	.49
Oil	.15	.37	.20	.28
Metals	.15	.46	.08	.31
Railroad	.19	.47	.08	.26
Utilities	.22	.23	.14	.41
Retail	.27	.23	.08	.42
Overall	.20	.31	.12	.37

Source: B. J. King, "Market and Industry Factors in Stock Price Behavior," *Journal of Business*, January 1966, pp. 139–190.

15-4   TIMING OF STOCK PURCHASES AND SALES

Some investors buy securities whose market prices are at or below the intrin-sic value they estimate and then hold these securities to obtain the long-run price appreciation and the dividends normally attained from common stocks. This is called a *buy-and-hold strategy*. It involves no attempt to "buy low and sell high" or otherwise outguess the market. Most life insurance companies, for example, follow a buy-and-hold strategy. They have millions of dollars of cash premiums flowing in every day, and they invest these funds as they come in and hardly ever liquidate. In contrast, some investors are *traders*; they try to outguess the rises and falls in the market so they will earn more profits by buying at cyclically low prices and selling at cyclically high prices. Traders hope to beat the buy-and-hold strategy.

Over the past years securities markets in Canada have periodically fallen precipitously, offering traders who can anticipate these turns ample opportunity to profit from timely security trading. Figure 9-6 showed the bull and bear markets that occurred in Canada over the past half century.

The evidence plainly shows that a trader who buys at market low points and sells at market high points can avoid capital losses and earn larger trading profits than a buy-and-sell strategy would earn. However, this is easier said than done. For example, studies of the performance of mutual funds that have the published objective of maximizing their investors' income by using "professional management" to trade actively reveal that they have been unable to earn a significantly higher rate of return than has been earned with a naive buy-and-hold strategy.[11] Mutual fund performance is examined in Chap. 26. Here the difficulties in forecasting the market's turns and the timing of security purchases and sales so as to earn trading profits are examined.

The purpose of this section is to discuss the tools a fundamental analyst who is an active trader can use to try to forecast the rises and falls in security markets. To predict the timing of security price movements, economic forecasts are utilized. Other approaches also are employed to anticipate the timing of rises and falls in security prices. A group of security analysts called *technical analysts* study charts of stock prices in order to predict the market's turns; they tend to ignore fundamental financial and economic factors. Technical analysis is explained in detail in Chap. 17. Of these two approaches to the timing problem, that of the fundamental analyst who studies the underlying economic forces is considerably more difficult because it requires formal training in macroeconomic forecasting. However, to utilize economic forecasts the security analyst need not be capable of actually preparing them.

15-4.1 Leading Indicators

It is important to be able to predict the course of the national economy because it affects corporate profits, investor optimism, and therefore security prices. Table 15-3 shows the manner in which gross national product (GNP), aggregate corporate profits before tax, and the TSE 300 Composite Index stocks average have varied together over time. These economic time series do not move exactly concurrently across time, however. Several economic variables rise and fall some months ahead of similar changes in the GNP; they are called *leading economic indicators*.

11 For Canadian evidence see A. L. Calvet and J. Lefoll, "The CAPM under Inflation and the Performance of Canadian Mutual Funds," *The Journal of Business Administration*, vol. 12, no. 1, Fall 1980, pp. 107–117. For U.S. evidence see William F. Sharpe, "Mutual Fund Performance," *Journal of Business*, January 1966, supplement, "Security Prices," pp. 119–138.

Statistics Canada prepares and publishes the Canadian Composite Leading Index, which contains ten leading indicators. These are

1. Average Work Week for Manufacturing
2. Residential Construction Index
3. The United States Composite Leading Index
4. New Orders for Durable Goods
5. Shipment to Inventory Ratio for Finished Goods
6. Price to Unit Labour Costs Ratio
7. Real Money Supply
8. Retail Trade in Furniture and Appliances
9. Retail Trade in New Motor Vehicles
10. TSE 300 Composite Index

Both the Royal Bank (Royal Bank Trendicator) and The Canadian Imperial Bank of Commerce (Commerce leading indicator) publish similar leading indexes.

15-4.2 Economic Forecasts

After viewing Table 15-3 and noting that the stock market *leads* the national economy, an investor may seem well advised not to bother to forecast the national economy but simply to follow those indicators that lead stock prices. This can be a valuable forecasting tool—especially in predicting bear markets. Home-building activity, durable goods orders, and the number of hours in the average workweek all usually turn down several months before a bear market begins. However, obtaining the most valuable information for making timing decisions in security trading requires a detailed sector forecast of the national economy that extends at least a year into the future.

Since the significant rises and falls (that is, the major bull and bear markets) in security prices have preceded the associated turns in the national economy by as much as eleven months in recent years, a forecast of the economy must extend more than eleven months into the future if it is to be useful in anticipating turns in the stock market. This prediction should thus extend at least one year into the future. Furthermore, the forecast should be broken down into a series of quarterly figures to give more insight into the timing of the expected changes.

A good economic forecast that discloses the timing of changes and provides some detail about inflation and other matters is useful in investment decisions. Much more detailed economic forecasts may be purchased from economic consultants. For example, some of the economic forecasting firms prepare ten-year economic projections showing the quarterly development of the Canadian economy broken down into intricate detail. These forecasts can usually predict the dollar amounts of economic activity in various sectors of the economy for a year into the future with only small errors. Such details are quite useful in pinpointing growth industries and other facts necessary in timing decisions for profitable investment. Table 15-7 (pages 382–383) lists the names and addresses of some of the better-known economic forecasting firms in the world. These firms may be hired for consulting work or some provide their periodic forecasts on a subscription basis.

Ultimately, the ability of an economic model to predict dollar quantities is not so important to the security analyst as the ability to foretell the *timing* and *direction* of the changes in the various rates of economic growth. Indications of shifts in the direction of the economy are most useful in anticipating similar changes in the stock market. This type of information allows portfolio managers to assume a defensive position when bear markets are foreseen and to assume an aggressive stance when bullish conditions are expected.[12]

Basis for Economic Forecasts   Economic forecasts that extend very far into the future and/or show very much detail within the national economy are always based upon a fairly detailed set of basic assumptions about the world situation and its impact on the fiscal and monetary policy of the nation. Assumptions about the particular industry in which a company is located and its competitors are also important to a security analyst who is estimating the impact of economic developments on a given industry or firm. Figure 15-6 shows the series of decisions that form the basis for any given forecast of the intrinsic value of a corporation's shares.

Since forecasting models rest squarely on assumptions about international, national, and industry conditions, a fundamental analyst trying to relate the effects of economic developments to security prices should take part in the formulation of these assumptions. This participation will ensure that factors such as large government contracts, labour relations, and technical development—all of which affect security prices—are considered. The economic forecasting services allow their customers to suggest their own assumptions on which to base a forecast (although an added fee may be charged).

Varying the Assumptions   Working with the economic forecasters allows the security analyst to ask the "what if" questions that are so important in the timing of investment decisions. For example, in the 1960s the Canadian government was considering a wide range of options for restructuring the federal income tax system. Each different assumption implied a different economic forecast and a different set of intrinsic values in Canadian securities markets. As shown in Fig. 15-6 (page 384), a wide array of intrinsic values are forecast for a given firm's share, depending upon the underlying assumptions about the world and the economy. Interaction between the security analyst and the economist will facilitate preparation of the best possible intrinsic value estimates. Multiple forecasts allow security traders to make immediate investment decisions as news is released because they will have estimates of the price implications of various possible economic developments.

In forecasting the times when any given security's price will rise above or fall below the intrinsic value that will prevail under normal market conditions, the fundamental analyst must ultimately estimate both (1) what each quarter's earnings per share will be and (2) what the earnings multipliers will be in each quarter.

**15-4.3
Crux of the
Timing
Question**

12 For an analysis of the ability of different security models to pick the best times to buy or sell see R. D. Arnott and W. A. Copeland, "The Business Cycle and Security Selection," *Financial Analysts Journal*, March–April 1985, pp. 26–33.

TABLE 15-7 A PARTIAL LISTING OF ECONOMETRIC SERVICE BUREAUS

COMPANY	CONTACT	MACRO FORECASTING	DATA ACCESS	CONSULTING	OTHER
1. Informetrica Limited P.O. Box 828, Station B Ottawa, Ontario Canada, K1P 5P9	Dr. Michael C. MCracken	Yes	Yes	Yes	Software application packages
2. A. Gary Shilling & Co. 111 Broadway New York, NY 10006 (212) 349-6000	Dr. Glenn C. Picou	Yes	No	Yes	Industry level analysis
3. Center for Economic Research Chapman College Orange, CA 92666	Dr. James L. Doti	Yes	Yes	Yes	
4. Chase Econometrics 150 Monument Road Bala Cynwyd, PA 19004 (215) 667-6000	Dr. Lawrence Chimerine	Yes	Yes	Yes	
5. Data Resources, Inc.* 29 Hartwell Ave. Lexington, MA 02173 (617) 816-0165	Mr. Geo. F. Brown, Jr.	Yes	Yes	Yes	
6. Economic Forecasting Georgia State University Atlanta, GA 30303 (404) 658-3282	Dr. Donald Ratajczak	Yes	No	Yes	Regional Analysis
7. Indiana University Bloomington, IN 47401	Dr. Eugene A. Brady	Yes	No	Yes	
8. Kent Econ. & Dev. Inst. Kent, Ohio 44242 (216) 672-2222	Dr. Vladimir Simunek	Yes	Yes	Yes	Special economic studies
9. Merrill Lynch Economics 165 Broadway New York, NY 10080 (212) 637-6211	Dr. Raymond Cosman	Yes	Yes	Yes	Special economic studies

Services Offered

10.	UCLA Business Forecasting Los Angeles, CA 91436 (213) 825-1623	Dr. Larry Kimbell	Yes	Yes	Yes	
11.	Wharton Econometric 3624 Science Center Philadelphia, PA 19104 (215) 386-9000	Mr. Petralia	Yes	Yes	Yes	
12.	Williams Trend Indicators 6 Devon Dr. Orangeburg, NY 10962 (914) 359-1129	Dr. Roger Williams	Yes	No	Yes	
13.	Centre for Economic Forecasting London Business School Sussex Place, Regents Park London, NW1 4SA England 01-262-5050	Dr. Bill Robinson	Yes	Yes	No	On-line access to large econometric model of the UK economy
14.	Henley Centre for Forecasting London, England 01-353-9961	Dr. Aleck Kellaway	Yes	Yes	Yes	Forecasting services & publications
15.	Phillips & Drew London, England 01-628-4444	Dr. Paul Neild	Yes	No	No	
16.	Institute of Economics Taipei, Taiwan Republic of China 115 782019	Dr. Paul K. C. Liu	No	Yes	Yes	
17.	Centre D'Observation Economique de la Chambre de Commerce et d'Industrie de Paris Paris, France 75008 561-99-00	Dr. Monsieru Devaud	Yes	Yes	No	
18.	Gama 2 Rue de Rouen Nanterre, France 92001 (1) 725-92-34	Dr. R. Courbis	Yes	No	Yes	Publishes quarterly global forecasts and annually global sectoral forecasts

Source: A. Migliaro and C. L. Jain, *An Executive's Guide to Econometric Forecasting* (Flushing, N.Y.: Graceway, 1983).
*Data Resources, Inc., is owned by McGraw-Hill.

FIGURE 15-6 The basic assumptions underlying economic forecasts have impact on intrinsic value estimates.

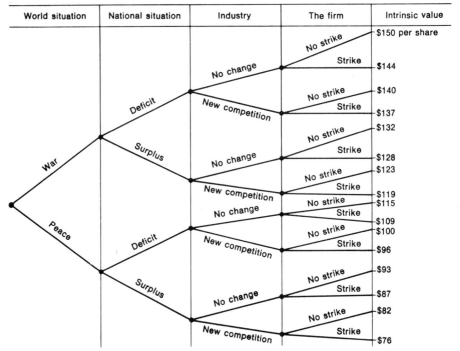

World situation	National situation	Industry	The firm	Intrinsic value

Forecasting Earnings Per Share Chapter 16 discusses the measurement of historical growth in a firm's earnings. Methods are suggested to adjust historical growth rates so they can be used to forecast earnings. The following basic relation is suggested for forecasting earnings:

$$e_t = (1 + g)^t e_0$$

where

e_t = earnings per share in period t

g = estimated earnings growth rate

This technique can be used to furnish one forecast of earnings per share. A second earnings forecast can be devised by using the economic forecast.[13]

---

13 Evidence exists that suggests that earnings per share fluctuate randomly. See J. Lintner and T. Glauber, "Higgledy Piggledy Growth in America," in J. Lorie and R. Bready (eds.) *Modern Developments in Investment Management*, 2d ed. (Hinsdale, Ill.: Dryden, 1978). Nevertheless, econometric models which rationalize a large proportion of earnings per share have been published. See J. C. Francis, "Analysis of Equity Returns: A Survey with Extensions," *Journal of Economics and Business*, Spring/Summer 1977, vol. 29, no. 3, pp. 181–192. Also, a different approach to forecasting a corporation's earnings is to use a simultaneous equation econometric model of the firm. See J. C. Francis and D. R. Rowell, "A Simultaneous Equation Model of the Firm for Financial Analysis and Planning," Spring 1978, *Financial Management*, pp. 29–44.

FIGURE 15-7   Sales-earnings per share regression for IBM useful in forecasting.

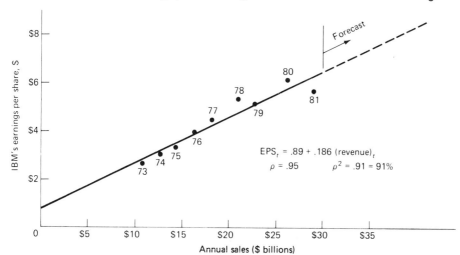

Detailed economic forecasts showing the quarter-by-quarter economic activity in the various industries comprising the national economy can be obtained. These industry sales forecasts can be broken down by company by using historical data on market shares and current information about new competitive developments. These sales forecasts can yield information about expected earnings.[14]

For example, the graph in Fig. 15-7 shows how earnings per share of IBM have varied with the firm's annual sales revenues over the nine years from 1973 to 1981. Note that an accurate sales forecast would have been able to explain 91 percent (that is, the correlation coefficient squared) of the variation in IBM's annual earnings per share. When stationary sales-earnings relationships exist, they can be used along with an economic forecast and sales projection to provide a second earnings forecast. Furthermore, information gained from interviews with the executives of a firm and its competitors can also be useful in forecasting earnings.

Forecasting Earnings Multipliers   The advance notice given by the leading economic indicators reveals that security prices have anticipated the economy from four to eleven months in Canada in recent years. This fact implies that an economic forecast for one year into the future can be expected to lead changes in the level of security prices from one to eight months. Since the time lag between changes in a one-year economic forecast and the associated

---

14 For an exploration of earnings per share forecasts and stock prices see E. H. Hawkins, S. C. Chamberlin, and W. E. Daniel, "Earnings Expectations and Security Prices," *Financial Analysts Journal*, September–October 1984, pp. 24–39. See also D. Givoly and J. Lakonishok, "The Quality of Analysts Forecasts of Earnings," *Financial Analysts Journal*, September–October 1984, pp. 40–48; E. J. Elton, M. J. Gruber, and M. N. Gultiken, "Professional Expectations: Accuracy and Diagnosis of Errors," *Journal of Financial and Quantitative Analysis*, September 1984, vol. 19, no. 4, pp. 351–364; N. Eckel, "An EPS Forecasting Model Utilizing Performance Expectations," *Financial Analysts Journal*, vol. 38, June 1982, pp. 68–77.

changes in security prices varies from four to eleven months, even the best economic forecasts cannot be expected to pinpoint the turn in the securities markets within much less than a three-month range. However, the economic forecast is still quite useful in indicating the direction of the market and in giving information about the extent of coming changes.

Forecasts of the market levels can be expressed most usefully for security analysis by stating them in terms of the average price-earnings ratio for the market. A study of past price-earnings ratios for some market average and the then-prevailing economic conditions will aid the fundamental analyst in converting the economic forecast into a forecast of the market's average earnings multiplier. Table 15-8 shows how the TSE 300 Composite Index earnings multipliers have varied in recent years.

After the analyst has forecast an average earnings multiplier, a scatter diagram such as the one shown in Fig. 15-8 can be used to convert this market

TABLE 15-8   P/E MULTIPLES AND THE TSE 300 COMPOSITE INDEX END OF YEAR CLOSING VALUES, 1956–1985

	P/E MULTIPLE	TSE 300 COMPOSITE INDEX
1956	15.80	564.97
1957	11.49	432.11
1958	15.96	547.72
1959	20.10	555.09
1960	16.48	544.74
1961	20.74	700.85
1962	17.65	628.99
1963	17.92	702.71
1964	20.50	853.53
1965	18.16	881.14
1966	14.59	789.51
1967	16.02	899.20
1968	18.63	1062.88
1969	16.25	1019.77
1970	15.37	947.54
1971	16.83	990.54
1972	17.79	1226.58
1973	12.95	1187.78
1974	6.58	835.42
1975	8.21	953.54
1976	9.01	1011.52
1977	8.24	1059.59
1978	8.87	1309.00
1979	8.72	1813.17
1980	8.81	2268.70
1981	8.57	1954.24
1982	19.12	1958.08
1983	22.41	2552.35
1984	15.24	2400.33
1985	14.54	2900.60

Source: Statistics Canada, Cansim Files, B0004237, B0004246. Reprinted with permission of the Minister of Supply and Services Canada.

FIGURE 15-8 IBM's price-earnings (P/E) ratio regressed on S&P 500 average price-earnings (P/E) ratio.

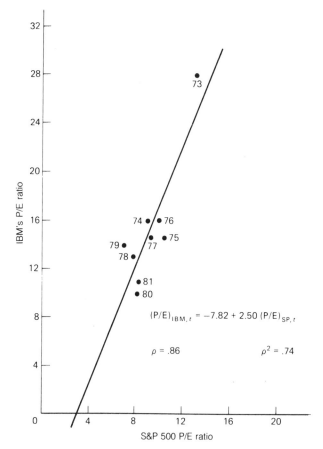

$$(P/E)_{IBM, t} = -7.82 + 2.50 \ (P/E)_{SP, t}$$

$$\rho = .86 \qquad \rho^2 = .74$$

forecast into earnings multipliers for individual securities. The price-earnings ratio may be viewed as an index of investor confidence. Since investors' confidence in all securities tends to rise and fall with the level of the market, useful relationships between the market's average earnings multiplier and individual securities earnings multipliers, such as IBM shows in Fig. 15-8, are not uncommon.[15] Note that 74 percent (that is, the correlation squared) of the variation in IBM's price-earnings ratio from 1973 to 1981 can be explained in terms of the Standard & Poor's 500 stocks average price-earnings ratio. Thus, a forecast of the market's average earnings multiplier has valuable implications for individual common stocks.

15 Refined estimates of the relationship between the price-earnings ratios of individual firms and the market averages (as well as a theoretical justification for their existence) may be found in J. C. Francis, "Analysis of Equity Returns: A Survey with Extensions," *Journal of Economics and Business*, Spring/Summer 1977, vol. 29, no. 3, pp. 181–192. This article is reprinted in *Readings in Investment*, edited by J. C. Francis, C. F. Lee, and D. E. Farrar (New York: McGraw-Hill, 1980).

**15-4.4
Conclusions
About Timing**

Because of the uncertainties involved in forecasting quarterly earnings per share, earnings growth rates, the risk of the firm, and the exact date when the market will begin expected changes in direction, it is difficult, if not impossible, to earn short-term trading profits that will exceed the returns from a buy-and-hold strategy after the forecasting expenses and commissions are deducted. To be more precise, it is usually not possible to earn trading profits over many trades by buying securities, holding them for less than six months, and selling them. Such short-term trading can yield a positive return. However, after the commissions are deducted, trading profits are almost always less than the return attainable with a buy-and-hold strategy based on fundamental analysis.

In Chap. 18 evidence is presented that suggests that short-term security price changes are unpredictable random movements — this is sometimes called the *random-walk theory* of security prices. Many securities salespersons and managers of ''go-go'' mutual funds disagree with this theory. However, their opinions are biased because of the fact that they derive their income from investors who seek short-term trading profits. In spite of the advertisements implying the contrary, few mutual funds earn a better rate of return than investors using a naive buy-and-hold strategy, as pointed out earlier.

For the long-run, say, for securities that are held over six months, forecasting security prices in order to make advantageously timed trades is easier and more profitable. After six months, market turns that were soundly forecast will usually come to pass, short-run random security price fluctuations will tend to average out to zero, and fundamental analysis will be profitable for those who are experienced professional fundamental security analysts. If these professional analysts are provided with good economic forecasts and the other information they need, they should be able to escape losses in bear markets and avoid the securities of corporations that go bankrupt. Thus, they should be able to earn returns on their portfolios in the long run that exceed the returns attainable from a naive (for example, selecting stocks with a dart) buy-and-hold strategy.

15-5 CONCLUSIONS ABOUT FUNDAMENTAL SECURITY ANALYSIS

As might be expected, it is not easy to find underpriced and overpriced securities. Professional fundamental analysts have usually forecasted changes in a corporation's income fairly accurately, and security prices have adjusted to the new intrinsic value before the latest income figures are announced to the public.

When significantly different earnings and dividends, which were *not* expected, are announced by a corporation, some analysts will reach buy or sell decisions immediately. By merely applying recent multipliers to the new income data and then comparing the intrinsic value estimates with the market price, it is possible to get some indication as to whether the security is priced correctly. This explains why security prices sometimes react noticeably to announcements of changed levels of income and/or dividends.[16]

Regardless of how sophisticated the techniques used, a complete, painstaking fundamental analysis, based on relevant facts, is a logical way to estimate the true value of a going concern. Understandably, fundamental analysis is the most widely used method of estimating security prices. Erroneous intrinsic value estimates can be attributed to several facts: (1) The analyst did not have all the relevant information. (2) The analyst simply did not do the necessary work thoroughly. (3) The market was in a temporary disequilibrium (for example, the election of the Parti Québécois in 1976 caused the stock market to drop temporarily, although fundamental values were unchanged). Hindsight is always better than foresight in these matters. Nevertheless, even under ideal conditions, fundamental analysis can suggest only a range of prices rather than a specific value.

QUESTIONS

1. "A fundamental analyst's estimate of intrinsic value is different from the present value of all income." Is this statement true, false, or uncertain? Explain.
2. Compare and contrast the earnings multiplier with the dividend multiplier. Why do they differ?
3. Does an increase in a firm's growth rate of earnings always mean an increase in its intrinsic value? Explain.
4. Why is the growth rate in dividends per share not a good measure of the firm's growth rate?
5. Can factors that are external to the firm, such as national economic conditions, affect the intrinsic value of a share of stock? Explain.
6. "An increase in a firm's liquidity ratios means that the firm is well-managed and safe. This will always increase its multipliers." Is this statement true, false, or uncertain? Explain.
7. Can fundamental analysis be used for quick, short-range value forecasts, or is it useful only for determining long-run equilibrium values? Explain.
8. Will accounting gimmicks (like accelerating depreciation) affect or distort the intrinsic-value estimates made by fundamental analysts?

16 P. Brown and R. Ball, "An Empirical Evaluation of Accounting Income Numbers," *Journal of Accounting Research*, Autumn 1968, pp. 159–178. P. C. Jain, "The Effect of Voluntary Selloff Announcements on Shareholder Wealth," *Journal of Finance*, March 1985, vol. 40, no. 1, pp. 209–223; J. D. Rosenfield, "Additional Evidence on the Relation between Divestiture Announcements and Shareholder Wealth," *Journal of Finance*, December 1984, vol. 39, no. 5, pp. 1437–1448; A. Kane, Y. K. Lee, and A. Marcus, "Earnings and Dividend Announcements: Is There a Corroboration Effect?" *Journal of Finance*, September 1984, vol. 39, no. 4, pp. 1091–1099; G. J. Alexander, P. G. Benson, and J. M. Kampmeyer, "Investigating the Valuation Effects of Announcements of Voluntary Corporate Selloffs," *Journal of Finance*, June 1984, vol. 39, no. 2, pp. 503–518.

9. An experienced fundamental security analyst claims that the intrinsic value estimating procedures used by members of the profession lead to realistic estimates of true value that are based on "all the facts" and realistic assumptions. Comment on this claim. *As close possible as we can if it still occur.*

10. The Blume Company is a small, growing manufacturer of lawn equipment that is planning to go public for the first time. Assume that Mr. Blume, the president of the firm, has hired you as a financial consultant to estimate the price per share at which stock should be sold. The Westerfield Corporation and the Pettit Corporation are also young lawn equipment manufacturers which have recently gone public and have similar product lines (they all even have the same accountant). Data on these three corporations are:

EARNINGS PER SHARE (EPS)	WESTERFIELD	PETTIT	BLUME'S TOTALS
Earnings per share 19 × 5	$ 5	$ 11	$1,000,000
Average EPS, 19 × 0 – 19 × 5	$ 5	$ 8	$ 780,000
Median market price, 19 × 5	$ 29	$ 145	?
Average price, 19 × 0 – 19 × 5	$ 27	$ 110	—
Dividends per share, 19 × 5	$ 3	$ 7.20	$ 500,000
Average dividends, 19 × 0 – 19 × 5	$280	$ 6.50	$ 390,000
Book value per share, 19 × 5	$ 81.23	$ 112.10	$ 131,500
Growth in EPS, 19 × 0 – 19 × 5	0	5%	6%
Debt-equity ratio, 19 × 5	9%	42%	45%
Current assets-current liabilities	3.1	1.9	2.0
Employees	180	90	80
Sales	$17,000,000	$9,800,000	$8,800,000

The sales, earnings, and stock prices of all lawn equipment manufacturers have followed rates of change in national income (that is, GNP) in the past few years. Historical data show that the two public firms have beta coefficients (of systematic risk) of about 1. The future for the lawn equipment industry is bright. Because of increased suburban living and rising affluence, it is expected that the market for lawn equipment will continue to expand. The economic outlook promises steady growth, and securities markets are normal. What data above will you ignore in pricing Blume's stock? If Blume issues one million shares, what price per share will you recommend?

11. The Archer corporation has a beta volatility coefficient (measuring its systematic risk) of 1, and as Fig. 15-3 leads us to expect, the market has been applying a $k = 10$ percent capitalization rate in valuing its earnings. Archer's normalized earnings of $2 per share are all paid out in cash dividends. Per-share earnings have been growing at 3 percent per annum for some time, and the current market price of $28.60 reflects this growth experience. However, because of a technological breakthrough, Archer's earnings are expected to grow at the increased rate of 6 percent per year for the foreseeable future. What effect do you think this technological innovation will have on Archer's market price per share when the news becomes public?

SELECTED REFERENCES

Brealey, R. A. *An Introduction to Risk and Return from Common Stocks*, 2d ed. Cambridge, Mass.: M.I.T., 1983. A readable, nonmathematical summary of various studies; chaps. 2 through 5 throw light on some issues relevant to fundamental analysis.

Chant, Peter. "Analyst's Forecasts of EPS." *Financial Research Foundation of Canada, Proceedings of the Fifth Conference*, Fall 1980, pp. 33–36. A discussion of the accuracy of analysts' earnings per share forecasts and the relationship between changes in the money supply, changes in the market, and future earnings per share behaviour of Canadian Companies.

Francis, Jack Clark. "Analysis of Equity Returns: A Survey with Extensions," *Journal of Economics and Business*, Spring/Summer 1977. Reprinted in J. C. Francis, C. F. Lee, and Donald E. Farrar, (eds.) *Readings in Investments*. New York: McGraw-Hill, 1980. Econometric analysis of earnings per share, price-earnings multipliers, and stock price changes reveals insights.

Graham, B., D. Dodd, and S. Cottle. *Security Analysis*. 4th ed. New York: McGraw-Hill, 1962. This nonmathematical book is used by most fundamental analysts; it should be read by anyone who aspires to be a fundamental analyst.

Malkiel, B. G. "The Valuation of Public Utility Equities," *The Bell Journal of Economics and Management Science*, 1970. A statistical test of the valuation model Eq. (15-3a).

Whitbeck, V., and M. Kisor. "A New Tool in Investment Decision Making." *Financial Analysts Journal*, May–June 1963. An easy-to-read empirical study of earnings per share and multipliers.

CHAPTER

16

Earnings Analysis

Chapter 8 explained that, in order to buy underpriced common stocks and sell overpriced stocks profitably, it is necessary to estimate the intrinsic economic *value* of the equity share and then compare the stock's price with its value. The present value model of Eq. (8-1) was introduced for this valuation work in Box 8-2 on page 163.

$$\text{Present value} = \sum_{t=1}^{\infty} \frac{\text{income}_t}{(1 + \text{discount rate})^t} \tag{8-1}$$

Chapter 8 went on to explain that, in order to use this model to value common stocks or other risky assets, one must answer two questions. First, what discount or capitalization rate should be used? The discussion of default risk in Secs. 9-2, 12-1, and 12-4 went into some detail answering this question. The second question is, how does the investor measure the income from common stocks, which, unlike bonds, do not clearly specify the stream of income payments in advance? Discussion of this income question is the subject of this chapter. The economist's concept of income is explained; then it is suggested that the concept of economic income is generally more suitable than reported accounting income for fundamental security analysis.

Economists define the *income of a firm* as the maximum amount that can be consumed by the owners of the firm in any period without decreasing their future consumption opportunities. This is more than a definition; it is an important concept[1] that financial analysts should keep in mind when they analyze income statements. The economist's definition of income is intuitively more appealing than the accountant's definition because it relates directly to the owner's real consumption. After all, what good is income that some accountant says you have if you cannot consume it?[2]

---

1 This concept of income is discussed in J. R. Hicks, *Value and Capital*, 2d ed. (New York: Oxford, 1965), chap. 14.

2 In addition to the accountants' definition of a firm's earnings and the economists' theory of income, a third income concept is employed by those economists who are macroeconomic model builders. For a capsule view of the differences between the accountants' earnings model and the macroeconomists' earnings concept, see G. Thomas Friedlob, ''How Economic Statisticians View Accounting Profits,'' *Journal of Accounting, Auditing and Finance*, Winter 1983, pp. 100–107.

The periodic income statements issued by a firm's accountants are the most highly visible and well-known source of income measurements. This chapter, therefore, examines the accountant's procedure for determining income. Accountants provide the basic figures an analyst typically uses when estimating a firm's economic income and intrinsic value.

16-1 THE ACCOUNTING INCOME STATEMENT

Table 16-1 outlines the essentials of the model underlying accountants income statements. Despite the model's seeming simplicity, in practice many questions arise concerning the definitions and measurements of the various items determining income. For decisions on these questions, the accounting profession can turn to several sources.

TABLE 16-1 MODEL OF ACCOUNTING INCOME STATEMENT

SALES	SALES
Less: Cost of goods sold	− COGS
Gross operating margin	GM
Less: Selling and administrative expenses and depreciation	− Op. Exp.
Net operating income (earnings before interest and taxes)	NOI (EBIT)
Less: Interest expense	− Int.
Taxable Income	T. Inc.
Less: Taxes	− Tax
Net Income	NI
Less: Dividends on preferred stock	− P. Div.
Net income for common equity	C. Inc.
Less: Dividends for common equity	− C. Div.
Retained earnings	Ret. E

In most cases, acceptable accounting procedures are determined by the general acceptance of the practicing accountants. As the phrase *general acceptance* readily suggests, more than one procedure may exist for reporting the same type of business transaction; that is, accounting principles are inexact. There are, however, limitations. The Canadian Institute of Chartered Accountants (CICA), through its Accounting Standards Committee, hands down opinions on which practices are acceptable and which are not. Often these opinions eliminate the less desirable (that is, the extreme or the completely ambiguous) alternatives while still allowing several accounting choices. The result is a narrowing of practices, but not the creation of uniform accounting. Thus, the same economic event can often legitimately be reported in several different ways.

The existing body of accounting practice has also been shaped by certain professional organizations, government agencies, and legislative acts. The most important institutions influencing accounting practices are the Canadian Securities Commission, the various provincial securities commissions, Revenue Canada-Taxation, the Canadian Institute of Chartered Accountants, the Society of Management Accountants of Canada, the Canadian Certified General Accountants Association, the Canadian Academic Accounting Association, the Securities and Exchange Commission (SEC), the American Institute of Certified Public Accountants (AICPA) of the United States,[3] and the International Federation of Accountants.

As of 1968, all Canadian accounting and auditing recommendations are contained in the *CICA Handbook*. The handbook sets out Canadian generally accepted accounting principles (GAAP) and is recognized as the legal and sole authority in Canada with respect to financial accounting standards and disclosure[4] as evidenced by its specific inclusion and identification in the major business and finance law statutes. For example, s.1. (3) of the Ontario Securities Act Regulations states that "where a recommendation has been made in the Handbook of the Canadian Institute of Chartered Accountants which is applicable in the circumstances, the terms 'generally accepted accounting principles,' 'auditor's report,' and 'generally accepted auditing standards' mean the principles, report, and standards, respectively, recommended in the Handbook." The Accounting Standards Committee (AcSC) of the CICA is responsible for the development of the recommendations contained in the handbook.

As of 1969, the CICA has required that any accounting practice that deviates from the handbook, must either be so indicated in the audit report of the accountant or disclosed in footnotes to the financial statement.[5] In addition to the handbook, the Steering Committee of the Accounting Standard's Committee publishes Guidelines that function much like the Interpretation Bulletins of Revenue Canada—Taxation. These Guidelines provide an interpretation of specific recommendations in the handbook. Revenue Canada-Taxation also limits the range of permissable accounting. If the Income Tax Act is silent on a particular matter (for example, the treatment of prepaid expenses), then the application of generally accepted accounting principles are deemed to apply.[6]

The securities commissions have also influenced accounting practices. The various Securities Acts require that companies which intend to offer securities to the public provide adequate disclosure so that the investing community can evaluate the investment merits of the issue. Furthermore, both the Securities Commissions and the Stock Exchanges require public companies to provide continuous and timely financial information to shareholders.[7]

Regulatory agencies establish accounting rules for the companies (like banks, trust companies, and public utilities) under their jurisdiction. These accounting rules are established so that the regulatory agency can determine the prices or rates that the company can charge its customers. In some cases,

---

3 U.S. accounting principles are more heavily codified than in Canada. Many U.S. principles are incorporated into Canadian GAAP without specific codification.

4 Donald E. Kieso, Jerry J. Weygandt, V. Bruce Irvine, and W. Harold Silvester "*Intermediate Accounting*," 2d Canadian ed., John Wiley & Sons Canada, 1986, p. 16. See also pages 12–17 for a detailed history of the development of accounting principles, practices, and procedures in Canada.

5 *CICA Handbook*, sections 1500.6 and 5500.20.

6 R. E. Beam, and S. N. Laiken, *Introduction to Federal Income Tax* (Don Mills, Ontario: CCH Canadian Limited, 1985–1986 edition), pp. 5 and 27; See also *Queen v. Metropolitan Properties Co. Ltd.*, 85 DTC 5128.

7 Chapter 4 provided a discussion of the financial disclosure requirements for public companies.

the accounting rules required may conflict with opinions promulgated by the CICA.

Persons unfamiliar with the complexity of accounting procedures understandably obtain the erroneous impression that the accounting income is a narrowly defined quantity. The neatly published financial statements in annual reports seem to imply that these statements are the last word and are not open to dispute. However, reference to an accounting textbook will reveal a multiplicity of generally accepted accounting procedures that may be used in many situations.

The following quotation opens the chapter entitled "Statement of Income and Retained Earnings" in a widely used intermediate accounting textbook. "The statement of income, or statement of earnings as it is frequently called, is the report that measures the success of enterprise operations for a given period of time. The business and investment community uses this report to measure investment value, credit worthiness, and income success, for instance. Whether this confidence is well-founded is a matter of conjecture, because derived income is at best a rough estimate, and great caution should be exercised not to give it more significance than it deserves."[8]

Although this quotation may come as a shock to neophyte accountants and fundamental analysts, experienced accountants and analysts have long recognized the vagaries in accountants' procedures for determining income.

The latitude of alternative, generally accepted procedures, which the accountant may follow in deriving a firm's income, is often not the cause of income reports by accountants, which differ significantly from the firm's economic income. The accountant needs some leeway in order to use a procedure that most clearly reports the true economic consequence of a business transaction. When accountants produce income statements that fundamental analysts find necessary to alter significantly in order to obtain income estimates the cause is usually (1) the accountant's use of an accounting procedure that is inappropriate for the relevant economic transaction and/or (2) pressure brought to bear on the accountant from top management to minimize the firm's income taxes or to "window dress" the corporation's financial statements. In order to explain most of the adjustments, the financial analyst may find it necessary to alter a firm's income statement; a numerical example is explained below.

16-2 CONTRAST OF INCOME STATEMENTS FROM IDENTICAL FIRMS

Table 16-2 shows income and expense statements for two companies that are identical in every way except for their accounting procedures. The statement on the left, for Firm B, tends to minimize taxable income. The income statement for Firm A, on the right, represents the economic income from both firms. The divergent accounting procedures followed in developing the

---

8 Donald E. Kieso, Jerry J. Weygandt, V. Bruce Irvine, and W. Harold Silvester, *"Intermediate Accounting,"* 2d Canadian ed. (John Wiley & Sons Canada, 1986), p. 145.

income statements for Firms A and B are legal, commonplace, and generally accepted by practising accountants. In essence, both income statements are correct on the basis of accounting practices, but only income statement A is "correct" in the sense that it provides a true picture of the economic results of the firm's transactions.

Firms A and B may be thought of as being two identical manufacturers whose identical sales are expected to remain constant in the future. The firms are assumed to be equally well managed, to have identical labour forces and identical assets, and to be carrying on identical research and development programs in search of cost reductions in their manufacturing process.

TABLE 16-2   TWO INCOME STATEMENTS FOR THE SAME YEAR

	COMPANY B, IN THOUSANDS OF DOLLARS		COMPANY A, IN THOUSANDS OF DOLLARS	KEY (SEE TEXT)
Sales revenue		$9,200	$11,000	
Less: Returns and allowances		−1,000	−1,000	
Net sales		8,200	10,000	(1)
Beginning Inventory	2,000		2,000	
Purchases and freight in	6,000		6,000	
Net purchases	8,000		8,000	
Less: Ending Inventory	−2,000		−3,000	(2)
Cost of goods sold		6,000	5,000	
Gross margin		2,200	5,000	
Operating expenses:	1,500		1,500	
Selling costs	500		300	(3)
Depreciation	100		20	(4)
Pension	200		50	(5)
Other costs	200		200	
Salaries	100		100	
Bonuses				
Total operating expenses		−2,600	−2,170	
Net operating expenses		(400)	2,830	
Less: Interest		− 100	− 100	
Pretax income (loss)		(500)	2,730	

Some firms prepare two different income statements, each statement being completely rational, legal in its own right, and compatible with the other. One income statement may be prepared for reporting purposes, and a second income statement may be kept confidential and used by management as a basis for decision making. Presumably, this second statement would be the better reflection of the firm's economic income. The two income statements A and B in Table 16-2 may alternatively be regarded, if so desired, as two different statements for the same firm instead of different statements for two identical firms.

The five items where statements A and B differ are keyed at the right margin of Table 16-2. These differences are explained below; they are a representative but far from exhaustive list of points where confusion and deception can enter into income measurements.

Where differences can arise:

Statement A includes in its sales item both cash sales and all current sales made on instalment contract. Both firms factor their accounts receivable as soon as they arise and thus realize the cash proceeds of the instalment contract sales immediately. But Company B does not recognize these sales until the customer's final cash payment is actually received and the factoring company has no potential bad debt claims against it. Both practices of instalment sales recognition are acceptable. However, the procedure shown in statement A is a truer reflection of the actual sales transaction and cashflow and should thus be used to obtain estimates of the firm's economic income. There are, however, some conditions that must be present before a cash-collection method may be used.

**16-2.1
Sales (1)**

Sales can be realized as early as the date the sales order is signed. Or, as with some long-term construction contracts, the sale may not be recognized until as late as the day the delivery is made; this may be years after the contract is signed. Between these extremes are many points in time when the accountant may choose to recognize the sales revenue in the financial statements.

In an attempt to improve current income, some firms have abused the revenue recognition principle. For example, real estate development corporations at one time reported the sale of land at the time of the sale even though the purchaser may have made only a small down payment. In the franchising business, a company that granted a franchise in exchange for a note rather than cash would report a sale in the current period for the total value of the transaction, a process called "front-end loading." In both instances, the collectibility of future payments from the purchaser raises questions about the appropriateness of recording the transaction as revenue in the current period.

According to the *CICA Handbook*, companies must now record transactions resulting in notes receivable at the fair market value instead of the face value of the note. In instances when the fair market value cannot be determined, the value of the note is taken as the present value of the future payments required by the issuer of the note. The discount rate is determined by the rate of interest that most appropriately reflects the credit rating of the issuer. Although this requirement reduces the value of the note in order to take into account the timing of cash receipt, it does not directly answer the question of when the sale should be recognized.

Statement A used the FIFO (*first in, first out*) method of inventory valuation while B used the LIFO (*last in, first out*) method. During periods of inflation, the FIFO method tends to result in higher reported profits.

**16-2.2
Inventory (2)**

Perhaps the easiest way to understand LIFO and FIFO is by an example. Imagine that one-ton steel ingots are the inventory items and that one ingot is always carried in inventory. Assume that, early in the accounting year represented in Table 16-2, the cost of ingots rose from $2,000 apiece to $3,000. The inventory is valued at cost, and the beginning inventory value of the one-ingot inventory is assumed to be $2,000 whether LIFO or FIFO is used. This value is shown in Tables 16-2 and 16-3.

If FIFO had been used, the ending inventory (of one ingot purchased for $3,000) would be valued at $3,000. This means that the cost of goods sold in Table 16-3 would be $5,000 if FIFO had been employed instead of LIFO.

TABLE 16-3   LIFO DURING INFLATION (FIRM B)

	INVENTORY VALUE
Beginning inventory (1 ingot at $2,000)	$2,000
Plus: purchases (2 ingots at $3,000 each)	6,000
Cost of goods available for sale	$8,000
Less: Ending inventory (1 ingot at $2,000)	−2,000 (undervalued)
Cost of goods sold	$6,000 (*overvalued*)

Some consideration of these methods reveals that FIFO incorporates inventory capital gains or losses into regular income, LIFO does not. Thus, the FIFO method often causes profit to be more volatile than the LIFO method. FIFO is assumed to be the most realistic (although least advantageous for tax purposes)[9] method of inventory valuation in this case for two main reasons: first, most manufacturers usually sell the oldest items in their inventories first. Second, profits and losses on the inventory are reflected in reported income as they occur.

Not only does the use of LIFO versus FIFO have different effects on income, but switching from one of these inventory valuation techniques to the other can result in some spectacular changes. Chrysler Corporation's 1970 income statement provides a good example of what switching from LIFO to FIFO can do to reported earnings.

**16-2.3
Depreciation
(3)**

Assuming that no new technology or unusually heavy use is likely to depreciate the value of the assets used by Firms A and B before they are worn out, the straight-line depreciation used by Firm A is more honest than the accelerated sum-of-the-digits depreciation procedure employed by Firm B.

Several depreciation techniques may be used in the financial statements that a firm reports to the public.

1. Straight-line method[10]
2. Units of production method
3. Double declining balance method
4. Sum-of-the-digits method

The third and fourth methods are accelerated methods of depreciation. The second method may be used to accelerate depreciation during a period of rapid production. To understand how depreciation affects profit, a numerical example using the first and fourth methods will be used.

Imagine an asset that costs $1,000 with an expected life of $n = 3$ years. By use of the straight-line method, depreciation is $333.33 (= $1000/3 = cost/

---

9 LIFO is generally not acceptable by Revenue Canada as the basis for inventory valuation for tax purposes.

10 The straight-line method is apparently the most widely used in Canada. See Canadian Institute of Chartered Accountants, *Financial Reporting in Canada*, Toronto, 1983.

n) for each of the 3 years. By use of the sum-of-the-digits method, the annual depreciation starts large and diminishes each year, because a decreasing fraction is multiplied by the cost of the asset (a stable amount) to determine each year's depreciation. The numerator of this fraction decreases by 1 each year, as shown below. The numerator represents the number of years left in the life of the asset. The denominator of the fraction remains stable; it is the sum of the years in the life of the asset (for example, if the life expectancy of an asset were 3 years, the denominator would be $1 + 2 + 3 = 6$).

YEAR	DEPRECIATION AS FRACTION OF COST	SUM-OF-THE-DIGITS ANNUAL DOLLAR DEPRECIATION
1	$n \div \sum\limits_{i=1}^{n=3} i = \dfrac{3}{6}$	$500.00
2	$n - 1 \div \sum\limits_{i=1}^{n=3} i = \dfrac{2}{6}$	$333.33
3	$n - 2 \div \sum\limits_{i=1}^{n=3} i = \dfrac{\frac{1}{6}}{1.0}$	$166.66 1000.00

Accelerated depreciation increases depreciation costs in the early years of a new asset's life; it thereby decreases profit, income tax, and net accounting profit when the asset is new. Accelerated depreciation postpones taxes on income. Postponing taxes is like obtaining an interest-free loan from the federal government. The total depreciation expense is unchanged; only the timing is altered. As Table 16-2 shows, however, it can affect any particular year's reported accounting income significantly. Depreciation accounting for tax purposes is an altogether different story.

For tax-reporting purposes, the Income Tax Act requires firms to explicitly assign all depreciable assets (called depreciable capital property) into one of thirty-five different classes (based theoretically on the life of the asset)[11] and then to depreciate the assets using the narrowly defined accelerated depreciation techniques specified in the income tax regulations. A maximum depreciation rate is specified for each class, and in most cases the diminishing balance basis is used to determine the depreciation expense (which is called capital cost allowance).[12] The accountant has no leeway in tax accounting for depreciation. As a result of the tax treatment of depreciation, there are disparities, sometimes quite wide, between the depreciation techniques used for financial reporting and those employed for tax reporting. The difference

11 In practice, the allowable maximum capital cost allowance rate for a class often bears little relationship to the estimated economic life of the asset.

12 See Chap. 5 for a more detailed discussion of this and other tax accounting issues.

gives rise to deferred income tax entries in the published public financial reports. This dichotomy between financial and tax reporting makes it a more complex problem for the financial analyst to unravel in an effort to discern the firm's true economic income.

16-2.4 Pension Costs (4)

The two firms used different bases for determining pension costs. Firm B uses the normal cost for current employee services, plus 10 percent of any unpaid past employee service costs and/or 10 percent of any change in prior service costs. Firm A uses the normal cost plus the equivalent of an interest payment on any unfunded prior employee service costs.

Firm B's cost is based on the notion that pension payments are due to individual employees. Firm A's cost is based on the idea that payments are put into a pension fund from which all present and all future retired employees can draw payment. The former recognizes prior services' expense during the life span of individuals (short time span), whereas the latter spreads it over the life of the pension plan (perhaps to infinity). On the assumption that the firms have a youthful labour force with few workers near the age when they will draw retirement benefits, Firm A's treatment of pension costs is the more forthright approach.

There are several methods of determining pension costs. For pension funds established in advance of the actual payment of the employees' benefits, these costs must be estimated. Usually an actuary analyzes a company's contractual pension liabilities, its labour turnover, the age pattern of the employees, the rate of return that can be earned on the funds invested, and the mortality rates of the pensioners. Based on these data, future costs are estimated. The pension costs deducted in any given year thus depend on both the accounting procedure and the actuary's estimates.

Although companies are required to disclose in a footnote to the financial statements the pension accounting and funding policy, the pension charge for the year, and the unfunded vested liability of the company, two important pieces of information are not provided. First, the company need not disclose the amount of unfunded past service obligations. Such obligations can exceed the net worth of a company. Second, the rate of return that the actuary assumes is not disclosed. If an unrealistically high rate of return is assumed to be earned on funds now invested in the pension plan, pension costs can be reduced on the income statement. Yet the company may then have to make large cash contributions in the future to make up any deficiency.

16-2.5 Expensing versus Capitalizing (5)

There are many items that the accountant may either (1) write off as current expenses or (2) capitalize and then amortize over a period of years. For example, motion picture production costs, oil well exploration costs, advertising campaign costs, and many other items are simply not clearly either an expense or an asset purchase; they are matters of managerial discretion that the fundamental analyst should scrutinize.

Statements A and B differ because some outlays were expensed by B but capitalized by A. A fundamental analyst would consider that practice in comparing the two income statements. If the outlays appear to be expenses, the analyst will adjust A's income statement accordingly.

Table 16-2 summarizes the five differences in accounting procedures which were just discussed and shows the effects on accounting income. These tax differences make it difficult to recall that both firms were identical except for the accounting procedures used. Thus, analysts and shareholders can be misled by the accounting income reported by the company. However, both firms would have little difficulty getting a chartered accountant to certify that their respective income statements were within current "generally accepted accounting principles."

Some financial executives and accountants take advantage of the discretionary leeway in the accounting procedures that were highlighted in Table 16-2. These persons use the variables at their discretion to manipulate their firms' income to suit their current purposes.

Many investors do not have the time or training to make the proper adjustments in reported income figures. Therefore, the accounting profession should continue to narrow the areas left to the discretion of firms in reporting their own incomes.[13] The numerical example summarized in Table 16-2 dramatically pinpoints major ambiguities in accountants' procedures for estimating income. The point-by-point discussion keyed to this table suggests how fundamental security analysts could derive estimates of a firm's true economic income from accounting statements that are misleading.

In interpreting this example, the reader should bear at least two caveats in mind. First, the true economic income that a firm earns may be less than its reported income (as represented by statement B, for example) instead of larger. The example in Table 16-2 is a teaching device and is not intended to show all possible misrepresentations.

Second, the amount difference between the reported earnings in statements A and B is not meant to be suggestive of some average amount of misrepresentation. In the final analysis, it is difficult to specify the amount of misrepresentation present in any given set of accounting procedures, since different analysts may interpret a given situation in quite different ways. However, well-trained, astute, but unethical financial managers can manage their accountants' and other affairs to make their firms' reported earnings come out to be any number they wish within a wide range. Thus, analysts should not use firms' reported income figures without due caution.[14]

16-2.6 Effects on Accounting Income

13 One study suggests that financial statements can be meticulously examined for the quality of corporate earnings in order to help increase the likelihood of avoiding stocks that will underperform the market. See Frank J. Fabozzi, "Quality of Earnings: A Test of Market Efficiency," *Journal of Portfolio Management*, Fall 1978, pp. 53–56.

14 There is a body of academic thought called the *efficient markets theory* that argues that the market prices of securities reflect all available public information; this thinking is explained in detail in Chap. 18. According to the efficient markets theory, it does not matter whether a firm accounts for its income using method A or B in the example above, because financial analysts will see through these accounting gimmicks and ferret out the underlying economic truth. As a result, the price of the stock should be the same, whether method A or method B is used. An experienced CPA argues against the efficient markets theory by providing salient contrary examples, see Arthur R. Wyatt, "Efficient Market Theory: Its Impact on Accounting," *Journal of Accountancy*, February 1983, pp. 56–65.

After a financial analyst has ferreted out and resolved the various ambiguities that may creep into a firm's income and expense statement, the income analysis work is not finished. The financial analyst should go on to examine the firm's income as it is reported on a per-share basis.

16-3   REPORTING EARNINGS PER SHARE

Investors should be concerned with earnings per share when they are estimating the value of the share. This figure measures the dollar amount of net income earned on a share of common stock during the reporting period.[15] If a company has convertible securities, warrants, stock options, or other contracts that permit the number of shares of common stock outstanding to be increased in future periods, more than one measure of earnings per share may be reported. Moreover, income or losses caused by extraordinary events will result in additional earnings per share measures being reported. The alternative measures of earnings per share[16] are discussed below.

**16-3.1
Potential
Dilution of
Earnings per
Share**

Although the total earnings of a company may increase over time, analysts are aware that an increase in the number of shares of common stock outstanding may *dilute* earnings per share. An increase in the outstanding common stock can occur because management elects to sell more shares or because of the existence of contracts which permit investors to purchase common stock from the company. Examples of such contracts are convertible bonds, convertible preferred stock, and options or warrants to purchase common stock.

If the potential dilution owing to the existence of convertible security contracts results in a nonmaterial decline in earnings per share, the potential dilution need not be reported. Only a single presentation of earnings per share need be made. For companies in which the impact of earnings per share is material, earnings per share will be presented two ways. First, basic earnings per share are shown using the simple calculation shown below as Eq. (16-1). Second, the maximum potential dilution of earnings per share must be reported in a footnote and cross-referenced to the income statement. This measure is termed *fully diluted earnings per share*. The calculation requires adjustments to both the numerator and denominator of Eq. (16-1). The accountant or analyst[17] should assume that all convertible securities are

---

15 Technically speaking, earnings per share on the common stock is net income after taxes, either before or after extraordinary items, less preferred stock dividend payments divided by the total number of common shares, or the weighted average number of shares of common stock outstanding. To compute the weighted average number of shares outstanding, the weights are determined by the length of time the shares are oustanding. For example, if there were 1.2 million shares outstanding for the first 8 months of the reporting year and 1.5 million shares in the last 4 months, then the weighted average number of shares is 1.3 million, determined as follows: (1.2 million shares × 8/12) + (1.5 million shares × 4/12) = 1.3 million shares.

16 When additional common shares have been issued within the year, the CICA recommends that the basic earnings per share figure be calculated on a weighted average of common shares oustanding. See *CICA Handbook*, s. 3500.20.

17 The method selected by the analyst need not necessarily conform to generally accepted accounting principles as set out in the CICA handbook.

actually exercised and then determine the new number of common shares that will then be outstanding. The firm's earnings must be adjusted to reflect the firm's reduced before-tax interest payment, if any (from exercise of convertible bonds) and the income earned, at some appropriate rate, such as the firm's before-tax cost of capital on the amounts received from the exercise of warrants, rights, or any other options that have exercise or striking prices. Eq. (16-2) shows the calculation of fully diluted earnings per share.[18]

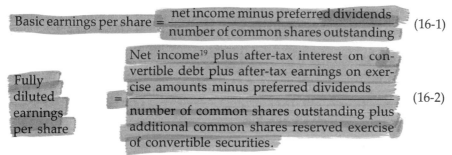

$$\text{Basic earnings per share} = \frac{\text{net income minus preferred dividends}}{\text{number of common shares outstanding}} \quad (16\text{-}1)$$

$$\text{Fully diluted earnings per share} = \frac{\text{Net income}^{19} \text{ plus after-tax interest on convertible debt plus after-tax earnings on exercise amounts minus preferred dividends}}{\text{number of common shares outstanding plus additional common shares reserved exercise of convertible securities.}} \quad (16\text{-}2)$$

Analysts attempt to estimate the future ''normal'' economic income of the companies they investigate. However, certain events may distort this ''normal'' economic income. For example, suppose a company takes a considerable loss by closing down an unprofitable division or wins a legal case in which a substantial award is received. How should the event be recorded?

16-3.2 Extraordinary Gains and Losses

Accountants have debated to treat extraordinary items on the income statement. On the one hand, some accountants took the view that extraordinary items should be reported on the income statement for the current period. The opposing view was that extraordinary items would distort income and hence should simply be charged or credited directly to retained earnings. In 1969, the controversy was virtually ended with the inclusion of consistent treatment for extraordinary items in the CICA Handbook.[20] The opinion requires that extraordinary items be reported separately in the income statement, net of taxes. The exception to this reporting rule was prior period adjustments, which the handbook[21] defines as

those material adjustments which (a) can be specifically identified with and directly related to the business activities of particular prior periods, and (b) are not attributable to economic events occurring subsequent to the date of the financial statements for the prior period, and (c) depend primarily on determinations by persons other than management, and (d) were not susceptible to reasonable estimation prior to such determination. Such adjustments are rare in modern financial accounting.

---

18 A study of the impact on financial statement users of the requirement in APB Opinion calling for reporting of fully diluted earnings per share indicates that investors do react to information on potential dilution. See Steven J. Rice, ''The Information Content of Fully Diluted Earnings per Share,'' *The Accounting Review*, April 1978, vol. LIII, no. 2, pp. 429–38.

19 Net income can be computed either before or after extraordinary items. If, paradoxically, there is a recurring nature to the extraordinary items, then the latter basis should be used. The most important principle for the analyst is consistency. The method adopted should be employed for both longitudinal and cross-sectional analysis.

20 See *CICA Handbook* s. 3480.

21 See *CICA Handbook* s. 3600, which is almost identical to the US APB Opinion 9, paragraph 23.

Examples of prior period adjustments are substantial settlements on lawsuits and adjustments or settlements of income taxes. Stringent requirements for an item to be classified as ''extraordinary'' are set out in the CICA Handbook. The opinion requires that the item be both unusual in nature and not expected to recur in the foreseeable future.[22] Two examples of extraordinary items are losses resulting from a major casualty, such as a flood, and losses resulting from an expropriation of business assets from foreign operations. Three examples of transactions or events that are not included as extraordinary items are the write-down of inventory, gains or losses because of foreign exchange fluctuations, and adjustments arising from the changes in the estimated useful life of fixed assets.

16-4 INFLATION AND EARNINGS

One major criticism of published financial statements in recent years is that they do not recognize the impact of inflation. Because profits are eroded as a result of inflation, the ability of a firm to maintain its operating capacity in the future is reduced. This occurs for two reasons: first, the profits retained in the corporation will have less purchasing power for replacing capital equipment; second, fewer dollars will be retained, since dividends and taxes are based on reported profits rather than on profits adjusted for inflation.

Two approaches have been suggested for adjusting for the impact of inflation on financial statements: general price-level accounting (GPLA) and current value accounting (CVA). The former deals with changes in the general price level; the latter adjusts for changes in individual items. The two approaches should be considered not as alternatives but rather as complementary responses to independent questions.[23] The U.S. history on the subject is quite revealing. In 1969, the Accounting Principles Board recommended that supplementary financial statements using GPLA be voluntarily presented by companies.[24] The motion was later dropped because few companies responded to the request. The Financial Accounting Standards Board, in December 1974, issued an exposure draft of a proposal, ''Financial Reporting in Units of General Purchasing Power,'' which would require that financial statements be disclosed on a general price-level adjusted basis.

Sidney Davidson and Roman Weil have estimated income by using general price-level accounting for thirty Dow Jones companies and a selected sample of other large companies for the years 1973 and 1974.[25] Their findings indicate that the effects of general price-level restatement differ significantly among

22 See *CICA Handbook* s. 3480.05.

23 Paul Rosenfield, ''The Confusion between General Price Level Restatement and Current Value Account,'' *Journal of Accountancy*, October 1972, pp. 63–68.

24 APB Accounting Series Release 3, ''Financial Statements Restated for General Price Level Changes,'' AICPA, June 1969.

25 Sidney Davidson and Roman L. Weil, ''Inflation Accounting: What Will General Price Level Adjusted Income Statements Show?'' *Financial Analysts Journal*, January–February 1975, pp. 27–31, 70–84. This article presents the results for 1973. The following article by the same authors presents the results for 1974: ''Impact of Inflation Accounting on 1974 Earnings,'' *Financial Analysts Journal*, September–October 1975, pp. 42–45.

firms. For almost all companies in the sample, adjusted income before monetary gain[26] was less than income as conventionally reported. However, when
monetary gains were included, the adjusted income was a high percentage
of reported income.

The SEC has supported the use of replacement cost accounting for financial reporting. Replacement cost accounting is one form of current value
accounting.[27] Beginning with the 1976 10-K forms,[28] the SEC has required
that certain registrants disclose current replacement cost for the cost of goods
sold and depreciation.[29] According to the SEC, replacement cost "is the lowest amount that would have to be paid in the normal course of business to
obtain a new asset of equivalent operating or productive capacity."

One major criticism of replacement cost accounting is that the SEC did
not provide specific guidelines for companies to estimate replacement cost.
Consequently, it is argued that it is difficult to compare companies because
of the alternative methods for measuring replacement cost. In a survey of
chief financial officers of the country's largest corporations conducted by the
National Association of Accountants to determine the usefulness of replacement cost data, many of the respondents indicated that they think that the
SEC requirement will mislead investors and further aggravate uncertainty
among the common stock analysts.[30] It was also felt that the requirement
would be too costly to implement.

A methodology for estimating replacement cost data and income was
developed by Angela Falkenstein and Roman Weil.[31] These two researchers

26 A monetary gain occurs when the company is, on balance, a net borrower and the price
level increases. There is a gain, since the company pays back creditors in cheaper dollars.
27 Davidson and Weil, in "Inflation Accounting: The SEC Proposal for Replacement Cost
Disclosures," *Financial Analysts Journal*, March–April 1976, p. 65, have described the essential
difference between general price-level restatement and replacement cost accounting as follows: "Replacement cost income measurements change in the timing, but not the ultimate
amounts, of income. Income over a sufficiently long period is still cash inflows less outflows.
General price-level-adjusted accounting changes the amounts, but not the timing, of reported
income."
28 The 10-K report is a detailed financial report that publicly held companies are required to
file with the SEC.
29 The requirement was set forth in Accounting Release 190, March 23, 1976. Companies that
have gross property and inventories which are valued at more than $100 million and which
represent more than 10 percent of total assets are required to disclose the necessary data.
30 Management Accounting Survey, "Corporations Doubt Usefulness of Replacement Cost
Data," *Management Account*, August 1976.
31 Angela Falkenstein and Roman Weil, "Replacement Cost Accounting: What Will Income
Statements Based on the SEC Disclosure Show?—Part 1," *Financial Analysts Journal*, January–
February 1977, pp. 46–56. Part II appears in the March–April issue. The estimates obtained
did not use the replacement cost increments provided in the 10-K forms, since prior to 1976
not much information was reported. Should the SEC continue to require that companies
provide replacement cost estimates, security analysts will need a methodology to construct
a time series of earnings based on replacement costs. A study of 1976 earnings by 17 companies in the pharmaceutical industry using the methodology developed by Falkenstein and
Weil and the replacement cost data provided in the 10-K forms found that for all firms the
income estimate using the reported replacement costs exceeded the income estimate using
the Falkenstein and Weil methodology. See also F. J. Fabozzi and Lawrence Shiffrin, "Replacement Cost Accounting: Application to the Pharmaceutical Industry," *Quarterly Review of Economics and Business*, Spring 1979, vol. 19, pp. 163–171.

applied their methodology to the financial statements of the thirty Dow Jones Industrials for 1975. They found that, for some companies that reported profits by using generally accepted accounting procedures (GAAP), losses occurred when replacement costs were used. Moreover, the payout ratio (that is, the percentage of earnings that is paid out in cash dividends) on a conventional basis was about 50 percent. However, when income was adjusted for replacement costs, the payout ratio was about 125 percent. A payout ratio in excess of 100 percent implies that new sources of funds will be required if the company is to operate at the same level it has operated at in the past; it is impossible for a firm to maintain a payout ratio in excess of 100 percent.

Realizing that a consensus could not be reached within the accounting profession about exactly how to report the effects of inflation on a business, the Financial Accounting Standards Board (FASB) issued its Statement 33 entitled "Financial Reporting and Changing Prices." This statement mandates inflation accounting disclosures in annual reports to shareholders of public corporations having either assets in excess of $1 billion or $125 million of inventories and gross properties. The following items are required to be reported under two fundamentally different measurement approaches.

CURRENT YEAR DATA	HISTORICAL COST-CONSTANT DOLLAR	CURRENT COST
1. Income from continuing operations	x	x
2. Purchasing power gain or loss on monetary assets and liabilities	x	x
3. Increases or decreases in the current costs of inventories and properties, net of inflation		x
4. Inventories and properties at year end		x
5. Five-year summary of selected data	x	x
6. Footnotes and narrative explanations	x	x

The historical cost-constant dollar accounting deals with general inflation (which must be measured by the Consumer Price Index, according to the FASB and the CICA in Canada in its modified approach); this technique is also popularly called price-level accounting. The current cost basis of accounting focuses on specific price changes for individual assets rather than on price changes caused by general inflation. Annual reports for years ending after December 24, 1980, are required to provide the new supplementary information about the effects of inflation according to FASB 33. The FASB expects to review Statement 33 and revise (and probably extend) it in the years ahead. That is, FASB 33 is viewed as merely a first step toward better reporting of price-level changes by the accounting profession.

In Canada, after a series of Exposure Drafts in the 1970s and a 1976 discussion paper, the Accounting Standards Committee's recommendations on price level accounting resulted in an experimental section added to the handbook in 1982.[32] Section 4510 requires that large, publicly held companies

---

32 It is interesting to note that this coincided with the zenith of inflation; price acceleration began to slow markedly shortly thereafter.

report supplemental information in their financial reports (in the form of statements, schedules, or notes) that provide current/constant dollar information for specific items. The following items are to be shown on a current cost basis:

Cost of goods sold; depreciation, depletion, and amortization of property, plant and equipment, changes in inventory, property, plant and equipment.

The following are shown on a constant dollar basis:

The purchasing power gain or loss on net monetary items, the amount of change during reporting periods in inventories, property, plant, and equipment attributed to general inflation.[33]

Thornton[34] examined the corporate response to section 4510 of the CICA Handbook and found that of the 380 firms that met the handbook criteria in 1983, only 73 complied, even partially. He concluded that Canadian firms disclose nonhistoric cost accounting data strictly on the basis of cost/benefit considerations, and that auditors play a role in influencing the disclosure.

16-5 HOW ACCOUNTING INCOME AFFECTS THE BALANCE SHEET

A *balance sheet* is a summary of account balances carried after the appropriate closing of the books. Income statements deal with *flows*, whereas the balance sheets deal with *stocks*. Of course, stocks are merely accumulations of flows. Thus, the vagaries that undermine the estimates of accounting income are cumulated in certain balance sheet items. Table 16-4 shows a model of the balance sheet.

TABLE 16-4 BALANCE SHEET MODEL

USES OF FUNDS	SOURCES OF FUNDS
Current assets	Current liabilities
Long-term assets	Long-term liabilities
Other assets	Net worth
Total assets	Total liabilities and N.W.

There is a great deal of debate in the accounting profession concerning the treatment of items in the balance sheet. The impact of inflation has made the balance sheet in its present form of questionable value to users of financial statements. Some of the reforms suggested or actually adopted for particular balance sheet items will be discussed below.

33 Donald E. Kieso, Jerry J. Weygandt, V. Bruce Irvine, and W. Harold Silvester,'' *Intermediate Accounting*,'' 2d Canadian ed. (John Wiley & Sons Canada, 1986), p. 1201. Chapter 25 provides considerable detail on the issues of price-level accounting in Canada.
34 Daniel B. Thornton, ''Current Cost Disclosures and Nondisclosers: Theory and Canadian Evidence,'' *Contemporary Accounting Research*, vol. 3, no. 1, Fall 1986, pp. 1–34.

**16-5.1
Asset
Reporting**

Two reforms have been suggested to improve the valuation of current assets on the balance sheet. For marketable securities it has been advocated that the value reported in the balance sheet should be the current market value. For inventories it has been proposed that all inventories should be valued at replacement cost (that is, what the company must pay in the current market to replenish inventories rather than the misleading inventory valuation methods presently permitted). Some worthwhile changes in the reporting of long-term assets are considered next.

Rather than reporting plant and equipment on the basis of historical cost less depreciation, it has been argued that this account should reflect how much it would take to replace the company's entire productive capacity. Adjustments to historical costs might be based on a variety of indexes. For land and natural resources, some accountants have suggested that these assets, since they are unique and cannot be reproduced, should be shown at net realizable value. This value represents current market price minus any future development, selling, or interest costs. There are other accountants who prefer a value based on the future expected cashflows from these assets, discounted at an appropriate interest rate. No professional consensus has emerged to specify exactly how to value the long-term assets.

**16-5.2
Business
Combination
Reporting**

A business *combination* can be accounted for by one of two accounting methods: purchase of assets or pooling of interest. Because of abuses that have resulted from permitting accountants leeway in selecting the method of handling business combinations for financial reporting, the CICA issued an opinion that sets forth the conditions under which each method must be used.[35] When the purchase-of-assets method is employed, the payment by one company of an excess amount for another company results in an intangible asset referred to as "goodwill." For reporting purposes, the company must amortize goodwill over its useful life or, at most, forty years.[36] However, some companies abuse the write-off requirement, with the result that goodwill is carried at an inflated value on the balance sheet and reported income is overstated.

**16-5.3
Reporting
Liabilities**

On the liabilities side of the balance sheet, there are three controversies facing accountants. The first surrounds the advantages that accrue to a company during an inflationary period when it has issued debt. Some accountants argue that since the company must repay the debt in the future in cheaper dollars (that is, dollars that have less purchasing power because of inflation), there is a gain to shareholders. This gain can be reflected in the financial statement by increasing net worth.

35 The purchase method is used wherever an "acquiring" company can be identified. In the (rare) instances that neither party can be identified as the acquiring company, the "pooling of interest" method may be used.
36 *CICA Handbook*, s. 1580.

A second controversy involves the treatment of deferred taxes. A deferred tax liability must be established when the company reports a lower income to Revenue Canada Taxation than to its shareholders. There is a question as to whether this amount should actually appear as a liability. Some argue that such an amount should be part of net worth if the company can continue to report lower earnings to Revenue Canada than it is reporting to shareholders. This can result if a company continually increases its capital expenditures and/or employs a greater rate for capital cost allowance purposes (tax reporting) than for depreciation (public reporting). In such cases, the deferred taxes will be, in effect, a long-term interest-free loan from the government that may not have to be repaid in the foreseeable future.[37]

The third controversy on the liability side of the balance sheet concerns the treatment of lease arrangements. The primary users of leases prior to 1960 were retail companies who leased their premises. The popularity of leases since 1960 has been such that lease financing now constitutes an important source of financing for different types of capital assets. Rather than borrow funds or raise equity to acquire capital assets, a company can elect to lease an asset from an asset leasing firm.

In the absence of uniformity in accounting for leases and disclosure of leases by lessees, comparisons of certain financial ratios of companies in the same industry may be inappropriate and misleading. For example, if Company X and Company Y are in the same industry and the former company *leases* its fixed assets whereas the latter firm *owns* its fixed assets, then an examination of the debt-equity ratio of the two companies would be misleading.[38]

Because a lease is a contractual agreement, the provisions of the lease may vary widely. The CICA has classified leases as either operating or capital (financing) leases.[39] The FASB has established criteria for classifying a lease as a capital lease. If at least one of the financing criteria is met, then the lease is classified as a capital lease. The criteria attempt to identify whether a transaction is a purely financing device for the purchase of the asset.

The accounting treatments of the two types of leases differ because it is necessary to portray the substance of each economic transaction. Rental payments on an operating lease are expensed. On the other hand, for a capital lease, the lessee records the lease as if an asset is being financed and an obligation is being created. More specifically, an asset and a liability of an amount equal to the present value of the minimum lease payments during the term of the lease are created on the balance sheet.[40]

---

37 In any event, the present value or discounted value of the deferred tax liability should in theory be recorded as a liability. The further into the future that this liability can be expected to be repaid, the lower the present value or discounted value of the liability.

38 For examples see A. Thomas Nelson, ''Capitalizing Leases—The Effects on Financial Ratios,'' *Journal of Accountancy*, July 1963, pp. 49–58.

39 *CICA Handbook*, section 3065.

40 There are several problems related to the determination of the recorded value. These problems involve the treatment of executory costs (for example, insurance, maintenance, and tax expenses), the discount rate for determining the present value, amortization of the leased asset, and the reduction of the liability over time.

16-5.4 Accounting Earnings Can Exaggerate Growth in Owners' Equity

The conventions the accounting profession uses for handling the balance item called retained earnings can mislead investors and unsophisticated financial analysts. For an example of the type of confusion that can arise, consider the equity section of the balance sheet shown in the hypothetical example below. Essentially, this section of the so-called right-hand side of the balance sheet contains the firm's nonliability sources of financing.

Common stock at $1 par (100,000 shares outstanding)	100,000
Paid-in surplus	900,000
Retained earnings	7,000,000
Total equity, or net worth	$8,000,000

There are three components of a corporation's net worth: (1) The par value of the outstanding common stock can only be increased if more shares are sold. Accountants define it to be the specified par value per share multiplied by the number of shares outstanding. (2) The paid-in surplus is the excess over and above the par value per share that the common stock investors paid for the stock when they originally bought it; this quantity is also fixed — unless more shares are sold. In the example above, for instance, it appears that the average share of stock was sold for $10 per share and thus contributed $9 per share to the paid-in surplus account. (3) Retained earnings, however, can increase or decrease every year for most corporations. Positive net earnings (that remain after all cash dividends are deducted) are added to retained earnings to increase it. Or, if the firm had a bad year, net losses are deducted from retained earnings to reduce it.

After the board of directors reaches its decision every quarter about how much of the corporation's quarterly accounting earnings to pay out in cash dividends, the remainder of the company's accounting earnings is designated as retained earnings, according to a deeply entrenched accounting convention. Since the average Canadian corporation pays out about 50 percent of its accounting earnings as cash dividends, the remaining 50 percent of the corporation's accounting earnings becomes retained earnings and gets added to the equity section of the corporate balance sheet. Thus, retained earnings increases in those years in which the corporation is profitable. Every time that retained earnings is increased, the corporation's total owners' equity (or net worth) account increases correspondingly, and this raises the corporation's book value per share. These are all merely accounting definitions that cannot be argued with and have some financial consequence only if financial analysts cannot discern the truth in the misleading cases. However, the way that retained earnings affect future years' earnings is a matter that can have more serious financial consequences.

Retained earnings initially show up in the corporate financial statements in some asset category to offset the equal increase on the other side of the balance sheet under the owners' equity heading. Retained earnings gets spent on something, call it "bricks and mortar" if there is a need for an example of a possible asset, which should make the corporation larger and more profitable in the years ahead. Two insights about these so-called retained earnings are worth noting here. First, retained earnings is not really economic income that the investor can spend at will. Since retained earnings are not really earnings available for the investors' consumption, it is wrong and misleading to label retained earnings as a form of "earnings" and thus imply that it is part of the investors' income.

A second important point is also worth noting about retained earnings. Retained earnings gets reinvested somewhere in the corporation so that some of the future earnings actually grow out of past earnings which were reinvested in retained earnings. This is circular. Part of a corporation's future earnings are actually only a return on past earnings that were reinvested under the heading of retained earnings. This is a form of double counting that inflates the accounting measure of corporate income.[41] In order to help investors see what is truly being done with the corporation's earnings, retained earnings should be renamed with a more descriptive title. Titles such as "involuntary reinvestment" or "usurped earnings" may sound overly dramatic; but these titles would be more likely to alert investors to the way that their corporation is actually being financed than would continued use of that misleading item called "retained earnings." In the final analysis, retained earnings is like a warrant or a stock rights offering that the board of directors forces its shareholders to purchase whether or not they want to.

16-6 HOW TO ADJUST A SERIES OF INCOME STATEMENTS

Since income is so important in determining the value of a security and since the concept of accounting profit is so vague, it is usually necessary to adjust or normalize the reported income figure to a more realistic value that is defined consistently from year to year.

The key word in analyzing a series of income statements from one firm is "consistency." Since there are so few clear-cut definitions in income accounting, some definitions must be adopted and used consistently. This is where the economists' concept becomes useful (see Box 16-1).

DEFINITION OF ECONOMIC INCOME FOR A PERSON A person's economic income is the maximum he or she can consume without diminishing a future period's consumption opportunities.

Box 16-1
A Person's
Economic
Income

The financial analyst's job is to detect misleading accounting statements and restate them consistently, using the definition of economic income (rather than some accountant's reported profit that may contain tax gimmicks or window-dressing manipulations). In this manner a company's true earning power can be analyzed and the *trend* in income can be detected. Typically, financial statements for several past years are gathered from the company's annual reports. Then, by referring to the notes to the financial statements,

---

41 For a more detailed explanation of how corporate investors are misled by the title and usage of "retained earnings" see the article by A. J. Merrett and Gerald D. Newbould entitled "CEPS: The Illusion of Corporate Growth," *Journal of Portfolio Management*, Fall 1982, pp. 5–10.

the various years' statements can be adjusted so the items in all years are consistently defined. After these adjustments, year-by-year comparisons of the share's economic income may be made. Box 16-2 defines the economic income from a share of stock.

Box 16-2
A
Shareholder's
Economic
Income

> **DEFINITION OF A STOCK SHARE'S ECONOMIC INCOME** The economic income from an equity share during a given period equals the maximum amount of real, physical consumption opportunities that can be withdrawn from the share during that period without diminishing the consumption opportunities that can be obtained from it in future periods.

The definition of an equity share's economic income furnishes the financial analyst a stable guiding light that suggests how to adjust a share of stock's reported (or accounting) income so that it is realistic, consistent, and suitable for informative comparisons with other years' incomes and other firms' incomes. Some key aspects of this guiding definition are worthy of further discussion.[42]

1. *Inflation adjustments.* The economic income definition's reference to "real, physical consumption opportunities" refers to inflation-adjusted dollars rather than to inflated (or nominal) dollars.
2. *Withdrawals.* An equity share's economic income does not actually have to be withdrawn and consumed, but the consumption *opportunity* must genuinely exist or the income is not real. For example, if a firm must retain some of its earnings to survive, then those retained earnings are not true economic income that the share's owner could consume without diminishing the share's future income.[43]
3. *Depreciation.* The economic income must be the income left after an allowance for wear and tear of the assets is deducted. This depreciation or depletion allowance must be reinvested in the assets to maintain their future productivity undiminished and is thus not consumable income.
4. *Market values.* A share's current economic income includes its current capital gains and losses at current market values, regardless of whether the gains and losses are realized. Thus, for example, if a supermarket firm discovered oil wells (which were totally unrelated to its basic food enterprise) on its customer parking lots, the appreciation that the firm enjoyed from the mineral deposits would constitute economic income regardless of whether the oil was sold.

The income statement for firm A in Table 16-2 provides an example of how some of the concepts above should be employed in an effort to delineate a firm's economic income.

---

42 Milton Friedman, *A Theory of the Consumption Function*, Princeton University Press, 1957. For a deeper discussion of many of the problems raised here, see R. K. Jaedicke and R. T. Sprouse, *Accounting Flows: Income, Funds and Cash* (Englewood Cliffs, N.J.: Prentice-Hall Foundations of Finance Series, Prentice Hall, 1965). Any intermediate accounting textbook will explain the details of the various procedures accountants use in handling different transactions.

43 For more discussion of how earnings are double-counted and mistaken for growth because retained earnings is erroneously called a source of income rather than a source of mandatory equity financing see "CEPS: The Illusion of Corporate Growth," *The Journal of Portfolio Management*, Fall 1982, pp. 5–10.

16-7   MEASURING AND PROJECTING EARNINGS STATISTICALLY

The preceding paragraphs discussed the concept of economic income and how to derive estimates of it from the accountant's income statements. After a firm's past accounting income figures have been normalized to yield a series of consistently defined estimates of the firm's economic income, the growth rate of a firm's economic income may be estimated. Knowledge of a firm's historical earnings growth rate is helpful when forecasting future earnings.[44]

---

44 The impact of reported accounting earnings on the market price of the corporation's stock has been actively researched. An easy-to-read article that surveys these studies and offers some suggestions is O. M. Joy and C. P. Jones, "Earnings Reports and Market Efficiencies: An Analysis of the Contrary Evidence," *The Journal of Financial Research*, vol. II, no. 1, Spring 1979, pp. 51–63. See the following studies for details: (1) R. Ball and P. Brown, "An Empirical Evaluation of Accounting Income Numbers," *Journal of Accounting Research*, Autumn 1968, pp. 159–178. (2) S. Basu, "The Information Content of Price-Earnings Ratios," *Financial Management*, Summer 1975, pp. 53–63. (3) S. Basu, "Investment Performance of Common Stocks in Relation to Their Price-Earnings Ratios: A Test of the Efficient Market Hypothesis, *The Journal of Finance*, June 1977, pp. 663–681. (4) W. Beaver, "The Information Content of Annual Earnings Announcements," *Journal of Accounting Research, Empirical Research in Accounting: Selected Studies*, 1968. (5) W. Breen, "Low Price-Earnings Ratios and Industry Relatives," *Financial Analysts Journal*, July–August 1968, pp. 125–127. (6) W. Breen and J. Savage, "Portfolio Distributions and Tests of Security Selection Models," *The Journal of Finance*, December 1968, pp. 805–819. (7) S. Brown, "Earnings Changes, Stock Prices and Market Efficiency," *The Journal of Finance*, March 1978, pp. 17–28. (8) D. Cassidy, "Investor Evaluation of Accounting Information: Some Additional Empirical Evidence," *Journal of Accounting Research*, Autumn 1976, pp. 212–229. (9) G. Foster, "Quarterly Accounting Data: Time-Series Properties and Predictive-Ability Results," *The Accounting Review*, January 1977, pp. 1–21. (10) J. C. Francis, "Analysis of Equity Returns: A Survey with Extensions," *Journal of Economics and Business*, Spring/Summer 1977, pp. 181–192. (11) J. C. Francis and D. R. Rowell, "A Simultaneous Equation Model of the Firm for Financial Analysis and Planning," *Financial Management*, Spring 1978, vol. 7, no. 1, pp. 29–44. (12) N. Gonedes, "Properties of Accounting Numbers: Models and Tests," *Journal of Accounting Research*, Autumn 1973, pp. 212–237. (13) P. Griffin, "The Time-Series Behavior of Quarterly Earnings: Preliminary Evidence," *Journal of Accounting Research*, Spring 1977, pp. 71–83. (14) C. Jones and R. Litzenberger, "Quarterly Earnings Reports and Intermediate Stock Price Trends," *The Journal of Finance*, March 1970, pp. 143–148. (15) O. Joy, R. Litzenberger, and R. McEnally, "The Adjustment of Stock Prices to Announcements of Unanticipated Changes in Quarterly Earnings," *Journal of Accounting Research*, Autumn 1977, pp. 207–225. (16) R. Kaplan and R. Roll, "Investor Evaluation of Accounting Information: Some Empirical Evidence," *The Journal of Business*, April 1972, pp. 225–257. (17) H. Latané and C. Jones, "Measuring and Using Standardized Unexpected Earnings," presented at the American Finance Association Meetings, New York, 1977. (18) H. Latané, O. Joy, and C. Jones, "Quarterly Data, Sort-Rank Routines, and Security Evaluation," *The Journal of Business*, October 1970, pp. 427–438. (19) H. Latané, C. Jones, and R. Rieke, "Quarterly Earnings Reports and Subsequent Holding Period Returns," *Journal of Business Research*, April 1974, pp. 119–132. (20) H. Latané and C. Jones, "Standardized Unexpected Earnings — A Progress Report," *The Journal of Finance*, December 1977, pp. 1457–1465. (21) R. Litzenberger, O. Joy, and C. Jones, "Ordinal Predictions and the Selection of Common Stocks," *Journal of Financial and Quantitative Analysis*, September 1971, pp. 1059–1968. (22) J. McWilliams, "Prices, Earnings and P. E. Ratios," *Financial Analysts Journal*, May–June 1966, pp. 137–142. (23) F. Nicholson, "Price Ratios in Relation to Investment Results," *Financial Analysts Journal*, January–February 1968, pp. 105–109.

It is necessary to estimate a stock's future income because the value of the share is the present value of its *future* economic income.[45] Chapter 17 discusses industry analysis and closes by explaining some tools that are valuable in analyzing a firm's earnings growth rate and in forecasting its future earnings.

For short-term forecasts (for example, one year or less in the future), a firm's earnings may usually be estimated from discussions with the firm's management and the firm's competitors, from publicly available information, and from other more-or-less subjective sources. A firm's long-run earning power is ultimately what determines its intrinsic value.

16-7.1 Forecasting Earnings per Share

Once the growth trend has been satisfactorily estimated, future values of earnings per share may be forecasted. First, the earnings trend line may be extrapolated. If the points do not "fit" fairly closely on the trend line, it may be difficult to obtain a good forecast. In this case a larger sample (change from annual to quarterly data and/or increase in the sample period) may help. Or Eq. (16-3) may be useful:

$$e_t = (1 + g)^t(e_0) \qquad (16\text{-}3)$$

where e_t denotes earnings per share at period t. These methods should be satisfactory for short forecasts of a few years into the future if no change in the firm's growth rate is anticipated.

16-7.2 Forecasting the Growth Rate for Earnings

Forecasting earnings per share may not be as simple as indicated in the preceding paragraph if the firm's rate of growth is expected to change. The rate of growth may change for several reasons. Products have life cycles, which can affect their earnings growth rates. Furthermore, old patents expire and/or new patents are obtained, competition becomes more or less aggressive, periods occur that are economically accelerating or depressed, or other factors cause growth rates to change. One of the purposes of fundamental analysis is to anticipate these factors accurately in order to make a good estimate of the growth rate of a firm's income.

16-7.3 Can Earnings Be Forecasted?

Methods for forecasting earnings are explained in the paragraphs above. However, an important question that the financial analyst should address is whether earnings can, in fact, be accurately forecasted by using historical earnings. Studies by both American and British researchers suggest that earnings per share follow a random walk.[46] That is, the study of successive

---

45 C. C. Holt, "The Influence of Growth Duration on Share Prices," *Journal of Finance*, September 1962, pp. 465–475. R. A. Haugen and D. W. Wichern, "The Elasticity of Financial Assets," *Journal of Finance*, September 1974, pp. 1229–1240.

46 This was first observed for British firms by Professor Ian M. D. Little, *Higgledy, Piggledy Growth*, vol. 24, no. 4 (Oxford: Institute of Statistics, November 1962). The results were supported in a later study with Professor A. C. Rayner entitled *Higgledy Piggledy Growth Again*, (Oxford: Blackwell, 1966). The following studies support the British findings. Joseph

changes in historical earnings per share suggests that they fluctuate randomly up and down and that they are not helpful in forecasting future changes.

The hypothesis that earnings per share follow a random walk does not imply that earnings per share cannot be predicted. What it simply means is that a security analyst will not usually improve the ability to forecast future earnings per share by simply projecting historical earnings.[47]

16-8 CONCLUSIONS ABOUT EARNINGS ANALYSIS

The economic income from an equity share is the maximum amount of consumption that the share can yield during some period such that the consumption opportunities from the share are undiminished at the end of the period. This economic quantity may not coincide with accountants' concept of income. Therefore, accounting income figures must be adjusted or normalized to obtain as nearly as possible a consistently defined series of economic income. The present value of this latter series is then taken to determine the value of that equity share. The procedures utilized by fundamental security analysts in determining the intrinsic value of an equity's economic income were explained in Chap. 15.

E. Murphy, Jr., "Relative Growth in Earnings per Share—Past and Future," *Financial Analysts Journal*, November–December 1966, pp. 73–76. John Lintner and Robert Glauber, "Higgledy Piggledly Growth in America?" Paper presented to the Seminar on the Analysis of Security Prices, University of Chicago, May 1967. Richard A. Brealey, *An Introduction to Risk and Return from Common Stocks*, 2d ed. (Cambridge, Mass.: M.I.T., 1983), chap. 5, "The Behavior of Earnings." W. S. Albrecht, L. L. Lookabill, and J. C. McKeown, "The Time-Series Properties of Annual Earnings," *Journal of Accounting Research*, Autumn 1977, vol. 15, pp. 226–244. R. J. Ball and R. Watts, "Some Time Series Properties of Accounting Income," *Journal of Finance*, June 1972, vol. 27, pp. 663–682. W. H. Beaver, "The Time Series Behavior of Earnings," *Empirical Research in Accounting: Selected Studies, Journal of Accounting Research* (supplement), 1970, vol. 8, pp. 62–99. R. A. Brealey, "Some Implications of the Comovement of American Company Earnings," *Applied Economics*, 1971, vol. 3, pp. 183–196. N. Dopuch and R. L. Watts, "Using Time-Series Models to Assess the Significance of Accounting Changes," *Journal of Accounting Research*, Spring 1972, vol. 10, pp. 180–194. L. L. Lookabill, "Some Additional Evidence on the Time Series Properties of Accounting Signals," *Accounting Review*, October 1976, vol. 51, pp. 724–738. R. L. Watts and R. W. Leftwich, "The Time Series of Annual Accounting Earnings," *Journal of Accounting Research*, Autumn 1977, vol. 15, pp. 253–271. In addition, the following book reviews the literature on the behavior and comovement of earnings: G. Foster, *Financial Statement Analysis* (Englewood Cliffs, N.J.: Prentice-Hall, 1978).

47 The value of earnings reported in interim financial statements for forecasting annual earnings has been debated in the investment literature. See David Green, Jr., and Joel Segall, "The Predictive Power of First-Quarter Earnings Reports," *Journal of Business*, January 1967, vol. 40, pp. 44–45, and Phillip Brown and Victor Niederhoffer, "The Predictive Content of Quarterly Earnings," *Journal of Business*, October 1968, vol. 41, pp. 488–497. The Francis model also has a high degree of explanatory power over the empirically observed quarterly earnings per share of NYSE stocks; see J. C. Francis, "Analysis of Equity Returns: A Survey with Extensions," *Journal of Business and Economics*, Spring-Summer 1977, vol. 29, no. 3, pp. 181–192. The Francis article is reprinted in J. C. Francis, C. F. Lee, and D. E. Farrar (eds.), *Readings in Investments* (New York: McGraw-Hill, 1980), pp. 459–470. For a discussion of the pitfalls of interim financial statements see Lee J. Seidler and William Benjes, "The Credibility Gap in Interim Financial Statements," *Financial Analysts Journal*, September–October 1967, pp. 109–115.

QUESTIONS

1. Write out the model used by accountants in determining taxable income.
2. How would reported assets, expenses, and accounting income be affected by a switch from LIFO to FIFO inventory valuation during an inflationary period? Explain.
3. Explain three ways in which a company can manipulate its earnings within the framework of generally accepted accounting principles.
4. "During an inflationary period the balance sheet of a firm may be of questionable value." Discuss.
5. How does basic earnings per share differ from fully diluted earnings per share? Will all firms report both statistics in financial statements?
6. Distinguish between an extraordinary item and a prior period adjustment.
7. What two approaches have been suggested for adjusting financial statements for the impact of inflation? Are these two methods alternative methods for handling inflation?
8. What is the present method of handling leases on a financial statement?
9. What are some accounting factors that could cause a firm's historical average growth rate to decrease in future years? To increase?
10. "Retained earnings are like a new issue of common stock that the old shareholders are forced to buy." True, false, or uncertain. Explain.

SELECTED REFERENCES

Briloff, Abraham. *Unaccountable Accounting*. New York: Harper & Row, 1972. A nonmathematical, case-by-case discussion, giving names of large corporations and large CPA firms, dates, and numerous actual examples of accounting entries that do not reflect the economic realities.

Canadian Securities Institute, *Advanced Interpretation of Financial Statements*, Part I, 1985. Canadian Securities Institute, Suite 360, 33 Yonge St., Toronto, Ontario. A straightforward treatment of basic accounting issues and financial statement analysis in Canada.

Davidson, Sidney, Clyde P. Stickney, and Roman L. Weil. *Inflation Accounting*. New York: McGraw-Hill, 1976. A book that illustrates the impact of inflation on reported earnings and presents the results of the author's research for specific companies.

Foster, George. *Financial Statement Analysis*. Englewood Cliffs, N.J.: Prentice-Hall, 1978. A new and modern approach to financial analysis that is based on economic theory and that uses simple econometrics is explained in this book.

Graham, B., D. Dodd, and S. Cottle. *Security Analysis*. 4th ed. New York: McGraw-Hill, 1962. This book is a standard reference of many practicing fundamental security analysts. It is a nonmathematical, detailed description of security analysis based on financial statements and other basic facts about the firm. Chapter 33 deals with earnings forecasting.

PART 5

SECURITY PRICE MOVEMENTS

CHAPTER 17 Technical Analysis

There are two main approaches to analyzing securities: technical analysis and fundamental analysis. This chapter introduces technical analysis.

A technical analyst is a particular kind of security analyst who prefers not to work through the infinite number of fundamental facts about the issuing corporation, such as the earnings of a company and its competitive products, or about forthcoming legislation that may affect the firm. Instead, technical analysts search for a quick-and-easy summary of these innumerable fundamental facts by studying the way that the market price of a security behaves. Over the past decades technical analysts almost totally focused their attention on *charts* of security market prices and a few related summary statistics about security trading. That is, technical analysts prepared and studied charts of various financial variables in order to make forecasts about security prices. Today, however, technical analysis includes the work of some nonchartists who use quantitative rather than graphical tools.[1] Dozens of different techniques are used by professional technical analysts. In this chapter, a few of the more prominent technical analysis tools are explained. Before the tools of technical analysis are examined, however, concepts that are at the core of all technical analysis are reviewed.

17-1 THE THEORY OF TECHNICAL ANALYSIS

Technical analysis is based on the widely accepted premise that security prices are determined by the supply of and the demand for securities. The tools of technical analysis are therefore designed to measure supply and demand. Typically, technical analysts record historical financial data on charts, study these charts in an effort to find meaningful *patterns*, and use these patterns to predict future prices. Some charting techniques are used to

---

1 One of the modern technicians is R. A. Levy, president, Computer Directions Advisors, Inc., Silver Spring, Md. Levy has stated his position in various articles and in a book: R. L. Levy, ''Conceptual Foundations of Technical Analysis,'' *Financial Analysts Journal*, July-August, 1966, p. 83; *The Relative Strength Concept of Common Stock Forecasting*, (Larchmont, N.Y.: Investors Intelligence, 1968). *Fortune* magazine reported that Levy's own work indicated that many technical analysis tools of the traditional charting type were worthless: *Fortune*, September 1970, p. 188.

predict the movements of a single security, some are used to predict movements of a market index, and some are used to predict both the action of individual securities and the market action.

Edwards and Magee[2] articulated the basic assumptions underlying technical analysis as follows:

1. Market value is determined solely by the interaction of supply and demand.
2. Supply and demand are governed by numerous factors, both rational and irrational.
3. In disregard of minor fluctuations in the market, stock prices tend to move in trends that persist for an appreciable length of time.
4. Changes in trend are caused by shifts in supply and demand.
5. Shifts in supply and demand, no matter why they occur, can be detected sooner or later in charts of market action.
6. Some chart patterns tend to repeat themselves.

In essence, technical analysts believe that past patterns of market action will recur in the future and can therefore be used for predictive purposes.

Chapters 15 and 16 explained how fundamental analysts estimate the intrinsic *value* of a security. Technical analysts, on the other hand, seek to estimate security *prices* rather than values; that is, they try to forecast short-run shifts in supply and demand that will affect the market price of one or more securities. They tend to ignore factors such as the firms' risks and earnings growth in favour of various barometers of supply and demand that they have devised.

One text[3] on technical analysis lyrically asserts that

It is futile to assign an intrinsic value to a stock certificate. One share of United States Steel, for example, was worth $261 in the early fall of 1929, but you could buy it for only $22 in June 1932. By March 1937, it was selling for $126 and just one year later for $38. . . . This sort of thing, this wide divergence between presumed value and actual value, is not the exception; it is the rule; it is going on all the time. The fact is that the real value of a share of U.S. Steel common is determined at any given time solely, definitely, and inexorably by supply and demand, which are accurately reflected in the transactions consummated on the floor of the . . . Exchange.

Of course, the statistics which the fundamentalists study play a part in the supply and demand equation—that is freely admitted. But there are many other factors affecting it. The market price reflects not only the differing fears and guesses and moods, rational and irrational, of hundreds of potential buyers and sellers, as well as their needs and their resources — in total, factors which defy analysis and for which no statistics are obtainable, but which are nevertheless all synthesized, weighted and finally expressed in one precise figure at which a buyer and seller get together and make a deal (through their agents, their respective brokers). This is the only figure that counts.

In brief, the going price as established by the market itself comprehends all the fundamental information which the statistical analyst can hope to learn (plus some which is perhaps secret to him, known only to a few insiders) and much else besides of equal or even greater importance.

2 R. D. Edwards and John Magee, Jr., *Technical Analysis of Stock Trends*, 4th ed. (Springfield, Mass.: Magee, 1958), p. 86.
3 R. D. Edwards and John Magee, Jr., *Technical Analysis of Stock Trends*, 4th ed. (Springfield, Mass.: Magee, 1958), p. 3.

The preceding quotation makes some strong assertions, stresses the impact of the investor emotion in an unscientific manner, and is an extremely flattering interpretation of one set of facts; but it does convey the spirit of technical analysis.

In defending their practices, most technical analysts do not accuse fundamental analysts of being illogical or conceptually in error. In fact, many technical analysts would agree with fundamental analysts that security prices do fluctuate around their true intrinsic values. Nevertheless, they assert the superiority of their methods over fundamental analysis by pointing out that technical analysis is easier and faster or that it can be simultaneously applied to more stocks than fundamental analysis. This latter claim is certainly true. Of course, if technical analysis does not accomplish what it is purported to do, its relative simplicity does not justify its use.

Many technical analysts would not say that fundamental analysis is worthless, but rather that it is just too troublesome to bother with. First, they point out that even if a fundamental analyst does find an underpriced security, he must wait and hope that the rest of the market recognizes the security's true value and bids its price up. Second, fundamental analysis is hard, time-consuming work. Technical analysis, on the other hand, requires less schooling and is easier to use. Third, technical analysts cite the inadequacy of the income statements produced by accountants (as discussed in Chap. 16) which form the basis for much fundamental analysis. Finally, technical analysts point out the highly subjective nature of the earnings multipliers used by fundamental analysts. In view of these deficiencies of fundamental analysis, consider some of the tools used by technical analysts to measure supply and demand and to forecast security prices.[4]

17-2   THE DOW THEORY

The Dow theory is one of the oldest and most famous technical tools; it was originated by Charles Dow, who founded the Dow Jones Company and was the editor of *The Wall Street Journal* around 1900. Mr. Dow died in 1902, and the Dow theory was developed further and given its name by members of *The Wall Street Journal* staff. Down through the years, numerous writers have altered, extended, and in some cases abridged the original Dow theory. Today, many versions of the theory exist and are used; it is the basis for many other techniques used by technical analysts.

The Dow theory rose to a peak of prominence during the 1930s. At that time, *The Wall Street Journal* published editorials written by its staff members that interpreted market action in terms of the theory. On October 23, 1929, *The Wall Street Journal* published a still-famous editorial, ''A Turn in the Tide,'' which correctly stated that the bull market was then over and a bear market had started. This forecast was based on the Dow theory. The horrendous

---

4 Although this chapter focuses on charting of common stock prices, technical analysis of other market indicators and other types of financial instruments is also widely practiced. For a favourable report about the profitability of technical analysis in commodity trading see Shawn Tully, ''Princeton's Rich Commodity Scholars,'' *Fortune*, Feb. 9, 1981, pp. 94–98.

market crash that followed the forecast drew much favourable attention to
the Dow theory.

The Dow theory is used to indicate reversals and trends in the market as a
whole or for individual securities. According to Mr. Dow himself, "The market is always considered as having three movements, all going at the same
time. The first is the narrow movement from day to day. The second is the
short swing, running from two weeks to a month or more; the third is the
main movement, covering at least 4 years in duration."[5] Dow theory prac-
titioners refer to these three components as: (1) daily fluctuations, (2) secondary movements, and (3) primary trends. The primary trends are
commonly called bear or bull markets. Secondary trends last only a few
months. The theory asserts that daily fluctuations are meaningless. However,
the chartist must plot the asset's price or the market average day by day in
order to outline the primary and secondary trends.

**17-2.1
How the Dow
Theory
Works**

FIGURE 17-1 A line chart of daily closing prices with Dow theory signals.

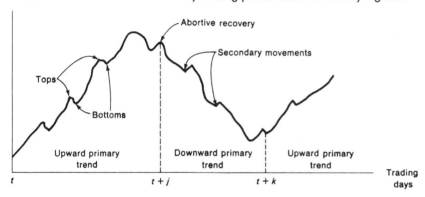

Figure 17-1 is a line chart that a Dow theorist might develop. This figure
shows a primary uptrend existing from period t to the peak price that
occurred just before day $t + j$. On trading day $t + j$, an "abortive recovery"
occurs, signalling a change in the direction of the market's primary movement. An abortive recovery occurs when a secondary movement fails to rise
above the preceding top. Before $t + j$, all the tops are ascending; but after
the abortive recovery, the tops are descending until just before day $t + k$.
At $t + k$, a secondary movement fails to reach a new bottom, signalling the
start of a bull market. Most Dow theorists do not believe that the emergence
of a new primary trend has been truly *confirmed* until the pattern of ascending
or descending tops occurs in both the industrial and transportation averages.[6]
Figure 17-2 shows graphs of various price patterns that Dow theorists
search for as signs of market tops and bottoms. Some of these patterns are
discussed in reference to other technical analysis theories.

5 *The Wall Street Journal*, Dec. 19, 1900.
6 A supportive empirical test of the Dow theory is reported by David A. Glickstein and Rolf
  E. Wubbels, "Dow Theory Is Alive and Well," *The Journal of Portfolio Management*, April
  1983, pp. 28–31.

FIGURE 17-2 Graphic illustrations of chart formations.

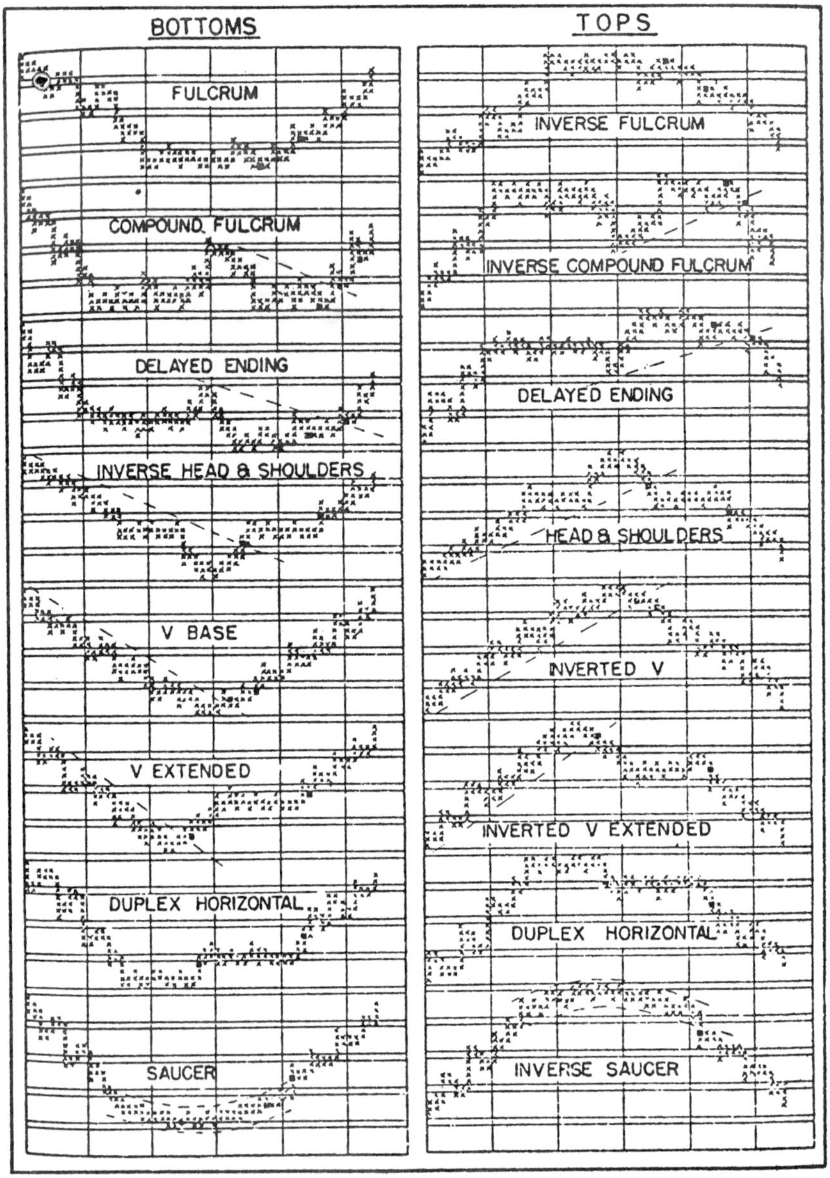

BOTTOMS	TOPS
FULCRUM	INVERSE FULCRUM
COMPOUND FULCRUM	INVERSE COMPOUND FULCRUM
DELAYED ENDING	DELAYED ENDING
INVERSE HEAD & SHOULDERS	HEAD & SHOULDERS
V BASE	INVERTED V
V EXTENDED	INVERTED V EXTENDED
DUPLEX HORIZONTAL	DUPLEX HORIZONTAL
SAUCER	INVERSE SAUCER

Source: *Commodity Year Book*, Commodity Research Bureau, Inc., New York.

17-3 BAR CHARTS

Technical analysts use three basic types of charts: (1) line charts, (2) bar charts, and (3) point and figure charts. Figure 17-1 shows a line chart; lines are used to connect successive days' prices. Figure 17-3 shows a bar chart. *Bar charts* have vertical bars representing each day's price movement. Each

FIGURE 17-3   Bar chart of head and shoulders top formation.

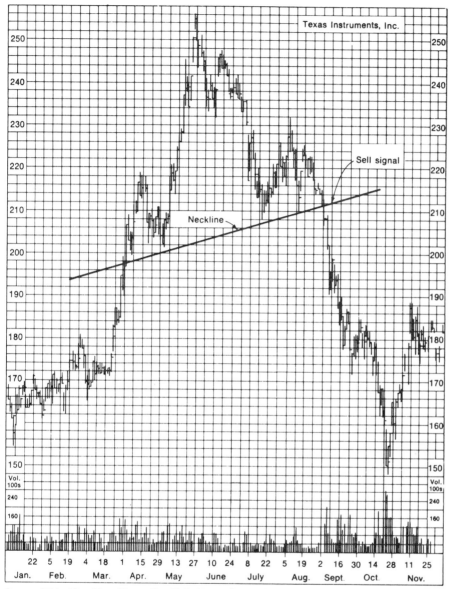

Source: W.L. Jiler, *How Charts Can Help You in the Stock Market*, Trendline, New York, p. 114.

bar spans the distance from the day's highest price to the day's lowest price; a small cross on the bar marks the closing price. Charts may be used to track the performance of both stocks and indexes. Figure 17-4 is a bar chart of the TSE 300 Composite Index.

Point and figure charts (PFCs) are made of X's and O's and are more complex than line and bar charts; they will be discussed in the next section.

Charts of the price movements of both individual assets and the market indexes are kept on all three types of charts.

FIGURE 17-4 Bar chart of the TSE 300 Composite Index.

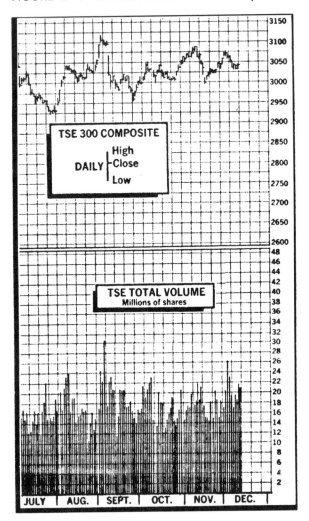

Line charts, bar charts, and PFCs usually have bar graphs along the bottoms of the charts showing the volume of shares traded at each price change. Figure 17-4 shows such volume data. Trading volume is of lesser importance to the chartists than the security prices themselves, but it is probably the second most important statistic they follow. As an example of how technical analysts try to relate stock price moves and the volume of shares traded, consider a pattern called the head and shoulders formation. Chartists find the head and shoulders pattern in line charts, bar charts, and PFCs for both individual assets and market indexes.

A head and shoulder top (HST) is a formation that signals that the security's price has reached a top and will decline in the future. As the name indicates the HST has a left shoulder and a right shoulder. The market action that forms an HST (see Fig. 17-3) can be broken down into four phases:

1. *Left shoulder* A period of heavy buying followed by a lull in trading pushes the price up to a new peak before the price begins to slide down.
2. *Head* A spurt of heavy buying raises a price to a new high and then allows the price to fall back below the top of the left shoulder.
3. *Right shoulder* A moderate rally lifts the price somewhat but fails to push prices as high as the top of the head before a decline begins.
4. *Confirmation or breakout* Prices fall below the neckline; that is, the line drawn tangent to the left and right shoulders. This breakout is supposed to precede a price drop and is a signal to sell.

Technical analysts have described numerous patterns that are supposed to indicate the direction of future price movements. Triangles, pennants, flags, channels, rectangles, double tops, triple tops, wedge formations, and diamonds are only some of the patterns for which chartists search. Figures 17-2 and 17-3 are charts with construction lines added by a chartist that illustrate some of these patterns.

17-4   POINT AND FIGURE CHARTS

Point and figure charts (PFCs) are more complex than line or bar charts. PFCs are not only used to detect reversals in a trend; they can also be employed to set actual price forecasts, called *price targets*.

The construction of PFCs differs significantly from the construction of line and bar charts in several respects. First, the construction of the chart varies with the price level of the stock being charted. Only ''significant'' changes are posted to a PFC. Thus, for high-priced securities, only three- or five-point (that is, dollar) price changes are posted, and, for low-priced securities, only one-point changes are posted. As a result, there are one-point PFCs, two-point PFCs, three-point PFCs, and five-point PFCs.

A second unusual feature of PFCs is their lack of a time dimension. On line and bar charts, each vertical column represents a trading day, but on a PFC, determining the days is sometimes impossible because each column represents a *significant reversal* instead of a trading day. As a result, a trading day in which the direction of the price made two significant reversals would generate two new columns on a PFC.

To set the price target (that is, forecasted price) that a stock is expected to attain, PFC chartists begin by finding ''congestion areas.'' A *congestion area* is a horizontal band of X's and O's created by a series of reversals around a given price level. Congestion areas are supposed to result when supply and demand are equal. A breakout is said to have occurred when a column of X's rises above the top of a congestion area. A *penetration* of the top of a congestion area is a signal for a continued price rise. Penetration of the bottom of a congestion area by a column of O's is a bearish signal.

Figure 17-5 shows PFCs where top and bottom penetrations have occurred. It shows that the PFC of the Standard & Poor's 500 composite average gave some sell signals late in the summer of 1969 as the 1969–1970 bear market began. The months of the year are indicated by the numbers from 1 through 12, which are used in place of an X or O when the first significant change occurs in a new month. At the end of 1969, some weak buy signals were given only to be followed by a strong sell signal in December 1969. If investors had followed all these signals, they would have been "whipsawed." That is, securities could have been sold, bought back at higher prices, and then later sold again at even lower prices for a considerable cumulative loss. In December 1969 when the PFC issued a strong sell signal, the bear market of 1969–1970 was already under way; so this signal merely pointed to something that was already obvious.

FIGURE 17-5 Point and figure chart of Standard & Poor's composite 500.

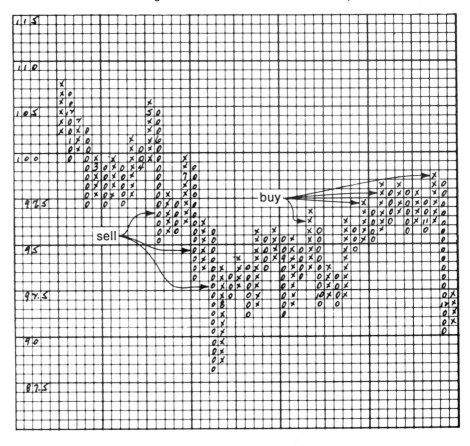

Source: A. W. Cohen, *Technical Indicator Analysis*, Chartcraft, Inc., Larchmont, N.Y.

To establish estimates of the new prices that a security should attain, PFC chartists measure the *horizontal count*—the horizontal width of a congestion area—as they watch for a breakout. *Breakout* refers to a price rise or fall in which the price rises above or falls below the horizontal band that contained the congestion area. When a breakout occurs, the chartist projects the horizontal count upward or downward in the same direction as the breakout to establish the new price target. The reason a particular price target is appropriate is not clear; even the PFC chartists themselves have difficulty explaining the establishment of price targets. John Schulz, a PFC chartist who has written columns for *Forbes* magazine, once wrote that ''on the question of where, in actual practice, measurements of lateral action should be taken, we are far from doctrinaire. . . . we advocate the utmost flexibility because this tends to obviate the dangerous rigidity of preconceived notions.''[7] Such flexibility also tends to obviate use of the technique.

**17-4.3
Establishing
Price
Targets**

17-5   CONTRARY OPINION THEORIES

The odd-lot theory is one of several theories of *contrary opinion*. In essence, the theory assumes that the average person is usually wrong and that a wise course of action is to pursue strategies contrary to popular thought. The odd-lot theory is used primarily to predict tops in bull markets, but also to predict reversals in individual securities.

Statistics on odd-lot trading are gathered in order to find out what ordinary people are doing. As mentioned previously, round lots are groups of 100 shares, and odd lots are groups of less than 100 shares. Since the sales commissions on odd lots are higher than the commissions on round lots, professional investors avoid odd-lot purchases. Most odd-lot purchases are made by investors with limited resources—that is, the average person who is probably a small, amateur investor.

**17-5.1
The Odd-Lot
Theory**

Odd-lot trading volume is reported daily in the United States. The odd-lot statistics are broken down into the number of shares purchased, sold, and sold short. Most odd-lot theorists chart the ratio of odd-lot sales to odd-lot purchases week by week. Some odd-lot chartists, however, chart only the odd-lot statistics from Mondays since odd-lot traders are believed to transact most of their trading on Mondays because of weekend conversations with their friends. In any event, if odd-lot sales exceed odd-lot purchases, the ''average'' person is selling more and buying less. If this difference is negative, then odd-lotters are net buyers. The odd-lot purchases-less-sales index is typically plotted concurrently with some market index. The odd-lotters' net purchases are used by chartists as a leading indicator of market prices. That is, positive net purchases are presumed to forecast falls in market prices, and net sales (or negative net purchases) are presumed to occur at the end of bear markets.

---

7 As quoted in D. Seligman, ''The Mystique of Point and Figure,'' *Fortune*, March 1962.

FIGURE 17-6 Graphs for odd-lot and short sales technical indicators.

Odd-lot trading and industrial stock prices

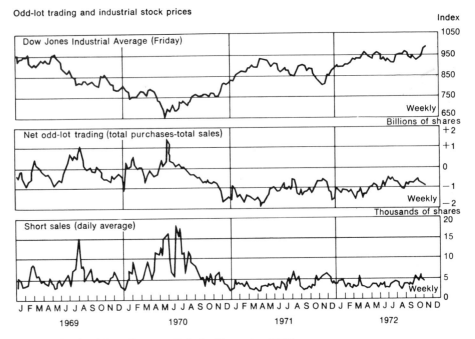

J F M A M J J A S O N D J F M A M J J A S O N D J F M A M J J A S O N D J F M A M J J A S O N D
1969　　　　　　1970　　　　　　1971　　　　　　1972

Source: Cleveland Trust Company Bulletin, November 1972.

Figure 17-6 shows data for the Dow Jones Industrial Average (DJIA) in the top panel; concurrent odd-lotter net purchases are shown in the centre panel for the period during and after the 1969–1970 bear market. Contrary to the odd-lot theory of contrary opinion, the odd-lotters were net buyers during low points in the DJIA. That is, the odd-lotters have ''bought low and sold high'' in recent years and thus have defied the theory about them.[8]

**17-5.2
The Short
Sellers
Theories**

Some chartists follow statistics on short sales. (Short sales are defined on pages 507 to 510.) Some short-sales theorists use aggregate statistics as an indicator of overall market sentiment, and some follow the short sales for individual securities in search of information about that security. However, both groups may interpret a high level of outstanding short sales (that is, uncovered short positions or short interest, as it is variously called) as a sign of increased future demand for securities with which to cover the outstanding short positions. Therefore, rising short sales foretell future demand for the security and thus increments in future prices. This is the *short sales contrary opinion* theory. The empirical data for 1970, graphed in the top and bottom

8 T. J. Kewley and R. A. Stevenson, ''The Odd-Lot Theory for Individual Stocks,'' *Financial Analysts Journal*, January–February 1969. This study suggests that the theory gives good ''buy'' signals, but not good ''sell'' signals. See also *Barron's*, ''Odd-Lot Short Sales,'' p. 21, August 25, 1986, for an indication that the ''theory'' is back in vogue.

panels of Fig. 17-6, tend to confirm the theory; the peak in short sales preceded the 1970 upturn in the DJIA. However, the indicator was wrong in July 1969.

In startling contrast to the short sales contrary opinion followers, another group of technical analysts believe that short sellers tend to be more sophisticated than the average investor. Therefore, this second group asserts, when short sales for the market as a whole or for an individual security are high, many sophisticated investors expect a price decline, and it should follow shortly. The top and bottom graphs in Fig. 17-6 for 1969 tend to support this second odd-lot theory in 1969, but not in 1970. It is not clear that either of the diametrically opposing groups of short sales followers has any valuable insights.[9]

17-6 THE CONFIDENCE INDEX

The confidence index is supposed to reveal how willing investors are to take a chance in the market. It is the ratio of high-grade bond yields to low-grade bond yields. When bond investors grow more confident about the economy, they shift their holdings from high-grade to lower-grade bonds in order to obtain the higher yields. This change bids up the prices of low-grade bonds, lowers their yields relative to high-grade bonds, and increases the confidence index.

Markets for bonds are frequented mostly by large institutional investors who are believed to be less emotional about their portfolio decisions than many investors in the stock market. In an effort to measure the market expectations of these ''smart money'' managers and assess their confidence in the economy, some chartists study the confidence index.

17-6.1 Calculating the Confidence Index

Barron's, the weekly financial and business newspaper, publishes figures on the confidence index regularly in its Market Laboratory section. The *Barron's* confidence index is the ratio of the average yield from its list of the ten highest-grade bonds over the average yield from the Dow Jones forty bonds. Equation (17-1) defines the *Barron's* confidence index (BCI).

$$\text{BCI}_t = \frac{\text{average yield of } Barron's, 10 \text{ highest-grade bonds at period } t}{\text{average yield of Dow Jones 40 bonds at time period } t} \tag{17-1}$$

The *Barron's* definition of the confidence index is widely used because it is published each week, but it has no intrinsic superiority over, say, the confidence index (CI) defined in Eq. (17-2).

$$\text{CI}_t = \frac{\text{average yield of Aaa bonds at time period } t}{\text{average yield of Baa bonds at time period } t} \tag{17-2}$$

Other valid definitions of the confidence index exist, too.

---

9 For an empirical report that is favourable to short interest technicians read Thomas J. Kerrigan, ''The Short Interest Ratio and Its Component Parts,'' *Financial Analysts Journal*, November–December 1974, pp. 45–49.

**17-6.2
Interpretation
of the
Confidence
Index**

The confidence index has an upper limit of unity (that is, $CI < 1.0$), since the yields on high-quality bonds will never rise above the yields on similar low-quality bonds. In periods of economic boom when investors grow optimistic and their risk-aversion diminishes, the yield spread between high- and low-quality bonds narrows and the confidence index rises. A rising confidence index is interpreted by chartists as an indication that the managers of the "smart money" are optimistic. On the assumption that the wisdom of these investors will be borne out, confidence index technicians predict that the stock market (where fewer sophisticated investors are assumed to trade) will follow the leadership of the smart money. Some confidence index technicians claim that the confidence index leads the stock market by two to eleven months. Thus, an upturn in the confidence index is supposed to foretell rising optimism and rising prices in the stock market.

Just as a rise in the confidence index is expected to precede a rising stock market, so a fall in the index is expected to precede a drop in stock prices. A fall in the confidence index represents the fact that low-grade bond yields are rising faster or falling more slowly than high-grade yields. This movement is supposed to reflect increasing risk-aversion by smart money managers who foresee an economic downturn and rising bankruptcies and defaults.

FIGURE 17-7   Point and figure chart of *Barron's* confidence index.

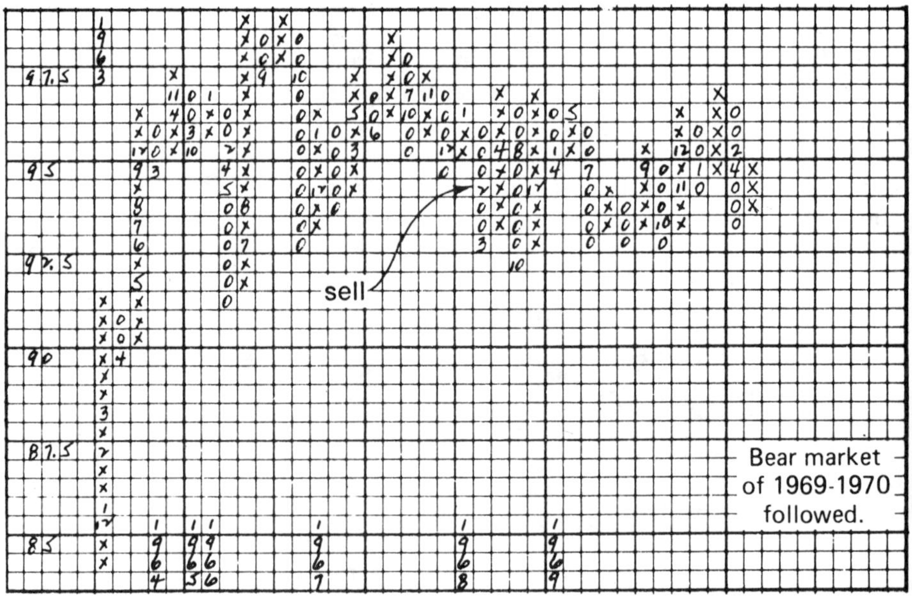

Source: Chartcraft, Inc., Larchmont, N.Y.

Figure 17-7 shows a point and figure chart of the *Barron's* confidence index plotted on the vertical axis at increments of half percentage points. Each block represents ½ of 1 percent. A change of 1½ percentage points in the opposite direction is considered a significant reversal that warrants starting a new column. The chart shows that the *Barron's* confidence index issued a weak sell signal when it broke out of the bottom of the congestion area in early 1968. This would have been a good sell signal to heed. A recession and bear stock market occurred soon after in the period 1969–1970. There is no question that the confidence index is positively correlated with the stock market. However, in view of the numerous other economic series that are also correlated with the stock market, this is of no unique value. The confidence index is usually, but not always, a leading indication. Furthermore, the confidence index has sometimes issued erroneous signals.

Many observers who have examined the confidence index conclude that it does measure what it is supposed to measure and thus that it conveys some worthwhile information. But, in view of its inconsistent lead-lag relationship with the stock market, if the confidence index is to be used it should be used in conjunction with other technical indicators or aids.

17-7   BREADTH OF MARKET

Breadth-of-market indicators are used to measure the underlying strength of market advances or declines. For example, it is possible that the Canadian Market Portfolio Index of only twenty-five blue-chip stocks that are very popular would still be rising for some time after the market for the majority of lesser known stocks had already turned down. Thus, to gauge the real underlying strength of the market, tools are needed to measure the *breadth* of the market's moves.

Numerous methods exist for measuring the breadth of the market. One of the easiest methods is to compare the number of issues that advanced in price and the number that declined on some particular market such as the Toronto Stock Exchange (TSE). More specifically, subtract the number of issues whose prices declined from the number of issues whose prices advanced each day to get *net advances or declines*. The data on advances and declines are published daily in most financial and national newspapers—a typical example is reproduced as Fig. 17-8.

17-7.1 Breadth-of-Market Calculations

FIGURE 17-8   Daily advances and declines.

TORONTO MARKET BREADTH

	Yester.	Prev.		Yester.	Prev.
Issues traded	1,162	1,160	52-week highs	19	28
Advances	305	331	52-week lows	51	46
Declines	476	435	Volume advances		6,473,000
Unchanged	381	394	Volume declines		7,341,000

The net advances or declines (sometimes called the *plurality*) are calculated newspaper excerpts, for example, as shown on page 433. Note that the top row of calculations starts from the most recent Tuesday data, shown in the right-hand column of Fig. 17-8.

FIGURE 17-9   Chart of stock market averages, trading volume, and advance-decline index, 1971–1984.

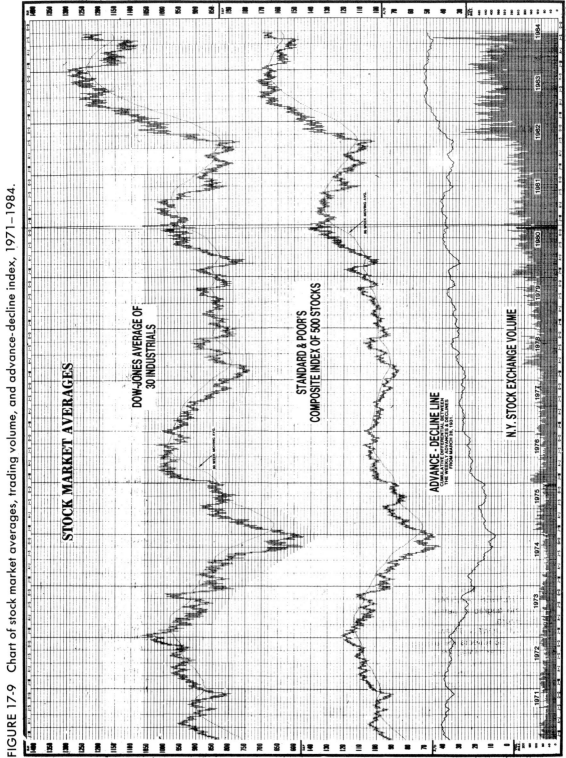

STOCK MARKET AVERAGES

DOW-JONES AVERAGE OF
30 INDUSTRIALS

STANDARD & POOR'S
COMPOSITE INDEX OF 500 STOCKS

ADVANCE-DECLINE LINE
CUMULATIVE DIFFERENTIAL BETWEEN
THE WEEKLY ADVANCES & DECLINES
FROM MARCH 28, 1931.

N.Y. STOCK EXCHANGE VOLUME

Source: Trendline's *Current Market Perspectives*, September 1984, p. 5.

DAY	ADVANCES	MINUS DECLINES EQUALS	NET ADVANCES AND DECLINES	BREADTH
Tuesday	331	435	−104	−104 (start)
Wednesday	305	476	−171	−275
Thursday	468	312	156	−119
Friday	255	468	−213	−332
Monday	669	87	582	250
Tuesday	582	122	460	710

These breadth-of-market statistics are obtained by simply cumulating the net advances and declines. The breadth statistics may become negative during a bear market, as they did in the example above. This is no cause for alarm, since the breadth level is entirely arbitrary; it depends on the date when the cumulative breadth series was begun. Only the direction, not the level, of the breadth-of-market statistics is relevant.

Breadth-of-market data are frequently plotted on line charts. Figure 17-9 shows a line chart of breadth data for the NYSE; the chart calls the breadth data the advance-decline line. Technical analysts compare the breadth of market with one of the market averages or, as done in Fig. 17-9, with two of them. The breadth and market averages usually move in tandem. What technical analysts watch for is breadth to follow a path that diverges from the path of a market average.

17-7.2 Interpretation of Breadth Data

Suppose the DJIA, with its thirty blue-chip stocks that are popular with amateur and professional investors alike, is moving upward. If breadth follows a divergent downward path, it indicates that many small stocks are starting to turn down while the blue chips continue to rise. This is an indicator of weakening market demand and signals a possible market downturn.

17-8   RELATIVE STRENGTH ANALYSIS

Dr. R. A. Levy suggests that the prices of some securities rise relatively faster in a bull market or decline more slowly in a bear market than other securities —that is, some securities exhibit *relative strength*. Relative strength technicians believe that by investing in securities that have demonstrated relative strength in the past, an investor will earn higher returns because the relative strength of a security tends to remain undiminished over time.[10]

---

10 Dr. Levy is one of the few technical analysts who has published a study of his techniques. The interested reader is directed to the following articles by Levy; all appeared in *Financial Analysts Journal*: (1) ''Conceptual Foundations of Technical Analysis,'' July–August 1966, pp. 83–89. (2) ''Random Walks: Reality or Myth,'' November–December 1967, pp. 69–76. An article by M. C. Jensen commenting on Levy's article follows directly in the same issue: ''Random Walks: Reality or Myth—Comment,'' November–December 1967, pp. 77–85. (3) ''Random Walks: Reality or Myth—Reply,'' January–February 1968, pp. 129–132. See also M. C. Jensen and G. A. Bennington, ''Random Walks and Technical Theories: Some Additional Evidence,'' *Journal of Finance*, May 1970, pp. 469–482.

**17-8.1
Measuring
Relative
Strength**

The relative strength concept may be applied to individual securities or to whole industries. Technicians measure relative strength in several ways. Some simply calculate rates of return and classify those securities with historically high average returns as securities with high relative strength. More frequently, technicians observe certain ratios to detect relative strength in a security or an industry. For example, consider the data for Anonymous Corp., denoted A, a hypothetical growth firm in the electronics industry, denoted EI, shown in Table 17-1.

TABLE 17-1   RELATIVE STRENGTH FOR ANONYMOUS CORP.

YEAR	PA*	PEIA	PTSE	PA/PEIA	PA/PTSE	PEIA/PTSE
19×3	30	17	2100	30/17 = 1.78	30/2100 = 0.0143	17/2100 = 0.0081
19×4	36	18	2500	36/18 = 2	36/2500 = 0.0144	18/2500 = 0.0072
19×5	72	20	2850	72/20 = 3.6	72/2850 = 0.0253	20/2850 = 0.0070

PA* = average price of Anonymous Corp. for the year.
PEIA = TSE 300 electrical/electronics subindex average for the year.
PTSE = TSE 300 Composite Index average for the year.

From 19×3 to 19×4, Anonymous did slightly better than most of the firms in the electronics industry, as evidenced by the fact that its price grew relatively more than the electronics industry average; the ratio *PA/PEIA* rose from 1.78 to 2. From 19×3 to 19×4, the electronics industry showed weakness relative to all industrial stocks: the ratio *PEIA/PTSE* declined from 0.0081 to 0.0072. Thus, Anonymous had to beat the electronics industry average merely to keep up (relatively speaking) with the rest of the market. From 19×3 to 19×4, Anonymous did not demonstrate any particular strength relative to the market average; the ratio *PA/PTSE* remained virtually unchanged. From 19×4 to 19×5, Anonymous showed considerable strength relative to its industry and to the market; during that time the electronics industry advanced at nearly as fast a rate as the market.

**17-8.2
Interpretation
of Relative
Strength Data**

A relative strength technician would typically plot the ratios of (1) the security relative to its industry and (2) the security relative to the entire market. A chart like the one shown in Fig. 17-10 might result for the Anonymous Corp.

Figure 17-10 shows that although the electronics industry is failing to keep pace with the market, the Anonymous Corp. is developing relative strength both in its industry and in the market. After preparing charts like this for numerous firms from different industries over a length of time, the technician would select certain industries and firms that demonstrated relative strength to be the most promising investment opportunities. Figure 17-11 (on pages 436–437) provides charts showing the TSE gold and oil and gas subindexes' relative strength to the TSE 300 Composite over the period 1978 to 1987.

FIGURE 17-10   Hypothetical relative-strength data for Anonymous Corp. and the electronics industry.

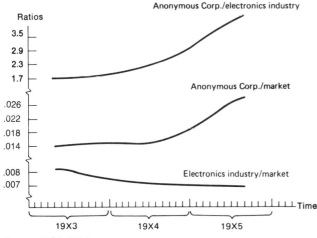

Source: Table 17-1.

17-9   CHARTING VOLUME OF TRADING DATA

On the day following each trading day many newspapers across Canada publish statistics giving the total number of shares traded in certain security markets. Some financial newspapers also publish the number of shares traded in selected individual issues. For example, Fig. 17-12 (on page 438) shows an excerpt from a typical financial newspaper giving data for the volume of shares traded for the TSE.

Many technical analysts believe that it is possible to detect whether the market in general and/or certain security issues are bullish or bearish by studying the volume of trading. Volume is supposed to be a measure of the intensity of investors' emotions. There is a Wall Street adage that "it takes volume to really move a stock" either up or down in price. This saying is often, but not always, true. Frequently, a large amount of trading volume tends to be associated with big security price changes. Thus it is reasonable for stock price chartists to study volume data in an effort to discern what might be the cause of specific stock price movements. However, the cause-and-effect relationship between the volume of shares traded and the price change in the traded security is vague and hard to unravel.[11]

---

11 Robert L. Crouch, "The Volume of Transactions and Price Changes on the New York Stock Exchange," *Financial Analysts Journal*, July–August 1970, pp. 104–109. Thomas W. Epps, "Security Price Changes and Transaction Volumes: Theory and Evidence," *American Economic Review*, September 1975, pp. 586–597. Paul C. Grier and Peter S. Albin, "Nonrandom Price Changes in Association with Trading in Large Blocks," *The Journal of Business*, July 1973, pp. 425–433. Seha Tinic, "The Economics of Liquidity Services," *Quarterly Journal of Economics*, vol. 86, February 1972, pp. 79–93.

FIGURE 17-11   Charts of market index and relative strength line 1978–1987.

T.S.E. GOLD/SILVER INDEX

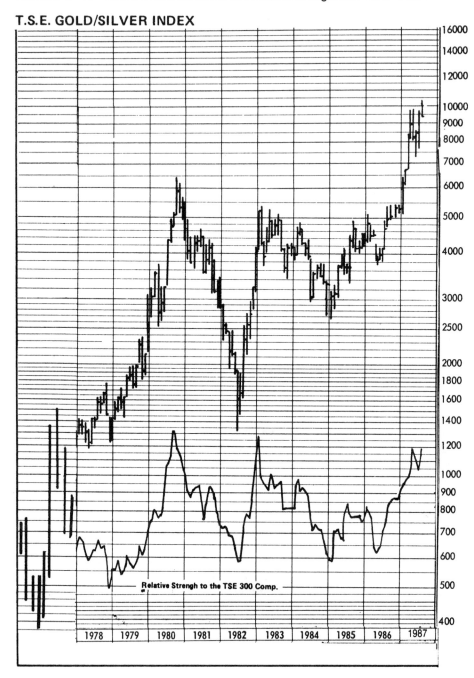

FIGURE 17-11 (continued)

T.S.E. OIL/GAS INDEX

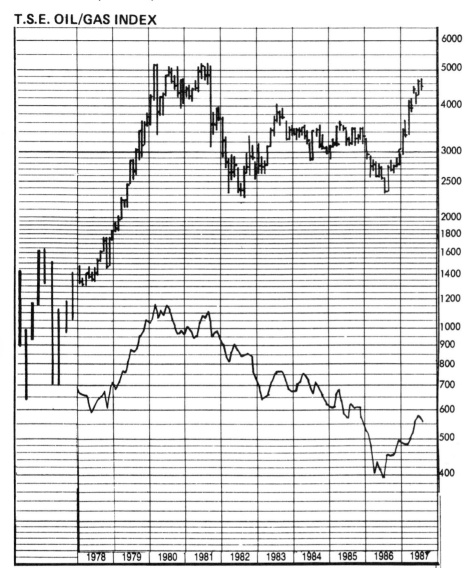

Source: Graphoscope 201, September 1987.

FIGURE 17-12 Volume data for the TSE from a representative newspaper.

TORONTO MOST ACTIVE STOCKS

Stock	Sales	High	Low	Close	Net Ch'g
INDUSTRIALS					
Husky	1557471	$11¼	11⅛	11⅛	
CTire A	622,454	$14¾	13¾	14⅜	+⅝
Nova A	609,217	$6⅜	6⅛	6¼	-⅛
IThomsn	583,430	$14½	13¾	13⅞	+⅛
Noranda	529,957	$21⅜	20⅞	21	-¼
MINES					
BlckHwk	167,600	65¢	52	55	-5
S[illegible]htA	108,327	$12	11⅛	11½	+⅜

Stock	Sales	High	Low	Close	Net Ch'g
SGordon	106,820	$6¼	6	6⅛	
Nthumbld	97,725	$1.30	1.15	1.24	
TVX	92,114	$5⅞	5⅛	5⅞	+¾
OILS					
UtdReef	143,850	$1.20	1.11	1.16	+5¢
Sienna	118,785	25¢	25	25	
Encor	113,168	$4.90	4.80	4.90	-5¢
Orbit	96,308	60¢	53	56	+6
Drumond	78,490	10¢	7½	10	+3

TORONTO MARKET BREADTH

	Yester.	Prev.
Issues traded	1,182	1,159
Advances	380	429
Declines	411	334
Unchanged	391	396

	Yester.	Prev.
52-week highs	32	30
52-week lows	21	26
Volume advances		8,427,000
Volume declines		9,241,000

DOLLAR TRADING		SHARE TRADING		TRANSACTIONS	
Industrials	269,297,150	Industrials	18,551,309	Industrials	12,998
Mines	21,603,534	Mines	3,088,404	Mines	2,589
Oils	4,784,246	Oils	1,539,386	Oils	941
Total	295,684,930	Total	23,179,099	Total	16,528

	Traded	Advances	Unchanged	Declines
Industrials	810	279	271	260
Mines	226	56	63	107
Oils	146	45	57	44

TORONTO VALUE LEADERS

INDUSTRIALS	Volume	Value	Last	Change	
Husky Oil	1,557,471	$17,329,596	$11⅛		
BCE	384,352	14,403,161	37⅜		
Cadillac Fairview	385,520	11,974,802	31	+	⅝
Noranda	529,957	11,215,242	21	—	¼
Alcan Aluminium	268,200	11,029,087	41⅛	+	⅛
Cdn Tire A	622,454	8,896,275	14⅜	+	⅝
Intl Thomson	583,430	8,184,402	13⅞	+	⅛
Dofasco	351,127	7,780,039	22¾	+	½
CP Ltd	425,378	7,510,448	17½	—	¼
Falconbridge	383,187	6,560,863	17¼	—	¼
MINES					
Placer	76,600	2,377,456	31⅛	—	⅛
Teck B SV	75,720	1,783,703	23¾		
Teck un	51,600	1,288,800	25⅛	+	⅛
Seabright A	108,327	1,244,125	11½	+	⅜
Intl Corona	41,960	1,227,332	29⅛	—	½
OILS					
Poco	63,942	697,114	10¾	+	¼
Encor	113,168	545,243	4.90	—	.05
Asamera	47,770	504,831	10½	+	⅛
Can Northwest	23,300	264,275	11⅜		
Westmin	33,545	255,262	7⅝	+	⅛

TSE 300 COMPOSITE INDEX

		Mkt. Volume
Net Change	+1.72	
Close	3072.56	23,179,099
3 p.m.	3074.99	18,124,238
2 p.m.	3073.81	15,699,035
1 p.m.	3073.22	13,994,056
Noon	3073.24	11,056,896
11 a.m.	3076.42	6,869,270
10 a.m.	3069.88	3,065,000
9:45 a.m.	3067.42	1,879,691
Previous Close	3070.84	26,297,612
Week Ago	3031.89	15,141,072
Month Ago	3070.78	16,934,154
Year Ago	2879.38	27,010,354

Yesterday's High	3076.42
Yesterday's Low	3067.42
1986 High	3134.49
1986 Low	2347.97
1985 High	2902.17
1985 Low	2347.49
P/E Ratio	17.21
Div. Yield	2.98
300 Volume	13,082,807
Total Return Index	4610.59

Volume technicians watch volume most closely on days when prices move, that is, on days when supply and demand move to a new equilibrium. If high volume occurs on days when prices move up, the overall nature of the market is considered to be bullish. If the high volume occurs on days when prices are falling, the market is bearish.

FIGURE 17-13 Chart of stock market average and trading volume.

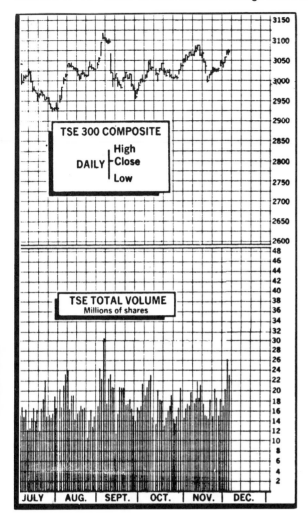

Figure 17-13 shows a bar chart of the TSE 300 Composite Index plotted with the daily volume on the TSE along the bottom of the chart.

There is one occasion when falling prices and high volume are considered bullish. When technicians feel the end of a bear market is near, they watch for a high volume of selling as the last of the bearish investors liquidate their holdings—this is called a *selling climax*. A selling climax is supposed to eliminate the last of the bears who drive prices down by selling, clearing the way for the market to turn up.

Some technicians also look for a speculative blowoff to mark the end of a bull market. A *speculative blowoff* is a high volume of buying that pushes prices up to a peak; it is supposed to exhaust the enthusiasm of bullish speculators and make way for a bear market to begin. Technicians who believe that a speculative blowoff marks the end of a bull market sometimes say "the market must die with a bang, not a whimper."

17-10   MOVING AVERAGE ANALYSIS

Moving average technicians, or rate-of-change technicians, as they are also called, focus on prices and/or a moving average of the prices. The *moving average* is used to provide a smoothed, stable reference point against which the daily fluctuations can be gauged. *Rate-of-change analysis* is used for individual securities or market indexes.

**17-10.1
Construction
of Chart**

Selecting the span of time over which to calculate the moving average affects the volatility of the moving average. Many technicians who perform rate-of-change analysis use a 200-day moving average of closing prices. The moving average changes each day as the most recent day is added and the two-hundred-and-first day is dropped. To calculate a 200-day moving average (MA_t) of the DJIA on day t, Eq. (17-3) is employed.

$$MA_t = \left(\frac{1}{200}\right)\sum_{j=1}^{200} TSE_{t-j} \tag{17-3}$$

Figure 17-14 shows the moving average of the TSE 300 Composite Index as a dotted line; the daily values of the index is represented by the bar chart. It is this relationship between the actual values and the moving average from which the technician obtains information.

**17-10.2
Interpreting
Rate-of-
Change
Charts**

When the daily prices penetrate the moving average line, technicians interpret this penetration as a signal. When daily prices move downward through the moving average, they frequently fail to rise again for many months. Thus, a downward penetration of a flattened moving average suggests selling. When actual prices are above the moving average but the difference is narrowing, this is a signal that a bull market may be ending. A summary of buy and sell signals followed by moving average chartists is given below.

Moving average analysts recommend buying a stock when (1) the 200-day moving average flattens out and the stock's price rises through the moving average, (2) the price of a stock falls below a moving average line that is rising, and (3) a stock's price that is above the moving average line falls but turns around and begins to rise again before it ever reaches the moving average line.

Moving average chartists recommend selling a stock when (1) the moving average line flattens out and the stock's price drops downward through the moving average line, (2) a stock's price rises above a moving average line that is declining, and (3) a stock's price falls downward through the moving average line and turns around to rise but then falls again before getting above the moving average line.

Adherence to the moving average trading rules over many months and many different stocks shows that sometimes profitable trades are signaled. However, the rules touch off unprofitable trades, too. This is why most tech-

FIGURE 17-14 Chart of TSE 300 Composite Index and moving average line.

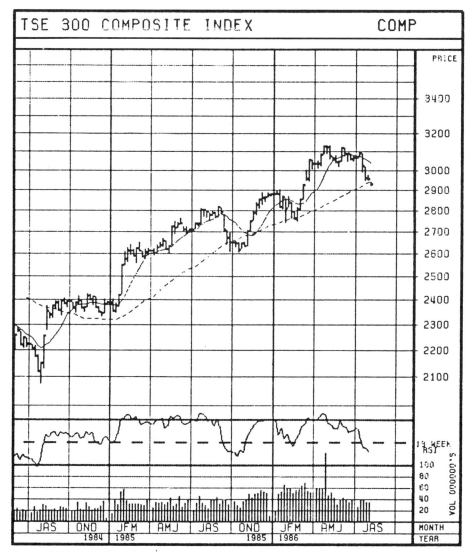

Source: Midland Doherty, *Market Dialogue*, August–October 1986.

nical analysts use more than one technique of technical analyis and compare the buy and sell signals issued by these different technical tools before they decide to trade securities.

17-11 CONCLUSIONS

Many more tools for technical analysis could be discussed; the discussion in this chapter has been limited to a mere sampling of the techniques.

All technical analysis tools have one thing in common: they attempt to measure the supply and demand for some group of investors. Technical analysis seems to presume that these shifts in supply and demand occur *gradually*, rather than instantaneously. More specifically, when shifting prices are detected, they are presumed to be the result of gradual shifts in supply and demand rather than a series of instantaneous shifts that all coincidentally happen to be moving in the same direction. Since these *shifts are expected to continue as the price gradually reacts* to news or other factors, the price change pattern is extrapolated to predict further price changes.

Many economists believe that technical analysis cannot measure supply and demand or predict prices. They suggest that security markets are efficient markets in which news is impacted into security prices instantaneously and without delay.[12] That is, news that causes changes in the supply and/or demand for a security is supposed to cause sudden once-and-for-all changes rather than gradual adjustments in supply and demand. As a result, economists believe that security *price changes* are a series of random numbers that occur in reaction to the random arrival of news. When a security's price moves in the same direction for several days, most economists interpret these movements as a series of independent changes in supply and/or demand— all of which coincidentally happen to move the price in the same direction. They assert that technical analysts are wrong in believing that supply and/ or demand adjust gradually, causing trends that may be used for predicting future prices. The evidence provided by economists to support their efficient markets hypothesis will be examined in Chap. 18.

QUESTIONS

1. "Fundamental analysts' estimates of intrinsic value are different from the security prices determined by supply and demand." True, false, or uncertain? Explain.
2. According to the Dow theory, what is the significance of an abortive recovery that follows a series of ascending tops?
3. What factual information is contained in the markings on a bar chart?
4. What does each column on a point and figure chart represent? How is the time dimension shown on a point and figure chart?
5. What significance is attributed to the volume of odd-lot trading by technical analysts?
6. Explain what the confidence index is supposed to measure. What relevance does this measure of confidence have for stock prices?
7. How are data on the number of shares that advanced and declined on a given trading day used by technical analysts?
8. Compare and contrast relative strength and systematic risk. What implications does high relative strength have for rates of return?
9. What are a *speculative blowoff* and a *selling climax*?
10. How is the moving average used in rate-of-change analysis?

---

12 Eugene F. Fama, "Efficient Capital Markets: A Review of Theory and Empirical Work," *Journal of Finance*, May 1970, pp. 383–417, and "The Behavior of Stock Market Prices," *Journal of Business*, January 1965, pp. 34–105.

11. Do most experienced technical analysts have one tool they believe in and follow closely? Explain.

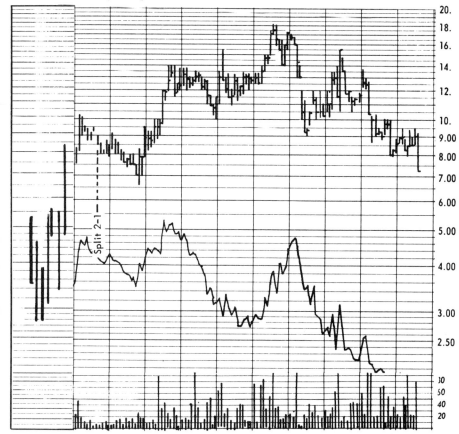

12. What type of pattern is found in the above chart? What is the implication of this pattern for price movements of Monendo?

SELECTED REFERENCES

Bookstaber, R., *The Complete Investment Book*. Glenview, Ill.: Scott Foresman & Co., 1985. Chapters 14–20 present computer programs for technical systems.

Edwards, R. D. and John Magee, Jr. *Technical Analysis of Stock Trends*, 5th ed. Springfield, Mass.: Trends Service, 1966. A book that has been used for years by technical analysts. Many different techniques are explained.

Jiler, William L. *How Charts Can Help You in the Stock Market*. New York: Trendline 1962. This popular book on charting explains many techniques and gives examples.

Levy, R. A. *The Relative Strength Concept of Common Stock Forecasting*. Larchmont, N.Y.: Investors Intelligence, 1968. This book explains some of the new nonchart-oriented quantitative technical tools.

Wu, Hsiu-Kwant and Alan Z. Zakon. *Elements of Investments: Selected Readings*. New York: Holt, 1965, sec. 5. This book of readings in investments devotes an entire section to technical analysis.

The Behaviour of Stock Market Prices

The economic model of capitalism, free markets, and private enterprise that the Canadian economy is patterned after requires (among other things) efficient capital markets that allocate investable funds where they are needed most so that they will be used most productively. Essentially, this requires that the highest bidder get the resource. Security prices must be allowed to fluctuate freely. If the prices are manipulated or controlled, financial capital will be misallocated to less productive uses.[1]

This chapter reviews empirical evidence about the capital markets in Canada and in the United States. Evidence is reviewed that suggests that the capital markets in the United States are free of price manipulation and are thus able to *allocate capital efficiently*. We make no similar claim for Canadian markets.[2] Some anomalous evidence is reported too. In effect, Chap. 18 treats the assertion that capital markets are efficient price setters as a testable hypothesis to be affirmed or denied with empirical evidence from scientific studies.

The investigation of security price movements that fills this chapter and its appendix is not undertaken solely to determine the *capital allocational efficiency* of security markets in Canada and the United States. The degree of efficiency with which a market allocates capital and how efficiently it sets prices also has implications for investment analysts. For example, if markets price their securities inefficiently, fundamental security analysis will be profitable because underpriced securities will await the perceptive analyst. Like-

---

1 A market may be considered *allocationally efficient* when prices adjust so that the risk-adjusted marginal rates of return are equal for all savers and all investors. As discussed in Chap 3, a securities market is *operationally efficient* when transactions costs are zero, or, more realistically, when transactions costs are kept down to a level where market-makers earn no economic profits. As suggested in Chap. 8, a market achieves *pricing efficiency* when its prices reflect all available information so that prices equal their underlying economic values. These three concepts of market efficiency are all interdependent. This chapter focuses on pricing efficiency.

2 The pioneering work on security price behaviour was conducted primarily with U.S. markets and securities data. Unfortunately, there are only a limited number of empirical studies published on Canadian security returns. We are unable to conclude at this time that the Canadian markets are indeed efficient.

wise, overpriced securities can be worthwhile to search for too, as they can be profitably sold short. Market pricing inefficiencies would also make it profitable to perform technical analysis. If security prices respond inefficiently to new information, learning lags that slow security price adjustments will cause trends that can be seen in charts and used to make trading profits. Also, if markets post inefficient prices, the risk-return analysis, which is based on the long-run equilibrium tendencies of a rational market, will not be a worthwhile pursuit. This chapter presents and reviews evidence about the efficiency of security prices with an eye toward reaching conclusions about these considerations.

18-1 THE MARKET MECHANISM

Before examining the facts about market efficiency, let us review the securities market mechanism. Securities markets are large institutions where many independent buyers and sellers meet. It is easy for newcomers to enter the market and for others to leave it. The existing securities regulations control price manipulation and require that security issuers disclose much information about themselves for the investing public. These factors are necessary for efficient markets, but they are not sufficient to guarantee market efficiency. However, additional aspects of the market mechanism are worthy of consideration.

News is generated in a random fashion. The various competing news services rush this news to the presses in an effort to "make the headlines." The news is not delayed or controlled in any systematic manner; it is widely dispersed and available to the public at virtually no cost. Public libraries contain current books published by the various financial services, and radio and television announcements are available at virtually no cost.

18-1.1 Dissemination of Information

There are no significant learning lags associated with news dissemination. That is, an investor in the Prairies or on the West Coast can obtain financial news as quickly as a resident of Montreal. Of course, different investors may develop different price forecasts based on the same news. Upon receiving financial news, some investors will underreact to it, while other investors will overreact. However, the reaction is immediate and continuous until the news is fully impacted into security prices.

Security prices are not controlled by any one buyer or seller. There are many independent buyers and sellers. Most security traders are not large enough to affect prices. The few institutions that are large enough to do so are restrained by law from manipulating prices (although they do sometimes reluctantly affect prices by their actions).

18-1.2 Prices Fluctuate Freely

There are many independent sources of opinion about security prices. Fundamental analysts and technical analysts develop expectations and valuation techniques that are widely divergent and independent of one another. Thus, at any moment, some "experts" will predict price rises for a security that other "experts" may consider overvalued.

**18-1.3
Fundamental
Analysis
Widespread**

There are many full-time fundamental analysts; over 12,000 are listed in the directory of the Financial Analysts Federation alone. These analysts follow the financial news and adjust their intrinsic value estimates accordingly. Many of them are in a position to affect prices through the buy or sell recommendations they make to their employers. Of course, all these analysts will never reach a uniform opinion about a security's intrinsic value, but they generally agree as to whether a given piece of news should tend to raise or lower prices.

**18-1.4
Continuous
Equilibrium
and
Degrees of
Disequilibrium**

If securities markets are perfectly efficient in allocating capital, the market will be in continuous equilibrium. This *continuous equilibrium* will not be static through time, however. Every time a new piece of news is released, one or more securities' intrinsic values will change, and the securities market prices will adjust toward their new values. It is the speed of this price adjustment process that gauges how efficient a market is. Since a *perfectly efficient market is in continuous equilibrium*, the intrinsic values of securities *vibrate randomly* and *market prices always equal the underlying intrinsic values at every instant* in time.[3] If any disequilibrium (of even a temporary nature) exists, then securities markets are less than perfectly efficient, and some capital will be misallocated as a result. Stated differently, allocational inefficiency results from irrational price movements.

18-2 TESTABLE HYPOTHESES ABOUT MARKET EFFICIENCY

When tests of the efficient markets hypothesis are being carried out, securities markets will be tested for varying degrees of efficiency. First, the *weakly efficient market hypothesis* is examined. The weakly efficient hypothesis says that *historical* price and volume data for securities contain no information that can be used to earn a trading profit above what could be attained with a naive buy-and-hold investment strategy.[4] This hypothesis suggests that technical analysis, which was discussed in Chap. 17, is merely well-recorded market folklore. Empirical evidence supports this hypothesis.

Also examined is the *semi-strong efficient market hypothesis*, which says that markets are efficient enough for prices to reflect all *publicly available* infor-

---

3 Paul Samuelson, "Proof That Properly Discounted Present Values of Assets Vibrate Randomly," *Bell Journal of Economics and Management Science*, Autumn 1973, pp. 369–374. See also Samuelson's article "Proof That Properly Anticipated Prices Fluctuate Randomly," *Industrial Management Review*, vol. 6, no. 2, pp. 41–49. The articles employ advanced mathematics.

4 The naive buy-and-hold strategy refers to the investment policy of randomly selecting securities (for example, with a dart), buying them, and holding them over the same time period as the alternative investment strategy is being tested while reinvesting all dividends. Studies indicate that about 10 or 11 percent per annum before taxes could have been earned in the New York Stock Exchange over the forty years by following a naive buy-and-hold strategy. L. Fisher and J. Lorie, "Rates of Return on Investments in Common Stock: The Year-by-Year Record, 1926–1965," *Journal of Business*, January 1964. Ibbotson Associates, *Stocks, Bonds, Bills and Inflation: 1985 Yearbook* (Chicago, Ill.: Capital Market Research Center.)

mation. Consequently, only a few insiders, trading on short-run price changes, can earn a profit larger than what could be earned by using a naive buy-and-hold strategy. It is concluded that securities markets in the United States are generally semi-strong efficient. The support for semi-strong efficiency in Canada, however, is thin. More empirical testing is necessary before definitive conclusions can be drawn.

Finally, the *strongly efficient market hypothesis* is examined; it claims that *no one* can consistently earn a profit larger than what could be earned with a naive buy-and-hold strategy by trading on short-run security price movements. The reason given is that security price changes are independent random variables and that *no one* has monopolistic access to valuable inside information. The strongly efficient market hypothesis is found to be not quite acceptable. A few cases of monopolistic profit making have been found that violate this hypothesis.

FIGURE 18-1   Illustration of different degrees of market price efficiency.

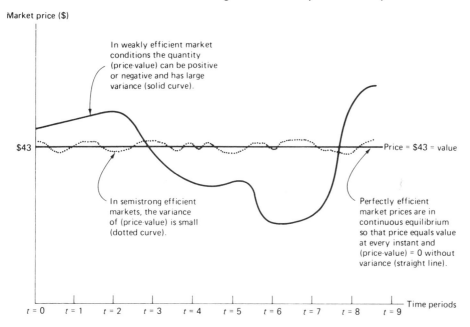

Differences in the degree of security price efficiency are contrasted graphically in Fig. 18-1. The three hypotheses about pricing efficiency are not mutually exclusive: They differ only in the *degree* of market efficiency they suggest. The review of evidence about pricing efficiency below begins with the weakest hypothesis and ends with evidence about the strongest hypothesis.[5] Some anomalous evidence is reviewed too.

5 Eugene F. Fama, "Efficient Capital Markets: A Review of Theory and Empirical Work," *Journal of Finance*, May 1970, pp. 383–417, and "The Behavior of Stock Market Prices," *Journal of Business*, January 1965, pp. 34–105.

18-3 THE WEAKLY EFFICIENT MARKETS HYPOTHESIS

In this section the hypothesis highlighted in Box 18-1, that markets are weakly efficient, is examined.

BOX 18-1
Definition of
Weakly
Efficient
Markets

Weakly efficient markets were defined to be markets in which past prices provide no information about future prices that would allow a short-term trader to earn a return above what could be attained with a naive buy-and-hold strategy. This definition does not mean that short-term traders and speculators will not earn a positive rate of return. It means that, on average, they will not beat a naive buy-and-hold strategy with information obtained from historical data.

Some lucky traders do beat the naive buy-and-hold strategy, and some unlucky ones lose everything they have. However, we will not illogically reason from these specific cases to reach general conclusions. Instead, we will scientifically analyze massive data in an effort to reach accurate general conclusions.

**18-3.1
Filter
Rules**

An x percent filter rule is a mechanical security trading rule that operates as defined in Box 18-2.

BOX 18-2
Definition
of a
Filter Rule

If the price of a security rises at least x percent, buy and hold the security until its price drops at least x percent from a subsequent high. Then, when the price decreases x percent, liquidate the long position, and assume a short position until the price rises x percent.

By varying the value of x, one can test an infinite number of filter rules. If stock price changes are a series of independent random numbers, filter rules should not yield more return than a naive buy-and-hold strategy. The filter rules should earn a significant profit, however, if some of the patterns chartists talk about (such as the primary trends of the Dow theory) actually exist.

Various studies have been conducted using different stocks and different filters. Filters as small as ½ of 1 percent (that is, $x = 0.005$), as large as 50 percent ($x = 0.5$), and many values between these extremes have been tested. The tests were performed with stock price data gathered at various intervals. One test used daily stock prices covering several years. Some of the filter rules earn a return above the naive buy-and-hold strategy if the commissions incurred in buying and selling are ignored. However, after commissions are deducted, no filter outperformed the naive strategy.[6] In fact, some ran up considerable net losses. If patterns do exist that can be used as bases for a profitable trading strategy, filter rules are unable to detect them. This is one piece of evidence in support of the weakly efficient markets hypothesis.

Security price changes do not appear to have significant momentum or inertia that causes changes of a given sign to be followed by changes of that same sign; the filter rules should have detected this pattern if it existed. However, security prices may follow some sort of *reversal* pattern in which price changes of one sign tend to be followed by changes of the opposite sign. Filter rules might not detect a pattern of reversals, but serial correlation tests should.

18-3.2 Serial Correlation

Serial correlation (or *autocorrelation*) measures the correlation coefficient between a series of numbers with lagging numbers in the same time series. Trends or reversal tendencies in security price changes can be detected with serial correlation. We can measure the correlation between security price changes in period t (denoted Δp_t) and price changes in the same security that occur k periods later and are denoted Δp_{t+k}; k is the number of periods of lag. Of course, there is a long-term upward trend in security prices; so if one ''period'' covers a number of years, a positive serial correlation should be observed. But long-term trends are of no interest; they were already known to exist, as shown in Table 7-2 on page 157. In question here is the existence of patterns in short-term (for example, daily, weekly, or monthly) price changes that can be used to earn a larger profit after commissions from aggressive trading than what the naive buy-and-hold strategy would yield. If such patterns exist, this would tend to indicate that security prices do not adjust to follow their randomly changing intrinsic values.

In effect, tests for serial correlation in a security's price changes are searching for patterns like the two in Fig. 18-2. The x's in Fig. 18-2 are what would occur if positive changes (denoted $\Delta p > 0$, or Δp^+) were followed by positive changes k periods later and/or if negative changes (denoted $\Delta p < 0$ or Δp^-) were followed by other negative changes k periods later. That is, the x's above the horizontal axis in Fig. 18-2 depict upward-trending prices, and the x's beneath the horizontal axis represent downward-trending prices. If prices kept reversing direction every kth period, the observations represented by the o's in Fig. 18-2 would result.

Various serial correlation studies about security prices have been published. Many different securities, many different lags (that is, different values of k), and many different time periods have been used from which to draw

6 S. Alexander, ''Price Movements in Speculative Markets: Trends or Random Walks,'' *Industrial Management Review*, May 1961, pp. 7–26. E. F. Fama and M. E. Blume, ''Filter Rules and Stock Market Trading,'' *Journal of Business*, January 1966, pp. 226–241. Readers who are interested in commodities trading may study the application of filter rules and other tests explained in this chapter to commodity prices. See Richard A. Stevenson and Robert M. Bear, ''Commodity Futures: Trends or Random Walks?'' *Journal of Finance*, March 1970, pp. 65–81.

FIGURE 18-2   Scatter diagram of price changes and lagged price changes in security.

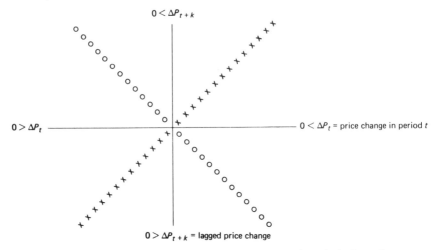

the data for the tests. The serial correlation studies failed to detect any significant trends (that is, any significant correlations).[7] Again, a scientific evaluation of stock price movements tends to support the weakly efficient markets hypothesis.

**18.3.3
Runs
Tests**

It is possible that security prices might fluctuate randomly but occasionally follow upward, sideways, or downward trends which filter rules and serial correlations could not detect as deviations from random wiggles. That is, price changes may be random most of the time but *occasionally* become serially correlated for *varying periods* of time. To examine this possibility, runs tests may be used to determine if there are runs in the price changes. A *run* occurs in a series of numbers whenever the changes in the numbers switch signs. For instance, six price *changes* that comprise four runs are listed below.

$\Delta p^+,\ \Delta p^+,\ 0,\ \Delta p^-,\ \Delta p^+,\ \Delta p^+$

The four runs illustrated above are positive, zero, negative, and positive. Runs vary in length from one to any large number. For example, in a bear market, a security price that declines for ten consecutive trading days will generate nine negative daily price changes but only one negative run.

7 Eugene F. Fama, "The Behavior of Stock Market Prices," op. cit. S. Alexander, op. cit. M. G. Kendall, "The Analysis of Economic Time Series, part I," *Journal of the Royal Statistical Society*, 1953, vol. 96, pp. 11–25. More recent studies that embrace a more heterogeneous sample of stocks and extend the previous serial correlation studies may be found in Gabriel A. Hawawini, "On the Time Behavior of Financial Parameters: An Investigation of the Intervaling Effect," unpublished doctoral dissertation, New York University, 1977. See also Robert A. Schwartz and David K. Whitcomb, "Evidence on the Presence and Causes of Serial Correlation in Market Model Residuals," *Journal of Financial and Quantitative Analysis*, June 1977, pp. 291–315. These more recent studies find significant positive serial correlations for one-day trends in some stocks.

Mathematical statisticians are able to determine how many positive, negative, zero, or total runs may be expected to occur in a series of truly random numbers of any size. Therefore, if a time series of security price changes has either a positive, negative, zero, or total number of runs which occur either more frequently or less frequently than would be expected in a series of random numbers, this is evidence that some kind of nonrandomness occurs. The runs tests which have been published suggest that the runs in the price changes of various securities are not significantly different from the runs in a table of random numbers.[8] It seems that short-run traders who search for various types of nonrandom trends from which to earn a profit will not be able to beat a naive buy-and-hold strategy, on average.

The preceding evidence suggests that studying charts of historical stock prices will not reveal any patterns that contain profitable insights about prices in the future. However, two patterns of minor proportion have been reported.

18-3.4 Anomalous Evidence about Weakly Efficient Markets

THE DAY OF THE WEEK (OR WEEKEND) EFFECT

One of the most interesting anomalies is a well-documented finding that there is a pattern to security returns by the day of the week; specifically, that the average returns on securities on Mondays, as measured by the closing price on the last trading day of the week to the closing price on Monday, are negative. Furthermore, it has been found that returns on the last trading day of the week are abnormally high.[9] This day of the week effect has been tracked back to 1928 on both exchange-traded and over-the-counter stocks in the U.S. equity market,[10] and has been identified on our Canadian markets as well as the Australian, Japanese, and United Kingdom bourses.[11]

This anomaly is variously described as the Monday Effect (abnormal low returns on Mondays), the Weekend Effect (price changes effectively occurring between the close at the end of the week and the opening on Monday), and in the most general form, the Day of the Week Effect (different and consistent

---

8 Eugene F. Fama, op. cit.; S. Alexander, op. cit. See also Table App. 18-A4.

9 See F. Cross, ''The Behaviour of Stock Prices on Fridays and Mondays,'' *Financial Analysts Journal* 29, November–December 1973, pp. 67–69, Kenneth R. French; ''Stock Returns and the Weekend Effect'', *Journal of Financial Economics* 10, March 1980, pp. 55–69; and Michael R. Gibbons and Patrick Hess, ''Day of the Week Effects and Asset Returns'', *Journal of Business* 54, October 1981, pp. 579–596.

10 Donald B. Keim and Robert F. Stambaugh, ''A Further Investigation of the Weekend Effect in Stock Returns'', *The Journal of Finance*, vol. 39, no. 3, July 1984, pp. 819–835. The authors found consistently negative Monday returns for the Standard & Poor's 500 Composite Index from 1928 (the day the daily history begins) to 1982 for actively traded over-the-counter stocks and for firms of all sizes.

11 Jeffrey Jaffe and Randolph Westerfield, ''The Week-End Effect in Common Stock Returns: The International Evidence'', *The Journal of Finance*, vol. 40, no. 2, June 1985, pp. 433–454. The authors also concluded that this international weekend effect was independent of both the weekend effect in the United States, and foreign exchange effects vis-à-vis the U.S. dollar.

average returns on each trading day). Jaffe and Westerfield examined daily returns in Canada using the Toronto Stock 300 Composite Index, from January 2, 1976, to November 30, 1983. They reported that the average daily percentage return on the index was .052 percent over this period. However they also found that the average daily returns were as shown below.[12]

Monday	Tuesday	Wednesday	Thursday	Friday
−.139%	.022%	.115%	.106%	.139%

Similar findings were reported for the other countries in the study. The magnitudes of this anomaly are not trivial. For example, although the average daily return in Australian stocks from March 1, 1973, to November 30, 1982 was .032 percent, the average return on Tuesdays and Thursdays was −.133 percent and .166 percent respectively.

A number of reasons for this pervasive effect have been explored. Thus far, the possibilities of settlement procedures and specialist bid-ask biases have been discarded. One possibility is that exdividend dates are clustered around Mondays causing a distortion to the rate of return calculations. Nevertheless, this interesting anomaly of a weekday seasonal trend implies that, ceteris paribus, the best time to buy stocks is Monday morning in Canada, the United States, and the United Kingdom, and Mondays or Tuesdays in Japan and Australia. And the best time to sell would be Friday in Canada, late Wednesday or Friday in the United States, Wednesday or Saturday in Japan, and Tuesday in the United Kingdom. However, the seasonality is unlikely to be of interest to retail investors as the profits gained would be too small to pay brokerage commissions.

THE YEAR-END (OR JANUARY) EFFECT

Another anomalous pattern in stock price movements is called the "year-end effect." Several researchers using U.S. data have discerned a tendency for stock prices, especially the prices of stock in small firms, to fall two or three percentage points late in December and then rise early in January.[13]

Morgan examined monthly returns of common stocks traded on the Toronto Stock Exchange over the period January 1963 to December 1982. He found some evidence of a January Effect in Canada, particularly evident for small firms that had sharply declined in value prior to January.[14] Brown et al.[15] found evidence of a similar seasonality for Australian securities. How-

12 Ibid., table 1, p. 435.

13 Ben Branch, "A Tax Loss Trading Rule," *Journal of Business*, April 1977, vol. 50, no. 2, pp. 198–207. Marc R. Reinganum, "The Anomalous Stock Market Behavior of Small Firms in January: Empirical Tests for Tax-Loss Selling Effect," *Journal of Financial Economics*, 1983, vol. 12, no. 1. Richard Roll, "The Turn of the Year Effect and the Return Premium on Small Firms," *Journal of Portfolio Management*, 1982.

14 I. G. Morgan, "Abnormal Returns and Recent Losses on Security Investments," Queen's University, working paper, May 1985.

15 Philip Brown, Donald B. Keim, Allan W. Kleidon, and Terry A. Marsh, "Stock Return Seasonalities and the Tax-Loss Selling Hypothesis: Analysis of the Arguments and Australian Evidence," *Journal of Financial Economics*, vol. 12, 1983.

ever, their results seem to indicate a "January/July Effect" as they reported that the December–January and July–August months earn consistently higher returns than do the other months, with the highest returns recorded in January and July.

It has been suggested that the year-end effect might result from last minute selling by those investors who have accumulated losses on stocks and who want to realize some of these losses to reduce their income taxes for the year. However, the cause of this second anomaly remains as much a mystery as the cause of the weekend effect. Some difficulties have been reported in getting accurate measurements too.[16] Whether or not someone will be able to devise a trading rule that profitably exploits the year-end effect on an after-commissions basis remains to be seen.

The two anomalies reported above make it difficult to conclude that stock prices conform completely to the weakly efficient markets hypothesis. However, they are not yet the basis for profitable trading strategies. Therefore, they appear to be of only limited significance.[17]

In testing the weakly efficient markets hypothesis, filter rules, serial correlations, and runs tests have been employed. Other tests could be reviewed, but their findings are similar.[18] These are scientific studies that support the weakly efficient hypothesis. Studies by unbiased scientists using analytical techniques that deny the weakly efficient hypothesis are conspicuously absent. Unscientific assertions that short-run security price changes are not random continue to emanate from persons who earn their living by selling

18-3.5 Weakly Efficient Markets Hypothesis Accepted

---

16 Marshall E. Blume and Robert F. Stambaugh, "Biases in Computed Returns: An Application of the Size Effect," *Journal of Financial Economics.* November 1983. Richard Roll, "On Computing Mean Returns and the Small Firm Premium," *Journal of Financial Economics*, November 1983, vol. 12, no. 3. These two studies reach similar conclusions.

17 Two studies reported a tendency for stock market prices to reverse and move in the opposite direction from one transaction to the next. This pattern does not suggest profitable trading schemes for people who do not own seats on the exchange so that they may trade without paying commissions. Victor Niederhoffer and M. F. M. Osborne, "Market Making and Reversal on the Stock Exchange," *Journal of American Statistical Association*, December 1966, vol. 61. Clive W. T. Granger and Oskar Morgenstern, "Spectral Analysis of New York Stock Market Prices," *KYKLOS*, vol. 16, 1963.

18 A. B. Larson reports that corn futures prices appear to fluctuate randomly in "Measurement of a Random Process in Futures Prices," Paul Cootner (ed.), *The Random Character of Stock Market Prices* (Cambridge, Mass.: MIT Press, 1964), pp. 219–230. Benoit Mandelbrot reports that spot cotton prices fluctuate randomly in "The Variation in Certain Speculative Prices," in Paul Cootner (ed.), *The Random Character of Stock Market Prices* (Cambridge, Mass.: MIT Press, 1964), pp. 307–332. Richard Roll documents random Treasury bill rates in *The Behavior of Interest Rates*, (New York: Basic Books, 1970). W. Schwert finds that the prices of seats on the NYSE fluctuate randomly in "Stock Exchange Seats as Capital Assets," *Journal of Financial Economics*, January, 1977, pp. 51–78. J. P. Stein's research uncovers randomly fluctuating prices for art in "The Monetary Appreciation of Paintings," *Journal of Political Economy*, October 1977, pp. 1021–1036. Several different commodity prices are found to fluctuate with little deviation from randomness by Richard Stevenson and Robert Bear, "Commodity Futures: Trends or Random Walks?" *Journal of Finance*, March 1970. Brad Cornell and David Mayers report that foreign exchange prices fluctuate randomly in "The Efficiency of the Market for Foreign Exchange under Floating Rates," *Review of Economics and Statistics*, February 1978.

charting services. However, the latter may be dismissed because of their bias and the paucity of scientific evidence they produce. Thus, a reasonable individual would have little trouble accepting the weakly efficient markets hypothesis.

18-4   THE SEMI-STRONGLY EFFICIENT MARKETS HYPOTHESIS

The semistrongly efficient markets hypothesis requires more evidence of market efficiency than the previous hypothesis. In essence, the weakly efficient hypothesis asserts only that security prices do not tend to follow patterns repetitively. Semistrongly efficient markets are defined in Box 18-3.

BOX 18-3 Definition of Semi-strongly Efficient Markets

> The semi-strongly efficient markets hypothesis requires that all *public* information be fully reflected in security prices. This means that information in *The Financial Post*, *The Globe and Mail*, and *The Wall Street Journal* publications, for example, is worthless to investors.

In a free and competitive market, prices adjust so that they equate supply and demand. When supply and demand functions do not change, an equilibrium price will emerge that represents a consensus of opinion. For securities this equilibrium price would be the intrinsic value. That price will prevail until supply and/or demand are changed by *new information*. When a new piece of information reaches the market, supply and/or demand will react, and a new price will be formed. The faster the news is assimilated and the new equilibrium price emerges, the more efficient the markets.

18-4.1 Learning Lags

In order for markets to be semistrongly efficient, there can be no lags as the latest news is disseminated to the public. Prompt news dispersion is important if prices are to reflect all relevant information immediately. Consider what would occur if learning lags existed.

Suppose that financial news released in Montreal did not spread beyond Quebec's boundaries on the day it was released because of some learning lag. If the news favourably affected some corporation's stock, the price would move up slightly as Montreal residents acted upon it. Then, on the second day after the announcement, suppose the news travelled as far west as Kenora near the Manitoba border. The rest of the eastern investors would bid the price up a bit further the second day. By the third day, suppose the news travelled as far west as the Rocky Mountains. As a result, prairie investors would bid prices up further as they learned the news. Finally, on the fourth day after the announcement, the news would spread to British Columbia. By that time, a price would be bid up for a fourth consecutive day. As a result of this hypothetical learning lag, two events would occur. First, there would be a 4-day trend in a security's price rather than one immediate effect. Second, for over three days the security's price would not have fully reflected all available information. The studies discussed in Sec. 18-3 revealed essentially no instances of trends such as the one just hypothesized. This lack of such trends indicates that financial news is widely and quickly disseminated. As a result, securities prices do tend to reflect all publicly available information at any moment.

The market may over- or underreact to news. However, as long as it reacts instantly and continuously in a series of unbiased movements around the true intrinsic value (or equilibrium price), the semistrong hypothesis is supported.

It is possible that securities prices fully reflect most news immediately but react imperfectly, irrationally, or slowly to a certain few kinds of news. Although investigating the reaction to every type of news is not possible, we can examine a few particularly interesting cases. One of the most important pieces of information determining a security's price is the earnings of the corporation that issued the security. If securities markets are semistrongly efficient, prices will reflect changes in firms' earning power.

18-4.2 Reaction to Earnings Announcements

A study by Ball and Brown analyzed the effects of the annual earnings announcements made by 261 corporations over a twenty-year period.[19] First, Ball and Brown estimated the simple linear regression Eq. (18-1) to measure each firm's changes in earnings.

$$\Delta eps_{it} = a_i + b_i(\Delta eps_{Mt}) + u_{it} \tag{18-1}$$

where

Δeps_{it} = change in the ith firm's earnings per share in the tth time period

Δeps_{Mt} = change in earnings per share averaged over all other firms

a_i and b_i = regression intercept and slope coefficient, respectively, for firm i

u_{it} = unexplained residual for firm i in period t

After Eq. (18-1) was estimated for each firm, respectively, Eq. (18-2) was derived from Eq. (18-1) to forecast the next year's earnings per share.

$$E(\Delta eps_{it}) = a_i + b_i(\Delta eps_{Mt}) \tag{18-2}$$

where

$E(\Delta eps_{it})$ = forecasted or expected change in eps for the ith firm in the tth time period

Δeps_{Mt} = change in the market average eps which actually occurred in time period t

19 R. Ball and P. Brown, ''An Empirical Evaluation of Accounting Income Numbers,'' *Journal of Accounting Research*, Autumn 1969, pp. 159–178. Ball and Brown acknowledged in their article that their results may be biased because the earnings were scaled by dividing them by market prices, a process that probably introduces spurious correlation. This possibility is evaluated by Nicholas J. Gonedes, ''Evidence of the Information Content of Accounting Numbers: Accounting-Based and Market-Based Estimates of Systematic Risk,'' *Journal of Financial and Quantitative Analysis*, June 1973, pp. 407–443.

Based on the one-year forecasts prepared with Eq. (18-2), each year's earnings for every firm were classified into two possible categories. First, there were those firms that did worse than expected — that is, the disappointing growth in earnings category. Second, there were the firms that did better than expected—that is, the category where growth in earnings was a pleasant surprise. The effects of these earnings changes on the common stock prices of the firms in each category were analyzed separately.

To determine the effects of the announcements on a security's price while holding other factors (namely, the market's movement) constant, Ball and Brown calculated characteristic lines relating the rate of change in the 261 firms' market prices to the rate of change in the level of the market.

$$r_{it} = a_i + b_i r_{Mt} + e_{it} \tag{10-1}$$

where

r_{it} = the ith stock's 1-month rate of return in time period t

r_{Mt} = the market's rate of return in month t

a_i and b_i = regression intercept and slope statistics, respectively, for the ith asset

e_{it} = the unsystematic residual return for stock i in month t which was left unexplained by the characteristic line

The number of percentage points above or below the firm's characteristic line where the actual rates of return occurred (that is, the residual error, denoted e_{it}) measures the portion of the price change that was caused by unsystematic factors other than the market's movements. The percentage points above or below the characteristic line were determined for all securities in the two categories—that is disappointing earnings or pleasantly surprising earnings—for each of the twelve months before and the six months after each firm's twenty annual earnings announcements. Equation (19-3) was employed to calculate the abnormal performance index (API) over the twelve months before and the six months after (for a total of eighteen months before and after) the earnings announcement for all 261 stocks.

$$\text{API} = \frac{1}{261} \sum_{i=1}^{261} (1 + e_{i,1})(1 + e_{i,2})...(1 + e_{i,18}) \tag{18-3}$$

Figure 18-3 shows the compounded rates of residual return averaged over all 261 firms in the sample. It shows that, on average, the market correctly anticipated earnings changes *before* they were announced to the public. That is, the firms that had disappointing earnings experienced unfavourable downward pressure on their prices in the months preceding the actual announcement to the market. Firms whose earnings were higher than expected enjoyed upward pressure on the prices of their securities in the months preceding the earnings announcement. On the average, only about 10 percent of the cumulative unsystematic price adjustment occurred *after* the

FIGURE 18-3   Average percentage price movements preceding and succeeding 20 annual earnings announcements of 261 firms.

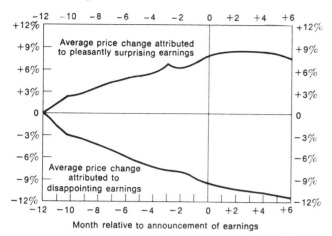

Month relative to announcement of earnings

earnings were announced. This was hardly enough of a price change to yield a net trading profit *after commissions*.

The analysis of earnings announcement effects supports the semistrongly efficient markets hypothesis. The securities prices reflected, and even anticipated, the new information about changes in firms' earnings.

Before going on to other subjects, we must pause to realize that the tendency of securities prices to anticipate changes in announced earnings does not result in *trends* in securities prices. First of all, earnings tend to change in a random manner, so that patterned reactions to earnings will not cause price patterns.[20] Second, none of the 261 firms in the sample experienced the smooth price changes indicated by the aggregate data shown in Fig. 18-3. Each individual firm's price moved up or down in a series of erratic random price changes that could not be predicted in advance. Only the cumulative unsystematic errors in the subsamples accumulated smoothly to nonzero sum over time.[21]

The discussion of interest rate risk in Chap. 9 explained why interest rates affect security prices. Essentially, market interest rates determine the appropriate discount rate to use in determining the security's present values. Therefore, changes in the discount rate announced by the Federal Reserve Board or the Bank of Canada may be expected to affect security prices. This

18-4.3 Announcement Effects from Changes in the Discount Rate

20 R. A. Brealey, *An Introduction to Risk and Return from Common Stocks* (Cambridge, Mass.: MIT Press, 1983), chap. 5. Chapter 5 discusses the randomness of earnings research.

21 Other studies have reached similar conclusions about the reaction of stock prices to earnings changes. J. Aharony and I. Swary, "Quarterly Dividend and Earnings Announcements and Stockholders Returns: An Empirical Analysis," *Journal of Finance*, March 1980, pp. 1–12. M. Joy, R. Litzenberger and R. McEnally, "The Adjustment of Stock Prices to Announcements of Unanticipated Changes in Quarterly Earnings," *Journal of Accounting Research*, Autumn 1977, pp. 207–225. R. Watts, "Systematic Abnormal Returns after Quarterly Earnings Announcements," *Journal of Financial Economics*, June–September 1978, pp. 127–150.

is particularly true because announcements of changes in the discount rate are so widely publicized by financial newspapers.

Research into the effects of discount rate changes has shown that the average security's price changes a tiny but significant amount (never exceeding ½ of 1 percent) on the first trading day following the public announcement by the Federal Reserve of a change in the discount rate.[22] This change is not enough to yield a trading profit. Most of the price change associated with the announcement seems to occur *before* the actual announcement. Thus, the semistrong hypothesis is again supported by the empirical facts.

18-4.4 Leading and Lagging Stocks

Some Wall Street veterans refer to General Motors as a "bellwether stock" because it is supposed to initiate, and sometimes lead, trends in the movements of stock prices. A diversified stock market average, like Standard & Poor's 500 stocks composite average, is thus an average of some leading and some lagging stocks, according to this thinking.

If some securities tended to lead market movements and other stocks tended to be laggers, economic logic suggests that profit-seeking price speculators would reduce these leads and lags to zero. These speculators would buy (sell) the lagging stocks whenever the leading stocks rose (fell) in price in order to profit from the price rise (to avoid losses on the price fall). As long as any stock tended to be a consistent leader or lagger, this simple rule would yield short-run trading profits.

The existence of consistent leading or lagging stocks would disprove the semistrongly efficient markets hypothesis, because consistent leads or lags must presumably be the result of some investors consistently getting valuable news before other investors. That is, leading and lagging security prices would result from the fact that for some securities (the leaders), new news that systematically affected all securities prices was impacted into their prices before the same news was reflected in the prices of other securities. Such intertemporal differences in the reaction of prices to new public information would refute the semistrong efficient markets hypothesis.

To test for leading and lagging stock prices, the modified characteristic regression line shown in Eq. (18-4) was estimated empirically by Dr. Jack Clark Francis.[23]

$$r_{it} = a_i + b_i(r_{m,t+k}) + e_t \tag{18-4}$$

Equation (18-4) is like the characteristic lines explained in Chap. 10 except that it also allows for leads and lags in the reaction of the *i*th security to

22 R. N. Waud, "Public Interpretation of Discount Rate Changes: Evidence on the 'Announcement Effect,' " *Econometrica*, 1971.

23 J. C. Francis, "Intertemporal Differences in Systematic Stock Price Movements," *Journal of Financial and Quantitative Analysis*, June 1975. A later study employing daily returns found some significant one-day leads and lags in NYSE and AMEX stocks—especially AMEX. See G. A. Hawawini and A. Vora, "Evidence of Intertemporal Systematic Risks in the Daily Price Movement of NYSE and AMEX Common Stocks," *Journal of Financial and Quantitative Analysis*, 1979. These leads and lags are so small, however, that they do not obviate the Francis conclusions.

systematic changes in the market, as measured by r_m. The subscript k, which is added to or subtracted from the time period subscript for r_m in Eq. (18-4), measures the lead or lag in months. For example, if Eq. (18-4) yielded a significant goodness of fit for the ith stock when $k = -2$, the ith stock would lead the rate of change in the market by two months. But if the regression had a significant correlation for $k = 4$, this would mean the stock's rate of price change r_i tended to lag four months behind the rate of change in the market index r_m. When $k = 0$, Eq. (18-4) is identical with the characteristic regression line, Eq. (10-1), with no leads or lags.

The leading-concurrent-lagging-characteristic regression line, Eq. (18-4), was estimated for values of $k = 6,5,4,3,2,1,0, -1, -2, -3, -4, -5$, and -6 months for 770 different NYSE stocks: that is (770 stocks $\times$ 13 leads and lags for each equals) 10,010 regressions were run on the sample. The model was estimated over two different three-year sample periods (that is, $t = 1, 2, ...,$ 36 months) to determine whether leaders or laggers existed over temporary short-run periods. Then the model was estimated over one 10-year (that is, $t = 1, 2, ..., 120$ months) sample to test for stocks that might consistently lead or lag in the long run. Thus, in total 30,030 ($= 3$ samples $\times$ 13 lags $\times$ 770 stocks) regressions were fitted.

Over the two 3-year sample periods, about 10 percent of the 770 stocks showed some statistically significant tendency to lead or lag the market in each sample period. But the stocks that tended to lead or lag in one 3-year sample usually did not show any tendency to lead or lag in the other 3-year sample. When the same 770 stocks were tested over a ten-year period, only 6 of them (that is, less than 1 percent of the sample) showed any significant tendency to lead or lag the market. Six significant regressions could be expected if 10,010 regressions on 770 stocks were run with *random numbers* simply because of coincidences called sampling errors.

The temporary leads and lags which were found in about 10 percent of the 770 stocks in one of the two 3-year subsamples help explain why chartists can think that some stocks lead or lag the market: They are observing spurious correlation errors which occur because of coincidence. But these temporary coincidences are not consistent enough to suggest that some stocks do in fact lead or lag the market or to violate the semistrong efficient markets hypothesis.

Stock splits and stock dividends are essentially paper-shuffling operations that do not change the total value of the firm or the owner's wealth. For example, a 100 percent stock dividend or a 2 for 1 stock split results in twice as many shares outstanding and in each share being worth half as much.[24]

**18-4.5
Effects of
Stock Splits**

---

24 To accountants, stock splits are different from stock dividends, the difference resulting from the treatment of the equity section of the balance sheet. With a stock split, the par value per share is decreased to reflect the splitting of the shares; the number of shares outstanding is simultaneously increased so as to leave the total amount in the capital account unchanged. With stock dividends, a portion of retained earnings equal to the value of the stock dividend is transferred from retained earnings to the capital account. Both adjustments are pure bookkeeping entries that leave total equity and total assets unchanged and hence have no real economic significance.

If security markets efficiently equate security prices with security values, the *total value* of the firm's outstanding shares will not be affected.

Some firms occasionally have stock splits to broaden the market for their shares. For example, if a firm's shares are selling for $120 each, a 3 for 1 stock split (or 200 percent stock dividend) will reduce the cost of a round lot (100 shares) from $12,000 to $4,000. Therefore, splitting the high-priced shares may be advisable if a firm is seeking to broaden its shareholder group to include families that may not have $12,000 but do have $4,000 to invest. This is particularly true because shareholders may make good customers. However, the additional small investors gained by such actions cannot be expected to control enough purchasing power to raise the price of the firm's shares significantly.

The study that will be discussed here is based on a sample of 940 stock splits and stock dividends that occurred on the NYSE between 1927 and 1959.[25] In essence, the study asked if stock splits or stock dividends had any influence on investors' one-period rates of return, as defined below.

$$r_t = \frac{\text{capital gains or loss} + \text{cash dividends}}{\text{purchase price}}$$

All the shares were adjusted for the stock splits and stock dividends before the rates of return were calculated. This adjustment ensured that only actual changes in the investor's wealth would be measured rather than the meaningless price changes which are associated with a stock dividend or split. For example, if a 2 for 1 split or 100 percent stock dividend occurred, the share prices would be halved before the stock dividend or split (or doubled afterward) so that no changes in the investor's wealth would be attributed to it in calculating rates of return.

The numerical example below shows how a share of stock, originally selling for $100 per share, can fall to $50 per share owing to a 2 for 1 split or

TIME PERIOD (T)	t = 1	t = 2	t = 3	t = 4
Market price per share	$100	$100	$50	$50
Cash dividend per share	$5	$5	$2.50	$2.50
Earnings per share	$10	$10	$5	$5
Number of shares held per $100 original investment	1	1	2	2
Rate of return per period	5%	5%	5%	5%

---

25 E. Fama, L. Fisher, M. Jensen, and R. Roll, "The Adjustment of Stock Prices to New Information," *International Economic Review*, February 1969, vol. 10, no. 1, pp. 1–21. The FFJR study was replicated with allowance for shifting beta statistics and similar results were obtained; see Sasson Bar-Yosef and Lawrence D. Brown, "A Reexamination of Stock Splits Using Moving Betas," *Journal of Finance*, September 1977, vol. XXXII, no. 4, pp. 1069–1080. More recently, it has been reported that stock splits increase the day-to-day and week-to-week price fluctuations approximately 30 percent. See James A. Ohlson and Stephen H. Penman, "Volatility Increases Subsequent to Stock Splits: An Empirical Aberration," *Journal of Financial Economics*, June 1985, vol. 14, no. 2, pp. 251–266.

100 percent stock dividend without changing the owner's 5 percent rate of return. The change in the unit of account (that is, the stock dividend or stock split) occurred between periods 2 and 3. Since the investor owns twice as many shares after the stock split but since each share has half the previous market price, the investor's wealth is unchanged. Moreover, the investor's income in this simple example is $5 of cash dividends per period per $100 of investment before and after the change in the unit of account, that is, a constant 5 percent rate of return.

Characteristic Line Used   In order to have a standard of comparison against which the rates of return may be evaluated, we must make adjustments for the differences in returns resulting from bull- or bear-market swings in price. The characteristic line, defined in Eq. (10-1), was calculated for each security studied in order to adjust for these changes in the market conditions. Each stock's characteristic line was fit using sixty monthly returns from the thirty months before and thirty months after the change in the unit of account.

Residual Errors   The residual errors e_t around the time of the stock split or stock dividend were the focus of the study. Figure 18-4 shows the characteristic line for some hypothetical firm.

FIGURE 18-4   Characteristic line.

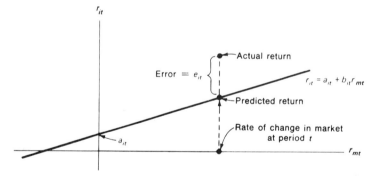

If the residual error at the time of stock split or stock dividend was zero, $e_{it} = 0$, the security's actual rate of return was right on the characteristic line, and the change had no positive or negative effects on an investor's normal pattern of returns. If the residual error was positive (that is, if it had a positive e_{it}) at the time of the change, then the actual return (that is, the r_{it}) was above the characteristic line, and the stock split or stock dividend was apparently boosting returns above the normal pattern. A negative residual error (that is, a negative e_{it}) occurs when the actual rate of return is below the characteristic line and some negative influence is affecting that period's rate of return. If the beliefs that most investors and businesspeople hold about stock splits and stock dividends somehow creating something of value are true, the residual errors will tend to be positive after the split or dividend because the value of the firm should increase at that time.

Monthly Residual Errors Averaged   The residual errors about the characteristic line are the results of many influences other than stock splits and stock dividends. Therefore, it is not practical to examine the residuals of *individual* firms following a split or dividend and draw conclusions. To overcome this problem, the residual errors averaged over 940 stocks were calculated for each month before and after the split or dividend. In effect, this approach averages the influences that are not due to the stock dividend or stock split to zero. If the *average* residuals are significantly different from zero in the months after the change, this disparity indicates that the change affected the value of the firm. Equation (18-5) defines the average residuals $\bar{e}_t$ for the tth month before or after the split or dividend month.

$$\bar{e}_t = \left(\frac{1}{940}\right)\sum_{i=1}^{940} e_{it} \qquad (18\text{-}5)$$

The average residual, say, six months before the split month is denoted $\bar{e}_{-6}$, for example.

Cumulative Average Residuals (CARs)   In order to measure the cumulative month-by-month effect that the stock dividend or split may have, the average monthly residuals from Eq. (18-5) were summed chronologically over sixty months. Equation (18-6) defines these cumulative abnormal (or unsystematic) average monthly residual returns, denoted CARs.

$$\text{CARs} = \sum_{t=-30}^{30} \bar{e}_t = \sum_{t=-30}^{30}\sum_{i=1}^{940} e_{it} \qquad (18\text{-}6)$$

Note that the cumulative abnormal residuals (CARs) graphed in Fig. 18-5 are increasing in the months *preceding* the stock split or stock dividend. This rise in returns in the few months prior to the change can be attributed to the information content of an *anticipated cash dividend*. In the majority of cases, a stock split or stock dividend is accompanied by an increase in the cash dividend. Thus, the stock split or stock dividend is interpreted by the market as evidence of an upcoming increase in cash dividends. These anticipated increases in the firm's cash dividends usually *contain information*. When a board of directors declares an increased cash dividend, this decision tends to indicate that the majority of the directors are confident that the sustainable earnings power of the firm has risen enough to maintain a higher level of future dividends. It is this implied earnings rise that is the basis for the higher returns preceding the stock split or stock dividend.

Interpreting the Results   The preceding explanation for the increasing cumulative abnormal residuals (CARs) prior to a stock dividend or split involves some complicated logic. Let us retrace this reasoning and examine it more closely. The cause-and-effect logic for positive residuals preceding the changes goes as follows. A stock dividend or split implies an increase in cash dividends; increased cash dividends imply a permanent rise in earnings; and

FIGURE 18-5   The average residual errors surrounding the item of a stock split or stock dividend.

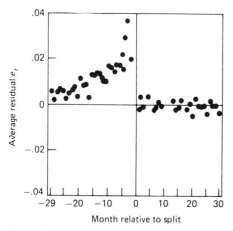

Source: E. Fama, L. Fisher, M. Jensen, and R. Roll, "The Adjustment of Stock Prices to New Information," *International Economic Review*, February 1969, vol. 10, no. 1, fig. 2a.

higher anticipated earnings cause capital gains, pushing returns up and causing positive residual errors. If this line of logic is correct, a firm that declares a stock dividend or split and subsequently fails to raise its cash dividend must be disappointing the market; its price and returns can be expected to rise in anticipation of the stock split or dividend and then fall when cash dividends and earnings fail to rise. Figure 18-6 shows graphs of the cumulative average residuals (CARs) for firms that had stock dividends or splits

FIGURE 18-6   The average residual errors before and after stock dividends and splits (a) average residuals for dividend "increases"; (b) average residuals for dividend decreases.

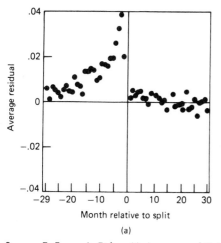

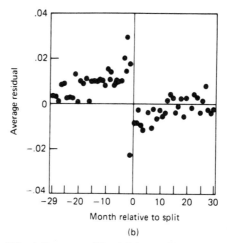

Source: E. Fama, L. Fisher, M. Jensen, and R. Roll, "The Adjustment of Stock Prices to New Information," *International Economic Review*, February 1969, vol. 10, no. 1, pp. 1–21.

and then either (1) increased their cash dividend or (2) decreased their cash dividend.

Figure 18-6a shows that firms that had stock dividends or splits and subsequently raised cash dividends had small positive residuals, on average, in the months after the stock dividend or split. This is an indication that the market had correctly anticipated the earnings rise and that most of the capital gains occurred before the earnings rise was announced. These stocks' increased cash dividends merely reflect the earnings rise. Thus, in the final analysis, the owners of the securities that split and also increased their earnings power enjoyed abnormally high returns, on average, during the months surrounding the stock dividend or split.

Those firms that had stock dividends or splits and also decreased cash dividends experienced high returns (that is, positive residuals, on average) until the cash dividend declined (presumably, because earnings were poor). Then the value of the stock fell, causing negative residuals, $e_{it} < 0$, after the stock dividend or split that was associated with lower earning power. Thus, investors who bought stocks that had stock dividends or splits followed by decreases in their cash dividends were worse off because the stocks experienced capital losses, on average, after the split month, as shown in Fig. 18-6b. Charest[26] conducted a similar study to that of Fama, Fisher, Jensen, and Roll using Canadian data. He examined the risk/returns behaviour on stocks traded on the Toronto Stock Exchange that split over the period 1963 to 1975. His results were surprising, as he found that investors would have realized large *negative abnormal* returns from the systematic purchases of split stocks. Charest concluded that the TSE was ''markedly inefficient'' with respect to split information.

Conclusions The evidence indicates that stock dividends and splits by themselves are worthless but that they may convey valuable information about the firm's earning power. Earning power is the basic source of stock values. Stock dividends and splits alone cause high returns only for several months before cash dividends are paid because the market expects an increase in dividends and, more basically, an increase in earnings. If the expected increase in dividends (and, also, in earnings) does not materialize, the information content of the stock dividend or split is discounted, and returns fall temporarily below normal before resuming their pattern along the characteristic line. In the final analysis, neither the market value of the firm nor the return to the investor is changed by stock splits and dividends. Such changes are essentially paper-shuffling operations that the market expects to convey information about earnings. Any effects from stock dividends and splits can be attributed to their implicit information content and nothing else.

If an investor can correctly anticipate stock dividends and stock splits, the data seem to indicate that it is possible to earn speculative capital gains. However, further studies of the average residuals show that the gains tend to be

---

26 Guy Charest, ''Returns to Splitting Stocks on the Toronto Stock Exchange,'' *Journal of Business Administration*, vol. 12, no. 1, Fall 1980, pp. 19–40.

zero after the announcement date of the stock dividend or split.[27] Therefore, speculation anticipating the announcement of stock dividends or stock splits should precede the public announcement if it is to be profitable. This is probably possible only by spending the capital gains before they are earned to detect announcements that are associated with increasing earnings. The investor would be better off by ignoring stock dividends and splits and instead concentrating on forecasts of the earning power of firms.

The study of stock dividends and splits furnishes additional support for the semistrongly efficient markets hypothesis that markets are efficient in the United States. The stock dividends and stock splits themselves had no discernible effects on prices. This evidence is impressive in view of the popular folklore about the importance of stock dividends and stock splits. It seems that the rational investors' evaluations prevailed over those of their less sophisticated counterparts. The unusual price changes which did occur near the time of the splits were attributable to rational investor reactions to changes in cash dividends and earnings.

The studies examined thus far provide strong support for semistrong market efficiency, at least in the United States. In the next sections the studies examined either refute the notion of semistrong efficiency in both the United States and Canada or provide ambiguous results.

Tests of dividend changes have focused on the speed and adjustment of security prices to changes in firms' cash dividends. Pettit, in a study of dividend change announcements of companies traded on the New York Stock Exchange over the period 1964 to 1968, found that the market anticipates, in part, dividend announcements and that prices quickly adjust to the impact of the announcement.[28] He found that when companies increase their dividends substantially (by 10 percent to 25 percent) there were abnormally high returns in the order of as much as 4 percent in the month of the dividend change (most of it occurring in a ten-day period prior to the announcement). However, he reported that the full impact of the change was imbedded in the month. There were no effects in preceding periods. Charest, however, in a study of New York Stock Exchange securities that changed dividends over the period 1947 to 1968, found that buying stocks of companies that announced dividend increases and selling short stocks that announced dividend decreases yielded a profitable trading strategy.[29]

Charest conducted a similar study using Canadian data.[30] He examined returns on dividend changing stocks for Toronto Stock Exchange listed securities over the period 1963 to 1976. Charest came to similar conclusions to his

18-4.6 Effects of Changes in Dividends

27 W. H. Hausman, R. R. West, and J. A. Largay, "Stock Splits, Price Changes, and Trading Profits: A Synthesis," *Journal of Business*, January 1971, pp. 69–77.

28 R. Richardson Pettit, "Dividend Announcements, Security Performance and Capital Market Efficiency," *Journal of Finance*, December 1972, pp. 993–1007. See also R. Richardson Pettit, "The Impact of Dividends and Earnings: A Reconciliation," *Journal of Business*, January 1976.

29 Guy Charest, "Dividend Information, Stock Returns and Market Efficiency-2," *Journal of Financial Economics* 6, 1978, pp. 297–330.

30 Guy Charest, "Returns to Dividend Changing Stocks on the Toronto Stock Exchange," *Journal of Business Administration*, volume 12, no. 1, Fall 1980, pp. 1–18.

U.S. data study. However, he expressed a caution in interpreting his results. He stated, ''On the surface, the TSE appears inefficient with respect to dividend information since our evidence indicates that abnormal returns from trading in dividend changing stocks, . . . could have been profitable. We could illustrate though that our results were unstable across time subperiods and rather sensitive to the method used for estimating normal returns.'' Charest went on to conclude, ''It is doubtful then that real systematic trading in dividend changing stocks on the TSE has been, or could be, profitable. Yet our results invite a try.''[31]

18-4.7
New Issues

Studies of new issues raise the question of whether investors who buy new issues of securities at the issue date, at the offering price, earn abnormal returns. Reilly found that this was precisely the case in the United States.[32] Investors who bought at issue earned positive excess returns although those who bought in the ''after-market'' earned normal returns. The implication is that underwriters slightly underprice new issues, thus providing excess returns to the primary issue investors, although the price quickly adjusts in the secondary market.

Shaw, however, in a Canadian study of new issues over the period 1956-1968 found that unseasoned new issues (first issue of public securities) provided investors with abnormally low rates of returns by comparison to simple market indexes.[33]

18-4.8
Shiller's
Findings

In 1981 Professor Robert J. Shiller dealt what some financial economists thought was a fatal blow to the efficient markets theory.[34] Shiller used inflation-adjusted empirical data that was detrended for per share cash dividends and stock prices, denoted d and p, respectively, for (1) the 1871 through 1979 Standard and Poor's 500 Composite Stocks index, and (2) the 1928 through 1979 Dow-Jones Industrial Average. Shiller compared the market prices with the present values. The present values, v, were calculated using the equation below.

$$v_t = \sum_{f=t+1}^{T} \frac{d_f}{(1 + k)^{f-t}} + \frac{p_T}{(1 + k)^{T-t}}$$

where the present time period is denoted t, the symbol T represents the terminal time period, and f indicates the number of time periods in the future that the expected cashflow occurs. Shiller used both constant and time-varying real interest rates for the discount rate, k, in different applications of the

31 Guy Charest, ''Returns to Dividend Changing Stocks on the Toronto Stock Exchange,'' *Journal of Business Administration*, volume 12, no. 1, Fall 1980, pp. 13–14.
32 Frank K. Reilly, ''New Issues Revisited,'' *Financial Management*, vol. 6, no. 4, Winter 1977, pp. 28–42.
33 David Shaw, ''The Performance of Primary Common Stock Offerings: A Canadian Comparison,'' *Journal of Finance*, December 1971, pp. 1101–1113.
34 R.J. Shiller, '' Do Stock Prices Move Too Much To Be Justified By Subsequent Changes in Dividends?'' *American Economic Review*, vol. 71, June 1981, pp. 421–436.

above equation. Figure 18-7 illustrates some representative findings about the divergence Shiller found between the market prices and the present values.

The theory of finance suggests that the true economic value of a security equals its present value. However, Figure 18-7*a* and *b* illustrates differences between the present value of the two indexes and their market values that is startling and flies in the face of the received theory. Various people reacted to Shiller's findings in different ways. In his presidential address to the American Economic Association in 1982, Gardner Ackley, for instance, said that ''Robert Shiller's recent (1981) paper appears to demolish the possibility that movements of U.S. stock prices can be explained by the rational expectations of shareholders.''[35]

FIGURE 18-7   Time series graphs of market prices and their concurrent present values for (a) Standard and Poor's 500 Composite Stocks and (b) Dow-Jones Industrial Average.

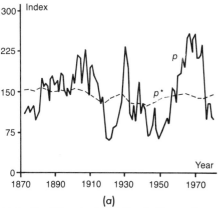
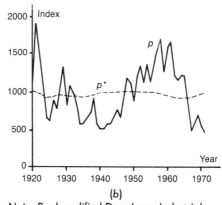

(a)

(b)

Note: Real Standard and Poor's Composite Stock Price Index (solid line *p*) and *ex post* rational price (dotted line *p**), 1871-1979, both detrended by dividing a long-run exponential growth factor. The variable *p** is the present value of actual subsequent real detrended dividends, subject to an assumption about the present value in 1979 of dividends thereafter.

Note: Real modified Dow Jones Industrial Average (solid line *p*) and *ex post* rational price (dotted line *p**), 1928-1979, both detrended by dividing by a long-run exponential growth factor. The variable *p** is the present value of actual subsequent real detrended dividends, subject to an assumption about the present value in 1979 dividends thereafter.

Source: R.J. Shiller, ''Do Stock Prices Move Too Much To Be Justified by Subsequent Changes in Dividends?'' *American Economic Review,* June 1981, vol. 71, figures 1 and 2, p. 422.

More recently, Marsh and Merton have faulted Shiller's findings by pointing out that corporate managers ''smooth'' the fluctuations in their cash dividend payments.[36] Marsh and Merton show that the present value of a time-series of smoothed cash dividend payments must necessarily fluctuate less

---

35 Gardner Ackley, ''Commodities and Capital: Prices and Quantity,'' *American Economic Review,* March 1983, p. 13.

36 T.A. Marsh and R.C. Merton, ''Dividend Variability And Variance Bounds Tests For The Rationality Of Stock Prices,''*American Economic Review,* June 1986, pp. 483–498.

than do the unconstrained market prices. Therefore, they conclude that their ''. . . analysis casts doubt in general over the use of volatility comparisons between stock prices and economic variables which are not also speculative prices, as a methodology to test stock market rationality.''[37]

Shiller replied to Marsh and Merton by admitting he made some relevant points about dividend smoothing.[38] At the same time Shiller cited independent research to support his assertion that the U.S. stock market prices were subject to bullish ascents that sometimes involved excessive optimism and bearish plunges that could be overwrought with pessimism.[39] In fact, Shiller's assertion that stock market prices are subject to irrational fads recalls to mind the similar view of investor behaviour that was set forth some years ago by an economist, and also a successful speculator, named John Maynard Keynes who stated that

> most of these persons are, in fact, largely concerned, not with making superior long-range forecasts of the probable yield of an investment over its whole life, but with forecasting changes in the conventional basis of valuation a short time ahead of the general public. They are concerned, not with what an investment is really worth to a man who buys it ''for keeps,'' but with what the market will value it at, under the influence of mass psychology, three months or a year hence. . . . For it is not sensible to pay 25 for an investment for which you believe the prospective yield to justify a yield of 30, if you also believe that the market will value it at 20 three months hence.
>
> Thus the professional investor is forced to concern himself with the anticipation of impending changes in the news or in the atmosphere of the kind that experience shows the mass psychology of the market is most influenced.[40]

Two anomalies in the semistrongly efficient markets hypothesis are noteworthy. First, there is a ''price-earnings ratio effect.'' Second, there is a ''size effect.'' Both of these anomalies have been found to cause statistically significant aberrations in stock prices as a result of publicly available information.

18-4.9 Anomalies in the Semi-strongly Efficient Markets Hypothesis

Stocks with Low Price-earnings Ratios   The use by fundamental security analysts of price-earnings ratios (or synonymously, earnings multipliers) was explained in some detail in Chap. 15. The following paragraphs present empirical evidence about a well-known and highly regarded investment scheme that is based on this form of analysis. The decision rule to employ the scheme is simple and easy to apply; buy stocks that have low price-earnings ratios in order to earn excessively high risk-adjusted rates of return. Respected investment advisory firms (for example, Value Line Investment Company of New York City) and money management firms use low price-

37 Ibid, p. 495.

38 R.J. Shiller, ''The Marsh-Merton Model of Managers' Smoothing of Dividends'', *American Economic Review*, June 1986, Volume 76, No. 3, pp. 499–503.

39 Lawrence H. Summers, ''Does The Stock Market Rationally Reflect Fundamental Values?'' *Journal of Finance*, vol. 41, no. 3, pp. 591–600.

40 John Maynard Keynes, *The General Theory of Employment, Interest, and Money* (New York: Harcourt Brace Jovanovich, 1936) pp. 154–155.

earnings ratios as investment criteria with acknowledged success.[41] Further, several academic researchers and financial analysts have published studies that advocate selection of stocks with low price-earnings ratios (called simply P/E's hereafter).[42] The most thorough study published recently that advocates the selection of low P/E stocks was done by Dr. S. Basu; it is explained below.[43]

Dr. Basu analyzed market data on over 750 NYSE listed stocks from the fourteen year period between September 1956 and August 1971. The first step in his analysis was to array all the stocks under analysis based on the values of their year-end P/E's. Second, Basu formed five equal-sized portfolios from the quintiles of each year's array of the stocks' P/E's. Third, the monthly rates of return of the five P/E quintile portfolios were calculated over the next year. Fourth, Basu computed the characteristic line in risk-premium form for each of the five quintile portfolios.

$$r_{pt} - R_t = A_p + B_p(r_{mt} - R_t) + u_{pt} \qquad (18\text{-}7)$$

where

$r_{pt} - R_t$ = the risk-premium on the pth P/E quintile portfolio in the tth month, also called excess return

$r_{mt} - R_t$ = the rate of return risk-premium in the tth month from the Lorie-Fisher market index

A_p = alpha regression intercept coefficient = Jensen's portfolio performance measure for the pth quintile portfolio

B_p = beta regression slope coefficient for portfolio p = an index of the pth portfolio's systematic risk

u_{pt} = residual return for portfolio p in month t that was left unexplained by the regression

41 Fischer Black, "Yes Virginia, There Is Hope: Tests of the Value Line Ranking System," *Financial Analysts Journal*, September-October 1973. T.E. Copeland and D. Mayers, "The Value Line Enigma, 1965-1978: A Case Study of Performance Evaluation Issues," *Journal of Financial Economics*, 1984. J. Shelton, "The Value Line Contest: A Test of Predictability of Stock Price Changes," *Journal of Business*, July 1967, pp. 251-269. W. Hausman, "A Note on the Value Line Contest: A Test of the Predictability of Stock Price Changes," *Journal of Business*, July 1969, pp. 317-320. R.S. Kaplan and R. Weil, "Risk and the Value Line Contest," *Financial Analysts Journal*, July-August 1973, pp. 56-60. L. Brown and M. Rozeff, "The Superiority of Analysts' Forecasts as Measures of Expectations: Evidence from Earnings," *Journal of Finance*, March 1978, pp. 1-16. C. Holloway, "A Note on Testing an Aggressive Strategy Using Value Line Ranks," *Journal of Finance*, June 1981, pp. 711-719.

42 Paul F. Miller and Ernest R. Widmann, "Price Performance Outlook for High and Low P/E Stocks," *1966 Bond and Stock Issue, Commercial and Financial Chronicle*, Sept. 29, 1966, pp. 26-28. Francis Nicholson, "Price Ratios in Relation to Investment Results," *Financial Analysts Journal*, July-August 1960, pp. 43-45. J. Peter Williamson, *Investments: New Analytic Techniques* (New York: Praeger, 1971) pp. 160-168. Volkert S. Whitbeck and Manown Kisor, Jr., "A New Tool in Investment Decision-Making," *Financial Analysts Journal*, May-June 1973, pp. 55-62.

43 S. Basu, "The Investment Performance of Common Stocks in Relation to Their Price-Earnings Ratios: A Test of the Efficient Markets Hypothesis," *Journal of Finance*, June 1977, vol. XXXII, no. 3, pp. 663-682. Basu used Jensen's characteristic line estimated in terms of risk premiums. M.C. Jensen, "Risk, the Pricing of Capital Assets, and the Evaluation of Investment Portfolios," *Journal of Business*, April 1969, vol. 42, no. 2, pp. 167-247. More recently, assertions

Basu replicated the four steps outlined above Eq. (18-7) each year for fourteen years. Table 18-1 contains summary statistics. Quintile portfolio 5 contains the 20 percent of the stocks with the highest P/E's. Portfolio 1 contains the stocks with the lowest P/E's and, purportedly, the highest risk-adjusted rates of return. Essentially, each of the quintile portfolios in Table 18-1 may be viewed as a mutual fund that has the policy of acquiring all NYSE stocks in a given P/E quintile (but no others) each year on April 1, holding the portfolio one year, and then liquidating and reinvesting in a similar P/E quintile portfolio on April 1 of next year.

The top three lines of Table 18-1 support the venerable folklore about P/E's. The first and second quintile portfolios, with their low median P/E's, earned much higher average rates of return and higher average risk-premiums than the other quintile portfolios with higher median P/E's. The inverse relationship between the P/E and the average return is clearly visible in the top three lines. However, these statistics in the top three lines ignore the effects of risk.

The fourth line of Table 18-1 lists the five quintile portfolios' beta systematic risk coefficients. There is no obvious relationship between the five portfolios' P/E's and their betas. Thus, it appears that the differences in returns documented in the second and third lines of Table 18-1 may be purely the result of P/E's.

The fifth and sixth lines in Table 18-1 present Treynor's and Sharpe's risk-adjusted investment performance measures, respectively. Treynor's measure is defined in Eq. (26-4) and illustrated in Fig. 26-7. Sharpe's portfolio performance measure is defined in Eq. (26-2) and illustrated graphically in Fig. 26-4. Both measures vary inversely with the P/E of the quintile portfolio. This is evidence that supports the notion that, on average, low P/E stocks earn better risk-adjusted rates of return than high P/E stocks. These results from two different investment performance measures, both of which measure return per unit of risk borne, are even more impressive than the simple return data shown in the first three lines of Table 18-1.

The resounding success of simply buying stocks with low P/E's, which is documented in Table 18-1, gave Dr. Basu some pause; it appeared to be too easy to beat the market. Furthermore, the superior risk-adjusted rates of return from low P/E stocks implies that the semistrongly efficient market hypothesis explained above was violated. Therefore, Dr. Basu pressed his inquiry further before jumping hastily to the conclusion that the semistrongly efficient markets hypothesis had been violated.

Basu simulated deducting the security analysis and portfolio management expenses that are appropriate for a large portfolio in order to determine the returns net of these costs that could have been earned from quintile portfolio 1. He deducted (1) the high, fixed NYSE commissions that existed during his sample period, (2) a research fee of ¼ of 1 percent each year, and (3)

---

that the P/E ratio subsumes the size effect are made by S. Basu, 'The Relationship Between Earnings Yield, Market Value, and the Return for NYSE Stocks: Further Evidence,'' *Journal of Financial Economics*, vol. 12, no. 1, 1983.

TABLE 18-1   PERFORMANCE MEASURES AND RELATED SUMMARY STATISTICS (APRIL 1957–MARCH 1971)

PERFORMANCE	Quintile P/E Portfolio*					Market Portfolio*
	5	4	3	2	1	S
Median P/E ratio†	35.8	19.1	15.0	12.8	9.8	15.1
Average annual rate of return r_p‡	0.0934	0.0928	0.1165	0.1355	0.1563	0.1211
Average annual excess return r'_p§	0.0565	0.0558	0.0796	0.0985	0.2260	0.0841
Systematic beta risk B_p	1.1121	1.0387	0.9678	0.9401	0.9866	1.0085
Treynor's reward-to-volatility measure ¶	0.0508	0.0537	0.0822	0.1047	0.1237	0.0834
Sharpe's reward-to-variability measure^a	0.0903	0.0967	0.1475	0.1886	0.2264	0.1526
Jensen's measure of average excess return, and	−0.0330	−0.0277	0.0017	0.0228	0.0467	0.0030
t value in parentheses	(−2.62)	(−2.85)	(0.18)	(2.73)	(3.98)	(0.62)

*5 = highest P/E quintile, 1 = lowest P/E quintile, S = total sample, and F = Fisher stock market index.

† = Based on 1957–1971 pooled data.

‡$\overline{r_p} = \left(\sum\limits_{t=1}^{168} r_{pt}\right)/14$, where r_{pt} is the continuously compounded return of portfolio p in month t (April 1957 to March 1971).

§$\overline{r'_p} = \left(\sum\limits_{t=1}^{168} r'_{pt}\right)/14$, where r'_{pt} is the continuously compounded excess return (r_{pt} minus r_{ft}) of portfolio p in month t (April 1957 to March 1971).

¶ Mean excess return on portfolio p divided by its systematic risk.

^{a} Mean excess return on portfolio p divided by its standard deviation.

Source: S. Basu, "The Investment Performance of Common Stocks Relative to Their Price-Earnings Ratios: A Test of the Efficient Markets Hypothesis," *Journal of Finance*, June 1977, table 1.

federal income taxes that were appropriate for an investor in the 50 percent tax bracket. After these costs were deducted from the quintile portfolio with the lowest P/E, Dr. Basu found that the portfolio earned from ½ of 1.0 to 2½ percent per annum more than a randomly selected portfolio (that is, selected without regard to the stocks' P/E's) in the same risk-class.

Basu's after-costs results are well worth considering when selecting common stocks, especially for tax-exempt investors and NYSE insiders who do not have to pay stock brokerage commissions. However, the one or two percentage points per year additional rate of return that the average (that is, commission- and tax-paying) investor could hope to attain from the lowest P/E portfolio hardly represents a breathtaking way to beat the market. Rather, the annual incremental return to be gained from selecting low P/E stocks could better be described as a slow, but fairly steady, little gain.[44]

The Size Effect—A Second Anomaly   Several studies were published in the early 1980s indicating that common stock investments in small-sized firms earned significantly higher rates of return than similar investments in medium- or large-sized corporations.[45] In one early study Banz, for instance, showed that NYSE-listed firms with market values of total common stock outstanding in the smallest 20 percent earned 19.8 percent per year more than the largest 20 percent of the firms in this NYSE sample.[46] There were times when the firms in the largest quintile outperformed the firms in the smallest quintile. However, the rates of return from common stock investments in the smallest quintile outperformed those in the larger quintiles by

44 Banz and Breen suggest that the effect of low-price earnings multiples on returns may be a function of the data base selected. They found support for the low price-earnings multiple effect when using data from the current COMPUSTAT file. However, when they used data from a sequentially collected COMPUSTAT file, they found no evidence of an independent "low P/E" effect. See Rolf W. Banz and William J. Breen, "Sample-Dependent Results Using Accounting and Market Data: Some Evidence," *The Journal of Finance*, vol. 41, no. 4, September 1986, pp. 779–793.

45 Rolf W. Banz, "The Relationship Between Return and Market Value of Common Stocks," *Journal of Financial Economics*, vol. 9, March 3–18, 1981. P. Brown, A.W. Kleidon, and T.A. March, "New Evidence on the Nature of Size-Related Anomalies in Stock Prices," *Journal of Financial Economics*, 1983, vol. 12, pp. 33–56. R.G. Ibbotson and R.A. Sinquefield, *Stocks, Bonds, Bills and Inflation: The Past and the Future* (Charlottesville, Va.: *Financial Analysts Research Foundation*, 1982). Donald Keim, "Size Related Anomalies and Stock Return Seasonality: Further Empirical Evidence," *Journal of Financial Economics*, June 1983, vol. 12, pp. 13–32. M.R. Reinganum, "Misspecification of Capital Asset Pricing: Empirical Anomalies Based on Earning's Yields and Market Values," *Journal of Financial Economics*, 1981a, vol. 9, pp. 19–46. M.R. Reinganum, "The Arbitrage Pricing Theory: Some Empirical Results," *Journal of Finance*, 1981b, vol. 36, pp. 313–321. M.R. Reinganum, "A Direct Test of Roll's Conjecture on the Firm Size Effect," *Journal of Finance*, 1982, vol. 37, pp. 27–35. M.R. Reinganum, "The Anomalous Stock Market Behavior of Small Firms in January: Empirical Tests for Tax-Loss Selling Effects," *Journal of Financial Economics*, 1983, vol. 12, pp. 89–104. M.R. Reinganum, "Portfolio Strategies Based on Market Capitalization," *Journal of Portfolio Management*, Winter 1983, vol. 9, pp. 29–36. R. Roll, "A Possible Explanation of the Small Firm Effect," *Journal of Finance*, 1981, vol. 36, 879–888.

46 Rolf W. Banz, "The Relationship Between Return and Market Value of Common Stocks," *Journal of Financial Economics*, March 1981, vol. 9, pp. 3–18.

an amount that was both economically and statistically significant over the longer sample intervals. Since the total market value of all common stock outstanding is a matter of public record for most corporations, the size effect appears to be a second flaw in the semistrongly efficient markets hypothesis.

Much research effort has gone into investigating the size effect. Statistical measurement problems have been encountered. Furthermore the economic rationale for the size effect has been difficult to unravel. It appears as if the size effect may be a proxy for one or more other fundamental economic determinants of common stock returns. For example, some researchers have found that small firms are typically riskier than larger firms. If so, economic theory suggests that riskier investments must yield higher returns to induce investors to assume the risk. Risk-adjusted rates of return (like those explained in Chap. 26) were calculated to see if the small firms yielded sufficiently high returns to compensate for their level of riskiness. These tests generally indicated that the small-sized firms outperformed the larger firms on a risk-adjusted return basis. However, some statistical problems in measuring the risk clouded these results.[47] Also, problems in measuring the investors' returns further obscured the results of the early tests of the size effect.[48]

Several different economic variables may ultimately be shown to be the cause of the size effect. The small firms may have low price-earnings ratios[49] or low market prices[50] or freedom from agency costs[51] — any of which may explain what appears at first to be a size effect. Or one of the other reasons

47 R. Roll, ''A Possible Explanation of the Small Firm Effect,'' *Journal of Finance*, 1981, vol. 36, pp. 879–888. Andrew A. Christie and Michael Hertzel, *Capital Asset Pricing Anomalies: Size and Other Correlations*, University of Rochester, 1981. M.R. Reinganum, ''Misspecification of Capital Asset Pricing: Empirical Anomalies Based on Earning's Yields and Market Values,'' *Journal of Financial Economics*, 1981, vol. 9, pp. 19–46.

48 Marshall Blume, and Robert F. Stambaugh, ''Biases in Computed Returns: An Application to the Size Effect,'' *Journal of Financial Economics*, November 1983, vol. 12, no. 3. R. Roll, ''On Computing Mean Returns and the Small Firm Premium,'' *Journal of Financial Economics*, November 1983, vol. 12, no. 3. H.R. Stoll and R.E. Whaley, ''Transaction Costs and the Small Firm Effect,'' *Journal of Financial Economics*, 1983, vol. 12, pp. 57–79.

49 S. Basu, ''The Investment Performance of Common Stocks in Relation to Their Price-Earnings Ratios: A Test of the Efficient Markets Hypothesis,'' *Journal of Finance*, June 1977, vol. XXXII, no. 3, pp. 663–682. S. Basu, ''The Relationship Between Earnings Yield, Market Value and the Return for NYSE Common Stocks: Further Evidence,'' *Journal of Financial Economics*, 1983, vol. 12, no. 1.

50 Some financial analysts have attached significance to the absolute dollar level of the price of a common stock, B. Graham, D.L. Dodd, and S. Cottle, *Security Analysis*, 4th ed. (New York: McGraw-Hill, 1962), p. 649. L.H. Fritzemeier, ''Relative Price Fluctuation of Industrial Stocks in Different Price Groups,'' *Journal of Business*, April 1936, pp. 113–154. M.E. Blume and F. Husic, ''Price, Beta, and Exchange Listing,'' *Journal of Finance*, May 1973, vol. 28, no. 2, pp. 283–299. Dan Galai and Benjamin Bachrach, ''The Risk-Return Relationship and Stock Prices,'' *Journal of Financial and Quantitative Analysis*, June 1979. More recent research, however, suggests that the low-priced stocks that earn the highest rates of return may be significantly positively correlated with the size and riskiness of the issuing corporation. Thus, the price level of the stock may really only be a proxy for the size and/or the riskiness of the issuing firm.

51 M. Jensen and W. Meckling, ''Theory of the Firm: Managerial Behavior, Agency Costs, and Ownership Structure,'' *Journal of Financial Economics*, October 1976, pp. 305–360.

cited above may explain the reason for the size effect. Further research may show that it is merely a statistical measurement error or some other logical economic variable that was simply difficult to discern in the early research into the size effect.[52] Nevertheless, the size effect stands as an anomaly in the semistrongly efficient markets hypothesis until a better explanation for its existence is determined.

This size effect anomaly has also been linked to the "January" or "Year-End Effect," discussed on page 452. Keim reported that at least one-half of the small firm/large firm return differential occurred in January over the period 1963 to 1979 in the United States.[53] Furthermore, over one-half of this January effect occurs in the first week of January.

Conclusions about the Semi-strongly Efficient Markets Hypothesis   The *Financial Post* Corporation Service reports, Moody's manuals, Standard & Poor's reports, and audited financial information filed with the provincial Securities Commissions and the Securities and Exchange Commission are readily available to investors across Canada and the United States. This background information about corporations provides the perspective needed to evaluate new information. Financial newspapers and the news services compete to deliver news as quickly as possible. As a result, investors can obtain the latest financial news quickly at minimal cost. They tend, on average, to interpret this news correctly. When news affects the value of a security, it will cause re-evaluations and security trading. This trading begins immediately after news is announced and affects prices at once. Prices adjust through a series of erratic but unbiased movements toward their intrinsic value. The studies reviewed above show that security prices not only usually react immediately and rationally to news; they often anticipate it. The weight of evidence at this time suggests that U.S. security prices reflect practically all publicly available information, as suggested by the semistrongly efficient hypothesis.

Nevertheless, the anomaly findings are disconcerting—particularly if an anomaly can be used to generate a trading program that generates abnormal returns. Painstaking empirical research into these and other anomalies will be conducted in the future. A curious phenomenon results. It is possible that the process of studying supposed market imperfections and the development of trading strategies to exploit the results will in itself eliminate these inefficiencies. That the Canadian market is the fourth largest in the world in trading value yet is still a relatively thin one[54] by comparison to the United

---

52 It has been suggested that stocks that are not widely held by institutional investors offer superior investment returns. This finding may be the result of underlying size effects, low P/E ratios, agency costs, or some other underlying factor. See Avner Arbel, Steven Carvell, and Paul Strebel, "Giraffes, Institutions and Neglected Firms," *Financial Analysts Journal*, May-June 1983, pp. 2–8.

53 Donald B. Keim, "Size-Related Anomalies and Stock Return Seasonality: Further Empirical Evidence," *Journal of Financial Economics* 12, June 1983, pp. 13–82. See also Richard Roll, 'Vas ist Das? The Turn of the Year Effect and the Return Premiums of Small Firms," *Journal of Portfolio Management*, Winter 1983, pp. 18–28.

54 See David J. Fowler, C. Harvey Rorke, and Vijay M. Jog, "Thin Trading and Beta Estimation Problems on the Toronto Stock Exchange," *Journal of Business Administration*, volume 12, no.

States, Japan, and the United Kingdom provides a rich forum for future research.

18-5   THE STRONGLY EFFICIENT MARKETS HYPOTHESIS

The strongly efficient markets hypothesis is defined in Box 18-4.

The strongly efficient markets hypothesis is that *all* (not just publicly available) information is fully reflected in security prices. This is sometimes called a *perfectly efficient market* in which prices and values are always equal as they fluctuate randomly together as new information arrives.

BOX 18-4
Definition of
the Strongly
Efficient
Markets
Hypothesis

Before looking at the evidence, common sense suggests that such an extreme hypothesis should be refutable: all that need be done would be to find one insider who has profited from inside information, and the hypothesis would be disproved. It is not hard, moreover, to find evidence that several investors have enough valuable inside information with which to earn trading profits.

Specialists on the organized U.S. security exchanges who make the markets in securities have valuable inside information. They keep a book of unfilled limit orders to buy and sell at different prices. This information allows them to see the outlines of the supply and demand curves for the securities in which they made a market. The specialists' book is kept confidential in order to stop possible price manipulation schemes by outsiders. As a result, specialists have monopolistic access to valuable information that they use to make a speculative trading profit.[55] This is one of the reasons why the seats on the NYSE sell for hundreds of thousands of dollars[56]

**18-5.1
Monopolistic
Access to
Valuable
Information**

Lawson examined a simple filter trading strategy (filters were discussed in 18-3.1) that was designed to track the performance of professional traders on the Toronto Stock Exchange. (Professional traders buy and sell securities on the floor for their own accounts and for the accounts of their brokerage firms).[57] He found that a simple, naive buy-and-hold strategy, on average,

**18-5.2
Professional
Trading
in Canada**

1, Fall 1980, pp. 77–90. They state on p. 88 in their conclusions: ''It has been demonstrated . . . that most of the stocks traded on the Toronto Stock Exchange exhibit thin or only sporadic trading.'' See also, V.M. Jog and A.L. Riding, ''Some Canadian Findings Regarding Infrequent Trading and Instability in the Single Factor Market Model,'' *Journal of Business Finance & Accounting* 13(1), Spring 1986, pp. 125–135.

55 V. Niederhoffer and M.F.M. Osborne, ''Market Making and Reversal on the Stock Exchange,'' *Journal of the American Statistical Association*, December 1966, pp. 897–916.

56 Another reason why seats have value is that members of the NYSE can also earn sales commissions by acting as floor brokers.

57 William M. Lawson, ''Market Efficiency: The Trading of Professionals on the Toronto Stock Exchange,'' *Journal of Business Administration*, volume 12, no. 1, Fall 1980, pp. 77–90.

yielded higher returns than the filter that obtained signals from the data on professional traders buying and selling activities. He concluded that there was no evidence that TSE professional traders exhibit superior timing in their transactions, thus supporting the notion of strong form market efficiency in Canada.

**18-5.3
Trading on
Inside
Information
in Canada
and the
United States**

Provincial securities legislation and federal and provincial corporations acts define insiders as directors, officers, persons who own directly or indirectly more than 10 percent of the voting shares of a company, and persons who receive specific confidential information from persons described in this clause.

Empirical tests of insider trading in Canada do not support strong form efficiency. Baesel and Stein studied the performance of insider trades on a sample of TSE stocks for the period 1968-1972.[58] They found that insiders outperformed other market traders; results that are consistent with the U.S. studies on insider trading are discussed below.

Various studies, actions taken by the SEC, and court cases also suggest that some corporate insiders are able to profit (sometimes illegally) from monopolistic access to information.

American federal law defines *insiders* as the directors, officers, significant shareholders, and any other persons who have access to valuable inside information about a firm. This section examines the profitability of trading on inside information.

Federal law requires all insiders to notify the Securities and Exchange Commissions (SEC) in writing of all trades they have made in their corporation's stock within one month. The SEC then publishes these insider trades in its monthly pamphlet *Official Summary of Insider Trading*, which is available to the public through the U.S. Government Printing Office. Professor Jeffrey F. Jaffe analyzed the *Official Summary* of many years to measure insiders' trading profits.[59] The capital asset pricing model (CAPM), or security market line (SML), furnished the engine for Dr. Jaffe's analysis of insiders' trading profits.

Using the CAPM for empirical work is complicated by the discontinuity that exists in going from the *ex ante* (that is, future-oriented) theoretical CAPM

---

58 Jerome Baesel and Garry Stein, "The Value of Information: Inferences From The Profitability of Insider Trading," *Journal of Financial and Quantitative Analysis*, September 1979, pp. 553–569. See also, for collaborative findings, David J. Fowler, C. Harvey Rorke, C. McLeary, and M. Pinter, "A Preliminary Examination of Insider Trading in Canada", paper presented at Canadian Association of Administrative Sciences Annual Conference, 1977; and C. Harvey Rorke and David J. Fowler, "Do Published Insider Trading Reports Contain Valuable Information?" Financial Research Foundation of Canada, Proceedings of the First Conference, October 1978, paper #3, unpaginated.

59 J.F. Jaffe, "Special Information and Insider Trading," *Journal of Business*, July 1974, pp. 410–428. Other studies about insider trading include the following: J.H. Lorie and V. Niederhoffer, "Predictive and Statistical Properties of Insider Trading," *Journal of Law and Economics*, April 1968, pp. 35–51. Joseph Finnerty, "Insiders and Market Efficiency," *Journal of Finance*, September 1976, pp. 1141–1148. S.H. Penman, "Insider Trading and the Dissemination of Firm's Forecast Information," *Journal of Business*, October 1982.

FIGURE 18-8 Security market lines estimated with ex post monthly returns measured from bull and bear markets.

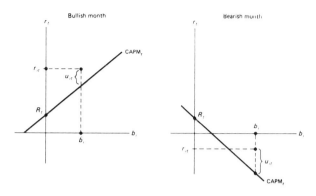

to the *ex post* (that is, observed in historical sample periods) CAPM. When dealing with the *ex post* data, the CAPM shifts every month. As shown in Fig. 18-8, the high beta stocks have the highest returns in bull markets and the lowest returns in bear markets.

Jaffe estimated the CAPMs for different months by first estimating the characteristic regression lines of all NYSE stocks, Eq. (10-1). Each stock's beta systematic risk coefficient and monthly returns were then taken from these first-pass regressions for the second-pass regression estimates of each month's CAPM. Regression Eq. (18-8) shows the regression model for the tth month's CAPM.

$$r_{it} = R_t + c_t(b_i) + u_{it} \quad \text{for } i = 1, 2, \ldots, n \text{ stocks} \quad (18\text{-}8)$$

The intercept R_t and slope c_t coefficients for month t's CAPM were found by regressing stocks' one-month rate of return in month t, r_{it}, on their beta systematic risk coefficients b_i. The ith stock's residual error from the CAPM in month t, denoted u_{it}, measures whether the stock did better or worse than the capital market theory (explained in Chaps. 10 and 24) suggests.

To see whether insiders' trades in their own corporation's stock were based on valuable insider information, Dr. Jaffe measured the residual errors for the ith stock in month t, as illustrated in Fig. 18-8. These residual errors are positive (that is, the observed monthly return is above the CAPM) if the stock beats the risk-adjusted market return. In other words, after allowing for current bullish or bearish market conditions and the stock's individual reaction to these conditions (as measured by its beta coefficient), the u_{it} term measures the ith stock's positive or negative unsystematic return in month t.

To discern which stocks were being actively traded by insiders, Dr. Jaffe studied each month's *Official Summary of Insider Trading* from the SEC. He selected the stocks in each month that had three more inside sellers than buyers; Jaffe labelled this event a *selling plurality* by insiders. Three more insiders buying than selling in the same month was called a *buying plurality*. Then he recorded the monthly residual errors u_{it} for each of these stocks in which the insiders seemed to exhibit some consensus about buying or selling.

After recording such facts for many stocks and for many years, Dr. Jaffe summed up the residual errors for all stocks traded actively by a plurality of insiders in the tth month. Equations (18-9) and (18-10) define the average residual error from the CAPM in month t for stocks that the plurality of insiders bought or sold, respectively. The upper limits of summation B and S refer to the number of stocks bought and sold, respectively, by the plurality of insiders in month t.

$$\text{Buyers' average plurality residual} = bu_t = \frac{1}{B}\sum_{i=1}^{B} u_{it} \tag{18-9}$$

$$\text{Seller's average plurality residual} = su_t = \frac{1}{S}\sum_{i=1}^{S} u_{it} \tag{18-10}$$

Combining the absolute values of the sums in Eqs. (18-9) and (18-10), as shown in Eq. (18-11), yields the average residual for all insiders' trades in month t; it is denoted U_t.

$$U_t = |bu_t| + |su_t| \tag{18-11}$$

The average residual from the CAPM for all insider plurality trading in month t is a measure of extra returns that these insiders earned, on average, from trades that are assumed to be motivated by inside information.

A 1 percent buying commission and a 1 percent selling commission were subtracted from each insider's trade to obtain net profit. Then the average residuals after commissions were cumulated over $C = 1$, 2, and 8 months after the month in which the plurality of insiders originally made its trades. This yielded the cumulative average residuals denoted U_{tc}, defined in Eq. (18-12) and shown in Table 18-2.

$$U_{tc} = \sum_{m=1}^{C=1,2,8} U_{t+m} \tag{18-12}$$

Table 18-2 shows that one month, $C = 1$, after a plurality of insider buying or selling, the insiders' net profit after commissions averaged ($-.0102$ equals a loss of) -1.02 percent of the value of the stock. After the stock was held two months (that is, $C = 2$), the insiders broke about even, $U_{tc} = .0009$. But only after eight months did the plurality of insiders' stocks experience

TABLE18-2   CUMULATIVE AVERAGE RESIDUAL MEASURES OF INSIDERS' PROFIT RATES, NET OF COMMISSIONS

MONTHS CUMULATED	CUMULATIVE AVERAGE RESIDUAL
$C = 1$	$U_{t1} = -.0102$
$C = 2$	$U_{t2} = .0009$
$C = 8$	$U_{t8} = .0307$

enough price change to pay the commissions and yield (.0307 =) 3.07 percent net profit. Statistically speaking, this rate of insiders' trading profit is significantly above zero. But practically speaking, the average insider certainly is not getting rich quick. Alas, investors aspiring to hitting the jackpot by using inside information must lower their sights and plan on working hard to earn a slightly better rate of return than they could by picking stocks with a dart.

The fact that specialists and some insiders can earn trading profits from their information refutes the strongly efficient markets hypothesis. However, discovery of these market flaws prompts one to wonder how many people have monopolistic access to valuable information. That is, given that there are imperfections that rule out strongly efficient markets, how deeply do these imperfections permeate the market?

18-5.4   Performance of Mutual Fund Managers in Canada and the United States

After an examination of corporate insiders and specialists, who undeniably have monopolistic access to valuable information, it would seem that a group of well-endowed professional portfolio managers should be examined next. That is, the latter group would seem to be the next most likely to be able to obtain and profit from valuable investment information before it is fully impacted into the market prices. Since mutual funds fall into this category, we shall examine them.

Calvet and Lefoll examined the performance of seventeen Canadian growth and fixed-income mutual funds (only funds with solely Canadian securities in the portfolios were included) over the period 1966–1975 and found that the funds did not outperform the market on a risk-adjusted basis in both nominal and real terms.[60] Grant, in an earlier study of the nominal performance of nineteen Canadian mutual funds (including some with global portfolios) over the period 1960–1974, came to an identical conclusion.[61] However, at present there are over 300 mutual funds in Canada, some of which have portfolio objectives and strategies that did not exist in the period examined by the Canadian studies. (For example, the Canadian Income Plus Fund invests in government bonds and writes covered options contracts against these holdings.) Furthermore, there are a now a number of funds with complete internationally diversified portfolios available in Canada. Given the small sample size and the different nature of the mutual fund industry, additional empirical research of mutual fund manager performance should prove fruitful.

In Chap. 26 various aspects of mutual fund performance are analyzed. Rankings of the annual returns achieved by thirty-nine U.S. funds showed (in Table 26-1) that no individual fund was able to earn a better-than-average return consistently over a ten-year period. This tended to indicate that no

---

60 Calvet and Lefoll, ''The CAPM under Inflation and the Performance of Canadian Mutual Funds,'' *Journal of Business Administration*, Fall 1980, pp. 107–117.

61 Dwight Grant, ''Investment Performance of Canadian Mutual Funds: 1960–1974,'' *Journal of Business Administration*, 8, Fall 1976, pp. 1–10. See also H.L. Dhinga, ''Portfolio Volatility Adjustments by Canadian Mutual Funds,'' *Journal of Business Finance and Accounting* 5, 1978, pp. 305–333.

individual fund (or funds) within the group had any relative advantage in obtaining valuable information. Plotting the performance of a sample of twenty-three mutual funds relative to the efficient frontier in risk-return space (in Fig. 26-3) showed that none was an efficient investment. In another sample, thirty-four mutual funds' performances were compared with the Dow Jones Industrial Average (DJIA) using Sharpe's portfolio performance index (which measures the risk-premium over risk). This comparison (which is illustrated in Fig. 26-5) showed that twenty-three out of the thirty-four funds ranked below the DJIA. These mutual fund studies all seem to point clearly to the fact that no funds possess any knowledge that is not already fully impacted into security prices.

Another study of 115 mutual funds over the decade from 1955 to 1964 showed similar findings. In particular, this study[62] concluded that

although these tests certainly do not imply that the strong form of the [efficient markets] hypothesis holds for all investors and for all time, they provide strong evidence in support of that hypothesis. One must realize that these analysts are extremely well endowed. Moreover they operate in the securities markets every day and have wide-ranging contacts and associations in both the business and financial communities. Thus, the fact that they are apparently unable to forecast returns accurately enough to recover their research and transactions costs is a striking piece of evidence in favour of the strong form of the [efficient markets] hypothesis.

18-6   CONCLUSIONS ABOUT SECURITY PRICES IN THE UNITED STATES

The weakly efficient and semistrongly efficient markets hypotheses are reasonably well supported by the facts. The strongly efficient markets hypothesis is not however. A few cases — namely, insiders and specialists — were found that violated the strongly efficient hypothesis. The evidence seems to indicate that, for all practical purposes, security markets in the United States are *intrinsic-value random-walk markets*. However, students should note with interest and caution the weak and semistrong anomalous findings uncovered, as well as the work of Shiller discussed in 18-4.8.

Dr. Paul Cootner has summarized this process and has suggested that security prices can be viewed as a series of constrained random fluctuations around the true intrinsic value.[63] He hypothesizes the existence of two groups of investors. The first group can be referred to as the "naive investors," those who have access only to the public news media for their information. They might be chartists, amateur fundamental analysts, dart throwers, or speculators; they base their investment decisions upon their interpretations of the public news and their financial circumstances. Naive investors will recognize

---

62 M. Jensen, "Risk, the Pricing of Capital Assets, and the Evaluation of Investment Portfolios," *Journal of Business*, April 1969, p. 170. Words in brackets added.

63 P.H. Cootner, "Stock Prices: Random versus Systematic Changes," *Industrial Management Review*, Spring 1962, pp. 24–45. E.F. Fama elaborated on his interpretations of the intrinsic-value random-walk market model on pp. 36–37 of "The Behavior of Stock Market Prices," *Journal of Business*, January 1965, pp. 34–105; essentially, he agreed with Cootner.

few, if any, divergences from intrinsic values.[64] They are more likely to invest on the basis of "hot tips" when they have excess liquidity, and at other more-or-less random times that may or may not be wise.

The second group of investors are the "professional investors" — those who have the resources to discover news and develop clear-cut estimates of intrinsic value. As a result, the professionals will recognize significant deviations from intrinsic value and initiate trading that tends to align the market price with the intrinsic value.

Figure 8-2, on page 166, shows how security prices might fluctuate over time in the market Cootner describes. The dashed lines represent the true intrinsic value of the security as estimated by the professional investors. Trading by the naive investors is not necessarily based on a correct interpretation of the latest news. As a result, naive investors may be buying securities whose market prices are above their intrinsic values, or vice versa. These naive traders are largely responsible for the aimless price fluctuations that can cause prices to diverge from intrinsic values.

When a security price does differ significantly from its true intrinsic value, the professional investors find it profitable to correct this disequilibrium. Small deviations will not be profitable to correct, but when prices are significantly out of line, the professionals will bid up low prices or liquidate over-priced securities. In effect, the professionals erect "reflecting barriers" around the true intrinsic value.[65] These reflecting barriers are represented by the solid lines above and below the intrinsic-value lines in Fig. 8-2. Prices will fluctuate freely within the reflecting barriers, but when they reach these barriers, the action of the professionals will cause prices to move toward their intrinsic value.

The intrinsic-value estimates of the professionals may change as the latest news is learned. The reflecting barriers around the intrinsic value will therefore change accordingly. As a result, it is not usually possible to observe the true intrinsic value or the reflecting barriers from charts of historical security prices. Price charts like the one in Fig. 8-2b will occur when a security experiences changes in its intrinsic value. The preceding evidence suggests certain investment policies.

18-7   CONCLUSIONS ABOUT SECURITY PRICES IN CANADA

We cannot make the same strong statements about market efficiency in Canada. The paucity of Canadian weak and semistrong studies and the generally small sample sizes of the few studies do not allow for responsible conclusions. It is also dangerous to casually extend the U.S. findings to the Canadian (or other markets for that matter) equity market. There are structural

---

64 Intrinsic-value estimation is discussed in Chap. 15.
65 William Feller, *An Introduction to Probability Theory and Its Applications*, vol. 1, 3d ed. (New York: Wiley, 1968) pp. 436–438. Provides a discussion of a random walk with reflecting barriers.

differences between the Canadian and U.S. markets. Furthermore, as pointed out earlier (see fn. 54) trading activity on the largest Canadian market, the Toronto Stock Exchange, is considerably lighter than that on the major U.S. exchanges. On the other hand, securities regulation, as discussed in Chap. 4, with its emphasis on full true and timely disclosure, is fairly tightly enforced in Canada, and the recent development of computer-assisted trading systems, including CATS on the TSE and COATS for over-the-counter trading, should theoretically lead to more efficient trading. Trading links forged between the Toronto Stock Exchange (TSE) and the American Stock Exchange, the TSE and Mid-West Stock Exchange, and the Montreal Exchange and Boston Stock Exchange in 1985–1986 may play a role as well.

A point made by Reinganum in 1984 with respect to the anomaly findings in the United States probably has major relevance for Canadian efficient markets research. "In the constant ebb and flow between theory and empirics, empirics currently holds the upper hand. While it would be foolish to proclaim that 'theory is dead' the anomalies signal that, at least in studies of equity markets, empiricism is currently the king."[66]

18-8 IMPLICATIONS OF THE EFFICIENT MARKETS THEORY

The implications of the theory are discussed below.

18-8.1 Fundamental Security Analysis

In an intrinsic-value random-walk market, fundamental analysis plays a major role in determining security prices. Expert fundamental analysts who discover new financial information and quickly interpret it correctly will earn higher-than-average returns, but most fundamental analysts will not earn a return above what could be achieved with a naive buy-and-hold strategy.

In an intrinsic-value random-walk market, security prices are unbiased estimates of the true intrinsic value and reflect all current public information. Searching for undervalued securities will therefore be largely unfruitful. Only the most expert fundamental analysts who have discovered new information will find it profitable to perform fundamental analysis, and any underpriced securities they discover will be bid up in price into line with their intrinsic value very quickly. Therefore, all but the few most expert fundamental analysts will not profit (above what a naive strategy would yield) from their activity. It will not be worthwhile for amateur investors to learn fundamental analysis in an intrinsic-value random-walk market. The amateur can expect to accumulate more wealth by selecting securities randomly and devoting the time that would have been spent on fundamental analysis to his or her own profession earning more wages or salary. The only fundamental analysts that will repeatedly earn unusual profits while experiencing few losses will be hard-working professional analysts with experience and resources to support their costly search for information.

---

66 Mark R. Reinganum, "Discussion: What the Anomalies Mean," *The Journal of Finance*, vol. 39, no. 3, July 1984, pp. 839–840.

The various tests to measure the randomness of stock price changes that were described earlier cannot detect absolutely every conceivable pattern that might be formed. Some extremely complex patterns might go undetected. However, technical analysts do not usually search for extremely complex patterns. Their concepts are simple at best. Therefore, the evidence that patterns do not exist tends to indicate that technical analysis will not be worthwhile to perform in an intrinsic-value random-walk market. Chartists can expect to earn an average rate of return, but they could expect to earn the same return by selecting securities with an unaimed dart. They would therefore be wiser to devote their time to more profitable activities and to select securities by some other method. There would be no reason for an institutional portfolio to employ a chartist in an intrinsic-value random-walk market.

**18-8.2
Technical
Analysis**

In an intrinsic-value random-walk market, most securities' rates of return will conform to probability distributions that are stationary over time. In such a market it will be worthwhile for investors to estimate the risk and return statistics for their investment alternatives. The investor can then select the investments with the maximum return in the preferred risk-class. In this manner investors can maximize their utility. Selecting the most efficient portfolio in the preferred risk-class will enable investors to attain their highest level of happiness from their investments. This investment may or may not earn an above-average rate of return; the outcome depends upon the risk-class the investor selects and when the investment is liquidated. Such analysis, however, will maximize the investor's expected utility (as defined in App. 25A).

**18-8.3
Risk-Return
Analysis**

Of course, risk-return relationships represent theoretical market equilibriums. In the real world of continuous dynamic disequilibrium, the positive relation between risk and average return can be expected to emerge only if investments are held for at least one *complete business cycle*. For example, risky assets purchased at the end of an inflated bull market and sold at the end of a long bear market will have had the *highest* risk and *lowest* rates of return during such a period. However, if risky assets are held over a complete market cycle (for example, from peak to peak), they will earn higher-than-averge returns and the positive relationship between risk and return will be evident.

The efficient markets theory is a very negative statement. It declares that no patterns exist in price changes, that technical analysis techniques that some persons have spent their lives developing are merely worthless folklore, and that the daily changes in the TSE 300 Composite Index that security sales representatives talk about are really random numbers containing no information. But it is not fruitful to try to reach general conclusions from a few specific cases. The efficient markets theory should be viewed as an unbiased scientific statement supported by a body of published evidence. The available data indicate that security markets in the United States and probably in Canada are intrinsic-value random-walk markets.

**18-8.4 The
Negativism
of the
Efficient
Markets
Theory**

**18-8.5
Internal Versus
External
Market
Efficiency**

Primarily as a result of large investments in "social overhead capital" that exists externally to the stock markets in the United States, the conclusion was reached that these markets are semistrongly efficient.[67] This *external market efficiency* or *pricing efficiency* differs from *internal efficiency*, or synonymously, *operational efficiency*.[68]

In order for a given securities market such as the TSE, the NYSE or the American Stock Exchange to be *internally efficient*, the securities traded there must be immediately marketable at low commissions to any investor-customer who wishes to trade. Internal market efficiency results from (1) publicly posted bid-and-ask prices that are backed by market-makers who stand ready to buy or sell large quantities at the posted prices, (2) brokerage commissions that are determined competitively rather than fixed at high levels that take large brokers' profits out of every trade, (3) market-makers who do not manipulate the prices of the securities in which they deal, and (4) a requirement that the companies whose securities are traded make public their audited financial statements. Since April 1983 when fixed commissions were abolished in Canada, the internal efficiency of the TSE has improved because its commission rates were driven down by healthy competition between competing market-makers and the different brokers.

If a particular market is terribly inefficient *internally* because its market-makers manipulate the prices of the securities in which they deal, or because its brokers charge unreasonably high commissions, or because it does not provide adequate information about the companies that issue its securities, or because all the preceding problems exist, then that market will probably not be *externally* efficient. In fact, some of the lesser developed foreign countries and some of the small, foreign securities markets such as Italy's Milan Stock Exchange are not externally efficient capital markets because of internal market problems. As long as competing market-makers exist and anticompetitive practices are forbidden by law, however, competition should lead to the development of externally efficient markets.

QUESTIONS

1. Explain the weakly efficient, semistrongly efficient, and strongly efficient markets hyphotheses.

2. "An investor who learned that Canadian Pacific's earnings per share had increased by an unusually large amount a few days before the news was announced publicly could probably buy CP stock and profit from a quick capital gain when the announcement was made." True, false, or uncertain? Explain.

---

67 The essential *social overhead capital* includes free public libraries; large international news services like UPI and AP; low-cost, publicly available investment advice publications like *The Financial Post*; good, inexpensive, daily financial newspapers; and an ample supply of qualified financial analysts who do the good financial research that should underlie all portfolio management decisions.

68 R.R. West, "On the Difference between Internal and External Market Efficiency," *Financial Analysts Journal*, November-December 1975, pp. 30–34. The phrases "internal efficiency" and "external efficiency" were defined and discussed in App. 3.

3. Characterize the nature and behaviour of stock prices in a large public securities market. That is, what do stock prices represent and what patterns do they follow? Why do stock prices behave in this manner? What does this imply about the investments management policies that should be followed?

4. Why are runs tests, serial correlation, and filter rules used in testing the random-walk hypothesis? What do these tests reveal?

5. "Stock prices are random numbers." Is this statement true, false, or uncertain? Explain.

6. "The managers of large institutional portfolios (such as mutual funds) should instruct their fundamental security analysts to collect and evaluate the "hot tips" that are discussed around the Stock Exchanges so their portfolios can profit from monopolistic access to this valuable information." True, false, or uncertain? Explain.

7. Suppose your long-time next-door neighbour is a business executive who watches the stars through a telescope and studies the physical sciences as a hobby. He has earnestly explained to you on several occasions that he has observed that the spots on the sun's surface are more active during bull markets. He has shown you books about sunspots to prove he can recognize them and records of his observations of sunspot activity and the stock market. If you believe and trust your neighbour, should you begin to study sunspot activity as a way to beat the stock market?

8. "If rates of return are distributed as a Paretian distribution with a characteristic exponent less than 2 (that is, theoretically infinite variance), then risk-return analysis is hopeless." To what problem is this statement referring? Is the statement true, false, or uncertain? Explain. *Hint*: See App. 18A.

9. "Rates of return conform to mathematical statisticians' random-walk model." True, false, or uncertain? Explain. *Hint*: See App. 18A.

10. Compare and contrast the random-walk theory of rates of return with the martingale model. *Hint*: See App. 18A.

11. "The Canadian dollar is typically weak at the end of the year reflecting dividend and interest payments and Canadian residents 'travelling abroad.' " Describe how you would develop evidence to support or refute this contention.

SELECTED REFERENCES

Brealey, R.A., *An Introduction to Risk and Return from Common Stocks*. 2d ed. Cambridge, Mass.: MIT Press, 1983. This book summarizes much current investments literature. The book is nonmathematical, easy-to-read, and relevant to the so-called random-walk theory.

Fama, Eugene F. "The Behavior of Stock Market Prices." *Journal of Business*, January 1965, pp. 34-105. This paper rationalizes the existence of an intrinsic-value random-walk market and shows various types of evidence in support of the theory. The stationary stable symmetric distribution with Paretian tails is discussed, and an appendix shows some theorems about such distributions. Mathematics and statistics are used.

Tinic, S.M. and R.R. West. *Investing in Securities: An Efficient Markets Approach.* Reading, Mass.: Addison-Wesley, 1979. This investments textbook is written from the viewpoint that securities markets are efficient. It rationalizes the determination of securities prices using joint tests of market efficiency in conjunction with various other asset pricing models.

For a collection of studies that weight against the efficient markets theory see "Symposium On Some Anomalous Evidence On Capital Market Efficiency", *Journal of Financial Economics*, June-September 1978.

Random-Walk and Martingale Models

A *model* is a simplified version of reality. It is a toylike construct that is "played with" in order to learn the essential nature of the more complex thing being modeled. Consider the random-walk model defined in Box App. 18A-1.

A *random-walk model* is a mathematical model in which a series of numbers are (1) independent and (2) identically distributed.

When introducing the random-walk model to a class, mathematical statistics professors sometimes use the aimless lurchings of an intoxicated person as an example. At each step the drunk's direction may be at any of the 180 degrees emanating from his location (assuming he cannot fall backward), and the distance of each step is a random variable with the range from zero to, say, four feet. Furthermore, the number of steps per minute is a random variable with a range from zero to dozens. If the probability distributions describing the direction, distance, and frequency of the drunk's steps are realistic, the random-walk model can tell the probability that the drunk reaches any given position at any point in time. This appendix examines the behaviour of security prices to see whether the random-walk model of mathematical statistics can be adapted to characterize their movements.

APP. 18A-1 PROBABILITY DISTRIBUTIONS FOR SECURITIES

Suppose that the market prices of certain common stocks were recorded at the close of each trading day for four years. If the relative frequency (that is, the objective historical probabilities) of each security's price were determined, a distribution of past prices could be prepared. Figure App. 18A-1 represents two hypothetical relative-frequency distributions for four years of common stock prices. One distribution is for the first two years, and the other distribution is for the second two years.

Distributions of security *prices* are of little value for two reasons that should be apparent after a glance at Fig. App. 18A-1. First, the distributions are not stable over time. Nearly all securities' prices increase with the passage of time at about 6 percent per year.[69] As a result, each year's relative-frequency distribution shifts a little farther to the right and has a higher mean price.

---

69 L. Fisher and J. Lorie, "Rates of Return on Investments in Common Stock: The Year-by-Year Record, 1926–1965," *Journal of Business*, January 1964, p. 315, table A2. The average NYSE stock's price rose 6.8 percent per annum from 1926 to 1960. This does not include cash dividends.

FIGURE APP. 18A-1 Hypothetical frequency distribution of a common stock's prices.

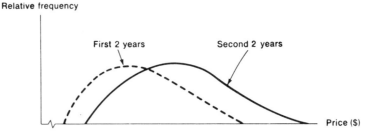

Second, the shape of the distribution changes each year. Each year, as the security's price rises, the distribution's tail on the right side grows a little longer. In statistical language, the positive skewness of a security's price tends to increase with the price.[70]

As a result of these two changes, the distributions of security prices are of little value: one year's distribution cannot be used to predict the probability that a certain price will occur in the next year. In statistical language, the distributions are not stable over time. This is unfortunate because stable distributions are the most useful in forecasting.[71]

Distributions of Price Changes Unstable In a search for stable distributions that could be useful in making probability statements about future security prices, analysts examined the price *changes* (denoted Δp) that occur daily, rather than the prices themselves. Figure App. 18A-2 shows two relative-frequency distributions of price changes for a hypothetical common stock like the one shown in Fig. App. 18A-1.

FIGURE APP. 18A-2 Frequency distributions of a hypothetical common stock's price changes.

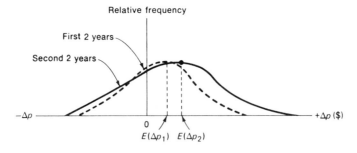

70 See Mathematical App. C for a definition and discussion of skewness. Essentially, positive skewness means that the distribution has an unusually long tail on the right side and is therefore lopsided.

71 The frequency distributions of historical security prices can be made more useful by adding subscripted time variables to the parameters of the distribution and building an appropriate growth rate into them. However, such complications should be avoided whenever possible by constructing stable probability distributions.

The distributions in Fig. App. 18A-2 represent four years of daily price changes. One distribution represents the first two years of daily changes, and the other distribution represents the second two years. The distributions of price changes for most securities have positive means because stock prices tend to drift upward with the passage of time.

Unfortunately, the frequency distributions of price changes are diminished in value because historical price changes tend to be unstable too. Security prices tend to fluctuate up and down in terms of a fixed range of *percentages*; so, as the security's price rises over time, the dollar amounts of the price changes grow, too. To see this intuitively, consider the variance of price changes before and after a stock split. If a $100 stock is split into two $50 shares, the variance of the stock price changes will be smaller after the split (unless the percentage price fluctuations increase, an occurrence that is highly unlikely).[72] As a result of this phenomenon, the mean and the standard deviation of price changes increase with the price of the security in most cases.

Although the distributions of price changes are not stationary, studying these distributions reveals that security prices tend to change by *percentages* that conform to a stable distribution. Let us denote the percentage price changes by the rate of change as defined in Eq. (App. 18A-1).

Stable Distributions of Rates of Return

$$r_t = \frac{p_{t+1} - p_t}{p_t}$$

$$= \frac{\Delta p_t}{p_t}$$

(App. 18A-1)

where

p_{t+1} = market price of asset at beginning of differencing period $t + 1$

p_t = beginning price at start of differencing period t

Δp_t = price change during differencing period $t = p_{t+1} - p_t$

The rates of change of daily, weekly, monthly, quarterly, semiannual, or yearly price changes tend to conform to a stable relative-frequency distribution as shown in Fig. App. 18A-3 if the price changes are drawn from at least one *complete* business cycle.

Dividends d_t, are sometimes included when rates of return are calculated, as shown in Eq. (App. 18A-2a).

$$r_t = \frac{p_{t+1} - p_t + d_t}{p_t}$$

(App. 18A-2a)

$$= \frac{p_{t+1} + d_t}{p_t} - 1$$

(App. 18A-2b)

---

72 In statistical language var$(2p)$ = 4 var(p), or in terms of standard deviations $\sqrt{\text{var}(2p)}$ = $2\sqrt{\text{var}(p)}$. This shows that higher-priced stocks (for example, twice as high for $2p$) have a larger variance of price changes (namely, four times larger).

FIGURE APP. 18A-3   Frequency distribution of historical rates of return and rates of change for a hypothetical security.

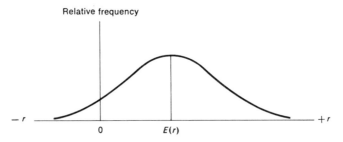

Most corporations pay the *same* dividends quarter after quarter, only occasionally increasing them slightly or cancelling them altogether; so dividends may be treated as a constant in dealing with most corporations. Thus, whether rates of return are calculated with Eq. (App. 18A-2*a*) or rates of change are calculated with Eq. (App. 18A-1), the distribution is shifted to the right by the amount of the dividend yield (that is, *d/p*) but has the same shape and stability.[73] It is better to use Eq. (App. 18A-2*a*) than Eq. (App. 18A-1) when measuring returns, so that the dividend income is considered in measuring the investor's income (and to compensate for the ex-dividend price drop-off).

Not every security has a relative-frequency distribution of historical rates of return that remains stationary. If the firm nears bankruptcy, changes products, enjoys major technological breakthroughs that confer a competitive advantage, or experiences other major changes, the distribution may shift. However, the distributions of returns for the vast majority of firms are fairly stationary over time if the distribution is observed over at least one complete business cycle. This is usually true even though the firm has executive shake-ups, enters new market areas, or alters its product line.

The existence of *stable* distributions of returns allows analysts to do several valuable things. First, probability statements may be made about the percentage price changes that may be expected to occur. Second, a security's historical average return and standard deviation of returns furnish estimates of the security's future risk and return. Thus, a stable random-walk model may be construed for rates of return (or rates of price change), although it is not possible to construct a stable distribution with the raw price data.

It will be recalled that for a series to be classified as random walk, the two major requirements are that the successive members in the series be (1) independent and (2) identically distributed. *Identically distributed* is a technical statistical phrase that means all the numbers conform to the same probability distribution. Since the probability distributions of historical rates of return

---

73 A third way to measure rates of return is to take the natural or Naperian logarithm of the value relatives. Symbolically $r_t = \ln (p_{t+1}/p_t) = \ln(p_{t+1}) - \ln (p_t)$.

tend to be stable for any given security, this fact indicates that the second condition necessary to classify securities as a random walk is fulfilled. The precise form of the probability distribution is considered below.

Advantages of Using Gaussian or Normal Distributions

Many researchers were hopeful that rates of change and rates of return are *normally distributed* for several reasons. First, normal distributions are completely described by only two statistics: the mean and the variance. Thus, skewness and kurtosis could be ignored.[74] Second, normal distributions have a finite variance; that is, their tails come down to the horizontal axis of the probability distribution. Figure App. 18A-4 compares a normal distribution, which has a finite variance (and standard deviation), with a distribution with infinite variance. It is highly desirable that a probability distribution possess a finite variance because statistics from populations possessing finite variance are dependable statistics that do not erratically vary from sample to sample.[75] Third, the normal distribution is well known and has a well-developed sampling theory.

FIGURE APP. 18A-4   Normal distribution compared with leptokurtic distribution with infinite variance.

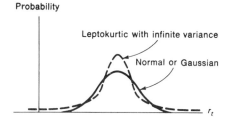

Probability

Leptokurtic with infinite variance

Normal or Gaussian

r_t

Infinite Variance

As computers analyzed larger files of accurate historical data, the normal distributions of rates of price change and rates of return were called into question. The occasional extremely large and extremely small rates of return that had previously been attributed to error or ignored repeatedly appeared in securities distributions. These extreme values lie beyond the tails of a normal distribution; they are sometimes referred to as *outliers.*

Closer examination of the distributions of returns indicated that they may not be normal or Gaussian, as had been thought. The distributions were

---

74 See Mathematical App. C for definitions and discussions of skewness and kurtosis.

75 Statistically speaking, an erratic statistic is said to be *inefficient*, a technical statistical word that means the statistic varies erratically from sample to sample. An *efficient* statistic varies less than any other statistic. Efficiency is a desirable statistical property. Statistics from populations with finite variances are more efficient than statistics from populations with infinite variances. Another advantage of having a finite variance is that the central limit theorem applies only to distributions with finite variances.

leptokurtic and had large variances. Drs. Benoit Mandelbrot and Eugene Fama published studies suggesting that the rates of return were distributed according to a stable symmetric distribution with *infinite* variance.[76] Of course, any sample of actual returns which was analyzed had a finite variance, since the actual rates of return were not infinitely large or infinitely small. Occasionally, however, outliers appeared that suggested that the probability distribution of returns implied a theoretically infinite variance. Figure App. 18A-4 outlines such a distribution with a dashed line and compares it with the normal distribution. The tails of the distribution represented by the dashed line are very long. As a result, there is a tiny probability that rates of return reach very large positive or negative values and cause the distribution to have a theoretically infinite variance.

Problems with Infinite Variance Populations

The existence of outliers and a theoretically infinite variance presents problems for risk-return analysis. Equation (App. 18A-3) shows the formula for calculating the standard deviation of returns from a sample of n observations.

$$\sigma = \sqrt{\frac{1}{n}\sum_{t=1}^{n}[r_t - E(r)]^2}$$

(App. 18A-3)

If risk is being estimated with Eq. (App. 18A-3) using historical returns, inefficient and erratic statistics will be obtained. Every time an extreme value of r_t (that is, an outlier) is included in the computation of the risk with Eq. (App. 18A-3), the standard deviation will increase erratically instead of smoothly approaching the true population value. Figure App. 18A-5 represents the problem graphically.

In order to develop efficient and unerratic risk statistics from a population with an infinite variance, some other financial risk surrogate may be used. Equation (App. 18A-4) defines the mean absolute deviation of returns (MAD).

$$MAD = \frac{1}{n}\sum_{t=1}^{n}|r_t - E(r)|$$

(App. 18A-4)

where

$|r_t - E(r)|$ = absolute value of the deviation from the mean

Since the deviations around the expected value are not squared in Eq. (App. 18A-4) as they are in Eq. (App. 18A-3), the MAD does not increase

---

[76] Benoit Mandelbrot, ''The Variation of Certain Speculative Prices,'' *Journal of Business*, October 1963, pp. 394–419. Eugene F. Fama, ''The Behavior of Stock Market Prices,'' *Journal of Business*, January 1965, pp. 39–105.

FIGURE APP.18A-5   Sequential values of the standard deviation and mean absolute deviation from population with infinite variance.

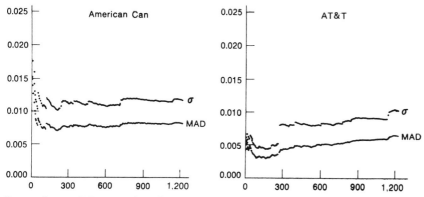

Source: Eugene F. Fama, "The Behavior of Stock Prices," *Journal of Business*, January 1965, p. 96.

dramatically as the standard deviation does when an outlier enters into the computations. Figure App. 18A-5 compares the MAD with the standard deviation in a sequential sampling experiment. The MAD is both smaller and less erratic than the standard deviation.

APP. 18-2   INDEPENDENCE OF SECURITY PRICE CHANGES

It will be recalled that the successive values in a random walk must be (1) identically distributed according to some stable distribution and (2) independent of preceding or subsequent observations. It has been explained that short-term rates of return are distributed according to a stable symmetric distribution, which fulfills the first requirement to classify rates of return as conforming to the random-walk model. However, in order for rates of return to fully conform to the random-walk model, they must also be independent. To be *independent*, the rates of price change and rates of return for a security must not possess any detectable cycle or other pattern.

   Next, some of the tests used to determine whether the rates of return from security price changes are a statistically independent series of numbers are examined. If these rates of return are independent, however, two conclusions may be drawn. First, a finding of perfect statistical independence will fulfill the requirements to classify the percentage changes of security prices as a random walk. Second, if the percentage changes in security prices are perfectly independent, then they are random. As a result, technical analysis will not be worth performing. Various statistical procedures are reviewed below in order to determine if rates of return and rates of price change are statistically independent.

Serial Correlation: A Test for Independence

Serial correlation is one of the many statistical tools used to measure dependence of successive numbers in a series. It has been widely used to measure possible dependence in security prices' rates of change. The linear regression model shown in Eq. (App. 18A-5) is the model for which the correlation coefficient is determined when measuring serial correlation in rates of return.

$$r_{i,t+k} = a_i + b_i r_{i,t} + e_{i,t} \qquad \text{(App. 18A-5)}$$

where

$r_{i,t}$ = rate of return from the ith asset during the tth period (that is, day, week, or year) as measured by Eq. (App. 18A-1) or (App. 18A-2)

$r_{i,t+k}$ = rate of return on the same security k periods later; k is called the lag

$e_{i,t}$ = a random error which averages zero

a_i and b_i = least-squares regression intercept and slope coefficient for asset i[77]

The correlation coefficient for model Eq. (App. 19A-5) is the serial correlation coefficient for a k-period lag. A simple graphical explanation should make this clearer.

FIGURE APP. 18A-6   Cyclical rates of return.

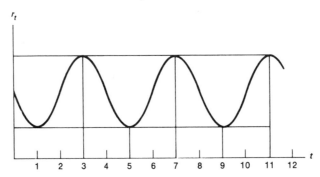

Figure App. 18A-6 is a graph of a time series of rates of return for some hypothetical security. These rates of return conform to a perfectly repetitive four-period cycle. If the lagged regression model Eq. (App. 18A-5) is fitted to the data graphed in Fig. App. 18A-6 the serial correlations (denoted ρ_k) will vary with the lag. For a four-period ($k = 4$) lag, the data graphed in Fig. App. 18A-6 will yield a perfect positive correlation ($\rho_4 = +1$), indicating the

---

77 Correct measurement of the serial correlation that is associated with regression Eq. (App. 18A-5) is possible only if var($r_{i,t}$) is constant over the period under examination; that is, homoscedasticity is essential.

existence of a four-period perfectly repetitive cycle. For a two-period lag, a perfectly negative serial correlation ($\rho_2 = -1$) will result, indicating that rates of return two periods apart move inversely. For a one-period lag ($k = 1$), zero serial correlation ($\rho_0 = 0$) will result, indicating that rates of return from adjoining periods move inversely half the time and directly the other half. The data would thus indicate that no pattern of dependence can be detected for $k = 1$; but for two- and four-period lags, complete dependence is implied by their correlations.

When performing serial correlation tests, the analyst tries all possible lags that may exist. For example, Table App. 18A-1 shows the serial correlation coefficients Fama found for each of the thirty securities in the Dow Jones Industrial Average for lags from one to ten days' length (that is, $k = 1,2,3,4,5,6,7,8,9,10$). It will be noted that few of the serial correlation coefficients in Table App. 18A-1 are significantly different from zero.[78] Fama and others have used serial correlation to test different securities and different lags. These studies detected no significant serial correlations that could be used to earn speculative profits. However, some significant serial correlations were found, particularly in the less actively traded stocks.[79]

Table App. 18A-2 presents serial correlations coefficients that are in some respects significantly different from Fama's statistics in Table App. 18A-1. Dr. Gabriel Hawawini used a more heterogeneous sample of securities to analyze than Fama used. Fama's sample was limited to actively traded, NYSE-listed, blue-chip stocks. Hawawini's more representative sample results shown in Table App. 18A-2 reveal many significant one-day serial correlations in both individual stocks and stock market indexes. For lags of three days and longer, however, Hawawini reports few significant serial correlations above what are expected to occur simply as a result of normal sampling error. Thus, some statistically significant serial correlation appears to exist, but it is of dubious economic significance. After all, how much after-commissions profit could a speculator earn if armed with the knowledge of some marginally significant one- and two-day serial correlations?

If rates of return were calculated by using long-enough differencing intervals (for example, one-period returns from five-year periods), then a positive serial correlation of returns would emerge owing to the upward trend in the market. The long-run trends can be seen with the naked eye in some graphs. The so-called random-walk theory, however, applies only to *short-run* rates of return from which speculative traders and technical analysts try

---

78 Correlation coefficents more than 1.96 standard errors from zero are significantly different from zero at the .05 level of significance if the underlying distribution is normal. Such coefficients are noted with an asterisk in Table App. 18A-1.

79 G.A. Hawawini, "On the Time Behavior of Financial Parameters; An Investigation of the Intervaling Effect,' unpublished doctoral dissertation, New York University, 1977. Robert A. Schwartz and David K. Whitcomb, "Evidence on the Presence and Causes of Serial Correlation in the Market Model Residuals," *Journal of Financial and Quantitative Analysis*, June 1977, vol. XII, no. 2, pp. 291–315, and "The Time-Variance Relationship: Evidence of Autocorrelation in Common Stock Returns," *Journal of Finance*, March 1977, vol. 1, no. 1, pp. 41–56.

TABLE APP. 18A-1 DAILY SERIAL CORRELATION COEFFICIENTS FOR LAG k = 1, 2, . . . , 10

STOCK	(1)	(2)	(3)	(4)	(5)	(6)	(7)	(8)	(9)	(10)
Allied Chemical	.017	-.042	.007	-.001	.027	.004	-.017	-.026	.017	-.007
Alcoa	.118*	.038	-.014	.022	-.022	.009	.017	.007	-.001	-.033
American Can	-.087*	-.024	.034	-.065*	-.017	-.006	.015	.025	-.047	-.040
AT&T	-.039	-.097*	.000	.026	.005	-.005	.002	.027	-.014	.007
American Tobacco	.111*	-.109*	-.060*	-.065*	.007	-.010	.011	.046	.039	.041
Anaconda	.067*	-.061*	-.047	-.002	.000	-.038	.009	.016	-.014	-.056
Bethlehem Steel	.013	-.065*	.009	.021	-.053	-.098*	-.010	.004	-.002	-.021
Chrysler	.012	-.066*	-.016	-.007	-.015	.009	.037	.056*	-.044	.021
Du Pont	.013	-.033	.060*	.027	-.002	-.047	.020	.011	-.034	.001
Eastman Kodak	.025	.014	-.031	.005	-.022	.012	.007	.006	.008	.002
General Electric	.011	-.038	-.021	.031	-.001	.000	-.008	.014	-.002	.010
General Foods	.061*	-.003	.045	.002	-.015	-.052	-.006	-.014	-.024	-.017
General Motors	-.004	-.056*	-.037	-.008	-.038	-.006	.019	.006	-.016	.009
Goodyear	-.123*	.017	-.044	.043	-.002	-.003	.035	.014	-.015	.007
International Harvester	-.017	-.029	-.031	.037	-.052	-.021	-.001	.003	-.046	-.016
International Nickel	.096*	-.033	-.019	.020	.027	.059*	-.038	-.008	-.016	.034
International Paper	.046	-.011	-.058*	.053*	.049	-.003	-.025	-.019	-.003	-.021
Johns Manville	.006	-.038	-.027	-.023	-.029	-.080*	.040	.018	-.037	.029
Owens Illinois	-.021	-.084*	-.047	.068*	.086*	-.040	.011	-.040	.067*	-.043
Procter & Gamble	.099*	-.009	-.008	.009	-.015	.022	.012	-.012	-.022	-.021
Sears	.097*	.026	.028	.025	.005	-.054	-.006	-.010	-.008	-.009
Standard Oil (Calif.)	.025	-.030	-.051*	-.025	-.047	-.034	-.010	.072*	-.049*	-.035
Standard Oil (N.J.)	.008	-.116*	.016	.014	-.047	-.018	-.022	-.026	-.073*	.081*
Swift & Co.	-.004	-.015	-.010	.012	.057*	.012	-.043	.014	.012	.001
Texaco	.094*	-.049	-.024	-.018	-.017	-.009	.031	.032	-.013	.008
Union Carbide	.107*	-.012	.040	.046	-.036	-.034	.003	-.008	-.054	-.037
United Aircraft	.014	-.033	-.022	-.047	-.067*	-.053	.046	.037	.015	-.019
U.S. Steel	.040	-.074*	.014	.011	-.012	-.021	.041	.037	-.021	-.044
Westinghouse	-.027	-.022	-.036	-.003	.000	-.054*	-.020	.013	-.014	-.008
Woolworth	.028	-.016	.015	.014	.007	-.039	-.013	.003	-.088*	-.008

*Coefficient is twice its computed standard error.

Source: Eugene F. Fama "The Behavior of Stock Market Prices," *Journal of Business*, January 1965, p. 72.

TABLE APP. 18A-2   EVIDENCE OF SERIAL CORRELATION IN SECURITIES AND MARKET RETURNS, JANUARY 1970–DECEMBER 1973

SECURITIES	ORDER OF SERIAL CORRELATION IN DAYS							
	1	2	3	4	5	10	15	20
Wayne Gossard	-.170*	-.040	-.034	.022	-.011	.025	-.001	.051
Mich. Seamless Tube	-.185*	.046	-.096*	.051	-.044	-.065*	-.024	-.011
Allied Products Corp.	-.368*	-.002	-.014	-.020	.014	.030	-.010	-.012
Maryland Cup Corp.	.201*	.091*	.011	-.014	-.012	-.038	-.007	-.005
Big Three Inds.	.145*	.074*	.047	.047	-.007	.010	-.014	-.019
Thomas & Betts Corp.	.145*	.061	.019	-.017	-.040	.043	.023	-.017
Cleveland Cliffs	.210*	.106*	.003	-.022	-.076*	-.030	.029	-.018
N.Y.S. Gas & Electric	-.137*	.076*	.004	.013	.019	-.010	-.010	-.029
Great West. Finance	.161*	.020	-.010	-.001	-.041	-.056	.029	-.040
Genuine Parts Co.	.126*	.001	-.031	-.060	-.085*	-.032	.004	.013
Union Electric Co.	-.155*	.037	.011	.048	-.001	.022	-.061	-.059
Searle, G. D.	.136*	.077*	-.038	-.031	-.060	-.020	-.060	-.020
Pacific Gas & Elec.	.154*	.080*	.037	.005	-.002	-.007	-.008	-.005
Shell Oil Co.	.123*	.022	-.020	-.033	-.001	-.026	.014	.003
Kresge, S. S. Co.	.143*	.015	-.064*	-.059	-.006	-.071	-.023	-.038
% of significant corr. for 50 securities	66%	20%	6%	6%	10%	8%	4%	4%
Market indexes								
Dow-Jones Industrial	.248*	.003	-.034	-.022	-.075*	-.049	.044	.005
Standard & Poor's Corp.	.285*	.043	.027	-.013	-.005	-.053	.047	.022
NYSE Composite	.338*	.048	.006	.007	-.002	-.052	.054	-.005

*Asterisks indicate correlations significantly different from zero.

Source: Gabriel A. Hawawini, "On the Time Behavior of Financial Parameters: An Investigation of the Intervaling Effect," unpublished doctoral dissertation, New York University, 1977.

to profit. The random-walk theory does not deny the existence of a long-run upward trend in security prices; it requires only that short-run price movements be random. The data reveal that short-run price changes and rates of return are not highly serially correlated. In essence, this means there is not a significant cycle or pattern in security price changes that repeats itself or that can be used to predict future security prices. The simple linear model underlying the serial correlation tests indicates that successive security price changes tend to behave somewhat like a series of random numbers. However, other more complicated patterns may exist.

Runs Tests

A runs test is a statistical tool used to detect the presence of occasional nonrandom trends in a series of numbers. For testing security prices, a *run* can be defined as a sequence of price changes of the same sign. Table App. 18A-3 shows how runs are determined from a series of daily closing prices. There are twelve price changes between the thirteen successive security prices p_t shown in the table. There are three runs of positive changes, one run of zero change, and two runs of negative changes for a total of six runs.

TABLE APP. 18A-3   DETERMINING RUNS IN A TIME SERIES OF HYPOTHETICAL SECURITY PRICES

TIME PERIOD (t)	SECURITY PRICES (p_t)	$\Delta p_t = p_{t+1} - p_t$	RUNS	TYPE RUN
1	$67	+1	1	positive
2	68	−5		
3	63	−3	2	negative
4	60	−3		
5	57	0	3	zero
6	57	0		
7	57	+3	4	positive
8	60	+1		
9	61	−1	5	negative
10	60	+2		
11	62	+1	6	positive
12	63	+2		
13	65			

A runs test is performed by comparing the number of runs in the data with the number of runs that would be present in a sample of random numbers. It is possible to determine the number of total runs, the number of positive-change runs, the number of zero-change runs, and the number of negative-change runs that can be expected in a series of random numbers of any length.[80] Then if the runs that were actually found in the data are significantly different (that is, either too few or too many) from the numbers that are expected from truly random numbers, it is inferred that the successive changes are dependent. Table App. 18A-4 shows some of the results of

80 Eugene F. Fama, op. cit., pp. 74–80. Fama explains the runs test and gives the formulas.

TABLE APP. 18A-4   RUNS ANALYSIS BY SIGN (DAILY CHANGES)

STOCK	Positive			Negative			No Change		
	ACTUAL	EXPECTED	ACTUAL-EXPECTED	ACTUAL	EXPECTED	ACTUAL-EXPECTED	ACTUAL	EXPECTED	ACTUAL-EXPECTED
Allied Chemical	286	290.1	− 4.1	294	290.7	3.3	103	102.2	0.8
Alcoa	265	264.4	0.6	262	266.5	− 4.5	74	70.1	3.9
American Can	289	290.2	− 1.2	285	284.6	0.4	156	155.2	0.8
AT&T	290	291.2	− 1.2	285	285.3	− 0.3	82	80.5	1.5
American Tobacco	296	300.2	− 4.2	295	294.0	1.0	109	105.8	3.2
Anaconda	271	272.9	− 1.9	276	278.8	− 2.8	88	83.3	4.7
Bethlehem Steel	282	286.4	− 4.4	300	294.6	5.4	127	128.0	− 1.0
Chrysler	417	414.9	2.1	421	421.1	− 0.1	89	91.0	− 2.0
Du Pont	293	300.3	− 7.3	305	299.2	5.8	74	72.5	1.5
Eastman Kodak	306	308.6	− 2.6	312	308.7	3.3	60	60.7	− 0.7
General Electric	404	404.5	− 0.5	401	404.7	− 3.7	113	108.8	4.2
General Foods	346	340.8	5.2	320	331.3	− 11.3	133	126.9	6.1
General Motors	340	342.7	− 2.7	339	340.3	− 1.3	153	149.0	4.0
Goodyear	294	291.9	2.1	292	293.0	− 1.0	95	96.1	− 1.1
International Harvester	303	300.1	2.9	301	298.8	2.2	116	121.1	− 5.1
International Nickel	312	307.0	5.0	296	301.9	− 5.9	96	95.1	0.9
International Paper	322	330.2	− 8.2	338	333.2	4.8	102	98.6	3.4
Johns Manville	293	292.6	0.4	296	293.5	2.5	96	98.9	− 2.9
Owens Illinois	297	293.7	3.3	295	291.2	3.8	121	128.1	− 7.1
Procter & Gamble	343	346.4	− 3.4	342	340.3	1.7	141	139.3	1.7
Sears	291	289.3	1.7	265	271.3	− 6.3	144	139.4	4.6
Standard Oil (Calif.)	406	417.9	− 11.9	427	416.6	10.4	139	137.5	1.5
Standard Oil (N.J.)	272	277.3	− 5.3	281	277.9	3.1	135	132.8	2.2
Swift & Co.	354	354.3	− 0.3	355	356.9	− 1.9	169	166.8	2.2
Texaco	266	265.6	0.4	258	263.6	− 5.6	76	70.8	5.2
Union Carbide	266	268.1	− 2.1	265	265.6	− 0.6	64	61.3	2.7
United Aircraft	281	280.4	0.6	282	282.2	− 0.2	98	98.4	− 0.4
U.S. Steel	292	293.5	− 1.5	296	295.2	0.8	63	62.3	0.7
Westinghouse	359	361.3	− 2.3	364	362.1	1.9	106	105.6	0.4
Woolworth	349	348.7	0.3	350	345.9	4.1	148	152.4	− 4.4

Source: Eugene F. Fama, "The Behavior of Stock Market Prices," *Journal of Business*, January 1965, p. 79.

a study of the thirty stocks in the DJIA. About 1400 daily stock prices from 1957 to 1962 were analyzed for each stock. Since the actual number of runs was not significantly different from the number of runs expected if the series were random, the test implies that stock price changes are random. Runs analyses of other securities by other analysts have also indicated that security price changes are a series of independent numbers.

Testing Independence with Filter Rules

A *filter rule* is a mechanical trading rule that can detect trends in data. An x percent filter rule operates as follows:

If the price of a security rises at least x percent, buy and hold the security until its price drops at least x percent from a subsequent high. Then, when the price decreases x percent or more, liquidate any long position and assume a short position until the price rises at least x percent.

By varying the value of x, an infinite number of filter rules can be tested. If stock price changes are a series of independent random numbers, filter rules should not yield more return than a naive buy-and-hold strategy.

Several analysts have applied filter rules to series of historical daily prices for various securities. The historical data were stored in the memory of a computer. Then, the computer was programmed to simulate trading activity using many different filters. Filters as small as ½ of 1 percent ($x = 0.005$) and as large as 50 percent ($x = 0.5$) were used. Each study showed that the filter rules were less profitable than a naive buy-and-hold strategy. If brokers' commissions are ignored, a few of the filter rules were able to earn a rate of return as high as 15 percent per year, a rate of return above what could have been achieved by using a naive buy-and-hold strategy during that period. Nevertheless, the vast majority of the filter rules earned very poor returns (that is, less than could be obtained with a naive buy-and-hold strategy) or even incurred losses. Many buy and sell transactions are generated by some filter rules (namely, $x = 0.005$). To perform a realistic test of a filter rule, sales commissions must be deducted to determine the *net* profitability of a trading technique. When allowance was made for sales commissions, the filter rules earned even poorer returns. No filter rule earned a rate of return above what a naive buy-and-hold strategy earned, and most filters resulted in losses after deduction of the commissions they generated.

Some studies of filter rules figured the rate of return from long positions and the return from short positions separately. Using a filter rule to select short positions nearly always resulted in losses even before allowance was made for commissions. Sometimes the long positions initiated by a filter rule earned positive returns. In fact, a ½ percent filter ($x = 0.005$) resulted in an annual return before commissions as high as 20 percent, according to one study. After sales commissions were deducted, however, a higher return could have been achieved by using a naive buy-and-hold strategy. In general, filter rules do not earn net rates of return as high as those that could be gained with a naive buy-and-hold strategy.

Thus far, the notions of a stable probability distribution and statistical independence have been developed in an effort to clarify the nature of a random walk. Before reaching conclusions, let us consider a simplified random-walk numerical example to pull these ideas together.

Simplified Numerical Example of Random Walk

Imagine a security whose rates of return either increase or decrease by one percentage point each period with equal probability. Denote the expected return of this security as $E(r_0)$. Table App. 18A-5 traces the course of all possible outcomes over several periods.

TABLE APP. 18A-5 SIMPLIFIED RANDOM WALK IN RETURNS

PERIOD (t)	0	1	2	3	4
Possible outcomes (and their probabilities)	$E(r_0)$	$E(r_0) + 1(\frac{1}{2})$ $E(r_0) - 1(\frac{1}{2})$	$E(r_0) + 2(\frac{1}{4})$ $E(r_0)$ $(\frac{1}{2})$ $E(r_0) - 2(\frac{1}{4})$	$E(r_0) + 3(\frac{1}{8})$ $E(r_0) + 1(\frac{3}{8})$ $E(r_0) - 1(\frac{3}{8})$ $E(r_0) - 3(\frac{1}{8})$	. . . .
$E(r_1)$	$E(r_0)$	$E(r_1) = E(r_0)$	$E(r_2) = E(r_0)$	$E(r_3) = E(r_0)$	. . .
$var(r_1)$	0	1	2	3	4

In this table the probability of any outcome is shown in parentheses following that outcome. Examination of the table will reveal the following characteristics. (1) The expected return is constant at $E(r_0)$ in every period and for every differencing interval. Thus, the expected return is stationary as the future unfolds and actual returns fluctuate around $E(r_0)$. (2) The variance of returns tends to increase with the length of the differencing period. (3) The probability distribution of possible returns is stationary although the actual returns vary randomly. That is, the actual rates of return over time are a series of independent values that can be assigned probabilities but cannot be predicted in advance.

The example shown in Table App. 18A-5 is a random walk in rates of return because the returns are independent and identically distributed. An examination of actual historical rates of return will reveal that characteristics 1 and 2 above also occur in the empirical data and that characteristic 3 is a rough approximation of a stable distribution to which the empirical data conform. Thus, this simple random-walk model is a good first approximation of the way rates of return actually perform.

Conclusions Regarding Independence

Some of the simplest and most common tests used to determine the independence of series of security price changes and rates of return have been presented. It was shown that the data are not *perfectly* statistically independent in every case. A few cases were found (namely, small serial correlations, actual runs not exactly equal to expected runs, a few filter rules that earned a small profit before commissions, and year-end and week-end anomalies) where variations from perfect statistical independence existed. These cases of dependence were found to be very slight; no profit could be earned from a knowledge of these small variations from pure independence. Nevertheless, a mathematical statistician would not say that rates of return are perfectly independent over time. Therefore, rates of return are not perfectly described by a rigorously defined random-walk model.

A practical businessperson need not adhere to the rigorous conventions of the mathematical statistician. Investors' criteria are simpler. As long as rates of return are sufficiently independent that profit cannot be increased by using whatever statistical dependency exists, it may be concluded that rates of return are independent for business purposes. Thus, as a first approximation, we may say rates of return follow a random walk as far as businesspeople need be concerned.

The random-walk conclusion casts serious doubts on the efficiency of technical analysis. It will be recalled that technical analysts' methods are largely based upon statistical dependency and patterns in security price changes. There is little doubt that some of the patterns described by the technical analysts actually exist; such patterns can also be found in series of random numbers or in ink blots. Also, some of the market indicators used by chartists (for example, the confidence index) are actually correlated with security market indexes. But technical tools *do not furnish dependable leading indicators*: they are frequently concurrent or lagging indicators, or they may even fail to formulate the proper signal at all. The patterns, moreover, are ambiguous. Different technicians interpret the same chart to mean different things. Furthermore, the charts issue erroneous signals about as frequently as they issue correct signals. The few studies that have been published in support of technical analysis are weak. The evidence presented by the random-walk advocates is more voluminous and more scientific than evidence presented by the technical analysts. A reasonable person who objectively studied the existing literature would most likely conclude that technical analysis tools were (in some cases) crude attempts to measure risk or (in most cases) not worth performing at all.

APP. 18A-3   MARTINGALE MODELS

The random walk is a mathematical model in which a series is both independent and identically distributed; it is a special, more narrowly defined

BOX APP.
18A-2
Definition of a
Martingale

> A martingale process is a mathematical process in which the conditional expectation of the $(n + 1)$st value equals the nth value in some set of data.[81]

81 William Feller, *An Introduction to Probability Theory and Its Implications*, vol. II (New York: Wiley, 1966); see pp. 210–212 for a more rigorous discussion of martingales.

case of a *martingale process*. A martingale does not require that successive members of the series be either independent or identically distributed. Box App. 18A-2 defines a martingale.

Symbolically, rates of return follow a martingale if Eq. (App. 18A-6) is not violated.

$$E(_jr_{t+1}|_jr_t, \ldots, _jr_{t-n}) = _jr_t \tag{App. 18A-6}$$

where

$_jr_t$ = return for security j at period t.

Equation (App. 18A-6) is a symbolic representation of the weakly efficient markets hypothesis. It says that knowledge of all historical returns of some security suggests only that the next period's return is expected to equal the last period's return.

A stronger form of the martingale exists if Eq. (App. 18A-7) is not violated.

$$E(_jr_{t+1}|N_t) = _jr_t \tag{App. 18A-7}$$

where

N_t = all the public news and information that existed at period t

This is the semistrongly efficient markets hypothesis. Equation (App. 18A-7) implies that all available news is already reflected in prices. Equations (App. 18A-6) and (App. 18A-7) imply that future returns are independent of past data, but they do not imply complete independence of the entire series of returns.[82] Security prices are a *submartingale* process, since they drift upward over time. Equation (App. 18A-8) defines the submartingale process followed by most security prices.

$$E(_jp_{t+1}|_jp_t, _jp_{t-1}, \ldots, _jp_{t-n}) > _jp_t \tag{App. 18A-8}$$

where

$_jp_t$ = price of security j at period t

In contrast to the martingale, the random-walk model is much more narrowly defined. Rates of return are a random walk if Eq. (App. 18A-9) is not violated.

$$f(_jr_{t+1}|_jr_t, _jr_{t-1}, \ldots, _jr_{t-n}) = f(_jr_t) \tag{App. 18A-9}$$

where

$f(_jr_t)$ = the probability distribution of returns for security j at period t

Equation (App. 18A-9) implies Eq. (App. 18A-6). Furthermore, Eq. (App. 18A-9) implies that rates of return are independent and identically distributed according to some stationary distribution.

[82] John T. Emery, ''The Information Content of Daily Market Indicators,'' *Journal of Financial and Quantitative Analysis*, March 1973, pp. 183–190.

Technically speaking, Eq. (App. 18A-9) is not true because the percentage price changes for securities are not all perfectly independent — only nearly so. Equations (App. 18A-6) and (App. 18A-8) are weaker assertions which are true, however.

The distinction between Eqs. (App. 18A-6) and (App. 18A-9) is not great where stock price changes are concerned. It took mathematicians and economists several years to determine that Eqs. (App. 18A-6) and (App. 18A-8) were true and that (App. 18A-9) was an overstatement. But, when using language precisely, it is best to refer to security prices as a submartingale and to rates of return as a martingale. The random-walk term is an exaggeration.

The efficient market hypothesis may be formalized by using the compact functional notation for probability distributions. Suppose that $f(p_{it}, p_{i,t-1}, p_{i,t-2}, p_{i,t-3}, \ldots | \phi_{t-1})$ is the joint probability distribution of the ith security's prices with all other securities prices in period t. Suppose further that this distribution is conditional upon ϕ_{t-1}, which is the set of *all information* that determines security prices in period t. Also, define $g(p_{it}, p_{i,t-1}, p_{i,t-2}, p_{i,t-3}, \ldots | \phi_{t-1}^M$ to be the joint probability distribution of the ith security's price with all other prices, which is conditional upon ϕ_{t-1}^M, the set of all information that the *market uses* to determine the security prices in period t. Capital markets are perfectly efficient if Eq. (App. 19A-10) is true.[83]

$$f(p_{it}, p_{i,t-1}, p_{i,t-2}, p_{i,t-3}, \ldots | \phi_{t-1}) = \qquad \text{(App. 18A-10)}$$

$$g(p_{it}, p_{i,t-1}, p_{i,t-2}, p_{i,t-3}, \ldots | \phi_{t-1}^M)$$

83 Stephen F. LeRoy, "Efficient Capital Markets: Comment," *Journal of Finance*, March 1976, vol. XXI, no. 1, pp. 139–141. E.F. Fama, "Reply," ibid, pp. 143–145. A study by Singh and Rahman indicated that Canadian security returns generally confirm the Martingale rather than the random walk process. See Balvir Singh and Abdul H. Rahman, "An Econometric Analysis of the Variability Security Returns," *Administrative Sciences of Canada Proceedings*, 1985 Conference, Finance Division, vol. 1, pp. 19–27.

PART 6

OTHER INVESTMENTS

Hedging and Options

This chapter introduces various speculative positions and assets. The short position, put and call options, warrants, and convertible securities are explained. Hedging is investigated as one of the uses for these speculative assets. Before exploring these positions, however, it is worthwhile to distinguish between three different economic activities: gambling, speculating, and investing.

A *gamble* involves the purchase of an opportunity to win some game of chance that will typically be completed in a few seconds. The results of a gamble are quickly resolved by the roll of the dice or a turn of a card. *Gambling differs from speculating and investing* in several respects. First of all, a gamble is completed much quicker than a speculation or an investment. Second, rational, risk-averse people undertake gambles as a form of entertainment, not as a way to earn an income. Casino gambling typically involves transactions that have a negative expected value for the gambler. Third, astute financial analysis cannot change the roll of the dice or the turn of a card. Essentially, the expected value of a gamble is invariant with respect to financial research insights.

Speculations last longer than gambles, but they have shorter durations than investments. *Speculation* involves the purchase of a marketable asset in hopes of making a profit from an increase in price that is expected to occur within a few weeks or months. Speculators can expect to avoid some unprofitable speculations and exploit some profitable ones by working to gain research insights. Unfortunately, speculating is perceived to be wasteful and unproductive by some observers. Actually, speculating is a productive economic activity that can benefit both the astute financial analyst and society in general.

Investing occurs when someone buys an asset and holds it in order to earn interest, dividends, or some other kind of income and, typically, in order to benefit from some long-term price appreciation. Financial analysts are employed to research out the investments with the best potential long-run investment rewards. There is no precise dividing line between the time involved in a speculation and an investment.

Speculators may assume a number of different financial positions that differ from the typical long-run investment position of buying a market asset, holding it, and hoping for price appreciation and other income. Each of these different speculative positions and assets can be used for different purposes: to obtain entertainment from a quick gamble, to profit from a short-run price change speculation, or to earn the long-run reward associated with successful investment. For example, bearish investors (that is, those who expect price declines) can assume short positions to profit from the price declines that they expect. These short positions can be taken for an hour-long gamble on a quick price drop or for a short-run speculation that the price will come down, or they can be held open for longer in order to profit from a long-run price decline in an investment asset. Another possibility is that short-run price speculators who want the breathtaking thrills that accompany highly leveraged positions may buy or sell puts, calls, strips, straps, spreads, straddles, warrants, or some combination of these options. Some of these positions are profitable if prices rise; some are profitable if prices fall; some are profitable if prices either rise or fall; and some are profitable if prices do not change at all. Further, some of the positions are best-suited for long-term investing, and some are tailor-made for short-term speculation. This chapter explains various positions from which speculators and investors may select. Whether the position turns out to be a speculation or an investment depends in each case on how long and why the position was kept open.

19-1 LONG AND SHORT POSITIONS

Investors may assume either or both of two basic positions in a market asset. A *long position* involves simply buying and holding the asset; this is the only position of which many investors are aware. The short position is more complicated.

19-1.1 The Short Position

A *short sale* occurs when one person sells a second person something that the first person does not yet own. Does it sound illegal? It is not. Short sales are routine transactions that just require more explanation than the buy-and-hold position.

Short sellers usually sell an asset (such as a stock or a bond) short because they expect its price to fall and they want to profit from that price fall. The short seller, therefore, actually sells an asset he or she does not own to a second party, who takes a long position in the asset; the long buyer expects the price to rise. Thus, a short sale requires a short seller who is bearish and a long buyer who is bullish (that is, one who expects price appreciation) about the same asset at the same time; it is a case of opposites attracting each other in search of profit. The short seller borrows the shares of stock (or whatever asset is involved) to be sold short from a third party in order to make delivery on the short sale. Then the short seller waits for the asset's price to fall so that the asset can be purchased at the anticipated lower price and so that the third party who loaned the asset can be repaid. If the asset's price does fall (rise), the short seller profits (loses) by the difference between the price paid for the asset to give to the third party and the price at which the asset was sold earlier to the long buyer, less any commission costs. Therefore, aside from the commission costs taken out of the transaction by the stockbroker, the short seller's profit equals the long buyer's loss — or vice versa, if the asset's price rises after the short sale. Table 19-1 outlines the parties, suggests some average times, and explains all the transactions in a hypothetical short sale.

A second reason to create a short position is to create another new position that is negatively correlated with an existing long position in order to reduce risk in the aggregate position. That is, a short position may be taken to establish a risk-reducing *hedged* portfolio comprised of an existing long position and the newly created offsetting short position. This risk-reducing strategy is discussed further in Sec. 19-2.

19-1.2 Complicated Aspects of Short Positions

Short sales are more complicated than the example in Table 19-1 may seem to indicate for several reasons. First, short sales of TSE common stocks, for instance, cannot be made below the price of the last sale of a board lot.[1] This is a TSE rule designed to keep short sellers from accenting a downturn in the price of a stock. A second complication involves dividends. If a common stock that is sold short pays a *cash dividend* while on loan to the short seller, the short seller must pay that dividend from personal funds to the third party who lent the shares. Third, the short seller may be required to put up *guarantee money* equalling as much as 200 percent of the value of the borrowed shares as collateral for the third party who lent the shares. A fourth problem that can arise with short sales is that the short seller can get "*closed out*" of the short position at any time if the third party who lent the shares demands them back. For example, if the price of the security that was sold short goes up so that the third party who lent the shares wants to sell and recognize a capital gain, the third party can call for the shares to be returned immediately. This can force the short seller, for example, to cover the short position by buying the shares at a disadvantageous higher price. This can throw the short seller for a loss unless the shares can be borrowed elsewhere (which they usually can).

19-1.3 Profit-Loss Illustrations for Long and Short Positions

Figure 19-1 illustrates the long and the short positions in a fashion that should help clarify the two concepts further. The vertical axis in these two profit-loss graphs shows the dollars of profit above the origin and the dollars of loss below the origin. The horizontal axis shows the market prices of the assets.

The profit-loss graph for the long position in Fig. 19-1a has a slope of positive unity, indicating that the person holding the long position makes a dollar of profit (loss) for each dollar the market price rises (falls). In contrast, the profit-loss graph for the short position in Fig. 19-1b has a slope of negative unity, indicating a dollar of loss (profit) for the short seller for each dollar the market price rises (falls).

---

1 However, short sales can be made below the price of the last sale of a board lot in a security interlisted with another stock exchange in Canada or the United States on a down-tick that occurs on the other exchange. See *The Toronto Stock Exchange Trading Manual*, s.11.27, p. 7-1.

TABLE 19-1   OUTLINE OF THE PARTIES AND TRANSACTIONS IN A HYPOTHETICAL SHORT SALE OF SECURITIES

DATE	MR. FIRST BULL	MR. BEAR	BROKER A	MR. SECOND BULL
January 15: An independent purchase is made.	First Bull buys 100 shares of XYZ on margin, leaves them in an account with Broker A, and retires to Kelowna. Broker A holds the shares in the brokerage's name without First Bull's knowing that he is doing so (a common practice).			
February 10: A short sale occurs.		Mr. Bear expects the price of XYZ to drop, and he calls Broker A and requests a short sale. So 100 shares of XYZ are sold short from Bear's account.	Broker A executes a short sale for Mr. Bear and a purchase for Mr. Second Bull, both for XYZ stock.	Mr. Second Bull buys 100 shares of XYZ through Broker A without knowing they are being sold by a short seller.
February 15: Delivery is made on short sale.	First Bull's 100 shares of XYZ are loaned to Bear by Broker A (without telling First Bull).	Bear makes delivery by borrowing First Bull's shares through Broker A. Now Bear is in a short position.	Broker A delivers First Bull's 100 shares of XYZ to Mr. Second Bull, collects cash for the shares, and marks Bear's account short 100 shares, which are owed to First Bull.	First Bull's 100 shares of XYZ are received by Second Bull without his knowing he has purchased them from a short seller.
March 3: The short position is covered.		Bear covers his short position by buying 100 shares of XYZ at today's market price and has Broker A return them to First Bull.	Broker A buys 100 shares of XYZ for Bear and places them in First Bull's safe deposit box. If these shares cost less (more) than the sale price on Feb. 10, Bear gets the profit (loss).	
March 8: Borrowed shares are replaced.	The 100 shares of XYZ are replaced in First Bull's account without his ever being aware they were gone.			

FIGURE 19-1   Profit Graphs: (a) long position; (b) short position.

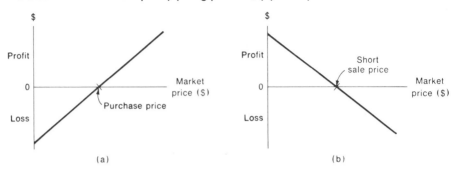

Short sales have been conducted on the floor of the Toronto Stock Exchange (amidst what is predominantly long trading) for decades. The volume of short sales is reported occasionally in the financial newspapers under the heading "Short Interest." The short interest is the total number of shares that brokers have listed in their accounts as being sold short. The short interest is usually below 2 percent of the total volume of shares traded.

There are different reasons why an individual may take a short position. First, and most obvious, is the desire to make a speculative gain from a short-term price fall. Second, a *risk-averse* investor may sell short to "hedge" against possible losses. Hedging is an important investment strategy that should be considered carefully.

19-2   HEDGING AND ARBITRAGE

Hedging may be defined as arranging for two different positions such that the potential losses from one of the positions tends to be, more or less, offset by profits from the other position. Alternatively, hedging can be defined as the establishment of offsetting long and short positions in order to diminish the portfolio's risk that could result from an adverse price movement. There are many different types of hedges. Some hedges are undertaken to reduce potential losses from adverse price movements. Other hedges are set up with the expectation of reaping profits. The easiest hedge of all to explain is discussed first; it is the perfect hedge from which no profits or losses can be earned. Figure 19-2 is a profit-loss graph that illustrates the position of an investor who is perfectly hedged.

Figure 19-2 is a profit-loss graph that combines the long position from Fig. 19-1a and the short position from Fig. 19-1b at the same purchase and sale price, respectively. The hedger is thus *perfectly hedged* so that the profits and the losses from these two positions sum up to zero at any value the market price may assume. Figure 19-2 might result, for instance, if an investor purchased a long position of 100 shares of the Alpha Corporation's common stock at $64 per share. Simultaneously, the investor sold 100 shares of Alpha's stock short at $64 per share. Figure 19-2 shows that if the market price of

FIGURE 19-2 The perfect hedge.

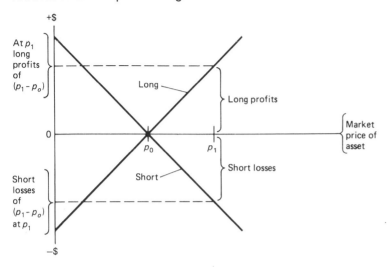

the hedged asset rises above the identical purchase price p_0 for the long position and sales price for the short position, to the higher price of, say, p_1
dollars, then the profit on the long position will be exactly offset by the loss
on the short position. The hedger, therefore, cannot earn either profits or
losses because the hedge is perfect.

The conditions essential for a hedge to be perfect are (1) equal dollar
amounts must be held in both the long and the short positions, and (2) the
purchase price for the long position must be identical to the sales price for
the short sale. Not all hedges are perfect.[2]

A hedge may be imperfect for either of two reasons. First, if the dollar commitments to the long and the short positions are not equal, the hedge will
be imperfect; or, second, a hedge will be imperfect if the short sales price is
not equal to the purchase price for the long position. This second imperfection often results from assuming the long and the short positions at different
points in time.

Figure 19-3 illustrates two *imperfect hedges*. Since the size of the dollar commitments to the long and the short positions cannot be illustrated in such
figures, let us assume that these dollar commitments are equal. Thus, the
two hedges are imperfect because their short sales price, denoted p_s, differs
from the purchase price for the long position, designated p_p in Fig. 19-3.

**19-2.1
Imperfect
Hedges**

---

2 Later it will be explained that the long and short positions do not have to be of equal dollar
magnitude to create a perfect hedge. For instance, an investment that involved only half as
many dollars in an offsetting short position that had twice the price volatility could result
in a perfect hedge too.

FIGURE 19-3 Imperfect hedges: (a) unprofitable hedge; (b) profitable hedge.

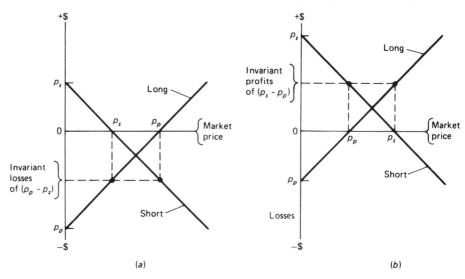

(a)   (b)

The hedge in Fig. 19-3a involves a purchase price for the long position, which is above the sales price for the short position, $p_p > p_s$. The resulting hedge will yield an *invariant loss* at whatever value the market price may assume. This loss will equal the excess of the purchase price over the short sale price, $(p_p - p_s)$.

The hedge in Fig. 19-3b is imperfect because its short sales price is above the purchase price for its long position. As a result, the hedge will yield an *invariant profit* equal to the excess of the short sale price over the purchase price. It is impossible for the imperfect hedge in Fig. 19-3b to do anything except yield a profit of $(p_s - p_p)$ regardless of what value the market price of the hedged asset assumes.[3]

19-2.2 Various Reasons for a Short Sale

As mentioned above, short sales are used to accomplish different objectives. First, they can be used by bearish speculators in search of profits from a price decline. Second, they can be used by risk-averse hedgers. For example, consider a hypothetical investor named Mr. Bell who owns a controlling interest in a corporation that he wishes to maintain. If Mr. Bell expects the price of his stock to fall because of inside information he has about the firm, he may hold his long position and sell short to establish a hedge that will minimize his anticipated loss.[4] If the price falls after Mr. Bell sets up a hedge, the losses on his long position are matched by gains on his short position. Thus, the investor has maintained control and hedged his loss. Since Mr. Bell always

---

3 For additional discussion of hedging see Frank J. Fabozzi and Gregory M. Kipnis, *Stock Index Futures* (Homewood Ill.: Down Jones-Irwin, 1984), chap.12.

4 In most Canadian jurisdictions the transaction described is illegal because "insiders" are not allowed to sell short. Thus, Mr. A. Bell of Bell Canada Enterprises, for instance, would be legally denied the privilege of selling Bell stock short against the box.

actually owned the shares (presumably they were in his safe-deposit box) that he sold short, he did what is commonly referred to as *selling short against the box*. Selling short against the box is not risky because the short seller is hedged against adverse price moves.

When selling short against the box, short sellers can borrow shares to use for delivery and then purchase shares to repay the loan, or they may simply deliver the shares they hold in their boxes. It is a common procedure to borrow shares. The borrower may give the lender cash to hold equal to the value of the shares borrowed. This protects the lender. The lender of the shares can use this cash at will while still benefitting from income from the shares. The lender of the shares may even be able to charge the borrower a fee for loaning the shares. Many brokers can arrange for such loans of shares in order to complete a short sale — the practice is common, and it may be unnecessary for the short seller to put up the cash collateral in some cases.

A fourth reason someone may be short in a security is to carry on arbitrage. *Arbitrage* involves simultaneously, or almost simultaneously, buying long and selling short the same, or different but related, assets in an effort to profit from unrealistic price differentials. Arbitrage may take place in the same or different markets. For an example of arbitrage between different markets consider Inco's common stock. If Inco stock is sold in Canada and also in the United States at different prices, arbitrage can be profitable. Profit seeking arbitrageurs facilitate enforcement of the economic *law of one price* by buying the stock in the market where its price is lowest and selling in the market where the stock's price is highest. Arbitrageurs will go on buying at the low price and selling at the high price until the price of Inco stock (adjusted for exchange-rate differences) is the same in all free markets around the world. The price of Inco stock may never be exactly identical in all markets because of transactions costs such as brokers' commissions, foreign exchange restrictions, long-distance telephone costs, mail costs, and other ''frictions'' that slow up arbitrage and erode arbitrage profits. However, with the exception of these transactions costs (of a few cents per share), Inco stock should cost the same no matter where in the world you buy it.

Some arbitrage is risky and some is riskless. In order to earn riskless trading profits, an arbitrageur simultaneously sells equal amounts of the security short in the market where its price is high and buys the security long in the market where the price is low. Figure 19-3*b* illustrates a profitable hedge of the type that arbitrageurs strive to establish. Arbitrageurs keep buying the security in the market where it is cheapest until they bid its price up to a higher level. Simultaneously, these same arbitrageurs keep selling everything they bought in the low-priced market in the market where the price is higher until they drive down the high price. As the short sale and the long purchase prices are thus driven together by the actions of profit-seeking arbitrageurs, the arbitrage pays off regardless of what other price fluctuations occur.

Short selling is also used by hedgers and arbitrageurs in foreign exchange markets and commodity exchanges, as explained in Chaps. 20, 21 and 22.

19-2.3 Arbitrageurs Are Hedged Short Sellers

It should be noted from the preceding examples that short sales are not always undertaken in order to attain a speculative profit. Short sales may be used like insurance to hedge away risks, or they may be used to maintain control, reallocate income tax burdens to later years, or arbitrage differential prices into equilibrium. Thus, risk-averse investors and risk-taking speculators both use short selling.

In addition to taking long, short, and hedged positions, market participants can buy and sell options. Options are financial instruments[5] which offer high leverage and limited liability to their buyers.

19-3 PUT AND CALL OPTIONS

Options are contracts giving their holder the right, but not the obligation, to buy or sell securities at a predetermined price. More specifically, options are marketable legal contracts that entitle their owner to buy or sell a stated number of shares (usually 100) of a particular security at a fixed price within a predetermined time period. There are two basic types of options. A *put* is an option to sell, that is, an option to "put" shares on someone else. It is a marketable contract giving the owner (or holder or buyer) the option to sell 100 shares of some security at any time he or she selects within a fixed period at a predetermined price. The predetermined price at which an option is to be exercised is variously called the *exercise price* or *contract price* or *striking price*.

A *call* is an option to buy, that is, an option to call in shares for purchase. It is a marketable contract giving its owner (or holder or buyer) the option of buying 100 shares of some security at a predetermined price within some specified time interval. The puts and calls traded on listed option exchanges are usually written for 30, 60, 90, 180, or 270 days.[6] *American options* may be exercised by their holder at any time before they mature. On the other hand, since they are marketable securities, instead of being exercised to obtain the gain, unexpired options can be sold in the secondary market in order to realize any gains in their market prices (or premiums). *European options* are identical to American options in every respect except one: the European options can be exercised only on the day when they expire. The term European options can be confusing, however, because many options traded in Europe are American options that can be exercised or bought or sold at any time during their life.

---

5 Although it may seem natural to call options and futures contracts "securities," this usage would offend some lawyers and regulatory bureaucrats who are embroiled in a jurisdictional dispute over which agency should exercise control over these different financial markets. The interests of certain parties are best served if the word *securities* is used only to refer to stocks and bonds.

6 Option contracts can be written to cover any length of time. The fact that no options with terms to maturity in excess of one year are written on the organized exchanges does not limit the ability of two parties to draw up an option contract of any duration they please. Only the standardized options originated there are actively traded on the exchanges, however.

Other kinds of options are a combination of puts and calls. However, these other options are discussed below, after the option markets are described.

Only a handful of firms make up the Canadian and U.S. over-the-counter option market. The exchanges where the standardized listed options are traded have taken most of the trading volume away from the older over-the-counter options market.

The over-the-counter put and call dealers publish lists suggesting premiums for options in the financial newspapers. This advertising is done to inform customers that they stand ready to do business. Interested option buyers and option writers contact the dealer, who acts as negotiator, helping a buyer and a writer who are interested in a given security to (1) settle on a mutually satisfactory premium, (2) settle on a contract price or exercise price at which the security may be put or called, and (3) determine what length of time they want the option contract to cover. To a certain extent these final arrangements depend upon the ''haggling power'' of the buyer and the writer of the options in the over-the-counter market for options. However, as a first approximation, the premium on 90-day calls averages around 9 percent of the cost of the 100 shares, while 6-month premiums average roughly 14 percent of the price of the round lot. These relative premiums vary considerably from stock to stock and from time to time depending on the degree of optimism or pessimism attached to any given security at that particular moment. However, in dollar terms, most premiums range from $137.50 to $1,000 per 100-share option. Today relatively few options are traded in the over-the-counter options market, compared to the exploding new markets for listed options.

19-3.1 Puts and Calls Markets— Over the Counter

In 1973 the Chicago Board of Options Exchange (CBOE) began operation. It was North America's first options exchange and organized secondary market for options. The CBOE began trading only call options on about two dozen stocks. Soon, trading volume flourished, and the CBOE expanded the number of options traded to over 200 by the early 1980s. To understand how the CBOE originated, it is helpful to know that it was originally established by the oldest and, contemporarily, the largest futures exchange in the United States—the Chicago Board of Trade. As a result, the CBOE clears its transactions through a clearing house that resembles the commodity futures contracts clearing house at the Chicago Board of Trade.

The today the organized market for listed equity options in the United States flourishes on the trading floors of the following five securities exchanges.

19-3.2 The Exchanges Where Listed Options Are Traded

1. The Chicago Board of Options Exchange (CBOE)

2. American Stock Exchange (AMEX)

3. Philadelphia Stock Exchange (PHLX)

4. Pacific Stock Exchange (PSE)

5. New York Stock Exchange (NYSE)

In 1975 the Ontario Securities Commission approved the trading of U.S. CBOE options in Ontario under the supervision of the Toronto Stock Exchange. In the same year, the Montreal Exchange introduced exchange-traded call-option contracts on a handful of Canadian companies. The contract specifications were similar to those on the CBOE. In 1976, the Toronto Stock Exchange also began options trading in Canadian companies and in 1977 the two exchanges merged their clearing corporations to form the Trans Canada Options Inc. (TCO). Put option contracts on Canadian companies were introduced on the TCO in 1979.

The Vancouver Stock Exchange, the third major exchange in Canada, joined the TCO in 1984. Each year, the three exchanges have a lottery to determine on which exchange new contracts are to be listed and traded. To be eligible for TCO stock option trading the shares of the underlying company must be listed on one of the three TCO member exchanges, must have in excess of 3,000 shareholders, have 3,600,000 or more shares outstanding, and a minimum market value of Cdn. $100,000,000.

As of the fall of 1986, stock option contracts (or as they are sometimes called, equity option contracts), are traded on sixty-nine different underlying companies in Canada.

Canadian exchange-traded equity-option contracts are standardized at 100 shares each of the underlying company. Contracts expire on the Saturday following the third Friday of an expiration month. Trading is conducted in expiry cycles as follows:

Cycle 1: January, April, July, October

Cycle 2: February, May, August, November

Cycle 3: March, June, September, December

Cycle 4: Next three consecutive months plus the two following months falling on cycle 3

For cycles 1, 2, and 3 the nearest three of the four contract months are traded at a time. In late January, for example, April, July, and October contracts are traded for cycle 1, February, May, and August are traded for cycle 2, and March, June, and September are traded for cycle 3. For cycle 4, five contract months are traded at a time.

The striking prices (the price at which the holder exercises the option) are set by the TCO at intervals of $1.00, $2.50, and $5.00 each, depending on the premium. Thus for any class of options there will usually be a number of different contracts, often as many as thirty, traded at one time, differentiated by striking price or expiry date.

Members of each respective exchange come together during the trading hours on the floor of the exchange and buy and sell options by open outcry. The phrase "open outcry" is used emphatically by exchange members to emphasize the fact that clandestine deals are not part of the price determination process in the options exchanges. Most of the trades that the members of the various option exchanges transact are done for the clients of securities brokerages — the members of the exchanges are essentially brokers for the brokerage firms.

The three security exchanges that make markets in listed options all clear their option transactions through the Trans Canada Options Inc. (TCO). The TCO has its headquarters in Montreal, but it is owned by the three security exchanges. The TCO is regulated by the securities commissions, as are all option markets in Canada.

The options traded at all three exchanges are issued by the TCO. The TCO does not write options. Instead, the TCO interposes itself between every option writer and every option buyer and acts as an *intermediary* and a clearing house for the options. In so doing, the TCO substitutes its ability to deliver in place of the option writer's ability to deliver.

Having the TCO as intermediary in every option transaction facilitates option trading by supplying the TCO's guarantee of financial integrity for every option contract it handles. This guarantee lowers transactions costs. For instance, transactions costs are lowered by eliminating the need for credit investigation that would be necessary if a reputable organization like the TCO did not stand behind every contract. Owners of options can choose to close out their positions at any time before the option expires by simply selling the option back to the TCO at the current market price for the option. The TCO then simply resells the position to another option buyer at that same current market price. Having the TCO as the centralized intermediary and clearing agent is fundamental to the maintenance of a smoothly functioning secondary market where options can be traded actively at any time before they expire.

The three organized options markets keep track of all of their trades in the memories of computers that are operated by the Trans Canada Options Inc. (TCO) and brokerage firms that are clearing members of the TCO. All buyers and sellers who may have owned the option at any time prior to its being closed out are successively crossed out of the computer's memory as they buy out the previous owner of the option. In addition to its clearing functions, the OCC also performs a guarantee function.

The TCO stands behind and guarantees every option it issues on the three options exchanges. Thus, if some option seller defaults on a contractual option obligation, the TCO steps in and delivers on the contract at its own expense. As a result of the TCO's guarantee, the options issued at the three organized options exchanges are perfectly marketable securities and the buyer need not check the credit of the party who wrote an option before buying it.

In order for speculators to buy an option, they need only examine the security prices and/or option prices published daily in most newspapers, and then call a few stockbrokers until an accommodating one is found. Figure 19-4 shows the prices of call options on Agnico Eagle, which is traded on the TSE. Options on securities not traded on the TSE may be bought or sold through one of the other organized options markets or through one of the over-the-counter options dealers[7].

---

7 The number of options and markets have proliferated in the 1980s. Many of the new contracts have thus far been remarkably unsuccessful in Canada. The open interest and trading volume, the two measures of trading activity, are extremely light for many of the exchange-

FIGURE 19-4 Explanation of representative newspaper quote of option prices.

SERIES	BID	ASK	LAST	VOL	OP INT
AGNICO EAGLE	C C31½				
A Feb $27½	D 560	E 585	F 560	G 10	H 19
$30	325	350	325	5	66
May $27½ P	130	140	130	20	20
B Nov $32½ P	205	230	225	1	5

A This shows a call option on 100 shares of Agnico Eagle.
   This option contract has an exercise price of $27.50 a share.
B This shows a put option on 100 shares of Agnico Eagle.
   This option contract has an exercise price of $32.50 a share.
C The closing price of Agnico Eagle common stock (called the underlying stock) on the Toronto Stock Exchange.
D Closing bid price of $5.60
E Closing ask price of $5.85
F Last trade price of $5.60
G Number of February 27½ call option contracts traded that day.
H Number of February 27½ call option contracts in existence that day.
   This is called the open interest.

**19-3.3
Profit-Loss
Graph for
a Call
Option**

The investor who thinks a security's price is likely to move upward (that is, a bull) may want to buy a call. If the security's price falls, only the premium (which is typically only about 15 percent of the value of the shares) is lost. However, if the security's price rises, the buyer of a call can (consider the premium paid, the commissions involved, and the probability of a timely execution of the trade by the floor broker, and then) decide whether to exercise the call and reap the capital gains from the price rise, less the transactions costs. Since the call buyer had only the amount of the writer's premium invested, he or she can earn a very large rate of return on the investment even if the price of the stock rises only moderately higher than the transactions costs to execute the transaction.

The market position of options buyers and writers can be depicted graphically. Figure 19-5 shows a profit-loss graph for the buyer and the writer of a call. Profit or loss is graphed on the vertical axis, and the market price of the optioned security is on the horizontal axis. The graph of the call option buyer's position shows a loss equal to the premium up to the point where the market price rises above the exercise price (also called the striking price or the contract price). Where the market price exceeds the exercise price by enough to cover the premium, the option buyer's profit is zero if he or she exercises the option; this is point Z in the graphs. The buyer might actually exercise the option at this zero-profit point in order to recoup the premium in the belief that the market price would not rise any more. If the market

---

traded equity options, particularly by comparison to CBOE trading. The Canadian precious metal, index, and bond options, discussed in the Appendix, are traded in very thin markets.

FIGURE 19-5 Profit graphs for a call option: (a) call buyer, (b) call writer.

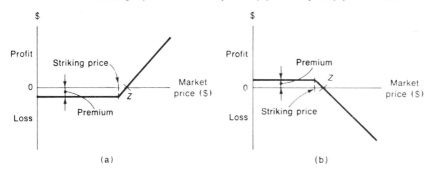

price rises above Z, the buyer reaps a profit (after the cost of the premium) by exercising the call.

19-3.4 Profit-Loss Graph for the Put Option

The profit positions of the writer and the buyer of a put option are shown in Fig. 19-6. The buyer of the put hopes the optioned security's price will fall, just as a short seller would. But unlike the short seller, the buyer has limited losses (that is, only the premium) if the security turns capricious and experiences a price rise. If the security's price falls, the put owner's profit cannot exceed the exercise price times 100 shares less the premium paid. Thus, the writer of the put has limited losses if the price falls. The put writer cannot lose more than 100 times the exercise price less the premium received. If the price of the security rises, the writer gains the premium and no more. Options writers' gains are always limited to their premiums.

FIGURE 19-6 Profit graphs for a put option: (a) put buyer; (b) put writer.

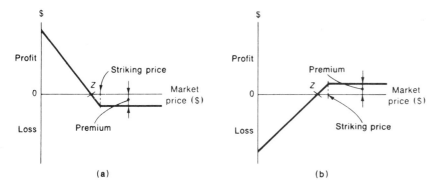

Any investor who wants to speculate that the price of some security will fall may choose between buying a put or selling short. The purchase of a put is usually more desirable than taking a short position for two main reasons. First, the investment in a put is limited to the premium, whereas a short seller usually must invest a larger sum. This means that the put option offers more *financial leverage* than the short position. Second, the holder of a put loses no more than the premium if the price of the optioned security rises, but a short seller's losses are unlimited if the security's price rises. A third reason that buying a put may be more desirable than selling short derives from the way cash dividends are handled. Short sellers must make up for any cash dividends the securities they borrowed may pay. That is, the short seller must pay from personal funds an amount of cash equal to any cash dividends that are declared on the borrowed stock to the party who lent the securities that were sold short.

Although the put option is a useful security, it is not always the preferred choice over a short sale. One of the big disadvantages of buying options is that they expire and become worthless. Therefore, if the speculator is not confident that the price of the security about which he or she is bearish will decline before the put expires, then a short position may be more advisable. Paying a series of put premiums while waiting for the price of the optioned security to decline is certainly not an optimal strategy. Each case must be judged on its own merits in the final analysis.

Put and call options can be used for four different types of financial activities: (1) gambles on immediate price changes, (2) speculations on short-run price changes, (3) long-run investments involving either long-term options or continuous reinvestment in a series of short-term options,[8] and (4) forming more complex options. The more complex options that can be formed from puts and calls are called *combinations* of options; they will be explained later in this chapter. Before examining these combinations however, let us consider what determines the prices (or premiums) for which put and call options sell.

19-4   THE DETERMINANTS OF PUT AND CALL PREMIUMS

Options need not be exercised to realize the profits from an advantageous price move in the underlying asset. Advantageous price moves in the underlying asset make the option itself worth more. Therefore, the option may be sold in the secondary options market before it matures in order to realize the profits. The price for which an option sells is called the *premium* for the option. In order to understand how to profit from selling unexpired options, let us consider the determinants of option premiums.

The option buyer pays the premium to some option writer to induce the writer to grant the option. The main factors that determine the price the option buyer must pay for an option are discussed below.

1. The *price of the optioned security*. It takes a larger premium to induce the option writer to assume the risks associated with 100 shares of high-priced stock because the possible losses are larger than for 100 shares of low-priced stock. For example, if market prices drop 10 percent, then the decrease in value of 100 shares of a $20 stock is only ($20 × 100 − $18 × 100 =) $200, whereas the 10 percent decrease

---

8 See Richard M. Bookstaber, *Option Pricing and Strategies in Investing* (Reading, Mass.: Addison-Wesley, 1981), chap. 10, for a discussion of how a portfolio manager can use options to reshape the probability distribution of returns from the portfolio.

in value of 100 shares of a $150 stock is ($150 × 100 − $135 × 100 =) $1500. The writers of both puts and calls must charge larger premiums to write options on high-priced securities because their potential losses are larger.

2. The *length of time the option remains open*. Writers of 6-month options charge about 40 percent higher premiums than they would to write the same three-month options on the security. The charge is higher simply because the probability that the option will be exercised and that the writer will lose money increases with the time the option remains open.

3. The *probability of a big price change in the optioned security*. A sizable change can make it profitable for the option owner to exercise the option. Several factors determine a security's potential for price volatility. The most important influences of volatility are:
   a. The historical price volatility of the security (for example, mining stocks have always been more volatile than public utility stocks).
   b. The trend of the market (that is, bullish or bearish).
   c. Recent news that may affect the security's price.
   Essentially, options on riskier securities enjoy higher premiums.

4. The *exercise price*. The exercise price (or striking price) of an option brackets the market price of the security on the day the option begins trading. Sometimes, however, the exercise price of a put or call is "points away" from the market price (that is, the exercise price is above or below the market price by several dollars). For example, if the exercise price of a call is several dollars above the optioned security's price, the probability that the call will be exercised is decreased. As a result, the call writer will be willing to accept a smaller premium.

Cash dividend payments and market interest rates also have some effect on the premium for which an option sells. These two factors are discussed later in this chapter.

19-4.1 The Call Option's Premium

Figure 19-7 illustrates the interaction between the various factors that determine the market price (or premium) for which a call option may be purchased. The dashed curves represent the prices for calls with different characteristics.

In the space below the (horizontal) stock price axis in Fig. 19-7, some phrases that are popular with security brokerage personnel are illustrated. They refer to the value of the call that is under discussion; they are defined as follows:

1. A call that is "out of the money" is worthless when it matures because the market price of the optioned security is less than the exercise price. That is,

   Exercise price$_{it}$ > market price of the optioned security$_{it}$

   for the ith optioned security at the tth instant in time. A call that is out of the money will probably still have a positive premium before its maturity date, however, because optimists expect that the price of the optioned security may rise before the option matures.

2. "At the market" a call option has a market price for the optioned security that is approximately equal to the call's exercise price; that is,

   Exercise price$_{it}$ = market price of the optioned security$_{it}$

FIGURE 19-7 The determinants of call prices (or premiums).

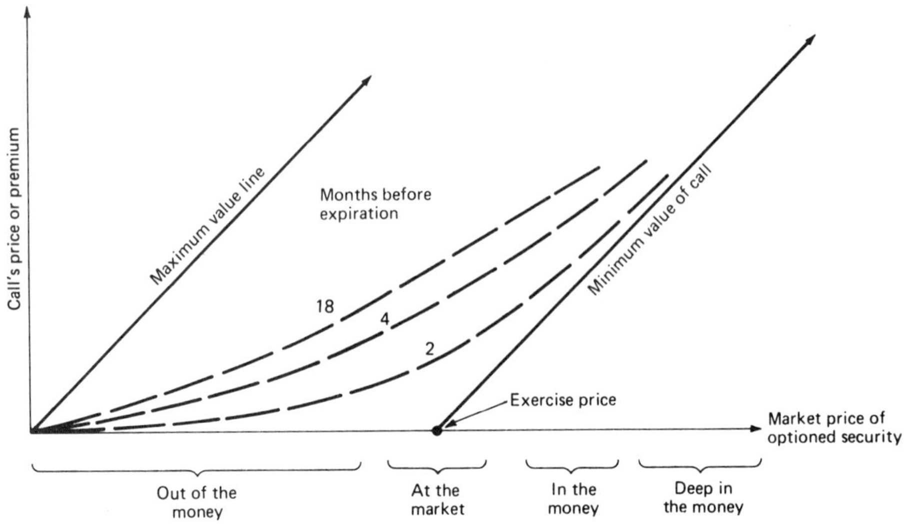

3. A call that is "in the money" has a market price for its optioned securities that has risen above the call's exercise price. A call that is "deep in the money" is highly valued because the market price of its optioned security is far above the call's exercise price; symbolically,

Exercise price$_{it}$ < market price of the optioned security$_{it}$

**19-4.2
A Call
Option's
Premium
Over
Intrinsic
Value**

The vertical distance between the minimum value line and the price curve for an option's premium is called the *premium over the intrinsic value*. Equation (19-1) defines the premium over intrinsic value for a call option.

$$\text{Premium over intrinsic value} = \text{call option's premium} + \text{exercise price} - \text{price of optioned stock} \qquad (19\text{-}1)$$

Observance of Fig. 19-7 shows that the premium over intrinsic value of a call option is greatest when the market price of the optioned asset equals the exercise price of the option. More specifically, the premium over intrinsic value of a call option (1) increases with the time-to-maturity value portion of a call's premium—that is, it increases with the length of time remaining until the call expires, (2) increases with the riskiness of the optioned security, (3) increases very slightly with the level of market interest rates, and (4) decreases with the payment of cash dividends by the optioned stock (because the price of the stock drops off by the amount of the cash dividend payout). The effects of the last three determinants cannot be illustrated in a graph like Fig. 19-7.

The CBOE has compiled an Options Index that measures the average premium paid for six-month options. The values of this CBOE Options Index stated as a percentage of the optioned security's market price—called relative option premiums and defined in Eq. (19-2)—are graphed in Fig. 19-8.

**19-4.3
Relative
Option
Premiums**

$$\text{Relative premium} = \frac{\text{dollar cost or premium for option}}{\text{market price of optioned security}} \qquad (19\text{-}2)$$

The index is an average relative price for options that have six months to maturity and have an exercise price equal to the market price of the optioned security. Note that the relative call premiums vary from about 8 to 14 percent. These variations reflect the market's consensus estimate of uncertainty. In uncertain times, the average call writer will require a higher relative call premium to be induced to grant the call option.

FIGURE 19-8 Relative option premiums for CBOE composite call and put indexes, 1979–1984.

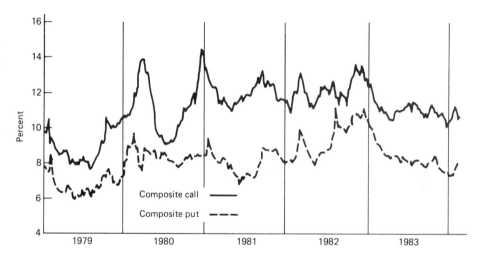

The call option is an interesting investment for a price speculator who is bullish. A bearish price speculator might wish to sell (or write) a call option but would not want to buy a call. On the other hand, the bear might buy a *put option* in order to profit from a security price decline. A put option offers profit possibilities which are similar in some respects to those derived from the short position, but the put option offers some additional benefits.[9]

9 For a discussion of option indexes see Walter L. Eckardt, Jr., and Stephen L. Williams, "The Complete Options Indexes," *Financial Analysts Journal*, July-August 1984, pp. 48–57, and Gary L. Gastineau and Albert Mandansky, "Some Comments on the CBOE Call Options Index," *Financial Analysts Journal*, July-August 1984, pp. 58–67.

**19-4.4
The Premium
for the
Put Option**

The market price (or synonymously, the premium) of a put option is determined by the four factors which were discussed a few paragraphs above in reference to the prices of call options. However, these four factors have completely different effects on put prices than they do on call prices. Figure 19-9 illustrates how put prices are determined by (1) the price of the optioned security, (2) the length of time the option remains open, and (3) the option's exercise price. Put premiums are also affected by (4) the riskiness (or volatility) of the optioned security's price, (5) the level of market interest rates, and (6) the payment of cash dividends, but these last three factors cannot be illustrated in a graph like Fig. 19-9.

FIGURE 19-9   The determinants of put prices (or premiums).

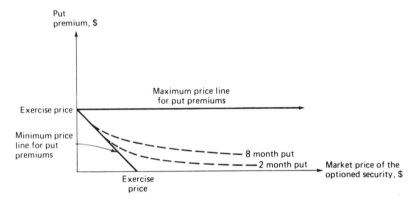

The *premium over instrinsic value* of a put option is calculated in Eq. (19-3).

$$\begin{matrix} \text{Premium over} \\ \text{intrinsic} \\ \text{value} \end{matrix} = \begin{matrix} \text{put's} \\ \text{premium} \end{matrix} + \begin{matrix} \text{price of} \\ \text{optioned} \\ \text{security} \end{matrix} - \begin{matrix} \text{exercise} \\ \text{price of} \\ \text{put} \end{matrix} \qquad (19\text{-}3)$$

A put's premium over its intrinsic value (1) increases directly with the riskiness or price volatility of the optioned asset, (2) increases with the length of time remaining until the put option expires, (3) increases with the exercise price, and (4) moves inversely with the level of market interest rates. The premium over intrinsic value is largest when the market price of the optioned asset is equal to the option's exercise price.

Put premiums fluctuate with call premiums as illustrated in Fig. 19-8. The relative put premiums for six-month puts range from 6 to 11 percent. These relative put and call premiums tend to fluctuate together because calls may be converted into puts, and thus there is a parity between the two premiums.[10]

---

10 There is a parity between put and call premiums that is maintained by an arbitrage process. This reasoning is explained by Hans R. Stoll, '' The Relationship between Put and Call Option Prices,'' *Journal of Finance*, December 1969, pp. 801–824. See also Robert A. Jarrow

The next section explains mathematical formulas with which to calculate option premiums.

19-5 THE BLACK-SCHOLES OPTION MODEL

Fischer Black and Myron Scholes have derived mathematical formulas for the values of put and call options.[11] These formulas are viewed as a formal theory called the Black-Scholes option valuation model; this theory is widely accepted. The mathematics used in deriving the Black-Scholes option valuation formulas are beyond the scope of this book. However, the final formulas are explained below.

The Black-Scholes call option pricing formula is shown as Eq. (19-4) in Box 19-1 (shown at the top of page 526). The call prices suggested by the Black-Scholes model are represented by the dashed curves in Fig. 19-7.

19-5.1 The Black-Scholes Call Valuation Formula

All that is needed to use the Black-Scholes model are (1) a table of natural logarithms and (2) a table of cumulative normal distribution probabilities. The values for $N(x)$ and $N(y)$ are shown in Table 19-2 (shown on page 527). Most algebra and statistics books contain tables of logarithms.

19-5.2 Numerical Example

To show an illustrative numerical example of how to apply the Black-Scholes model, the following data are used: $p_s = \$60$, $p_e = \$50$, $d = .333$ (which represents 120 days out of a 360-day year), $R = .07$ (which represents 7 percent per annum), and $var(r_i) = .144$. The quantity x is evaluated below using Eq. (19-5).

$$x_i = \frac{\ln(60/50) + [.07 + .5(.144)](.333)}{\sqrt{.144}\sqrt{.333}}$$

$$= \frac{.182 + .142(.333)}{.379(.577)} = \frac{.2296}{.2191} = 1.048$$

---

and Andrew Rudd, *Option Pricing* (Homewood, Ill.: Irwin, 1983), chaps. 4, 5, and 6. Or see E.J. Elton and M.J. Gruber, *Modern Portfolio Theory and Investment Analysis*, 2d ed. (New York: Wiley, 1984) pp. 534–537. The formula for this parity is:

$$\begin{bmatrix} \text{Price of} \\ \text{optioned} \\ \text{security} \end{bmatrix} + \begin{bmatrix} \text{premium} \\ \text{or price} \\ \text{on put} \end{bmatrix} - \begin{bmatrix} \text{exercise} \\ \text{or striking} \\ \text{price} \end{bmatrix}(1+r)^d - \begin{bmatrix} \text{premium} \\ \text{on} \\ \text{call} \end{bmatrix}$$

[11] F. Black and M. Scholes, "The Pricing of Options and Corporate Liabilities," *Journal of Political Economy*, May-June 1973, pp. 637–654. The Black-Scholes model was derived by assuming that the optioned security's prices are lognormally distributed so that the continuously compounded one-period rates of return $r_{it} = \ln(p_{it}|p_{i,t-1})$ are normally distributed with a constant known variance. J.C. Francis and S.H. Archer, *Portfolio Analysis*, 2d ed. (Prentice-Hall Foundations of Finance Series, 1979), chap. 14, for a discussion of continuously compounded rates of return and the log-normal distribution of prices.

BOX 19-1
The Black-Scholes Call Formula

$$c_i = p_{si}N(x_i) - p_{ei}[e^{(-Rd_i)}]N(y_i) \tag{19-4}$$

where x and y are defined below.

$$x_i = \frac{\ln(p_{si}/p_{ei}) + [R + .5\,\text{var}(r_i)]d_i}{[\text{var}(r_i)]^{1/2}d_i^{1/2}} \tag{19-5}$$

$$y_i = x_i - [\text{var}(r_i)]^{1/2}d_i^{1/2} \tag{19-6}$$

where

c = the call's price or premium

p_s = market price of the optioned stock

p_e = exercise or striking price

$\ln$ = natural (base e) logarithm

e = the exponential number = 2.7183 = antiln

$\text{var}(r_i)$ = variance of the rates of price change for the ith optioned stock, a risk measure

R = riskless rate of interest

d_i = duration or time until expiration of the ith call, stated as a fraction of 1 year (for example, 1 month means $d = 1/12$)

$N(x)$ = cumulative normal-density function of the argument x; $N(x)$ gives the probability that a value of less than x will occur in a normal probability distribution which has a mean of zero and a standard deviation equal to unity: $N(-\infty) = 0$, $N(0) = .5$, and $N(+\infty) = 1.0$, for instance

The formula was derived from the heat exchange equation from physics and requires the following assumptions for its implementation.

1. No dividends on the underlying asset (modifications have been developed to allow for dividends on the underlying asset; see 19-5.5)

2. No transaction costs

3. The continuously compounded one-period rate of return on the underlying asset is lognormally distributed

4. The risk-free rate is constant

5. Securities markets are efficient

6. There are no restrictions on short selling

7. The option contract is European; i.e., exerciseable at maturity only. (If there is no dividend payable on the underlying asset, American options should never be exercised early and thus can be treated as European options.)

TABLE 19-2   VALUES OF N(x) FOR GIVEN VALUES OF x FOR A CUMULATIVE NORMAL DISTRIBUTION WITH ZERO MEAN AND UNIT VARIANCE

x	$N(x)$	x	$N(x)$	x	$N(x)$	x	$N(x)$	x	$N(x)$	x	$N(x)$
		−2.00	.0228	−1.00	.1587	.00	.5000	1.00	.8413	2.00	.9773
−2.95	.0016	−1.95	.0256	−.95	.1711	.05	.5199	1.05	.8531	2.05	.9798
−2.90	.0019	−1.90	.0287	−.90	.1841	.10	.5398	1.10	.8643	2.10	.9821
−2.85	.0022	−1.85	.0322	−.85	.1977	.15	.5596	1.15	.8749	2.15	.9842
−2.80	.0026	−1.80	.0359	−.80	.2119	.20	.5793	1.20	.8849	2.20	.9861
−2.75	.0030	−1.75	.0401	−.75	.2266	.25	.5987	1.25	.8944	2.25	.9878
−2.70	.0035	−1.70	.0446	−.70	.2420	.30	.6179	1.30	.9032	2.30	.9893
−2.65	.0040	−1.65	.0495	−.65	.2578	.35	.6368	1.35	.9115	2.35	.9906
−2.60	.0047	−1.60	.0548	−.60	.2743	.40	.6554	1.40	.9192	2.40	.9918
−2.55	.0054	−1.55	.0606	−.55	.2912	.45	.6736	1.45	.9265	2.45	.9929
−2.50	.0062	−1.50	.0668	−.50	.3085	.50	.6915	1.50	.9332	2.50	.9938
−2.45	.0071	−1.45	.0735	−.45	.3264	.55	.7088	1.55	.9394	2.55	.9946
−2.40	.0082	−1.40	.0808	−.40	.3446	.60	.7257	1.60	.9452	2.60	.9953
−2.35	.0094	−1.35	.0885	−.35	.3632	.65	.7422	1.65	.9505	2.65	.9960
−2.30	.0107	−1.30	.0968	−.30	.3821	.70	.7580	1.70	.9554	2.70	.9965
−2.25	.0122	−1.25	.1057	−.25	.4013	.75	.7734	1.75	.9599	2.75	.9970
−2.20	.0139	−1.20	.1151	−.20	.4207	.80	.7881	1.80	.9641	2.80	.9974
−2.15	.0158	−1.15	.1251	−.15	.4404	.85	.8023	1.85	.9678	2.85	.9978
−2.10	.0179	−1.10	.1357	−.10	.4602	.90	.8159	1.90	.9713	2.90	.9981
−2.05	.0202	−1.05	.1469	−.05	.4801	.95	.8289	1.95	.9744	2.95	.9984

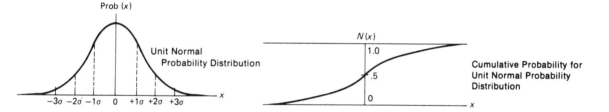

The quantity y_i is evaluated using Eq. (19-5).

$$y_i = x_i - (\sqrt{.144}\,\sqrt{.333}) = 1.048 - .2191 = .829$$

Substituting the values from above in Eq. (19-4) yields the figures below:

$$c_i = \$60[N(1.048)] - \$50\{antiln[-.070(.333)]\}\,[N(.829)]$$

Looking up the values of the antilog for natural logs and the cumulative normal distribution in tables and completing the calculations yields the results below:

$$c_i = \$60(.851) - \$50(.9769)(.800) = \$51.060 - 39.076 = \$11.98$$

The calculations indicate that the ith call option's intrinsic value is $11.98. As a result of slight differences in the way various people interpolate between the values in Table 19-2, slightly different answers are possible. Another place where different estimates can arise when using the Black-Scholes model is in the risk statistic, var(r_i). Because the risk statistic must be estimated different analysts are likely to develop differing estimates of it.[12]

**19-5.3
The Hedge
Ratio**

The *hedge ratio* of an option may be defined as the dollar change in the option's premium (or price) that is associated with a one-dollar change in the price of the optioned asset. Graphically speaking, the hedge ratio is the slope of the dashed call price curve in Fig. 19-7.

From the standpoint of the risk-averse investor, the optimal hedge ratio is the ratio of shares of optioned stock per 100-share option that must be held to fully hedge against movements in the stock's price. Mathematically, this optimal hedge ratio is given by the value of the quantity $N(x)$ in the Black-Scholes call Eq. (19-4), as shown below.

$$N(x) = \Delta c / \Delta p = \text{slope of call price curve} = \text{hedge ratio} \qquad (19\text{-}7)$$

If an investor uses the hedge ratio so that $(-1)N(x)$ times as much stock is held in a position opposite to the option position, then any movement in the value of the stock position will be exactly offset by an opposite and equal movement in the value of the option position. For instance, if a call option for 100 shares of ABC stock is owned in a long position and the hedge ratio based on the current price of ABC is $N(.808) = -.790$, the 79 shares of ABC should be sold short in order to establish a perfect hedge.[13]

Unfortunately, the hedges formed using the hedge ratio are perfect only as long as the price of the optioned stock does not change. As soon as the stock's price changes, then the value of $N(x)$ changes, and the hedge has to be recomputed. After the new hedge ratio is computed, the securities position has to be correspondingly rebalanced.[14]

---

12 Computer programs are available to calculate the prices of puts and calls using the Black-Scholes model. One such program is the TK!Solver program produced by Software Arts Inc. Software Arts is a computer software manufacturer that is probably best known for its spreadsheet program named Visi-Calc. The TK!Solver program is a sophisticated equation processor that is totally different from the Visi-Calc program. TK!Solver will solve virtually any equation for the value of any variable in the equation if the values of all other variables are known. Hand calculators are also available to solve the Black-Scholes formula.

13 The hedge ratio is discussed in Richard M. Bookstaber, *Option Pricing and Strategies in Investing*, (Reading, Mass.: Addison-Wesley, 1981), chap. 8.

14 Mr. Gary L. Gastineau, vice president, Webster Management, a subsidiary of Kidder, Peabody and Co., 20 Exchange Place, New York, has developed a competing option valuation model. Gastineau's model is explained in an article he authored, "An Index of Listed Option Premiums," *Financial Analysts Journal*, May-June 1977, pp. 3–8, see especially the appendix. Or see G.L. Gastineau, *The Stock Options Manual*, 2d ed. (New York: McGraw-Hill, 1979), chap. 7, pp. 254–264. Other option valuation models that have been derived include the following: J. Cox and S. Ross. "The Valuation of Option for Alternative Stochastic Processes," *Journal of Financial Economics*, March 1976, vol. 3, pp. 145–166. Also see J. Cox, S. Ross, and M. Rubinstein, "Option Pricing: A Simplified Approach," *Journal of Financial Economics*, October 1979, vol. 7, pp. 229–264. See also R. Roll, "An Analytic Method for Valuing American Call Options on Dividend Paying Stocks," *Journal of Financial Economics*, November 1977, vol. 85, pp. 251–258. See also M. Rubinstein, "Displaced Diffusion Option Pricing," *Journal of Finance*, March 1983, vol. 38, pp. 213–218. These and other approaches to valuing

Since the Black-Scholes model's derivation presumes a normal distribution of continuously compounded rates of one-period return, the variance of continuously compounded rates of return should be used as a risk measure.[15] Equation (19-8) shows the definition for the one-period continuously compounded rate of return.

19-5.4 Estimating Risk for the Optioned Stocks

$$r_t = \ln_e \frac{p_{st}}{p_{s,t-1}}$$ \hfill (19-8)

The noncompounded one-period rate of return of Eq. (2-2) furnishes an acceptable approximation to Eq. (19-8), especially for small rates of return— that is, for short periods. Regardless of how the rates of return are calculated, the variance of returns is defined in Eqs. (C-3a) and (C-3b) of Mathematical App. C.

TABLE 19-3 SOME HISTORICAL ANNUALIZED VARIANCE STATISTICS

OPTIONED STOCK	ANNUAL VARIANCES
McDonald's	0.50
Northwest Airlines	0.35
Delta Airlines	0.25
International Harvester	0.15
Sears, Roebuck & Co.	0.10

Table 19-3 presents some annualized variances for optioned New York Stock Exchange common stocks that are traded on the Chicago Board of Options Exchange to be used as a guideline. However, these risk statistics may change with the passage of time, and thus they need to be rechecked every time they are used.[16] One common way to obtain current risk statistics is to (1) estimate the variance using recent empirical returns and then (2) subjectively adjust the empirically estimated variance to reflect expected changes in the optioned security's risk that are not reflected in the historical statistics.[17]

---

puts and calls are analyzed by R. Geske and K. Shastri, "Valuation by Approximation: A Comparison of Alternative Option Valuation Techniques," *Journal of Financial and Quantitative Analysis*, March 1985, vol. 20, no. 1, pp. 45–72.

[15] Although systematic (or beta or covariance) risk is relevant in analyzing individual assets with the Security Market Line (SML) or Capital Asset Pricing Model (CAPM), only *total* risk is relevant in the Black-Scholes model.

[16] J.C. Francis, "Statistical Analysis of Risk Surrogates for NYSE Stocks," *Journal of Financial and Quantitative Analysis*, December 1979. H. Latane and R.J. Rendelman, Jr., "Standard Deviation of Stock Price Ratios Implied in Option Prices," *Journal of Finance*, May 1976, pp. 369-381. M. Brenner and D. Galai, "On Measuring the Risk of Common Stocks Implied by Option Prices: A Note," *Journal of Financial and Quantitative Analysis*, December 1984, vol. 19, no. 4, pp. 403–404.

[17] For a discussion about estimating risk statistics, see Michael Parkinson, "The Extreme Value Method for Estimating the Variance of the Rate of Return," *Journal of Business*, January 1980, vol. 53, no. 1, pp. 61–67, and (in the same issue) Mark B. Garman and Michael J. Klass, "On the Estimation of Security Price Volatilities from Historical Data," pp. 67–78.

After the value of a call option has been estimated, this value may need to be adjusted to reflect the effects of cash dividends. The next section shows how to adjust for a cash dividend.[18]

**19-5.5
The Effects
of Cash
Dividends**

When the board of directors of a corporation declares that all stockholders on a certain date are to receive a cash dividend, that date is called the *date of record* in legal discussions. Anyone who buys the stock after the date of record is not entitled to the cash dividend; the stock is then said to be selling *ex-dividend*. When a stock opens trading on its first day of trading ex-dividend, its market price drops by an amount almost exactly equal to the cash dividend per share that was paid to shareholders on the date of record. This ex-dividend price *drop-off* decreases the value of any call options against the stock and should therefore be considered in determining when to exercise an American call. Since European calls can be exercised only on their maturity dates, the decision to exercise these options before they trade ex-dividend is not relevant.

Figure 19-7 illustrates the minimum call boundary and the Black-Scholes value curve for some hypothetical American call option. The minimum-value line (or stock price parity line) establishes the minimum value of the call if it is exercised at any time. Upon its exercise, the call is said by option traders to be "dead". The curve gives the option's value if it is still "alive" (that is, if it has not been exercised prior to maturity). An American call is always worth at least as much alive as dead if it has any time remaining before it expires. The vertical distance between the minimum value (or dead or parity) line and the live value curve measures the value of the time remaining until the option expires. The graph is useful in illustrating some key considerations involved in deciding whether to exercise a call before the stock goes ex-dividend.

FIGURE 19-10   Security values before and after ex-dividend trading.

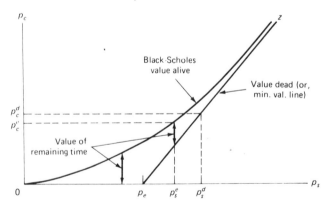

18 Computer programs for the Black-Scholes model and various option pricing statistics are available for microcomputers from Dr. Richard Bookstaber, Morgan Stanley Co., New York. These programs may be purchased at a fraction of the price of some commercially available programs.

If a call on an optioned security with a market price of p_s^d is exercised, this call's value of p_c^d is given by reference to the minimum value boundary Op_eZ in Fig. 19-10. If the optioned stock goes ex-dividend, its price will drop off from p_s^d to p_s^e. However, the option's premium will not fall as much as the price of the optioned stock if the option is alive. At an ex-dividend market price for the optioned stock of p_s^e, the value of the live call is p_c^e. The Black-Scholes formula can be used to find the value of live calls. If the option's drop-off of $(p_c^d - p_c^e)$ dollars when exercised ex-dividend is less than the amount of the cash dividend, then the call should be kept alive to maximize the investor's wealth. The call should be exercised before it goes ex-dividend if inequality (19-9) is true.[19]

$$\text{Cash dividend per share}_{it} < (p_c^d - p_c^e)_{it} \qquad (19\text{-}9)$$

Black and Scholes derived a formula for pricing European puts—that is, puts that may only be exercised on their expiration date. However, no one has been able to analytically derive a formula for valuing American puts (that may be exercised on any day of their life) that is as accurate as the numerical approximation techniques available to value American puts.[20] Therefore, some people use the put-call parity formula in Eq. (19-10a) to derive the value of a put option after the value of a call option on the same security has been determined.[21]

19-5.6 Valuing the Put Option

$$\begin{array}{ccccc}
\text{Premium} & \text{premium} & & & \text{price of} \\
\text{or price} & = & \text{or price} & + & \left[\left(\begin{array}{c}\text{exercise} \\ \text{or striking} \\ \text{price}\end{array}\right)/(1+r)^d\right] & - & \text{optioned} \\
\text{on put} & & \text{of call} & & & \text{security}
\end{array} \qquad (21\text{-}10a)$$

r = a short-term market interest rate (such as the 90-day Treasury bill rate) which is used to find the present value of the exercise price

d = the time until the option expires

---

19 Rational call premium adjustments to reflect the payment of cash dividends and other factors are analyzed by Robert C. Merton, ''The Theory of Rational Option Pricing,'' *Bell Journal of Economics and Management Science*, Spring 1973, pp. 141–183. Also see R.E. Whaley, ''Valuation of American Call Options on Dividend Paying Stocks: Empirical Tests,'' *Journal of Financial Economics*, March 1982. Also see C.A. Ball and W.N. Torous, ''On Jumps in Common Stock Prices and Their Impact on Call Pricing,'' *Journal of Finance*, March 1985, vol. 40, no. 1, pp. 155–174.

20 M. Parkinson, ''Option Pricing: The American Put,'' *Journal of Business*, January 1977, pp. 21–36. See also M. Brennan and E. Schwartz, ''The Valuation of American Put Options,'' *Journal of Finance*, May 1977, pp. 449–462. See also J. Cox, S. Ross, and M. Rubinstein, ''Option Pricing: A Simplified Approach,'' *Journal of Financial Economics*, September 1979, pp. 229–263.

21 There is a parity between put and call premiums that is maintained by an arbitrage process. This reasoning is explained by Hans R. Stoll, ''The Relationship between Put and Call Option Prices,'' *Journal of Finance*, December 1969, pp. 801–824. See also Robert A. Jarrow and Andrew Rudd, *Option Pricing* (Homewood, Ill.: Richard D. Irwin, 1983), chaps. 4, 5, and 6. Or see E.J. Elton and M.J. Gruber, *Modern Portfolio Theory and Investment Analysis*, 2d ed. (New York: Wiley, 1984), pp. 534–537.

The Put-call parity formula can be developed as follows. Consider an investor who holds one share of stock at a price of p_{so}. The investor can establish a riskless portfolio by buying a put option and selling a call option on this same stock. The striking prices on the options must be identical, but not necessarily equal to the price of the share.

p_{so} = Price of common share at time 0

p_{sm} = Price of common share at maturity

Put_o = Price of put option at time zero

p_m = Price of put option at maturity

x_o = Price of call option at time zero

x_m = Price of call option at maturity

p_e = Exercise price on put option; call option

R = Risk-free rate

d = Time until the option expires, stated as a fraction of one year

The investor's cash outflow at time zero on this riskless portfolio is

$$p_{so} + Put_o - x_o$$

The investor's cash inflow at maturity can be calculated as

STOCK PRICE	CALL OPTION	PUT OPTION	STOCK	PORTFOLIO
	value	value	price	value
rises	$-[p_{sm} - p_e]$	0	p_{sm}	p_e
falls	0	$[p_e - p_{sm}]$	p_{sm}	p_e

Therefore the investor received p_e whether the stock rises or falls; in fact, he/she will receive p_e in all states of the world. The present value of the investor's future payoff on this "portfolio" at time zero $= p_e/(1+r)^d$.

Since the investor has created a riskless portfolio, his profit on this strategy should be zero, and the sum of the outflow at time zero is equal to the present value of the inflow:

therefore $p_{so} + Put_o - x_o = p_e/(1 + r)^d$

therefore $Put_o = x_o + p_e/(1 + r)^r p_{so}$

and

$$x_o = Put_o + p_{so} - p_e/(1 + r)^d$$

The same values from the numerical example of how to apply the Black-Scholes call valuation model are employed to determine the value of a put option on the same stock. The following data are used: p_s = \$60, p_e = \$50,

$d = .333$ (which represents 120 days out of a 360-day year), $R = .07$ (which represents 7 percent per annum), and $var(r_i) = .144$. The Black-Scholes model placed a value on this 4-month call of $11.98. The value of the put is calculated below by substituting these values into Eq. (19-10a).

$$(\$11.98) + [(\$50) / (1.0 + .07)^{.333}] - (\$60) = \qquad (19\text{-}10b)$$

$$(\$11.98) + [(\$50) / (1.0227)] - (\$60) =$$

$$(\$11.98) + (\$48.89) - (\$60) =$$

$$\$60.87 - \$60 = 87 \text{ cents}$$

If the optioned stock recently paid a cash dividend, the market price of the stock probably experienced an *ex-dividend drop-off* that exactly equalled the amount of the cash dividend. In this case, the amount of the recent cash dividend should be added back into the current market price of the stock, and this total amount should be used in place of the stock's price in valuing the put option. For instance, if the stock just paid a 25-cent cash dividend, then the $60 stock price should be increased to $60.25 in Eq. (19-10$b$) for valuing the put.

19-5.7 Option Market Efficiency

Halpern and Turnbull[22] studied call option trading on the Toronto Stock Exchange for the period January 3, 1978, to December 31, 1979. The option data used was taken from the TSE computer Toronto Option Tape as compiled by Turnbull and Halpern.[23]

The authors identified the lower bounds for the value of the TSE call options. The basic lower boundary condition is that the price of an American call option cannot be less than its intrinsic value. Two other lower bounds allow for the adjustment to option values for dividend payments. They identified through their empirical study numerous examples of violations of the three lower boundary conditions, particularly for deep in the money options. They also found that the average dollar size of the violations was a positive function of both the time to expiry and the number of dividends paid before the exercise date. The results indicated that arbitrage opportunities were presented to investors who could trade both the underlying stock and the option contract. However, these arbitrage profits were insufficient to compensate most retail investors for transaction costs of trading. Thus, a "free lunch" was only available to investors who did not have to pay transaction costs.[24] They cautiously concluded that the TSE option market was inefficient over the period 1978–1979, possibly because of the rapid growth of the market and the failure of the infrastructure to keep pace. They cautioned that "whatever

---

22 Paul J. Halpern and Stuart M. Turnbull, "Empirical Tests of Boundary Conditions For Toronto Stock Exchange Options," *The Journal of Finance*, vol. 40, no. 2, June 1985, pp. 481–500. See also: Dan Galai, "Boundary Conditions for CBOE Options," *Journal of Financial Economics* 6, pp. 187–211, for a similar study of option trading on the Chicago Board Options Exchange.

23 Stuart M. Turnbull and Paul J. Halpern, "The Toronto Option Tape," working paper, Institute For Policy Analysis, University of Toronto.

24 Market makers are the only option-market participants that pay minimal transaction costs.

inefficiencies observed should not be generalized to current periods when the option market has matured and its growth has levelled off."[25]

19-6   COMBINATIONS

Straddles, strips, spreads and straps are the names of option positions that are constructed from various combinations of puts and calls. These combinations are analyzed below.

19-6.1
Straddles

The buyer of a straddle is actually simultaneously purchasing both a put and a call on the same optioned asset. The buyer thus pays a premium for a straddle that equals the sum of the premiums for both a put and a call purchased separately. Straddle buyers are willing to pay the large premium for a put plus a call because they are reasonably confident that the price of the optioned security will deviate, either up or down, from the exercise price. The straddle buyer gains if the price of the optioned asset makes either an upward, a downward, or both an upward and a downward price move. The writer of a straddle has the opposite view. Straddle writers are sufficiently confident that the security's price will not vary before the option matures that they are willing to write a contract that guarantees it will not move, if they are paid the straddle premium as an inducement.

FIGURE 19-11   Profit graphs for a straddle option: (a) straddle buyer; (b) straddle writer.

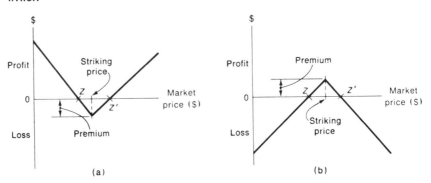

(a)   (b)

The profit positions of the buyer and the writer of a straddle are depicted in Fig. 19-11. Since a straddle is a put and a call at the same exercise price, the profit positions for the straddle in Fig. 19-11 are merely Figs. 19-5 and 19-6 added for the case when the exercise prices of the put and the call are identical.

Figure 19-11 shows that the straddle writer loses if the optioned security's price either rises or falls. For taking this large risk, the straddle writer receives a premium that is equal to a put premium plus a call premium. In fact, there

25 Paul J. Halpern and Stuart M. Turnbull, "Empirical Tests of Boundary Conditions For Toronto Stock Exchange Options," *The Journal of Finance*, June 1985, vol. 40, no. 2, p. 26.

may be two writers to a straddle, both a put writer and a call writer. This could occur if the puts and calls dealer is not able to find one person to write the entire straddle.[26] Or, the person desiring to buy a straddle might buy a put and a call separately on the same security in order to create a straddle position.

The buyer of a strip is speculating that the price of some security will change from the exercise price, but strip buyers believe that the security's price is more likely to fall than it is to rise. Figure 19-12 represents the profit positions for the buyer and the writer of a strip.

19-6.2 Strip

FIGURE 19-12   Profit graphs for a strip: (a) strip buyer; (b) strip writer.

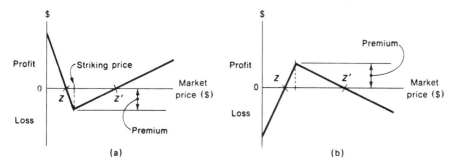

Since a strip equals two puts and one call on the same asset, the buyer evidently believes a decrease in the price of the optioned security is more probable than an increase. The premium for writing a strip usually equals the premium for writing two puts plus one call. In order for the buyer to recoup this large premium, the market price of the optioned security must either drop to Z or rise to Z' as shown in Fig. 19-12. The drop from the exercise price to Z is only half as far as the rise from the exercise price to Z' because the line through Z has twice as steep a slope as the line through Z'. Figure 19-12, representing the strip, is quite similar to Fig. 19-11 for the straddle. The only differences are in the size of the premium and the slope of the line through point Z'.

Figure 19-13 represents the profit position of the buyer and the writer of a spread and is similar to Fig. 19-11 for the straddle. The difference between these two figures is that the exercise price of the spread is "points away" from the market. The exercise price for the put portion of the spread is point A in Fig. 19-13. The market price for the optioned security when the option was written is represented by point B. Point C is the exercise price for the

19-6.3 Spread

---

26 The dealer probably owns a seat on one or more of the options exchanges and earns income either (1) from being a broker for other parties who are willing to write options, or (2) by selecting some of the options to be written by him- or herself in order to earn the premium income for writing.

FIGURE 19-13   Profit graphs for a spread: (a) spread buyer; (b) spread writer.

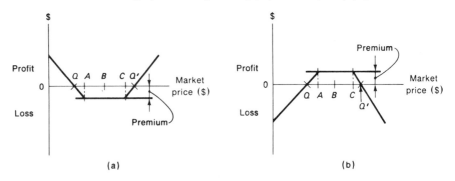

(a)   (b)

call portion of the spread. The premium on the spread is less than the premium on the straddle because the market price of the security that is optioned with a spread must rise or fall more than if it were optioned with a straddle in order for the option buyer to profit. Graphically, this means the distance from Z to Z' in Fig. 19-11 is less than the distance from Q to Q' in Fig. 19-13. Symbolically, $(Z' - Z) < (Q' - Q)$.

**19-6.4
Strap**

Straps consist of two calls and one put on the same security at the same exercise price. Thus, a strap is like a strip that is skewed in the opposite direction. The buyer of a strap evidently foresees bullish and bearish possibilities for the optioned security, with a price rise being more likely. Graphs of the profit positions for the buyers and sellers of a strap are left as an exercise for the interested reader to construct.[27]

Other Options   In addition to the strips, straps, spreads, and straddles that can be formed from puts and calls, numerous other option packages can be developed. For example, the *down-and-out option* is basically a call option with two complications added. The first complication is that the option expires any time the market price of the optioned security falls below some specified price level. The second complication is that the call's writer will return a portion of the purchase price paid for the call option if the call is exercised prior to its maturity. There is also the *up-and-out option*, which is a put option with two added provisions: (1) The option expires and becomes worthless if the market price of the optioned security rises above some prespecified level. (2) If the option is exercised prior to its maturity, the writer must refund some prespecified portion of the premium received for writing the up-and-out option. These less popular options will not be analyzed here.[28] However,

27 The combination position called a strap is discussed and graphically illustrated in William W. Welch, *Strategies for Put and Call Option Trading* (Cambridge, Mass.: Winthrop, 1982), p. 163.

28 The down-and-out option is analyzed by R.C. Merton, ''The Theory of Rational Option Pricing,'' *Bell Journal of Economics and Management Science*, Spring 1973, vol. 4, no. 1, sec. 6. The down-and-out option, compound options, options on more than one security, options on futures and other options are discussed in chap. 7 of *Options Markets* by J.C. Cox and M.

there is a more popular option strategy involving the basic positions that is worthwhile to consider; it is called "writing covered calls."

Sometimes options writers buy the security on which they are writing the option. When they do so, they are said to have *covered* themselves. For example, consider a woman who wrote a call. This call writer might buy 100 shares of the security on which she is writing the call if she expects (as does the call's buyer) that the price of the optioned security might rise. Then, if the security's price does rise and the call is exercised, the writer will simply deliver the shares she has already purchased and not suffer any loss. Assuming that the call writer's interest expense and commissions incurred by covering herself are less than the premiums she received, both the call writer and the buyer may be able to gain from the price rise. If this call writer has covered herself with securities purchased on margin, she may earn a handsome rate of return on her invested capital. On the other hand, if the security's price falls, then the call buyer loses the premium and the covered call writer loses on her long position. However, at least the call writer's security price losses are offset by the premium she received.[29]

Figure 19-14 represents writing covered calls graphically. At points Z the buyer and the writer have zero profit. Note, however, that point Z for the buyer is above the striking price by the amount of the premium, whereas point Z is below the striking price for the writer.

An option writer who writes a call against some security without owning that security is said to be *writing naked* or *writing against cash* or *writing uncovered*. Figure 19-5*b* shows the profit position for a call writer who was writing naked. That is, this particular call writer had not covered himself by buying the securities for which he wrote the option. In this case, the call buyer's

**19-6.5
Writing
Covered
and
Uncovered
(or Naked)
Options**

FIGURE 19-14   Profit graphs for a call: (a) call buyer; (b) covered writer.

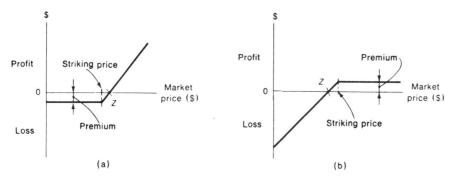

(a)   (b)

Rubinstein (Englewood Cliffs, N.J.: Prentice-Hall, 1985). The appendix to chap. 23 of this book also discusses options on futures. Warrants and convertibles are the topic of the appendix to this chapter.

29 C.R. Grube, D.B. Panton, and T.J. Michael, "Risks and Rewards in Covered Call Positions," *Journal of Portfolio Management*, vol. 5, 1979.

profits are the call writer's losses. A comparison of the call writer's exposure to loss in Fig. 19-5*b* and 19-14*b* shows that writing calls *naked* is risky in a bull (rising) market and that writing calls *covered* is risky in a bear (falling) market.

The writers of options may write any option naked or choose to cover themselves. The final decision depends on the particular option being written and the option writer's beliefs about the direction of the market. In any event, the naked option writer's profits are limited to the premium, while the naked writer's potential losses are unlimited.[30]

The exchanges' margin requirements mandate that option sellers who write options naked put up the appropriate initial margin; in recent years this has been at least 30 percent of the total market value of the optioned shares. Thus the leverage attainable by writing naked is not infinite, but it is more leverage than can be obtained in nonmargined long or short transactions. Option writers who have an offsetting position in the security on which the option is being written (that is, covered writers) on deposit at their brokers' offices are not required to put up any additional margin.

In the final analysis, it is not correct to assume that covered option writers always gain from their activity. Covered call writers will gain from their call writing only if the price of their optioned stock remains almost unchanged so that it is never exercised. If the price of the stock advances significantly, the covered call writer would have been better off not to have written the options because the appreciating securities are called away at a lower price. If the price of the optioned stock declines, the covered call writer suffers the loss in market value just as if the call had never been written; however, the loss from the price drop is at least partially offset by the premium income.

Mandron[31] found that the returns to covered in-the-money call writing in Canada over the period October 1977 to April 1983 averaged 3.0 percent per quarter, as compared to a 4.1 percent return on a long position in the corresponding stocks. However, the dispersion on the covered-call strategy (6.9 percent) was considerably less than that of the naked position in stocks (11.1 percent).

**19-6.6
Federal
Income Taxes
and Options**

The cost of an option is a nondeductible capital expenditure, and the option represents a capital asset in the hands of the holder. Gain or loss occurring upon the sale of an option in a closing sale transaction constitutes a capital gain or loss. If an option is allowed to expire, it is treated as having been sold on the expiration date. Upon the exercise of an option, its cost is added to the exercise price to determine the adjusted cost base of the underlying stock acquired.

---

30 For a discussion of how the manager of an options portfolio can reshape the probability distribution of returns attainable from the various options see Richard M. Bookstaber and Roger G. Clarke, *Option Strategies for Institutional Investment Management* (Reading, Mass.: Addison-Wesley, 1983).

31 Alix Mandron, "Risk and Returns on Covered Call Strategies in Canada," *Financial Research Foundation Proceedings*, Fall Conference, October 1985, pp. 21–23.

The premium received for writing an option is included in the writer's taxable income as a capital gain at the time of receipt (when the option is written). The writer's obligation may terminate (1) by the passage of enough time for the option to expire, (2) by delivery of the underlying stock pursuant to the terms of the option, or (3) the writer may sell the written call to another call writer for a premium which may be more, the same, or less.

If the option is exercised against the writer, he will reverse the treatment of the premium as a capital gain and will instead treat the premium as part of the proceeds of disposition of the underlying asset. For example, suppose Mr. A owns 100 shares of Bell Enterprises Ltd. and in October 1987 sells (writes) a Bell August 40 call option at a premium of $7.00 per share, when the Bell Enterprises common stock is selling for $39.00. Assume that when Mr. A files his income tax return the following April the option has not been exercised. Mr. A will include in income for the taxation year ended December 31, 1987, $700 as a capital gain. In June 1988, the call option is exercised against Mr. A by the holder. Mr. A can file an amended tax return for taxation year 1987, eliminating the $700 capital gain. Instead, for taxation year 1988, Mr. A will have proceeds of disposition of $4,000 (the exercise price), plus $700 (the option premium), or a total of $4,700. His capital gain will be the $4,700 minus his adjusted cost base on the 100 shares minus the commissions paid on the closing transaction.

19-7 SUMMARY AND CONCLUSIONS

Research by one of the Nobel Prize winners in economics has shown that resources within a nation can be allocated better if there are more different contingent claims on assets than are provided by only the long position.[32] That is, the existence of short positions, hedges, and options actually increases the nation's average per capita wealth, regardless of whether every person owns securities. Stated differently, the existence of short positions and options increases the chances that an investor will find a set of financial claims that are consistent with his or her preferences, thus inducing the investor to make a comfortable increase in investment. This additional investment can create more jobs and more goods for consumption and also shape security prices so that they more clearly reflect investors' wishes and forecasts. This scientific finding refutes the naive notion that speculation is some worthless form of gambling.

The people who buy and sell put and call options have obligations and rights that are summarized in Table 19-4.

The spectrum of possible positions that participants in securities markets may assume is wide. For example, individuals who want to speculate that the market price of an asset will rise or fall may set themselves up to profit

---

[32] Kenneth Arrow, ''The Role of Securities in the Optional Allocation of Risk-Bearing,'' *Review of Economic Studies*, April 1964, pp. 91–96.

TABLE 19-4 THE BUYERS AND SELLERS OF OPTIONS HAVE DIFFERENT RIGHTS AND OBLIGATIONS

	CALL OPTION	PUT OPTION
Buyer or owner	Right to buy on or before the expiration date at the exercise price	Right to sell on or before the expiration date at the exercise price
Writer or seller	Obligation to sell at the exercise price on or before the expiration date	Obligation to buy at the exercise price on or before the expiration date

from such moves, if they materialize, by assuming a long or short position, respectively. If a speculator desires more financial leverage and/or wants only a limited liability—which are not obtainable with the long and short positions —then call or put options are appropriate. On the other hand, a speculator who thinks that the price of some security will not change and wants to profit from this expectation can do so. By writing strips, straps, and straddles, the person can profit if the security's price remains stationary. Positions exist from which thoughtful individuals may profit from practically every other situation too. The existence of such profitable opportunities encourages good securities research, helps keep securities prices aligned with their true intrinsic values, and makes securities markets more efficient allocators of capital.

Both risk-taking speculators and risk-averse hedgers use options. Risk-averse investors who must maintain a long (short) position during a period of time when they expect the price of the asset to decline (rise) may buy put (call) options or take the opposite position to protect themselves from the adverse price movements. Thus, options perform an important risk-reducing function, somewhat analogous to the function performed by insurance.

Other kinds of options exist. Appendix 19A delves into Warrants and Convertible Securities—both of which are essentially options added to other securities. In addition, following Chaps. 20 and 21, which introduce futures contracts, 21A explains options on futures contracts.

QUESTIONS

1. "Risk-averters do not sell short. Short selling is done by speculators." Is this statement true, false, or uncertain? Explain.
2. Who are the parties to put and call options and what function is performed by each party?
3. What are the main factors determining put and call premiums?
4. Graph the profit positions showing the positions of the buyer and the writer of a strap.
5. Compare and contrast writing a call naked and selling a common stock short.

6. Is it possible to create a short position from options? Explain.
7. Compare and contrast call options and warrants.
8. Does the Montreal Exchange ever trade options of any type with the same expiration date but different exercise prices? Why?
9. Should the price of a strip option bear any relation to the prices of put and call options? Explain.
10. Is there any kind of basic relation between the prices of puts and calls on the same security which may be expected to exist permanently? Explain.
11. Use the Black-Scholes call option pricing formula to find the value of call options on the following optioned stocks:

	ABC STOCK	XYZ STOCK
Time to maturity	4 months	88 days
Standard deviation	30	40
Exercise price	$40	$60
Price of optioned stock	$40	$68
Interest rate	.12	.06

SELECTED REFERENCES

Black, F., and M. Scholes. '' The Pricing of Options and Corporate Liabilities.'' *Journal of Political Economy*, June 1973, pp. 637–654. A seminal mathematical paper that develops a static equilibrium pricing model for options.

Bookstaber, R. M. *The Complete Investment Book*. Glenview, Illinois: Scott, Foresman and Company, 1985. Chapter 3 discusses cash-futures arbitrage. Chapter 5 discusses interest rate arbitrage. Chapter 23 discusses the Black-Scholes option pricing formula. Chapter 24 discusses Black's commodity options pricing model. Chapter 25 discusses volatility estimation using historical data. Chapter 26 discusses the implied volatility statistics derived from option prices. Each chapter contains a computer program to perform the calculations.

Brown, B. ''Trading Options: A Market Makers View,'' Financial Research Foundation, Proceedings of the 1982 Conference, 1982, unpaginated. This paper presents a professional's view of how professional trading is conducted on the floor of the TSE.

Cox, J.C. and M. Rubinstein. *Options Market*. Englewood Cliffs, N.J.: Prentice-Hall, 1985. This comprehensive book covers both the institutional material and option theory in detail.

Gastineau, Gary L. *The Stock Options Manual*, 2d ed. New York: McGraw-Hill, 1979. The first six chapters contain easy-to-read descriptions of options and option markets. Chapters 7 through 10 discuss quantitative call-pricing models, options on bonds and commodities, and other topics.

For a description of how the short selling process works, see: E.F. Kirzner and Stuart Turnbull, ''Buying on Margin and Short Selling: How Does It Work?'' *Common Sense Economics*, vol. 6, no. 1, University of Waterloo, Fall 1981, pp. 15–20.

Warrants, Convertibles, and the Newer Options

The options industry has enjoyed explosive growth since the organized option exchanges opened in the 1970s. Moreover, this growth is continuing into the 1980s as entirely new types of options are created and as more of the traditional options on securities are listed and traded. Options on commodities, options on financial indexes, and options on futures contracts are all exciting new products. Understanding these new products well enough to sell them has been straining the capacity of the securities industry since the 1980 decade started. In contrast, warrants and convertible bonds are well-known option-type securities. Let us consider them first.

APP. 19A-1 WARRANTS

Stock purchase warrants, or more simply, warrants, are options to buy shares of stock. They are like *calls* to the extent that they are options to buy a fixed number of shares at a predetermined price during some specified time period. However, warrants are different from calls in certain respects. Warrants are written by the corporation to whose stock they apply rather than by an independent option writer. They are given as attachments to the corporation's issue of bonds or preferred stock. Warrants are "sweeteners" given with an issue of senior securities in order to increase the proceeds of the issue and thereby lower the interest cost. These options may expire at a certain date or they may be perpetual. They are usually detached from the securities with which they were issued and traded as separate securities.

Warrants are widely used by Canadian companies. As of December 31, 1984, there were 148 warrant series outstanding, issued by 136 different companies listed on the Toronto, Alberta, and Vancouver Stock Exchanges and the Montreal Exchange. This represents a much higher proportion of warrant issues to listed companies than in the United States.

The price stated on the warrant, which the owner must pay to purchase the stated number of shares, is called the *exercise price*. The minimum value of a warrant, denoted MVW, may be calculated with Eq. (App. 19A-1).

$$MVW = (p_s - p_e)N \qquad \text{(App. 19A-1)}$$

where

p_s = market price per share of the optioned stock

p_e = conversion or exercise price

N = number of shares of common stock obtained with one warrant

For example, a warrant that entitles its owner to buy two shares (that is, N = 2) of stock at an exercise price of $50 per share ($p_e$ = $50) while the market price is $60 per share ($p_s$ = $60) has a minimum value of [($60 — $50)(2) =]

FIGURE APP. 19A-1   The determinants of a warrant's price.

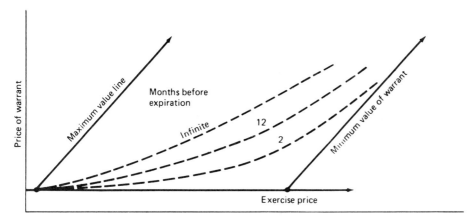

$20 per warrant. Figure (App. 19A-1) depicts Eq. (App. 19A-1) graphically as the minimum-value line. The slope of the MVW line is N.

Figure App. 19A-1, depicting the determination of warrant prices, is also appropriate to explain the price of calls since call options and warrants are identical except for some minor details. Figure App. 19A-1 shows that when the market price of the optioned security is above the exercise price, the warrant has some positive minimum value. The actual market price of the warrant actually follows the dashed curves in Fig. App. 19A-1 (like call prices). This shows that warrants typically have a market value above the MVW. The excess of a warrant's price over its minimum value (p_w - MVW) is determined by expectations about future stock prices in a similar way that call option premiums are determined.[33]

However, warrants differ from exchange-traded stock options in that exercise of the warrant causes dilution (increases the number of common shares outstanding) and injects cash into the underlying company. Therefore the Black-Scholes option pricing model must be modified to allow for this difference.[34]

The terms governing a warrant are set out in detail in the warrant certificate that the purchaser receives. This certificate sets out important details such as when and how the warrant can be exercised.

---

33 J.P. Shelton, "The Relation of the Pricing of a Warrant to the Price of Its Associated Common Stocks," *Financial Analysts Journal*. This two-part article is in the May-June 1967 issue and also the July-August 1967 issue. Also see D. Leabo and R.L. Rogalski, "Warrant Price Movements and the Efficient Market Model," *Journal of Finance*, March 1975; A.H.Y. Chen, "A Model of Warrant Pricing in a Dynamic Market," *Journal of Finance*, December 1970; A.J. Boness, "Elements of a Theory of Stock-Option Value," *Journal of Political Economy*, April 1964.

34 See David Emanuel, "Warrant Valuation and Exercise Strategy," *Journal of Financial Economics*, 12, 1983, pp. 211–235. Blazenko has derived a Black-Scholes variant valuation equation for warrants. See George W. Blazenko "Valuation of Call Options on Firms with Warrants," working paper, University of Waterloo, 1986.

Most warrants are like long-term American call options; that is, they may be exercised anytime within their life of five or ten years. A few warrants have perpetual lives, and a few other warrants are like European calls and may be exercised only at specific points in time.

Most warrants are protected against stock splits and stock dividends. Thus, if the security to which the warrant applies undergoes a 2 for 1 split, for instance, the warrant likewise is adjusted so that it entitles its owner to two of the new split shares (which are worth half of what the old shares would have been worth if they had not been split). However, most warrants are not protected against the eroding effect of cash dividends on the price of the optioned security. Thus, when a common stock starts to trade ex-dividend, its market price drops off by an amount approximately equal to the cash dividend that was just paid. This ex-dividend price drop-off moves the price of the optioned stock further below the exercise price of the warrant and thus tends to decrease the value of the warrant.

Some warrants are *nondetachable*, which means that they cannot be detached from their associated securities. However, many warrants are detachable, and they may be separated from the securities to which they were attached as sweeteners and traded separately as independent financial instruments. The warrant agreement outlines all such rights and provisions for its particular issue of warrants.

Commodity, currency, and bond purchase warrants have been issued in Canada in recent years. These interesting instruments pose a particular valuation problem in that the value of the warrant is not only a function of the usual option parameters but is also dependent on the ability of the underlying firm to meet its obligations. For example, Echo Bay Mines, a major Canadian gold producer, issued in 1982, as part of a package underwriting, four series of European-style gold purchase warrants that allow the holder to acquire the cash equivalent of 0.01765 ounces of gold at an effective exercise price of U.S. $297.50 per ounce as of January 31, 1986, 1987, 1988, and 1989, respectively. However, the warrants are exercisable only if the price of gold is above $625 per ounce, at the exercise date. It is possible to think of cases where the price of gold is above $625 per ounce, yet the firm is unable to honour its agreement because of financial difficulty. In this and all cases where the issuer of a commodity, currency, or financial instrument warrant is a risky firm, the Black-Scholes equation must be modified to provide for this contingency.[35]

APP. 19A-2 CONVERTIBLE BONDS

Convertible bonds are corporate debt securities, usually debentures. However, convertible bonds are unlike most other bonds because, at the option of the bondholder, they may be *converted* into equity shares in the same corporation that issued the convertible bonds, if certain conditions are met.

---

35 See Phelim P. Boyle and E.F. Kirzner, "Pricing Complex Options: Echo Bay Ltd. Gold Purchase Warrants," *The Canadian Journal of Administrative Sciences*, vol. 2, no. 2, December 1985, pp. 294–306.

However, from their investors' point of view, most convertible bond issues are encumbered by an unfortunate call provision. That is, most convertible bond issues have provisions in their indenture contracts which allow their issuers to call them in before maturity. When an issuer calls in an outstanding issue, this action is taken for the issuer's benefit, and whatever the issuer gains from the conversion essentially comes out of the investors' pockets. These call and conversion requirements and their implications are discussed at length in Sec. 2-9.

Essentially, a convertible bond may be viewed as a combination of two different securities that were both issued together by the same corporation: (1) a nonconvertible bond and (2) a nonmarketable warrant. These nonmarketable warrants that are attached to convertible securities are sometimes called *latent warrants*. Viewed as a two-part package, a convertible bond investment offers (*a*) fixed coupon interest payments until such time as the bond defaults, or until it may be called by the issuer or converted by the investor, (*b*) bond price fluctuations that result from changes in market interest rates, (*c*) bond price fluctuations that result from changes in the price of the common stock into which the bond may be converted (these are actually changes in the value of the latent warrant that is viewed as being "attached" to the bond), (*d*) downside risk protection provided by a "floor" or "safety net" under the investment's price that equals the present value of the nonconvertible bond's coupon payments, and (*e*) cashflows from the bond coupons that would normally exceed the cash dividend cashflows from a common stock investment of equal size. Calculating a value for such a package is a complicated task. To make matters even worse, as mentioned above, most convertible bond issues are callable at the issuer's discretion. Figure App. 19A-2 (on page 546) illustrates the general principles that are applicable in valuing convertible bonds.[36]

Figure App. 19-A2*a* illustrates how the value of a noncallable, nonconvertible bond increases directly with the value of the issuing corporation's common stock price. This relationship derives from the fact that as the corporation prospers and its common stock's value rises, the probability decreases that bonds issued by the same corporation might fall into default. However, an upper limit or "ceiling" on the bond's price is established by the fact that the bond can never be worth more than a default-free bond with similar coupon and maturity provisions.

Figure App. 19A-2*b* shows that the value of the *latent warrant* that is implicit in every convertible security package rises in value directly with the value of the common stock into which it might be converted. Adding together the values indicated in Fig. App. 19A-2*a* and *b* results in the series of values illustrated in Fig. App. 19A-2*c*. Figure App. 19A-2*c* indicates how the value of a noncallable convertible bond varies directly with the price of the underlying common stock. However, life is usually more complicated than even Fig. App. 19A-2*c* reveals.

---

36 Valuing convertible bonds is discussed by M.J. Brennan and E.S. Schwartz, "Convertible Bonds: Valuation and Optimal Strategies for Call and Conversion," *Journal of Finance,* December 1977, vol. XXXII, no. 5, pp. 1699–1716.

FIGURE APP. 19A-2 The elements of value in a convertible bond.

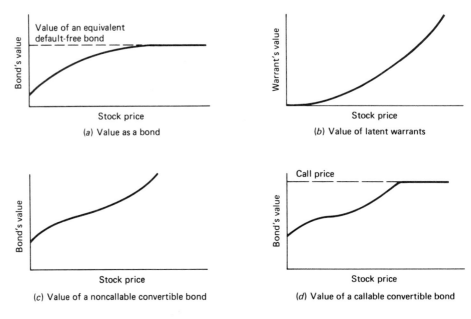

(a) Value as a bond

(b) Value of latent warrants

(c) Value of a noncallable convertible bond

(d) Value of a callable convertible bond

As mentioned before, most convertible bonds are callable by the issuer at some call price that is prespecified in the indenture contract governing the bond issue. This call price imposes some sort of "ceiling effect" that limits the callable, convertible bond's price rise. To see how the "ceiling effect" works, consider a hypothetical corporation that starts to enjoy prosperity. Suppose this prosperity pushes up the prices of the corporation's common stock and convertible bonds. Eventually the corporation will probably call the convertible bonds, in order to force their owners to convert them into common stock. After all, the corporation does not want an overhanging issue of convertible bonds that limits its ability to issue new securities. Therefore, when the market price of the convertible bonds rises to about 125 percent of the call price, the issuing corporation usually calls the issue. Figure App. 19A-2*d* summarizes all of this; it is merely Fig. App. 19A-2*c* redrawn with a constraint or ceiling equal to the price the market thinks will cause the bonds to be called inserted as a "lid" on the price of the callable convertible bond.

APP. 19A-3 OPTIONS ON COMMODITIES AND ECONOMIC INDEXES

Table App. 19A-1 lists options on assets that were never optioned until the 1980s. Options on oil stocks, debt instruments, and economic indexes are exciting new opportunities to speculate on the values of important variables that differ from the stock price options that dominated the option market for decades. Furthermore, options contracts on futures contracts are another new development. Options on futures are discussed at length in App. 21A.

TABLE APP. 19A-1 OPTIONS ON COMMODITIES, FINANCIAL INSTRUMENTS, AND ECONOMIC INDEXES

Canadian Contracts

UNDERLYING ASSET	EXCHANGE	TRADING UNIT
Foreign currencies	ME	
British pound	ME	£100,000 in US$
Canadian dollars	ME	CDN$50,000 in US$
Deutsche marks	ME	US$100,000 in Dm
Japanese yen	ME	US$100,000 in ¥
Swiss francs	ME	US$100,000 in Sfr
U.S. dollars	ME	US$100,000 in CDN$
Debt Instruments		
Government of Canada bonds	ME, TSE, TFE	$25,000 face value at maturity
T-bill index	ME	$250,000
Market Indexes		
TSE 300 Composite Index	TSE	($100 × index)/20
TSE 35 Index	TSE	$100 × index
Canadian Market Portfolio Index	ME	$100 × index
Canadian Banking Index	ME	$100 × index
Precious Metals		
Gold	ME*, VSE*	10 oz
Silver	TFE	100 oz
Silver	VSE*	250 oz
Platinum	ME*, VSE*	10 oz

* Internationally linked with the European Options Exchange of Amsterdam and the Sydney Stock Exchange of Australia. Contracts opened on one exchange can be traded on the other exchanges.

U.S. Contracts

Foreign Currencies		
Australian dollar	PHLX	A$50,000
British pound	PHLX	£12,500
Canadian dollars	PHLX	CDN$50,000
Deutsche marks	PHLX	DM62,500
French francs	PHLX	Ffr125,000
Japanese yen	PHLX	¥6,250,000
Swiss francs	PHLX	Sfr62,500
ECU (European Currency Unit)	PHLX	ECU62,500
Debt Instruments		
Treasury bonds	CBOE	US$20,000 and US$100,000
Treasury notes	AMEX	US$100,000
Treasury bills	AMEX	US$1,000,000
GNMAs	CBOE	US$100,000
Market and economic indexes		
S&P 100	CBOE	US$100 × Index
S&P 500	CBOE	US$100 × Index

U.S. Contracts (continued)

UNDERLYING ASSET	EXCHANGE	TRADING UNIT
S&P OTC 250 Index	CBOE	US$100 × Index
AMEX Market Value Index	AMEX	US$100 × Index
NYSE Composite Index	NYSE	US$100 × Index
Financial News Composite	PSE	US$100 × Index
Value Line Index	PHLX	US$100 × Index
National O-T-C Index	PHLX	US$100 × Index
Subindexes		
Computer technology	AMEX	US$100 × Index
Oil and gas	AMEX	US$100 × Index
International Oils	CBOE	US$100 × Index
Institutional	AMEX	US$100 × Index
Airline	AMEX	US$100 × Index
Telephone	NYSE	US$100 × Index
Gold/Silver	PHLX	US$100 × Index
Technology	PSE	US$100 × Index
Computer and business equipment	CBOE	US$100 × Index
Technology	PSE	US$100 × Index
Utilities	PHLX	US$100 × Index
Beta	NYSE	US$100 × Index

LEGEND:
AMEX-American Stock Exchange
CBOE-Chicago Board Options Exchange
CBT-Chicago Board of Trade
ME-Montreal Exchange
NYSE-New York Stock Exchange
PSE-Pacific Stock Exchange
PHLX-Philadelphia Stock Exchange
TFE-Toronto Futures Exchange
TSE-Toronto Stock Exchange
VSE-Vancouver Stock Exchange

For options on futures contracts see App. 21A.

Commodity Futures Contracts

CHAPTER 20

As the name suggests, commodity futures contracts are legal contracts. The terms of a futures contract stipulate the type of commodity covered by the contract, the future date for which delivery of the goods is scheduled, the sales price per unit for the commodity, the number of units (that is, the quantity) of the commodity that was sold, the quality specifications of the commodity that must be delivered under the contract, and related details. These stipulated details cannot be changed once a contract is executed because the futures contracts traded on any particular commodity in any given market are all standardized contracts that vary only with respect to the price and quantity of the particular sale covered by that specific contract.

The *uniformity* of the futures contract makes it more marketable to new buyers. For example, rapid trading is expedited if a homogeneous commodity is uniformly specified in all the futures contracts traded in a given market. Nevertheless, the second, third, and later buyers of any futures contract can, and usually do, pay a different price per unit for the contracted commodity than was agreed upon in the original contract. A futures contract is traded at successively different prices by transferring the contract through a third party called the *clearing house*. The clearing house inserts itself between every buyer and every seller. That is, the clearing house pays the original commodity seller the current price for the agreed-upon quantity and then turns around and sells a new, but identical, futures contract to the new buyer at the same current price. As a result of the clearing house positioning itself as the *intermediary* in every trade, a commodity contract may be resold at a price per unit that differs from the originally contracted unit price. The ultimate future delivery price and deliverer are reassigned by the clearing house each time the contract is resold. Thus, commodity futures contracts are *marketable financial instruments* that are actively traded on commodity futures exchanges.

Commodity futures contracts are usually called simply *futures*. Futures should be viewed as another type of financial instrument that portfolio managers may wish to consider.[1] Commodity futures contracts are useful to both

1 C.V. Harlow and R.J. Tewles, ''Commodities and Securities Compared,'' *Financial Analysts Journal*, September-October 1972, pp. 67–70. Futures contracts and securities are different financial instruments. Securities include stocks and bonds; the SEC oversees the securities markets in the United States. Futures contracts are not called securities. In the United States, futures markets are governed by the CFTC. In Canada, both securities and futures trading are governed by the provincial securities commissions except for Winnipeg Commodity Exchange grain futures, which are subject to the Federal Grain Futures Act. However, the bulk of futures trading in Canada is on U.S. futures exchanges, and Canadian traders are subject to CFTC regulations for their U.S. trades. See John E. Hore, *Trading on Canadian Futures Markets*, 2d ed., the Canadian Securities Institute, Toronto, 1985, pp. 144–150, for a discussion of the Canadian regulatory situation for futures trading.

risk-taking speculators and risk-averse hedgers in ways that are explained in the chapter that follows. The opportunities to earn a diverse mix of returns from a portfolio made up of stocks, bonds, options, and futures are too rich to ignore.

20-1 COMMODITIES TRADING

Commodities include farm products such as wheat, rapeseed, cotton, soybeans, hogs, and their derivatives, like soybean meal, soybean oil, and pork bellies (which refers to unsliced bacon). Other homogeneous raw materials, such as silver and copper, are also actively traded commodities.

Commodity prices are determined by the supply of and the demand for the underlying commodity. Commodity supplies are subject to all such capricious acts of nature as fire, flood, disease, insects, and drought, plus various unpredictable governmental acts like import-export quotas, subsidies, and foreign exchange revaluations. In contrast to erratic supply, the demand for most commodities is fairly steady. Farm products are traded in what economists call nearly perfect markets where there are many small sellers (namely, farmers) and many buyers—none of whom is large enough to affect prices.

The physical commodities are traded in what are synonymously called the cash, physicals, or actuals markets. Grain elevators and stockyards where farmers deliver and sell their products for cash are examples of *cash markets*. Large cash markets exist in the cities of Regina and Saskatoon in Canada and Kansas City and Minneapolis in the United States, but no commodity futures contracts are traded at those cash markets. The commodity futures contracts are traded at markets for financial instruments called *futures exchanges*. Some cash markets are supplemented by associated futures contract markets, but most cash markets are not associated directly with a futures exchange.

Since the supply of harvested new crops arrives erratically to meet a demand function that is typically not so seasonal, some commodities must be stored for future delivery. Perhaps that is why contracts to deliver stocks of stored commodities came to be called commodity futures contracts. No one knows for sure where the word "futures" gained its first usage in the commodities business. Technically speaking, commodity futures contracts that do not fall due for delivery in the next few days are called *futures contracts*. Futures contracts that are near expiration and ready for the commodity to be delivered instantaneously are usually called *spot contracts* instead of futures contracts in Canada and the United States.[2] In spite of the fact that they are different, however, some people (in particular, the British) equate the spot market and the cash market in their market vernacular. Maybe the British refer to the physicals or cash market as the "spot market" because spot contracts are due to be delivered instantaneously and, thus, to be turned into the physical or cash commodity. In Canada and the United States both spot and futures contracts are traded on commodity exchanges. The physical or cash commodity, however, is never traded on a commodity exchange in either country.

2 Futures contracts are not traded in spot market transactions. Bills of lading and warehouse receipts are used in the spot market transactions.

TABLE 20-1   COMMODITIES

Canadian Futures Exchange

COMMODITY & EXCHANGE	TRADING HOURS (LOCAL TIME)	CONTRACT UNIT	Minimum Price Change PER UNIT	Minimum Price Change PER CONTRACT	VALUE OF 1¢/1$/£1 MOVE	Maximum Daily PRICE CHANGE	Maximum Daily PRICE RANGE	CONTRACT VALUE OF MAXIMUM MOVE
Barley, domestic feed (WCE)	9:30–1:15	100 tons (bd lot) / 20 tons (job lot)	10¢ ton	$10 / CDN $2	$100 / $20	$5	$10	CDN $500 / $100
Flaxseed (WCE)	9:30–1:15	100 tons (bd lot) / 20 tons (job lot)	10¢ ton	$10 / CDN $2	$100 / $20	$10	$20	$1,000 / $200
Oats, domestic feed (WCE)	9:30–1:15	100 tons (bd lot) / 20 tons (job lot)	10¢ ton	$10 / CDN $2	$100 / $20	$5	$10	$500 / $100
Rye (WCE)	9:30–1:15	100 tons (bd lot) / 20 tons (job lot)	10¢ ton	$10 / CDN $2	$100 / $20	$5	$10	$500 / $100
Rapeseed; Vancouver (WCE)	9:30–1:15	100 tons (bd lot) / 20 tons (job lot)	10¢ ton	$10 / CDN $2	$100 / $20	$5	$10	$1,000 / $200
Wheat, domestic feed (WCE)	9:30–1:15	100 tons (bd lot) / 20 tons (job lot)	10¢ ton	$20 / $100	$100 / $20	$5	$10	$500 / $100
Treasury bills (90 days) (TFE)	9:00–3:15	$1,000,000 board lot	1 B.Pt. .005*	CDN $24	100 B.Pt. = $2500*	Pt. 60	120	$1,440
Gold (WCE)	8:25–1:30	20 oz	10¢ oz	$2	$20	$25	$50	$500
Silver (WCE)	8:40–1:25	200 oz	1¢ oz	$2	$2	.50¢	$1	$100
Long-term Canada bonds (TFE)	9:00–3:15	$100,000 face value	1/32 pt	$31.25	32/32 = $1,000	64/32nds	128/32nds	$2,000
TSE Composite 300 Index (TFE)	9:30–4:15	$10 × index	1 pt	$10	100 pts = $1,000	150 pts	300 pts	$1,500
TSE Composite 300 Spot Index (TFE)	9:20–4:10	$10 × index	1 pt	$10	100 pts = $1,000	None	None	—
TSE Oil and Gas Index (TFE)	9:30–4:15	$10 × index	1 pt	$10	100 pts = $1,000	250 pts	500 pts	$2,500
TSE Oil and Gas Spot Index (TFE)	9:20–4:10	$10 × index	1 pt	$10	100 pts = $1,000	None	None	—
U.S. Dollar (TFE)	8:30–4:00	US$100,000	CDN$.0001	$10	CDN$.01 = $1,000	CDN$.01	CDN$.02	$1,000
Eastern Lumber (ME)	9:00–15:00	130,000 bd.ft	US$.10 /1,000 bd.ft	US$13	US$130	US$5 /1,000 bd.ft	US$10 /1,000 bd.ft	$650
Gold (cash-settled) (ME)	9:00–15:00	100 oz	US$.10/oz	US$10	US$100	US$50	US$100	US$5,000
Gold (IMM)	8:00–1:30	100 oz †	10¢ oz	$10	$100	$50	$100	$5,000
Gold (MACE)	8:00–1:40	33.2 oz †	2.5¢ oz	83¢	$33.20	$25	$50	$830
GNMA CDR (CBT)	8:00–2:00	$100,000	1/32 pt	$31.25	1 pt = $1,000	64/32nds	128/32nds	$2,000
Heating oil, no. 2 NY (NYMEX)	10:00–2:45	42,000 US gal	$.0001 gal	$4.20	$420	2¢	4¢	$840
Heating oil, no. 2 (CBT)	10:00–2:45	42,000 US gal	$.00025 gal	$10.50	$420	3¢	6¢	$1,260
Hogs, live (CME)	9:10–1:00	30,000 lb	2½¢/100¢ lb	$7.50	$300	1½¢	3¢	$450
Hogs, live (MACE)	9:10–1:15	15,000 lb	0.025¢ lb	$3.75	$150	1½¢	3¢	$225
Lumber (CME)	9:00–1:05	130,000 board ft	10¢ MBF	$13.00	$130	$5	$10	$850
NYSE Composite Index (NYFE)	10:00–4:15	$500 × futures price	0.05	$25.00		none	none	none
Oats (CBT)	9:30–1:15	5,000 bu	¼¢ bu	$12.50	$50	6¢	12¢	$300
Oats (MACE)	9:30–12:30	5,000 bu	⅛¢ bu	$6.25	$50	6¢	12¢	$300
Palladium (NYMEX)	9:00–2:20	100 oz †	5¢ oz †	$5.00	$100	$6	$12	$600
Platinum (NYMEX)	9:10–2:30	50 oz †	10¢ oz †	$5.00	$50	$20	$40	$1,000

TABLE 20-1 COMMODITIES (continued)

United States Commodity Exchange

COMMODITY & EXCHANGE	TRADING HOURS (LOCAL TIME)	CONTRACT UNIT	Minimum Price Change PER UNIT	Minimum Price Change PER CONTRACT	VALUE OF 1¢/1$/£1 MOVE	Maximum Daily PRICE CHANGE	Maximum Daily PRICE RANGE	CONTRACT VALUE OF MAXIMUM MOVE
Cattle, feeder (CME)	9:05–12:45	44,000 lb	$.000025 lb	$11	$440	1½¢	3¢	$660
Cattle (CME)	9:05–12:45	40,000 lb	2½/100¢ lb	$10	$400	1½¢	3¢	600
Cattle (MACE)	9:05– 1:00	20,000 lb	$.00025 lb	$5	$200	1½¢	3¢	$300
Certificates of deposit (CBT)	7:30– 2:00	$1,000,000	1 B.Pt.* .01	$25	100 B.Pt. = $2500*	80 B.Pt.*	160 B.Pt.*	$2,000
Certificates of deposit (IMM)	7:30– 2:00	$1,000,000	1 B.Pt.* .01	$25	100 B.Pt. = $2500*	80 B.Pt.*		$2,000
Citrus (FCOJ) (NYCE)	10:15– 2:45	15,000 lb	5/100¢ lb	$7.50	$150	5¢	10¢	$750
Cocoa (NYCSC)	9:30– 3:00	10 ††	$1 ††	$10	$10	88¢	$176	$880
Coffee C (NYCSC)	9:45– 2:28	37,500 lb	1/100¢ lb	$3.75	$375	4¢	8¢	$1,500
Copper (COMEX)	9:50– 2:00	25,000 lb	05/100¢ lb	$12.50	$250	5¢	10¢	$1,250
Corn (CBT)	9:30– 1:15	5,000 bu	¼¢ bu	$12.50	$50	10¢	20¢	$500
Corn (MACE)	9:30– 1:15	1,000 bu	¼¢ bu	$1.25	$10	10¢	20¢	$100
Cotton (NYCE)	10:30– 3:00	50,000 lb	1/100¢ lb	$5	$500	2¢	4¢	$1,000
Cotton (NOCE)	9:15– 2:00	50,000 lb	$.0001 lb	$5	$500	2¢	4¢	$1,000
Currencies, foreign (IMM)								
British pound	7:30– 1:24	25,000	$.0005	$12.50				
Canadian dollar	– 1:26	100,000	$.0001	$10				
Deutsche mark	– 1:20	125,000	$.0001	$12.50				
Dutch guilder	– 1:30	125,000	$.0001	$12.50				
French franc	– 1:28	250,000	$.0005	$12.50				
Japanese yen	– 1:22	12,500,000	$.00001	$12.50				
Mexican peso	– 1:18	1,000,000	$.00001	$10				
Swiss franc	– 1:16	125,000	$.0001	$12.50				
Eurodollar CDs	7:30– 2:00	$1,000,000	1 B.Pt.* .01	$25	100 B.Pt. = $2500*			
Crude oil, sour (NYMEX)		1,000 bbl	$.01 bbl	$10	$10	$1	$2	$1,000
Crude oil, sweet (NYMEX)		1,000 bbl	$.01 bbl	$10	$10	$1	$2	$1,000
Crude oil, sweet (CBT)		1,000 bbl	$.01 bbl	$10	$10	$1	$2	$1,000
Gasoline, leaded NY (NYMEX)	9:30– 3:30	42,000 gal	$.001	$4.20	$420	2¢	4¢	$840
Gasoline, leaded (CBT)		42,000 gal	$.00025 gal	$10.50	$420	3¢	6¢	$1,260
Gasoline, unleaded Gulf (CBT)	8:30– 2:30	42,000 gal	$.00025 gal	$10.50	$420	3¢	6¢	$1,260
Gasoline, leaded (CME)		42,000 gal	$.00025 gal	$10.50	$420	2¢	4¢	$840
Gasoline unleaded (CME)		42,000 gal	$.00025 gal	$10.50	$420	2¢	4¢	$840
Gold (CBT)	8:00– 1:30	100 oz †	10¢ oz	$10	$100	$40	$80	$4,000
Gold (COMEX)	9:00– 2:30	100 oz ††	10¢ oz	$10	$100	$25	$50	$2,500
Pork bellies (CME)	9:10– 1:00	40,000 lb	$.00025 lb	$10.00	$400	2¢	4¢	$800
Potatoes, white round (NYME)	9:45– 2:00	50,000 lb	1¢ cwt	$5.00	$5	50¢	$1	$250
Propane (LPG) (NYCE)	9:45– 2:35	42,000 gal	$.001	$4.20	$420	1¢	2¢	$420
Rice, milled (NOCE)	9:45– 1:45	1,200 cwt	$.005 cwt	$6.00		50¢	$1	$600
Rice, rough (NOCE)	9:45– 1:45	2,000 cwt	$.005 cwt	$10.00		30¢	60¢	$600
Silver, NY (COMEX)	9:05– 2:25	5,000 oz †	10/100¢ oz	$5.00	$50	50¢	$1	$2,500
Silver, Chicago (CBT)	8:05– 1:25	5,000 oz †	10/100¢ oz	$5.00	$50	50¢	$1	$2,500
Silver, Chicago (CBT)	8:05– 1:25	1,000 oz †	10/100¢ oz	$1.00	$10	50¢	$1	$500
Silver, Chicago (MACE)	8:05– 1:40	1,000 oz †	.005¢ oz	$.50	$5	50¢	$1	$500
Silver, NY (MACE)	8:30– 1:40	1,000 oz †	$.001 oz	$1.00	$10	50¢	$1	$500
Soybeans (CBT)	9:30– 1:15	5,000 bu	¼¢ bu	$12.50	$50	30¢	60¢	$1,500
Soybeans (MACE)	9:30– 1:30	1,000 bu	¼¢ bu	$1.25	$10	30¢	60¢	$300
Soybeans (NOCE)	9:30– 1:15	5,000 bu	$.0025 bu	$12.50	$50	30¢	60¢	$1,500
Soybean meal (CBT)	9:30– 1:15	100 tons (200,000 lb)	10¢ ton	$10.00	$100	$10	$20	$1,000
Soybean oil (CBT)	9:30– 1:15	60,000 lb	1/100¢ lb	$6.00	$600	1¢	2¢	$600

S & P 500 stocks index (CME)	9:00–3:15	$500 × futures price	.05	$25.00		none	none	$500.00
Sugar, no. 11 (NYCSC)	10:00–1:43	112,000 lb	1/100¢ lb	$11.20	$1,120	1¢	2¢	$1,120
Sugar, no. 14 (NYCSC)	10:00–1:43	112,000 lb	1/100¢ lb	$11.20	$1,120	1¢	2¢	$1,120
Sugar, refined (MACE)	9:00–1:00	40,000 lb	1/100¢ lb	$4.00	$400	½¢	1¢	$200
Treasury bills (90-day) (IMM)	8:00–2:00	$1,000,000	1 B.Pt0.01*	$25.00	100B.Pt.=$2,500*	60 B.Pt.*	120 B.Pt.*	$1,500
Treasury bonds (CBT)	8:00–2:00	$100,000	1/32 pt.	$31.25	32/32nds=$1,000	64/32nds	128/32nds	$2,000
Treasury bonds (NYFE)	9:00–3:00	$100,000	1/32 pt.	$31.25	32/32nds=$1,000	96/32nds		$3,000
Treasury notes (10-year) (CBT)	8:00–2:00	$100,000	1/32 pt.	$25.00	32/32nds=$1,000	64/32nds		$2,000
Value Line composite index (KCBT)	9:00–3:15	$500 × futures price	0.05	$25.00	$500	none	none	
Wheat (CBT-KC-MPLS)	9:30–1:15	5,000 bu	¼¢ bu	$12.50	$50	20¢	40¢	$1,000
Wheat (MACE)	9:30–1:30	1,000 bu	⅛¢ bu	$1.25	$10	20¢	40¢	$200

CME = Chicago Mercantile Exchange
MACE = Mid-America Commodity Exchange
CBT = Chicago Board of Trade
IMM = International Monetary Market of the CME
NYCE = New York Cotton Exchange
NYCSC = New York Coffee, Sugar and Cocoa Exchange
COMEX = Commodity Exchange, N.Y. City
NOCE = New Orleans Cotton Exchange
NYMEX = New York Mercantile Exchange
KCBT = Kansas City Board of Trade
WCE = Winnipeg Commodity Exchange
TSE = Toronto Stock Exchange
*B.Pt.—basis point
††—metric tons
‡ oz †—troy ounces
TFE = Toronto Futures Exchange
ME = Montreal Exchange

Table 20-1 lists the major commodity exchanges in Canada and the United States and the commodity futures contracts that are traded at each. The Chicago Board of Trade, now more than a century old, is the largest commodity exchange in North America. Interestingly, there are no significant cash markets for commodities in Chicago, although two of the largest commodity futures exchanges in the world, the Chicago Board of Trade and the Chicago Mercantile Exchange, operate in that city. Since it is very expensive to accept delivery on a futures contract in Chicago, the commodity exchanges in Chicago primarily support trading by hedgers and speculators instead of farmers.

Figure 20-1 shows a floor plan of a trading room found in a typical commodity exchange. There are usually several trading rooms at an exchange, and only the exchange members may enter them. Trading actually occurs in the *trading ring*, or *trading pit*, shown in Fig. 20-1. Exchange members who want to buy or sell futures in some commodity go to the appropriate trading room, step into the trading pit, and indicate by *open outcry* or by making appropriate hand signals that are visible to all who are present their intention to transact business. This is how commodity buyers and sellers get together to consummate a legitimate trade on domestic futures exchanges in Canada and the United States. When the buyer and the seller settle on the contract terms, news of the latest price is posted to the board on the trading room wall and also sent out by wire to the boardrooms of brokerage houses around the world.

FIGURE 20-1 Trading floor of a commodity exchange.

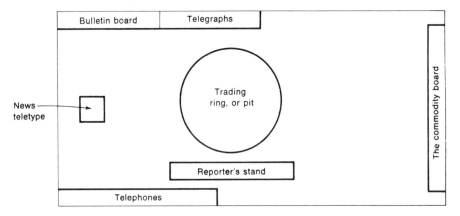

Floor brokers are independent members of the commodity exchange who transact most of the trading on the exchange floor. For a commission, they buy and sell futures for their customers. Orders to buy and sell come into the exchange by telephone and/or telegraph to the floor brokers from their customers. The floor brokers step into the appropriate pit, execute the trades, and then notify their customers. The *independents*, as these floor brokers are called, execute orders for the public and for their own accounts as well; this is called *dual trading*.

Figure 20-2 indicates who the people who trade commodity futures contracts interact with, where some of the more important of these contracts occur, and how the news of the trades is channelled around the world. Figure 20-2 is an event flowchart that traces out the flow of events and information that accompany every commodity futures trade.

FIGURE 20-2   Flowchart of events in the origination of one futures contract.

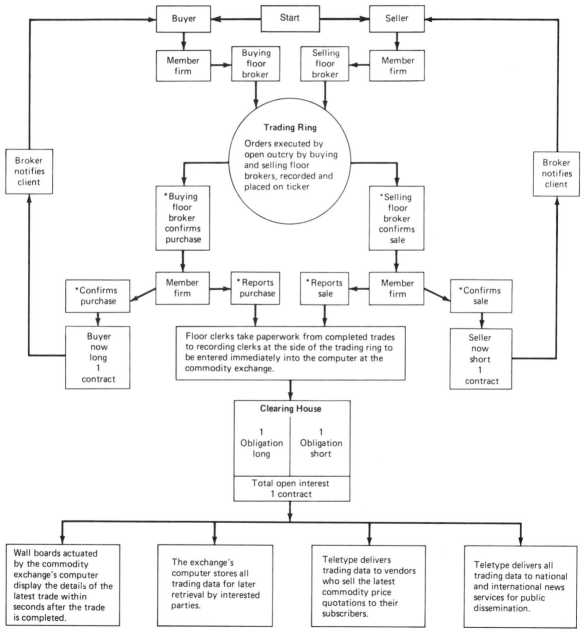

*Gives the price, quantity, delivery month, and time of transaction.

20-1.1 Futures Contracts The phrase "commodity exchange" can be misleading, because the commodities themselves are not traded at commodity exchanges. It is the commodity futures contracts that are actively traded at the exchanges. Today, the futures contracts themselves are not even traded. *Trading cards* are what are actually traded. Modern futures contracts are, in fact, a set of legal contract provisions, rules, regulations, and exchange bylaws that govern every transaction that flows through a futures exchange. Years ago, however, preprinted contractual forms were traded on the floors of the commodity exchanges.

In years past, a different commodity futures contract form existed for each commodity that specified the standard trading unit for the commodity in pounds, bushels, or whatever unit was appropriate; what grade of commodity was to be delivered; where the commodity was to be delivered; and what penalties would be imposed if the delivery were made at another place or in another grade. When a futures contract was signed, the buyer and the seller merely filled in blanks on the contract specifying their names, the date,

FIGURE 20-3   Futures contract for Brazilian coffee from yesteryear.

CONTRACT "B" (new)
(BRAZIL COFFEE CONTRACT)
(Variable Differentials)
Montreal _____ 19_____

_____ (has) this day (sold)
(have)   (bought)

and agreed to (deliver to) _____
                 (receive from)

32,500 lbs. (in about 250 bags) of Brazilian COFFEE shipped through the ports of Santos, Paranagua, Angra dos Reis or Rio de Janeiro, grading from No. 2 to No. 6 inclusive, provide the average grade shall not be above No. 3, nor below No. 5. Nothing in this contract, however, shall be construed as prohibiting a delivery averaging above No. 3 at the premium for No. 3 grade. No premium shall be allowed for Softish Coffee grading above No. 4.

At the price of _____ cents per pound for Santos No. 4, Strictly Soft, Fair to Good Roast, Solid Bean with additions or deductions for grades, ports of shipment and description (quality) according to the differentials established or to be established by the Committee on Coffee of the New York Coffee and Sugar Exchange for the delivery month specified below in accordance with Section 88(8) (a) of the By-Laws of said Exchange. The delivery must consist of Coffee from one port only.

The Coffee to be Fair to Good Roast, Solid Bean, and the description (quality) to be Strictly Soft, Soft, or Softish. No delivery permitted of Hard Coffee.

Deliverable from licensed warehouse in the Port of New York between the first and last days of _____inclusive, the delivery within such time to be at the seller's option upon either five, six or seven days' notice to the buyer as prescribed by the Trade Rules.

Either party may call for margin as the variations of the market for like deliveries may warrant, which margin shall be kept good.

This contract is made in view of, and is in all respects subject to, the By-Laws, Rules and Regulations of the New York Coffee and Sugar Exchange, Inc.

(Across the face is the following):   *(Brokers)*
*For and in consideration of One Dollar to_____
in hand paid, receipt whereof is hereby acknowledged,_____
accept this contract with all its obligations and conditions.*

the quantity, the price, and the month in which delivery was to be made. Figure 20-3 shows a blank futures contract from the "old days," before computer memories were used to store the details of all the "open interest" futures contracts.

For any given commodity there are several delivery months that may be specified in the futures contract. The price of the futures in any given commodity varies with the month in which the commodity is to be delivered. Thus, March No. 3 grade Canada western red spring wheat deliverable at Thunder Bay, Ontario, has a different price per bushel from the price of the same type of wheat delivered at the same place in May. As a result, commodity futures prices are listed on a *commodity board* like the one shown in Table 20-2.

20-1.2 The Commodity Board

TABLE 20-2 COMMODITY BOARD FOR WINNIPEG WHEAT

DELIVERY MONTHS	DECEMBER	MARCH	MAY	JULY	OCTOBER
Open	96.50	95.00	95.00	81.00	83.50
Range	94.10–98.50	93.20–96.80	93.10–96.50	79.00–81.00	79.80–83.70
High	98.50	96.80	96.50	81.00	83.70
Low	94.10	93.20	93.10	79.00	79.80
Trades	410	337	212	88	55
4th	94.60	93.90	93.90	81.00	83.40
3rd	94.40	93.80	93.80	80.90	82.20
2nd	94.70	93.90	93.60	80.10	81.30
Last	94.30	93.30	93.20	80.20	80.70
Change	−1.20	−1.30	−1.10	−0.40	−0.70
Stlmt. price	94.40	93.30	93.30	80.10	80.80
Season high	262.7	245.5	279.00	104.00	85.10
Season low	75.8	77.5	79.00	78.70	77.20

The top line of the commodity board gives the delivery months. It will be noted that the Winnipeg wheat futures, like most futures, are not available for delivery every month. The delivery months are determined by the commodity exchange with the approval of the Canadian Grain Commission for Winnipeg commodity futures contracts and the provincial securities commissions for Toronto and Montreal futures contracts. The second line of the board gives the opening price of the commodity. All prices are in dollars per metric ton for this commodity. The third line provides the range between the high and low price for the day. The fourth and fifth lines give the high and low prices at which the commodity had traded thus far that day. The sixth line is the number of contracts traded in the day to that point. The next four lines provide the fourth, third, and second-last trades, and the last trade in the commodity for each of its delivery months. The eleventh line gives the change in the price thus far that day relative to the settlement price of the previous day. The settlement price shown in the twelfth line is the closing price for the day, the price that is used for settling all trader and customer accounts. This price is determined by the exchange officials, based on price activity and bids, and offerings at the close of trading, and is generally, but not always, close to the final trade for the day. The final two lines give the highest and lowest prices at which that particular commodity has ever been traded since the contract's inception.

The commodity board is kept current by clerks employed by the exchange. The current prices are transmitted electronically on a worldwide communications network.

20-1.3 Price Fluctuations in Canada and the United States

Commodity futures prices have both minimum and maximum price limit fluctuations imposed on them by the commodity exchanges. The fifth column of Table 20-1 lists the *minimum price fluctuations* on the major commodities. New bids must be higher than the old (or existing) bids, and new asked (or offering) prices must be less than the old (or existing) asked prices by at least the amount of the minimum fluctuation limit; otherwise the exchange will not accept the new bid or asked price. The minimum price limit fluctuations are designed to prevent bids involving price changes that are not significantly different from zero.

Column seven of Table 20-1 lists the *maximum price fluctuations* permitted on most commodities. The purpose of these maximum limits is to prohibit large and potentially destabilizing price changes. Thus, if a commodity's price rises the *day's limit*, trading in that commodity for the remainder of the day cannot exceed that day's maximum price. Trading may thus be stopped. The next day, trading resumes at the previous day's high price but still cannot rise higher than the daily maximum or trading will be halted again. Luckily, the maximum price fluctuation limits seldom halt trading in any commodity. Some economists suggest that price restrictions distort natural supply and demand relationships and thus misallocate resources when they do come into play. However, there is a perennial debate among market economists about whether the price change limits do more good than bad.

20-1.4 The Clearing House

In addition to the buyer and the seller, there is a third party to every futures contract, the *clearing house*, which guarantees that every futures contract will be fulfilled even if one of the parties defaults. Every commodity exchange has a clearing house.

The clearing house acts as buyer if the buyer defaults or as seller if the seller defaults. The clearing house thus provides a performance guarantee for every futures contract. It saves part of the fees it collects for insuring futures contracts in a guarantee fund. When one of the parties to a futures contract defaults, the clearing house pays whatever costs are necessary to carry out the contract from this fund. This provision frees futures traders from checking one another's credit every time they transact a trade and thus helps make the futures contract a freely negotiable financial instrument.

The clearing house also facilitates trading of futures contracts before they are due for delivery. If the original buyer of a future sells the contract to reverse the trade, and if the second buyer in the series sells the contract to reverse that trade, and then if a third buyer in the series sells the contract to reverse that trade, the clearing house keeps track of this series of buyers.

Then, when the time comes to deliver on the contract, the clearing house arranges for the original seller of the contract to make delivery to the last buyer of the contract. In practice, the clearing house actually rewrites every futures contract as two separate contracts and substitutes its name into both. That is, the clearing house becomes the seller from which all buyers obtain delivery and the buyer to whom all sellers make delivery. Thus, when several subsequent buyers are involved in a given futures contract, these various buyers and sellers do not even need to know each other's names to ensure that the contract gets delivered.[3] The clearing house keeps track of these details and deals directly with each buyer and seller separately, as shown in Fig. 20-4.

FIGURE 20-4 Flowchart of a series of trades of one futures contract which is reversed.

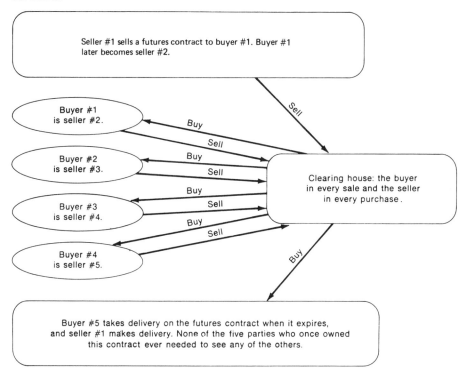

Futures traders need not be involved in a business utilizing the commodities they trade; they need not ever see the commodities. Commodity traders usually start by opening a trading account with a futures commission merchant (FCM hereafter) at a brokerage house that deals in commodities. The brokerage firm will either purchase or lease a *membership* at a commodity

**20-1.5
The
Mechanics
of Trading
Commodity
Futures**

3 Technically, the traders on the floor of a commodity exchange make it a point to know the names of the other sides of all their trades in order to expeditiously clear up any mistakes, called *out trades*. By knowing the other party that was part of the out trade, the trader can negotiate a settlement of the mistake directly. Such direct negotiation avoids costly and inconvenient arbitration of the out trade.

exchange, or the FCM will make arrangements with a floor trader who is a member of a commodity exchange to carry out the trades.

The major full-service brokerage firms like Merrill Lynch and Davidson Partners have commodities departments or subsidiaries (such as Merrill Lynch Futures Inc.) to assist the general public in trading futures. Some firms like Conti-Commodity and Phibro specialize in being FCMs and dealers for the larger buyers of commodities. In addition, there are discount brokers in the commodity futures business. Like the discount brokers in the common stock markets, the discount FCMs do not provide free research, nice offices for clients to visit, and other expensive amenities. As a result, the FCMs charge their clients commissions that are about one-quarter as much as one of the full-service FCMs would charge for the same transaction. FMG Commodity Services in Canada and Lind-Waldock, Macro-Source, Murias Commodities Inc., and Jack Carl Associates in the United States are all discount FCM firms. The discount FCMs are not as large as the full-service FCM firms, do not have offices in as many cities, and do very little advertising. However, almost all of them have offices in market centres and can be contacted by telephone from anywhere in the world.

Futures contracts are denominated in a specified quantity of a commodity. For example, on the Winnipeg Commodity Exchange, wheat contracts consist of 20 and 100 metric tons, while on the Chicago Board of Trade, 100 tons is one unit or one contract of soybean meal, a wheat contract consists of 5000 bushels, and a unit of soybean oil is 60,000 pounds. Table 20-1 shows the standard contract units for every major commodity in the third column. To sell a futures contract, the trader notifies the broker. The broker obtains all the needed details about whether the customer wants to sell futures (that is, to take a short position) or buy futures (to assume a long position); what the current prices, margin requirements, relevant unit, and total costs are; and in what trading months the future may be bought and sold.

The broker prepares the order and transmits it to the commodity exchange. For example, if the customer wanted to go short 200 tons of wheat until May, the broker could notify the floor trader at the wheat trading room of the Winnipeg Commodity Exchange to "sell two May wheats." This message would be transmitted by telephone or direct wire to the floor trader. This floor trader would probably execute the order and send word back to the broker that the transaction had been consummated — all within a few minutes. At that time the customer would be required to put up the initial margin requirement of approximately 5 to 10 percent. Then, anytime before May, when the wheat contract expired and came due to be delivered, the broker's short-selling customer could either buy back the contract in the futures market or buy physical wheat in the cash market and deliver it to fulfill the futures contract. If the short seller defaulted on the contract, the clearing house would carry out the contracted delivery of 200 tons of wheat as scheduled and initiate a lawsuit against the defaulted short seller. Actually, very few commodity market traders ever make delivery on their futures contracts; most settle by "rolling over" their position into a later delivery month or reversing the trade so that they are left without a position.

20-2 ACTIVELY TRADED COMMODITIES

Commodities that are actively traded in the futures markets in North America include both the traditional (for example, agricultural products) and the newer financial instruments.

Agricultural Commodities   Some of the actively traded farm commodities include meats (unsliced bacon and live cattle), grains (wheat, corn, flaxseed and soybeans), and other commodities (coffee, sugar, rice, and cotton).

Various other traditional commodities that have been traded for a long time exist too; these include metals (gold and silver) and wood (stud lumber).

The farm goods and other traditional commodities mentioned above were the earliest commodities traded. Investors started trading them centuries ago in crude markets. The most recent items traded at commodities exchanges are financial futures contracts.

Financial Futures   The financial commodities traded in futures markets are contracts on foreign currencies (such as the British pound, the Canadian dollar, the Swiss franc, and the Japanese yen), contracts on bonds (such as Government of Canada bonds, U.S. Treasury bonds, U.S. Treasury bills, and commercial paper), and contracts on financial indexes (a stock market index).[4]

It is natural to have financial futures markets because money is a commodity. Like wheat or corn or any other commodity, money has one price for current delivery and a different price for future delivery. The difference between the current price and the future price of money is essentially the market interest rate, or basis, for the commodity called money.

When we say a given commodity is ''traded successfully,'' we are speaking from the point of view of the commodity exchange. *Successfully traded* commodity futures contracts are those that enjoy sufficient trading volume (or, what is a closely related measure, the open interest) to make active markets for the contract and generate sufficient trading fees to pay the commodity exchange's cost of keeping the market operating. In general, the following list of statements apply to actively traded commodities.

- The commodity should be gradable into *homogeneous quality categories*. This means that one lot of any commodity (such as a boxcar load of sugar) should be interchangeable with any other lot of that commodity.
- *Raw materials* (such as wheat) are traded successfully more frequently than finished goods (such as flour). Money is also a raw material; it is used to produce a finished product called profits.
- The commodity's cash market price should be determinable by a *clear price discovery process*; there should be no arbitrariness about the price. For example, the price should be determined by supply and demand facts rather than by the whim of an individual or by a nonmarket process.
- *Storability* is important; perishable commodities (for example, lettuce or fresh flowers) cannot be stored or shipped easily. Since commodity hedgers endeavour to

**20-2.1
The
Traditional
and the New
Commodities**

**20-2.2
Characteristics
of Actively
Traded
Commodities**

4 Financial futures are the topic of Chap. 21 of this book.

buy at a low price and sell at a high price, they want commodities they can hold in storage cheaply until prices rise.

- The commodity must exist in *volume*. Rare objects (for example, art objects) cannot generate the trading volume needed to sustain an active market.
- Large amounts of *risk capital* must be committed to carrying the risky inventories needed to make liquid markets. That is, hedgers must be willing to invest millions of dollars in inventories that will fluctuate in value. Then, when the parties investing in inventories of physicals enter the futures market to hedge, they, in turn, create more needs for risk capital to finance the speculators' positions that bear the risk the hedgers are hedging.
- The futures contract should be *conveniently written* for both buyer and seller. Contracts cannot be written in such dense legal language that only lawyers can read them.
- The commodity should be *cheaply transportable*. The marketability of a commodity is maximized if it can be shipped inexpensively to buyers.
- The commodity should be *readily describable*. There can be no ambiguity about what is going to be delivered.
- The *price* of the commodity must be *volatile*. The more that the price of a commodity fluctuates, the more risk-averters will want to hedge their inventories and, in turn, the more speculative trading will occur to create these hedges.
- A liquid cash market where the physical commodity is traded should be active before trading in commodity futures contracts is begun. The *prior existence of a viable cash market* means that the price discovery process for the commodity already exists and is discernible.
- The public, and the risk-averse manufacturers who will want to hedge their inventories, need to be *educated* about the commodity and its futures contract. No one will invest in something they do not understand.

Most of these statements apply to most actively traded commodities. However, not every one of the statements above applies to every successfully traded commodity. For example, although most Canadian and U.S. farm commodities are not easily gradable into homogeneous quality categories, both governments nevertheless grade and inspect these commodities. The above list merely suggests what is usually required to trade a contract successfully.[5]

Usually, any given commodity is traded successfully at only one North American commodity exchange. For example, the Chicago Mercantile Exchange (nicknamed the "Chicago Merc") is primarily a meat market, although it also successfully trades other commodities. There are exceptions to this tendency, however; wheat and several other commodities are traded successfully on various U.S. commodity exchanges. No foreign commodity exchanges are as large as the ones in the United States, but several are nevertheless efficient commodity exchanges.

20-3 PRICES AND RETURNS

Commodity prices are determined by the supply of and the demand for the commodity. However, the relationships between the cash price, spot price,

---

5 Lester Telser and Harlow Higginbotham, "Organized Futures Markets: Costs and Benefits," *Journal of Political Economy*, October 1977, pp. 969–1000. Henry Bakken, *Futures Trading in Livestock—Origins and Concepts* (Madison, Wis.: Mimir, 1970).

and futures price for any given commodity at any given instant are determined by different factors.

For any storable commodity on a given day, the futures price is normally higher than the spot price.[6] The excess of the futures price over spot price is called the *premium*, or the *positive basis*. In *normal markets*, the premium is just sufficient to cover storage, inspection, interest expense, insurance, and the other carrying charges incurred while holding a commodity for future delivery. This premium is necessary to compensate hedgers like grain elevator operators for buying commodities when their cash prices are low (for example, at harvest time) so that they will store them until their prices are bid higher, at which time they will sell the commodity to fill the excess demand. Such storage by grain elevator operators and other similar commodity dealers provides a supply of commodities all year long, although the entire crop in the commodity may be harvested in one month of the year. It is so common for futures prices to exceed spot prices by the amount of carrying charges in commodity markets that this situation is called a *normal carrying charge market*.

20-3.1 Normal and Inverted Markets

More generally, the difference between futures and spot prices on the same commodity at a given moment is called the *basis*. If futures exceed spot prices, this situation is called a positive basis, a premium, or *contango*.[7] However, a negative basis, or *discount* situation, can also occur.

$$\text{Basis} = (\text{futures price}) \text{ less } (\text{spot price}) \tag{20-1a}$$

A *normal market* is defined as one in which the basis, as measured in Eq. (20-1a), is a positive amount that equals the carrying cost.[8]

The premium of futures prices over spot prices may be slightly less than the cost of carrying the commodity in inventory if a "convenience yield" exists.[9]

---

6 Some commodities (such as fresh eggs, fresh potatoes, and live cattle) are not storable. For these nonstorable commodities it is not uncommon for spot prices to exceed futures prices. Also, just before harvest time when current supplies of a storable commodity are short but the forthcoming new crop is expected to be large, inverted markets are not unusual for storable commodities. Holbrook Working, "Theory of the Inverse Carrying Charge in Futures Markets," *Journal of Farm Economics*, February 1948, vol. XXX, and also, "The Theory of Price of Storage," *American Economic Review*, December 1949, vol. XXXIX. Furthermore, if excess demand develops in the spot market for nonagriculturals, inversion may occur. A market that is subject to occasional bouts of inversion is copper.

7 J.M. Keynes was first observed to use the word *contango* in an article he wrote for the *Manchester Guardian Commercial* in 1923. The word is more popular in England than in the United States today. However, the word *contango* seems to be used more frequently by silver futures traders than others for some unknown reason — perhaps because silver is such an international commodity.

8 If the basis is restated as shown in Eq. (20-1b), then the basis is negative and has an absolute value equal to the carrying costs in normal markets.

$$\text{Basis} = (\text{spot prices}) \text{ less } (\text{futures price}) \tag{20-1b}$$

9 The convenience yield concept was first introduced by Nicholas Kaldor, "Speculation and Economic Stability," *Review of Economic Studies*, 1939, vol. 7, pp. 1–27.

The "convenience" yield can be defined as the sum of extra advantages (other than appreciation in the market value) which a manufacturer may derive from carrying stocks above his immediate requirements rather than holding the equivalent value in cash and buying stocks at a later date.[10]

The higher selling price that a manufacturer could obtain by being a dependable supplier of substantial quantities of some raw material is one example of how a convenience yield is obtained from carrying a commodity in inventory. Some users of the commodity would be willing to pay the dependable supplier's higher selling price simply to establish a good relationship with the supplier and thus free themselves of worry about suffering from a costly and troublesome out-of-stock condition.

Occasionally the market in some storable commodity becomes "inverted." In an *inverted market* the futures price is less than the spot price. This excess of spot over futures prices is called a *discount*. Futures can sell at a discount to spot, for example, when the current supply of a commodity is very low, keeping cash and spot prices high, but the currently growing crop is expected to yield a large harvest, so that future supplies will be plentiful and futures prices low.

20-3.2 One Risk-Averter Plus One Speculator Can Equal One Futures Contract

Between most risk-averting hedged sellers and most risk-averting hedged buyers is a risk-taking speculator. This speculator dislikes risk, too. However, like an insurance company, the professional speculator takes many risks in both buying and selling. If the majority of the speculator's decisions are based on correct forecasts, he or she earns a trading profit over many transactions.

Professional speculators may or may not be members of a commodity exchange. Speculators prepare commodity forecasts and then, on the basis of their forecasts, either sell short to or buy futures contracts from hedging sellers or other speculators. For instance, one hedging seller and one speculator might consummate a trade that created one hedged inventory position for the hedger who sold the contract and one long futures position for the speculator who bought the contract. Later, the speculator might liquidate the long futures position by selling the contract to, say, a futures buyer who was hedging a short position in the physical commodity. As a result of this second transaction, one speculator with a futures contract to sell and one hedging futures buyer can create another hedged position.

The final result is that the hedging buyer and the hedging seller have passed the risks they sought to avoid on to the professional speculator (who is probably well hedged and earns a profit for providing insurance). However, if the number of hedging buyers does not exactly equal the number of hedging sellers (and it rarely will), the speculator is left holding some long or short positions that are unhedged. In such situations, speculators hope that the price forecasts on which they based their decisions are correct. The

10 Gerda Blau, "Some Aspects of the Theory of Futures Trading," *Review of Economic Studies,* 1944–1945, vol. XII, no. 1, pp. 9–14. See also M.J. Brennan, "The Supply of Storage," *American Economic Review,* volume 48, March 1958, pp. 50–72.

fact that commodity exchanges have been growing for over a century suggests that, typically, many parties to these arrangements profit from them.

Not all trades need take place between a hedger and a speculator. Sometimes speculators can trade with each other (through the clearing house) merely because of differing price expectations.

Financial economists are not all in agreement about exactly how large the basis should be in normal market conditions with storable commodities. Let us consider the determination of the size of the basis in more detail.

Two famous English economists, Keynes and Hicks, have argued independently that futures prices (*fp*) for storable commodities should normally be slightly less than the expected spot prices, *E(sp)*, by the amount of an insurance premium they called "normal backwardation."[11] The Keynes-Hicks viewpoint can be represented symbolically as Eq. (20-2).

20-3.3 The Argument About Normal Backwardation

$$fp - E(sp) - \text{a tiny positive "insurance premium"} \qquad (20\text{-}2)$$

Since the *expected spot price* is expected to occur at the *future* delivery date, it can never really be observed and measured. Thus, the Keynes-Hicks hypothesis does not yield to direct empirical testing.

Keynes and Hicks hypothesize that speculators provide a valuable insurance function for hedgers, and thus, hedgers must pay a risk-premium called *normal backwardation* in order to induce speculators to assume the risks associated with providing this insurance. More specifically, Keynes and Hicks argue that hedgers will usually be long the physical commodity and thus hedge themselves with offsetting short positions in the futures markets. This hedging activity, according to Keynes and Hicks, will force speculators, in the *aggregate*, to hold a net long position in futures contracts. Keynes and Hicks reasoned that in order to entice speculators to perenially take the net long positions that they envisioned, the futures markets would have to allow speculators to buy futures at prices that were slightly below their expected spot price. The difference between the futures price and the expected spot price is the insurance premium paid by the hedgers to the speculators. Stated differently, the normal backwardation theory implies that there is a positive net cost for hedgers to use the futures markets.

Mr. C.O. Hardy has suggested that the Keynes-Hicks theory is wrong. In contrast to Hicks and Keynes, Hardy argues that futures prices should normally be at a slight premium over the expected spot prices.[12] Mr. Hardy hypothesizes[13] that special types of "speculative insurance" have been developed to meet the need for

---

11 J.M. Keynes, *A Treatise on Money*, vol. II, and also *The Applied Theory of Money* (London: Macmillian, 1924). J.R. Hicks, *Value and Capital*, 2d ed. (Oxford: Clarendon, 1946), chaps. IX and X, expecially pp. 136–139.

12 C.O. Hardy and L.S. Lyon, "The Theory of Hedging," *Journal of Political Economy*, April 1923, vol. 31, no. 2, pp. 276–287.

13 C.O. Hardy, *Risk and Risk Bearing*, Chicago, 1923, pp. 67–69.

protection against various types of loss where no proper distribution of risk can be obtained. In this type of contract, a large group of private insurers enters into a contract by which they agree to recompense the insured for his loss, dividing the cost between themselves. If the individual insurer writes many policies, and none are large, he secures a combination of risks that protect him against excessive loss. But there is a large speculative element involved in fixing the premium rates.

Mr. Hardy's speculators are like gamblers who are willing to pay for the opportunity to gamble. Furthermore, it appears as if Mr. Hardy's speculators view futures markets as being somewhat like gambling casinos that exist for their enjoyment. As a result, Hardy hypothesizes that speculators will bid futures prices up above what they actually expect the spot prices to be in the future. Mr. Hardy's hypothesis is summed up by Eq. (20-3).

$$fp = E(sp) + \text{a tiny ''gamblers fee''} \tag{20-3}$$

Some of the opponents of Mr. Hardy argue that his view is inappropriate for futures prices because diversification is not very useful at reducing the insurer's risk exposure against *systematic* fluctuations in futures prices. Thus, the situation envisioned by Mr. Hardy is not economically self-perpetuating.

Professors Telser[14] and Cootner[15] formulated empirical tests that were intended to discern whether futures prices were biased estimates of their expected spot prices. However, the results of these tests are not decisive. Thus, the debate about whether futures prices normally lie a little above or a little below their expected spot prices is still unresolved. Fortunately, the amount of this discrepancy is a modest amount for any given commodity contract.

20-3.4 The Relationship Between Spot and Futures Prices

The market prices for storable commodities conform to Eq. (20-4) when the markets are normal.

$$fp_t \leqslant sp_0 + tC \tag{20-4}$$

where

fp_t = the market price of a futures contract that provides delivery t time periods in the future

sp_0 = the current (that is, at time $t = 0$) market price of a spot contract

C = the total carrying cost for the commodity for one month. This varies from commodity to commodity, but it is the sum of items like the following: (1) storage costs, (2) insurance, (3) insect spray,

---

14 Lester G. Telser, ''Future Trading and the Storage of Cotton and Wheat,'' *Journal of Political Economy*, June 1958, vol. LXV, pp. 233–255. Telser was not testing Hardy's hypothesis; his study was instead directed at disproving the normal backwardation theory of Keynes and Hicks.

15 Paul H. Cootner, ''Returns to Speculators: Telser versus Keynes,'' *Journal of Political Economy*, no. 4a, August 1960, vol. LXVIII. See also Cootner's ''Rejoinder'' to Telser's ''Reply,'' in the same issue. A recent piece of evidence supporting the Hicks-Keynes position was reported by Eric C. Chang, ''Returns to Speculators and the Theory of Normal Backwardation,'' *Journal of Finance*, March 1985, vol. 40, no. 1, pp. 193–208.

(4) interest expense (either direct or imputed) for financing the inventory, plus (5) whatever else is appropriate, minus (6) the commodity's convenience yield (if any exists)

t = the number of months the commodity is stored for future delivery

Note the inequality sign in Eq. (20-4). The inequality implies that futures prices cannot normally rise above the combination of spot prices plus the carrying costs. This inequality results from the fact that current inventories can be carried into future months for consumption at a later date merely by paying the carrying cost. On the other hand, the reverse is not possible. Future harvests cannot be consumed before they are harvested. Therefore, futures prices for storable commodities increase by the amount of the monthly carrying costs each month under normal market conditions.

The logic of inequality (20-4) can be extended to explain the difference between the prices of two futures contracts on the same storable commodity that have different expiration (or delivery, or unwinding) dates. Under normal market conditions, inequality (20-5) can be used to establish limits on the spot-futures price relationship.

$$fp_{t2} \leqslant fp_{t1} + C(t_2 - t_1) \tag{20-5}$$

The time period subscript t_2 is assumed to occur further in the future than time subscript t_1 so that $t_2 > t_1$. Thus, the quantity $(t_2 - t_1)$ measures the time difference between the expiration dates of the two futures contracts.

If inequality (20-5) was ever violated (namely, if it were reversed), profit-seekers would quickly and profitably restore its integrity by simultaneously performing the following transactions at the instant the violation is observed (some time before t_1). (1) Take a long position in the futures contract for delivery at time period t_1. (2) Take a short position in the contract for delivery at time t_2. (3) Take delivery at time t_1 at price fp_1 and store the commodity for C cents per month per bushel (or barrel, or pound, or whatever is appropriate). (4) At time t_2 deliver the stored commodity at a price of fp_2 to reap a certain profit. (5) Keep doing this transaction for as many times as you can because you will earn a riskless profit until such time as inequality (20-5) is restored. Actually, this five-step arbitrage process is such an easy "money pump" that Eq. (20-5) is not frequently violated.

The one-period rate of return from purchasing a futures contract in period t and selling it in period $t + 1$ is defined in Eq. (20-6). Essentially, the rate of return is the rate of price fluctuation. The price of the futures contract in period t is denoted p_t.

**20-3.5
One-Period
Futures
Returns and
Margins**

$$r_t = \frac{p_{t+1} - p_t}{p_t} \tag{20-6}$$

$$= \frac{\text{net income or loss from price change}}{\text{invested cash capital (that is, 100\% margin)}}$$

Equation (20-6) ignores the broker's commission; commissions should be deducted from the numerator to reduce the holding period return.[16]

Speculators buy and sell futures contracts with the hope of profiting from price changes. They usually never hold a futures contract long enough for the delivery date to arrive. Instead, they trade contracts actively and only make small down payments, called the initial (or original) *margin*, to bind their purchase or sales agreements.[17] Margin requirements are set and enforced by the commodity exchanges to accomplish several objectives. First, margin requirements are supposed to help maintain the integrity of futures contracts and futures traders by limiting their risk exposure. Second, margins are supposed to control the pyramiding of debt that could contribute to a market crash.

All major commodity exchanges in North America require purchasers or short sellers of futures contracts to put up margin money to guarantee that they perform as contracted. *Initial margin* requirements of 5 and 10 percent are common.[18] The initial margin is like a deposit or performance bond that is supposed to be sufficient to guarantee payment by the speculator unless the margined commodity's price falls by more than the maintenance margin on a long position (or rises by more than the maintenance margin on a short position). If adverse price fluctuations decrease the value of the trader's initial margin too much, then the trader receives a margin call to put up additional margin money, which is called the maintenance (or variation) margin.

Maintenance margin or *variation margin* requirements are additional amounts of guarantee money that margin traders may be required to pay to their brokerage to ensure their performance of the futures contract if the price of the commodity fluctuates adversely. For example, if a speculator buys a futures contract long on 5 percent initial margin and then the commodity's price falls 5 percent, the speculator's original margin is wiped out. In this case the broker will ask the speculator to put up some maintenance margin money. If the speculator does not quickly put up the maintenance margin money, the

16 Dusak defines the return in Eq. (20-6); Katherine Dusak, "Futures Trading and Investor Returns: An Investigation of Commodity Market Risk Premiums," *Journal of Political Economy,* December 1973, pp. 1387–1406. Fischer Black, in contrast, argues that it is not possible to define the rate of return for a highly leveraged futures contract in "The Pricing of Commodity Contracts," *Journal of Financial Economics,* January 1976. Returns on margined futures contracts are defined by Zvi Bodie and Victor Rosansky, "Risk and Return in Commodity Futures," *Financial Analysts Journal,* May-June 1980, pp. 38–39. Professor Lester Telser argues that margins affect the rates of return but he does not explicitly show how he thinks they should be measured. L. Telser, "Margins and Futures Contracts," *Journal of Futures Markets,* 1981, vol. 11, no. 2.

17 Commodity brokerages define a client's margin to be equal to the equity value in the client's account. The equity equals the sum of the following amounts: (1) cash, (2) cashlike securities (namely U.S. or Canadian Treasury bills that are left on deposit at the broker's office), and (3) the net total of the unrealized gains on open positions less the unrealized losses (that is, net "paper profits," that may be positive or negative).

18 Note that commodity futures margins are much lower than the common stock margin requirements. Common stock margin requirements were 50 percent while futures margins were about 5 to 10 percent for initial margins in 1987, for instance. Futures margins are always described as a dollar amount per contract rather than a percentage.

broker will liquidate the client's future positions. In order to avoid the losses and ill feelings that can result from a *margin call*, the clearing house requires the broker to do what is called "mark to the market." Then, the broker will, in turn, force the speculator to "mark to the market." A futures trader or futures brokerage firm is said to *mark to the market* when they pay the additional margin money, called the maintenance margin, to keep from having a futures position liquidated to pay off losses.[19]

Varying the use of margins changes futures traders' financial leverage and risk. Equation (20-6) is rewritten as Eq. (20-7) to show mr_t, the one-period rate of return to a margined buyer of a long position when the initial margin is the fraction, $0 < m < 1.0$, of the purchase price.

$$mr_t = \frac{p_{t+1} - p_t}{p_t m_t} \tag{20-7}$$

The variability of return, or risk, in margin trading increases, as shown by Eq. (20-8), as the margin decreases. The r_t term was defined in Eq. (20-6).[20]

$$\text{var}(mr_t) = \left(\frac{1}{m_t}\right)^2 \text{var}(r_t) \tag{20-8}$$

Equation (20-8) shows that trading on $(m = .1 =)$ 10 percent margin increases the margined trader's variance of return $[(1/m)^2 = (1/.1)^2] = 100$ times larger than the nonmargin trader's. Clearly, margin trading can be breathtaking.

20-3.6 Using T-Bills to Meet Margin Requirements

Clients of most commodity brokerages are allowed to give the brokerage either cash or an interest-bearing Canadian or U.S. Treasury bill or some combination of both to meet their margin requirement. This is good for the client and bad for the brokerage. It is bad for the brokerage because the broker loses cash deposits on which no interest was being paid and in its place receives the client's T-Bill, which pays interest to the client rather than to the brokerage. This is good for the client because the brokerage's loss is the client's gain.

Suppose that a commodity investor buys a T-bill and asks the broker to hold it in order to meet the margin requirement. If the commodity client buys T-bills that are worth p_1 and p_2 dollars at the beginning and end of the invest-ment period, respectively, the client has an average of $[(p_1 + p_2)/2]$ dollars

---

[19] Maintenance margins are approximately 75 percent of the initial margins at most commodity brokerage firms; however, this relationship varies from broker to broker. In any event, any time the customer's equity falls below the required maintenance margin, the customer receives a margin call. Maintenance margin is allowed on the Winnipeg Commodity Exchange, but not on the Toronto Futures Exchange. Margins are discussed more fully in Thomas A. Hieronymus, *Economics of Futures Trading*, Commodity Research Bureau Inc., New York, chap. 3, p. 63—a detailed numerical example of how maintenance margins are calculated.

[20] See Mathematical App. B. Theorem B-2, for proof of Eq. (20-8).

invested during that period. Equation (20-9) shows how much income the T-bill will receive during the period if the interest rate on T-bills is the riskless interest rate, denoted R.

$$\text{Interest Income} = R[(p_1 + p_2)/2] \tag{20-9}$$

Equation (20-9) can be combined with Eq. (20-6), as shown in Eq. (20-10). Equation (20-10) defines the total rate of return from both the interest income on the T-bill and the commodity investment for the owner of the margined commodity account; it is noted br.

$$br = \frac{1}{p_t}(p_{t+1} - p_t) + R\frac{(p_1 + p_2)}{2} \tag{20-10}$$

A commodity investor can earn a one-period rate of return from a commodity account in three different ways; they are defined in Eqs. (20-6), (20-7), and (20-10). Equation (20-6) is for a cash (that is, it is like a 100 percent margin) account, and Eqs. (20-7) and (20-10) are appropriate for margin accounts.[21]

20-4 COMMODITY HEDGING

People who wish to limit their losses from an adverse move in commodity prices may do so by hedging. That is, hedgers "cover" themselves in anticipation of an adverse price movement so that they are not later forced to make a disadvantageous purchase or sale. Hedging is not an activity that is designated to maximize profits. Hedging results in less than maximum profits; this is the cost of averting a possible loss. *Hedging* may be defined as arranging (or synchronizing) a requirement to coincide with its fulfillment. There are basically three types of hedges: the so-called "perfect" hedge, a buying hedge, and a selling hedge.

**20-4.1
The So-Called
Perfect
Commodity
Hedge**

Someone who owns identical long and short positions has a position that is sometimes called a *perfectly hedged position* or *perfectly hedged portfolio*.[22] The owner of a perfectly hedged position has contracted to buy and to sell the same goods at the same price at the same time. Thus, future price fluctuations cannot affect holders of a perfect hedge. The owner of a perfectly hedged position is contractually bound to a zero profit and zero loss situation.

21 The mathematical relationship between the three different holding period rates of return for commodity positions is shown below.

$$1.0 + br_t = (1.0 + R_t)(1.0 + r_t)$$

See footnote 16 for more details about the rate of return measure.

22 No commodity futures hedge is a truly perfect hedge. Unavoidable risks called "basis risks" introduce small elements of risk into every commodities hedge. These "basis risks" are explained later in this section, after the concept of the so-called perfect hedge is introduced. Perfect and imperfect hedges are analyzed graphically in Sec. 19-2, starting at p. 510.

Discussions of a perfectly hedged options position may be interpreted to refer to an option hedge ratio of unity, as explained in Sec. 19-5 beginning at p. 525.

For an example of what might be called a perfectly hedged position, consider a hypothetical silverware manufacturer. Suppose that as of July 198X this silversmith owns a futures contract that obligates her to take delivery on 10,000 ounces (two contracts on the New York Comex) of silver in July 198X. Stated differently, the silverware manufacturer is long silver futures to guarantee that needed raw materials will be supplied. Further, suppose that our hypothetical silversmith is also obligated by another futures contract to sell 10,000 ounces of silver in July 198X; she is now short physical silver. This manufacturer is perfectly hedged against changes in the level of silver prices and also is assured of needed supply. In effect, a perfectly hedged position is like having no position or holding cash until such time as the hedge is lifted. Before July 198X, the silverware manufacturer can lift the hedge by taking delivery of the silver needed to produce the firm's product and buying back the July 198X futures contract. If the price level of silver has changed, the profits on one position will be exactly offset by the losses on the other position, and so the silverware manufacturer can neither suffer losses nor enjoy gains from the price change in silver bullion.[23]

Figure 20-5 illustrates the profit from a long and a short position that offset each other to form a perfect hedge.

FIGURE 20-5   Profit graphs of (a) long position, (b) short position, and (c) perfect hedge.

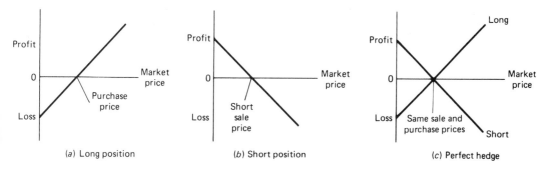

(a) Long position   (b) Short position   (c) Perfect hedge

A *buying hedge* is a purchase of futures to protect against price rises. Many people call a buying hedge a *long hedge*, because the hedger is long the futures contract. Breakfast cereal manufacturers who buy grain commodities, shoe manufacturers who buy hides, and other commodity users frequently use buying hedges to protect themselves from price fluctuations in the commodities that are their raw material. For example, consider the plight of a manufacturer of breakfast cereals who has contracted to deliver fixed quantities of breakfast cereals to supermarkets at a fixed price every month for a year. Essentially, this cereal manufacturer has contracted to be short physical cereal. If the price of the grain used to manufacture the cereal rises above the price for which the cereal manufacturer has contracted to sell it, the cereal

**20-4.2
Buying
Hedges**

---

23 If the silver manufacturer negotiated a sales contract that tied the delivery prices of the finished silverware advantageously above the market price of the raw silver bullion, then the manufacturer has also "locked in" profits and "locked out" price fluctuation risks.

manufacturer would be legally obligated to perform under a contract that entailed losses and perhaps even resulted in bankruptcy. To be free of this risk, the cereal manufacturer need only buy grain futures providing for delivery of the quantity of grain needed to fill the orders at a cost that allows a margin for profit. The cereal manufacturer has thus hedged away the buying risks and can earn the profit needed to survive by concentrating on *manufacturing* cereal efficiently. The speculator who sells the grain futures contract to the cereal manufacturer will bear all the risks of an increase in the price of the grain.

Hedging reduces both potential losses and, unfortunately, potential profits. To see how a hedger's profits are reduced, consider what happens if the price of the hedged commodity falls. If the price of a commodity drops, a hedged buyer (like the cereal manufacturer in the paragraph above) cannot gain from the price decline. The speculator who sold the futures contract captures the profit from a price drop or absorbs the loss from a price rise, respectively, whichever the case may be. Thus, commodity markets allow specialization of the risk-taking function. The manufacturers who use commodities may hedge away their commodity risks and concentrate on manufacturing efficiently, and the commodity speculators can concentrate on forecasting commodity prices and specialize in assuming the risks of commodity price fluctuation; thus, they perform an insurance function.[24]

20-4.3 Selling Hedge

A *selling hedge* (or *short hedge*, as it is also called) involves selling futures to avoid losses from possible price declines on an item carried in inventory. Commodity handlers who buy commodities in the cash markets frequently use selling hedges to protect themselves from losses in inventory values. For example, the operator of a grain elevator may own the tons of grain that are stored in the company facility. Now suppose that during the spring the elevator operator hears rumors that a foreign country is dumping large quantities of grain on the domestic markets. To protect the firm from losses if its inventory falls in value, the elevator operator can sell grain futures to hedge its inventories. By selling grain futures equal in quantity to this inventory at a price that will allow a profit, the grain elevator operator has hedged away some of its selling risks. The speculator who buys the grain futures will assume some of the risks of a price drop.

If the price of the grain in the example above rises in the future, the hedged sellers may not profit from the rising value of their inventories. A selling hedge removes some of the profit from a price rise as well as the possibility of loss from a price fall. There are many risk-averse commodity processors who prefer to earn their income from manufacturing operations rather than commodity speculation and therefore use selling hedges regularly.[25]

---

24 For a theoretical analysis of hedging see L.L. Johnson, ''The Theory of Hedging and Speculation in Commodity Futures,'' *Review of Economic Studies*, vol. 27, no. 3, pp. 139–151.

25 All the incentive to hedge is not subsumed under the aegis of risk-aversion. Many hedges are profitable—in addition to reducing the risk from an adverse price fluctuation. However, since risk-aversion is the central purpose of most hedging activity, the profits to be gained from hedges are not discussed here for the sake of expedition.

Consider how farmers might sell a growing crop before it is harvested to protect themselves from uncertainty. They commonly use the transaction called a selling hedge as a safeguard against losses if the market value of their crop falls. Unfortunately, hedging can also limit the hedged farmer's potential profits if the market value of the crop goes up.

Suppose, for example, a wheat producer named Mr. Brown can profitably produce at least 400 metric tons of wheat if, at the time of planting, he is assured of a price of $200 per metric ton. Farmer Brown expects to harvest his crop in late June, and notices that the present futures price of July wheat on the Winnipeg Commodity Exchange is $200 per metric ton. To assure himself of this price, he decides to sell futures (that is, take a short position in the futures market) for 400 metric tons of wheat. Assume that in June, when Mr. Brown harvests and markets his crop, the cash price of wheat has fallen to $187.50 per metric ton. Since futures and cash prices converge near the contract expiration date, the futures price will also be near $187.50 per metric ton. At the same time that farmer Brown sells his crop in the cash market for $187.50 per metric ton, he executes a buy order in the futures market for the same price, thus cancelling (or reversing) his earlier July contract committing him to delivery in July. He realizes a net gain of $12.50 per metric ton on his futures transactions while the cash market value of wheat was $12.50 per metric ton less than the price upon which he based his planting plans. Excluding the brokerage commissions, the three transactions (the cash sales and the two futures contracts) have the net result that farmer Brown receives the $200 per metric ton he anticipated. This is all summarized in Table 20-3. Note that if farmer Brown had not hedged his harvest against a price change, he would have lost $12.50 per metric ton. Unfortunately, not all hedges are profitable; some only neutralize risk, at best.

TABLE 20-3   ADVANTAGEOUS SELLING HEDGE

IN CASH MARKET		IN FUTURES MARKET		FARMER'S ACTION
October 1, 19X1 Expected harvest: Expected price: (at harvest)	400 metric tons $200/metric ton	October 1, 19X1 Sells: Price:	400 metric tons July futures $200/metric ton	Lays down hedge
July 1, 19X2 Sells: Price: Loss:	400 metric tons $187.50/metric ton $12.50/ metric ton	July 1, 19X2 Buys: Price: Gain:	400 metric tons July futures $187.50/metric ton $12.50/metric ton	Lifts hedge

Hedged position: No net gain or loss from expected price of $200 per metric ton because cash losses equal future gains.

**20-4.4
Disadvanta-
geous Selling
Hedge**

While a well-constructed hedge should always lessen the hedger's risk exposure, few if any hedges are able to totally eliminate all risks. For example,
farmer Brown's hedge, shown in Table 20-3, might not have worked out quite
so advantageously. If the cash price increases during the production season,
as in the similar example shown in Table 20-4, then farmer Brown would be
worse off than if he had not hedged. The important point is that the farmer
has, within fairly narrow limits, protected himself from *downside* price risk
by hedging some fraction of his anticipated crop at the time it was planted.

TABLE 20-4   DISADVANTAGEOUS SELLING HEDGE

IN CASH MARKET		IN FUTURES MARKET		FARMER'S ACTION
October 1, 19X1 Expected harvest: Expected price: (at harvest)	400 metric tons $200/metric ton	October 1, 19X1 Sells: Price:	400 metric tons July futures $200/metric ton	Lays down hedge
July 1, 19X2 Sells: Price: Gain:	400 metric tons $212.50/metric ton $12.50/ metric ton	July 1, 19X2 Buys: Price: Loss:	400 metric tons July futures $212.50/metric ton $12.50/metric ton	Lifts hedge

Hedged position: No net gain or loss from expected price of $200 per metric ton because cash
losses equal future gains.

If farmer Brown had not hedged in the rising market example shown in
Table 20-4, he would have made $12.50 per metric ton additional profit. On
400 metric tons, the possible $5,000 profit was lost because of the disadvan-
tageous hedge.

**20-4.5
Reversing or
Unwinding a
Position**

In both the advantageous and the disadvantageous examples of a selling
hedge above, our wheat farmer, Mr. Brown, lifted the hedge with a *reversing
trade*. That is, farmer Brown purchased another July wheat futures that was
as *similar as could be obtained* to the one that was originally sold. Figure 20-4
illustrates a series of futures trades that might represent the wheat contract's
life. In spite of the fact that the selling hedge may reduce farmer Brown's
risk-exposure to price declines, there are other risks that are still inherent in
every hedge. These risks, called *basis risks*, are listed and defined below. As
a result of any of these four different basis risks, a commodity's basis may
become larger (or smaller) rather than remain constant. If the basis changes,
the hedger can suffer losses (or reap gains) of a few dollars per metric ton.
These losses (or gains) can be substantial over a position of several units (that
is, thousands of metric tons of grain, for example).

1. *Quantity risk.* The unit of measurement used in a futures contract may not correspond to the amount of commodity that has to be hedged. Since the futures contracts are all uniform and cannot be tailormade, the hedged quantities may not always correspond exactly. As a result, any unhedged quantity is exposed to risk.
2. *Quality risk.* An undesirable grade of the commodity may be all that is available for sale in the future market. If so, the party who sold the futures contract will deliver the undesirable grade and be forced to pay a penalty fee to the buyer. Nevertheless, the satisfactory grade of the desired commodity may be unavailable at any price. This possibility could cause the buyer who received the unsatisfactory grade of the commodity considerable expense.
3. *Location risk.* The only futures contracts that are available to be purchased may provide for delivery at an undesirable location. Thus, the buyer could incur unexpected shipping costs that contribute to basis risk.
4. *Expiration date risk.* A futures contract that offers delivery in the month the goods are needed may not exist. For instance, reconsider the example of farmer Brown's July wheat contract from a few paragraphs above. In this case, if a July wheat contract was nonexistent, the wheat farmer would be forced to buy a wheat contract for delivery in the nearest possible month to July. Such a contract might sell at a significantly different price than the desired contract. This price difference is a source of basis risk.

As a result of the four types of basis risks listed above, the perfect hedge is in fact a rarity. The truth is that hedging will reduce the large risks associated with a price-level change but will not always eliminate the four basis risks described above. In fact, the basis risks can be so substantial that some speculators earn their livings by doing what is called *trading on the basis risks*. Of course, the unskilled speculators can also go bankrupt at trading on the basis.

20-5 INFORMATION FOR COMMODITY SPECULATORS AND INVESTORS

Having current information that is accurate can mean the difference between gains or losses to active investors and speculators.[26] Therefore, let us consider some sources of commodity information.

Spot and futures prices are largely determined by supply and demand expectations. Since demand is fairly steady, it is usually not too difficult to forecast. Forecasting commodity supplies is more difficult and requires accurate, up-to-date information. In particular, profitable speculation in commodities requires information about inventories held in storage, current harvests, exports and imports, and any changes in the government's policies that will affect supply. The main sources of commodity information follow.

**20-5.1
Sources of
Information**

26 Michael Gorham, ''Public and Private Sector Information in Agricultural Commodity Markets,'' *Economic Review*, San Francisco Federal Reserve Bank, Spring 1978. Copies of this study of the determinants of grain prices are available free upon request from the bank's research department.

Government Reports   Agriculture Canada and the provincial Ministries of Agriculture and the U.S. Department of Agriculture (USDA) issue periodic crop reports and news bulletins for farm commodities. These reports are released to the public and are quite accurate. The USDA also gathers and publishes information from U.S. embassies abroad about the commodity situation in foreign lands. These foreign agriculture bulletins are typically more accurate than official commodity reports issued by the foreign governments themselves.[27]

The agricultural information disseminated publicly by some foreign governments is sometimes untrue and self-serving. For instance, consider a hypothetical South American country whose main export is coffee. If this hypothetical country experiences a bumper coffee crop one year, that country's government might be tempted to tell public lies and announce to foreign newspapers (in Canada, to make this example more specific) that the coffee crop was expected to be small. The hypothetical country's lies might drive up the price of coffee and help that country's balance of trade and its balance of payments.

Situation Reports   Various magazines discuss the major price-making influences in specific commodities. For example, two of the many situation reports are *The Poultry and Egg Situation* and *The Wheat Situation*. Situation reports are available for every major commodity; they discuss any issue that might affect prices. Since there are so many factors to consider in commodity speculating, most speculators specialize in contracts for only a few commodities. Such speculators would subscribe to the situation reports about the commodities in which they specialize.

Commodity Research Organizations   Some research companies publish newsletters, price analyses, supply and demand statistics, and analyses of current news, and some even publish buy and sell recommendations about commodities. The Commodity Research Bureau in New York City is the largest of these services. However, there are many other commodity advisory services.

Brokerage Houses   Most brokerage houses that handle commodity trading have commodity research departments that issue newsletters to customers. One of the more sophisticated is Friedberg's Commodity and Currency Comments, Friedberg Commodity Management Inc., 347 Bay Street, Toronto, Ontario.

Newspapers   *The Journal of Commerce* has what many people consider to be the best newspaper coverage of commodity market developments; it has an

---

27 G. Gunnelson, W.D. Dobson, and S. Pamperin, "Analysis of the Accuracy of USDA Forecasts," *American Journal of Agricultural Economics*, November 1972. For a review of the price determining factors for all the major commodities, see Perry J. Kaufman, *Handbook of Futures Markets*, a Wiley-Interscience Publication (New York: John Wiley and Sons, 1984). A commodity information company that sells subscriptions for up-to-the-minute price graphs is Commodity Perspective, Suite 1200, 30 South Wacker Drive, Chicago, Ill. 60606.

entire section devoted to commodities. *The New York Times, The Wall Street Journal, and Barron's* publish valuable commodity news, too.

In reading these various sources of information, the commodity speculator should watch for news about factors that can influence commodity prices. The major news items that affect these prices are cited in the following paragraphs.

Changes in the Government's Agricultural Program   Changes in government subsidies, acreage allotments, marketing quotas, export programs, and commodity "loan" programs have a major impact on commodity prices.

International News   International tensions have a strong effect on prices of imported and exported commodities. Currency restrictions, war rumours, or loss of imports can touch off a wave of stockpiling that will send prices skyrocketing.

General Business Conditions   Commodity prices tend to rise and fall with the general price level. Moreover, the level of business activity affects both the inflation rate and the demand for some commodities.

Agricultural Production News   Unusual weather in areas where a commodity is produced can cause changes in the price of the commodity. Planting crop reports should be followed closely for news of changes in the number of hectares under cultivation, news of insect damage, or news of disease in the crop. Harvest reports should be compared with previous expectations to see if the supply and demand expectations upon which current prices are based were correct.

Successful speculation is based on fast and accurate information processing. After all, prices are determined by buyers' and sellers' *expectations.* Only by studying the information that shapes these expectations can speculation be profitable in the long run.

One of the more widely watched commodity futures statistics is called the *open interest.* Many daily newspapers publish both the commodity futures prices, as shown in Fig. 20-6 and Fig. 20-6a and the open interest statistics for every commodity contract, as shown in Fig. 20-7.

When a new futures contract of any kind is originated and the first contract is sold, the open interest advances from zero to one. During the early months of a contract's trading life (of one year for most grain commodities, for example) many contracts are opened, and the open interest soars to become thousands of contracts within a few months. Later, as the contract's delivery date nears, more positions are closed out with reversing trades. Thus, the open interest declines back to zero on the delivery date. Only about a few percent of all the futures contracts that are opened are ever actually delivered; all the rest disappear as reversing trades wipe them out. The typical pattern of a futures contract's lifetime open interest is shown in Fig. 20-8a for several grain contracts.

FIGURE 20-6 Futures price quotations from a representative newspaper.

Futures Prices

Open Interest Reflects Previous Trading Day.

—GRAINS AND OILSEEDS—

CORN (CBT) 5,000 bu.; cents per bu.

	Open	High	Low	Settle	Change	Lifetime High	Lifetime Low	Open Interest
Sept	....	....	....	....	....	....	....	80
Dec	284¼	284¾	282½	283¼	− 1	330	275¼	95,222
Mar85	287¾	288½	286½	287½	− ¾	325½	283¾	25,387
May	290½	292½	290	291¼	− ½	330	289¾	8,176
July	292	293½	291	292¼	....	331	291	7,701
Sept	284	284	282½	283¾	+ ¼	321½	282½	433
Dec	274	275½	273½	275½	+ 1½	295	273½	1,002
Mar86	282½	282½	282½	282½	+ ½	288	282	2

Est vol 25,500; vol Mon 23,912; open int 138,003, +685.

CORN (MCE) 1,000 bu.; cents per bu.

	Open	High	Low	Settle	Change	Lifetime High	Lifetime Low	Open Interest
Dec	284¼	285	282½	283¼	− 1	330	275¼	6,172
Mar85	287¾	288¾	286½	287½	− ¾	325¼	284	671
May	291¾	292¼	290	291¼	− ½	328	290	170
July	292¼	293¼	291	292¼	....	330	291	171
Sept	....	....	....	283¾	+ ¼	315½	285	24
Dec	275¾	275¾	274	275½	+ 1¼	290	274	103

Est vol 650; vol Mon 885; open int 7,311, +141.

OATS (CBT) 5,000 bu.; cents per bu.

	Open	High	Low	Settle	Change	Lifetime High	Lifetime Low	Open Interest
Dec	175¾	177¼	175¾	176¼	− ½	193¼	168½	3,064
Mar85	174½	175½	174½	174¾	− ¾	196½	173	1,152
May	172½	172½	172½	172½	− ½	191	171	320
July	170½	171¼	170½	171¼	+ ¼	178½	169½	143

Est vol 400; vol Mon. 352; open int 4,679, +43.

SOYBEANS (CBT) 5,000 bu.; cents per bu.

	Open	High	Low	Settle	Change	Lifetime High	Lifetime Low	Open Interest
Nov	593	599	590	597½	+ 5¾	772¼	568½	34,983
Jan85	604	609	600	608¼	+ 6½	779	580½	10,484
Mar	615	621	613	619¾	+ 4¼	790½	593½	4,890
May	626	631½	624	631	+ 5¾	797	601	1,806
July	630	635	626½	634½	+ 4¾	799	607	2,657
Aug	628	633	627	633	+ 3	756	610½	292
Sept	621	625	620	625	+ 3	667	605	147
Nov	620	623½	618	623	+ 2	660	602	930

Est vol 35,400; vol Mon 19,763; open int 56,189, +810.

SOYBEANS (MCE) 1,000 bu.; cents per bu.

	Open	High	Low	Settle	Change	Lifetime High	Lifetime Low	Open Interest
Nov	592½	599	590	597½	+ 5¾	772¼	568	11,038
Jan85	603½	609½	600	608¼	+ 6½	779	580	1,038
Mar	615	620½	614	619¾	+ 4¼	788	596	555
May	626	630	625	631	+ 5¾	796½	602	202
July	630	635	628	634½	+ 4¾	798	609	271
Aug	632	632	631	633	+ 3	672⅛	612	50
Sept	....	....	....	625	+ 3	647	624	12
Nov	621⅜	624	620	623	+ 2	660	602	68

Est vol 1,650; vol Mon 2,901; open int 13,234, −497.

SOYBEAN MEAL (CBT) 100 tons; $ per ton.

	Open	High	Low	Settle	Change	Lifetime High	Lifetime Low	Open Interest
Oct	146.00	147.00	145.20	146.90	+ .30	240.00	141.00	12,153
Dec	152.00	153.20	151.50	153.00	+ .40	227.00	148.00	19,808
Jan85	154.60	156.20	154.50	155.80	+ .40	208.00	151.30	8,244
Mar	159.50	161.00	159.00	160.20	+ .50	209.00	155.50	3,609
May	163.70	165.00	163.30	164.00	− .50	205.00	160.00	1,501
July	168.00	168.00	166.50	167.50	− .30	196.50	163.20	948
Aug	167.00	167.00	166.00	166.80	− .70	176.00	163.50	252
Sept	167.00	167.00	166.00	166.00	− .50	175.00	163.00	37
Oct	....	....	....	165.60	− .40	177.00	163.50	36

Est vol 11,000; vol Mon 10,079; open int 46,588, −1,100.

SOYBEAN OIL (CBT) 60,000 lbs.; cents per lb.

	Open	High	Low	Settle	Change	Lifetime High	Lifetime Low	Open Interest
Sept	....	....	....	....	....	....	....	23
Oct	25.00	25.28	25.00	25.28	+ .21	33.05	23.50	14,390
Dec	24.15	24.52	24.13	24.47	+ .24	30.90	22.74	16,861
Jan85	24.05	24.40	24.00	24.37	+ .27	30.50	22.85	5,468
Mar	23.95	24.13	23.85	24.15	+ .23	30.40	22.95	3,516
May	23.80	24.10	23.75	24.00	+ .25	30.10	22.80	1,567
July	23.55	23.80	23.45	23.75	+ .12	30.02	22.70	734
Aug	....	....	....	23.40	− .20	27.00	22.50	250
Sept	....	....	....	23.08	+ .14	24.75	22.50	67
Oct	....	....	....	22.75	....	26.00	22.00	50

Est vol 10,500; vol Mon 11,285; open int 42,926, −513.

WHEAT (CBT) 5,000 bu.; cents per bu.

	Open	High	Low	Settle	Change	Lifetime High	Lifetime Low	Open Interest
Sept	....	....	....	....	....	....	....	1
Dec	352	352½	350½	350¾	− 1¾	418	337½	26,963
Mar85	357½	359	357	357½	− ¾	404	344	9,750
May	355	356½	355	355	− ¾	405	350	3,569
July	340	340¾	339½	339¾	− 1	390	335	1,500
Sept	....	....	....	343½	− 1	376½	340½	83
Dec	355½	355½	355½	355½	− ½	356	355½	1

Est vol 6,300; vol Mon 5,947; open int 41,867, −286.

WHEAT (KC) 5,000 bu.; cents per bu.

	Open	High	Low	Settle	Change	Lifetime High	Lifetime Low	Open Interest
Dec	373¾	374½	373¼	373½	− ¼	397	355	18,523
Mar85	370½	371¾	370	371	+ ¼	407½	362	9,473
May	360¼	361½	359¼	359¾	....	384½	356½	1,135
July	349½	349½	348	348	− ¼	373½	346¼	526
Sept	....	....	....	354	....	358	356¾	2

Est vol 2,879; vol Mon 305; open int 29,659, +213.

WHEAT (MPLS) 5,000 bu.; cents per bu.

	Open	High	Low	Settle	Change	Lifetime High	Lifetime Low	Open Interest
Dec	376¾	378½	376½	378¼	+ 1½	414	366½	4,361
Mar85	384¼	387	384	386¾	+ 2¾	413½	380¾	2,364
May	....	....	....	391½	+ 2½	412	386	390
July	....	....	....	386	+ 1	407	381	43

Est vol 1,436; vol Mon 1,628; open int 7,158, −93.

WHEAT (MCE) 1,000 bu.; cents per bu.

	Open	High	Low	Settle	Change	Lifetime High	Lifetime Low	Open Interest
Dec	352½	352½	350¼	350¾	− 1¾	408¾	340	5,676

	Open	High	Low	Settle	Change	Lifetime High	Lifetime Low	Open Interest
Dec	65.00	65.29	64.90	65.17	+ .21	78.40	64.43	12,109
Mar85	66.55	66.95	66.55	66.84	+ .25	79.35	66.36	5,591
May	67.65	68.00	67.65	67.90	+ .20	79.20	67.60	580
July	69.10	69.15	69.00	69.05	+ .15	79.85	68.70	728
Oct	69.50	69.50	69.50	69.55	+ .40	77.50	69.20	55
Dec	69.90	69.90	69.67	69.85	+ .10	73.00	69.67	620
Mar86	....	....	....	70.36	+ .06	70.60	70.60	6

Est vol 1,500; vol Mon 1,798; open int 20,792, −122.

ORANGE JUICE (CTN)—15,000 lbs.; cents per lb.

	Open	High	Low	Settle	Change	Lifetime High	Lifetime Low	Open Interest
Sept	....	....	....	....	....	....	....	603
Nov	181.60	181.70	180.15	181.00	− 1.35	185.65	107.50	3,125
Jan85	182.20	182.80	181.10	182.60	− .55	185.60	109.00	3,269
Mar	182.25	182.95	181.30	182.90	+ .15	185.50	118.50	1,777
May	182.10	182.80	181.60	182.80	− 1.00	185.00	151.00	974
July	182.00	182.00	182.00	183.15	+ .15	184.80	155.00	665
Sept	180.50	180.50	180.00	180.50	− .90	181.50	165.00	142
Nov	179.00	179.00	179.00	179.90	....	181.00	164.50	46

Est vol 1,500; vol Mon 2,478; open int 10,601, +167.

SUGAR—WORLD (CSCE)—112,000 lbs.; cents per lb.

	Open	High	Low	Settle	Change	Lifetime High	Lifetime Low	Open Interest
Oct	3.90	4.05	3.87	4.04	+ .03	15.30	3.80	14,330
Jan85	4.60	4.80	4.59	4.75	+ .09	13.10	4.41	1,024
Mar	5.15	5.30	5.13	5.30	+ .08	13.60	4.94	47,702
May	5.52	5.70	5.49	5.70	+ .15	10.50	5.25	9,734
July	5.82	6.05	5.81	6.05	+ .17	9.95	5.57	3,380
Sept	6.15	6.40	6.15	6.40	+ .21	9.75	5.86	274
Oct	6.30	6.55	6.30	6.54	+ .19	9.05	6.03	5,869
Jan86	6.75	6.75	6.69	6.85	+ .15	7.45	6.45	82

Est vol 13,570; vol Mon 8,483; open int 82,395, −2,253.

SUGAR—DOMESTIC (CSCE)—112,000 lbs.; cents per lb.

	Open	High	Low	Settle	Change	Lifetime High	Lifetime Low	Open Interest
Nov	21.45	21.45	21.45	21.45	− .01	22.19	21.43	1,142
Jan85	21.55	21.62	21.55	21.61	+ .07	22.20	21.54	2,104
Mar	21.80	21.80	21.76	21.79	+ .02	22.30	21.70	3,400
May	21.97	21.99	21.95	21.97	....	22.40	21.75	1,740
July	22.10	22.15	22.10	22.13	+ .03	22.43	21.85	2,064
Sept	22.10	22.10	22.10	22.10	....	22.23	21.90	1,071
Nov	21.94	21.97	21.94	21.95	− .05	22.15	21.90	1,784
Jan	22.00	22.00	22.00	22.00	+ .02	22.00	21.95	10

Est vol 413; vol Mon 610; open int 13,315, +160.

—METALS & PETROLEUM—

COPPER (CMX)—25,000 lbs.; cents per lb.

	Open	High	Low	Settle	Change	Lifetime High	Lifetime Low	Open Interest
Sept	56.20	56.20	56.00	56.05	− .40	90.80	54.95	89
Oct	56.00	56.00	56.00	56.05	− .45	61.45	56.00	50
Dec	57.50	57.70	56.90	57.35	− .40	92.70	55.90	47,933
Jan85	....	....	....	57.95	− .40	92.00	57.05	270
Mar	59.25	59.50	58.90	59.15	− .40	93.20	57.75	18,306
May	60.45	60.45	60.30	60.30	− .40	92.50	59.45	6,064
July	61.45	61.45	61.45	61.45	− .40	88.25	60.25	3,470
Sept	62.65	62.75	62.50	62.60	− .40	82.10	61.15	3,564
Dec	64.70	64.70	64.15	64.35	− .45	84.25	63.20	1,950
Jan86	....	....	....	64.90	− .45	84.20	69.50	73
Mar	66.30	66.30	66.25	66.05	− .45	80.00	64.70	695
May	....	....	....	67.15	− .45	74.00	66.20	397
July	68.50	68.60	68.50	68.25	− .45	72.55	68.50	231

Est vol 6,500; vol Mon 7,983; open int 83,092, +714.

GOLD (CMX)—100 troy oz.; $ per troy oz.

	Open	High	Low	Settle	Change	Lifetime High	Lifetime Low	Open Interest
Sept	345.50	345.50	345.50	345.70	+ .20	354.80	334.50	9
Oct	345.00	346.80	344.50	345.90	+ .10	597.00	335.50	8,272
Dec	351.20	353.30	351.20	352.40	+ .10	608.00	341.60	47,437
Feb85	357.50	359.50	357.20	358.90	+ .10	522.00	348.00	26,921
Apr	363.50	366.00	363.50	365.30	+ .20	514.50	355.00	26,644
June	371.90	371.90	371.90	372.20	+ .20	510.00	362.70	16,463
Aug	379.00	379.00	379.00	379.10	+ .20	485.00	370.00	7,750
Oct	....	....	....	386.30	+ .20	493.00	377.00	3,321
Dec	393.40	393.40	393.00	393.80	+ .20	489.50	383.90	5,476
Feb86	401.00	401.00	401.00	401.60	+ .20	485.50	392.00	3,710
Apr	....	....	....	409.40	+ .20	496.80	401.80	2,123
June	....	....	....	417.90	+ .20	433.50	407.00	504

Est vol 23,000; vol Mon 36,834; open int 148,630, +467.

PLATINUM (NYM)—50 troy oz.; $ per troy oz.

	Open	High	Low	Settle	Change	Lifetime High	Lifetime Low	Open Interest
Sept	....	....	....	324.50	+ 2.80	356.00	320.50	0
Oct	322.00	326.00	321.50	325.20	+ 2.60	463.00	316.50	4,980
Dec	....	....	....	330.70	+ 2.60	337.50	332.00	2
Jan85	330.70	335.00	330.50	334.40	+ 2.70	447.00	325.00	7,273

	Open	High	Low	Settle	Change	Lifetime High	Lifetime Low	Open Interest
Nov	126.20	129.20	125.30	127.30	+ 1.50	229.00	120.20	4,314
Jan85	137.00	139.00	135.50	137.70	+ 1.70	221.30	130.30	1,913
Mar	147.50	149.30	146.30	147.90	+ 1.20	220.40	139.30	965
May	156.30	157.70	155.30	156.10	+ .40	225.00	147.40	298
July	165.00	166.20	164.50	166.00	+ .50	230.50	153.00	284
Sept	170.60	171.70	170.50	171.10	+ .80	197.50	157.50	200
Nov	173.60	174.60	173.60	174.00	....	186.10	167.30	66
Jan86	....	....	....	181.50	....	182.00	176.50	13

Est vol 3,154; vol Mon 2,023; open int 8,020, −147.

—FINANCIAL—

BRITISH POUND (IMM)—25,000 pounds; $ per pound

	Open	High	Low	Settle	Change	Lifetime High	Lifetime Low	Open Interest
Dec	1.2345	1.2405	1.2330	1.2375	− .0085	1.5100	1.2145	16,483
Mar85	1.2400	1.2445	1.2360	1.2405	− .0090	1.5170	1.2155	598
June	....	....	....	1.2440	− .0095	1.3050	1.2240	26
Sept	....	....	....	1.2490	− .0095	1.2735	1.2450	7

Est vol 4,951; vol Mon 7,005; open int 17,114, +898.

CANADIAN DOLLAR (IMM)—100,000 dlrs.; $ per Can $

	Open	High	Low	Settle	Change	Lifetime High	Lifetime Low	Open Interest
Dec	.7584	.7584	.7574	.7580	−.0003	.8048	.7451	5,264
Mar85	.7577	.7577	.7550	.7573	−.0005	.8050	.7443	1,364
June	.7574	.7574	.7574	.7573	−.0005	.7835	.7483	185

Est vol 569; vol Mon 1,093; open int 6,813, −27.

JAPANESE YEN (IMM) 12.5 million yen; $ per yen (.00)

	Open	High	Low	Settle	Change	Lifetime High	Lifetime Low	Open Interest
Dec	.4111	.4118	.4108	.4114	−.0019	.4663	.4074	17,362
Mar85	.4175	.4175	.4165	.4167	−.0019	.4695	.4133	598
June	.4225	.4230	.4218	.4230	−.0019	.4570	.4205	107
Dec		....	....	.4355	−.0019	.4483	.4370	3

Est vol 5,546; vol Mon 10,268; open int 18,070, −81.

SWISS FRANC (IMM)—125,000 francs-$ per franc

	Open	High	Low	Settle	Change	Lifetime High	Lifetime Low	Open Interest
Dec	.4008	.4033	.4008	.4031	−.0021	.5000	.3938	18,290
Mar85	.4078	.4098	.4073	.4096	−.0021	.5035	.3995	496
June	.4160	.4160	.4145	.4160	−.0021	.4900	.4102	58
Sept	.4200	.4215	.4195	.4215	−.0020	.4830	.4175	11
Dec	.4275	.4280	.4260	.4280	new	.4280	.4260	0

Est vol 12,693; vol Mon 16,967; open int 18,855, −1,372.

W. GERMAN MARK (IMM)—125,000 marks; $ per mark

	Open	High	Low	Settle	Change	Lifetime High	Lifetime Low	Open Interest
Dec	.3305	.3313	.3289	.3303	−.0042	.4080	.3204	34,422
Mar85	.3355	.3355	.3333	.3348	−.0043	.4110	.3244	1,241
June	.3400	.3405	.3395	.3401	−.0044	.3710	.3338	86
Sept		....	....	.3460	−.0045	.3460	.3424	1

Est vol 20,795; vol Mon 30,633; open int 35,750, −1,191.

EURODOLLAR (LIFFE)—$1 million; pts of 100%

	Open	High	Low	Settle	Change	Lifetime High	Lifetime Low	Open Interest
Dec	88.61	88.76	88.59	88.74	+ .07	89.36	85.92	5,767
Mar85	88.33	88.48	88.32	88.46	+ .03	88.85	85.49	3,014
June	88.06	88.25	88.03	88.19	+ .02	88.58	85.66	1,512
Sept		....	....	87.97	+ .02	88.39	85.50	424

Est vol 3,803; vol Mon 3,631; open int 10,717, +151.

STERLING DEPOSIT (LIFFE)—£250,000; pts of 100%

	Open	High	Low	Settle	Change	Lifetime High	Lifetime Low	Open Interest
Dec	89.65	89.71	89.59	89.71	− .01	90.91	88.13	3,147
Mar85	89.61	89.67	89.60	89.70	− .02	90.86	87.85	1,456
June	89.49	89.59	89.47	89.55	− .05	90.60	87.94	457

Est vol 986; vol Mon 1,017; open int 5,108, −87.

LONG GILT (LIFFE)—£50,000; pts of 100%

	Open	High	Low	Settle	Change	Lifetime High	Lifetime Low	Open Interest
Sept	106-16	107-05	106-14	107-05	+ 0-15	109-12	97-27	617
Dec	105-28	106-18	105-22	106-17	+ 0-16	108-31	97-06	1,990
Mar85		....	....	105-28	+ 0-15	108-19	96-21	41
June	105-06	105-06	105-06	105-25	+ 0-15	105-26	96-17	101
Sept		....	....	108-28	+ 0-15	101-01	99-00	0

Est vol 2,929; vol Mon 1,802; open int 2,749, +39.

EURODOLLAR (IMM)—$1 million; pts of 100%

	Open	High	Low	Settle	Chg	Yield Settle	Yield Chg	Open Interest
Dec	88.39	88.48	88.36	88.37	− .03	11.63	+ .03	40,406
Mar85	88.11	88.21	88.07	88.09	− .04	11.91	+ .04	22,035
June	87.92	87.92	87.76	87.77	− .07	12.23	+ .07	11,157
Sept	87.62	87.65	87.51	87.51	− .07	12.49	+ .07	3,174
Dec	87.38	87.41	87.27	87.27	− .06	12.73	+ .06	1,994
Mar86	87.19	87.20	87.06	87.07	− .05	12.93	+ .05	209
June	86.95	87.00	86.88	86.90	− .04	13.10	+ .04	11

Est vol 17,965; vol Mon 19,000; open int 78,985, +202.

GNMA 8% (CBT)—$100,000 prncpl; pts. 32nds. of 100%

	Open	High	Low	Settle	Chg	Yield Settle	Yield Chg	Open Interest
Sept	....	....	....	....	....	....	....	159
Dec	67-08	67-14	66-29	66-31	− 7	13.846	+ .052	7,725
Mar85	66-15	66-20	66-05	66-06	− 7	14.034	+ .053	2,260
June	65-25	65-25	65-14	65-14	− 8	14.218	+ .062	679
Sept	....	....	....	64-27	− 9	14.365	+ .070	196
Dec	64-25	64-25	64-10	64-10	− 9	14.499	+ .071	310
Mar86	64-09	64-09	63-27	63-27	− 9	14.619	+ .072	344
June	63-27	63-27	63-15	63-15	− 9	14.715	+ .072	522

Est vol 2,500; vol Mon 2,169; open int 12,195, +45.

TREASURY BONDS (CBT)—$100,000; pts. 32nds of 100%

	Open	High	Low	Settle	Chg	Yield Settle	Yield Chg	Open Interest
Sept	....	....	....	....	....	....	....	18,092
Dec	67-13	67-21	66-30	66-30	− 12	12.547	+ .071	134,655
Mar85	66-25	67-02	66-11	66-12	− 12	12.655	+ .072	22,388
June	66-11	66-18	65-28	65-28	− 12	12.753	+ .073	6,734
Sept	65-27	65-28	65-15	65-15	− 12	12.833	+ .074	6,001
Dec	65-15	65-25	65-03	65-03	− 13	12.908	+ .081	7,721
Mar86	65-11	65-14	64-25	64-25	− 13	12.971	+ .082	6,482

CBT—Chicago Board of Trade; CME—Chicago Mercantile Exchange; CMX—Commodity Exchange, New York; CRCE—Chicago Rice & Cotton Exchange; CSCE—Coffee, Sugar & Cocoa Exchange, New York; CTN—New York Cotton Exchange; IMM—International Monetary Market at CME, Chicago; KC—Kansas City Board of Trade; LIFFE—London International Financial Futures Exchange; MCE—MidAmerica Commodity Exchange; MPLS—Minneapolis Grain Exchange; NYFE—New York Futures Exchange, unit of New York Stock Exchange. NYM—New York Mercantile Exchange; WPG—Winnipeg Commodity Exchange.

FIGURE 20-6a Canadian futures price quotations.

WINNIPEG COMMODITY EXCHANGE GRAIN

—Contract— High Low		High	Low	Settle	Chg.	Open Int.
WHEAT — 20 metric tons; $ a ton						
262.70 75.80 Dec		96.50	82.50	95.90	− 1.20	2,264
245.50 77.50 Mar		95.00	81.50	94.40	− .60	2,968
279.00 79.00 May		95.00	82.70	94.30	− .50	1,533
104.00 81.00 Jul		81.00	81.00	94.50	− .40	75
85.00 85.00 Oct		83.50	83.50	83.50	− 1.50	
Wed.'s sales 1,046.						
Wed.'s open int 6,840, up 198.						
OATS — 20 metric tons; $ a ton						
85.50 75.60 Dec		82.90	82.30	82.50	− .80	313
83.00 75.60 Mar		81.50	81.40	81.50	+ .10	532
82.00 77.80 May				80.80	+ .10	87
81.50 81.00 Jul		81.00	81.00	81.00		
Wed.'s open int 932.						
BARLEY — 20 metric tons; $ a ton						
99.50 80.30 Dec		83.60	83.30	83.40	− .50	2,522
91.40 81.50 Mar		82.90	82.40	82.50	− .30	4,329
89.90 83.00 May		83.00	82.70	82.70	− .50	1,053
855.00 83.00 Jul		83.20	82.20	83.80	+ .50	420
85.00 85.00 Oct		83.50	83.50	83.50	− 1.50	
Wed.'s sales 905.						
Wed.'s open int 8,324, off 111.						
RAPESEED — 20 metric tons; $ a ton						
352.00 137.90 Nov		252.20	249.50	249.50	− 3.50	1,157
354.90 224.30 Jan		261.50	254.00	254.10	− 3.60	18,977
318.50 245.00 Mar		262.50	260.00	260.00	− 3.70	7,530
291.50 240.70 Jun		271.70	269.00	269.00	− 3.50	625
281.00 265.00 Sep				279.00	− 3.00	95
Wed.'s sales 5,600.						
Wed.'s open int 28,384, off 1,134.						
FLAXSEED — 20 metric tons; $ a ton						
325.00 227.10 Dec		236.50	233.20	233.40	− 3.60	1,973
287.60 235.70 Mar		243.50	241.70	241.90	− 3.20	1,763
280.00 241.70 May		247.70	247.00	247.00	− 2.90	225
253.00 250.50 Jul				252.00	− 1.00	2
Wed.'s sales 2,294.						
Wed.'s open int 3,963, off 140.						

—Contract— High Low		High	Low	Settle	Chg.	Open Int
RYE — 20 metric tons; $ a ton						
127.40 96.00 Dec		98.00	96.60	98.00	+ .70	1,252
111.40 95.50 Mar		101.50	101.20	101.50	+ .70	1,195
105.50 97.00 May				101.80	+ .50	297
102.00 102.00 Jul		102.30	102.30	102.30	+ .30	50
Wed.'s sales 210.						
Wed.'s open int 2,794, up 27.						

TORONTO FUTURES EXCHANGE

—Contract— High Low		High	Low	Settle	Chg.	Open Int.
TSE 300 COMPOSITE INDEX; 10 times index **Change of 1 index point equal to $10 a contract**						
	SPOT 3070		3054	3070	+ 10	
3150 2966 Nov 86	3074		3070	3068	− 4	434
3093 2976 Dec 86	3078		3076	3075	− 2	136
3083 3045 Jan 87				3081	+	163
3081 3081 Feb 87				3086	+	18
3106 3094 Mar 87	3106		3106	3096	+ 5	10
closing				3070.8	+ 10.1	
sales 638						
prev day open interest 753 + 129						
91-DAY TREASURY BILLS **$1-million; multiples of 1 cent**						
91.45 91.10 Dec 86	.00		.00	91.50	+ .00	24
sales						
prev day open interest 24						
GOVERNMENT OF CANADA BONDS II **9% $100,000 princ.; price is % of par value**						
98 − 16 88 − 08 Sep 86	− 00		− 00	− 00	− 00	
96 − 06 86 − 16 Dec 86	− 00		− 00	95 − 06	− − 11	30
sales						
prev day open interest 30 − 1						

FIGURE 20-7 Statistics on open interest from a representative newspaper.

Open Interest

Wednesday, August 30
(Changes from Tuesday)

WHEAT (CBT): Sept. 5,278, Dec. 23,196, March'79, 8,842, May 7,297, July 2,166. Sept. 10. Total: 46,789, down 459. **CORN**: Sept. 10,415, Dec. 59,230, March'79, 25,692, May 10,426, July 3,507, Sept. 172. Total: 109,442, down 2,710. **OATS**: Sept. 1,060, Dec. 5,254, March'79, 1,033, May 923, July 6. Total: 8,276, up 150. **SOYBEANS**: Aug. 1, Sept. 6,271, Nov. 35,983, Jan.'79, 18,574, March 17,172, May 12,922, July 6,070, Aug. 834. Total: 97,827, up 493. **SOYBEAN MEAL**: Sept. 4,441, Oct. 12,111, Dec. 18,882, ... 4,719, Mar... 1,067. Aug.

1,785, Dec. 348. Total ... up 1,264. **FEEDER CATTLE**: Aug. 8, Sept. 1,620, Oct. 4,565, Nov. 3,703, Jan.'79, 1,817, March 2,517, April 2,108, May 2,223, Aug. 4. Total: 28,609, down 498. **EGGS**: Sept. 671, Oct. 94, Nov. 112, Dec. 390, Jan.'79, 14, Feb. 9. Total: 1,290, down 91. **HOGS**: Aug. 7, Oct. 5,442, Dec. 5,486, Feb.'79, 2,361, April 1,863, June 633, July 299, Aug. 139, Oct. 86, Dec. 5. Total: 16,-

321, down 97. **FROZEN PORK BELLIES**: Aug. 16, Feb.'79, 5,805, March 1,281, May 259, July 125, Aug. 104. Total: 7,590, up 88. **LUMBER**: Sept. 2,579, Nov. 2,692, Jan.'79, 1,685, March 749, May 309, July 18. Total: 8,032, down 48. **TREASURY BILLS**: Sept. 2,901, Dec. 5,257, March'79, 4,817, June 5,174, Sept. 4,714, Dec. 5,298, March'80, 3,550, June 2,590. Total: 34,301, up 781.

MAINE POTATOES: Nov. 2,241, March'79, 2,305, April 558, May 6,417. Total: 11,521, down 43. **COCOA**: Sept. 299, Dec. 2,516, March'79, 1,368, May 640, July 264, Sept. 125, Dec. 196. Total: 5,408, up 208. **WORLD SUGAR NO. 11**: Sept. 1,139, Oct. 10,840, Jan.'79, 117, March 14,205, May 4,323, July 1,562, Sept. 831, Oct. 1,188. Total: 34,205, up 100. **COFFEE**: Sept. 294, Dec. 1,687, March'79, 1,085, May 469, July 253, Sept. 57, Oct. 55. Total: 3,900, down 2. **COTTON**: Oct. 3,590, ... March'79 ... 1,345.

942, May ... July 27,926, Sept. ..., Dec. 31,... Jan.'80, 12,571, March 10,837, May 2,517. Total: 212,996, down 1,828. **SILVER** (CBT): Aug. 18, Sept. 28, Oct. 8,069, Nov. 1, Dec. 12,729, Feb.'79, 24,790, April 46,464, June 37,850, Aug. 35,954, Oct. 23,570, Dec. 13,030, Feb.'80, 8,719, April 5,841, June 5,369, Aug. 3,064, Oct. 509, Dec. 321, Feb. 6. Total: 226,332, down 293.

FIGURE 20-8   (a) Average open interest and time to maturity for grains; (b) Average volume and time to maturity for grains.

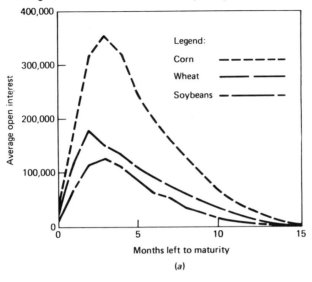

(a)

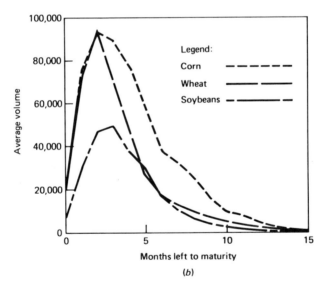

(b)

Source: Nikolaos T. Milonas. "Liquidity Price Variability, and Storage Asymmetry: Prices in Futures Markets." Ph.D. dissertation. Baruch College, City University of New York, 1984.

Figure 20-8*b* illustrates the average volume of contracts traded per month for the same three grain contracts shown in Fig. 20-8*a*. Note that there is a high positive correlation between the monthly average open interest and the monthly average volume of contracts traded for any specific commodity futures contract. Similar patterns also exist for other commodity futures contracts.

During the life of a futures contract the futures price rises and falls in unison with the underlying commodity's cash (or physicals) price. Throughout these positively correlated price fluctuations, however, the futures price remains above the cash price by the amount of the carrying charges in normal markets. However, as the delivery date nears, the futures price converges with the cash price. This occurs because as the futures contract expires, it becomes a substitute for holding the physical commodity. Even after the contract expires and the commodity is delivered, however, the futures prices and the cash prices are still affected by carrying costs because many futures traders "roll their hedges forward" again and again rather than take delivery on them. Restated in market vernacular, the "basis strengthens" (that is, the basis shrinks) in a normal market as the delivery date draws nearer, but the cash and the futures prices still co-vary closely. Finally, on the last permissible delivery date (when the contract will cease to exist), the futures price converges with the cash price because the basis reflects almost nothing except an allowance for the tiny remaining carrying costs. Essentially, the spot and the futures prices interact so closely that they are determined simultaneously. Figure 20-9 illustrates how futures prices and spot prices move together through time for a storable commodity.

FIGURE 20-9   Market prices of oats contracts with different delivery dates.

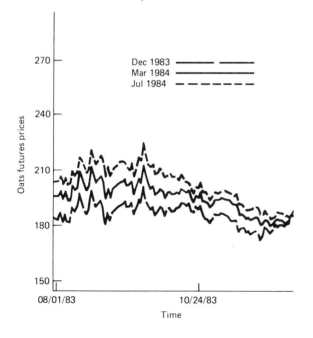

To see the manner in which spot and futures prices are determined simultaneously, consider a hypothetical example of some commodity that is easily stored, such as coffee, sugar, cocoa, or cotton. Imagine that this year's new crop of, say, coffee is very small. Nearly all coffee comes from Latin America. The scarcity could occur for several reasons: if international trade relations

20-5.4 The Simultaneous Determination of Spot and Futures Prices

with Latin America become poor because of political tensions; if foreign exchange restrictions were raised by Latin America; if Latin American revolutionaries burned the coffee crop; or if the coffee crop was wiped out by insects, drought, disease, or flood, existing inventories would have to last until the next new crop became available. Current coffee inventories would become more valuable as soon as news arrived that the new crop would not be forthcoming.

The rise in spot prices would decrease current coffee consumption and cause coffee processors to process their supplies more carefully to minimize waste. Speculators would bid up coffee futures prices in order to profit from expected price rises. Coffee futures, as a result, would stay at a premium above the rising spot prices, and higher premiums would provide for higher coffee storage expenses. As a result, coffee inventories would receive unusually good care. Some coffee inventories might be moved to better leakproof, fireproof, humidity-controlled storage facilities and would be treated with insect repellent. Thus, the current supply would be conserved. Spot and futures prices could rise until consumption was cut back to a level that existing inventories could be expected to meet. Then supply and demand would be equated in both the spot and futures markets, and coffee prices would stabilize at a new higher level.

The speculators who were first to obtain, interpret, and act upon the news indicating that future commodity supplies would be decreased would earn a speculative profit. By buying both spot and futures contracts before the news spread and prices were bid up, they would obtain inventories of the spot commodity and futures contracts that could later be sold at a profit (after news of the shortage spread and prices were bid up).

20-6 DIVERSIFICATION AND COMMODITY RETURNS

Unsystematic risk was defined (in Chap. 10) as variability of return caused by factors that are unique to an asset; it is *diversifiable* risk. Since the prices of many commodities are primarily influenced by natural disasters (such as droughts, floods, and insect hordes), the weather during the growing season, and political considerations (such as wars, import quotas for foreign goods, and space allotments for domestically grown commodities), there is a good reason to suspect that commodity prices are independent of security prices, which are mainly determined by business earnings and other financial factors. In order to evaluate the degree of interdependence between commodity returns and the returns from a diversified stock market index, the characteristic line and its related statistics were estimated. The characteristic line in risk-premium form was employed; it is shown below as Eq. (20-11).

$$r_{it} - R_t = A + B(r_{mt} - R_t) + u_{it} \qquad \text{for } E(u_{it}) = 0 \qquad (20\text{-}11)$$

The dependent variable in Eq. (20-11) is the excess of the ith spot commodity's one-period rate of return, Eq. (20-6), over the riskless rate (namely, a 15-day Treasury bill rate) in the tth time period. The explanatory variable is the risk-premium for Standard & Poor's 500 Composite Stock Index rate of return in time period t. Two-week time periods were employed in calculating all returns. The regression intercept of A and the slope coefficient of B are simple regression statistics. The u_{it} term is an unexplained residual return that has an expected value of zero.

Dr. Katherine Dusak estimated Eq. (20-11) over the lives of different futures contracts on corn, soybeans, and wheat during a sample period from 1952 to 1967.[28] Over the different contracts for each of these commodities the highest beta systematic risk statistic she found had a value of only $b = .119$. Practically none of the beta coefficients she estimated by regressing the spot commodity returns onto the stock market average returns was significantly different from zero. Moreover, the largest coefficient of determination she found had a value of only $R^2 = .011$; it was for the same soybean contract that had the highest beta. This soybean statistic of $R^2 = .011$ suggests that at least $(1.0 - .011 - .989 =)$ 98.9 percent of the total risk of most agricultural commodities is unsystematic risk. This type of risk can be easily diversified away to zero in a portfolio of diversified common stocks and commodities. Thus, common stock investors who are seeking the risk-reducing benefits of diversification would be well-advised to consider putting some of their investment funds into commodities.

Over the different commodity investments that she examined, Dr. Dusak found that the commodity spot contracts earned average rates of return that were only about as large as the riskless rate of return, R. This is the rate of return that the capital asset pricing model (CAPM) suggests is appropriate for market assets with beta values of approximately zero (a reassuring piece of evidence for those who may wonder if the risk-return analysis is appropriate for commodity analysis). This finding, however, also has implications for commodity speculators who may hope to "get rich quick" in the commodity markets. It suggests that only those few commodity speculators who do their homework carefully and then exercise their trades expeditiously can expect to earn rates of return above what they could earn by putting their money in a riskless savings account. That is, commodity speculation does not appear to be a likely place for reckless playboys who hope to "strike it rich" and "get something for nothing" merely by gambling in commodities. Only the experts with years of experience who work hard can expect to enjoy large returns from commodity speculation.

20-7   IS COMMODITY SPECULATION HARMFUL?

"Speculation" is a word that has undesirable connotations to some people who do not understand speculation and who may erroneously identify it with

28 Katherine Dusak "Futures Trading and Investor Returns: An Investigation of Commodity Market Risk Premiums," *Journal of Political Economy*, December 1973, pp. 1387–1406. See Dusak's table 3 for the beta estimates. The characteristic line in risk-premium form used by Dusak is very similar to the traditional characteristic line in one-period rates of return that is explained above in Chap. 10. The characteristic line in risk-premiums is explained by M.C. Jensen, "Risk, the Pricing of Capital Assets, and the Evaluation of Investment Portfolios," *Journal of Business*, April 1969.

market corners or similar activities. Market corners are socially and economically undesirable. These and other price manipulation schemes use the brute force of centrally controlled wealth to destabilize prices so that a few unethical people can profit therefrom; such results are clearly not beneficial. In fact, laws have been passed making the obviously harmful commodity price manipulation schemes and fraud illegal in Canada. On the other hand, the legal forms of speculation discussed here are socially and economically desirable. Consider the costs and benefits to the community that result from speculation.[29]

**20-7.1
Speculation
May
Destabilize
Prices**

Only one issue has been seriously suggested by economists considering the undesirable effects of futures and options speculation, that is, price destabilization. There is an unresolved academic debate on this point.[30] Some economists have argued that profitable speculation in commodities or other investments must stabilize the price of the asset. In essence, this group argues that, to earn a profit, the speculator must "buy low and sell high" and that this activity will be stabilizing. Purchases made at low prices, such as point L in Fig. 20-10, will tend to drive prices up, and sales at high prices, like point H, will tend to lower prices. The overall effect of such speculation will be to (1) maximize speculators' profits and (2) stabilize prices. It is reasoned that speculators who do not "buy low (L) and sell high (H)" will remain a near-bankrupt, nonpowerful force and that their destabilizing effects will be small.

FIGURE 20-10   Graph of price fluctuations across time.

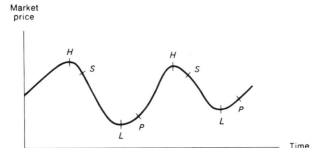

29 A study of financial futures which found no price destabilization was reported by Kenneth C. Froewiss, "GNMA Futures: Stabilizing or Destabilizing," *Economic Review*, Spring 1978, Federal Reserve Bank of San Francisco, pp. 20–29.

30 M. Friedman, "In Defense of Destabilizing Speculation," in R.W. Pfouts, *Essays in Economics and Econometrics*, pp. 133–141; W.J. Baumol, "Speculation, Profitability and Stability," *Review of Economics and Statistics*, August 1957; L.G. Telser, "A Theory of Speculation Relating Profitability and Stability," ibid., August 1959, pp. 295–301; W.J. Baumol, "Reply," ibid.; J.L. Stein, "Destabilizing Speculation Can Be Profitable," ibid., August 1961. More recently, studies have been published providing new evidence that speculation is a beneficial social activity. See William L. Silber, "Marketmaker Behavior in an Auction Market: An Analysis of Scalpers in Futures Markets," *Journal of Finance*, September 1984, vol. 39, no. 4, pp. 937–953. See also Robert Forsythe, Thomas R. Palfrey, and Charles R. Plott, "Futures Markets and Informational Efficiency: A Laboratory Experiment," *Journal of Finance*, September 1984, vol. 39, no. 4, pp. 955–981.

The second group of economists disagrees. They assert that it is possible for speculation to be both profitable and destabilizing at the same time. These economists assert that purchases can be made after prices have started to rise (at points like purchase point P in Fig. 20-10), which accents the price rise. They also point out that sales can be made after prices have started to fall (at points like sale point S in Fig. 20-10), causing prices to fall faster and perhaps further. Yet as long as the purchase price is below the sales price, symbolically, $P<S$, a speculative profit will result. In this case, speculation will be both profitable and destabilizing.

Unnecessarily unstable prices are undesirable because they increase business executives' uncertainty, frustrate planning, discourage long-range investment programs, and cause capital to be allocated to projects that yield only short-run profits with very little risk. Furthermore, as speculators destabilize the prices of futures contracts, this might destabilize the prices in the cash markets for the commodity.

Unfortunately, no empirical tests have been published to substantiate either the claim that speculation is destabilizing or the claim that it is a stabilizing influence. The conclusion that can be drawn is that speculation can destabilize prices if the speculator is not adept at maximizing profit (that is, buying at or near the lowest price and selling at or near the highest price). However, such inept speculators will probably not become very powerful in the price formation process.

Several desirable economic benefits result from speculation. For example, society enjoys the following benefits from speculation:

20-7.2 Socially Desirable Effects of Speculation

1. Consumption is expeditiously allocated over time.
2. Some risks may be hedged away.
3. Publicly available forecasts are contained in futures prices.
4. Prices adjust more efficiently.
5. Resources are allocated more efficiently.
6. Active markets provide liquidity for traders.
7. Arbitrage helps ensure uniform prices.

These points are advantageous in the following ways:

Allocation of Consumption Over Time   Commodities and most investments are items that may be used either now or later. The price at which an item is expected to sell later, relative to the current price, will largely determine when the item is used. For example, if the premium on some commodity exceeds its carrying costs, it will be profitable to stockpile the commodity for use later.

Speculators prepare the forecasts and conduct the activity that help determine spot and futures prices. Thus, speculators help allocate consumption over time. It is fairly well recognized that futures speculators are necessary to keep farm prices from dropping to near zero at harvest time (that is, during the new-crop month), to store goods for the future, and to sell goods at reasonable prices long after the harvest and during years when the harvest is poor.

Risks Hedged Away   In the preceding pages, buying hedges and selling hedges were discussed. It was explained how futures contracts are utilized by risk-averters to hedge away risk. Speculators can relieve business executives of their buying and selling risks and leave them free to concentrate on efficient production. Thus, speculation allows separation and specialization of the risk-bearing function, and thus expedites efficient production.

Public Forecasts Speculators' fortunes depend on their ability to forecast. As a result, professional speculators devote considerable time, expense, and efforts to forecasting the supply of and demand for commodities and other investments. Such speculators actively search out news. Any new information contains a profit potential if it will affect the price of an asset in which they are prepared to speculate. After the new information becomes public and prices adjust accordingly, the information is worthless to the speculators' efforts to earn a profit. Therefore, in order to maximize their profits, speculators act upon such new information *immediately*.

Speculators' forecasts and news discoveries enable them to make timely profit-oriented purchases and sales. As a result, the prices of speculative assets reflect the latest information — frequently even before it reaches the news media. These prices are widely published. Therefore, the general populace may avail itself of a free, up-to-the minute, expert forecast of the future price of any commodity simply by observing the published prices of futures contracts.

Efficient Price Adjustment Efficient prices may be defined as prices that react immediately and continuously to all relevant information so that prices at every instant fully reflect the latest relevant facts. Efficient prices are characterized by continuous, unpredictable moves. Although seasonal or other trends may be evident in efficient prices, the day-to-day price changes should be random as they adjust to the random arrival of news.

Although unnecesary price movement of the type caused by price manipulation is undesirable, the price movement characterizing efficient markets is valuable. Only if prices reflect all the latest information about supply and demand may resources be allocated in such a manner as to maximize society's welfare. Efficient prices may overreact or underreact to any given piece of information. Nevertheless, it is essential that prices react continuously as they pursue an ever-changing equilibrium price. Efficient prices may be imperfect estimates of equilibrium prices (or, if you prefer, the intrinsic economic value of the commodity), but they are *unbiased* estimates that fluctuate around the equilibrium price. Since stable equilibriums with constant prices are impossible in this world of uncertainty, efficiently fluctuating prices are the best that can be hoped for.

Efficient prices are partially the result of profit-maximizing speculators. These persons will uncover the relevant facts about supply and demand and act upon them without delay in an effort to maximize their profits.[31] This action causes continuous, unbiased price adjustments.

Efficient Resource Allocation The supplies of resources that are available in the world at any time are limited. If these resources are not allocated in

31 Aggressive forecasting and news prospecting do not necessarily earn a profit for the speculator. These activities are necessary merely to avoid bankruptcy. Only the experts will profit from their forecasts. Empirical research suggesting that commodity prices are random has

an optimum manner, the welfare of society cannot attain its full potential. In order for these limited resources to be allocated to the proper place at the proper time, they must be mobile and must react swiftly to changing demands.

In a market such as that in Canada, resources tend to go to the highest bidder. Thus efficient resource allocation requires (1) efficient prices and (2) resources that may be readily shifted between places and time periods. The activities of speculators facilitate these needs by (1) making prices adjust in an efficient manner and (2) making inventories available when and where demand is high.

Liquidity for Traders   The existence of a commodity market provides a place where commodity producers, speculators, and users all can meet and enjoy free entry and exit (perhaps through their brokers) to the market. If the trading activity on the commodity exchange is flourishing, liquidity (of both long and short positions) is increased.[32] This liquidity reduces cash budgeting problems and frees business executives to transact their primary business.

Arbitrage to Ensure Uniform Prices   As explained before, if the prices of a given commodity sold in different markets differ by more than the transportation costs between the two markets, arbitrage will bring the prices together. A speculator can buy the commodity in the market where its price is low and simultaneously sell it where the price is high. This transaction will yield a riskless profit and may be continued until the two prices differ by no more than the transportation costs between the two markets. A uniform price between markets will ensure that a commodity is not in excess supply and that it is not being wasted in one place because its price is low while the same commodity is in short supply in another place.[33]

---

been published. R.A. Stevenson and R.M. Bear, "Commodity Futures: Trends or Random Walks," *Journal of Finance*, March 1970. T.F. Cargill and G.C. Rausser, "Time and Frequency Domain Representations of Futures Prices as a Stochastic Process," *Journal of the American Statistical Association*, March 1972. S. Smidt, "A Test of the Independence of Price Changes in Soybean Futures," *Food Research Institute Studies*, 1965, vol. 5, no. 2. A.B. Larson, "Measurement of a Random Process in Futures Prices," *Food Research Institute Studies*, 1960, vol. 1, no. 3. D.J.S. Rutledge, "A Note on the Variability of Futures Price," *Review of Economics and Statistics*, 1976, vol. LVIII, no. 1, pp. 118–120. P.A. Samuelson, "Is Real-World Price a Tale Told by the Idiot of Chance?" *Review of Economics and Statistics*, 1976, vol. LVIII, no. 1, pp. 120–123. Thomas Cargill and Gordon C. Rausser, "Temporal Price Behavior in Commodity Futures Markets," *Journal of Finance*, September 1975.

32 William L. Silber, "Marketmaker Behavior in an Auction Market: An Analysis of Scalpers in Futures Markets," *Journal of Finance*, September 1984, vol. 39, no. 4, pp. 937–953.

33 Pure arbitrage can be defined as taking identical long and short positions at the same time and in the same quantities so that the resulting position involves no risk. Quasi-arbitrage involves selling items from an existing portfolio in order to obtain the funds to buy similar but different goods in an equivalent portfolio at a lower price. For an example of quasi-arbitrage in the financial futures markets see Richard J. Rendelman, Jr., and Christopher E. Cabrini, "The Efficiency of the Treasury Bill Futures Market," *Journal of Finance*, September 1979, vol. 34, no. 4, pp. 895–914. Quasi-arbitrage is just as useful as pure arbitrage at stopping equivalent goods from selling at different prices. See Sec. 19-2 for more information about arbitrage.

**20-7.3
Speculation
Is Beneficial**

The preceding review of the undesirable and desirable effects of commodity speculation points fairly clearly to the conclusion that speculation is beneficial to the public welfare. The probability does exist that prices will occasionally be destabilized by some speculator who ineptly tries to maximize profits. However, this seems to be a small cost to pay in comparison with the benefits society derives from speculation.

QUESTIONS

1. Compare and contrast selling a futures contract without owning an inventory in the commodity and selling a common stock short.
2. What functions are performed by the clearing house in a commodity futures contract?
3. Define an inverted market and suggest how it might occur.
4. "Futures prices are determined after spot prices are known. Adding carrying costs to spot prices yields futures prices." Is this statement true, false, or uncertain? Explain.
5. Explain what a selling hedge is, and give an example.
6. "Speculation is an evil pastime for wealthy playboys. It destabilizes prices and misallocates resources, and it should be declared illegal." True, false, or uncertain? Explain.
7. The following data are reported on the commodity prices of wheat futures:

June	$3.49 per bushel
September	$3.57
December	$3.69¼
March	$3.81½
May	$3.88
June	$3.75⅞
September	$3.84

   From these data, estimate (a) the cost of storing a bushel of wheat per month and (b) the month in which wheat is harvested. Explain how you obtain these estimates.
8. Explain why there are no futures markets for coal, raisins, and salt. Does the absence of such markets mean that no speculation in these commodities occurs?
9. If wheat futures were selling at $3 per bushel and some event occurred which changed wheat's new equilibrium price to $3.50 per bushel, what would this do to trading in the relevant wheat future?
10. Assume that you are hired by the Toronto Futures Exchange (TFE) to manage its New Products Committee. You are directed to do research to discern new commodities in which the TFE might advantageously initiate trading in futures contracts. List and explain six criteria you would adopt for screening commodities in order to select high-volume possibilities for the TFE to consider trading.

11. Define and discuss the determinants of the basis in commodity trading.
12. What factors prevent any hedge from being a perfect hedge? Explain.
13. Define the one-period rate of return for a commodity investor who purchased a futures contract on margin and gave the commodity broker a Treasury bill to hold as the margin.

SELECTED REFERENCES

Hore, John E. *Trading on Canadian Futures Markets*. 2d ed. Toronto, Ontario: The Canadian Securities Institute, 1985. A descriptive text on futures trading in Canada. The focus is on the characteristics of Canadian futures contracts. Students will find the examples of hedging with futures contracts particularly useful

Kaufman, Perry J. *Handbook of Futures Markets*. New York: Wiley-Interscience, John Wiley and Sons, 1984. A thick volume that discusses a comprehensive range of commodity topics nonmathematically.

Labys, W.C. and C.W.J. Granger. *Speculation, Hedging and Commodity Price Forecasts*. Lexington, Mass.: Heath, Lexington Books, 1970. An econometric study of commodity price fluctuations.

Peck, Anne E. *Selected Writings on Futures Markets*, vols. 1 and 2. Chicago Board of Trade, 1977. These two volumes contain scholarly articles that were compiled by Anne Peck of the Food Research Institute at Stanford University. The first volume contains only papers written by Dr. Holbrook Working. The second volume contains papers by selected writers. Mathematics is used in most of the papers. The Chicago Board of Trade has also prepared other volumes.

Pring, Martin J. *The McGraw-Hill Handbook of Commodities and Futures*. New York: McGraw-Hill, 1985. A comprehensive text on the nature and mechanics of futures trading. Considerable detail is provided on the fundamental and technical analysis of most major commodities.

Tewles, R.J., H.L. Stone, and C.V. Harlow. *The Commodity Futures Game*. New York: McGraw-Hill, 1977. A nonmathematical textbook that explains various facets of commodity futures trading.

Appendix 20A

Fundamental Determinants of Storable Agricultural Commodity Prices

This appendix supplements the material in Chap. 20 with an explanation of the principal factors that determine the market prices of storable agricultural commodities and their futures contracts.[34]

APP. 20A-1 ANALYSIS OF SPOT PRICES

The market prices of spot commodities are determined by the demand for and the supply of the physical commodity.[35] For agricultural commodities the supply comes from essentially two aggregate sources:

1. Harvests (H) of new crops
2. Inventories (I) carried forward in storage

The demand for commodities comes from two types of aggregated needs:

1. Consumption (C) demand
2. Demand for a storable quantity (Q) for inventory

The market for a given spot commodity is in static equilibrium when the prices have no tendency to change because the aggregate supply of physicals (that is, $H + I$) equals the aggregate demand for physicals (that is, $C + Q$), as shown in Eqs. (App. 20A-1a) and (App. 20A-1b).

$$\text{Supply} = \text{Demand} \qquad\qquad \text{(App. 20A-1a)}$$

$$H + I = C + Q \qquad\qquad \text{(App. 20A-1b)}$$

At any given instant in time the aggregate supply of a commodity is a constant; this is illustrated in Fig. App. 20A-1 by the vertical supply function denoted S_0. The aggregate demand function, in contrast to the inelastic supply function, is negatively sloped to indicate that consumption increases at lower prices. At harvest time the quantity of a given physical commodity that is available increases by H units (such as bushels or barrels or whatever unit is used to measure quantity). This is represented in Fig. App. 20A-1 by the rightward shift of the before-harvest supply function, denoted S_0, to the after-harvest supply function S_1. The demand function is presumed to remain fixed through time because the commodity is consumed at a rate that is an unchanging function of the commodity's price.

---

34 This appendix draws heavily on Paul Samuelson, ''Intemporal Price Equilibrium: A Prologue to the Theory of Speculation,'' *Weltwirtschaftliches Archiv*, 1957, vol. 79, pp. 181–219, reprinted in *Collected Scientific Papers of Paul A. Samuelson*, vol. II, edited by J.E. Stiglitz, MIT Press, 1966, chap. 73, pp. 946–984.

35 This section draws on J.L. Stein, ''The Simultaneous Determination of Spot and Future Prices,'' *American Economic Review*, December 1961, pp. 1012–1025.

590

FIGURE APP. 20A-1   Static equilibrium analysis of a commodity harvest.

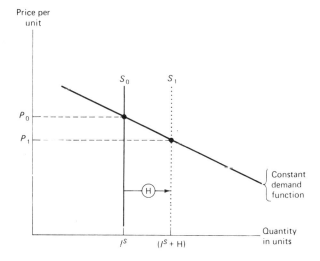

In order to present clear-cut examples of how the price of a given commodity fluctuates as the quantity available for sale varies, some simplifying assumptions are necessary. Assume that

1. The aggregate demand function shown in Fig. App. 20A-1 never shifts.
2. An aggregate quantity of H units of the commodity is harvested each year.
3. The entire harvest is gathered on July 15 of each year.
4. A carrying cost of four cents per bushel per month is incurred regardless of how many bushels of the given commodity are stored.
5. Speculators will buy the commodity and carry it in their inventory to earn a speculative profit if, and only if, they expect the commodity's price to increase by at least the carrying charge (of 4 cents per bushel per month).
6. The price of the commodity will not rise more than an amount equal to the carrying charge per period for the commodity because, if it did, speculators, in order to maximize their profits, would buy all the commodity and hold it for later sale at a higher price until none was left for sale. As a result of this hoarding, the price would be quickly bid up until storing more inventory was no longer profitable. Sales would then resume at a new, higher price level, and this price would then increase slowly at a normal rate per month equal to the carrying charge.
7. Finally, risk and uncertainty are assumed away. This allows clear-cut graphs to be drawn; the graphs need not have the wild and erratic price fluctuations caused by uncertain transactions that are later reversed in a world confused by uncertainty.

Dynamic Analysis of Equal Annual Harvests

Figure App. 20-2*a* and *b* illustrates how the aggregate quantity of the commodity carried in inventory and the market price of the spot commodity will vary together under the preceding seven simplifying assumptions. Figure App. 20A-2*a* shows that the *aggregate inventory* increases by H bushels on the harvest day of July 15 each year and then is consumed at a steady rate. Figure App. 20A-2*b* shows that the commodity's *price* drops each year on July 15 when the new crop increases the aggregate supply. Then, after July 15, the

FIGURE APP 20A-2   The interaction of price and aggregate inventory for a commodity with equal annual harvests: (a) aggregate inventory; (b) price per unit.

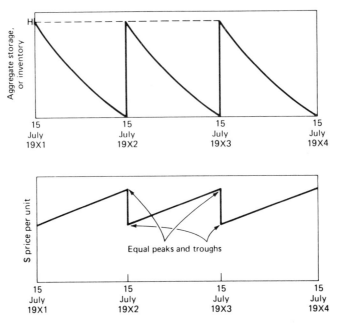

market price rises steadily by 4 cents per bushel per month until the next harvest. Figure App. 20A-2a and b depicts the simplest possible case. Next consider what happens if the size of the harvest changes every year; this is a more complex case.

Dynamic Analysis of Increasing Harvests

Let the second simplifying assumption be changed as indicated in Eq. (App. 20A-2).

$$H_t = H_{t-1} + h \qquad \text{(App. 20A-2)}$$

Equation (App. 20A-2) suggests that the size of each year's harvest increases by h bushels. This modified assumption means that the vertical supply functions in Fig. App. 20A-1 shift further to the right at each harvest. This more realistic situation is analyzed in Fig. App. 20A-3a and b.

Figure App. 20A-3a illustrates how the aggregate inventory increases, on July 15 of each year, to a new peak that is h bushels higher than the previous inventory peak. The commodity's price reacts to this situation by falling to a new lower level each year on July 15 and then rising steadily by 4 cents per bushel per month until the next harvest. However, each year's price peak is lower than the previous year's peak because each year's aggregate supply available for sale is larger.

FIGURE APP. 20A-3   The interaction of price and aggregate inventory for a commodity with increasing annual harvests: (a) aggregate inventory; (b) price per unit.

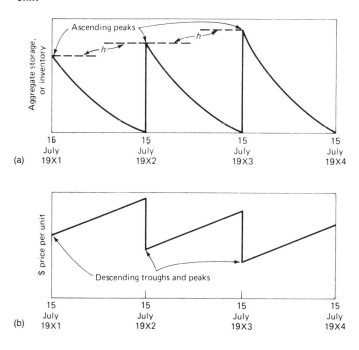

To analyze what may happen if each year's harvest decreases, Eq. (App. 20A-2) is rewritten as Eq. (App. 20A-3).

$$H_t = H_{t-1} - h \qquad\qquad \text{(App. 20A-3)}$$

Dynamic Analysis of Decreasing Annual Harvests

Equation (App. 20A-3) suggests that each harvest's vertical supply function in Fig. App. 20A-1 shifts further to the left as the successive harvests dwindle in the face of unchanging demand. Figure App. 20A-4a and b illustrates one possible outcome from successively smaller harvests that occur while demand is invariant.

Figure App. 20A-4a shows that the amount of commodity carried forward increases to a series of successively lower peaks at each year's harvest. However, it is also assumed that, because of one or both of the two following reasons, the aggregate inventory levels never fall all the way to zero.

Minimum Inventory Maintained

1. Speculators never let their inventories fall all the way to zero in case some natural catastrophe (for example, locusts or a drought) destroys the growing crop and causes the commodity's price to skyrocket and yield large profits as their inventory appreciates.

FIGURE APP. 20A-4   The interaction of price and aggregate inventory for a commodity with decreasing harvests and inventory carryover: (a) aggregate inventory; (b) price per unit.

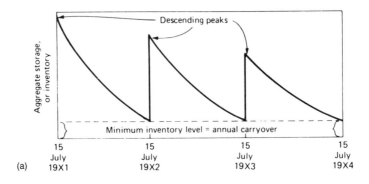

(a)

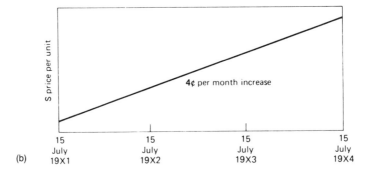

(b)

2. Some commodity processors always maintain a minimum inventory level in order to keep their production lines running without delays in case some shortages develop. That is, the commodity processors obtain some "convenience yield" from carrying minimum levels of inventory and thus are willing to incur some losses if necessary in order to maintain a minimum inventory level.[36]

As a result of the continual existence of some inventory carry-over into each new year's ever-tightening supply situation, the price of the commodity increases steadily by 4 cents per bushel per month year after year. The price does not fall at harvest time because the price speculators, who expect continued price gains, and/or the commodity processors, who obtain a convenience yield from maintaining their inventories, buy the entire harvest at current prices and store it for the future at a cost of 4 cents per bushel (or whatever the unit may be) per month.

If Inventory Can Fall to Zero

If it is assumed (1) that there are no price speculators to buy and hold inventories in the hope of earning profits and (2) that no one obtains a convenience yield from maintaining some minimum level of inventory, then the inventory level can fall to zero. In this case, Fig. App. 20A-5a and b (rather than Fig.

36 The concept of a convenience yield was developed by Nicholas Kaldor, "Speculation and Economic Stability," *Review of Economic Studies*, 1939, vol. VII, p. 6.

FIGURE APP. 20A-5   The interaction of price and aggregate inventory for a commodity with decreasing harvests and zero inventory carryover: (a) aggregate inventory; (b) price per unit.

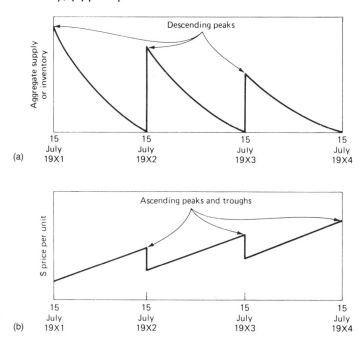

App. 20A-4a and b) illustrates the results of decreasing harvests. Figure App. 20A-5a shows a series of descending aggregate inventory peaks as each year's smaller harvest is gathered. Moreover, after each year's harvest, all the commodity carried in storage is consumed before the next harvest. As a result, the price rises steadily by the amount of the carrying charge each month, as shown in Fig. App. 20A-5b. Then on July 15 of each year, the price drops back in a series of ascending trough prices as the supply situation shrinks each year and demand continues undiminished.

APP. 20A-2   MORE REALISTIC HARVESTS AND STORAGE COSTS

In order to gain realism, consider the effects of relaxing the third and fourth simplifying assumptions while the harvests are constant, as shown in Fig. App. 20A-2a. First, the third assumption is relaxed; later, the fourth will be relaxed too. Instead of assuming that all the harvest occurs on July 15, suppose that it begins on July 15 and continues until August 15. This modifies the example depicted in Figure App. 20A-2a and b to become the more realistic situation illustrated in Figure App. 20A-6a and b.

Figure App. 20A-6a shows that the amount of inventory starts increasing on July 15, when the harvest begins each year. This increase continues every day for one month until the harvest ends on August 15 and the aggregate

Month-Long Harvests

FIGURE APP. 20A-6   The interaction of price and aggregate inventory for a commodity with equal annual month-long harvests: (a) aggregate inventory; (b) price per unit.

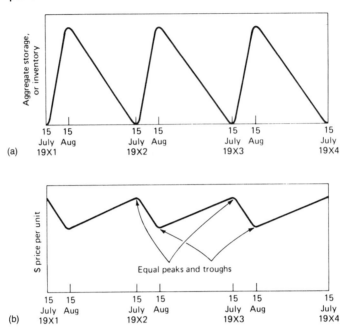

inventory reaches its annual peak. Then the inventory is steadily consumed until it reaches a low point just before the next year's harvest. As a result, the inventory graphed in Fig. 20A-6a reaches *curved peaks* (rather than the pointed peaks caused by the one-day harvests that were illustrated in the preceding figures).

The month-long harvest smooths the inventory fluctuations somewhat, and this in turn dampens the price reactions. Figure App. 20A-6b shows how the commodity's *price fluctuations are smoothed by the longer harvest periods.* Figure App. 20A-6b is more realistic than its counterpart Figure App. 20A-2b, which was developed under the third simplifying assumption that all the harvest occurred on one day. Next, the fourth assumption will be realigned to reflect more realistic circumstances.

Nonconstant Storage Costs

The fourth simplifying assumption, that storage costs are constant, could be represented graphically by a perfectly horizontal line, such as the one shown in Fig. 20A-7a. In fact, the S-shaped curve shown in Fig. App. 20A-7b is more realistic than the simple assumption of a horizontal line.

Figure App. 20A-7b illustrates what is referred to as the *supply-of-storage curve.*[37] It relates the aggregate amount of any given physical commodity that

37 See Holbrook Working, "The Theory of Price of Storage," *American Economic Review*, December 1949, pp. 1254–1262 for the original theory. See M.J. Brennan, "The Supply of Storage," *American Economic Review*, March 1958, for empirical evidence.

FIGURE APP. 20A-7 Two different supply-of-storage functions: (a) constant storage cost per unit; (b) increasing storage cost per unit.

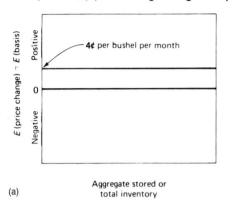

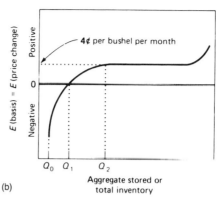

(a)

(b)

is carried in inventory (that is stored) to the basis (that is, the price change) expected for that commodity. The supply-of-storage curve slopes upward to reflect the fact that speculators (such as grain elevator operators) will store more of a commodity when they think its price will increase more rapidly. The curve is horizontal over its midrange because some of the storage space available for wheat can be rented to store corn, for example, without bidding up the rent for storage space. This represents the normal market condition in which the expected basis equals the typical carrying cost for storage (for example, the basis for grain of 4 cents per bushel per month equals the carrying cost for the grain). The right-hand side of the supply-of-storage curve does slope more steeply upward, however, to reflect the fact that large carrying costs—and thus price changes which are large and positive—are necessary to induce price speculators to store large inventories. The most difficult portion of the supply-of-storage curve to explain is the left-hand side.

To the left of the quantity Q_2 the supply-of-storage curve drops down to the point denoted Q_1 because lower-cost storage facilities become available when only small quantities of aggregate inventory are in storage. Then, strange as it may seem, the supply-of-storage curve drops off steeply at quantities below Q_1, into areas where the expected price changes (that is, basis) are negative. This area between the quantities Q_0 and Q_1 indicates that some minimum quantity of aggregate inventory, denoted Q_0, will be carried even if the cost of carrying the inventory exceeds the carrying costs (that is, money is lost in carrying the inventory). The minimum level of aggregate inventory that is maintained in spite of losses on the carrying charges Q_0 is explained by the *convenience yield*. Some commodity processors (for example, food manufacturers who make flour from wheat) maintain some minimum level of inventory at any cost because they find it convenient and economical to keep their production process running smoothly rather than be forced to shut down their plants because of, say, delayed raw material deliveries. This valuable convenience obtained from maintaining minimum levels of inventory is called the convenience yield; it is the reason minimum inventories are maintained even on a loss basis.

FIGURE APP. 20A-8   The interaction of price and aggregate inventory for a commodity with equal annual month-long harvests and increasing storage costs: (a) aggregate inventory; (b) price per unit.

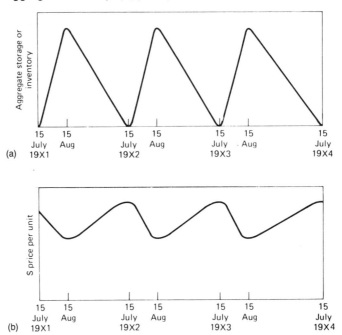

As a result of the nonconstant storage costs indicated by the supply-of-storage curve, it is necessary to modify Fig. App. 20A-6a and b as shown in Fig. App. 20A-8a and b; Fig. App. 20A-8a is similar to Fig. App. 20A-6a. However, Fig. App. 20A-8b differs from Fig. App. 20A-6b because the constant storage cost assumption was dropped. Allowing for the supply-of-storage schedule of Fig. App. 20A-7b causes the commodity prices in Fig. App. 20A-8b to fall less at low inventory levels and rise less at high inventory levels (namely at harvest time) and thus demonstrate smoother curves than the analogous price graph in Fig. App. 20A-6b.

Figure App. 20A-8a and b represents the most realistic examples of aggregate inventory and price interactions for commodities in the spot market that have been developed in this appendix. However, they were drawn with the seventh simplifying assumption, that uncertainty was absent, so that all speculators would visualize the same forecasts of supply, demand, and prices. This seventh assumption can make the price graphs appear deceptively simplistic.

If the *actual market prices* of spot contracts for a given commodity were graphed, the graphs would exhibit random price fluctuation rather than the clear-cut pattern shown in Fig. App. 20A-8b.[38] Compare the spot corn prices

38 T.F. Cargill and G.C. Rausser, "Time and Frequency Domain Representations of Futures Prices as a Stochastic Process," *Journal of the American Statistical Association*, March 1972, pp. 23–30. T.C. Cargill, "Temporal Behavior in Commodity Futures Markets," *The Journal of Finance*, September 1975, vol. 30, no. 4, pp. 1043–1053.

FIGURE APP. 20A-9   Market price fluctuation of corn.

CORN

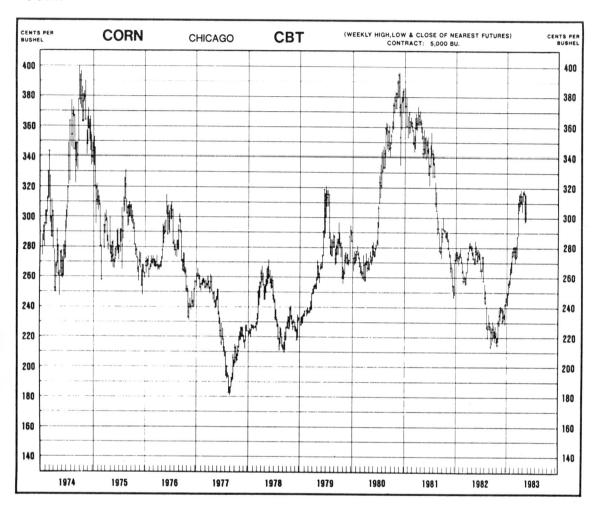

shown in Fig. App. 20A-9 with those shown in Fig. App. 20A-8*b*. The random and sometimes wild price changes visible in graphs of actual commodity prices result from new information about supply and demand conditions that affect the commodity prices in an unpredictable fashion. For example, if news of a drought destroying a growing grain crop or news of a foreign exchange complication that affected coffee prices became public, the prices of the affected commodity would be disrupted and would react instantly to the important news. It is the continual arrival of good and bad news that causes commodity speculators to adjust supply and demand estimates and thus causes commodity prices to resemble the random-walk staggerings of an intoxicated person rather than follow simple seasonal patterns. The prices of both the spot and futures contracts fluctuate randomly together in this manner, as shown in Fig. 20-9 on page 581.

CHAPTER 21

Financial Futures Contracts*

Financial futures contracts are a new category of commodity futures contract; they were first traded in the United States in 1972.[1] They were introduced in Canada in 1980.[2] Financial futures contracts, usually called *financial futures*, have rapidly grown in popularity since their inception. Figure 21-1 illustrates the growth of financial futures trading at the Chicago Board of Trade (CBT). The graph indicates that the aggregate number of T-bond futures, T-note futures, GNMA futures, and options on bond futures grew from 0.5 million contracts in 1977 to 23.7 million contracts in 1983. The cash market value of those 23.7 million contracts was over $2 trillion. Other commodity exchanges also enjoyed soaring rates of growth in new financial futures contracts they introduced during this time period.

FIGURE 21-1   S&P 500 stock index futures contract price quotations from a newspaper excerpt.

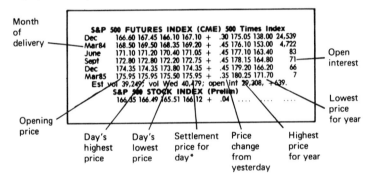

*The settlement price is sometimes the same as the closing price. However, if there were several trades made at the closing bell's ring, then the most representative of these closing prices is selected as the settlement price on which mark-to-the-market computations are calculated for that day.

*Chapter 21 presumes a knowledge of the material in Chaps. 2, 19, and 20. Chapter 21 has an appendix entitled "Options on Futures" that presumes a mastery of Chap. 21.

1 Foreign exchange futures started trading at the International Monetary Market (IMM) of the Chicago Mercantile Exchange in 1972 — the United States' first financial futures contract. Previous to this almost all foreign exchange in the United States was traded informally through an interbank forward market.

2 Ninety-one day Canada Treasury bills, 18-year long-term Canada bonds and year mid-term bond futures contracts were introduced on the Toronto Stock Exchange in 1980. The T-bill and long-term bond (slightly modified) contracts have survived and are currently traded on the Toronto Futures Exchange.

TABLE 21-1   ANNUAL VOLUME OF FINANCIAL FUTURES TRADING ON THE TORONTO FUTURES EXCHANGE, 1980–1986

YEAR	91-DAY TREASURY BILLS	LONG-TERM BONDS 1	LONG-TERM BONDS 2	TSE 300 COMPOSITE INDEX	TSE OIL AND GAS INDEX	TSE 300 SPOT INDEX	TSE OIL AND GAS SPOT INDEX	U.S. DOLLAR	TOTAL
1980	1,242	3,597							4,839
1981	2,018	30,691							32,709
1982	14,774	40,871							55,645
1983	15,820	19,603							35,423
1984	13,312	30,115		19,014				21,865	84,306
1985	9,463	25,224	9,036	25,050	3,307	23,680	424	9,032	105,216
1986	9,802		2,315	51,491	795	75,081	67	18	139,569
Total	66,431	150,101	11,351	95,555	4,102	98,761	491	30,915	457,707

Source: The Toronto Futures Exchange, *Notice To Members,* various months.

In Table 21-1, annual volume of trading on the Toronto Futures Exchange is shown. Although growth from 1980 to 1986 as a percentage has been substantial, total trading volume is extremely light, and at this stage the TFE is best described as a local and minor futures exchange. Canadian speculator interest remains focused on the liquid and active U.S. markets, while Canadian financial futures hedging activity is either extremely modest or also conducted with U.S. financial futures through cross hedges.

21-1 FINANCIAL FUTURES DEFINED

Financial futures are standardized futures contracts whose market prices are established through open outcry and hand signals in a regulated commodity exchange. Like all futures contracts, financial futures represent a legally enforceable commitment to buy or sell a prespecified quantity and quality of a specific financial instrument during a predetermined future delivery month. Unlike the traditional commodity futures contracts, however, delivery is not made in a voluminous physical commodity. Instead, either financial securities or a cash settlement are delivered to fulfill a financial futures contract. The physically small financial security or cheque to be delivered, and also the economic variables that determine the market price of the financial future are two principal factors that differentiate these new contracts from the traditional futures contracts.

Financial futures contracts are traded on the following financial securities, precious metals and economic indexes. The number(s) after each financial futures item refer to one or more of the exchanges, listed below on p. 604, where the contract is traded.

FINANCIAL INSTRUMENTS

Canada
Canadian long-term bonds (15 year) (7)
Canadian T-Bills (91 days) (7)
Canadian T-Bill index (14)

United States
U.S. Treasury bonds (1, 5, 9, 11)
U.S. Treasury notes (6½-10 years) (1)
U.S. Treasury notes (2 years) (1)
U.S. Treasury bills (90-days) (2, 5)
Eurodollar time deposits (3-months) (2, 17)
Municipal bond index (1)
GNMA (cash-settled) (1)
GNMA collateralized deposit receipts (CDR) (1)
Domestic U.S. certificates of deposit (3-months) (2)
5-year U.S. Treasury index (15)

Other
20-year U.K. gilt interest rate (9)
Short gilts (9)

3-month Eurodollar interest rate (9, 11)
3-month sterling interest rate (9)
90-day bank accepted bills of exchange (11)

CURRENCIES

Australian dollar (2, 16)
West German mark (2, 5, 9, 16)
Canadian dollar (2, 5, 16, 17)
French franc (2, 16)
Swiss franc (2, 5, 9, 16)
Dutch guilder (2)
British pound (2, 5, 9, 16, 17)
Japanese yen (2, 5, 9, 16, 17)
U.S. dollar (7, 11)
U.S. dollar index (15)
European Currency Unit (ECU) (2, 15, 16)

STOCK INDEXES

Canada
TSE 300 Composite Index (7)
TSE 300 Composite Spot Index (7)
TSE 35 Index (7)
TSE Oil and Gas Index (7)
TSE Oil and Gas Spot Index (7)

United States
Standard & Poor's 500 Stock Composite Index (3)
Standard & Poor's 100 Stock Index (3)
Standard & Poor's Over-the-Counter Index (3)
Value Line Stock Index (4)
Mini Value Line Stock Index (4)
NYSE Composite Stock Index (6)
NYSE Financial Stocks Index (6)
NYSE Beta Index (6)
Major Market Index-Maxi (1)
NASDAQ-100 Index (1)
National Over-the-Counter Index (16)

OTHER

Financial Times Stock Exchange 100 Index (9)
Nikkei-Stock Index (17)
All-Ordinaries Share Price Index (11)

PRECIOUS METALS

Silver (1, 5, 8, 12)
Gold (1, 5, 8, 10, 11, 12, 17)

Platinum (5, 18)
Palladium (18)

ECONOMIC INDEXES

Consumer Price Index (13)
CRB Futures Price Index (6)

The list of financial futures contracts now being traded is growing rapidly. The financial futures on additional securities and economic indexes that are awaiting approval of various regulatory bodies is almost as long as the list above.

The financial futures contracts listed above are traded at the commodity exchanges listed below. Slightly different versions of the same financial futures contract are traded on more than one exchange in some cases.

1. Chicago Board of Trade
2. International Monetary Market (IMM) of the Chicago Mercantile Exchange
3. Index and Option Market (IOM) of the Chicago Mercantile Exchange
4. Kansas City Board of Trade
5. Mid-America Commodity Exchange
6. New York Futures Exchange (NYFE)
7. Toronto Futures Exchange
8. Winnipeg Commodity Exchange
9. London International Financial Futures Exchange (LIFFE)
10. International Futures Exchange (INTEX) of Bermuda
11. Sydney Futures Exchange Ltd. (of Australia)
12. Commodity Exchange (COMEX) in NYC
13. New York Coffee, Sugar and Cocoa Exchange (NYCSC)
14. Montreal Exchange
15. New York Cotton Exchange
16. Philadelphia Board of Trade
17. Singapore International Money Exchange (SIMEX)
18. New York Mercantile Exchange

21-2   FINANCIAL FUTURES CONTRACTS ON MARKET INDEXES

In February 1982, the Kansas City Board of Trade introduced the Value Line Index futures contract, a contract for future settlement of a portfolio of about 1,700 underlying stocks. Shortly after, the Chicago Mercantile Exchange began trading the Standard and Poor's 500 Stocks Composite Index (S&P 500), and the New York Futures Exchange introduced the NYSE Composite Index future. In October 1982, the Toronto Stock Exchange received permission from the Ontario Securities Commission to begin trading a futures contract based on a ten-share equally weighted portfolio. The contract was an abysmal failure, since virtually no trading interest developed, speculative or otherwise, and was quickly withdrawn. In 1984, the Toronto Futures Exchange introduced a new index futures contract, the TSE Composite Index Futures. Let us investigate this ingenious new financial future because it is interesting both in its own right and as a way to learn about financial futures in general.

Some investors feel more adept at forecasting the trend of the stock market's average price than they do at selecting individual issues. These investors may take one of two basic positions with the TSE 300 futures contract.

21-2.1 Long or Short the Contract?

1. Bullish traders should buy the TSE 300 futures contract — that is, they should take a *long position*. If their optimistic expectations are borne out, they will profit in proportion to the increase in the index's value.
2. Bearish investors should sell the TSE 300 Composite futures contract. By selling the contract *short*, pessimistic investors can gain earnings in proportion to the decrease in the TSE 300 Composite Index.

Almost all futures contract buyers close out their long positions by selling their contract before it matures — this is called making a *reverse transaction* — rather than holding the contract until it expires and then taking delivery. Essentially, these buyers take their profits or losses at a time they think is advantageous for them, rather than waiting for their contract to expire. However, a small fraction of futures contract buyers hold their contracts until they expire and take delivery on the contracted commodity. The natural question is, ''What do buyers of a TSE 300 futures contract *receive* if they hold the contract until its delivery (or expiration) date?''

Like the other stock market index futures traded, the TSE 300 Composite Index future is a cash settlement contract—only cash may be used to ''make delivery'' on the expiring contract. Each TSE 300 Composite Index future is quoted at $10 times the value of the TSE 300 Composite Index. For instance, if the TSE 300 Composite Index reaches $2,850 then the underlying index for the contract has a value of $28,500 at that instant in time. If an investor buys a TSE 300 Composite Index futures at $2,710 and sells it at $2,850, then the investor makes a profit of $1,400, as shown below.

21-2.2 What Is Delivered on the TSE 300 Composite Index Futures Contract?

VALUE OF TSE 300 COMPOSITE INDEX	×	$10	=	CONTRACT'S MARKET VALUE	DESCRIPTION
2850		$10		$28,500	Selling price
2710		$10		−$27,100	Buying price
				$ 1,400	Profit

If, instead of taking a long position, our hypothetical trader had first sold TSE 300 Composite Index futures short at 2710, the story would have ended differently. A short sale would have resulted in a $1,400 loss from the ensuing rise in the index, as shown below.

VALUE OF TSE 300 COMPOSITE INDEX	×	$10	=	CONTRACT'S MARKET VALUE	DESCRIPTION
2850		$10		−$28,500	Bought to cover short
2710		$10		$27,100	Sold short
				$ 1,400	Loss

The example of the long and short positions above make it clear that no attempt is made to deliver the TSE 300 Composite Index. Instead, the profit or loss on a financial futures contract held to maturity is resolved by cash settlement.

21-2.3 Delivery Months and Margins

The TSE 300 Composite Index *futures months traded* are the current month and next four months. There is also a TSE 300 Composite spot contract that has daily expiration. The U.S. index futures, by contrast, trade for March, June, September, and December expiries plus, in some cases, the current and next two or three months. The three major U.S. indexes, the S&P 500, the Value Line Stock Index, and the NYSE Composite Stock Index have the same four delivery months to facilitate hedging and spreading transactions betwen them.

When investors buy a futures contract, they may either pay cash or use credit to guarantee the purchase. If a security of any kind is purchased on credit, the customer must post a performance bond, which is called the *margin*. Margins on commodity futures contracts are much less than most margins required in the security markets. (For instance, margins are about one-half the value of the transaction for common stocks.) Margins on futures contracts range from 2 to 10 percent of the contract's market value. This margin money must be posted ''up front'' by both long buyers and short sellers to ensure that they will make good any losses on their positions.

If a trader buys one December 19X9 TSE 35 Index futures contract (the new TFE contract introduced in 1987) on July 18, 19X9, when the value of the index is 150 and a 5 percent *initial margin* is required, the trader must pay $3,750 (equals .05 times 150 times $500) to the broker, for example. If the market value of the contract does not change, the required margin remains constant. When the contract is liquidated the initial margin is returned if the contract's price remains unchanged. However, additional margin may be either demanded from or paid to the trader if the market price of the contract fluctuates adversely or beneficially, respectively.

21-2.4 Settlement Prices and Marking to the Market

Variation margin is the additional margin required as a result of fluctuations in the market value of a futures contract; this is sometimes also called the *maintenance margin*.[3] If the futures trader has a long (short) position and the contract's market value increases, then the position is earning (losing) money, and margin payments (demands called *margin calls*) are made to (upon) the trader. When a brokerage house demands that one of its customers immediately pay cash to bring the margin level back up to an acceptable level, this is referred to as a *variation margin call*. If the customer doesn't meet this demand quickly, the brokerage house may liquidate the account rather than take a chance of suffering uncompensated losses if the value of the margined accounts suffers declines that more than wipe out the initial margin.

---

3 Maintenance margins are allowed for contracts traded on the Winnipeg Commodity Exchange; however, at present all losses must be covered in full each day for trades on the Toronto Futures Exchange, i.e. there is no provision for maintenance margin.

Variation margin requirements are based on the *closing (or settlement) price* of every commodity futures account every day. Thus, every day computers or margin clerks at all brokerage houses in Canada calculate every client's required margin and then issue variation margin calls in those cases where losses have reduced the customer's margin (or equity) in the account to unacceptable levels. A numerical example should clarify this daily procedure.

Suppose that Mr. Samuel Speculator is bullish about the outlook for common stock prices in general. As a result, let us further assume that Sam bought one December 19X1 futures contract on the TSE 35 Index on July 18, 19X1, when the value of the index was 150. Mr. Speculator's initial margin requirement would be (.05 times $500 times 150 equals) $3,750. Sam holds this long position open for four trading days and then liquidates it on July 21, 19X1, for a net profit of $5,000 before brokerage commissions and income taxes. Mr. Speculator receives this $5,000 net gain over the four-day period in the form of the following outflows and inflows:

DATE	SAM'S CASHFLOW	EXPLANATION
7/18	− $3,750	Initial margin
7/19	− $1,900	Variation margin call
7/20	+ $1,900	Variation margin payment
7/21	+ $8,750	Liquidating value
	$5,000	Net gain over 4 days

The cashflows above are explained in Table 21-2.

TABLE 21-2   MR. SAM SPECULATOR'S MARGINED POSITION IN THE TSE COMPOSITE 300 CONTRACT FOR 4 DAYS

ITEM NUMBER AND TITLES	Daily Dates Position Open			
	7/18	7/19	7/20	7/21
1 TSE 35 index settlement price	150	146	150	160
2 Value of one contract [= item 1 × $500]	$75,000	$73,000	$75,000	$80,000
3 $ value of change in contract's value (= daily change in item 2)	NA	($2,000)	$2,000	$5,000
4 Daily owner's margin (= item 3 + previous day's values in items 4 and 6)		$3,750 ($2,000) $0 $3,750	$1,750 $2,000 $1,900 $1,750	$5,650 $5,000 ($1,900) $5,650
	$3,750	$1,750	$5,650	$8,750
5 5% margin requirement (= .05 × item 2)*	$3,750	$3,650	$3,750	$4,000
6 Variation margin call or (excess margin) [= item 5-item 4]†	0	$1,900	($1,900)	($4,750)

*   The numerical example shown in Table 21-1 is oversimplified to make it easier to explain. In actuality, the margin requirements are more complicated than the constant 5 percent used in the table. Initial margins are expressed as a dollar amount and are higher than the maintenance margin requirements.

†   Payments to clients are shown as negative amounts in item 6.

Commodity futures traders are required to *mark to the market* each trading day. This means that at the close of trading each day cashflows to and from the brokerage must be paid or received, respectively, to maintain the variation margin requirements. The $1,900 variation margin call that Sam Speculator had to pay on July 19, 19X1, is an example of how Sam's position was "marked to the market." And the $1,900 and $4,750 excess margins that Sam withdrew from his account on July 20 and 21, 19X1, respectively, are examples of how marking to the market can generate cashflows for a trader if his or her position is profitable.

21-2.5 A Short Hedge to Eliminate Undiversifiable Risk

Financial futures on stock market indexes like the TSE 300 Composite Index are excellent vehicles for constructing hedges that can eliminate some of the undiversifiable stock market risks that result from bull and bear market swings.[4] An example should clarify the value of a hedge to eliminate undiversifiable stock market risks.

Hedging a Portfolio Assume that a financial manager is responsible for a $40 million portfolio that is diversified across thirty different blue-chip stocks from ten different industry groups. The portfolio's manager is concerned about the prospect of an upcoming bear market that could drive down the market value of the portfolio significantly. To avoid such losses the manager is considering a hedge to protect the $40 million investment's value.

Since the $40 million portfolio is made up of thirty blue-chip stocks from ten different industry groups, it occurs to the portfolio's manager that the portfolio is behaving similarly to the Dow Jones Industrial Average (DJIA). The DJIA is an average of thirty blue-chip stocks which, as shown in Table 21-3, is highly correlated with the other stock market indexes.[5] Thus, the portfolio's manager concludes (correctly) that the S&P 500 futures contract should experience fluctuations in market value that are similar to the $40 million portfolio's fluctuations. Stated differently, the S&P 500 financial futures contract is an excellent financial instrument with which to hedge away some of the undiversifiable market risk from systematic market swings that affect almost all stocks' prices simultaneously.

The portfolio manager is satisfied with the thirty stocks in the portfolio. Liquidating the portfolio and buying it back after the bear market decline passes would be costly in terms of brokerage commissions alone. Therefore, the manager decides to sell short $40 million worth of S&P 500 index financial futures. Being short the S&P 500 index futures in an amount equal to the value of the long position in the stock market should substantially hedge the portfolio's value against bear market declines. If the market does decline as expected, the short position in the S&P 500 financial futures should earn about a dollar for each dollar of portfolio value that is lost in a systematic market decline. As a result, the combined value of the portfolio's long posi-

4 Chapter 10 defines undiversifiable risk, diversifiable risk, and the beta coefficient.
5 Chapter 7 analyzes the DJIA in some detail and compares it to other market indexes.

tion and the short position in financial futures should remain unchanged at about $40 million until the futures contract expires, regardless of whether the stock market advances or declines. This futures transaction to minimize potential losses from an expected decline in the value of the portfolio will entail much smaller commission costs than selling the shares of stock and repurchasing them at a later date.

Savings in Commission Costs The savings to a portfolio in commission costs alone are, in most cases, sufficient to justify using futures contracts to hedge a common stock position — rather than using the common stock directly to form an offsetting position. Consider the round-turn (that is, both the buy and the sell) commissions for the $40 million portfolio, (which is modest in size by Wall Street standards).

Assuming that $40 million of common stock can be sold and repurchased at a total round-turn commission cost of 1 percent suggests that this transaction would involve $400,000 in commission costs. In contrast, the round-turn commission cost for a futures contract on the Standard & Poor's 500 index is only about $80 per contract. Since 500 of these futures contracts would be needed to hedge the $40 million portfolio, the total commission cost of using the futures contracts would be (500 contracts times $80 commission apiece equals) $40,000. The estimated commission savings is ($400,000 less $40,000 equals) $360,000 from using the futures contracts to hedge the $40 million portfolio of common stocks. The disadvantage of hedging with futures contracts is that after some months the contracts reach their delivery date. So, after the contracts expire a new hedge with new hedge costs must be established if the need for the hedge remains.

The portfolio hedging transaction hypothesized above in which the trader hedges a long position by selling futures short is called a *short hedge*. The risks inherent in this strategy are the basis risks that result (1) because the basis between the S&P 500 index and the portfolio will not remain constant as their values fluctuate similarly but not in perfect harmony, and (2) if the futures contracts expire before the expected systematic market decline is past. The example provided was simple; more sophisticated hedging procedures exist.[6]

The S&P 500 index financial futures contract is not the only financial future based on a stock market index. Table 21-3a provides details on the five Canadian stock market index futures contracts while Table 21-3b lists details about three similar but different U.S. stock market index futures contracts. The primary difference between the three U.S. contracts is the indexes on which they are based.

21-2.6 Spreading Between Different Stock Index Futures

---

6 See Frank J. Fabozzi and Gregory M. Kipnis, *Stock Index Futures*. Homewood, Ill.: Dow Jones-Irwin 1984. See also Nancy H. Rothstein (ed.), *Handbook of Financial Futures*. New York.: McGraw-Hill, 1983, chaps. 9-12. See Allan M. Loosigian, *Interest Rate Futures*. Homewood, Ill.: Dow Jones-Irwin, 1980; Allan M. Loosigian, *Foreign Exchange Futures*. Homewood, Ill.: Dow Jones-Irwin, 1981.

TABLE 21-3a CANADIAN STOCK INDEX FUTURES CONTRACT SPECIFICATIONS

CONTRACT	EXCHANGE	PRICE QUOTATION	MINIMUM FLUCTUATION (TICK) VALUE	MAXIMUM FLUCTUATION (LIMIT) VALUE	INITIAL MARGIN	TRADING HOURS	CONTRACT DELIVERY MONTHS	SETTLEMENT (DELIVERY) DATE(S)	DELIVERY INVOICING METHOD	LAST TRADING DAY
Toronto Stock Exchange Composite 300 Index	Toronto Futures Exchange (TFE)	$10 times TSE Composite 300 Index	1 index point $10	150 index points $1,500	Speculative: $1,500 Hedge: $1,000	9:30 –4:15 EST	Next five months	First business day following last day of trading	Cash settlement using TSE 300 Composite Index as cash settlement price to two decimal places	Third Friday of the delivery month.
Toronto Stock Exchange Composite 300 SPOT Index	Toronto Futures Exchange (TFE)	$10 times TSE Composite 300 Index	1 index point $10	None	Speculative: $1,500 Hedge: $1,000	9:20 –4:10 EST	Daily	Next morning at 9:00	Cash settlement using TSE 300 Composite Index as cash settlement price to two decimal places	Same day
Toronto Stock Exchange Oil and Gas Index	Toronto Futures Exchange (TFE)	$10 times TSE Oil and Gas Index	1 index point $10	250 index points $2,500	Speculative: $2,500 Hedge: $1,500	9:30 –4:15 EST	Next three months	First business day following last day of trading	Cash settlement using TSE Oil and Gas Index as cash settlement price to two decimal places	Third Friday of the delivery month.
Toronto Stock Exchange Oil and Gas SPOT Index	Toronto Futures Exchange (TFE)	$10 times TSE Oil and Gas Index	1 index point $10	None	Speculative: $2,500 Hedge: $1,500	9:20 –4:10 EST	Daily	Next morning at 9:00	Cash settlement using TSE Oil and Gas Index as cash settlement price to two decimal places	Same day
Toronto Stock Exchange 35 Index	Toronto Futures Exchange (TFE)	$500 times TSE 35 Index	.02 index point $10	9 index points $4,500	Speculative $4,500 Hedge: $3,000	9:15 –4:15 EST	Next three months	Next morning at 9:00	Cash settlement using TSE 35 Index as cash settlement price to two decimal places	Thursday before third Friday of the delivery month

TABLE 21-3b U.S. STOCK INDEX FUTURES CONTRACT SPECIFICATIONS

CONTRACT	EXCHANGE	PRICE QUOTATION	MINIMUM FLUCTUATION (TICK)/VALUE	MAXIMUM FLUCTUATION (LIMIT)/VALUE	MARGIN INITIAL/MAINTENANCE	TRADING HOURS	CONTRACT DELIVERY MONTHS	SETTLEMENT (DELIVERY) DATE(S)	DELIVERY INVOICING METHOD	LAST TRADING DAY
New York Stock Exchange Composite Index (NYSE Composite Index)	New York Futures Exchange (NYFE)	$500 times the NYSE Composite Index	.05 (5 BP)* $25	None	Speculative: $3,500/$1,500 Hedge: $1,500/$750	10:00–4:15 EST	Mar., June, Sept., Dec.	Last business day in settlement month	Cash settlement based on the value of the NYSE Composite Index at close of trading at NYSE on the last trading day	Business day prior to last business day in settlement month
Standard & Poor's 500 Stock Index (S&P 500 Index)	Index and Options Market (a division of the Chicago Mercantile Exchange)	$500 times the Standard & Poor's 500 Index	.05 (5 BP)* $25	None	Speculative: $6,000/$2,500 Hedge: $2,500/$750	9:00–3:15 CST	Mar., June, Sept., Dec.	Last day of trading	Cash settlement based on closing quotation of Standard & Poor's Price Index on last day of trading	3d Thurs. of contract month
Value Line	Kansas City Board of Trade (KCBT)	500 times futures price in units of Value Line Composite average	.01 (1 BP)* $5	None	Speculative: $6,500/$5,100 Hedge: $3,500/$3,500	9:00–3:15 CST	Mar., June, Sept., Dec.	First business day of month immediately following contract month	Cash settlement via wire transfer through clearing house	Last business day of contract month

*BP stands for basis points, or hundredths of the $500.

The correlation coefficients in Table 21-4 above indicate that the prices of the three different stock market futures should move together, since the indexes on which they are based are highly correlated. Since none of the correlations are equal to 1, however, none of the stock market futures should move together in perfect unison—small differences remain. These differences are basis risk differences similar to the differences in grain prices that may exist, for instance, because different qualities of the same grain are delivered under similar grain contracts.

TABLE 21-4 CORRELATION COEFFICIENTS BETWEEN DAILY CHANGES IN STOCK MARKET INDEX, 1971–1982

	S&P 500	VALUE LINE	NYSE*	DJIA†
S&P 500	1.0			
Value Line	.88	1.0		
NYSE	.98	.93	1.0	
DJIA†	.73	.51	.64	1.0

* New York Stock Exchange.
† Dow Jones Industrial Average.

Other types of basis risk exist too. Even though three similar financial futures contracts on different stock market indexes have the same delivery months, the fact that their delivery days differ slightly will introduce additional small elements of basis risk between the contracts. These small basis risks provide the incentive for a form of arbitrage that is referred to as *intermarket spreading*.[7]

An intermarket spread could be set up by (1) taking a long position with the S&P 500 index contract and (2) *simultaneously* selling short an equal quantity of financial futures on the NYSE Composite Index that have the same delivery months, for instance. Any changes in the market values of these long and short positions will almost, but not quite, offset each other. However, the basis risk associated with the small spread between the two different contracts is what provides the profit opportunity that motivates the spread. The spreader's goal is to gain more on one "leg" of the spread than is lost on the other "leg."

Some people say that spreading is less risky than taking an unhedged long or short position alone.[8] However, the appearance of the safe hedge can be misleading. Since the two hedged contracts are likely to move in fairly close tandem (as indicated in Table 21-1), the commodity exchanges and brokerages have smaller margin requirements on hedged positions than on unhedged positions. Therein lies the danger. The lower margin percentage requirements allow the spreader to take a larger position than would have been permitted

---

7 Arbitragers create different kinds of spreads—intermonth spreads, butterfly spreads, intercommodity spreads, and intermarket spreads. For a discussion see James M. Little, "Strategies for Speculation" in Nancy H. Rothstein (ed.) *Handbook of Financial Futures*. New York: McGraw-Hill, 1983, chap. 9, especially pp. 145-153.

8 Mark Castelino and Ashok Vora, "Spread Volatility in Commodity Futures: The Length Effect," *Journal of Futures Market*, Spring 1984, vol. 4, no. 1, pp. 39-46.

without the hedge if the same amount of initial margin money were invested. Because of the larger hedged position the spreader may enter, the risk exposure with the spread may be greater than the risk exposure with the seemingly safer unhedged position of lesser size.

The prices of all actively traded futures contracts are published in the next day's news by large national newspapers like *The Globe and Mail, The New York Times* and *The Wall Street Journal*; the S&P 500 futures is one of those published. Figure 21-1 is a newspaper excerpt showing the S&P 500 index futures contract price quotations for one trading day.

21-2.7 Price Quotations in Newspapers

The market price of the S&P 500 contract is 500 times the value of the S&P 500 index. Thus, when the S&P 500 index is 170.5, for instance, the price of one contract is a much larger number, as shown below.

$$170.5 \quad \text{Hypothetical Standard \& Poor's 500 index value}$$
$$\underline{\times\ 500} \quad \text{The multiplier of 500 times}$$
$$\$85,250.00 \quad \text{Resulting value of S\&P 500 futures contract}$$

In order to conserve newspaper space, the excerpt in Fig. 21-1 shows that only the value of the index is published, not the larger value of the contract's prices. The notes in Fig. 21-1 explain the meanings of the values of the numbers in each column. Each row of the figure represents a S&P 500 futures contract with a different expiration month. At the bottom of the price quotations in Fig. 21-1 are statistics about the volume of contracts traded and the next day's values for the S&P 500 index. The Canadian indexes are quoted in Fig. 21-2.

FIGURE 21-2 TSE 300 Composite Index futures contract quotation from a newspaper excerpt.

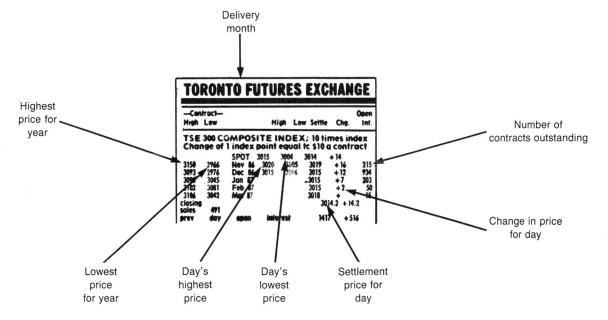

In addition to the stock market index contracts, bond market index contracts also exist.[9]

21-3 FINANCIAL FUTURES ON GOVERNMENT SECURITIES

The wide fluctuation in interest rates in the 1970s provided the impetus for the development of interest rate futures contracts. Financial futures on government securities were first available in the United States in 1976, with the introduction on the International Monetary Market of the Chicago Mercantile Exchange of the 91-day Treasury bill futures contract. A similar contract was introduced in Canada in 1980.

Tables 21-5a and 21-5b lists financial futures on government securities of various types traded in Canada and the United States.

Financial futures on stock market indexes differ from the futures contracts on Treasury securities in two major respects. First, the contracts on government securities are called *interest rate futures*, because their prices are determined by market interest rates. In contrast, interest rates are only one of many factors that affect the prices of common stocks. The second major difference between stock index futures and interest rate futures is that government securities, unlike the stock market indexes, may actually be delivered when the contract expires. Interest rate futures are not cash settlement contacts, as are the stock index futures. In addition to these two major differences, there are a number of other significant differences. Let us consider futures contracts on government securities in more detail.

Treasury bills are the single most important money market security traded. There are over $300 billion in T-bills outstanding in the United States, and futures contracts on this underlying security are traded actively in liquid markets. Over $3 billion worth of T-bills are traded on an average day as their prices fluctuate throughout each trading day. Figure 21-4 on page 620 shows one day's T-bill quotations from a daily newspaper.

---

9 For additional discussion of the determinants of the value of financial futures consult the following articles: G.M. Constantinides, ''Capital Market Equilibrium with Personal Tax,'' *Econometrica*, 1983; B. Cornell and M.R. Reinganum, ''Forward and Futures Prices: Evidence from the Foreign Exchange Markets,'' *Journal of Finance*, 1981, vol. 36, pp. 1035-1045; B. Cornell and Kenneth R. French, ''The Pricing of Stock Index Futures,'' *Journal of Futures Markets*, 1983, vol. 3, no. 1, pp. 1-14; B. Cornell and K.R. French, ''Taxes and the Pricing of Stock Index Futures,'' *Journal of Finance*, June 1983, pp. 675-694; J.C. Cox, J.E. Ingersoll, and S. A. Ross, ''The Relation Between Forward and Futures Prices,'' *Journal of Financial Economics*, 1981, vol. 9, pp. 321-346; E. Elton, M. Gruber, and J. Rentzler, ''Intra-day Tests of the Efficiency of the Treasury Bill Futures Markets,'' *Review of Economics and Statistics*, vol. 66, no. 1, pp. 129-137; Frank J. Fabozzi and Gregory M. Kipnis, *Stock Index Futures*, Homewood, Ill: Dow Jones-Irwin, 1984; K.R. French, ''The Pricing of Futures and Forward Contracts,'' Ph.D. dissertation, University of Rochester, 1982a; K.R. French, ''A Comparison of Futures and Forward Prices,'' working paper, UCLA, 1982b; R.A. Jarrow and G.S. Oldfield, ''Forward Contracts and Futures Contracts,'' *Journal of Financial Economics*, 1981, vol. 9, pp. 373-382; R.J. Rendleman and C.E. Carabini, ''The Efficiency of the Treasury Bill Futures Market,'' *Journal of Finance*, 1979, vol. 34, pp. 895-914; S.F. Richard and M. Sundaresan, ''A Continuous Time Equilibrium Model of Forward Prices and Futures Prices in a Multigood Economy,'' *Journal of Financial Economics*, 1981, vol. 9, pp. 347-372.

In Canada there are over $60 billion in T-bills outstanding; however, the Toronto Futures Exchange T-bill contract is surprisingly quiescent, failing thus far to attract even a fraction of that of its U.S. counterpart.

The first column of Fig. 21-3 shows the maturity date of each T-bill issue. The term to maturity for each T-bill is calculated by counting from November 17, 19X3, the date of the quotations, to the maturity date. No price data are shown in Fig. 21-3; the prices must be computed from the bid yields and asked yields shown in the second and third columns, respectively. The *T-bill yields* shown in columns two and three are calculated with Eq. (21-1a).

**21-3.1
Reading U.S.
T-Bill Price
Quotations**

FIGURE 21-3   Treasury bill quotations for November 17, 19X3.
(*Source:* November 18, 19X3 newspaper excerpt).

U.S. Treas. Bills Mat. date	Bid	Asked	Yield Discount	Mat. date	Bid	Asked	Yield Discount
-19X3-				-19x4-			
11-25	7.90	7.80	7.94	3- 8	8.86	8.76	9.15
12- 1	8.38	8.30	8.46	3-15	8.85	8.75	9.15
12- 8	8.28	8.20	8.37	3-22	8.90	8.82	9.24
12-15	7.90	7.80	7.97	3-29	8.90	8.82	9.26
12-22	8.24	8.12	8.31	4- 5	8.94	8.86	9.32
12-29	8.38	8.30	8.51	4-84	8.98	8.90	9.38
-19X4-				4-19	8.99	8.91	9.41
1- 5	8.45	8.35	8.58	4-26	8.99	8.91	9.43
1-12	8.48	8.40	8.65	5- 3	8.97	8.89	9.42
1-19	8.62	8.54	8.81	5-84	9.04	8.96	9.51
1-26	8.69	8.61	8.89	5-17	9.01	8.99	9.57
2- 2	8.78	8.70	9.00	6-14	9.01	8.95	9.54
2- 9	8.80	8.72	9.04	7-12	9.01	8.97	9.58
2-16	8.84	8.82	9.16	8- 9	9.09	9.01	9.66
2-23	8.88	8.80	9.16	9- 6	9.13	9.07	9.77
3- 1	8.86	8.76	9.13	10- 4	9.12	9.04	9.79
				11- 1	9.12	9.06	9.86

$$\text{T-bill yield} = \frac{[(\text{face value} - \text{price}) \times 360]/\text{days to maturity}}{\text{face value}} \qquad (21\text{-}1a)$$

The T-bill yield is synonymously called the *discount yield* and the *bank discount rate*. This is an annualized yield.

For example, a $1,000,000, 91-day T-bill with a price of $984,833.33 would have a T-bill yield 6 percent, as shown below.

$$\frac{[(\$1,000,000 - \$984,833.333) \times 360]/91}{\$1,000,000} = .06 = 6.0\% \qquad (21\text{-}1b)$$

Newspaper readers who want to know either the bid price or the asked price can algebraically solve Eq. (21-1a) for the price, as shown in Eq. (21-2a), substitute in the appropriate values from the newspaper, and calculate the price.

$$\text{Price} = \left[1 - \left(\frac{\text{days to maturity} \times \text{T-bill yield}}{360} \right) \right] \text{face value} \qquad (21\text{-}2a)$$

TABLE 21-5a   CANADIAN INTEREST RATE FUTURES CONTRACTS

CONTRACT	EXCHANGE	CONTRACT SIZE	PRICE QUOTATION METHOD	MINIMUM FLUCTUATION (TICK)/ VALUE	MAXIMUM FLUCTUATION (LIMIT)/ VALUE	INITIAL MARGIN	TRADING HOURS	CONTRACT DELIVERY MONTHS	SETTLEMENT (DELIVERY) DATE(S)	DELIVERABLE GRADE	LAST TRADING DAY
91-day Government of Canada Treasury bills	Toronto Futures Exchange (TFE)	$1,000,000 face value	Annualized discount yield: 100-yield = price	0.01 index point $24	0.60 index points $1,440	Speculative: $1,500 Hedge: $1,000	9:00 –3:15 EST	Mar. June Sept. Dec. plus spot month	Any of the last three Fridays of the delivery month	Government of Canada Treasury bills with maturities ranging from 89 to 93 days	11:00 a.m. on the day of the Bank of Canada auction preceding the last Friday of the delivery month
Long-term Government of Canada Bonds 11	Toronto Futures Exchange (TFE)	$100,000 face value	% of par quoted in 32ds of a point	1/32d of a point $31.25	2 points $2,000	Speculative: $2,000 Hedge: $1,000	9:00- 3:15 EST	Mar. June Sept. Dec.	Fifth business day following the last day of trading	Government of Canada bonds which do not measure and are not callable for at least 15 years from date of delivery	Sixth last business day of the delivery month.

TABLE 21-5b INTEREST RATE FUTURES CONTRACTS ON U.S. TREASURY SECURITIES

CONTRACT	EXCHANGE	CONTRACT SIZE	PRICE QUOTATION METHOD	MINIMUM FLUCTUATION (TICK)/VALUE	MAXIMUM FLUCTUATION (LIMIT)/VALUE	MARGIN INITIAL/MAINTENANCE	TRADING HOURS	CONTRACT DELIVERY MONTHS	SETTLEMENT (DELIVERY) DATE(S)	DELIVERABLE GRADE	DELIVERY INVOICING METHOD	LAST TRADING DAY
U.S. Treasury bonds (20-year)	Chicago Board of Trade (CBT)	$100,000 principal	% of par quoted in 32ds of a pt	1/32d of a point $31.25	64/32 (2 pts) $2,000	Speculative: $4,500/$3,000 Hedge: $3,000/$3,000	8:00–2:00 CST	Mar. June Sept. Dec.	Any business day during month	U.S. Treasury bonds with not less than 15 years to call or maturity	(Conversion factor × futures price × $1,000) + accrued interest	7 business days prior to last business day of month
U.S. Treasury bonds (20-year)	MidAmerica Commodity Exchange (MIDAM)	$50,000 principal $15.62	% of par quoted in 32ds of a pt	1/32d of a point $15.62	64/32 (2 pts) $1000	$1,500/$1,000	8:00–2:10 CST	Mar. June Sept. Dec.	Any business day during month	U.S. Treasury bonds with not less than 15 years to call or maturity	(Conversion factor × futures price × $1,000) + accrued interest	7 business days prior to last business day of month
U.S. Treasury bills (90-day)	International Monetary Market (IMM)	$1,000,000 face value	Annualized discount yield: 100–discount yield–price	1/100 of 1% (1 BP) $25.00	60/100 of 1% (60 BP) $1,500	$2,500/$2,000	8:00–2:00 CST	Mar. June Sept. Dec.	3-day period beginning 1st Thurs. after 3d weekly bill auction in the delivery month	13-week U.S. Treasury bills with $1,000,000 face value	Wire transfer vs. deposit in one of 4 Chicago banks of a registered New York bank	2d day following 3d weekly T-bill auction in contract month
U.S. Treasury bills (90-day)	MidAmerica Commodity Exchange (MIDAM)	$500,000 face value	% of par quoted in 32ds of a pt	1/100 of 1% (1 BP) $12.50	64/32 (2 pts) $1,000	$1,250/$1,000	8:00–2:15 CST	Mar. June Sept. Dec.	Weds. following 3d Mon. of contract month	Cash settlement. No delivery	Based on settlement price of IMM T-bill contract	2d day following 3d weekly T-bill auction in contract month
U.S. Treasury notes (10-year)	Chicago Board of Trade (CBT)	$100,000 principal	Annualized discount yield: 100–discount yield–price	1/32d of a point $31.25	60/100 of a point (60 BP) $750	Speculative: $3,000/$2,000 Hedge: $2,000/$2,000	8:00–2:00 CST	Mar. June Sept. Dec.	Any business day during month	U.S. Treasury notes with maturity of 6½–10 years	(Conversion factor × futures price × $1,000) + accrued interest	7 business days prior to last business day of month

The fourth column of Fig. 21-3 gives the *bond-equivalent yield*, which is based on asked prices, as defined in Eq.(21-3).

$$\text{Bond equivalent yield} = \frac{[(\text{face value} - \text{asked price}) \times 365]/\text{days to maturity}}{\text{price}} \tag{21-3}$$

There are two significant differences between Eqs. (21-1*a*) and (21-3).[10] The T-bill yield definition uses a 360-day year, whereas the bond equivalent yield uses a 365-day year. The second difference is the denominators. Equation (21-3) realistically bases the yield on the *actual* price. In contrast, Eq. (21-1*a*) is based on the face value—a less realistic yield measure results.

Equation (21-4) defines the yield to maturity, denoted r, for a T-bill (or any zero coupon bond).[11] This measure needs to be annualized to facilitate yield comparisons.

$$\text{Price} = \frac{\text{face value}}{(1.0 + r)^t} \tag{21-4}$$

Algebraically solving Eq. (21-4) for the yield to maturity results in Eq. (21-5), which is computationally more handy.

$$r = \sqrt[t]{\frac{\text{face value}}{\text{price}}} - 1.0 \tag{21-5}$$

Equations (21-1*a*), (21-3), and (21-5) are all similar rate-of-return measures. But all three differ slightly, and these differences should not be overlooked.

21-3.2 The IMM's T-Bill Futures Contract

The International Monetary Market (IMM) of the Chicago Mercantile Exchange (CME) started trading the first futures contract with T-bills as the underlying commodity in 1976. Although competing T-bill contracts have been introduced by other exchanges since 1976, the IMM contract remains the most actively traded. Therefore, we will discuss the IMM contract in detail—the concepts also apply to other T-bill futures, although the similar contracts traded on other exchanges have slightly different delivery dates and differ in other details.

The IMM's T-bill futures contract has a $1 million face value. This means that whoever is short the contract must deliver T-bills with $1 million face value when the contract expires. The long buyer, in contrast, buys the con-

---

10 Equation (21-3) is true for maturities of less than 182 days. For instruments with maturities in excess of 182 days see Marcia Stigum, *Money Market Calculations: Yields, Break-Evens and Arbitrage.* Homewood, Ill.: Dow Jones-Irwin, 1981, pp. 33-35. See also Bruce D. Fielitz, "Calculating the Bond Equivalent Yield for T-Bills," *Journal of Portfolio Management*, Spring 1983, pp. 58-60.

11 The yield to maturity for coupon bonds was discussed at length in Sec. 11-3 of Chap. 11. Equation (21-4) measures the same compound rate of return when no coupons exist.

tract at a fluctuating market price that varies inversely with market interest rates.[12]

Consider how the price of a T-bill futures contract is derived. It is traditional in securities markets for bid prices (that is, the highest bid made by a potential purchaser) to be lower than the offering price (namely, the lowest price at which any potential seller will sell). Because of the inverse relationship between interest rates and bond prices, it is also traditional and logical for bid yields (not bid prices) to be higher than offer yields. Thus, if a T-bill is sold at a greater yield, its price declines.

When the T-bill futures contract was being written a unique value called the *IMM index* was defined to make the IMM T-bill futures prices conform with all the traditional pricing relationships. The IMM index is defined in Eq. (23-6a).

$$\text{IMM index} = 100.0 - (\text{T-bill futures yield}) \qquad (21\text{-}6a)$$
$$94.0 = 100.00 - 6.0 \qquad (21\text{-}6b)$$

Note that the T-bill yield defined in Eq. (21-1a) is used in the IMM index rather than one of the other rate-of-return measures. It is also worthwhile to observe that the IMM index is not an actual price of a 90-day bill since the T-bill yield [Eq. (21-1a)], from which the IMM index is calculated, is an *annualized* interest rate. This annualization facilitates comparison of the yields and IMM index values of T-bills with different maturities (for example, a 3-month T-bill and a 6-month T-bill), but it does not yield actual market prices for the contracts.

To continue the example of the 6 percent 91-day T-bill from Eq. (21-1b), Eq. (21-6b) above indicates an IMM index value of 94.0 for the T-bill. The IMM index produces results that conform to the traditional quotation procedures listed below.

1. Bond prices and yields move inversely.
2. Bid prices are always lower than asked prices.
3. Bid yields are always higher than asked yields (as shown in Fig. 21-3, for example).

The final step is to convert the IMM index to an actual T-bill price. Equation (21-2a) is used to calculate the price because it considers: (1) the number of

---

12 The minimum yield change for T-bill futures contracts is 1 basis point, as indicated in column five of Table 21-5b above. The following formula is used to determine the dollar value of the smallest price change associated with a yield change of 1 basis point.

[(1/100) of 1.0%] × [face value] × [fraction of year to maturity] = [$value of 1 basis point]

Example 1: a full (360-day) year's contract for $1,000,000

$$.0001 \times \$1,000,000 \times \frac{360}{360} = \$100$$

Example 2: a 90-day T-bill contract on IMM

$$.0001 \times \$1,000,000 \times \frac{90}{360} = \$25$$

The formula above shows that the relationship between basis point changes in yields and dollar changes in the price of a contract depends on both the face value and the term to maturity for the contract.

days to maturity, (2) the T-bill yield, and (3) the face value of the T-bill in question. All three values are essential price determinants. The price of $1 million face value T-bill with 91 days to maturity and a 6 percent T-bill yield is $984,833.33, as shown below in Eq. (21-2b).

$$\text{Price} = \left[1.0 - \left(\frac{\binom{\text{days to}}{\text{maturity}} \times \binom{\text{T-bill}}{\text{yield}}}{360} \right) \right] \binom{\text{face}}{\text{value}} \tag{21-2a}$$

$$\$984,833.33 = \left[1.0 - \left(\frac{91 \times .06}{360} \right) \right] (\$1,000,000) \tag{21-2b}$$

To see how gains or losses are calculated, suppose a speculator expects market interest rates to drop from the T-bill yield of 6 percent shown in Eq. (21-1b) and (2l-2b), to 4 percent. Further assume that this speculator therefore purchases a T-bill future in order to profit from the expected decline in interest rates. If this speculator's expectations are suddenly fulfilled as interest rates drop in the same day the T-bill future is purchased, the speculator enjoys a gain of $25 per basis point, as shown in column five of Table 21-4 for the IMM T-bill contract. Thus, the 200 basis point drop in the yield (times $25 per basis point) equals a $5,000 total gain.

**21-3.3
Price
Quotations
for the IMM
T-Bill
Contract**

Figure 21-4 shows an excerpt from a newspaper reporting the preceding day's prices for the IMM T-bill contract. The first column lists the delivery months of the contracts traded. Note that the contracts' expiration dates extend up to two years into the future. As indicated above in the far right-hand column of row three in Table 21-5b, trading in the expiring T-bill contracts terminates two business days after the third weekly 3-month T-bill auction of the delivery month. These auctions are held almost every Monday at the Federal Reserve Bank of New York City, but the contracts expire in only the third week of every third month. So, there are no T-bill futures contracts expiring near the dates of more than 90 percent of the weekly T-bill auctions.

The values of the IMM index calculated with Eq. (21-6) are shown in columns two, three, four, and five of Fig. 21-4 for the day's opening value, the day's highest value, the day's lowest value, and the day's settlement price,

FIGURE 21-4   Treasury bill futures contract's price quotations for November 17, 19X3.

TREASURY BILLS (IMM)—$1 mil.; pts. of 100%					Discount	Open
	Open	High	Low	Settle	Chg	Settle Chg	Interest
Dec	91.00	91.03	90.97	91.02	− .05	8.98 + .05	26,004
Marx4	90.59	90.61	90.55	90.60	− .06	9.40 + .06	18,742
June	90.29	90.29	90.25	90.28	− .06	9.28 + .06	4,637
Sept	90.03	90.03	89.99	90.03	− .06	9.97 + .06	1,565
Dec	89.81	89.81	89.78	89.81	− .06	10.19 + .06	470
Marx5	89.61	89.62	89.58	89.61	− .06	10.39 + .06	178
June	89.41	89.41	89.37	89.41	− .07	10.59 + .07	124
Sept	.....	.....	.....	89.32	+ .02	10.68 − .02	12

Est vol 12,489; vol Wed 14,475; open int 51,732, −749.

(*Source:* November 18, 19X3 newspaper excerpt.)

respectively.[13] The "Chg" heading over column six refers to the change in the settlement price from the preceding day's settlement price.

Columns seven and eight of Fig. 21-4 fall under the word "Discount." Column seven shows the T-bill discount yield calculated with Eq. (21-1*a*) based on the day's settlement price for the IMM index. Column eight gives the change in this T-bill discount yield from the preceding trading day. Column nine, headed "Open Interest," shows the total number of open contracts for each different T-bill contract. Below the price quotations in Fig. 21-4 are figures for the day's estimated volume of contracts traded, the preceding day's volume, the total open interest over all IMM T-bill contracts (that is, the total of column nine), and the change in the total open interest since the preceding trading day.

When any IMM T-bill future expires and it is time for the contract's seller to make delivery, a specific procedure is followed. The contract buyer and the contract seller each have a responsibility to perform certain steps in the delivery procedure.

Commodity brokerages or full-service security brokerages like E.F. Hutton, Merrill Lynch, Bache, or Paine Webber are members of the IMM's clearinghouse. Every buyer and every seller is represented by one of these so-called "clearing members."

21-3.4 Delivery Procedures for the T-Bill Future

The Seller's Delivery Commitment   The clearing member representing the seller of a T-bill future is responsible for delivering a seller's delivery commitment to the IMM clearinghouse by noon of the last trading day. This delivery commitment must specify the name of a Chicago bank (1) that is a member of the Federal Reserve System, (2) at which the seller has a bank account, and (3) which must be registered with the IMM. No later than 12:45 P.M. on the delivery day the seller must transfer from his or her prespecified bank account the T-bills to fulfill the delivery obligation. The seller is responsible for seeing that these T-bills reach the bank selected by the buyer by 12:45 P.M. and bear whatever costs are incurred to complete the delivery.

The Buyer's Delivery Commitment   The buyer's broker must deliver a buyer's delivery commitment to the IMM clearinghouse by noon of the last trading day of the T-bill contract. This document must specify a bank account to which the T-bills can be transferred. The buyer's clearing member must present to the seller's designated agent a wire transfer of federal funds to pay in full for the purchase by 11 A.M. on the delivery day.

---

13 The settlement price is selected by the clearinghouse of the commodity exchange after every trading day. This settlement price is used in determining net gains or losses, margin requirements, and the next day's price limits. The term *settlement price* is also often used as an approximate equivalent to the term *closing price*. The close in futures trading refers to a brief period of time at the end of the trading day during which transactions frequently take place quickly and at a range of prices. The settlement price is the closing price if there is only one closing price. When there is a *range* of closing prices, the settlement price is as near the midpoint of the closing range as possible, consistent with the contract's price change increments. Thus, the settlement price can be used to provide a single reference point for analysis of marking to the market.

The Role of the Clearinghouse   The IMM clearinghouse matches the buyer's and seller's delivery commitments and also communicates to the buyer's bank and the seller's bank the instructions needed to complete the delivery transaction. The clearinghouse also monitors these delivery procedures to ensure the timely transfer and payment between the buyer and seller. Should either party default in any way, the clearinghouse will complete the transaction on schedule at its own expense. Later, the clearinghouse will collect damages from the defaulted party. As a result of the clearinghouse's role, no IMM contract has ever failed to be delivered on schedule.

As shown in Table 21-5b, the IMM is not the only financial futures exchange that makes a market in Treasury securities. Each different exchange's futures contract on a Treasury security is unique in some respect, and each exchange's clearinghouse follows a different delivery procedure. However, all these competing futures markets function smoothly and are growing.

**21-3.5
The Toronto
Future's
Exchange
T-Bill Futures
Contract**

The Toronto Future's Exchange T-bill futures contract was first introduced on the Toronto Stock Exchange in 1980. In 1984 the contract was transferred to the new Toronto Futures Exchange. In 1985 a new T-bill futures contract with modified specifications, the Canadian T-bill II futures was introduced and traded side by side with the existing one. The original contract has since ceased trading, and only the specifications of the Canadian T-bill II futures contract are discussed below.

The Canadian T-bill futures contract is a CDN $1,000,000 nominal value contract for delivery of 89 to 93-day T-bills with an appropriate adjustment in price to provide the same T-bill yield as a 91-day bill. Prices are quoted as an index, i.e., 100 minus the yield. Hence, a price quotation of 91.50 means an annualized yield of 8.5 percent. A year is assumed to be 365 days, in contrast to the 360 day year used in the U.S.

The minimum yield change for a T-bill futures contract is one basis point or 1/100 of 1 percent. The dollar value of such a change is calculated as: $0.0001 \times$ price of contract $\times 91/365 = 0.00002493 \times$ price of contract. Hence if the T-bill contract were trading at 96.00 or $960,000, the value of this minimum move would be $0.00002493 \times \$960,000 = \$23.93$. If it were trading at 92.50 or $925,000 this would translate to $0.00002493 \times \$925,000 = \$23.06$. For simplicity the Toronto Futures Exchange has set the value of a minimum tick at $24.00. This is in contrast to the IMM's method set out in section 21-3.2 where a minimum tick is calculated as $0.0001 \times 1,000,000 \times 90/360 = \$25.00$. As you can see, the Toronto Future's Exchange calculation is based on the percentage of market price change, whereas the IMM is based on the face value.

To convert the T-bill index value to an actual price, an equation that considers the number of days to maturity , the T-bill yield and the face value of the T-bill is used. To illustrate assume that the index value is 91.50 representing an annual yield of 8.5 percent.

The price of such a $1,000,000 face value T-bill with ninety-one days left to maturity and an 8.5 percent T-bill yield is $979,247.99 as shown on page 623 in Eq. (21-2c).

$$\text{Price} = \frac{\text{Face value}}{1 + (\text{yield} \times \text{days to maturity}/365)} \qquad (21\text{-}2c)$$

$$\text{Price} = \frac{1,000,000}{1 + (.085 \times 91/365)} = \$979,247.99 \qquad (21\text{-}2c)$$

The daily limit or maximum amount by which the T-bill futures contract is allowed to rise or fall above or below the previous day's close in a single trading day is 0.60 points. This translates to $1,440 per contract as follows:

value of 1 basis point change (as set by the TFE) x 60

= 24 × 60 = $1,440

The seller is obligated to deliver Treasury bills that mature ninety-one days from the delivery date; however the Toronto Future's Exchange allows the substitution of T-bills with maturities ranging from eighty-nine to ninety-three days. This provides the "short" with a wider range of deliverable T-bills and thus adds a small increment to the value of the short's position; a quality option.

The minimum margin set by the TFE for T-bill positions, both long and short, is $1,500 for speculators and $1,000 for hedgers. Some brokerage firms, however, will set their required margins for customers above these exchange minimums. This provides the brokerage firm with added protection against a customer default. Furthermore, the firms that insist on margins in cash only earn interest income on the difference between the amount required of the client and the amount that they must supply to the clearing corporation.

21-3.6 Speculating on Interest Rate Changes

Futures contracts on government securities provide a useful vehicle for speculating on forecasted changes in market interest rates. Hedging strategies, spreads of various types, and arbitrage opportunities can be profitably exploited if the speculator can correctly forecast market interest rates. A few possibilities are discussed below.

A Long Hedge to Lock in High Current Rates Assume that on February 15, 19X1, a manager of a manufacturing corporation's cash position expects short-term interest rates to decline in the months ahead. The expected decline troubles this manager, who knows that the corporation will receive a $1 million lawsuit settlement in the form of cash on May 15, 19X1. The cash position manager fears that if the $1 million is invested on May 15, 19X1, it will earn a lower rate of return than it could earn if it were invested sooner, because declining interest rates are foreseen between February 15 and May 15 of 19X1.

In order to "lock in" the opportunity to invest at the high interest rate that exists on February 15, 19X1, the cash position manager establishes a long hedge. A long hedge occurs when futures contracts are purchased to protect against future price rises. More specifically, the cash position manager buys one 90-day T-bill contract that has a June delivery. This contract has a value that is as close to the $1 million cash receipt due May 15, 19X1, as can be obtained.[14] This allows the cash position manager to "lock in" the high current yield four months before the $1 million cash is actually received and available to be invested. Table 21-6 summarizes the results of such a profitable long hedge.

The long hedge in Table 21-6 was reversed (or unwound) when the cash available for investment arrived as scheduled on May 15, 19X1. If the cash position manager invested the cash without simultaneously selling the T-bill future, the portfolio would have been "doubled up"; that is, the portfolio would have had simultaneous long positions in T-bill futures and in T-bills. Doubling up is sloppy hedge administration—it should be avoided because it exposes the portfolio to double the risk and provides no hedge as protection.

TABLE 21-6   RESULTS OF A LONG HEDGE IN 90-DAY T-BILL FUTURES

CASH MARKET	FUTURES MARKET	SUMMARY OF DAY	
February 15, 19X1: no transaction occurs, but 90-day T-bills are yielding 7.60%	February 15, 19X1: cash position manager buys 90-day T-bill future maturing in June for 91.90	Long hedge laid down to "lock in" high yield of 8.1 percent	February 15, 19X1
May 15, 19X1: $1 million cash received and used to purchase one 90-day T-bill yielding 6.80%	May 15, 19X1: cash manager sells June 90-day T-bill future contract for 92.80	Hedge lifted when cash invested at an effective yield of 7.7%	May 15, 19X1
80 basis points less interest income earned because cash not invested sooner, an opportunity loss	90 basis point profit earned on one T-bill contract (= 92.80 − 91.90)	Effective yield is 7.7% (= 6.8% + 90%) because of hedge	Overall summary

No cash was lost in this example. But Table 21-6 shows that an opportunity loss of 80 (= 7.60% − 6.80%) basis points occurred in the cash market for T-bills by (unavoidably) delaying the investment. This opportunity loss was more than offset by a gain of 90 (= 92.80 − 91.90) basis points on the T-bill future, however. Thus, an effective yield of 7.7 percent is earned even though the T-bill rate had fallen down to 6.8 percent (as had been forecasted).

The Difference Between Practice and Theory   Unfortunately, interest rate forecasts are not always correct. First of all, if short-term interest rates had increased, instead of decreased as the cash manager had predicted, an out-of-pocket loss would have been suffered in the futures market. A second, but smaller risk occurs because the market value of the June 90-day T-bill future contract on May 15, 19X1, was not exactly equal to the $1 million

14 For directions on how to establish the proper *hedge ratio* see the following: P. Bacon and R. Williams, "Interest Rate Futures: New Tools for the Financial Manager," *Financial Management*, Spring 1976, pp. 32-38; Robert W. Kolb and Raymond Chiang, "Improving Performance Using Interest Rate Futures," *Financial Management*, Autumn 1981, p. 77; Sarkis J. Khoury, *Investment Management*, New York: Macmillan, 1983, pp. 454-455.

amount being hedged. Since fractions of future contracts cannot be obtained, perfect hedges for the exact amount needed are rare.

Figure 21-5 illustrates the objectives that long (or buying) hedgers idealistically seek when they employ interest rate futures contracts. But a long hedge based on a faulty interest rate forecast could work out differently.

FIGURE 21-5 The objectives of a long hedge with interest rate futures when declining interest rates are expected.

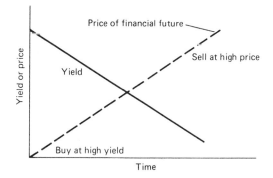

As explained briefly in Chap. 8 and in more detail in Chap. 18, an *efficient price* fluctuates around its underlying *value* less than does an *inefficient price*. Tests of market efficiency are of interest because market inefficiencies can be profitably exploited. Let's consider a case in point.

21-3.7 Market Efficiency and Quasi-Arbitrage

One of the basic axioms of economics is that the same good cannot sell at two different prices. If such a price inequality emerged, riskless arbitrage profits would occur until the same good sold at the same price around the world (after allowance is made for differences in the transportation cost). For example, suppose that $1 million T-bills from the same issue (which were perfect substitutes) were selling for $1 million in Toronto, and only $999,999 in Montreal—a tiny $1 difference. This situation could not endure because profit-seeking arbitragers would keep buying millions of dollars of T-bills in Montreal and then instantly resell them in Toronto. The arbitragers would make a $1 profit per T-bill without taking any risk because they would be perfectly hedged with a short position in Toronto that was offset by a long position in Montreal. Using wire transfers, the arbitragers could quickly make many dollars of riskless profits—except for one thing that would surely occur to stop the arbitrage profits: the price of the Montreal T-bills would be bid upward by the constant purchases in Montreal and/or the price of the identical T-bills in Toronto would be driven down by continual price-depressing sales pressure. When the Toronto and the Montreal prices were equal, the arbitrage would cease, and the T-bill market would enjoy efficient prices as the *law of one price* prevailed.

The pure arbitrage model above should extend to include quasi-arbitrage too. That is, quasi-arbitrage should ensure that a real T-bill and an equivalent position involving a synthetic duplicate T-bill should both sell at the same price too.

Pure arbitrage refers to shorting one asset to fund a position in an economically equivalent asset at a lower price. *Quasi-arbitrage* refers to selling securities from an existing portfolio to fund an economically equivalent synthetically created position at a lower price. Quasi-arbitrage is explained in more detail in the following paragraph.

Quasi-Arbitrage With T-Bill Futures William Pool and Donald Puglisi have argued that it is possible to create a *synthetic* T-bill position that mimics a genuine T-bill position.[15] For example, Poole and Puglisi reason that a long position with a genuine 6-month T-bill is no different from a synthetic 6-month T-bill long position created by combining a genuine 3-month T-bill with a 3-month T-bill futures contract. More specifically, assume that an investor purchases a 6-month T-bill and a 3-month T-bill that both originate on the same date. In addition, the investor purchases a futures contract. This futures contract entitles its owner to take delivery of a 3-month T-bill that originates on the exact date that the other 3-month T-bill expires. Thus, the investor has created a synthetic 6-month T-bill by linking a genuine 3-month T-bill with a 3-month T-bill futures contract that delivers a second genuine T-bill to follow immediately after the first genuine 3-month T-bill.

More formally, let's adopt the following three conventions (which are somewhat similar to the conventions used to define the expectations theory about the term structure of interest rates in Chap. 13).

$_0R_3$ = the market interest rate on a genuine 3-month T-bill purchased in the cash market that originates at time $t = 0$ and matures at time $t = 3$.

$_0R_6$ = the market interest rate on a genuine 6-month T-bill purchase in the cash market that originates at time $t = 0$ and matures at time $t = 6$. Note that both this 6-month T-bill and the 3-month T-bill originate at the same time.

$_3r_6$ = the rate of return earned on a 3-month T-bill futures contract that delivers a 3-month T-bill originating at time $t = 3$ and maturing at time $t = 6$. Note that this latter 3-month T-bill originates on the same date that the other 3-month T-bill expires, and it matures on the same date as the 6-month T-bill.

The relationship between these three rates of interest defined above can be stated as shown in Eq. (21-7).

$$(1.0 + {_0R_6}) = (1.0 + {_0R_3})(1.0 + {_3r_6}) \tag{21-7}$$

$$\begin{pmatrix} 1.0 + \text{interest rate} \\ \text{on genuine 6-month T-bill} \end{pmatrix} = \begin{pmatrix} 1.0 + \text{interest rate on} \\ \text{synthetic 6-month T-bill} \end{pmatrix}$$

The right-hand side of Eq. (21-7) represents the rate of return from the synthetic 6-month T-bill. If the T-bill futures market is efficient, the return from the genuine 6-month T-bill, on the left-hand side of Eq. (21-7), should exactly equal the return on the synthetic 6-month T-bill because they are perfect substitutes (assuming we ignore whatever differences in taxes and

---

15 William Poole, "Using T-Bill Futures to Gauge Interest Rate Expectations," *Economic Review*, Federal Reserve Bank of San Francisco, Spring 1978. Also see Donald J. Puglisi, "Is the Futures Market for Treasury Bills Efficient?" *Journal of Portfolio Management*, Winter 1978, vol. 4.

transactions costs may exist). If the equality of Eq. (21-7) were an inequality, quasi-arbitrage would occur until such time as the equality were restored.

Quasi-arbitrage could be done with zero initial investment. First, the genuine 6-month T-bill could be sold short. Then, the proceeds from this short sale could be used to purchase a long position in a synthetic 6-month T-bill in a long position. Equation (21-8) indicates that the profit from this quasi-arbitrage should be zero if T-bill futures markets are efficient.

$$[(1.0 + {}_0R_3)(1.0 + {}_3r_6)] - (1.0 + {}_0R_6) = 0$$

$$\underset{\text{return}}{\text{Long position's}} - \underset{\text{position's}}{\underset{\text{short}}{\text{position's}}} = \underset{\text{quasi-arbitrage}}{\text{return from}}$$

Empirical Tests Of T-Bill Futures Market Efficiency   Different researchers have constructed various forms of empirical tests to determine if quasi-arbitrage of the type outlined above can actually generate profits. Although the results were mixed, it seems that the T-bill futures market is sufficiently efficient to deny quasi-arbitragers the opportunity to get rich quick.

Some inefficiencies were discovered, however. Anthony Vignola and Charles Dale concluded that the T-bill futures market is slightly inefficient and that this inefficiency has not diminished as the market has grown and matured.[16] Poole analyzed only short-term T-bill futures and concluded that the market is efficient.[17] However, Poole's test included an inappropriate assumption about using T-bills to meet margin requirements. Richard Lang and Robert Rasche reviewed Poole's results; their own results did not suggest that all T-bill futures contracts are efficiently priced. They found that only the contracts closest to delivery, which were the contracts Poole found to be efficient, are efficient.[18] Lange and Rasche went on to conclude that

on the basis of this evidence, we cannot conclude that the differences between the futures and forward rates have been narrowing consistently over time as the futures market for Treasury bills have become more developed.

Richard Rendelman and Christopher Carabini tested observed IMM index values to see if they fall within their expected price range. Their conclusion was that

to the extent that quasi-arbitrage opportunities have existed in the market, there appears to have been a tendency for the market to become less efficient over time. The pricing of the near term contract has become less efficient while the pricing of

16 Anthony J. Vignola and Charles J. Dale, "Is the Futures Market for Treasury Bills Efficient?" *Journal of Portfolio Management*, Winter 1979, vol. 5.

17 William Poole, "Using T-Bill Futures to Gauge Interest Rate Expectations," published by Federal Reserve Bank of San Francisco, *Economic Review*, Spring 1978.

18 Richard W. Lang and Robert H. Rasche, "A Comparison of Yields on Futures Contracts and Implied Forward Rates," *Review*, Federal Reserve Bank of St. Louis, December 1978. Reprinted in *Interest Rate Futures: Concepts and Issues*, Gerald D. Gray and Robert W. Kolb (co-editors) Richmond, Va: Robert F. Dame, Inc., 1982, chap. 8. Several of the other articles about quasi-arbitrage referenced here are also reprinted in the book.

the third contract has become more efficient. However, it is doubtful that these inefficiencies have been large enough to induce portfolio managers to alter their investment policies.[19]

Additional empirical evidence about the efficiency of T-bill futures prices is forthcoming.[20]

The conclusion that quasi-arbitrage profits are not substantial does not necessarily imply that the T-bill futures market is efficient. Quasi-arbitrage profits are the easiest to detect and the most blatant form of market inefficiency. Additional research into other, more subtle market strategies is needed before conclusions about the efficiency of T-bill futures prices can be attained.

In addition to stock market index futures and Treasury bill futures, there are other actively traded financial futures contracts.

21-4   T-BOND AND T-NOTE FUTURES CONTRACTS

Tables 21-5*a* and 21-5*b* above list the specifications for futures contracts on two different Treasury bond futures, one Treasury note future and the one Canadian government bond future. U.S. Treasury bonds and notes are similar coupon interest-paying debt securities that differ primarily with respect to the length of time until they mature. T-bonds have longer lives than the T-notes (as explained in Chap. 2).

21-4.1 Contract Specifications of the Long-Term Government of Canada Bond Futures Contract

At present only one bond futures is traded in Canada, the long-term Government of Canada Bond II futures contract on the Toronto Futures Exchange. (A Winnipeg Commodity Exchange futures contract on long-term bonds is dormant).

The contract calls for delivery of $1,000,000 face value Government of Canada bonds with a 9 percent coupon rate and fifteen years or more to maturity or earliest call date from the date of delivery. The TFE allows other long-term government bonds to be delivered by the seller at appropriate discounts or premiums, thus increasing the supply of deliverable bonds. The exchange regularly publishes a list of acceptable bonds for delivery against the contract. The table on page 629 sets out the list of Government of Canada bonds that are eligible for delivery against the futures contract as of March 1986. The conversion factor is the premium that each bond commands on delivery relative to the basis grade, a 9 percent coupon bond.

19 Richard J. Rendleman, Jr., and Christopher E. Carabini, ''The Efficiency of the Treasury Bill Futures Market,'' *Journal of Finance*, September 1979, vol. 34.

20 Ben Branch, ''Testing the Unbiased Expectations and Theory of Interest Rates,'' *The Financial Review*, Fall 1978, vol. 13, pp. 51-66; Brian G. Chow and David J. Brophy, ''The U.S. Treasury Bill Futures Market and Hypotheses Regarding the Term Structure of Interest Rates,'' *The Financial Review*, Fall 1978, vol. 13, pp. 36-50; Dennis P. Capozza and Bradford Cornell, ''Treasury Bill Pricing in the Spot and Futures Markets,'' *Review of Economics and Statistics*, November 1979, vol. 61, no. 4.

TABLE 21-7 LONG CANADA BOND II FUTURES CONVERSION FACTORS

O/S AMT (MILLION $)	BOND COUPON	MATURITY	Deliverable Canada Issues					
			JUNE/ 1986	SEPT./ 1986	DEC./ 1986	MARCH/ 1987	JUNE/ 1987	SEPT./ 1987
1,850	10%	May 1, 02	1.0830	1.0827	1.0818	1.0814	1.0805	1.0801
1,625	11¼%	Dec 15, 02	1.1915	1.1899	1.1889	1.1872	1.1861	1.1843
2,700	11¾%	Feb 1, 03	1.2341	1.2321	1.2308	1.2289	1.2275	1.2255
2,200	10¼%	Feb 1, 04	1.1091	1.1082	1.1078	1.1068	1.1064	1.1054

Source: Toronto Futures Exchange, Notice to Members, no. TF86-17. March 20, 1986.

21-4.2 U.S. Contract Specifications

The prices of both the underlying T-bonds and T-notes and the futures contracts on them are all quoted in thirty-seconds of one percentage point. For example, 94.16 means 94 16/32 percent of face or par value. Thus, a $100,000 T-bond or T-bond future quoted at 94.16 would have a market price of 94.5 percent of $100,000, or $94,500.

Both the T-bond and T-note contracts come in $100,000 denominations. And both require that 8 percent coupon securities be tendered for delivery. However, T-bonds or T-notes with coupon rates that differ from 8 percent can be delivered if suitable price adjustments are made — the price adjustments are defined in the futures contract.

The T-note and T-bond contracts have longer maturities than the money market securities on which futures contracts are traded (such as T-bills, CDs, commercial paper, and banker's acceptances). Therefore, the futures contracts on T-notes and T-bonds may be used for different purposes than T-bill futures. Consider an example of how T-bond futures have been used to short hedge a long position in corporate bonds.

21-4.3 An Investment Banker Short Hedges an Underwriting

Consider the dilemma of a large investment banking firm, Salomon Brothers in this example, when they underwrite a huge bond issue for a big corporation. Salomon Brothers agreed to buy and distribute a primary issue of IBM debt securities made up of (a) $500 million of seven-year notes and (b) $500 million of twenty-five year debentures. On October 4, 1979, Salomon paid IBM $990 million for this issue of blue chip. The prospect of unstable market interest rates at that time worried the managers of the underwriting. The investment bankers were worried that after they paid the IBM Corporation $990 million for the long-term bond issue, but before they could sell the bonds to the public for $1 billion, market interest rates might rise and decrease the market value of the bonds while they were trying to distribute them. In order to foreclose such possible losses, let us suppose that Salomon Brothers laid down the short hedge that is summarized in Table 21-8 on page 630.

The investment banker paid for legal possession of a long position in bonds that, if market interest rates stayed constant, had a market value of $1 billion on October 4, 1979. To hedge the possibility that a sudden rise in market

TABLE 21-8 AN UNDERWRITER'S SHORT HEDGE OF A CORPORATE BOND ISSUE

CASH MARKET	FUTURES MARKET	EVENT
Oct 4, 1979, at 11 A.M. Salomon Brothers gives IBM a $990 million cashier's cheque to purchase a primary bond issue worth $1 billion.	11 A.M. Oct 4, 1979, Salomon Brothers sells short 10,000 T-Bond futures contracts with a $1 billion total value.	A short hedge is laid down.
October 10, 1979 at 2 P.M. Salomon sells $350 million of the bonds for $348 million so its overnight inventory has a $650 million face value. A rise in market interest rates caused an opportunity loss of $2,000,000 on the IBM bonds sold.	October 10, 1979 at 2 P.M. Salomon buys back $350 million worth (or 350 contracts) for $347 million. It retains a $650 million short position in futures market. A $3,000,000 gain on the futures position resulted from rising interest rates.	The short hedge is balanced so the long cash and short futures positions are equal. A net gain of $1,000,000 was earned.
October 11, 1979, Salomon sells its remaining $650 million inventory of IBM bonds for $647 million because interest rates have stayed high. An opportunity loss of $3,000,000 results.	October 11, 1979, Salomon buys 650 T-Bond contracts with $650 million face value for $645 million because interest rates rose higher. A gain of $5,000,000 on the futures position results.	The last part of the short hedge is lifted and a net gain of $2,000,000 is realized.
$2,000,000 plus $3,000,000 equals a total opportunity loss of $5,000,000 on the inventory of IBM bonds because market interest rates rose.	$3,000,000 plus $5,000,000 equals $8,000,000 total profit from short futures as market interest rates rose and remained high.	$8,000,000 gain less $5,000,000 opportunity loss equals $3,000,000 net benefit from the short hedge.

interest rates wipe out all or part of their $10 million spread between the purchase price and the resale price, the investment banker sold $1 billion worth of T-Bond futures short. T-Bond futures were used because the managers of the underwriting felt that the T-Bond futures price would be more highly correlated with any changes in the price of the IBM bonds than would the price of other futures contracts they might have used to create their hedge.

By October 10, 1979, the underwriters' syndicate had been able to distribute only $350 million of the issue of IBM bonds.[21] IBM bonds with a par

21 This underwriting example is taken from a true story. See, for example, *Business Week*, October 29, 1979, p. 50. Also see "Prices Drop Further As Record IBM Offer Encounters Surprising Buyer Resistance," *Wall Street Journal*, October 5, 1979, p. 37. There actually was a $1 billion IBM bond issue on October 4, 1979, underwritten by Salomon. However, the facts have been simplified here to expedite the teaching points. One of the largest simplifications is that Salomon Brothers handled the large IBM underwriting without the aid of an underwriting syndicate. In fact, a syndicate of 227 investment banking firms participated in the IBM bond issue, and Merrill Lynch helped Salomon manage the underwriting.

value of $650 million had to be carried in Salomon Brothers overnight inventory at risk. In order to avoid being short $350 million worth of unhedged T-Bond futures, Salomon Brothers covered (or bought back or unwound or reversed) $350 million of their $1 billion short position in T-Bond futures. This transaction rebalanced the $650 million hedged position in IBM bonds. As indicated in Table 21-8, the investment banker sold the last of the IBM bond issue on October 11, 1979. At that time, the remaining $650 million short position in T-Bond futures was reversed with a purchase of $650 million of futures contracts to lift the hedge.

In this partially simplified underwriting example, it was assumed that Salomon Brothers' advance fears of rising market interest rates were vindicated. As a result, the investment banker suffered an opportunity loss of $2 million between October 4, and October 10, 1979. This opportunity loss occurred when IBM bonds with a par value of $350 million could only be sold for $348 million. However, the T-Bond futures simultaneously also dropped in price. So, when Salomon Brothers covered $350 million of its short T-Bond position, these contracts were repurchased for $347 — or $3,000,000 less than the amount received when the short position was established. This $3 million gain in the futures market more than offset the investment banking firm's $2 million opportunity loss on the IBM bonds so that a net gain of $1 million occurred.

Table 21-8 further indicates that market interest rates continued to rise. As a result, the investment bankers $650 million of remaining inventory in IBM bonds had to be sold for $647 million, resulting in an opportunity loss of $3 million on October 11, 1979. As with the preceding days, however, the $650 million short position in T-bond futures profited as market interest rates rose. So, Salomon made a $5 million gain on the T-Bond futures by buying back the still outstanding $650 million of futures contracts for $645 million. This $5 million gain more than offset the $3 million opportunity loss that occurred on October 11, 1979—$2 million more net gain resulted.

Overall, the investment banker's short hedge in Table 21-8 was well-executed and profitable. The hedge protected the value of the long position in IBM bonds and, since it was not a perfect hedge, was able to earn a $8 million total gain on the T-Bond futures. This profit more than compensated for the $5 million opportunity loss incurred when the issue of IBM bonds with a face value of $1 billion could not be sold for the full amount of their face value.

21-4.4 Generalizations about Short Hedges

Figure 21-6 at the top of page 632 illustrates what Salomon Brothers and every other short hedger idealistically *hopes* to accomplish when establishing a short hedge. Compare the idealistic Fig. 21-6 with the IBM Salomon case in Table 21-8 for further insight into the short hedge.

In the Salomon's case, the loss they incurred from their cash position in IBM bonds was more than compensated for by the gain from their short position in T-bond futures. However, consider what would have happened if market interest rates had fallen instead of rising as Salomon (correctly) feared. If interest rates had fallen instead of rising, Salomon's profits and losses on their futures and cash positions, respectively, would have been

FIGURE 21-6   The objectives of a short hedge with financial futures when rising interest rates are forecasted.

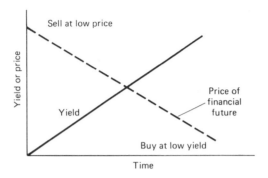

reversed. More specifically, there would have been a gain from appreciating IBM bonds in the inventory and a loss on the short futures position, leaving Salomon's net position largely unchanged. This effect is the essence of hedging with interest rate futures: interest rate risk is reduced or eliminated.

21-5   CHAPTER SUMMARY AND CONCLUSIONS

The volume of financial futures contracts traded every day is exploding. Furthermore, there are new financial futures contract applications waiting to be approved by various government agencies. The financial futures business is one of the most rapidly growing parts of the financial community.

Section 21-1 of this chapter listed dozens of financial futures contracts already being actively traded at over a dozen different commodity exchanges. There are simply too many different financial futures contracts in existence to be discussed in this chapter. Only the more popular contracts were explained to provide familiarity with these new financial instruments.

Stock market averages and indexes, indicators that track the average price of the securities in a given market, were explained in Chap. 7. And Chap. 20 introduced futures contracts and explained how commodity exchanges work. Section 21-2 of this chaper (1) brought this preceding material together and introduced futures contracts on stock market indexes; (2) explained the use of the TSE 300 Composite Index and the Standard & Poor's 500 Stocks Composite Average, not as deliverable commodities, but as indicators for cash settlement futures contracts; (3) reviewed initial margins, variation of maintenance margins, and the requirement that exists in all commodity exchanges to mark to the market at the close of each day's trading; (4) examined various strategies available to those who foresee either bull or bear markets and want to speculate accordingly; and (5) discussed strategies for risk-averse hedgers.

Interest rate futures are financial futures, too. But unlike the stock market index futures, whose prices are determined by numerous factors, the prices of the interest rate futures are determined by one primary factor—market interest rates. Market interest rates determine bond prices, as explained in Chaps. 11 and 13. Interest rate futures, however, have bonds or other interest rate-sensitive assets as the deliverable commodity. This chapter examined different speculative and hedging strategies and the delivery process for interest rate futures used at the Chicago Mercantile Exchange's International Monetary Market (IMM). It also introduced quasi-arbitrage, which was used to analyze the efficiency of the T-bill futures market.

Canadian government bonds, Treasury notes, and Treasury bonds are different from Treasury bills in two major respects. First, T-bills are short-term money market securities, while T-notes are intermediate-term assets and Canadian Government bonds and T-bonds are long-term assets. A second important difference is that T-bills are issued on a discount basis and pay no coupons. In contrast, Canadian Government bonds, T-notes, and T-bonds all pay periodic coupons (as previously explained in Chap. 2). Futures contracts on Canadian Government bonds, T-notes, and T-bonds are popular instruments that can be used by both speculators and hedgers. Therefore, this chapter briefly reviewed the Canadian Government bond, T-note, and T-bond contracts, and their use was demonstrated by an investment banking example. Financial futures contracts are still a fairly new product on the North American scene; new products are rapidly emerging, and much remains to be learned.[22]

22 The research articles listed below and other articles published in the same periodicals may be informative.

Fisher Black, "The Pricing of Commodity Contracts," *Journal of Financial Economics*, January-March 1976; vol. 3, no. 1.

Marcelle Arak and Christopher J. McCurdy, "Interest Rate Futures," *Quarterly Review*, Federal Reserve Bank of New York, Winter 1979-1980.

Peter W. Bacon and Richard E. Williams, "Interest Rate Futures: New Tool for the Financial Manager," *Financial Management*, Spring 1976; vol. 5, no. 1.

Robert W. McLeod and George M. McCabe, "Hedging for Better Spread Management," *The Bankers Magazine*, July-August 1980, vol. 163, no. 4.

Richard W. McEnally and Michael L. Rice, "Hedging Possibilities in the Flotation of Debt Securities," *Financial Management*, Winter 1979, vol. 8, no. 4.

Louis H. Ederington, "The Hedging Performance of the New Futures Markets," *Journal of Finance*, March 1979, vol. 34.

Charles T. Franckle, "The Hedging Performance of the New Futures Markets: Comment," *Journal of Finance*, December 1980, vol. 35, no. 5.

Gerald D. Gay and Robert W. Kolb, "The Management of Interest Rate Risk," *Journal of Portfolio Management*, Winter 1983, pp. 65-70.

Robert W. Kolb and Raymond Chiang, "Improving Hedging Performance Using Interest Rate Futures," *Financial Management*, August 1981, pp. 72-79.

Edward J. Kane, "Market Incompleteness and Divergences between Forward and Futures Interest Rates," *Journal of Finance*, May 1980, vol. 35, no. 2.

Michael A. MacKenzie and John L. Playfair, "Interest Rate Futures—Not For Idle Speculation," *CA Magazine*, November 1981, pp. 40-49.

Edward Miller, "Tax-Induced Bias in Markets for Futures Contracts," *The Financial Review*, vol. 15, pp. 35-38.

J.E. Hilliard, "Hedging Interest Rate Risk with Futures Portfolios under Term Structure Effects," *Journal of Finance*, December 1984, vol. 39, no. 5, pp. 1547-1570.

James G. O'Brien, "Tax Topics: Interest Rates Futures—Commercial Banks," *The Banking Law Journal*, March 1981, vol. 98, no.2.

James Kurt Drew, "Bank Regulations for Futures Accounting," *Issues in Bank Regulation*, Spring 1981.

(continued on next page)

In conclusion, it is informative to review the difference between option contracts and futures contracts. Table 19-4 on page 540 summarizes the rights and obligations of the buyers and sellers of both put and call options. The primary difference between options and futures is the difference between the rights and obligations of the buyers of these two different financial instruments. The buyer of a futures contract is legally obligated to perform. In contrast, the option buyer has the right *but not* the obligation to perform. The sellers of both options and futures are obligated to perform; it is only the option buyers who are not obligated to do anything after they pay the premium to buy their option. The appendix to Chapter 21 explains option contracts on futures contracts.

QUESTIONS

1. Define the "basis" for an interest rate future contract. What determines the basis on interest rate futures?
2. Why might speculators prefer futures markets over the cash market in the underlying asset?
3. Forward contracts were the predecessor of futures contracts. Why didn't speculators and hedgers use forward contracts as much as they use futures contracts?
4. "The existence of two almost identical T-bill futures contracts traded at competing commodity exchanges is economically undesirable because it fragments the market." Is the preceding sentence true, false, or uncertain? Explain.
5. Define "spreading." (*Hint*: You might check one of the books referenced in this chapter for more spreading information.) Why do some commodity speculators use spreading strategies rather than simply take a long or short position?
6. Do you expect trading in stock market index futures contracts to have any impact on stock market prices? Explain.
7. If an investor buys a Government of Canada bond in a long position and then realizes that the Government of Canada bond price is going to decline because of a previously unforeseen turn in interest rates, what

Robert C. Lower and Scott W. Ryan, "Futures Trading by National Banks," *The Banking Law Journal*, March 1981, vol. 98, no. 3.

Phillip Cagan, "Financial Futures Markets: Is More Regulation Needed?" *Journal of Futures Markets*, Summer 1981, no. 2.

Louis H. Ederington, "Living with Inflation: A Proposal for New Futures and Options Markets," *Financial Analysts Journal*, January-February 1980.

"Ready or Not, Here Come Financial Futures," *Institutional Investor*, March 1983, pp. 51-66.

Victor Niederhoffer and Richard Zeckhauser, "Market Index Futures Contracts," *Financial Analysts Journal*, January-February 1980.

J.C. Francis and Mark Castelino, "Basis Speculation in Commodity Futures: The Maturity Effect," *Journal of Futures Markets*, 1982, vol. 2, no. 2, pp. 195-206.

Many of the papers above, and others as well, have been published in Gerald D. Gay and Robert W. Kolb (eds.), *Interest Rate Futures*, Richmond, Va: Robert F. Dame, Inc., 1982.

can the investor do to avoid losses? Describe more than one way to avoid the imminent loss.

8. Compare and contrast a long position in futures contracts with owning a call option position of the same size on the same asset. (*Hint*: Refer to Chap. 19 about call options.)

9. Suppose that long-term Treasury bonds are currently yielding higher interest rates than Treasury notes — that is, the yield curve is sloping upward. Assume that your research makes you confident that the yield curve will flatten out, causing the yield spread between T-notes and T-bonds to narrow. How can you profit from this flattening of the yield curve if your expectations are borne out?

10. Is quasi-arbitrage riskier than pure arbitrage? Explain.

SELECTED REFERENCES

Commodity futures exchanges. Each exchange will gladly provide free printed material describing its products and procedures.

Frank J. Fabozzi and Gregory M. Kipnis (eds.) *Stock Index Futures*. Homewood, Ill: Dow Jones-Irwin, 1984. An easy-to-read collection of articles about different aspects of stock index futures written by experts in their respective segments of the subject.

John E. Hore. *Trading on Canadian Futures Markets*. The Canadian Securities Institute, 1985. An easy-to-read nonmathematical description of the futures markets and interest rate futures contracts.

Robert W. Kolb. *Understanding Futures Markets*. Glenview, Ill: Scott, Foresman, and Company, 1985. This college-level textbook starts by describing the institutions of futures markets, explains the present value calculations that permeate financial futures work, and analyzes various aspects of market efficiency, speculation, and hedging in financial futures contracts. Algebra and statistics are used, but the book is easy to read.

Allan M. Loosigian. *Foreign Exchange Futures*. Homewood, Ill: Dow Jones-Irwin, 1981. A nonmathematical description of the foreign exchange aspect of the financial futures markets. This book comprehensively reviews international economic agreements, defines the foreign exchange vocabulary, discusses the futures markets, and reviews numerous hedging and speculation applications.

———. *Interest Rate Futures*. Homewood, Ill: Dow Jones-Irwin, 1980. An easy-to-read, nonmathematical description of the commodity exchanges and the major interest rate futures contracts, with details about brokerage services, speculation, hedging, arbitraging, and the determinants of market interest rates.

Nancy H. Rothstein (ed.). *The Handbook of Financial Futures*. New York: McGraw-Hill, 1984. This collection of essays written by businesspeople uses virtually no mathematics, is easy to read, and is replete with examples. The book contains a comprehensive discussion of institutional arrangements and examples of applications.

Andrew D. Seidel and Philip M. Ginsberg. *Commodities Trading*. Englewood Cliffs, N.J.: Prentice-Hall, 1983. A comprehensive, advanced undergraduate-or MBA-level textbook about options and commodity futures. The book uses mathematics. The main focus of the book is on financial futures.

Options on Futures

Chapter 19 defined put and call options. Chapter 20 introduced commodity futures contracts. And Chap. 21 went on to explain financial futures contracts. This appendix considers all these elements at once as it discusses a financial instrument that is a combination of options and futures contracts—it is called an option on a futures contract or a commodity option.

Options on futures were traded actively in London and Canada before World War II. And some options on futures were traded on the Chicago Board of Trade until 1934. But options on futures were outlawed in the United States by some 1936 amendments to the Grain Futures Trading Act. Then, in 1982 commodity exchanges in the United States began trading options on a few futures contracts under the supervision of a Commodity Futures Trading Commission (CFTC) pilot program. Table App. 21A-1 provides a description of a few of the options on futures currently traded. At present there are no options on futures contracts traded in Canada, only options on actual commodities.

APP. 21A-1 CHARACTERISTICS OF OPTIONS ON FUTURES

All options on futures are two steps removed from the underlying asset. First, there is the futures contract on the underlying asset. Second, there is the put or call option on the futures contract. At first, this seems complicated. But options on futures are actually like ordinary futures contracts that have only limited liability and different margin procedures.

Buying or Selling an Option on a Future The *buyer* of one option on a future may exercise the option to assume a position in one future. But the position assumed depends on whether the option buyer purchases a put or a call. If a *call option is purchased*, the buyer has the right to exercise the call option by purchasing a long (but not a short) position in the specified future at the exercise (or striking) price stipulated in the option contract. In contrast, if a *put option is purchased*, the buyer has the option to exercise that put by establishing a short (not a long) position in the specific future at the exercise price stipulated in the put option contract. Put and call options must be exercised before some maturity date agreed upon when the option seller sells the option to the option buyer or else the option expires and becomes worthless. The buyers of put and call options on futures have the right, but are under no obligation of any kind, to exercise the options they have purchased. Options need not be exercised to be profitable, however. Options are marketable financial instruments. Therefore, owners of profitable put and call options often choose to realize their profits by selling the option for a higher price than they paid for it instead of exercising its privileges and entering a futures market position.

TABLE 21A-1 OPTIONS ON FUTURES CONTRACTS

OPTION	U.S. TREASURY BOND FUTURES	GOLD FUTURES	STANDARD & POOR'S 500 STOCK INDEX FUTURES
Exchange	Chicago Board of Trade	Commodity Exchange, Inc. (COMEX)	International Monetary Market (IMM), a division of Chicago Mercantile Exchange
Trading unit	$100,000 face value U.S. Treasury bond futures contract	100 troy ounces	One S&P 500 stock index futures contract
Price quotation method	Points & 64ths of a pt Each full point = $1,000 1/64 = $15.63 (e.g. 2-16 = 2 pts and 16/64 $2,500)	Dollars per ounce (e.g., a quote of 2.45 means $2.45 per ounce, or $2,450 per option)	Quoted in index points, i.e., each .01 point (1 BP) Each BP is worth $5 (e.g. a quote of 2.45 represents $1,225)
Strike price interval	Integral multiples of 2 points ($2,000) per T-bond futures contract (e.g. 68, 70, 72, etc.)	If the strike price is between $300 & $500, intervals are $10; if between $500 & $800, interval is $30; if over $800, strike prices trade in intervals of $40.	Integer divisible by 5 without remainder (e.g. 110, 115, 120)
Minimum fluctuation (tick value)	Multiples of 1/64 of 1% of a $100,000 T-bond futures contract ($15.63)	10¢ per ounce ($10)	.05 index points (i.e., 5 BP) ($25)
Maximum fluctuation (limit value)	Same as limit for T-bond futures, currently 2 points (128/64 = $2,000)	No limit	No limit
Trading hours	8-2 CST	9:25-2:30 EST	9:00-3:15 CST
Trading months	Same as CBT T-bond futures: Mar., June, Sept., Dec.	Apr., Aug., Dec. (4-month cycle)	Mar., June, Sept., Dec. (4-month cycle)
Exercise	Buyer may give notice by 8 P.M. any business day prior to expiration; clearing corporation will establish future position for buyer (long if a call, short if a put) & opposite position for seller prior to opening on next business day	Until 3 P.M. on any business day on which the option is trading	Until last day of trading (i.e., 3d Thurs. of contract month for underlying futures contract)
Last day of trading	12 P.M. on 1st Friday preceding by at least 5 business days the first notice day for the T-bond futures contract	2d Friday of month prior to expiration of underlying contract month; 2:30 P.M.	Last trading day of underlying contract (i.e., 3d Thurs. of contract month)
Expiration	10 A.M. on first Saturday following last day of trading	2d Friday of month prior to expiration of underlying futures contract	Last day of trading of underlying contract (i.e., 3d Thurs. of contract month)

Consider the irrevocable obligation of the seller, or writer, of the option on the future. Unlike the option buyer, the option writer has a legal *obligation* to perform—the writer has no other option. What the option writer is obligated to perform, however, depends on whether he or she sold a put or a call option.

If the seller or *writer of one call option* on a futures contract is notified that the buyer is exercising the option, the call seller must instantly assume a short position in the particular futures contract that was optioned. More specifically, the call seller must deliver the optioned futures contract at the stipulated exercise price. If the writer of the option does not have a long position in the underlying instrument when the option is exercised the writer must assume a short position in the optioned futures contract by paying the initial margin.

Now let's consider the position of someone who writes a put option on a future. If the *writer of one put option on a futures contract* is notified that the buyer is exercising the option, the put seller is obliged to instantly assume a long position. That is, the put writer must let the option buyer put (that is, deliver) the optioned commodity futures contract to him or her at the exercise price (which is typically above the current market price or the put would not be profitable to exercise).

Graphs to illustrate the gains or losses of the various positions involved may be helpful. These graphs illustrate the expiration date profits attainable by exercising an option to enter a position in the futures market. The profits that may be attained from simply selling the option for more than its purchase price are considered later in this appendix, when the determinants of option prices are analyzed.

Illustrations of the Various Positions' Gains and Losses

Figure App. 21A-1 illustrates the profit position of the option buyer on a financial future. Movements in financial option prices are determined by changes in the prices of the underlying asset. In Fig. App. 21A-1, the buyer of an option contract gains as the price of the option rises. For a call option on an interest rate future, such gains occur when interest rates fall, or for a put option, when interest rates rise. As the option price falls, however, the buyer's maximum loss is limited to the premium paid. In Fig. App. 21A-2

FIGURE APP. 21A-1 Option buyer's position.

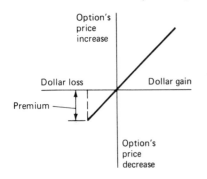

FIGURE APP. 21A-2 Option writer's position.

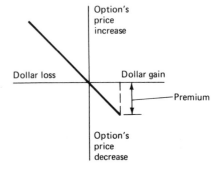

FIGURE APP. 21A-3 Position of a future's buyer.

FIGURE APP. 21A-4 Position of a future's seller.

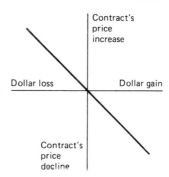

the position of an option writer on a financial futures contract is illustrated. This option writer loses as the price of the option rises, but if the option price falls the maximum gain is limited to the initial premium received.

Figure App. 21A-3 shows that the buyer of a futures contract on an underlying financial asset gains as the price of the contract rises. In the lower left quadrant of Fig. App. 21A-3, losses occur as the price of the contract falls. In Fig. App. 21A-4, the short seller of a financial futures contract gains as prices fall and loses as prices rise.

APP. 21A-2 RIGHTS VERSUS OBLIGATIONS FOR THE OPTION PARTIES

Options are *unilateral* contracts—this is an important way in which they differ from the bilateral futures contract. Any party who buys an option on a futures contract acquires the right—but not the obligation—to assume a long or a short position in one futures contract at the prearranged exercise price at any time during the life of the option, if it is an American option. (European options can be exercised only on the final day of the contract, and they are usually written on forward contracts.) Since option buyers have no obligation to perform after their premium is paid, they are not required to mark to the market as are the sellers of futures options contracts (although this rule may be changed in the future).

In contrast to option buyers, anyone who writes an option contract on a future undertakes a firm (legally enforceable) commitment to assume a long (for a call) or a short (for a put) position in the futures market at the striking price if the buyer exercises the option. Since option writers are required to perform, these writers are required to deposit an initial margin when a position is opened. Furthermore, this margin is marked to the market daily to reflect changes in the value of the option.

The buyer of an option on a futures contract may exercise the option at any time before it expires merely by notifying the clearinghouse at the appropriate commodity exchange. All this takes is a quick phone call to the buyer's broker, who then notifies the clearinghouse (or clearinghouse member, if the broker is not a member of the clearinghouse). Then the clearinghouse will proceed to establish a futures position for the buyer. At the same time, the seller of the option is obliged to instantly assume the opposite futures position at the prearranged exercise price.

In the large exchanges, a computer assigns a particular option writer to respond to an option buyer who decides to exercise a put or call option; the assignment is given randomly on a first-in-first-out basis. The clearinghouse computer, which keeps an inventory of writers, typically selects the clearinghouse member with the largest number of positions in an option that expires in the relevant month. Then the oldest outstanding written option within that clearinghouse member's inventory is selected to fulfill the demands of the exercising option buyer. The option buyer and writer need never know each other's identity. The clearinghouse acts as intermediary between the buyer and the writer.

How the writer of the option on the futures contract responds depends on the particular underlying financial instrument. If the instrument is a U.S. Treasury bond, the relevant bond can be delivered to fulfill the contract if the contract is obtained and held for delivery. But if the futures contract underlying the option is on some stock market index, then a cash settlement is the only possible mode of delivery if the contract is obtained and held for delivery. Delivery on stock market futures contracts is explained in Sec. 21-2 of this chapter.

The option writer's response to notification that the option is being exercised depends on whether the writer was writing "naked" or "covered," as explained in Sec. 19-6. If the option writer owns the underlying financial instrument, then that position can be delivered to fulfill the buyer's demand for it — if such a demand ever emerges. If the option writer was writing naked, then, delivery of the contract is ultimately demanded, the writer is placed in a short position.

App. 21A-2.1 OPTIONS ON FUTURES SPECIFICATIONS FOR T-BONDS

As indicated in Tables App. 21A-1 and 21-5*a* & *b*, the expiration months for options on T-bond futures are identical to the T-bond futures delivery months — March, June, September, and December of each year, for two years into the future.

The market prices of both T-bonds and T-bond futures are quoted in terms of percentage points followed by thirty-seconds of a percentage point. For example, a T-bond quoted at 99-16 is worth 99 16/32 or 99.5 percent of the bond's face value. Thus a $100,000 T-bond quoted at 99-16 is worth $99,500. Each full percentage point is worth $1,000 of market value, and each thirty-second of a point is worth $31.25.

Unlike T-bond futures, options on T-bond futures are quoted in sixty-fourths of a percentage point. Thus, for instance, a premium of 2-32 represents a premium of $2,500. Each sixty-fourth is worth $15.63. The next section explains how the premiums on options on T-bond futures are determined.

For the sake of clarity, consider an option on a T-bond futures contract that has an exercise (or striking) price of exactly 60 percentage points of face value. Figure App 21A-5 illustrates the determination of this option's price or premium. When the underlying T-bond futures contracts are trading at 62-00, the call option on these contracts has a *minimum value* of 2 points, denoted 2-00. However, option prices (or premiums) rise farthest above their minimum value line when the price of the optioned asset lies near the exercise (or striking) price, as shown in Fig. App. 21A-5. Thus, the premium (or price) on this call option is 3-00 points (that is, $3,000) because the premium is 1 point above its minimum value when the T-bond future's price is 62-00.

Determinants of Premiums for a Call on T-bond Futures

FIGURE APP. 21A-5 Price breakdown for call option on T-bond future.

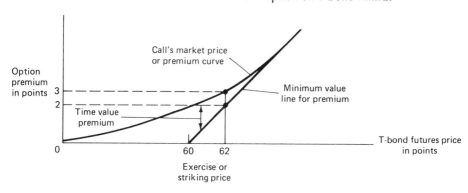

The vertical distance between the minimum value line and the curve representing the market price of the call option is called the *time value* of the option. The time value of a call option is calculated as follows:

$$
\begin{pmatrix} \text{Time} \\ \text{value} \\ \text{of call} \end{pmatrix} = \begin{pmatrix} \text{call} \\ \text{option's} \\ \text{premium} \end{pmatrix} + \begin{pmatrix} \text{exercise} \\ \text{price} \end{pmatrix} - \begin{pmatrix} \text{market} \\ \text{price of} \\ \text{underlying} \\ \text{asset} \end{pmatrix}
$$

$$
(1) \quad = \quad (3) \quad + \quad (60) \quad - \quad (62)
$$

The time value for a call option on a financial futures contract increases directly with the riskiness (namely, the price volatility) of the underlying futures contract and the time remaining until the call option expires, if all other factors are held equal. Essentially, the same factors that explained the premiums of options on common stocks in Chap. 19 determine the values of options on futures contracts.

Figure App. 21A-6 (at the top of page 642) illustrates the primary determinants that influence premiums for a put option on a T-bond future when the exercise (or striking) price is 60-00. If the underlying T-bond future is trading at 58-00 (that is, $58,000 for a $100,000 T-bond), the put option's premium is 3-00 points (namely $3,000). This 3-00 point market price is comprised of

Determinants of Premiums for a Put on T-Bond Futures

FIGURE APP. 21A-6   Price breakdown for put option on T-bond future.

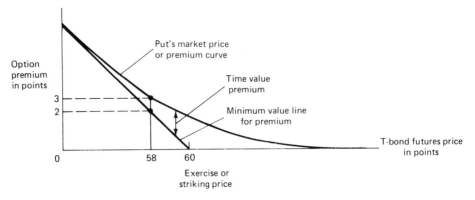

a minimum value of 2-00 plus a time value premium of 1 point, as calculated below.

$$
\begin{pmatrix} \text{Time} \\ \text{value} \\ \text{put} \end{pmatrix} = \begin{pmatrix} \text{put's} \\ \text{premium} \\ \text{or price} \end{pmatrix} + \begin{pmatrix} \text{put's} \\ \text{market} \\ \text{price} \end{pmatrix} - \begin{pmatrix} \text{put's} \\ \text{exercise} \\ \text{price} \end{pmatrix}
$$
$$
(1) \quad = \quad (3) \quad + \quad (58) \quad - \quad (60)
$$

The time value premium over the minimum value line is illustrated by a vertical arrow in Fig. App. 21A-6. The factors that determine the size of the time value premiums on puts also determine the time value premiums on calls.

APP. 21A-3   THE ADVANTAGES AND DISADVANTAGES OF OPTIONS ON FUTURES

After considering options on futures for a while, the question arises: "Are there any advantages to buying options on futures instead of simply buying the same futures contract directly?" The answer is: "Yes, there is an advantage." Speculators who buy options on futures enjoy a so-called safety net that inherently keeps the buyer of an option on a futures contract from losing more than the premium paid for the put or call option.

Speculators who buy futures contracts directly must put down an initial margin and then mark to the market based on each day's settlement price — this requirement is explained in this chapter. As a result, the owner of a futures contract can lose much more than the cost of an option's premium. Figure App. 21A-1 illustrates the fact that option buyers' losses are limited to the premium they paid to purchase the option. Of course, option buyers do not enjoy this safety net or limited liability for free. Options do not become profitable until the price of the underlying asset moves far enough in the appropriate direction to cover the cost of the option's premium. As a result

TABLE APP. 21A-2 OPTIONS ON FUTURES CONTRACTS

COMMODITY	CONTRACT SIZE	EXCHANGE
All Ordinaries Share Price Index	A$ 100 × Index	Sydney Futures Exchange (SFE)
British pound	£25,000	Chicago Mercantile Exchange (CME)
British pound	£25,000	London International Financial Futures Exchange (LIFFE)
Canadian dollar	CDN 100,000	CME
Cocoa	10 metric tons	Coffee, Sugar, and Cocoa Exchange (CSCE)
Coffee	37,500 lb.	CSCE
Copper	25,000 lb.	Commodity Exchange Inc. (COMEX)
Corn	5,000 bu	Chicago Board of Trade (CBT)
Cotton	50,000 lb.	New York Cotton Exchange (CTN)
Crude Oil	1000 bbl	New York Mercantile Exchange (NYME)
European Currency Unit	ECU 100,000	CTN
Eurodollar Time Deposit	US$ 1,000,000	CME
Eurodollar	US$ 1,000,000	LIFFE
Gold	100 oz	COMEX
Gold	33.2 oz	Mid-America Commodity Exchange (MA)
Japanese yen	¥ 12,500,000	CME
Live Cattle	40,000 lb.	CME
Live hogs	30,000 lb.	CME
NYSE Composite Stock Index	US$ 500 × Index	New York Futures Exchange (NYSE)
Ninety Day Bank bills	A$ 500,000	SFE
Orange juice	15,000 lb.	CTN
Pork bellies	40,000 lb.	CME
Silver	1,000 oz	CBT
Silver	5,000 oz	COMEX
Soybeans	1,000 bu	MA
Soybeans	5,000 bu	CBT
Standard & Poor's 500 Composite Index	US$ 500 × Index	CME
Sugar	112,000 lb.	CSCE
Swiss franc	Sfr 125,000	CME
U.S. Dollar	US$ 100,000	SFE
U.S. Dollar Index	US$ 500 × Index	CTN
U.S. T-Bills	US$ 1,000,000	CME
U.S. T-Bonds	US$ 100,000	CBT
U.S. T-Bonds	US$ 100,000	LIFFE
U.S. T-Notes	US$ 100,000	CBT
Ten-Year T-Bonds	A$ 100,000	SFE
Twenty-Year U.K. Gilts	£50,000	LIFFE
West German mark	DM 125,000	CME
Wheat	5 × 1,000 bu	MA
Wheat	5,000 bu	Kansas City Board of Trade (KCBT)
Wheat	5,000 bu	Minneapolis Grain Exchange (MGE)
Wheat	5,000 bu	CBT

of this built-in difference, speculators who forecasted the market's move correctly will always make a larger gain from a futures contract than they would have if they had used an option on the same futures contracts.

When considering the desirability of using options on futures, it would also be appropriate to inquire: "Is there any reason to buy an option on a futures contract instead of simply buying an option on the underlying asset directly?'' The answer is: ''Yes. The advantage from using options on futures is that less cash may be required.'' This advantage becomes evident only when a comparison is made after the two different options have been exercised. When a direct option is exercised on the underlying asset, the underlying asset must be purchased with cash—this is a large outlay. In contrast, a speculator who exercises an option on a futures contract need only pay enough cash to cover the cost of the required initial margin—the entire value of the contract need not be expended simply to exercise the option. However, this exercising advantage may be valueless to some speculators. After all, the options need not be exercised to be profitable. Options that have appreciated over their initial premium can simply be sold to another speculator in the secondary market in order to realize the gain. Buying the option on a future rather than buying the direct option is advantageous primarily to buyers who may not want to exercise the option to recognize a gain.

Options on different futures contracts are similar. Table App. 21A-1 lists the options on futures that were initially traded in 1982. Table App. 21A-2 lists the current options on futures traded worldwide.

SELECTED REFERENCES

Michael T. Belongia and Thomas H. Gregory. ''Are Options on Treasury Bond Futures Priced Efficiently?'' *Review*. St. Louis Federal Reserve Bank, January 1984, vol. 66, no. 1, pp. 5–13.

Fischer Black. ''The Pricing of Commodity Contracts.'' *Journal of Financial Economics*, January 1976, vol. 3, no. 1 and 2, pp. 167–79.

Eugene Moriarity, Susan Phillips, and Paula Tosini. ''A Comparison of Options and Futures in the Management of Portfolio Risk.'' *Financial Analysts Journal*, January-February 1981, pp. 61–67.

Avner Wolf. ''Fundamentals of Commodity Options on Futures.'' *Journal of Futures Market*, 1982, vol. 2, no. 4, pp. 391–408.

CHAPTER 22

International Investing

The corporate form of business ownership with multiple owners, limited liability for investors, and separate debt and equity securities exists in some form in most industrial countries of the world. International investing is a routine transaction at many banks and stock brokerage firms. So let's begin our exploration of the opportunities available to international investors by considering the financial economics of international investing.

22-1 MULTINATIONAL DIVERSIFICATION

The possibility of investing in different countries of the world introduces another dimension to diversification. Portfolio theory is a useful tool with which to analyze these possibilities.

The initial application of portfolio theory in an international context was by Herbert Grubel.[1] Grubel's model assumes that there are two countries that are economically isolated. In each of these countries, there are three types of wealth: real assets, money, and marketable bonds. The model explores what happens when the initial economic barriers are removed, assuming that only marketable bonds and consumer goods (such as food) are traded. In this model a portfolio of marketable bonds from both countries would have an expected return that is determined by the expected returns in each country and the proportion of assets invested in each country, as specified in Eq. (22-1a).

**22-1.1
Grubel's
Classic
Analysis**

$$E(r_p) = (x)E(r_1) + (1 - x)E(r_2) \qquad (22\text{-}1a)$$

where

$E(r_p)$ = expected return on an international portfolio of marketable bonds from countries 1 and 2

$E(r_1)$ = expected return on bonds in country 1

$E(r_2)$ = expected return on bonds in country 2

x = proportion of assets invested in country 1, where $1.0 > x > 0$

$(1 - x)$ = proportion of assets invested in country 2

---

1 Herbert Grubel, ''Internationally Diversified Portfolios: Welfare Gains and Capital Flows,'' *American Economic Review*, December 1968, pp. 1299–1314.

The conventions employed in Eq. (22-1a) are all presumed to be adjusted to reflect foreign exchange risk, or else it is assumed that the foreign exchange rates are pegged. (Foreign exchange risk will be treated separately, later in this chapter.)

The variance of this two-country bond portfolio, var(r_p), would be determined by the variances of returns in each country, denoted var(r_1) and var(r_2), respectively, the proportion of assets in each country, x and $(1 - x)$, respectively, and the correlation of returns between both countries' bonds, denoted $\rho_{1,2}$, as shown in Eq. (22-2a)

$$\text{var}(r_p) = x^2 \text{var}(r_1) + (1 - x)^2 \text{var}(r_2) \tag{22-2a}$$
$$+ 2(x)(1 - x)(\sigma_1)(\sigma_2)(\rho_{1,2})$$

where

var(r_1) = variance of returns in country 1 = σ_1^2

var(r_2) = variance of returns in country 2 as seen from country 1 and adjusted for any changes in the foreign exchange rate = σ_2^2

$\rho_{1,2}$ = correlation coefficient between the two countries' bond returns

Box 22-1 illustrates the risk reduction benefits available to the international investor as the correlation between the two countries' bond portfolios varies. The correlation between international investment returns is seen to be the key to risk reduction through international diversification. Table 22-1 presents empirical estimates of the correlations between common stock portfolios in

BOX 22-1 The Impact of Intercountry Return Correlations ontheVariance from an International Portfolio	
$E(r_1) = E(r_2) = 10\% = $ expected returns in the two countries	
$\sigma_1^2 = \sigma_2^2 = 16\% = $ variance of expected returns	
$(x) = (1 - x) = .50 = $ proportion of assets invested in	
each country, $x > 0$	
$E(r_p) = (x)E(r_1) + (1 - x)E(r_2)$	(22-1a)
$E(r_p) = (.5)(.1) + (1.0 - .5)(.1) = .1 = 10.0\%$	(22-1b)
$\text{var}(r_p) = x^2 \text{var}(r_1) + (1 - x)^2 \text{var}(r_2) +$	
$+ 2(x)(1 - x)(\sigma_1)(\sigma_2)(\rho_{1,2})$	(22-2a)
$\text{var}(r_p) = (.5)^2(.16)^2 + (1.0 - .5)^2(.16)^2 +$	(22-2b)
$+ 2(.5)(1.0 - .5)\sqrt{(.16)}\sqrt{(.16)}(\rho_{1,2})$	
$\text{var}(r) = .08 + .08(\rho_{1,2})$	(22-2c)

NUMERICAL ILLUSTRATION OF THE PORTFOLIO'S VARIANCE REDUCTION

CORRELATION, ρ	+1.0	+.50	0.0	-.50	-1.0
var(r_p)	.16	.12	.08	.04	0

TABLE 22-1   SUMMARY OF INTERCOUNTRY CORRELATIONS STUDIES

COUNTRY	(1)	(2)	
Australia	.58	.57	
France	.44	.41	
Hong Kong	.79	.23	
Italy	.27	.39	
Japan	.23	.34	
Netherlands	.55	.39	
Singapore	.60	.42	
Switzerland	.35	.50	
United Kingdom	.36	.60	
United States	.71	.77	
West Germany	−.04	.39	
Author	**Sampled period**		**Publication**
(1) R.G. Ibbotson, R.C. Carr, and A.W. Robinson	1960–1980 monthly		1982 *FAJ*
(2) Daiwa Securities	1982		*Daiwa Securities Report*, 1983

Canada and various foreign countries; these estimates can be used to quantify and refine the claim of potential risk reduction.

Table 22-1 shows that estimates of the correlation between the Canadian stock market and foreign stock markets have ranged from as high as .79 with the Hong Kong market to as low as −.04 with the West German market. The correlations from Table 22-1 in the risk analysis model shown in Box 22-1, for example, demonstrate that equal investments in Canada and the United States would produce a portfolio variance of only 13.68 percent versus 16.00 percent for a total investment in Canada. Or for equal investments in Canada and Japan, the portfolio variance would be only 9.84 percent. These statistics suggest that international diversification could aid Canadian investors and foreign investors as well.[2]

It is possible to analyze the effect of multinational diversification on the Markowitz efficient frontier using Grubel's model. As might be expected, as the number of countries in which investments are made increases, more desirable efficient frontiers bcome attainable. That is, as the number of countries in the investment universe increases, the rate of return for any given level of risk increases, or conversely, the level of risk attainable at any given rate of return decreases.

22-1.2   The International Investor's Efficient Frontier

2 Monthly rates of return from foreign investments in common stocks that are adjusted to reflect changes in the foreign exchange rate can be calculated with Eq. (22-3) below.

$$\text{Effective monthly rate of return} = \left(\frac{\dfrac{\text{annual cash dividend}}{12\,\text{mo.}} + p_t}{p_{t-1}} \right)^{12} - 1.0 \tag{22-3}$$

where

p_t = market price of the foreign security (or foreign stock market index) that existed at the end of the period

p_{t-1} = market price at the beginning of that period

Point *F* in Fig. 22-1 indicates the risk level and rate of return for the U.S. stock market alone. Efficient frontier *E* shows the risk and return combinations available from investing in only developing countries; this option is dominated by all the other investment alternatives illustrated in Fig. 22-1.

FIGURE 22-1 Various efficient frontiers derived from different investment opportunities.

A–28 countries
B–16 high-income countries
C–11 western European countries
D–5 Common-market countries
E–9 Developing countries
F–United States

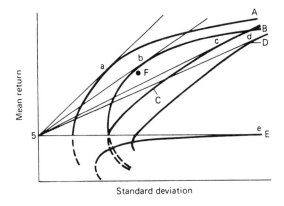

Source: H. Levy and M. Sarnat, "International Diversification of Investment Portfolios," *American Economic Review*, September 1970, pp. 668–675.

Even though point *F* in the figure represents a portfolio that is fully diversified within the United States, this portfolio is not efficient in an international context. Efficient frontier *D* indicates the efficient frontier if investments are limited to the countries in the European Economic Community (EEC)—that is, the Common Market countries. If the investment universe is expanded beyond the EEC to include all western European countries, efficient frontier *C* becomes attainable. When all high-income countries are considered, the possibilities expand to efficient frontier *B*. Finally, when all countries, including the developing countries, are allowed into the solution, efficient frontier *A* is reached. Efficient frontier *A* dominates all other investment opportunities in Fig. 22-1. This analysis suggests that the portfolio with the highest rate of return in whatever risk class is selected should be composed of investments from many countries, if possible. As a practical matter, however, barriers to capital flows (such as government-imposed foreign exchange restrictions or actual prohibitions on nonresident trading[3]) may not make the theoretically optimal portfolio feasible.

3 The South Korean, and Indian capital markets, for example, are closed to nonresident investors.

The key factor that accounts for the change in the risk-return opportunities available in an open international capital market is the low correlation between the different countries' securities markets. For international diversification the relevant market index changes; that is, a domestic market index is replaced by a *world market index*. As a result, the correlation of each security with the broader world is lower.[4] Table 22-2 shows empirical statistics about what percent of each domestic portfolio is explained by a worldwide investment index.

22-1.3 Correlations for the Multinational Investor

TABLE 22-2 PERCENTAGE OF THE VARIANCE OF DIFFERENT COUNTRIES' STOCK MARKET INDEXES EXPLAINED BY A WORLDWIDE INDEX*

COUNTRY	R-SQUARED FOR A MARKET VALUE WEIGHTED INDEX, %	R-SQUARED FOR AN EQUALLY WEIGHTED INDEX, %
Australia	11.1	20.2
Austria	4.5	20.1
Belgium	26.2	50.1
Canada	66.7	38.2
Denmark	0.8	11.6
France	9.6	40.2
Germany	22.3	49.0
Italy	6.2	25.6
Japan	7.9	15.5
Netherlands	45.4	52.7
Norway	2.0	22.2
Spain	0.4	8.9
Sweden	13.1	28.5
Switzerland	29.5	54.5
United Kingdom	16.9	22.6
United States	88.0	30.0
Simple Average	21.9	30.6

* Monthly returns from January 1959 to October 1973 were used.

Source: Donald R. Lessard, "World, Country and Industry Relationships in Equity Returns: Implications for Risk Reduction through International Diversification," *Financial Analysts Journal*, January–February 1976, pp. 2–8.

The statistics in Table 22-2 are the coefficient of determination (that is, the correlation squared, or the *R*-squared, as it is also called) for the international characteristic line shown in Eq. (22-4).

$$r_{ct} = a_c + b_c r_{wt} + e_{ct} \tag{22-4}$$

4 Correlation and regression are introduced in Mathematical App. D. The characteristic line is introduced in Chap. 10.

In Eq. (22-4) the symbol r_{ct} is the dependent variable in this simple linear regression model—it is the one-period rate of return from country c in time period t. The independent variable is r_{wt}, the one-period rate of return in time period t from a portfolio that is diversified worldwide and is therefore not highly correlated with the portfolio from any one individual country. The regression intercept for country c is denoted a_c, and its regression slope (or beta) coefficient is b_c. This regression slope coefficient is a *country-world beta*. The unexplained residual return for country c in time period t is denoted e_{ct}.

The coefficient of determination for regression Eq. (22-4) is inversely related to the desirability of investing in each country. Stated differently, the countries with the lowest R-squared statistics are the most desirable for the purposes of obtaining beneficial international diversification.

**22-1.4
Fundamental
Reasons for
Low
Intercountry
Correlations**

The intercountry correlations between security markets are not low merely because random good or bad luck strikes different countries at different times. There are sound economic reasons why the different countries and their economic prospects are not tied closely together.

Different countries have different political systems (for example, capitalism versus socialism), different currencies (such as French francs and Japanese yen), different foreign exchange regulations (for example, fixed versus floating exchange rates), different trade restrictions (such as import and export limitations and tariffs), different political alliances (such as the Communist block countries), and various other different kinds of barriers to international trade. Furthermore, different countries may be at different phases in their business cycle (for example, Canada may be starting a recovery just as some other countries are in the trough of a recession), undergoing foreign exchange rate changes (because of different intercountry inflation rates, interest rates, monetary policies, and/or fiscal policies), or in differing military postures (such as peace versus cold war versus hot war) at the same time. As a result of all these important differences, the different countries' security markets are not expected to be highly synchronized or highly positively correlated with each other.[5]

Figure 22-2 illustrates how the inflation rates and security market indexes of the major industrial countries of the world move together through time. The various panels of the figure highlight the differences in different countries' economic conditions.

22-2 DIVERSIFICATION IN DIFFERENT COUNTRIES

Multinational diversification is beneficial if there are barriers to investment such as restrictions on currency flows, lack of English translations of foreign financial statements, lack of information about local accounting conventions,

5 R.A. Cohn and J.J. Pringle, "Imperfections in International Financial Markets: Implications for Risk Premia and the Cost of Capital to Firms," *Journal of Finance*, March 1973, pp. 59–66.

FIGURE 22-2 International comparisons of inflation rates and stock prices.

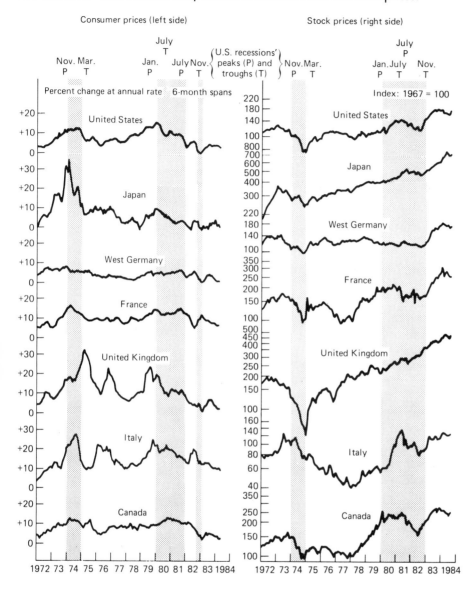

lack of information about social and cultural differences, or markets that are thin with respect to volume of trading or number of traders.[6] If such barriers do exist, the international market structure will be segmented and diversification will be beneficial. If such barriers to international diversification do

6 Gunter Dufey and Ian Giddy, *The International Money Market*, Englewood Cliffs, N.J.: Prentice-Hall, 1978.

not exist, the markets will be *homogeneous*.[7] Multinational diversification would not be expected to offer any beneficial risk-reducing opportunities if the international markets were homogeneous.[8]

Because individuals have limited funds, the amount of diversification that is possible is limited. Even large investment companies may experience limits to effective diversification. Consequently, it is valuable to know how best to diversify across countries for an international portfolio. Using weekly returns for eight different countries from 1966 to 1971, Bruno Solnik calculated the proportion of variance that could be eliminated from portfolios by increasing the number of assets included in the portfolio. For each country, portfolios of various sizes were constructed from randomly selected stocks from that country and the variances of these portfolios were calculated. These variances were averaged for each portfolio size.[9] In each country, average portfolio variance declined rapidly until portfolios of approximately twenty randomly selected securities were attained, at which point little additional reduction in average portfolio variance was achieved with additional portfolio size. Table 22-3 and Fig. 22-3 show the proportion of the average common stock's total variance for each country; undiversifiable systematic risk ranges from a low of 19 percent in Belgium to a high of 44 percent in Switzerland. Stated differently, the average portfolio of domestic stocks achieved with only simple diversification (that is, random selection) in, say, Belgium, has 19 percent as much risk as the typical individual stock's risk in that country.

TABLE 22-3   RANDOMLY DIVERSIFIED PORTFOLIO'S VARIANCE AS PERCENT OF VARIANCE OF THE AVERAGE INDIVIDUAL STOCK

USA	27.0%
UK	34.5%
France	32.7%
W. Germany	43.8%
Italy	38.0%
Belgium	19.0%
Netherlands	24.1%
Switzerland	44.0%
International	11.7%

Source: Bruno H. Solnik, "Why Not Diversify Internationally?" *Financial Analysts Journal*, July–August 1974, pp. 48–54.

7 The recent trend of market trading links, such as that between the American Stock Exchange and the Toronto Stock Exchange, is moving the world toward greater market homogeneity.

8 Jorion and Schwartz examined the issue of integration versus segmentation of the Canadian equity market relative to a global North American market. Using data from the Laval Securities Tape for the period January 1963 to December 1982, they found evidence of segmentation in the pricing of Canadian stocks. See Philippe Jorion and Eduardo Schwartz, "Integration and Segmentation in the Canadian Stock Market," *The Journal of Finance*, vol. 41, no. 3, July 1986, pp. 603–616.

9 Solnik was, essentially, applying the methodology originally developed by John L. Evans and Stephen H. Archer in "Diversification and the Reduction of Dispersion: Empirical Analysis," *Journal of Finance*, December 1968. The Evans-Archer results are presented in Sec. 23-2 on page 671.

FIGURE 22-3 Diversification within various countries.

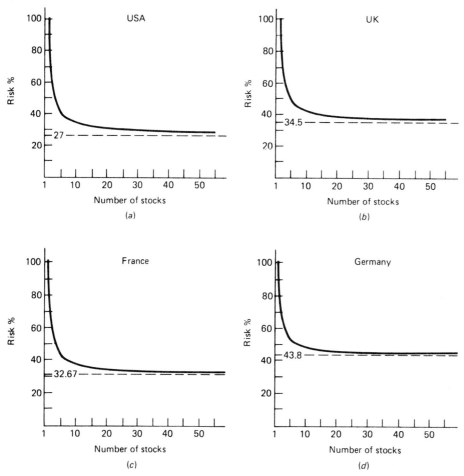

Source: Bruno H. Solnik, "Why Not Diversify Internationally?" *Financial Analysts Journal,* July-August 1974, pp. 48–54.

Also of note is the fact that an *internationally diversified* portfolio of randomly selected stocks had only 11.7 percent as much variance as the typical individual international stock. This statistic implies that it may be possible to reduce a portfolio's domestic systematic risk by multinational diversification. Panels *a* through *c* of Fig. 22-4 illustrate some risk reduction possibilities. Unfortunately, the benefits from Solnik's study cannot be taken too literally because his study did not make adjustments to hold the rates of return *equivalent* from country to country as diversification was employed to reduce the risk. That is, the international investor may have had to suffer undesirably low rates of return to obtain the variance reduction that the Solnik study suggests.

To determine how best to diversify, three strategies of selecting different numbers of randomly selected common stocks were examined. Stocks were

FIGURE 22-4   Illustration of results from different diversification strategies.

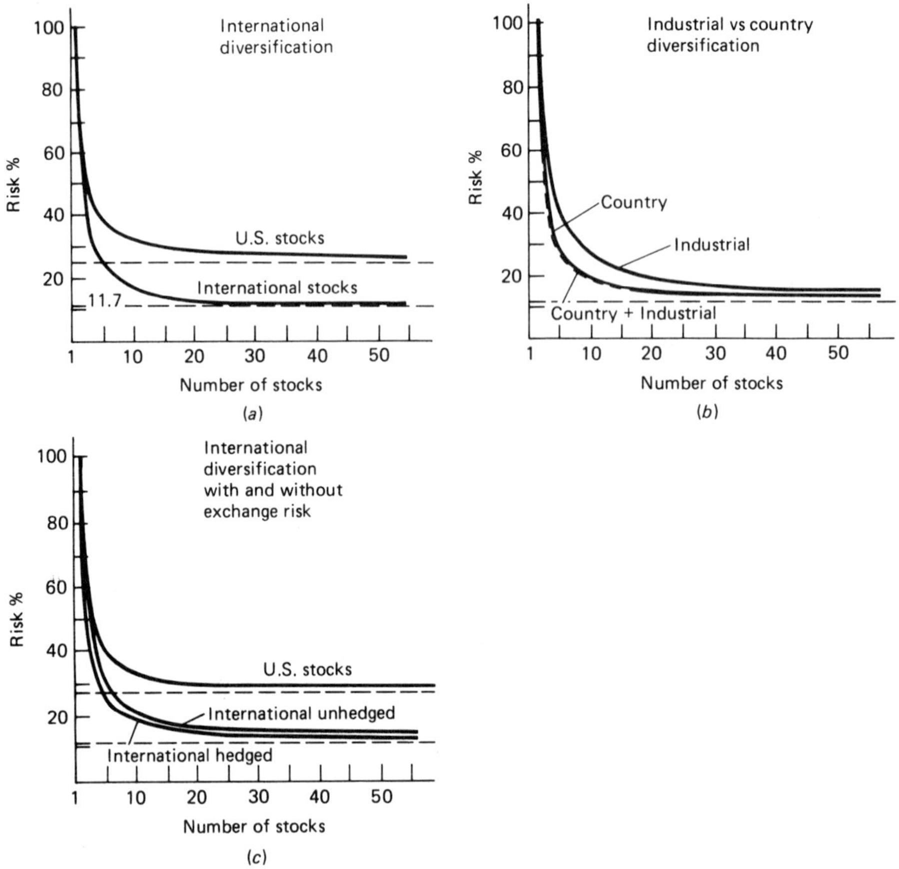

(a)

(b)

(c)

Source: Bruno H. Solnik, "Why Not Diversify Internationally?" *Financial Analysts Journal,* July-August 1974, pp. 48–54.

selected (1) across countries, (2) across industries, and (3) across both countries and industries. Panels *a, b,* and *c* of Fig. 22-4 illustrate that both selection across countries and selection across countries and industries are superior strategies to selecting only across industries. These experiments with random diversification suggest that the optimal portfolio should contain approximately twenty common stocks diversified across countries.[10]

An important consideration of investors in foreign securities is foreign exchange risk. However, panel *c* of Fig. 22-4 indicates that a substantial portion of the risk-reducing value of multinational diversification occurs whether or not international portfolios are hedged against foreign exchange losses. Although the hedged portfolio has lower risk than the unhedged portfolio,

10 One simple way to diversify internationally without bumping into problems with foreign languages and foreign accounting conventions is to simply buy shares in one large corporation that is active multinationally, and has most of its sales outside Canada.

unfortunately its total return is also greatly reduced. Thus, the value of international diversification exists with or without a concurrent currency hedge.[11]

Let's consider the foreign exchange risk more closely.

22-3   THE EFFECTS OF FOREIGN EXCHANGE RATES THAT VARY

If we view the rate of return on the multinational common stock portfolio in terms of capital gains and cash dividend yield, the investor's one-period rate of return, r_t, is the difference between the portfolio value at the beginning of the period, p_{t-1}, and the portfolio's value at the end of the period, p_t, plus any cash distributions during the period, d_t, all divided by the portfolio's beginning value. This well-known relationship is restated as Eq. (22-5a).

$$r_t = (p_t - p_{t-1} + d_t)/p_{t-1} \tag{22-5a}$$

The rate of return in local currency (LC) for multinational investment, denoted $R(N,LC)$, is equal to the terminal value of the investment, denoted $V1'$, less the initial value of the investment, $V0'$, plus any distributions during the period, $D1'$, all divided by the initial investment, $V0'$. All these terms are denominated in local currency in Eq. (22-6).

$$R(N,LC) = (V1' - V0' + D1')/V0' \tag{22-6}$$

Note that Eqs. (22-5a) and (22-6) are similar, except that Eq. (22-6) restates any foreign returns into local currency amounts.[12]

If the exchange rate between dollars and local currency, at time period $t = 0$, denoted $S0$, is constant over the period, there will be no foreign exchange effect, as the amounts $V0$, $V1$, and $D1$ will all be converted to dollars at an exchange rate that remains invariant throughout the period. In this case Eqs. (22-5a) and (22-6) produce identical results.

In the case when the exchange rate remains unchanged we can substitute the identities $[(S1)(V1)] = (V1')$, $[(S0)(V0)] = (V0')$, and $[(S1)(D1)] = (D1')$ into Eq. (22-6) to obtain Eq. (22-7a). Equations (22-6) and (22-7a) are mathematically equivalent. Equation (22-7a) assumes the local currency is dollars.

$$R(N,\$) = \frac{(S1)(V1) - (S0)(V0) + (S1)(D1)}{(S0)(V0)} \tag{22-7a}$$

However, if the current exchange rate $S1$ changes to $S1$ at the end of one period, then $V1$ and $D1$ will be converted at the $S1$ exchange rate and $V0$ will

[11] The capital asset pricing model (CAPM) or security market line (SML) for the international investor has been worked out in a seminal article by Rene Stulz, "On the Effects of Barriers to International Investment," *Journal of Finance*, vol. 36, no. 4, September 1981, pp. 923–934.

[12] The discussion assumes that all local currency cashflows remain unchanged — an oversimplification in many cases. For a detailed and comprehensive discussion of all possible cases see David K. Eiteman and Arthur I. Stonehill, *Multinational Business Finance*, 3d ed. (Reading, Mass.: Addison-Wesley, 1982), chap. 14. See also Gunter Dufey and S.L. Srinivasuler, "The Case for Corporate Management of Foreign Exchange Risk," *Financial Management*, Fall 1983.

be converted into dollars at the *S0* exchange rate. Thus, the rate of return on multinational investment, in dollar terms, changes because the foreign exchange rate changes, as shown below. Rearranging Eq. (22-7*a*) above yields Eqs. (22-7*b*) and (22-7*c*).

$$R(N,\$) = \frac{[(S0 - S0 + S1)(V1)] - [(S0)(V0)] + [(S0 - S0 + S1)(D1)]}{[(S0)(V0)]}$$ (22-7*b*)

Rearranging Eq. (22-7*b*) above yields the following equivalent equations.

$$R(N,\$) = \frac{[(S0)(V1 - V0 + D1)]}{[(S0)(V0)]} + \frac{[(S1 - S0)(V1 + D1)]}{[(S0)(V0)]}$$ (22-7*c*)

$$R(N,\$) = R(N,LC) + [1 + R(N,LC)]\left(\frac{S1 - S0}{S0}\right)$$ (22-7*d*)

= (pure nominal rate of return) + (foreign exchange factor)   (22-7*e*)

The dollar return on foreign investment is determined by two elements that are visible in Eqs. (22-7*d*) and (22-7*e*)—they are (1) the return on assets in local currency, $R(N,LC)$, plus (2) a foreign exchange factor. Thus, we have seen algebraic proof that the investor's rate of return is explicitly affected by the foreign exchange factor. For example, assume that a portfolio is composed of $100 of investment in a foreign market at an exchange rate of 20 units of local currency for $1, denoted 20 LC = $1. The total investment thus costs 2,000 units of local currency. One year later, the value of the investment is 2,200 LC and, in addition, a 200-LC dividend is paid. If the exchange rate is still 20 LC:$1, the return on investment is 20 percent, as shown below using Eq. (22-7*a*).

$$\frac{(20{:}1)(2,200\,LC) - (20{:}1)(2,000\,LC) + (20{:}1)(200\,LC)}{(20{:}1)(2,000\,LC)} = .2 = 20\%$$

The amounts in Eq. (22-7*a*) above may be equivalently restated using the 20 to 1 exchange ratio; the results are restated below in terms of Eq. (22-5*a*).

$$\frac{\$110 - \$100 + \$10}{\$100} = .2 = 20\%$$ (22-5*b*)

Consider an *x* percent change in the foreign exchange rate; this quantity is defined below.

$$\frac{S1 - S0}{S0} = \text{an } x \text{ percent change in the exchange ratio}$$

If the exchange rate falls (rises) by 5 percent, the new return on investment in dollars will be 26.3 percent (14.3 percent), as shown below.

First, let's consider the 5 percent increase from (20:1) to (21:1) in terms of Eq. (22-7*a*), as shown below.

$$\frac{(21{:}1)(2,200\,LC) - (20{:}1)(2,000\,LC) + (21{:}1)(200\,LC)}{(20{:}1)(2,000\,LC)} = .143$$

The formula above is equivalently restated below in terms of Eq. (22-5a) by adjusting with the two different exchange rates.

$$\frac{\$104.7619 - \$100 + \$9.523}{\$100} = \frac{\$14.28}{\$100} = .143 = 14.3\% \qquad (22\text{-}5c)$$

Next, let's evaluate the 5 percent decrease in the exchange rate from (20:1) to (19:1) in terms of Eq. (22-7a), as shown below.

$$\frac{(19\text{:}1)(2,200\,\text{LC}) - (20\text{:}1)(2,000\,\text{LC}) + (19\text{:}1)(200\,\text{LC})}{(20\text{:}1)(2,000\,\text{LC})} = 0.263$$

The values above are equivalently restated in terms of Eq. (22-5a) by using the two different exchange rates.

$$\frac{\$115.789 - \$100 + \$10.526}{\$100} = \frac{\$26.315}{\$100} = .263 = 26.3\% \qquad (22\text{-}5d)$$

The two preceding numerical examples of appreciation and depreciation in the exchange rate were informative. The two examples showed that a foreign investment with a 20 percent rate of return in the foreign country could pay either a 14.3 or a 26.3 percent rate of return to the multinational investor if the foreign currency's exchange rate varied by 5 percent in either direction. Foreign exchange risk is thus seen to be an additional risk consideration of significant importance to multinational investors.

As the volatility of the exchange rate increases, swings in return due to the foreign exchange factor may also increase—this can be seen explicitly in the right-hand side of Eq. (22-7d). Thus, if the foreign exchange rate change is a random variable with an expected value of zero, $E(S1 - S0) = 0$, the rate of return for a multinational investment will become more variable (that is, risky) as the probability that the exchange rate change equals zero decreases. Since it has been shown that changes in the foreign exchange rate follow a random walk, the return for a multinational portfolio should become more variable under floating foreign exchange rates, unless the returns from the investment are negatively correlated with the changes in the foreign exchange rates.[13]

Figure 22-5 illustrates the fluctuations in some of the major foreign exchange rates around the world.[14]

---

[13] Gunter Dufey and Ian Giddy, ''The Random Behavior of Flexible Exchange Rates: Implications for Forecasting,'' *Journal of International Business Studies*, Spring 1975, vol. 6, no. 1, pp. 1–32. Gunter Dufey, ''Corporate Finance and Exchange Rate Variations,'' *Financial Management*, Summer 1972, pp. 51–57.

[14] Options on foreign currencies are traded on the Montreal Exchange (British pound, Japanese yen, Swiss franc, West German mark, and U.S. dollar) and the Philadelphia Stock Exchange (British pound, Canadian dollar, European currency unit, French franc, Japanese yen, Swiss franc, West German mark). The availablility of active markets in these major currencies provides investors a better chance to hedge the foreign exchange risk they undertake in

FIGURE 22-5   Movements in exchange rates.

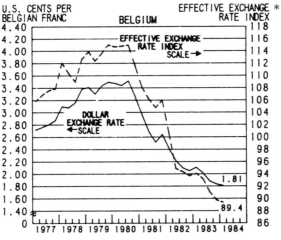

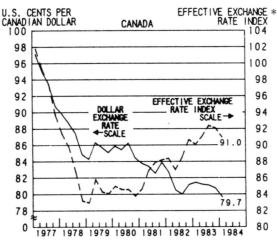

FIGURE 22-5 (*continued*)

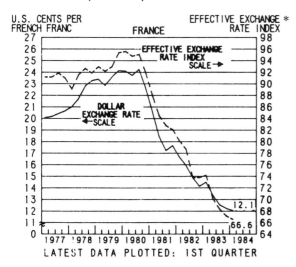

LATEST DATA PLOTTED: 1ST QUARTER

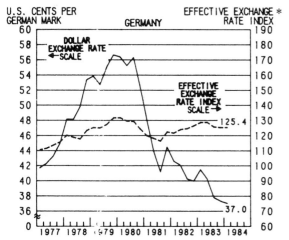

*The *effective exchange rate index* is based on a basket of 17 diversified currencies with 1980 as a base year value of 100.

Source: International Economic Conditions, Federal Reserve Bank of St. Louis, August 1984, pp. 2 and 3.

multinational investing. Prior to the opening of the PHLX currency options market, foreign exchange hedgers were forced to buy forward contracts in an informal interbank market that was less convenient for nonbankers.

For more information, the following pamphlet may be obtained free by writing to the Federal Reserve Bank of Philadelphia, Research Dept., 10 Independence Mall, Philadelphia, Pa. 19106; ask for Brian Gendreau, "New Markets in Foreign Currency Options," *Business Review*, July-August 1984, pp. 3–12.

The Montreal Exchange publishes a monthly brochure called *Montreal Options*, a strategy supplement. This can be obtained by writing the Montreal Exchange, P.O. Box 61, 800 Victoria Square, Montreal, Quebec, H4Z 1A9.

22-4 EXPANDED OPPORTUNITY SET

An additional feature of international investment is the expansion of the investor's opportunity set. There are a number of investment and hedging instruments that are not at this time available in Canadian capital and derivative markets and can only be purchased abroad. Thus, by expanding the investment horizon, the investor creates a more robust investment opportunity set. The very exotic nature of some of the instruments described below would make them ideal instruments for specific hedgers or investors attempting to accomplish some particular purpose. For example, stock index linked bonds can provide the holder with *long-term* options on foreign equity market indexes. Some of these instruments include:

Stock Index Linked Bonds Euphemistically called "heaven and hell" bonds, the indexed-linked bonds provide payments at maturity that are linked to the performance (or closing level) of a market index. The holder has a stream of coupon payments plus a market index call or put option. Swedish Export Corporation issued 5-year stock-indexed linked bonds in 1986. The redemption proceeds on the bond are tied to the level of the Nikkei Dow index at maturity. The proceeds are at par if the index is at 25,606 at maturity and at a premium (discount) if the Nikkei-Dow is higher (lower) at maturity. Thus an investor can obtain a form of long-term option contract on the Japanese equity market with this bond.

Performance Warrants Performance warrants are options whose exercise price is a function of some particular measure of management performance, such as a specified level of income by a specified period. Medcomp Technologies Inc. of the United States issued performance warrants in 1985. Each warrant entitles the holder to acquire one common share of Medcomp up to July 31, 1987, and thereafter from one-half to four Medcomp common shares based on Medcomp's net income for its fiscal years ending April 30, 1986, and 1987.

"Bunny Bonds" Bunny bonds are multiplier bonds that allow the holder the option of receiving the annual interest payment in cash or in additional bonds of the same class. The holder thus has a coupon stream plus a call option on a coupon-bearing bond. Chrysler Corporation of the United States issued ten ¾ percent "Bunny Bonds" in 1986. For the first five years of the bond's life, the holder may receive interest in cash or 10¾ percent bonds maturing in 1991.

Flip Flop Bonds Flip flop bonds are bonds that can be converted into bonds with different terms and then either converted back into the original bond or put to the issuer on pre-arranged terms. The World Bank issued a flip flop perpetual floater in 1985. Each bond allows the holder to convert back and forth between a perpetual floating rate note and a fixed-rate fixed-term note. Specifically after September 1985, investors can convert their "flip flop" into a three-month note carrying the 91-day U.S. Treasury bill rate flat. The holder can then convert back into the perpetual or sell the note back to the World Bank at par value.

Bond Purchase Warrants   Bond purchase warrants are normally attached to a new bond issue and allow the holder to purchase a bond with a pre-specified coupon rate. If the exercise of the warrant does not change the face value of the outstanding debt of the issuer, the warrant is called a harmless warrant. If exercise of the warrant does affect the face value of outstanding debt, the warrant is called a harmful warrant. Gas de France issued harmless warrants in 1985, attached to its 10-year bond issue. The bonds are callable after five years. The warrants allow the holder to buy otherwise identical noncallable bonds from the company. For the first five years the warrants are married to the bond; to exercise the warrant the holder must sell the original bond back to the issuer. The warrants are divorced from the bond over the last five years.

22-5   TRANSACTIONS IN FOREIGN SECURITIES

Investors who wish to diversify their portfolios internationally can either trade directly in securities on foreign markets, or indirectly through American Depositary Receipts, or global, international, or specific country mutual funds.

There are a number of methods by which Canadians can buy or sell foreign securities directly. These are described below.

Canadian Brokerage Firms   The full-service Canadian brokerage firms, such as Merrill Lynch Canada Inc. and McLeod Young Weir, will place buy and sell orders for clients for foreign securities, typically for a relatively large commission that will reflect the commission schedule on the foreign stock market as well as an increment for the Canadian broker. Investors should expect some time delay since the broker may have to wire abroad for a quote on the security. One- and two-day lags between the time the order is placed and a confirmation from the broker is received are not at all uncommon for foreign security transactions. Canadian brokerage firms can buy or sell American Depositary Receipts for clients as well.

Foreign Banks and Brokerage Firms   Many of the foreign banks and brokerage firms will accept trades from nonresidents. In general, however, this is a cumbersome method of trading in foreign securities, since it will require the search for a reputable firm, making appropriate custody arrangements, foreign currency conversions, and other inconveniences.

Canadian Branches of Foreign Banks   The domestic branches of foreign banks will normally handle foreign security transactions for clients, including initial foreign currency conversions, delivery and custody arrangements, and currency conversion at time of sale. Typically, however, the banks set minimum transaction amounts at $100,000.

Investors wishing to reduce or minimize search costs and trading frictions associated with foreign investment can alternatively transact in American Depositary Receipts (ADR's) and mutual funds.

**22-5.1
Direct
Transactions
in Foreign
Securities**

**22-5.2
Indirect
Transactions**

American Depositary Receipts These ADR's are negotiable receipts representing ownership of a specific number of shares. They are issued by large U.S. banks (such as Citibank and Morgan Guaranty) who purchase securities in a foreign corporation (Sony Corporation, for instance) for a client. The bank keeps these securities in the vault of its foreign branch, registered in the bank's own name. The client is issued an ADR stating that the bank is holding (Sony, in this example) securities for the client. The bank collects cash dividends or coupon interest for the client and either reinvests the money or converts it into U.S. dollars and pays it out to the client—whichever alternative is requested — for a modest fee of a penny or two out of each security's cash payment. The bank also stores the foreign securities in a safe place where they may be sold quickly.

Although most of the corporations represented by banks' ADRs are large and reputable, these issuers enjoy a kind of diplomatic immunity from most of the rules and regulations of the U.S. Securities and Exchange Commission (SEC). But this immunity hasn't hurt the marketability of these foreign securities. Every day hundreds of thousands of foreign shares represented by ADRs are traded in the organized security exchanges and over the counter in the United States. In fact, sometimes more shares of a popular stock (like Sony) are traded using ADRs in the United States than are traded in the issuer's homeland. ADR's are freely available to Canadians.

In conclusion, ADR holders receive all the benefits that someone who owns the underlying security would receive without paying any additional brokerage commission, without losing any marketability, and without being bothered with collecting cash dividends in a foreign currency.

Global, International, and Specialized International Investment Funds Probably the easiest route through which the investor can achieve international diversification is the purchase of global, international and specialty country mutual funds. These funds sell shares to the public and invest their funds in a portfolio of securities. Global funds (such as Templeton Growth Fund) invest in the securities of various countries, including their own; international funds (such as Bolton-Tremblay International Fund), in the securities of foreign countries only; and specialized funds (such as the Korea Fund traded on the New York Stock Exchange), invest only in the securities of a specific country.

22-6 CHAPTER SUMMARY AND CONCLUSIONS

International investors face all the same risks that domestic investors face, plus four additional risks — international marketability risk, international political risk, foreign exchange risk, and the risk of being forced to work with inferior investment information.

Many foreign markets lack the efficiency of our reasonably liquid Canadian securities markets. Billions of dollars change hands in Canadian security markets daily without most of the sellers being forced to give up large price markdowns or pay large commissions to sell their investments. Dealing with these marketability risks in a foreign market can be an unpleasant new experience. Furthermore, there is the added marketability risk in some foreign countries—security price manipulation that is illegal in Canada may be permitted or go unnoticed in some foreign markets.

International political risk and foreign exchange risk are usually interrelated. Many of the foreign exchange rates in the world are fixed by the governments of the countries that issue the currencies, rather than being freely floating exchange rates determined by supply and demand. And since the administration of every country is some form of political organization, the foreign exchange rate authorities are typically high-level bureaucrats who are subject to political pressures from their country's top administrators.

The risk of being forced to compete against foreign investors who have inside information, who have faster access to the public information about their country, and who may even be able to manipulate security prices in their country places the outside investor at a distinct disadvantage in terms of information. Some large institutional investors have foreign offices that manage investments in the host country and are partly staffed by the local citizens of the foreign country. Such foreign nationals not only are low-cost employees, but they may also be able to gather valuable information for their employer. Or, a foreign investor can simply purchase a highly diversified portfolio of securities in the foreign country without doing intensive investments research—buying shares in an index fund is an example of this passive kind of investment management. Such a passive international investor is essentially investing in the overall economic prospects of the foreign country.

Investors may be willing to assume the international political risk, the foreign exchange risk, and the information risks in order to obtain the impressive risk reduction available in the international security markets. That is, the risk-reducing benefits from international investing may more than offset the disadvantages from possible traumas arising from political considerations, the risk that the investment be harmed by a currency devaluation, and/or the disadvantage that the foreign investor may suffer relative to the domestic investors in the foreign country when it comes to getting valuable information in a timely fashion.

The correlations between the securities markets in different countries are usually lower than the correlations available to the purely domestic investor. As a result, multinational investing opportunities offer a more dominant efficient frontier of investment opportunities from which to choose.

QUESTIONS

1. How might a multinational investor based in Canada use foreign exchange futures to hedge against the risk that the foreign exchange rate changes? (*Hint*: Some of the material about financial futures in Chap. 21 may be helpful.)

2. Are there any risks that are peculiar to international investing? Stated differently, what factors in addition to the usual investment risks should be of particular concern to the multinational investor?

3. What are the advantages that induce investors to invest internationally when they have to face additional new risks peculiar to multinational investing?

4. Does every international investment opportunity provide the investor with new investment opportunities that dominate the old opportunities in a risk-return analysis?

5. What factors explain why the intercountry correlations between securities markets are low? (*Hint*: You may benefit from consulting an international economics textbook or an international finance textbook.)

6. What do the following mutual funds have in common? Explain each fund's investment objective.
   (*a*) International Investors Incorporated
     New York City
   (*b*) Research Capital Fund
     San Mateo, California
   (*c*) Templeton Growth Fund
     Toronto, Ontario
     (*Hint*: Consult the latest edition of a book entitled *Investment Companies*, published each year by Warren, Gorham, and Lamont.

7. If an investor is interested in multinational diversification but does not have the time or expertise to select individual foreign securities in which to invest, is there another way this investor can invest internationally?

8. Since the intercountry correlation between securities markets plays such an important role in international diversification, consider the trend in these statistics. Do you think that, in general, these correlations should increase, stay the same, or decrease with the passage of time? Explain why?

SELECTED REFERENCES

Kalman J. Cohen, Steven F. Maier, Robert A. Schwartz, and David K. Whitcomb. *The Microstructure of Securities Markets*. Englewood Cliffs, New Jersey: Prentice Hall, 1986. This book contains comparisons of world equity markets, electronic trading, trading orders, beta estimation in thin markets, and market links. Substantial theory is included in a nonmathematical manner.

Gunter Dufey and Ian Giddy. *The International Money Market*. Englewood Cliffs, N.J.: Prentice-Hall, 1978. This book analyzes international business finance from a monetary economics viewpoint with liberal usage of empirical data. No mathematics.

Edwin J. Elton and Martin J. Gruber (eds.) *Studies in International Capital Markets*. Amsterdam: North-Holland, 1978. A collection of studies that analyze international finance in terms of modern portfolio theory and efficient markets. Mathematics and statistics are used.

Charles N. Henning, William Pigott, and Robert Haney Scott. *International Financial Management*. New York: McGraw-Hill, 1978. Three monetary economists present their analysis of international business finance. The discussion is supplemented with some empirical data. No mathematics.

Roger G. Ibbotson, Richard C. Carr, and Anthony W. Robinson. "International Equity and Bond Returns," *Financial Analysts Journal*, July/August, 1982, pp. 61–83. A comprehensive analysis of equity and bond returns for eighteen countries over the period 1960 to 1980.

Lynette J. Kemp. *The Wardley Guide to World Money and Securities Markets*. London: Euromoney Publications, Nestor House, Playhouse Yard, 1984. The book contains detailed reference information on money and capital markets, transactions costs, financial and monetary systems, withholding taxes, and exchange controls for a large number of countries.

Eric F. Kirzner and John R. Dickinson. *Guide to International Investing*. Don Mills, Ontario: CCH Canadian, 1985, 1986. This is a reference book that is updated monthly. The book provides economic, political, banking information, and equity, bond, futures, options, and money market details for fourteen countries.

Maurice Levi. *International Finance*. New York: McGraw-Hill, 1983. A discussion of international finance that uses algebra and empirical data. Modern portfolio theory and the efficient markets theories are employed.

PORTFOLIO THEORY

CHAPTER 23 — Diversification and Portfolio Analysis explains why and how wealth-seeking, risk-averse investors should diversify. Portfolios, rather than individual securities, are shown to be the objects of choice for rational investors.

CHAPTER 24—Capital Market Theory explicates models for the determination of the prices of risky marketable securities.

CHAPTER 25 — Different Investment Goals rationalizes the coexistence of both daring and timid investors and shows their common, rational grounds by using utility analysis to analyze investment decisions.

CHAPTER 26 — Portfolio Performance Evaluation introduces the tools used to evaluate the performance of the managers of investment portfolios; mutual fund data are analyzed.

CHAPTER 27—Multiperiod Wealth Maximation explains how to use the one-period Markowitz portfolio analysis in the long-run context involving multiple planning horizons.

In Part 7 the focus shifts from individual assets to portfolios of assets. The concepts essential to portfolio management are introduced and analyzed.

Diversification and Portfolio Analysis *

Dictionaries explain that *efficient* things produce the desired result with a minimum of waste. This chapter shows how to apply the concept of efficiency to investment management. The desired result investors seek is returns, or income. And the waste they seek to avoid is lost returns—that is, they seek to minimize their investment's *variability of return*. Diversification is essential to the creation of an efficient investment because diversification reduces variability of the investment returns.

The portfolio manager seeking efficient investments works with two statistics—the expected return and risk statistics. The expected return and risk statistics for individual stocks and bonds serve as input data that are analyzed in order to develop a diversified portfolio having the maximum rate of return that can be expected at whatever level of risk is deemed appropriate. All information available to the security analyst is supposed to be summarized in the risk-return statistics for the stocks and bonds that are under consideration. These statistics furnish the input information for the portfolio analysis. This chapter explains how the portfolio manager selects which assets to buy and how much of each one to purchase based only on each asset's risk and expected return statistics.

23-1 DOMINANCE AND EFFICIENT PORTFOLIOS

When a portfolio manager is confronted with the expected return and risk statistics of hundreds of different bonds, stocks, options, mortgages, and whatever other assets that are investment candidates, he or she may select the assets worthy of investment by using the dominance principle.

**23-1.1
Dominance
Principle**

The *dominance principle* states that (1) among all investments with any given expected rate of return, the one with the least risk is the most desirable or (2) among all the assets in a given risk-class, the one with the highest expected rate of return is the most desirable.

Application of the dominance principal to the assets in Table 23-1 reveals that Fairyear Tire and Rubber (FTR) is dominated by Canadian Telephone Works (CTW) because they both have the same risk (σ = 3 percent), but CTW

* Chapter 23 presumes a knowledge of Chaps. 9 and 10.

TABLE 23-1   THE RISK AND EXPECTED RETURN OF FIVE ASSETS

SECURITY	EXPECTED RETURN, $E(r)$, %	RISK , %
Canadian Telephone Works (CTW)	7	3
General Auto Corporation (GAC)	7	4
Fuzzyworm Tractor Co. (FTC)	15	15
Fairyear Tire and Rubber Co. (FTR)	3	3
Hotstone Tire Corporation (HTC)	8	12

has a higher expected return than FTR. Figure 23-1 shows this graphically. That is, FTR can be eliminated from consideration because it is a *dominated investment*. CTW dominates General Auto Corporation (GAC); their expected returns are the same, but CTW has less risk. So GAC is dominated and can be ignored too.

Use of the dominance principle shows FTR and GAC to be inferior investments. The nondominated assets are Fuzzyworm Tractor Co. (FTC), Hotstone Tire Corporation (HTC), and CTW. Part of the work of investment decision making seems to be done, since the investment choices have been narrowed from five to three. However, this example is simplified because it has ignored diversification and assets called portfolios.

Although HTC is a nondominated asset, a close examination of Fig. 23-1 shows that its relative risk and return opportunities are somehow not as appealing as those of CTW and FTC. The reason is that *portfolios* have not been considered.

23-1.2 Efficient Portfolios

FIGURE 23-1   Five assets in risk-return space.

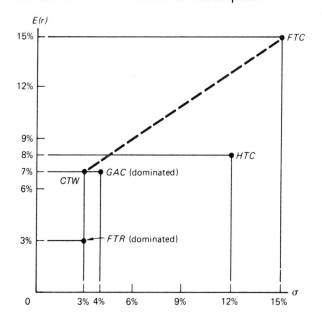

Suppose a portfolio were constructed of CTW and FTC. The portfolio's expected return is simply the weighted average of the expected rates of return of the assets in the portfolio. Equation (23-1) defines the expected return for a portfolio, denoted $E(r_p)$ for an n-asset portfolio.

$$E(r_p) = \sum_{i=1}^{n} x_i E(r_i) \tag{23-1}$$

where x_i is the fraction of the total value of the portfolio invested in the ith asset (the x_i's are called *weights* or *participation levels*) and $E(r_i)$ denotes the expected rate of return from the ith asset. It is assumed that the weights sum to 1 (that is, $\sum_{i=1}^{n} x_i = 1$), since it is pointless to account for more or less than 100 percent (which is equal to 1.0) of the funds in the portfolio.

To be more specific, suppose that seven-eighths of the portfolio's funds are put into CTW and the other one-eighth into FTC. In this case $n = 2$; the weight in CTW is $x_{ATW} = \frac{7}{8}$; and the weight in FTC is $x_{FTC} = \frac{1}{8}$. The computations for this two-asset portfolio's expected return are as follows:

$$E(r_p) = x_{CTW}E(r_{CTW}) + x_{FTC}E(r_{FTC})$$

$$= \frac{7}{8}(7\%) + \frac{1}{8}(15\%)$$

$$= .875(.07) + .125(.15)$$

$$= .08 = 8\%$$

The two-asset portfolio with seven-eighths in CTW and the other one-eighth in FTC has the same expected rate of return as HTC. The dashed line from CTW to FTC in Fig. 23-1 represents the risk and return of all possible portfolios that can be formed from various proportions of CTW and FTC.[1] HTC is a dominated asset if portfolios are considered as possible assets; that is, the dashed line from CTW to FTC dominates HTC in Fig. 23-1.

It appears that the concept of dominant assets should be extended to include portfolios. Hereafter, dominant assets will be called *efficient portfolios* whether they contain one or many assets. An efficient portfolio, then, is any asset or combination of assets that has: (1) the maximum expected return in its risk-class, or conversely, (2) the minimum risk at its level of expected return.

The objective of portfolio management is to develop efficient portfolios. As the dashed line in Fig. 23-1 shows, there are a number of efficient portfolios. The group of all efficient portfolios will be called the efficient set of portfolios, or, simply, the *efficient set*. The efficient set of portfolios composes the efficient frontier in risk-return space (if borrowing and lending are

---

[1] The linear opportunity locus representing portfolios composed of CTW and FTC ignores beneficial diversification effects, which will be explained later in this chapter.

ignored). The *efficient frontier* is the locus of points in risk-return space having the maximum return at each risk-class.

The efficient frontier dominates all other assets. Consider how different kinds of diversification can be used to reduce a portfolio's risk and improve the efficient frontier from which a rational, risk-averse, wealth-seeking investor will select his or her investments.

23-2 SIMPLE DIVERSIFICATION

Simple diversification can be defined as ''not putting all the eggs in one basket,'' or ''spreading the risks.'' These vague definitions are analyzed in the paragraphs below.

Simple diversification implies that a portfolio made up of 200 different securities is 10 times more diversified than a portfolio made up of 20 different securities. (It will be shown later in this chapter that this is not true.) Simple diversification can usually be expected to reduce the risk of a portfolio somewhat. As the number of securities added to a simply diversified portfolio increases to ten or fifteen, the portfolio's risk will usually decrease toward the systematic level of risk in the market. After the portfolio's assets have been spread across more than about fifteen randomly selected securities, further decreases in portfolio risk usually cannot be attained, on average, simply by investing in additional securities.

23-2.1 Effects of Simple Diversifi- cation

Several studies have shown that the total risk of most securities, as measured by their variance in rates of return over time, can be divided into two parts.[2] The exact proportions of systematic and unsystematic risk vary from

---

2 Given the *i*th security's characteristic line,

$$r_{it} = a_i + b_i r_{mt} + e_{it}$$

the variance of the security's returns can be partitioned as follows:

$$\text{var}(r_{it}) = \text{var}(a + b r_{mt} + e_{it})$$
$$= b_i^2 \text{var}(r_{mt}) + \text{var}(e_{it})$$
$$= \text{systematic risk} + \text{unsystematic risk}$$
$$= \text{total risk}$$

Here $\text{var}(e_{it})$ is the residual variance and $\text{var}(r_{it})$ is the total variance. Independent studies show that systematic risk is typically between one-fourth and one-third of a security's total risk. J. Evans and S.H. Archer, '' Diversification and the Reduction of Dispersion: An Empirical Analysis,'' *Journal of Finance*, December 1968, pp. 761–767. K.H. Johnson and D.S. Shannon have extended the Evans-Archer study in ''A Note on Diversification and the Reduction of Dispersion,'' *Journal of Financial Economics*, December 1974, pp. 365–372. See also W.H. Wagner and S. Lau, ''The Effect of Diversification on Risk,'' *Financial Analysts Journal*, November-December 1971, pp. 48–53. More recent research has shown that it may take a few more securities to achieve a satisfactory level of diversification than the pioneering empirical studies indicated. See E. Elton and M. Gruber, ''Risk Reduction and Portfolio Size: An Analytical Solution,'' *Journal of Business*, October 1977, pp. 415–437; T. Tole, ''You Can't Diversify without Diversifying,'' *Journal of Portfolio Management*, Winter 1982, pp. 5–11. Lorie demonstrated that even for portfolios of fifty and one hundred securities, annual return could vary significantly from market index returns. See J. Lorie, ''Diversification: Old and New,'' *Journal of Portfolio Management*, Winter 1975, pp. 25–28.

security to security and industry to industry, but for a large number of Canadian common stocks, systematic risk has been shown to compose about one-quarter of the securities' total risk on average.[3]

systematic variability of return	25%
Plus: unsystematic variability of return	75%
Equals: total variability of return	100% of total risk

Simple diversification will usually decrease the unsystematic portion of total risk toward zero until approximately fifteen to thirty securities are added to the portfolio, because unsystematic risk is (by definition) uncorrelated with the market. That is, the unsystematic variabilities in different firms' rates of return are independent with an average value of zero, and therefore they average out to zero when added together into a portfolio. Adding more than about fifteen securites to a portfolio cannot be expected to reduce its unsystematic risk (or to increase it, in most cases).[4]

FIGURE 23-2   Naive diversification reduces risk to the systematic level in randomly selected portfolios.

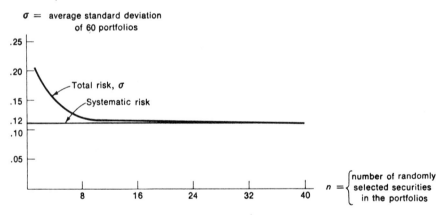

Source: J.H. Evans and S.H. Archer, "Diversification and the Reduction of Dispersion: An Empirical Analysis," *Journal of Finance*, December 1968, pp. 761–767.

3 James E. Hatch and Robert W. White, *Canadian Stocks, Bonds, Bills and Inflation: 1950–1983.* The Financial Analysts Research Foundation, Monograph 19, 1985, p. 121. However, in an earlier study, Morin found an average level of systematic risk of only 17 percent for a different sample of Canadian stocks. See Roger A. Morin, "Market Line Theory and the Canadian Equity Market," *Journal of Business Administration*, Fall 1980, chap. 4, pp. 57–76.

4 Lawrence Kryzanowski et al. have shown that portfolios of 30 securities were required, on average, to obtain domestic Canadian diversification in terms of the reduction of the mean and the variance of monthly portfolio return variances. See Lawrence Kryzanowski, Abdul Rahman, and Al Boon Sim, "Diversification, the Reduction of Dispersion, and the Effect of Canadian Regulations and Self-Imposed Limits on Foreign Investment," working paper, Faculty of Commerce, Concordia University, June 1985.

Figure 23-2 shows the manner in which simple diversification works. Drs. Evans and Archer prepared the figure using empirical data on 470 common stocks from the NYSE. The figure shows that the average standard deviation of returns for all 470 stocks was .21. The level of systematic risk in the market was estimated at. 12 (that is, σ_m = 12 percent).

For preparation of Fig. 23-2, sixty different portfolios of each size were constructed randomly, that is, sixty one-security portfolios, sixty two-security portfolios, sixty three-security portfolios, and so on up to the forty-security portfolios. Every portfolio was constructed from randomly selected stocks. These portfolios were constructed so that each *randomly selected* security was allocated an *equal weight* in all the random portfolios. Then the average standard deviation of returns was calculated for the sixty portfolios of each size. Figure 23-2 shows these average standard deviations at each size of portfolio. From it we can see that, on the average, randomly combining ten to fifteen stocks will reduce the portfolio's risk to the systematic level of variation found in the market average, but spreading the portfolio's assets over twice or three times as many stocks cannot be expected to further reduce risk.

23-2.2 Diversifying Across Industries

Some investment counselors advocate selecting securities from different and unrelated industries to achieve better diversification. It is certainly better to follow this advice than to select all the securities in a portfolio from one industry. But it turns out that diversifying across industries is not much better than simply selecting securities randomly. Either procedure is simple diversification—as explained below.

Studies of the rates of return of securities in many industries have shown that nearly all industries are highly correlated with one another. This *systematic variability* of return cannot be diversified away merely by selecting securities from different industries.

One study sought to test the effectiveness of diversifying across different industries and also of increasing the number of different assets in the portfolio. Portfolios containing 8, 16, 32, and 128 common stocks, all listed on the NYSE, were formed by two separate techniques. Technique 1 involved simple random selection of assets (for example, with a dart). Technique 2 drew each asset in the portfolio from a different industry. Numerous portfolios were constructed in this study, and statistics were tabulated about the portfolio's rates of return.[5]

Table 23-2 presents the findings of the study. The rates of return were calculated from portfolios constructed in each of twenty consecutive years.

The two main conclusions that may be drawn from Table 23-2 are that (1) diversification across industries is not better than random diversification and

---

5 The study actually investigated wealth relatives, or link relatives, as they are sometimes called, rather than the rates of return.

Wealth relative = p_t/p_{t-1} = $1 + r_t$ = link relative

However, the variance of the wealth relatives is the same as the variance of the percentage price change over the same period since var$(1 + r)$ = var(r). See Mathematical App. B for proof.

TABLE 23-2   STATISTICS OBTAINED BY USE OF DIFFERENT DIVERSIFICATION TECHNIQUES

STOCKS IN PORTFOLIO	TECHNIQUE USED TO DIVERSIFY	20TH, AND 80TH PERCENTILES (THE MIDDLE 60%)	MIN. RETURN	MAX. RETURN	MEAN RETURN	AVERAGE STD. DEV. OF RETURNS
8	Random	.94-1.29	53	2.64	1.13	.22
	Across industries	.94-1.30	53	2.58	1.13	.22
16	Random	.94-1.28	63	2.21	1.13	.21
	Across industries	.94-1.28	65	2.21	1.13	.21
32	Random	.95-1.27	69	1.98	1.13	.20
	Across industries	.95-1.27	71	1.93	1.13	.20
128	Random	.96-1.27	71	1.76	1.13	.19

Source: L. Fisher and J. Lorie, "Some Studies of Variability of Returns on Investments in Common Stocks," *Journal of Business*, April 1970, p. 112, table 5.

(2) increasing the number of different assets held in the portfolio above eight does not substantially reduce the portfolio's risk.

23-2.3 Superfluous Diversification

Simple diversification will ordinarily reduce risk to the systematic level in the market (as indicated by Fig. 23-2). However, portfolio managers should not become overzealous and spread their assets over too many assets. If ten or fifteen different assets are selected for the portfolio, the maximum benefits from simple diversification most likely have been attained. Further spreading of the portfolio's assets is *superfluous diversification* and should be avoided. Superfluous diversification will usually result in the following poor portfolio management practices:

1. *Purchasing lackluster performers.* The search for numerous different assets to buy will ultimately lead to the purchase of investments that will not yield an adequate rate of return for the risk they bear.
2. *Using out-of-date securities information.* If the portfolio contains dozens of different securities, the portfolio's management cannot hope to stay informed on the status of them all simultaneously.
3. *Incurring higher search costs.* The larger the number of assets to be selected for the portfolio, the more expensive the search for potential investments.
4. *Incurring high transaction costs.* Frequent purchases of small quantities of shares will result in larger broker's commissions than will less frequent purchases of larger quantities.[6]

Although more money is spent to manage a superfluously diversified portfolio, there will most likely be no concurrent improvement in the portfolio's performance. Thus, superfluous diversification may lower the net return to the portfolio owners after the portfolio management expenses are deducted.

---

6 As the full service and discount brokers compete, negotiated brokerage commissions continue to be chiselled down on larger trades.

23-3 MARKOWITZ DIVERSIFICATION

Named after its originator, Harry M. Markowitz, *Markowitz diversification* may be defined as the process of combining assets that are less than perfectly positively correlated[7] in order to reduce portfolio risk without sacrificing any portfolio returns.[8] It can sometimes reduce risk below the systematic level. Markowitz diversification is more analytical than simple diversification and considers assets' correlations (or covariances). The lower the correlation between assets, the more it will be able to lower risk.[9]

The simplest way to see the benefits of combining securities with low correlations is by numerical example. Consider what happens when two assets, denoted X and Y, which have perfectly negatively correlated rates of return, are combined into a portfolio. Table 23-3 shows the results.

**23-3.1
Numerical
Example**

TABLE 23-3 NUMERICAL EXAMPLE OF MARKOWITZ DIVERSIFICATION WITH INVERSE CORRELATION

TIME PERIOD	$t = 1$	$t = 2$	$t = 3$	$t = 4$	var(r)*
Return from X	$r_{x_1} = 5\%$	$r_{x_2} = 10\%$	$r_{x_3} = 15\%$	$r_{x_4} = 5\%$	$\sigma_x^2 = .0015$
Return from Y	$r_{y_1} = 25\%$	$r_{y_2} = 20\%$	$r_{y_3} = 15\%$	$r_{y_4} = 25\%$	$\sigma_y^2 = .0021$
Return for portfolio of half X and Y	$\dfrac{25 + 5}{2} = 15\%$	$\dfrac{10 + 20}{2} = 15\%$	$\dfrac{15 + 15}{2} = 15\%$	$\dfrac{5 + 25}{2} = 15\%$	$\sigma_p^2 = 0$

*$\text{var}(r_x) = \Sigma\ \frac{1}{4}(r_s - .008)^2 = .00612/4 = .00153$
$\text{var}(r_y) = \Sigma\ \frac{1}{4}(r_y - .2125)^2 = .0085/4 = .00212$
$\text{var}(r_p) = \Sigma\ \frac{1}{4}(r_p - .15)^2 = .0$

The portfolio of half asset X and half Y has *zero variability of returns*. This complete reduction of risk is due to the perfect negative correlation of the rates of return of X and Y; their returns move inversely so that the gains on one asset offset the losses on the other.

Numerical examples represent only specific cases. It is a well-known (but often made) error in logic to draw general conclusions from specific cases. Therefore, a more general mathematical analysis of Markowitz diversification is needed. Consider the risk and return of a simple two-asset portfolio as the correlation coefficient between the two assets varies. Table 23-4 gives the risk and return of two hypothetical common stocks issued by the Apex and Bean Corporations.

**23-3.2
General
Two-Asset
Analysis of
Markowitz
Diversifi-
cation**

---

7 Mathematical App. D, in Part 9, defines correlation and discusses it briefly.
8 H. Markowitz, ''Portfolio Selection,'' *Journal of Finance*, March 1952, p. 89.
9 There is a trade-off between risk and return in the market. But at any given level of expected return, Markowitz diversification can reduce risk lower than can simple diversification. This reduction in risk need not be accompanied by a reduction in the portfolio's expected rate of return.

TABLE 23-4   STATISTICS FOR APEX AND BEAN

STOCK	EXPECTED RETURN E(r), %	RISK, %
Apex	5	20
Bean	15	40

Formula for Portfolio Return   For the Apex and Bean stocks, Eq. (23-2a) is a special case of Eq. (23-1) that defines the two-asset portfolio's expected return.

$$E(r_p) = x_A E(r_A) + x_B E(r_B) \qquad (23\text{-}2a)$$

$$= x_A(5\%) + x_B(15\%)$$

$$= .05x_A + .15x_B \qquad (23\text{-}2b)$$

The portfolio's return formula is a linear function, since the weight variables in Eq. (23-2a) or Eq. (23-2b) have exponents of unity. The portfolio risk formula is more complex.

Risk Formula   Total risk, as measured by the standard deviation of returns from a portfolio made up of n assets, is defined for the general n-asset case by Eq. (23-3a).

$$\sigma_p = \sqrt{\sum_{i=1}^{n}\sum_{j=1}^{n} x_i x_j \sigma_{ij}} \qquad (23\text{-}3a)$$

$$= \sqrt{\sigma_i^2 x_i^2 + \sigma_j^2 x_j^2 + 2x_i x_j \sigma_{ij}} \qquad \text{if } n = 2 \qquad (23\text{-}3b)$$

where

$$\sigma_p = \text{standard deviation of the portfolio's rates of return}$$

$$\sigma_i^2 = \sigma_{ii} = \text{variance of returns of the } i\text{th asset, that is, the stan-}$$

$$\text{dard deviation squared}$$

$$\sigma_{ij} = \text{cov}(r_i, r_j) = \text{covariance of returns for assets } i \text{ and } j^{[10]}$$

The covariance is related to the correlation coefficient, as shown in Eq. (23-4).[11]

$$\sigma_{ij} = (\sigma_i)(\sigma_j)(\rho_{ij}) \qquad (23\text{-}4)$$

where ρ_{ij} is the correlation coefficient between variables i and j.

The covariance measures how two variables covary. If two assets move together, their covariance is positive. For example, most common stocks have a positive covariance with each other. If two variables are independent, their covariance is zero. If two variables move inversely, their covariance is negative.

---

10 Mathematical App. B, in Part 9, explains the covariance, σ_{ij}.
11 Mathematical App. D explains correlation and the correlation coefficient in more detail.

Equation (23-3) defines a portfolio's risk. For the two-asset portfolio of Apex and Bean, Eq. (23-5) gives the standard deviation of returns.[12]

$$\sigma_p = \sqrt{x_A^2\sigma_A^2 + x_B^2\sigma_B^2 + 2x_Ax_B\sigma_{AB}} \tag{23-5}$$

Substituting Eq. (23-4) into (23-5) yields (23-6a), which shows exactly how the correlation between the returns from Apex and Bean affects the portfolio's risk.

$$\sigma_p = \sqrt{x_A^2\sigma_A^2 + x_B^2\sigma_B^2 + 2x_Ax_B\rho_{AB}\sigma_A\sigma_B} \tag{23-6a}$$

$$= \sqrt{x_A^2(20\%)^2 + x_B^2(40\%)^2 + 2x_Ax_B\rho_{AB}(20\%)(40\%)} \tag{23-6b}$$

$$= \sqrt{.04x_A^2 + .16x_B^2 + .16x_Ax_B\rho_{AB}}$$

Figure 23-3a, b, c, and d is a set of graphs in risk-return space of the two assets Apex and Bean and the portfolios that can be formed from them at

FIGURE 23-3(a)   Two perfectly positively correlated assets generate linear portfolio investment opportunities; (b) two zero correlated assets generate a curve of portfolio possibilities; (c) two perfectly negatively correlated assets can create a riskless portfolio; (d)the asset's correlation affects the portfolio's risk.

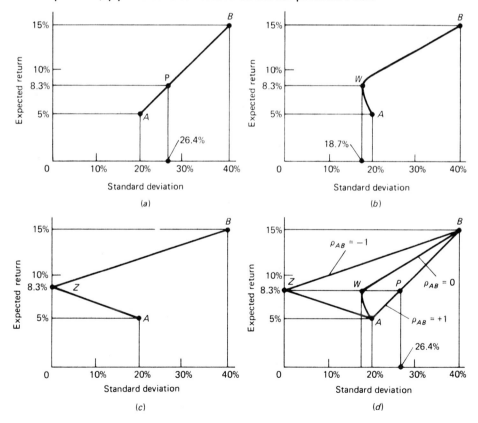

12 The portfolio risk formula shown in Eqs. (23-5) and (23-6) and elsewhere is derived and explained in Mathematical App. E.

three different values for their correlation coefficient, ρ_{AB} = −1, 0, and +1. These four figures were prepared by plotting the risk and return of the various portfolios composed of Apex and Bean stocks for which the participation levels summed to unity (that is, $x_A + x_B = 1$) and for three different correlation coefficients, ρ_{AB} = −1.0, 0, and +1.0.

In order to understand Fig. 23-3, it is informative to verify a few points in the figures by substituting some appropriate numbers into Eq. (23-2b) and (23-6b) and calculating the portfolio's expected return and risk. For example, for the portfolio that has x_A = ⅔ and x_B = ⅓, the expected return is fixed at 8.3 percent regardless of what value the correlation coefficient assumes.

$$E(r_p) = \sum_{i=1}^{2} x_i E(r_i)$$

$$= x_A E(r_A) + x_B E(r_B)$$

$$= x_A(.05) + x_B(.15)$$

$$= \frac{2}{3}(.05) + \frac{1}{3}(.15) = .083 = 8.3\%$$

The risk for this portfolio with x_A = ⅔ and x_B = ⅓ varies with the correlation coefficient, ρ_{AB}.

$$\sigma_p = \sqrt{x_A^2 \sigma_A^2 + x_B^2 \sigma_B^2 + 2x_A x_B \rho_{AB} \sigma_A \sigma_B} \qquad (23\text{-}6a)$$

$$= \sqrt{(\tfrac{2}{3})^2(20\%)^2 + (\tfrac{1}{3})^2(40\%)^2 + 2(\rho_{AB})(\tfrac{2}{3})(\tfrac{1}{3})(20\%)(40\%)}$$

$$= .0175 + .0175 + .035(\rho_{AB}) \qquad (23\text{-}6c)$$

$$= .035 + .035(\rho_{AB})$$

**23-3.3
Perfectly
Positively
Correlated
Returns,
Fig. 23-3a**

Portfolio analysis of the two-asset portfolio illustrated in Fig. 23-3a shows that diversification does not reduce portfolio risk when the returns are perfectly positively correlated, ρ_{AB} = +1.0. When the correlation coefficient between the rates of return from assets A and B is at its maximum value of positive unity, the linear risk-return relationship in Fig. 23-3a results. This straight line between assets A and B in risk-return space is derived by first setting ρ_{AB} to positive unity in Eq. (23-6a). Next the values of the two asset's weights are varied from zero to 1 (that is, $0.0 < x < +1.0$) inversely so that they always sum to positive unity (namely, $x_A + x_B = 1.0$). Finally, the infinite number of pairs of values for x_A and x_B values (such that $x_A + x_B = 1.0$ for $0 < x_A < + 1.0$ and $0 < x_B < + 1.0$) are substituted into the portfolio risk formula, Eq. (23-6a), and the portfolio return formula, Eq. (23-2a). The infinite number of risk and return statistics for the two-asset portfolio are thus derived, and they trace out the straight line in Fig. 23-3a when ρ_{AB} = +1.0.

**23-3.4
Uncorrelated
Assets,
Fig. 23-3b**

If the rates of return from Apex and Bean stocks are zero-correlated, substantial risk reduction benefits can be obtained from diversifying between the two assets. This beneficial risk reduction can be seen analytically by noting what happens to portfolio risk Eq. (23-6a) when ρ_{AB} equals zero. The last quantity on the right-hand side of the equation becomes zero and thus disappears when $\rho_{AB} = 0$. This reduces the portfolio's risk level below what it was when this correlation was a larger value (for example, when $\rho_{AB} = +1.0$).

The results of the uncorrelated returns are illustrated in Fig. 23-3b. The portfolio's expected return is unaffected by changing the correlation between assets — this is because ρ_{AB} is not a variable in the portfolio return Eq. (23-2a.) All differences between the portfolios generated when $\rho_{AB} = +1.0$ and the portfolios generated when $\rho_{AB} = 0$ are risk differences stemming from Eq. (23-6a). Figure 23-3b shows that the portfolios with $\rho_{AB} = 0$ have less risk at every level of expected return than the same portfolios with $\rho_{AB} = +1.0$ in Fig. 23-3a.

The substantial risk reductions available by diversifying across uncorrelated assets are readily available to all investors. Empirical research has shown that common stock price indexes, bond price indexes, and commodity price indexes all tend to be uncorrelated.[13] Thus, any investor who diversifies across these different market assets can expect to benefit from the diversification between uncorrelated assets as indicated in Fig. 23-3b.

The lowest possible value for any correlation coefficient is negative unity. When the correlation coefficient in portfolio risk Eq. (23-6b) reaches negative unity, the last term on the right-hand side of the equation assumes its maximum negative value for any given pair of values for x_A and x_B. In fact, the portfolio's risk can be reduced to zero risk when $\rho_{AB} = -1.0$ for one set of portfolio weights. For example, for the portfolio made of Bean and Apex stocks, Fig. 23-3c shows that when $x_A = \frac{2}{3}$ and $x_B = \frac{1}{3}$ and $\rho_{AB} = -1.0$, the portfolio's risk vanishes to zero. For all other weights the portfolio's risk is above zero, but portfolio risk is always at its lowest possible level over all possible sets of portfolio weights when $\rho_{AB} = -1.0$.

If it seems dubious that two perfectly negatively correlated *risky assets* like Apex and Bean can be combined in just the correct proportions to form a *riskless portfolio* like the one at $x_A = \frac{2}{3}$ and $x_B = \frac{1}{3}$ in Fig. 23-3c, reconsider the example in Table 23-3.

**23-3.5
Perfectly
Negatively
Correlated
Returns,
Fig. 23-3c**

Figure 23-3d summarizes the three illustrated examples from Fig. 23-3a, 23-3b, and 23-3c. To summarize, Fig. 23-3a shows that at point P, $x_A = \frac{2}{3}$ and $x_B = \frac{1}{3}$ and, for a correlation of $\rho_{AB} = +1$, the portfolio's total risk is $\sigma_p = \sqrt{.07} = 26.4$ percent. Figure 23-3b shows that if $\rho_{AB} = 0$, then $\sigma_p = \sqrt{.035} = 18.7$ percent at point W. And Fig. 23-3c illustrates the case when $\rho_{AB} = -1$; then $\sigma_p = \sqrt{0} = 0$ at point Z. Figure 23-3d was constructed by plotting all the points (like P, W, and Z, respectively) from Fig. 23-3a, 23-3b, and 23-3c together in risk-return space.

**23-3.6
Analysis
Using
Markowitz
Diversification**

13 James E. Hatch and Robert W. White, *Canadian Stocks, Bonds, Bills and Inflation: 1950–1983,* The Financial Analysts Research Foundation, Monograh 19, 1985, table 29, p. 102. R.G. Ibbotson and R.A. Sinquefield, *Stocks, Bonds, Bills, and Inflation: The Past (1926–1976) and the Future (1977-2000),* Financial Analysts Research Foundation, 1977, exhibit 7; K. Dusak, "Future Trading and Investor Returns: An Investigation of Commodity Risk Premiums," *Journal of Political Economy,* December 1963, vol. 81, no. 6, pp. 1387–1406.

Markowitz diversification can lower risk below the systematic level if the security analyst can find securities whose rates of return have low enough correlations. Unfortunately, there are only a precious few securities that have low correlations. Therefore, using Markowitz diversification requires a data bank of financial statistics for many securities, and a computer.

Applying Markowitz diversification to a collection of potential investment assets with a computer is called *Markowitz portfolio analysis*. It is a scientific way to manage a portfolio, and its results are quite interesting. Since Markowitz portfolio analysis considers both the risk and return of dozens, or hundreds, or thousands of different securities simultaneously (the number is limited only by the size of the computer and the number of securities for which one has risk and return statistics), it is a more powerful method of analyzing a portfolio than using one's head or selecting investments with a committee. A person's mind (even the mind of a genius) or an investment committee cannot simultaneously evaluate hundreds of different investment opportunities and balance the risks and returns of them all with one another to find efficient portfolios that dominate all other investment opportunities. Markowitz portfolio analysis is essentially a mathematics problem requiring that many different equations be solved simultaneously. This can be done on a large scale only by using a computer program that does what is called quadratic programming. *Quadratic programming* minimizes the portfolio's risk (a quadratic equation) at each level of average return for the portfolio.[14]

The type of portfolio manager who is not sufficiently analytical to use quadratic programming is sometimes lightly referred to as a "financial interior decorator."

Financial Interior Decorating   Many investment counsellors are financial interior decorators, meaning that they *design* portfolios of securities to match the investors' personalities. Thus, an elderly widow completely dependent on the income from a modest fixed investment (such women are referred to as "Aunt Janes" in the brokerage industry) would be advised to invest in low-risk, low-return assets like bonds and utility stocks on the assumption that they would minimize risk. The financial interior decorator would give little or no consideration to the correlation coefficients among assets. On the other hand, a young professional man or woman with a promising future would be advised to invest in high-risk, high-return securities. A financial interior decorator would make this suggestion on the oversimplified assump-

---

14 Computer programs to perform portfolio analysis and other forms of investment analysis are publicly available. See William B. Riley, Jr., and Austin H. Montgomery, Jr., *Guide to Computer Assisted Investment Analysis*. New York: McGraw-Hill, 1982. Chapter 8 contains a simplified Markowitz portfolio analysis computer program that can be run on a personal computer. This and other programs can be purchased from McGraw-Hill on a floppy disk called "Investpak" for about $40. For information write to: Investpak, McGraw-Hill Book Co., 27 Floor, 1221 Avenue of the Americas, New York, NY 10020. Also see chap. 10 of *The Complete Investment Book* by Richard Bookstaber (Glenview, Ill.: Scott, Foresman, and Company), 1985. The chapter lists a quadratic program written in Basic language on pp. 119–126. Dr. Bookstaber's computer programs may be purchased on floppy disks to run on personal computers for a modest fee, as explained on page 142.

tion that the high-risk stocks must combine to make a portfolio with the highest long-run rate of return, an assumption that is not necessarily true.

In spite of the superficial intuitive appeal of the financial interior decorating approach to portfolio management, the preceding analysis reveals its weakness. A Markowitz diversified portfolio of risky assets will earn a higher average return in the long run than a simply diversified portfolio because it will not experience the large losses that periodically hurt the long-run performance of a simply diversified portfolio. Or, on the other hand, two high-risk, high-return securities might yield the minimum risk portfolio if they are negatively correlated.

23-4 CONVEXITY OF THE EFFICIENT FRONTIER

If the risk and return of all individual assets on all security exchanges were plotted in risk-return space, they would be dominated by portfolios. Figure 23-4 represents the set of investment opportunities available in the securities markets. The escalloped, quarter-moon-shaped opportunity set in this figure contains individual assets (stocks and bonds) represented by dots in the lower right-hand side of the opportunity set. The efficient frontier is represented by the heavy dark curve from E to F. Only portfolios will lie along the efficient frontier. Portfolios will always dominate individual assets because of the risk-reducing benefits of diversification that portfolios enjoy. Only the highest-return portfolio F in Fig. 23-4 is likely to be a one-asset efficient portfolio.

FIGURE 23-4   The set of investment opportunities.

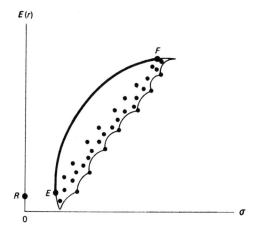

The opportunity set is constructed of curves that are all convex toward the $E(r)$ axis. This is because all assets have correlation coefficients between positive unity and negative unity. As shown in Fig. 23-3, this fact results in a locus of portfolios that traces a curve convex to the $E(r)$ axis in $[\sigma, E(r)]$ space. Only perfectly positively correlated (that is, $\rho = +1$) assets will generate linear combinations of risk and return; under no circumstances will a portfolio possibility locus ever curve away from the $E(r)$ axis in $[\sigma, E(r)]$ space.

Not all portfolios will lie on the efficient frontier; some will dominate others. For example, Markowitz diversification will generate portfolios that are more efficient than simply diversified portfolios. If Markowitz diversification is applied to all marketable assets, the resulting portfolios are the efficient set of portfolios that forms the efficient frontier in Fig. 23-4. Appendix 23A shows how to perform the portfolio analysis required to find the efficient frontier when more than two assets are involved.

23-5 DERIVATION OF THE CAPITAL MARKET LINE

Earlier in this chapter the concept of the efficient frontier was examined. It was explained that the efficient frontier that can be constructed without borrowing or lending is rarely a straight line. Rather, it is a curve that is convex toward the $E(r)$ axis in risk-return space. However, if borrowing and lending opportunities are included in the analysis, a linear set of investment opportunities called the *capital market line* (CML) emerges.

**23-5.1
One Riskless
Asset
Assumed**

If investors were surveying *all* investment opportunities, they would find that opportunities to borrow and lend exist. Figure 23-4 depicts a *riskless asset* at a point R on the expected-return axis. Point R might represent U.S. Treasury bonds that are held to maturity. Such an investment yields a positive return and has zero variability of return. Symbolically, $\sigma_R = 0$ represents this riskless condition.

After considering the opportunities shown in Fig. 23-4, a thoughtful investor would realize that it is possible to create more investment opportunities. By combining the riskless asset with a risky asset, new portfolios can be created that are not shown in this figure.

The expected return of a portfolio composed of one risky and one risk-free asset is shown in Eq. (23-7a).

$$E(r_p) = x_R R + x_i E(r_i) \tag{23-7a}$$

$$= x_R R + (1 - x_R)E(r_i) \quad \text{since } x_i = (1 - x_R) \tag{23-7b}$$

R denotes the expected return of the riskless asset, and $E(r_i)$ is the expected return of some risky asset. The risk of a portfolio of R and a risky asset is shown in Eq. (23-8a).

$$\sigma_p = \sqrt{x_R^2 \sigma_R^2 + x_i^2 \sigma_i^2 + 2x_R x_i \sigma_{iR}} \tag{23-8a}$$

$$= 0 + x_i \sigma_i + 0 \quad \text{since } \sigma_R = \sigma_{iR} = 0 \tag{23-8b}$$

The opportunity locus in risk-return space representing the portfolios that can be formed from a risky asset and R is a straight line since Eqs. (23-7a) and (23-8b) are both linear. Figure 23-5 shows four of the infinite number of opportunity loci representing portfolios containing R and a risky asset. These

FIGURE 23-5   Several portfolio possibility lines for portfolios containing risk-free asset R.

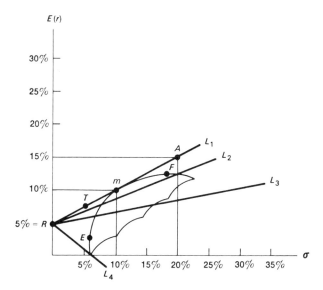

opportunity loci all start at R and pass through the opportunity set of risky assets.

In Fig. 23-5 the portfolios between R and the efficient frontier (point T, for example) represent portfolios containing both R and the risky asset m; that is, part of the portfolio is invested in the riskless asset. But those portfolios lying on the section of the opportunity loci above point m on the line $RTmAL_1$ (point A, for example) contain negative amounts of R, $x_R < 0$. A negative amount of R may be interpreted as borrowing at interest rate R to buy more of a risky asset like m—buying on margin. Thus, an aggressive investor might create a leveraged portfolio like A in Fig. 23-5 to increase his or her expected return. Of course, financial leverage also increases the financial risk, as shown in the figure.

Suppose one share of investment m costs \$1,000 and offers a 50-50 chance of returning either \$1,000 or \$1,200. The expected return for the holding period is 10 percent, as shown below.

23-5.2 Numerical Example of a Leveraged Portfolio

$$E(r_m) = \sum_{i=1}^{2} p_i r_i$$

$$= .5\left(\frac{1,000 - 1,000}{1,000}\right) + .5\left(\frac{1,200 - 1,000}{1,000}\right)$$

$$= .5(0) + .5(20\%)$$

$$= 0 + 10\% = 10\%$$

The standard deviation of returns is 10 percent for m (still assuming the zero and 20 percent outcomes are equally likely).

$$\sigma_m = \sqrt{\Sigma p_i[r_i - E(r)]^2}$$
$$= \sqrt{.5(0 - .1)^2 + .5(.2 - .1)^2}$$
$$= \sqrt{.5(.01) + .5(.01)}$$
$$= \sqrt{.01}$$
$$= .1 = 10\%$$

Now if an investor borrows \$1,000 at $R = 5$ percent and buys a second share of $m, x_m = 2$ and $x_R = -1$. In this case the investor has a 50-50 chance of receiving \$950 or \$1,350 on the \$1,000 of original equity, as shown below.

	Two Alternative Outcomes	
	BAD	GOOD
Original equity	\$1,000	\$1,000
Principal amount borrowed at 5%	1,000	\$1,000
Total amount invested in m	\$2,000	\$2,000
Return on two shares of m	\$2,000	\$2,400
Repayment of loan principal	(1,000)	(1,000)
Payment of interest at 5%	(50)	(50)
Net return on original equity	\$ 950	\$1,350
Probability of outcome	.5	.5

Thus, the expected return on m leveraged is 15 percent. The calculations follow.

$$E(r) = \sum p_i r_i$$
$$= .5\left(\frac{950 - 1,000}{1,000}\right) + .5\left(\frac{1,350 - 1,000}{1,000}\right)$$
$$= .5(-5\%) + .5(35\%)$$
$$= -2.5\% + 17.5\%$$
$$= 15\%$$

The standard deviation of returns on the leveraged portfolio is 20 percent, as follows.

$$\sigma = \sqrt{\Sigma p_i[r_i - E(r_i)]^2}$$
$$= \sqrt{.5(-5\% - 15\%)^2 + .5(35\% - 15\%)^2}$$
$$= \sqrt{.5(-20\%)^2 + .5(20\%)^2}$$
$$= \sqrt{.5(.04) + .5(.04)}$$

$$= \sqrt{.02 + .02}$$

$$= \sqrt{.04}$$

$$= .2 = 20\%$$

These results are shown graphically in Fig. 23-5 as portfolios m and A on line L_1. Equations (23-7a) and (23-8b) may be checked by substituting in the values from this example.

Rational investors who use Markowitz diversification will recognize the various opportunities shown in Fig. 23-5. These investors will also recognize that the opportunity locus designated L_1 dominates *all* other opportunities. The portfolios that can be created from R and risky assets other than m (along lines L_2, L_3 and L_4, for example) and even most of the efficient set of portfolios (along curve EF) are dominated by the opportunities represented by the line L_1 in Fig. 23-5. Therefore, investors will all want the portfolio denoted m in Fig. 23-5 because this is the risky asset needed to generate the dominant opportunity locus L_1. Hereafter, L_1 will be called the capital market line (CML). The CML is a separate and distinct relation from the security market line (SML), or capital asset pricing model (CAPM), which was developed in Chap. 10. The CAPM or SML is a linear relationship between expected return and *systematic risk* for portfolios and individual assets. The CML, on the other hand, is a linear relationship between expected return and *total* risk on which *only portfolios* will lie.[15]

**23-5.3
The CML
Emerges**

Imagine a capital market, such as the ones shown in Fig. 23-5 and 23-6, that is at equilibrium. By the definition of an economic equilibrium in a market, supply and demand are equal for all goods. So every security in the market must be held by some owner. Since all investors unanimously want m, it follows that, in equilibrium, m must be a huge portfolio containing all securities in the proportions x_i^* where

**23-5.4
The Market
Portfolio**

$$x_i^* = \frac{\text{total value of the } i\text{th firm's securities}}{\text{total value of all securities in the market}}$$

Let m be designated as the *market portfolio*, the unanimously desirable portfolio containing all securities in exactly the proportions in which they are supplied.[16] The return on the market portfolio is the weighted average return

---

15 The rationale for the CML and CAPM (or SML) and the assumptions underlying them both are explained in detail in chap. 24.

16 For the original discussion of the market portfolio see E. Fama, ''Risk, Return and Equilibrium: Some Clarifying Comments,'' *Journal of Finance* March 1968, pp. 32–33. For empirical estimates of the market portfolio see Roger G. Ibbotson and Carol L. Fall, ''The United States Market Wealth Portfolio,'' *Journal of Portfolio Management*, Fall 1979. See also Roger G. Ibbotson,

FIGURE 23-6   The capital market line (CML) tangent to the efficient frontier.

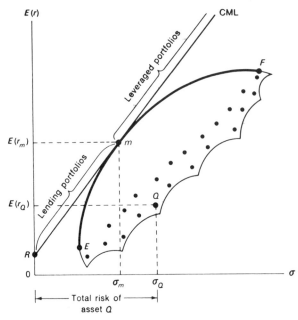

on all securities in the market. In equilibrium R must be the interest rate that equates the supply of and demand for loanable funds.

In reality there is no market portfolio. However, it is a useful theoretical construct, since the return on m is the return the TSE 300 Composite Index, the Canadian Market Portfolio Index, Dow Jones average, the Standard & Poor's average, the NYSE index, and others are estimating.[17] The return on m would be the optimum market index.

23-5.5
Lending and
Leveraged
Portfolios
on the CML

In Figure 23-6, portfolio m is the only portfolio on the CML that is not utilizing the opportunity to borrow or lend at the riskless rate R(that is, $x_R = 0$ for m). The portfolios along the CML between R and m are *lending portfolios*. They all have some money invested in the riskless asset R; that is, they are lending money at the rate R. Symbolically, $x_R > 0$ for lending portfolios.

The portfolios above m on the CML are all *leveraged or borrowing portfolios*. They were constructed by borrowing at the rate R and investing the proceeds

Lawrence B. Siegel and Kathryn S. Love, "World Wealth: Market Values and Returns," *Journal of Portfolio Management*, Fall 1985, pp. 4–23.

The geometric shape of the opportunity set in risk-return [that is, $(\sigma, E(r))$] space has been analyzed by R.C. Merton, "An Analytic Derivation of the Efficient Portfolio Frontier," *Journal of Financial and Quantitative Analysis*, September 1972, pp. 1151–1172.

17 Probably the "best" measure of return on the market portfolio is the World Composite Index, as published by Morgan Stanley Capital International SA. The portfolio is a weighted index of over twenty countries, and returns are published in U.S. dollars, British pounds, and local currencies.

in m, increasing the portfolios' expected return on equity and risk, as shown by the upper portions of the CML. Leveraged or borrowing portfolios on the CML have $x_R < 0$.

23-5.6 Systematic Risk

When borrowing and lending opportunities (at the riskless rate R) are considered, the true efficient frontier is the straight line called the CML. These investment opportunities dominate the portfolios lying on the curve EF in Fig. 23-6. It was shown in Fig. 23-3a that when assets form a linear opportunity locus in risk-return space, they are perfectly positively correlated. This means that the returns from portfolios on the CML must all vary together systematically. These portfolios along the CML have had their unsystematic risk reduced to zero by diversification. Only the undiversifiable systematic risk remains. Their returns are perfectly positively correlated because of systematic variability in returns.

Individual assets represented by dots like point Q in Fig. 23-6 are not efficient because their total risk includes both systematic and unsystematic risk. These individual assets have not had their total risk reduced by diversification. The total risk of asset Q is equal to the distance from 0 to σ_Q along the horizontal axis of Fig. 23-6. The total risk can be partitioned into two pieces—systematic and unsystematic risk.[18] As explained in Chap. 10, the systematic part of an asset's total risk is due to the systematic parts of market risk, purchasing power risk, interest rate risk, managerial risk, industry risk, default risk, and whatever other systematic factors may exist.[19]

23-5.7 CML Is Simplified but Realistic

The preceding analysis is a simplified version of reality. The CML was mathematically derived from the efficient frontier by unrealistically assuming that money could be freely borrowed or lent at the risk-free rate R. Of course, private citizens cannot borrow money at the same low rate as the federal government, that is, at interest rate R. Such assumptions, however, keep the model simple and manageable. In spite of the simplifications used to derive the market model shown in Fig. 23-6, it is still realistic. Most portfolios' rates of return are highly positively correlated and lie along a curve like the efficient frontier EF in Fig. 23-6.

Table 23-5 lists the risk and return statistics of thirty-four mutual funds. These portfolios' average returns were regressed on their risk. The results are shown in Fig. 23-7.

---

18 Partitioning the total risk of asset Q statistically proceeds as shown below:

$$\text{var}(r_Q) = \text{var}(a_Q + b_Q r_m + e) \quad \text{since } r_Q = a + b_Q r_m + e$$
$$= b_Q^2 \text{var}(r_m) + \text{var}(e_Q)$$
$$= \text{systematic} + \text{unsystematic risk}$$
$$= \text{total risk of asset } Q$$

19 B.F. King, op. cit., pp. 139–190. King partitions the risk of 316 stocks listed on the NYSE from 89 different industrial categories. Factor analysis is used. The factors that make up an asset's systematic risk are discussed further in chap. 28 entitled "Arbitrage Pricing Theory."

TABLE 23-5 PERFORMANCE OF 34 MUTUAL FUNDS, 1954–1963

	AVERAGE ANNUAL RETURN, %	STD. DEV. OF ANNUAL RETURN, %
Affiliated Fund	14.6	15.3
American Business Shares	10.0	9.2
Axe-Houghton, Fund A	10.5	13.5
Axe-Houghton, Fund B	12.0	16.3
Axe-Houghton, Stock Fund	11.9	15.6
Boston Fund	12.4	12.1
Board Street Investing	14.8	16.8
Bullock Fund	15.7	19.3
Commonwealth Investment Company	10.9	13.7
Delaware Fund	14.4	21.4
Dividend Shares	14.4	15.9
Eaton and Howard, Balanced Fund	11.0	11.9
Eaton and Howard, Stock Fund	15.2	19.2
Equity Fund	14.6	18.7
Fidelity Fund	16.4	23.5
Financial Industrial Fund	14.5	23.0
Fundamental Investors	16.0	21.7
Group Securities, Common Stock Fund	15.1	19.1
Group Securities, Fully Administered Fund	11.4	14.1
Incorporated Investors	14.0	25.5
Investment Company of America	17.4	21.8
Investors Mutual	11.3	12.5
Loomis-Sales Mutual Fund	10.0	10.4
Massachusetts Investors Trust	16.2	20.8
Massachusetts Investors — Growth Stock	18.6	22.7
National Investors Corporation	18.3	19.9
National Securities — Income Series	12.4	17.8
New England Fund	10.4	10.2
Putnam Fund of Boston	13.1	16.0
Scudder, Stevens & Clark Balanced Fund	10.7	13.3
Selected American Shares	14.4	19.4
United Funds — Income Fund	16.1	20.9
Wellington Fund	11.3	12.0
Wisconsin Fund	13.8	16.9

Source: William F. Sharpe, "Mutual Fund Performance," *Journal of Business*, January 1966 suppl., p. 125.

The correlation coefficient for the regression line shown in Fig. 23-7 is high and positive. The empirical data indicate that the trade-off of risk for return available in the market does resemble the theoretical CML model shown in Fig. 23-6.

23-6 CONCLUSION: RATIONAL INVESTORS DIVERSIFY

In the preceding pages of this chapter, it was shown how the dominance principle could be used to delineate desirable assets. Then various diversification practices were reviewed. It was seen that simple diversification of even the most naive variety (for example, selecting securities with a dart) was

FIGURE 23-7   Empirical test of the capital market line (CML).

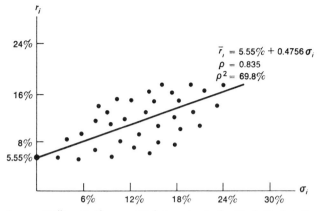

$$\bar{r}_i = 5.55\% + 0.4756\,\sigma_i$$
$$\rho = 0.835$$
$$\rho^2 = 69.8\%$$

Source: William F. Sharpe, ''Risk Aversion in the Stock Market: Some Empirical Evidence,'' *Journal of Finance*, September 1965, pp. 416–422.

beneficial in reducing risk. Markowitz diversification was seen to be the most effective way of attaining risk reduction.

After derivation of the efficient frontier was explained in terms of Markowitz diversification, borrowing and lending opportunities were introduced. It was seen that the dominant assets were always portfolios (as opposed to individual assets) and usually involved lending or leverage. Thus, we reach the conclusion that *diversification is essential* to the investment program of a rational, risk-averse, wealth-seeking investor. Furthermore, Markowitz diversification helps the investor attain a higher level of expected utility (or happiness) than any other risk reduction technique. Thus, rational investors will be concerned with the *correlation* between assets, in addition to the assets' expected returns and standard deviations.

After investors somehow (that is, by using either simple or Markowitz diversification) delineate the most dominant investment opportunities to be found (that is, their own most efficient frontier), they still must select one in which to invest their funds. Essentially, once the efficient frontier is delineated, portfolio selection is a personal choice.

QUESTIONS

1. Write a few sentences explaining the mathematical calculations used to find the portfolio's expected return.
2. What is assumed about the weights or participation levels of the assets in a portfolio? Why?
3. Define an efficient portfolio.
4. Define simple diversification. Will simple diversification reduce total risk? Unsystematic risk? Systematic risk?
5. Define superfluous diversification. What problems frequently result from superfluous diversification?

6. Define Markowitz diversification. Draw a graph of a two-asset portfolio's risk and return possibilities and explain how Markowitz diversification can reduce risk.

7. What does it mean to say that two variables are perfectly positively correlated? Uncorrelated or independent? Inversely correlated? Graph realistic examples of each and explain. (*Hint*: Mathematical App. D may be helpful reading.)

8. Define financial interior decorating and explain the shortcoming of this popular approach to portfolio management.

9. Why are all the curves in the opportunity set drawn convex rather than concave to the expected return axis?

10. "A portfolio of many different assets from many different industries will be a well-diversified portfolio." Is this statement true, false, or uncertain? Explain.

11. "Apart from negatively correlated stocks, all the gains from diversification come from 'averaging over' the independent components of the returns and risks of individual stocks. Among positively correlated stocks, there would be no gains from diversification, if independent variations [unsystematic risk] were absent." Quotation from John Lintner, "Security Prices, Risk, and Maximal Gains from Diversification," *Journal of Finance*, December 1965, p. 589 (bracketed words added). Explain this statement.

Note: The following questions are more technical and presume a knowledge of the appendixes to this chapter.

12. What assumptions describe an investor who prefers to use Markowitz portfolio analysis?

13. What is the objective of portfolio analysis?

14. What statistical inputs are required for a portfolio analysis of four assets?

15. Expand the following formula for a portfolio's variance of returns for four assets into a form showing all four assets' variances and covariances.

$$\text{var}(r_p) = \sum_{i=1}^{n}\sum_{j=1}^{n} x_i x_j \sigma_{ij} \quad \text{for } n = 4$$

16. Below are the possible rates of returns for two assets:

r_1, %	r_2, %	prob. (r_1 and r_2)
15	15	$\frac{1}{3}$
30	12	$\frac{1}{3}$
45	9	$\frac{1}{3}$
$E(r_1) = 30\%$	$E(r_2) = 12\%$	1.0

Assume that a security analyst has forecasted these returns, based on three different possible rates of economic growth. Also assume that the analyst has also calculated the expected return for each asset. Calculate the two variances and $\text{cov}(r_1, r_2)$. If assets 1 and 2 are combined 50-50 into a portfolio, what is the variance of this portfolio? Show your formulas and calculations.

SELECTED REFERENCES

Gordon Alexander and J.C. Francis. *Portfolio Analysis*. 3d ed. Englewood Cliffs, N.J.: Prentice-Hall, 1986. The CML and other more sophisticated models are developed. Graphical utility analysis, statistics, and advanced mathematics are used.

H. Markowitz. *Portfolio Selection*. New York: Wiley, 1959. Chapters 1 through 5 present the foundations for portfolio analysis. Chapters 7 and 8 present different techniques for performing portfolio analysis. Algebra is used.

F. Modigliani and G.A. Pogue. ''An Introduction to Risk and Return: Concepts and Evidence,'' part 1. *Financial Analysts Journal*, March-April 1974, vol. 30, no 2. Part 2, ibid., May-June 1974. An easy-to-read tutorial article explaining Markowitz diversification and its various implications. Important research is reviewed.

Mathematical Portfolio Analysis

Markowitz portfolio analysis performed graphically cannot handle more than a few securities. The graphical analysis does serve well as an introduction to portfolio analysis and may result in a better understanding of the analysis and of the solution obtained.[20] However, a more efficient solution technique for portfolio analysis that uses differential calculus and linear algebra is explained in this appendix.

APP. 23A-1 A CALCULUS RISK MINIMIZATION SOLUTION: GENERAL FORM

Calculus can be used to find the minimum risk portfolio for any given expected return E^*. Mathematically, the problem involves finding the minimum portfolio variance. That is,

$$\text{Minimize: } \text{var}(r_p) = \sum_{i=1}^{n}\sum_{j=1}^{n} x_i x_j \sigma_{ij} \qquad \text{(App. 23A-1)}$$

subject to two Lagrangian constraints. The first constraint requires that the desired expected return E^* be achieved. This is equivalent to requiring the following equation:

$$\sum_{i=1}^{n} x_i E(r_i) - E^* = 0 \qquad \text{(App. 23A-2)}$$

The second constraint requires that the weights sum to unity. This constraint is equivalent to requiring the following equation:

$$\sum_{i=1}^{n} x_i - 1 = 0 \qquad \text{(App. 23A-3)}$$

Combining these three quantities yields the Lagrangian objective function of the risk minimization problem with a desired return constraint:

$$z = \sum_{i=1}^{n}\sum_{j=1}^{n} x_i x_j \sigma_{ij} + \lambda_1 \left(\sum_{i=1}^{n} x_i E(r_i) - E^* \right) + \lambda_2 \sum_{i=1}^{n} x_i - 1 \right) \qquad \text{(App. 23A-4)}$$

---

[20] Informative examples of Markowitz portfolio analysis performed graphically may be found in: Harry Markowitz, *Portfolio Selection* (New York: Wiley, 1959), chap. 7; J.C. Francis and S.H. Archer, *Portfolio Analysis*, 2d ed. (Englewood Cliffs, N.J.: Prentice-Hall, 1979), chap. 5; J.C. Francis, *Investments: Analysis and Management*, 3d ed. (New York: McGraw-Hill, 1980), apps. A and B to chap. 18. App. B contains a short Fortran computer program to plot the isovariance ellipses.

The minimum risk portfolio is found by setting $dz/dx_i = 0$ for $i = 1, \ldots$ n and $dz/d\lambda_i = 0$ for $i = 1, 2$ and then solving the system of equations for the x_i's. The number of assets analyzed, n, can be any positive integer. Martin solved this problem and has shown the relationship between the solution and the graphical critical line solution in a well-written article.[21]

APP. 23A-2   CALCULUS MINIMIZATION OF RISK: A THREE-SECURITY PORTFOLIO

For a three-security portfolio, the objective function to be minimized is shown below.

$$z = x_1^2\sigma_{11} + x_2^2\sigma_{22} + x_3^2\sigma_{33} + 2x_1x_2\sigma_{12} + 2x_1x_3\sigma_{13} + 2x_2x_3\sigma_{23} \qquad \text{(App. 23A-5)}$$
$$+ \lambda_1(x_1E_1 + x_2E_2 + x_3E_3 - E^*) + \lambda_2(x_1 + x_2 + x_3 - 1)$$

Setting the partial derivatives of z with respect to all variables equal to zero yields equation system (App. 23A-6).

$$\frac{dz}{dx_1} = 2x_1\sigma_{11} + 2x_2\sigma_{12} + 2x_3\sigma_{13} + \lambda_1E_1 + \lambda_2 = 0$$

$$\frac{dz}{dx_2} = 2x_2\sigma_{22} + 2x_1\sigma_{12} + 2x_3\sigma_{23} + \lambda_1E_2 + \lambda_2 = 0$$

$$\frac{dz}{dx_3} = 2x_3\sigma_{33} + 2x_1\sigma_{13} + 2x_2\sigma_{23} + \lambda_1E_3 + \lambda_2 = 0 \qquad \text{(App. 23A-6)}$$

$$\frac{dz}{d\lambda_2} = x_1 + x_2 + x_3 - 1 = 0$$

$$\frac{dz}{d\lambda_1} = x_1E_1 + x_2E_2 + x_3E_3 - E^* = 0$$

This system is linear, since the weights (x_i's) are the variables and they are all of degree one; thus the system may be solved as a system of linear equations. The matrix representation of this system of linear equations is shown below as matrix Eq. (App. 23A-7), a Jacobian matrix.

$$\begin{matrix} \begin{bmatrix} 2\sigma_{11} & 2\sigma_{12} & 2\sigma_{13} & E_1 & 1 \\ 2\sigma_{21} & 2\sigma_{22} & 2\sigma_{23} & E_2 & 1 \\ 2\sigma_{31} & 2\sigma_{32} & 2\sigma_{33} & E_3 & 1 \\ 1 & 1 & 1 & 0 & 0 \\ E_1 & E_2 & E_3 & 0 & 0 \end{bmatrix} & \cdot & \begin{bmatrix} x_1 \\ x_2 \\ x_3 \\ \lambda_1 \\ \lambda_2 \end{bmatrix} & = & \begin{bmatrix} 0 \\ 0 \\ 0 \\ 1 \\ E^* \end{bmatrix} \\ C & & x & = & k \end{matrix} \qquad \text{(App. 23A-7)}$$

21 A.D. Martin, Jr., "Mathematical Programming of Portfolio Selections," *Management Science*, January 1955, pp. 152–166. Reprinted in E.B. Frederickson, *Frontiers of Investment Analysis* (Scranton, Pa.: International Textbook, 1965), pp. 367–381.

This system may be solved several different ways. With matrix notation, the inverse of the coefficient matrix, denoted C^{-1}, may be used to find the solution (weight) vector x as shown below. I denotes the identity matrix.

$$Cx = k$$
$$C^{-1}Cx = C^{-1}k \qquad \text{(App. 23A-8)}$$
$$Ix = C^{-1}k$$
$$x = C^{-1}k$$

The solution will give the n ($n = 3$, in this case) weights in terms of E^*.

$$x_1 = a_1 + d_1 E^*$$
$$x_2 = a_2 + d_2 E^* \qquad \text{(App. 23A-9)}$$
$$x_3 = a_3 + d_3 E^*$$

where the a_1 and d_1 are constants. For any desired E^* the equations give the weights of the minimum-risk portfolio. These are the weights of a portfolio in the efficient frontier. By varying E^* the weights may be generated for the entire efficient frontier. Then the risk, $\text{var}(r_p)$, of the efficient portfolios may be calculated, and the efficient frontier may be graphed.

As a numerical example, the data from the three-security portfolio problem indicated in Table 23A-1 are solved to obtain the following coefficients matrix.

TABLE APP. 23A-1   STATISTICAL INPUTS FOR PORTFOLIO ANALYSIS OF THREE COMMON STOCKS

ASSET	$E(r_i)$	$\text{var}(r_i) = \sigma_{ii}$	$\text{cov}(r_i, r_j) = \sigma_{ij}$
Homestake Mining	$E(r_1) = 5\% = .05$	$\sigma_{11} = .1$	$\sigma_{12} = -.1$
Kaiser Aluminum	$E(r_2) = 7\% = .07$	$\sigma_{22} = .4$	$\sigma_{13} = 0$
Texas Instruments	$E(r_3) = 30\% = .3$	$\sigma_{33} = .7$	$\sigma_{23} = .3$

$$
\begin{bmatrix}
2\sigma_{11} & 2\sigma_{12} & 2\sigma_{13} & E_1 & 1 \\
2\sigma_{21} & 2\sigma_{22} & 2\sigma_{23} & E_2 & 1 \\
2\sigma_{31} & 2\sigma_{32} & 2\sigma_{33} & E_3 & 1 \\
1 & 1 & 1 & 0 & 0 \\
E_1 & E_2 & E_3 & 0 & 0
\end{bmatrix}
=
\begin{bmatrix}
2(.1) & 2(-.1) & 2(0) & .05 & 1 \\
2(-.1) & 2(.4) & 2(.3) & .07 & 1 \\
2(0) & 2(.3) & 2(.7) & .3 & 1 \\
1 & 1 & 1 & 0 & 0 \\
.05 & .07 & .3 & 0 & 0
\end{bmatrix}
= C
$$

Multiplying the inverse of this coefficents matrix by the constants vector (k) yields the weights vector ($C^{-1}k = x$) as shown below in matrix Eq. (App. 23A-10).

$$
\overset{C^{-1}}{
\begin{bmatrix}
.677 & -.736 & .059 & .789 & -1.433 \\
-.736 & .800 & -.064 & .447 & -2.790 \\
.059 & -.064 & .005 & -.236 & 4.223 \\
-1.433 & -2.790 & 4.223 & .522 & -15.869 \\
.789 & .447 & -.236 & -.095 & .552
\end{bmatrix}}
\overset{k}{
\begin{bmatrix}
0 \\ 0 \\ 0 \\ 1 \\ E^*
\end{bmatrix}}
=
\overset{x}{
\begin{bmatrix}
x_1 \\ x_2 \\ x_3 \\ \lambda_1 \\ \lambda_2
\end{bmatrix}}
\qquad \text{(App. 23A-1)}
$$

Evaluating the weights vector yields the system of Eq. (App. 23A-11), below.

$$x_1 = .789 - 1.433E^*$$
$$x_2 = .447 - 2.790E^*$$
$$x_3 = -.236 + 4.223E^*$$

$x_1 + x_2 + x_3 = 1$ for any given E^*

(App. 23A-11)

$$\lambda_1 = .522 - 15.869E^*$$
$$\lambda_2 = -.095 + .522E^*$$

The weights in the first three equations in (App. 23A-11) sum to unity are a linear function of E^* and represent the weights of the three securities in the efficient portfolio at the point where $E(r_p) = E^*$. Varying E^* generates the weights of all the efficient portfolios.

Stochastic Dominance

Stochastic dominance selection rules utilize every bit of information in the probability distributions rather than simply focusing on the probability distribution's first two moments (that is, the expected return and the variance). As a result, stochastic dominance selection rules can sometimes yield portfolios that maximize expected utility, are not Markowitz efficient portfolios, and (sometimes) dominate Markowitz efficient portfolios.

Figure App. 23B-1 shows the locations of three assets, denoted A, B, and C, in relation to the efficient frontier. Figure App. 23B-2 shows three uniform probability distributions of returns for these three assets. Figure App. 23B-3 shows cumulative probability distributions for the three assets. In terms of the logic of stochastic dominance, inefficient portfolio A is more desirable than efficient portfolio B, for example. This example demonstrates that portfolio analysis methods that consider only the first two moments may waste some information that could be used to maximize investors' expected utility.

Probability distribution A is said to stochastically dominate probability distribution B if the cumulative probability of achieving any rate of return up to some specified level for distribution A is less than or equal to that same cumulative probability for asset B and, at least at one point, the less than inequality holds. This means that the chances of earning a low rate of return from asset A are lower than the chances of earning a low return from asset B.

Figure App. 23B-3 graphically depicts how portfolio A stochastically dominates portfolio B even though A is an inefficient portfolio. For any given rate of return, the cumulative probability that asset B earns up to that return is larger than the cumulative probability that A earns up to that same return. This is obvious since portfolio A's lowest return (of 100 percent) equals portfolio B's highest possible return.[22]

The advantages of selecting investments with the stochastic dominance criteria instead of risk-return criteria are:

1. Stochastic dominance orderings do not presume a certain form of probability distribution.
2. Fewer restrictions on the investor's utility function are implied by use of the stochastic dominance criteria.
3. Undesirable portfolios, such as those on the lower section of the efficient frontier, can be eliminated from further consideration.[23]
4. The stochastic dominance selection criteria do not waste information about the probability distribution; every point is considered.

[22] More rigorous mathematical statements are usually used to define stochastic dominance. Some writers distinguish between first-degree, second-degree, and third-degree stochastic dominance. In the interest of brevity these distinctions are not developed here. For a more detailed discussion, see J.P. Quirk and R. Saposnik, ''Admissibility and Measurable Utility Functions,'' *Review of Economic Studies*, 1962, vol. 29, pp. 140–146.

[23] W.J. Baumol, ''An Expected Gain-Confidence Limit Criterion for Portfolio Section,'' *Management Science*, October 1963, pp. 171–182.

FIGURE APP. 23B-1   Points in risk-return space.

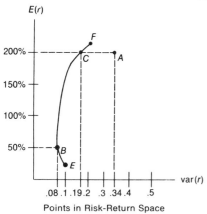

Points in Risk-Return Space

FIGURE APP. 23B-2   Uniform probability distribution for three assets.

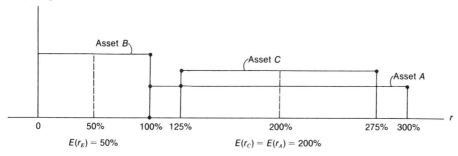

FIGURE APP. 23B-3   Cumulative probability function: for the three risky assets the graphs are uniform probability distributions from b to c. It is well known that the expected value of such distribution is $E(r) = (b + c)/2$; the variance is $\sigma^2 = (c - b)^2/12$; and the cumulative probability of a return less than or equal to r_c is $F(r_0) = (r_0 - b)/c - b)$.

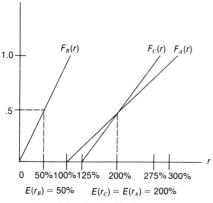

Cumulative Probability Functions

Although stochastic dominance selection rules are logically superior to simpler selection criteria, their practical value is dubious, since they require knowledge of *every point* on the probability distribution rather than, for example, merely the first two moments. It requires rather heroic confidence to try to estimate every point on a probability distribution in this world of uncertainty and changing expectations. The cost of estimating the entire probability distribution not only exceeds the cost of estimating the first two moments, but this cost probably is not justified in terms of the additional benefits it could realistically be expected to yield. This is an empirical question that has not yet been resolved.

SELECTED REFERENCES

M.M Ali. ''Stochastic Dominance and Portfolio Analysis.'' *Journal of Financial Economics*, 1975, vol. 2, pp. 205–229.

V.S. Bawa. ''Optimal Rules for Ordering Uncertain Prospects.'' *Journal of Financial Economics*, 1975, vol. 2, pp. 95–121.

————. ''Safety-First, Stochastic Dominance and Optimal Portfolio Choice.'' *Journal of Financial and Quantitative Analysis*, 1978, vol. 13, pp. 255–271.

P.A. Diamond and J.E. Stiglitz. ''Increases in Risk and in Risk Aversion.'' *Journal of Economic Theory*, 1974, vol. 8, pp. 337–360.

J. Hadar and W.R. Russell. ''Diversification of Interdependent Prospects.'' *Journal of Economic Theory*, 1974, vol. 7, pp. 231–240.

————and ————. ''Rules for Ordering Uncertain Prospects.'' *American Economic Review*, 1969, vol. 59, pp. 25–34.

————and ————.''Stochastic Dominance and Diversification.'' *Journal of Economic Theory*, 1971, vol. 3, pp. 288–305.

————, ————, and K. Seo. ''Gain from Diversification.'' *Review of Economic Studies*, 1977, vol. 44, pp. 363–368.

W.H. Jean. ''The Geometric Mean and Stochastic Dominance.'' *Journal of Finance*, March 1980.

O.M. Joy and R.B. Porter. ''Stochastic Dominance and Mutual Fund Performance,'' *Journal of Financial and Quantitative Analysis*, 1974, vol. 9, pp. 25–31.

R.C. Kearns and R.C. Burgess. ''An Effective Algorithm for Estimating Stochastic Dominance Efficient Sets.'' *Journal of Financial and Quantitative Analysis*, September 1979.

H. Levy and G. Hanoch. ''Relative Effectiveness of Efficiency Criteria for Portfolio Selection.'' *Journal of Financial and Quantitative Analysis*, 1970, vol. 5, pp. 63–76.

H. Levy and Y. Kroll, ''Efficiency Analysis with Borrowing and Lending: Criteria and Their Effectiveness.'' *Review of Ecnomics and Statistics*, February 1979.

H.M. Markowitz. ''An Algorithm for Finding Undominated Portfolios.'' In H. Levy and M. Sarnat (eds.) *Financial Decision Making Under Uncertainty*. New York: Academic Press, 1977.

R.B. Porter. ''An Empirical Comparison of Stochastic Dominance and Mean-Variance Choice Criteria.'' *Journal of Financial and Quantitative Analysis*, 1973, vol. 8, pp. 587–608.

————. ''Semi-Variance and Stochastic Dominance: A Comparison.'' *American Economic Review*, 1974, vol. 64, pp. 200–204.

―――― and R.P. Bey. "An Evaluation of the Empirical Significance of Optimal Seeking Algorithms in Portfolio Selection." *Journal of Finance*, December 1974.

―――― and R.C. Pfaffenberger. "Efficient Algorithms for Conducting Stochastic Dominance Tests on Large Numbers of Portfolios: Reply." *Journal of Financial and Quantitative Analysis*, 1975, vol. 10, pp. 181–185.

R.C. Scott and P.A. Horvath. "On the Direction of Preference for Moments of Higher Order than the Variance." *Journal of Finance*, September 1980.

G.A. Whitmore, "Third Degree Stochastic Dominance." *American Economic Review*, 1970, vol. 60, pp. 457–459.

CHAPTER 24

Capital Market Theory

This chapter discusses five aspects of the capital market theory, some of which have been touched on previously.

1. The assumptions that underlie the theory
2. The definition of the market portfolio
3. The capital market line (CML)
4. The capital asset pricing model (CAPM)—or the security market line (SML), as it is also called
5. What happens to the theory when the underlying assumptions used to simplify the theory are dropped

Capital market theory is an economic equilibrium theory about asset valuation. The theory considers all marketable investments—that is, thousands of stocks, bonds, options, commodities, warrants, and other things—simultaneously and explains how their prices should behave. Parts of this theory have already been introduced in this book. The notions of a security's total risk, systematic risk, and unsystematic risk were explained and the concept of the CAPM, or SML, was presented in Chap. 10. Then in Chap. 23, when the discussion turned to portfolios instead of individual assets, the CML emerged as a portfolio pricing model. The present chapter pulls all these ideas together and shows how they interact to form one unified economic theory.

24-1 INVESTMENT OPPORTUNITIES IN RISK-RETURN SPACE

Chapter 23 explained how to determine the efficient frontier for a group of assets. Suppose that all investment assets in the world were analyzed; stocks,

FIGURE 24-1 The opportunity set without borrowing and lending opportunities.

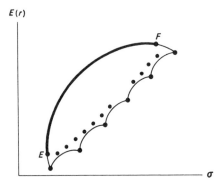

bonds, paintings, entrepreneurships, foreign exchange, commodities, and many other marketable assets would be considered. By use of a large computer and advanced mathematics, it is possible to perform portfolio analysis upon these thousands of assets and thus to determine the efficient frontier. Figure 24-1 shows the investment opportunities that might be shown to exist by undertaking such a massive analysis.

24-1.1 The Efficient Frontier

All the thousands of investment opportunities in the world are assumed to be represented by the escalloped quarter-moon-shaped design in Fig. 24-1. The individual assets lie along the *bottom* of this set of investment opportunities and are represented by the dots.

Individual assets (like stocks, bonds, and other securities) contain both systematic risk and unsystematic risk and are not efficient. Only *portfolios* using Markowitz diversification have had the unsystematic risk reduced to zero and can attain the curved efficient frontier. The efficient frontier is represented by the heavy dark curve from *E* to *F* in Fig. 24-1. The portfolios lying on the efficient frontier contain only systematic risk caused by variations in the economic, political, and sociological environment, which simultaneously affects nearly every asset in some way. As a result, the efficient assets along the curve *EF* in Fig. 24-1 are highly positively (but not perfectly) correlated.

24-1.2 Borrowing and Lending at a Riskless Rate

The investment opportunities shown in Fig. 24-1 may be extended by considering the possibilities of borrowing and lending. To keep the model simple and easy to conceptualize, suppose that all investors can borrow or lend at one riskless rate of return, denoted *R*. By definition, the riskless asset has no variability of return, var(*R*) = 0.

Figure 24-2 represents the investment, borrowing, and lending opportunities that would exist in equilibrium if all investors were Markowitz portfolio analysts, could borrow or lend at rate *R*, and had homogeneous expectations. The term *homogeneous expectations* means that all investors visualize the same expected return, risk, and correlation statistics for any specific asset in the world. Different assets can and will be perceived differently. But, any particular asset will be perceived homogeneously. Assuming homogeneous

FIGURE 24-2   Borrowing, lending, and investment opportunities in a market of Markowitz diversifiers.

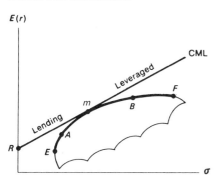

expectations allows us to represent the investment opportunities visualized by every investor with just one graph; we are spared the work of drawing separate graphs to represent differences of opinion over the risk and return statistics of specific assets. The capital market line shown in Fig. 24-2 is specified mathematically in Eq. (24-1).

$$E(r_i) = R + \left[\frac{\{E(r_m) - R\}}{\sigma_m} \right] \sigma_i \tag{24-1}$$

where

$E(r_i)$ = expected rate of return from the ith portfolio (and its total risk is measured by the standard deviation σ_i)

R = riskless rate of interest

$E(r_m)$ = expected rate of return from the market portfolio, denoted M

σ_m = market portfolio's standard deviation of returns

The market portfolio is defined in more detail in the following paragraph.

24-1.3 The Market Portfolio

Portfolio m in Fig. 24-2 is a huge portfolio containing all assets in the world in the proportions x_i^* where

$$x_i^* = \frac{\text{total value of the } i\text{th security}}{\text{total value of all securities in the market}}$$

Let m be designated as a *market portfolio*. It contains all securities in exactly the proportions they are supplied in equilibrium because it is the one unique portfolio that all investors would buy. The return on the market portfolio is the weighted average return on all securities in the market.[1]

Of course, there is no real-life analogue to the market portfolio, but it is a useful theoretical construct, since the return on m is the return that the TSE 300 Composite index, the Canadian Market Portfolio index, the Dow Jones average, the Standard & Poor's average, and the New York Stock Exchange index are estimating.

---

1 The market portfolio was originally Eugene Fama's concept. See E. Fama, "Risk, Return and Equilibrium: Some Clarifying Comments," *Journal of Finance*, March 1968, pp. 32–33. However, William Sharpe had previously published the conclusions discussed in this chapter before anyone else, without the market portfolio notion. See W. Sharpe, "Capital Asset Prices: A Theory of Market Equilibrium under Conditions of Risk," *Journal of Finance*, September 1964, pp. 425–552. For empirical estimates of the market portfolio see R.G. Ibbotson, Laurence B. Siegel, and Kathryn S. Love, "World Wealth: Market Values and Returns," *Journal of Portfolio Management*, Fall 1985, pp. 4–23. For an explanation of the critical role of the market portfolio in empirical tests of the capital market theory see Richard Roll, "A Critique of the Asset Pricing Theory's Tests," *Journal of Financial Economics*, March 1977, pp. 129–176. Roll's critique is made in a general-equilibrium context. Thus, Roll's critique does not obviate the usefulness of empirical characteristic line statistics based on some narrowly defined market index—this is partial-equilibrium analysis rather than general-equilibrium analysis.

24-2   ASSUMPTIONS UNDERLYING CAPITAL MARKET THEORY

Capital market theory is based on the assumptions underlying portfolio analysis. The theory consists essentially of the logical, mathematical, and economic implications of portfolio analysis. The following assumptions form the basis for performing Markowitz portfolio analysis to delineate the efficient frontier:

1. The rate of return from an investment adequately summarizes the outcome from the investment, and investors see the various possible rates of return in a probabilistic fashion (that is, they visualize a probability distribution of rates of return, either consciously or subconsciously).
2. Investors' risk estimates are proportional to the variability of return (namely, the standard deviation or variance) they perceive for a security or portfolio.
3. Investors are willing to base their decisions on only two parameters of the probability distribution of returns: the expected return, and the variance (or its square root, the standard deviation) of returns. Symbolically, $U = f\{E(r), \sigma\}$ where U denotes the investors' utility.
4. For any risk-class, investors prefer a higher rate of return to a lower one. Symbolically, $\delta U/\delta E(r) > 0$. Conversely, among all securities with the same rate of return, investors prefer less rather than more risk. Symbolically, $\delta U/\delta\sigma < 0$.

Investors who conform to the preceding assumptions will prefer efficient portfolios. Such investors will be referred to as *Markowitz diversifiers*. With this background information, it is possible to begin to discuss capital market theory. The assumptions necessary to generate the capital market theory are listed below.

1. All investors are Markowitz efficient diversifiers who delineate and seek to attain the efficient frontier. Thus, the four assumptions in the preceding list are also part of the assumptions on which the capital market theory is constructed.
2. Any amount of money can be borrowed or lent at the risk-free rate of interest R. The return on short-term Canadian Treasury bills may be used as a proxy for R. Essentially, this assumption allows investors to have idealized margin accounts. No other borrowing is permitted.
3. *Idealized uncertainty* prevails; that is, all investors visualize identical probability distributions for the future rates of return on any specific asset. They have *homogeneous expectations*. This assumption does not imply that different assets are not perceived to have different risk and/or rate-of-return statistics, however.
4. All investors have the same "one- period" time horizon.
5. All investments are infinitely divisible; fractional shares may be purchased in any portfolio or any individual asset.
6. No taxes and no transaction costs for buying and selling securities exist. Thus, trading is "frictionless."
7. No inflation and no change in the level of interest rates exist (or all changes are fully anticipated).
8. The capital markets are in equilibrium.

Readers unaccustomed to economic analysis are probably confused and discouraged by a theory based upon a list of unrealistic assumptions, but they should not be. The assumptions provide a concrete foundation upon which a theory can be derived by applying the forces of logic, intuition, and mathematics. Without these assumptions, the analysis would degenerate into a polemical discussion of which historical facts, folklore, and institutions are significant, which are insignificant, what their relationships are, and what conclusions might be reached by a "reasonable person." Such discussions are usually not productive.

Traditionally, economists have based their analyses on as few and as simple assumptions as possible. Then a theory is derived with conclusions and implications that are incontestable, given the assumptions. Later, the assumptions are relaxed to determine what can be expected in more realistic circumstances. In the final analysis, the test of a theory is not how realistic its assumptions are; rather, it is the predictive power of a model that should be judged. Later in this chapter, the assumptions underlying the capital market theory are aligned with reality in order to see whether the implications of the model are changed. Before this alignment is made, however, the parts of the capital market theory will be examined in a unified presentation.

24-3   THE CAPITAL ASSET PRICING MODEL (CAPM)

Thus far in this chapter, the analysis has determined that in an equilibrium situation characterized by the given assumptions, the expected return of a *portfolio* is a linear function of the portfolio's standard deviation of returns. This linear relation has been called the CML. Thus far, however, the discussion has ignored the determination of the equilibrium rate of return on *individual assets* (such as individual stocks and bonds). Reconsider the rationale lying behind the CAPM, or SML, to understand how the prices of the individual assets are determined.

**24-3.1
Covariance
with the
Market**

The variance of a two- security portfolio is given in Eq. (24-2*a*).

$$\text{var}(r_p) = x_1^2 \text{var}(r_l) + x_2^2 \text{var}(r_2) + 2x_1 x_2 \text{cov}(r_1, r_2) \qquad (24\text{-}2a)$$

For an *n*-security portfolio, the variance is given by Eq. (24-2*b*).

$$\text{var}(r_p) = \sum_{i=12}^{n} x_i^2 \text{var}(r_i) + \sum_{i=1}^{n}\sum_{j=1}^{n} x_i x_j \sigma_{ij} \quad \text{for} \neq j \qquad (24\text{-}2b)$$

Note that within the expression for the risk of a portfolio of any size are covariance terms between all possible pairs of securities in the portfolio. The essence of Markowitz diversification is to find securities with low positive covariances or negative covariances. As a result, demand will be high for individual securities or portfolios that have low positive covariance or negative covariance of returns with the market portfolio. Securities that have high covariance with the market portfolio, that is, high systematic risk, will experience low demand. As a result, the prices of securities with high systematic risk will fall, and prices of securities with low systematic risk will be bid up. Since equilibrium rates of return move inversely with the price of the security, securities having a high covariance with the market will have *relatively* low prices (that is, low relative to their income but not necessarily low in absolute dollars) and high expected returns. Conversely, securities with low or negative covariances will have relatively high prices and therefore experience low expected rates of return in equilibrium. This relationship is depicted in Fig. 24-3.

FIGURE 24-3 The CAPM in terms of the covariance.

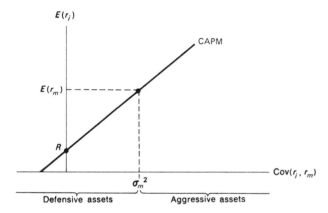

Equation (24-3a) is a mathematical statement of the CAPM, or SML, in terms of the covariance.[2]

$$E(r_i) = R + \left[\frac{E(r_m) - R}{\sigma_m^2}\right] \text{cov}(r_i, r_m) \qquad (24\text{-}3a)$$

where
$$E(r_m) - R]/\sigma_m^2 = \text{slope of CAPM} = \text{the market price of systematic risk}$$
$$R = \text{riskless rate of return}$$
$$\text{cov}(r_i, r_m) = i\text{th asset's covariance of returns with market}$$
$$E(r_i) = \text{equilibrium expected return for } i\text{th asset}$$

2 For the first rigorous mathematical derivation of the CAPM, or SML, see W.F. Sharpe, "Capital Asset Prices: A Theory of Market Equilibrium under Conditions of Risk," *Journal of Finance*, September 1964, vol. XIX, no. 3, footnote 22. For a review of several different mathematical derivations of the CAPM, or SML, as it is also called, see J.C. Francis and S.H. Archer, *Portfolio Analysis*, 2d ed. (Englewood Cliffs, N.J.: Prentice-Hall, 1979), appendix to chap. 8. Jack L. Treynor also developed the CAPM, or SML, model in an unpublished paper he prepared at about the same time that W.F. Sharpe prepared his "Capital Asset Prices . . ." paper. Treynor was working alone and mailed copies of his paper to various interested people; for example, W.F. Sharpe acknowledges Treynor's paper in the sixth footnote of "Capital Asset Prices . . ." Unfortunately, Treynor never did publish his paper. Later developments of the CAPM can be found in John Lintner, ""The Valuation of Risk Assets and the Selection of Risky Investments in Stock Portfolios and Capital Budgets," *The Review of Economics and Statistics*, February 1965, pp. 13–27. For a different formulation of the same model see Jan Mossin, "Equilibrium in a Capital Asset Market," *Econometrica*, October 1966, pp. 768–783.

The expected return $E(r_i)$ is the appropriate discount rate to use in valuing the ith security's income; it is the cost of capital for that security's amount of systematic risk.

Expressed in words, Fig. 24-3 and Eq. (24-3a) say that in equilibrium an individual security's or a portfolio's expected return is a linear function of its covariance of return with the market. That is, the expected return from any market asset is an increasing function of its systematic risk. Since systematic risk is the portion of a security's total risk that hinders rather than helps diversification, the relationship is intuitively appealing. The more risk a security has that cannot be eliminated by diversification, the more return investors will require to induce them to hold that risky security in their portfolios.

**24-3.2
Components
of Expected
Return**

The expected rate of return, which the CAPM suggests is appropriate for any asset, is made up of two separate components:

1. The CAPM's intercept R represents the *price of time*. This component of the ith asset's expected rate of return compensates the investor for delaying consumption in order to invest.
2. The CAPM's *market price of risk*. This component is measured by the slope of the CAPM, $[E(r_m) - R]/\sigma^2_{im}$.

The market price of risk is multiplied by the ith asset's systematic covariance risk, as shown in Eq. (24-3a). The product of this multiplication determines the appropriate *risk-premium* that should be added to the riskless rate to find the appropriate expected rate of return for the ith asset. This risk-premium is what induces investors to invest in risky instead of riskless assets.

The locus of equilibrium-expected returns shown in Fig. 24-3 is the CAPM, or SML; it is a separate and distinct relation from the CML shown in Fig. 24-2.

In equilibrium, an *individual* security's expected return and risk statistics will lie on the CAPM, or SML, and *off* the CML. Likewise, in equilibrium, efficient *portfolios* $[E(r), \sigma]$ pairs will lie *on* the CML, and portfolio $[E(r), \mathrm{cov}(r_i, r_m)]$ pairs will lie on the CAPM. Thus, even under idealistic assumptions and at static equilibrium, the CML will not include all points if portfolios and individual securities are plotted together on one graph. Individual securities and inefficient portfolios will not lie on the CML.

The returns of individual securities and portfolios are not determined by *total* risk. The unsystematic risk of a security is not particularly undesirable since it washes out to zero in a portfolio. Unsystematic risk is the stuff that makes simple diversification useful.

**24-3.3
Defensive
and
Aggressive
Securities**

In Fig. 24-3, the portion of the horizontal axis representing low or negative covariances is marked as including *defensive securities*. These securities are defensive in the sense that they offer the opportunity to reduce portfolio risks by including them in a portfolio that is correlated with m (as nearly all portfolios will be). Defensive assets have less than average covariance with the market. Symbolically, $\mathrm{cov}(r_i, r_m) < \mathrm{cov}(r_m, r_m) = \sigma_m^2$ for defensive assets.

The *aggressive securities* are those that offer opportunities for speculation; their dividend and price reactions to changes in market conditions are more dramatic and volatile than the reactions of defensive securities. Aggressive assets have more than average covariances with the market; that is, $\text{cov}(r_i, r_m) > \text{cov}(r_m, r_m) = \sigma_m^2$ for aggressive assets.

In the discussion of systematic risk in Chap. 10, the regression coefficient b_i from Eqs. (10-1) and (10-10) was suggested as an *index* of systematic risk. The covariance of returns with m was suggested as a *measure* of systematic risk earlier in this chapter. Two methods of defining the CAPM are possible. In Fig. 24-4a, the CAPM, or SML, is defined in terms of the beta regression coefficient b_i. In terms of b_i, defensive and aggressive securities can be delineated more simply. It is intuitively appealing to think of securities with $b_i < 1$ as being defensive and aggressive securities as having $b_i > 1$.

**24-3.4
The CAPM
Restated**

FIGURE 24-4   The CAPM restated in terms of (a) the beta coefficient, (b) the covariance.

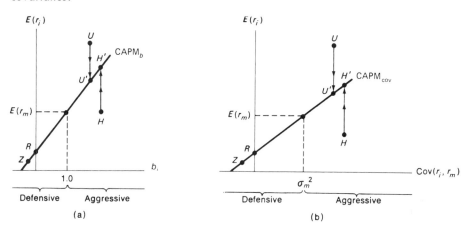

The CAPM in terms of the $\text{cov}(r_i, r_m)$ is shown in Fig. 24-4b. The two presentations of the CAPM in Fig. 24-4 are equivalent. The only difference between the two graphs of the CAPM is that the horizontal scale of the CAPM in terms of the beta coefficient is $1/\sigma_m^2$ times the length of the horizontal scale of the other graph. This is due to the definition of the slope coefficient shown in Eq. (24-4).

$$b_{(i|m)} = \frac{\text{cov}(r_i, r_m)}{\sigma_m^2}$$

$$= \text{cov}(r_i, r_m)\left(\frac{1}{\sigma_m^2}\right).$$

(24-4)

where $1/\sigma_m^2$ is constant for all assets. Equation (24-3a) may be equivalently restated in terms of the beta coefficient as shown in Eq. 24-5).

$$E(r_i) = R + \left[\frac{E(r_m) - R}{\sigma_m{}^2}\right]\text{cov}(r_i, r_m) \tag{24-3a}$$

$$= R + [E(R_m) - R]\left[\frac{cov(r_i, r_m)}{\sigma_m{}^2}\right] \tag{24-5}$$

$$= R + [E(r_m) - R]b_i$$

Equation (24-5) is the CAPM graphed as in Fig. 24-4a. But, Fig. 22-4a is equivalent to the graph in Fig. 24-4b, which represents Eq. (24-3a). Note that when $b_{(i|m)} = 1$, then cov $(r_i, r_m) = \sigma_m{}^2$. This relation reveals why the divisions between defensive and aggressive securities in the two graphs in Fig. 24-4 are comparable.

24-3.5 Overpriced and Underpriced Indications

The CAPM, or SML, has asset pricing implications for both portfolios and individual securities. Points between the CAPM, or SML, and the $E(r)$ axis like point U in Fig. 24-4 represent securities whose prices are lower than they would be in equilibrium. Since points like U represent securities with unusually high returns for the amount of systematic risk they bear, these securities enjoy strong demand that will bid their prices up until their equilibrium rate of return is driven back onto the CAPM or SML at point U'.

Likewise, assets lying between the CAPM, or SML and the systematic risk axis represent securities whose prices are too high. The asset at point H in Fig. 24-4 does not offer sufficient return to induce rational investors to accept the amount of systematic risk it bears. As a result, the asset's price will fall because of lack of demand. The prices of such assets will continue to fall until the denominator of the rate-of-return formula is low enough to allow the expected return to reach the CAPM at a point like H'.

$$E(r) = \frac{E(\text{capital gains or losses} + \text{dividends})}{\text{purchase price}} \tag{24-6a}$$

$$= \frac{[E(p_t) - p_{t-1}] + E(d_t)}{p_{t-1}} \tag{24-6b}$$

Then the capital loss will cease, and an equilibrium purchase price will emerge until a change in the firm's systematic risk, a change in R, or some other change causes another disequilibrium. These asset pricing implications of the *security market line* model are why it is often called the *capital asset pricing model*.

24-3.6 Negative Correlation with Portfolio m

Consider point Z in Fig. 24-4; it represents a defensive security with an equilibrium rate of return *below* the return on riskless asset R. Upon observing rates of return that were consistently below R, the traditional financial analyst would typically attribute the low return to a high price for the security, which was bid up in expectation of growth. But capital market theory provides a second rationalization of points like Z: Their price is maintained at high levels by the Markowitz diversification benefits they offer (an example is Homestake

Mining stock, which is listed on the NYSE). Asset Z is negatively correlated with the market portfolio.

This analysis implies that equilibrium *expected* returns are determined by *expected* risk—this is called the *ex ante theory*. Historical, or *ex post*, returns are not used by investors as a basis for their decisions about the future, although their expectations can be affected by ex post behavior. Their investment plans for the future are based on their expectations about the future. Thus it should be noted that a ''jump'' is made in going from the capital market theory, which is stated in terms of expectations, to actual historical data. If the probability distribution of historical returns has remained fairly stable over time, then historical average returns and variances can be used to estimate expected returns and expected variances. However, historical data play *no role* in the theory itself.

To test capital market theory, expectations must be observed—an impossible task if conducted on a meaningful scale. Of course, expectations may be formed from historical observations, but unless investors' past expectations were always correct, historical data will not be satisfactory to validate or deny the theory.

24-4 RELAXING THE ASSUMPTIONS

The assumptions underlying capital market theory will now be aligned more closely with conditions existing in the ''real world.'' First, assumption 2 on page 703, that one riskless interest rate exists at which everyone may borrow or lend, will be relaxed.

In a more realistic model, the borrowing rate B is higher than the lending rate L. In Fig. 24-5, this is represented by two unchanging rates (that is, $\sigma_L = \sigma_B = 0$) at points L and B. The lines emerging from points L and B represent the dominant lending and borrowing opportunities, respectively. The dashed portions of these two lines do not represent actual opportunities and are included merely to indicate the construction of the figure. Two tangency portfolios, denoted m_L and m_B, are shown for lenders and borrowers, respectively.

FIGURE 24-5 The capital market line (CML) when borrowing and lending rates differ.

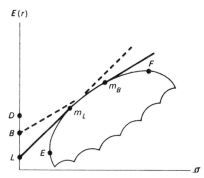

They replace the market portfolio. The kinked line formed by the solid sections of the two lines and a section of the opportunity locus is the relevant efficient frontier when the borrowing and lending rates differ. As a result, the CML has a curved section between m_L and m_B in Fig. 24-5. The curved section is part of the efficient frontier.[3]

Of course, not all investors can borrow at rate B; those with poor credit ratings must pay a higher borrowing rate than those with good credit ratings. The proverbial *deadbeat* might be able to borrow money only by paying rate D in Fig. 24-5. Obviously, the greater the difference between the lending and the various borrowing rates, the greater the curve of the CML. Furthermore, the CML will change for each individual as that person's credit rating changes, and the CML for the market in general will change with credit conditions, that is, as the borrowing and lending rates change. The reader may graph these complications as an exercise.

In Fig. 24-5 points m_L and m_B are two separate tangency portfolios for lending and borrowing, respectively, if one lending rate and one borrowing rate are recognized. The existence of two tangency portfolios creates problems. Equation (24-3) is a mathematical representation of the CAPM in terms of the covariance.

$$E(r_i) = R + \left[\frac{E(r_m) - R}{\sigma_m^2}\right]\text{cov}(r_i, r_m) \tag{24-3a}$$

where $[E(r_m) - R]/\sigma_{im}^2$ is the slope that measures the market price of risk.

If separate borrowing B and lending L rates are assumed to exist, two CAPM's emerge:

$$E(r_i) = B + \left[\frac{E(r_{mB}) - B}{\sigma_{mB}}\right]\text{cov}(r_i, r_{mB}) \quad \text{for } E(r_i) > E(r_{mB}) \tag{24-3b}$$

$$E(r_i) = L + \left[\frac{E(r_{mL}) - L}{\sigma_{mL}{}^2}\right]\text{cov}(r_i, r_{mL}) \quad \text{for } E(r_i) < E(r_{mL}) \tag{24-3c}$$

These two CAPMs will have not only different vertical axis intercepts, but also different slopes, since $[E(r_m) - R]/\sigma_m^2$ will be different. Also, since their covariances are measured with respect to two different tangency portfolios (namely, m_L and m_B), even their covariances differ. As a result, two CAPMs emerge. Figure 24-6 shows the relationship between $CAPM_L$ and $CAPM_B$. Since further relaxation of assumption 2 would clutter Figs. 24-5 and 24-6 without yielding any additional insights, this task is left to the reader.

---

3 K.L. Hastie, "The Determination of Optimal Investment Policy," *Management Service*, August 1967, pp. B757–B774. Hastie was the first analyst to study relaxing the assumptions. See also M.J. Brennan, "Capital Market Equilibrium and Divergent Borrowing and Lending Rates," *Journal of Financial and Quantitative Analysis*, December 1971, vol. 6, no. 5, pp. 1197–1206. Brennan shows that, under certain assumptions, a weighted average of the borrowing and lending rates would emerge as a single rate.

FIGURE 24-6   Two CAPM's when borrowing and lending rates differ.

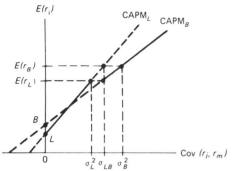

If assumption 6 (which assumes away transaction costs) is dropped, the CML and CAPM have "bands" on their sides, as shown in Figs. 24-7 and 24-8. Within these bands, it would not be profitable for investors to buy and sell securities and generate the price revisions necessary to attain equilibrium; transaction costs would consume the profit that induces such trading. As a result, the markets would never reach the theoretical equilibrium described earlier, even if the other assumptions were retained.

**24-4.2
Transaction
Costs**

FIGURE 24-7   Transaction costs obscure the capital market line (CML).

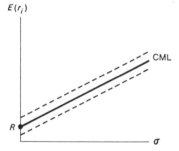

FIGURE 24- 8   Transaction costs obscure the capital asset pricing model (CAPM).

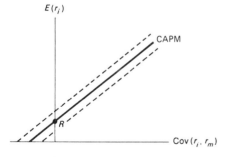

The effects of simple diversification, which were explained in Sec. 23-2, show that investors need not diversify over many securities to obtain portfolios near the CML. Instead they may buy larger quantities of fewer different market assets and thereby obtain the lower brokerage fees associated with large block transactions. Therefore, the effect of transaction costs need not be particularly detrimental to the attainment of equilibrium; that is, the "bands" around the CML and CAPM may not be wide.

24-4.3 General Uncertainty of Heterogeneous Expectations

To jettison assumptions 3 and 4 about homogeneous expectations over a common planning horizon would require drawing an efficient frontier, CML, and CAPM composed of "fuzzy" curves and lines. The more investors' expectations differed, the fuzzier and more blurred all lines and curves would become. In effect, they would become bands. As a result of general uncertainty, the analysis becomes determinate only within limits. Only major disequilibriums will be corrected. Statements cannot be made with certainty, and predictions must contain a margin for error.

24-4.4 Different Tax Brackets

Recognition of the existence of different tax rates on ordinary income and capital gains would also blur the picture. The after-tax rate of return atr_t is defined as follows:

$$atr_t = \frac{\text{capital gains} \times (1 - T_G) + \text{dividends} \times (1 - T_O)}{\text{price at beginning of holding period}} \tag{24-7}$$

where T_G is the capital gains tax rate and T_O is the tax rate applicable to ordinary income. In terms of after-tax returns, every investor would see a slightly different CML and CAPM depending on his or her particular tax situation. Thus, a static equilibrium could never emerge under existing tax laws even if all the other assumptions were rigorously maintained.

24-4.5 Indivisibilities

If all assets were not infinitely divisible, that is, if assumption 5 were discontinued, the CAPM would degenerate into a dotted line. Each dot would represent an opportunity attainable with an *integral* number of shares. Little profit is to be gained from further examination of this trivial problem.

24-4.6 Varying Rates of Inflation

The interest rates observed in reality are nominal interest rates or, equivalently, yields to maturity (ytm) on marketable bonds rather than real interest rates (rr). The market ytm of a bond is determined by several factors, as indicated below.

$$ytm_t = rr + E\left(\frac{\Delta P}{P}\right) + \theta + f(n) \tag{24-8}$$

where

ytm_t = nominal yield to maturity in period t for a bond that is published in the news media

rr = real rate of return or real rate of interest per period

$E(\Delta P/P)$ = expected percentage change in the general price level per period, that is, the expected rate of inflation or deflation

θ = risk-premium

$f(n)$ = function of the number n of years until the bond's maturity.

This discussion will omit the impact of risk-premiums, transaction costs, and the term structure of interest rates in determining the market yields to maturity, ytm_t. One of the primary factors that makes market yields to maturity and other market interest rates fluctuate is changes in the rate of inflation. The rate of inflation fluctuates with the level of investment, monetary policy, fiscal policy, and other factors. Thus, it follows that ytm_t fluctuates, too.

Relaxing assumption 7 means that even if ytm_t is the market interest rate on default-free Canadian government Treasury bills, for instance, it must nevertheless *vary* in both the money and the real sense. Thus, there is no true riskless asset, $\text{var}(R) > 0$; even default-free Canadian government securities will experience some variability of real return.[4]

Graphically, this means point R in Fig. 24-9 ceases to exist as a lending possibility and is replaced by a risky nominal interest rate at a point like Z. The efficient frontier is now the curve from S to K or from S' to K, assuming all money is borrowed at rate Z. Portfolio S or S' is the minimum-risk portfolio —it may or may not contain default-free securities, and it may not actually have zero risk, as S' does. A point like S will be the minimum-variance portfolio if returns on Z and m are uncorrelated but not perfectly negatively correlated.[5] If borrowing at rate B rather than at rate R is considered, the efficient frontier becomes SmJ or $S'mJ$, depending on whether S or S' is the minimum-variance portfolio. If it is assumed that funds may be lent (but not borrowed)

FIGURE 24-9 Lack of riskless rate obscures the capital market line (CML).

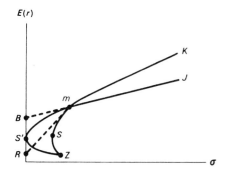

4 K.L. Hastie, op. cit., pp. B-771 and B-772. More recently, Black has extended Hastie's work by developing a portfolio, called the zero-beta portfolio (ZBP), which is free of systematic risk. Black derived the ZBP mathematically and derived some theorems about it (see Fischer Black, "Capital Market Equilibrium with Restricted Borrowing," *Journal of Business*, 1972, vol. 45, pp. 444–445). Empirical estimates of the returns on the ZBP were also prepared by F. Black, M.C. Jensen, and M. Scholes [see "The Capital Asset Pricing Model: Some Empirical Tests," in M.C. Jensen (ed.), *Studies in the Theory of Capital Markets*, (New York: Praeger, 1972)]. Essentially, the ZBP is an all-equity portfolio with positive variance but zero correlation with the market portfolio. Borrowing and lending at some riskless interest is an unneeded assumption if it is instead assumed that funds may be borrowed (for example, by short selling) and lent (that is, invested) in the ZBP.
5 See Fig. 23-4 and the accompanying discussion of how the correlation coefficient determines the degree of convexity.

at rate R, then the efficient frontier becomes the nonlinear set of opportunities through points RmK (unless point S' exists).

24-4.7 Zero-Beta Portfolio

Point Z in Fig. 24-9 will be called the *zero-beta portfolio* hereafter. Portfolio Z has a beta of zero, in spite of its positive variance, because its variability of return is all unsystematic risk that is uncorrelated with the returns from the market portfolio. The existence of portfolio Z causes the CML to bend. The CAPM is still linear when Z is employed, as shown in Fig. 24-10.

FIGURE 24-10   the CAPM shifts with portfolio Z.

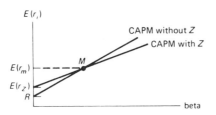

The CAPM derived with portfolio Z is a slightly different asset pricing model. The CAPM remains linear when the portfolio Z is employed (instead of the riskless rate R) because the expected return and beta risk of all portfolios are *linear* weighted averages of the expected returns and betas from assets m and Z. The portfolio expected rate of return formula is shown in Eqs. (24-9a) and (24-9b).

$$E(r_p) = x_1E(r_1) + x_2E(r_2) + \ldots + x_nE(r_n) \tag{24-9a}$$

where $\sum_{i=1}^{n} x_i = 1.0$. But for a two-asset portfolio comprised of assets Z and

m, Eq. (26-9a) can be equivalently rewritten as Eq. (24-9b).

$$E(r_p) = x_mE(r_m) + x_Zb_Z \tag{24-9b}$$

where $x_Z = (1.0 - x_m)$.

The beta of a portfolio is also a linear weighted average of the beta of the assets in the portfolio.

$$b_p = x_1b_1 + x_2b_2 + \ldots + x_nb_n \tag{24-10a}$$

where $\sum_{i=1}^{n} x_i = 1.0$. But for a two-asset portfolio made up of assets denoted

Z and m the portfolio's beta can be equivalently rewritten as Eq. (24-10b).

$$b_p = x_mb_m + x_Zb_Z \tag{24-10b}$$

where $x_Z = (1.0 - x_m)$. Thus, if it is assumed that funds may be raised by selling portfolio Z short (that is, let x_Z be negative), then the new linear CAPM with a flatter slope, illustrated in Fig. 24-10, emerges.

Thus far, all the assumptions underlying capital market theory except the first have been relaxed. Finally, let us relax this first assumption — that all investors are Markowitz diversifiers. Simply diversified investors would most likely adjust asset prices until returns were proportional to the *total* risk (as measured by the variance or standard deviation) of an asset. They will not delineate the efficient frontier and therefore will not recognize that portfolio *m* in Fig. 24-2 is the single most desirable portfolio. Only the Markowitz diversifiers will recognize that *m* is the most desirable asset; they will bid up the price of portfolio *m*. Consequently, the purchase price of an asset *m* will rise, and its expected return will be lower after these temporary capital gains cease if systematic risk is unchanged (because the expected return moves inversely to the purchase price).

$$E(r) = \frac{E(\text{capital gains} + \text{dividends})}{\text{purchase price}} \tag{24-11}$$

The prices of portfolios other than *m* (for example, *A* and *B* in Fig. 24-2) will tend to remain constant as they are held by simple diversifiers who do not realize the unique desirability of *m*. After some temporary capital gains for portfolio *m*, a new, higher equilibrium purchase price and a lower rate of return emerge. Thus, prices and expected returns are revised, asset *m* falls downward in $[\sigma, E(r)]$ space, and the CML swings downward until portfolios *A*, *m*, and *B* are all tangents to the CML.

As a result of these price revisions, which occur in a market where some investors are simple diversifiers, a condition represented by Fig. 24-11 emerges. Several portfolios lie along the CML in Fig. 24-11, all those along the line segment *AmB*. Equilibrium is attained when all assets are included in combinations lying along *AmB*, and they are included in such proportions as they are supplied to the market.

FIGURE 24-11 Market equilibrium with simple diversification.

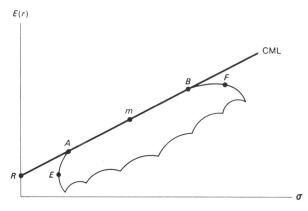

Consider the implications of the equilibrium shown in Fig. 24-11. It was shown that when two or more assets plot in a straight line in $[\sigma, E(r)]$ space, they must be perfectly positively correlated. Thus, assets like *A*, *m*, and *B*

and all other combinations of assets along *AmB* must be perfectly positively correlated. The risky combinations of assets along *AmB* vary because of some common cause, such as variation in the overall economic, psychological, and market situations. The returns on combinations *A*, *m*, and *B* will vary together *systematically*. All other variability of return (namely, unsystematic risk) resulting from causes unrelated to movements in market conditions has been reduced by diversification. Only undiversifiable risk remains in the assets on the efficient frontier.

In a capital market partially inhabited by simple diversifiers, an equilibrium such as the one shown in Fig. 24-11 is expected to emerge.[6] In this model the efficient frontier is flattened out along the CML, since simple diversifiers cannot delineate the efficient frontier. This suggests that the regression line shown in Eq. (24-12) should fit the empirical data for portfolios and yield high correlations.

$$r_i = R + c\sigma_i \text{ for } i = 1, 2, \ldots, n \text{ portfolios} \tag{24-12}$$

In Eq. (24-12), r_i and σ_i are the historical average return and risk statistics for portfolio *i*, and *c* is the regression slope coefficient, a positive constant. In fact, it was explained in Chap. 23 (see Fig. 23-7 on page 689) that such a simple linear regression, using a sample of 34 mutual funds, yielded a +.83 correlation coefficient.[7] The inclusion of individual assets in this regression would decrease the correlation because the individual assets are not efficient enough to lie on the CML.

24-4.9 Infinite Borrowing and Lending Opportunities

Suppose that assumption 2, that infinite amounts of money could either be borrowed or lent at the riskless rate of interest, were true. This outcome is unlikely because there are legal margin requirements, capital adequacy requirements for brokerage houses, short sales restrictions, and other impediments to restrict investors' ability to either borrow or lend without limit. However, if these restrictions were somehow not binding, the opportunity set in [σ, $E(r)$] space would extend infinitely far.[8] As illustrated in Fig. 24-12, even with divergent borrowing and lending rates of interest, infinite extensions of the upper and lower boundaries of the investment opportunity set are indicated by the arrowheads—an interesting but unlikely consideration.

6 If all investors were simple diversifiers who focused only on total risk, all assets (that is, both portfolios and individual assets) would lie on the CML in equilibrium. The CAPM, or SML, would cease to exist because simple diversifiers would not recognize the importance of undiversifiable systematic risk.

Empirical data supporting an equilibrium such as the one shown in Fig. 24-11 could also arise from heterogeneous expectations. That is, if each investor delineated a different efficient frontier, each would seek to attain a different market portfolio. As a result, many portfolios could lie along a ray like *AmB* in Fig. 24-11.

7 William F. Sharpe, "Risk Aversion in the Stock Market: Some Empirical Evidence," *Journal of Finance*, September 1965, pp. 416–422; W.F. Sharpe, "Mutual Fund Performance," *Journal of Business*, January 1966, pp. 123–125.

8 R.C. Merton, "An Analytic Derivation of the Efficient Portfolio Frontier," *Journal of Financial and Quantitative Analysis*, September 1972, pp. 1151–1172.

FIGURE 24-12 Unrestricted short sales and leverage leave risk and return unbounded on the right-hand side in [σ, $E(r)$] space.

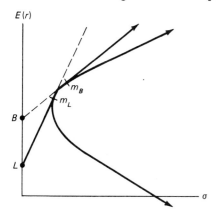

24-5 CHAPTER SUMMARY

Capital market theory is an economic equilibrium theory that explains how the market prices of stocks, bonds, mutual fund shares, and other assets are determined. Assuming that investors are risk-averse, the theory is derived from the distinction between diversifiable and undiversifiable risk. Since unsystematic risk may be easily eliminated through diversification, it has no effect on the rates of return that risk-averse investors should expect in equilibrium. The capital asset pricing model shows that expected returns are a linear function of only one kind of risk—the undiversifiable risk.

The capital market theory was derived with the aid of some simplifying assumptions. However, all the assumptions underlying the theory were relaxed one at a time. In each case the implications of the model were slightly obscured. If all were relaxed simultaneously, the result would be even less determinate. However, the fact that the analysis is not exactly determinate under realistic assumptions does not mean it has no value. The analysis still rationalizes much observed behaviour, explains such hitherto unexplained practices as diversification, and offers realistic suggestions about the directions that prices and returns should follow when they deviate significantly from equilibrium. The theory is a powerful engine for analysis.[9]

QUESTIONS

1. Compare and contrast the two terms *dominant asset* and *efficient asset*. Use graphs to show what you mean.

---

[9] Capital market theory has been extended into the international securities markets. See a book of readings edited by E.J. Elton and M.J. Gruber, *International Capital Markets* (Amsterdam: North Holland, 1975.) In particular, see Rene Stulz, "On the Effects of Barriers to International Investment," *Journal of Finance*, September 1981, no. 4, pp. 923–934; Joanne Hill and Thomas Schneeweis, "International Diversification of Equities and Fixed-Income Securities," *The Journal of Financial Research*, vol. VI, no. 4, Winter 1983, pp. 333–343.

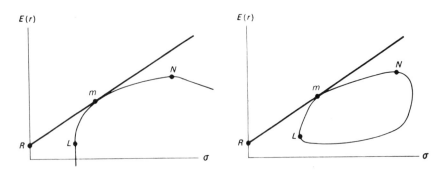

2. Which of the two graphs above is incorrect? Why?

3. Draw a graph in risk-return space showing the various parts of the total risk for one inefficient asset. Hint: See Fig. 23-6 on page 686 for a start.

4. Define the market portfolio.

5. "Since the assumptions underlying portfolio analysis are unrealistic, the theory is not a valid description of reality." True, false, or uncertain? Explain.

6. Compare and contrast your conception of the characteristic lines for a highly leveraged tool manufacturer's common stock and a cigarette manufacturer's common stock.

7. Compare and contrast the CML and the CAPM, or SML. What assets lie on both lines in equilibrium? What assets should never lie on the CML?

8. John Lintner said that the "best portfolio will never be the one in the Markowitz efficient set with the lowest attainable risk."[10] Explain Lintner's remark.

9. Compare and contrast the behaviour of aggressive securities and defensive securities in a bear market.

10. Explain how you would find the beta coefficient for some firm using historical data. What data would you need? What would you do with the data? What can you use this beta for? Graph two different models in which the beta coefficient is an important factor and explain them.

11. Given the assumptions underlying capital market theory, rationalize the following *separability theorem*: The investment decision of which asset to buy is a separate and independent decision from the financing decision of whether to borrow or lend.

12. What does it mean to assume that all investors have "homogeneous expectations" or that "idealized uncertainty" exists? Why is this assumption necessary to capital market theory?

13. Basic Scientific Research, Inc. (BSRI) is composed of a group of scientists working to develop new products that can be patented, manufactured, and sold to obtain large monopolistic profits. Investors in BSRI stock are told that the corporation has a small chance of inventing a highly lucrative product like Xerox or Polaroid. They are also told that, quite frankly, it

---

10 In "Security Prices, Risk, and Maximal Gains from Diversification," *Journal of Finance,* December 1965, p. 589.

is much more likely that BSRI will simply consume its original capital with no payoff at all. The best possible outcome is the long shot that BSRI's research will be fruitful and thus will turn their investment into a multimillion-dollar capital gain. Use risk-return analysis to evaluate this investment opportunity.

SELECTED REFERENCES

The reader who wishes to follow the original development of capital market theory is directed to the following articles, especially the second one by Sharpe. All use calculus and probability theory. This list is not exhaustive.

Gordon Alexander and J. C. Francis. *Portfolio Analysis*. 3d ed. Englewood Cliffs, N.J.: Prentice-Hall, 1986. This monograph derives the capital market theory mathematically using consistent notation.

Harry Markowitz. *Portfolio Selection*. Cowles Foundation Monograph 16. New York: Wiley, 1959. Footnote 1 on page 100 appears to be the first seed of the capital market theory.

William F. Sharpe. "Capital Asset Prices: A Theory of Market Equilibrium under Conditions of Risk." *Journal of Finance*, September 1964, pp. 425-552. Reprinted in J. C. Francis, C. F. Lee and D. Farrar. *Readings in Investments*. New York: McGraw-Hill, 1980, pp. 109-126.

————. "A Simplified Model for Portfolio Analysis." *Management Science*, January 1963, pp. 277-293. See especially part 4 on the diagonal model, later called the characteristic line.

James Tobin. "Liquidity Preference as Behavior Towards Risk." *Review of Economic Studies*, vol. 26, no. 1, February 1958, pp. 65–86. This article derived a seminal market equilibrium model from Markowitz's portfolio analysis theory. Sharpe's work is based on the Markowitz and Tobin models.

25

Different Investment Goals

This chapter deals with the economic analysis of risky decision making. The economist's concept of "utility" is used to explain why different investors select different investments in an effort to maximize their happiness. In particular, the investor's expected utility from investment returns is defined and analyzed in this chapter.[1]

Utility means about the same thing as happiness; thus, utility is a measure of psychic gain. Punishment, for example, is designed to decrease the recipient's level of utility; it yields disutility. The recipient would pay money in order to avoid the punishment. On the other hand, eating sweet fruit increases utility for most people. They would pay money for the psychic gain to be derived from eating, say, a grape. Every activity provides some level of utility. If eating an apple is more enjoyable than eating a grape and eating a grape is preferable to receiving punishment, this situation can be represented symbolically as follows;

$$U(\text{apple}) > U(\text{grape}) > U(\text{punishment})$$

where $U(\text{apple})$ denotes the utility from an apple, etc.

Investors' basic reason for investment activity is to maximize their personal happiness or utility. They hope to increase their happiness by investing so they will have more money to buy things they want. This is summarized in Eq. (25-1).

$$\max U = g(w) \tag{25-1}$$

where

U = investor's utility

w = personal wealth

g = some positive function

---

1 The utility analysis in Chap. 25 is a more well-defined and rigorous concept than the dominance concept, which was initially used in Chap. 23 to explain why some investments are more desirable than others. And for readers who wish to see a more formal statement of the utility theory, the appendix to Chap. 25 presents some basic mathematics about utility analysis of choices involving risk.

so the investor's utility rises as that wealth increases ($dU/dw = g' > 0$, mathematically speaking).[2]

Essentially, Eq. (25-1) says that an investor's happiness is a function of how much wealth the investor has. This does not mean that all wealthy people are necessarily happy. Instead, it means that persons can be happier (that is, achieve a higher level of utility) if they have more wealth with which to buy the things that bring them happiness.

25-1   MAXIMIZING UTILITY

Maximizing an investor's utility-of-wealth function, like $U(w) = g(w)$ in Eq. (25-1), is related to the investor's one-period rate of return because the rate of return measures the percentage change in wealth, $r = h(w)$, as shown explicitly in Eq. (25-2a).

Maximize: One-period rate of return from invested wealth, r:

$$\text{Maximize: } r = h(w) = \frac{w_T - w_0}{w_0} \tag{25-2a}$$

where w_O is the beginning level of wealth and w_T is the terminal wealth, or wealth at the end of period; and the symbol h denotes the one-period rate of return from wealth function of Eq. (25-2a). Equation (25-3) is the inverse function of Eq. (25-2a)—it states terminal wealth as a function, denoted $f(r)$, of the rate of return.

$$w_T = f(r) = w_0(1.0 + r) \tag{25-3}$$

In Eqs. (25-2a) and (25-3), maximizing $r = h(w)$ is equivalent to maximizing $w = f(r)$. Stated differently, if $w_T > w_O$, this implies $r > 0$, and vice versa. For example, if an investor invests \$75 of beginning wealth and one period later liquidates the investment for \$100 of terminal wealth, the rate of return from the invested wealth is 33 percent.

$$r = \frac{\$100 - \$75}{\$75} = 33\% \tag{25-2b}$$

Conversely, if $w_T < w_O$, then, $r < 0$ because the invested wealth diminishes. In summary, there is a one-to-one correspondence between the investor's terminal wealth and the investor's one-period rate of return.

It is better to discuss the rates of return from investments than it is to discuss the dollar amount of their gain or loss, because the rates of return

---

2 The functional notation may be unfamiliar. Functions f, g, and h are some unspecified functions performed on the variables in parentheses. The symbols f, g, and h represent three different functions. Three examples of the form a function in the variable w might assume are

$U = aw$ a linear function denoted $U = f(w)$
$U = a + bw^2$ a second-degree equation denoted $U = g(w)$
$U = a + b [\log (cw)]$ a logarithmic function denoted $u = h(w)$
where a, b, and c are some constants in the explicit formulas.

from different assets are in directly *comparable units*. But dollar amounts are *not comparable* between assets with different price levels. For example, consider a different investment that also has a 33.3 percent rate of return but costs twice as much to purchase as the investment of Eq. (25-2b). This higher-priced asset's rate of return is shown in Eq. (25-2c).

$$r = \frac{\$200 - \$150}{\$150} = 33\% \tag{25-2c}$$

These two different investments had vastly different dollar gains, $25 and $50, from the mathematically equivalent Eq. (25-2b) and (25-2c), respectively. But the investment of Eq. (25-2c) may simply represent twice as many shares of the same stock represented by Eq. (25- 2b). The different-sized dollar gains hinder recognition of the fact that the two similar investments have the same rate of return and are equally desirable. This example shows that it is better to discuss different assets' rates of return because they are directly comparable, whereas the dollar amounts are hard to compare.

The mathematical relationships between the investor's utility function (or happiness function), denoted U; the investor's utility (or happiness) from the terminal value of the invested wealth, denoted $U(w_T) = g(w_T)$; and the investor's terminal wealth stated as a function of the one-period rate of return, denoted $w_T = f(r)$, are all summarized in Eq. (25-4a), below.

$$\max U(w_T = g[w_T] \tag{25-1}$$
$$= g[f(r)] \tag{25-4a}$$
$$= \text{some function of rate of return, } r \tag{25-4b}$$

Equation (25-4a) follows from substituting the quantity $w_T = f(r)$ from Eq. (25-3) for w_T in Eq. (25-1). Essentially, Eq. (25-4a) shows that maximizing the investor's happiness is simply a function of the investor's rate of return.

In an uncertain world, investors cannot know in advance which investment will yield the highest return. Even if investors have a hot tip or inside information about an investment, they are still uncertain whether the tip is true or precisely how to act upon it. In an *uncertain* world, investors can maximize only their *expected* utility. Expected utility is determined by the function denoted c of expected return and risk. Symbolically, this is summarized in Eq. (25-5).

$$\max E(U) = c[E(r), \text{risk}] \tag{25-5}$$
$$= c[E(r), \sigma]$$

where

$E(U) =$ expected utility

$E(r) =$ expected return

risk $=$ defined as variability of returns and measured by the standard deviation of return (denoted σ)

$c =$ some mathematical function

An increase in expected return will increase the investor's expected utility if risk does not also increase. Mathematically speaking, this means that the following partial derivative is positive, $\delta E(U)/\delta E(r) > 0$. A decrease in risk, denoted σ, will increase expected utility if expected return does not decrease simultaneously. That is, $\delta E(U)/\delta\sigma < 0$. The two preceding statements (that are both restated as partial derivatives) together mean that the investor will prefer efficient investments over inefficient ones. Such utility-maximizing behaviour is analyzed graphically by using utility (or happiness) isoquants to measure investor utility in risk and expected return space (Fig. 25-1).

25-2   INDIVIDUAL'S INVESTMENT GOALS

Investment goals are determined in large part by the age and socio-economic status of the individual investor. For example, consider the fictitious Aunt Jane, a little, old, frail widow who is all alone in the world. Aunt Jane lives modestly on a government pension from the Canada Pension Plan, an old age security supplement, and the income from a small portfolio. She is terrified, and rightfully so, of the prospect of a decrease in the value of her portfolio. She does not know how to manage the portfolio for herself and has no idea how to gain maximum benefit from it. In order to conserve her meager wealth, she consumes only the income from her portfolio and none of the principal.

In marked contrast to Aunt Jane is Dr. Swift, an aggressive young man who can expect a successful professional career.[3] Dr. Swift's income began at a comfortable level shortly after he completed a medical degree, and it can be expected to rise in years to come if he works hard. The financial future for this person is fairly secure.

Dr. Swift has different investment objectives from those of Aunt Jane. He is willing to take risks in order to gain a larger return. If his risky investments are wiped out, his family will not suffer—he may merely have to work a few more years before retirement or do without some luxuries. However, Dr. Swift is not a reckless person. He dislikes risk and is willing to assume it only because he wants the high returns that might be attained. Thus, Aunt Jane and Dr. Swift are both risk-averters, and Aunt Jane is the more risk-averse of the two.

The investment preferences of these two hypothetical investors are represented graphically in Fig. 25-1, which shows three families of *indifference curves* representing three investors' investment preferences. Each indifference curve is an *expected utility isoquant* showing all the various combinations of risk and return that provide an equal amount of expected utility for the investor. Aunt Jane's indifference curves are steeply sloped, reflecting the fact that it would take a large increase in expected return to induce her to assume a small increase in risk. Dr. Swift's indifference curves are less steep,

25-2.1 Indifference Maps in Risk-Return Space

3 Both Aunt Jane and Dr. Swift represent stereotypes in the investment world; there are also plenty of helpless widower Uncle Stans and upwardly mobile women.

FIGURE 25-1 Different investment preferences in risk-return space.

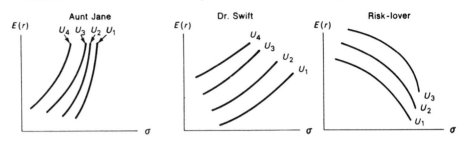

indicating that he is more willing to assume risk to attain an increase in his expected return than Aunt Jane.

The indifference map of a risk-lover is also shown in Fig. 25-1. The risk-lover's indifference curves are negatively sloped, indicating a willingness to give up expected return in order to gain risk. The authors have never actually observed this type of behaviour; it is graphed only as an intellectual exercise.

In order to see how the three investment preferences shown in Fig. 25-1 will result in different investments, they must be graphed with some investment opportunities in risk-return space. Figure 25-2 shows a hypothetical set of investment opportunities in $[\sigma, E(r)]$ space. These opportunities might represent all the stocks, bonds, real estate, and art objects in the world at a given point in time, plus the opportunity to borrow or lend at R.

Aunt Jane's utility isoquants are $AJU_4 > AJU_3 > AJU_2 > AJU_1$ and appear in the lower left portion of Fig. 25-2. Aunt Jane will maximize her expected utility by selecting the low-risk, low-return portfolio at point J on the capital market line (CML). Portfolio J is the weighted average of investments R and M.

FIGURE 25-2 Selection of an investment in $[\sigma, E(r)]$ space

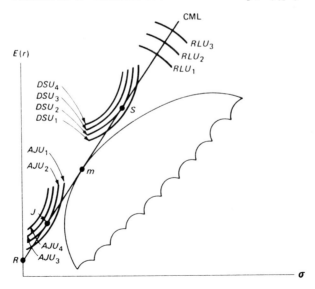

Dr. Swift maximizes his expected utility higher on the CML by purchasing portfolio S, which will provide him with the level of expected utility represented by his indifference curve DSU_2. This is the highest level of utility he can hope to achieve, given the investment opportunities shown in Fig. 25-2.

In contrast with rational investors, risk-loving investors will maximize their expected utility by borrowing all that they can to leverage themselves as high on the CML as possible.

Thus far, the discussion has focused on investors' preferences at a point in time. People's preferences change with the passage of time; so we shall see how this tendency can affect their investment decisions.

For most young couples, the first three investments are life insurance, an emergency fund, and a home—in about that order.

**25-2.2
The Typical
Family's
Changing
Investment
Preferences**

Life Insurance   Most newly married people are advised that they should make provisions to care for their spouse, any children, and any large expenses in the event that they die or are killed. This is advice that most couples follow. However, the newly married person must by wary not to buy (or be sold) more life insurance than necessary to meet family needs.

After the amount of coverage is determined, the question arises as to whether term insurance or whole-life insurance with cash values is best. After looking at the facts, many young people find that decreasing term insurance that has no cash value other than the death payment is a good buy. However, life insurance sales agents prefer to sell whole-life or endowment policies because the sales commissions are larger than for term insurance. And the whole-life insurance policies are also more profitable for the life insurance companies because the policies allow an insurance company to invest the cash values in whole-life or endowment policy until the policy is cashed in, while paying the policyholder a smaller rate of interest for the funds. Thus, most life insurance buyers are better off purchasing term insurance and investing the money they saved by not buying an equal amount of whole-life or endowment life insurance.

A *term insurance policy* is essentially a bet with the insurance company that the insured will not die — nothing more, no frills or savings plans. The insured pays the insurer a premium to issue a contract that legally binds the insurer to pay if the insured dies within some specified time period. If the insured does not die within the time span of the policy, the policyholder and the beneficiaries receive nothing from the insurer. When the term insurance policy expires, a new policy must be purchased. As the insured grows older, the probability of dying increases; therefore, the cost of a given amount of term insurance increases with the age of the insured. When the insured reaches old age, term insurance will be very expensive, and it should be discontinued. Table 25-1 shows some typical costs of term insurance at various ages. This is the type of insurance policy that is best for many people; it is the cheapest, simplest type. By purchasing term insurance instead of more expensive policies, the insured will save hundreds of dollars each year.

TABLE 25-1 COSTS PER $1,000 OF TERM LIFE INSURANCE PER YEAR AT VARIOUS AGES

AGE	ANNUAL COST PER $1,000, $*
20	3.66
25	3.71
30	3.78
35	3.89
40	4.44
45	6.04
50	9.06
55	14.41
60	21.56
65	32.06

*These figures are the averages of several rates quoted by large insurance companies.

If these savings are saved at compound interest, they will grow to thousands of dollars by the time the insured reaches old age. At that time, the insured can cancel the term insurance because the accumulated savings on insurance premiums will exceed the face value of the term life insurance policy.

If the insured does not have the self-discipline to save the difference in cost between term insurance and the whole-life or endowment policies, he or she should consider those policies that include contractual savings plans.

Whole-life and *endowment insurance policies* are a combination of decreasing term insurance and rising cash values. These policies are more expensive than term insurance. Table 25-2 shows the costs of various types of cash value life insurance purchased at different ages. The cash values associated with these policies arise because the insurance company invests the extra revenue from whole-life and endowment policies in the insured's name, and it grows at a

TABLE 25-2 ANNUAL PREMIUM COST PER $1,000 OF VARIOUS TYPES OF LIFE INSURANCE WITH CASH VALUES*

AGE	5-YEAR TERM RENEWABLE AND CONVERTIBLE, $	STRAIGHT OR ORDINARY LIFE, $	LIFE PAID UP AT 65, $	20-PAY LIFE, $	20-YEAR ENDOWMENT, $
25	4.33	12.35	13.86	21.07	41.69
30	4.41	14.65	16.83	23.73	42.01
35	5.04	17.61	20.93	26.93	42.63
40	6.61	21.55	26.68	30.80	43.76
45	9.08	26.58	35.49	35.49	45.67
50	13.40	32.81	49.66	41.19	48.65
55	21.05	40.37	78.10	48.25	53.14

*Averages of several quoted rates.

low rate of interest. Figure 25-3 graphically depicts how the $123.50 annual premium on a straight-life policy paying a $10,000 death benefit, purchased at age 25, will be divided between actual insurance costs and savings.

FIGURE 25-3 Whole- or straight-life insurance policy is a combination of term insurance and a savings plan; the figures are the average of several quoted rates.

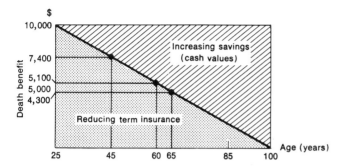

The interest paid by the insurer on the cash values is low and may not equal inflation in some years.[4] But the insured who lacks self-discipline to buy term insurance and invest the money so saved should buy the more expensive policies that have automatic savings provisions. In this manner the insured will have a paid-up insurance policy with cash values.

An Emergency Fund and a Home The new family also needs an emergency fund to cover unforeseen problems not covered by insurance. This fund should be held in a form that is liquid and available if needed. After a new family has life insurance, an emergency fund, and some furniture, it usually invests in a home. Home ownership can be a good investment. There are positive economic benefits for home owners. The home owner builds equity in the home; this equity can be recovered if the house is sold at a price advantageous to the seller. In addition, a home is an inflation hedge because the values of houses tend to rise during inflation while the real value (in terms of purchasing power) of the fixed mortgage debt decreases. Furthermore, the capital gains earned by home owners on their principal residence are specifically exempt from income tax [Income Tax Act S.40(2)(b)].

Most of the disadvantages of home ownership are difficult to assess in money terms. Home ownership decreases many people's willingness to move to a new job even if it offers better pay and opportunities. Home and yard care often consumes time that could be used more productively elsewhere — such as taking a self-improvement course in night school, for instance. Home owners make "home-improvements" that are sometimes poor investments when viewed from a purely financial point of view. Home ownership involves the risk that the neighbourhood may depreciate in value. All in all, it is difficult to base home-ownership decisions purely on investment criteria unless the house is to be used solely as a rental property. Home

---

4 For example, during several recent time periods the rate of inflation has been over 10 percent. During some of these same time periods the interest that some older life insurance policies were paying on cash values was about 3 or 4 percent. Savings accounts at some banks and savings and loan associations were paying about 6 percent. Thus, these types of savings lose purchasing power. Furthermore, if the policyholder has any investment skills, higher rates of return are available.

owners who live in their homes obtain "psychic income" that can obscure the dollar economics of the home purchase.

One of the purposes of the low-risk, low-return investments of life insurance, an emergency fund, and a home is to assure the young family of some fixed minimum-level financial support and security. After these basic investments are made, and if no health or education expenses are straining the family budget, the family's willingness and ability to undertake risky investments increase. Figure 25-4 shows the risk and return preferences for a hypothetical family as it matures.

FIGURE 25-4 Investment preferences: (a) a young family; (b) a mature family.

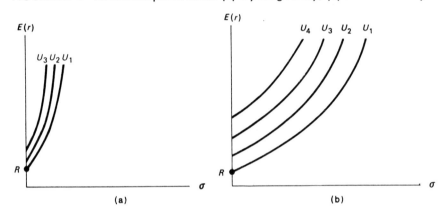

The investment in life insurance and an emergency fund are represented by point R. After the young family has accumulated sufficient wealth, typically it purchases a home. In the next few years, families mature and their preferences for risk and return shift. The indifference map in Fig. 25-4b represents the typical risk-averse, wealth-maximizing behaviour of most mature families whose homes are paid for and whose children are educated. At retirement, the families' risk-return preferences will shift again. Most families in retirement will have investment preferences similar to those of Aunt Jane; they become very risk-averse after their income ceases. They move back to an attitude like the one shown in Fig. 25-4a.[5]

25-3 INSTITUTIONAL INVESTORS

Many of the marketable securities in Canada are managed by institutional investors, such as insurance companies, pension funds, and trusts, although they are owned by individuals. Furthermore, the trend toward institutional participation has been increasing in recent years in Canada. From 1979 to 1986, for example, the institutional percentage of equity trading on the Toronto Stock Exchange increased from 43.8 percent to 54.2 percent.[6] As of

---

5 Franco Modigliani, "Life Cycle, Individual Thrift, and the Wealth of Nations," *American Economic Review*, June 1986.
6 The Toronto Stock Exchange, *Fact Book*, 1983, 1985, p.17; 1986, p. 32.

1983, approximately 11.3 percent of Canadians owned shares, a surprisingly low number when compared to the 22.0 percent of U.S. citizens that are equity holders. By 1986, approximately 18 percent of the Canadian adult population were shareholders. Table 25-3 shows the characteristics of the individuals who are Canadian shareholders.

TABLE 25-3   SELECTED CHARACTERISTICS OF INDIVIDUAL CANADIAN SHAREOWNERS, 1983

AGE	PERCENTAGE OF ALL SHAREHOLDERS	PERCENTAGE OF POPULATION
18–24	10.7	5.4
25–34	24.5	9.7
35–44	22.5	12.4
45–54	17.6	11.4
55 and over	24.7	9.1
Total	100.0	

EDUCATION		
Elementary/public school	1.0	0.7
Partial high school	13.3	5.5
High school graduate	23.5	8.0
Partial community college CEGEP, or technical school	7.1	10.6
Community college, CEGEP or technical school graduate	11.2	12.2
Partial university	12.2	15.0
University graduate	31.7	23.8
Total	100.0	

OCCUPATION		
Professional & executives	37.4	17.9
Other white collar	18.2	12.7
Skilled blue collar	10.1	7.2
Unskilled blue collar	5.1	6.9
Homemaker	12.1	5.4
Student	2.0	3.7
Retired	12.1	8.0
Unemployed	2.0	2.7
Other	1.0	12.5
Total	100.0	

HOUSEHOLD INCOME		
Under $15,000	5.4	2.9
$15,000–24,999	8.2	4.1
25,000–34,999	16.2	9.3
35,000–49,999	21.8	13.2
50,000 and over	28.4	20.4
Not stated	20.0	10.0
Total	100.0	

Source: The Toronto Stock Exchange, *Canadian Shareowners: Their Profile and Attitudes*, April, 1984, pp. 11–14.

Because institutional investors manage such a large quantity of financial assets, many portfolio management job opportunities exist within these institutions. Consider the type of investments that some institutional investors select and the reasons.

**25-3.1
Mutual
Funds**

The provincial securities commissions require that all mutual funds (that is, open-ended investment companies) state their investment policies and objectives as explicitly as possible in their prospectus or selling document. (For example, in Ontario, by form 15 S.50-569, item 7 of the Ontario Securities Act, mutual funds are instructed to describe "Aims such as long-term capital appreciation or current income and the types of the securities in which the issuer will invest.")

The funds are expected to follow these stated objectives so investors will know what kind of investment management services they are buying. The main categories of mutual funds can be delineated by these statements of objectives:

1. Common stock funds:
   (a) *Income and growth funds*. The income and growth funds take a middle-of-the-road approach in selecting between high returns and low risk. They keep the vast majority of their invested capital in blue-chip common stocks. Capital gains and dividend income are sought, but these funds do not invest in high-risk situations in an effort to maximize their rates of return.
   (b) *Growth funds*. Growth funds, which are also called "go-go" speculative or performance funds, seek to maximize their returns. The prospectuses of these funds usually refer to the fact that risks will be assumed in pursuit of high capital gains. Dividend income is desired by the performance funds, but it is second to price appreciation.
   (c) *Index funds*. Index funds have appeared in recent years as the mutual fund industry began to admit publicly that it was unable to achieve rates of return that were as good as most stock market indexes could report. Although index funds do not have to limit their investments to common stocks, they have tended to do so as they typically sought to emulate a market index such as the TSE 300 Composite Index. All the other types of mutual funds utilize an *active management*, which works to find the best investments available in the market. In contrast, index funds have a *passive management*, which does little more than try to keep the fund's investments aligned with the securities that make up the market index the fund is seeking to emulate.[7]
   (d) *Specialized common stock funds*. These funds specialize in certain types of common stocks. For example, such a fund might specialize in stock in gold companies (for those who think that a gold investment has special advantages), real estate, energy, shares in "sinless product" manufacturers (for religious investors who do not want their money invested in cigarette or liquor stocks, for example), shares in "ethical" companies that are not involved in the armaments industry, or pollution-control companies' stock (for the ecology-oriented investor).

---

7 For an analysis of passive portfolio analysis rendered scientifically, see Andrew Rudd, "Optimal Selection of Passive Portfolios," *Financial Management*, Spring 1980, vol. 9, no. 1, pp. 57-66. For a discussion of active versus passive portfolio management see the following: Keith P. Ambachtsheer and James L. Farrell, "Can Active Management Add Value?" *Financial Analysts Journal*, November-December 1979. Walter Good, R. Ferguson, and Jack Treynor, "An Investor's Guide to the Index Controversy," *Financial Analysts Journal*, November-December 1976.

2. Special-purpose funds:
  (a) *Balanced funds*. A balanced fund typically holds invested assets in bonds preferred and common stocks. The other part of the fund's investment is usually
  diversified over many different common stocks. Balanced funds stress risk
  minimization and conservation of principal. These funds are conservatively
  managed and do not seek high-return investments that are risky. The fund
  manager changes the mix of debt/equity instruments with changing times
  (b) *Money market funds*. These mutual funds began as a result of double-digit inflation and the related double-digit interest rates that started late in the 1960s.
  Money market funds typically invest entirely in money market assets (that is,
  loans with less than one year to maturity). Thus, they own large-denomination
  certificates of deposit issued by large commercial banks, Treasury bills, and
  commercial paper, which all pay rates of interest in excess of the current inflation rate.
  (c) *Area mutual funds*. The objective of these is to invest only in specifically stated
  geographic areas of the world (such as Japan or the Pacific Rim). They have
  recently become popular with some investors.
  (d) *Fixed income funds*. These invest their portfolio assets in bonds, mortgages,
  preferred shares, and other fixed income securities. The fixed income funds
  stress high yields and safety of principal, although they can become relatively
  volatile in a period of fluctuating interest rates.

Figure 25-5 shows indifference maps characterizing the risk-return preferences of the three main types of mutual funds. The actual operating performances of mutual funds are analyzed in Chap. 26.

FIGURE 25-5 Different mutual fund objectives represented in $[\sigma, E(r)]$ space.

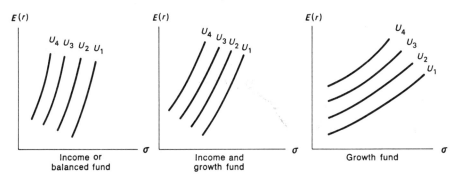

The banks' activities are highly regulated because the federal government
allows them to create money by making loans against fractional deposits. If
banking activities are not stable, the nation's money supply and the national
economy cannot be stable either.

25-3.2 Charter Banks

Constraints on Bank Managers Banks must remain liquid and continuously able to instantly repay any funds that demand depositors (that is,
checking-account depositors) wish to withdraw from their accounts. Bank
examiners regularly inspect banks to ensure that they are holding the legally
required reserves in vault cash and non-interest-earning deposits at other
banks (primarily the Bank of Canada). The government regulates bank liquidity in this fashion to prevent another money panic and run on the banks

like the catastrophic event that occurred in the early 1930s during the Great Depression. As a result of this legal liquidity requirement, banks must hold more of their assets in noninterest-earning required reserves than they wish. Of course, this hurts the banks' profitability: this is an important fact. In addition to required reserves, there are other assets that are not totally within the control of a bank's management.

Some of the substantial asset items are commercial and personal loans, mortgages, and leasing receivables. These are only partially controlled by the bank. For example, the quantity of commercial loans demanded by businesses depends on the rate of business expansion and market interest rates. The interest rates on commercial loans are largely determined by economic conditions. Mortgage loans are long-term loans, the demand for which varies with credit conditions and home-building activity. Management of those portions of a bank's investments represented by commercial loans and mortgages largely involves evaluating customers' credit-worthiness and collateral at the time the loans are made. Risk can be assessed only subjectively for most of a bank's assets that are direct loans. Furthermore, some mortgages are insured with the Canada Mortgage and Housing Corporation or National Housing Administration. This all makes risk-return analysis difficult. Asset and liability management within a bank are further complicated by credit conditions, which vary over the business cycle.

It is common for banks' liquidity to alternate with economic conditions. During an economically slow period, banks may be saturated with liquidity for which they cannot find borrowers. During an economic boom, banks may be rationing loans, raising loan rates, and liquidating reserves to meet loan demand. In effect, the opportunities open for adept investment management are limited mainly to anticipating shifts in interest rates in the bond markets and so operating as to minimize income taxes. Banks are so highly *constrained by regulations* that only their investment departments need be concerned with seeking an efficient frontier that is not highly constrained.

Portfolio Analysis of Bank Balance Sheets   In spite of the legal constraints and other external forces touched upon above, it is still possible to delineate an efficient banking frontier and select an efficient portfolio of bank assets and liabilities. This efficient banking frontier will be dominated by other efficient frontiers, selected from more assets and not constrained by banking regulations. But the constrained risk-return analysis is still a worthwhile bank management exercise. A U.S. study can be used for illustration.

Figure 25-6 shows the risk and return statistics for the average large U.S. bank's major asset categories, major liability categories, and its owner's equity. The dotted curve marked *UU* in the figure represents the unconstrained efficient banking frontier that Markowitz portfolio analysis can delineate from the assets and the liabilities. These efficient bank balance sheets contain no required reserves, for example, and are thus not realistically feasible. The curve *CC* illustrates the more realistic constrained efficient banking frontier. The bank balance sheets along the *CC* efficient frontier offer the minimum risk at each level of return on equity that can be attained while

FIGURE 25-6   Unconstrained and constrained efficient banking frontiers for average large bank.

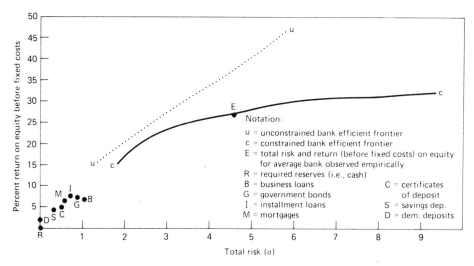

Source: J. C. Francis, "Portfolio Analysis of Asset and Liability Management in Small- Medium-, and Large-Sized Banks," *Journal of Monetary Economics*, August 1978, vol. 4, no. 3, figs. 1 and 2.

holding the required legal reserves, and also while relying on only a realistic amount of demand deposits as a source of funds (that is, the bank is constrained not to do all its borrowing through interest-free checking deposits). The average large bank's actual balance sheet is at point *E* in risk-return space, just below the *CC* efficient frontier in Fig. 25-6.

It is impossible to construct an indifference map in risk-return space that represents the investment preferences of a group of people. And in this case in particular, it is thus not possible to rationalize the preferences of bank owners in this fashion. Therefore, Fig. 25-6 contains no utility isoquants. Point *E*, however, does represent the bank shareholders' revealed preference within the various legal and competitive constraints which impinge upon banks. This is a portfolio worthy of further examination.

The average large bank's portfolio of assets and liabilities (that is, point *E*) lies far above the eight dots that lie in the lower left corner of Fig. 25-6. These eight dots represent the characteristics of the five assets and the three liabilities that make up bank balance sheets. At first it may seem strange that point *E* lies so far above the risk and return statistics of the component assets and liabilities that make up the balance sheet. This difference between risk and return is easily explained in terms of *financial leverage*. The average large bank's debt-to-equity ratio is 9.5 to 1.0, whereas most Canadian nonfinancial corporations have debt-to-equity ratios of less than unity. It appears that most bank investors are willing for their banks to undertake considerable financial leverage to generate rates of return on equity sufficient to reward them for investing in the banks' equity shares.

The investment activities that financial institution trust departments undertake in managing other people's investment funds are less constrained and therefore easier to analyze than the banks' investments of their own funds.

25-3.3 Trusts A *trust* is a fiduciary agreement in which a trustee or trustees administer assets placed in trust by a creator (donor, or grantor). In general, trusts are established to place responsibility for the administration of a person's estate or assets into the hands of someone other than the creator or the beneficiary of the trust. They are managed by trust companies, the trust departments of chartered banks, or insurance companies. Trust contracts are called *fiduciary agreements*.

Personal trusts may be set up by a deceased person's will (a testamentary trust), or a living person may put assets in trust (a living trust) for some designated beneficiary. *Living trusts* may be classed as either revocable or irrevocable. Irrevocable trusts have tax advantages not available through revocable trusts.

About one-third of all employee pension funds are set up as common trusts in which the retired employees are the beneficiaries. Some banks' trust departments also have *common trusts* in which many small accounts are commingled and managed as one. *Endowment trusts* are also set up; these trusts may designate schools, research facilities, libraries, art groups, and others as beneficiaries. Under most of these arrangements, the trustee has the power of attorney to buy and sell the assets of the trust in any manner he or she chooses as long as (1) the transactions are conducted in accordance with any provisions stated in the trust agreement and (2) the trustee (man or woman) acts as what the courts interpret to mean a "prudent man."[8]

Under some personal trusts the trustee acts only as an adviser and caretaker of the trust; in these situations some other person, usually the beneficiary, holds the ultimate decision power over the way the trust is managed. The trustee receives a fee for his or her services that ranges from ¼ of 1 percent to 2 percent per year on the value of the assets in trust, depending mainly upon the size of the trust.

In some cases, an entire business or other asset will be turned over to a trustee to administer. However, most assets held in trusts are marketable securities. Trust funds are managed in accordance with the provisions set out in the trust agreement. Most trusts specify maintenance of principal as the main objective. The trustee can violate the trust agreement only under penalty of law; that is, the trustee's own personal risk-return preferences should not affect the manner in which the trust is managed. The risk-return preferences used in trust management are specified by the creator of each trust

---

8 The "prudent man" legal guidelines that govern trust portfolio managers are discussed in C. W. Buck, "Managing Our Trusts as Prudent Men Would Do," *Commercial and Financial Chronicle*, Mar. 3, 1960. Reprinted in H. Wu and A. Zakon (eds.), *Elements of Investments* (New York: Holt, 1965), reading 4.3. See also Peter Westaway, "Prudence and the Trust Industry," Financial Research Foundation of Canada, *Proceedings of the Spring Conference*, May 1986, pp. 11-14.

and usually reflect that creator's risk-return preferences and the purpose for which that trust was created. Thus, no single preference map in risk-return space is suitable for all the trust portfolios at one bank.

In addition to the individual trust accounts for substantial individuals, financial institution trust departments may operate a commingled or *common trust fund*. A common trust fund operates in a manner similar to that of a mutual fund. Numerous investors place their funds in a commingled port-folio that the bank's trust department manages for a fee. Every investor in a common trust fund is treated the same and earns the same rate of return. Large bank and trust company trust departments operate these commingled accounts for small investors who do not have enough funds to start private trust accounts of their own but still need investment management services. Most bank trust departments require a minimum of $100,000 to open a private trust account. The common trusts are also used by some corporations that want professional money management for their pension funds. Some bank trust departments even have several different common trust funds. One might be managed as a growth portfolio, one might be managed as a bond portfolio, and one might be managed as a real estate portfolio. The individual investors in a common trust have no voice in the management of their port-folio — they are typically told in advance of investing what investment goal is used to govern the portfolio. Thus, selecting a common trust fund is like selecting a mutual fund to manage your money.

25-3.4 Life Insurance Companies

Most life insurance policies are more than mere insurance policies—they are combinations of insurance and savings plans. As the insured grow older, their risk of death mounts and their insurance rates rise. But by this time the savings portions of most life insurance policies (other than term insurance) have attained cash values that can offset the purchase of increasingly expen-sive insurance. The investment activities performed by life insurance com-panies arise from a need to invest the savings portion of the whole-life or endowment life insurance policies that represent cash values to the insured.

Life insurance companies pay a small fixed rate of dividends or interest on the cash value of the savings. Then they invest these funds at a higher rate of return. Table 25-4 shows the balance sheet of a typical life insurance company.

The balance sheet in common-sized percentages in Table 25-4 shows that life insurance companies invest heavily in interest-income-bearing assets, that is, bonds and mortgages. The companies enjoy a very favourable treatment under the income tax laws; among other things, these laws make life insur-ance companies indifferent between interest and capital gains income. Thus, these companies can earn satisfactory after-tax returns on their investments by specializing in corporate bonds and mortgages rather than by seeking the more risky capital gains.

Life insurance companies are the largest institutional holders of govern-ment bonds with the exception of the chartered banks. They are such large purchasers of corporate bonds that they sometimes capture part of the bro-ker's commissions from the bond market by buying *entire* bond issues directly from the issuer. *Direct placements*, as these purchases of an entire bond issue are called, allow the issuer to avoid the delays, uncertainties, red tape, and underwriting costs of a public bond issue. Instead, the issuer sells the entire issue directly to a life insurance company at an interest rate slightly above the appropriate market rate. Thus, the issuer of the bonds passes along some of the savings of the direct placement to the purchasing life insurance company by paying the slightly higher interest rate.

TABLE 25-4   TYPICAL BALANCE SHEET FOR A LIFE INSURANCE COMPANY

ASSETS	PERCENTAGE	LIABILITIES	PERCENTAGE
Cash and demand deposits	0.7	Actuarial reserves	52.9
Term deposits and short-		Liabilities held for business	
term paper	3.0	outside Canada	24.9
Mortgages	22.8	Amounts left on deposit	3.2
Government bonds	15.0	Other liabilities	5.9
Other bonds	12.5		
Preferred shares	1.0	Net Worth	
Common shares	3.0	Share capital, contributed	
Investments outside Canada	0.3	surplus, and reserves	5.2
Assets held for business		Retained earnings	5.5
outside Canada	29.1	Head office accounts	2.4
Other assets	12.6		
		Total liabilities	
Total assets	100.0	and Net Worth	100.0

Source: Adopted from Statistics Canada, *Financial Institutions*, Catalogue 61-006, vol. 23, no. 4 Fourth Quarter, 1985.

Some large life insurance companies have also developed very efficient mortgage investment operations. These companies employ full-time forces of agents who go into the field and originate mortgages, with the life insurance company lending home buyers the money they need. Small- and medium-sized life insurance companies whose volume of mortgage credit in any given area is not large enough to justify the expense of originating their own mortgages simply buy them from *mortgage bankers* who originate the mortgages and then resell them to life insurance companies and other mortgage investors.

It is interesting to note insurance companies' lack of interest in common stocks. Even though the Canadian Federal Insurance Act allows life insurance companies to hold up to 25 percent of their total assets in common stocks,[9] a few companies do not even own any common stock. Their reluctance to hold common stocks is particularly unusual in view of their lack of need for liquidity. They usually have premium inflows that exceed their outflow for loans, death payments, and operating expenses and thus are in the enviable position of being able to wait for favourable market conditions to buy and

9 The "basket clause" under the federal Insurance Act allows insurance companies to invest up to 7 percent of their total assets in other investments that do not fall within the authorized investment classes.

sell common stocks. In fact, there is a controversy in the life insurance industry as to whether more or less common stock should be purchased. This discussion revolves around technicalities involving legal reserves and the treatment of capital gains.

Another reason life insurance companies do not invest more aggressively in common stock is the ''authorized list'' restrictions imposed on them. According to the Federal Insurance Act, the company can buy only common stocks which (1) have paid dividends continuously for over five years and (2) have paid dividends from current earnings rather than borrowed funds. Furthermore, a company cannot purchase more than 30 percent of the common shares of any corporation, invest more than 25 percent of its total (book) assets in common shares, or purchase shares of other Canadian insurance companies. Common stocks that meet these and other restrictions are included on the *authorized list* of stocks in which life insurance companies are permitted to invest. Such arbitrary restrictions have caused life insurance companies to invest their funds in other sources. Some have been putting funds into sale-and-lease-back arrangements that involve some risk and a higher return. In any event, the rigid investment restrictions imposed on life insurance companies make it impossible to accurately represent their investment preferences in terms of risk and return statistics.

Life insurance companies also administer about one-third of all pension fund assets. Most of these portfolios are heavily invested in common stock, but these assets are separate from the assets that provide backing for life insurance policies' cash values. These pension fund portfolios can be viewed as being a separate group of assets aside from the insurance companies' own assets, which are invested in different ways. The life insurance companies manage these pension funds for a fee somewhat in the way a mutual fund is managed. A company may operate one or more commingled funds, each of which contains funds from several different clients' pension funds. Or it may manage a separate and independent portfolio for each of its large clients; in that case each client can dictate the investment goal to the insurance company's investment managers.

25-4 CONCLUSIONS ABOUT INVESTMENT PREFERENCES

Institutional investors' investment choices are often severely constrained by federal and provincial law. Thus, it is often impossible to represent the investment objectives of these institutions by preference maps in risk-return space. Mutual funds, whose investment practices are only moderately constrained, are one of the few institutional investors whose investment objectives may be represented by an indifference map.[10]

---

10 Unfortunately, mutual funds' published statements of investment objectives do not always align with the investment preferences implied by their actual investments. This latter problem is one of the points taken up in Chap. 26 where the ability of mutual funds to maximize their shareholders' expected utility is evaluated.

An individual investor's preferences can be represented with an indifference map in risk-return space. The point at which an investor's highest indifference curve is just tangent to the efficient frontier is the portfolio that will maximize the investor's expected utility. When investment preferences change, this may be represented by drawing a new set of indifference curves in risk-return space.

QUESTIONS

1. Draw an indifference map in risk-return space for an investor who is absolutely fearless but loves high returns. Have you ever known anyone who actually had such investment preferences? Explain.
2. "Term insurance is the best buy for the person who has the self-discipline for regular savings." Is this statement true, false, or uncertain? Explain.
3. "Life insurance companies' holdings of common stocks are predominantly in low-risk stocks." Is this statement true, false, or uncertain? Is the investment area, as implied by your answer, the desirable one? Explain.
4. Define a trust and explain the roles of the parties to a trust. Do trusts tend to be managed conservatively, or do they tend to seek high risks and high returns?
5. Explain what difficulties you would have in constructing the indifference map for an institutional investor like a bank or life insurance company.
6. Do you think that the legislators and government policymakers who developed the investment regulations for publicly owned institutional investors understood Markowitz diversification? Explain your view.

SELECTED REFERENCES

Marshall E. Blume and Jack P. Friedman (eds.) *Encyclopedia of Investments*. Boston: Warren, Gorham and Lamont, 1982. This nonmathematical volume explains numerous financial securities, real assets, and other investment vehicles appropriate for various investors.

David E. Bond, Ronald A. Shearer, and Donald Chant. *The Economics of the Canadian Financial System: Theory, Policy and Institutions*. Scarborough Ontario: Prentice-Hall, 1985. A well-written text on the Canadian financial system with considerable detail and background on financial institutions. Unlike many of the money, banking, and financial institution texts, this is more than merely descriptive. The authors, for example, pay careful attention to portfolio theory and its implications for portfolio management and investment decisions.

Lawrence J. Gitman and Michael D. Joehnk. *Fundamentals of Investing*. New York: Harper & Row, 1981. Chapters 14 through 18 of this elementary investments textbook discuss different investment programs that are suitable to achieve different investment objectives.

Lawrence Kryzanowski and Minh Chau To. "Revealed Preferences for Risky Assets in Imperfect Markets." *Canadian Journal of Administrative Sciences*, vol. 3, no. 2, December 1986, pp 329-47. This paper sets out the findings of an extensive study of over 12,000 Canadian households with respect to their utility functions.

John L. Maginn and Donald L. Tuttle (eds.) *Managing Investment Portfolios*. Boston: Warren, Gorham and Lamont, 1983. This easy-to-read volume explains how to set an investment goal, what assets are appropriate for different investment objectives, and how to monitor an investment to see that it progresses according to plan.

Arthur Pedoe and Colin E. Jack. *Life Insurance, Annuities and Pensions, A Canadian Text*. Toronto: University of Toronto Press, 1978. (This book is used as the text for the courses of the Life Underwriters Association of Canada and is a comprehensive examination of life insurance principles and practices in Canada.)

Herbert Phillips and John C. Ritchie. *Investment Analysis and Portfolio Selection*, 2d ed. Cincinnati: South-Western Publishing Company, 1983. Chapters 25 through 29 of this investments textbook discuss the merits of different types of investments in light of differing investor goals.

Appendix 25A

Utility Analysis

Utility analysis and decision making in uncertainty are complex. To discuss all the important issues in the field would take several volumes.[11] Therefore, Chap. 25 has merely touched on the main points necessary to understand (1) what utility is; (2) how utility is related to consumption, wealth, and the rate of return; and (3) how a utility map in risk-return space may be used to maximize investor utility. This appendix extends that analysis and shows proof of several of the important assertions made in the chapter about single-period utility maximization. Multiperiod utility analysis is discussed in Chap. 27.

APP. 25A-1 GRAPHICAL UTILITY ANALYSIS

The principal elements of utility analysis underlying investments management are explained graphically in the following few pages. To begin with, a utility-of-wealth function is a formula or a graph of a formula that shows how much utility (how many utils, or how much happiness) a person derives from different levels of wealth. A utility-of-wealth function might be mathematically written as $U = g(w)$, or simply $U(w)$, for example. Figure App. 25A-1 shows a graph of a utility-of-wealth function. The notion of marginal

FIGURE APP. 25A-1   Diminishing marginal utility of wealth.

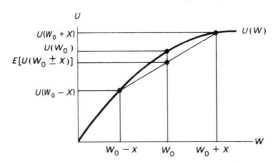

11 Here is some of the important literature: S. Archer and C. D'Ambrosio, *The Theory of Business Finance: A Book of Readings* (New York: Macmillan, 1967), readings 2-4, 39, and 40; Harry Markowitz, *Portfolio Selection*, Cowles Foundation Monograph 16 (New York: Wiley, 1959), chaps. 10-13; and J. L. Bicksler and P. A. Samuelson, *Investment Portfolio Decision-Making* (Lexington, Mass: Lexington Books, 1974), readings 1-8 and 14-18. See also, Tracy LeMay, "The Challenge of the Timid Investor," *The Financial Post*, September 21, 1985, p. 19, for a survey of the priorities influencing Canadian investors.

utility is a little more complex; it involves segments of the utility-of-wealth function. In words, *marginal utility* of wealth may be defined as the additional utility a person enjoys from a change in his or her wealth. Mathematically, marginal utility is the first derivative of the utility function—that is, $dU/dw = U'(w)$. To determine whether marginal utility is rising or falling, the slope of the utility function or the sign of the second derivative of the utility function must be observed. Decreasing marginal utility is present when the utility function rises at a less steep rate or when the second derivative of the utility function is negative, $d^2U/dw^2 < 0$, or equivalently $U''(w) < 0$.

Utility analysis is useful for analyzing the logic, or lack of it, in decisions involving risk. The analysis of such decisions is based on the expected-utility principle (see Box App. 25A-1).

Decision makers make decisions that maximize their *expected* utility.

BOX APP. 25A-1 Expected- Utility Principle

Maximizing *expected* utility is different from simply maximizing utility if the possible outcomes are risky. To understand the difference, consider the definition of expected utility. (Mathematical App. B explains the mathematical expectation.) The expected utility from a decision to undertake some risky course of action is the weighted average of the utils from the possible outcomes calculated, using the probability of each outcome as the weights. For example, if you decide to enter into a coin-tossing gamble, you have made a decision to undertake a risky course of action. There are two possible outcomes—heads or tails. The probability of heads is denoted $P(\text{heads})$ and the probability of tails is written as $P(\text{tails})$. The utility from the gamble that results if heads turns up is represented by $U(\text{heads})$ and the utility of getting tails is $U(\text{tails})$. Thus, the expected utility of the gamble is written symbolically as

$$E[U(\text{coin toss})] = P(\text{head}) \times U(\text{head}) + P(\text{tail}) \times U(\text{tail})$$

To understand this more clearly, consider some more specific examples.

Risk-averse behaviour will result if the investor has diminishing marginal utility of wealth of returns. Diminishing marginal utility- of-wealth and utility-of-returns functions are graphed in Figs. App. 25A-1 and App. 25A-2, respectively. They are both concave to the horizontal axis.[12]

App. 25A-1.1 Diminishing Marginal Utility and Risk- Aversion

12 By definition, a function U is concave if and only if $U(x) \geq \alpha U(x - y) + (1 - \alpha) U(x + y)$ for $1 \leq \alpha \leq 0$. A concave (to the horizontal axis) utility function results in risk-aversion.

FIGURE APP. 25A-2 Diminishing marginal utility of returns.

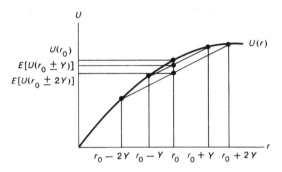

Diminishing marginal utility of wealth or of returns leads to risk-avoiding behaviour since, from any point on the utility-of-wealth or utility-of-returns curve, a risky investment has a lower expected utility than a safe investment with the same expected outcome. That is, if an investment offers a 50-50 chance of increasing or decreasing a given level of starting wealth by X dollars, the loss of utility from the bad outcome is larger than the gain in utility from the favourable outcome. Symbolically, $.5U(W_0 - X_u + .5U(W_0 + X) \leq U(W_0)$. Thus, the person with diminishing utility of wealth would prefer to keep W_0 rather than make a risky investment or bet to attain $W_0 + X$ or $W_0 - X$ with equal probability. Figure App. 25A-1 represents this situation graphically. Since the utility of the certain starting wealth $U(W_0)$ is larger than the expected utility of an equal amount of uncertain wealth $E[U(W_0)]$, the risk-averter prefers not to assume the risk, $U(W_0) > E[U(W_0)]$. The risk-averter prefers simply to hold W_0 cash rather than assume risks in an effort to increase this wealth. If the chance for gains from the risky investment were large enough, however, the risk-averse investor would find it sufficient compensation to assume the risk. Thus, risk-averters may gladly accept risky investments if they feel the odds are in their favour. People everywhere commonly exhibit diminishing marginal utility of wealth (for example, people require higher wages per hour to work overtime).

App. 25A-1.2 Equality of Wealth and Return Utility Functions

Utility preference orderings are *invariant* under a positive linear transformation of the utility function. Graphically speaking, this means that any utility curve (such as the ones in Fig. App. 25A-1 and App. 25A-2) can be raised or lowered (that is, can have a constant added or subtracted), can be scaled down without having its shape changed (that is, can be divided by a positive constant), or can be expanded without changing its curvature (that is, can be multiplied by a positive constant) without changing the way the utility curve would rank the desirability of a set of investment opportunities. These transformations would change the number of utils assigned to any given outcome, but the preference rankings would be invariant under a positive linear transformation. Since the one-period rate of return is just a positive linear transformation of the investor's wealth, this implies that a given investor's utility-of-returns function is simply a linear transformation of his or her utility-of-wealth function, and the two will yield the same preference orderings for any given group of investment opportunities. Thus, the investor's utility curves shown in Figs. App. 25A-1 and App. 25A-2 are merely linear transformations of each other and result in *identical preferences* for single-period changes in wealth or equivalent one-period rates of return. The positive linear transformation between one-period changes in wealth and the rate of return is

$$r_t = \frac{w_T - w_0}{w_0}$$

where

w_0 = beginning-of period wealth (a positive constant)

w_T = end-of-period wealth (a random variable)

r_t = one-period rate of return (also a random variable)

Suppose, for example, that an investor can earn a rate of return of r_0 with certainty or can invest in a risky investment that will return $r_0 + y$ or $r_0 - y$ with equal probability. Symbolically, $P(r_0 - y) = P(r_0 + y) = \frac{1}{2}$. Both the riskless and the risky investment have an expected return of r_0.

App. 25A-1.3 Graphical Analysis

$$E(r) = P_1(r_0 + y) + P_2(r_0 - y)$$

$$= \frac{1}{2}(r_0 + y) + \frac{1}{2}(r_0 - y)$$

$$= r_0$$

Since the expected returns are the same, a risk-averse investor will prefer the sure return because the risk-averter's diminishing marginal utility will cause the disutility from a return of $r_0 - y$ to exceed the gain in utility from a return of $r_0 + y$.

Furthermore, suppose that this risk-averter had a third investment opportunity in an even riskier investment expected to yield either $r_0 - 2y$ or $r_0 + 2y$ with equal probability. This latter investment is riskier (that is, has more variability of return) than the other risky investment, but it offers the same expected return. The calculations at the top of page 744 show that the two risky investments have equal expected returns. A risk-averse investor will rank the desirability of the riskiest investment last, since its expected return is the same as the other two investments but it entails more risk. Therefore, the riskiest investment will have the least expected utility. Symbolically, $U(r_0) > E[U(r_0 \pm y)] > E[U(r_0 \pm 2y)]$. This is shown graphically in Fig. 25A-2.

$$\overbrace{E(r) = P_1(r_0 - y) + P_2(r_0 + y)}^{\text{Small risk}} = r_0$$

$$\overbrace{E(r) = P_1(r_0 + 2y) + P_2(r_0 + 2y)}^{\text{Larger risk}}$$

$$= \frac{1}{2}(r_0 - 2y) + \frac{1}{2}(r_0 + 2y) = r_0$$

App. 25A-1.4 Expected Utility, Expected Return, and Risk Formulas

In an uncertain world, expected utility is determined by expected return *and* risk.[13] Symbolically, this is summarized in Eq. (App. 25A-1a)

$$E(U) = f[E(r), \text{risk}] \qquad \text{(App. 25A-1a)}$$

$$= f[E(r), \sigma] \qquad \text{(App. 25A-1b)}$$

where

$e(U)$ = expected utility

$E(r)$ = expected return

risk = variability of returns, measured by the standard deviation of returns

(denoted σ)

f = some unspecified mathematical function

An increase in expected return will increase the investor's expected utility if risk does not also increase. Or a decrease in risk will increase expected utility if expected return does not decrease simultaneously.[14] Expected returns and expected utility are defined in Eqs. (App. 25A-2) and (App. 25A-3), respectively.

$$E(r) = \sum_i^N p_i r_i \qquad \text{(App. 25A-2)}$$

where

p_i = probability of ith outcome

r_i = ith possible rate of return

N = number of possible outcomes

13 The standard deviation of returns is, of course, only a risk surrogate rather than a risk synonym, as this discussion implies. See Chap. 9 for a more complete discussion of risk. Throughout this book, σ is used as a symbol standing for *total* risk. Sometimes it is convenient to use the variance σ^2 rather than the standard deviation. Both are used interchangeably to denote total risk.

14 Technically, expected utility is a function of $E(r)$ and σ only if the utility function is quadratic or if the distribution of terminal wealth is a two-parameter distribution (such as a normal distribution).

Expected utility is calculated as follows:

$$E(U) = \sum_{i}^{N} p_i U_i \qquad \text{(App. 25A-3)}$$

where U_i = utility of ith outcome.

The expected value is like a weighted average of the possible outcomes where the probabilities are the weights.[15]

Measurement of total risk was examined in detail in Chap. 9. Equation (App. 25A-4) shows the formula used to calculate the standard deviation of returns for the ith security from expected rates of return.[16]

$$\sigma = \sqrt{\sum_{t=1}^{T} P_t [r_{it} - E(r_i)]^2} \qquad \text{(App. 25A-4)}$$

Before the utility analysis of risky investment alternatives can be performed, the investment analyst must be supplied with probability distributions of outcomes and a utility function in order to find the expected utility for each object of choice. For example, in selecting among alternative investments, a probability distribution of returns representing the possible investment outcomes and their probabilities is required. And a utility function assigning utils to each possible rate of return that the investment might earn is also needed. Only after the utility function and the probability distributions are known can utility analysis proceed.

**App. 25A-1.5
Numerical
Example**

Consider three objects of choice, say, investments A, B, and C, with probability distribution of returns as defined in Table App. 25A-1.

TABLE APP. 25A-1   PROBABILITY DISTRIBUTIONS OF RETURNS FOR THREE INVESTMENTS

INVESTMENTS	OUTCOMES	INVESTMENT OUTCOMES AND THEIR PROBABILITIES						CHARACTERISTICS	
		−3%	0	3%	6%	9%	$\Sigma p = 1$	$E(r)$	
A	↑	.5		+		.5	1	$E(r_A) = 3\%$	$\sigma_A = 0$
B	Probabilities		.5	+	.5		1	$E(r_B) = 3\%$	$\sigma_B = 3$
C	↓			1			1	$E(r_C) = 3\%$	$\sigma_C = 0$

15 Mathematical App. B discusses the mathematical expectation.

16 When calculating the standard deviation of returns from historical rates of return, the probabilities become relative frequencies, so substitute $P = 1/T$ and rewrite Eq. (App. 25A-4) as (App. 25A-4a)

$$\sigma \sqrt{\sum_{t=1}^{T} \left(\frac{1}{T}\right) [r_t - E(r)]^2} \qquad \text{(App. 25A-4a)}$$

Figures App. 25A-3 to App. 25A-5 represent the utility functions for a risk-averting, a risk-indifferent, and a risk-seeking investor, respectively. Since investments *A*, *B*, and *C* all offer the same expected return of 3 percent, it is clear that the three investors will rank these three investments differently *purely* because of their differences in risks.

FIGURE APP. 25A-3 Risk-averter's quadratic utility-of-returns function.

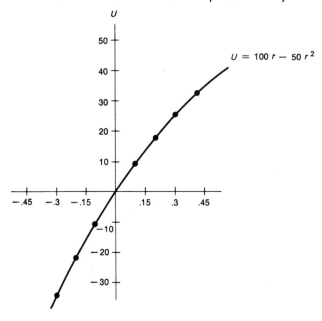

$$U = 100\,r - 50\,r^2$$

FIGURE APP. 25A-4 Risk-indifferent investor's linear utility-of-returns function.

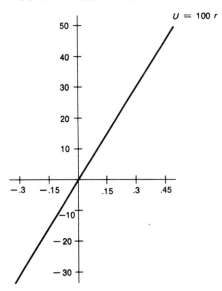

$$U = 100\,r$$

FIGURE APP. 25A-5   Risk-lover's quadratic utility-of-returns function.

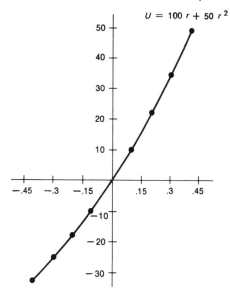

The risk-averter's expected utility from A, B, and C is calculated thus:

$$E[U(A)] = \sum_{i=1}^{2} P_i U(r_i)$$

$$= \frac{1}{2}[U(-0.03)] + \frac{1}{2}[U(0.09)]$$

$$= \frac{1}{2}(-3.045) + \frac{1}{2}(8.595)$$

$$= 2.785 \text{ utils}$$

$$E[U(B)] = \frac{1}{2}[U(0)] + \frac{1}{2}[U(.06)]$$

$$= 0 + \frac{1}{2}(5.82)$$

$$= 2.91 \text{ utils}$$

$$E[U(C)] = 1[U(.03)]$$

$$= 1(2.955)$$

$$= 2.955 \text{ utils}$$

The risk-averter derives the most satisfaction from investment C, which has the least variability of return.

The risk-indifferent investor's expected utils from the three investments are calculated below:

$$E[U(A)] = \frac{1}{2}[U(-(.03)] + \frac{1}{2}[U(.09)]$$

$$= \frac{1}{2}(-3) + \frac{1}{2}(9)$$

$$= 3 \text{ utils}$$

$$E[U(B)] = \frac{1}{2}[U(0)] + \frac{1}{2}[U(0.06)]$$

$$= 0 + \frac{1}{2}(6)$$

$$= 3 \text{ utils}$$

$$E[U(C)] = 1[U(0.03)]$$

$$= 1(3)$$

$$= 3 \text{ utils}$$

Since investments A, B, and C differ only with respect to their risk, the risk-indifferent investor assigns the same utility to all three. Symbolically, $E[U(A)]$ = $E[U(B)]$ = $E[U(C)]$ for the risk-indifferent investor.

The risk-lover's utility calculations follow.

$$E[U(A)] = \frac{1}{2}[U(-0.3)] + \frac{1}{2}[U(0.09)]$$

$$= \frac{1}{2}(-2.055) + \frac{1}{2}(9.405)$$

$$= 3.225 \text{ utils}$$

$$E[U(B)] = \frac{1}{2}[U(0)] + \frac{1}{2}[U(0.06)]$$

$$= 0 + \frac{1}{2}(6.18)$$

$$= 3.09 \text{ utils}$$

$$E[U(C)] = 1[U(0.3)]$$

$$= 1(3.045)$$

$$= 3.045 \text{ utils}$$

The risk-lover prefers the large variability of return exhibited by investment A. The three investors' expected utilities are summarized in Table App. 25A-2.

Investments A, B, and C all have identical expected returns of 3 percent, $E(r)$ = 3 percent; only their variability of returns differs. The lower expected

TABLE APP. 25A-2   DIFFERENT INVESTMENT PREFERENCES FOR RISKY INVESTMENTS

INVESTOR	ASSET A—MOST RISKY $E(r_A) = 3\%, \sigma_A = 6\%$	ASSET B $E(r_B) = 3\%, \sigma_B = 3\%$	ASSET C—LEAST RISKY $E(r_C) = 3\%, \sigma_C = 0$
Risk-averter	$E[U(A)] = 2.785$	$E[U(B)] = 2.91$	$E[U(C)] = 2.955$
Risk-indifferent	$E[U(A)] = 3$	$E[U(B)] = 3$	$E[U(C)] = 3$
Risk-lover	$E[U(A)] = 3.225$	$E[U(B)] = 3.09$	$E[U(C)] = 3.045$

utilities assigned to A and B by the risk-averse investor are due to their larger variability of returns, which seems distasteful. And the larger expected utility the risk-lover associates with investments A and B reflects this investor's preference for risk. Thus, the two parameters—mean and variance of returns —are *both* reflected in expected utility. In all cases, expected utility measures the effects of both $E(r)$ and σ. Symbolically, $E(U) = f[\sigma, E(r)]$.

The preceding numerical example showed how a rational, risk-averse, wealth-seeking investor will select investments that minimize risk at any given level of expected return and thus maximize expected utility in a world of uncertainty.

Given the investor's utility function, we have seen how an individual will be able to select investment assets (either consciously or subconsciously) in terms of the investments' expected return and risk. Figure App. 25A-6 shows graphically how an investor will select between investments by examining only their expected returns and risk. The exhibit is a graph in risk-return space of the seven hypothetical securities listed at the top of page 750.

App. 25A-1.6 Selecting Investments in Terms of Risk and Return

FIGURE APP. 25A-6   Opportunities and preferences in risk-return space.

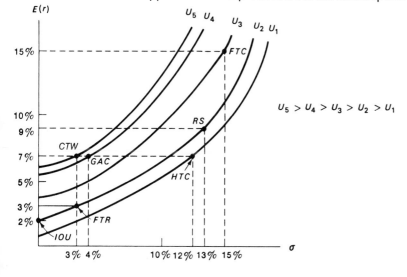

$U_5 > U_4 > U_3 > U_2 > U_1$

NAME OF SECURITY	EXPECTED RETURN, E(r), %	RISK, σ, %
Canadian Telephone Works (CTW)	7	3
General Auto Corporation (GAC)	7	4
Fuzzyworm Tractor Company (FTC)	15	15
Fairyear Tire & Rubber (FTR)	3	3
Hotstone Tire Corporation (HTC)	7	12
Rears and Sawbuck Co. (RS)	9	13
Treasury IOUs (IOU)	2	0

Figure App. 25A-6 also shows a utility map in risk-return space representing the preference of some risk-averse investor (like the one whose utility from rates of return curve was shown in Fig. App. 25A-3). In this indifference map the investor's utility is equal all along each curve. These curves are called *utility isoquants* or *indifference curves*. The graph is called an *indifference map in risk-return space*. Since investments RS, IOU, and FTR are all on the same indifference curve (that is, U_2), the investor obtains equal expected utility from them although their expected returns and risk differ considerably.

An infinite number of indifference curves could be drawn for the risk-averter depicted in Fig. App. 25A-6, but they would all be similar in shape and would all possess the following characteristics:

1. Higher indifference curves represent more investor satisfaction. Symbolically, $U_5 > U_4 > U_3 > U_2 > U_1$, because the investor likes higher expected return and dislikes higher risk.
2. All indifference curves slope upward. This is because the investor requires higher expected returns as an inducement to assume larger risks. Consider, for example, the investor's indifference between FTR, IOU, and RS. This indifference results from the fact that RS's expected return is just enough above the expected return of FTR to compensate the risk-averse investor for assuming the additional risk incurred in going from FTR to RS. Riskless investment IOU has just enough reduction in risk below the risk of FTR to compensate the investor for accepting IOU's lower rate of return and still be as happy as with FTR or RS. Investment IOU is called the *certainty equivalent* of investments FTR and RS because it involves no risk.
3. The indifference curves grow steeper at higher levels of risk. This reflects the investor's diminishing willingness to assume risk as returns become higher.

Given the investment opportunities and the investor preferences shown in Fig. App. 25A-6, we see that the investor prefers CTW over any of the other investments since CTW lies on a higher indifference curve than any other investment. In fact, Fig. App. 25A-6 shows that

$$U(CTW) > U(GAC) > U(FTC) > U(IOU) = U(RS) = U(FTR) > U(HTC)$$

App. 25A-1.7 Unusual Risk Attitudes The indifference map graphed in Fig. App. 25A-6 represents rational normal, risk-averse preferences. Figure App. 25A-6 is implied by a utility-of-returns function like the one in Fig. App. 25A-3. Figures App. 25A-4 and App. 25A-5 represent *radically* different investment preferences, the preferences of a risk-indifferent investor and of a risk-loving investor, respectively.

Figure App. 25A-7 is simply another way of representing the utility-of-returns function graphed in Fig. App. 25A-4, and Fig. App. 25A-5 results

FIGURE APP. 25A-7   Risk-indifferent wealth maximizer's preferences in risk-return space.

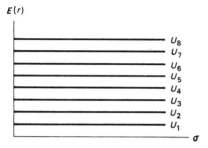

FIGURE APP. 25A-8   Risk-lover's preferences in risk-return space.

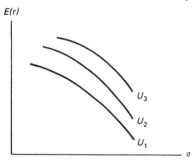

from a utility function like the one in Fig. App. 25A-8. These two pathological cases of investment preferences are presented merely as intellectual curiosities. They do not represent rational, risk-averse behaviour.

APP. 25A-2   MATHEMATICAL UTILITY ANALYSIS

For quadratic utility functions it may be shown that expected utility is determined by expected return $E(r)$ and risk (as measured by the variance of returns σ^2 or standard deviation σ). This finding can be generalized to other utility functions if the probability distribution of returns is a two- parameter distribution.

Consider the quadratic utility of wealth and return functions (App. 25A-5) and (App. 25A-6).

App. 25A-2.1 Quadratic Diminishing Marginal Utility Functions

$$U = w - aw^2 \quad w < \left(\frac{1}{2a}\right) \quad \text{for } a > 0 \qquad \text{(App. 25A-5)}$$

$$U = r - br^2 \quad r < \left(\frac{1}{2b}\right) \quad \text{for } b > 0 \qquad \text{(App. 25A-6)}$$

Equations (App. 25A-5) and (App. 25A-6) are graphed in Figs. App. 25A-9 and App. 25A-10, respectively. Figures App. 25A-9 and App. 25A-10 also show the marginal-utility curves; they are denoted MU. The marginal utility diminishes as larger returns are obtained.

FIGURE APP. 25A-9   Diminishing quadratic utility-of-wealth function.

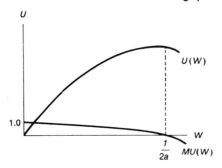

FIGURE APP. 25A-10   Diminishing quadratic utility-of-returns function.

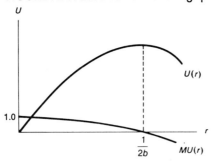

The preference orderings of a utility function are invariant under a positive linear transformation of the basic random variable.[17] This implies that the diminishing quadratic utility-of-wealth function (App. 25A-5) is equivalent to the diminishing quadratic utility-of-returns function (App. 25A-6), since one variable is a positive linear transformation of the other.

Expected utility is a function of $E(r)$ and σ for quadratic utility functions. Taking the expected value of Eq. (App. 25A-6) yields Eq. (App. 25A-7a). (See Mathematical Expectation Theorem B-2, in Part 9, for proof.)

$$\begin{aligned} E(U) &= E(r - br^2) \\ &= E(r) - bE(r^2) \\ &= E(r) - b\sigma^2 - bE(r)^2 \qquad \text{since } E(r^2) = \sigma^2 + E(r)^2 \qquad \text{(App. 25A-7a)} \\ &= f[E(r), \sigma^2] \qquad \text{(App. 25A-7b)} \end{aligned}$$

Equation (App. 25A-7b) shows that expected utility is a function of expected return and risk as measured by the variance of returns. Expected utility varies directly with $E(r)$ and inversely with risk, since

---

17 J. von Neumann and O. Morgenstern, *Theory of Games and Economic Behavior*, 3d ed., Princeton, N.J.: Princeton University Press, 1953, pp. 22-24.

$$\frac{dE(U)}{dE(r)} = 1 - 2bE(r) > 0$$

and

$$\frac{dE(U)}{d\sigma} = -2b < 0$$

for the values to which b and r are constrained. Thus, investors with diminishing quadratic utility of wealth from returns desire both higher $E(r)$ and less risk.

Solving Eq. (App. 25A-7a) for σ^2 yields Eq. (App. 25A-8a).

$$\sigma = \left(\frac{E(r)}{b}\right) - E(r)^2 - \left(\frac{E(U)}{b}\right) \qquad \text{(App. 25A-8a)}$$

$$= \left(\frac{E(r)}{b}\right) - E(r)^2 - \text{constant} \qquad \text{(App. 25A-8b)}$$

Varying the constant term in Eq. (App. 25A-8a) generates the quadratic indifference map in $[E(r), \sigma]$ space shown in Fig. App. 25A-11. Figure App. 25A-11 shows that investors whose utility is well approximated by Eqs. (App. 25A-6) and (App. 25A-7a) will maximize their expected utility by selecting investments with the maximum return in some risk-class, that is, by selecting efficient portfolios.

FIGURE APP.25A-11   Indifference map for risk-averter.

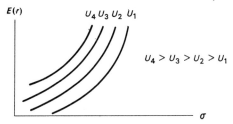

It can be shown that if the probability distribution of rates of return or wealth is a two-parameter distribution and the investor has a diminishing single-period utility function, the investor can maximize expected utility by selecting investments with the minimum risk at each rate of return (or, conversely, the maximum return at each risk-class).[18]

App. 25A-2.2 Quadratic Utility not Required for $[E(r), \sigma]$ Analysis

$$E[U(r)] = U(r)f(r\,|\,m_1, m_2)dr \qquad \text{(App. 25A-9a)}$$

$$= F(r\,|\,m_1, m_2) \qquad \text{(App. 25A-9b)}$$

18 J. Tobin, "Liquidity Preference as Behavior Towards Risk," *Review of Economic Studies*, February 1958, pp. 65-86, and M. K. Richter, "Cardinal Utility, Portfolio Selection of Taxation," *Review of Economic Studies*, June 1960, pp. 152-160.

where $f(r|m_1, m_2)$ is a two-parameter probability distribution of returns that is completely specified by m_1 and m_2. For example, if Ms. Investor has logarithmic utility function (that is, diminishing marginal utility) and if the probability distribution is a two-parameter distribution (such as a normal distribution), she will maximize her expected utility by maximizing returns at any given risk-class, since $dE(U)/dE(r) = dF/dm_1 > 0$ and $dE(U)/\sigma^2 = dF/dm_2 < 0$. Thus, selection of investments in terms of $E(r)$ and σ does not require a quadratic utility function.

APP. 25A-3   CONCLUSIONS

This book deals with investors who have diminishing but positive marginal utility of wealth and/or returns. Such investors, this chapter has shown, prefer more wealth to less wealth but prefer less risk to more risk. In an uncertain world, these investors will maximize the expected utility from their investment activities by selecting assets that have (1) the maximum expected return in their risk-class, or conversely, (2) the minimum risk at any particular level of expected return.

The objective of rational investment management, then, is to delineate and select those investments that have the maximum expected return within the risk-class the investor prefers over the investor's single-period planning horizon. The investor need not always select an individual asset. He or she can construct a portfolio that yields higher expected utility than an individual asset.

QUESTIONS

1. If people's utility is determined largely by what they consume, how do investors derive utility from the rates of return on their investments? After all, a rate of return cannot be eaten.

2. Draw a graph of the utility-of-wealth function for a risk-lover. What are the characteristics of a risk-lover's marginal utility of wealth?

3. If their risk is the same, is investment A or B better? Show how you choose between them.

	A	B
Cost at time $t = 0$	$W_0 = \$500$	$W_0 = \$40$
Proceeds at time $t > 0$	$W_T = \$800$	$W_T = \$95$

4. How does risk affect utility? Use formulas and/or graphs to explain.

5. Rank the desirability of the investments at the top of page 755. Show your work graphically.

6. Write down your social insurance number. Assume that you can purchase a risky investment that will pay one of two equally likely rates of return. This investment will pay the rate of return indicated by the last digit in your social insurance number with a 0.5 probability and the rate of return

INVESTMENT	E(r), %	σ,%
A	10	5
B	10	10
C	5	5
D	12	10

indicated by the next-to-last digit with a 0.5 probability. Calculate the expected return of this investment. For example, for the social insurance number 307-383-152, the expected return is 0.5(5%) + 0.5(2%) = 3.5% = E(r). If you were the risk-averse investor shown in Fig. App. 25A-3, would you rather have a certain (that is, one riskless) investment paying the expected return calculated from the last two digits of your social insurance number, or the risky investment based on the equal probability of the last two digits? Explain. Explain what the risk-indifferent investor in Fig. App. 25A- 4 and the risk-lover in Fig. App. 25A-5 would do if confronted with this same choice between a certain expected return and a risky investment with the same expected return.

SELECTED REFERENCES

M. Friedman and L. J. Savage. "The Utility Analysis of Choices Involving Risk." *The Journal of Political Economy*, August 1948, pp. 279-304. A classic paper rationalizing choice in uncertainty with the expected-utility hypothesis. Only algebra is used.
H. Markowitz. *Portfolio Selection*. New York: Wiley, 1959. Chapters 10 through 13 discuss the utility theory underlying the selection of efficient assets. Most of the mathematics is first-year college algebra.

26 Investment Performance Evaluation

Billions of dollars are kept invested in marketable securities in Canada. Most of these funds are managed by professional investment managers (or money managers) who earn their living by providing portfolio management services for fees. The largest and most popular types of publicly available portfolio management services are provided by the *institutional investors* below.

1. The trust departments of large, big-city chartered banks
2. Investment advisory services (which are usually subsidiaries of mutual fund management companies, security brokerage firms, or investment newsletter services)
3. The investment management departments of life insurance companies
4. Investment companies (primarily, the open-end companies called mutual funds)

The publicly available portfolio management services receive the funds they manage from the following major sources of investable wealth.

1. Pension funds
2. Substantial individuals (for example, wealthy widows and orphans)
3. University endowments
4. Charitable foundations

These investors own and ultimately control the funds, but they frequently turn temporary control of the investment decisions over to some external portfolio management service. Before delegating the investment management function to a hired consultant, however, they have asked themselves two questions. First, should they try to manage the funds themselves? Most of them have decided to seek investment management services externally in the hope of obtaining expert advice that would more than pay for itself in better returns for their portfolios. This leads to the second question: Which portfolio management service should be selected?

This chapter addresses itself to the question of how to select the "best" portfolio management service. The tools taught in this chapter are also useful to the portfolio managers themselves, if they wish to be able to evaluate and improve their own money management skills. The remainder of the chapter explains both good and bad ways to evaluate the portfolio performance of the hundreds of bank trust departments, investment advisers, investment management departments of life insurance companies, mutual funds, and other money managers. Tools that can be used to rank the historical performance of all these different portfolios will be explained. Some naive methods and some logical methods of portfolio performance will be considered and compared.

All the logical methods are derived from various parts of the risk-return analysis presented in Chaps. 9 and 10. Regardless of whether the old, naive methods or the newer, more logical methods of portfolio performance are used, however, one common problem exists: data availability. Historical rate of return data are required in order to evaluate the investment performance of any portfolio. Unfortunately, not all portfolio management services make adequate data about their past performance publicly available.

The performance of dozens of mutual funds is evaluated in this chapter. Mutual funds are examined rather than other portfolios because, by law, mutual funds must publicly disclose their operating results. Also, provisions of the provincial securities acts, provincial business corporations acts, the Canadian Business Corporations Act, and the code of practice of the Investment Funds Institute, limit mutual funds' use of leverage[1] (that is, issuing debt), buying on margin, taking more than 9 percent of the proceeds from the sales of new shares for sales commissions, selling the funds' shares on margin, and short selling. These requirements ensure a certain amount of similarity among mutual funds. Because of these similarities, plus the requirements that they disclose their holdings and income, and their popularity with investors, mutual funds make an interesting subject for study. Before evaluating the investment performances of the mutual fund managers, however, let's first investigate the organizations and objectives of mutual funds.

26-1 INVESTMENT COMPANIES DEFINED

Investors with modest amounts to invest may not be well advised to buy securities because they have insufficient funds to buy a diversified portfolio. Since investors should buy stock in lots of 100 shares or more to incur lower stockbroker round-lot commissions, and since the average Toronto Stock Exchange (TSE) stock costs about $15 per share, it takes, on average, $1,500 per issue (100 shares times an average price of $15 per share), to buy one round lot of stock. Fifteen hundred dollars per stock issue multiplied by thirty different stock issues (which are needed to obtain diversification) gives $45,000 (30 issues times $1,500 per issue) as the minimum needed to begin investing in individual securities in a diversified manner. Diversification is, of course, valuable as a means of reducing investment risks.[2]

---

1 Companies that are federally chartered and who use borrowed funds for investment purposes must be registered under the Investment Companies Act, which is administered by the Superintendent of Insurance.

2 Selection of the number 30 as the minimum number of stock issues needed to obtain diversification is discussed analytically in Chap. 23. The discussion is based on the work by John H. Evans and S. H. Archer, "Diversification and the Reduction of Dispersion: An Empirical Analysis," *Journal of Finance*, December 1968, pp. 761-67.

Since millions of aspiring investors lack (1) sufficient capital to buy a diversified portfolio, (2) the expertise to manage a portfolio, and/or (3) the time to manage a portfolio, enterprising portfolio managers have created public portfolios of diversified securities in which investors can buy a small or large number of shares. These public portfolios, called investment companies, typically assume one of two basic forms: (1) the open-end investment company, usually called a mutual fund, and (2) the closed-end investment fund.

26- 1.1 Mutual Funds

About 1.5 million people own shares in over 300 open-ended investment companies in Canada.[3] The size of these accounts ranges from a child's single share, valued at only a few dollars, to a multimillion dollar investor's share in several different mutual funds. Likewise, the total asset holdings of individual mutual funds range from only a few million dollars to hundreds of millions.

Mutual funds are conduits from savings to investment. The funds pool the savings of many people by commingling them into one large, diversified investment portfolio. Many mutual funds own over one hundred different issues of stocks and/or bonds. But no single investor owns any particular asset. Instead, an investor who has purchased a certain percentage of the mutual fund's total shares outstanding owns that percentage of every asset and every liability the fund obtains. Investors can cash in their shares in the fund whenever they wish, at the net asset value per share on that day. The *net asset value per share* equals the value of the fund's total net assets after liabilities divided by the total number of shares outstanding on that day. Thus, the net asset value per share fluctuates every time any asset experiences a change in its market price.

The Canadian Income Tax Act draws a distinction between mutual fund corporations and mutual fund trusts. Investment companies are treated as mutual fund trusts if the entity is unincorporated; if at least 80 percent of its portfolio consists of Canadian securities, rental or royalty interests in resource properties; if at least 95 percent of its income is derived from these assets; and if no more than 10 percent of its portfolio consists of shares, bonds or securities of any one corporation or debtor other than the federal or provincial governments.[4] A mutual fund trust does not pay tax; all income and gains of the trust are treated as if they were earned directly by the investor.[5]

Mutual fund corporations,[6] on the other hand, are subject to corporate income tax on their income and capital gains. Dividends distributed by the corporation are taxable as dividends in the unit-holders hands, unless the source of the distribution was a capital gain. In this event the dividend is a

---

3 Marianne Tefft, ''Mutual Admiration Society,'' *Moneywise Magazine,The Financial Post*, December 1986, p. 41.

4 Income Tax Act, s.108(2).

5 And thus subject to the appropriate income and capital gain treatment. See Chap. 5.

6 Canadian open-ended investment companies other than mutual fund trusts. See Income Tax Act, s.131(8).

capital-gain dividend to the shareholder and treated as a capital gain for tax purposes.

By law,[7] open-ended investment companies are required to publish and adhere to a statement of the fund's investment objective. Figure 26-1 shows a typical set of fund objective provisions. These statements are typically one or two paragraphs long and can be grouped under the following main categories:

Growth Funds   These funds tend to invest only in common stock and assume some risks to obtain stocks that are expected to yield higher returns.

Income Funds   Investment in stocks and bonds that pay high cash dividends and coupon interest is the objective of income funds. Risky stocks offering higher potential capital gains tend to be avoided in favour of "blue-chip" stocks (that is, those of large, old, stable companies).

Balanced Funds   These funds divide their holdings between fixed-income securities and low-risk common stocks in order to avoid the risk of loss. Their primary objective is stability of returns. Typically, the fund manager maintains a balance between fixed income securities and equities that range from 30 percent to 70 percent either way.

Money Market or Liquid Asset Funds   These mutual funds invest in money-market instruments such as Treasury bills, certificates of deposit, deposit receipts, short-term government bonds, and commercial paper. One of the main assets of some money-market funds is 91- and 182-day Treasury bills, which usually pay one of the highest rates of interest available on default-free instruments. These liquid asset funds started in the 1970s when interest rates rose above 10 percent. Their objective is to earn high rates of interest from liquid low-risk, short-term instruments.

Fixed Income   Fixed income funds have all of their assets in bonds, mortgages and money-market instruments. Their objective is to earn moderate to high after-tax income and provide relative stability to their returns.

Specialty Funds   These funds invest their assets in a defined industry or sector. These include oil and gas funds, precious metal funds, and high technology funds.[8]

Global and International Funds   These funds hold a portfolio of assets that is not limited by any geographical boundaries. Global funds, such as Templeton Growth Fund, invest in securities anywhere in the world, including at times, Canada. International funds, such as Bolton Tremblay International, invest strictly in securities outside Canada. Figure 26-2 contains the Templeton Growth Fund statement of objectives.

U.S. Funds   These funds, such as Bullock American, invest all or substantially all, of their assets in U.S. securities.

---

7 For example, see Ontario Securities Legislation—Regulations, Form 15, Item 7.
8 Although these funds typically hold diversified portfolios of securities within the target sector, they are not *per se* diversified funds within the Markowitz definition. They may however be included by investors in the development of a Markowitz diversified portfolio.

FIGURE 26-1 Mutual fund objectives.

PROVISIONS OF SELECTED FUNDS

A.G.F. Management Limited

Head Off. — 50th fl., Toronto-Dominion Bank Tower, Toronto, Ont. M5K 1E9. **Telephone** — (416) 367-1900.

INVESTMENT FUNDS

AGF HiTech Fund Limited — (Can. 1983). Com. stk. fund with an objective of above-average long term growth of capital through investment in cos. engaged in businesses which are expected to benefit from the development of high technologies. Licensed to sell in all provinces. Manager — A.G.F. Management Limited.

Purchase Plans: (1) Cash Purchases — Units may be purchased at net asset value plus a sales commission. (2) Systematic Withdrawal Plan — Regular withdrawals may be made with a charge of 50¢ for each regular withdrawal, $1.50 for each special withdrawal. Admin. fee $10 p.a. and termination fee of $2.50. (3) Periodic Purchases — By way of pre-authorized checks — monthly, quarterly or s.a.; min. $500.

Reinvestment Privilege — See Canadian Trusteed Income Fund.

Transfer Privilege — See Canadian Trusteed Income Fund.

Sales Commission — See Canadian Trusteed Income Fund.

Management Fee — 1% of aver. net asset value of fund during the yr., computed and pd. monthly.

Redemption Policy — Redeemable at net asset value as of the close of business on the day on which the application is received. Payment within 7 days.

Distributions — Income distributed quarterly to unitholders and capital gains distributed on annual basis. Automatically pd. by check unless reinvestment requested.

AGF Japan Fund Limited — (Can. 1969). Com. stk. specialty fund with primary objective of l.-t. growth of capital through invest. in well-established cos. operating in important Japanese industries. Offered for sale in all provinces. Manager — A.G.F. Management Limited.

Purchase Plans: (1) Cash Purchases — Mutual fund shs. may be purchased at net asset value plus a sales commission. (2) Systematic Withdrawal Plan — Regular withdrawals may be made with a charge of 50¢ for each regular withdrawal, and $1.50 for each special withdrawal. Admin. fee $10 p.a. and termination fee of $2.50. (3) Periodic Purchases — By way of pre-authorized checks — monthly, quaterly or s.a.; $100 min.

Reinvestment Privilege — Shldrs. who redeem shs. may, within 60 days, reinvest all or part of the proceeds into shs. of the fund at net asset value (without sales charge). Admin. fee $25.

Transfer Privilege — Shs. may be exchanged for shs. or units of any other fund managed by A.G.F. Management Ltd. (with the exception of AGF Money Market Fund and AGF Preferred Income Fund) on pay. of a commission per sh. or unit not to exceed 2% of offering price.

Sales Commission — Not to exceed 9% of offering price. On purchases under $10,000 charge is a max. of 9%, then declining by steps to 2% on $300,000 to $499,000. Commissions are negotiable but no commission shall be less than 2% except on purchases of $500,000 and over, when commission is fully negotiable.

Management Fee — Monthly fee based on the following: 1/12 of 1⅜% of the first $100,000,000 of the average net asset value of the fund during the mo., plus 1/12 of 1% of the amt. by which the aver. net asset value of the fund during the month exceeds $100,000,000.

Redemption Policy — Mutual fund shs. may be redeemed at net asset value as of the close of business on the next market day following the day a written request for redemption has been received. Payment will be made within 4 market days. Fee payable if redemp. made within 90 days of purchase.

Dividends — No divds. pd. to date.

AGF Money Market Fund — (Estab. 1975). Money market trusteed mutual invest. fund, whose principal objective is to achieve as high a level of current inc. as is consistent with the preservation of capital and liquidity. Qualifies as an invest. for RRSPs, RRIFs and RHOSPs. Offered for sale in all provinces. Manager — A.G.F. Management Limited.

Purchase Plans: (1) Cash Purchases — Units may be purchased at net asset value without sales charge. Min. initial invest. is $2,500, with subsequent invests. of at least $1,000. (2) RRSPs — Min. initial deposit of $100, subsequent deposits $50. Units of the fund may also be deposited with the trustee in min. lots of 25 units. Trustee entitled to s.a. admin. fee of 1/5 of 1% of value of assets of each plan, pay. Jan. and July. Min. annual admin. fee $15; max. $50. Termination fee of $15. Trans. fee of $15 on trans. of funds from another registered plan the trustee for which is not Montreal Trust Co. (3) RRIFs — Trustee entitled to s.a. admin. fee of 1/5 of 1% of value of assets of each plan, pay. Jan. and July. Min. annual admin. fee $15; max. $50. Termination fee of $15. Trans. fee of $15 on trans. of funds from another registered plan the trustee for which is not Montreal Trust Co. (4) RHOSPs — Min. initial deposit and subsequent deposits of $100. Units of the fund may also be deposited with the trustee in min. lots of 25 units. Trustee entitled to s.a. admin. fee of ¼ of 1% of value of assets of each plan, pay. Jan. and July. Min. annual admin. fee $10; max. $25. Termination fee $20.

Fee of $10 payable if units are redeemed within 30 days of purchase. Account admin. fee $1.50 per month.

Management Fee — Annual fee of ½ of 1% of the fund's average net assets computed and pd. in monthly instalments.

Redemption Policy — Units redeemed at the option of the holder at net asset value following notification to the fund by mail or, under certain conditions, by telephone or telex. Payment normally made on next business day after notification received but not later than 7 days thereafter.

Distributions — Inc. of the fund is credited on a daily basis to unitholders of record as of the close of business on the preceding business day. Net capital gains credited on the last business day of the year to unitholders of record at the close of the preceding day. On the last business day of each month, the total amount credited to the unitholder's account, less acct. admin. fee, will be reinvested in additional units of the fund at net asset value unless pay. requested in cash.

AGF Option Equity Fund — (Ont. 1979). An open-end mutual fund investing primarily in securities of well-managed, financially sound United States and Canadian companies and, when deemed appropriate, to write exchange-traded covered call options on such securities. Offered for sale in all provinces. Manager — AGF Management Limited.

Purchase Plans: (1) Cash Purchases — Units may be purchased at net asset value plus a sales commission. (2) Systematic Withdrawal Plan — Regular withdrawals may be made with a charge of 50¢ for each regular withdrawal, $1.50 for each special withdrawal. Admin. fee $10 p.a. and termination fee of $2.50. (3) Periodic Purchases — By way of pre-authorized checks — monthly, quarterly or s.a.; min. $500.

Reinvestment Privilege — See Canadian Trusteed Income Fund.

Transfer Privilege — See Canadian Trusteed Income Fund.

Sales Commission — See Canadian Trusteed Income Fund.

Management Fee — 1% of aver. net asset value of fund during the yr., computed and pd. monthly.

Redemption Policy — Redeemable at net asset value as of the close of business on the day on which the application is received. Payment within 7 days.

Distributions — Income distributed quarterly to unitholders and capital gains distributed on annual basis. Automatically pd. by check unless reinvestment requested.

AGF Preferred Income Fund — (Ont. 1984). An open-end mutual fund investing primarily in high quality preferred shares of taxable Canadian corporations for the purpose of obtaining maximum divd. income. Manager — AGF Management Ltd.

Purchase Plan — Offered on a continuous basis at an amount equal to the net asset value plus an acquisition cost not exceeding 4% of the offering price. On purchase under $25,000, charge not to exceed 4% then declining by steps to not more than 2% on $100,000 to $499,999; and 1% on amounts of $500,000 and above.

Management Fee — Payable monthly at annual rate of ½ of 1% of the aver. net assets value of the fund during the yr.

Redemption — Redeemable at net asset value at the close of business on the day on which the application is received. Payment within 7 days.

Distributions — Made monthly in amts. estimated by manager to equal 1/12 of anticipated net income of fund for the calendar yr. Net realized capital gains, if any, distributed in last month of each calendar yr. Automatically pd. by check unless reinvested in additional shares requested.

AGF Special Fund Limited — (Can. 1968). Com. stk. mutual fund investing in special situations both technical and non-technical. Objective is above avge. growth of capital. Shs. of the fund are offered in all provinces of Canada. Manager — A.G.F. Management Limited.

Provisions — See AGF Japan Fund Limited for details of Purchase Plans, Reinvestment Privileges and Sales Commissions.

Management Fee — See American Growth Fund Limited.

Redemption Policy — Mutual fund shs. may be redeemed at net asset value at close of business on the day application for redemption is received. Payment will be made within 5 days. Fee may be payable if redemption is made within 90 days of purchase.

Dividends — Automatically reinvested in additional shs. unless payment requested in cash.

American Growth Fund Limited — (Can. 1957). Com. stk. mutual invest. fund, investing primarily in securities listed on the NYSE, particularly growth co.'s considered likely to attain above average earnings increases. Objective is l.-t. growth of capital and inc. Offered for sale in all provinces of Canada. Manager — AGF Management Ltd.

Provisions — See AGF Japan Fund Limited for details of Purchase Plans, Reinvestment Privileges and Sales Commissions.

Fees — Management Fee — Manager entitled to a fee charged monthly at the rate of 1/12 of 1¼% on the first $100,000,000 of avge. net assets for each month plus 1/12 of 1% of amt. over $100,000,000.

Redemption Policy — Mutual fund shs. may be redeemed at net asset value as at the close of business on the day shs. are presented to the trustee if the NYSE is open or, if closed, at the close of business on the next day the Exchange is open. Payment made in 7 days. A fee may be payable if shs. redeemed within 90 days of purch.

Dividends — Automatically reinvested in additional shs. unless pay. requested in cash.

Canadian Gas and Energy Fund Limited — (Ont. 1960). Com. stk. mutual fund with objective of l.-t. growth of capital. Invests in Cdn. cos. engaged in discovery, development and extraction of natural gas, oil and metals. Qualifies as an invest. for

The Financial Post

INFORMATION SERVICE

Survey of Funds

Source: *The Financial Post* Information Service, "Survey of Funds," September 30, 1986.

FIGURE 26-2 Templeton Growth Fund.

Dec., distributions will be automatically reinvested without charge, unless investors request payment in cash.

Templeton Management Ltd.

Head Off. — 1500, 44 Victoria St., Toronto, Ont. M5C 1Y2. **Telephone** — (416) 364-4672.

INVESTMENT FUNDS

Templeton Growth Fund, Ltd. — (Estab. 1954). Operates as a com. stk. fund investing in all types of securities issued by companies or governments of any nation. Objective is l.-t. growth of capital. Licensed to sell in all provinces and territories. Manager — Templeton Investment Counsel Limited.

Purchase Plans — (1) Lump Sum Purchases — Min. initial purchase is $500. (2) An investor may make an agreement to invest at least $12,000 in the fund over not longer than 13 mos. with each part of the invest. qualifying for the discount from the regular offering price which would apply if the total invest. were made at one time. (3) Cash Withdrawal Plan — Investors with holdings of at least $12,000 may request regular quarterly or monthly withdrawals providing a fixed sum. Plan can be terminated at any time. Additional shs. of the fund can be purchased in the program in a min. amount of $25.

Fees — Com. shs. may be purchased at net asset value plus an acquisition charge of not more than 8½% of the offering price. On purchases under $12,000 charge is 8½% then declining by steps to ½% on $2,400,000 and more. Management Fee — Manager entitled to fee of 0.125% quarterly on the avge. daily net asset value during the quarter preceding each payment up to US$200,000,000. The fee is reduced on the average daily net asset value in excess of $200,000,000.

Redemption Policy — Com. shs. may be redeemed at net asset value as of the close of business on the day notice of redemption is received. Payment made within 7 days.

Dividends — Fund will distribute not less than 90% of ordinary income. Dividends and capital gains automatically reinvested in additional shs. without charge unless payment requested in cash.

Templeton Canadian Fund — (Estab. 1983). Open-end mutual fund investing mainly in Canadian equity securities. Objective of the fund is to achieve maximum growth consistent with reasonable security. Licensed to sell in all provinces and territories. Manager — Templeton Management Ltd.

Purchase Plans — (1) Lump Sum Purchases — Min. initial purchase is $500. (2) An investor may use a pre-authorized purchase plan where the min. invest. is $50 per month. (3) Cash Withdrawal Plan — Investors with holdings of at least $10,000 may request regular monthly, quarterly or yearly withdrawals. (4) Qualifies as an invest. for RRSPs.

Fees — Units may be purchased at net asset value plus an acquisition charge of not more than 9% of the offering price. On purchases under $10,000 charge is 9% then declining by steps to 1% on $2,000.00 and more. Management Fee — Manager entitled to monthly fee of 1/12 of 1¼% net asset value of fund up to $100,000,000 and 1/12 of 1% on amounts over $100,000,000. Trustee of RRSP entitled to s.a. admin. fee equal to 1/5 of 1% of the fund subject to min. of $7.50 and max. of $25.

Redemption — At net asset value as of the close of business on the day of notice of redemption is received. Payment made within 7 days.

Dividends — Automatically reinvested in additional units without charge unless payment requested in cash.

Timvest Fund Management

Head Off. — 2050, Place du Canada, Montreal, Que. H3B 2N2. **Telephone** — (514) 875-7040. **Trans. Agent** — The Royal Trust Co., Montreal, Charlottetown.

INVESTMENT FUNDS

Timvest Growth Fund (formerly Beaubran Inc.) — (P.E.I. 1947). Mutual investment fund investing in Cdn. securities to provide l.-t. growth of capital as well as current income. Qualifies as an investment for RRSP. Shs. are sold in Quebec, New Brunswick and P.E.I. Fund Managers — Beaubran Management Inc., Montreal; Timmins & Assoc. Ltd., Toronto.

Purchase Plans: Lump Sum Purchases — Shs. may be purchased at net asset value. Retirement Savings Plan — Shs. may be purchased for RRSP under the Income Tax Act.

Fees — Acquisition charge of not more than 8% of the offering price. On purchases under $9,999, charge is 8%, then declining by steps to 5% for amts. of $500,000 to $99,999. On amts. over $100,000, charge is subject to negotiation. Trustee entitled to a s.a. admin. fee of ⅛ of 1% of the net asset value of ord. shs. held; min. annual fee is $6 and max., $24. No redempt. fee unless shs. are redeemed within 90 days of purchase. Management Fee — Fee of 1/16 of 1% of the value of the fund's portfolio at each mo.-end.

Redemption Policy — Shs. are redeemable at the option of the holder at net asset value at the close of business on the day following the day of acceptance of the request for redemption. Payment will be made within 5 business days.

Timvest Bond Fund (formerly Beaubran Bond Fund) — (Estab. 1972). Open-end fund, operating as a fixed inc. invest. fund. Primary objective is inc. and security of capital through invests. in bonds and debs. of govts., institutions and corps. Qualifies as investment for RRSP and DPSP. Managers - Beaubran Management Inc., Montreal; Timmins & Assoc. Ltd., Toronto.

Purchase Plans: Lump Sum Purchases — Min. initial invest. of $200, with subsequent purchases of $50. Offering price net asset value plus acquisition charge. Open Account Plans — Min. initial invest. of $200, with subsequent monthly purchases of $50 minimum. Monthly payments through post-dated of pre-authorized cheques. RRSP — Same conditions as Lump Sum Purchases and Open Account Plans. DPSP — Details available from distributor. Systematic Withdrawal Plan — Provides for payments monthly of a special amount. Min. invest. of $10,000, and min. monthly withdrawal of $50.

Fees: No transfer or redemption fees. Lump Sum Purchases — Acquisition charge of not more than 1%. Volume discounts available on $25,000 or more. Open Account Plan — Administrative fee of 50 cents on each pre-authorized cheque. RRSP — Trustee is entitled to a $5 fee for establishing plan, and to an annual admin. charge of ½ of 1%, with a max. annual charge of $25. Termination fee is $10.

Management Fee — Manager is entitled to a monthly fee equal to 1/16% of 1% of net asset value calculated on the last business day of the month.

Timvest Income Fund (formerly Beaubran Mortgage Fund) — (Estab. 1974) Open-end fund which operates as a fixed inc. invest. fund. Primary objective is to provide inc. by investing in first mtges. Investments can also be made in securities issued or guaranteed by the governments of Canada or the provinces and in interest bearing bank accounts in any chartered bank or by deposit with a trust company. Qualifies as an invest. for RRSP and DPSP. Licensed to sell in Quebec. Managers — Beaubran Management Inc., Montreal; Timmins & Assoc. Ltd., Toronto.

Purchase Plans: Lump Sum Purchases, Open Account Plan, RRSP and DPSP — See Timvest Bond Fund for details.

Fees: No transfer or redemption fees. For fees on plans available, see Timvest Bond Fund.

Management Fee — Manager is entitled to a monthly fee equal to 1/10 of 1% of the net asset value calculated on the last business day of the month.

The Toronto-Dominion Bank

Head Off. — Toronto-Dominion Bank Centre (P.O. Box 1), Toronto, Ont. M5K 1A2. **Telephone** — (416) 866-8222.

INVESTMENT FUND

Toronto Dominion Mortgage Fund — (Estab. 1973). Open-end fund which invests primarily in mtge. insured or guaranteed by the Cdn. or provincial govts., and conventional 1st mtges. with minimum equity of 25%.Qualifies as an invest. for RRSP's and RRIF's. Licensed to sell in all provinces.

Offered at net asset value per unit on the last business day of the month in which application is made.

Fees — Administrator is entitled to a monthly fee equal to the sum of: 5/48 of 1% of the net asset value on the last business day of each month up to $10,000,000; plus 1/12 of 1% on the next $90,000,000; and 1/16 of 1% on assets over $100,000,000.

Redemption Policy — Units may be redeemed at net asset value without charge as determined on the last business day of each month provided at least 10 days' notice has been given prior to that date. A fee of 1% may be charged if units are redeemed within 60 days of purchase. The fund may require a balance of at least 25 units be maintained in each account. Payment will be made within 7 days of valuation date to the unitholder or to the RRSP trustee, as applicable. Units may be transferred into a registered retirement savings deposit instrument offered by the manager. Units will be redeemed at their net asset value without transfer fees.

Income — Income is allocated to unitholders' accounts monthly and distributed quarterly. Distributions are automatically reinvested in additional units of the fund without charge.

Trimark Investment Management Inc.

Head Off. — Suite 935, One First Canadian Place (P.O. Box 189), Toronto, Ont. M5X 1A6. **Telephone** — (416) 362-7181.

INVESTMENT FUNDS

Trimark Fund — (Ont. 1981). Open-end investment trust with the objective of strong growth of capital and a high degree of reliability over the long run. Manager — Trimark Investment Management Inc. Licensed to sell in all provinces.

Puchase Plans: (1) Lump Sum Purchases — Min. initial invest. $500. (2) Open Account Plan — Min. initial invest. $500 with min. subsequent invest. of $100. (3) Pre-Authorized Cheque Account — Regular monthly purchases having a $50 min. (5) Systematic Withdrawal Plan — Unitholders having asset value of $5,000 or more may estab. predetermined monthly or quarterly cash payments through automatic redemption of units. (5) Trimark 50/50 Plan — Based on 50 purchases over a 50-month period. Min. initial purch. $50 and min. subsequent purch. of $50 per month.

Fees — Acquisition fees not to exceed 9% of total amt. pd. by purchaser. On purchases up to $24,999 charge is 9%, then declining by steps to 1% on amts. over $1,000,000. Reduced rates apply to additional purchases. Management Fee — Payable monthly at rates equal to 1/12 of 1.75% of net assets of the funds up to $100,000,000; 1/12 of 1.5% of net assets over $100,000,000 and up to $200,000,000; 1/12 of 1.25% of net as-

The Financial Post

INFORMATION SERVICE **Survey of Funds**

Source: *The Financial Post* Information Service, "Survey of Funds," September 30, 1986.

Japan Funds   These funds, such as AGF Japan, invest all or substantially all of their assets in Japanese securities.[9]

**26-1.2
The Investors
Return From
Mutual Fund
Investing**

Investors obtain three types of income from owning mutual fund shares: (1) cash dividend or interest disbursements, denoted d, (2) capital gains disbursements, denoted c, and (3) change in the fund's net asset value (*nav*) per share from capital gains and cash dividends that were not distributed to the owners, denoted by $(nav_{t+1} - nav_t)$ for the tth period. The one-period rate of return for a mutual fund share is defined in Eq. (26-1).

$$r_t = \frac{c_t + d_t + (nav_{t+t} - nav_t)}{nav_t} \tag{26-1}$$

Mutual fund investors do not receive the entire rate of return defined in Eq. (26-1) because of two deductions. First, the fund's management fee of from 0.5 to 1.5 percent per year of the net asset value is deducted to pay the portfolio's management expenses. And second, some mutual funds, called *load funds*, deduct from 1 to 9.0 percent (the average is about 5 percent) of the mutual fund owner's original investment to pay a commission to the mutual fund salesperson. *No load funds* are mutual funds that sell their shares by mail without sales representatives and charge their investors no sales commission.

All mutual funds are called open-ended because they can keep selling more shares and thus keep growing larger as long as investors will buy more shares. Fund managers want their funds to grow larger so they can charge their management fee percentage on a larger amount of total assets and thus pay themselves higher salaries. The investment performance of actual mutual funds is analyzed later in this chapter, where the rates of return, risk, and overall performance of funds are evaluated and ranked.

**26-1.3
Closed-
Ended
Funds**

Closed-ended investment companies are like mutual funds to the extent that both are publicly owned investment portfolios. But closed-ended funds differ in several important respects. First, as their name implies, a closed-ended fund cannot sell more shares after its initial offering — thus, its growth is limited. Second, the shares of closed-ended funds are not redeemable at their net asset value,[10] as are the shares in a mutual fund. Instead, the shares of the closed-ended funds trade on stock exchanges at market prices that may be above or below their net asset values.[11] These two distinctions between

9 Global, international, U.S., and Japan funds are not RRSP eligible investments as they hold more than 10 percent of their assets in foreign securities.

10 If the fund will redeem shares on a continuous basis, the fund is called, in some countries, a unit trust; if it does not redeem shares, it is a closed-ended investment company. Unit trusts are most commonly used in Europe. *Fixed-unit investment trusts* in the United States are typically locked in portfolios; the managers secure the portfolio and freeze it for life locking in for the investor.

11 For a discussion of the prices of closed-end shares see Rex Thompson, "The Information Content Of Discounts And Premiums On Closed-End Fund Shares," *Journal of Financial Economics*, vol. 6, 1978.

closed-ended and open-ended funds are essentially the best way to define the closed-ended funds. Closed-ended funds have diversification and investment objectives that differ over a much wider range than the open-ended funds, making them very difficult to describe. Closed-ended fund shares sell at a market-determined price that is rarely the net asset value. Most typically this price is at a discount to the fund's net asset value. In the United States, for example the discount has *averaged* 10 to 20 percent in recent years.

One might immediately conclude that a well-managed fund of high quality, reasonably liquid securities, selling at a substantial discount to net asset value, represents good investment value. Such funds may be particularly valuable if the underlying portfolio contains a high proportion of dividend-paying securities, since the investor thus has a higher dividend yield than the implicit rate in the secondary market. Furthermore, the recent policy of "open-ending," i.e., groups buying closed-ended companies and receiving permission to change them to open-ended thus pushing the price directly to the net asset value, makes closed-ended funds interesting speculations.[12] But it is important to note that the discount to net asset value can prevail indefinitely.

The question of why closed-ended funds typically sell at prices other than net asset value (and usually a discount) has perplexed researchers and practioners for years. Numerous reasons have been put forth; some simplistic, others more subtle.

To explain this anomaly, we must first identify a paradox. Start with a closed-ended fund selling at a price other than net asset value. Whether it is a premium or discount, it is easy to see that this introduces an additional element of uncertainty into the investment, since the *amount (or percentage)* of the premium or discount can change over time—and presumably in random fashion. The investor thus has two sources of risk and return; that associated with the portfolio itself and that associated with the variance about the premium or discount. A fundamental concept of investments that we examined in Chap. 25, is that of risk aversion: when faced with two investments offering identical expected returns, the risk averter selects the one with the smaller risk or variance. Studies indicate that the vast majority of investors are risk averters. Thus if we compare two funds with identical portfolios, one open-ended, the other closed-ended, we would expect the closed-end fund to sell at a lower price. This is why some funds sell at a premium.

Arguments that have been put forth to explain the typical prevailing discount include the following:

1. The closed-ended fund discount reflects the cost of liquidating the portfolio and distributing the proceeds to investors. However, this cannot explain a discount of the magnitude of 10 to 20 percent, nor would it explain the differential pricing of open- and closed-ended funds since the former is also subject to (identical) liquidation costs.

---

12 See Pamela Sebastian, "Closed-End Fund Premiums Dismay Some Experts," *Wall Street Journal*, June 9, 1986, p. 31.

2. Closed-ended fund discounts reflect the implicit management/advisory fees or other expenses of the funds. If so, we would expect to find higher percentages of such expenses in the closed-ended fund over the open-ended counterpart.
3. Since commissions are typically lower for closed-ended funds than for open-ended ones, brokers have an incentive to sell the latter, thus reducing the relative demand for closed-ended funds.
4. Closed-ended funds are not promoted by a sales team, like their open-ended counterpart.
5. Closed-ended funds are not awarded the favourable tax treatments of their open-ended counterparts. This however, is certainly not the case in a number of countries.
6. Closed-ended funds have unrealized tax liabilities that must someday result in taxes payable.

These arguments are, at this stage, conjecture. And none would explain the *premium* over net asset value observed for some funds. In late 1986, for example, the Korea Fund, publicly traded in the U.S. on the New York Stock Exchange, sold for premiums over its new asset values of 45 percent while other single country closed-ended funds such as the Japan and the France funds sold at discounts.

With the recent proliferation of closed-ended fund issues, particularly specialized country offerings, the importance of further research into this phenomenon is underscored.

Table 26-1 contains a list of single country closed-ended funds and their respective premiums or discounts to net asset value as of fall, 1986.

TABLE 26-1   CLOSED-ENDED SINGLE COUNTRY FUNDS

All prices in U.S. dollars except as indicated

FUND NAME	EXCHANGE	ISSUE DATE	1986 PREMIUM (DISCOUNT) TO NET ASSET VALUE
First Australia Fund	American Stock Exchange (AMEX)	1985	−21.4%
France Fund	New York Stock Exchange (NYSE)	1986	−5.2%
Germany Fund	NYSE	1986	−10.7%
Italy fund	NYSE	1986	−27.9%
Japan fund	NYSE, Pacific Stock Exchange	1963	−27.6%
Korea Fund	NYSE	1984	34.1%
Mexico fund	NYSE	1981	−42.7%
Scandinavia Fund	AMEX	1986	−12.0%

Since closed-ended funds are essentially marketable shares of common stock, their one-period rates of return are calculated by using Eq. (2-1), just like common stock returns.

The rest of this chapter analyzes mutual fund returns data. These data are analyzed in order to show how (1) investment performance analysis can be accomplished and (2) to see if the mutual fund managers can earn returns for their investors that exceed the returns available from other investment alternatives.

26-2 RANKING FUNDS AVERAGE RETURNS

When an investor considers the purchase of shares in mutual funds, the first question to be asked is: "Can the mutual funds earn a higher return for me than I can earn for myself?" Table 26-2 shows performance data for thirty-nine U.S. mutual funds for the decade from 1951 to 1960 inclusive.[13]

Column 1 of Table 26-2 shows the average rate of return for each mutual fund. These returns are what would have been earned if a tax-exempt investor had purchased shares in each fund on January 1, 1951, held them ten years while reinvesting the dividends, and sold the shares at the end of December 1960. It will be noted that only eighteen of the mutual funds (that is, less than half of them) were able to earn a rate of return above the 14.7 percent that the investor could have expected to earn by picking stocks listed on the New York Stock Exchange with a dart or using some other naive buy-and-hold strategy.[14]

Of the thirty-nine funds, the best performance exceeded the average by only four percentage points. The data indicate that, on the average, the mutual funds did not earn returns for investors that a naive investor could not attain alone at less cost.

Columns 2 through 11 of Table 26-2 show the rankings of the thirty-nine funds' yearly rates of return. The most striking feature of the ranking is their lack of consistency. None of the thirty-nine funds was able to consistently outperform the naive buy-and-hold strategy over the decade.

Now let's examine some Canadian data. Table 26-3 sets out the ten-, five-, three-, and one-year average compounded rates of returns for a large number of Canadian mutual funds, grouped into three categories by objec-

---

13 For a ranking of mutual fund performances from 1970 to 1979, see Jack Clark Francis, *Management of Investments*, McGraw-Hill, 1983, table 27-1, p. 588.

14 A naive buy-and-hold strategy means randomly selecting securities (for example, with an unaimed dart), buying them, and holding them regardless of what information becomes available about them or the market. The naive buy-and-hold strategy is used as a standard of comparison because it represents an investment that someone with no skill should be able to earn with average luck—no unusual good luck or unusual bad luck is involved. The actual returns from a naive buy-and-hold strategy have been estimated by different researchers. See J. Lorie and L. Fisher, "Rate of Return on Investments in Common Stocks: The Year-by-Year Record, 1926-1965," *Journal of Business*, July 1968, pp. 291-316. See Table 25-1 for the actual returns. See also R. G. Ibbotson and R. A. Sinquefield, *Stocks, Bonds, Bills, and Inflation: The Past and the Future*. Charlottesville, Virginia: Financial Analysts Research Foundation, 1982. Also see *Stocks, Bonds, Bills and Inflation: 1985 Yearbook*, by Ibbotson Associates, published by the Capital Market Research Center, 8 South Michigan Avenue, Suite 707, Chicago, Illinois, 60603. See also Roger G. Ibbotson, Laurence Siegel, and Kathryn S. Love, "World Wealth: Market Values And Returns," *Journal of Portfolio Management*, Fall 1985. Also see R. G. Ibbotson, R. C. Carr, and A. W. Robinson, "International Equity And Bond Returns," *Financial Analysts Journal*, July-August 1982.

TABLE 26-2 YEAR-BY-YEAR RANKING OF INDIVIDUAL FUND RETURNS

Fund	AVERAGE ANNUAL RETURN (1)	1951 (2)	1952 (3)	1953 (4)	1954 (5)	1955 (6)	1956 (7)	1957 (8)	1958 (9)	1959 (10)	1960 (11)
Keystone Lower Price	18.7	29	1	38	5	3	8	35	1	1	36
T Rowe Price Growth	18.7	1	33	2	8	14	15	2	25	7	4
Dreyfus	18.4	37	37	14	3	7	11	3	2	3	7
Television Electronic	18.4	21	4	9	2	33	20	16	5	4	20
National Investors Corp.	18.0	3	35	4	19	27	4	5	15	8	1
De Vegh Mutual Fund	17.7	32	4	1	8	14	4	8	5	23	36
Growth Industries	17.0	7	34	14	17	9	9	20	4	6	11
Massachusetts Investors Growth	16.9	5	36	31	11	9	1	23	5	9	4
Franklin Custodian	16.5	26	2	4	13	33	20	16	15	9	4
Investment Co. of America	16.0	21	15	14	11	17	15	23	27	15	15
Chemical Fund Inc.	15.6	1	39	14	11	3	33	1	11	4	23
Founders Mutual	15.6	21	13	25	27	2	20	16	20	13	28
Investment Trust of Boston	15.6	6	3	25	8	14	26	31	25	29	20
American Mutual	15.5	14	13	4	3	14	13	16	11	25	4
Keystone Growth	15.3	29	15	25	22	1	1	39	27	13	38
Keystone High	15.2	10	7	3	1	1	36	5	27	25	11
Aberdeen Fund	15.1	32	23	9	27	23	7	10	18	7	30
Massachusetts Investors Trust	14.8	8	9	14	25	9	15	20	20	32	28
NYSE Market Average*	14.7										
Texas Fund, Inc.	14.6	3	15	9	32	23	26	5	27	37	7
Eaton & Howard Stock	14.4	14	9	4	17	20	15	13	37	29	17
Guardian Mutual	14.4	21	26	25	34	31	29	13	20	15	2
Scudder, Stevens, Clark	14.3	14	23	14	19	27	15	29	9	15	30
Investors Stock Fund	14.2	8	28	21	22	27	20	23	5	29	23
Fidelity Fund, Inc.	14.1	21	26	25	34	31	29	13	20	15	23
Fundamental Investment	13.8	14	15	31	16	9	11	31	18	25	30
Century Shares	13.5	14	28	35	25	3	20	23	31	34	2

Bullock Fund Ltd.	13.5	29	9	21	19	14	9	20	34	34	20
Financial Industries	13.0	26	15	31	13	19	29	34	20	9	35
Group Common Stock	13.0	38	8	25	27	27	33	8	20	34	17
Incorporated Investors	12.9	14	13	37	6	3	13	37	11	18	39
Equity Fund	12.9	14	27	21	32	31	33	13	31	18	23
Selected American Shares	12.8	21	15	21	31	23	20	23	15	32	30
Dividend Shares	12.7	32	7	14	34	20	32	4	37	37	11
General Capital Corp.	12.4	10	28	9	38	35	39	23	34	13	23
Wisconsin Fund	12.3	32	26	4	37	35	38	10	34	18	7
International Resources	12.3	10	37	39	22	35	1	37	39	1	11
Delaware Fund	12.1	36	23	25	27	39	26	29	9	23	30
Hamilton Fund	11.9	38	28	9	34	35	36	10	31	18	17
Colonial Energy	10.9	10	15	35	39	20	4	36	20	39	10

* The NYSE market average represents what a tax-exempt investor could have expected to earn by randomly picking (for example, with a dart) a large number of stocks listed on the NYSE and holding them 10 years while reinvesting the dividends. The data were published by L. Fisher and J. Lorie. "Rates of Return on Investments in Common Stock," *Journal of Business*, January 1964, pp. 1–21.

Source: Eugene F. Fama, "The Behavior of Stock Prices," *Journal of Business*, table 18, p. 93, January 1965.

TABLE 26-3   AVERAGE CANADIAN MUTUAL FUND PERFORMANCE RELATIVE TO AN INDEX, 1976–1986

CATEGORY/NUMBER OF FUNDS/INDEX	10 YEAR	5 YEAR	5 YEAR	1 YEAR
Equity Funds—average compounded rate of return	15.1%	13.5%	9.9%	16.3%
Number of funds	83	91	97	106
TSE 300 composite total return index	16.1%	14.0%	9.8%	16.7%
Fixed Income funds	11.6%	17.4%	13.3%	13.0%
Number of funds	59	65	66	78
McLeod Young Weir 40 Bond Index	12.5%	26.1%	18.1%	18.9%
Balanced Funds	11.2%	13.9%	8.9%	13.6%
Number of funds	7	10	11	16
Balanced index*	14.3%	20.1%	14.0%	17.8%

* Arithmetic average of TSE total return index and McLeod Young Weir 40 index.

Source: The Financial Post Information Service, "Survey of Funds," September 30, 1986.

tives, over the period 1976 to 1986. Each set of returns culminates in 1986. For example, the five-year rate of return spans the period 1981 to 1986. The average compounded rate of return is the arithmetic mean of the funds in the category. For each category a benchmark index is provided, representing a reasonable proxy for investors' alternate investment opportunities. In every case, except for the five-year returns for equity funds, the benchmark outperformed the average return of the funds in the category. These results are similar to those provided in Table 26-2 for the United States. We therefore conclude that the average or typical Canadian mutual fund does not outperform a naive buy-and-hold strategy of holding the "market" or representative index.[15]

Table 26-4, however, provides some interesting results. The annual compounded rates of return of Canadian resident International and Global Funds that had been in existence for at least ten years are presented on a ten-, five-, three-, and one-year basis for the period 1976 to 1986. The results are compared to that of the Toronto Stock Exchange 300 composite total return index, and the Standard & Poor's 500 composite total return index in Canadian dollars. Only one of the nine funds (Bolton Tremblay International) outperformed both indexes over all time periods. However, what is revealing is that the average return of the nine funds exceeded the return on the TSE over each measurement period. One can argue that the appropriate benchmark index is that of a world portfolio (such as the Morgan Stanley Capital International World Portfolio Index) that has similar characteristics to a typical

---

15 Canadian research studies of the performance of mutual funds were cited in Chap. 18. All of these studies found that Canadian mutual funds and mutual fund managers did not earn excess returns, i.e., returns in excess of that expected on a risk-adjusted basis. See A. L. Calvet and J. Lefoll, "The CAPM Under Inflation and the Performance of Canadian Mutual Funds," *Journal of Business Administration*, Fall 1980, pp. 107-117, and Dwight Grant, "The Investment Performance of Canadian Mutual Funds, 1960-1974," *Journal of Business Administration*, Fall 1976, pp. 136-145.

TABLE 26-4   CANADIAN RESIDENT INTERNATIONAL AND GLOBAL FUNDS PERFORMANCE RELATIVE TO THE TSE 300 COMPOSITE TOTAL RETURN INDEX AND THE S&P 500 TOTAL RETURN INDEX IN CANADIAN DOLLARS

FUND/INDEX	10 YEAR (%)	5 YEAR (%)	3 YEAR (%)	1 YEAR (%)
Bolton Tremblay International	20.7	25.1	22.4	36.8
Dixon Krogseth International	14.1	7.2	6.3	21.5
Eaton/Bay International	20.4	19.4	15.3	26.5
Guardian World Equity	17.6	13.7	13.4	24.0
Investors International Mutual	14.1	16.4	9.9	19.5
Montreal Trust International	16.0	19.1	18.2	36.7
Royal Trust A Fund	12.4	15.3	10.2	28.9
Templeton Growth Fund	23.1	22.1	19.6	27.6
United Accumulative	18.1	18.4	20.2	22.7
Average	17.4	17.4	15.1	27.1
TSE Composite 300 Index	16.1	14.0	9.8	16.7
S&P 500 (CDN$)	17.5	23.5	21.1	32.9

Source: *The Financial Post* Information Service, "Survey of Funds," September 30, 1986.

global or international fund. On the other hand, a Canadian investor who is contemplating the alternative of a mutual fund investment to the purchase of self-selected portfolio of *Canadian* equities might well consider examining the performance of international and global funds in light of these results.

26-3   EFFICIENCY AND RELIABILITY OF THE FUNDS' PERFORMANCES

One might question whether the mutual funds are really as poor at managing investments as the data in Tables 26-2 and 26-3 indicate. After all, they might be maximizing their returns in a very low risk-class where high returns were not available. This would mean the funds were efficient investments along the bottom portion of the efficient frontier. Figure 26-3 shows the actual performance of twenty-three mutual funds in risk-return space relative to the efficient frontier (that is, the curve EF) that existed at that time.

Figure 26-3 was prepared from monthly data on the twenty-three mutual funds from 1946 to 1956. It shows that none of the funds was an efficient asset, and only a few had average returns that were within one percentage point of the efficient frontier. It is interesting to note, however, that the funds tended to cluster into groups. The funds that sought growth and were willing to assume risk to attain it formed a cluster that tended to lie above that of the less aggressive funds, and the income-growth funds clearly lay above the risk-avoiding balanced funds. Mutual fund managers evidently are able to distinguish the risk and return characteristics of their investments and stay in some preferred risk class fairly consistently. Unfortunately, they do not all seem to be able to follow their published objectives very well.

FIGURE 26-3   Performance of 23 mutual funds from 1946 to 1956 in risk-return space.

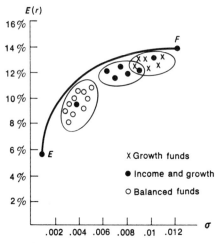

Source: Donald E. Farrar, *The Investment Decision Under Uncertainty* (Englewood Cliffs, N.J.: Prentice-Hall, 1962) p. 73.

According to the provincial securities acts, mutual funds must publish a written statement of their investment objectives and make it available to their shareholders. This objective can be changed only if the majority of the shareholders consent in advance to the new objective. These investment objectives can be classified into the following four categories.

1. Growth
2. Growth and income
3. Income and growth
4. Income, growth, and stability (called a balanced fund)

These objectives are listed in descending order with respect to the aggressiveness with which the fund's management implies it will seek high average rate of return and assume the corresponding risks.

The stated objectives that mutual funds issue to their shareholders are not dependable; that is, there is sometimes no relation between the stated investment objectives and the actual performance of some mutual funds. Although the funds shown in Fig. 26-1 tended to remain in fairly consistent risk-return groupings over time, the risk-return grouping did not align with the funds' stated objectives in some cases. As a matter of fact, quantitative risk measures give a clearer picture of the funds' investment objectives than what the fund management say in their published statements.

**26-3.1
Portfolio
Risk-
Classes**

All average rates of return for portfolios vary widely over time as the market alternates between bullish and bearish periods. Therefore, average rates of return are not satisfactory measures with which to classify mutual fund risk and return. Certain quantitative risk measures, however, are fairly stationary over time. And, since risk and return are positively related, they also furnish an indication of whether the portfolio can be expected to earn a high, medium, or low rate of return in the long run — that is, over at least one complete business cycle.

Two quantitative risk surrogates are appropriate for measuring the historical risk of portfolios. First, the standard deviation of historical rates of return may be used to measure total risk. Second, beta coefficients for portfolios from their characteristic lines (which were fit with historical data) may be used to measure systematic or undiversifiable risk. Either of these risk surrogates is satisfactory for categorizing portfolio risk. Examples of both will be explained later in this chapter.

Mutual funds' beta coefficients may be classified as explained in Table 26-5. Table 26-6 shows the relationship between the two risk surrogates and the average rates of return for 103 mutual funds. The data for these statistics were gathered from January 1960 to June 1968. Table 26-6 shows the two risk surrogates are highly positively related with each other and with the portfolios' average rates of return.

TABLE 26-5 PORTFOLIO SYSTEMATIC RISK MEASURES DEFINED

RANGE OF BETA	LEVEL OF RISK	DESCRIPTION OF PRICE VOLATILITY
.5 to .7	Low	Share prices vary about half the rate of the market index
.7 to .9	Medium	Share prices rise about 80% of the rate of the market index
.9 to 1.3	High	Share prices vary directly with the rate of change in the market index.

TABLE 26-6 RISK-RETURN RELATIONSHIPS FOR MUTUAL FUNDS

RISK CLASS	RANGE OF BETAS	NUMBER OF MUTUAL FUNDS	AVERAGE BETA	AVERAGE 2 VARIANCE σ	AVERAGE RATE OF RETURN
Low	.5 to .7	28	.619	.000877	.091 = 9.1%
Medium	.7 to .9	53	.786	.001543	.106 = 10.6%
High	.9 to 1.1	22	.992	.002304	.135 = 13.5%

Source: Irwin Friend, Marshall E. Blume, and Jean Crockett, *Mutual Funds and Other Institutional Investors: A New Perspective* (New York: McGraw-Hill, 1970), p. 150.

Table 26-7 compares portfolio published investment objectives with quantitative risk and average return statistics. It shows that the standard deviations and beta coefficients of portfolios were much better indicators of their actual performance than their published statements. The data in the table also show that the betas and standard deviations for the portfolio vary together positively.

TABLE 26-7 COMPARISON OF MUTUAL FUNDS PERFORMANCES WITH THEIR STATED OBJECTIVES JANUARY 1960 TO JUNE 1968*

	Number of funds in category				Average rate of return, %			
BETA COEFFICIENT	GROWTH	GROWTH & INCOME	INCOME & GROWTH	INCOME, GROWTH, & STABILITY	GROWTH	GROWTH & INCOME	INCOME & GROWTH	INCOME, GROWTH, & STABILITY
.5 to .7	3	5	4	16	6.9	10.1	9.7	9.1
.7 to .9	15	24	7	7	11.2	10.0	10.0	12.2
.9 to 1.1	20	1	0	1	13.8	9.5		13.5

* Investment objectives as classified by Arthur Wiesenberger Services in 1967.

Source: Irwin Friend, Marshall E. Blume, and Jean Crockett, *Mutual Funds and Other Institutional Investors: A New Perspective* (New York: McGraw-Hill, 1970), p. 150.

26-4 SHARPE'S PORTFOLIO PERFORMANCE MEASURE

In assessing the performance of a portfolio, it is necessary to consider *both* risk and return. Ranking average returns on portfolios ignores the skill with which they minimize risk and is therefore an oversimplified performance measure. Determining the relative efficiency of a portfolio (Fig. 26-1), is a more comprehensive analysis of a portfolio's performance. However, it is often desirable to be able to *rank* a portfolio's performance. The real need is for an index of portfolio performance that is determined by both the return and the risk of that portfolio. Equation (26-2) defines a single parameter portfolio performance index that calculates its index number from both the risk and return statistics.

**BOX 26-1
Sharpe's
Portfolio
Performance
Index**

Dr. William F. Sharpe has devised an index of portfolio performance, denoted S_i, which is defined in Eq. (26-2) for the ith portfolio.

$$S_i = \frac{\text{risk-premium}}{\text{total risk}} = \frac{\bar{r}_i - R}{\sigma_i} \qquad (26\text{-}2)$$

where $\bar{r}_i$ = average return on ith portfolio
σ_i = standard deviation of returns for portfolio i
R = riskless rate of interest

The numerator of Eq. (26-2) $\bar{r}_i - R$ is called the risk-premium for portfolio i. The *risk-premium* is that return over and above the riskless rate that is paid to induce investors to assume risk.

Sharpe's index of performance generates one (ordinal) number that is determined by both the risk and the return of the portfolio (or other investment) being assessed. Figure 26-4 graphically depicts Sharpe's index. S_i measures the slope of the solid line starting at the riskless rate R in Fig. 26-4 and running out to asset i. Thus $S_C > S_B > S_A$ indicates that asset C is a better

FIGURE 26-4   Sharpe's index of portfolio performance measures the ratio of risk-premium to total risk.

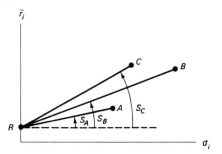

performer than asset *B,* and *B* is better than *A.* The fact that the portfolios have different average returns or risks does not hinder a direct comparison with Sharpe's performance index.[16] Sharpe gathered data on the risk and return of thirty-four mutual funds for the decade from 1954 to 1963 inclusive and ranked their performances. Table 26-8 lists the average return, standard deviation, and Sharpe's performance for the Dow Jones Industrial Average (DJIA) to use as a standard of comparison in evaluating the performance of the funds. The DJIA is a sample of thirty stocks of large, old, blue-chip firms

FIGURE 26-5   Frequency distribution of Sharpe's risk-premium-to-risk ratio for a sample of 34 mutual funds, 1954-1963.

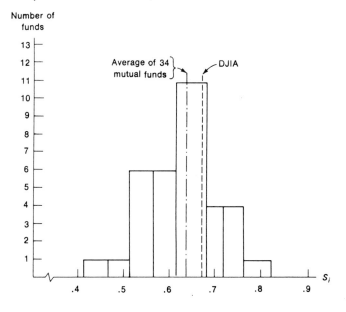

16 I. Friend and M. Blume, "Measurement of Portfolio Performance under Uncertainty," *American Economic Review,* September 1970, pp. 561-575. This study questions portfolio performance measures.

that are popular with investors. Figure 26-5 shows a frequency distribution of the S_i's for the thirty-four mutual funds listed in Table 26-8 and the DJIA.

TABLE 26-8 PERFORMANCES OF 34 MUTUAL FUNDS, 1954–1963

MUTUAL FUND	AVERAGE ANN. RETURN, %	STD. DEV. OF ANN. RETURN, %	RISK-PREMIUM* TO STD. DEV. RATIO = S_i
Affiliated Fund	14.6	15.3	.75896
American Business Shares	10.0	9.2	.75876
Axe-Houghton, Fund A	10.5	13.5	.55551
Axe-Houghton, Fund B	12.0	16.3	.55183
Axe-Houghton, Stock Fund	11.9	15.6	.56991
Boston Fund	12.4	12.1	.77842
Broad Street Investing	14.8	16.8	.70329
Bullock Fund	15.7	19.3	.65845
Commonwealth Investment Company	10.9	13.7	.57841
Delaware Fund	14.4	21.4	.53253
Dividend Shares	14.4	15.9	.71807
Eaton and Howard, Balanced Funds	11.0	11.9	.67399
Eaton and Howard, Stock Fund	15.2	19.2	.63486
Equity Fund	14.6	18.7	.61902
Fidelity Fund	16.4	23.5	.57020
Financial Industrial Fund	14.5	23.0	.49971
Fundamental Investors	16.0	21.7	.59894
Group Securities, Common Stock Fund	15.1	19.1	.63316
Group Securities, Fully Administered Fund	11.4	14.1	.59490
Incorporated Investors	14.0	25.5	.43116
Investment Company of America	17.4	21.8	.66169
Investors Mutual	11.3	12.5	.66451
Loomis-Sales Mutual Fund	10.0	10.4	.67358
Massachusetts Investors Trust	16.2	20.8	.63398
Massachusetts Investors— Growth Stock	18.6	22.7	.68687
National Investors Corporation	18.3	19.9	.76798
National Securities— Income Series	12.4	17.8	.52950
New England Fund	10.4	10.2	.72703
Putnam Fund of Boston	13.1	16.0	.63222
Scudder, Stevens & Clark Balanced Fund	10.7	13.3	.57893
Selected American Shares	14.4	19.4	.58788
United Funds— Income Funds	16.1	20.9	.62698
Wellington Fund	11.3	12.0	.69057
Wisconsin Fund	13.8	16.9	.64091

*S_i = (average return − 3 percent)/variability. The ratios shown were computed from original data and thus differ slightly from the ratios obtained from the rounded data shown in the table.

Source: William F. Sharpe, "Mutual Fund Performances," *Journal of Business,* Supplement, January 1966, p. 125.

Of the thirty-four funds shown in Fig. 26-5, eleven had risk-premium to risk ratios above the .667 of the DJIA.[17] The average of the thirty-four funds' ratio is .633, which is below .667 for the DJIA. This means that the DJIA was a more efficient portfolio than the average mutual fund in the sample. When one considers that (1) the sales commission of 8 percent paid on the purchase of mutual fund shares exceeds the commissions incurred in purchasing securities directly (that is, creating your own portfolio) and (2) the efficiency of the average mutual fund investment is below that of the DJIA, it follows that most investors would be better off by creating their own portfolios of randomly selected blue-chip stocks than buying mutual funds.

In calculating the data in Table 26-8, which are shown in Fig. 26-3, the management expenses of the mutual funds were deducted to determine net returns to the funds' investors. If the management expenses of the thirty-four funds are ignored, nineteen of them had better performance index scores than the DJIA. The sample data indicate that before management expenses, the average mutual fund performs about as well as a market average such as the DJIA, but the returns to the funds' shareholders (after the funds' operating expenses are deducted but ignoring the sales commission paid by fund investors) were less than those of the DJIA. It seems that salaries for mutual fund managers and other professional management expenses lowered the net returns to shareholders because these costs were larger than the increase in returns they generated.

26-5 TREYNOR'S PORTFOLIO PERFORMANCE MEASURE

Mr. Jack Treynor conceived an index portfolio performance that is based on systematic risk, as measured by portfolios' beta coefficients, rather than on total risk, like Sharpe's measure. To use Treynor's measure, the characteristic regression lines of portfolios must first be calculated by estimating Eq. (26-3):

$$r_{pt} = a_p + b_p(r_{mt}) + e_{pt} \quad t = 1, 2, \ldots, T \tag{26-3}$$

where r_{pt} = rate of return on pth portfolio in tth time period

$\quad\quad r_{mt}$ = return on market index in period t

$\quad\quad e_{pt}$ = random error term for portfolio p in period t

$\quad\quad a_p$ = intercept coefficient for portfolio p

$\quad\quad b_p$ = portfolio's beta coefficient

---

[17] The average return of the DJIA over the period was 16.3 percent, and its standard deviation was 19.94 percent. Thus $S_{DJIA} = (16.3 - 3)/19.94 - 13.3/19.94 = .667$. Another study of data for 38 mutual funds from 1958 to 1967 showed similar but not identical results. This study showed that only 18 out of the 38 mutual funds outperformed the Standard & Poor's (SP) 500 stocks average, but the average risk-premium to risk ratio for the 38 funds was slightly above the SP 500's ratio. K. V. Smith and D. A. Tito, "Risk Return Measures of Ex Post Portfolio Performance," *Journal of Financial and Quantitative Analysis*, December 1969, pp. 464-465.

Figure 26-6 shows typical characteristic lines for two portfolios with different management policies toward risk.

FIGURE 26-6 Characteristic lines for portfolios.

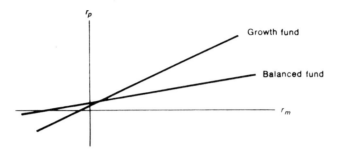

Chapter 10 discussed characteristic regression lines and the beta coefficient as an index of systematic risk in some detail. As with individual assets, the beta coefficient from a portfolio's characteristic lines is an index of the portfolio's systematic or undiversifiable risk. Using only naive diversification, the unsystematic variability of returns of the individual assets in a portfolio typically average out to zero, and the portfolio is left with only systematic risk. Therefore, Treynor suggests measuring a portfolio's return relative to its systematic risk rather than relative to its total risk, as does the Sharpe measure.

26-5.1 The Treynor Index

Equation (26-4) defines Treynor's index of portfolio performance, denoted T_p for the pth portfolio.[18]

BOX 26-2
Treynor's Portfolio Performance Index

Treynor's single parameter investment performance index number for ranking purposes is defined in equation (26-4).

$$T_p = \frac{\text{risk-premium}}{\text{systematic risk index}} = \frac{r_p - R}{b_p} \qquad (26\text{-}4)$$

where r_p = average rate of return on portfolio p

b_p = beta coefficient for portfolio p

R = riskless rate

Graphically, T_P is a measure of the slope of the line from R to the pth portfolio as shown in Fig. 26-7. As this figure demonstrates, portfolio P is more desirable than portfolio Q because P earned more risk-premium per unit of systematic risk; that is, $T_p > T_q$.

18 J. Treynor, "How to Rate Management of Investment Funds," *Harvard Business Review,* January-February 1965, pp. 63-75.

FIGURE 26-7   Treynor's portfolio performance measure in $(b_p, \bar{r}_p)$ space.

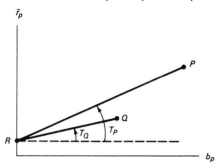

26-6   JENSEN'S PORTFOLIO PERFORMANCE MEASURE

Dr. Michael C. Jensen has modified the characteristic regression line to make it useful as a one-parameter investment performance measure.[19] The basic random variables in Jensen's model are risk-premiums, as defined in Eq. (26-5).

$$rp_{it} = r_{it} - R_t \qquad (26\text{-}5)$$

where rp_{it} = risk-premium for asset i in period t

r_{it} = one-period rate of return from asset i in time period t

R_t = riskless rate observed in period t

Jensen restates the original characteristic line of Eq. (10-6) in risk-premiums instead of returns. Equation (26-6) defines Jensen's characteristic line in risk-premium form.

$$r_{it} - R_t = A_i + B_i (r_{mt} - R_t) + u_{it} \qquad (26\text{-}6)$$

$$rp_{it} = A_i + B_i (rp_{mt}) + u_{it} \qquad (26\text{-}6a)$$

where rp_{mt} = $r_{mt} - R_t$ = risk-premium for the market portfolio (or its empirically observed surrogate) for time period t

    = the regression's explanatory variable

  A_i = alpha = ordinary least-square (OLS) regression intercept

    = Jensen's investment performance measure for the ith asset

19 M. C. Jensen, "Risk, the Pricing of Capital Assets, and the Evaluation of Investment Portfolios" Ph. D. dissertation, University of Chicago, 1968. M. C. Jensen, "The Performance of Mutual Funds in the Period 1945-64," *Journal of Finance*, vol. XXIII, no. 2, May 1968, pp. 389-416. M. C. Jensen, "Risk, the Pricing of Capital Assets and the Evaluation of Investment Portfolios, *Journal of Business*, vol. 42, April 1969, pp. 167-247.

$$B_i = \text{cov}[(r_{it} - R_t)(r_{mt} - R_t)]/\text{var}(r_{mt} - R_t), \qquad (26\text{-}7)$$
regression slope coefficient = a beta
systematic risk index

$u_{it} =$ the residual risk-premium for the ith asset
in the tth time period which is left
unexplained by the regression; it has a
zero expected value, $E(u_{it}) = 0)$

As illustrated in Fig. 26-8, the capital asset pricing model (CAPM) may be restated in terms of Jensen's beta. And even though Jensen's beta, Eq. (26-7), is different from the original beta systematic risk coefficient of Eq. (10-6), these two different betas will have very similar numerical values for the same assets.

FIGURE 26-8   Security market line (SML) in risk-premium form and several assets' investment performance.

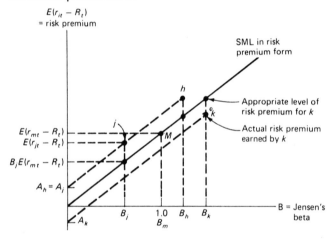

Taking the mathematical expectation of Eq. (26-6) or (26-6a) results in Eq. (26-8).

$$E(r_{it} - R_t) = A_i + B_i E(r_{mt} - R_t) \qquad (26\text{-}8)$$

since $E(u_{it}) = 0$.

Equation (26-8) is represented graphically in Fig. 26-8 as the capital asset pricing model (CAPM) reformulated in risk-premiums.

**26-6.1
Explanation
of Jensen's
Alpha
Measure**

The alpha intercept in Jensen's characteristic line in risk-premium form is a (positive, zero, or negative) regression estimate of the excess returns from the ith asset. This alpha estimates the excess returns averaged over the sample period used to estimate the characteristic line in risk-premium form regression. If the ith asset was correctly priced so that it yielded no returns either in excess of the appropriate risk-premium or less than the appropriate risk-premium, $E(r_{it} - R_t) = 0$, then the alpha intercept will have a value of zero, $A = 0$. But if the ith asset has rates of return in excess of its appropriate risk-premium, so that inequality (26-9) is true, then this ith asset's alpha intercept will be positive and will provide an empirical estimate of these excess returns averaged over the sample period used to estimate the regression.

$$\text{If } E(r_{jt} - R_t) > B_j(r_{mt} - R_t) \text{ then } A_j > 0 \tag{26-9}$$

The positive excess return, $A_j > 0$, shown in inequality (26-8), measures a vertical distance above the CAPM reformulated in risk-premium form. This quantity is the jth asset's excess returns; it is depicted graphically in Fig. 26-8. Essentially, any individual asset or portfolio that has a positive alpha has earned an average rate of return over the sampled period that exceeds what is appropriate for its level of systematic risk.

If the kth asset is incorrectly overpriced so that it yields risk-premiums that are inappropriately low for its level of systematic risk over some sample period, this asset's alpha will be negative, $A_k < 0$, for a regression estimated over that sample period. This unhappy situation is mathematically specified by inequality (26-10). The inadequate return situation represented by inequality (26-10) is illustrated in Fig. 26-8 too.

$$\text{If } E(r_{kt} - R_t) < B_k E(r_{mt} - R_t) \text{ then } A_k < 0 \tag{26-10}$$

The alpha regression intercept term in Jensen's characteristic line reformulated in risk-premiums can be used to evaluate the investment performance of assets. For example, if the jth asset outperformed the market, as represented by $A_j > 0$, if asset M earned returns that were exactly appropriate for its level of systematic risk, $A_M = 0$, and if the kth asset performed poorly, $A_k < 0$, then the three assets investment performances could be ranked as shown in inequality (26-11).

$$A_j > 0 = A_M > A_k \tag{26-11}$$

First, consider two assets named h and j. Suppose these two assets' excess returns measured over the same sample period are identical, that is, $A_h = A_j$. Further, suppose that asset h has more systematic risk than asset j, $B_h > B_j$, as shown in Fig. 26-8. Could it be concluded that these two assets performed equally well simply because their alphas are identical? The answer is negative. To see why, reconsider Treynor's investment performance ranking device, defined in Eq. (26-12).

26-6.2 Two Caveats About Jensen's Alpha Measures

$$T_j = \frac{E(r_{jt} - R_t)}{B_j} > \frac{E(r_{ht} - R_t)}{B_h} = T_h \tag{26-12}$$

Equation (26-11) utilizes Treynor's performance ranking device to show that asset j's performance surpassed asset h's performance, although their Jensen alpha measures were identical, $A_j = A_h$. The teaching point here is that Jensen's alpha cannot be used to *rank* the performance of different assets unless it is risk adjusted. Inequality (26-13) shows how to risk adjust Jensen's alpha —by dividing it by beta to make it suitable for performance ranking purposes.

$$\text{Risk-adjusted alphas:} \frac{A_j}{B_j} > \frac{A_h}{B_h} \tag{26-13}$$

Thus the first caveat is against using Jensen's alpha for ranking purposes. Jensen's alpha has asset-pricing implications, and it measures excess returns empirically. But it is not suitable for ranking purposes until it has been divided by beta.

The second caveat is about the interpretation of the alpha intercept term from the original characteristic line, which is estimated with rates of return rather than risk-premium, that is, a_i in Eq. (10-6). This original alpha is different from Jensen's alpha, $a_i \neq A_i$. More important, the original alpha should not be used for investment performance evaluation; it has no direct asset-pricing implications.[20]

26-7 McDONALD'S EMPIRICAL RESULTS

Using 120 monthly rates of return from the decade 1960 to 1969, Dr. John G. McDonald analyzed the performance of 123 mutual funds. The Sharpe and Treynor performance measures were used in the slightly reformulated manner shown in Eqs. (26-2a) and (26-4a) below.

$$S_P = \frac{E(r_{pt} - R_t)}{\sigma_P} \tag{26-2a}$$

$$T_P = \frac{E(r_{pt} - R_t)}{b_p} \tag{26-4a}$$

Dr. McDonald used monthly observations of the 30-day commercial paper rate as a surrogate for the riskless rate; this is why the R's in Eqs. (26-2a) and (26-4a) have subscripts of t for $t = 1, 2, \ldots, 120$ months. These monthly observations of R_t were subtracted from each portfolio's monthly rate of return to obtain monthly risk-premiums, denoted $r_{pt} - R_t$. Then the average risk-premium, denoted $E(r_{it} - R_t)$ over the 120 months, was divided by the appropriate risk measure to compare the portfolios' performances. Table 26-9 shows a summary of the statistics.

McDonald found that, on average, the funds with more aggressive objectives took more risk and earned higher returns, as was found earlier (see Table 26-6) in the Friend-Blume-Crockett study. The McDonald study also found that a few funds departed from their stated objective; similar results were reported (see Table 26-7) in the Friend-Blume-Crockett study and elsewhere.

Concerning the investment performance of the 123 funds, McDonald's study reported that slightly over half the 123 mutual funds (that is, 67 out of 123) had values for Treynor's performance index that exceeded the stock market average. Using Sharpe's performance measure, about 31.7 percent

20 See J. Michael Murphy, "Why No One Can Tell Who's Winning," *Financial Analysts Journal*, May-June, 1980, pp. 49-57 for another critique of the alpha measure.

TABLE 26-9 PORTFOLIO PERFORMANCE STATISTICS, 1960–1969, FOR 123 MUTUAL FUNDS

FUND'S STATED OBJECTIVE (SAMPLE SIZE)	AVERAGE BETA	AVERAGE STD. DEV.	AVERAGE E(r − R)	AVERAGE SHARPE	AVERAGE TREYNOR	AVERAGE JENSEN
Maximum capital gain (18)	1.22	5.90	.693	.117	.568	.122
Growth (33)	1.01	4.57	.565	.124	.560	.099
Growth income (36)	.90	3.93	.476	.121	.529	.058
Income growth	.86	3.80	.398	.105	.463	.004
Balanced (12)	.68	3.05	.214	.070	.314	−.099
Income (12)	.55	2.67	.252	.094	.458	−.002
Total sample (123)	.92	4.17	.477	.133	.510	0
Market average				.133	.510	

Source: John G. McDonald, "Objectives and Performance of Mutual Funds," *Journal of Financial and Quantitative Analysis,* June 1974, table 1, p. 319.

(that is, 39 out of 123) of the funds outperformed the stock market average. Thus, using a slightly different specification of the Sharpe and Treynor portfolio performance measures—and a more recent sample—did not yield any significantly different conclusions. On average, mutual funds perform about as well as a naive buy-and-hold strategy. All the studies of mutual fund performance reach essentially the same conclusions.

26-8 COMPARING INVESTMENT PERFORMANCE MEASURES

The Treynor, Sharpe, and Jensen investment performance measures may be compared and contrasted from several perspectives.

The Sharpe measure is suitable for evaluating portfolios; it is less appropriate for evaluating the performance of individual assets because it measures total risk instead of systematic risk. Stated differently, Sharpe's measure evaluates assets relative to the capital market line (CML) that is only a portfolio pricing model, while the Treynor and Jensen measures are formulated in the capital asset pricing model (CAPM) context that analyzes both portfolios and individual assets. Thus, the Treynor and Jensen measures are more suitable for a wider range of performance evaluation problems than the Sharpe measure.

Equation (26-6) is suitable to evaluate the performance of both portfolios and individual assets. If the asset is priced correctly, then the $[B_i, E(r_i - R)]$ pairs from equation (26-6) for all assets should fit on the CAPM of equation (26-8). Jensen's alpha can be viewed as a measure of disequilibrium in equation (26-8).

Treynor's single-parameter performance measure can be derived from equation (26-8) by dividing both sides of that equation by its beta to obtain equation (26-14).

26-8.1 Algebraic Relationships

$$T_i = E(r_i - R)/B_i = A_i/B_i + E(r_m - R) \tag{26-14}$$

Equation (26-8) shows that the Treynor is simply a positive linear transformation of Jensen's measure since the $E(r_m - R)$ term is a constant over all assets. Sharpe's portfolio performance measure may also be derived from equation (26-8) by substituting the definition of the beta coefficient from equation (26-15) into equation (26-8) as shown in equation (26-8a).

$$B_i = (\sigma_m)(\sigma_i)(\rho_{im})/(\sigma_m{}^2) \text{ by definition} \tag{26-15}$$

$$E(r_i - R) = A_i + [(\sigma_m)(\sigma_i)(\rho_{im})/(\sigma_m{}^2)]E(r_m - R) \tag{26-8a}$$

For portfolios that are well-diversified $\rho_{im} \cong + 1.0$. Therefore we can drop the correlation coefficient from equation (26-8a) for well-diversified portfolios, and, after also dividing it by σ_i, we obtain Sharpe's portfolio performance measure, equation (26-16).

$$S_i = E(r_i - R)/\sigma_i = A_i/\sigma_i + E(r_m - R)/(\sigma_m) \tag{26-16}$$

Since the $E(r_m - R)/(\sigma_m)$ term is constant over all assets, Sharpe's portfolio performance measure is shown to be an approximately positive linear transformation of Jensen's alpha measure. Explicitly, Sharpe's S_i = Jensen's A_i/σ_m + (constant).

A final comparison can be made between T_i and S_i by remembering that $T_i = E(r_i - R)/B_i$ and substituting $(\sigma_m) (\sigma_i) (\rho_{im}) = B_i$. This algebra results in $T_i = E(r_i - R)/[(\sigma_i) (\rho_{pm})]\sigma_m$, so for well-diversified portfolios that have $\rho_{im} \cong + 1.0$ we have the approximation shown in equation (26-17).

$$T_i \cong S_i\sigma_m \tag{26-17}$$

Equation (26-17) shows that S_i and T_i are approximately linear transformations of each other, too. Sharpe confirmed this result in an empirical study where he found that S_i and T_i were .97 correlated with each other over a sample of thirty-four mutual funds.[21]

26-8.2 General Discussion of the Performance Measurement Tools

When analyzing and comparing the merits of alternative investments, two classes of problems are usually considered—selectivity problems and timing problems.[22]

Selectivity problems   This asset specific category of problems focuses on information that is idiosyncratic to individual assets. The Sharpe, Treynor, and Jensen evaluation tools are well-suited for analyzing this class of problems.

---

[21] William F. Sharpe, "Mutual Fund Performances," *Journal of Business*, Supplement, January 1966, page 125.

[22] A third class of problems that is considered less frequently is how to evaluate the performance of returns from a non linear model (such as a call option that is deep in the money) using linear tools (such as the CAPM). Some intractable problems arise with this third class of investment evaluations.

Timing problems   This category of problems focuses on how particular investment assets react or adapt to changes in the state of nature. These problems cannot be analyzed within the framework provided by the Treynor, Sharpe, and Jensen evaluation tools unless the underlying theoretical framework (namely, the CML and/or CAPM) is extended.[23]

26-9   EVALUATING INVESTMENT TIMING DECISIONS

In an effort to discern whether or not some portfolio managers were able to foresee the market's bullish up-turns and the bearish down-turns, Treynor and Mazuy[24] reformulated the characteristic regression line with a second-order term added, as shown in equation (26-18).

$$r_{it} = a_i + b_{1i} (r_{mt}) + b_{2i} (r_{mt}^2) + e_{it} \tag{26-18}$$

where equation (26-18) is a time-series multiple regression model estimated over $t = 1, 2, \ldots, T$ time periods,

r_{it} = rate of return from investment i in tth time period,

r_{mt} = return on market index in period t,

e_{it} = random error term for investment i in period t,

a_i = intercept coefficient for investment i,

b_{1i} = beta coefficient for market returns from investment i, and,

b_{2i} = beta coefficient for squared market returns from investment i.

---

23 The arbitrage pricing theory (APT) model is somewhat more suitable to analyzing timing-oriented problems than the CAPM because the APT admits multiple explanatory variables. The APT can thus analyze new states of nature as one of the explanatory variables. The APT is discussed in Chap. 28.

   For a highly pro-CAPM discussion see David Mayers and Edward Rice, "Measuring Portfolio Performance And The Empirical Content Of Asset Pricing Models." *Journal of Financial Economics*, March 1979, pp. 3-28. For an extremely anti-CAPM discussion see Richard Roll, "A Critique Of The Asset Theories Tests, Part I: On Past And Potential Testability Of The Theory," *Journal of Financial Economics*, March 1977, pp. 129-176. For an analysis that reports both shortcomings and strengths of the CAPM see Philip H. Dybvig and Stephen A. Ross, "Differential Information And Performance Measurement Using A Security Market Line (aka CAPM)," *Journal of Finance*, vol. XL, no. 2, June 1985, pp. 383-399.

   For details about market timing studies see Roy D. Henriksson and Robert C. Merton, "On Market Timing And Investment Performance, II. Statistical Procedure For Evaluating Forecasting Skills," *Journal of Business*, October 1981, vol. 54, pp. 513-533. See also Roy D. Henriksson, "Market Timing And Mutual Fund Performance: An Empirical Investigation," *Journal of Business*, vol. 57, January 1984, pp. 73-96. Also see Ravi Jagannathan and Robert A. Korajczyk, "Assessing The Market Timing Performance Of Managed Portfolios," Part 1, *Journal of Business*, vol. 59, no. 2, April 1986, pp. 217-235.

24 Jack L. Treynor and Kay K. Mazuy, "Can Mutual Funds Outguess the Market?" *Harvard Business Review*, vol. 44, no. 4, July-August 1966, pp. 131–36. F. J. Fabozzi and J. C. Francis, "Mutual Fund Systematic Risk for Bull and Bear Markets: An Empirical Examination," *Journal of Finance*, vol. 34, no. 5, December 1979, pp. 1243–50.

Suppose that the ith asset is a mutual fund managed by a person who is able to predict bull- and/or bear-market conditions. In order to maximize this portfolio's gains, this gifted portfolio manager shifts the portfolio into high beta securities as bull markets begin. Then, when the bullish advance is complete and a bearish decline is starting, the manager will liquidate the high beta assets and buy low beta securities (and/or sell high beta assets short) to further profit from his superior *market timing* abilities. As a result of such adept investment timing decisions, the portfolio would have $b_{2i} > 0$. In contrast, if the portfolio manager were unsuccessful in his attempts to outguess the market turns, b_{2i} would equal zero (and not be significantly different from zero, statistically speaking).

Treynor and Mazuy estimated equation (26-18) for fifty-seven mutual funds —thirty-two balanced funds and twenty-five growth funds—over ten annual returns. After finding that fifty-six of these mutual funds had $b_{2i} = 0$ and only one had a slightly positive value for b_{2i}, Treynor and Mazuy concluded that none of the mutual funds in their sample had the ability to foresee either bull- or bear-market conditions. Essentially, all fifty-seven of the mutual funds appeared to have linear characteristic regression lines that fit their data better than the curvilinear model shown at Eq. (26-18).

26-10   CONCLUSIONS

The preceding discussion explained certain risk-return portfolio performance tools. These tools were applied to mutual funds to provide examples of their use. Some conclusions can be drawn regarding mutual funds and the tools used to evaluate portfolio performance.

26-10.1 Conclusions About Mutual Fund Investing

The preceding portfolio performance analysis of mutual funds suggests that many investors who own or are considering buying mutual fund shares could expect higher rates of return and less risk if they invested their own funds by selecting securities blindly with a dart and then simply holding them. This statement does not mean that all mutual fund shares represent poor investment decisions. Mutual funds can perform some valuable services for some investors.

Consider an average, amateur investor who has $3,000 or less to invest. If we suppose that this small investor will purchase only round lots (to avoid paying the higher odd-lot trading cost) and that the securities have an average cost of $15 per share, this investor would probably be well-advised to invest in a good mutual fund. Such an investor would be able to buy only two securities, as the following computations show.

$15 × 100 shares = $1,500 per round lot

$3,000 total investment = ($1,500 per round lot) × (2 round lots)

Since two is too few securities to minimize the portfolio's unsystematic portion of total risk, this investor would probably look for a mutual fund. Furthermore, the small private investor cannot usually find time and/or does not have the skills needed to perform the economic and financial analysis that should precede any investment decision.

Although mutual funds do not typically earn high rates of return, they are usually able to reduce their risk to the systematic level of the market fluctuations. So, the fortunes of a mutual fund investor are not tied to the fortunes of only a few individual securities. Therefore, unless investors have the resources at their disposal to perform Markowitz diversification (namely, access to an electronic digital computer, a data file for many securities, and the ability to analyze data with the computer), they might be better off investing in a mutual fund.

The majority of mutual funds earn long-run average rates of return that exceed the returns paid by insured savings accounts. Thus, investors receive some added return for assuming risk (unless they are forced to liquidate their holdings in a period of depressed prices).

Finally, mutual funds can help an investor stay in some preferred risk-class (although that risk-class is not necessarily the one the fund says it will pursue in its statement of investment objectives). By examining mutual funds' quantitative risk coefficients, an investor can find a fund that will fairly consistently maintain a given level of risk. Table 26-5 explained the risk implications of various portfolio risk measures. As mentioned before, mutual funds do tend to stay in a given risk-class and select assets that earn a mediocre return for that level of risk.[25] This is a valuable service that amateur or part-time investors might not be able to provide for themselves.

26-10.2 Conclusions About Portfolio Performance Measures

Ranking portfolio yearly rates of return reveals whether any of them are consistently able to outperform their competitors. However, such rankings may make an efficient low-risk portfolio appear to be doing poorly. To evaluate a portfolio adequately, the level of risk it assumes must be considered *with* its rate of return. Unfortunately, some portfolio managers' statements about the degree of risk (and concurrent expected returns) they will seek are sometimes erroneous. In contrast, empirically measured risk coefficients of portfolios furnish more stationary indexes of the level of risk a portfolio undertakes. If the standard deviation is used, portfolio standard deviations and average rates of return may be plotted in $[o, E(r)]$ space and compared with the efficient frontier. Sharpe's index of portfolio performance measures the risk-premium per unit of risk borne by individual portfolios. This index considers both risk and return and yields one index number for each portfolio; these index numbers may be used to rank the performances of a group of portfolios or individual assets.

Some analysts prefer Treynor's portfolio performance measure because systematic risk is more relevant than total risk in certain applications and because Treynor's measure can be used to compare both individual assets

25 R. S. Carlson, ''Aggregate Performance of Mutual Funds, 1948-1967,'' *Journal of Financial and Quantitative Analysis*, March 1970, pp. 1-32. T. Kim, ''An Assessment of the Performance of Mutual Fund Management: 1969-1975,'' *Journal of Financial and Quantitative Analysis*, vol. 13, no. 3, pp. 385-407, September 1978.

and portfolios. On the other hand, Treynor's performance measure has the disadvantage that it is sensitive to the market index used, and it is not clear which market index is "best." The Treynor index uses portfolio beta systematic risk coefficients and average returns to compare portfolio performance in [b,E(r)] space. The Treynor, Jensen, and Sharpe investment performance measures all tend to rank mutual funds similarly.

26-10.3 Conclusions About Portfolio Management Practices

There are several common traps a portfolio manager may fall into that can shackle the portfolio's performance. An aimless search for undervalued securities is not likely to yield returns that exceed those that could be attained by using a naive buy-and-hold strategy (unless the portfolio manager resorts to illegal practices like using inside information). So the portfolio manager should try to limit the portfolio's holdings to a small number of securities so that each one may be watched carefully. Superfluous diversification across dozens of securities is not good diversification, and it reduces the portfolio's flexibility and diminishes the portfolio's expected return. Portfolio management could benefit from an accurate, detailed economic forecast to improve both the selectivity and timing aspects of investment decisions. Such an economic forecast will reveal the growth industries in the economy and furnish various indicators that are necessary to allocate capital in an optimal manner. Finally, a good economic forecast will provide advance warning of economic downturns and thus of the bear markets that precede them. This advance notice will allow the portfolio manager to shift the portfolio's assets to financial instruments that are advantageous to hold in a bear market. In order to be efficient, a portfolio's funds must be shifted among various unrelated securities (such as stocks, bonds, options, and precious metals) in order to take full advantage of Markowitz diversification and to maximize the expected return. Judging from the performance statistics reviewed above, all mutual fund managers have room for improvement.[26]

QUESTIONS

1. "Closed-end investment companies redeem their shares at the current net asset value." Is this statement true, false, or uncertain? Explain.
2. How is the income of an open-end investment company taxed?
3. "Rankings of portfolios' average returns show that, although the average mutual fund does not outperform the market, a few truly superior funds consistently beat the market." Is this statement true, false, or uncertain? Explain.
4. Why is ranking mutual funds by their rates of return a poor way to evaluate their performance?
5. How well does the mutual fund industry perform relative to some naive buy-and-hold strategy?

---

26 For an analysis of the principal-agent sharing rule problems that arise when portfolio managers are hired to manage investments, see Sudipto Bhattacharya, "Delegated Portfolio Management," *Journal of Economic Theory*, vol. 36, 1985, pp. 1-25.

6. Assume you have been put in charge of a mutual fund with a large staff of fundamental analysts and millions of dollars of assets spread over more than 100 different securities. The fund's gross return is about average for the industry, but its management expenses are high, so its net yield to its investors is slightly below average. The previous management did not try to specialize as a growth or safety fund, but ran the firm as a general-purpose fund. What do you plan to do with your fund? Explain why.

7. Consider the following investment advice: "Put your money in the trust department of a good trust company. Trust companies will manage your investments better than the mutual funds, and they won't charge you a load fee." Is this statement true, false, or uncertain? Explain.

8. Consider the following summary statistics about five investment portfolios.

PORTFOLIO	AVERAGE RETURN	STANDARD DEVIATION	BETA
Alpha (A)	7%	3	0.4
Beta (B)	10%	8	1.0
Gamma (γ)	13%	6	1.1
Delta (Δ)	15%	13	1.2
Epsilon (E)	18%	15	1.4

Assume that the riskless rate of interest is 3.0 percent.

a. Which of the portfolios performed the best according to Sharpe's measure? The worst?

b. Which performed the best according to Treynor's performance measure? The worst?

c. Assume that the riskless rate of interest was 6.0 percent. Under this new assumption, which portfolio ranks the best according to Sharpe's measure? According to Treynor's measure? Show your calculations and draw graphs to illustrate the work. Label all variables in your calculations and graphs.

SELECTED REFERENCES

Fama, E. F. "Components of Investment Performance." *Journal of Finance*, June 1972, pp. 551-568. This paper uses mathematical statistics to analyze and extend the Sharpe and Treynor portfolio performance evaluation tools.

Jensen, Michael C. "The Performance of Mutual Funds in the Period 1945-64."*Journal of Finance*, May 1968, pp. 389-416. An analysis of the performance of mutual funds which uses regression analysis.

Sharpe, William F. "Mutual Fund Performance." *Journal of Business*, Supplement on Security Prices, January 1966, pp. 119-138. This risk-return analysis of mutual fund performance uses correlation, regression, and statistical inference.

Alexander, Gordon and Jack Clark Francis. *Portfolio Analysis*, 3rd ed. Prentice-Hall, 1986. Chapter 13 uses advanced statistics and discusses different investment performance evaluation techniques and problems.

27 Multiperiod Wealth Maximization*

The portfolio management process presented in Chaps. 23, 24, and 25 is a "one-period" form of analysis. At the beginning of each period the following portfolio management process must be repeated.

Step one: *Security analysts* prepare estimates of the one-period risk and return statistics for every asset that is an investment candidate.

Step two: The *portfolio analyst* uses Markowitz portfolio analysis (explained in Chap. 23) to delineate the one-period efficient frontier from all the individual assets' risk and return statistics.

Step three: *Portfolio selection* is made by choosing one of the portfolios on the efficient frontier and making a one-period investment in it.

The length of the one period that a Markowitz efficient portfolio is designed to span is arbitrary. One or two years is a likely length of time for the period to encompass, however, because it is difficult to estimate the risk and return statistics over very short or very long time periods. After the portfolio management staff defines the length of their planning horizon period, the risk and return statistics for every individual asset that is being analyzed must be estimated for this *single period*.

Since security analysts have increasing difficulty as they try to estimate expected risk and return statistics further in the future, the length of one period cannot be extended indefinitely. It is difficult to imagine predicting, for example, a security's expected risk and return statistics as far as five years ahead. And ten year forecasts are even more unimaginable. So, what does the portfolio manager do in the *long run*?

When the one-period planning horizon on which a portfolio is constructed comes to its end, the old portfolio must almost always be *revised* for several reasons. First, more current information has probably caused the security analysts to revise their input statistics on which the single-period portfolio analysis is based. Second, even if no new information causes the efficient frontier to be revised, price changes and the receipt of cash dividends and coupon interest have passively modified the weights of the assets held in the

---

* Chapter 27 presumes a knowledge of Chaps. 23, 24, 25, and 26 and Mathematical App. F.

portfolio. So, long-term investing requires that the one-period portfolio analysis be performed every year or so to calculate the weights in the new efficient portfolios, and then a new portfolio must be selected from the revised efficient frontier. The question to which Chap. 27 addresses itself is: "What kind of investment management policy is appropriate for long-run investing over *multiple periods?*" For example, suppose you should inherit millions of dollars at the age of twenty and you expect to bequeath it to charity when you are seventy years old. Or suppose you are involved in the management of a multimillion-dollar portfolio for a life insurance company, and it is not expected that any of this portfolio need be liquidated within the next two decades. In such real-life situations that involve decades—that is, they clearly involve *multiple periods*—the question naturally arises as to whether the *one-period* Markowitz portfolio analysis procedure is relevant. And if the Markowitz model is relevant for multiple-period investment management, how is portfolio analysis over one period applied to multiple periods?

27-1 UTILITY OF TERMINAL WEALTH

The proper multiperiod or long-run investment policy is assumed to be the one that will maximize the investor's utility (that is, happiness) from his or her consumption in each period, as shown in Eq. (27-1).

$$\max U(C_1, C_2, \ldots, C_T) \tag{27-1}$$

The symbol C_t denotes consumption in the tth period, and the Tth period is the terminal period or last period. For the average person, C_1 and C_2 would probably involve more wining and dining and less geriatric medical care than C_T, for example. Since a person's acquisition of wine, companionship, and geriatric medical care can be expedited with money, economists typically assume that maximizing a person's wealth in each period is equivalent to maximizing the utility from consumption.

If a person owns a portfolio of securities and other market assets, he or she can obtain money for consumption purposes in each period by liquidating part of these assets to finance current consumption.[1] Therefore, let us make the simplifying assumption that investing in order to maximize the terminal value w_T of a portfolio at the end of T periods (for example, at the end of someone's lifetime or at the end of an insuranace company's long-run planning horizon), as shown in Eq. (27- 2a), is equivalent to maximizing utility of consumption, Eq. (27-1).[2] Equation (27-2a) represents this long-run investment objective.

$$\max U(w_T) \tag{27- 2a}$$

---

[1] By pledging the portfolio as collateral, the investment owner can borrow about as much as the portfolio's current value. However, borrowing against an asset involves penalty costs, which complicate the analysis. Since the owner can simply liquidate part of the portfolio to finance consumption, this simpler alternative is employed.

[2] The relationship between consumption and investment decisions over multiple periods is analyzed by E. F. Fama, "Multiperiod Consumption-Investment Decisions," *American Economic Review*, March 1970, pp. 163-174

The investor's *beginning wealth* at time period $t = 0$ may be denoted w_0. This allows Eq. (27-2a) to be rewritten equivalently as Eq. (27- 2b), since $w_T = w_0(1 + r)^T$, where r denotes the *average compounded rate of return* over T periods.

$$\max U[w_0(1 + r)^T] = \max [U(w_T)] \qquad (27\text{-}2b)$$

In the world of uncertainty, an investor cannot expect to foresee the future clearly. Therefore, *expected* (rather than known with certainty) utility must be maximized to acknowledge the existence of risk. This is represented by rewriting Eq. (27-2b) with an expectation operator (discussed in Mathematical App. B and the appendix to Chap. 25), as shown in Eq. (27-3a).

$$\max E[U(w_T)] = \max E\{U[w_0(1 + r)^T]\} \qquad (27\text{-}3a)$$

**27-1.1
Geometric
Mean Return**

The compounded rate of return r equals the geometric mean of the T one-period rates of return r_t for $t = 1, 2,...,T$, as shown in Eqs. (27- 4a) and (27-4b). (See Mathematical App. F at the end of this book for a more detailed explanation of the *geometric mean return*.)

$$(1 + r)^T = \frac{w_T}{w_0} \qquad (27\text{-}4a)$$

$$= (1 + r_1)(1 + r_2)\ldots(1 + r_T) \qquad (27\text{-}4b)$$

Equation (27-4a) shows that maximizing the geometric mean return is *equivalent* to maximizing the ratio of terminal wealth over beginning wealth. Essentially, maximizing the geometric mean also maximizes terminal wealth.

Since the geometric mean return as defined in Eq. (27- 4a) is a factor in the utility-of-wealth function, Eq. (27- 3a), it can be seen that increases either in terminal wealth or in the geometric mean return help increase the investor's expected utility. And in the special case in which initial wealth w_0 is a fixed constant that is separable and independent from the geometric mean return, maximizing the geometric mean is equivalent to maximizing the investor's expected utility of terminal wealth. In fact, w_0 is separable and independent of r if the investor's utility is logarithmic.[3]

---

3 Separability occurs in log utility functions
$$U(w) = \ln (w)$$
as shown in Eq. (27-5c). For an analysis of these cases, see E. J. Elton and M. J. Gruber, "On the Optimality of Some Multi-Period Portfolio Selection Models," *Journal of Business*, April 1974, pp. 231-243.

Other cases are analyzed by Samuelson and Merton: Paul A. Samuelson, "Lifetime Portfolio Selection by Dynamic Stochastic Programming," *Review of Economics and Statistics*, August 1969, pp. 239-246; and Robert C. Merton, "Lifetime Portfolio Selection under Uncertainty: The Continuous Time Case," ibid., pp. 247-257. The papers by Merton and Samuelson are companion pieces.

For the sake of concreteness, assume utility equals the logarithm of wealth, or equivalently, the logarithm of returns. The investor's beginning wealth w_0 is separable from the rate of return r as shown in Eq. (27-5c).

27-1.2 Logarithmic Utility of Terminal Wealth

$$U(w_T) = \ln(w_T) \qquad (27\text{-}5a)$$

$$= \ln[w_0(1 + r^T)] \qquad 27\text{-}5b)$$

$$= \ln(w_0) + T[\ln(1 + r)] \qquad (27\text{-}5c)$$

Since the rate of return is *separable* from wealth, this shows that at least the Markowitz procedure of confining the analysis to the rate of return and ignoring the dollar value of the investor's wealth is logical and satisfactory for logarithmic utility functions.

As the analysis focuses explicitly on the log utility function, the plausibility of this popular form is reviewed before proceeding further. Figure 27-1 shows a graph of Eq. (27-5a). This utility function is realistic because, first, it exhibits positive marginal utility of wealth. That is, more terminal wealth always increases utility; this means that investors never get tired of more wealth.

FIGURE 27-1   The natural or Naperian logarithm utility function of terminal wealth.

w_T	$U = \ln(w_T)$
$1	0 utils
5	1.60
10	2.30
100	4.60
500	6.21
2,000	7.59
10,000	9.20
100,000	11.50
250,000	12.42
1,000,000	13.80

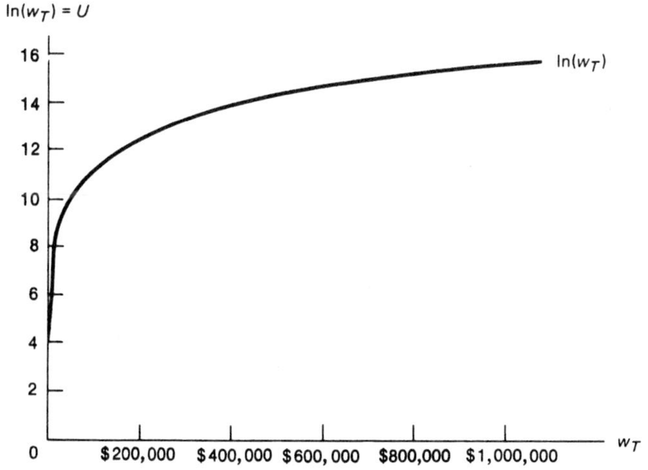

Second, utility function Eq. (27-5a) is realistic because it has diminishing marginal utility of wealth. In other words, each additional wealth increment increases its recipient's happiness less than each preceding increment of the same size. The log utility function possesses other properties that are desirable for analysis, too.[4]

**27-1.3
Positive
Linear
Transfor-
mations**

The log utility function yields an invariant preference ordering over a set of objects (for example, investments) if the function undergoes any positive linear transformation. That is, if a and b are positive constants, Eq. (27-6a) is true.

$$\text{Preference ordering } [\ln (w_T)] = \text{preference ordering } [a + b \ln (w_T)] \quad (27\text{-}6a)$$

For a more pragmatic and relevant example of transformations that leave the preference ordering invariant, consider the positive constant initial wealth, w_0. If w_0 is subtracted from w_T and the difference is divided by w_0, this is a positive linear transformation of the basic random variable w_T. As shown in Eq. (27-7), it transforms the random variable terminal wealth into a rate of change in wealth or one-period rate of return.

$$r = \frac{w_T - w_0}{w_0} \quad (27\text{-}7)$$

Equation (27-7) means that ranking investments based on the log of their expected terminal values or their expected returns will yield identical preference rankings. This is summarized succinctly in Eq. (27-6b).

$$\text{Preference ordering } [U(\ln \{w_T\})] = \text{preference ordering } [U(\ln \{r\})] \quad (27\text{-}6b)$$

Other positive linear transformations can be used to vary the shape of the log utility function. The logarithmic utility function can even be transformed to create approximations of nonlogarithmic utility functions.[5] Therefore, the conclusions obtained here with the log utility function are also roughly true for some other classes of utility functions—most particularly, the quadratic utility function. That is, in spite of the fact that a mathematical economist can prove that a quadratic and a logarithmic utility function yield different investment preferences, for example, these differences might be so slight or might be present in such extreme cases that a business investment executive would never notice or encounter them. Furthermore, many business invest-

---

4 J. W. Pratt, ''Risk Aversion in the Small and in the Large,'' *Econometrica*, April 1964, pp. 122- 136.

5 Harry Markowitz, *Portfolio Selection*, New York: Wiley, 1959, pp. 120-125. Markowitz shows how the quadratic function can approximate the log function. In particular, he shows that the following equation is a very close approximation over the range of relevant returns.
$\ln (1 + r) = r - .5r^2$

ment decisions are made by committees, and it is not possible to specify one utility function for a group of people. Thus, selecting efficient portfolios must be done without reference to a utility function for group decision making.

Regardless of the numerous business situations for which utility analysis is inappropriate, it is still useful for analyzing the logic of various economic decisions. So, to gain more insights into the proper long-term investment strategy, log utility function Eq. (27- 5a) is rewritten in terms of the one-period rates of return below.

Substituting the logarithmic Eq. (27-5b) into the investor's long-term expected utility objective function Eq. (27- 3a) produces Eq. (27-3b)

$$\max E[U(w_T)] = \max E\{U[w_0(1 + r)^T]\} \qquad (27\text{-}3a)$$

$$= \max E\{\ln [w_0(1 + r)^T]\} \qquad (27\text{-}3b)$$

**27-1.4
One-Period
Returns and
Utility of
Terminal
Wealth**

Substituting Eq. (27-4b) into objective function (27-3b) yields Eq. (27-3c), which shows explicitly how utility of terminal wealth relates to the T different single-period rates of return $r_1, r_2, \ldots r_T$.

$$\max E[U(w_T)] = \max E\{\ln [w_0(1 + r)^T]\} \qquad (27\text{-}3b)$$

$$= \max E\{\ln [w_0(1 + r_1)(1 + r_2)\ldots(1 + r_T)]\} \qquad (27\text{-}3c)$$

One of the insights that can be obtained by restating the investor's long-term objective as Eq. (27-3c) is the effect of taking risks period after period. Suppose that in the tth period the investor selects a risky asset that has a one-period rate of return of $r_t = -100$ percent. The link relative for period t becomes zero since -100 percent $= -1.0$ and thus $1 + r_t = 1 - 1 = 0$. This might happen, for example, if an investor becomes too greedy and impatiently speculates in a nondiversified venture that is not prudent in hopes of ''getting rich quick.''

If any one link relative becomes equal to zero, the investor loses all the wealth that had been accumulated up to period t. When this situation occurs it is commonly called *bankruptcy*. The bankrupt party's utility of returns [namely, Eq. (27-3c)] becomes as low as it can possibly be—it becomes the utility of zero, mathematically speaking. This shows that some risk-aversion (that is, the fear of bankruptcy) is essential to maximize expected utility of terminal wealth over multiperiod reinvesting. Merely buying high-risk assets or ''taking long shots'' at the racetrack will not automatically yield riches or happiness. Quite to the contrary, the assumption of high risks period after period means that $r_t = -100$ percent $(= -1.0)$ may occur in one period and cause the terminal wealth to become zero. Such outcomes were what allegedly caused some Bay and Wall Street speculators to jump from their office windows to their deaths during the Great Crash of the early 1930s.

**27-1.5
The Utility
from Being
Bankrupt**

27-2 SINGLE-PERIOD PORTFOLIO MANAGEMENT

Thus far, three long-run investment strategies have been shown to be equivalent: (1) maximizing the logarithmic utility function, (2) maximizing the geometric mean rate of return, and (3) maximizing terminal wealth.[6] The analysis of these multiperiod objectives ultimately focused on the individual *one-period* rates of return r_t, which are the focal point of Markowitz single-period portfolio analysis. It has been shown at various places in this book (for example, see the CAPM, or SML, and the CML, or the efficient frontier) that the portfolio manager must undertake some risks of investing in order to obtain significant positive returns. However, it was also shown earlier in this chapter [namely, in the bankruptcy discussion that followed Eq. (27-3c)] that it is foolhardy to undertake large risks and expect to maximize multiperiod terminal wealth. To go a step further and reach a conclusion about exactly how the portfolio manager should select a portfolio, it is necessary to assume that the one-period rates-of-return distribution may be described by the two-parameter normal distribution. In fact, there is good evidence that returns are normally distributed.[7]

The *normal probability distribution* is completely defined by its two parameters: the expected value (or mean) and the variance (or standard deviation). Information about higher-order statistical moments is irrelevant when analyzing the normal distribution. The rational investment policy is therefore to select a portfolio with the maximum expected return at whatever level of risk is deemed appropriate—that is, to select an efficient portfolio.[8] The optimum multiperiod strategy is to select any efficient portfolio between the low-return-and-low-risk segment and the high-risk-and-high-return segment that seems likely to maximize terminal wealth in light of the current facts. Coincidently, this is *identical* with the optimal single-period investment strategy.

---

6 Footnote 5 showed that a fourth utility function, a specific quadratic function, is also essentially equal.

7 Randolph Westerfield, ''The Distribution of Common Stock Price Changes: An Application of Transaction Time and Subordinated Stochastic Models,'' *Journal of the American Statistical Association*, December 1977; R. C. Blattberg and N. J. Gonedes, ''A Comparison of the Stable and Student Distributions as Statistical Models for Stock Prices,'' *Journal of Business*, April 1974, pp. 244–280; E. Fama, *Foundations of Finance* (New York: Basic Books, 1976). Fama suggests the normal distribution in chaps. 1 through 4.

8 Mathematical proof that expected utility of terminal wealth is a function of the expected return, $E(r)$, and variance, σ^2, if rates of return are normally distributed, is outlined below. Mathematical statisticians will be able to fill in the missing steps of the proof.

$$E[U(w_T)] = \int U(r|w_0)f[r|E(r), \sigma^2]dr$$
$$= E[U(r)|w_0, E(r), \sigma^2]$$

where

r = rate-of-return random variable
U = a logarithmic utility function
$f[r|E(r), \sigma^2]$ = a normal probability distribution of rates of return

The vertical bars indicate that the variables after them are given. The full proof is omitted because it is lengthy and involves integral calculus. See eqs. (3.5), (3.6), (3.7), et al., in James Tobin, ''Liquidity Preference as Behavior Towards Risk,'' *The Review of Economic Studies*, February 1958.

It is not possible to specify in advance how much risk is wise to undertake when seeking to maximize terminal wealth.[9] However, a study by Sharpe and Cooper throws some light on the question.[10] Over a 36-year sample, they found that large portfolios of New York Stock Exchange (NYSE) stocks with beta systematic risk coefficients slightly above unity had the highest geometric mean rate of return. Table 27-1 shows the average betas for portfolios made from NYSE stocks, constructed from homogeneous *risk deciles*. The table also shows the geometric mean returns for each of the portfolios from the ten different risk-classes.

TABLE 27-1   BETA SYSTEMATIC RISK COEFFICIENTS AND GEOMETRIC MEAN RETURNS FOR 10 NYSE STOCK PORTFOLIOS, 1931–1967

RISK-CLASS	PORTFOLIO'S BETA	GEOMETRIC MEAN RETURN, %
1	1.42	14.52
2	1.18	14.21
3	1.14	14.79
4	1.24	15.84*
5	1.06	13.80
6	0.98	15.06
7	1.00	14.69
8	0.76	12.14
9	0.65	12.40
10	0.58	9.89

*Highest geometric mean return.

The statistics in Table 27-1 tend to indicate that portfolios composed of stocks with beta coefficients between about 1.0 and 1.25 were the most lucrative. A search for either low-risk stocks with betas below about 0.6 or high-risk stocks with betas above about 1.3 appears to be a counterproductive strategy. However, the stocks for this Sharpe-Cooper study were selected only on the basis of their beta coefficients. Selecting stocks with the aid of an expert security analyst and/or an economic forecaster could change the results in Table 27-1. In the final analysis, the experience of the decision maker and the ''luck of the draw'' can also be significant factors in investment selection.

The only aspect of multiperiod portfolio management left to be discussed is the question, ''How and when should the single-period efficient portfolios be *revised* to take advantage of new information that becomes available during the multiperiod horizon?''

27-3   PORTFOLIO REVISION

As bull- and bear-market periods pass in succession, new stocks are offered, and old securities go bankrupt, the efficient frontier shifts, making portfolio

9 Richard Roll, ''Evidence on the Growth Optimum Model,'' *Journal of Finance*, June 1973, pp. 551-566. Harry Markowitz, ''Investment for the Long Run: New Evidence for an Old Rule,'' *Journal of Finance*, December 1976, vol. 31, no. 5, pp. 1273-1286.

10 W. F. Sharpe and G. M. Cooper, ''Risk-Return Classes of N.Y.S.E. Common Stocks, 1931-1967,'' *Financial Analysts Journal*, March-April 1972, p. 46.

revision necessary. Furthermore, the portfolio will receive cash dividends and interest income that need to be reinvested. Also, new information will arrive continually, causing securities risk and return statistics to change. For these reasons, a multiperiod portfolio strategy will involve *portfolio revision* even though the investor's utility function may never change.

Investors do not usually desire a portfolio that changes its risk-class, even if it shifts along the efficient frontier. For example, a poor, elderly widow would probably not be happy to have her life savings in a "go-go" mutual fund even if it were efficient, like portfolio C in Fig. 27-2. Instead, the widow would probably prefer a less risky balanced fund, like portfolio E' in Fig. 27-2, even though it is not on the efficient frontier.[11] Thus, the practical objective of portfolio management in most business and personal situations typically becomes one of simple return maximization in a particular risk-class when the investor's utility map (or indifference curves) is unknown.

FIGURE 27-2 Portfolio revision possibilities.

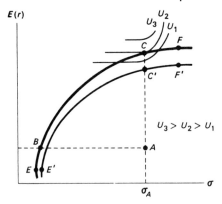

For another example, suppose a mutual fund has become suboptimal at point A in Fig 27-2. This portfolio's manager should not seek just any portfolio that has less risk and/or more expected return, such as the portfolios in the triangle bounded by points A, B, and C. Instead, only portfolios in or near the mutual fund's traditional risk-class (that is, σ_A, which its owners presumably prefer) that have higher expected returns should be sought. Such portfolios lie along the dotted line $AC'C$ in Fig. 27-2—this dotted line is evidently the *risk-class* that the investor prefers.

27-3.1 Revision Costs Make True Efficient Frontier Unattainable

Portfolio revision is a costly process. When a portfolio is revised, some previously purchased securities may have to be liquidated at a loss. The expense of updating the risk and return statistics for many securities and the computer operation necessary to determine the new efficient frontier are not trivial. And the commissions on any securities bought or sold must be paid, too.

As a result of these costs, it is not possible for a revised portfolio to attain the true efficient frontier along the curve $EBCF$ in Fig. 27-2. Instead, the con-

11 The indifference curve representation of the investment preferences of Dr. Swift and Aunt Jane in Fig. 25-1 shows why the widow would prefer portfolio E' instead of C.

strained efficient frontier along the curve *E'C'F'* represents the optimum attainable investments. The vertical difference between the unattainable efficient frontier curve *EBCF* and the *optimum attainable efficient frontier* curve *E'C'F'* equals the revision costs as a percentage of the portfolio's total assets.[12] In Fig. 27-2, the optimum attainable efficient frontier is closer to the true efficient frontier for low-risk, low-return portfolios than for efficient portfolios with higher returns because the low-risk, low-return portfolios presumably contain many bonds, and the sales commissions for buying and selling bonds are lower than for stock.

In situations like the one depicted in Fig. 27-2, portfolio *A* should be revised to attain point *C'*. Revisions of this nature should occur as often as they are possible—a month, a quarter, or longer after portfolio *A* was originally purchased.[13] There is no optimum time schedule for portfolio revision. Because of revision costs, it is impossible to attain the most efficient portfolio, *C*, in the desired risk-class, σ_A. But there is no reason that portfolio *C'* should not be obtained directly and immediately if it yields net profit after the revision costs.

27-4   CONCLUSIONS

When all things are considered, there are unusual circumstances that could arise in selecting an investment portfolio that would make a Markowitz efficient portfolio inadvisable.[14] However, as a pragmatic matter, myopically selecting a one-period Markowitz efficient portfolio in each successive period can maximize expected utility of terminal wealth over a planning horizon that extends many periods into the future, or over a single period.

This discussion about long-run portfolio strategies encompassing multiple periods tends to draw attention away from the portfolio managers who are managing small and/or short-term portfolios. These managers must consider liquidating their portfolios and consuming the wealth, using the money for an emergency, using the proceeds to finance some expenditure for which they were accumulating wealth over one period, ad infinitum. These portfolio managers are not in the position to look more than one period into the future. But they, too, should seek efficient portfolios to maximize their expected utility.[15] Thus, whether portfolio managers are looking one period or multiple periods into the future, they should seek the efficient frontier.

12 A. H. Chen, F. C. Jen, and S. Zionts, "The Optimal Portfolio Revisions Policy," *Journal of Business*, January 1971, pp. 51-61.

13 K. H. Johnson and D. S. Shannon, "A Note on Diversification and the Reduction of Dispersion," *Journal of Financial Economics*, December 1974, vol. 1, no. 4, pp. 365-372. For evidence about a workable portfolio revision algorithm, see John Schreiner, "Portfolio Revision — A Turnover-Constrained Approach," *Financial Management*, December 1979; reprinted in J. C. Francis, C. F. Lee, and D. Farrar (eds.), *Readings in Investments* (New York: McGraw-Hill, 1980).

14 Nils H. Hakansson, "Capital Growth and the Mean-Variance Approach to Portfolio Selection," *Journal of Financial and Quantitative Analysis*, January 1971, pp. 517-555.

15 E. F. Fama, "Multiperiod Consumption-Investment Decisions," *American Economic Review*, March 1970, pp. 163-174.

QUESTIONS

1. Why maximize *expected* utility rather than simply the utility of wealth?
2. Find a utility function with positive but diminishing marginal utility that is incompatible with the logarithmic function and graph it. Compare and contrast this function (for example, a quadratic function over its upward-sloping range) with the logarithmic function. Can you make positive linear transformations on the log function so that it closely approximates the other function?
3. Assume a portfolio manager has taken *large risks* to attain large returns and has been so successful at this strategy that she has quadrupled her wealth every year for the past ten years. Now this portfolio manager offers to manage your life savings along with her own funds for free. What do you think of this free chance to get rich quick and retire early?
4. Suppose investor *A* had as his investment strategy the maximization of a one-period logarithm of returns utility function. In contrast, his twin brother, *B*, maximized the log of multiperiod terminal wealth. If *A* and *B* were choosing among the same assets from which to form their portfolios, how should their portfolios differ?
5. Compare and contrast the marginal utility of an investor with a log utility function with the quadratic utility function of another investor.
6. If investor *P* had to pay brokerage fees to trade securities when she revised her portfolio but her twin sister, *F*, could trade without paying brokerage fees, how should their portfolios differ after a few periods?

SELECTED REFERENCES

Eugene F. Fama. ''Multiperiod Consumption-Investment Decisions.'' *American Economic Review*, March 1970, pp. 163-174. This article uses integral calculus to show that selecting one-period Markowitz efficient portfolios will yield an optimal multiperiod investment strategy if the investor has current consumption as an alternative to reinvestment each period and if the capital markets are perfect. A knowledge of utility and portfolio theory is presumed.

H. A. Latane, D. L. Tuttle, and C. R. Jones. *Security Analysis and Portfolio Management*. 2d ed. New York: The Ronald Press Co., 1975. This investments textbook suggests how to make investment decisions so as to maximize the geometric mean rate of return or terminal wealth.

Harry Markowitz. ''Investment for the Long Run: New Evidence for an Old Rule.'' *Journal of Finance*, December 1976, vol. 31, no. 5, pp. 1273-1286. Mathematical statistics are used to show that maximizing the geometric mean is compatible with Markowitz's portfolio analysis.

John Schreiner. ''Portfolio Revision—A Turnover-Constrained Approach.'' *Financial Management*, Spring 1980. This article uses algebra and statistics to explain a mathematical portfolio revision algorithm. Numerical results are also discussed.

PART 8

ARBITRAGE PRICING THEORY

CHAPTER 28 — Arbitrage Pricing Theory (APT) *presents a powerful new investments theory that first emerged in 1976 and went relatively unnoticed for several years. It is a comprehensive theory in that it embraces different risk factors but yet includes the capital asset pricing model (CAPM) as a special case. APT is also a simple theory that can be derived with only the most modest assumptions about the underlying utility function and the probability distribution of assets' returns. The theory and initial empirical evidence are presented in Chapter 28. Chapter 28 presumes that the material in Chap. 9, 10, and 19 has been mastered.*

28

Arbitrage Pricing Theory (APT)

The modern portfolio theory (MPT) of Harry Markowitz, William Sharpe, Jack Treynor, and others is the most widely accepted investments theory — it was explained previously, in Chaps. 23 through 26.[1] However, Doctor Stephen Ross's arbitrage pricing theory (APT) is a new investments theory that competes with the MPT for the attention of financial researchers.[2] Section 28-1 introduces the APT in a simple two-asset context that is intuitive.

28-1 AN INTRODUCTION TO ARBITRAGE PRICING THEORY (APT)

An *arbitrage opportunity* is a perfectly hedged portfolio that can be acquired at a cost of zero, but that will have a positive value with certainty at the end of the investment period.

1 Portfolio theory was explained above in Chaps. 23 through 26 inclusive. The modern portfolio theory originated in the following articles. H. M. Markowitz, ''Portfolio Selections,'' *Journal of Finance*, March 1952, pp. 71-91; H. M. Markowitz, *Portfolio Selection: Efficient Diversification of Investments* (New York: Wiley, 1959). The single-index model, or the market model, as it is also called, was first published on page 100 of Markowitz's 1959 monograph. Later, additional research on the model was published by Markowitz's student W. F. Sharpe, ''A Simplified Model for Portfolio Analysis,'' *Management Science*, January 1963, pp. 277-293. Today's factor models are simply these earlier index models with their names changed. Then, the CAPM was developed independently by Jack Treynor and W. F. Sharpe: W. F. Sharpe, ''Capital Asset Prices: A Theory of Market Equilibrium under Conditions of Risk,'' *Journal of Finance*, September 1964, pp. 425-442; W. F. Sharpe: ''Mutual Fund Performance,'' *Journal of Business*, January 1966, pp. 119-138; J. L. Treynor, ''Toward a Theory of the Market Value of Risky Assets,'' unpublished manuscript, 1961; and, J. L. Treynor, ''How to Rate Management of Investment Funds,'' *Harvard Business Review*, January-February 1965, pp. 63-75. Many later researchers contributed to the development of the MPT.
2 S. A. Ross, ''The Arbitrage Pricing Theory of Capital Asset Pricing,'' *Journal of Economic Theory*, December 1976, pp. 344-360; S. A. Ross, ''The Current Status of the Capital Asset Pricing Model,'' *Journal of Finance*, June 1978, pp. 885-901; and Richard Roll and Stephen A. Ross, ''An Empirical Investigation of the Arbitrage Pricing Theory,'' *Journal of Finance*, December 1980, vol. 35, no. 5, pp. 1073-1103.

Box 28-1

An arbitrage opportunity is expressed more formally in Eqs. (28-1), (28-2a), and (28-3) below. These three equations are all *dollar*-denominated.

$$\sum_{i=1}^{N} w_i = 0 \tag{28-1}$$

$$E(w_p^T) = \sum_{i=1}^{N} E(w_i^T) > 0 \tag{28-2a}$$

$$0 = \sum_{i=1}^{N} \sum_{j=1}^{N} \sigma_{ij}$$

where

   w_i = dollars of initial wealth invested in the ith asset

$E(w_i^T)$ = mathematical expectation of terminal wealth (or value)

   of asset i,

   σ_{ij} = covariance between assets i and j

In this case, the expected dollar profits from the arbitrage portfolio are positive, as indicated in Eq. (28-2a).

No money was invested to create this profitable arbitrage portfolio because some securities were sold short to obtain cash inflow (that is, $w_i > 0$) while other securities cost money (that is, $w_j < 0$) when they were purchased to hold in a long position. Essentially, investors are assumed to receive the proceeds (that is, positive cash inflows) from their short sales to invest in their long positions (that cost negative cash outflows) so that Eq. (28-1) is not violated. Eqs. (28-1), (28-2a), and (28-3) define the type of arbitrage opportunity that leads to the arbitrage pricing theory (APT).[3]

In the next section the discussion changes from dollar quantities to *rates of return* in order to achieve a higher level of generality.

APT is based on the law of one price. The *law of one price* says that the same good cannot sell at different prices. If the same good sells at different prices, arbitrageurs will buy the good where it is cheap (and bid up that low price) and simultaneously sell the good wherever its price is higher (and drive down the high price). Arbitrageurs will continue this activity until the different

28-1.1   The Returns That Underlie the APT

3 S. Ross, ''The Arbitrage Pricing Theory of Capital Asset Pricing,'' *Journal of Economic Theory,* December 1976, pp. 344-360. This mathematical essay derives the APT model. Richard Roll and S. Ross, ''An Empirical Investigation of the Arbitrage Pricing Theory,'' *Journal of Finance,* December 1980, vol. 35, pp. 1073-1103. This second article reviews the APT model and presents initial empirical tests of the APT.

prices for the good are all equal. Equivalently, the law of one price says that securities with identical risks must have the same expected rate of return. Most specifically, one of the fundamental theorems of APT says that assets with the same stochastic behaviour must have the same expected returns. Consider, for instance, the one-period rates of return from two assets with the *equally risky* cashflows indicated in Eq. (28-4a) and (28-4b).

$$r_1 = E(r_1) + e = (w_1^T/w_1) - 1.0 \tag{28-4a}$$

$$r_2 = E(r_2) + e = (w_2^T/w_2) - 1.0 \tag{28-4b}$$

The random variable e in equation series (28-4) is assumed to have a mathematical expectation of zero, $E(e) = 0$, and be identical for the two assets.

In order to prevent arbitrage, the expected returns from equally risky assets one and two must be equal, $E(r_1) = E(r_2)$. However, suppose that these expected rates of return are not equal and $E(r_1) > E(r_2)$. In this case a shrewd investor can create a profitable arbitrage portfolio by taking the proceeds of w_2 dollars from a short sale of asset two and investing this amount in a long position of equal size in asset one. Mathematically, $| - w_1| = w_2$. This arbitrage portfolio requires no initial investment since $- w_1 + w_2 = 0$, as specified in Eq. (28-1). The portfolio is hedged to zero risk, as indicated by Eq. (28-3). The portfolio is also perfectly hedged to zero risk because any gains (or losses) on the long position will be exactly offset by the simultaneous losses (or gains) from the short position of equal size. But, nevertheless, the arbitrage portfolio has positive expected profits with certainty, as specified by Eq. (28-2a), since $[E(r_1) - E(r_2)] > 0$. Thus, this arbitrage portfolio conforms to Eqs. (28-1), (28-2a), and (28-3).

28-1.2 Undiversifiable Risk from a Common Factor

Suppose that the one-period rates of return for two assets are generated by a single *factor* denoted F in accordance with the linear model of Eq. (28-4c) and Eq. (28-4d).

$$r_{it} = a_1 + b_1 F_t \tag{28-4c}$$

$$r_2 t = a_2 + b_2 F_t \tag{28-4d}$$

Let F_t be a random variable with an expected value of zero, $E(F_t) = 0$. For instance, F_t might be the percentage change in the GNP, the TSE 300 Composite Index, or the price of oil. The b_1 coefficient in Eq. (28-4c) is a measure of undiversifiable risk—it indicates how sensitive the asset is to the common source of variations. According to the law of one price, two risky assets with equal values of b_i must have the same expected rate of return; Eq. (28-5) states this condition formally.

$$E(r_i) = a_i \quad \text{for } i = 1, 2, \ldots \quad \text{since } E(F_t) = 0 \tag{28-5}$$

The two asset's expected rates of return should be equal, $E(r_1) = E(r_2)$, because these assets are equally responsive, $b_1 = b_2$, to the common risk factor F. But suppose that $b_1 \neq b_2$. When the riskiness of the two assets differs, the arbitrageur can earn riskless profits by investing a fraction x of the arbitrage portfolio's total wealth in asset one and $(1.0 - x)$ in asset two, where $0 < x < + 1.0$. Equation (28-6a) defines this portfolio's weighted average rate of return.

$$r_{pt} = xr_{1t} + (1 - x)r_{2t} \qquad (28\text{-}6a)$$

$$= x(a_1 + b_1F_t) + (1 - x)(a_2 + b_2F_t) \qquad (28\text{-}6b)$$

$$= x(a_1 - a_2) + a_2 + [x(b_1 - b_2) + b_2]F_t \qquad (28\text{-}6c)$$

If the value of the investment proportion x is selected so that $x^* = [b_2/(b_2 - b_1)]$, then this quantity can be substituted into Eq. (28-6c) for x to obtain, after some rearranging, Eq. (28-7).

$$r_p = \frac{a_2 + b_2(a_1 - a_2)}{b_2 - b_1} \qquad (28\text{-}7)$$

In Eq. (28-7) the portfolio's return is riskless since the random systematic factor F drops out of the equation. In perfect capital markets, a certain investment must yield a risk-free rate of return, denoted R. This allows us to say that $r_p = R$, and it also allows us to rewrite Eq. (28-7) as Eq. (28-8).

$$R = \frac{a_2 + b_2(a_1 - a_2)}{(b_2 - b_1)} \qquad (28\text{-}8)$$

Multiplying both sides of Eq. (28-8) by the quantity $(b_2 - b_1)$ and rearranging leads to Eq. (28- 9a).

$$\frac{(a_1 - R)}{b_1} = \frac{(a_2 - R)}{b_2} \qquad (28\text{-}9a)$$

From Eq. (28-5) we know that $E(r_i) = a_i$. Substituting for a_i allows Eq. (28-9a) to be restated as Eq. (28-9b).

$$\frac{(a_i - R)}{b_i} = \frac{E(r_i) - R}{b_i} = \lambda = \frac{(\text{risk-premium})}{(\text{risk-measure})} \qquad (28\text{-}9b)$$

Equations (28-9a) and (28-9b) define a constant called lambda, denoted λ, that represents the *factor risk-premium*.

Equation (28-9b) can be equivalently rewritten as Eqs. (28-10a) and (28-10b) to obtain the *arbitrage pricing line*. Substituting from Eqs. (28-5) and (28-9b) allows Eq. (28-10a) to be stated below.

**28-1.3
The Arbitrage
Pricing Line**

$$E(r_i) = R + b_i\frac{E(r_i) - R}{b_i} \qquad (28\text{-}10a)$$

$$E(r_i) = R + b_i\lambda \qquad (28\text{-}10b)$$

Equation (28- 10b) was derived by substituting from the definition in Eq. (28-9b). Figure 28-1 illustrates the arbitrage pricing line of Eq. (28-10a).

FIGURE 28-1 The APT model for one factor.

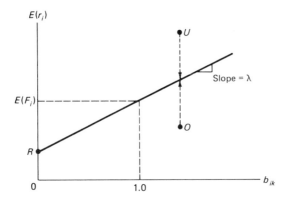

The factor risk-premium, λ, can be interpreted as the *excess rate of return*, $[E(r_i) - R]$, for a risky asset with $b_i = 1.0$. Equation series (28-10) is the essence of the APT. Equations (28-10a) and (28-10b) say that, in the absence of profitable arbitrage opportunities, the expected rate of return from any risky asset equals the risk-free rate of return plus a risk-premium that is proportional to the asset's sensitivity, b_i, to the common risk factor, F. This sensitivity is measured by the *factor loading*, b_i, for the ith asset.

The arbitrage pricing line shown in Fig. 28-1 is a risk-return relationship. Risk is measured along the horizontal axis of Fig. 28-1. The APT considers all assets that are in the same risk-class, such as assets O and U in Fig. 28-1, to be perfect substitutes that should yield the same rate of return. Assets' expected rates of return are measured along the vertical axis of Fig. 28-1. The arbitrage pricing line intersects the vertical axis at point R, the riskless rate of interest.

**28-1.4
Over- and
Under-Priced
Assets**

Consider two assets in the same risk-class, like the two assets at points U and O in Fig. 28-1. Assets U and O both violate the law of one price because they are both in the same risk-class but do not have the same expected rate of return on the arbitrage pricing line. In the economic equilibrium all assets should lie on the arbitrage pricing line. The forces of supply and demand will drive all assets to lie on the arbitrage pricing line as arbitrageurs work to profit from assets that violate the law of one price. The arbitrage process that will tend to move all assets onto the arbitrage pricing line follows.

As investors investigate before they invest, some of them will discover that asset O in Fig. 28-1 offers potential investors a lower rate of return than asset U, even though they both involve *equal* amounts of risk. Therefore, risk-averse investors will sell asset O because it is a less desirable investment. The resulting excess of supply over demand for asset O will drive down its market price. As the price of asset O is driven down, the one-period expected rate of return for asset O will rise; this price-adjustment process is indicated by the arrows in a common stock's expected rate of return equation at the top of page 805.

$$\uparrow E(r) = \frac{[E(p_{t-1}) - p_t] + d_t}{\downarrow p_t} = \frac{[\text{price change}] + [\text{cash dividend, if any}]}{\downarrow \text{purchase price}}$$

Risk-averse investors will continue to sell asset O until its price is driven down and its expected rate of return rises up onto the arbitrage pricing line in Fig. 28-1. The upward-pointing arrow in Fig. 28-1 traces the path that asset O's expected rate of return should follow until it reaches its equilibrium point on the arbitrage pricing line.

Smart investors will not only sell asset O if they own any of it, they will also sell asset O short and use the cash proceeds they obtained from the short sale to buy a long position in asset U. Investors will buy asset U in order to enjoy its expected rate of return, which lies above the arbitrage pricing line in Fig. 28-1 and also above the expected return from asset O. As these profit-seekers buy asset U in order to obtain its high return, they will bid up its price. And, as the price of asset U is bid higher, its expected rate of return will come down. This process can be traced by reversing the direction of the arrows in the common stock's expected rate of return equation above.

The basic economic assumption that most people prefer more wealth to less wealth will assume that asset U will experience more buyers than sellers until its purchase price is bid so high that its expected rate of return is lowered down onto the arbitrage pricing line in Fig. 28-1, as indicated by the downward-pointing arrow in the figure. When the expected rate of return from asset U is driven down onto the arbitrage pricing line, the asset's price will be in equilibrium.

The price adjustment process outlined in the preceding paragraphs will work for all assets in all risk-classes. This means that every asset that plots *above* the arbitrage pricing line in Fig. 28-1 is underpriced, and its price will adjust upward in the same way that the price of asset U rose. Likewise, every asset that plots *below* the arbitrage pricing line is overpriced, and its price will fall by the same market mechanism that lowered the price of asset O in Fig. 28-1.

In an effort to maximize the profits they can derive from their research finding, the smartest investors will sell asset O short and *simultaneously* buy a long position of equal dollar value in asset U. These smartest investors will have zero cash invested in their *arbitrage portfolio* made up of a short position in asset O combined with an equal long position in asset U. They will not need to invest a cent of their own funds because they can take the cash proceeds from the short sale of asset O and use these short sale proceeds to buy a long position of equal value in asset U. Furthermore, these smartest investors will not be exposed to any risk because their arbitrage portfolio is perfectly hedged with long and short positions of equal value that offset each other's gains and losses. And finally, the *arbitrage portfolio* will earn a riskless profit of $[E(r_U) - E(r_O)]$. The arbitrage portfolio earns this profit by raising funds from the short sale on which the arbitrageur must pay a rate of return of $E(r_O)$ and, simultaneously, investing these funds in the long position at a

**28-1.5
The
Arbitrage
Portfolio**

higher rate of return of $E(r_U)$. This profit is riskless because the *arbitrage port-folio* is perfectly hedged.

In summary, the *arbitrage portfolio* will (1) have zero money invested, (2) be a riskless investment undertaking, and, (3) earn a predetermined positive profit. Most investors in the world will not even know what the word ''arbitrage'' means. But, if only a few aggressive investors run arbitrage portfolios for themselves, their actions will be sufficient to generate the APT equilibrium condition illustrated in Fig. 28-1.

28-1.6
Implications
and
Extensions of
the APT

Note that the capital asset pricing model (CAPM), which happens to be equal to Eq. (28-10*b*), is a special case of the APT.[4] Furthermore, in the case when only one factor exists, that single factor must be the *market portfolio* from the capital market theory of Chap. 24.

Another significant aspect of the APT is that it can be extended to include several different common factors. For example, factors like F_1, F_2, and F_3 (or even more factors) could be included as different sources of variation that affect market assets. Much empirical work remains to be done to determine the number of relevant factors that determine asset returns and the identity of these factors. But, before considering the empirical evidence, the APT is developed further in the section below.

28-2 A MORE GENERAL DERIVATION OF THE APT MODEL

Equation (28-11) below may be thought of as an extended characteristic line with k different economic indexes as explanatory variables.[5] It is a single asset, time-series return-generating model.

$$r_{it} = a_i + b_{i1}F_{1t} + b_{i2}F_{2t} + \ldots + b_{ik}F_{kt} + e_{it} \tag{28-11}$$

where

r_{it} = one-period rate of return from ith asset in time period t

a_i = expected rate of return for an asset if all risk factors have a value of zero, that is, $a_i = E(r_i)$

F_{jt} = jth risk factor (or communality) that impacts on assets' returns, where $j = 1, 2, \ldots, k$ different risk factors exist. This risk factor has a mathematical expectation of zero, $E(F_{jt}) = 0$

---

4 William F. Sharpe, ''Capital Asset Prices: A Theory of Market Equilibrium under Conditions of Risk,'' *Journal of Finance*, September 1964, pp. 425-442. The CAPM is derived in this paper. Robert Jarrow and Andrew Rudd, ''A Comparison of the APT and CAPM,'' *Journal of Banking and Finance*, June 1983, vol. 7, pp. 295-303.

5 The characteristic regression line from Chap. 10, Eq. (10-1), is reproduced below as an orientation for those who may already be familiar with it.

$$r_{it} = a_i + b_i r_{mt} + e_{it}. \tag{10-1}$$

Although Eqs. (10-1) and (28-11) are different return-generating functions, they have enough in common to make a comparison insightful.

b_{ij} = sensitivity indicator (or factor loading) that measures how
responsive returns from asset i are to index j for $j = 1, 2,...,k$ indexes.[6]

e_{it} = random-error term for asset i in period t that measures
unexplained residual return, which has expected value of zero
and variance of σ_{ei}

Two statistical conditions must be true of the return-generating function
in Eq. (28-11).

1. The unexplained residuals between all assets must be independent, $E(e_i e_j) = 0$
   where $i \neq j$.
2. All factors must be independent (or orthogonal) with respect to all assets, $E[e_i\{F_j - E(F_j)\}] = 0$ for all i and j.

Let us derive the APT from a return-generating process like Eq. (28-11).

A linear additive return-generating process like Eq. (28-11) underlies all APT. It is nevertheless possible to discuss the APT without ever referring to this return-generating model. But we will derive a simple APT model with two indexes in order to see how the theory is derived. Equation (28-12) is a simple return-generating process with two unidentified risk factors.

**28-1.2
A Two-Factor
Return-
Generating
Process**

$$r_{it} = a_i + b_{i1}F_{1t} + b_{i2}F_{2t} + e_{it} \tag{28-12}$$

If you want concrete examples, you may imagine that the first risk factor in Eq. (28-12) is the rate of change in the TSE 300 Composite Index and the second risk factor as being an index of cash dividend payout rates. The APT gives us *no clue* as to what indexes could be relevant—this is unlike the capital market theory, which is based on a unique index called the *market portfolio*.

Consider three risk-averse investors who form portfolios that each contain n assets, where (1) the number of assets (n) must exceed the number of indexes ($K = 2$, in this example), and (2) n is some large number. The return on such a portfolio is defined in Eq. (28-13a) as r_p. The x_i term is the weight or participation level for the ith asset in the portfolio.

**28-2.2
Three Widely
Diversified
Portfolios**

$$r_{pt} = \sum_{i=1}^{n} x_i r_{it} \tag{28-13a}$$

$$= \sum_{i}^{n} x_i a_i + \sum_{i=1}^{n} x_i b_{i1}F_{it} + \sum_{i=1}^{n} x_i b_{i2}F_{2t} + \sum_{i=1}^{n} x_i e_i$$

---

6 The b_{ij} term is called a factor loading if it is estimated using factor-analytic procedures, or it is called a regression coefficient if it is estimated using regression analysis.

Equation (28-14) is the *balance sheet identity*, which cannot be violated if the investor's portfolio is to have any rational financial interpretation. This equation requires that the weight add up to unity (or 100 percent).

$$\sum_{i=1}^{n} x_i = 1.0 \tag{28-14}$$

In a widely diversified portfolio the unsystematic residual risk is *diversifiable* and hence will average out to zero, as indicated in Eq. (28-15).

$$\sum_{i=1}^{n} x_i e_i = 0 \tag{28-15}$$

As a result of Eq. (28-15), Eq. (28-13a) will contain only systematic risk and can thus be written as Eq. (28-13b).

$$r_{pt} = \sum_{i=1}^{n} x_i a_i + \sum_{i=1}^{n} x_i b_{i1} F_{1t} + \sum_{i=1}^{n} x_i b_{i2} F_{2t} \tag{28-13b}$$

The systematic risk in portfolio p thus equals $\sum_i x_i b_{i1} = b_{p1}$ and $\sum_i x_i b_{i2} = b_{p2}$

from risk factors one and two, respectively.

Table 28-1 shows the risk and return statistics for the three hypothetical widely diversified portfolios.

TABLE 28-1   RISK AND RETURN STATISTICS FOR THREE PORTFOLIOS

PORTFOLIO	EXPECTED RETURN	b_{p1}	b_{p2}
B	$E(r_B) = 16.0\%$	1.0	.7
C	$E(r_C) = 14.0\%$	.6	1.0
D	$E(r_D) = 11.0\%$	.5	.4

28-2.3   The APT Model

Equation (28-16) shows the general form of the APT model which can be derived from the two-factor return-generating function of Eq. (28-12). The two sensitivity values, b_{i1} and b_{i2}, are the explanatory variables in Eq. (28-16a).

$$E(r_i) = \lambda_0 + \lambda_1 b_{i1} + \lambda_2 b_{i2} \tag{28-16a}$$

$$E(r_i) = 5.629 + 7.777 b_{i1} + 3.703 b_{i2} \tag{28-16b}$$

Equation (28-16b) shows the specific APT model that can be derived from the numerical values in Table 28-1. The mathematical derivation of the values of λ_0, λ_1, and λ_2 in Eq. (28-16a) is explained below.

Any three points, like $E(r_i)$, b_{i1}, and b_{i2}, for example, define a plane in geometry. Equation (28-16b) is the formula for a specific three-dimensional plane that is an asset pricing model for the three portfolios in Table 28-1.[7] Figure 28-2 illustrates the APT plane of Eq. (28-16a). Substituting the numerical value for any of the three portfolios in Table 28-1 into Eq. (28-16b) proves numerically that the three points all fit this APT plane.[8]

28-3 THE ARBITRAGE PORTFOLIO

In equilibrium, the risks and return of every asset should conform to the APT model of Eq. (28-16a) and Fig. 28-2. Consider a specific case where one asset

FIGURE 28-2 APT plane for two-factor model.

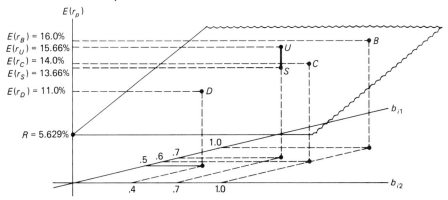

[7] For other derivations of APT models see Phillip H. Dybvig, "An Explicit Bound on Individual Assets' Deviations from APT Pricing in a Finite Economy," *Journal of Financial Economics*, December 1983, pp. 483-496; Mark Grinblatt and Sheridan Titman, "Factor Pricing in a Finite Economy," *Journal of Financial Economics*, December 1983, vol. 12, no. 4, pp. 497-507.

[8] This footnote shows the mathematical derivation of eq. (28-16b) and the plane in Fig. 28-2. The APT model of Eq. (28-16a) can be rewritten for the three assets (namely, the portfolios) in Table 28-1, as shown below.

$$E(r_i) = \lambda_0 + \lambda_1 b_{i1} + \lambda_2 b_{i2} \tag{28-16a}$$
$$16.0 = \lambda_0(1.0) + \lambda_1(1.0) + \lambda_2(.7) \tag{28-16c}$$
$$14.0 = \lambda_0(1.0) + \lambda_1(.6) + \lambda_2(1.0) \tag{28-16d}$$
$$11.0 = \lambda_0(1.0) + \lambda_1(.5) + \lambda_2(.4) \tag{28-16e}$$

Equations (28-16c), (28-16d), and (28-16e) are three equations in three unknowns (namely, the λ_0, λ_1, and λ_2), which are equivalently rewritten in matrix Eqs. (28-17a) and (28-17b) below.

$$\begin{bmatrix} 16.0 \\ 14.0 \\ 11.0 \end{bmatrix} = \begin{bmatrix} 1.0 & 1.0 & 0.7 \\ 1.0 & 0.6 & 1.0 \\ 1.0 & 0.5 & 0.4 \end{bmatrix} \begin{bmatrix} \lambda_0 \\ \lambda_1 \\ \lambda^2 \end{bmatrix} \tag{28-17a} \tag{28-17b}$$
$$R \quad = \quad\quad C$$

The matrix (or, more technically, the vector) of unknowns, λ, is evaluated by, first, finding the inverse of the coefficients matrix, C. This inverse is denoted C^{-1}. Second, premultiplying the inverse of matrix C times the return vector, R, yields the values of the vector of unknowns, λ, as shown below in Eqs. (28-18a) and (28-18b).

$$\begin{bmatrix} -.9629 & -.1851 & 2.1481 \\ 2.2222 & -1.1111 & -1.1111 \\ -.3703 & 1.8518 & -1.4814 \end{bmatrix} \begin{bmatrix} 16.0 \\ 14.0 \\ 11.0 \end{bmatrix} = \begin{bmatrix} 5.629 \\ 7.7777 \\ 3.7037 \end{bmatrix} = \begin{bmatrix} \lambda_0 \\ \lambda_1 \\ \lambda_2 \end{bmatrix} \tag{28-18a} \tag{28-18b}$$
$$C^{-1} \quad\quad\quad R \quad = \quad \lambda \quad = \quad \lambda$$

The values for the lambdas in matrix Eq. (28-18a) are used in APT Eq. (28-16b).

is mispriced to see why the APT has asset pricing implications. Suppose that a wealth-seeking, risk-averse investor analyzed portfolio U in Table 28-2 and discovers that it is underpriced. In order to make this security analysis discovery the investor had to create portfolio S (on paper, without any real transactions). Portfolio S is made up of three equal part investments of one-third each in portfolios B, C, and D from Table 28-1. The two sensitivities and the expected return of portfolio S are calculated below and reported in Table 28-2.

$$E(r_S) = \frac{1}{3}E(r_B) + \frac{1}{3}E(r_C) + \frac{1}{3}E(r_D) \tag{28-19}$$

$$13.66\% = \frac{1}{3}(16.0\%) + \frac{1}{3}(14.0\%) + \frac{1}{3}(11.0\%)$$

$$b_{S1} = \frac{1}{3}(b_{B1}) + \frac{1}{3}(b_{C1}) + \frac{1}{3}(b_{D1}) \tag{28-20}$$

$$.7 = \frac{1}{3}(1.0) + \frac{1}{3}(.6) + \frac{1}{3}(.5)$$

$$b_{S2} = \frac{1}{3}(b_{B2}) + \frac{1}{3}(b_{C2}) + \frac{1}{3}(b_{D2}) \tag{28-21}$$

$$.7 = \frac{1}{3}(.7) + \frac{1}{3}(1.0) + \frac{1}{3}(.4)$$

TABLE 28-2   RISK-RETURN STATISTICS FOR TWO PORTFOLIOS

PORTFOLIO	$E(r_p)$, %	b_{i1}	b_{i2}	IDENTITY
S	13.66	.7	.7	(⅓)B + (⅓)C + (⅓)D
U	15.66	.7	.7	Underpriced

Portfolios S and U in Table 28-2 have identical risk statistics, but they have different expected rates of return. According to the *law of one price*, the same good should never sell at two different prices. Since portfolios S and U have identical risks, they are perfect investment substitutes. So, according to the law of one price, investors should buy portfolio U in order to get more return at the same risk as portfolio S. No rational investor would want to buy portfolio S and get less return for the same risk that portfolio U bears.

Some shrewd investor will use the law of one price to earn riskless arbitrage profits. By setting up a hedge with portfolios S and U the shrewd investor can create a profit without investing any money or without taking any risks. Table 28-3 illustrates how a shrewd investor can initially (1) sell $100 (or any other amount) of portfolio S short and (2) take the $100 from the short sale and buy a long position in portfolio U. Note that the shrewd investor has a position in the arbitrage portfolio without investing a single penny.

TABLE 28-3 THE ARBITRAGE PORTFOLIO

PORTFOLIO	INITIAL CASHFLOW	ENDING CASHFLOW	b_{i1}	b_{i2}
S = Short	+$100	−$113.66	−.7	−.7
U = Underpriced (long)	−$100	$115.66	.7	.7
A = Arbitrage (hedged)	0	+$2.00	0	0

This no-money-invested (shown in the second column of Table 28-3) characteristic of the arbitrage portfolio can be formalized as Eq. (28-22).[9]

$$0 = \sum_{p=1}^{p=2} x_p \tag{28-22}$$

Table 28-3 shows how the shrewd investor has set up a riskless *arbitrage portfolio*, denoted A, which is both long and short assets with identical risks. These identical long and short positions create a riskless hedge that cannot profit or lose from any price changes, because the equal-sized gains and losses from the long and short positions exactly offset each other. The two types of zero-systematic-risk-of-any-kind characteristic of the arbitrage portfolio are formalized in Eq. (28-23) and (28-24), respectively.[10]

$$0 = \sum_{p=1}^{p=2} x_p b_{p1} \tag{28-23}$$

$$0 = \sum_{p=1}^{p=2} x_p b_{p2} \tag{28-24}$$

At the end of the investment period the closing cash flows sum up in favour of the arbitrageur. This shrewd investor can sell portfolio U and collect the $100 investment plus the 15.66 percent return for a total of $115.66 cash inflow. And, at the same time, the shrewd investor can spend $113.66 to cover the $100 short position in portfolio S and pay the 13.66 percent interest (or cash dividend) that the person who bought $100 worth of S expected to receive for making this risky investment. After these cashflows, the shrewd

---

9 Note that Eq. (28-22) is different from Eq. (28-14). They differ because Eq. (28-14) is summing across the *n* assets that make up portfolio *p* while, in contrast, Eq. (28-22) is summing across only portfolios S and U in Table 28-3. Conceptually, however, the two equations are identical.

10 Note that although they may appear similar at a glance, Eqs. (28-23) and (28-24) are different from Eqs. (28-20) and (28-21) because Eqs. (28-20) and (28-21) are summing across B, C, and D while (28-23) and (28-24) are summing across the objects in the arbitrage portfolio — portfolios S and U.

investor earns $2 profit without investing any money or without taking any risk. Shrewd arbitrageurs will bid up the price of the underpriced portfolio U and therefore drive down its expected return, as indicated in Eq. (28-25).

$$\downarrow E(r_U) = \frac{E(\$15.66 \text{ income per period})}{\uparrow \text{purchase price (bid upward)}} \tag{28-25}$$

The arbitrage will continue until portfolio U is priced so that it lies on the APT plane at point S in Fig. 28-2. In fact, if you think about it, similar arbitrage will cause the price of every asset to be revised until its expected return and risk statistics align with the APT model of Eq. (28-16b).

28-4 RECONCILING THE CAPM AND APT

Various aspects of the APT can be given economic interpretations that are insightful. For instance, the intercept term, λ_0, in Eq. (28-16a) must equal the return on a riskless asset when an asset with zero sensitivities to all the indexes is considered. The derivation of the APT is in no way dependent upon the existence of a riskless asset. However, if we define the return on a zero beta or riskless asset to be R, then if such an asset exists, $\lambda_0 = R$. Using this equality allows the APT model of Eq. (28-16a) to be equivalently rewritten in *risk-premium form*, as shown in Eqs. (28-26a) and (28-26b).

$$E(r_i) - \lambda_0 = \lambda_1 b_{i1} + \lambda_2 b_{i2} \tag{28-26a}$$

$$E(r_i) - R = \lambda_1 b_{i1} + \lambda_2 b_{i2} \quad \text{since } \lambda_0 = R \tag{28-26b}$$

The lambda coefficient associated with the risk sensitivity to the jth index, denoted λ_j, measures the increase in expected return the market requires to induce investors to assume a one-unit increase in b_{ij} risk. The λ_j coefficient thus measures the *market price of risk* for whatever risk is measured by b_{ij}.

**28-4.1
The CAPM**

When $b_{i1} = 1.0$ and $b_{i2} = 0$ then APT Eq. (28-26b) reduces to Eqs. (28-27a) and (28-27b).

$$E(r_i) - R = \lambda_1 b_{i1} \tag{28-27a}$$

$$E(r_i) = R + \lambda_1 b_{i1} \tag{28-27b}$$

Equation (28-27b) is simply the capital asset pricing model (CAPM) with λ_1 defined in Eq. (28-28) and b_i as the beta coefficient from the characteristic line of Chap. 10. That is, Eq. (28-27b) is the CAPM.

$$\lambda_1 = E(r_m) - R \text{ in Eq. (28-27b)} \tag{28-28}$$

This interpretation of the APT shows that the CAPM is merely a special case of the APT. The derivation of the CAPM in Eq. (28-27b) from the APT model of Eq. (28-26a) shows that the CAPM and the APT theories do not contradict each other.[11]

11 Robert Jarrow and Andrew Rudd, ''A Comparison of the APT and CAPM,'' *Journal of Banking and Finance*, June 1983, vol. 7, no. 2, pp. 295-303.

The k-factor return-generating process of Eq. (28-11) was abbreviated to Eq. (28-12) for the sake of expedition. If this simplification were not employed, the k-factor APT model shown in Eq. (28-29) would have been derived instead of the two- factor APT model of Eq. (28-16a).

$$E(r_i) = \lambda_0 + \lambda_1 b_{i1} + \lambda_2 b_{i2} + \ldots + \lambda_k b_{ik} \tag{28-29}$$

Equation (28-29) is the APT in a k-dimensional hyperplane that has all the implications suggested for the two-factor APT model above. In particular, Eqs. (28-22), (28-23), (28-24), and (28-25), which define the arbitrage portfolio, are also true in the k-dimensional hyperplane.

28-5 COMPARING APT WITH MPT

The modern portfolio theory (MPT) of Markowitz and Ross's more recent APT are competing for the attention of the finance profession. Let us compare and contrast these two theories so we can understand why proponents of the new APT suggest its superiority over the older and more widely accepted MPT.

The capital asset pricing model (CAPM), which was discussed in Chaps. 10 and 24, is probably the single most important aspect of the MPT. It has been shown that MPT's important CAPM is merely a special case of the APT. Thus, APT may be viewed as a logical extension, generalization, and natural outgrowth of the MPT. Other comparisons of the two theories are reviewed in this section as a way to obtain a better perspective on the APT.

All economic theories are based on one or more simplifying assumptions. Economic theories based on fewer and more realistic assumptions are more popular than more highly contrived theories because they are easier to learn, apply, and explain. APT and MPT both employ simplifying assumptions. One of the arguments favouring APT over MPT is that the APT's greater generality is accomplished in spite of the fact that APT is based on fewer simplifying assumptions.

Like MPT, APT assumes that investors prefer more wealth over less wealth. Both theories also assume that investors dislike risk. Stated in terms of the utility theory (explained in the appendix to Chap. 25), both theories assume that all investors have positive but diminishing marginal utility of wealth (or returns) and make investment decisions that will maximize their expected utility. These are realistic assumptions.

Other MPT simplifying assumptions (explained in Chap. 24) that are shared by APT are (1) that capital markets are perfect and (2) that investors have homogeneous expectations. *Perfect markets* is an assumption which is widely used by economists, and it is easy to accept. By assuming that the capital asset markets are perfect, economists assume away the possibility that prices are manipulated or distorted away from the equilibrium values established by supply and demand.

28-4.2
The k-Dimensional APT Hyperplane

28-5.1
APT Is More General than MPT

28-5.2
APT Employs Fewer Assumptions

28-5.3
The Underlying Assumptions

Homogeneous expectations is a more heroic assumption. *Homogeneous expectations* implies that all investors share the same risk and return perceptions for any given asset. The MPT and APT theories both assume that investors have different assessments for different assets. But, investors are assumed to all have the same risk and return perceptions for any particular asset to obviate the need to complicate the model with differences of opinion over how investors view a particular investment opportunity.

Supporters of APT argue its superiority over MPT because of the following assumptions that MPT requires but are not needed in the APT. Unlike MPT, APT is (1) not restricted to a one-period planning horizon; (2) not restricted to rates of price change that conform to a normal empirical probability distribution of returns; (3) not dependent on any strong assumptions about investors' utility functions in order to generate a two-parameter model; (4) not based on a market portfolio that is a uniquely desirable investment; and (5) not based on any requirement for riskless borrowing and lending.

Although the APT requires fewer assumptions than the more specific and restrictive MPT model, the APT does depend on one unique and fairly unrealistic assumption. The APT no-money-invested assumption, Eq. (28-22), presumes that the arbitraging short sellers are able to obtain 100 percent of the proceeds from their short sales to finance the purchase of their equal and offsetting long positions. Realistically, only a few professional investors (such as NYSE specialists) are able to achieve anything approaching this utopian situation. However, it only takes a few well-funded investors who are arbitrageurs to maintain the "law of one price" on which the APT is based.

28-6 EMPIRICAL TESTS OF APT

Empirically testing the APT involves a two-step process. This process employs two different phases of statistical estimates. It is informative to recall how the CAPM is estimated in order to see how the APT tests are structured —the two differing models employ somewhat analogous empirical estimation procedures.

CAPM EMPIRICAL TEST PROCEDURE Empirically testing the CAPM begins with a "first-pass" time-series regression for each different asset, to estimate the characteristic line and the beta coefficient for each asset sampled. Essentially, a list (or vector) of one-period rates of return from the ith asset,

$$[r_{it}, r_{i,t+1}, r_{i,t+2}, r_{i,t+3}, \ldots, r_{i,t+T}]$$

are regressed onto a list of concurrent market returns.

$$[r_{mt}, r_{m,t+1}, r_{m,t+2}, r_{m,t+3}, \ldots, r_{m,t+T}]$$

The market returns are the independent variable that is used to explain the behaviour of the ith asset's returns in a simple regression of the form shown below.

$$r_{it} = a_i + b_i r_{m,t} + e_{i,t} \tag{10-1}$$

where $e_{i,t}$ is a normally distributed random variable with a mean value of zero and a constant variance. After the time-series regression above is estimated for many different assets, one "second-pass" cross-sectional regression is used to measure the risk-return relationship between the average rates of return and the beta risk coefficients for the sampled assets. This second-pass simple regression is of the form below.

$$\begin{pmatrix} \text{Average rate of} \\ \text{return for asset } i \end{pmatrix} = A + B \begin{pmatrix} \text{beta for} \\ \text{asset } i \end{pmatrix} + u_i \tag{28-30}$$

The cross-sectional regression above is an empirical estimate of the CAPM.

APT EMPIRICAL TEST PROCEDURE USING FACTOR ANALYSIS To test or estimate the APT model a statistical methodology called factor analysis is frequently used. *Factor analysis* simultaneously performs two functions in its "first-pass" computation. The factor analysis algorithm analyzes time-series data of $T + 1$ periods' rates of return over a cross section of N different assets and statistically *extracts* those risk factors that systematically affect the returns from the sampled assets. Essentially, factor analysis simultaneously analyzes all the returns from N assets over $T + 1$ time periods—that is, all the data in the matrix below—in the "first-pass" computation.

$$\begin{bmatrix} r_{1,t}, r_{1,t+1}, r_{1,t+2}, \dots, r_{1,t+T} \\ r_{2,t}, r_{2,t+1}, r_{2,t+2}, \dots, r_{2,t+T} \\ \cdot \\ \cdot \\ \cdot \\ r_{N,t}, r_{N,t+1}, r_{N,t+2}, \dots, r_{N,t+T} \end{bmatrix}$$

Factor analysis produces or extracts its own explanatory variables, called *factors*, from the matrix of returns above. The purpose of factor analysis is to reduce the N by $T + 1$ matrix of returns to a smaller k by $T + 1$ matrix that explains all or most of the variation in the matrix of returns. The k factors extracted by factor analysis have *factor scores* like the $F_{i,t}$ value for the ith factor in time period t, shown in the factor matrix below.

$$\begin{bmatrix} F_{1,t}, F_{1,t+1}, F_{1,t+2}, \dots, F_{1,t+T} \\ F_{2,t}, F_{2,t+1}, F_{2,t+2}, \dots, F_{2,t+T} \\ \cdot \\ \cdot \\ \cdot \\ F_{k,t}, F_{k,t+1}, F_{k,t+2}, \dots, F_{k,t+T} \end{bmatrix}$$

The factor scores in the matrix above are used as the independent variables in the second part of the "first-pass" factor analysis computations.

In the second stage of the "first-pass" computation to estimate the APT model empirically, regression analysis is used to estimate the b_{ij} coefficients for the ith asset's sensitivity to the jth factor. These $b_{i,t}$ coefficients are called *factor loadings*. Time-series regressions of the form at the top of page 816 yield estimates of the factor loadings.

$$r_{it} = a_i + b_{i1} F_{1t} + \ldots + b_{ik} F_{kt} + e_{it} \qquad (28\text{-}31)$$

To be more specific about what is obtained, factor analysis yields factor scores in the first portion of the *first-pass* computation that are employed in a regression to get estimates of the factor loadings, denoted b_{ij} in Eqs. (28-10b) and (28-16a) in this chapter, for instance. Thus, in the "first pass" the factor analysis computes factor loadings for each asset ($i = 1, 2,\ldots N$) and every risk factor ($j = 1, 2,\ldots k$). These factor loadings are somewhat like the betas obtained from the "first-pass" characteristic line estimates when testing the CAPM.

A "second-pass" regression yields estimates of the APT *factor risk-premiums*, denoted λ_j. The cross-sectional model below is used to regress the assets' average returns, $\bar{r}_i$, on their factor loadings, b_{ij}, and obtain estimates of the λ regression statistics.

$$\bar{r}_i = \lambda_0 + \lambda_1 b_{i1} + \lambda_2 b_{i2} + \ldots + \lambda_k b_{ik} + u_i \qquad (28\text{-}32)$$

This second-pass regression also produces separate statistics (called t statistics) for each value of lambda, λ, that indicate whether or not the estimated risk-premiums are statistically significant. If these risk-premiums are significantly different from zero, then the jth factor is said to be "priced" or valued by the market in the determination of market prices. The second-pass regression's goodness-of-fit statistics (such as the correlation coefficient) also indicate how well the factors explain the securities' average returns. Let us consider specific empirical studies.

28-7 AN INITIAL STUDY BY ROLL AND ROSS IN 1980[12]

Factor analysis is a technique of statistical analysis with which most financial analysts were unfamiliar in 1976, when Stephen A. Ross's seminal article introducing APT was published.[13] As a result, few empirical tests of the new APT were published soon after the theory's 1976 introduction.[14] Here we will

---

12 R. Roll and S. Ross, "An Empirical Investigation of the Arbitrage Pricing Theory," *Journal of Finance*, December 1980, vol. 35, pp. 1073-1103.

13 S. Ross, "The Arbitrage Pricing Theory of Capital Asset Pricing," *Journal of Economic Theory*, December 1976, pp. 344-360.

14 Some of the earliest empirical studies were A. Gehr, "Some Tests of the Arbitrage Pricing Theory," *Journal of the Midwest Finance Association*, 1978. An interesting factor analysis study not directly related to APT was published by Benjamin F. King, "Market and Industry Factors in Stock Price Behavior," *Journal of Business*, January 1966, supp., vol. 39, pp. 139-190. More recently published APT studies include the following: Nai-fu Chen, "Some Empirical Tests of the Theory of Arbitrage Pricing," *Journal of Finance*, December 1983, vol. 38, no. 5, pp. 1393-1414; Stephen A. Ross, "Return, Risk, and Arbitrage," in Irwin Friend and James Bicksler (eds.) *Risk and Return in Finance*, vol. 1, (Cambridge, Mass.: Ballinger, 1977); S. Brown and M. Weinstein, "A New Approach to Testing Asset Pricing Models: The Bilinear Paradigm," *Journal of Finance*, 1983, vol. 38, pp. 711-743; J. D. Jobson, "A Multivariate Linear Regression Test for the Arbitrage Pricing Theory," *Journal of Finance*, September 1982, vol. 37, no. 4, pp. 1037-1041; Phillip H. Dybvig, "An Explicit Bound on Deviations from APT Pricing in a Finite Economy," *Journal of Financial Economics*, December 1983, pp. 483-495; Marc R. Reinganum, "The Arbitrage Pricing Theory: Some Empirical Results," *Journal of Finance*, May 1981, vol. 36, no. 2; B. Lehman and D. Modest, "Testing the Arbitrage Pricing Model," University of Columbia working paper, July 1985.

review some of the major findings of an initial inquiry prepared by Stephen Ross and Richard Roll (RR hereafter).

RR employed factor-analytic techniques to analyze 1,260 NYSE stocks divided into forty-two groups containing thirty stocks each. Daily stock price returns from 1962 through 1972—that is, 2,619 trading days of returns for each stock—were analyzed. After the factor loadings were estimated in the first step of their tests, RR used multiple regression to perform the second step of their study. RR ran a separate cross-sectional multiple regression for each of the forty-two groups of stocks. The factor loadings, b_{ij}, from the first step of the analysis were the independent variables in the multiple regressions of the second step. The cross-sectional regression coefficient, λ_j, for the jth factor loading is an empirical estimate of that factor's risk-premium. One or more of these regression coefficients should be statistically significantly different from zero if APT is to be substantiated. Tables 28-4 and 28-5 summarize some of RR's findings.

TABLE 28-4   RESULTS FROM 42 CROSS-SECTIONAL REGRESSIONS FOR EQ. (28-26b),
$$[E(r_i) - 6\%] = \lambda_1 b_{i1} + \lambda_2 b_{i2} + \ldots$$

NUMBER OF SIGNIFICANT FACTORS AT 95% LEVEL	NUMBER OF GROUPS (OUT OF 42) WITH AT LEAST AS MANY SIGNIFICANT FACTORS AS INDICATED IN COLUMN ONE	PERCENTAGE OF 42 GROUPS THAT WERE SIGNIFICANT	EXPECTED PERCENT DUE TO CHANCE IF ALL $\lambda_i = 0$
One factor	37	88.1%	22.6%
Two factors	24	57.1%	2.6%
Three factors	14	33.3%	0.115%
Four factors	7	16.7%	0.003%
Five factors	2	4.8%	0.00003%

Source: R. Roll and S. Ross, "An Empirical Investigation of the Arbitrage Pricing Theory," *Journal of Finance,* December 1980, p. 1092, table III.

TABLE 28-5   RESULTS FROM 42 CROSS-SECTIONAL REGRESSIONS FOR EQ. (28-29),
$$[E(r_i) = \lambda_0 + \lambda_1 b_{i1} + \lambda_2 b_{i2} + \ldots$$

NUMBER OF SIGNIFICANT FACTORS AT 95% LEVEL	NUMBER OF GROUPS (OUT OF 42) WITH AT LEAST AS MANY SIGNIFICANT FACTORS AS INDICATED IN COLUMN ONE	PERCENTAGE OF 42 GROUPS THAT WERE SIGNIFICANT	EXPECTED PERCENT DUE TO CHANCE IF ALL $\lambda_i = 0$
One factor	29	69.0%	22.6%
Two factors	20	47.6%	2.6%
Three factors	3	7.1%	0.115%
Four factors	2	4.8%	0.003%
Five factors	0	0	0.00003%

Source: R. Roll and S. Ross, "An Empirical Investigation of the Arbitrage Pricing Theory," *Journal of Finance,* December 1980, p. 1094, Table IV.

Table 28-4 presents the estimates of the APT model of Eq. (28-26b), assuming the riskless rate was 6 percent ($R = 6.0\%$) in order to calculate the securities' risk-premiums. At least one of the five risk factors (λ_j for $j = 1, 2,...,5$) tested was statistically significant at the 95 percent level of significance for thirty-seven out of the forty-two (that is, 88.1 percent of the groups). Table 28-4 also shows that two or more factors were significant for twenty-four out of the forty-two groups—that is, 57.1 percent. And, at least three factors were significant for one-third of the forty-two groups. About one-sixth of the forty-two groups had four or more factors that were significant. Two (or 4.8 percent) of the forty-two groups had five significant factors. Two out of forty-two groups may not seem like very many—until the fourth column of Table 28-4 is considered. Column four gives the percentage of the forty-two groups that are expected to have the indicated number of significant groups if, in fact, none of the groups were actually significant (that is, due solely to random sampling error). In all five cases, the percent that were actually significant far exceeded the percent that would result from only sampling error. Even though these test results suggest that the APT-based factor analysis can explain a significant amount of common stock returns, RR reformulated their test slightly in order to obtain additional evidence.

Table 28-5 shows the results of RR's test of APT Eq. (28-29). The only difference between RR's test results in Table 28-4 and the results in Table 28-5 is in the riskless rates of interest used in the two tests. The results in Table 28-4 used a 6 percent ($R = 6.0\%$) riskless rate of interest to calculate the excess returns, $[E(r_i) - 6.0\%]$, which served as the independent variable. In contrast, RR used a multiple regression algorithm that estimated its own intercept coefficient, λ_0, to serve as an estimate of the rate of return from an asset that has no systematic risk. The same NYSE common stock data were used for both tests.

The results in Table 28-5 show that twenty-nine out of the forty-two groups (that is, 69 percent) had a least one statistically significant factor at the 95 percent level of statistical significance. For twenty of the forty-two (or 47.6 percent) groups, at least two factors were significant. For 7 percent (or three out of forty-two) of the groups at least three of the risk factors were significant. And four factors were significant for two (or 4.8 percent) of the groups. Although these results do not furnish evidence that is quite as strong as the results in Table 28-4, the results in both tables are much more than would occur merely as the result of normal sampling error.

The results in Table 28-4 suggest that three or possibly even four risk factors exist that systematically influence common stock returns. RR say that the statistically significant risk factors are "priced"—that is, their impact is reflected in the security prices to some statistically significant extent. The results in Table 28-5 support the existence of two statistically significant risk factors. That is, only two risk factors are "priced" according to the results in Table 28-5.

The coefficients of determination (that is, the squared multiple correlation coefficients) associated with RR's cross-sectional regression results in Tables 28-4 and 28-5 were in the range of 50 to 60 percent. This means that the factor loadings explained over half the variance in the common stock's returns. This is a high percentage for individual securities. In comparison, King found that the single-factor characteristic line model explained slightly less than 30 percent of the average common stock's returns.[15]

In an earlier study using longer time periods and different sample data, Gehr found two and possibly three significant risk factors.[16] The high coefficients of determination reported by RR and the similar results of Gehr lend empirical support to the validity of the APT.

28-8 EMPIRICAL TESTS OF THE APT USING CANADIAN DATA

Tests of the arbitrage pricing theory, using Canadian data, have been conducted by Hughes, Kryzanowski and To, Fisher and Boyle, and Fisher.[17]

Support for the APT in Canada were found in all cases although the characteristics varied somewhat from the U.S. findings. Hughes, in the first study using Canadian data, found that there were three or four price factors underlying Canadian security returns. Kryzanowski and To[18], using both Canadian and U.S. data, found a larger number of common factors with Canadian as compared with the U.S. data. However, they concluded that only about two factors were significant in both countries. Fisher[19], and Boyle and Fisher,[20] using Canadian monthly return data based on the Laval TSE Return File for the period 1963 to 1982, found that as many as fifteen factors are relevant in explaining the variances on Canadian security returns. However, they also found that only six or seven factors were economically relevant. Most important, the authors conclude that at this embryonic stage of APT development, "We do *not* know what the common factors [in Canada] are, or how they are related to broad economic forces."[21]

28-9 PROBLEMS WITH APT EMPIRICAL TESTS

Although the initial empirical tests of the APT by Gehr and by Roll and Ross (RR) are supportive, their findings are also clouded by several problems.

15 B. F. King, "Market and Industry Factors in Stock Price Behavior," *Journal of Business*, January 1966, pp. 139-190.

16 A. Gehr, Jr., "Some Tests of the Arbitrage Pricing Theory," *Journal of the Midwest Finance Association*, 1978, pp. 99- 106.

17 Patricia J. Hughes, "A Test of the Arbitrage Pricing Theory Using Canadian Security Returns," working paper, Graduate School of Management, University of California, Los Angeles, August 1981 (revised January 1984).

18 Lawrence Kryzanowski and Minh Chau To, "General Factor Models and the Structure, of Security Returns," *Journal of Financial and Qualitative Analysis*, vol. 18, March 1983, pp. 31-52.

19 K. Fisher, "Testing the Arbitrage Pricing Theory: Some Empirical Results," paper presented at the Western Finance Association Meetings, Phoenix, Arizona, June 1985.

20 Phelim P. Boyle, and Kathy Fisher, "The Mystery and the Reality of the Arbitrage Pricing Theory," manuscript, University of Waterloo. This paper also contains a prologue that draws an interesting parallel between the progression of the modern asset-pricing models from CAPM to APT and the writings of two ancient Greek philosophers. Interested students can see how creative thinking and research can remove the finance discipline from its narrow confines into the broader structure of philosophy and the other humanities.

21 Ibid., p. 17.

These problems are essentially problems with factor analysis, not problems with the APT model.

First, one problem inherent in any empirical application of factor analysis is that the statistical procedure is not capable of testing rigorously specified hypotheses. Regression analysis, in contrast, is a statistical tool that can be used to rigorously test specific models and indicate whether or not the data support the model being tested. But factor analysis is such a *flexible procedure*, it is capable of accidentally furnishing support for models that are illogical and/or erroneous because sampling errors may influence the results.[22]

A second problem with the APT tests is that the ability of the factor-analysis process to delineate risk factors to explain securities' returns is highly *dependent upon the sample* of securities being analyzed. Thus, for example, each of the forty-two groups of thirty stocks used by RR could conceivably contain different risk factors. Stated differently, if two significant risk factors were found in each of RR's forty-two groups, for instance, this hypothetical finding might actually represent as many as eighty-four different factors, or as few as two factors, or any number between two and eighty-four. The way to reduce this problem is to increase the sample size so that it becomes equal in size to the population size. This is a costly process, at least, and is simply impossible in some circumstances. Furthermore, it can be so difficult to identify the delineated factors that distinguishing among them can be another whole problem in itself.

Third, *"errors in the variables"* is a statistical problem that results because the factor loadings are statistical estimates that may contain sampling error. As a result, the second-pass cross-sectional regression used in APT tests is likely to have downward-biased goodness-of-fit statistics and regression coefficients.

Fourth, the *signs* on the factor loadings have no logical meaning. The signs of the b_{ij} sensitivity coefficients may be either positive or negative for essentially the same factor from one sample to the next. This, in turn, causes the signs of the λ_j coefficients in the second-pass regression to have no rational economic meaning—since the λ_j's are based on the b_{ij}'s. Furthermore, there is also a scaling problem. If the b_{ij} is halved, then as a result the associated λ_j is doubled.

22 Jay Shanken, ''The Arbitrage Pricing Theory: Is It Testable?'' *Journal of Finance*, December 1982, vol. 37, no. 5, pp. 1129-1140. See also M. Reinganum, ''The Arbitrage Pricing Theory: Some Empirical Results,'' *Journal of Finance*, May 1981, vol. 36, pp. 313-321. Both of these studies are critical of the ability of APT to be tested and measured empirically. A comment that disagrees with the nontestability hypothesis is Phillip H. Dybvig and Stephen A. Ross, ''Yes, the APT Is Testable,'' *Journal of Finance*, September 1985, vol. 40, no. 4, pp. 1173-1188. Other critical discussions are furnished by: Phoebus J. Dhrymes, Irwin Friend, and N. Bulent Gultekin, ''A Critical Reexamination of the Empirical Evidence on the Arbitrage Pricing Theory,'' *Journal of Finance*, June 1984, vol. 39, no. 2, pp. 323-346; Phoebus Dhrymes, ''Arbitrage Pricing Theory,'' *Journal of Portfolio Management*, Summer 1984, pp. 35-44. See also Richard Roll and Stephen A. Ross, ''A Critical Reexamination of the Empirical Evidence on the Arbitrage Pricing Theory: A Reply,'' *Journal of Finance*, June 1984, pp. 347- 350. D. C. Cho, E. J. Elton, and M. J. Gruber, ''On The Robustness of the Roll and Ross Arbitrage Pricing Theory,'' *Journal of Financial and Quantitative Analysis*, March 1984, vol. 19, no. 1, pp. 1-10.

Identification is a fifth problem present in most factor-analytic studies. Identifying the factors that are statistically delineated by the factor analysis procedure is one of the most interesting, and also one of the most difficult, aspects encountered with empirical tests of APT.[23]

A sixth problem involves the availability of large and heterogeneous *data* banks and computers that can handle such massive empirical data. The findings of Kryzanowski and To suggest that the number of significant factors delineated by the initial studies was too small because the data sampled were inadequate.

First, the larger the sample size in terms of time periods, the simpler is the factor structure in terms of the number of relevant factors, and the relatively more "important" is the first factor. Second, the larger the number of securities in the sample studies, the greater is the number of relevant factors. These two biases might help to explain the smaller number of factors found by authors who used a larger sample size and a smaller number of securities.[24]

Our economic intuition can suggest unanticipated risk factors that we think should be delineated by the factor-analysis tests of the APT. Unfortunately, the initial empirical studies of the APT have done very little to identify the factors that significantly influence security prices.[25] In fact, the APT

---

23 Some preliminary empirical work on factor identification includes the following: George S. Oldfield, Jr., and Richard J. Rogalski, "Treasury Bill Factors and Stock Returns," *Journal of Finance*, May 1981, vol. 36, no. 2, pp. 337-353; H. Russell Fogler, Kose John, and James Tipton, "Three Factors, Interest Rate Differentials and Stock Groups," *Journal of Finance*, May 1981, vol. 36, no. 2, pp. 323-335; William F. Sharpe, "Factors in New York Stock Exchange Security Returns," *Journal of Portfolio Management*, Summer 1982, pp. 5-19; R. Roll and S. Ross, "The Arbitrage Pricing Theory Approach to Strategic Portfolio Planning," *Financial Analysts Journal*, May-June 1984, pp. 14-26. In the preceding *FAJ* article Roll and Ross suggest that their empirical research has identified four factors: (1) unanticipated changes in inflation; (2) unanticipated changes in industrial production; (3) unanticipated changes in risk-premiums (as measured by the yield spread between low-grade and high-grade bonds); and (4) unanticipated changes in the slope of the yield curve.

24 Lawrence Kryzanowski and Minh Chau To, "General Factor Models and the Structure of Security Returns," *Journal of Financial and Quantitative Analysis*, March 1983, vol. 18, no. 1, pp. 48-49.

25 Various studies have independently suggested different risk factors that may have a significant impact on security prices. The price-earnings ratio has been suggested by S. Basu, "Investment Performance of Common Stocks in Relation to Their Price- Earnings Ratio: A Test of the Efficient Market Hypothesis," *Journal of Finance*, June 1973, pp. 643-682. Industry factors was suggested by B. F. King, "Market and Industry Factors in Stock Price Behavior," *Journal of Business*, January 1966, pp. 139-190. Farrell suggested more broadly based stock groups: J. L. Farrell, Jr., "Analyzing Covariation of Returns to Determine Homogeneous Stock Groupings," *Journal of Business*, April 1974, pp. 186-207. Some studies of the market reaction to dividend announcements include G. Charest, "Dividend Information, Stock Returns and Market Efficiency—II," *Journal of Financial Economics*, June-September 1978, vol. 6, pp. 297-330; R. R. Pettit, "Dividend Announcements, Security Performance and Capital Market Efficiency," *Journal of Finance*, December 1972, vol. 27, pp. 993-1007; R. H. Litzenberger and Krishna Ramaswamy, "The Effect of Personal Taxes and Dividends on Capital Asset Prices: Theory and Empirical Evidence," *Journal of Financial Economics*, June 1979, pp. 117-162; and others.

The following papers examine the relationship between returns and firm size: R. W. Banz, "The Relationship between Return and Market Value of Common Stocks," *Journal of Financial Economics*, March 1981, vol. 9, pp. 3-18; M. R. Reinganum, "Misspecification of

tests reported above have not given us a clue as to what risk factors might influence security prices. This is an area where further work is needed.[26]

Many empirical investigations of new APT will doubtless emerge during the decade of the 1980s to clarify our understanding. Currently, APT tells us that linear combinations of unspecified risk factors determine securities' expected returns. The initial research by Roll and Ross and by Gehr suggested that two, three, or four factors were all that were significant. However, the study by Kryzanowski and To suggested that a larger number of factors may be significant.[27] From the investment managers' viewpoint, identifying the significant factors is the most important aspect of APT research. This latter task will keep many financial researchers busy for the next few years.[28]

28-10   AN ALTERNATIVE APPROACH TO ESTIMATING THE APT

There is an old debate among financial analysts and economists about whether the power of economic theory and mathematics should be used to

---

Capital Asset Pricing: Empirical Anomalies Based on Earnings, Yields and Market Values,'' *Journal of Financial Economics*, March 1981, vol. 9, pp. 19-46.

Some studies of stock prices and the money supply are: R. D. Auerbach, ''Money and Stock Prices,'' *Monthly Review Federal Reserve Bank of Kansas City*, September-October 1976, pp. 3-11, R. V. L. Cooper, ''Efficient Capital Markets and the Quantity Theory of Money,'' *Journal of Finance*, June 1974, vol. 29, pp. 887-908; M. J. Hamburger and L. A. Kochin, ''Money and Stock Prices: The Channels of Influence,'' *Journal of Finance*, May 1972, vol. 27, pp. 231-249; K. E. Homa and D. M. Jaffee, ''The Supply of Money and Common Stock Prices,'' *Journal of Finance*, December 1971, vol. 26, pp. 1045-1066; M. W. Keran, ''Expectations, Money and the Stock Market,'' *Review of the Federal Reserve Bank of Saint Louis*, June 1971, pp. 16-31; M. Palmer, ''Money, Portfolio Adjustments and Stock Prices,'' *Financial Analysts Journal*, July-August 1970, vol. 26, pp. 19-22; J. E. Pesando, ''The Supply of Money and Common Stock Prices: Further Observations on the Econometric Evidence,'' *Journal of Finance*, June 1974, vol. 29, pp. 909-922; R. J. Rogalski and J. D. Vinso, ''Stock Prices, Money Supply and the Direction of Causality,'' *Journal of Finance*, September 1977, vol. 32, pp. 1017-1030; Tom Urich and Paul Wachtel, ''Market Response to the Weekly Money Supply Announcements in the 1970s,'' *Journal of Finance*, December 1981, vol. 36; and others. In addition, many other risk factors exist that might by significant.

26 Part of the problem involved in identifying the factors delineated by the factor analysis is related to the esoteric mathematical algorithm employed. Factor analysis simultaneously analyzes N assets' returns over T time periods and ''extracts'' the ''commonalities'' we call risk factors. The extraction process is not simple. There are many methods of mathematically extracting orthogonal (that is, essentially, uncorrelated) factors. But they all end up with a maximum of one factor for each variable; each factor represents the ''loadings'' of the different variables' commonalities on that factor. Interpreting these factors, even the statistically significant ones, is difficult because they are contrived linear combinations of the returns from selected assets. Although factor analysis tells the researcher which assets' returns contributed to each factor, this list of assets' names does not clearly identify the resulting extracted factor. Furthermore, after the first factor is extracted the remaining data are mathematically manipulated (that is, rotated to create either new orthogonal or new oblique residual factors), so these derived factors can be indirect and abstruse.

27 Lawrence Kryzanowski and Minh Chau To, ''General Factor Models and the Structure of Security Returns,'' *Journal of Financial and Quantitative Analysis*, March 1983, vol. 18, no. 1, pp. 48-49.

28 Many preliminary APT research studies exist that are not published or are not in a quotable form at the date of this writing.

derive a rigorous theoretical model before the model is tested empirically—as in the case of the CAPM, for instance. Those who take the other side in this debate argue that the empirical data should be analyzed to see what relationship can be found on which to base a theory—like factor analysis does in delineating the APT, for example. One relevant consideration is that without a prespecified theoretical model, the statistical tests that can be employed to validate or reject a theory are weaker and harder to interpret. For instance, in the case of the very general APT model, we have no idea about what risk factors to test, or what values the risk-premiums on these risk factors should be expected to have. All we can say in advance of empirically estimating the APT model is that we expect some unknown number of unspecified risk-premiums to emerge and be statistically significant. It is difficult to reject such a vague model.

Economics discussions in the earlier chapters of this book defined the following types of investment risk factors that factor analysis might be expected to delineate empirically if it were employed to estimate an APT model.

28-10.1 Economic Theory Suggests Risk Factors

Default risk factor
Interest rate risk factor
Market risk factor
Purchasing power risk factor
Management risk factor
Callability risk factor
Convertibility risk factor
Marketability risk factor
Political risk factor
Industry factors

Chapters 9, 10, 16, and the appendix to Chap. 9 discuss these investment influences, review the underlying economic theory about each factor, and present empirical evidence to help identify the different risk factors. All these risks are well known and widely recognized.[29]

Economic intuition suggests that some of the risk factors listed above might be delineated by the factor-analysis tests of the APT. And various studies of the influences that affect security prices have suggested some more specific factors that we might expect empirical estimates of the APT model to find.[30] Unfortunately, the initial empirical studies of the APT have done very little to identify the factors that significantly influence security prices. In fact, the APT tests reported above have not given us a clue as to what risk factors

---

[29] Harry Sauvain, *Investment Management* (Englewood Cliffs, N. J.: Prentice- Hall, 1973). Sauvain's investments textbook devotes several chapters to discussing the risk factors covered in Chap. 9 of this book. Other books also discuss these different types of investment risk factors.

[30] Some preliminary empirical work on factor identification includes the following: George S. Oldfield, Jr., and Richard J. Rogalski, "Treasury Bill Factors and Stock Returns," *Journal of Finance*, May 1981, vol. 36, no. 2, pp. 337-353; H. Russell Fogler, Kose John, and James Tipton, "Three Factors, Interest Rate Differentials and Stock Groups," *Journal of Finance*, May 1981, vol. 36, no. 2, pp. 323-335; William F. Sharpe, "Factors in New York Stock Exchange Security Returns," *Journal of Portfolio Management*, Summer 1982, pp. 5-19.

have a significant influence over security prices. This is an area where further work is needed.[31]

**28-10.2
An
Alternative
to Factor
Analysis**

Most of the initial APT empirical researchers have used factor analysis to endogenously estimate the indexes (or risk factors) and the sensitivity coefficients (or factor loadings) for the indexes. Some people even argue that factor analysis (or a similar statistical procedure called principal components analysis) is the only satisfactory way to test the APT model empirically. However, some financial analysts and economists prefer to estimate an APT model using a different empirical testing procedure — a two-step procedure somewhat like the procedure used to empirically estimate the CAPM.[32]

Risk factors that may affect security prices can be developed from exogenous economic theory rather than by endogenous factor-analytic techniques. Developing the risk factors exogenously from economic theory is the first step in the two-step procedure that differs from the factor-analysis approach usually employed to estimate APT models. Then cross-sectional regression analysis can be used in the second step of the empirical work to verify or reject the hypothesized economic variables.

Two basic types of economic theories can be employed to develop indexes (or risk factors) in the first step of the two-step alternative to using factor analysis to delineate risk factors. First, macroeconomic theory can be used to develop risk factors like interest rate risk, purchasing power risk, market risk, and other risks of the type defined in Chaps. 9 and 16. Second, the economic theory of the firm can be used to delineate factors such as Macaulay's duration for a firm's securities; a firm's cash dividend yield; the beta coefficient from the characteristic line for a firm's securities; a numeric surrogate for securities' quality ratings, and other similar indexes. After some economically logical explanatory variables are hypothesized in the first step of the alternative APT estimation procedure, these variables can be tested empirically in the second step by using a cross-sectional regression to estimate an APT model like Eq. (28-16a) or (28-29) from this chapter.

The two-step estimation procedure proposed as an alternative to using factor analysis to estimate an APT model has already been employed by various researchers.[33] Some of these empirical studies were published before the

---

31 See footnote 25.

32 Edwin J. Elton and Martin J. Gruber, for instance, argue in favour of using indexes with theoretical economics foundations in empirical APT investigations, rather than using indexes manufactured by the factor-analysis algorithm. See Elton and Gruber's *Modern Portfolio Theory and Investment Analysis*, 2d ed. (New York: Wiley, 1984). pp. 357- 366.

33 See E. Fama and J. MacBeth, ''Risk, Return and Equilibrium: Empirical Tests,'' *Journal of Political Economy*, May-June 1973, vol. 81, no. 3, pp. 607-636; J. C. Francis, ''Skewness and Investors: Decisions,'' *Journal of Financial and Quantitative Analysis*, March 1975; J. C. Francis, ''Analysis of Equity Returns: A Survey with Extensions,'' *Journal of Economics and Business*, Spring-Summer 1977, vol. 29, no. 3, pp. 181-192; F. J. Fabozzi and J. C. Francis, ''Industry Effects and the Determinants of Beta,'' *Quarterly Review of Economics and Business*, Autumn 1979, vol. 19, no. 3, pp. 61-74; F. J. Fabozzi and J. C. Francis, ''Mutual Fund Risk Statistics for Bull and Bear Markets: An Empirical Examination,'' *Journal of Finance*, December 1979, vol. 34, no. 5, pp. 1243-1250; C. F. Lee, F. J. Fabozzi, and J. C. Francis, ''Generalized Functional Form for Mutual Fund Returns,'' *Journal of Financial and Quantitative Analysis*,

development of the APT, and thus, APT is not mentioned in the reports of those empirical estimates. However, these published tests and extensions of these efforts provide an alternative way to estimate APT models, like Eq. (28-29), without using factor analysis.

28-11   CHAPTER SUMMARY

The APT is a new theoretical model that suggests how to price market assets. Prior to the development of the APT, the capital asset pricing model (CAPM) was the newest financial theory to explain the prices of market assets. So, it is natural to compare and contrast these two important theories.

The APT requires fewer underlying assumptions and admits more different variables into the analysis than the CAPM. Therefore, the APT is a more general and more flexible theory than the CAPM. In fact, it can be shown that the CAPM is a special case of the APT. Thus, the two theories do not contradict each other. In fact, the theories are somewhat similar because both theories delineate *systematic influences* that generate *undiversifiable covariances* between market assets as their basis for risk-premiums.

Since the APT model has been in existence a relatively short time, it has not been tested extensively with empirical data. The results of the initial empirical tests that have been published are favourable—these tests tend to suggest that the APT has more explanatory power than the CAPM. Roll and Ross have stated that

the well-known Capital Asset Pricing Model asserts that only a single number—an asset's "beta" against the market index—is required to measure risk. Arbitrage Pricing Theory asserts that an asset's riskiness, hence its long-term rate of return, is directly related to its sensitivities to unanticipated changes in four economic variables—(1) inflation, (2) industrial production, (3) risk premiums, and (4) the slope of the term structure of interest rates. Assets, even if they have the same CAPM beta, will have different patterns of sensitivities to these systematic factors.[34]

Whether these factors are also relevant for Canada is an unanswered question at this time. As Boyle and Fisher conclude, "…the existence of a relationship in United States equity markets does not necessarily imply that it also holds in Canada."[35]

December 1980, vol. 15, no. 5, 14 journal pages; C. F. Lee and J. C. Francis, "Investment Horizon, Risk Proxies, Skewness, and Mutual Fund Performance: A Theoretical Analysis and Empirical Investigation," in Haim Levy (ed.), *Readings in Finance*, vol. 4, J.A.I. Press, Greenwich, Conn., 1983, pp. 1-19. See also P. Casabona, A. Vora, and J. C. Francis, "Risk and Security Prices," *Review of Business*, Spring 1983, pp. 14-26; R. H. Litzenberger and K. Ramaswamy, "The Effects of Personal Taxes and Dividends on Capital Asset Prices: Theory and Empirical Evidence," *Journal of Financial Economics*, 1979, vol. 7, pp. 163-196; W. F. Sharpe, "Factors in NYSE Security Returns, 1931-1979," *Journal of Portfolio Management*, Summer 1982, vol. 8, no. 2, pp. 5-19.

34 Richard Roll and Stephen A. Ross, "The Arbitrage Pricing Theory Approach to Strategic Portfolio Planning," *Financial Analysts Journal*, May-June 1984, p. 14.

35 Phelim P. Boyle, and Kathy Fisher, "The Mystery and the Reality of the Arbitrage Pricing Theory," manuscript, University of Waterloo, p. 17.

While some people may expect to discover more risk factors with different identities in later empirical research, the point about multiple patterns of sensitivities that Roll and Ross assert nevertheless makes sense.[36]

QUESTIONS

1. The riskless rate of interest plays a key role in APT. True, false, or uncertain? Explain.
2. Compare and contrast the role of the market portfolio in modern portfolio theory (MPT) with its role in APT.
3. What does APT tell us about the risk factors that should determine the returns from assets?
4. Why is it claimed that APT is a more general theory than MPT?
5. Why is the word ''arbitrage'' in the name of APT?
6. Does this textbook give you any clues or suggestions as to what risk factors you might expect to be relevant in APT? Explain. (*Hint:* Consult other chapters.)
7. Compare and contrast the beta coefficient from the characteristic regression line with the sensitivity coefficient (or factor loading) in APT.
8. The capital asset pricing model (CAPM) and the arbitrage pricing theory (APT) models are very similar. True, false, or uncertain? Explain.
9. Empirical estimates of the riskless rate of interest obtained from estimates of the APT are far from realistic. True, false, or uncertain? Explain.
10. What problems cloud the results of empirical tests of the APT?

SELECTED REFERENCES

Andrew L. Comrey. *A First Course in Factor Analysis*. New York: Academic Press, 1973. A mathematical statistics book that uses matrix algebra supplemented with easy-to-read examples to explain the various approaches to factor analysis.

Phoebus Dhrymes. ''Arbitrage Pricing Theory.'' *Journal of Portfolio Management*, Summer 1984, pp. 35-44. An empirical study and critique of the APT that uses no rigorous mathematics.

Richard Roll and S. Ross. ''An Empirical Investigation of the Arbitrage Pricing Theory.'' *Journal of Finance*, December 1980, vol. 35, pp. 1073-1103. This article reviews the APT model and presents initial empirical tests of the APT. Matrix algebra is used.

S. Ross. ''The Arbitrage Pricing Theory of Capital Asset Pricing.'' *Journal of Economic Theory*, December 1976, pp. 344-360. This mathematical essay derives the APT model.

Jay Shanken. ''The Arbitrage Pricing Theory: Is It Testable?'' *Journal of Finance*, December 1982, vol. 37, no. 5, pp. 1129-1140. This article critiques the empirical application of the new APT. Some matrix algebra is used.

Financial Research Foundation of Canada. ''Putting New Investment Theories Into Practice.'' *Fall Conference Proceedings*, October 1985. See pp. 5-12 for a discussion of recent developments in APT by Stephen Ross (pages 5-7) and a report on Arbitrage Pricing in Canada by Phelim Boyle (pages 8-11).

---

[36] William F. Sharpe, ''Factor Models, CAPMs, and the APT,'' *Journal of Portfolio Management*, Fall 1984, vol. 11, no. 1, pp. 21-25. Sharpe compares and contrasts the CAPM and the APT and reaches some significant conclusions.

PART 9

MATHEMATICAL APPENDIXES

MATHEMATICAL APPENDIX A—The Present Value Concept explains how the time value of money affects security values.

MATHEMATICAL APPENDIX B—The Expected-Value Operator defines the mathematical expectation and derives some relevant theorems.

MATHEMATICAL APPENDIX C—Statistical Moments defines the first four statistical moments of a probability distribution of returns.

MATHEMATICAL APPENDIX D—Elements of Correlation and Regression Analysis defines the simple correlation coefficient, simple regression, and related terms.

MATHEMATICAL APPENDIX E—Mathematical Derivation of Formulas for Portfolio Risk and Expected Return shows how the risk and return of the individual assets combine to determine the portfolio's risk and return statistics.

MATHEMATICAL APPENDIX F—Geometric Mean Return is explained as the way to measure multiperiod rates of return.

These mathematical appendixes define various terms, concepts, and operations that may become unclear if not used recently.

The Present Value Concept

A dollar to be received in one year is not worth as much as a dollar to be received today—even if there is no doubt the dollar will be paid in one year. This is because a dollar received now can be invested in, say, a 5 percent savings account and $1.05 can be withdrawn in one year.

The Time Value of Money

The time value of money can be represented symbolically. Let v_t represent the terminal value of money at the end of time period t, p_0 represent the present value, and r represent the interest rate per period which may be earned on money that is saved for T periods starting at time $t = 0$, that is, the present time.

$$p_0(1 + r)^1 = v_1 \tag{A-1}$$

$$\$1,000(1 + .05)^1 = \$1,050$$

Equation (A-1) is only a "one-period" formula. If money is invested and left for T periods, then Eq. (A-2) shows the results.

$$P_0(1 + r)^T = v_T \tag{A-2}$$

$$\$1,000(1 + .1)^2 = \$1,210 \text{ if } T = 2$$

The numerical example above shows that $1,000 saved at $r = 10$ percent for $T = 2$ periods will grow in value to $1,210.

Present Value

Equations (A-1) and (A-2) can be used to find the *present discounted value* of money to be received at time period t. Dividing both sides of (A-2) by the quantity $(1 + r)^T$ yields (A-3).

$$p_0 = \frac{v_T}{(1 + r)^T} \tag{A-3}$$

$$\$1,000 = \frac{\$1,210}{(1 + .1)^2} = \frac{1,210}{1.21}$$

The calculations above show that the present value of $1,210 to be received $T = 2$ periods in the future is $1,000, if the interest rate or discount rate is $r = 10$ percent. The quantity $1/(1 + r)^T$ is called the *discount factor* and will sometimes be written $1/(1 + r)^T = DT_r$. For example, $500 to be received $T = 2$ periods in the future has a present value of $347.22 when $r = 20$ percent, as shown at the top of page 829:

$$p_0 = \frac{v_T}{(1 + r)^T} = v^T D_r^T \tag{A-3}$$

$$\$347.22 = \frac{\$500}{1.2^2} = \$500 D_{.2}^2$$

Equation (A-3) is a point-input-point-output present value model. This is a very simple transaction. Equation (A-4) is a more general present value model which allows for simultaneous inflows and outflows at multiple points in time. Let c_t denote the cashflow at time period t.

$$p_0 = \sum_{t=1}^{T} \frac{c_t}{(1 + r)^t} \tag{A-4}$$

$$= c_1 D_r^1 + c_2 D_r^2 + \ldots + c_T D_r^T$$

Symbols

The discussion of the time value of money that makes up this appendix utilizes the following symbols:

i = stated or coupon interest rate; this is not necessarily the total yield earned from holding the asset. i is an interest rate per period which is printed on a new bond and may bear little relation to the market rate of interest.

p_0 = present value in dollars, or the cost of the asset.

v_T = terminal or ending value in dollars.

T = the number of time periods which the investment lasts.

c_t = net cashflow in period t = cash inflow in period t less cash outflow in period $t = I_t - 0_t$.

t = the time period counter index.

D_r^T = $1/(1 + r)^T$ = the discount factor for T periods in the future at discount rate r.

k = the *appropriate* discount rate. Determining the appropriate discount rate is discussed in Chap. 9. Suffice it to say, the higher the risk, the higher k should be. The symbol k is the cost of capital; it is the discount rate which is appropriate to find the present value of an investment. This k is determined by the asset's risk and the opportunity cost of the investment. The value of k can be determined before the cashflows are estimated.

r = the yield to maturity = the internal rate of return = the market rate = the nominal yield. The value of r will typically vary with credit conditions and other factors. The symbol r is the discount rate which equates the present value of all net cashflows to the cost of the investment. Therefore, r can be determined only after all cashflows and the cost are known.

F = face or par value of a security.

iF = the dollar interest payable per period = the coupon interest rate i multiplied by the face value F.

Present Value Table

It is quite tedious to evaluate all the discount factors, $D_r^T = 1/(1 + r)^T$, when performing present value calculations. To save the analyst this trouble, present value tables have been calculated and printed. Table A-1 is a present value table. This table shows the values of D_r^T for many values of T and r. The

TABLE A-1   PRESENT VALUE TABLE*

PERIOD	1%	2%	3%	4%	5%	6%	7%	8%	9%	10%	12%	14%	15%	16%	18%	20%	24%	28%	32%	36%
1	.9901	.9804	.9709	.9615	.9524	.9434	.9346	.9259	.9174	.9091	.8929	.8772	.8696	.8621	.8475	.8333	.8065	.7813	.7576	.7353
2	.9803	.9612	.9426	.9246	.9070	.8900	.8734	.8573	.8417	.8264	.7972	.7695	.7561	.7432	.7182	.6944	.6504	.6104	.5739	.5407
3	.9706	.9423	.9151	.8890	.8638	.8396	.8163	.7938	.7722	.7513	.7118	.6750	.6575	.6407	.6086	.5787	.5245	.4768	.4348	.3975
4	.9610	.9238	.8885	.8548	.8227	.7921	.7629	.7350	.7084	.6830	.6355	.5921	.5718	.5523	.5158	.4823	.4230	.3725	.3294	.2923
5	.9515	.9057	.8626	.8219	.7835	.7473	.7130	.6806	.6499	.6209	.5674	.5194	.4972	.4761	.4371	.4019	.3411	.2910	.2495	.2149
6	.9420	.8880	.8375	.7903	.7462	.7050	.6663	.6302	.5963	.5645	.5066	.4556	.4323	.4104	.3704	.3349	.2751	.2274	.1890	.1580
7	.9327	.8706	.8131	.7599	.7107	.6651	.6227	.5835	.5470	.5132	.4523	.3996	.3759	.3538	.3139	.2791	.2218	.1776	.1432	.1162
8	.9235	.8535	.7894	.7307	.6768	.6274	.5820	.5403	.5019	.4665	.4039	.3506	.3269	.3050	.2660	.2326	.1789	.1388	.1085	.0854
9	.9143	.8368	.7664	.7026	.6446	.5919	.5439	.5002	.4604	.4241	.3606	.3075	.2843	.2630	.2255	.1938	.1443	.1084	.0822	.0628
10	.9053	.8203	.7441	.6756	.6139	.5584	.5083	.4632	.4224	.3855	.3220	.2697	.2472	.2267	.1911	.1615	.1164	.0847	.0623	.0462
11	.8963	.8043	.7224	.6496	.5847	.5268	.4751	.4289	.3875	.3505	.2875	.2366	.2149	.1954	.1619	.1346	.0938	.0662	.0472	.0340
12	.8874	.7885	.7014	.6246	.5568	.4970	.4440	.3971	.3555	.3186	.2567	.2076	.1869	.1685	.1372	.1122	.0757	.0517	.0357	.0250
13	.8787	.7730	.6810	.6006	.5303	.4688	.4150	.3677	.3262	.2897	.2292	.1821	.1625	.1452	.1163	.0935	.0610	.0404	.0271	.0184
14	.8700	.7579	.6611	.5775	.5051	.4423	.3878	.3405	.2992	.2633	.2046	.1597	.1413	.1252	.0985	.0779	.0492	.0316	.0205	.0135
15	.8613	.7430	.6419	.5553	.4810	.4173	.3624	.3152	.2745	.2394	.1827	.1401	.1229	.1079	.0835	.0649	.0397	.0247	.0155	.0099
16	.8528	.7284	.6232	.5339	.4581	.3936	.3387	.2919	.2519	.2176	.1631	.1229	.1069	.0930	.0708	.0541	.0320	.0193	.0118	.0073
17	.8444	.7142	.6050	.5134	.4363	.3714	.3166	.2703	.2311	.1978	.1456	.1078	.0929	.0802	.0600	.0451	.0258	.0150	.0089	.0054
18	.8360	.7002	.5874	.4936	.4155	.3503	.2959	.2502	.2120	.1799	.1300	.0946	.0808	.0691	.0508	.0376	.0208	.0118	.0068	.0039
19	.8277	.6864	.5703	.4746	.3957	.3305	.2765	.2317	.1945	.1635	.1161	.0829	.0703	.0596	.0431	.0313	.0168	.0092	.0051	.0029
20	.8195	.6730	.5537	.4564	.3769	.3118	.2584	.2145	.1784	.1486	.1037	.0728	.0611	.0514	.0365	.0261	.0135	.0072	.0039	.0021
25	.7798	.6095	.4776	.3751	.2953	.2330	.1842	.1460	.1160	.0923	.0588	.0378	.0304	.0245	.0160	.0105	.0046	.0021	.0010	.0005
30	.7419	.5521	.4120	.3083	.2314	.1741	.1314	.0994	.0754	.0573	.0334	.0196	.0151	.0116	.0070	.0042	.0016	.0006	.0002	.0001
40	.6717	.4529	.3066	.2083	.1420	.0972	.0668	.0460	.0318	.0221	.0107	.0053	.0037	.0026	.0013	.0007	.0002	.0001	†	†
40	.6080	.3715	.2281	.1407	.0872	.0543	.0339	.0213	.0134	.0085	.0035	.0014	.0009	.0006	.0003	.0001	†	†	†	†
60	.5504	.3048	.1697	.0951	.0535	.0303	.0173	.0099	.0057	.0033	.0011	.0004	.0002	.0001	†	†	†	†	†	†

* Present value of $1 received at the end of T years $= D_r^T = \dfrac{1}{(1+r)^T}$

† The factor is zero to four decimal places.

D_r^T values are not perfectly accurate because of rounding at the fifth decimal place.

British consols are perpetual bonds; that is, the bearer of the consol will **Perpetuities** receive periodic interest to perpetuity, but the principal will never be repaid.

To value a consol, assume that the appropriate discount rate is k. The coupon rate i on bonds almost always differs from the discount rate. The coupon rate is the interest rate paid on the face value of the bond. The face value and coupon rate are printed on the bond itself and never change once the bond is issued. Let F and i denote the face value and coupon rate, respectively. Then iF is the cashflow, which is a fixed constant. The present value of a consol may be determined with Eq. (A-4). The bar over c denotes that it has a fixed constant value.

$$p_0 = \sum_{t}^{T} \frac{c_t}{(1+k)^t} \tag{A-4}$$

$$p_0 = \sum_{t=1}^{T=\infty} \bar{c}D_k^t \quad \text{for a consol, since } T = \infty \text{ and } c_t = \bar{c} = iF$$

$$p_0 = \frac{\bar{c}}{k} \tag{A-5}$$

$$= \frac{iF}{k}$$

It is difficult (to say the least) to evaluate the sum D_k^t an infinitely large number of times, as required above. However, this problem is easily overcome by using Eq. (A-5), which shows how to find the present value p_0 of a *perpetual stream* $(T = \infty)$ of *constant cashflows*. When $T = \infty$ and the cashflows are constant, Eqs. (A-4) and (A-5) are equivalent,[1] but Eq. (A-5) saves much computation.

---

1 Equation (A-5) is derived from (A-4) as follows:

$$p_0 = \sum_{t}^{T} \bar{c}D_k^t \tag{A-4}$$

$$= \bar{c}\sum_{t}^{T} D_k^t \quad \text{since } \sum ax = a\sum x$$

$$p_0 = \bar{c}D_k^1 + \bar{c}D_k^2 + \bar{c}D_k^3 + \ldots + \bar{c}D_k^T \tag{A-4a}$$

$$p_0(1+k) = \bar{c} + \bar{c}D_k^1 + \bar{c}D_k^2 + \ldots + \bar{c}D_k^{T-1} \tag{A-4b}$$

$$p_0(1+k) - p_0 = \bar{c} - \bar{c}D_k^T \quad \text{by subtracting (A-4a) from (A-4b)}$$

$$p_0 + kp_0 - p_0 = \bar{c} - \bar{c}D_k^T$$

$$kp_0 = \bar{c} \quad \text{since } D_k^T \to 0 \text{ as } T \to \infty, \text{ the } \bar{c}D_k^T \text{ term becomes zero}$$

$$p_0 = \bar{c}/k \tag{A-5}$$

Thus, (A-5) is derived from (A-4) for the case when $T = \infty$.

TABLE A-2   THE PRESENT VALUE OF SOME ANNUITIES*

NUMBER OF PAYMENTS	1%	2%	3%	4%	5%	6%	7%	8%
1	0.9901	0.9804	0.9709	0.9615	0.9524	0.9434	0.9346	0.9259
2	1.9704	1.9416	1.9135	1.8861	1.8594	1.8334	1.8080	1.7833
3	2.9410	2.8839	2.8286	2.7751	2.7232	2.6730	2.6243	2.5771
4	3.9020	3.8077	3.7171	3.6299	3.5460	3.4651	3.3872	3.3121
5	4.8534	4.7135	4.5797	4.4518	4.3295	4.2124	4.1002	3.9927
6	5.7955	5.6014	5.4172	5.2421	5.0757	4.9173	4.7665	4.6229
7	6.7282	6.4720	6.2303	6.0021	5.7864	5.5824	5.3893	5.2064
8	7.6517	7.3255	7.0197	6.7327	6.4632	6.2098	5.9713	5.7466
9	8.5660	8.1622	7.7861	7.4353	7.1078	6.8017	6.5152	6.2469
10	9.4713	8.9826	8.5302	8.1109	7.7217	7.3601	7.0236	6.7101
11	10.3676	9.7868	9.2526	8.7605	8.3064	7.8869	7.4987	7.1390
12	11.2551	10.5753	9.9540	9.3851	8.8633	8.3838	7.9427	7.5361
13	12.1337	11.3484	10.6350	9.9856	9.3936	8.8527	8.3577	7.9038
14	13.0037	12.1062	11.2961	10.5631	9.8986	9.2950	8.7455	8.2442
15	13.8651	12.8493	11.9379	11.1184	10.3797	9.7122	9.1079	8.5595
16	14.7179	13.5777	12.5611	11.6523	10.8378	10.1059	9.4466	8.8514
17	15.5623	14.2919	13.1661	12.1657	11.2741	10.4773	9.7632	9.1216
18	16.3983	14.9920	13.7535	12.6593	11.6896	10.8276	10.0591	9.3719
19	17.2260	15.6785	14.3238	13.1339	12.0853	11.1581	10.3356	9.6036
20	18.0456	16.3514	14.8775	13.5903	12.4622	11.4699	10.5940	9.8181
25	22.0232	19.5235	17.4131	15.6221	14.0939	12.7834	11.6536	10.6748
30	25.8077	22.3965	19.6004	17.2920	15.3725	13.7648	12.4090	11.2578
40	32.8347	27.3555	23.1148	19.7928	17.1591	15.0463	13.3317	11.9246
50	39.1961	31.4236	25.7298	21.4822	18.2559	15.7619	13.8007	12.2335
60	44.9550	34.7609	27.6756	22.6235	18.9293	16.1614	14.0392	12.3766

* Present value of \$1 per year for T consecutive years $= \sum_{t=1}^{T} D_k^t = \sum_{t=1}^{T} \frac{1}{(1 + k)^t}$

Present Value of n Equal Cashflows

Sometimes an equal amount is to be received for T consecutive periods, for example, an annuity. Equation (A-4) can be used to find the present value of T equal cashflows ($c = c_t$ for all t).

$$p_0 = \sum_{t}^{T} \frac{c_t}{(1 + k)^t} \qquad \text{(A-4)}$$

$$= c_t(D_i^1) + c_2(D_i^2) + \ldots + c_n(D_k^T) \qquad \text{(A-6)}$$

$$= \bar{c}(D_i^1 + D_i^2 + D_i^3 + \ldots + D_i^T) \quad if\, c_t = \bar{c} = \text{constant}$$

$$= c \sum_{t=1}^{T} D_k^t$$

When $c_t = \bar{c}$ for n periods, Eq. (A-6) is a convenient simplification of (A-4). The sum of the D_k^t quantities in (A-6) is merely the sum of part of a column

9%	10%	12%	14%	15%	16%	18%	20%	24%	28%	32%
0.9174	0.9091	0.8929	0.8772	0.8696	0.8621	0.8475	0.8333	0.8065	0.7813	0.7576
1.7591	1.7355	1.6901	1.6467	1.6257	1.6052	1.5656	1.5278	1.4568	1.3916	1.3315
2.5313	2.4869	2.4018	2.3216	2.2832	2.2459	2.1743	2.1065	1.9813	1.8684	1.7663
3.2397	3.1699	3.0373	2.9137	2.8550	2.7982	2.6901	2.5887	2.4043	2.2410	2.0957
3.8897	3.7908	3.6048	3.4331	3.3522	3.2743	3.1272	2.9906	2.7454	2.5320	2.3452
4.4859	4.3553	4.1114	3.8887	3.7845	3.6847	3.4976	3.3255	3.0205	2.7594	2.5342
5.0330	4.8684	4.5638	4.2883	4.1604	4.0386	3.8115	3.6046	3.2423	2.9370	2.6775
5.5348	5.3349	4.9676	4.6389	4.4873	4.3436	4.0776	3.8372	3.4212	3.0758	2.7860
5.9952	5.7590	5.3282	4.9464	4.7716	4.6065	4.3030	4.0310	3.5655	3.1842	2.8681
6.4177	6.1446	5.6502	5.2161	5.0188	4.8332	4.4941	4.1925	3.6819	3.2689	2.9304
6.8052	6.4951	5.9377	5.4527	5.2337	5.0286	4.6560	4.3271	3.7757	3.3351	2.9776
7.1607	6.8137	6.1944	5.6603	5.4206	5.1971	4.7932	4.4392	3.8514	3.3868	3.0133
7.4869	7.1034	6.4235	5.8424	5.5831	5.3423	4.9095	4.5327	3.9124	3.4272	3.0404
7.7862	7.3667	6.6282	6.0021	5.7245	5.4675	5.0081	4.6106	3.9616	3.4587	3.0609
8.0607	7.6061	6.8109	6.1422	5.8474	5.5755	5.0916	4.6755	4.0013	3.4834	3.0764
8.3126	7.8237	6.9740	6.2651	5.9542	5.6685	5.1624	4.7296	4.0333	3.5026	3.0882
8.5436	8.0216	7.1196	6.3729	6.0472	5.7487	5.2223	4.7746	4.0591	3.5177	3.0971
8.7556	8.2014	7.2497	6.4674	6.1280	5.8178	5.2732	4.8122	4.0799	3.5294	3.1039
8.9501	8.3649	7.3658	6.5504	6.1982	5.8775	5.3162	4.8435	4.0967	3.5386	3.1090
9.1285	8.5136	7.4694	6.6231	6.2593	5.9288	5.3527	4.8696	4.1103	3.5458	3.1129
9.8226	9.0770	7.8431	6.8729	6.4641	6.0971	5.4669	4.9476	4.1474	3.5640	3.1220
10.2737	9.4269	8.0552	7.0027	6.5660	6.1772	5.5168	4.9789	4.1601	3.5693	3.1242
10.7574	9.7791	8.2438	7.1050	6.6418	6.2335	5.5482	4.9966	4.1659	3.5712	3.1250
10.9617	9.9148	8.3045	7.1327	6.6605	6.2463	5.5541	4.9995	4.1666	3.5714	3.1250
11.0480	9.9672	8.3240	7.1401	6.6651	6.2492	5.5553	4.9999	4.1667	3.5714	3.1250

of Table A-1. This sum of T consecutive values of D_k^t is then multiplied by the constant $\bar{c}$ to find the present value of the T equal cashflows. Table A-2 shows

the sums of T consecutive D_k^t quantities, $\displaystyle\sum_{t=1}^{T} D_k^t$, for several values of T and k.

This table is useful in finding the present value of T equal cashflows. It shows the present value of \$1 received each period for T periods when the discount rate is k.

Sometimes it is appropriate to compound the interest factor several times per period. Let b denote the number of times per period the interest is compounded. Equation (A-7) may be used for such present value problems.

Compounding Several Times per Period

$$p_0 = \sum_t^T \frac{c_t}{(1 + r/b)^{bt}} \tag{A-7}$$

Equation (A-7) takes $1/b$ times the interest rate r (that is, r/b) and compounds it b times as frequently (that is, bt) as is done when interest is compounded once a year. Since $(1 + r/b)^b > (1 + r)$, compounding more frequently yields different values. More frequent compounding decreases the present value. For example, at $r = 4$ percent the present value of $1 received in 5 years and compounded annually is $0.82193, as calculated with (A-3) below. But at $r = 4$ percent, the present value of $1 received in 5 years and compounded semiannually (that is, $b = 2$) is $0.82035. The difference is due to compounding semiannually.

$$p_0 = \frac{v_5}{(1 + r)^5}$$

$$= \$1(.82193) \tag{A-3}$$

$$= 82.193¢$$

$$p_0 \left(\frac{v_5}{(1 + r/b)^{5b}} \right)$$

$$= \$1(.82035) \tag{A-7}$$

$$= 82.035¢$$

Equation (A-7) is a popular approximation that does not yield consistent or exact values because of approximations that are demonstrated in the following inequalities.

$$\left(1 + \frac{r}{4}\right)^4 \neq (1 + r) \neq \left(1 + \frac{r}{2}\right)^2$$

For instance, consider the three following numerical examples when $r = 4.0$ percent.

QUARTERLY, $b = 4$	ANNUAL, $b = 1$	SEMIANNUAL, $b = 2$
$\frac{.04}{4} = 0.01$	$\frac{.04}{1} = .04$	$\frac{.04}{2} = 0.02$
$(1.01)^4 = 1.040604$	$(1.04)^1 = 1.04$	$(1.02)^2 = 1.0404$

None of the three values obtained in the numerical examples above are equal. Stated differently, we have employed approximations that have produced inconsistent values. To be exact the correct discount rate to be compounded b times per year should be the quantity below.

$$[(1 + r)^{1/b}] = r' \quad \text{where } r' < r$$

The two following numerical examples demonstrate the consistent way to calculate the quarterly and semiannual values.

$$[(1.04)^{1/4}]^4 = (1.0098534)^4 = 1.04 \quad \text{for quarters}$$
$$[(1.04)^{1/2}]^2] = (1.0198039)^2 = 1.04 \quad \text{for semiannual}$$

The widespread availability of computers and calculators should have made the approximations that were developed in the days of hand computation obsolete. However, many still use Eq. (A-7)[2].

---

[2] For additional discussion see Philip A. Horvath, ''A Pedagogic Note on Intra-Period Compounding and Discounting,'' *The Financial Review*, February 1985, vol. 20, no. 1, pp. 116–118.

The Expected-Value Operator (E)

An expectation is like an "average" value. For example, for one toss of a fair coin for $1, we can say the expected value of the outcome is the probability of heads times the $1 loss plus the probability of tails times the $1 gain. Symbolically,

$$\text{Expected value} = P(\text{heads})(-\$1) + P(\text{tails})(+\$1)$$
$$= .5(-1) + .5(+1) = 0$$

The above symbols are a very definite statement of what is meant by the phrase "we expect that fair gambles will break even." Writing the expression for expected value in even more general form, we say:

$$E(x) = \sum_{i=1}^{n} P_i x_i \tag{B-1}$$
$$= P_1 x_1 + P_2 x_2 + \ldots + P_n x_n$$

In words, the expected value of the variable x (for example, x might be the $1 outcome of the gamble or any other number resulting from an experiment involving chance which has n possible outcomes) equals the sum of all n products of $(P_i)(x_i)$, where P is the probability of the ith outcome [$P(\text{heads})$ = P_i = ½ in the coin example] and x_i is the ith outcome [x_i = $1 or $-$1 in the example].

Mathematicians say that the letter E as used in Eq. (B-1) is an *operator*, meaning that the letter E specifies the operation of multiplying all outcomes times their probabilities and summing those products to get the expected value.

Finding the expected value is roughly analogous to finding the weighted average by using probabilities for weights. Do not be confused, however; although the arithmetic is the same, an average is conceptually different from an expectation. An expectation is determined by its probabilities, and it represents a hypothesis about an unknown outcome; but an average is a summarizing measure. There is no conceptual connection between an average and an expectation; there is only the mechanical similarity of the calculations.

The operator E can be used to derive several important formulas. Therefore, let us consider several elementary properties of expected-value operations.

1. The expected value of a constant number is that constant. Symbolically, if c is any constant number (for example, c = 2, $-$ 99, or 1,064),

$E(c) = c$

Proof of this is given below.

$$E(c) = \sum_{i=1}^{n} P_i c = P_1 c + \ldots + P_n c$$

$$= c \sum_{i=1}^{n} P_i = c(1) = c$$

2. The expected value of a constant times a random variable equals the constant times the expected value of the random variable. Thus, if x is a random variable (for example, the -1 or $+1$ outcome of the gamble) and c is a constant (namely, the number of dollars bet on each toss),

$E(cx) = cE(x)$

The proof follows.

$$E(cx) = \sum_{i=1}^{n} P_i(cx_i) = P_1(cx_1) + \ldots + P_n(cx_n)$$

$$= P_1 cx_1 + \ldots + P_n cx_n$$

$$= c(P_1 x_1 + P_2 x_2 + \ldots + P_n x_n) = c \sum_{i=1}^{n} P_i x_i = cE(x)$$

3. The expected value of the sum of n independent random variables is simply the sum of their expected values. For example, if $n = $ two random variables called, say, x and y,

$E(x + y) = E(x) + E(y)$

The proof follows.

$$E(x + y) = \sum_{i=1}^{n} P_i(x_i + y_i) = P_1(x_1 + y_1) + P_2(x_2 + y_2) + \ldots + P_n(x_n + y_n)$$

$$= P_1 x_1 + P_1 y_1 + P_2 x_2 + P_2 y_2 + \ldots + P_n x_n + P_n y_n$$

$$= [P_1 x_1 + P_2 x_2 + \ldots + P_n x_n] + [P_1 y_1 + P_2 y_2 + \ldots + P_n y_n$$

$$= \sum_{i=1}^{n} P_i x_i + \sum_{i=1}^{n} P_i y_i = E(x) + E(y)$$

where P_i is the *joint probability* of x_i and y_i occurring jointly.

4. The expected value of a constant times a random variable plus a constant equals the constant times the expected value of the random variable plus the constant. Symbolically, if b and c are constants and x is a random variable,

$E(bx + c) = bE(x) + c$

The proof is a combination of the three preceding proofs. These four properties of the expected-value operator may be used to derive the following useful theorems.

Theorem B-1 The variance of a random variable equals the expected value of the squared random variable less the expected value of the random variable squared.[1]

Stated in equation form,

$$\text{var}(x) = E(x^2) - [E(x)]^2$$

Proof

$$
\begin{aligned}
\text{var}(x) &= E[x - E(x)]^2 \quad \text{by definition of var}(x) \\
&= E\{x^2 - 2xE(x) + [E(x)]^2\} \\
&= E(x^2) - 2E(x)^2 + [E(x)]^2 \\
&= E(x^2) - [E(x)]^2 \quad\quad\quad\quad\quad\quad\quad\quad\quad \text{Q.E.D.}
\end{aligned}
$$

Theorem B-2 The expected value of a squared random variable equals the variance of the random variable plus its expected value squared.

Stated in equation form,

$$E(x^2) = \text{var}(x) + [E(x)]^2$$

Proof

$$
\begin{aligned}
\text{var}(x) &= E(x^2) - [E(x)]^2 \quad \text{by Theorem B-1} \\
[E(x)]^2 + \text{var}(x) &= E(x^2) \quad\quad\quad\quad\quad\quad\quad\quad \text{Q.E.D.}
\end{aligned}
$$

Theorem B-3 The variance of a linear transformation of the random variable is not affected by adding or subtracting a constant, but multiplying the random variable by a constant increases the variance of the product by the square of the constant.

Stated in equation form,

$$\text{var}(ax + b) = a^2 \, \text{var}(x) \quad \text{for any constants } a \text{ and } b$$

Proof

$$
\begin{aligned}
\text{var}(ax + b) &= E[ax + b - E(ax + b)]^2 \text{ by definition} \\
&= E[ax + b - aE(x) - b]^2 \\
&= Ea^2[x - E(x)]^2 \\
&= a^2E[x - E(x)]^2 = a^2 \, \text{var}(x) \quad\quad\quad \text{Q.E.D.}
\end{aligned}
$$

Theorem B-3 implies that the standard deviation of $ax + b$ equals $a\sigma_x$, the square root of $a^2 \, \text{var}(x)$.

Theorem B-4 If two random variables are independent, the expected value of the product of the two random variables equals the product of their expectations.

---

[1] Note that Theorem B-1 implies a computationally efficient way to compute the variance in a real-valued problem. That is, finding the average of the deviations

Stated in equation form,

$E(xy) = E(x)E(y)$ if x and y are independent

Proof

$$E(xy) = \sum_i \sum_j [P(x_i \text{ and } y_i)(x_i)(y_i)]$$

but

$P(x \text{ and } y) = P_x P_y$ if x and y are independent

Therefore

$$E(xy) = \sum_i \sum_j (P_{xi} P_{yj} x_i y_j)$$

$$= \sum_i (P_{xi} x_i) \sum_j (P_{yj} y_j)$$

$$= E(x)E(y) \qquad\qquad \text{Q.E.D.}$$

Theorem B-5 The covariance of two random variables equals the expected value of their product less the product of their expectations.

Stated in equation form,

$\text{cov}(x,y) = E(xy) - E(x)E(y)$

Proof

$$\text{cov}(x,y) = E\{[x - E(x)][y - E(y)]\} \quad \text{by definition}$$

$$= E\{[(xy - xE(y) - yE(x) + E(x)E(y)]\}$$

$$= [E(xy) - E(x)E(y) - E(y)E(x) + E(x)E(y)]$$

$$= E(xy) - E(x)E(y) \qquad\qquad \text{Q.E.D.}$$

Theorem B-6 The covariance of a random variable with any constant is zero.

Stated in equation form,

$\text{cov}(x,c) = 0$ where c is a constant

Proof

$$\text{cov}(x,c) = E(xc) - E(x)E(c) \quad \text{by Theorem B-5}$$

$$= cE(x) - cE(x) = 0 \qquad\qquad \text{Q.E.D.}$$

$$\frac{1}{n}\sum_{i=1}^{n}(x_i - \bar{x})^2 = \text{var}(x)$$

requires more computation than subtracting the mean squared from the mean of the squares:

$$\frac{1}{n}\sum_{i=1}^{n} x_i^2 - \bar{x}^2 = \text{var}(x)$$

The other theorems also imply similar computational shortcuts which are useful in performing hand calculations or in writing efficient computer programs.

Theorem B-7   The covariance of linear transformations of two random variables (x and y) is not affected by adding or subtracting constants to one or both of the variables, but the covariance is increased by a multiple equal to any constants which were multiplied by the random variables.

Stated in equation form,

$$\text{cov}(ax + b, cy + d) = ac\,\text{cov}(x,y) \quad \text{where } a, b, c, \text{ and } d \text{ are constants}$$

Proof

$$\text{cov}(ax + b, cy + d) = E\{[ax + b - E(ax + b)][cy + d - E(cy + d)]\}$$
$$\text{by the definition of the covariance}$$
$$= E\{[ax + b - aE(x) - b][cy + d - cE(y) - d]\}$$
$$= E\{a[x - E(x)]c[y - E(y)]\}$$
$$= acE\{[x - E(x)][y - E(y)]\}$$
$$= ac\,\text{cov}(x,y) \qquad \text{Q.E.D.}$$

Theorem B-8   The covariance of a sum of random variables with another variable x equals the sum of their covariances with variable x.

Stated in equation form,

$$\text{cov}(x, y + z) = \text{cov}(x,y) + \text{cov}(x,z)$$

Proof

$$\text{cov}(x, y + z) = E[x(y + z)] - E(x)E(y + z) \quad \text{by Theorem B-5}$$
$$= E(xy + xz) - [E(x)E(y) + E(x)E(z)]$$
$$= E(xy) + E(xz) - [E(x)E(y) + E(x)E(z)]$$
$$= E(xy) - E(x)E(y) + E(xz) - E(x)E(z) \quad \text{using B-5 again:}$$
$$= \text{cov}(x,y) + \text{cov}(x,z) \qquad \text{Q.E.D.}$$

Theorem B-9   If the random variables x and y both undergo a linear transformation (for example, $ax + b$ and $cy + d$, where a, b, c, and d are constants), their correlation coefficient ρ_{xy} is invariant.

Symbolically,

$$\rho(x,y) = \rho(ax + b, cy + d)$$

Proof

$$\rho(ax + b, cy + d) = \frac{\text{cov}(ax + b, cy + d)}{(\sigma_{ax+b})(\sigma_{cy+d})} \quad \text{definition of } \rho_{xy}$$

$$= \frac{ac\,\text{cov}(xy)}{a(\sigma_x)c(\sigma_y)} \quad \text{by Theorems B-3 and B-7}$$

$$= \frac{\text{cov}(x,y)}{\sigma_x \sigma_y}$$

$$= \rho(x,y) \qquad \text{Q.E.D.}$$

Theorem B-10 The variance of a sum of random variables equals the sum of their variances plus the sum of all their covariances.

Stated in equation form.

$$\text{var}(\Sigma x_i) = \Sigma \sigma_i^2 + \sum_i \sum_j \sigma_{ij} \quad \text{for } i \neq j$$

Proof

$$\text{var}(\Sigma x_i) = E\left(\sum_i x_i - \sum_i u_i\right)^2 \quad \text{where } u_i = E(x)$$

$$= E\left[\sum_i (x_i - u_i)^2\right]$$

$$= E\left[\sum_i \sum_j (x_i - u_i)(x_j - u_j)\right]$$

$$= \sum_i \sum_j E[(x_i - u_i)(x_j - u_j)]$$

$$= \sum_i \sum_j \sigma_{ij}$$

$$= \sum_i \sigma_i^2 + \sum_i \sum_j \sigma_{ij} \quad \text{for } i \neq j$$

Q.E.D.

Theorem B-11 The third statistical moment is a simple linear additive sum of the first three moments about the origin, denoted $E(x^n)$ for $n = 1, 2$, and 3.

Symbolically,

$$M_3 = E[(x - E(x)]^3 = E(x^3) - 3E(x^2)E(x) + 2[E(x)]^3$$

Proof

$$M_3 = E[x - E(x)]^3$$

$$= E\{[x^3 - 2x^2E(x) + x[E(x)]^2 - x^2E(x) + 2x[E(x)]^2 - [E(x)]^3\}$$

Since

$$(a - b)^3 = (a^3 - 2a^2b + ab^2 - a^2b + 2ab^2 - b^3)$$

$$= E[x^3 - 3x^2E(x) + 3x[E(x)]^2 - [E(x)]^3]$$

$$= E(x^3) - 3E(x^2)E(x) + 3E(x)[E(x)]^2 - [E(x)]^3$$

$$= E(x^3) - 3E(x^2)E(x) + 2[E(x)]^3$$

Q.E.D.

This theorem generalizes to the nth statistical moment.

Statistical Moments

Some probability distributions (such as the uniform and normal) may be completely described by their "statistical moments." The moments of a probability distribution are statistical measures.[1]

The Expected Return and Mean

For a probability distribution of returns, the first moment about the *origin* is defined as shown in Eqs. (C-1) and (C-1a).

$$E(r) = \sum_{i=1}^{n} P_i r_i \quad \text{for future returns} \tag{C-1}$$

$$\bar{r} = \frac{1}{T} \sum_{i=1}^{T} ri \quad \text{for historical returns} \tag{C-1a}$$

where

$E(r)$ = expected return

n = number of different returns possible

$\bar{r}$ = mean return

r_i = ith possible rate of return

$P_i = 1/n$ = relative frequency of ith return = $1/T$

T = terminal time period

It is always assumed that $\sum_{i}^{n} P_i = 1$. The first moment about the origin of a distribution is the same as its expected value or mean. The first moment about the origin is a measure of location or central tendency for the distribution.

Probability Distributions and Relative-Frequency Distributions

Equation (C-1) is similar to Eq. (C-1a). The only difference in them is that (C-1) is stated in terms of probabilities and therefore applies to future returns (denoted r_i), whereas Eq. (C-1a) is stated in terms of T historical rates of return (denoted r_t) and relative frequencies (denoted $1/n$). Thus, (C-1a) defines the mean of a historical relative-frequency distribution.

---

1 For a more rigorous discussion of moments, see J. E. Freund, *Mathematical Statistics*. (Englewood Cliffs, N. J.: Prentice-Hall, 1962), chap. 4. For a more elementary discussion of moments and various approximations for moments *see* S. B. Richmond, *Statistical Analysis*, 2d ed. (New York: Ronald, 1964), chap 4. For those probability distributions (for example, Cauchy) having no moments, this discussion is, of course, irrelevant.

Equations (C-1) and (C-1a) both define first moments about the origin, but (C-1) defines a first moment about the origin of an (expected) probability distribution, while (C-1a) defines the first moment about the origin of a (historical) relative-frequency distribution.

Moments about the mean are different from *moments about the origin*. The *first moment* about the mean is defined by Eqs. (C-2) and (C-2a).

First Moment About the Mean Always Zero

$$M_1 = \sum_{i=1}^{n} P_i[r_i - E(r)] = 0 \quad \text{for future returns} \tag{C-2}$$

$$M_1 = \frac{1}{T}\sum_{t}^{T} [r_t - \bar{r}] = 0 \quad \text{for historical returns} \tag{C-2a}$$

The first moment about the mean is always zero. However, higher-order moments about the mean, called *statistical moments*, are useful in security and portfolio analysis.

The *second moment* about the mean of a distribution of returns is defined by Eqs. (C-3) and (C-3a).

Variance or Second Moment

$$\sigma^2 = \sum_{i}^{n} P[r_i - E(r)]^2 \quad \text{for future returns} \tag{C-3}$$

$$\sigma^2 = \frac{1}{T}\sum_{t}^{T} [r_t - \bar{r}]^2 \quad \text{for historical returns} \tag{C-3a}$$

Second statistical moment is a synonym for *variance*. The second statistical moment measures the distribution's dispersion or wideness. The square root of the variance is the *standard deviation*.

The *third moment* of a distribution of returns is defined in Eqs. (C-4) and (C-4a).

The Third Moment and Skewness

$$M_3 = \Sigma P_i[r_i - E(r)]^3 \quad \text{for future returns} \tag{C-4}$$

$$M_3 = \frac{1}{T}\sum_{t}^{T} [r_t - \bar{r}]^3 \quad \text{for historical returns} \tag{C-4a}$$

The third statistical moment measures the lopsidedness of the distribution; it is normalized by dividing it by the standard deviation cubed. This puts the third moments of different distributions in terms of a relative measure of lopsidedness which is called *skewness*. Equation (C-5) defines the skewness of a distribution of returns.

$$sk(r) = \frac{M_3}{\sigma^3}$$

$$= \frac{\Sigma P[r_i - E(r)]^3}{\{\sqrt{\Sigma P[r_i - E(r)]^2}\}^3} \tag{C-5}$$

Figure 9-2 on page 176 shows three probability distributions with the three possible types of skewness — positive, zero, and negative. A distribution which is skewed left (*a*) will have a long left tail, a negative third moment, and negative skewness. A symmetrical distribution (*b*) will have a third moment and skewness of zero.[2] Distributions which are skewed right (*c*) will have positive third moments, positive skewness, and longer right tails.

Fourth Moment and Kurtosis

The *fourth moment* M_4 measures the peakedness of a probability distribution. For a probability distribution of returns, the fourth moment is defined by Eqs. (C-6) and (C-6*a*).

$$M_4 = \Sigma P_i[r_i - E(r)]^4 \quad \text{for future returns} \tag{C-6}$$

$$M_4 = \frac{1}{T}\sum_{t}^{T}[r_t - \bar{r}]^4 \quad \text{for historical returns} \tag{C-6a}$$

Figure C-1 shows three probability distributions of returns, leptokurtic (*a*), platykurtic (*b*), and normal or mesokurtic (*c*). Although all three of these distributions may have first, second, and third moments which are identical, they would all have different fourth moments.

FIGURE C-1   Peakedness of kurtosis of distributions (a) leptokurtic; (b) platykurtic; (c) normal or mesokurtic.

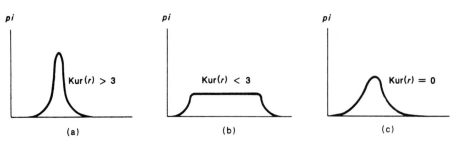

2 Skewness may be zero for nonsymmetrical distributions in a few pathological situations. P. G. Hoel, *Introduction to Mathematical Statistics*, 3d ed. (New York: Wiley, 1962), pp. 76–77. Skewness can also be difficult to measure econometrically, as shown by J. C. Francis, "Skewness and Investors' Decisions," *Journal of Financial and Quantitative Analysis*, March 1975, pp. 163–172.

The fourth moment of a probability distribution is usually normalized by being divided by the standard deviation raised to the fourth power, allowing direct comparisons of the peakedness of different distributions. This normalized fourth moment is called a *measure of kurtosis*. Kurtosis is defined by Eq. (C-7).

$$\text{kur}(r) = \frac{M_4}{\sigma^4}$$

$$= \frac{\Sigma p[r - E(r)]^4}{\{\sqrt{\Sigma p[r - E(r)]^2}\}^4}$$

(C-7)

Appendix D

Elements of Correlation and Regression Analysis

Correlation and regression are classical statistical tools used to analyze the interrelation between variables. In this appendix we shall examine simple linear models of correlation and regression.

D-1 Regression

We shall denote the *independent* or *control variable* as x and the *dependent variable* as y. As an example, x and y might be observations of returns on a market index such as the TSE 300 Composite Index, and the concurrent returns on some security, respectively. Of course, then we would be discussing the characteristic line—a particular regression line. Or x might represent the average number of cigarettes smoked per month and y might represent the number of chest colds and other respiratory illnesses the smoker suffered per month. Eq. (D-1) shows the basic regression model we shall examine here.

$$y = \alpha + Bx + e \tag{D-1}$$

where

α = intercept coefficient, alpha

B = slope coefficient, beta

e = random error term, epsilon; this is the residual portion

   of the y value which is left unexplained by the regression =

   $[y_i - (\alpha + Bx_i)]$

Figure D-1 shows a scatter diagram and the form of Eq. (D-1) which seems to "fit the data best."

FIGURE D-1   Graphs of simple linear regression. (a) scatter diagram of (x,y) observations; (b) least-squares line through scatter of observations.

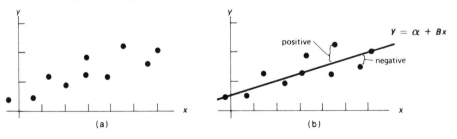

(a)   (b)

The Sample Data

Regression analysis begins with n observations of (x_i, y_i) pairs: $(x_1 y_1)$, $(x_2 y_2)$, ..., $(x_n y_n)$. These n observations may be graphed as a scatter diagram like the one in Figure D-1. For the characteristic line, the n observations represent observations from n different time periods all for the same asset. For the analysis of the effects of smoking on health, the n observations represent n persons' experiences (or n periods of experience by one person).

The objective of regression analysis is to find the line through the points in (x,y) space which "fits the observations." The objective is to minimize the sum of the squared errors around the regression line, or, more specifically, to minimize SSQ in Eq. (D-2).

Fitting the Regression Line

$$\min SSQ = \sum_{i=1}^{n}[y_i - (\alpha + Bx_i)]^2 \qquad\text{(D-2)}$$

$$= \sum_{i=1}^{n}e_i^2$$

$$= \sum_{i=1}^{n}(y_i - \hat{y}_i)^2$$

$$= \text{the sum of the errors squared}$$

Here, $\hat{y}_i = \alpha + Bx_i$ = a predicted value of y given that x equals the ith value of x. That is, $\hat{y}_t$ denotes some point lying on the regression line, y_i is an actual observed value of the variable y, and $(y_i - \hat{y}_i) = e_i$ = the ith error. Differential calculus is used to find the formulas for the regression coefficients α and B which "fit a line" through the n observations in such a manner that SSQ is minimized.[1] This line is called a least-squares regression line, or an ordinary least-squares (OLS) line.

The formula for the least-squares regression slope coefficient B is defined in Eq. (D-3).[2]

The Regression Coefficients

$$B = \frac{\text{cov}(x,y)}{\text{var}(x)} \qquad\text{(D-3)}$$

[1] The partial derivatives $\partial(SSQ)/\partial\alpha$ and $\partial(SSQ)/\partial B$ are set to zero, and the two resulting linear equations in two variables are solved simultaneously for α and B.

[2] Simplified, computationally efficient formulas for the regression slope coefficient are

$$B = \frac{\sum_i (x_i - \bar{x})(y_i - \bar{y})}{\sum_i (x_i - \bar{x})^2} \qquad\text{(D-3a)}$$

$$B = \frac{n\sum_i x_i y_i - \sum_i x_i \sum_i y_i}{n\sum_i x_i^2 - \left(\sum_i x_i\right)^2} \qquad\text{(D-3b)}$$

Equations (D-3), (D-3a) and (D-3b) are equal. The means of x and y, denoted $\bar{x}$ and $\bar{y}$, are required to calculate (D-3) and (D-3a) but not (D-3b). Therefore, (D-3b) is computationally the simplest formula to use.

The formula for the least-squares regression intercept coefficient α is defined in Eq. (D-4).

$$\alpha = \bar{y} - B\bar{x} \tag{D-4}$$

B from (D-3) is required before α may be determined. After α and B are determined, the line $y = \alpha + Bx$ may be graphed in (x,y) space. This is the least-squares line or line of best fit.

Properties of Least-Squares Regression Lines

All least-squares regression lines meet the following three conditions if they are calculated correctly.

1. They pass through the centroid $(\bar{x},\bar{y})$.
2. The sum of the squared errors is minimized: SSQ = minimum.
3. The sum of the errors is zero: $\Sigma_{i=1}^{n} e_i = 0$.

If all three of these conditions are not met, some error has been made in calculating the least-squares line intercept and slope coefficients.

D-2 CORRELATION

A correlation coefficient can vary as follows: $-1 \le \rho \le +1$. If $\rho_{xy} = +1$, then x and y are perfectly positively correlated; they move in the same direction in unison. If $\rho_{xy} = 0$, the two variables x and y are uncorrelated; they show no tendency to follow each other. If $\rho_{xy} = -1$, x and y vary inversely; they are perfectly negatively correlated. The definition of ρ_{xy} is given in Eq. (D-5).[3]

$$\rho_{xy} = \frac{\text{cov}(x,y)}{\sigma_x \sigma_y} = \rho_{yx} \tag{D-5}$$

Pure Correlation Analysis

The correlation coefficient for x and y may be determined whether or not any regression of y and x is performed. Correlation analysis makes no assumptions as to which variable is the independent variable and which is dependent. The correlation coefficient is a *standardized* measure of the way two variables covary.

A Closeness-of-Fit Measure

If the regression of y onto x (or x onto y) is performed, the correlation coefficient has a second interpretation; the correlation coefficient is a measure of the *closeness of fit* of the observed points to the regression line. Figure D-2 shows some scatter diagrams to which least-squares regression lines have been fitted.

[3] A computationally efficient formula for the correlation coefficient is

$$\rho_{yx} = \rho_{xy} = \frac{n\Sigma xy - \Sigma x \Sigma y}{\{[n\Sigma x^2) - (\Sigma x)^2][(n\Sigma y^2) - (\Sigma y)^2]\}^{.5}} \tag{D-5a}$$

Equation (D-5a) is equivalent to (D-5). Neither formula adjusts for degrees of freedom.

FIGURE D-2   The correlation coefficients for various scatter diagrams.

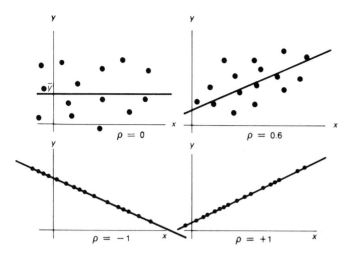

When the (x_iy_i) points do not follow any linear model of the form shown in Eq. (D-1), the correlation coefficient is zero. If all the (x_iy_i), points lie exactly on some regression line, the correlation coefficient equals either positive or negative unity, depending on the slope of the line. If the points tend to follow the line but do not lie exactly on the line, the correlation is nonzero and its sign depends on the slope of the regression line.

The correlation coefficient does not vary whether x is regressed onto y or vice versa, although the regression coefficients α and B vary (unless $p = +$ 1 or -1). Denote the regression slope coefficient for regressing y onto x as $B_y|_x$. Equation (D-6) shows the relation of the beta or slope coefficients and the correlation coefficient.

$$\rho_{xy} = \sqrt{(B_x|_y)(B_y|_x)} = \rho_{yx} \tag{D-6}$$

The correlation coefficient squared is called the *coefficient of determination* and denoted ρ^2. The coefficient of determination gives the percentage of variation in the dependent variable which can be explained by concurrent variance in the independent variable.

Coefficient of Determination

The serial correlation coefficient measures the tendency of time series data to run in trends or cycles. If x_t are observations of some variable x at different points in time, then x_t for $t = 1, 2, \ldots, T$ is a *time series* over T periods. The serial correlation or autocorrelation coefficient for a time series of a variable x is defined in Eq. (D-7).

Serial Correlation

$$\rho_k = \frac{\text{cov}(x_t x_{t+k})}{(\sigma x_t)(\sigma x_{t+k})} \tag{D-7}$$

ρ_k is a serial correlation coefficient of order k, where k is the number of periods of lag which is being examined.

D-3   TOTAL AND UNEXPLAINED VARIANCE

The total variance of the dependent variable in regression model (D-1) is defined in Eq. (D-8).

$$\sigma_y^2 = \frac{1}{n}\sum_{i=1}^{n}(y_i - \bar{y})^2 \tag{D-8}$$

Residual Variance

Equation (D-9) defines the residual variance.

$$\sigma(\sigma_y^2|x) = \frac{1}{n}\sum_{i=1}^{n}(y_i - y_i)^2 \tag{D-9}$$

$$= \frac{1}{n}\sum_{i=1}^{n}[y_i - (\alpha + bx_i)]^2 \quad \text{since } \hat{y}_t = \alpha + bx_i$$

$$= \frac{1}{n}\sum_{i=1}^{n}e_i^2$$

The difference between Eqs. (D-8) and (D-9) is that they measure deviations from different points. Equation (D-8) measures deviations of y around the mean of y, whereas (D-9) measures deviations of y around the regression line. If the regression line explains any relation between x and y (that is, if $\rho_{xy} \neq 0$), then the residual variance must be less than the total variance because the regression line is a better estimator of y than the mean, $\bar{y}$. The square root of the residual variance is called the *standard error* of the regression estimate.

The percentage of variance in y unexplained by regression y onto x is defined in Eq. (D-10).

$$\frac{\sigma^2_{(y|x)}}{\sigma_y^2} = \text{percent of var}(y) \text{ unexplained by regression} \tag{D-10}$$

The coefficient of determination is simply unity (100 percent) less the percentage of variance unexplained.

$$\rho^2 = 1 - \frac{\sigma^2_{(y|x)}}{\sigma_y^2} = \text{coefficient of determination} \tag{D-11}$$

D-4   REGRESSION ASSUMPTIONS

Thus far in this appendix we have been discussing least-squares regression lines. Least-squares regression lines are ''better'' if the following four conditions pertaining to the random error term e exist:

1. e is a random variable with a mean of zero; that is, the error term is unbiased.

2. e has some variance which is constant throughout the length of the regression line. This is called *homoscedasticity*.

3. e_i and e_{i+k} do not covary for any values of k so that $\text{cov}(e_{i+k}) = 0$; that is, the errors are uncorrelated.

4. e_i and x_i do not covary so that $\text{cov}(e_i x_i) = 0$; that is, the errors are independent.

If the preceding four conditions are met, the regression line not only minimizes the squared errors, but the following two desirable properties are also obtained (the Gauss-Markov theorem):

1. $E(y|x) = \alpha + Bx$; that is, the regression line is an unbiased, linear estimator of y.

2. y_i and y_{i+k} are not serially correlated. Serial correlation can cause the regression coefficients α and B to vary erratically from sample to sample.

If the error term is unbiased and uncorrelated and has homoscedasticity and, in addition, e is a *normally distributed* random variable, the following two additional desirable properties apply to the regression line.

1. e_i and e_{i+k} are independent. This is a stronger condition than being uncorrelated.

2. Probability statements can be made about the various regression statistics. For example, it is possible to draw confidence limits aound the regression line.

SELECTED REFERENCES

Brennan, M. *Preface to Econometrics*, 3d ed. Cincinnati: South-Western Publishing Co., 1973. An elementary mathematics and statistics text that gives intuitive nonmathematical explanations of complex topics.

Folger, H. R. and S. Ganapathy. *Financial Econometrics*. Englewood Cliffs, N.J.: Prentice-Hall, 1982. This is an econometrics book that employs numerical examples from financial applications.

Pindyck, R. S. and D. L. Rubinfeld. *Econometric Models and Economic Forecasts*, 2d ed. New York: McGraw-Hill, 1981. An easy-to-read intermediate-level econometrics textbook which uses elementary calculus and matrix algebra. The use of real empirical data and numerical examples make this book interesting.

Mathematical Derivation of Formulas for Portfolio Risk and Expected Return

This appendix explains the risk and return formulas for portfolios and relates them to the risk return formulas for individual assets.

E-1 RISK AND RETURN FORMULAS FOR INDIVIDUAL ASSETS

The expected return from the ith asset is defined as follows:

$$E(r_i) = \sum_{t=1}^{n} P_t r_t$$

where

P_t = probability of tth rate of return   (E-1)

r_t = tth rate of return

n = number of different rates of return possible

It is assumed that the probabilities sum to 1; that is, $\sum_{t=1}^{n} P_t = 1$. The expected-value operator is discussed in Mathematical Appendix B.

In a discussion of investments, it is assumed that the rate of return is the single most meaningful outcome associated with an investment's perform-ance. Thus, discussion of the risk of a security focuses on dispersion of the security's rate of return around its expected return. Following Markowitz, risk is defined as "variability of return."[1] In any event, the standard deviation of rates of return or variance of rates of return is a possible measure of the phenomenon defined above as the risk. Symbolically, for the ith asset,

$$\text{var}(r_i) = \sigma_i^2 = \sigma_{ii} = \sum_{t=1}^{n} P_{it}[r_{it} - E(r_i)]^2 = E[r - E(r)]^2 \qquad \text{(E-2)}$$

Equation (E-2) defines the variance of returns for asset i. The value of σ_{ii} is in terms of a "rate of return squared." The standard deviation of returns is

1 Harry Markowitz, *Portfolio Selection*, Crowles Foundation Monograph 16 (New York: Wiley, 1959), p. 14.

more intuitively appealing, since it is the square root of the variance. It is defined in Eq. (E-3).

$$\sigma \quad \text{or} \quad \sigma_i = \sqrt{\sum_{t=1}^{n} P_{it}[r_{it} - E(r_i)]^2}$$

$$= \sqrt{E[r - E(r)^2}$$ (E-3)

$$= \sqrt{\sigma_{ii}}$$

The covariance of returns between assets i and j is denoted by σ_{ij} or $cov(r_i, r_j)$.

$$\sigma_{ij} = E\{[r_i - E(r_i)][r_j - E(r_j)]\}$$ (E-4)

$$= \sum_{t=1}^{T} P_t\{[r_{it} - E(r_i)][r_{jt} - E(r_j)]\}$$

where r_{it} is the tth rate of return for the ith asset. It can be shown that the covariance may also be defined as shown in Eq. (E-4a).

$$\sigma_{ij} = (\rho_{ij})(\sigma_i)(\sigma_j)$$ (E-4a)

where ρ_{ij} denotes the correlation coefficient between the returns of assets i and j. Mathematical Appendix B defines the covariance.

Equations (E-1) to (E-4) define the expected return, risk, and covariance of an individual asset. The expected return and risk of a portfolio are broken down in terms of these four components in the following subsection.

E-2 RISK AND RETURN FORMULAS FOR PORTFOLIOS

Assuming that all funds allocated for portfolio use are to be invested, the following constraint is placed on all portfolios.

$$\sum_{i=1}^{n} x_i = 1$$ (E-5)

where x_i denotes the weight, participation level, or fraction of the portfolio's total equity invested in the ith asset. In words, the n fractions of the portfolio's equity invested in n different assets sum up to 1 (or 100 percent). Cash can be one of the assets in the portfolio. Equation (E-5) is a constraint which cannot be violated in portfolio analysis; if it is, the analysis has no rational economic interpretation.

Let r_p denote some actual return from a portfolio, and let $E(r_p)$ denote the expected return for the portfolio. The expected return for the portfolio can be restated in terms of the assets' expected return as is shown at the top of page 854:

$$E(r_p) = \sum_{i=1}^{n} x_i E(r_i)$$

$$= \sum_{i=1}^{n} x_i \left(\sum_{t=1}^{T} p_{it} r_{it} \right) \tag{E-6}$$

$$= x_1 E(r_1) = x_2 E(r_2) + \ldots + x_n E(r_n)$$

In words, the expected return of a portfolio is the weighted average of the expected returns from the n securities in the portfolio.

Following the *dispersion of outcome* or *variability of return* definitions of risk, the risk of a portfolio is defined as the variability of its return, that is, the variability of r_p. By denoting the variance of r_p by var(r_p), it is possible to derive an analytical expression for var(r_p) in terms of the r_i's of all securities in the portfolio. This is the form of the expression suitable for portfolio analysis.

Substituting r_p for r_i in Eq. (E-7) yields Eq. (E-8), which defines the variance of the portfolio's rates of return, denoted var(r_p).

$$\sigma_i^2 = \sigma_{ii} = E[r_i - E(r)]^2 \tag{E-7}$$

$$= \sum P_i[r_i - E(r)]^2 \tag{E-7a}$$

$$\sigma_p^2 = \text{var}(r_p) = E[r_p - E(r_p)]^2 \tag{E-8}$$

$$= \sum_i P_i[r_p - E(r_p)]^2 \tag{E-8a}$$

A simple two-security portfolio will be used to illustrate the derivation of the formula for the risk of a portfolio. However, the results are general and follow for an n-security portfolio, where n is any positive integer. Substituting the quantity $(x_1 r_1 + x_2 r_2)$ for the equivalent r_p into Eq. (E-8) yields (E-9).

$$\text{var}(r_p) = E[r_p - E(r_p)]^2 \tag{E-8}$$

$$\text{var}(r_p) = E(x_1 r_1 + x_2 r_2) - E(x_1 r_1 + x_2 r_2)]^2 \tag{E-9}$$

Removal of the parentheses and use of property 2 in Mathematical Appendix B for the expectation operator results in an equivalent form:

$$\text{var}(r_p) = E[x_1 r_1 + x_2 r_2 - x_1 E(r_1) - x_2 E(r_2)]^2$$

Collecting terms with like subscripts and factoring out the x_i's gives

$$\text{var}(r_p) = E\{x_1[r_1 - E(r_1)] + x_2[r_2 - E(2r_2)]\}^2$$

Since $(ab + cd)^2 = (a^2 b^2 + c^2 d^2 + 2abcd)$, the above squared quantity can likewise be expanded by letting $ab = x_1[r_1 - E(r_1)]$ and $cd = x_2[r_2 - E(r_2)]$, which gives

$$\text{var}(r_p) = E\{x_1^2[r_1 - E(r_1)]^2 + x_2^2[r_2 - E(r_2)]^2$$
$$+ 2x_1x_2[r_1 - E(r_1)][r_2 - E(r_2)]\}$$

Bringing the E operator inside the braces (by property 2) yields

$$\text{var}(r_p) = x_1^2 E[r_1 - E(r_1)]^2 + x_2^2 E[r_2 - E(r_2)]^2$$
$$+ 2x_1x_2 E\{[r_1 - E(r_1)][r_2 - E(r_2)]\}$$

Recalling Eqs. (E-2) and (E-4), which define σ_{ii} and σ_{ij}, we recognize that the above expression is equivalent to

$$\text{var}(r_p) = x_1^2\sigma_{11} + x_2^2\sigma_{22} + 2x_1x_2\sigma_{12} \tag{E-10}$$
$$= x_1^2\text{var}(r_1) + x_2^2\text{var}(r_2) \quad 2x_1x_2 \, \text{cov}(r_1r_2)$$

Equation (E-10) shows that the variance of a weighted sum is not always simply the sum of the weighted variances. The *covariance* term may increase or decrease the variance of the sum depending on its sign.

The derivation of Eq. (E-10) is repeated in a more coherent manner thus:

$$\sigma_p^2 = \text{var}(r_p) = E[r_p - E(r_p)]^2$$
$$= E[x_1r_1 + x_2r_2 - E(x_1r_1 + x_2r_2)]^2 \quad \text{by substitution for } r_p$$
$$= E[x_1r_1 + x_2r_2 - x_1E(r_1) - x_2E(r_2)]^2$$
$$= E\{x_1[r_1 - E(r_1)] + x_2[r_2 - E(r_2)]\}^2 \quad \text{by collecting like terms}$$
$$= E\{x_1^2[r_1 - E(r_1)]^2 + x_2^2[r_2 - E(r_2)]^2 + 2x_1x_2[r_1 - E(r_1)][r_2 - E(r_2)]\}$$
$$= x_1^2 E[r_1 - E(r_1)]^2 + x_2^2 E[r_2 - E(r_2)]^2 + 2x_1x_2 E[r_1 - E(r_1)][r_2 - E(r_2)]$$
$$= x_1^2\text{var}(r_1) + x_2^2\text{var}(r_2) + 2x_1x_2\text{cov}(r_1r_2) \tag{E-10}$$

An understanding of Eq. (E-10) is essential to a true understanding of diversification and portfolio analysis. Next, Eq. (E-10) is expanded (without proof) to measure the risk of more realistic portfolios, that is, portfolios with more than two securities. However, even in its more elaborate versions, this equation is still simply the sum of the weighted variances and covariances.

Equation (E-10) is sometimes written more compactly using summation signs as shown below:

$$\text{var}(r_p) = \sum_i^n x_i^2\sigma_{ii} + \sum_j^n \sum_i^n x_ix_j\sigma_{ij} \quad \text{for } i \neq j \tag{E-10a}$$

where $n = 2$ or any other positive integer.

To clarify this notation, consider the following table of terms. The subscript i is the row number, and j is the column number.

	COL. 1	COL. 2	

$$\mathrm{var}(r_p) = \quad +x_1x_1\sigma_{11} + \qquad +x_1x_2\sigma_{12} + \qquad \text{row 1}$$

$$+x_2x_1\sigma_{21} + \qquad +x_2x_2x_{22} \qquad \text{row 2}$$

$$= x_1x_1\sigma_{11} + x_1x_2\sigma_{12} + x_2x_1\sigma_{21} + x_2x_2\sigma_{22}$$

$$= x_1^2\sigma_{11} + 2x_1x_2\sigma_{12} + x_2^2\sigma_{22} \quad \text{since } x_1x_2\sigma_{12} = x_2x_1\sigma_{21}$$

$$= \sum_{i=1}^{2} x_i^2\sigma_{ii} + \sum_{j=1}^{2}\sum_{i=1}^{2} x_ix_j\sigma_{ij} \quad \text{for } i \neq j \tag{E-10a}$$

$$= \sum_{j}^{2}\sum_{i}^{2} x_ix_j\sigma_{ij} \quad \text{since } \mathrm{cov}(r_i, r_i) = \mathrm{var}(r_i) \tag{E-10b}$$

$$= \sum_{i=1}^{2} x_i^2\sigma_{ii} + \sum_{i=1}^{2}\sum_{j=1}^{2} x_ix_j\rho_{ij}\sigma_i\sigma_j \quad \text{since } \sigma_{ij} = \rho_{ij}\sigma_i\sigma_j \quad \text{for } i \neq j \tag{E-10c}$$

The three factors which determine the risk of a portfolio are the weights of the securities, the standard deviation (or variance) of each security, and the correlation coefficient (or covariance) between the securities.

Expressions of $\mathrm{var}(r_p)$ for a large number of securities take the following form:

COL. 1	COL. 2	COL. 3		COL. $n-1$	COL. n	
$\mathrm{var}(r_p) = x_1x_1\sigma_{11}$	$+\ x_1x_2\sigma_{12}$	$+\ x_1x_3\sigma_{13}$	$+\ \ldots$	$x_1x_{n-1}\sigma_{1,n-1}$	$+\ x_1x_n\sigma_{1n}$	row 1
$+\ x_2x_1\sigma_{21}$	$+\ x_2x_2\sigma_{22}$	$+\ x_2x_3\sigma_{23}$	$+\ \ldots$	$x_2x_{n-1}\sigma_{2,n-1}$	$+\ x_2x_n\sigma_{2n}$	row 2
$+\ x_3x_1\sigma_{31}$	$+\ x_3x_2\sigma_{32}$	$+\ x_3x_3\sigma_{33}$	$+\ \ldots$	$x_3x_{n-1}\sigma_{3,n-1}$	$+\ x_3x_n\sigma_{3n}$	row 3
.				.	.	
.				.	.	
.				.	.	
$+\ x_nx_1\sigma_{n1}$	$+\ x_nx_2\sigma_{n2}$	$+\ x_nx_3\sigma_{n3}$	$+$	$x_nx_{n-1}\sigma_{n,n-1}$	$+\ x_nx_n\sigma_{nn}$	row n

These data comprise a matrix, which can be represented more compactly using Eq. (E-10a) or (E-10b) above. A matrix can be regarded as an array of numbers or a table of numbers. The matrix above represents the weighted sum of all n variances plus all $n^2 - n$ covariances. Thus, in a portfolio of 100 securities (that is, $n = 100$), there will be 100 variances and $100^2 - 100 = 9{,}900$ covariances. The security analyst must supply all these plus 100 expected returns for the securities.

Notice that the elements of the matrix containing terms with identical subscripts form a diagonal pattern from the upper left-hand corner to the lower right-hand corner. There are the n weighted variance terms of the form $x_ix_i\sigma_{ii}$.

All the other boxes contain the $n^2 - n$ weighted covariance terms (that is, terms of the form $x_i x_j \sigma_{ij}$, where $i \neq j$). The variance-covariance matrix is symmetric since $x_i x_j \sigma_{ij} = x_j x_i \sigma_{ji}$; each covariance is repeated twice in the matrix. The covariances above the diagonal are the mirror images of the covariances below the diagonal. Thus, the security analyst must actually estimate only $\frac{1}{2}(n^2 - n)$ unique covariances.

Geometric Mean Return

When dealing with the average of several *successive rates of rates of return*, the distinction between various multiperiod average rates of return and the *geometric mean* return should be recognized.

F-1 THE MISLEADING ARITHMETIC MULTIPERIOD AVERAGE RETURN

Consider asset A, purchased at $40. Suppose asset A's price rises to $60 at the end of the first period, then falls back to $40, and the asset is sold at that price at the end of the second period. The *arithmetic average rate* of return is the average of 50 percent and -33.3 percent, which is 8.35 percent.

$$\frac{50\% + (-33.3\%)}{2} = 8.35\% = \text{arithmetic average return on } A$$

Next consider asset B, which also has an original price of $40. But asset B's price falls to $20 at the end of one period. Then it rises back to $40 at the end of period 2. The arithmetic average rate of return for asset B is the average of -50 percent and 100 percent, which is 25 percent.

$$\frac{-50\% + 100\%}{2} = 25\% = \text{arithmetic average return for } B$$

The *behaviour of assets* A and B prices over the two periods is summarized graphically in Fig. F-1.

FIGURE F-1 Prices of two assets over two periods.

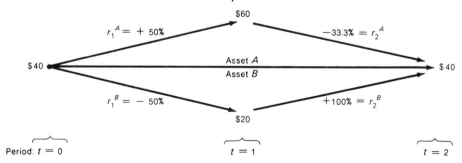

An asset purchased for $40 and sold for $40 two periods later did not return 8.35 percent or 25 percent; it clearly earned *zero* return. The arithmetic average of successive one-period returns is obviously not equal to the *true* average rate of return over *multiple periods*.

F-2   THE DOLLAR-WEIGHTED RATE OF RETURN

In classes about capital budgeting (or capital expenditures or corporation finance, as it is variously called), the rate of return from a multiperiod investment is defined to be the discount rate which equates the present value of all cashflows c_t to the cost of the investment c_0, as shown below.

$$c_0 = \sum_{t=1}^{T} \frac{c_t}{(1 + r)^t} \qquad\qquad \text{(F-1a)}$$

This rate of return is also sometimes called the *dollar-weighted rate of return*, or the *internal rate of return*. It is represented by the symbol r in Eq. (F-1a).

For only a one-period investment, $n = 1$, the internal rate of return is equivalent to the one-period rate of return, Eq. (2-2), as shown below.

$$c_0 = \frac{c_1}{1 + r}$$

$$c_0 r = c_1 - c_0 \qquad\qquad \text{(F-1b)}$$

$$r = \frac{c_1 - c_0}{c_0} \quad \text{equivalent to Eqs. (2-2) and (2-1)}$$

The quantity $c_1 - c_0$ equals capital gains or losses plus cash dividends or interest for stock or bonds, respectively, as in Eqs. (2-2) and (2-1) in Chap. 2.

For multiperiod investments involving only one cash inflow—namely, the cost of the asset, or c_0—and one cash outflow, c_t, the internal rate of return yields the same solution as the (average compounded or) geometric mean rate of return. For example, for asset A the cashflows were $c_0 = \$40$ and $c_2 = \$40$, which yields $r = 0$, as shown in Eq. (F-1c).

$$\$40 = \frac{\$40}{(1 + r)^2} \quad \text{only if } r = 0 \qquad\qquad \text{(F-1c)}$$

The internal rate of return is different from the (average compounded or) geometric mean rate of return for multiperiod investments which involve *multiple* cash inflows or outflows, however.

The internal rate of return is also called the dollar-weighted rate of return because it is influenced by how many dollars remain invested in a multiperiod investment. Thus, the dollar-weighted rate of return is not useful for comparing the rates of return for, say, two mutual funds which experience different cashflow patterns over time. The *time-weighted rate of return* is the true (average compounded or geometric mean) rate of return, which is useful for such comparisons because it is not affected by the size of an investment's cash inflows and/or outflows.

F-3   FORMULAS FOR GEOMETRIC MEAN RETURN

The true rate of return over n periods is called average compounded rate of return or geometric mean return (gr) and is defined in Eq. (F-2a). The $1 + r$ terms are called *link relatives* or *value relatives*.

$$gr = \sqrt[T]{(1 + r_1)(1 + r_2) \ldots (1 + r_T)} - 1 \tag{F-2a}$$

$$= \left[\prod_{t=1}^{T} (1 + r_t) \right]^{1/T} - 1 \tag{F-2b}$$

For a common stock, the link relative is the ending price plus dividends divided by the beginning price. Symbolically,

$$1 + r_t = \frac{p_{t+1} + d_t}{p_t} = \text{price plus dividend value relative} \tag{F-3}$$

It is cumbersome to evaluate a Tth root, not to mention the fact that there may be T different roots to consider. The logarithmic transformations may be used to expedite computation of the geometric mean return. Equation (F-4a) shows a computationally efficient formula for calculating the geometric mean of T different one-period returns by using logarithms.[1]

$$gr = \left\{ \text{antilog} \left[\frac{1}{T} \sum_{t=1}^{T} \log (1 + r_t) \right] \right\} - 1 \tag{F-4a}$$

Returning to the two-period numerical example, we can calculate the geometric mean with Eq. (F-4a). The natural logs of the value relatives for asset B are shown on the bottom line of Table F-1 which appears at the top of page 861. The geometric mean return for asset B is zero, as shown below.

$$e^{(1/2)(.693 - .693)} - 1 = 0 \tag{F-4b}$$

since $e^0 - 1 = 0$. Obviously, the true rate of return for asset B is the geometric mean return of zero and not the arithmetic average return of 25 percent. The same thing is true for asset A; its geometric mean of zero is calculated below in Eq. (F-4c).

$$e^{(1/2)(.405 - .405)} - 1 = 0 \tag{F-4c}$$

1 Either common base-10 logarithms or Naperian, base-e, logarithms may be used; they yield the same geometric return. But natural logs are preferred because the natural log of the value relative is a measure of rate of return. For example, if r = 10 percent = .1, then $1 + r$ = 1.1 and ln 1.1 = .095 = 9.5 per cent continuously compounded rate of return.

TABLE F-1 MULTIPERIOD MEAN RETURN COMPUTATIONS

TIME PERIODS	$t = 0$	$t = 1$	$t = 2$
A $\begin{cases} \text{Market value of asset } A \\ \text{One-period return} \\ \text{Natural logarithm of } (1 + r) \end{cases}$	$p_0 = \$40$	$p_1 = \$60$ $r_1 = 50\%$ $\ln(1 + .5) = .405$	$p_2 = \$40$ $r_2 = -33.3\%$ $\ln(1 - .333) = -.405$
B $\begin{cases} \text{Market value of asset } B \\ \text{One-period return} \\ \text{Natural logarithm of } (1 + r) \end{cases}$	$p_0 = \$40$	$p_1 = \$20$ $r_1 = -50\%$ $\ln(1 - .5) = -.693$	$p_2 = \$40$ $r_2 = 100\%$ $\ln(1 + 1) = .693$

F-4 COMPARISON OF ARITHMETIC AND GEOMETRIC MEAN RETURNS

The arithmetic average of successive one-period rates of return is defined in Eq. (F-5).

$$\bar{r} = \frac{1}{T}\sum_{t}^{T} r_t \qquad \text{(F-5)}$$

The arithmetric average return $\bar{r}$ is an approximation of the true multi-period rate of return. The arithmetric average always overstates a positive geometric return. As the variance of the r_t's grows smaller, this approximation becomes better. Equation (F-6) shows the nature of this approximation.

$$\bar{r} \approx [gr^2 + \mathrm{var}(r)]^{1/2} \qquad \text{(F-6)}$$

F-5 THE IMPACT OF CASH INFLOWS AND OUTFLOWS ON RATE-OF-RETURN MEASURES

If the owner of investment funds is a different person from the manager of the invested funds, the manager of the investment portfolio typically experiences cash inflows when additional money is invested and cash outflows when some of the invested funds are withdrawn by their owner. The managers of most institutional investment portfolios (such as the managers of mutual funds, trust departments of banks, and other large investment programs) can have their investment rate-of-return measurements significantly affected by cash inflows and outflows if they are not analyzed properly. In order to correctly measure the rate of return for an investment portfolio that experiences cashflows in and out of the portfolio, the geometric mean rate of return must be employed. This so-called time-weighted rate of return can yield correct multiperiod rate-of-return measurements if applied properly. In contrast, the internal (or dollar-weighted) rate of return will produce incorrect rate-of-return measurements if any cash inflows or outflows occur in the time period during which the rate of return of the investment portfolio is being measured. A numerical example should clarify the nature of the possible errors that can be caused by analyzing cash inflows and outflows improperly when measuring an investment portfolio's rate of return over multiple time periods.

Consider the rates of return from a hypothetical mutual fund over two consecutive one-year investment periods. Suppose that the shares in this mutual fund, let us call it asset B, earn a one-period rate of return of -50 percent in the first year and 100 percent in the second year. This hypothetical mutual fund is simply case B indicated in the lower branch of Fig. F-1 above. If the mutual fund has a constant amount of total funds invested over the two-year period, then the portfolio's geometric mean rate of return is zero — as shown in the lower section of Table F-1.

Let us now consider the more realistic (and more problematical) case that occurs when cash inflows and outflows cause the amount of total funds invested to change. Suppose that our hypothetical mutual fund, or asset B, starts out with a total of $200 million invested in it at the beginning of the first time period. But, at the end of period one the $200 million of total assets declines in market value to only $100 million because the portfolio suffers a -50 percent one-period rate of return in the first of the two-years being evaluated here. Then, at the end of the first year, or, synonymously, at the start of the second year, $100 million of net purchases of shares by investors in the mutual fund cause an unanticipated cash inflow that raises the total funds invested at the start of the second year to a total of $200 million. And finally, during the second year the mutual fund earns an annual rate of return of 100 percent, pushing its total market value up from $200 million to $400 million at the end of the second period. This pattern of market values and cash flows is illustrated in Fig. F-2. Essentially, there are three cashflows: (1) the original positive amount of $200 million, (2) the $100 million inflow before period two, and (3) $400 million available to be withdrawn at the end of period two, which can be treated as a negative cashflow. The question to be answered here is, "Given this fact situation, what is this mutual fund's multi-period rate of return over two years?"

FIGURE F-2   Cash value of a mutual fund's portfolio over two years.

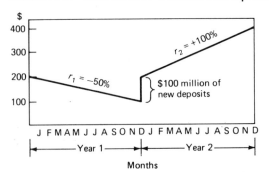

If the inappropriate dollar-weighted (or internal) rate-of-return measure were employed, an erroneous rate-of-return measure of about 20 percent (or 18.6 percent, to be more exact) would be obtained. That is, the dollar-weighted rate of return would indicate that the beginning $200 million was invested at about 20 percent per year for two years, and the additional net investor purchases of $200 million that occurred between the first and the second years were also invested at about 20 percent for the second year. But this answer is obviously in error. If an investment of any amount loses half its value (namely, −50 percent) in one year and then doubles in value (that is, + 100 percent) in the second year, such an asset wound up earning an annual average rate of return that is closer to zero than it is to 20 percent. In any event, it is difficult to argue plausibly that such an investment earned about 20 percent per year for two consecutive years.

Our hypothetical mutual fund actually earned a rate of return of zero compounded over the two-year period. To see this intuitively, consider the fortunes of one of the *original dollar bills* invested at the start of the two-year period. One of these original dollars fell in value to 50 cents at the end of the first year. Then, during the second year, this fallen investment's 50-cent value grew to be worth a dollar — the same value it started with two years earlier. Thus, we see that the invested dollar earned zero over the two-year period. This correct answer could have been obtained analytically with the geometric mean rate-of-return formulas. In fact, the calculations for asset *B* shown in the lower section of Table F-1 are also appropriate for our hypothetical mutual fund. Now you see that the geometric mean rate of return is not affected by cashflows that determine how much money the investment manager has to manage. The geometric mean rate of return is a *time-weighted rate of return* that weights equal time periods equally, regardless how much money is invested in each time period. This is the correct rate-of-return measure to use to evaluate the rate of return for investment managers who have cashflows into and out of the portfolio.

F-6   MAXIMIZING GEOMETRIC MEAN RETURN AS A GOAL

Dr. H. A. Lantane has suggested that maximizing the geometric return is a good investment goal.[2] This suggestion is well taken, since maximizing gr involves maximizing the r_t's each period while minimizing var(r) — that is, risk. To see this more clearly, solve Eq. (F-6) for the geometric mean return.[3]

$$gr = [\bar{r}^2 - var(r)]^{1/2} \tag{F-7}$$

Equation (F-7) shows that minimizing risk [var(r)] and maximizing the arithmetic average return ($\bar{r}$) will tend to maximize the geometric mean return. Such a policy is equivalent to maximizing terminal wealth because the ratio of terminal wealth, denoted w_r, to beginning wealth, denoted w_0, is simply

---

2 H. A. Lantane, ''Criteria for Choice among Risky Ventures,'' *The Journal of Political Economy*, April 1959, pp. 144–155.

3 William E. Young and Robert H. Trent, ''Geometric Mean Approximations of Individual Security and Portfolio Performance,'' *Journal of Financial and Quantitative Analysis*, June 1969, pp. 179–199.

$(1 + gr)^T = w_T/w_0$. This shows that maximizing the geometric mean return is equivalent to maximizing the ratio of terminal to beginning wealth.

Some financial economists have suggested that maximizing the terminal wealth or geometric mean return of a portfolio is an investment objective which may be preferable to maximizing the portfolio's expected return in a selected risk-class each period. Although this suggestion may be true for some investors, it is not true for all of them. The portfolio which maximizes the geometric mean return or terminal wealth is just one portfolio on or near the efficient frontier.[4] It is shown in Chap. 25 that as an investor's planning horizon and risk-aversion varies, the point on the efficient frontier preferred by that investor varies considerably. Chapter 27 discusses multiperiod portfolio management.

4 Nils H. Hakansson, ''Capital Growth and the Mean-Variance Approach to Portfolio Selection,'' *Journal of Financial and Quantitative Analysis*, January 1971, pp. 517–557; and Jan Mossin, ''Optional Multi-Period Portfolio Policies,'' *Journal of Business*, April 1968, pp. 215–229; E. F. Fama, ''Multi-Period Consumption-Investment Decisions,'' *American Economic Review*, March 1970, pp. 163–174; Harry M. Markowitz, ''Investment for the Long-Run: New Evidence for an Old Rule,'' *Journal of Finance*, December 1976, vol. 31, pp. 1273–1286.

INDEX